MW00586140

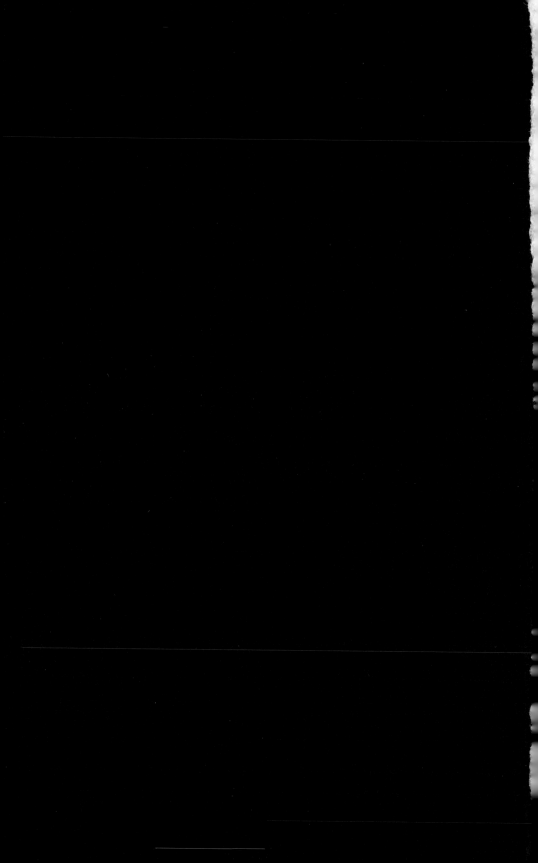

Praise for the revised and expanded edition of
Perdurabo: The Life of Aleister Crowley

"In this revised edition of *Perdurabo,* Richard Kaczynski takes readers through the Beast's amazing life and work in a sympathetic and compelling fashion. It is an effective combination of erudition and accessibility that will remain the standard biography of Crowley for years to come."

> —Henrik Bogdan, PhD, author of *Western Esotericism and Rituals of Initiation*

"If you're a collector of Crowley biographies, this is an essential addition to your collection. If you can only afford one Crowley biography, this is the one to get."

> —Sabazius, X°, National Grand Master, Ordo Templi Orientis, USA

"This is not only the most carefully researched, detailed, and informative biography of Crowley yet written but also a remarkable insight into the nature of magic itself."

> —Ronald Hutton, author of *The Triumph of the Moon* and *Blood and Mistletoe: The History of the Druids in Britain*

"This new edition is essential reading for anyone wanting to understand the Great Beast."

> —Clive Harper, author of *Notes towards a Bibliography of Austin Osman Spare*

"*Perdurabo* is the result of many years of painstaking research. Dr. Kaczynski has been able to uncover a host of previously unexplored sources that cast new light on Aleister Crowley's life and works. It is an achievement that deserves praise, and I am sure the book will be an indispensable reference for scholars and students for many years to come."

> —Marco Pasi, assistant professor at the Center for the History of Hermetic Philosophy and Related Currents, University of Amsterdam, and author of *Aleister Crowley and the Temptation of Politics*

"The blurb on the front of the dust jacket [of the new edition] says: *The definitive biography of the founder of modern magick.* Having read the first edition of *Perdurabo,* and every other biography of this controversial figure, I readily agree."

> —Oz Fritz, music producer and engineer

"Richard Kaczynski's *Perdurabo: The Life of Aleister Crowley* is a meticulously researched biography of a person whose reputation has been distorted by rumors and misinformation. Crowley will probably remain a controversial figure for many, but the readers of *Perdurabo* will be in a position to assess his life and work based on evidence, and Kaczynski should be congratulated for providing it in abundance."

> —Gordan Djurdjevic, sessional lecturer, Simon Fraser University

Praise for the first edition:

"Several recently-published biographies of Crowley do justice, for the most part, to his life and works. But their offerings now stand like skeletal frames of unfinished houses next to Kaczynski's magnificently constructed edifice. Every brick is set in place with the mortar of meticulous research and insight. Thank you, Dr. Kaczynski. I've waited thirty-five years for this."

> —Lon Milo DuQuette, author of *The Magick of Aleister Crowley*

"At long last, the world has a balanced and readable biography that reflects how magick shaped every facet of Aleister Crowley's life. And Dr. Kaczynski doesn't dismiss magick as humbug or mumbo-jumbo but validates it as a legitimate method of spiritual development meriting serious study."

> —Christopher S. Hyatt, PhD, author of *Undoing Yourself*

"Dr. Kaczynski brings two unique qualifications to this massive biography of the prophet and master of magick Aleister Crowley: he is both a university professor who moves comfortably in research institutions (and the masses of data contained therein) and a practicing adept of [Crowley's] Thelemic magical system. This is a magnificent book and is highly recommended."

> —James Wasserman, author of *The Militia of Heaven* and *Art and Symbols of the Occult.*

"*[Perdurabo]* is the best and most rigorous treatment of Crowley's life ever published. Essential reading for anyone who wants to know more about this remarkable man."

> —*Cardiff University Pagan Society* magazine

RICHARD KACZYNSKI

PERDURABO

THE LIFE OF ALEISTER CROWLEY

REVISED AND EXPANDED EDITION

North Atlantic Books
Berkeley, California

Published by
North Atlantic Books
Berkeley, California

Cover photo courtesy of Ordo Templi Orientis
Cover design by Paula Morrison
Printed in the United States of America

Quotations from the works of Aleister Crowley © Ordo Templi Orientis, International Headquarters, Postfach 33 20 12, D-14180 Berlin, Germany.

Perdurabo: The Life of Aleister Crowley is sponsored and published by the Society for the Study of Native Arts and Sciences (dba North Atlantic Books), an educational nonprofit based in Berkeley, California, that collaborates with partners to develop cross-cultural perspectives, nurture holistic views of art, science, the humanities, and healing, and seed personal and global transformation by publishing work on the relationship of body, spirit, and nature.

North Atlantic Books' publications are available through most bookstores. For further information, visit our website at www.northatlanticbooks.com or call 800-733-3000.

Library of Congress Cataloging-in-Publication Data

Kaczynski, Richard.
    Perdurabo : the life of Aleister Crowley / Richard Kaczynski. — Rev. and expanded ed.
        p. cm.
    ISBN 978-1-55643-899-8
    1. Crowley, Aleister, 1875–1947. 2. Occultists—Great Britain—Biography.
3. Authors, English—20th century—Biography. I. Title.
    BF1598.C7K33 2010
    130.92—dc22
    [B]   2010014721

6 7 8 9 SHERIDAN 20 19 18

Printed on recycled paper

North Atlantic Books is committed to the protection of our environment.
We partner with FSC-certified printers using soy-based inks and
print on recycled paper whenever possible.

Acknowledgments

The twenty-first century has witnessed a major reassessment of Aleister Crowley's place in modern culture, making this updated biography most timely. Evidence of Crowley's popularity is ubiquitous. BBC Two's 2002 poll for the *100 Greatest Britons* ranked Crowley at seventy-three, just ahead of Robert the Bruce; since then, his portrait has been added to London's National Portrait Gallery. When *Rolling Stone* asked Paul McCartney what accounts for the Beatles' enduring popularity, he answered:

> I think it's basically magic. There is such as thing as magic, and the Beatles were magic.
>
> It depends on what you believe life is. Life is an energy field, a bunch of molecules. And these particular molecules formed to make these four guys, who then formed into this band called the Beatles and did all that work. I have to think that was something metaphysical. Something alchemic. Something that must be thought of as magic—with a *k*.[1]

Actor Robert Downey Jr. offered a remarkable description of how he prepared for his *Iron Man* audition through a combination of ceremonial magic and compulsive rehearsal of every possible delivery of his lines:

> I had amendments and ancillaries and pop-ups for every part of the scene—if it went off in one direction I could add A, B, or C. It was madness, but also the most positively reinforced ritual I've ever performed. If Aleister Crowley had a younger brother—it was that type of s---.[2]

Comic book author and self-professed magician Alan Moore—whose *Watchmen* made *Time* magazine's list of "All-Time 100 Greatest Novels"—features Crowleyan themes prominently in *Promethea* (1999–2005) and *The League of Extraordinary Gentlemen, Volume III: Century* (2009–2011). Meanwhile, Martin Hayes and Roy Huteson Stewart's graphic novel *Crowley: Wandering the Waste* will be released in late 2010. And on television, the first balanced documentary on him, *Aleister Crowley: The Beast 666,* aired in Canada in 2007 and the United States in 2009.[3]

The result of all this exposure is that Crowley's works are in high demand, landing him on the American Book Exchange's list of the top ten best-selling authors.[4] His desirable first editions were also the subject of a 2008 article in *Book and Magazine Collector* and the 2009 coffee-table book *The Wickedest Books in the World*.[5] Similar interest in his artwork is attested by two 2008 exhibitions: at the Palais de Tokyo from May 29 to June 29, and at the Pompidou Center from June 5 to June 29.

In academia, where magic has become an accepted area of religious studies, Crowley was the subject of several papers in the first decade of the twenty-first century,[6] and an anthology of new academic papers on Aleister Crowley has been prepared under the editorship of Henrik Bogdan and Martin P. Starr. On April 16, 2008, the first academic panel devoted entirely to Aleister Crowley was held at the conference "Twenty Years and More: Research into Minority Religions, New Religious Movements and 'the New Spirituality.'" Outside of religious studies, Crowley has also turned up in studies of politics,[7] science,[8] and drug culture.[9] These subjects—including current perspectives on his careers in mountain climbing and theater—are reflected in this revised and expanded edition of *Perdurabo*, along with a great deal of new original research.

This new edition would not have been possible without the kind assistance of many people. The full list goes back to 1987, when I undertook writing the first edition. It is personally overwhelming. I feel truly blessed, and wish to express my greatest appreciation and gratefulness to the following people:

Hymenaeus Beta—my friend, counsel and comrade from the very beginning—granted me free access to the OTO Archives, permitted me to quote from the published and unpublished works of Aleister Crowley, allowed me to reproduce pictures of and by Crowley, and helped in countless other ways. This book would never have happened without his help.

L. Page Brunner was my navigator and an indispensable research assistant both in London and during the Great Road Trip of 1990. Both she and Kate McPherson offered encouragement, moral support, and friendship during the years of writing the first draft. Kevin Saari did tremendous detective work and uncovered important legal documents at the National Archives.

Clive Harper generously shared photocopies, sent scans, exchanged currency, and provided many helpful comments on both the original and expanded editions; I am grateful for his continued friendship and fine madness.

Both help and hospitality were kindly offered by Nicholas Culpeper and family, Tony Ianotti, Martin Starr, Jan Henson Dow and Robert Schroder.

The following people generously shared their knowledge with me: T. M. Caldwell, Jerry Cornelius, Lloyd Currey, Andrew Dickos, Christina Foyle, R. A. Gilbert, Ian Glover, Kenneth Grant, Amy Hale, George M. Harper, Christina Oakley Harrington, Bill Heidrick, Michael Holroyd, Andrew Jones, P. R. König, Mishlen Linden, Richard Londraville, Robert Lund, Sheila Mann, Louis Martinié, Michela Megna, Keith Richmond, Phyllis Seckler,

Leslie Shepard, Paul Sieveking, Ken Spencer, Timothy d'Arch Smith, Roger Staples, Gerald Suster, Brad Verter, Clint Warren, Oliver Wilkinson and John Yorke. Kenneth Walters at Wayne State University helped me identify and translate Catullus.

Access to the archival, rare book, and manuscript collections of their respective institutions was facilitated by: Glyn Hughes (Alpine Club); Jeff Twine (American Society for Psychical Research); Charles Greifenstein and Earle E. Spamer (American Philosophical Society); Marguerite Gillezeau (Ascham School); John Jordan and Margaret J. Cox (BBC); C. M. Hall and Elizabeth Wells (British Library); Margaret E. Pamplin (Cambridge University); Jennie Bradshaw (Christ Church, Oxford); John L. Sorger (Cleveland Public Library); Tony Scott (Climbers' Club); Bernard Crystal (Columbia University); Averil J. Kadis (Enoch Pratt Free Library); Emil P. Moschella (FBI Freedom of Information–Privacy Acts Section); Martin Cherry (Freemason's Hall, London); Amy Daugherty and Carolyn A. Davis (George Arents Research Library); Hannah Westall (Girton College); Marilyn Jones (Grand Lodge of Michigan); Jane Philpot, Alys Blakeway and Jane Harris (Hampshire Archives); Elspeth Healey, Linda Briscoe Myers and Cathy Henderson (Harry Ransom Humanities Research Center); Pamela Madsen, Micah Hoggatt and Susan Halpert (Harvard Theatre Collection); Claire Sawyer (Henry Moore Institute); Roberta Carew (Kambala); Nigel Walsh (Leeds Art Gallery); Chuck Kelly (Library of Congress); Patricia Methven and I. Hunter (Liddell Hart Centre for Military Archives); Saundra Taylor (Lilly Library); Glen Longacre (National Archives, Chicago); David Pfeiffer (National Archives, College Park); Megan Williams (National Library of Australia); D. B. Lloyd (National Library of Wales); Valerie Wingfield, Lola L. Szladits, John D. Stinson and Dorothy Swerdlove (New York Public Library); R. Russell Maylone (Northwestern University); Charles Mann (Pennsylvania State University); Debby Cramer (Presbyterian Ladies' College); Charles Greene and Jean F. Preston (Princeton University); Kathy Lazenbatt (Royal Asiatic Society); Rachel Rowe (Royal Commonwealth Society Library, Cambridge); Joy Wheeler (Royal Geographical Society); Robin Campbell (Scottish Mountaineering Club); David C. Braasch and David Koch (Southern Illinois University at Carbondale); Jim Andrighetti, Warwick Hirst and John Murphy (State Library of New South Wales); Tony Marshall (State Library of Victoria); Helen Fisher (University of Birmingham); Lesley Hart (University of Cape Town); Ann Caiger, Michael Olson and Dorothy (UCLA); Nancy Shawcross (University of Pennsylvania); Dr. H. Rorlich (University of Southern California); Lara Wilson and John Frederick (University of Victoria); Jack Rossi and Robin D. Wear (University of Virginia); Sharon Snow (Wake Forest University); W. F. Ryan and Patricia Killiard (Warburg Institute); Kevin Ray (Washington University in St. Louis); and Pat Sewell (West Yorkshire Archive, Calderdale), as well as the staff of the Beinecke Rare Book and Manuscript Library at Yale

University, Harvard University, Virginia University, University of Illinois at Urbana–Champaign, and Archibald Stevens Alexander Library.

The following people either granted or helped with photo clearances and permissions: William Breeze (Ordo Templi Orientis); Adam Garel-Frantzen (Getty Images); Scott Hobbs (Cameron Foundation); J. D. Holmes; Cara Jones (Rogers, Coleridge & White Literary Agency); Kathy Lazenbatt (Royal Asiatic Society); Sarah Lewin (Hampshire Records Office); Pamela Madsen (Harvard Theatre Collection); Kappy Mintie (Curatorial Assistance); Carmella Napoleone (Harvard Imaging Services); Tony Naylor; François Quiviger (Warburg Institute Archives); Keith Richmond; Timothy d'Arch Smith; Tony Stansfeld-Jones; Adi Warring (Swiss Foundation for Alpine Research); Joy Wheeler (Royal Geographical Society); and Francis Wyndham.

My bibliographic quests were abetted by many book dealers; exceptional assistance came from J. D. Holmes, Glen Houghton, Paul Hudson, Michael Kolson, Darcy Küntz, Tony Naylor, Todd Pratum, Helen Parsons Smith, Dr. Paul P. Ricchio, Keith Richmond, Marilyn Rinn, and Robert Thibodeau.

Kristin Frasier read the original manuscript and provided many helpful suggestions. Rafael Aguilar, Kenneth Blight, Kayla Block, Craig Dickson, Paul Feazey, Christian Hartman, Robert Paul Howard, W. Adam Mandelbaum, Jason Michaelson, Holy Pardieu, David A. Poole, Phyllis Seckler, Martin P. Starr, Evan Verbanic, and Clint Warren brought corrections to my attention.

Dr. Chris Hyatt and Jim Wasserman made the first edition of this book happen.

I extend my deepest appreciation to all the wonderful people at North Atlantic Books who recognized that the time was right to update Crowley's biography, including my editor, Erin Wiegand; copy editors Christopher Church and Jordan Tulin; art director Paula Morrison; and also Doug Reil, Philip Smith, Kat Engh, and Susan Bumps.

Finally, I give thanks to my wife Kerry Kurowski, whose unconditional support and enthusiasm helped to see me through the huge undertaking of this revision.

Contents

Birthday	1
A Place to Bury Strangers	32
The Golden Dawn	56
The Mountain Holds a Dagger	81
A Rose by Any Other Name	109
The Five Peaks	131
The Great White Brotherhood	157
Singer of Strange and Obscene Gods	177
The Vision and the Voice	191
Aleister Through the Looking Glass	216
Ordo Templi Orientis	249
Chokmah Days	277
Amalantrah	320
The Abbey of Thelema	355
Adonis	381
Eccentrics in Exile	397
The French Connection	423
Beast Bites Back	444
The Black Magic Libel Case	472
The War of the Roses (and the Battle of the Book)	482
The Book of Thoth	500
The Great Turkey Tragedy: Or Heirs Apparent	524
Epilogue	553
Notes	563
References	669
Picture Credits	683
Index	685

CHAPTER ONE

Birthday

Darkness swallowed the unfamiliar room as two men pulled a hood over his head. The floor was cold and hard beneath his knees, and through the door he could hear the muffled sounds of knocking and speaking. He counted two … three … four voices at least, followed by silence: a heavy stillness filled only by his breath. Aleister Crowley feared for his life.

London's Euston Road was far from the safe, nurturing campus of Trinity College; farther from his Redhill, Surrey, home; and farther still from the Swiss Alps, where training on the Schönbühl Glacier resulted in his fateful meeting with the man who sent him into this ordeal. For Crowley, the chain of events leading to this situation was every bit as real and confining as the rope now wound about his waist. The sensation of the tightening restraints stilled the images of his life and snapped him to the present. When tumblers fell and hinges creaked, excitement replaced his fear. It began.

"Child of Earth," commanded the man beside him, "arise and enter the Path of Darkness."

Blindfolded and bound, Crowley staggered awkwardly to his feet, advancing but a step before the sensation of a sharp rap striking the floor in front of his feet froze him in place. A voice from the doorway replied, "Very Honored Hierophant, is it your pleasure that the candidate be admitted?"

"It is," the Hierophant intoned solemnly from the room beyond. "Fratres Stolistes and Dadouchos, assist the Kerux in the admission."

The one blocking the doorway, evidently the Kerux, addressed Crowley in a loud clear voice. "Child of Earth, unpurified and unconsecrated, thou canst not enter our Sacred Hall."

A wet finger reached under the hoodwink and traced a cross on his forehead as a new voice declared, "Child of Earth, I consecrate thee with water." Next, smoky incense, sweet and thick, wafted over his masked face. "Child of Earth," another announced, "I purify thee with fire." Once the officers Stolistes and Dadouchos finished these appointed tasks, an unknown hand pulled him

1

forward and led him stumbling blindly through the room. Finally, he heard the voice of the Hierophant entreat him with grave authority. "Child of Earth, why dost thou request admission to this Order?"

Prompted by his guide, Crowley stammered, "My soul is wandering in darkness, seeking for the light of occult knowledge."

"Thou wilt kneel on both knees. Give me your right hand, which I place on this sacred and sublime symbol." The Child of Earth heard several others step close as the Hierophant guided his hand onto a wooden triangle on the table before him. "Place thy left hand in mine, bow thy head, repeat thy full name at length, and say after me."

He swallowed dryly as the achievements of his short life— from publishing his first book of poetry to setting records for sea cliff and mountain climbing— paled in comparison to the weight of this moment. Crowley parted his lips and spoke. "I, Aleister Crowley, in the presence of the Lord of the Universe and of this Hall of Neophytes of the Order of the Golden Dawn in the Outer, do of my own free will and accord hereby and hereon most solemnly pledge myself to keep secret this Order, its name, the name of its members, and the proceedings which take place at its meetings, from all and every person in the whole world who is outside the pale of the Order. I furthermore promise and swear that I will divulge nothing whatsoever concerning this Order to the outside world, in case either of my resignation, demission, or expulsion therefrom, after the completion of my admission.

"I will not suffer myself to be hypnotized, or mesmerized, nor will I place myself in such a passive state that any uninitiated person, power, or being may cause me to lose control of my thoughts, words, or actions. Neither will I use my occult powers for any evil purposes. These points I generally and severally, upon this sacred and sublime symbol, swear to observe without evasion, equivocation, or mental reservation of any kind whatsoever; under the no less penalty on the violation of any or either of them of being expelled from this Order, as a wilfully perjured wretch, void of all moral worth, and unfit for the society of all right and true persons."

Parched, he whispered the oath's solemn and stunning conclusion. "And in addition, under the awful penalty of voluntarily submitting myself to a deadly and hostile current of will set in motion by the chiefs of the Order, by which I should fall slain and paralyzed without visible weapon." A sharpened steel blade pressed against the nape of his neck as he spoke these words, then withdrew just as suddenly. "So help me the Lord of the Universe and my own higher soul."

The Hierophant commanded, "Let the candidate rise." He did. "Child of Earth, long hast thou dwelt in darkness. Quit the night and seek the day."

Someone whisked the hoodwink from his head, and amid the images that burst onto his vision, he saw the scarlet-robed Hierophant. He was in his midforties, but clad in mystic robes and insignia, he might as well have been immortal. He fixed the young man with his eye, raised his staff above the candidate's head, and proclaimed, "Frater Perdurabo, we receive thee into the Order of the Golden Dawn." *Perdurabo* was the Latin motto Crowley had chosen to describe his spiritual aspirations in the order. It was Latin for "I shall endure to the end," from Mark 13:13: "but he that shall endure unto the end, the same shall be saved."

Standing in this temple of the Order of the Golden Dawn, beaming with relief and joy, he knew he had discovered the Secret Sanctuary. On Friday, November 18, 1898, Aleister Crowley—mountaineer, poet, and Seeker of the Light—was reborn as Frater Perdurabo.[1]

Four generations before Aleister Crowley was born, his great-great-grandfather Thomas Crowley (c. 1713–1787) rebelled against his parents' religion, self-published his tracts and poetry, and sought to avert the American Revolution by pitching his political schemes to Benjamin Franklin. Thomas was a general merchant who lived in London with his wife and seven children at 73 Gracechurch Street, with a country estate in Walworth. As a "religious controversialist and political writer,"[2] Thomas Crowley penned over thirty books, booklets, and broadsheets, many criticizing his Quaker faith and its opposition to tithes and taxes. Works like *Dissertations on the Pecuniary Testimonies of the People Called Quakers, Relative Their Refusing to Pay Tithes and Church-Rates, as also Fines or Assessments Respecting the Militia or Military Service* (c. 1773) and *To the Superstitious Priests, Lovers of Their Own Power, and to Their Silly Tools of Priestcraft, Quacks and Money-mongers, among the Misled People Called Quakers* (no date) did not endear him to church leadership. Indeed, Smith's bibliography of Quaker-authored works disclaimed that "Few (if any) of the publications of this Friend were approved of, but rather disapproved of and testified against;"[3] in February of 1774, Thomas Crowley was disowned by the Devonshire House monthly meeting.[4] That same month, his daughter Ann (1757–1774) died short of her seventeenth birthday after a prolonged illness; inspired by her pious sickbed statements, Thomas published these as *Some Expressions of Ann Crowley.*[5] He blazed his own religious path, although "regretting that his unorthodox tendencies made life difficult for his family, who maintained their Quaker association."[6]

Many of his political writings, appearing under the nom de plume "Amor Patriæ" (Latin, "a lover of his country"),[7] addressed the taxation without representation disputes between the crown and the American colonies. Despite disparaging the colonists' protests as shortsighted, he agreed in principle with their objections, and urged giving parliamentary seats to colonial representatives lest war result. He advocated this message through works like *Observations and Propositions for an Accommodation between Great Britain and Her Colonies* (1768) and *Dissertations, on the Grand Dispute between Great-Britain and America* (1774). He also corresponded with Benjamin Franklin in an effort to mediate the escalating political tensions.[8] Franklin ultimately dismissed him as hopelessly obsessed, even though his concerns about war proved prescient. After the Revolutionary War, Crowley's political writing ceased.

Thomas Crowley died a widower at Walworth on December 17, 1787, leaving his children an estate in land, buildings, stocks, and cash valued at several thousand pounds.[9]

Although his son Thomas has been described as "a successful business man,"[10] Aleister's great-grandfather Thomas Crowley (1753–1809) first appears in London's business directories in 1777 in the decidedly unpleasant and hazardous trade of currier, tanner, and leatherworker at 35 Camomile Street. Eleven years later, in 1788, he became bankrupt; 1790 was his last appearance in the directories.[11] From these humble beginnings, four of Thomas Crowley's eight children would establish the family fortune that would be such a formative influence on Aleister Crowley's life.[12]

Three of his sons—Abraham (1795–1864), Charles Sedgefield (c. 1798–1868), and Henry (1793–1857)[13]—followed very similar paths. Like their father, and his father before him, they supported the abolition of slavery.[14] All three married into the Curtis family of Alton: Abraham married Charlotte Curtis (1801–1892) in 1822; Charles took her younger sister Emma (1804–1845) as his second wife in 1838; and Henry married their sister Elizabeth (1806–1900) in 1845.[15] Together these brothers formed a business partnership to purchase, on August 28, 1821, the Brewhouse in Turk Street, Alton; it had been founded in 1763 by James B. Baverstock (1741–1815), who pioneered the use of scientific instrumentation in brewing (he was the first person to use a hydrometer) and laid the foundation for saccharometry (measuring the amount of sugar in a solution).[16] The Crowley family's Quaker faith opposed the production and consumption of hard spirits and intemperance through any kind of liquor, but there were no prohibitions against brewing, and at least a dozen Quakers in the eighteenth century were prominently involved in the industry.[17] Indeed, Grey notes that the family already owned a brewery at Waddon, near Croydon, Surrey, which had been in operation for two hundred years.[18]

Under the name A. C. S. & H. Crowley, the new brewery established itself in Croydon and Alton and boomed with the opening of its Alton ale houses. By offering a glass of ale and a sandwich (ham was a specialty) for four pence, the Crowleys not only competed with the four-penny ale offered by brewers like Mann of Mile End Road,[19] but in doing so they also essentially invented the pub lunch. Their shops were "for the most part open-fronted with a clean marble counter with four or five handsome brass engines; small plates and glasses were provided with a display of bread, biscuits, cakes, etc."[20]

No less than Charles Dickens noted the growing popularity of Crowley's ale houses, writing that Alton's growth boom included "a feeding place, 'established to supply the Railway public with a first-rate sandwich and a sparkling glass of Crowley's Ale.'"[21] Similarly, the 1863 article "Tales out of School" recounts a sixteen-year-old's first visit to the shop:

The libation was obtained at a little shop hard by, where 'Alton Ale' was advertised in large black letters on a ground of white canvas, with a further announcement that you might have a glass of ale and a sandwich for fourpence. It arrived in two bright pewter pots with spouts, and was accompanied with three tall and narrow glasses, three to a pint, which would give four glasses of ale to each of us.[22]

Yates's *Recollections and Experiences* recounted lunching at Crowley's Alton ale house, whose shops were "exceedingly popular with young men who did not particularly care about hanging round the bars or taverns."[23] Crowley's pub lunches offered high-quality food, and in time added other items like Banbury cakes. This prompted competitors to introduce the "Melton Mowbray Pork Pie," and ultimately the luncheon counter and grill room.[24]

The tremendous success and spread of the Alton ale houses also inspired parodies, with a beer shop in City Road announcing "A Glass of Ale and an Electric Shock for Fourpence."[25] In response to their imitators, the Crowleys ran the following notice in the *Times:*

CROWLEYS' ALTON ALE.—Being desirous that the public should not be deceived in purchasing a spurious article for their Alton ale, A.C.S. and H. Crowley beg to inform them that they have no Alton ale stores or any agent in London, except at their ALTON ALE WHARF, Upper Fore-street, Lambeth. And whereas houses have been opened in imitation of their customers on the new "ale and sandwich plan," they further state that they do not supply ale to any such house unless the name of Crowley is conspicuously written up.—Alton, June, 1843.[26]

In subsequent years, Crowley's ale stores expanded into London locations like Bishopsgate, Kensington Park Terrace, London Bridge, Kingston, Fenchurch Street, and Wandsworth Road,[27] with distribution channels to match. Their barge Amelia carried product along the Thames, while *In Praise of Ale* declared "the LSWR [London and South Western Railway] transports 'Alton Ale' in large quantities to London."[28] Indeed, their commercial success was so great that one city newspaper joked:

Some sensation was excited in the city towards the close of the day (yesterday), in consequence of a report that government intends to legalize the sale of the Bank of England, and that a celebrated purveyor of ham and beef had made the directors a liberal offer on behalf of an Alton ale brewer; but we think the rumor is premature.[29]

The British census provides a fairer picture of the company's growth: In 1851, Abraham Crowley described himself as a "brewer and maltster employing forty-six men."[30] A decade later, he employed three foremen, eight maltsters, and forty-nine laborers (or sixty men in all).[31]

Abraham Crowley's is the name most closely associated with the family brewing business. As a young man, he apprenticed to the Quaker brewer Thomas Ashby (1762–1841) of Staines, who was married to his cousin Kitty (1760–1796).[32] On December 7, 1821—four months after buying the Baverstock brewery—Abraham and his brothers partnered with Thomas and Charles Ashby on a ninety-nine-year counterpart lease for the Barley Mow Public House in Alton.[33] Abraham's career branched out around 1839, when he became one of the first emigration agents employed by the newly founded New Zealand Company, which promoted the systematic colonization of British settlements in Wellington, Nelson, Wanganui, and Dunedin. New Zealand was a new and untested emigration destination at the time, but under Abraham Crowley's agency, his hometown of Alton had the highest rate of applications in all of England.[34] As a highly successful businessman, he gave back to his community by supporting both boys' and girls' schools.[35] With the acquisition of expansive hops gardens near Alton, the family began to hold annual "hop parties," a tradition that his widow, Charlotte, continued after his death.[36]

Abraham Crowley (1795–1864), founder of A. C. S. & H. Crowley.

His sons continued the family business, with Abraham Curtis (1823–1878) and Frederick (1825–1910) tending to the Alton brewery, while Alfred (1824–1876) and Philip (1837–1900) partnered in its Croydon location.[37] Frederick attended University College, London; was a member of the Alton Local Board for thirty years, and chairman of the twelve-member Local Board of Alton (and its successor, the Alton Urban District Council) for thirty-seven years; and donated, on May 1, 1867, a school at the northeast end of High Street large enough for 150 children.[38] Abraham's son Philip distinguished himself through avid interests in, and generous patronage of, horticulture and natural history. His collections of exotic butterflies and over four thousand bird eggs were considered the world's finest. He was also a writer on entomology, lecturer at the Society of Arts, president of the Croydon Natural History and Scientific Society, treasurer of the Royal Horticultural Society, master of the Gardeners' Company, vice chairman of the British Ornithologists' Club, fellow of the Linnean, Zoological, and Entomological societies, and a member of the Croydon Microscopical Club. He died on December 20, 1900, and was buried on Christmas Eve in Shirley, near Croydon. He bequeathed his bird egg collection to the Natural History Museum in South Kensington.[39]

Frederick Crowley (1825–1910, left) and Philip Crowley (1837–1900, right).

On March 24, 1877—when Aleister Crowley was seventeen months old—the family sold their business to Abraham Curtis Crowley's future son-in-law, Harry Percy Burrell (1852–1938), who continued to run the family business as Crowley & Co.[40] Watney Combe Reid & Co. acquired Crowley & Co. in 1947, the year that Aleister Crowley died.

The most relevant of Thomas Crowley's sons, however, is Aleister's grandfather, Edward Crowley (c. 1788–1856). He was Thomas Crowley's first son, the third of eight children. He wed Mary Sparrow (1788–1868) of West Hill, Wandsworth, in London on August 21, 1823,[41] and together they had four children: Jonathan Sparrow (1826–1888), Mary Elizabeth (c. 1828–1880), Sarah Maria (1829–1856), and Aleister's father, Edward (c. 1830–1887).[42]

Together with his brother Charles Sedgefield Crowley, Edward Crowley Sr. diversified the family's wealth into railways as early as 1836–1837.[43] Throughout the 1840s and into the 1850s, both brothers served as directors of many emerging railways: Charles Sedgefield Crowley directed the Direct London and Portsmouth Railway; London and South Western Railway; Colchester, Stour Valley, Sudbury and Halstead Railway; London and Croydon Railway; and its successor, the London, Brighton and South Coast Railway. Edward Crowley, meanwhile, was deputy chairman of the London and Brighton Railway, and a director of the Brighton and Chichester Railway and Brighton, Chichester and Portsmouth Railway. All three companies were part of the 1846 merger that formed the London, Brighton and South Coast Railway, which Edward directed along with his brother. In addition, he directed the Isle of Wight Railway and the Dublin, Belfast and Coleraine Junction Railway. He was also provisional director of three proposed railways: the London, Warwick, Leamington and Kidderminster Railway; the London Central Railway Terminus Company; and the Irish North Midland Railway.[44] He even held shares in the Great Western Railway of Canada.[45] A Private Bill Office list of 1846 railway subscribers reflects their wealth: that year, Edward Crowley had invested £97,408, while his brother had invested £56,850.[46]

Edward and Charles Sedgefield synergized the family brewing and railway interests. Mere days passed between Edward Crowley's appointment to the London and Brighton Railway and A. C. S. & H. Crowley's "beware of imitators" ad in the *Times*.[47] Writing about the British railway system, Henry O'Neil describes a placard with the slogan: "In the course of my excavations I have brought to light a board whereon is painted in large letters these words: ESTABLISHED TO SUPPLY THE PUBLIC WITH CROWLEY'S ALTON ALE.'"[48] In 1846, Director Charles Sedgefield Crowley vocally supported the London and South West Railway's proposed line between Farnham and Alton, which would connect Alton to London. He "spoke of the great want of a line to Alton" and "considered that the prosperity of Alton depended on the obtaining this line."[49] Four years later, the debate among the directors continued. For instance, Sergeant Gazelee

> remembered the glowing picture which on a former occasion the chairman drew of the vast quantities of Crowley's Alton ale which would be conveyed to London by this proposed line, and he remembered how he trembled for the London brewers with such a dismal prospect before them [laughter]; but he never heard of any other traffic they were likely to get besides the Alton ale. Would they get a single passenger more by extending the line from Farnham to Alton?[50]

The plan eventually passed, with a gala on Monday, July 26, 1852, as a train ran from London to Farnham, then continued the nine miles on to Alton for the first time. Thereafter, as *In Praise of Ale* noted, the London and South Western Railway shipped large quantities of Alton ale to London.[51]

In October 1854, in his sixty-sixth year, Edward Crowley delivered an address to the Clapham Athenæum, *The Age We Live In: High Art No Evidence of a High State of Civilization*. A reflection on the great civilizations of the past that have crumbled, Edward Crowley cautioned that, without God, modern civilization is subject to the same fate; particularly worrisome trends included smoking, drinking, gambling, cursing, slavery, socialism, spiritualism, labor strikes, women's rights, women's bonnets, dancing saloons, and children referring to their parents as "governor."[52] A little over a year later—on February 16. 1856—Edward Crowley died at his house in Lavender Hill, Surrey, appointing as his executors his sons Jonathan Sparrow and Edward, his son-in-law John Thrupp, and his friend Joseph Prestwick.[53]

When Charles Sedgefield Crowley, the last of his four brothers, died in 1868, he left his nephews—Abraham Crowley's four sons, Abraham, Alfred, Frederick, and Philip, all co-owners of the family brewery and executors of his will—£48,000, his shares in the Great Western Railway, and his mines in Mexico. His remaining nieces and nephews—including Aleister's father, Edward—divided the rest of his estate. Charles's cellar of over two hundred cases of wine—old sherry, port, champagne, and the like—was auctioned off on May 1, 1868.[54] Shortly thereafter, Aleister's grandmother, Mary, succumbed to liver disease after twenty years and died on May 29, 1868, at age eighty.[55]

Jonathan Sparrow Crowley, a civil engineer, entered the railway business following a November 1, 1852, collision on the Brighton railway managed by his father, Edward Crowley.[56] Jonathan was at the railway's London terminal when he learned that an express passenger train had crashed with a freight train. Rumors of horrible injuries stoked fears for his father's welfare, until a telegram assured him that Edward Crowley was safe at dinner (and no other serious injuries had resulted from the crash). To ensure that such accidents never happened again, Jonathan quickly invented "Crowley's Safety Switch and Self-acting Railway Signals." On November 8—a week after the accident—he received provisional protection for his "improvements in the means of, or apparatus for, working the signals and switches on railways."[57] He became a member of the Institution of Civil Engineers,[58] and a fellow of both the Ethnological Society of London and the Royal Geographical Society of London.[59] Jonathan Sparrow Crowley married Agnes Pope of Marylebone on May 14, 1853[60] and had three children: Jonathan Edward (b. 1854, died in infancy), Agnes (1856–1916), and Claude Edmund (1865–1937).[61] Their mother died of tuberculosis in 1869 at age forty-three,[62] leaving him with a three-year-old son and thirteen-year-old daughter. Within three years, he married the children's governess, Anne Higginbotham (1840–1921), on April 4, 1872.[63]

Of Edward and Mary's second child, Mary Elizabeth, Aleister Crowley makes no mention. Born around 1828, she married Charles Ebeneezer Burgess

(c. 1833–1890) in 1869, and lived in Leamington, Warwickshire, until her death in 1880.[64] Given that she lived near Aleister Crowley's childhood home, it is likely that he knew this aunt.[65]

However, Aleister Crowley would never meet his aunt Sarah, who died around age twenty-seven, nearly two decades before he was born. She was the third child of Edward Crowley senior, marrying the widower John Thrupp (1817–1870) on September 21, 1854[66] and, tragically, dying within seventeen months.[67] Thrupp was a solicitor and writer who began practicing in 1838, and in the early 1840s published a series of historical law tracts; he evidently remained cordial with the Crowleys despite remarrying: he was an executor of his father-in-law's will, and—in partnership with Robert Dixon—represented the Crowley family in 1865.[68]

Edward Crowley (c. 1830–1887), father of Aleister Crowley.

Although Edward Crowley Jr. is described in the 1851 census as an engineer like his older brother Jonathan, Aleister Crowley noted that his father "was educated as an engineer, but never practised his profession."[69] Indeed, one wonders if he ever worked at all: Edward Crowley appears in postal directories and membership lists as "esquire," indicating that he was upper gentry. The 1861 census lists his occupation/social status as "freeholder, householder," while in 1881 he was "receiving income from houses and dividends."[70]

Around 1853, the brothers Edward and Jonathan partnered with Robert White, a zinc oxide manufacturer of King William Street, to form the company Crowley, White & Crowley. According to a notice in the *Times,* Robert White's business partner, Langston Scott, had a patented process for manufacturing zinc oxide, which was a safe and economical substitute for white lead in the manufacture of paint; on his retirement on October 13, 1853, Scott vested the rights with Crowley, White & Crowley.[71] Despite having won prizes at the Great Exhibition in Hyde Park in 1851 and securing the prestigious patronage of the Admiralty and the French government, the partnership dissolved in 1855.[72] It is possible that Aleister Crowley alluded to his father's business venture when he wrote in his commentary on *The Book of the Law,* "'white' is 'what champaks, zinc oxide, sugar, etc., report to our eyesight.'"[73]

Shortly after dissolving this partnership, Edward Crowley, aged twenty-six, retired to devote himself to religion. He had been a devout Quaker from childhood, the dying utterance of the family's servant Anne—"Lost, lost, lost"— demonstrating to him the fate of those souls not saved by Jesus.[74] Breaking from his family's traditional Quaker roots, he became an Anglican clergyman,[75] but eventually converted to the fundamentalist evangelical sect known as the Plymouth Brethren or Darbyists.[76] By April 1861, he authored the tracts *Letters Stating Sundry Reasons for Not Returning to the Church of England* and *Cease to Do Evil, Learn to Do Well.* These were but the first of over one hundred that Edward Crowley would publish over the years as a preacher for the Brethren, earning him a mention in Knapp's 1932 *History of the Brethren.*

Notorious for frequent internal schisms, the Brethren movement ironically began with one man's protest against denominationalism. Edward Cronin (d. 1882), a Roman Catholic, moved to Dublin in 1825 and declined to affiliate with the local Anglican Church of Ireland. At a time when society judged men by their congregational membership, Cronin found himself ostracized by his neighbors. Citing Matthew 18:20 ("Where two or three are gathered together in my name, there am I in the midst of them"), Cronin claimed anyone could celebrate the Lord's supper, and thus began breaking bread with other religious outcasts. He claimed clerics, ministers, and priests were not only superfluous but also contrary to the will of God, since Matthew 18:20 clearly instructed worshipers to gather in the name of *God,* not of a priest.

Within two years (1827), his meetings attracted a follower in John Nelson Darby (1800–1882), who became so influential that his name was synonymous with the movement. In 1830, Darby left the Anglican priesthood to devote himself to the group, and his tract "The Nature and Unity of the Church of Christ" helped spread their message. In 1832, B. W. Newton invited Darby to organize his assembly in Plymouth and share its ministry. This he did, and Plymouth quickly became the movement's center.

While Darby spent much of his time traveling to support the Brethren, Plymouth attracted 1,200 members by 1845, including generals and admirals, scholars and linguists, and even English lords and other nobility—including a cousin of Queen Victoria. When he returned to Plymouth in 1845, Darby discovered Newton attempting to establish an independent church with himself as pastor. This contradicted the nondenominational and nonclerical ethos of the Brethren, and ultimately, Darby excommunicated Newton and his followers.

Within two years, the Brethren split into two factions: the Open Brethren, who broke bread with good people of other faiths, and the Exclusive Brethren, led by Darby, who shunned all non-Brethren as sinners. It was but the first of a series of schisms that led the Exclusive Brethren to refuse friendship with adherents of other Brethren variants, earning them the distinction of being "the narrowest and most bigoted sect on earth."[77] In 1879, the Exclusive Brethren went so far as to excommunicate their founder, Edward Cronin. Today, various branches are known by the names Darbyites, Newtonites, Mullerites, Grantites, Kellyites, Stuartites, Ravenites, Taylorites, etc.[78]

The Brethren believed the Bible—particularly the translation made by Darby—was divinely inspired and literally true. The faith was also pretribulational and premillenial: believers expected Jesus to return at any moment to rescue the faithful from the period of darkness about to begin. Long-term plans—including retirement and life insurance—disclosed lack of faith in Jesus' imminent arrival. All answers lurked within the Bible, the inevitable "It is written" or "Thus saith the Lord" with which they settled disputes, earning the Brethren the sarcastic designation of "walking Bibles."

Edward Crowley was a devout Exclusive Brother and a fiery, articulate clergyman. He distributed thousands of copies of his tracts through the mail and on the streets. He routinely took walking tours throughout England, where he would preach to the masses and draw large crowds for whom, at the time, proselytizing was a respected fad. At other times, he would simply stop unsuspecting fellows on the street and ask what they were doing; after they answered, he would reply, "and then?" This question would repeat until the other inevitably answered with something like, "Well, I suppose I shall die." This was the opening Crowley waited for, when he would interject the phrase he was known for: "Then you'd better *get right with God!*"[79] He would then add the wretched soul's name and address to his book and for years afterward send religious literature. Edward Crowley traveled so extensively that he could tell a person's hometown from his accent.

Eventually, he sold his shares in both the railway and the family brewery, reinvesting them in Amsterdam's waterworks. This move was evidently prompted by his religious convictions: Aleister Crowley reported that "my father would refuse to buy railway shares because railways were not mentioned in the Bible"[80] and later quoted his father as quipping sardonically that "he had been an abstainer for nineteen years, during which he had shares in a brewery. He had now ceased to abstain for some time, but all his money was invested in a waterworks."[81] The specific waterworks investments are unknown, but a likely contender is the highly successful Amsterdam Water Works Company, founded by English businessmen in 1865 and whose 1872 expansion drew thousands of workers to the company.

His new investment interests were quite likely what first brought him to the baths, spas, and waterworks of Leamington.

Emily Bertha Crowley, née Bishop (1848–1917).

To Emily Bertha Bishop (1848–1917), life must have felt like a fantasy. The youngest daughter of farmer John Bishop (c. 1793–1854) and his second wife Elizabeth Cole (1808–1896), Emily had gone from working in 1871 as governess for Kensington brewer Alexander Gordon to marrying, on November 19, 1874, the devout and independently wealthy Edward Crowley. The marriage took place at the register office in Kensington, witnessed by her brother Tom Bond and her half-sister Anne, along with the families of Edward's two siblings (Jonathan came with his daughter Agnes and second wife, Anne, while Mary came with her husband, Charles).[82] Because of her slight form and vaguely Asian appearance, she was dubbed "the little Chinese girl" at school. She had a talent with watercolors but, despite academic training, never pursued art as a career. Now she was joining her husband to raise a family in the beautiful and affluent health resort town of Leamington Spa. Warwickshire's spa on the river Leam was at the peak of a growth spurt that had transformed a sleepy little borough of just over five hundred into a newly incorporated town of 26,000 in 1875. Visitors flocked to its artesian wells and saline springs, which were advertised to relieve the symptoms of gout, rheumatism, "stiffness of tendons," and "other paralytic conditions." The gardens outside the Jephson and Royal Pump Rooms were likewise botanical spectacles. Emily was already into her third trimester of pregnancy late that summer when she moved to 30 Clarendon Square, about four blocks from the Leam.

Within six weeks, a sudden gale turned her idyll into a nightmare. On the Saturday morning of October 8, 1875, a violent storm struck Warwickshire, uprooting trees, breaking telegraph lines, and blocking roads. Flash floods turned fields into lakes, inundated the baths and gardens, and spewed a two-foot-deep river into the town's Great Western railroad station. The flood damaged crops, killed large numbers of livestock, and drowned two people. While it is unknown whether Emily was among those forced to flee in boats, it is doubtful her property escaped flood damage.[83]

When the storm abated and the flood slowly began to recede, she went into labor. On Tuesday, October 12, 1875, between the hours of eleven and midnight, Emily Crowley delivered a son to her husband. They dubbed him Edward, after his father and the father before him, with the middle name taken from his father's friend Alexander. Edward Alexander Crowley would not change his name to Aleister until adulthood, and to his family the child was simply known as Alick. He was tongue-tied, and within the first few days of his birth, a doctor cut the frenum that connected his tongue to the bottom of his mouth. Despite the intervention, he would never pronounce the letter *r* correctly. Within his first three months of life, he was baptized into the Plymouth faith.

Although previous biographers have portrayed Aleister Crowley's childhood as marred by religious intolerance, physical frailty, and the British school system, Crowley's accounts reveal a happy boyhood through age ten, and he enjoyed the privileges of wealth throughout childhood. Granted, marriage required his mother to convert; and despite the Bishop family being evangelical Christians, the Crowleys in true Exclusive form only associated with other Brethren. This estranged Emily from her two siblings, Tom Bond (1839–1920) and Ada Jane (1842–1896), and—from her father's first marriage—three half-siblings, John (1821–1900), William (b. 1822), and Anne (1824–1890). Likewise, Aleister recalled that "My father's religious opinions had tended to alienate him from his family."[84] Thus, Aleister Crowley's childhood recollections—primarily from his *Confessions* and his indictment of Victorian society, *The World's Tragedy*—are largely populated by his parents, the family servants, and other Brethren, such as his first governess, Mary Arkell (1838–1892), "a grey-haired lady with traces of beard upon her large flat face and a black dress"; Mary Carey (born c. 1813), the "orange-coloured old lady … who used to bring him oranges"; Emma (born c. 1829) and Susan Cowper (born c. 1838), "Plymouth sister old maids" whom he never particularly liked; and portly Sister Musty, who had delayed a prayer meeting for an hour by politely eating the food that Alick kept offering her.[85]

As the son of Exclusive Brethren, his was a Spartan childhood. The Crowleys did not celebrate the pagan festival of Christmas. Likewise, Brethren prohibitions forbade toys. When he learned to read at age four, Alick's primary text was the Bible. Recalling his father's sermon on the word *but*, Alick once read through the book, circling every occurrence of the word.[86] He idolized his father. Although they shared little sympathy or understanding, Alick would grow up to be more like him than he would ever realize.

Although he described Emily Crowley as "the best of all possible mothers,"[87] he was normally aloof toward her, regarding her as just another one of the servants.

Servants were but one of the luxuries Alick enjoyed as a child. Although most middle-class families in Victorian England had a servant—at the very least a "step girl" who scrubbed the front steps on Saturday mornings as a display of affluence for the neighbors—doctors, lawyers, and other professionals kept staffs of at least three: a cook, a parlor maid, and a house maid.[88] The Crowley household had four servants, identified in census records as Mary Gough (age thirty-one), Elizabeth Hanad (age twenty-six), Fanny Maples (age twenty-two), and William Soden (age seventeen).[89] This fourth servant would have filled the typical role of manservant to the household. While landed gentry and larger household estates boasted up to twenty servants, the Crowleys' employment of more servants than there were household members reveals their affluence.

Likewise, Crowley's accounts of his various residences, private tutors and boarding schools gives away the luxuries to which he was privy. Indeed his entire childhood is set among some of Britain's most notable locales. The family lived for five years in the resort town of Leamington Spa, stayed a while in Surrey near the Thames, then moved between various residences in and around London. Meanwhile, young Crowley attended boarding schools in places like Cambridge and Tonbridge (where he almost certainly attended the Tonbridge Schools, one of England's top educational institutions). While not at boarding school, he stayed with private tutors in locales like that international haven for the rich and famous, Torquay, in the English Riviera. Similarly, his teens were full of vacations climbing the hills, cliffs, and mountains of the Isle of Skye (Scotland), Beachy Head (England), Tyrol (Austria), and the Swiss Alps.

Crowley was unreservedly upbeat about his first decade of life. He fondly recalled the landmarks around Leamington Spa and Warwick such as Guy's Cliffe and Warwick Castle; memories of the weir, or dam, on the Leam river remained especially fond, so that weirs forever after took him home again. Crowley particularly recalled walks with his father down main street and through the green fields. On one occasion, his father warned him away from a clump of stinging nettles. "Will you take my word for it, or would you rather

learn by experience?" the patriarch cautioned his boy. The exuberant child
retorted, "I would rather learn by experience," and dove headlong into the
nettles. This pattern of chasing blindly after whatever captured his interest also
typified much of his adult life.

Equally formative in Crowley's life were the family's daily Bible readings:
after breakfast each morning, the three Crowleys and their four servants gathered in the dining room and took turns reading biblical verses aloud. Alick was
captivated by the unusual sounding names—such as those in his favorite chapter, Genesis 5—and voraciously absorbed his father's sermons on those familiar
passages. Nevertheless, it was the woman whom he regarded as little more than
one of the servants, his mother, who inspired Alick's greatest fascination with
the Bible: In moments of exasperation with her son, she would say he was the
beast prophesied in the Book of Revelation. This curious assertion piqued his
curiosity. The precocious youngster scurried back to his Bible and marveled at
its apocalyptic conclusion, describing the tribulations to befall mankind; the
appearance of the great beast 666, who branded his number on the foreheads of
his followers; and the war in heaven between the woman clothed with the sun
and the devouring beast. Heaven's angels, harps and miracles paled beside the
dragon, false prophet, and scarlet woman. He speculated on the message of this
story. And he pondered what it meant if his mother was right.

Alick was four years old on February 29, 1880—a leap year—when his sister,
Grace Mary Elizabeth, was born. She suffered convulsions and lived only four
hours.[90] When he was taken that day to see her body, Alick, too young to
understand the joys of birth and the loss of death, was indifferent. He could do
nothing about his sibling's demise, and failed to understand why his parents
bothered him with it.[91] Nevertheless, Alick would feel Grace Crowley's death
through the subsequent changes in his life. Barely three months later, at the end
of May, Edward Crowley left his home on the northwest side of Leamington.
Although his whereabouts during this time are unknown, over a year later, on
June 11, 1881, the Crowleys moved away from their painful memories to the
Grange in Redhill, Surrey, which Aleister would later recall as "really an
awfully nice place."[92]

Their new home stood in a long garden that ended in woods overhanging
the road. The sand pit across the road provided Alick with hours of amusement
with his cousin Gregor Grant, who became a frequent visitor and playmate. He
was six years older than Alick, who remembered him as a Presbyterian "very
proud of his pedigree."[93] The Crowleys tolerated him because he was a relative;
otherwise, all of Alick's playmates were children of local Brethren. These carefree times he recalled as perpetual happiness.

The Grange, the Crowley family home in Redhill, Surrey.

When Alick turned eight, his father declared him old enough for boarding school. So Edward Crowley packed up his child to Hastings, where Henry Theodore Habershon (c. 1828–1885) and his sons Henry Earnest (b. 1861) and Arthur Herbert (b. 1864), as Messrs. Habershon & Sons, ran the White Rock School at 10 Pevensey Road in St. Leonards on Sea.[94] Although not Brethren, they were extreme evangelicals, and as such were entrusted with Alick's education … but not with his virtue. Before depositing his son at the school, Edward Crowley gave him one last lesson from Genesis, this time chapter nine:

> And Noah began to be an husbandman, and he planted a vineyard: And he drank of the wine, and was drunken; and he was uncovered within his tent. And Ham, the father of Canaan, saw the nakedness of his father, and told his two brethren without. And Shem and Japheth took a garment, and laid it upon both their shoulders, and went backward, and covered the nakedness of their father; and their faces were backward, and they saw not their father's nakedness. And Noah awoke from his wine, and knew what his younger son had done unto him. And he said, Cursed be Canaan; a servant of servants shall he be unto his brethren.

He closed the Bible, looked sternly into his son's eyes, and enjoined him, "Never let anyone touch you there." Although the rendition greatly impressed Alick, the reference to sodomy was lost on the boy, who thought little of the injunction at the time.

Alick's time passed without replication of the story of Noah, and in 1885—following the death of Theodore Habershon[95]—he transferred to a school for sons of the Brethren. Located at 51 Bateman Street, Cambridge, its thirty-one-year-old headmaster, Reverend Henry d'Arcy Champney (1854–1942), seemed just the man to teach Alick: he had received his master of arts degree from Corpus Christi College, Cambridge, and although ordained an Anglican in 1878, he converted to the Brethren faith four years later, writing hymns for the faithful. A true zealot, he voted for Parliament by crossing out the candidates' names and writing in "I vote for King Jesus." According to Crowley, Champney was so pious he claimed never to have had marital relations with his wife. At the time, such claims meant no more to Alick than his father's warning against sodomy.

Extracurricular activities at the school were rigorously religious. Although the boys played cricket, scoring was forbidden lest they commit the sin of emulation. Prayers, ceremonies, meetings, Bible readings, and sermons filled each Sunday, with only two hours allocated for other activities, such as reading books sanctioned for Sundays. On Monday nights, "Badgers' Meetings" opened the big schoolroom to feed and proselytize the residents of Cambridge's slum, Barnswell; alas, the visitors often left a bit of themselves behind, resulting in epidemics of ringworm, measles, and mumps at the school. Champney regarded illness among the boys as God's punishment for some undisclosed sin.

"Alec," as he now called himself, was initially happy at this school, writing exuberant letters home. Following in his father's footsteps, Alec decided to be the most devoted servant of Jesus in the whole school:

> I perceived a difficulty in the Scriptures. The beginning of my fall? I could not see how any one could be three days and three nights in the grave between Friday night and Sunday morning. I took my trouble to one of the masters, who admitted his own perplexity upon the point … he simply said that no one had been able to explain it. Then and there I resolved to astonish the world. Alas for boyish ambitions; the problem is still unsolved.[96]

He excelled in academics, and received White's Selbourne prize for being at the top of his class in "religious knowledge, classics and French."[97]

Around 1886, Alec also began writing his first poems. One of his earliest efforts, "Death of a Drunkard," reveals that the boy's exposure to poetry had been confined to Brethren hymns:

> Just what the parson had told me when young:
> Just what the people in chapel have sung:
> "Wine is a mocker, strong drink is raging."[98]

Bright and amiable, the other boys liked and admired him, and he made many friends.

Nearly a year passed before Alec was suddenly called home in the middle of his spring 1886 term.

Edward Crowley was sick. Ironically, Dr. Paget had diagnosed the preacher with cancer of the tongue and recommended immediate surgery. The Crowleys couldn't have asked for a more qualified opinion. Sir James Paget (1814–1899) had served as Queen Victoria's surgeon in 1858, nearly three decades previously. He had since gone on to describe the second most common bone disease—subsequently called Paget's disease—in 1876. He became a baronet in 1871, and by the time Edward Crowley became his patient in 1886, Paget presided over various professional medical societies.

The Brethren gathered to decide the Lord's will in this matter, and Alec was brought home for moral support. In the end, they decided against surgery. Instead, Edward Crowley began seeing Count Cesare Mattei (1809–1896), inventor of electrohomeopathy, which purports to treat ailments through the therapeutic bioenergy in plant extracts. This new form of treatment generated interest in England at the time: Dr. A. S. Kennedy of St. Saviour's Hospital in London had just published *Notes on Count Mattei's Electro-Homeopathic Remedies* (1886), which advertised a cure "for Cancer and Kindred Diseases."[99] The Crowleys sold the Grange and moved to Glenburnie in Southampton to be closer to the Count.[100]

Although the doctors were optimistic and his father experienced no pain, the specter of death haunted Alec back at school. About a year later, on March 5, 1887, Alec woke from a disturbing dream about his father's death. The next day he learned his father had died the very night of his dream. Edward Crowley, at age fifty-two, was worth £150,000, equivalent to roughly $6 million by modern standards.[101] He left his forty-one-year-old widow one-third of his estate; Alec would inherit another third—$2 million—when he came of age; and the final third went to other relatives, to whom Alec was legatee.

Alec's "boyhood in hell," as he later called it, began after the funeral. That was when everything changed: Emily adopted Edward Crowley's cause, dutifully sending Brethren literature to the people in her husband's address book. She also sold their house and spent the next year or two living in various hotels. Beneath the surface, however, she also changed as a person. This transformation resulted from yet another schism in the Exclusive Brethren. Known as the Raven Division after brother Frederick Edward Raven (1837–1903), it bitterly sundered friends and families over a doctrinal point regarding baptism: whether one was reborn into eternal life, or whether eternal life was attained through faith alone.[102] Emily Crowley took the minority view and wilfully cut herself off from her dissenting intimates. Despite the love she once professed for them, none, she now believed, would reach heaven. Sadly, just as Edward Crowley's faith had estranged Emily from most of her family, her own fanaticism now separated her from her friends.

How people could number among God's chosen one day and collectively
join the legions of the damned the next perplexed Alec. Reflecting on the
images of his childhood, he saw Mary Carey, the Cowpers, Sister Musty, and
others who were practically relatives now condemned to hell. In the boy's eyes,
his mother became "a brainless bigot of the most narrow, logical, and inhuman
type."[103] Or, as he explained elsewhere, perhaps a bit more kindly, she was
"marred beyond belief by the religious monomania which perhaps started in
what one may call 'Hysteria of Widowhood.'"[104] For all that widowhood
changed his mother, the religious schism among the Brethren demonstrated to
Alec the problems of his faith. For an adolescent challenging and rejecting all
that his parents held dear, he found Plymouth piety to be hypocritical.

Despite belonging to the Exclusive Brethren, Emily reestablished contact
with her family after Edward's passing, and they appear for the first time in
Aleister Crowley's various accounts of his childhood. Emily's brother, with
whom she often stayed in London, ought to have made a natural surrogate parent for Alec. Tom Bond Bishop (1839–1920) had moved to London around the
time his own father had died of natural causes in 1854. He worked in the civil
service as a customs clerk, advancing to a lucrative position. Known in philan-
thropic circles as an evangelical Christian, "T. B. B." founded the Children's
Special Service Mission in 1867, which quickly grew to include the Children's
Scripture Union and *Our Own Magazine,* a one-penny monthly magazine of
inspirational stories for children that he edited for many years. He was also a
founding member of Civil Service Prayer Union, serving on its committee
from July 1881 until he resigned in 1889 from "over work."[105] He was every
bit as devoted to God as Edward Crowley. However, while Edward's devotion
garnered Alec's respect, Uncle Tom's earned nothing but scorn. A rigid and
devout man, he represented all that Crowley came to hate about religion, and
he remembered his uncle bitterly. "No more cruel fanatic, no meaner villain,
ever walked this earth," he wrote in his memoirs.[106] He attributed *White Stains,*
his Decadent book of erotic verse, to a fictional character bearing Tom's family
name. In later years, Crowley published his uncle's obituary prematurely,[107] and
verbally attacked him while reviewing his book *Evolution Criticised.*[108]

Whereas the death of Alec's sister barely registered on his consciousness at
all, the passing of his father changed his life. In 1887, psychology was still in its
infancy and no grief counselors were available to help the boy adjust to his loss.
In Alec's situation, typical adolescent coping strategies were unavailable: no
family member felt close enough for him to talk to. The latest Brethren schism
had cut him off from most social contact, and Emily had become, in his own
words, hysterical. He could not turn to religion for comfort because he connected the Brethren faith with his difficulty. At age eleven, the boy found himself compelled to leave his carefree existence behind and become the man of
the household. As biographer Martin Booth notes, it is at this point in his *Confessions* that Crowley begins referring to himself in the first person.

While grieving children experience feelings of isolation and loneliness, for Aleister Crowley it was genuine. Research indicates that parental death doesn't directly affect long-term child adjustment, but short-term symptoms like anxiety, delinquency, and psychosomatic illness are common.[109] Within three weeks of his return to Bateman Street, Alec made his first of many visits to the headmaster's office. While Crowley fails to describe his misdeeds, he admits the first infractions were minor and were dismissed as an expression of grief. Soon, punishment became more severe: fifteen strokes "on the legs, because flogging the buttocks excites the victim's sensuality!—15 minutes prayer, 15 more strokes of the cane—and more prayer to top it!"[110] Then, one day after prayer time, Alec found himself in Champney's office, not knowing why.

One of the children had described Crowley's latest misdeed, and Champney wanted a confession. To his dismay, he received only protestations of innocence. "Come, come, Crowley," the headmaster prodded impatiently. "You know that the Lord has a special care of this school, and he brings to light that which is done in darkness." Champney offered a sermon peppered with fire and brimstone—not to mention several threats for good measure—before his patience reached an end. "Confess, boy," he insisted, his eyes bulging like blisters on his face. At that point, Alec would have admitted to anything just to be rid of Champney. But not even knowing the charges, his only answer was silence. His sentence for refusing to come clean was placement in "Coventry," meaning that no master or boy could speak to Alec nor he to them. During play hours, he would work; during work hours, he would wander the empty school yard. Social contact was forbidden, and in his isolation he would receive only bread and water. To end it, all Alec had to do was confess.

Uncle Jonathan Crowley was a striking contrast to Alec's father. He had two children from a previous marriage, and his present wife was the children's former governess. Like his brother Edward, he inherited both the family fortune—managing to live well without being ostentatious—and good looks. As Crowley wrote:

> The tremendous brow, the eagle eyes, the great hooked arrogant nose, the firm mouth and the indomitable jaw combined to make him one of the most strikingly handsome men that I have ever seen.[111]

Clearly, for Alec the Crowley side of the family tree basked in Edward's halo, while the Bishop branch was tainted with the same bigotry with which he painted his mother.

Alec looked unnaturally pallid and weak when Jonathan Crowley visited him at school during the following term. Although the boy made no complaints, his mistreatment was obvious. Hearing about the Badgers' Meeting and subsequent ringworm outbreaks, Jonathan bristled. He confronted Champney and, threatening to call in the authorities, forced him to discontinue the prac-

tice. He then arranged for his nephew to see Justice Stirling in order to determine any other mistreatment at the school. This move intimidated Alec, who
did not understand the legal system and feared that complaints could mean
prison sentences for his mother or Uncle Tom. He insisted unconvincingly that
he was perfectly happy at school, and so he was sent back.

By the time he went home that Christmas, Alec's health had deteriorated
so badly that even Emily asked questions. This time, Alec described his mistreatment, and she promised to take care of it. Her solution was to take Alec for
a visit to her brother's house, where unbeknownst to the child, Champney
awaited. When he stepped inside Uncle Tom's, Alec's blood ran cold and his
skin paled even more. He hid in the corner and uttered no complaints. After
the holiday, he returned to school to complete his sentence.

The next term was nearly over when, during a visit by Uncle Tom, Alec
described being placed in "Coventry" for something he had supposedly done.
Tom, in what Crowley later called "a lucid interval,"[112] marched over to
Champney's office and insisted on knowing the charges. Accusations of drunkenness and sodomy convinced Tom to take Alec home. Shortly thereafter, several other parents reached the same conclusion about Champney, and the
school reportedly closed.[113] For Alec, however, the damage—both physical
and psychological—had already been done: the doctor confirmed that Alec
was indeed very ill. He had albuminuria—traces of albumin in his urine, suggesting kidney disease—and it was so serious that Alec was expected never to
reach adulthood. The physician could only offer a prescription for country air.

This news must have been staggering. For Emily, she had lost her husband
and now her only child had been handed a death sentence. Jonathan Sparrow
Crowley had suffered from albuminuria for the past twenty years; right around
this time, he would have begun vomiting blood and, after three weeks, would
die on September 13, 1888.[114] This could only have added gravity to Alec's
prognosis. And the boy lost another respected male role model in his life.

Emily Crowley moved in with her brother Tom in what is now Drayton Gardens. When Alec's interest turned to books, he found his choices proscribed by
the dogma of his mother and uncle: Charles Dickens's *David Copperfield* (1850)
was forbidden because of the character named Emily, lest Alec grow to disre-
spect his mother. Sophocles' *Oedipus Rex* was plain inappropriate, even though
he had been expected to learn it in school. Worst of all was Samuel Taylor Coleridge's *The Rime of the Ancient Mariner* (1798) because the mariner's encounter
with the water snakes ends with the words "And I blessèd them unaware"[115] ...
and *everyone* knew snakes were cursed in Genesis. This was a far cry from
Edward Crowley, who once defended Alec's reading of Robert Michael Ballantyne's children's book *Martin Rattler: A Boy's Adventures in the Forests of Brazil*
(1869) on a Sunday by telling Emily, "If the book is good enough to read any
other day, then why not on Sunday? Every day is the Lord's Day. The Jews

observe a Sabbath, not us." Those days were over, and now Alec had to sneak books home under his coat and lock himself in the bathroom to read them.

Alec at age fourteen.

The whole business of religion became intolerable. As he later put it, "I did not hate God or Christ, but merely the God and Christ of the people whom I hated.... The Christianity of hypocrisy and cruelty was not true Christianity."[116] All his woes came down to one word: sin. He lived in constant fear of it, stood accused and punished in its name, and lived miserably by its avoidance.

No more, he concluded. If everybody was so mistaken about God, they could also be wrong about sin. Thus, he decided to become a sinner. But not just any sinner: with the same zeal he showed over the theological poser of Christ's three days in the grave, Alec decided to become the world's best sinner. Petty transgressions like theft wouldn't do. Instead, he contemplated the ultimate spiritual wrong: the only sin that could not be forgiven, the sin against the Holy Ghost. Nobody knew what it was, and even to guess was considered blasphemy. Maybe he couldn't prove how Jesus was three days and three nights upon the cross from Friday to Sunday; but he vowed to solve *this* riddle. Once he discovered what this sin was, he resolved to do it, and thoroughly.

But what might it be? Was there a clue in the story his father told him about Noah? Did it have something to do with that mysterious activity Champney never engaged in with his wife? How did the accusations made against him at school fit in? He had a lot to learn about this business of sin.

Until he either died or was well enough to return to school, it was decided Alec would be taught by tutors handpicked by his Uncle Tom. In qualifications, academic credentials ranked second to religious faith, with the ability to engage Alec in his health-building regimen of travel, climbing, and fishing a distant third. His tutors were consequently fundamentalist degree-holders from minor Cambridge colleges. Alec considered them all to be his physical and intellectual inferiors and, compelled to get the better of them, watched tutors come and go so quickly that he soon lost count.

In the spring of 1891, at age fifteen, he embarked on a rest cure for whooping cough that consisted of a bicycle trip[117] to the seaside resort of Torquay in the southwest of England. Although it would later become famous as the birthplace of Agatha Christie (a year earlier, in 1890), Torquay—along with Paginton and Brixham—was known as the English Riviera and enjoyed an international reputation as a haven for the rich and famous. Alec's latest tutor and chaperone was James Archibald Douglas (b. 1866), a twenty-five-year-old teacher of arts and philosophy from Sheffield, Yorkshire.[118] Alec collapsed twenty-eight miles outside of London, too ill to proceed, so the pair continued by train to their destination at 5 Cary Parade.

Despite the journey's failure, the vacation proved most educational. As an Oxford University graduate and Bible Society missionary, Douglas had much to teach Alec, but most important was his refreshing—and surprising—normality. This tutor smoked and drank. He also played cards and billiards. And he thought women were a welcome pleasure in life, not vehicles of sin. Most importantly, however, he demonstrated one could safely enjoy these things in moderation. Far from his stifling home life, Alec found a completely new outlook. Crowley records, "He taught me sense and manhood, and I shall not easily forget my debt to him."[119]

During the first ten days of his rest cure, Alec fell in love with a girl from the local theater. Together they retreated into a field to explore their attraction. Savoring the feeling of the spring breeze, sunshine, and soft skin against him, the fifteen-year-old lost much more than his virginity. He realized sex was not a subject of evil and sin; he understood its joy and beauty. And in that awakening he shed his obsession with sin like a heavy winter jacket.

Alec was soon well enough to attend part time a Streatham day school south of London. Here he discovered smoking, one of the top two on his Uncle Tom's hit parade of sin. He recalled with amusement his uncle's attempt to convey to him the moral of an article that he had written for *Boys' Magazine* on the evils of drinking and smoking, "The Two Wicked Kings." "Alec, my lad," he summoned the boy over.

"Yes, Uncle?"

Tom replied predictably: "'O my prophetic soul! mine uncle!'"

Alec knew this response well and, having by now learned *Hamlet,* quickly completed the quote: "'Ay, that incestuous, that adulterate beast.'"

"Do you know of the two wicked kings?" Tom continued, undaunted. After a pause, he answered for Alec. "Drin-king and smo-king?"

Alec, having read the article, pointed out, "But, Uncle, you have forgotten to mention a third, the most dangerous and deadly of all."

Uncle Tom pondered the riddle for a moment and drew a blank. Alec's crude but astute identification—whether it was fuc-king or wan-king he does not say—stunned him.

To Alec, this "wicked king" business was just another example of Uncle Tom's misguided enthusiasm. Papa had drunk wine, claiming he would rather preach to miserable drunkards than self-righteous teetotalers. Drinking, therefore, couldn't be a serious offense. But Papa had also said, "If God had intended man to smoke, He would have supplied a chimney at the top of his head." The observation did nothing to deter the habit Alec had learned at Streatham.

In recovery, Alec became a handsome young man. His hair was neatly cropped and his eyes dark, penetrating, brooding. Expressive lips and a wide square chin supported his features. His body possessed the sinew and virility of a young man in his prime. Suddenly, he found himself desirable to young women.

Alec thrilled when the new parlor maid[120] flirted with him, but, too inexperienced to know how to respond, he shied away until, on her night off, he worked up the courage to flirt with her during a cab ride. Then, one Sunday, when Alec made some excuse not to join the family at church, he led the maid into his mother's bedroom. For Alec, the thrill of seducing her on the bed of his pious mother was more than just an adolescent expression of oedipal urge; it was a victory over religious oppression.

Alec understood the maid's flirting as simply an attempt to gain a better position in the household. However, when she complained to Tom Bond Bishop of how his nephew had corrupted her innocence, she found herself dismissed without references. Confronted with the story, Alec flatly denied the allegations. On the condition that he not be punished, he confessed that on one of the nights in question he was at the tobacconist's with wicked school companions who had led him astray. Although he got off by pleading guilty to a lesser charge, the lie haunted him:

> First we have a charming girl driven to attempt blackmail, next a boy
> forced to the most unmanly duplicity in order to exercise his natural rights
> with impunity, and incidentally to wrong a woman for whom he had
> nothing but the friendliest feelings. As long as sexual relations are compli-
> cated by religious, social and financial considerations, so long will they
> cause all kinds of cowardly, dishonourable and disgusting behaviour.[121]

The best thing to come of this unfortunate circumstance was Uncle Tom's
decision that Streatham provided a poor example for Alec.

On November 5, 1891, less than a month after his sixteenth birthday, Alec
brought a ten-pound jar home from the grocer and filled it with two pounds of
gunpowder. This he topped with metallic salts, sugar, and potassium chlorate.
He dug a hole in the ground, inserted the jar, and lit the concoction. The
explosion shattered windows nearby and left a large crater in the ground. Alec
fell unconscious on the ground without ever hearing the boom, countless
pieces of gravel embedded in his face. It would be Christmas before his eyes
healed enough to be briefly exposed to light. Of focusing on his other senses
without benefit of eyesight, he later recalled, "I did learn quite a lot from my
famous Guy Fawkes day, when the bandages were on my eyes for 40 days."[122]

Tom realized Alec had too much time on his hands—and idle hands were,
after all, the devil's playthings—and decided once again to send him to school.
Thus, in the spring of 1892, Alec went to stay in Huntingdon's No. 4 in Malvern, Worcestershire, a small town in the English Midlands. Here he enrolled in
a militia, the First Worcestershire Artillery Volunteers.[123] The school had a
name in sports, and Alec—not well enough to participate—became the butt
of abuse. He grew painfully familiar with two great pastimes of bullies everywhere: greasing (spitting into someone's face) and pill-ragging (clenching
someone's testicles). At the school, Crowley recalled, "Buggery was the
rule";[124] his study companion even made money as a prostitute. He parlayed
this information into a speedy transfer for the following year.

Alec spent his summer vacationing with his mother on Scotland's Isle of
Skye, whose main attraction is the hilly terrain known as the Black Cullins.
Here Alec met Sir Joseph Lister (1827–1912) at the Sligachan Inn. Lister,
although remembered as the physician who introduced antisepsis to surgery,
was also an avid mountaineer, and he persuaded a group of climbers to take
Alec up the 3,162-foot Sgurr-nan-Gillean. Crowley was hooked by the experience, which marked the first of many competitive climbs. During his vacation
in Skye that September, he also climbed Sgurr a' Ghreadaidh (3,192 feet), Bruach na Frìthe (3,143 feet), Am Basteir (3,064 feet), Sgurr a' Mhadaidh (3,012
feet), and the Bloody Stone (33 feet).[125]

That fall of 1892, he transferred to the Tonbridge School in Kent, where
his house was Ferox Hall.[126] Located in historic Tonbridge with its thirteenth-
century motte-and-bailey castles, Tonbridge School was one of the nation's top

schools. Founded in 1553 by Sir Andrew Judde (c. 1492–1558), it rested on 150 acres at the north edge of Tonbridge; it had been largely rebuilt as the school grew in size and status in the second half of the nineteenth century.

Early in his fall term, Alec again took ill. As he recalls cryptically in *The World's Tragedy*:

> My health broke down; partly, one may say, through what would have been my own fault or misfortune if I had been properly educated; but, as it was, was the direct result of the vile system that, not content with torturing me itself, handed me over bound and blindfold to the outraged majesty of Nature.[127]

A marginal note in his personal copy of the book clarifies: he "caught the clap from a Glasgow prostitute."

Boarding school seemed too strenuous for Alec, so his mother sent him to Eastbourne to live with a Brethren tutor named Lambert. There he enjoyed more freedom than he expected from a Darbyist. He wrote more poetry, which he contributed to both the *Eastbourne Gazette* and *The Christian*.[128] He also spent much of his free time playing chess, easily beating the best players in town, and eventually writing the "Chess Notes" column for the *Eastbourne Gazette* under the pseudonym Ta Dhuibh.[129] That spring and summer, he climbed literally dozens of peaks in Snowdonia, Wales, and in England's Lake District.[130] His passions for poetry, chess, and mountain climbing blossomed.

With chalk cliffs rising 575 feet above sea level, Beachy Head is the highest headland on England's south coast. Its crumbling edifice projects into the English Channel from its location in East Sussex on the east end of South Downs. British mountaineer Edward Whymper (1840–1911) and his brother nearly killed themselves trying to climb it in the mid-1800s.

Victorian England birthed and buried the craze of chalk-cliff climbing. It originated with some bright alpinist's contention that Britain's sea cliffs made great practice mountains when, in fact, their chalk faces crumbled too readily to be climbed safely. After he had become a seasoned climber, Crowley wrote, "English rock climbing is the most severe and difficult in the world."[131] Walter Parry Haskett Smith's (1859–1946) guidebook *Climbing in the British Isles: England*[132] declared that the chalk cliffs of Sussex were climbable only up to twenty feet above high-water mark. Similar claims were made by Albert Frederick Mummery (1855–1895), whom the *Encyclopaedia of Mountaineering* calls "the foremost climber of the second half of the last century, with justifiable claims to be regarded as the founder of modern Alpinism."

Crowley, looking upon Beachy Head in 1894, doubted these estimates. Having spent the previous summer climbing in England with his cousin Gregor Grant—whom he described as someone "who considers climbing for climbing's sake as stupid, if not actually sinful"[133]—Crowley believed they could conquer this unclimbable cliff. He surveyed the edifice and noted its most conspicuous pinnacles: the peak closest to the sea was known as the Devil's Chimney and consisted of two pinnacles separated by a gap: the Needle was the outermost peak, and the Tooth was innermost. Further inland beside it was Etheldreda's Pinnacle, with the Cuillin Crack's two-hundred-foot cliff overhanging it. They began climbing on April 4.

Passing to the top of the grassy slope that ran along the base of the Devil's Chimney, they marveled at the beautiful sight of the sunlit cliffs before them, the sea behind, and the clouds above. To the right of the Cuillin Crack was a cleft, which Crowley named Etheldreda's Walk after his dog,[134] that ran "round Etheldreda's Pinnacle, to the foot of Grant's Chimney." Etheldreda's Pinnacle was accessible by twin chimneys—deep grooves in the cliff wall—that stretched before him like chalk incarnations of Castor and Pollux. He liked the analogy and thus dubbed the chimneys after the Greek twins. Crowley began climbing Castor, the north access way, until its chalk face gave way and buried his legs in a cloud of rubble. Undeterred, he wriggled free of the debris and pressed on. Progress was slow, even glacial, to avoid further mishaps; to the *Scottish Mountaineering Club Journal,* Alec described his ascent as "a chemical combination of the writhe, the squirm, and the slither." Arriving at the top and sitting upon its square summit, he could feel Etheldreda's Pinnacle teeter and sway beneath him. Cleare and Collomb, in their account of sea-cliff climbing in Britain, write, "The traverse on a chalk and grass slope of 50 degrees' steepness below the cliff proved to be a nightmare of insecurity. One can therefore only marvel at Crowley and his friends who managed to effect a traverse on this slope."[135]

They returned three months later, on July 4, to tackle the Devil's Chimney, conquering several landmarks and deeming others unclimbable. Of climbing the Tooth, Crowley reported,

> Both the N[orth] and E[ast] faces were coated with loose layers of chalk, which came away with a single touch, but the E[ast] had the advantage of being less vertical. ... The laborious nature of the climbing is evidenced by the fact that two hours and more were required to overcome a vertical height of only thirty feet.[136]

Subsequent climbs took place on July 11 and 13 and on October 1. Despite having deemed the Needle unclimbable from his promontory atop Etheldreda's Pinnacle, Crowley set his sights on its peak on July 13. Proceeding into the gap that separated the twin peaks of the Tooth and the Needle, Alec sought a surface solid enough to climb. Cutting steps into the nearly vertical walls proved futile. After five failed attempts, Alec finally scooped out a hole in the wall, planted his chin in it, and used his free hands to haul himself up. Using this unconventional tactic, he emerged on the other side of the gap, after which ascent of the Needle was easy. While Gregor waved the Union Jack from the Tooth's pinnacle, Crowley gazed proudly from the top of the Needle, surveying the landscape below. They stood where no one else had ever stood, achieved what no climber had before. They had conquered the Devil's Chimney.

The Devil's Chimney at Beachy Head, July 13, 1894, showing Gregor
Grant atop the Tooth (right) and Aleister Crowley atop the Needle (left).

Their October 1 attempt on Cuillin Crack was less successful. Crowley
judged this ascent "the finest and most difficult piece of climbing that I have yet
found in the whole neighbourhood."[137] Consequently, after scaling the first
sixty feet or so of its two-hundred-foot height, he became too exhausted either
to climb further or to pull up Gregor. Thus Alec remained wedged in the crack
while his cousin fetched the coast guard to lower a rope and help pull him out.

These ascents are best understood in retrospect. The sport of chalk-cliff
climbing is esoteric, and its Victorian period "would have been inconsequential
were it not for Aleister Crowley."[138] Etheldreda's Pinnacle, though only
twenty-five feet high, is rated a "very severe" climb, and Cleare and Collomb
dubbed Crowley's ascent "a remarkable achievement and in concept years
ahead of its time."[139] Crowley's attempt of Cuillin Crack—probably omitted
from his memoirs because its abortive attempt required his rescue—was nevertheless so important that the feature is now called Crowley's Crack. Although
others soon repeated the climbs, sea-cliff climbing died out within six years.

No other ascents were recorded until the sport experienced a rebirth in the 1980s; today, the upper part of the Devil's Chimney has collapsed into the sea.

If history accords Crowley a place for his climbs, this was not the case at the time. The initial response to his achievements left Alec cold. A local newspaper began its coverage of the climb with the words, "Insensate folly takes various forms." Mummery initially dismissed Crowley as a braggart. Before long, however, these climbing records on Beachy Head were verified, and Alec established himself as a pioneer of the short-lived sport of sea-cliff climbing.

Shortly after this victory, Gregor announced his engagement and that he could no longer climb on Beachy Head with his cousin, but Alec's love of climbing continued unabated. He traveled to Tyrol, Austria, with his tutor and attempted his first Alpine climbs. Unable to find a satisfactory guide, he set out with A. E. and M. W. Maylard and climbed the Schrötterhorn nearly to the top, despite the bad snow, as well as Vertainspitze. In the Italian Alpine village of Sulden he made solo ascents of Monte Cevedale (12,382 feet), Suldenspitze (11,076 feet), Tschengglser Hochwand (11,073 feet), Gran Zebrù (12,635 feet), Thurwieserpitze (11,982 feet), Ortler (12,812 feet), and others.[140] While climbing the Ortler, he reached its peak by the Hintere Grant in only six and a half hours, where he met an American and his guide, who, he learned, had climbed up the other side … the easy side. Alec never again climbed with guides, feeling safer relying on his own instincts and natural talent. The Alps proved unforgettable, and Alec would return regularly for the next four years.

In September 1894 he applied for membership in the Scottish Mountaineering Club. He was balloted for and elected at their December 7 meeting.[141]

Returning to Eastbourne from the Alps, Alec found relations with his tutor strained. One day, he and Lambert got into an argument that turned critical when Lambert began throwing punches; Alec caught him in a hammerlock with one arm and pounded his tutor's face with the other. Another incident involved Lambert's daughter, Isabelle, whom Crowley described as "the only pretty and decent member of the family."[142] Over breakfast, Alec watched her parents forbid her to see her fiancé because he would not convert to the Brethren faith; when their admonishments and abuse drove her to tears, Alec interrupted to tell her parents how revolting and cruel he found them. Another blowup ensued, and Lambert telegraphed Tom Bishop to fetch his nephew.

The family row that Alec expected over this incident never materialized. His mother, grateful to see Alec prosper in manhood rather than dying as the doctors had predicted when they first diagnosed him with albuminuria, eased her stranglehold. And when he expressed his interest in the sport that had helped turn him into a strapping young man, she sent him back to the Alps sans chaperone. He had come of age.

If only in sheer numbers of ascents, 1895 was his best year for climbing.[143] Returning to the Bernese Alps in south-central Switzerland, Alec scaled many of its peaks, including the Eiger (13,025 feet), which he conquered alone. Noting no record of an ascent of Trift (7,667 feet) from the Mountet side, he and an "intelligent-looking young Englishman"[144] named Ellis climbed it in half a day. Other victories included the peaks of the Jungfrau (13,642 feet), Mönch (13,474 feet), and the Wetterhorn (12,113 feet). Many alpinists—H. V. Read, W. Larden, O. Eckenstein, A. E. Maylard, and H. Solly among them— recognized AC, as Alec had become known, as a promising young climber, and several took him under their wings. Among them was Dr. John Norman Collie (1859–1942), whom he later described as "unquestionably the finest all-round climber of his generation."[145] Collie was about to embark on his fateful expedition to Nanga Parabat, in which A. F. Mummery, with whom AC corresponded about Beachy Head, would be lost. However, Collie proposed Crowley for membership in the Alpine Club, with Sir Martin Conway (1856–1937)—who would later preside over the Alpine Club from 1902 to 1904— seconding the motion; the application, however, was rejected. From that time, Crowley would have nothing but scorn for the club. Founded in London in 1857, it was the world's first mountaineering club, and in those days it had many charateristics of a gentlemen's club—staid, exclusive, superior, and authoritarian—making it an easy target for Crowley's scorn.[146]

Another of Collie's interests was the occult. Whether it was mysticism, magic, alchemy, or folklore, the unexplainable fascinated him. He believed in the Loch Ness Monster and reported being followed on Scotland's highest summit, Ben Macdui (4,295 feet), on Easter of 1891—whether by a ghost or by the legendary Am Fear Lias Mòr (Scotland's Sasquatch, the Big Grey Man) he did not speculate, but he remarked that "No power on earth will ever take me up Ben Macdui again." This, along with tales of old Gaelic mountain gods and goddesses, he would often relate to friends around campfires or in his den, according to his biographer Christine Mill, "no one quite knowing how much he was believing himself."[147] As Crowley recalled, "Norman Collie, of all people, by the way, was very keen on alchemy in the days when we climbed rocks together."[148] That Collie was also a scientist—an organic chemist at University College, later department chair and, after his 1928 retirement, professor emeritus—no doubt made a great impression on Crowley, who would many years later define magick as an art and science, coining the phrase "the method of science, the aim of religion" and dubbing his methodology "scientific illuminism." Not long after meeting Collie, Crowley would begin to consider himself a young authority on alchemy, expounding the subject to anyone who would listen. Most remarkably, Collie was but the first of three highly influential climber-chemists that Crowley would meet in as many years.

A telegram from home cut short AC's perambulations upon the Bernese Oberland. Mother and Uncle Tom were sending him to Trinity College, Cambridge, and entrance exams were a week away.

CHAPTER TWO

A Place to Bury Strangers

The halls of Trinity College, Cambridge, opened to AC in October 1895. There he took a room in 16 St. John's Street, far from the relatives who would have liked to choose his friends, teachers, and diversions. Instead, no Plymouth tutor monitored his actions for moral probity, and no censor told him what to do or read. Plus, as an adult, he was finally entitled to £50,000 in discretionary funds—equivalent to $2 million by today's standards—from his father's estate. As he would describe one of his own students many years later, he was free, white, and twenty.

Gone was Edward Alexander Crowley, for, as a free man, he had no desire to go by his given name. Gone too was the boy's name Alec. So how should the chess, poetry, and mountaineering wunderkind be appropriately addressed? A cursory examination of his surname led him to conclude that Crowley derived from the common Irish O'Crowley. With poets W. B. Yeats and George Moore making Ireland and all things Irish fashionable at that time, AC naturally wished to participate in the Celtic revival. He therefore tried the Gaelic form of Alexander: Aleister.

He pondered it a moment and recalled reading that for fame, the best combination of stressed and unstressed syllables were a dactyl followed by a spondee: the pattern of one long or accented syllable, two short, one long, one short … like Algernon Swinburne. Aleister Crowley. It fit the pattern. He liked it. And so he became known.

Ranking highly among his first acts of independence was his refusal to attend chapel, lecture, or hall. He told the junior dean that chapel—obligatory Sunday morning religious services—was forbidden by his Plymouth upbringing as being outside his faith, and that "the seed planted by my father, watered by my mother's tears, would prove too hardy a growth to be uprooted."[1]

When a political economics professor described the subject as very difficult due to lack of reliable data, Aleister, favoring the discipline of mathematics and chemistry to what sounded like superstition, closed his notebook and returned to class only for exams, which he passed easily. Finally, Cambridge's 8:30 dinner hour was untenable as it broke up what could otherwise be a productive evening. Raised in isolation from his peers, the thought of sitting in a dining hall filled with his classmates was at best uncomfortable. Thus Aleister arranged with the kitchen to send food to his room at his convenience.

Before long, he fell into a pattern of beginning work—reading, writing, and studying—at midnight, an hour he was certain no social calls could interrupt him, and continuing straight through until dawn. When tired of toiling during these long nights, he wandered the campus alone, pondering how many great men had walked in Neville's Court; or watched from Garret Hostel Bridge as mist rolled over the river below; or, from his room, simply watched the sun rise over the tower of St. John's Chapel.

While his nocturnal lifestyle left him with few friends at Cambridge, the tale of fellow undergraduates throwing Crowley into Trinity's fountain[2] is apocryphal at best. Cambridge's debating society, the Magpie and Stump, attracted his attention from 1895 to 1897, but he ultimately found it "absurd for these young asses to emit their callow opinions on important subjects."[3] A better fit was the Cambridge University Chess Club, where, in his first term, he beat its president, William Vawdrey Naish (1873–1956), and was humbled by Henry Ernest Atkins (1872–1955), future nine-time British chess champion.[4] Crowley ultimately became the chess club's president. Representing Cambridge in intervarsity matches, he usually won, as he did on March 27, 1896, when he came out of a lost position to beat N. H. Robbins of Oxford, or in a February 20, 1897, match against the City of London Chess Club, where he bested Edward Bageshott Schwann (1872–1902), who had received the Wills prize for an interclub record of twelve wins, three draws, and no losses. However, fortune wasn't always on Crowley's side: in an April 2, 1897, match against Oxford at the British Chess Club in Covent Garden, his opponent, E. George Spencer-Churchill (c. 1876–1964)—Winston Churchill's cousin—came from behind to win the match. Similarly, in a November 20, 1897, match between the Chess Club and the Senior Club, Crowley lost against William Hewison Gunston, MA (1856–1941), a fellow of St. John's College, Cambridge, and well-known chess player.[5]

His most influential friend at this time, however, was a senior named Adamson. AC left no record of him, probably because they were casual acquaintances, but the *Alumni Cantabrigienses* lists a student named Henry Anthony Adamson (1871–1941), who matriculated to Trinity College in 1889 and received his BA in 1892 and his MA in 1896.[6] He profoundly changed Crowley's life by introducing him to the poetry of Percy Bysshe Shelley (1792–1822). For Crowley the budding poet, Shelley's lyrical style and unique expressive language represented the perfect marriage of poetry and music. This was indeed a far cry from Plymouth devotional verse.

Realizing he had never read real poetry before, Crowley lost all interest in history, geography, and botany. He stopped studying altogether, voraciously consuming whatever poetry and literature he could find: in addition to poets like Robert Browning and Algernon Swinburne, he also devoured the works of writers like playwright William Shakespeare, satirist Jonathan Swift, essayist Thomas Carlyle, novelist Henry Fielding, historian Edward Gibbon, and adventurer-scholar Sir Richard Burton. "I was influenced by Ruskin's[7] imbecile remark that any book worth reading was worth buying, and in consequence acquired books literally by the ton."[8] Before long, floor-to-ceiling bookcases lined his apartment. Shelley nevertheless remained Crowley's lifelong favorite,[9] influencing not only his writing but also his emulative passion for life.

Aleister Crowley as a young poet.

By 1896, AC was wearing a poet's silk shirt with floppy hat and bow tie, constantly writing poetry. Everything—even campus landmarks—inspired a Shelleyan passion in his own lyrical soul.

> My poetic instincts, further, transformed the most sordid liaisons into romance ... I found, moreover, that any sort of satisfaction acted as a powerful stimulus. Every adventure was the direct cause of my writing poetry.[10]

His verse frequented Cambridge's student publications *The Granta, Cambridge Magazine,* and *Cantab.*[11] Fortunately when one of Crowley's instructors, Greek scholar Arthur Woollgar Verrall (1851–1912), confronted him about his absence from lecture and heard his student explain his newfound love for English literature, Verrall allowed him to pursue this interest unimpeded.

AC spent his 1896 winter vacation alone, sometimes secluded in the mountains and sometimes enjoying the long nights and cold clear air of northwestern Europe. "I loved to wander solitary in Holland, Denmark, Norway, and Sweden. There was a mystery in the streets and a spontaneous gaiety in the places of amusement, which satisfied my soul."[12] Over Easter, he was one of thirty-two members of the Scottish Mountaineering Club in Fort William for a wet and rainy meet.[13] In the end he returned to Britain's sea cliffs at Wastdale Head. There he reunited with Norman Collie, who had mentored Crowley's Alpine climbs the previous summer. He was back from his tragic Himalayan climb in which A. F. Mummery (who had skeptically received AC's correspondence about Beachy Head) was killed. Crowley and Collie's reunion was nevertheless happy; together they demonstrated the puttees that Collie had brought back from Nanga Parabat. These leather leggings, secured by winding laces around the calf, were handy for keeping snow out of one's boots. Also at this time, John Wilson Robinson (c. 1853–1907),[14] who pioneered climbing in Cumbria's lake district, showed AC some of Wastdale Head's easier climbs; snowy gales prevented more difficult ascents. AC commemorated these climbs with the poem "A Spring Snowstorm in Wastdale."[15]

That summer he also returned to the Bernese Oberland, making the first guideless ascent of the Mönch (13,474 feet) on July 14, commemorated in his poem "A Descent of the Moench."[16] Other solo unguided ascents at this time included the Aiguille de la Za (12,051 feet); Aiguilles Rouges d'Arolla (11,929 feet), immortalized in his poem "The Traverse of Aiguilles Rouges";[17] and the Vuibez Séracs, an icefall that had probably never before been passed. Crowley would later attribute this last accomplishment to his "quite uncanny faculty" to "divine the one possible passage through the most complex and dangerous icefall."[18] In addition, he and a companion made an unguided ascent of the Trifthorn (12,231 feet), as well as a new descent down its northwest face.[19]

Despite his literary interests, Crowley took Cambridge's honors examination (the Moral Science Tripos) and tentatively chose the diplomatic service as his profession. His training included an 1897 stint learning Russian in St. Petersburg. Uninspired by the experience, he stopped on his return trip to attend a chess congress in Berlin. The roomful of stodgy old masters convinced him that chess, despite his own skill and passion for the game, could be nothing more than a hobby for him—albeit one he would enjoy through his last days. He

came to the same realization about mountaineering—during 1897 he climbed
the Pic Coolidge (12,385 feet), crossed the Brèche de la Meije (11,014 feet),
returned to the Aiguille de la Za, and traversed Mont Collon (11,932 feet)[20]—
and his educational options looked no more promising.

These observations culminated in an existential crisis in October 1897.
Although death had been omnipresent ever since his childhood struggle with
albuminuria, now he pondered: what would he have to show for his lifelong
struggle when he died? Would his career in the diplomatic service be quickly
forgotten like that of most politicians? What use was his beloved poetry when
his Cambridge peers had never heard the name Aeschylus? And even if he succeeded as a great politician or poet—a Caesar or Shakespeare—his eminence
would eventually perish with the death of mankind.

Crowley determined to "find a material in which to work which is
immune from the forces of change,"[21] concluding that only spiritual pursuits
had eternal implications. Then and there he renounced the diplomatic service
in favor of the spirit. Over thirty years later, asked why he did not seek fame,
Crowley would reply cryptically, "Who was our representative at the Sublime
Porte, say, eight years ago?"

Crowley's experience of the First Noble Truth, however, was not that simple, as evidenced by another major awakening in his life.

A year earlier—in December 1896—Crowley had been in Stockholm during
the Christmas holiday. There, at midnight of New Year's Eve, he joined what
he called the Military Order of the Temple. As he later described it:

> I was awakened to the knowledge that I possessed a magical means of
> becoming conscious of and satisfying a part of my nature which had up to
> that time concealed itself from me. It was an experience of horror and
> pain, combined with a certain ghostly terror, yet at the same time it was
> the key to the purest and holiest spiritual ecstasy that exists.[22]

Crowley was never one to mince words about his mystical experiences, and the
couched euphemisms of this passage recall the polite if incomprehensible
description of contracting venereal disease that he gives in *The World's Tragedy*.
It appears that the "Military Order of the Temple" was a euphemism for Crowley's awakening to his bisexuality, simultaneously stirring up feelings of horror
from his upbringing along with quiescent relief. His poem "At Stockholm"
addresses a secret forbidden love:

> We could not speak, although the sudden glow
> Of passion mantling to the crimson cheek
> Of either, told our tale of love, although
> We could not speak.[23]

He wrote of events at this time that he "Hunted new Sins till October, '97, when one of them turned to bay, and helped me to experience the 'Trance of Sorrow.'"[24] Similar reference to sin appears in an early poem from this period:

> He who seduced me first I could not forget.
> I hardly loved him but desired to taste
> A new strong sin. My sorrow does not fret
> That sore. But thou, whose sudden arms embraced
> My shrinking body, and who brought a blush
> Into my cheeks, and turned my veins to fire,
> Thou, who didst whelm me with the eager rush
> Of the enormous floods of thy desire,
> Thine are the kisses that devour me yet,
> Thine the high heaven whose loss is death to me,
> Thine all the barbed arrows of regret,
> Thine on whose arms I yearn to be
> In my deep heart thy name is writ alone,
> Men shall decipher—when they split the stone.[25]

This "new strong sin" was his friendship with H. C. J. Pollitt.

Herbert Charles Pollitt (1872–1942) was the son of *Westmorland Gazette* proprietor Charles Pollitt (born c. 1837) of Thorny Hills, Kendal, and his wife Jane, née Hutchinson (c. 1837–1892).[26] Born on July 20, 1871, he, like Crowley, was a gentleman of leisure owing to his family's fortune and, around the time of their October 1897 meeting, took the Christian name Jerome, by which he preferred to be called. He had matriculated to Trinity College, Cambridge, in 1889, receiving his BA in 1892 and his MA in 1896. Although he failed to qualify as a doctor, he later appeared in London's 1901 census as a "medical servant, own means" and would go on to serve during the Great War as a Lance-Corporal in the Royal Army Medical Corps, entering the 9159th regiment on August 27, 1914.[27]

As early as 1892, Pollitt was a member of the Footlights Dramatic Club, where he wowed audiences as a female impersonator. Although his stage name "Diane de Roughy" was an homage to French actress-courtesan Liane de Pougy (1869–1950), American avant-garde dancer Loie Fuller (1869–1928) was the model for his trademark serpentine scarf dance, which became so famous at Cambridge that it featured in two of Arthur Pilkington Shaw's plays: *The Mixture* and *The Mixture Remixed*.[28] Pollitt's performances would reputedly "make many women green with envy."[29] According to Hobbs,[30] Pollitt was, in his day, one of the most talked-about undergraduates at Cambridge, his rooms hung with the works of Rops, Whistler, and Beardsley, and his bookshelves stocked with the Decadents.

Decadence was a fin de siècle literary and artistic movement dealing with social and physical decay, originating in Paris with Theophile Gautier's *Mademoiselle de Maupin* (1834), which juxtaposed beauty against gross and corrupt events. A generation later, Gustave Flaubert—best known for *Madame Bovary*

(1857)—populated his series of set pieces in *The Temptation of Saint Anthony* (1874) with androgynes, sphinxes, paganism, and the devil such that the pieces, taken as a whole, formed a cohesive tale. In 1884, two more influential offerings focused on moral decay, sexual perversity, materialism, Satanism, and nihilism: the Rosicrucian Joséphin Péladan's *Le Vice Suprême* and Joris-Karl Huysman's classic *A Rebours (Against Nature)*. The movement became so influential that many authors contemporary with Crowley—Arthur Symons (1865–1945), Oscar Wilde (1854–1900), and 1923 Nobel laureate W. B. Yeats (1865–1939)—incorporated Decadent themes into their work.[31]

Herbert Charles Jerome Pollitt (1872–1942), in and out of stage costume.

Pollitt was not only a close friend but also a patron of Decadent artist Aubrey Beardsley (1872–1898), collecting many of his originals, including drawings from *Lysistrata* (1896). Beardsley, meanwhile, designed a bookplate for his friend Pollitt. It is probably through Pollitt that Crowley met the ailing Beardsley and commissioned a bookplate from him;[32] he also asked Beardsley to provide a cover illustration for one of his books, for that December the artist wrote to Pollitt, "Your Cambridge bard must indeed be decorated and issued from the Arcade. I will protect him with the finest cover."[33] Alas, Beardsley died in January 1898, before he could finish either commission. (Coincidentally, Beardsley's father had worked for Crowley's ales as personal assistant to Edward Crowley up until the time the business was sold in 1877.)[34] Pollitt and Beardsley had a mutual friend in Leonard Charles Smithers (1861–1907), publisher of Beardsley and Oscar Wilde; from him Pollitt sometimes purchased items for his sizable collection. According to Low, Pollitt

> always bought three copies of his favourites. Two of these would have the
> bookplates designed for him by Beardsley, one of these he would read, and

the other keep mint. The third copy was to lend and give away, as Pollitt was sure he would have to.[35]

Beardsley, on his deathbed, sent an urgent message to Smithers, "I implore you to destroy *all* copies of *Lysistrata* and bad drawings. Show this to Pollitt and conjure him to do the same. By all that is holy *all* obscene drawings."[36] Being collectors, neither Smithers nor Pollitt complied.

Pollitt was also a collector and patron of American expatriate artist James McNeil Whistler (1834–1903). Around September 1896, and again in July through September 1897, he sat for sketches and portraits by Whistler; although "splendidly begun," the portrait was ultimately destroyed. However, copies of two lithographic sketches survive.[37]

Edward F. Benson's 1897 novel *The Babe B.A.* paid tribute to Pollitt's Cambridge celebrity by modeling its title character after him:

> The Babe was a cynical old gentleman of twenty years of age, who played the banjo charmingly. In his less genial moments he spoke querulously of the monotony of the services of the Church of England, and of the hopeless respectability of M. Zola. His particular forte was dinner parties for six, skirt dancing and acting, and the performances of the duties of half-back at Rugby football. His dinner parties were selected with the utmost carelessness, his usual plan being to ask the first five people he met, provided he did not know them too intimately. With a wig of fair hair, hardly any rouge, and an ingénue dress, he was the image of Vesta Collins, and that graceful young lady might have practised before him, as before a mirror ...
>
> The furniture of his rooms was as various and as diverse as his accomplishments. Several of Mr. Aubrey Beardsley's illustrations from the Yellow Book, clustering round a large photograph of Botticelli's Primavera, which the Babe had never seen, hung above one of the broken sofas, and in his bookcase several numbers of the Yellow Book, which the Babe declared bitterly had turned grey in a single night, since the former artist had ceased to draw for it, were ranged side by side with Butler's *Analogies,* Mr. Sponge's *Sporting Tour,* and Miss Marie Corelli's *Barabbas.*[38]

On the book's publication in early 1897, Beardsley wrote excitedly, "Have you seen Dodo Benson's new novel? It contains three immortal references to your humble servant. There will be a statue yet."[39]

Crowley met Pollitt at Cambridge in October 1897, in the midst of his trance of sorrow. Jerome lived in a Kendal, Westmoreland, house called the Green Window, and had returned to his alma mater to dance again for the Footlights Dramatic Club. Offstage he wore a plain and tragic face: his most striking features were afflicted lips and starved eyes, framed by a pale golden mane; but, onstage, he resembled "one of Rossetti's women brought to life."[40] Crowley thought he was beautiful.

Jerome, who was twenty-six to Crowley's twenty-two, soon became the first intimate friend in AC's sheltered life. They saw each other daily, enjoying, as Crowley put it, "that ideal intimacy which the Greeks considered the great-

est glory of manhood."[41] His personal copy of the book clarifies the thinly
veiled metaphor with the handwritten note, "I lived with Pollitt as his wife for
some six months and he made a poet out of me."

AC was certainly no stranger to the notion of homosexuality: his father had
warned him against it upon his introduction to boarding school; he had been
accused of it at Champney's school for Plymouth brethren; a Plymouth tutor
had attempted to seduce him; and Malvern housed among its star athletes a
host of sodomites. But there was something different about Pollitt. Jerome was
an artist, an educated man, someone he respected and learned from. And Cambridge represented unlocked doors, boundless horizons, and open minds.
Although Crowley was a passionate artist, his upbringing left him tremendously
naive. He doubtlessly proved to be an easy, if not willing, conquest.

Christmas vacation 1897 found Crowley in Amsterdam, the spiritual emptiness
and hunger he began experiencing just two months before now at its peak. He
was restless, sleepless. On December 23, having walked the streets all day, he
watched the sun set by the docks, cradling in his hands his crucifix, pondering
the martyred God, and finding no comfort therein.

> I contemplate the wound
> Stabbed in the flanks of my dear silver Christ.
> He hangs in anguish there; the crown of thorns
> Pierces that palest brow; the nails drip blood;
> There is the wound; no Mary by Him mourns,
> There is no John beside the cruel wood;
> I am alone to kiss the silver lips;
> I rend my clothing for the temple veil;
> My heart's black night must act the sun's eclipse;
> My groans must play the earthquake, till I quail
> At my own dark imagining; and now
> The wind is bitter; the air breeds snow;
> I put my Christ away.[42]

He was having a crisis of faith, seeking spiritual truths but afraid of releasing the
sacred creed of his upbringing. So he struggled with reverence and disillusion-
ment, writing two days later a cynical account of "The Nativity."[43]

Turning his back on the God and Jesus of his upbringing, the only alternative he knew was the devil himself. Thus in March 1898, Crowley visited a
Deighton Bell bookshop and purchased a likely sounding reference: A. E.
Waite's (1857–1942) *The Book of Black Magic and of Pacts* (1898). The book, he
soon discovered, was no Satanic primer, but a sensationally titled anthology of
medieval books on magic. The text described a spiritual alternative hitherto
unknown to the sheltered poet. Moreover, Waite's introduction was riveting;
salted throughout were pieces of a larger picture:

> There stood the source of such authority, the school or schools that issued,
> so to speak, the certificates of title which the records of the expounding
> master are supposed to shew that he possessed ... That there was, as there
> still is, a science of the old sanctuaries.[44]

The idea was anything but clear, but he caught the gist: there existed a school
of mystic knowledge that throughout the ages instructed seekers after spiritual
truth. He sent a letter to the author requesting more information.

Waite's kind reply came in April, urging Crowley to prayer and purity. He
also encouraged him to read German mystic Karl von Eckartshausen (1752–
1813), whose *Der Wolke vor dem Heiligthume* (1802) had recently been translated
as *The Cloud upon the Sanctuary* (1896). Although Crowley always seemed to
have a disparaging word or twenty about Waite's occult scholarship,[45] he admitted Waite's impact upon his own life at this juncture:

> Waite certainly did start a revival of interest in Alchemy, Magic, Mysticism,
> and all the rest. That his scholarship was so contemptible, his style so over-
> loaded, and his egomania so outrageous does not kill to the point of
> extinction the worth of his contribution. If it had not been for Waite, I
> doubt if, humanly speaking, I should ever have got in touch with the
> Great Order. You may of course, if you like, go one step further, back to
> Anna Kingsford and Edward Maitland,[46] but their work, superior as it is to
> him, lacked one great asset. They gave us no idea of the bulk of medieval
> literature. To go back further still, H. P. B.,[47] genius as she was, was far too
> "oriental" to produce the necessary effect. Waite occupies a position not
> unlike that of Samuel Johnson. There is an omnivalence about him, which
> did just what was necessary at the time.[48]

Crowley took the man's advice and purchased a copy of the book to read during Easter vacation.

That holiday at Wastdale Head with Pollitt was clumsy and awkward.
Although they walked the fells together, they spent much of their time apart.
Pollitt refused to join AC in any climbing, and Crowley spent the rest of his
spare time reading. Although he admired Crowley's mind, Pollitt feared that his
spiritual pursuits would drive them apart. As Crowley recalled, Jerome "fought
most desperately against my increasing preoccupation with the aspiration in
which he recognized the executioner of our friendship."[49]

That hangman was Eckartshausen's book. Written in the form of six letters,
The Cloud upon the Sanctuary spelled out the existence of the mystic academy
that Waite had hinted at. Toward the end of the first letter, AC read:

> A more advanced school has always existed to which the deposition of all
> science has been confided, and this school was the community illuminated
> interiorly by the Saviour, the Society of the Elect, which has continued
> from the first day of creation to the present time; its members, it is true,
> are scattered all over the world, but they have always been united by one
> spirit and one truth.

The second letter was more explicit:

> This community possesses a School, in which all who thirst for knowledge
> are instructed by the Spirit of Wisdom itself; and all the mysteries of God
> and of nature are preserved therein for the children of light.[50]

In this school, knowledge was presented dressed in symbol and ceremony, so
the student learned spiritual truths by degrees. It was exactly what he wanted.
But how to find it? Crowley took the only tack he could imagine: he prayed
and petitioned to God and the masters to lead him to the Sanctuary. As if on
cue, he met Oscar Eckenstein (1859–1921)—a skilled mountaineer seventeen
years older than Crowley—who would unwittingly set him on the right path.

Oscar Johannes Ludwig Eckenstein was born in Canonbury, Islington, on
September 9, 1859, to the German Jewish refugee Frederick Gottlieb Eckenstein (c. 1821–1891) and his wife Julie Amalie Antonia Helmke (born c.
1831).[51] Frederick fled Bonn in 1848 to avoid prosecution for his socialist
activities,[52] and in London he started the firm Kumpf & Eckenstein, exporting
seeds, grain, oil paints, turpentine, and machinery to continental European cities like Antwerp, Paris, Bordeaux, and Hamburg.[53] Oscar was the sixth of seven
children,[54] attending University College School and studying chemistry in both
London and Bonn. Although he worked as a chemist, Eckenstein is better
known as a civil engineer with the International Railway Congress Association.[55] According to H. W. Hillhouse, he was "years ahead of the times in
thought and scientific invention of devices for the betterment of railroading."[56]
Crowley's *Confessions* recount several of Eckenstein's professional anecdotes.[57]
His line of work indeed gave Eckenstein something in common with Crowley's
uncle Jonathan, but it was his skill as a mountaineer that first impressed Aleister.

Below the Pen Y Pass youth hostel in North Wales sits the Eckenstein
Boulder. As a new climber, Oscar Eckenstein applied his engineering skills and
fascination with arithmetic puzzles to this modest-sized object, and in doing so
he pioneered the hold and balance techniques that would later revolutionize
the sport of climbing. Although he scaled his first mountain in 1872, his first
Alpine climbs aren't recorded until 1886.[58] He evidently made up for lost time,
and in 1887 made numerous first ascents with various climbers, including the
famous Alpine guide Matthias Zurbriggen (1856–1917). Many of these peaks
are documented in *The Alpine Portfolio*, an album of one hundred heliotype
photographs of the Swiss Alps edited by Eckenstein and August Lorria.[59]
Around this time he also began the first of several first ascents of Y Lliwedd
(2,946 feet) in North Wales.

By most accounts, Eckenstein met art historian and mountaineer William
Martin Conway (1856–1937) while climbing at Zermatt in 1891. However,
Oscar's sister Lina—a feminist polymath and budding cultural historian in her
own right—had already been working for Conway as a transcriber and translator on *The Literary Remains of Albrecht Dürer*,[60] and this connection may well
have played a role in the climbers' meeting. Conway invited Eckenstein to join
his 1892 expedition to the Karakorams, which was being subsidized by the

Royal Geographical Society and the Royal Society.[61] Their mutual acquaintance Zurbriggen was also part of the team, and Eckenstein gladly accepted. Alas, Oscar wound up leaving the expedition early and returning to London. Conway consistently reported that Eckenstein was forced to leave the expedition due to ill health.[62] However, Eckenstein's account in *The Karakorams and Kashmir: An Account of a Journey* (1896) reveals there had been tensions between the conservative Conway and the unorthodox Eckenstein. Ultimately, Eckenstein felt that they spent too much time reconnoitering and not enough climbing in their two and a half months among the mountains, and in a meeting with Conway it was decided that he should leave the expedition.[63] A tacit competition brewed after that, with Conway knighted in 1895 while Eckenstein remained in relative obscurity.

Those who knew Eckenstein agreed that he was "cultured but eccentric," an opinionated and sometimes didactic individual with no interest in conforming to convention.[64] It was at the root of his conflict with Conway. It was the reason he, like Crowley, disdained the Alpine Club, which he perceived as staid and conventional. It was even clear from his dress: he preferred his full beard, straw sandals, and old fisherman's hat to well-appointed clothes, leading more than one acquaintance to the mistaken conclusion that he was poor.

One characteristic of Eckenstein that would prove very influential on Crowley was his love of the works of Sir Richard Francis Burton (1821–1890). According to Guy Knowles (1879–1959), Eckenstein—with whom he climbed the Weisshorn (14,780 feet), Lyskamm (14,852 feet), Dent Blanche (14,291 feet), and Matterhorn (14,692 feet) in 1898—was an avid collector of Burtonania, buying it whenever he came across any.[65] Indeed, Eckenstein's collection of Burton documents and first editions (including rare variants of the first editions) was so significant that N. M. Penzer relied upon it when compiling his Burton bibliography; it was posthumously donated to the Royal Asiatic Society's Burton memorial in 1939 by Lewis C. Lloyd and was referenced for the first time by a Burton biographer in Godsall's *The Tangled Web*.[66] Dean considers it unlikely that the men ever met, pointing out that "Burton died in 1890, aged sixty-nine, when Eckenstein was 31; and during the previous eighteen years Burton had been consul at Treiste."[67] Nevertheless, Hillhouse asserts that his friend had indeed met Burton:

> O. E. often spoke of him [Sir Richard Burton] to me, in our talks about the philosophies of India and the East, and I do know that it was O. E.'s and Burton's intense interest in Eastern philosophies, especially mental telepathy, which brought them together at one time.[68]

This statement is doubly significant: First, it indicates that Eckenstein was the second mountain-climbing chemist with mystical tendencies to cross Crowley's path. Second, Crowley was also a great admirer of Burton, who would inspire Crowley's subsequent adventures in the middle and far east, as well as his book *The Scented Garden* (1910). In later years, Crowley would recommend Burton's

The Book of the Thousand Nights and a Night and *Kasidah* to students in *Magick in Theory and Practice* (1929), and even canonize Burton as a saint in his Gnostic Mass (1918). Crowley's *Confessions* don't reveal how he first discovered Burton, but it may have been through Eckenstein ... much as Crowley's classmate H. A. Adamson introduced him to Shelley. Regardless, Crowley certainly equated the two men: Burton and Eckenstein were two of the "Three Immortal Memories" to whom he dedicated his *Confessions,* and within its pages he would say, "Sir Richard Burton was my hero and Eckenstein his modern representative."[69]

A 1894 portrait of Oscar Eckenstein (1859–1921) by Alphonse Legros.

Eckenstein's neat, logical, and tactical approach to climbing provided the perfect foil for skilled but undisciplined AC. Short and stocky, Eckenstein was a complete athlete with seemingly limitless stamina and an uncanny sense of direction. His right arm was so strong that he could grab a ledge and pull himself up with just a few fingers. As Crowley later reported to hill-climber and writer Joseph Henry Doughty (1889–1936), "Eckenstein, provided he could get 3 fingers on something that could be described as a ledge by a man far advanced in hashish, would be smoking his pipe on the aforesaid ledge a few seconds later and none of us could tell how he had done it."[70] Also enamored of puzzles, Eckenstein quickly solved climbing conundrums with great success.

Together they climbed Wastdale Head, discussing mountaineering, the Alpine Club, and the lack of a true challenge. Eckenstein was determined to return to the Himalayas and conquer the Baltoro Glacier; to succeed where

Conway failed. Crowley eagerly bought into the plan, agreeing to tackle the Himalayas some day, but only after sufficient training.

During these animated encounters on Wastdale Head, Crowley saw a rift open between Pollitt and himself like that in the Devil's Chimney. Not only did they seem to share little in common, but Pollitt proved an impediment to his spiritual quest. Thus, when Crowley began composing "Jezebel"[71] during the vacation, he snuck off to Maidenhead to be alone to write. When Pollitt finally tracked him down, the poet at work was angry and resentful. "I have given my life to religion," Crowley told him, "and you don't fit into the scheme."

Regret sank in soon afterward. Crowley realized his error and weakness, and drafted a letter of apology that he couldn't bring himself to send. Thus they parted on those terms, speaking only occasionally thereafter until, one day, they passed each other on Bond Street; Crowley didn't notice, while Pollitt took it as a personal slight and never spoke to him again.

Crowley carried bittersweet memories of Pollitt for many years, leaving scattered literary remnants as testimony to their friendship. The dedication of Crowley's first book, which was in press about this time, refers to Pollitt as his "Lover and Lord."[72] Later, he wrote two scathing sonnets on Pollitt, published in his *Works of Aleister Crowley* with the apologia:

> The virulence of these sonnets is excusable when it is known that their aim was to destroy the influence in Cambridge of a man who headed in that University a movement parallel to that which at Oxford was associated with the name of Oscar Wilde. They had their effect.[73]

Over a decade later, he published *The Scented Garden* (1910), a parody of Sir Richard Burton's essays on Middle Eastern sexuality. References to homosexuality occur throughout, while Chapter XLI, "The Riddle," teases the reader:

> Habib hath heard; let all Iran
>   who spell aright from A to Z
> Exalt thy fame and understand
>   with whom I made a marriage-bed ...

The solution to the riddle is easy enough: the first letter of each line spells out the name of Herbert Charles Jerome Pollitt. Lest there be any uncertainty, the next poem, Chapter XLII's "Bagh-i-Muattar," contains an acrostic spelling Aleister Crowley in reverse. The tender feelings survived four years later, when, arriving in America in 1914, he wished in his diary for a companion like Pollitt.[74] In "Not the Life and Adventures of Sir Roger Bloxham," written three years later in 1917, the character Hippolytus is H. Pollitt, while Sir Roger Bloxham is Crowley himself.[75] Finally, in his *Confessions,* he recalls his break with Pollitt with the words, "It has been my lifelong regret, for a nobler and purer comradeship never existed on this earth."[76]

> Then Judas, which had betrayed him, when he saw that he was con-
> demned, repented himself, and brought again the thirty pieces of silver to
> the chief priests and elders, saying, I have sinned in that I have betrayed the
> innocent blood. And they said, What is that to us? see thou to that. And
> he cast down the pieces of silver in the temple, and departed and went and
> hanged himself. And the chief priests took the silver pieces, and said, It is
> not lawful for to put them into the treasury, because it is the price of
> blood. And they took counsel, and bought with them the potter's field to
> bury strangers in. Wherefore that field was called, The field of blood, unto
> this day.
>
> —Matthew 27:3–8

The soil of Potter's Field in Jerusalem, according to tradition, could consume a corpse in twenty-four hours. Its Hebrew name, Aceldama, means "field of blood." In 1218 boatloads of its soil were shipped to the Campo Santo in Pisa. In 1898 it became the title of Crowley's first book.

Aceldama: A Place to Bury Strangers In was a poem in thirty-two stanzas brimming with passion and ranging from the erotic to the divine. It reveals the author's delirious struggle with base emotions and the trance of sorrow while striving for a glimpse of his guru upon the spiritual pinnacle:

> This was a dream—and how may I attain?
>   How make myself a worthy acolyte?
>   How from my body shall my soul take flight,
> Being constrained in this devouring chain
>   Of selfishness? How purge the spirit quite
>   Of gross desires
> That eat into the heart with their corrupting fires?
>
> Old Buddha gave command; Jehovah spake;
>   Strange distant gods that are not dead today
>   Added their voices; Heaven's desart way
> Man wins not but by sorrow...[77]

The book appeared in an edition of one hundred copies. Of these, two were on outsize vellum, ten on Japanese vellum, and eighty-eight on handmade paper. Copies sold for half a crown. Because of its small print run, and because copies did not go out for review, his debut garnered little press reaction. One rare reviewer wrote apprehensively:

> Induced by we know not what course of reading, the book is not one that
> can be recommended to the young, for though its stanzas are sufficiently
> musical, there runs through them a vein of scepticism and licentiousness
> which requires to be treated with caution.[78]

Crowley, of course, assessed the book more generously. "I attained, at a bound, the summit of my Parnassus. In a sense, I have never written anything better."[79]

College influences are readily apparent in *Aceldama*. The author of the book is given as "a gentleman of the University of Cambridge" in homage to Shelley, who published his *St. Irvyne; or the Rosicrucian: A Romance* (1811) as "a gentleman of the University of Oxford." The book's flowing, lyric style is likewise modeled after Shelley. Pollitt's influence is visible not only in the dedication to his "Lover and Lord," but also in the introduction, which smacks of the Decadent literature to which Pollitt had introduced him:

> It was a windy night, that memorable seventh night of December, when this philosophy was born in me. How the grave old Professor wondered at my ravings! I had called at his house, for he was a valued friend of mine, and I felt strange thoughts and emotions shake within me. Ah! how I raved! I called to him to trample me, he would not. We passed together into the stormy night. I was on horseback, how I galloped round him in my phrenzy, till he became the prey of a real physical fear! How I shrieked out I know not what strange words! And the poor good old man tried all he could to calm me; he thought I was mad! The fool! I was in the death struggle with self: God and Satan fought for my soul those three long hours. God conquered—now I have only one doubt left—which of the twain was God? Howbeit, I aspire!

Although to conclude from this dramatic account that Crowley was a Satanist would be missing the point entirely, the passage does reflect his inner conflict over religion, just as the poem itself describes his aspiration for enlightenment. Crowley's Decadent mindset is evident when one considers that he inscribed one of the two outsized vellum copies to Beardsley.[80] Alas, the artist died before AC could present it. Another copy of the book he inscribed to his publisher: "To Leonard Smithers from Aleister Crowley hys fyrst booke."[81]

Smithers, as mentioned earlier, was a friend of Pollitt and Beardsley. He possessed an incongruous mixture of admirable and repugnant traits. Learned and generous, vulgar and irresponsible, he drank brandy excessively—although he favored absinthe—and was notoriously unfaithful to his wife. Oscar Wilde wrote of him, "He loves first editions, especially of women: little girls are his passion. He is the most learned erotomaniac in Europe. He is also a delightful companion and a dear fellow."[82] He was a lawyer who, in 1891 or 1892, entered into a bookselling and publishing partnership, issuing some of the most beautiful books ever produced. Admirers called Smithers the cleverest publisher in London. He supplemented his income with erotic literature such as *Teleny, or, The Reverse of the Medal* (1893).[83] In 1894 he started his own successful book business, offering titles such as Sir Richard Burton's *The Carmina of Caius Valerius Catullus* (1894), Ernest Dowson's *Verses* (1896), Alexander Pope's *Rape of the Lock* (1896), Arthur Symons's *Amoris Victima* (1897), and Ben Jonson's *Volpone* (1898).

Crowley first met him in 1897 as part of Pollitt's Decadent circle. Although finely crafted books no longer sold well—nor did clandestinely published erotica—Smithers remained committed to publishing fine editions despite financial hardship. He published Beardsley's *Book of Fifty Drawings* (1897), *A Second Book of Fifty Drawings* (1899), and the periodical *The Savoy* (1898). After Oscar Wilde's trial, he was the only publisher willing to handle Wilde's last three books: *The Ballad of Reading Gaol* (1898), *An Ideal Husband* (1899), and *The Importance of Being Earnest* (1899).

"I'll publish anything the others are afraid of," he bragged to Crowley, who took the statement as an invitation. Smithers had already taught him how publishing deluxe editions can bolster a book's collectability; given him an appreciation for Japanese vellum as book stock; and introduced him to erotica with a copy of *Teleny*. Crowley regarded the publisher, his pale face framed by a straw hat on one end and a blue tie on the other, and determined to produce a book for Smithers to publish. Whence *Aceldamaworks*.

Portrait artist and Royal Academy President Sir Gerald Festus Kelly (1879–1972) was just another Cambridge student when *Aceldama* appeared. He purchased it at a specialty bookshop that carried the book as a courtesy because Crowley spent so much money there on first editions. The book, particularly its quotation from Swinburne's "The Leper," fascinated Kelly. He wished to meet the mysterious "gentleman of the University of Cambridge," so the bookseller arranged it.

Their meeting in May 1898 went wonderfully. They discovered many common experiences: Both had suffered debilitating childhood illnesses. Both came from affluent families. Both were reacting against clerical fathers. Both identified with their Irish ancestry. And both were passionate artists.

Gerald Kelly was the grandchild of Frederic Festus Kelly, His Majesty's Inspector of Inland Letter Carriers who, in 1835, began publishing Kelly's Directories, which were essentially the Victorian version of the yellow pages. Gerald was the third child and only son of the Reverend Frederic Festus Kelly (1838–1918), Vicar of Camberwell, and his wife, Blanche Bradford (born c. 1845). He had two older sisters, Rose Edith (1874–1932) and Eleanor Constance Mary (born 1877). Gerald enjoyed the benefits of affluence, and in 1896, at age seventeen, sailed with Rose for South Africa to recuperate from a liver abscess. Macey, his cabinmate, praised Gerald's early watercolors and urged him to study painting in Paris. Although he and Macey saw each other only occasionally after they arrived in Cape Town, the notion of becoming a painter consumed the young man.

When he eventually returned home with a clean bill of health, Gerald announced his intention to become a painter. "Rot" his father said. "No member of my family ever showed the slightest talent." Mrs. Kelly, who adored Gerald, defended his decision, and after six months' argument they reached an agreement: if Gerald went to Cambridge as his father had,[84] then Reverend Kelly would allow him to become a painter.

In 1897, Gerald matriculated to Trinity Hall. He had no intention of following a regular course of study; he was simply there to pass time and enjoy himself. Thomas Thornely (1855–1949), lecturer in moral and historical sciences, was disappointed to find the Kelly heir uninterested in history, but did his best to expose the lad to poetry. Gerald would spend the next three years reading poetry in a desultory manner, leading eventually to Crowley. Four years younger than Crowley, Kelly saw a worldly and charming role model in the poet, and they immediately became close friends. Reflecting on this time more than fifty years later, Kelly mused, "Aleister and I were great friends for several years," and "I liked him; we made each other laugh ... he was certainly a delightful companion."[85]

Smithers was the logical publisher for Crowley's next book, *White Stains* (1898). Although tame by today's standards, some of its pieces—such as "A Ballad of Passive Paederasty," "With Dog and Dame," and "Necrophilia"—required the seasoned hands of an underground publisher. Because of its content, Smithers sent the book to Amsterdam to be typeset by Binger Bros. Crowley published it anonymously, and as with *Aceldama,* only one hundred copies were printed.

The book, with the descriptive subtitle "The literary remains of George Archibald Bishop, a neuropath of the Second Empire," was a reaction to Austrian police doctor Richard Freiherr von Krafft-Ebing's (1840–1902) study of sexual aberrations, *Psychopathia Sexualis* (1893): the book that coined the term *masochism* after the fiction of fellow Austrian Leopold Ritter von Sacher-Masoch (1836-1895). Although Krafft-Ebing translated the racier sections of his text into Latin, the book became a sensation among erudite pornographers everywhere. Crowley, determined to do a better job of explaining the nature of sexual deviance, wrote a story from the perspective of a poet who goes astray, taking on various vices and ultimately committing murder. Crowley later clarified, "The work is entirely one of imagination, as he had no actual experience, even by hearsay, of the subject on which he was writing."[86]

Although *White Stains* has been hastily dubbed pornographic, it actually belongs to Decadent literature, with poetry a natural style for Crowley to choose. Swinburne's Decadent poem "Tannhauser" impressed him so much that he would later re-tell the tale in his own book of the same title. And Reed's description of Decadence, although applied to Flaubert's *The Temptation of Saint Anthony,* also applies to *White Stains:*

> a sequence of set pieces rendered in a complicated and ornate self-advertising style. The segments of the work are detachable, yet when read in sequence they create an anticipatory mood like that of musical composition.[87]

Other Decadent themes incorporated into *White Stains* include the pursuit of pleasure, irreverence toward religion, and repugnant subject matter.

Crowley's third manuscript, *Green Alps,* was next in Smithers's hands. It contained "Two Sonnets in Praise of a Publisher": two poems for Smithers with little praise and much shocking imagery. This collection of poetry never appeared. A fire at the printers destroyed the sheets and Smithers went bankrupt shortly thereafter. Proofs of the dedication and pages 81–107 are known to have survived, although Crowley published some of these poems later.[88]

With Smithers defunct, Pollitt out of the picture, Beardsley dead, and Crowley at the end of his senior year, it was time to move on. Just as the diplomatic service, like all other mortal aspirations, was an exercise in futility, so was a Cambridge degree. It was merely window dressing for one's pride. Although he had successfully completed his coursework and exams up to this point, Crowley never appeared for the second part of his finals. He felt he had mastered the subjects, and that was good enough for him. In the tradition of Byron, Shelley, Swinburne, and Tennyson, he left the university without a degree and pursued his own star.

The entire month of July 1898 passed camped in a tent above the Alpine snow line at 11,500 feet, below the Dent Blanche (14,291 feet) and beside the Schönbühl Glacier.[89] Crowley was training with Eckenstein in techniques necessary to attempt the Himalayas. "You never know when you'll have to jump in an emergency," Eckenstein instructed, and, by way of preparation, Eckenstein ran his student through grueling training. Early on, he made Crowley slide headfirst down a snowy incline, with instructions to do nothing to stop himself until given the word; then he had to the count of five to stop and end up standing. From there, the training became increasingly difficult and dangerous, with glissades from various positions and slopes.[90]

He also taught Crowley how to use crampons, or ice claws. Eckenstein attempted to introduce them to British mountaineers, insisting that they made cutting steps with ice axes unnecessary; but English and Scottish climbers panned them for years as "artificial aids" before finally accepting them. In 1908 he would invent a hinged ten-point crampon that would become commercially available in 1910, known today as the Eckenstein crampon. Another of Eckenstein's later innovations was to turn the typical ice ax, or alpenstock, into a one-handed implement by shortening it by five inches and making the head smaller; while poorly received in England, it proved to be most effective in combination with his crampon designs. Both were offered by A. Hupfauf of Einsiedeln, Switzerland.[91]

The indifference of the climbing establishment to Eckenstein's innovations typified his clash with the Alpine Club. To him, the club was merely a means for mediocre climbers to congratulate themselves for lame achievements. Like Crowley, he found their Alpine guides useless and their recommended routes hardly more than a scramble. When the Club condemned their guideless ascents as reckless, AC accused the Club of "virulent, dishonest, envious intrigues against guideless climbing and climbers."[92] Eckenstein, meanwhile, joked sardonically that he could take a cow up the Matterhorn if he tied its legs. He wrote in his "Hints to Young Climbers,"

The aspirant is confronted by real trouble—that is, if he really wishes to become good; for he is compassed about with a great cloud of witnesses— "expert witnesses"—who are all quite, or nearly quite, as ignorant of mountain craft as the veriest beginner, and are Great Authorities on Climbing and Mountaineering. Climbing is, as far as I know, the only sport in which the absolute humbug can reign supreme without instant exposure....

Believe nothing that is told you about mountain craft, unless you have absolute proof that a real expert is speaking. If a *soi-disant* "Authority" tells you that no man can walk up an ice slope of 60 degrees without cutting steps; that no one can see a crevasse when it is covered with snow; that guides are vastly superior to amateurs; believe him not. Go and try for yourself; if you find you cannot do any of these things, find some one who can, and then take *his* statements for gospel ...

How, you will ask, are you to distinguish this sublime person at sight? Thus. Ask him if he uses claws; if he is better than most first-class Swiss guides; if he can sit on one leg on a smooth hard ice slope of 70 degrees without a step having been cut; if he has led on more than six good guideless expeditions in the Alps (successful ones!); if he is a better rock-climber than almost any guide he ever met—he must answer "Yes" to all these queries and be prepared to provide his words, or he is a beginner in the Art.[93]

This article gives a good glimpse of what training with Eckenstein must have been like for Crowley. Indeed, this maverick instructor even acknowledged his protégé's unconventional technique: "For example, the outer pinnacle of the Devil's Chimney at Beachy Head was only climbed with the assistance of a definite pull from an unshaven chin!"[94]

Perhaps what was difficult for the club to bear was that these dissident climbers were good. Competent and respected Eckenstein struck out on his own; under his wing was the outspoken and independent Crowley, who, after astonishing everyone by climbing Beachy Head, proceeded to set other climbing records both on the Alps and on Britain's sea cliffs. Arnold Lunn (1888–1974)—British skier, Alpine Club president, and creator of the alpine slalom race—reluctantly admitted they were both technically excellent climbers,[95] and mountaineer Thomas George Longstaff, after a demonstration of the new crampons on August 24, called Crowley

a fine climber, if an unconventional one. I have seen him go up the dangerous and difficult right (true) side of the great icefall of the mer de Glace below the Géant alone, just for a promenade. Probably the first and perhaps the only time this mad, dangerous and difficult route had been taken.[96]

During free moments on the glacier, Crowley studied S. L. MacGregor Mathers's (1854–1918) *The Kabbalah Unveiled* (1887), which he had been reading since July. It was a translation of Knorr von Rosenroth's (d. 1689) Latin tome *Kabbala Denudata* (1677–1684), itself a translation of that classic of Hebrew mystic literature, *The Zohar*. Crowley recognized a wealth of information in the book but could not grasp it. For that reason it intrigued him even more. He pined increasingly for the teacher he had prayed for at Wastdale. Little did he realize that Eckenstein had brought him to just the right place.

In August 1898, Crowley descended the glacier for a much needed break, packing up his book and staying in the village of Zermatt. There, the impetuous student of mysticism found himself in a beer hall one night discussing alchemy. Having passed Cambridge's special exam in chemistry with a second class, Crowley felt himself quite the expert in present company, and lectured with cocksureness. He was wrong. After the discussion, a man introduced himself to Crowley as Julian L. Baker, analytical chemist. Baker recognized a well-read and sincere student of the mysteries beneath AC's arrogant exterior and discussed the fine points of alchemy while escorting Crowley back to his hotel.

Science records the name of Julian Levett Baker (1873–1958) as an English chemist, educated at the City of London School until a bout of scarlet fever over Easter 1888 prevented his return. His father arranged for academic coaching, and Baker passed the next entrance exam to Finsbury Technical College, where he studied chemistry for three years (because he was so young at entry, they kept him an extra year beyond the customary two). In 1891, at age nineteen, he became assistant chemist—and later chief chemist—to the London Beetroot Sugar Association under Arthur Robert Ling (1861–1937), future professor of brewing at Birmingham, with whom he collaborated.[97] In April 1899, Baker was proposed as a fellow of the Society of Public Analysts;[98] he was also a fellow of the Imperial College and of the Chemical Society.[99] In 1900 he became the first chemist appointed to a London brewery—the Stag Brewery at Pimlico, operated by Watney, Combe, Reid and Co. Ltd.—where he would remain until his retirement forty-six years later.[100] Indeed, he is best known for his contributions to brewing chemistry—an interesting coincidence given the Crowley family's roots. Baker became honorary secretary of the London section of the Society of Chemical Industry in 1905, where his responsibilities included the program of its ambitious annual meetings.[101] As a founding member of the Institute of Brewing, he also authored *The Brewing Industry* (1905), followed by his chapter on "Malt and Malt Liquors" in *Allen's Commercial Organic Analysis* (1909), and the article on "Fermentation" in *Encyclopædia Britannica* (1911).[102] He quickly established a reputation as "one of the foremost English exponents of brewing chemistry.... In him are combined two attributes which are seldom found together, namely a finely trained and rigidly scientific mind with practical knowledge and action."[103]

Baker would author some fifty papers over his career. He would also serve his profession as honorary secretary of the Institute of Brewing (1908–1918), followed by a forty-year term as its vice president; publication committee member for the *Journal of the Society of Chemical Industry;* editor of *The Analyst* (1907–1920) and *Journal of the Institute of Brewing* (1920–1949); and an examiner in brewing to both the City and Guilds of London Institute (1908–1911) and the University of Birmingham (1928–1931). On November 6, 1924, he delivered the Streatfield Memorial Lecture at his alma mater, the Finsbury Technical College.[104] Other career honors included his 1944 election to the City and Guilds of London Institute, and his 1948 receipt of the Horace Brown medal, the highest award of the Institute of Brewing.[105] He was well known in the business; his colleague George Cecil Jones noted that, among a crowd of chemists, "Baker seems to know everyone here and everyone knows Baker."[106] Another colleague described him, "His character was essentially his own and he possessed an old world courtesy that was as charming as it was natural."[107]

In 1898, however, Baker was still a chemist with the Beetroot Sugar Association, where he discovered his interest in sugars and starches.[108] Thus Crowley had just met the third of three climber-chemists with a mystical bent.

Crowley sat in his room that night, pondering his luck. Baker was an alchemist, but was he the master he had asked for? If so, how ironic that fatigue and vanity were the devices of his discovery. Kismet, he decided: in the morning, he would ask Baker if he *was* a master.

By the time Crowley asked after him, however, Baker had already left the hotel. AC frantically telegraphed all over the valley, desperate not to let his one link to the Sanctuary vanish. After searching the local hotels and railroad stations, he finally found Baker and told him of his search for the Secret Sanctuary. Then he asked the big one: "Are you a Master?"

Baker smiled and shook his head. "No, but on our return to London, I'll introduce you to a man who is much more of a magician than I."

His health declined throughout the summer, finally forcing Crowley to leave Eckenstein's camp and return to London under a physician's care. He took a room in the Cecil Hotel during his convalescence, writing the poetic play *Jephthah* and corresponding with Baker about the Secret Sanctuary.

When Baker introduced Crowley to George Cecil Jones (1873–1960) that October, everything fell neatly into place. Jones was an industrial chemist of 58 Cliddesden Road, Basingstoke, who, like Baker, was still early in his career. Although Crowley called him Welsh,[109] Jones was actually born in Croydon, Surrey, on January 10, 1873.[110] Educated from 1889 to 1893 at the City and Guilds of London Central Institute, he worked for eighteen months as assistant to the eminent London analytical chemists Messrs. Helbing and Passmore.[111] From there, he transferred to the Dowson Economic Gas and Power Company, Basingstoke, in late 1894. At that time, he was also balloted and elected to the Chemical Society, and in 1896 became a member of the Society of Chemical Industry.[112] In 1896 the *Chemical News and Journal of Industrial Science* listed him as one of eighteen alumni of the City and Guilds of London Institute "whose subsequent careers merit notice."[113]

In the years after meeting Crowley, Jones would work as managing chemist at Free, Rodwell & Co. Ltd.—maltsters of Misty, Essex—from 1902, then five years later start his own consulting practice, which he would run until his 1939 retirement. Other professional accomplishments include passing the Associate of the Institute of Chemistry's branch "A" examination in mineral chemistry; serving on the London committee of the Society of Chemical Industry (for which Baker was secretary); nomination to the Society of Public Analysts and Other Analytical Chemists; and being an abstractor for *The Analyst* and an auditor for the Chemical Technology Examination Board.[114] Over his career he authored a number of papers and reviews in trade journals like *The Analyst* and the *Journal of the Institute of Brewing and Distilling*.[115] Along with Baker, he contributed to *Allen's Commercial Organic Analysis* (1909), with chapters on "Alcohols," "Wines and Potable Spirits," and "Non-Glucosidal Bitter principles."[116] He also reported on the state of "Analytical Chemistry" in 1915.[117]

Jones was known for his gentle, tolerant, and self-effacing character, his sound judgement, and moral courage.[118] Slight and lean, with long hair, beard, and mustache, he looked like Jesus incarnate. "I am not an appreciator of poetry," he told Crowley, "and I have no Keats";[119] but he was well read in magic, which he investigated empirically. Most medieval books on the subject, he explained, were purposely unintelligible to prevent the profane from penetrating their secrets. Only a proper instructor could decipher their meaning.

Once a student was ready, Jones continued, he could contact a teacher in the manner described in the medieval book *The Book of the Sacred Magic of Abramelin the Mage;* the process involved a six-month retirement from the cares of daily living, spent instead in constant prayer and meditation unto one's holy guardian angel. Jones tipped Crowley to a modern translation and interpretation of the book that had just been published that February; the translator, coincidentally, was Samuel Liddell Mathers. AC instantly recognized this as the translator and expositor of that other mysterious and impenetrable tome, *The Kabbalah Unveiled,* and resolved to find a copy. Jones, like Baker, recognized Crowley's vast magical potential and offered to introduce him to a body of initiates that could prepare him for the sacred magic of Abramelin.

In response, Crowley secretly took a flat at 67 and 69 Chancery Lane under the identity of Count Vladimir Svareff. His reasons for adopting this outlandish pseudonym were twofold, as he explains:

> 1) I had resolved to perform the operation of the *Sacred Magic of Abramelin the Mage*. In that book, the aspirant is warned that his family will oppose his actions and seek to interfere. The assumption of this name was one of my precautions against any such nonsense.
> 2) I had just come back from Russia, where I had been to learn the language for the Diplomatic Service, and I thought it would be fun to observe the reactions of Londoners to a foreign nobleman. It was.[120]

Despite advice to wait, he dedicated two rooms to the sacred magic.

Meanwhile, Baker and Jones taught Crowley the technique of astral projection. The practice resembles a controlled out-of-body experience, where one's consciousness leaves its physical confines and travels in the imagination. The first step involved drawing a protective circle around one's body, simultaneously preventing other entities from invading it and isolating the practitioner from ambient distractions. Next, the room was purged of undesirable energies by means of a formula called the Lesser Banishing Ritual. Prayer or meditation followed, and finally, projection. All visions were critically examined, tested, and recorded for agreement with known facts about the astral realm. Unusual as the technique was, it strove for the same systematic and empirical standards that made science possible.

Crowley's first experience was unusually vivid, and his second sight quickly surpassed Baker's. In two months' instruction, Crowley logged a total of eighteen visions, including attending a performance of Beethoven's Fifth at Queen's Hall. The visions, which survive in his diaries and were later partly published in *The Equinox,* are fascinating. One in particular merits description:

Traveling down a long gold-purple column that opened into a scarlet cavern, the student found his astral body besieged by lost souls attempting to break through the protective barrier of his magic circle. Among these, he recognized Pollitt's face. "Who are these?" Crowley asked.

A voice said, "They are the souls of those whom thou hast caused to sin."

Truth or lie, it was an ugly sight. He raised an imaginary sword in outrage, and as he did, a hideous deformed giant lunged out of the shadows and threw its black form repeatedly at the circle. To AC's disbelief, the barrier nearly yielded, and he prepared to smite the creature. But a voice interrupted and warned that the monster was his own evil persona, and he ought not to banish it.

Although the magician commanded his persona to stop tormenting him, the shadow responded more furiously than before. The circle yielded dramatically, allowing the figure perilously close to Crowley, who was confused about how to react. Finally, he raised his magic sword, traced a protective pentagram between himself and his alter ego, and intoned the Tetragrammaton, or sacred four-lettered name of God: Yahweh. In response the hulk sullenly withdrew.

Crowley mournfully considered his dark half, extended his left arm, and instructed the beast to kiss his hand and repent. However, the wary magician extended his hand only part way, and the monstrosity bent only slightly toward it. Aleister Crowley's two sides confronted each other that night and could not meet halfway. That dark half would resurface over the years, presenting its ugly face at the most inopportune moments, leaving people with a demonic impression of AC. But for now, the astral traveler returned to his physical body.[121]

His quick progress convinced Jones and Baker of both his sincerity and ability. They agreed: it was time Aleister Crowley joined the Order of the Golden Dawn.

CHAPTER THREE

The Golden Dawn

William Wynn Westcott (1848–1925) was a gentle, friendly man, born in Crowley's hometown of Leamington. His life was like two parallel streams, flowing side by side but never crossing. One river was the medical profession, the other his spiritual journey. His father, the surgeon Peter Westcott of Oundle, died when Wynn was about ten, and he was subsequently raised by his uncle, Dr. Richard Westcott Martyn of Martock, Somerset. Following in the footsteps of his family, Westcott attended University College, London, passing the University of London's second division MB exam in 1869, and on April 14, 1870, passing his exam at Apothecaries' Hall to receive a certificate to practice medicine.[1] By age twenty-three—four years before Crowley was born—he became a partner in his uncle's medical practice in Martock, Somersetshire. Shortly thereafter, he married Eliza Burnett (c. 1851–1921), with whom he had five children.[2] Beginning around 1883 he held the post of deputy coroner for central Middlesex and central London until he was appointed coroner of northeast London in 1894.[3] In this capacity, he held over twenty-one inquests per week into deaths reported in his region[4] until his 1918 retirement. His professional service included stints as president of the Society for the Study of Inebriety, vice president of the Medico-Legal Society, vice president of the National Sunday League, and councillor of the Coroners' Society. Although he published professionally—authoring the book *Suicide: Its History, Literature, Jurisprudence, Causation, and Prevention* (1885) and the paper "Twelve Years' Experience as a London Coroner" (1907) and coediting fifteen editions of *The Extra Pharmacopœia* from its original 1883 publication[5]—the bulk of his literary output concerned the occult.

Hermetic philosophy always fascinated Westcott, leading him to study kabbalah, alchemy, and Rosicrucianism. These pursuits led him in 1871—about the time he partnered with his uncle—to join the Parrett and Axe Masonic Lodge, over which he would preside as Worshipful Master in 1877. He also pursued the higher degree rites of Freemasonry, advancing to the Royal Arch and the Rose Croix degrees in 1873 and by 1878 reaching the thirtieth degree of the Ancient and Accepted Scottish Rite.[6] On December 2, 1886, he was admitted to the prestigious Masonic research lodge, Quatuor Coronati; seven years later, in 1893, he was unanimously elected and installed in a one-year term as its master.[7]

Dr. W. Wynn Westcott (1848–1925), cofounder of the Golden Dawn.

Westcott also joined other initiatory organizations, both allied and irregular. On January 7, 1880—just before becoming Deputy Coroner—he joined London's prestigious Rosicrucian fraternity, Societas Rosicruciana in Anglica (SRIA). He served as Supreme Grand Secretary of the Swedenborgian Rite, a hermetic revival of an earlier fraternal order based on the teachings of Christian mystic Emanuel Swedenborg (1688–1772). And he joined the Esoteric Section of H. P. Blavatsky's (1831–1891) Theosophical Society (TS). The results of his scholarly research into hermeticism took the form of several dozen contributions to Masonic journals *Ars Quatuor Coronatorum* and *The Freemason,* to the *Transactions of the Metropolitan College* of the SRIA, and to Theosophical journals *The Theosophist, Lucifer,* and *Theosophical Siftings.* He also wrote books like *Numbers: Their Occult Power and Mystic Virtue* (1890), translated the *Sepher Yetzirah* (1893) and *The Magical Ritual of the Sanctum Regnum* (1896) into English, and cowrote and edited a series of ten monographs issued by the TS as *Collectanea Hermetica* (1893–1896).[8]

In 1887, Westcott discovered in the musty SRIA library an old manuscript written in cipher. Decoding its contents, he discovered ritual fragments and the address of Fräulein Anna Sprengel, a German Rosicrucian adept. Writing her, he was surprised to receive authorization to start an English branch of the esoteric school known as "Die Goldene Dämmerung," thus marking the inception of the Golden Dawn (GD), the organization that counted England's intelligentsia amongst its members. This, at least, is the legend.

Whatever the origin of the Cipher Manuscript, the Isis-Urania branch (or, formally, Temple) of the GD was founded in 1888. Like the other societies he had encountered, the GD espoused no particular religious belief, merely transmitting knowledge gained from comparative study of religion and philosophy the world over. Westcott invited two SRIA associates—W. R. Woodman and Samuel Liddell Mathers—to form the ruling triumvirate.

Dr. W. R. Woodman (1828–1891) was a retired physician twenty years Westcott's senior. He had also studied kabbalah, Egyptian antiquities, gnosticism, philosophy, astrology, alchemy, and tarot. Having begun as SRIA's secretary in 1867, he advanced in eleven years to the post of supreme magus. Upon his death in 1891 (three years after founding the GD), Westcott would succeed him as SRIA's head.

Samuel Liddell Mathers (1854–1918) was the most colorful of the GD's founders. Born in Hackney, he was the son of commercial clerk William M. Mathers. His father died young, and his mother raised him alone at Bournemouth. After her death in 1885 he moved to London. As an adult he maintained a firm athletic build from boxing and fencing. He also spent countless hours in the British Museum reading room, studying both magic and warfare. He joined the SRIA around 1877, where he met both Woodman and Westcott. In 1887—while Westcott was reputedly deciphering the Cipher Manuscript—he published *The Kabbalah Unveiled,* a translation of Christian Knorr von Rosenroth's treatise on the *Zohar, Kabbala Denudata* (1677–1684), prefaced with his own exposition on the subject. He dedicated the book to Anna Kingsford (1846–1888), past president of the London TS and one of the first English women to obtain a degree in medicine; highly influenced by her and her book *The Perfect Way* (1882), Mathers became a staunch vegetarian and anti-vivisectionist.[9] At the reading room, Mathers made two friends who would become major players in the GD saga: Mina Bergson and W. B. Yeats.

Mina Bergson (1865–1928) was the younger sister of Nobel Prize–winning philosopher Henri Bergson (1859–1941).[10] A sweet, attractive woman with springy hair and blue eyes, she was a London art student by age fifteen. She met Mathers in 1888 while studying Egyptian art at the British Museum. The mysterious scholar, eleven years her senior, fascinated her, and they wed two years later. She called him Zan, after the protagonist in Bulwer-Lytton's mystic novel *Zanoni* (1842). He called her Moïna, his Highland redaction of her name.

William Butler Yeats (1865–1939) placed mysticism second in his life only to poetry. By 1887 he had joined Kingsford's Hermetic Students and, between 1889 and 1890, organized the Esoteric Section of the TS. He met Mathers in the British Museum reading room around 1889, and came to idolize the man he later characterized as having "much learning" but "little scholarship."[11] Yeats split with the Theosophists because they discouraged the practice of magic; on March 7, 1890, he joined the GD.

Golden Dawn cofounder Samuel Liddell MacGregor Mathers (1854–1918) in 1911.

After losing his job in London and moving to Paris with his wife, Mathers became increasingly eccentric. Rekindling his childhood love of Celtic symbology, he adopted all its trappings: He claimed descent from the clan MacGregor, the name of which had been suppressed under penalty of death and in 1603 changed to Mathers. He adopted pseudonyms like Comte de Glenstrae, Comte MacGregor, and Samuel Liddell MacGregor; rode his bicycle through the Paris streets in full Highland dress; and reputedly performed the sword dance with a knife in his stocking. Back in London, rumor had it Mathers believed himself to be the reincarnation of Scottish wizard king James IV.

That same year, Woodman died; with Westcott succeeding him as supreme magus of the SRIA, he essentially became a silent partner in the GD. This left Mathers as de facto head of the order, and he seized the opportunity to assert his dominance, claiming direct contact with the Secret Chiefs—those mysterious and disembodied masters who ran the order—and managing the London temple from Paris.

When high-ranking members tired of answering to an invisible hand, Mathers responded with a pronunciamento dated October 29, 1896: the Secret

Chiefs had appointed him supreme ruler of the GD; as such, Mathers demanded all members sign and return to him an oath of loyalty. He would meet all refusals with expulsion.

Ousted in the shakedown was high-ranking member Annie Horniman. The wealthy daughter of a tea merchant, her £200 annual stipend to Mathers was the only thing standing between his obscure translations—such as *The Sacred Book of Abramelin the Mage*—and poverty. The expulsion, of course, meant the end of his allowance. Many of the London temple's 323 members were outraged by Horniman's suspension and assembled a petition to reinstate her. Mathers refused to yield.

Coincidentally, matters forced Westcott to further distance himself from the GD at this time. Within days of Mathers's last visit to London, Westcott's employers confronted him: someone (in retrospect, presumably Mathers or an ally) had left a GD instructional paper on a carriage with Westcott's name and business address on it. Learning of Westcott's outside interests, his superiors told him, "A coroner should bury bodies, not dig them up." Westcott gladly pulled back from the order, finding Rosicrucians much easier to deal with than ceremonial magicians.

In this agitated political environment, Crowley found himself a Neophyte.

A member of that ages-old college of occultism described by Eckartshausen, Perdurabo set out to learn all he could. Upon entering the grade of Neophyte (cryptically denoted 0°=0□, where the first digit represented the grade and the second digit the corresponding position on the Hebrew Tree of Life), he discovered that, like any other school, the GD contained grades through which students passed after examination. Four grades awaited: the Zelator (1°=10□), Theoricus (2°=9□), Practicus (3°=8□), and Philosophus (4°=7□); then he would enter the Portal grade to the mysterious Second Order.

His first lessons as an occultist gravely disappointed him. They were neither new nor arcane. His teachers asked him to learn the Hebrew alphabet, the 10 spheres or *sephiroth* of the Hebrew Tree of Life, and the attribution of the seven planets to the seven days of the week. The secrets he swore to keep inviolable were trivia he had already known for months, gleaned from countless other books of magic. Jones and Baker were supportive, advising him not to judge the GD until he reached the Second Order.

Equally disappointing was the order's membership. Expecting to encounter spiritual giants, he discovered a group of nonentities. Crowley was not alone in this opinion. GD member and Irish feminist Maud Gonne (1866–1953) characterized the order as "the very essence of British middle-class dullness. They looked so incongruous in their cloaks and badges at initiation ceremonies."[12] Even Jones called it "a club, like any other club, a place to pass the time and meet one's friends."[13] Despite these views, the GD attracted its share of luminaries. Over the years, it claimed among its membership authors Arthur

Machen (1863–1947) and Algernon Blackwood (1869–1951); the aforementioned poet W. B. Yeats and his uncle George Pollexfen; and Constance Mary Wilde (1859-1898), wife of Oscar Wilde. In addition to these better-known names, the GD also hosted men of learning, including chemists (Baker and Jones), physicians (Westcott, Woodman, Bury, Berridge, Felkin, and others), and occult scholars (Waite, Mathers, Bennett). In 1898, Dr. Bury even invited Sir Arthur Conan Doyle (1859-1930) to join, but he declined.

Despite his protestations, Crowley's initiation deeply impressed him. He wrote the poem "The Neophyte"[14] about the experience and, like Yeats, would forever after show its influence in his writing and life.

Jezebel and Other Tragic Poems (1898)[15] was a twenty-three-page booklet with a vellum wrapper, privately printed at the Chiswick Press with twelve copies on vellum and forty on handmade paper. Published under his Russian pseudonym of Vladimir Svareff,[16] it featured an introduction and epilogue by Aleister Crowley and a dedication to his Cambridge friend Gerald Kelly.

While Crowley had an excellent printer in the Chiswick Press, he had no way to distribute and sell his books. Smithers introduced him to the London firm of Kegan Paul, Trench, Trübner and Company, printers and booksellers, and he chose them to sell his next book, *Tale of Archais* (1898). Appearing in January 1899, the edition consisted of one hundred copies which sold for five shillings apiece. One-fourth of the print run was sent out for reviews, which ranged from "a certain command of facile rhythm" to "spurious romanticized mythology."[17] As early as 1905, Crowley regretted publishing the piece.[18] Later, Crowley recalled it as "simply jejune; I apologize."[19]

Songs of the Spirit (1898) continued Crowley's association with Kegan, Paul, Trench, Trübner and Company. Although Crowley contracted this edition around December 1898, it appeared after *Tale of Archais*. Finishing at 109 pages, AC dedicated the volume to Julian L. Baker in gratitude for introducing him to the GD. He issued one copy on vellum and fifty signed, besides the print run of three hundred. This mixed bag of poems, largely dating from 1897, garnered mixed reviews from the press. While the *Manchester Guardian* admired its intense spirituality and technical superiority, the *Athenaeum* considered it to be "difficult to read, and where they touch definite things, more sensual than sensuous."[20] *The Outlook* called Crowley "a poet of fine taste and accomplishment" and his book "contains much that is beautiful."[21] By the end of the year, half the print run had sold.

Realizing how easy it was to publish his poetry, Crowley continued turning it out as quickly as the presses could print it.

A cold chill filled the room, but not because it was January. Magical energy charged the temple, but not because of the ritual. No, it was that haggard man with dark wild eyes that put everything out of sorts. AC didn't know who he was but felt his unsettling energy throughout the ceremony. Crowley anxiously disrobed in the changing room, anticipating a lungful of open air.

As he adjusted his floppy silk bow tie, his heart pounded with the sound of approaching footsteps. The man pierced him with his eyes. He had a thick brow and an almost fanatical gaze. If not for his pallor and the physical suffering exuded by his presence, he might have been handsome. For now, Crowley found him intimidating. "Little Brother," he observed, "you have been meddling with the *Goetia*."

Crowley stared into his burning eyes, transfixed. "No, I haven't." It was a lie. He had been playing with magical tomes like *Abramelin* and the *Goetia* or *Key of Solomon* ever since he moved into his Chancery Lane flat. Just the other night, he and Jones watched as semimaterialized figures and shadows paraded endlessly around the temple.

"In that case," the man continued, "the *Goetia* has been meddling with you." Then he was gone again.

The figure was Frater Iehi Aour ("Let there be light"), affectionately known as the White Knight after *Through the Looking-Glass*. GD members ranked him second only to Mathers as a magician. They told the story of how, at a party, someone ridiculed the notion of a blasting wand as described in medieval texts on magic; Iehi Aour took offense, produced a long glass prism, and pointed it at the offender. Fourteen hours later, doctors revived the skeptic.

Other gossip described an altercation about Hinduism between Mathers and Iehi Aour. Mathers had rejected Frater IA's contention that, by calling upon Shiva, one could cause the god to open his eyes and thereby destroy the world. To prove his point, IA plopped down on the floor of Mathers's living room in lotus position and began chanting, "Shiva, Shiva, Shiva ... " Mathers, already agitated by the argument, stormed out of the room. Returning half an hour later to find his guest still at it, he erupted, "Will you stop blaspheming?" The mantra continued. Mathers drew his revolver. "If you don't stop, I'll shoot you." The mantra continued. Moïna entered the room just in time to end the argument, saving not just the White Knight but also the universe.

The man behind the legend of Frater Iehi Aour was Allan Bennett (1872–1923). Born Charles Henry Allan Bennett during the Franco-Prussian war, his widowed mother raised him a strict Catholic. According to Crowley, he led a sheltered life, still believing at age sixteen that angels brought babies to earth. When classmates showed him an obstetrics manual, he found the facts of human reproduction so offensive and degrading that he lost faith in a benevolent God and abandoned Catholicism. At eighteen he briefly experienced the yogic trance of *Shivadarshana,* wherein the entire universe is united and all sense of self annihilated. Although he knew nothing of yoga, the vision was so profound that he vowed, "This is the only thing worth while. I will do nothing else in all my life but find out how to get back to it." Thus he dedicated himself to the study of Buddhist and Hindu scriptures. By 1894 he had joined the GD and performed many legendary ceremonies. In one of these, he created a talisman for rain that required water to work; he lost it in a sewer, and London had one of the wettest summers on record. By twenty-five his magical prowess was renowned throughout the order.

Allan Bennett (1872–1923), Frater Iehi Aour.

Like Baker and Jones, he was an analytical chemist. He was tall, but asthma had reduced him to a stoop. Opium, morphine, cocaine, and chloroform each rotated for two months as his antihistamine and inadvertently showed him the ability of certain drugs to open pathways to higher consciousness.

Crowley was stunned to find Bennett living in a south London tenement with Charles Rosher, GD member, inventor, sportsman, and jack of all trades. Such a great scholar ought not to live in squalor, Crowley believed. Realizing that Bennett could teach him more in a month than anyone else could in five years, he proposed a solution: since he needed a teacher and Bennett needed a benefactor, the White Knight could share Crowley's flat in exchange for lessons in magic. Bennett accepted, and under his tutelage, Crowley progressed rapidly.

Possessing all the order's papers, Bennett provided his acolyte with a preview of the material he would receive. He also demonstrated his infamous wand:

> With this he would trace mysterious figures in the air, and, visible to the ordinary eye, they would stand out in a faint bluish light. On great occasions, working in a circle and conjuring the spirits by great names ... he would obtain the creature ... in visible and tangible form. On one occasion he evoked [the angel] Hismael and through a series of accidents, was led to step out of the circle without effectively banishing the spirit. He was felled to the ground, and only recovered 5 or 6 hours later.[22]

In private moments Bennett insisted, "There exists a drug whose use will open the gates of the World behind the Veil of Matter." This introduced Crowley to the controlled use of drugs for mystical purposes.

Theirs was one of the strongest friendships Crowley would ever know. He always spoke of Bennett with great respect. "There never walked a whiter man on earth," Crowley described him. "A genius, a flawless genius."[23]

In the months following his initiation, Crowley advanced steadily through the GD's grades, graduating to Zelator in December 1898; Theoricus in January 1899; and Practicus in February. After an obligatory three-month interval, Frater Perdurabo reached the highest grade in the GD's hierarchy, Philosophus, in May 1899. He stood at the gates of the Second Order, where the great secrets of magic awaited. Soon he would advance to the Portal.

It was time he met the head of the order, known in the First Order by the motto Frater 'S Rioghail Mo Dhream ("Royal is my tribe"), in the Second Order as Frater Deo Duce Comite Ferro ("With God as my leader and the sword as my companion"), and, in the mundane world, as Samuel Liddell MacGregor Mathers. He and Crowley shared many common interests. Both were athletic. Both basked in the romance of the Celtic revival, inventing romantic lineages for themselves; Mathers of the clan MacGregor and Crowley from the family O'Crowley. Both were driven by aspirations to spiritual greatness, and both were scholars of recondite wisdom. Mathers saw great potential in Crowley and approved of Bennett's accelerated instruction.

By summer, Crowley was notorious in the order.

In befriending Bennett and Mathers, he inspired suspicion, uneasiness, and envy among senior members. The best magicians in the order had taken him under their wings. Crowley was sharp, moving easily and briskly through the grades, and grew arrogant about his aptitude. Bennett, although respected, was also a figure of awe and, to some, fear; thus Crowley's tutelage under the White Knight seemed darker still. Moreso, Perdurabo's friendship with Mathers allied him in a camp where loyalties were quickly dividing. Mathers was increasingly viewed as a despot, and Crowley became guilty by association.

Part of his bad reputation traced to his friendship with Elaine Simpson (b. 1875), known in the order as Semper Fidelis ("Always faithful"). Born in Kussowlie, West Bengal, she was the daughter of Rev. William Simpson and Alice (née Hall); Elaine's grandfather was Sir John Hall (1795–1866), a British military surgeon from 1818 to 1857 and Inspector General of Hospitals. Alice Simpson was born in Mahableshwar, India; the family's temporary move to Germany during the 1860s "laid the foundation of the training in music and languages which enabled her later in life to become a musician of repute and a linguist of considerable fame."[24] In 1873 she married Rev. Simpson of the Indian Anglican Ecclesiastical Establishment, living with him for some time in India. The Simpsons had two daughters: Elaine was the eldest, while the younger daughter, Beatrice, would move to New York, where she would establish herself as an actress and poet under the stage name Beatrice Irwin.[25] Both Alice and Elaine belonged to the order; although Crowley found Elaine charming, he had nothing nice to say about her mother, whom he described as "a horrible mother, a sixth-rate singer, a first-rate snob, with dewlaps and a paunch; a match-maker, mischief-maker, maudlin and muddle-headed."[26] The hard feelings stem from a rumor spread by Mrs. Simpson that Crowley had visited her daughter's bedroom at night in astral form. Both Aleister and Elaine denied the charge (but a few years later it inspired an experiment between them).

Finally, even Crowley's lifestyle fell under scrutiny. The older, staid members believed that a magician should abstain from sex, drink, and drugs to keep his mind clear, and Crowley's libertine ways went against the grain on all counts. Under Bennett's guidance, he drank and took all manner of drugs— the members could only guess which ones. And his promiscuity quickly became legend: gossip linked Crowley not only to Elaine Simpson but also to the Praemonstrix (acting head), Florence Farr, and even Bennett himself. Still others suggested that "he lived under various false names and left various districts without paying his debts."[27]

Yeats and Crowley should have gotten along, considering how much they had in common: the Celtic revival, magic, Decadence, and poetry.[28] However, Crowley's notoriety made him a difficult figure for Yeats to embrace when they met in the summer of 1899. As Crowley's friend Gerald Yorke later recalled,

> Crowley objected to Yeats on the grounds that he had deserted the Great Work for literature. Yeats of Crowley that he had prostituted the Great Work and was a 'Black Magician.' Both verbally to me. I think they were both mistaken, but both had fairly legitimate reasons for their opinion.[29]

Instead of becoming friends, circumstances made them rivals in three areas dear to their hearts: love, magic, and poetry.

If there is but one iota of truth to the contention that they were rivals in "at least one romantic affair"[30]—Florence Farr—this alone could have made them mortal enemies. Florence Beatrice Farr (1860–1917) was an early GD friend of

Crowley's, possibly through the astral projection study group she ran. The daughter of a successful doctor, she abandoned college at age eighteen to pursue an acting career. After an unsuccessful marriage to Edward Emery, she became George Bernard Shaw's (1856-1950) mistress in 1889. She joined the GD a year later and, attracted to Yeats, found herself torn between two loves: Shaw and Yeats, drama and magic. She chose magic, attaining prominence in both the GD hierarchy and Yeats's affections. Crowley possessed "affectionate respect tempered by a feeling of compassion"[31] for her. Farr's biographer maintains that, while "There is no doubt that Florence and 'The Beast'… shared some sort of rapport for a short while,"[32] they were not romantically linked.

Another rivalry—magic—posed an obstacle to friendship with Yeats. Long a close friend of Mathers, Yeats visited him and exchanged friendly correspondence after his move to Paris. Suddenly, a brash young upstart arrived, apparently brownnosing the order's head. At the very least, Crowley became the friend to Mathers that Yeats felt he should have been.

If Crowley is to be believed, Yeats was also jealous of his talent as a poet. While correcting the proofs to *Jephthah; and Other Mysteries, Lyrical and Dramatic* (1899), Crowley asked Yeats his opinion of the piece. Looking it over, Yeats replied politely, but Crowley detected rage and jealousy in his reply. If the critics are right, Crowley may have been somewhat correct: most reviewers received *Jephthah* with praise. The *Manchester Guardian* wrote, "If Mr. Swinburne had never written, we should all be hailing Mr. Aleister Crowley as a very great poet indeed," while the *Aberdeen Journal* thought "He has caught the spirit in the style of Swinburne, and in some respects the pupil is greater than his master."[33] *The Outlook* effused:

> Mr. Aleister Crowley possesses uncommon gifts. As behoves a person so blest, he devotes himself to poesy. And there is no department of the sad mechanic exercise in which he fails of a kind of mastery. That is to say, his blank verse is almost unexceptionable; he will rhyme you fair sound rhymes from now to Candlemas; he is good at your strophe, your antistrophe, your chorus, your semi-chorus, your sonnet, your ode, your set of verses of all lengths; and he can build a pleasure-house of sweet words upon the inane.[34]

Nevertheless, it would be Yeats, not Crowley, who would go on to win a Nobel prize for literature.

Regardless of the reasons, these rivals in matters of love, magic and poetry strongly disliked each other. Yeats admitted Crowley was handsome, but suspected he was mad. "[W]e did not think a mystical society was intended to be a reformatory," he wrote of Crowley.[35] As a poet, Yeats felt Crowley had "written about six lines, amid much foul rhetoric, of real poetry."[36] Meanwhile, Crowley gave Irish writer George Moore (1852–1933) a book with the inscription: "You write of Yeats as 'a poet in search of a pedigree'—but who told you he was a poet? Read ME!"[37]

Accusations of black magic finally emerged from this rivalry. Crowley describes one incident in "At the Fork in the Roads" (1910):[38] During the summer of 1899, AC was visited by Irish poet and artist Althea Gyles (1867–1949), who had drawn the cover of Yeats's *The Secret Rose* (1897), *Poems* (1899), and *The Wind among the Reeds* (1899)[39] and whose work Yeats praised:

> Miss Gyles' images are so full of abundant and passionate life that they remind one of William Blake's cry, "Exuberance is Beauty," and Samuel Palmer's command to the artist, "Always seek to make excess more abundantly excessive." One finds in them what a friend, whose work has no other passion, calls "the passion for the impossible beauty" ... [H]er inspiration is a wave of a hidden tide that is flowing through many minds in many places, creating a new religious art and poetry.[40]

Despite being perceived as naive and spiritual—even Crowley remarked on "her steely virginal eyes"[41]—she was also working, and having an affair, with Leonard Smithers, much to the chagrin of her friends. Mackenzie, in her thinly disguised novel about Gyles, wrote that she,

> after treating reasonable admirers with prudish contempt, had fallen into the arms of an abominable creature of high intelligence, no morals, and the vivid imagination which was perhaps what she had been waiting for. He had the worst of reputations even among the Paris set. Ariadne lost caste, and when the affair ended after more than a year of heady intoxication, and with a certain amount of inspired work, she collapsed.[42]

According to "At the Fork in the Roads," after a discussion on clairvoyance, Gyles put on her coat to leave and, in so doing, inadvertently scratched Crowley with her brooch. The next day, when Crowley awoke feeling weak, Gyles admitted that Yeats was using black magic to destroy him. With Crowley, distinguishing fact from fancy in his fiction is nearly impossible; when he calls the account true in "every" detail, the claim wants for caution. It is unlikely Gyles gave Crowley such a confession; if she did, we don't know if it was volunteered or extracted. Regardless, enough happened for Crowley to write of himself (in the third person):

> His house in London became charged with such an aura of evil that it was scarcely safe to visit it. This was not solely due to P[erdurabo]'s own experiments; we have to consider the evil work of others in the Order ... who were attempting to destroy him. Weird and terrible figures were often seen moving about his rooms, and in several cases, workmen and visitors were struck senseless by a kind of paralysis and by fainting fits.[43]

Similarly, Yeats claimed "Crowley has been making wax images of us all, and putting pins in them."[44]

Neither one of them imagined a real magical war would soon begin.

"As life burns strong, the spirit's flame grows dull," Crowley wrote in his first book. Now the life flame of his spiritual beacon Allan Bennett was wracked by spasmodic asthma, was crumbling. Medicine had failed to cure him. Drugs had ceased to help. Something needed to be done.

His only chance was to flee the "old grey country" of England in favor of a warm, dry climate … providing he lived long enough to move. Crowley and Jones recognized the failure of conventional avenues to cure their beloved Frater Iehi Aour, and journeyed down an alley they trusted more than the thoroughfares: magic. In an effort to prolong Bennett's life enough for him to reach a healthier climate, Crowley and Jones turned to the *Goetia.*

The temple was thick with dittany of Crete burning in the censer in the south. An acacia altar, twice as tall as it was square, sat within the protective circle. Outside the circle, the Triangle of the Art awaited the appearance of the summoned spirit. With everything prepared, they conjured Buer, an infernal president who, according to the *Goetia,* "healeth all distempers in man." It was a modest working, for Buer, although he commanded fifty legions of spirits, was but a president in rank: neither a king, duke, prince, prelate, nor marquis.

As they conjured, they noticed the clouds of incense dispersing unevenly, hanging in clumps in the air. In places, the smoke became almost opaque. As Fratres Perdurabo and Volo Noscere proceeded, the room cleared of incense except around the censer, where it accumulated thick and heavy in a distinct pillar of smoke. A shape began materializing in the smoke. With their apparent success, the magicians proceeded to the "Stronger and More Potent Conjuration" from the *Goetia,* which caused parts of the figure to grow vaguely distinct. They made out a helmet, part of a tunic, and solid footgear.

It was all wrong. It contradicted the *Goetia's* description of Buer. Crowley and Jones shot glances at each other, and decided against learning what they had inadvertently summoned. Before the materialization completed, they banished and closed the temple.

Foyers was just another vacation for Crowley, an opportunity to scale the rocks overlooking Loch Ness. He reposed on the north side of the Loch, across from the ruins of Urquhart Castle, one of Scotland's largest castles until it was bombed in 1692 to prevent the Jacobites from using it. Conquering cliff after cliff, rock after rock, Crowley reached the pinnacle of an outcropping and looked down at the countryside. Precipitous rocks juxtaposed hills of heather. The earth sloped up gently from the Loch. A larch- and pine-covered hillock filled one spot; upon its mound he saw a house.

Named Boleskine, it was a huge one-story lodge, built in the late eighteenth century by the Honourable Archibald Fraser (1736-1815) and passed through the Fraser family ever since. The manor boasted a pillared entranceway and terrace, a large formal garden, lodge, stable, boat house, and sacred well. It overlooked the Fraser burial grounds, a seventeenth-century graveyard enclosed by a spear-tipped wrought-iron fence. A long driveway wound away from the house, through low-hanging trees, and toward the road that led to Foyers, 1.5

miles south, and Inverness, eighteen miles north. The house, he thought, was perfect for the Abramelin operation. *The Book of the Sacred Magic of Abramelin the Mage* stipulated that one's oratory have windows opening onto an uncovered terrace, plus a lodge to the north. The building met these requirements.

"I must have it," he thought.

He rang the owner, Mary Rose Burton, and explained his interest. She told him Boleskine was not for sale. He insisted he must have it, and offered her £2,000—twice its market value.[45] She said it was a deal. By November, Boleskine was Crowley's.

Boleskine, Crowley's home on Loch Ness.

In the time between Boleskine's discovery and sale, Crowley kept busy with magic and poetry. He eagerly discussed magic with Gerald Kelly, and one letter on the subject is particularly illuminating in light of his later philosophy of the True Will:

> Conjure up the image of your father in your mind's eye. When you have got him standing before you almost as solid as if you were there, say, 'I *will* go to A.C. at Boleskine, Foyers, Iverness' in the most determined voice. Let every incident of the day remind you of your *will,* and devote any spare moment to the imagination formula as well. In a very few days of this, interspersed with frequent letters home stating your *will,* will certainly have the desired effect.[46]

On Halloween 1899, Kelly became Frater Eritis Similis Deo ("You will be like God") on his introduction to the GD G. C. Jones sponsored Kelly, as he had

Crowley. Kelly found Jones sincere and likable; however, unimpressed by its other members, Kelly never advanced beyond the grade of Neophyte.

In November, Mathers authorized Crowley to act as his London agent concerning publication and distribution of his Abramelin translation. Around this same time, AC also arranged to publish five hundred copies of his own *An Appeal to the American Republic* (1899). Reviews of this twelve-page booklet are not preserved, but the poem was later reprinted in *The English Review*. He also wrote an essay on the magical significance of numbers; though never published in his lifetime, this fragment represents his first paper on a magical subject.

A happy homeowner, Crowley plunged more than ever into the trappings of his Scottish surroundings. He took long walks over the moors, hunted red deer and grouse, and called himself Laird Boleskine. On the edges of his land, he hung signs reading "Beware of the Ichthyosaurus!" and "The Dinotheriums are out today!"[47] Taking the lead of his GD mentor, he also donned the red plaid kilt of the MacGregor tartan, and affected the name Aleister MacGregor.

With the perfect place in which to retire for the Abramelin operation, he was ready to advance through the portal from the First Order to the Second Order of the GD. He thus applied to the Second Order with all eagerness and sincerity. Their refusal stunned him. Crowley was being made an example for the order. It was nothing personal, as Farr liked Crowley and, several years later, would defend him in the *New Age;* but she deemed Crowley unfit. It was an example of Farr playing the part of Praemonstrix, "a role which she assumed with occasional outrageous officiousness."[48]

Some time between the ritual for Bennett's health and Crowley's rejection by the Second Order, Crowley received another in a series of plaintive letters from one of his lovers. Lilian Horniblow was the wife of Colonel Frank Herbert Horniblow of the Royal Engineers, who was stationed in India at this time.[49] The affair ended when Perdurabo devoted himself to the Abramelin operation and observed the spiritual and physical conditions of abstinence. She pleaded to see him again and invited him to her hotel. Although he had dismissed her previous requests, he agreed to this one because he had a plan.

He arrived at her room, confronted her coolly, and told her: "You are making a mess of your life by your selfishness. I will give you a chance to do an absolutely unfettered act. Give me £100. I won't tell you whom it's for, except that it's not for myself. I have private reasons for not using my own money in this matter. If you give me this, it must be without hoping or expecting anything in return."[50] Crowley's private reasons are curious: Bennett needed £100 to leave England. Crowley refused to give the money himself not out of greed but because he feared the transaction would ruin their friendship. Although Crowley provided Bennett with free room and board, he did so in exchange for lessons in magic. Thus both parties retained their dignity.

One hundred pounds. His mistress pondered, and handed it over. Crowley took it and beat a hasty retreat from her life.

The Buddhist monasteries were Bennett's destination. Magic was useless to him there, so on his departure he gave his GD notes to Crowley.[51] Then he was gone. On Bennett's departure, AC wrote:

> O Man of Sorrows: brother unto Grief!
>> O pale with suffering, and dumb hours of pain!
>> O worn with Thought! thy purpose springs again
> The Soul of Resurrection: thou art chief
> And lord of all thy mind: O patient thief
>> Of God's own fire! What mysteries find fane
>> In the white shrine of thy white spirit's reign,
> Thou man of Sorrows: O, beyond belief![52]

Meanwhile, Crowley's jilted mistress had more than a cold shoulder in mind when she handed over £100 for mysterious purposes. When all she received was a hurried thank-you, she protested. Word got around, and that January, Laird Boleskine invited her to stay at his new home. He offered to pay her expenses as compensation for the money in dispute. She accepted and made the journey.

No doubt precipitating this invitation, Horniblow had warned Crowley that he was about to find himself in what he, in his diary, referred to as "Great Trouble." The nature of this trouble varies: one account has Horniblow complaining to the police about her loss of £100, and some of Yeats's letters (quoted below) support this theory. Another connects this to Crowley's relationship with Pollitt back at Cambridge. Supporting this homosexual scandal theory, he received two letters on January 15, 1900, warning that the police were watching him and his friends at 67 Chancery Lane because of something related to the "brother of a college chum."[53] When refused entry into the GD's Second Order, the reason was suspicion of "sex intemperance on Thomas Lake Harris lines in order to gain magical power—both sexes are here connoted."[54] Indeed, both scandals may have come into play.

That night, Crowley continued on to Paris and visited Mathers. On Tuesday, January 16, Mathers initiated him into the grade of Adeptus Minor (5°=6□), the first grade of the GD's Second Order. While the First Order was known as the Order of the Golden Dawn in the Outer, the Second Order was called the *Rosea Rubea et Aurea Crucis* (Ruby Rose and Cross of Gold).

Like all GD initiations, this one involved dramatic ritual. It drew heavily upon Rosicrucian symbolism and Mathers's connections with the SRIA. The initiate was instructed by officers, then dressed in a black Robe of Mourning and draped with the Chain of Humility. Next, he was tied to the Cross of Suffering, and took the following tenfold oath:

> (1) I, [the candidate's motto is used here], a member of the body of Christ, do this day, on behalf of the Universe, spiritually bind

myself, even as I am now bound physically unto the Cross of Suffering:

(2) That I will do the utmost to lead a pure an unselfish life.

(3) That I will keep secret all things connected with this Order; that I will maintain the Veil of strict secrecy between the First and Second Order.

(4) That I will uphold to the utmost the authority of the Chiefs of the Order.

(5) Furthermore that I will perform all practical work connected with this Order, in a place concealed; that I will keep secret this inner Rosicrucian Knowledge; that I will only perform any practical magic before the uninitiated which is of a simple and already well-known nature, and that I will show them no secret mode of working whatsoever.

(6) I further solemnly promise and swear that, with the Divine permission, I will from this day forward apply myself unto the Great Work, which is so to purify and exalt my spiritual Nature that with the Divine Aid I may at length attain to be more than human, and thus gradually raise and unite myself to my higher and divine Genius, and that in this event I will not abuse the Great Power entrusted unto me.

(7) I furthermore solemnly pledge myself never to work at any important Symbol or Talisman without first invoking the Highest Divine Names connected therewith; and especially not to debase my knowledge of Practical magic to purposes of Evil.

(8) I further promise always to display brotherly love and forbearance towards the members of the whole Order.

(9) I also undertake to work unassisted at the subjects prescribed for study in the various practical grades.

(10) Finally, if in my travels I should meet a stranger who professes to be a member of the Rosicrucian Order, I will examine him with care, before acknowledging him to be so.[55]

The Robe of Mourning and Chain of Suffering were removed from the candidate, who next learned the history of the Rosicrucian Order: it began with Christian Rosenkreuz, a mythical German noble who was initiated into the Mysteries in Arabia in 1393. He traveled and studied the teachings of world religions until 1410, when he and four Masons whom he had initiated founded a temple of the Rosy Cross. After Rosenkreuz died he was buried in a vault within the temple undisturbed until, over a century later, a brother who had been repairing the temple discovered a secret door inscribed with the words POST CXX ANNOS PATEBO (I will be found after 120 years). The rediscovery of the vault occurred precisely 120 years after Rosenkreuz's death.

The name Crowley chose as an Adeptus Minor was one he guarded closely all his life. He recorded this motto in only one notebook as Christeos Luciftias. In the Enochian angelic language, it means "let there be light." Allan Bennett's motto meant the same thing in Hebrew; the reference to his friend and mentor is clear. Crowley's motto is also interesting as its surface resemblance to Western

Christian terms contrasts and unites the names of Christ and Lucifer.[56] Its only appearance in print is as the "translator" of "Ambrosii Magi Hortus Rosarum," a satirical Rosicrucian essay included in his *Works*.

The initiation marked a milestone for Crowley. Dissatisfied with the instructions of the First Order, he had followed advice to wait until he reached the Second Order before judging the system. The First Order, he had learned, served only to prepare the student; the Second Order taught the application of magic. Now he was ready for the real secrets. The initiation was also a victory for Mathers. While the order in London had refused to advance Crowley, Mathers overruled Farr's decision. The war had begun.

While in Paris, Crowley asked Mathers for advice on the legal trouble brewing in London. Mathers examined Crowley's astrological chart and, based on the date of the letters of warning, concluded there was real danger. However, his Saturn on the cusp of Capricorn mitigated things. "You are strong and the end of the matter is good," Mathers counseled. "By all means, avoid London."[57]

Using the lunar pantacle from the *Key of Solomon* in order to avoid trouble, Crowley took his chances and briefly returned to London to check in with his associates. While Bennett, Jones, and Eckenstein believed his concerns were unfounded, GD member W. E. H. Humphrys warned Crowley that he was indeed wanted, and that the danger was greatest just before Easter.

Crowley left London and reached Boleskine safely on February 7. In his absence, Horniblow had left without warning or explanation. The reason lies in one of Yeats's letters about the GD's activities at this time:

> We found out that his [Mathers's] unspeakable mad person [Crowley] had a victim, a lady who was his mistress and from whom he extorted large sums of money. Two or three of our thaumaturgists ... called her up astrally, and told her to leave him. Two days ago (and about two days after the evocation) she came to one of our members (she did not know he was a member) and told a tale of perfectly medieval iniquity—of positive torture, and agreed to go to Scotland Yard and there have her evidence taken down. Our thaumaturgist had never seen her, nor had she any link with us of any kind.[58]

Nothing would ever come of this, although the gossip would haunt Crowley years later in the yellow press.

Crowley waited langorously in his tranquil new neighborhood for things to quiet down in London. On Saturday, February 24, he began recording his preparations for the Abramelin working, starting with his Oath of the Beginning:

> I, Perdurabo, Frater Ordinis Rosae Rubeae et Aureae Crucis, a Lord of the Paths in the Portal of the Vault of the Adepts, a 5°=6□ of the Order of the Golden Dawn; and an humble servant of the Christ of God; do this

day spiritually bind myself anew:
    By the Sword of Vengeance:
    By the Powers of the Elements:
    By the Cross of Suffering:
    That I will devote myself to the Great Work: the obtaining of Communion with my own Higher and Divine Genius (called the Guardian Angel) by means of the prescribed course; and that I will use my Power so obtained unto the Redemption of the Universe.
    So help me the Lord of the Universe and mine own Higher Soul![59]

With these words, he also took an Obligation of the Operation, which he adapted from his Adeptus Minor oath.

From the outset, circumstances seemed to oppose this working. Jones was the obvious choice for Crowley's assistant, but he was unable to come to Boleskine. Therefore, Crowley summoned Bennett's old roommate, Charles Rosher; he helped for a while but sneaked off early one morning and caught a steamer to Inverness, never to return. Rosher's replacement was an old Cambridge friend, who also came and left suddenly. Finally, Boleskine's teatotalling lodge-keeper went on a three-day drinking binge and tried to kill his wife and children. This and similar phenomenon convinced Crowley that the daily prayers and conjurations which constituted the Abramelin working were also attracting malevolent forces.[60]

Florence Farr, troubled by her schism with Mathers, resigned as both Praemonstrix of the Isis-Urania temple and as his London representative. Mathers feared her resignation indicated Westcott's attempt at a coup: on February 16 he sent her a letter claiming that Westcott

> has never been *at any time* either in personal or in written communication with the Secret Chiefs of the Order, he having *either himself forged or procured to be forged* the professed correspondence between him and them, and my tongue having been tied all these years by a previous Oath of Secrecy to him.[61]

The accusation was devastating. If Mathers was telling the truth, then she had been living a lie for years, initiating people under false pretenses.

To sort out her feelings, Farr returned to her childhood home of Bromley, where, after much contemplation and soul-searching, she decided to share the letter with six other members of the Second Order. On March 3, these seven formed an informal committee to quietly decide what they should do about Mathers's accusations. The committee included Farr, Yeats, and Jones, as well as Mr. and Mrs. E. A. Hunter, M. W. Blackden, and P. W. Bullock.

On March 18, Bullock wrote Mathers on behalf of the committee, expressing shock over the letter's implications and requesting proof of its accusations. Mathers shot an angry letter to Farr, refusing to recognize any committee formed "to consider my *private* letter to you … All these complications could have been avoided had you written me an open straightforward letter at the beginning of the year, saying you wished to retire *from office*."[62]

Two days later, Yeats contacted Westcott. The Rosicrucian Supreme Magus's response was noncommittal:

> Speaking *legally,* I find I cannot prove the details of the origin of the knowledge and history of the G.D., so I should not be just nor wise to bias your opinion of them.
>
> Mr. M. may insinuate and claim the authorship because I cannot disprove him. How can I say *anything* now, because if I accepted this new story, then Mrs. Woodman would rightly charge me with slandering her dead husband's reputation, for he was answerable for the original history; and if I say M.'s new story is wrong I shall be open to violent attack by him and I shall have to suffer his persecution.
>
> I must allow you to judge us both to the best of your judgement, and to decide on your responsibility.[63]

On March 23, Mathers sent poison pen letters to Farr and Bullock, again expressing umbrage at having his letter shown to others and refusing to recognize their committee. Calling on the vows of obedience to him which all members signed in 1896, he forbade the committee to meet and ordered them to abandon the inquiry. He also dismissed Farr as his representative.

The next day, the committee met to decide on a plan of action, and Bullock wrote apologetically to Mathers, stating that his letter forbidding meetings reached him after the committee had already met. Mathers wrote back to Bullock on April 2 and threatened the committee. "And for the first time since I have been connected with the Order," he wrote, "I shall formulate my request to Highest Chiefs for the Punitive Current to be prepared, to be directed against those who rebel."[64]

The situation in London had continued for over a month when Crowley made his first contact with the lodge since his initiation by Mathers. From Boleskine, he wrote Maud Cracknell, assistant secretary of the Second Order, whom he bitterly called "an ancient Sapphic crack, unlikely to be filled."[65] As an Adeptus Minor in the GD, he requested the instructional papers to which he was entitled, but Cracknell told him he needed to deal directly with Mrs. Hunter, his superior in the order. Crowley's letter to her couldn't have been worse timed. Hunter was on the investigative committee and unkindly disposed to Mathers. On March 25, Mrs. Hunter sent Crowley a reply wherein she refused to recognize his initiation into the Second Order. "The Second Order is apparently mad," he mused. In Crowley's mind, Mathers was

> unquestionably a Magician of extraordinary attainment. He was a scholar and a gentleman.... As far as I was concerned, Mathers was my only link with the Secret Chiefs to whom I was pledged. I wrote to him offering to place myself and my fortune unreservedly at his disposal; if that meant giving up the Abra-Melin Operation for the present, all right.[66]

A week later, Mathers accepted the offer. In his diary, Crowley noted,

> D.D.C.F. accepts my services, therefore do I again postpone the Operation
> of Abramelin the Mage, having by God's Grace formulated even in this a
> new link with the Higher, and gained a new weapon against the Great
> princes of the Evil of the World. Amen.[67]

On Tuesday, April 3, Crowley stopped in London to ask his oldest friends
in the order their opinion of the rebellion. Baker told Crowley he was sick of
all the politicking in the order, while Jones insisted that, without Mathers,
there was no GD. Elaine Simpson also took Mathers's side. Crowley also consulted Kelly and Humphrys, but their reactions are unrecorded.

That Saturday, Crowley appeared at the Second Order's meeting room at
36 Blythe Road. His plan was to reconnoiter the order's property for Mathers,
but he found the vault locked and Miss Cracknell on duty. "I insist I be allowed
inside," he pressed her.

"The Vault is closed by order of the committee, and no one can go in
without its consent," she told the intruder coolly.

"Have you a key?"

"I'm a new member and don't have a private key," she lied.

"Can you go in yourself?"

"No," she lied again. "Perhaps you'd better go to Mrs. Emery, or Mr.
Hunter or Mr. Blackden."

"On the contrary. It is *they* who should come to *me*." At that, he dramatically stormed out of the room. Satisfied with his observation of the situation in
London, he proceeded to France.

Crowley returned to 28 rue St. Vincent on Monday, April 9, and proposed
a strategy to the Matherses: Crowley should return to London and summon the
members of the Second Order individually to headquarters. There, they would
encounter a masked man (Crowley) and his scribe. They would answer
whether they believed in the truth of the teachings of the Second Order and
were willing to stop the revolt; then they would sign a vow of obligation to the
GD. Any refusal would mean expulsion.

Mathers accepted the plan. On April 11 he penned letters of authorization
for Crowley. The next day, Crowley entered the following oath into his diary:

> I, Perdurabo, as the Temporary Envoy Plenipotentiary of Deo Duce
> Comite Ferro & thus the Third from the Secret Chiefs of the Order of the
> Rose of Ruby and the Cross of Gold, do deliberately invoke all laws, all
> powers Divine, demanding that I, even I, be chosen to do such a work as
> he has done, at all costs to myself. And I record this holy aspiration in the
> Presence of the Divine Light, that it may stand as my witness.[68]

Crowley left Paris at 11:50 a.m. on April 13. For protection, Mathers gave
him a Rose Cross, the Rosicrucian talisman. He warned Crowley to expect
magical attack, and know that sure signs were mysterious fires or fires refusing
to burn. It was the best he could do to prepare Crowley for the fight ahead.

Back in London, Crowley's first tactic was to contact GD members loyal to Mathers. He hired a cab to take him to two of these members, Mrs. Simpson and Dr. Berridge. During the ride, the paraffin lights on the carriage caught fire and the cab could go no further. Most mysterious, Crowley thought, in light of Mathers's warning about fires. He hailed another cab, and as he rode along the horse bolted inexplicably.

When he finally arrived at Mrs. Simpson's, Crowley noted the refusal of her hearth fire to remain lit, while his rubber raincoat, nowhere near the fire, spontaneously combusted. Mathers appeared to be correct about the fires: when they should have burned, they did not; when they were burning, they behaved mysteriously; when they should not be, they appeared. Crowley concluded he was under magical attack.

Taking out the Rose Cross, Crowley clenched the protective talisman given to him by Mathers and noticed something unusual about it. Its color was bleaching out, fading. In one day's time, the talisman was nearly white.

During this time as Mathers's plenipotentiary, Crowley also had his one and only contact with Supreme Magus William Wynn Westcott:

> I only saw the old boy once in my life, and then merely on an errand from Mathers to tell him he had incurred a traitor's doom. And I only wrote to him once, and that to demand that he should deposit the famous Cypher Manuscripts with the British Museum as their secrecy was being used for purposes of fraud.[69]

Westcott was less receptive to Crowley's communications than he was to Yeats's.

Thirty-six Blythe Road was the rebel base. As the Second Order's London headquarters, it was the source of the insurrection's power. Without it, they would be dead in the water.

On Monday, April 16, Crowley met C. E. Wilkinson, landlord of the room, and convinced him that he had authority to enter and occupy the premises. The next day, he returned with Elaine Simpson to wrest headquarters from the dissidents. They found Cracknell in the room, repeating her statement that the rooms had been closed by Farr's order. As Mathers's plenipotentiary, Crowley gleefully expelled the Sapphic Crack from the order. She rushed off and sent a telegram to E. A. Hunter: "Come at once to Blythe Road, something awful has happened."

When Hunter arrived, he was shocked to encounter resistance in entering the room. Then he found Crowley in the supposedly locked premises, having apparently forced open the doors and changed the locks. Crowley proudly declared, "We have taken possession of headquarters by the authority of MacGregor Mathers." He handed over his letters of authority.

Hunter looked the papers over. "The authority of that gentleman has been suspended by a practically unanimous vote by the members of the society," he replied dryly.

Undaunted, Crowley turned his attack to Cracknell, who had entered the room with Hunter. Jabbing a finger in her direction, he continued. "That woman must leave the room. She has been suspended from membership."

Hunter shook his head. "I will not allow it. Not without her consent."

Meanwhile, Farr appeared with a constable. Unfortunately, the authorities were powerless to help her. The landlord was not present to verify ownership of the premises, and Farr had not put into writing her orders for the rooms to be closed. Crowley was technically in possession of the rooms.

Victorious, AC proceeded according to plan. To cancel the proposed meeting of the renegade Second Order on April 21 and to summon all members for their test of allegiance, he sent the following telegram:

> You are cited to appear at Headquarters at 11:45 am on the 20th inst.
> Should you be unable to attend, an appointment at the earliest possible moment must be made by telegraphing to 'MacGregor' at Headquarters.
> There will be no meeting on the 21st inst.
> By the order of Deo Duce Comite Ferro,
> Chief of the S∴O∴[70]

Two days later, on April 19, Yeats and Hunter found Wilkinson, the landlord. Since members came and went regularly, he explained, he assumed Crowley was as welcome as any other. However, he agreed that Farr, who paid the bills, could do whatever she wanted with the rooms. They thereupon showed him a letter from Farr, authorizing them to change her locks.

At 11:30 that same morning, Crowley's figure cut a spectacle through the shop below. He appeared in Highland dress with a plaid over his head and shoulders, a huge gold cross around his neck, and a dagger at his waist. According to plan, he wore a black mask over his face to conceal his identity.[71] Crowley marched past the shop clerk, who notified Wilkinson. The landlord—having passed word along to Yeats, Hunter, and the constable—stopped Crowley in the back hall and forbade him from entering the premises. When the constable arrived, he advised Crowley to get a lawyer.

Yeats and Hunter spent the rest of the day refusing as "name unknown" the flood of telegrams which arrived for "MacGregor." This was interrupted at 1 o'clock by the arrival of a burly fellow who had been wandering the London streets for two hours trying to find 36 Blythe Road. Crowley had hired him outside Alhambra, a Leicester Square pub, for thirteen shillings four pence. The man had no idea why he was wanted there: he thought some sort of entertainment would be provided.

Later that day, the committee met and suspended Mathers, Berridge, and Mrs. and Miss Simpson from the Second Order. They further moved "no person shall be deemed to belong to the London branch who has not been initiated by that body in London." It was a smack in Crowley's face. The Mathers loyalists were unamused by their suspension. On Friday, April 20, Dr. Berridge (c. 1843–1923) replied to the committee upon learning of his expulsion:

> I am in receipt of your note of yesterday in which you convey to me the decision of the self-appointed and unauthorised committee of your new Archaeological Association.
>
> I have read it carefully but am at present unable to decide where impudence or imbecility is its predominant characteristic.
>
> As I have never been a member of your new Society I cannot be suspended from such non-existent membership.[72]

The next day, the committee reached a decision about Mathers: if his accusations of forgery were true, then he was guilty of fraud. If he was lying, then he was guilty of slander against a brother of the order. In either case, Mathers's word was worthless.

Even at this point the battle raged. Crowley summonsed Farr to appear before the police magistrate of the West London Police Court on April 27 on charges of "unlawfully and without just cause detaining certain papers and other articles, the property of the Complainant."[73] He wanted either the items returned or £15 remuneration. Appealing to friends in high places, the Second Order rebels hired as their representative Charles Russell, son of the Lord Chief Justice. Yeats feared his name would be dragged into the case and, awaiting the court hearing, wrote:

> The case comes on next Saturday, and for a week I have been worried to death with meetings, law and watching to prevent a sudden attack on the rooms. For three nights I did not get more than 4½ hours sleep any night. The trouble is that my Kabbalists are hopelessly unbusinesslike and thus minutes and the like are in complete confusion.[74]

To their advantage, however, they learned Crowley had been blacklisted by the Trades' Protection Association for a bad debt; so they called in a trade union representative to testify in their defense.

Cracknell sent a letter to Crowley's counsel in an effort to clear matters up. She explained that Farr was president and Hunter treasurer of the order; Mathers acted only as honorary head, but had never been in 36 Blythe Road, let alone contributed financially to its upkeep. She also described how Crowley broke into the premises, adding, "certain things of pecuniary value to the society were found to be missing."[75]

The day of the trial, Yeats—having just been elected the GD's new leader—sat at home like an expectant mother, awaiting the news. He wrote to Lady Gregory:

> I do not think I shall have any more bother for we have got things into shape and got a proper executive now and even if we lose the case it will not cause any confusion though it will give one Crowley, a person of unspeakable life, the means to carry on a mystical society which will give him control of the conscience of many.[76]

He finished and sealed the letter but, before he could mail it, the news arrived. They had won. Crowley's solicitor, concluding they had no case, feared the GD would claim their losses exceeded £15, thus taking the case to a higher court. To avoid this complication, they withdrew charges for a £5 penalty.

Easter had passed, and it was thus too late for Crowley to resume the Abramelin operation. He returned to Boleskine for a few somber days, then returned to Mathers in Paris. Berridge, he learned, had joined Westcott to set up a new branch of Isis-Urania under Mathers's direction.[77] Evidently the controversy did not prevent Mathers and Westcott from collaborating.

During his visit, Crowley convinced Mathers to unleash the punitive current against the rebels. He thus spent a Sunday afternoon watching Mathers baptize dried peas in the names of the rebels and rattling them around inside a sieve. Crowley, unimpressed, recorded, "nobody seemed a penny the worse."[78]

Thus ended the revolt in the GD, with Mathers believing he had been the victim of a conspiracy, and Yeats regretting the loss of a friend. Shortly after the break, Yeats recalled Mathers respectfully: "MacGregor apart from certain definite ill doings and absurdities ... has behaved with dignity and even courtesy."[79] Years later, he recalled his old friend in a poem:

> I call MacGregor Mathers from his grave,
> For in my first hard spring-time we were friends,
> Although of late estranged.
> I thought him half a lunatic, half knave,
> And told him so, but friendship never ends ...[80]

In 1925 he fondly dedicated his book *A Vision* to Moïna. Although they parted bitterly, the Matherses' influence upon him never faded.

CHAPTER FOUR

The Mountain Holds a Dagger

When Count and Countess MacGregor of Glenstrae stepped onto the stage of the Bodinière Theater in Paris, clothed in Egyptian raiment, they became the High Priest Rameses and the High Priestess Anari in public celebrations of the Rite of Isis. Beginning around October 1899, these public ceremonies involved both Rameses and Anari invoking the goddess Isis. A Parisian dancer in long white robes next performed invocations of the four elements: the *danse des fleurs* (earth), *danse du miroir* (water), *danse de la chevelure* (fire), and *dance des parfums* (air). Finally, offerings of flowers or wheat were thrown upon the altar by female and male attendees, respectively. "The ceremony was artistic in the extreme," remarked reporter Frederick Lees. The object of these rites was to generate interest in their mystery school, and in this they were apparently successful: the receptions and celebrations hosted at their residence—"amongst the most interesting in Paris"—attracted "scientists, doctors, lawyers, painters, and men and women of letters, besides persons of high rank."[1]

Crowley, while attending these rites, met American soprano Susan Strong (1870–1946). Born in Brooklyn, she inherited a fortune when her father, lawyer and former New York State Senator Demas Strong (1820–1893), died of heart failure on November 9, 1893. He had been part of the California gold rush in 1849 and, accumulating a fortune, returned home to Brooklyn and entered politics.[2] With her older siblings married, Susan, aged twenty-two, moved to London and studied singing for her own amusement at the Royal Academy of Music under Hungarian composer and teacher Francis Korbay (1846–1913). Both her vocal and acting ability convinced Korbay that she could be a great diva, and he encouraged her to audition for the English Opera Company. Although she sang as Elsa in *Lohengrin* (1893), her big-stage debut at Covent Garden two years later as Sieglinde, in an English-language version of *Die Walküre,* made her an overnight star.[3] *The Academy* called her performance "a veritable triumph,"[4] while the *Times* raved, "artistic as her singing is it is thrown into the shade by her wonderful skill as an actress. Gifted with a fine physique and an unusually dignified stage presence, her command of beautiful and appropriate gesture is such as the most experienced singers rarely attain."[5] In a highly uncharacteristic gesture of appreciation noted by the *Times,* she was given numerous bouquets at the conclusion of the first act.

American soprano Susan Strong (1870–1946) in her breakout role as Sieglinde from Wagner's *Die Walküre.*

Based on this performance, Strong was engaged for the 1896 season at Bayreuth, followed by her New York debut later that fall. In the years that followed she toured America and regularly returned to London. By the time Crowley met her, Strong's repertoire had expanded to include the demanding roles of Marguerite (Gounod's *Faust,* in 1896), Aïda (Verdi's *Aïda,* in 1897–1898), Brünnhilde (Wagner's *Siegfried,* in 1898), Donna Anna (Mozart's *Don Giovanni,* in 1900), Freïa (Wagner's *Das Rheingold,* in 1900), and Gutrune (Wagner's *Götterdämmerung,* in 1900). She originally performed as Venus at Covent Garden in *Tannhäuser* in June 1899, and reprised both the role and the venue in May–June 1900, which matches the time in which Crowley says he saw her portray Venus at Covent Garden.[6]

From her attending Mathers's public ritual, one wonders to what degree she shared Crowley's interest in the occult; indeed, AC identifies her as "a member of the Order."[7] She took him "by storm," he punned, and a relationship sprung up between them. He summarized his relationship with Strong, "She courteously insisted on my sampling the goods with which she proposed to endow me. The romance of an intrigue with so famous an artist excited my imagination"[8] They fell in love and soon became engaged. The only delay was supposedly the disposal of her husband, then in Texas. The marriage never materialized.[9] Crowley had the good fortune of knowing Strong at the height of her career; after a few more years of singing, she retired from the stage to open a high-class London laundry on Baker Street called Nettoyage de Linge de Luxe.[10] Despite the rave reviews she received at the time, the *New Grove Dictionary of Opera* accords Strong a less illustrious place in history: "Her few recordings, mostly of songs, show an imaginative artist with a voice probably not meant by nature for the heavy roles she undertook."[11]

Another pair of Mathers's Parisian friends, recounting tales of their Mexico vacation, reminded Crowley of Eckenstein's invitation to climb mountains there. With GD business settled and the Abramelin operation postponed, his time was free and his wallet cumbersome. One can't help but wonder whether Crowley's legal troubles back in London also motivated him. Regardless, in June 1900 England became just another port as the SS *Pennsylvania,* Crowley's new home, sailed for the United States. On Independence Day, still en route, he wrote a commemorative poem:

> The ship to the breezes is bended;
> The wind whistles off to the lee;
> The sun is arisen, the splendid!
> The sun on the marvellous sea!
> And the feast of your freedom is ended,
> O sons of the free![12]

The poem's critical tone shows Crowley was prepared to dislike the States. What he found when he arrived around July 6 made disdain even easier.

Like much of the northeastern United States (and Europe soon thereafter), New York was at the peak of a record-breaking heat wave that began in late June. On July 1, both New York and Philadelphia recorded the hottest day on record at 98 and 102 degrees respectively, with similar temperatures reported from Washington, D.C., to St. Louis. By the time Crowley arrived, there were over four hundred heat-related deaths in Manhattan alone, eight hundred throughout the metropolitan area, and hundreds more in New Jersey and New England. Even more were hospitalized with heat prostration, taxing the health care system.[13] The temperature and humidity left Crowley, like so many others, prostrated. Miles of glass and concrete accentuated the heat, and he found the constant bustle repellent. He thought to himself, "The people tend to behave like the Madrileños ... 'Festina lente' and 'More haste, less speed' ought to be painted up at every street corner."[14] After only two or three days, he caught a train for Mexico City.

Crowley preferred Mexico. Although hot, it was nowhere near as humid as New York. He rented part of a house overlooking the Alameda and hired a young local woman as his maid. That summer, he bought an orange pony in Iguala and went sightseeing until a bout of malaria forced him to rest in a luxurious former palace, the Hotel Iturbide.

Mexico's rustic simplicity and stability provided a prolific phase for Crowley. The mass of poetry written at this time runs the gamut, from haunting confessions of desperate loneliness to travelogues and mystical ecstasy. "The Growth of God" is of the chilling variety:

> Even as beasts, where the sepulchral ocean
>   Sobs, and their fins and feet keep Runic pace,
> Treading in water mysteries of motion,
>   Witch-dances: where the ghastly carapace
> Of the blind sky hangs on the monstrous verge:
>   Even as serpents, wallowing in the slime;
> So my thoughts raise misshapen heads, and urge
>   Horrible visions of decaying Time.[15]

Other poems from this period—all later published in *Oracles* (1905)—include "Assumpta Canidia," "March in the Tropics," "Metempsychosis" and "Night in the Valley," and "Venus." The latter work expresses feelings of longing, regret, and even insecurity for his Venus, Susan Strong:

> MISTRESS and maiden and mother, immutable mutable soul!
> Love, shalt thou turn to another? Surely I give thee the whole!
> Light, shall thou flicker or darken? Thou and thy lover are met.
> Bend from thy heaven and hearken! Life, shalt thou fade or forget?
>
> I know thee not, who art naked; I lie beneath thy feet
> Who hast called till my spirit ached with a pang too deathly sweet.
> Thou has given thee to me dying, and made thy bed to me.
> I shiver, I shrink, and, sighing, lament it cannot be.
>
> O Goddess, maiden, and wife! Is the marriage bed in vain?
> Shall my heart and soul and life shrink back to themselves again?
> Be thou my one desire, my soul in day as in night!
> My mind the home of the Higher! My heart the centre of Light![16]

Similar echoes of Strong appear in one of Crowley's more paradoxical creations. On the heels of a torrid afternoon in a slum, his lover left him unsatisfied; thinking of his former fiancée, he wrote his own version of *Tannhäuser* in sixty-seven uninterrupted hours of writing. It is a piece that by its nature juxtaposes sex and creativity, England and Mexico, actress and lover. Despite inspired moments, it is ultimately long and difficult, although Crowley considered it the pinnacle of the first phase of his poetry.

In addition to writing, Crowley also began testing the GD instruction on invisibility. Based on the formula used in the Neophyte initiation, the ritual to bestow this power involved banishing the area: He began by energizing and grounding the energy centers of his body, giving the sign of the kabbalistic cross and intoning the Hebrew words for "Thine is the kingdom, the power and glory unto the ages, amen." Next, he traced a circle in the air around himself, stopping at the east, south, west, and north quadrants to draw a protective pentagram and to call on one of the sacred Hebrew names of God. Calling upon the archangels Raphael, Gabriel, Michael, and Uriel to oversee and protect him, the ritual space would be duly purified. A recitation of the first Enochian Key—reputedly written in the language of the angels and passed down from Elizabethan magician John Dee—followed. Finally, Crowley invoked the powers of concealment. The magician, visualizing a shroud about his or her body, should gradually and partially turn invisible ... or so they said. The key to the illusion was neither optical nor physical, since the magician never truly disappeared. However, he *did* take advantage of distraction, one of the oldest principles of sleight of hand: the invisible magician affected about himself an aura which made his presence ordinary, subliminal, almost chameleonlike. When Crowley saw his reflection begin to flicker like a motion picture, he knew he was on to something. He considered himself successful when he was able to stroll through Mexico City in a golden crown and scarlet robe without attracting any attention.

On November 14 and 17 he experimented further with the Enochian evocations of Doctor John Dee. In Dee's system, the spiritual world was stratified into thirty Aethyrs, each with its own name and conjuration. By reading the key and gazing into his crystal, Crowley unlocked the moods and visions of that sphere, writing them down as they happened. His results are surrealistic, apocalyptic, and bear the stamp of his evangelical upbringing:

> An immense eagle-angel is before me. His wings seem to hide all the Heaven.
> He cried aloud saying: The Voice of the Lord upon the Waters: the Terror of God upon Mankind. The voice of the Lord maketh the Skies to tremble: the Stars are troubled: the Aires fall. The First Voice Speaketh and saith: Cursed, cursed be the Earth, for her iniquity is great. Oh Lord! Let Thy Mercy be lost in the great Deep! Open thine eyes of Flame and Light, O God, upon the wicked! Lighten thine Eyes! The Clamour of Thy Voice, let it smite down the Mountains![17]

He knew only limited success, however, for he was not yet advanced enough to pass through or comprehend any Aethyrs beyond the first two (working his way up from the thirtieth to the twenty-ninth).

Shortly afterward he met an old man named Don Jesus de Medina-Sidonia, a high-ranking chief in Scottish Rite Freemasonry (apparently unbeknownst to

Crowley, this was "a miniscule irregular body").[18] Crowley's knowledge of the
mysteries so impressed Don Jesus that the Mason conferred upon him the 33°,
the highest grade in the Scottish Rite of Freemasonry. In commensurate spirit,
Crowley used his authority from Mathers to initiate *in partibus* and founded a
new magical order—the Lamp of Invisible Light (LIL)—in Guanajuato with
Medina as its first Imperator.[19] Prior to his Enochian visions—in October
1900—the mysteries of LIL had revealed themselves to Crowley, and indeed
the name of this order seems influenced by those Enochian visions, as LIL is the
name ascribed by Dee to the first, or highest, Aethyr.[20] The order set up a perpetual flame that was invoked daily with appropriate elemental, planetary, and
zodiacal forces to make it a center of light and enlightenment. The letters LPD
represented its philosophical, scientific, and moral principles: liberty, power,
duty; light, proportion, density; law, principle, *droit*. Naturally, these letters also
had other secret meanings. Unfortunately, Crowley's interest in ceremonial
magick waned shortly thereafter, and he dropped out of touch with Medina;
the fate of LIL is unknown.[21]

Eckenstein joined Crowley in Mexico in December 1900, taunting him for
wasting time on poetry and occultism when he could be climbing. Nevertheless, Crowley confided in him that after searching so long for the truth, he was
troubled to find dramatic ritual dissatisfying. Fully expecting some belittling
jibe, his friend's thoughtful reply jolted him. "Do you know what your problem is? You're unable to control your thoughts. You're scattered, and you waste
energy. You have to learn how to *concentrate*." This comment struck Crowley
with such clarity and truth that he wondered whether Eckenstein was a master
in disguise. He recalled, back at Wastdale Head, begging the gods to send him
a tutor; instead, he began to suspect, they sent two: Baker and Eckenstein.
    Although the mountaineer considered himself no master, he devised a
course of study for Crowley. His instructions on concentration involved visualizing objects, beginning with simple forms and advancing with practice to
more complicated ones, such as moving objects or human beings. He also
assigned similar tasks for the other senses. Eckenstein monitored and commented on Crowley's progress, and when too zealously pursued, told him
when to back off,[22] which they did by mountain climbing.
    At that time, there was scarcely any published account of previous climbs in
Mexico. Furthermore, the locals had little interest in the mountains around
them. The exception was geologist Ezequiel Ordóñez (1867–1950) of the State
Geological Survey, after whom the rhyolite crystal Ordóñezite is named and
who would later that year discover the first petroleum deposits in Mexico. He
had written extensively on the mountains and volcanoes of Mexico[23] and, having climbed many of them, facilitated Crowley and Eckenstein's ascents.[24]
    They began in January 1901 in the town of Amecameca, thirty-six miles
southeast of Mexico City. It rested between the bases of two volcanoes. The

first of these, Ixtacíhuatl, the White Lady of Mexico, was a triple-peaked extinct volcano rising to Ixtacíhuatl (17,343 feet) and is the only Central American mountain with a permanent glacier. Its neighbor, Popocatépetl (17,802 feet), was an active volcano with a crater half a mile wide. Requiring a couple of good men with mules, they met with the *jefe politico* or mayor of Amecameca, courted him with cigars and liquor, and explained their intent to climb Ixtacíhuatl. After four days' negotiation, he agreed to help.

Eckenstein and Crowley found only sketchy and dubious records of previous ascents, and concluded Ixtacíhuatl had never been fully explored. The warning of I. R. Whitehouse, the previous person to attempt a climb, that "I doubt if it would be possible to reach the summit or summits by any other route than the one we took, as on all sides, as far as I could discover, there were sheer ice walls and precipices,"[25] only enticed, rather than dissuaded, them. Unsure what to expect, they cautiously began on its lower slopes. The sun was relentless, and nowhere did they encounter the streams they expected to find running down from the glacier. Dehydration threatened, but they finally located a spring, checked their provisions, and prepared to finish the climb. Setting up camp at 15,807 feet, they spent the next three weeks scaling the White Lady's slopes from every side.

On January 19, they ascended the icy summit of Panza, the central summit of Ixtacíhuatl, from the east-northeast, overcoming a 220-foot rock wall along the way. On the 24th they crossed "some of the worst walking we had ever encountered"[26] to the snowy northern summit of Cabeza (16,883 feet); its flat snowy surface concealed gaps between giant hunks of ice which had fallen from an avalanche, so that some steps fell on solid ice while others sank into deep pits of snow. On the 28th they tackled Panza from a different approach.[27] The north ridge of Panza was Ixtacíhuatl's great challenge: its shadow kept the area bitterly cold, with frostbite a serious threat; and the ridge's seventy-foot ice wall rose at a steep incline of fifty-one degrees, and was so rotten that the surface ice needed to be chopped away before their crampons could find a satisfactory hold. Nevertheless, they managed to ascend at a rate Crowley says "beat the record for similar altitudes very easily."[28] Eckenstein reported this ascent as 2,687 feet in two hours at the lower altitudes, and 907 feet per hour (including stops) between altitudes of 13,717 and 17,343 feet.[29] By the last three days of the climb, the intrepid adventurers were living on nothing but champagne and Danish butter. This was not uncommon among mountain climbers, as the body expended so much energy both climbing and staying warm that maintaining one's weight was frequently a challenge.

Returning to Amecameca in understandably high spirits, they sought the *jefe politico* for a celebration, only to find a dour official. He regretfully informed them of Queen Victoria's death on January 22. To his surprise, the pair shouted for joy and broke into dance. Later, Crowley explained, "To us, Queen Victoria was sheer suffocation."[30]

They next rode nineteen hours by rail to Guadalajara, followed by another two days to Zapotlán, the town nearest where the Sierra Madre and a chain of volcanic mountains converged. Here they found more peaks to conquer, including the Nevado de Colima with its two summits of 14,239 feet (southwest) and 14,039 feet (northeast); and its neighbor to the south, the Colima volcano (14,206 feet), the most active and dangerous volcano on the continent. Three days' rough traveling from Zapotlán took them to the horseshoe-shaped ridge at the base of the Nevado de Colima, where they struck camp. On March 3 they tackled the twin peaks: the first was an easy scramble and climb, and they were evidently the first ever to reach the top; the higher southwestern summit was even easier, and they could tell it had been climbed before.

Next, they hacked and marched their way through the forest toward Volcán di Colima for two days until, twelve miles from their destination, the volcano erupted. Its hot ash, carried by the wind, landed on them and burned through their clothes. They camped on the crest of a ridge directly north of the volcano and observed over a dozen eruptions over the course of twenty-four hours. Approach was impossible; as Eckenstein wrote, "it presented the cheerful alternatives of death by bombardment or by cremation."[31] So Crowley and Eckenstein made the most of the situation by climbing the neighboring mountain and watching the volcano for a pattern in its eruptions. After a week's vigil, they detected no pattern whatsoever and decided to take their chances and begin climbing the peak. The futility of their attempt soon became clear when the soles of their boots burned through.

Volcán di Colima (14,206 feet) ten seconds after erupting at 4 p.m. on March 7, 1901.

Eckenstein and Crowley's next goal was Citlaltépetl (Pico de Orizaba), located in Veracruz on the Gulf of Mexico. At 18,491 feet, its inactive volcanic peak was the highest point in Mexico and the third highest in North America.

Setting out from Mexico City on April 3, they arrived in Chalchicomula to find further transport impossible due to local saints' days for the next five days. Facing what, even at this distance, was obviously an easy scramble, the pair gave up. Crowley bitterly watched vultures swoop about the landscape:

> Dim goes the sun down there behind the tall
> And mighty crest of Orizaba's snow:
> Here, gathering at the nightfall, to and fro,
> Fat vultures, foul and carrion, flap, and call
> Their ghastly comrades to the dome'd wall
> That crowns the grey cathedral. There they go—
> The parasites of death, decay and woe,
> Gorged with the day's indecent festival.[32]

They next traveled from Mexico City to Toluca, and from there to Calimaya, the city nearest the inactive volcano Nevado de Toluca (also known as Xinantécatl or Cinantécatl, 15,354 feet), whose crater was the basin for lakes of melting snow. This was the site of their camp; from here, it was difficult to tell which of the two most visible peaks on the ridge of the crater was tallest: Pico del Fraile (the Friar's Peak) or El Espinazo del Diablo (the Devil's Backbone), so they climbed both. On April 10 they scaled Pico del Fraile; Eckenstein was sick the next morning,[33] so Crowley ascended El Espinazo alone.

While the mountaineers puzzled out an ascent of Volcán di Colima, Kegan Paul, Trench, Trübner and Company prepared Crowley's next opus, *The Soul of Osiris*. It was the second half of *The Mother's Tragedy,* which was so long that Kegan Paul had suggested splitting it into two separate works. It appeared on March 7 in an edition of five hundred copies, plus six on India paper. The book garnered mixed reviews. The *Westminster Review* wrote, "it cannot be denied that Aleister Crowley is a true poet—a poet of the school of Baudelaire and Poe."[34] Most notable was by up-and-coming writer G. K. Chesterton (1874–1936), who wrote in the June 18 *Daily Mail:*

> We have all possible respect for Mr. Crowley's religious symbols and we do not object to his calling upon Shu at any hour of the night. Only it would be unreasonable of him to complain if his religious exercises were generally mistaken for an effort to drive away cats....
>
> If Mr. Crowley and the new mystics think for one moment that an Egyptian desert is more mystic than an English meadow, that a palm tree is more poetic than a Sussex beech, that a broken temple of Osiris is more supernatural than a Baptist Chapel in Brixton, then they are sectarians...But Mr. Crowley is a strong and genuine poet, and we have little doubt that he will work up from his appreciation of the Temple of Osiris to that loftier and wider work of the human imagination, the appreciation of the Brixton Chapel.[35]

Despite Chesterton's ideological reservations, it was proof that even the Atlantic Ocean was not wide enough to stop the flow of Crowley works.

Crowley and Eckenstein began their final Mexican climb on April 17. However, the route up the second highest peak in Mexico, Popocatépetl (17,802 feet), was actually more like "walking up very objectionable scree, or rather volcanic debris, lying at practically the critical angle."[36] The mountain's claim to fame was that its ascent in 1521 by Francisco Montaño was arguably the earliest record of any high ascent on a mountain. On their climb 380 years later, Eckenstein and Crowley brought along a Chicago-based newspaper writer who reported the climb as his syndicated alter ego, "Mr. Dooley," who commented humorously on political and social issues in a thick Irish accent (written phonetically). While neither Crowley nor Eckenstein identify this writer, "Mr. Dooley" wass the immensely popular creation of Finley Peter Dunne (1867–1936); his article "Mr. Dooley Climbs Popo" recounted his adventures with "me former counthrymon, the Shivvyleer O'Rourke, an' his parthner-in-crime, Bar-ron von Eckenstein."[37] Greeting the climbers on this last adventure was an amazing display of *nieves penitentes,* formations of ice flakes that were two to four feet high and up to eighteen inches thick, running diagonally in parallel rows up the mountain over several acres.

Eckenstein left Mexico on April 20, bound for England to arrange an expedition that, if successful, would place them in the history books.

When Allan Bennett left London, so did Crowley. Likewise when Eckenstein left Mexico, Crowley did too. After nine months of Mexico he prepared to visit GD alumni Elaine Simpson and Allan Bennett in Asia. On April 22 he journeyed to San Francisco, where he spent a week. The Bay City for him was "rank and gross, without a touch of subtlety."[38] On May 3, he set sail for Honolulu on the *Nippon Maru.* Having solemnly pledged to pursue magic again, he passed the voyage honing his concentration skills. His diaries from this period show a strong influence of Theosophy: his May 8 entry mentions Adyar-Theosophy's cofounder Bishop Charles Webster Leadbeater (1854–1934), and elsewhere he writes of his determination to look up the local Theosophists. He landed in Hawaii on May 9, noting this was also "White Lotus Day," in honor of TS founder H. P. Blavatsky (1831–1891). In actuality, the commemoration of Blavatsky's death was a day earlier, May 8.

Waikiki Beach became, for a month, the center of Crowley's outpourings, immortalized in "On Waikiki Beach."[39] He also wrote Book One of *Orpheus* (1905)—which he dedicated to Eckenstein. "What a hell scene I can write," he reported eagerly to Gerald Kelly. "You wait."[40]

On May 10, he met Mary Alice Rogers (née Beaton)[41] of Salt Lake City at his hotel. Of Scottish descent, she was ten years older than Crowley and married to a lawyer. She had come to Honolulu with her thirteen-year-old son, Blaine, to escape hay fever. The boy was bright and intelligent, yet, to Crowley's astonishment knew no language other than English and was equally unskilled in math, history, and geography. He thought it criminal that school provided no grist for such a bright child's mill.[42] Mary was one of the sweetest, most beautiful women Crowley had ever known. From the beginning, he calculated an affair and breakup with her to inspire his poetic muse; this premeditation is evident in his diaries where, early on, he begins referring to her as "Alice," the pseudonym to which Crowley would ultimately address a series of love poems collectively titled *Alice: An Adultery* (1903). All the while he mused how absurd it was for him to come all the way to Hawaii "only to fall in love with a white woman."[43]

Crowley convinced her to accompany him to Japan. With boy in tow, they sailed on the *American Maru*. On the thirteenth day of their acquaintance, they kissed for the first time, his diary noting that he "told her I loved her; kissed and was kissed."[44] Still, the relationship advanced at a slower pace than Crowley preferred. On May 23, his diary reads, "Kissing all evening.... All this should prepare a superb Eurydice lament when we part." Two days later, he entered in his diary, "Promised not to do anything against her will, so we lay together about an hour on my bed kissing." He dismantled the temple in his cabin the next day: "Took down my shrine.... The 'affaire' seems designed by the devil to take up maximum of time and virility."[45] All the while he promised himself,

> Another month to be a man,
> Another month to kiss her and be kissed,
> And then—all time to Magic and to Art![46]

They wrestled with guilt—"The silly 'Thus far and no farther,'"—but appetite overcame chastity, and the affair commenced. Even as it did, Crowley confided in his journal, "don't much care what happens really. Love is good, but so is freedom."[47] Mary was equally conflicted about her infidelity. Some nights she locked her cabin door and refused to see Crowley; on others, she accommodated him. Before the month was over, their relationship ended. On June 29, 1901, Crowley noted in his diary, "Finished with *that* foolishness. Alice sailed at noon. Thirty-eight days from when we kissed all wasted—or all *rest*." Thus, he was free to chase after magic and art in Shanghai while she rejoined her home and husband in Utah. Crowley summarized, in much kinder terms than his diary's, this liaison in a letter to Gerald Kelly:

> We loved, and loved chastely...
>   On the boat we fell to fucking, of course, but—here's the miracle!—
> we won through and fought our way back to chastity and far deeper, truer
> love.[48]

The fifty days between their meeting and parting inspired Crowley to commemorate their relationship in a series of fifty sonnets, one for each of those days. The book *Alice: An Adultery* (1903) testifies to the most puzzling aspect of Crowley's relationships: when he loved, he did so with his whole being, but the passion was typically short-lived. Like the prototypical double-ended candle, his emotions burned more fiercely, and his losses seemed twice as dark. He expressed his anguish over losing this forbidden paramour in another poem from this period:

"I am so faint for utter love I sigh and long to die."[49]

Despite his heartache, Crowley, as ever, found in the encounter the energy and inspiration for new works: his thirty days as a man being up, he returned dutifully to magic and poetry, neither of which he had truly abandoned so much as neglected during this time. Proofs for *Tannhäuser* awaited in a Hong Kong post office, and he continued writing "Book II" of *Orpheus,* which he dedicated to Mary Beaton, "whom I lament." In a letter to Kelly, Crowley described his state of mind at the time: "my ideas are changing and fermenting. You will not recognize my mind when I get back. I am calm and happy and thoroughly energetic at the same time."[50]

By July, a new manuscript went into production. Despite slow sales of previous works, he remained undaunted. *The Mother's Tragedy* came out in an edition of five hundred copies. Press opinions were again divided on this volume: while *Oxford Magazine* wrote, "Mr. Crowley has a claim to recognition as a true poet … Magnificent poems—pagan in their intensity and vividness of colouring," the *Athenaeum* wrote, "If the reader can form a conception of a wind-bag foaming at the mouth, he will get some notion of 'The Mother's Tragedy,' and other Poems (privately printed)."[51] The *Westminster Review* noted "The love of a man for his own mother, not according to a moral but a sexual standard, is not quite a novel idea, but Mr. Crowley handles the subject in a revolting fashion," while *The Academy* noted that Crowley "frequently expressed things with all his uncompromising completeness, which poetry (to our mind) had better leave unexpressed."[52]

Back in April, while scaling mountains and volcanoes in Mexico, Crowley began corresponding with Elaine Simpson. She had been his ally in the GD dispute, one of the few members loyal to Mathers, and helped him seize head-quarters. Inspired by Mrs. Simpson's accusation that Crowley had visited her daughter's bedroom in astral form, they agreed to an experiment: every week-end they would visit each other on the astral plane. Recording their results, their diaries could later be compared for accuracy. On April 17, the evening following Crowley and Eckenstein's return to Amecameca from Nevado de Toluca, it began. Crowley visualized himself traveling to Hong Kong, where she now lived, within an egg of white light. In a green and white room, he met Fidelis, who dressed in a soft, white wool gown with velvet lapels. *"Ave, Soror,"* he greeted her in Latin, and conversed for a while. Thus it started.

Even during his tryst with "Alice," Elaine Simpson, the former Soror Fidelis, was on his mind. On May 19, 1901, his diary records a bad dream: "Broken images in my Shrine—reconciliation with [Florence Farr] Emery—some foulest sexual ideas—& Fidelis running like a golden cord throughout." Now proceeding to Shanghai, Crowley's thoughts were consumed with Simpson, whom he had visited on the astral plane every Saturday evening for the past months. She was one of the only people who could understand the psychological changes he was experiencing. And she could help him forget "Alice."

Meeting her a continent away from the Isis-Urania Temple, she looked just the way he remembered. Her place was also as he had pictured it; after all, he had *been* there, in astral form. His vision had been correct in every detail, right down to the cloisonne vase he had tried lifting off the shelf with an invisible hand. Nevertheless, she proved to be a disappointment. She had married the Hong Kong merchant Paul Harry Witkowski on May 8, 1900,[53] and practically abandoned magic. And although he howled when he heard her tale of wearing her adept's robes and regalia to a fancy dress ball and winning first prize, Crowley was disappointed to draw no compassion or inspiration from Fidelis.

Disillusioned, he crossed Singapore and the southern coast of India en route to the island Ceylon, the British colony known today as Sri Lanka. Arriving in Ceylon's capital, Colombo, on August 6, he saw firsthand how much the White Knight thrived in his new environment. The climate improved his health, eradicating his wheezing and drug dependency. He was now the Bhikkhu Ananda Metteya, an aspiring Buddhist monk. Ceylon's Solicitor General Ponnambalam Rámanáthan (1851–1930), also known as the orthodox Shaivite guru Sri Parananda, employed Bennett as a tutor for his children in exchange for instruction in yoga and Hinduism. As part of Ceylon's Buddhist revival, Parananda allied with Theosophist Henry Steel Olcott (1832–1907) to advocate Buddhist education in schools. He also authored *On Faith or Love of God* and *An Eastern Exposition of the Gospel of Jesus According to St. Mathew*; the following year, he would continue the argument in his *An Eastern Exposition of the Gospel of Jesus according to St. John* that Christ was simply teaching yoga.[54] His Biblical expositions were well received, with *Metaphysical Magazine* writing "we know of no more deserving and practical Commentaries on the Holy Scriptures," while *The Theosophist* called their study "very interesting and very profitable"; interest in his writings would eventually lead to an American teaching visit.[55] Thus two mystical mentors, Bennett and Rámanáthan, gave Crowley "my first groundings in mystical theory and practice."[56]

His new environs—the Cinnamon Gardens, an affluent suburb of Colombo—inspired the poem "Dance of Shiva" and many of the other pieces that would appear in *Oracles* (1905). He nevertheless felt ambivalent about Colombo, and by August 17 he and Bennett moved about sixty miles northeast to Kandy, one of Ceylon's principal cities, where they took a furnished bungalow surrounded by ancient palaces and crypts, beautiful mountains and lakes, and Buddhist and Brahman temples.

Sri Parananda, Ceylon's solicitor general Ponnabalam Rámanáthan (1851–1930).

Crowley busied himself with literary preparations. He wrote "Sonnet for a Picture,"[57] and Kandy cropped up again in *Why Jesus Wept*. He also finished revising *Tannhäuser,* wrote its introduction, and sent it to Kegan Paul, who produced five hundred copies to sell for five shillings apiece. Reviewers received it coldly, and even Bennett found it obscure, long, and motiveless—comparing unfavorably to *The Soul of Osiris.* Crowley typically considered it the pinnacle of his achievements up to that point. "What the hell do you mean by a motive?" the crushed poet argued, heaping torrents of abuse upon his guru.

Bennett explained that the piece lacked the literary transmigration of a moral. He clarified with an analogy: a moral is to a fable what a motive is to an epic poem.

With a scowl and hrumph, Crowley defended, "It's the history of a soul: my soul; every soul; no soul!"

"I ought to do yoga instead of exciting my favorite pupil to filthy and blasphemous language."[58]

Crowley agreed, and proceeded to wrap up business so he could forget it. On the literary front, he moved his next book, *Carmen Sæculare,* into production. With respect to climbing, he wrote to Eckenstein on August 23, placing £500 at his disposal for organizing their proposed expedition to climb a mountain higher than anyone had climbed before. On August 28, 1901, Crowley commenced instruction under Bennett, beginning with a ceremonial vow of silence for three days to facilitate introspection. His studies involved yogic postures *(asana)*, controlled breathing *(pranayama)*, vocal repetition *(mantra)*, concentration *(dharana)*, and meditation. After two weeks of this discipline, the ascetic's life proved too much, and Crowley disappeared for a week, doubtlessly in search of women, alcohol, or some other diversion. At this time, AC sent Kelly a telling bit of advice on how to become a great painter:

> A slut for your mistress, a gamin for your model, a procuress for your land-
> lady and a whore for your spiritual guide! That is the only way to become
> a great artist![59]

Crowley contended that asceticism's major drawback was its failure to purge distracting impulses. Rather than submerging these buoys in the subconscious, after which they inevitably surfaced with greater force than before, he favored indulging and satiating his impulses, leaving his mind free from distraction. Thus, he returned from his hiatus prepared to immerse himself in study. Crowley diligently pursued yogic discipline, his reward coming on October 3: after eight hours of breathing at a reduced rate of once a minute, he experienced the "Golden Dawn":

> I became conscious of a shoreless space of darkness and a glow of crimson
> athwart it. Deepening and brightening, scarred by dull bars of slate-blue
> cloud arose the Dawn of Dawns. In splendour not of earth and its mean
> sun, blood-red, rayless, adamant, it rose, it rose! Carried out of myself, I
> asked not "Who is the Witness?" absorbed utterly in contemplation of so
> stupendous and so marvellous a fact.... And this, then, is *Dhyana!*[60]

In *Book Four* (1911), his classic text on yoga and magic, Crowley explained the trance of *dhyana* in clearer language:

> In the course of our concentration we noticed that the contents of the
> mind at any moment consisted of two things, and no more: the Object,
> variable, and the Subject, invariable, or apparently so. By success in *Dha-
> rana* the object has been made as invariable as the subject.
> Now the result of this is that the two become one.... All the poetic
> faculties and all the emotional faculties are thrown into a sort of ecstasy by
> an occurrence which overthrows the mind, and makes the rest of life seem
> absolutely worthless in comparison.[61]

Crowley received an update from Eckenstein in a letter of September 20 and a cable of October 3. Crowley transferred another £500 to Eckenstein's budget, bringing to £1,000—equivalent to roughly $42,000 by today's standards—his commitment to the slowly developing venture. On October 12, at Kandy, he signed a formal agreement for the climb. They set their sights on Mt. Godwin Austen, the second highest mountain in the world. It was the highest point available to Westerners at the time, with Mount Everest remaining inaccessible and therefore unclimbed by Europeans until 1921.

Spiritual success drained Crowley, so the pupil and his teacher suspended work for pilgrimages to Buddhism's sacred cities. Their voyage began in Kandy, where they participated in Perahera, the annual celebration and circus in honor of the alleged tooth of Buddha—which Crowley was sure came from a dog or crocodile. "This celebration is no more Buddhist than the carnival at Nice is Christianity," he mused, and shrugged his shoulders. "Io Pan!" However, the jovial display disillusioned Bennett, who believed sorrow to be the primary human condition. They moved on to the Buddhist temple at Dambulla, Sri Lanka's largest and best-preserved complex of cave temples with statues and paintings of Lord Buddha; Crowley called it "one of the most extraordinary works of human skill, energy and enthusiasm in the world."[62] Sticking up above the jungle, the unclimbable Rock of Sigiri distracted Crowley, who determined to climb it until he realized that approaching it required cutting through miles of dense foliage. Thwarted, he instead wrote the poem "Anima Lunae"[63] about King Zohra's encounter with the spirit of the moon.

Stopping by a shallow lake, Crowley and Bennett spotted two cows and a bull. Much to the ascetic's dismay, Crowley reached for his Mauser .303 rifle, and began a stealthy approach to this big game. When he got within one hundred yards, the bull suddenly stampeded toward him. Crowley acted quickly and, without thinking, raised his rifle, hastily aimed, and fired. But nothing happened. The cartridge didn't explode. "Balls!" he muttered under his breath as the bull charged up. It ran right past Crowley and off into the distance. Luckily it fled rather than gore the intruder. Crowley was dumbfounded. "No question about it," he snorted. "I need a double-barreled rifle."

The pair journeyed north by coach through desolate, monotonous plains of vegetation to Anuradhapura, one of Ceylon's ancient capitals. This city was important to the history of Buddhism, being the place where the Ceylonese ruler converted around 250 BC; it was also the place Crowley wrote "The House,"[64] based on a recurring anxiety dream that Bennett was having about a house on a moor on a dark and stormy night.

By mid-November the magicians parted ways. Bennett pursued the ascetic life of a Buddhist monk, not in Ceylon "where the sodden corruption of the Sangha sickened his sincerity,"[65] but in Akyab (today called Sitwe), the port and chief city on the western coast of Burma, where he took the yellow robe at the Lamma Sayadaw Kyoung monastery. Crowley, more interested in Hinduism, pressed on to Madura in southern mainland India, en route to the Himalayas. Here he determined to see the enormous rock temples that were forbidden to Europeans. Taking a leaf from his idol Sir Richard Burton, Crowley went incognito by donning a loincloth and begging bowl. He fooled no one, but the authorities, moved by the Englishman's sincerity, permitted him entrance to some shrines, where he sacrificed a goat to the goddess Bhavani.

On November 16 and 17, Browning's poems "Christmas Eve" and "Easter Day" inspired Crowley to write "Ascension Day" and "Pentecost." Crowley used Browning's work as a stylistic model to express the philosophical issues he'd been wrestling with in magic, Christianity, Buddhism, and Hinduism. Despite the weighty and serious issues explored, Crowley did so in a highly mercurial way, lacing his work with wordplay and puns. His whimsy also expressed itself by finding good rhymes for seemingly impossible words such as courtesan, Euripides, and Abramelin. These and other pieces written at this time would become *The Sword of Song* (1904).

Crowley continued to the temple of the Shivalingam and the "sleepy, sticky and provincial" city of Madras (now Chennai)[66] before a bout of malaria laid him up in Calcutta in January 1902. He befriended and stayed with two fellow Westerners: Harry Lambe, an Anglo-Indian whose friendship with Crowley was based on twelve hours' previous association, and Edward Thornton, an artist who always carried a sketch pad and *kukuri* knife at his side. In his convalescence, Crowley unsuccessfully tried to learn Hindustani and Balti in order to act as interpreter on the Himalayan expedition. On January 8 he attended as a guest the monthly meeting of the Asiatic Society of Bengal, at which he heard the papers "On Trilokanātha in the Kandā Valley," "On the Secret Words of the Çūlūās," and "On the Organization of Caste by Ballala Sen."[67] Around January 14, Crowley tired of the study of Vedanta and Hinduism, yearning again for Buddhism and Allan Bennett. Two months after they parted, it appeared that a reunion was in order.

On January 21, 1902, a healthy Crowley set off to rejoin his Buddhist friend, with Thornton as his companion. The most direct route to Akyab required him to sail from Calcutta to Rangoon and cross the Arakan range. Crowley's malaria flared up again in Rangoon, leaving him to live on quinine and iced champagne. Crowley adopted a passive attitude toward his condition, no longer caring whether he recovered or died. He merely subsisted, and thereby acquired a new sympathy for Allan. Pressing ahead on January 25, they journeyed 150 miles north to Prome, Burma, where they hired a thirty-five-foot boat and sailed toward Akyab. Crowley, still sick with malaria, sat at the stern, rifle in hand, shooting at everything in sight.

He finally reached the Lamma Sayadaw Kyoung monastery in Akyab at 8 o'clock on the evening of February 14. Fortunately, the first man he encountered took him by carriage to the monastery, where he found Bennett in his bungalow, entranced, rigid, and sitting on his head like an overturned statue; his breathing exercises apparently caused his body to involuntarily leap into the air while in lotus position, landing the oblivious yogi on his head. Otherwise, he was the same old gentle Allan, a giant among his diminutive Burmese *fratres*. Refreshed, Crowley wrote the poem *"Sabbé Pi Dukkham"*[68] (Pali, "All is sorrow") that night. Allan found Aleister's enthusiasm for the Buddhist faith refreshing, spending days discussing how best to spread Buddhism into Europe.

Following his 1902 ordination as a Bhikkhu into the Theravada tradition—he was only the second Englishman so recognized—he would found the Buddhasasana Samagama, or International Buddhist Society, and begin publishing *Buddhism: An Illustrated Quarterly Review,* with six issues appearing between 1903 and 1908. Allan would then return to England, carrying on his work there as a Buddhist missionary and serving as one of the key figures responsible for Buddhism's spread into the West.

Like the other exotic locations of his journey, Akyab inspired the poet in Crowley. Under its spell, he wrote "Ahab" and began working on "The Argonauts" and Book III of *Orpheus.* All these pieces show the residue of his studies in Hinduism and Shaivite mysticism. Crowley, reciting portions of his works to see how they would read, was surprised by the potency of *Orpheus.*

> O triple form of darkness! Sombre splendour!
>   Thou moon unseen of men! Thou huntress dread!
>   Thou crowne'd demon of the crownless dead!
> O breasts of blood, too bitter and too tender!
> …
> I hear the whining of thy wolves! I hear
>   The howling of the hounds about thy form
>   Who comest in the terror of thy storm,
> And night falls faster ere thine eyes appear
>   Glittering through the mist.
>   O face of woman unkissed
>   Save by the dead whose love is taken ere they wist!
> Thee, thee I call! O dire one! O divine![69]

As he recited this invocation of Hecate, he had a vision of her in the form of Bhavani, the goddess to whom he had sacrificed a goat in Madura. For the poet, Akyab's magic was strong indeed.

On February 23, Crowley bid farewell to the Bhikkhu and boarded the SS *Kapurthala.* He had travelled a long distance not only physically but spiritually as well. "I suppose by this time I may consider myself a pretty confirmed Buddhist," he thought, "with merely a metaphysical hankering after the consoling delusions of Vedanta."[70] Returning to Calcutta, he collected his mail and received the awaited news: Eckenstein's Himalayan expedition was meeting in Rawalpindi, Pakistan, in late March. Crowley passed the time until then writing: he composed "St. Patrick's Day"[71] on the 17th, and completed Book III of *Orpheus* the following day. Over March 20 and 21 he wrote "Crowleymas Day," later published as *Berashith* (1903), taken from the first word of Genesis. Subtitled "An Essay in Ontology," it seeks to unite Christianity, Hinduism and Buddhism by subjecting their ontological beliefs to mathematical analysis.

On March 23, he boarded a train for Rawalpindi. Coincidentally, Eckenstein and his four men were heading to Rawalpindi on the same train, so Crowley joined them in their carriage for introductions.

Guy Knowles (1879–1959) was a young climber who first visited the Alps in 1893, at age fourteen, where he scaled the Piz Roseg (12,917 feet) and other nearby mountains. His résumé included the Wetterhorn (12,113 feet) and Jungfrau (13,642 feet) in 1895, and the Matterhorn (14,692 feet), Gabelhorn (13,330 feet), and Wellenkuppe (12,805 feet) in 1896. In 1898, Eckenstein accompanied him on ascents of the Weisshorn (14,780 feet), Lyskamm (14,852 feet), Dent Blanche (14,291 feet), and Matterhorn by the Zmutt arête.[72] Although Crowley considered him, at age twenty-two, "far too young for work of this kind,"[73] Eckenstein's firsthand experience with the climber convinced him otherwise; the fact that he was able to help finance the expedition made up for any lack of mountaineering experience.[74] Guy John Fenton Knowles was the second son of Charles Julius Knowles and his wife Loyse (née Essinger) of Kensington, who were friends with many English and French artists of the era and patrons of painter and etcher Alphonse Legros (1837–1911). They started Guy in art collecting while he was still a schoolboy at Rugby, introduced him to Rodin in Paris (Rodin gifted him with the first bronze cast made of his sculpture *Sœur et frère*), and even arranged for Legros to give Guy lessons in drawing and sculpting. He matriculated to Trinity College in June 1898, just missing Crowley; dividing his time between engineering, rowing, and the Fitzwilliam museum (where he said he passed many of the most profitable and enjoyable quieter hours of his undergraduate life), he took a Second Class in Part I of the Mechanical Sciences Tripos, receiving his BA in 1901, the year before the K2 expedition.[75] Crowley found him cheerful and willing to follow directions, "the best companion I could have wished."[76]

Dr. Heinrich Pfannl (1870–1929) was at age thirty-one the best rock climber in Austria, having climbed extensively on the Swiss, Ennstal, and Julian Alps. Indeed, he would in later years become the president of the Austrian Alpine Club. Born in Trumau, Lower Austria, he studied law in Vienna, received his Doctor of Laws in 1894, and in 1896 passed the exam to become an Austrian judge. In 1894, at age twenty-four, he began hiking and climbing as a spiritual retreat from the covetous, acquisitive world of law and lawyers; for him, climbing was a way to fulfill his will, of playing on death's own border, where the only laws were those of nature.[77] Thus in March 1896, when his brother Josef, also a climber, was one of three killed in an avalanche on Lower Austria's Rax mountain over the Reistalersteig, it did not dissuade Heinrich from climbing: the same year, he made the first ascent of the Hochtor (7,772 feet) from the north, considered at that time impossible. He developed a reputation for his systematic approach and guideless climbs, giving him much in common with Eckenstein's methodical and antiestablishment ways. Pfannl made a guideless ascent of Mont Blanc (15,404 feet), the highest Alpine mountain, in 1899. In 1900, he recorded an ascent of Aiguille de Triolet and the first free climb of Dent du Géant (or Dent del Gigante, the Giant's Tooth, 13,165 feet), and in 1901 conquered the northern face of the Reichstein in Austria's

Ennstal Alps.[78] "Superb climber as he was," Crowley noted, "he was totally incapable of realising the magnitude of the task we had set out to perform."[79]

Drs. Heinrich Pfannl (1870–1929), left, and Jules Jacot-Guillarmod (1868–1925), right.

His regular climbing companion was Austrian barrister Dr. Victor Wessely (born c. 1870) of Linz. Wessely, Hans Lorenz, and W. Merz were the first to ascend the Dolomite rock ridge Langkofelkarspitze (9,268 feet) in 1892.[80] He was Pfannl's frequent climbing partner, joining him, for example, on his 1896 first ascent of the Hochtor-Norwand (7,861 feet), and his 1899 ascent of Mont Blanc; on December 27, 1900, the two of them climbed the Hoch Arn (10,676 feet) in snowshoes.[81] Crowley found him myopic (he was the only one in the party who wore glasses), and was revolted by his eating habits, which he likened to hunching over a plate and shoveling food into one's mouth. Perhaps in response to this unflattering characterization, Wessely, in his account of the expedition, fails to mention Crowley at all.[82]

Doctor Jules Jacot-Guillarmod (1868–1925) acted as the expedition's physician and photographer; since the purpose of the expedition was ostensibly to determine the effect of prolonged exposure to rarefied air on mountain climbers,[83] his professional acumen was vital to the mission. Born in La Chaux-de-Fonds, Switzerland, on Christmas Eve 1868, he was one of four children to Jules (a prominent professor, wildlife painter, and art teacher) and Adèle Emma Courvoisier. From 1888 to 1897, he studied medicine in Lausanne and Zürich, obtaining his PhD and working as a general physician in Corsier, Geneva, from 1898 to 1902. During his studies in Zürich, he became acquainted with the mountains of central Switzerland and developed passions for both climbing and photography. He climbed every year from 1891 through 1901, and is best known for his ascent of Mont Blanc, which he and several doctor colleagues climbed without a guide on June 12, 1897. Other guideless ascents that year included Mont Chemin (5,774 feet), Cornettes de Bise (7,979 feet), Col d'Emaney (8,077 feet), the Dom (14,911 feet), Col de Fenêtre (7,365 feet), La Ruinette (12,713 feet), Col du Mont Rouge (10,961 feet), Col de Seilon (10,499 feet), Pas de Chèvres (9,354 feet), Col des Maisons Blanches (11,240 feet), Pointe du Mountet (12,720 feet), and Monte Rosa (15,203 feet).[84] In 1890 he joined the Diablerets section of the Swiss Alpine Club, the French Alpine Club in 1898, and in 1899 he became a senior member of the Academic Alpine Club of Zurich.[85] Aged thirty-three, his climbing skills were, in Crowley's opinion, marginal, but his congenial nature did wonders for morale. Crowley described him as "certainly worth his place in the party, and more, for his constant cheerfulness and the fun we could always have with him."[86]

The K2 party (from left to right): Victor Wessely, Oscar Eckenstein, Jules Jacot-Guillarmod, Aleister Crowley, Heinrich Pfannl, and Guy Knowles.

Towering over the Karakoram range north of India at a height of 28,251 feet, the second-highest mountain in the world was known variously as K2, Chogo Ri, Mount Godwin Austen, and Dapsang. Its sheer walls of ice, jutting sharply out of the landscape, were considered unclimbable. Despite Godwin Austen's nineteenth-century survey, Conway's 1892 Karakoram expedition, and Freshfield's 1899 snow-aborted attempt, K2 and its surrounding mountains remained relatively unexplored. Conway did ascend the lesser neighboring pinnacles

Crystal Peak and Pioneer Peak, but Eckenstein, who was in the expedition, knew the facts: Crystal Peak was a minor summit, nine thousand feet smaller than its neighbor K2, while Pioneer Peak was not even a peak but the top of a ridge whose summit Conway could not climb. He scorned the achievements on which the new president of the Alpine Club built his reputation, knowing he could do better with the four climbers he recruited, none of whom belonged to the club.

On March 29, they set out with three tons of baggage, 150 porters, and seventeen ekkas (two-wheeled carts drawn by horses, oxen, or similar animals), spending the night in Tret. The next morning, Crowley awoke to find a smartly dressed young man sitting attentively at his bedside. He was a police inspector sent to detain the expedition. Baffled, Crowley referred him to Eckenstein. Later that morning, Rawalpindi's deputy commissioner told Crowley, "The rest of your party can do as it pleases. Mr. Eckenstein, however, cannot enter Kashmir." Eckenstein, fearing this complication would fatally delay the expedition, asked Crowley to lead them into Srinagar while he sorted things out. So, for the next three weeks, Crowley led the march toward the mountain.

Pfannl trained constantly. As Crowley wrote, "After a fifteen-mile march he would have a little tiffin, and then go off in the afternoon up the mountainside to keep himself in condition!"[87] He enjoyed marching ahead of the others and, when everyone caught up, proudly announced how many hours he had been waiting. Crowley was sure Pfannl would make himself sick.

Guillarmod, meanwhile, oversaw the cooks, trying to teach them a thing or two about preparing meals. He was good-humored, not even minding being the butt of jokes. For this, the natives invented the saying *Yahan Doctor Sahib tahaan tamasha:* "Where the Doctor Sahib is, there is amusement."

Eckenstein found himself accused of being a spy. Interpreting this as an attempt by his rival, Conway, to use his influence to interfere with their expedition, Eckenstein boldly went to Delhi and confronted the ranking British official: if he was blocked from Kashmir, he would go to the *Daily Telegraph* and expose Conway's machinations. On April 22 a suddenly unimpeded Eckenstein caught up to his comrades in Srinagar, the capital of Kashmir.[88] An ancient city rich with pagodas and mosques, it offered very few familiar Western comforts; it reminded Guillarmod of Venice, but with a breathtaking mountain panorama visible from virtually every direction.[89]

On April 28 they proceeded north toward the Karakorams, daily hiring porters to carry their gear. The government, in an effort to make amends for detaining Eckenstein, provided additional food, porters, and permissions to aid the expedition.[90] Seventeen days' march brought them to Skardu, the capital of Baltistan, on May 14. Crossing the Indus river by ferry, they continued toward Askole. Then trouble began.

While most of the world's great peaks were populated near their bases, K2 was not: Askole, ten days from the mountain's base, was the last village along the way. This meant carrying an extra twenty days' provisions for everyone in the caravan. Since a porter could carry thirty days' rations at best, bringing enough provisions for the entire length of the expedition became a problem. The solution: They cut their baggage back to forty pounds per person, bought every pound of food in the valley, and hired every available man—about 250— to carry it. Crowley's insistence on bringing along his library drove Eckenstein into uncharacteristic anger. The poet shrugged his shoulders and told Eckenstein flatly, "I would rather bear physical starvation than intellectual starvation. Either I take my books with me or I leave the expedition."[91]

On June 5, ten days after arriving in Askole, the expedition proceeded in four teams. Crowley set out first, followed a day later by Wessely and Pfannl, then by Knowles and Guillarmod another day behind. Eckenstein planned to join them after Crowley set up a base of operations on the glacier.

Crowley's team consisted of about twenty hand-picked porters, his library, and a mobile farmyard of fifteen sheep, thirty goats, and various fowl. The hired help was trying: Baltis traveled for days to sneak into the porters' pay line and expect their ten cents without working. At nightfall, porters made off with supplies. Through it all, AC tried to treat them fairly and on terms he believed their culture understood. When a porter tested his authority by straggling, he responded by ignoring the offender until the end of the day, then humiliated him in front of his friends with a whipping.[92] Conversely, when a Pathan porter cheated a Kashmiri servant of his tattered clothing, Crowley mediated the dispute. He heard the evidence and conceded that, by native justice, the clothes belonged to the Pathan. However, Crowley added a twist to the judgment: "Hassan's coat certainly belongs to you, but the coat *you* are wearing belongs to me." Thus Crowley dressed the servant in the new coat he had bought for each of his porters, while the bully slunk off in rags that were far too small for him. Finally, when he arrived at Paiyu's open plateau on June 8 and discovered the servants had stolen his fowl and nearly all the sugar, he fired them all. According to Rowell,[93] this was only the first of many expeditions to search in vain for competent high-altitude porters in the Karakorams.

Finally, on June 16—seventy-nine days after setting out from Pindi— Crowley greeted the Baltoro Glacier with awe. Its wall of ice dwarfed the Swiss Alps, jutting over one thousand feet into the sky, and this from an altitude of 16,000 feet. AC spent the next four hours marching where no one had set foot before. At an altitude of 16,592 feet on the southeast ridge that would later be known as the Abruzzi Ridge, Crowley set up Camp 8. His survey from this point indicated that the ridge was the best approach to the summit of K2. Subsequent expeditions would confirm that Crowley lucked upon the best, and possibly only, way up K2.

Crowley's team proceeded up the south face of the mountain to 17,332 feet, where the glacier rose sharply. Not wishing to endanger his porters, Crowley set up Camp 9 and halted the group. He climbed another 1,400 feet alone to set up Camp 10, the main camp, then sent his porters home and awaited the others.

Pfannl and Wessely reached Camp 10 with their group on June 19. With their arrival came the persistent snow that marred the expedition. While the weather didn't keep Knowles, Guillarmod, and the rest of the third team from arriving the next day, it soon turned into a furious blizzard. A week passed before Eckenstein could ascend with fresh meat and bread.

A view of Camp 10.

Eckenstein and Knowles were both ill, with Knowles showing signs of altitude sickness. So Crowley, Pfannl, and Guillarmod started up the mountain. High winds kept them busy trying to keep their tents secure, and Crowley awoke the next morning with snow blindness. Wessely and Pfannl went ahead on July 1 to set up Camp 11 at 20,000 feet. They concluded K2 could be climbed not by the Abruzzi Ridge but by the northeast ridge, an unrealistic plan that Eckenstein vetoed. Snow fell for the next five days.

The climbers soon found that, living on the mountain, their body temperature and weight made a depression in the ice beneath their tent, forming a spot for water to collect and soak everything. On July 5, when two men arrived with two copies of *Tannhäuser* from the publisher, Crowley wrote in his diary, "We wished they had been 2,000 as then we should have something dry to put tents on."[94] Crowley spent the next day floating paper boats in the small lake inside his tent. The snow and moisture earned this site the nickname "Camp Misery."

When Eckenstein proposed moving to Camp 11, Crowley objected strenuously, believing Abruzzi Ridge to be the best route up the mountain. Eckenstein feared the porters couldn't manage the climb, so, on July 8, Crowley, Wessely, Pfannl, and Guillarmod moved to Camp 11, which Crowley dubbed Camp Despair, while Eckenstein and Knowles held back at Camp 10. Crowley went climbing the next day, reaching heights of 21,500 to 22,000 feet, only to relapse into illness on his return. The next day, an avalanche showered Camps 10 and 11 with snow.

Over the next days, Eckenstein and Knowles joined the others at Camp 11. Pfannl and Wessely established Camp 12 at an estimated height of 21,000 feet.

By July, K2 took its toll on the expedition: the weather was inhospitable, the altitude beyond acclimation, and the strain debilitating. At this altitude, water boiled at 194 degrees Farenheit—eighteen degrees lower than normal; it took two hours to make lukewarm tea, and the whole day to boil mutton. Knowles lost thirty-three pounds, and Guillarmod dropped down to 147; both were constantly ill with the flu. Crowley, meanwhile, was down with malaria. Locked in his tent on the mountain, with a fever of 102.9 degrees, the magician worked on *The Sword of Song*. Later, delirious with fever, Crowley pulled his Colt revolver on Knowles, who disarmed him with a sharp blow to the stomach. In later years, the gun would occupy Knowles's mantel beside artworks of Degas, Rodin, Whistler, and Guardi.

When news came down from Camp 12 that Pfannl was ill, the doctor took notice. Pfannl had suffered bronchitis on the Finsteraarhorn (14,022 feet) in 1898 and had requried a period of convalescence at that time,[95] so Jacot-Guillarmod monitored him closely. His condition worsened the next day, so the doctor examined him and brought him back down to Camp 11. He had edema of both lungs, triggered by the high altitude. It was a common occurrence in mountaineering, but at that time, fluid in the lungs was usually diagnosed as pneumonia; the correct diagnosis is to Guillarmod's credit.[96] On morphine, Pfannl babbled incoherently and explained his illness to Crowley: "The others are brutes and cannot understand. But you are a poet, you can see. There are three of me: two are well, but the third is a mountain, which holds a dagger. I am afraid it will stab me." On July 21, after the latest snowstorm passed, Wessely took Pfannl down to Rdokass. Five days passed before the others realized Wessely had taken most of the emergency rations with him.

On August 1 the Austrians sent word from Rdokass that a cholera epidemic had broken out in the Bralduh Nala valley, and that the government had sealed off their return route. Eckenstein and Knowles were alarmed. Forty-nine days after Camp 10 was established, Eckenstein wrote to climber Douglas Freshfield (1845–1934):

Since then, we've had eight partially fine days (no three consecutive) and
the rest of the time continuous snow storms. Our present storm has gone
on for over 96 hours, and shows as yet no sign of abatement. At our camp
here there are over five feet of fresh snow. Our prospects of ascending a
high mountain, or any mountain, are consequently practically nil on this
occasion.[97]

Crowley assessed the situation in very similar terms:

Of the 68 days which I spent on the glacier, only eight were fine; it was
impossible even to start on any serious climb, easy as the mountain was,
judged by the standard of technical difficulty. Pluck and perseverence are
all very well; but they make no impression on deep powdery snow. A novice and a coward to boot will do as well—or as badly—as the best climber
in the world with the temperament of Achilles.[98]

Perhaps more concisely, Crowley wrote these lines at Camp Despair:

So now the Earl was well a-weary of
The grievous folly of this wandering.[99]

At a long meeting the team evaluated their options. Their money was spent,
everyone was sick, the snow was relentless, and a cholera epidemic threatened.
Even if the weather miraculously cleared, the plateaux would require at least a
week before they could be climbed, and the team had only a fortnight's supplies to see them back to civilization. They decided unanimously to descend.

They tore down Camp 11 on August 3 and began their descent the next
day. On the lower Baltoro Glacier, which they found dry of snow, Crowley
stopped near a spring and washed for the first time since they began; he was
rewarded with a head cold the next day. The team rejoined Pfannl and Wessely
on August 11 in Rdokass, where they were surprised to find their rations gone.
Crowley raved, "there were no sheep, the Austrians having managed to eat
eight in sixteen days, in addition to fowls, etc!"[100] At another meeting the team
expelled the two climbers.

Alarmed by the cholera epidemic, Knowles and Eckenstein dumped the
expedition's tea and other provisions into the river and left the region before
they could be infected. Neither Crowley nor Guillarmod bought into the
panic and left the region at a leisurely pace. On August 20, 1902, Crowley
recorded, "My constant sorrow at having ever been born was interrupted by
moments of something very like indifference as to whether I was alive or not.
It needed, in fact, a very few days to plunge me into the moral abyss of actually
liking life."[101] On September 1 they arrived at Gurais, where Crowley and
Guillarmod enjoyed a hot bath and cooked food. On September 6 the two
climbers continued to Srinagar and parted. One hundred and thirty-two days
after it started, the world's first expedition up K2 was over.

Crowley bathing in a spring on the lower Baltoro Glacier, 1902.

It is necessary to put this expedition into perspective because it is often over-looked by historians. The oversight is intentional, because the team's two principals were very unpopular among Alpinists: Eckenstein disdained what he considered glory-grabbing tactics of the Alpine Club, so that Conway was knighted while Eckenstein died in obscurity in 1921.[102] Crowley, on the other hand, because of his colorful reputation, was too notorious to receive credit for any achievement, however well deserved. Thus, many histories of K2 fail to mention this expedition at all; for instance, Sir Francis Younghusband's (1863–1942) account[103] merely states that the Swiss doctor, Jacot-Guillarmod, explored the region.

So what did the team accomplish? While it did not reach the top of K2, it was the first to set foot on the mountain; only the weather prevented their reaching the pinnacle. Even so, Guillarmod and Wessely performed reconnais-sance up to 23,000 feet, a Himalayan record.[104] Guillarmod also performed sci-entific measurements, recording not only the daily high and low temperatures, but also the altitudes at which vegetation ended (13,500 feet), ibex ascended (16,000 feet), and jackdaws flew overhead (18,000 feet). Eckenstein pioneered the use of successive depots and camps for climbing the great mountains of Asia.[105] The expedition also stayed on the glacier for sixty-eight days, living at an altitude of 20,000 feet for longer than was thought possible; none but Knowles complained about the thin air. All this by a team of what some have called amateurs, using very primitive equipment by today's standards. It would be over fifty years before the party lead by Italian climber Professor Ardito Desio (1897–2001) became first to reach K2's summit in 1954.

From Srinagar, Crowley returned home by stages: first to Baramula, where he hunted bears for a week; then to Bombay, his ambition for sightseeing withered by sickness and exhaustion. On October 4, he sailed for five days to Aden, where Yemini authorities quarantined him in case he had caught cholera in Bombay. By the time he reached Cairo on October 14, his ennui had swelled: he had been away from London for sixteen months, climbing mountains, learning mysticism, and writing poetry. Although he felt certain he had attained greatness in all three areas, he found no comfort in the knowledge when pondering his next move. Rather than see the pyramids, Crowley visited Cairo's flesh pots, muttering "I won't have 40 centuries looking down on *me*." On November 5, 1902, after three weeks in Cairo, Crowley resumed life in France.

He called on Mathers, who, in the process of moving to Butte Montmartre, received him warmly. Crowley eagerly described his journeys, only to find Frater SRMD uninterested in tales of mountaineering, concentration, and yoga. Disappointed with his master, he concluded they had grown apart. Moreover, he believed Mathers had lost contact with the Secret Chiefs, and with it any mystical power or authority he may have claimed.

CHAPTER FIVE

A Rose by Any Other Name

While Crowley circled the globe, Gerald Kelly moved to Paris to become an artist. As early as 1900, William Dalton, principal of the Camberwell School of Arts and Crafts, had advised Rev. Kelly, "Let your son go to Paris; you'll never regret it." Once he accepted the idea of his son being a painter, the clergyman supported Gerald's endeavors. The budding artist arrived alone in Paris in 1901 and took a studio on the rue Campagne-Première in Montparnasse. He rubbed elbows with local luminaries like Monet, Degas, Rodin, and Renoir, finding himself a portrait painter, a realist, in the Impressionistic hotbed. At the urging of a friend, he reluctantly submitted his first two portraits—both of his sister Rose—to the Salon, where they were put on display. From there, he quickly gained a reputation as a talented painter with an encyclopedic knowledge of art, and in 1903 the French government bought one of his pictures. Gerald Kelly had arrived. So, too, did Crowley, who decided to stay with him.

Crowley's empty feeling about his achievements wilted into what he called his "cynical bonhomie" phase. He completed "Ahab" on December 9 and dedicated it to G. C. Jones, his mentor in the GD. From the manuscript, he printed the sonnet "New Year, 1903" in gold capital letters on a folded sheet with a crimson border. It bore the message, "From Aleister Crowley, wishing you a speedy termination of existence." His next publication was an edition of two hundred copies of *Berashith,* his first published work on magic. The Paris printing firm Clarke & Bishop did the job.

His nihilistic attitude emerged from a desire for the trance of nonexistence—of union with the godhead. This sentiment runs through his works from this period, including "Science and Buddhism," "The Excluded Middle," and his disenchanted treatment of Buddhism, "Summa Spes":

> Existence being sorrow,
>   The cause of it desire.
> A merry tune I borrow
>   To light upon the lyre:

> If death destroy me quite,
>> Then, I can not lament it;
> I've lived, kept life alight,
>> And—damned if I repent it!
>
> Let me die in a ditch,
>> Damnably drunk,
>> Or lipping a punk,
> Or in bed with a bitch!
>> I was ever a hog;
> Muck? I am one with it!
>> Let me die like a dog;
> Die, and be done with it!

This poem, like *Berashith,* appeared in early 1903, with *Alice: An Adultery* following it into production. He showed the manuscript of *Alice* to several acquaintances, one of whom was aspiring artist Sybil Meugens (born c. 1877), who was helping to distribute his books.[1] To Crowley's surprise, both she and Kelly claimed no lady would kiss her suitor so early as the thirteenth day of his wooing. He felt vindicated when, shortly thereafter, Sybil's lover went to Brussels for a week and she became intimate with Kelly. The artist was, in fact, so smitten that he proposed. Only a hasty visit from his sister Rose, who warned him his allowance would be cut off if he went ahead with the marriage, caused him to wait. Eager to put a twist onto the situation, Crowley offered to match the allowance if Gerald were to go ahead and marry her. By then, the matter had degenerated to the point that Gerald reconsidered matrimony altogether.

Meanwhile, Crowley found himself enamored of an Irish friend of Gerald's from the Slade School of Fine Art, Eileen Gray (1878–1976). Kathleen Eileen Moray Gray had come to Paris to study art at the Académie Julian and Académie Colarossi, and she lived near Montparnasse. Kelly was painting her portrait, so she spent a good deal of time in his studio, where she met Crowley. Something about the poet with silk shirts, floppy bow ties, and ostentatious rings appealed to her. Perhaps it was his sense of luxury, or his fashionable interest in occultism, or because she thought "he was very lonely."[2] For whatever reason, she patiently sat and listened to his discourses on magic, while he denied Kelly's assumption that they were lovers: "She was never anything of the sort, nor within a million miles of it. Never wished it, nor she."[3] Regardless, Crowley soon proposed and gave her a diamond brooch.

One day, while sitting for Kelly, Eileen asked about her intended. Reading in *The Sword of Song* that Crowley had read Lévi and the cryptic Coptic, she wondered, "What does *Coptic* mean?" The painter told her, "It's the language spoken by the ancient Copts." When she asked, "What does *cryptic* mean?" he stopped painting and smirked. "The language spoken by the ancient Crypts."

Much of Crowley's writing from this period concerns his fiancée: In *Rosa Mundi and Other Love Songs,* poems 3, 14–16, 18, and 21–28 are all about Gray. Even poem 13 of the "Lover's Alphabet" series is titled "Eileen." In number 27, her full name appears as an acrostic. Like Kelly's hasty proposal to Sybil Meugens, Crowley's marriage to Eileen Gray failed to materialize. Although Gray would go on to become a successful furniture designer and architect, the importance of her reputation and contributions are only recently being appreciated: At a February 25, 2009, auction from Yves Saint Laurent's art collection, Gray's "Fauteuil aux dragons" armchair sold for a record £19.4 million, the highest price ever paid for a piece of twentieth-century design.[4] Likewise, the *Irish Times* quipped that 2009 "might be called The Year of Eileen Gray."[5]

Another of Crowley's works, "The Star and the Garter," commemorated his entire circle of women at the time: fiancée Eileen Gray was the star, while the garter was three other ladies, most likely Kelly's fiancée, Sybil Meugens; model Nina Olivier; and sculptress Kathleen Bruce. Olivier—of whom, as Crowley wrote, "I loved and loved so well and sang so passionately"[6]—would reappear in "The Ordeal of Ida Pendragon" and in *Rodin in Rime,* while Bruce, as will be seen, featured in numerous works.

Kathleen Bruce (1878-1947)—born Edith Agnes Kathleen Bruce—was Eileen Gray's close friend. The youngest of eleven children, she was orphaned in infancy, raised in Edinburgh by a strict grand-uncle, and sent to an equally strict convent school from age fourteen to eighteen. She became an art student at age twenty-one and in 1901 began attending the Académie Colarossi in Paris. Starting with paint—she loved the work of Augusts John—she soon discovered clay was her medium. As a friend and pupil of Rodin, etched in her memory was the day she went from being called *chère élève* (dear student) to *chère collègue* (dear colleague). Within months of graduating with the Colarossi's highest honors, her sculptures were displayed by the Salon.

During a sitting, Kathleen Bruce's Highland flamboyance and seductive beauty captivated Crowley. Characterized by some biographers as a misogynist because the frailties of her female friends exasperated her, Bruce was not the easy conquest Crowley had hoped. "She took delight in getting married men away from their wives," Crowley wrote bitterly, and "initiated me into the torturing pleasures of algolagny on the spiritual plane."[7] Of their "sexless love," Crowley remarked that she "made me wonder, in fact, if the secret of puritanism was not to heighten the intensity of love by putting obstacles in its way."[8] As it turns out, she was simply remaining chaste until she found Mr. Right: As she recalled her artist friends and potential lovers in Paris, "I kept my goal, my star, firmly fixed. None of these was the right, the perfect father for my son."[9] Crowley's later poems "The Black Mass," "The Adept," and "The Vampire" recount his ambivalence toward her with lines like:

> Spit in my face! I love you. Clench your fists
> And beat me! Still, I love you. Let your eyes
> Like fiery opals or mad amethysts
> Curse me! I love you. Let your anger rise
> And your teeth tear bleeding bits of flesh
> Out of my body—kill me if you can![10]

After she married Antarctic explorer Captain Robert Scott (1868–1912) in 1908, Crowley concluded he had always disliked her. Bruce bore her husband a son, Peter, in 1909; Scott and three others died tragically on his second Antarctic expedition, two months after reaching the South Pole.

Whatever Crowley's feelings about her may have been, Kathleen Bruce nevertheless commanded much attention in his writings: His later books *Why Jesus Wept* and *Rodin in Rime* would bear dedications to Kathleen Bruce, as would his poems "The Muse" and "Song"[11] and the short story "The Vitriol Thrower."[12] The namesake of "The Ordeal of Ida Pendragon"[13] was based in part on her, as were the poems "Ovariotomy" and "The Gilt Mask."[14] Much of his later work *Clouds without Water,* although not overtly dedicated to her, was written in her memory.

Near the Gare Montparnasse, a circle of artists and writers clustered into Le Chat Blanc, a restaurant in rue d'Odessa with a reputation for excellent yet inexpensive food. The clique was closed, the same people dining nightly around the horseshoe-shaped configuration of tables that claimed most of the first floor. Those outsiders who unwittingly visited the English, American, and French painters quickly found themselves unwelcome. Gerald Kelly was part of the "in" crowd at Le Chat Blanc, and introduced Crowley to the assorted personalities who frequented it.

One of these was a young doctor named Willie who aspired to be a writer. Although he had recently published *Mrs. Craddock* (1902)—and his first book, *Liza of Lambeth,* in 1897—the name William Somerset Maugham (1874–1965) would not enter the ranks of literary greats for some years. Maugham was brother-in-law to one of Rose Kelly's best friends, and through Gerald gained an introduction to Le Chat Blanc's circle. Maugham was fond of Kelly, finding him talented, loquacious, and enthusiastic. When he wrote *Of Human Bondage* (1915), Maugham based the character Lawson on Kelly, creating a knowledgeable and aggressive artist who says, "Raphael was only tolerable when he painted other people's pictures. When he painted Peruginos or Pinturichios he was charming; when he painted Raphaels he was … Raphael."[15] Maugham, however, was not so impressed with Crowley, writing of him:

> I took an immediate dislike to him, but he interested and amused me. He was a great talker and he talked uncommonly well. In early youth, I was told, he was extremely handsome, but when I knew him he had put on weight and his hair was thinning. He had fine eyes and a way, whether natural or acquired I do not know, of so focusing them that, when he looked at you, he seemed to look behind you. He was a fake but not entirely a fake.… He was a liar and unbecomingly boastful, but the odd thing was that he had actually done some of the things he boasted of.[16]

Despite his reservations, Maugham admired the boastful yet worldly raconteur in Crowley enough to base the title characater of *The Magician* (1908), Oliver

Haddo, on Crowley. This unflattering parody—discussed later—is balanced by a more sympathetic portrait of him as Cronshaw in *Of Human Bondage*.[17] Cronshaw was a poet, an extraordinary fellow and an excellent talker. He was at his best when drunk, but taking "a devil of a time to get drunk." Despite his worldliness—he knew everyone worth knowing—he spoke French with an abominable accent. Stout but not fat, his round head was so small compared to the rest of his body that it "looked like a pea poised uneasily on an egg." Maugham describes one incident which is typically Crowley:

> "I wrote a poem yesterday." Without being asked he began to recite it, very slowly, marking the rhythm with an extended forefinger.[18]

Whether or not he liked Crowley, Maugham thought enough of him to portray his character in two books.

Another acquaintance was Marcel Schwob (1867–1905), French author, translator and one of the great scholars of the nineteenth century. Although Schwob reputedly called Crowley "ridiculous and a bad poet,"[19] the poet himself says Schwob called *Alice: An Adultery* a little masterpiece. Crowley considered him one of his best friends in Paris, and greatly admired him. Although Schwob was only eight years older than Crowley, he was quite sickly and would die two years after their meeting, at age thirty-seven.

Through Schwob, Crowley met novelist Arnold Bennett (1867–1931) and writer and poet William Ernest Henley (1849–1903), both natives of England. Crowley had read and admired Bennett's recent *The Grand Babylon Hotel* (1902) and was surprised to find Bennett somehow offended by his praise; he concluded Bennett was "very ill at ease to find himself in Paris in polite society."[20] Henley—the original of Robert Louis Stephenson's Long John Silver—was ailing from tuberculosis, but nevertheless invited Crowley to his house near Woking for a lunch of Chablis and roast lamb. Crowley appreciated the consideration Henley showed to a young unknown writer. He died three weeks after the visit, and Crowley recalled him fondly:

> And here his mighty and reverend high-priest
> Bade me good cheer, an eager acolyte,
> Poured the high wine, unveiled the mystic feast ...[21]

Best known for the poem "Invictus" (1875), Henley had several books of poetry, including *A Book of Verses* (1888), *Poems* (1898), *Hawthorn and Lavender* (1901), *A Song of Speed* (1903), and *In Hospital* (1903). However, the work that Crowley admired most was the one he edited with John Stephen Farmer: *Slang and Its Analogues, Past and Present: A Dictionary, Historical and Comparative, of the Heterodox Speech of All Classes of Society for More than Three Hundred Years; with Synonyms in English, French, German, Italian, etc.*, was privately published in 1903 for subscribers only, and its catalog of vulgarities ceaselessly entertained him.

He also met Dr. Ivor Gordon Back (1879–1951), an observer and appreciator of the circle of writers and artists. Crowley described him as a "great surgeon, and true gentleman.... Handsome as a god, with yet a spice of devil's laughter lurking there, he would sit and enjoy the treasures of the conversation, adding at the proper interval his own rich quota of scholarly jest."[22] Like Crowley, his friendship with Kelly gained him an introduction to Maugham and the rest of the circle. British author Frank Arthur Swinnerton (1884–1982) remembered him as "solid and dark," "a racy talker without illusions or moral refinement," and possessing a curious habit: Whenever they met, the doctor would approach, point to his chest, and say, "Back. I met you at Willie Maugham's," even though Sinnerton had never been to Maugham's.[23]

Dr. Ivor Back (1879–1951).

Back was one of Crowley's few Paris acquaintances with whom he continued a friendship after returning to England, dedicating *In Residence: The Don's Guide to Cambridge* (1904) to him. Back was a proud descendant, through his grandmother, of the Duke of Wellington, to whom he bore a striking resemblance. Entering Trinity College, Cambridge, in 1898, he graduated with his BA in 1901, and when he met Crowley he was doing his clinical training at St. George's Hospital. As a colleague recalled,

> Ivor Back came to St. George's from Cambridge with a great reputation as an anatomist, as those who attended his admirable demonstrations in the dissecting-room at St. George's in his early days have good cause to remember. From the first he decided to become a surgeon and his desires came to fruition by his early appointment to the surgical staff.[24]

He was also an avid Mason—whether he joined before or after meeting Crowley is unclear; he would go on to reach a high grade in Freemasonry and eventually be Past Master of the Lanesborough Lodge. His wide range of interests—including literature, criminology, and fly-fishing—earned him a reputation as a superb after-dinner speaker. "Whenever one met him," another colleague remembered, "there was the ever-ready spontaneous friendly smile and greeting which would banish gloom and depression."[25]

Crowley made various other acquaintances in the Le Chat Blanc circle. Painter Eugène Carrière (1849–1906), recovering from an operation for throat cancer when they met, told him, "If it comes back, I shall kill myself." Norwegian landscape painter Frits Thaulow (1847–1906), whom he met several times, he recalled as a "jolly, bearded senior on whom life had left no scars."[26] Canadian painter James Wilson Morrice (1865–1924) was "invariably mellow drunk all day and all night."[27] And he would parody sculptor Paul Wayland Bartlett (1865–1925) in *Snowdrops from a Curate's Garden* (1904) as a "brilliant but debauched sculptor, caustic of wit, though genial to his friends."[28]

When Crowley met Auguste Rodin (1840–1917), the gray-haired, sixty-two-year-old artist was being attacked for his sculpture of Balzac, which Crowley considered "the most interesting and important thing he did."[29] He was so impressed that he wrote a sonnet praising it:

> Giant, with iron secrecies ennighted,
> Cloaked, Balzac stands and sees. Immense disdain,
> Egyptian silence, mastery of pain,
> Gargantuan laughter, shake or still the ignited
> Stature of the Master, vivid.[30]

After returning unfulfilled from his world travels, he finally had a cause to get behind. Just as he fought for Mathers and Eckenstein, he now defended a great artist from ignorant critics. Crowley presented his poem, along with a sonnet titled "Rodin," to the artist. Rodin read English no better than he spoke it, but based on reviews by his friends, Rodin gave them to Schwob to translate.[31] Schwob's rendering of the laudatory poems, especially their "unexpected flower of violence, good sense and irony,"[32] pleased Rodin. The author published these poems privately as "Balzac: Hommage à Auguste Rodin," with eighteen copies on Japanese vellum and six on China paper. They also appeared in *Maîtres Artistes* later that year, causing "a considerable stir in Paris."[33]

Rodin invited his champion to stay with him at Meudon and write poetry about his best works. Crowley accepted, with many of the poems appearing in the *Weekly Critical Review,* a bilingual periodical devoted to literature, music, and the fine arts edited by Arthur Bles and published in Paris from 1903 to 1904 alongside contributions from luminaries like W. B. Yeats, Havelock Ellis, and H. G. Wells.[34] When Crowley finally left Meudon, Rodin presented him with ten nude drawings, seven of which Crowley used as illustrations when he published the poems four years later as *Seven Lithographs by Clot from the Watercolours of Auguste Rodin, with a Chaplet of Verse* (1907), also known as *Rodin in Rime.*

By spring of 1903, Crowley tired of Paris and its provincialism and cliqu-
ishness. Wrapping up business, he completed *The Sword of Song* and left it with
Parisian printer Philippe Renouard on 19 rue des Saints-Pères for private publication. Then he sent copies of "Summa Spes" to his friends and returned to
Boleskine for another go at the Abramelin operation.

Back in Scotland, having decided against marrying Eileen Gray, Crowley put
his energies instead into the Abramelin operation. An old family friend, L. C.
R. Duncombe-Jewell, a.k.a. Ludovic Cameron, had come to Boleskine for a
week's visit but, according to Crowley, "managed somehow or other to settle
down there as my factor."[35] He was a sportsman, poet, chess enthusiast, and
advocate of the Cornish language; as a Plymouth Brother turned Catholic who
wore a kilt and advised visitors to speak Gaelic, he was a perfect fit for Crowley's Highland home.

Louis Charles Richard Jewell (1866–1947) was born on September 10,
1866, the eldest son of Richard and Mary Jewell of 112 Barras Street, Liskeard,
Cornwall. His father was a bank manager, but later become an accountant and
moved his family first to 25 Granville Road, London, then to Beech Villa on
Barrow Road, Streatham, just a few blocks from the Crowley and Bishop families.[36] As Duncombe-Jewell recalled, "I have known Edward Alexander Crowley—which is his correct name, though he has gone under many aliases—since
he was a boy of 14: his mother and uncle having been friends of my father and
mother."[37] The friendship was natural, since the Jewell family were Plymouth
Brethren; like Crowley, he was taught by private tutors.

Jewell tried his father's line of work but soon abandoned banking for writing, publishing in 1881 "a jejune railway novel."[38] In 1893 he began to write
on foreign politics and military subjects (being a lieutenant in the 3rd Volunteer
Battalion of the Royal Fusiliers), contributing successively to the *St. Jame's
Budget,* the *Sketch,* the *Globe, Black and White,* and the *Pall Mall Gazette.* In
November 1895 he assumed the surname Duncombe in accordance with his
grandmother's will, and married Mary Amy Slaughter (1870–1904).[39]

Around the time of his marriage he edited *The Royalist,* a journal dealing
with Irish and Welsh Jacobitism and Cornish identity. It was subsidized by
Celtic-Cornish scholar and activist Henry Jenner (1848–1934). Both the magazine and Jenner were part of a larger Legitimist movement that sought dynasty
change by restoring to the throne Don Carlos VII of Spain and Charles XI of
France, among others. Jenner and Duncombe-Jewell had a long acquaintance,
and both were actively involved in Legitimism.[40] Ironically, Duncombe-Jewell
was also Spanish correspondent to *The Times* (1898–1899), covering the Carlist
uprising at the same time he was participating in it. Crowley too was involved
around 1899; for instance, his poem *Carmen Sæculare* contains the Carlist verse:

> O piteous fallen tyranny of Spain!
> What dogs are tearing at thy bowels yet?

> Let thine own King, saith God, resume his reign!
> Loyal and happy seasons may forget
> The ancient scars. Thy moon is on the wane?
> Thy sun may never set!

As Crowley elaborated in his *Confessions:*

> My cousin Gregor had made me a romantic Jacobite.... I actually joined a conspiracy on behalf of Don Carlos, obtained a commission to work a machine gun, took pains to make myself a first-class rifle shot and studied drill, tactics and strategy. However, when the time came for the invasion of Spain, Don Carlos got cold feet. The conspiracy was disclosed; and Lord Ashburnham's yacht, which was running the arms, fell into the hands of the Spanish navy.[41]

Here Crowley refers to the June 17, 1899, seizure by the Spanish government of Lord Ashburnham's British yacht *Firefly* off the coast of Arcachon in the Bay of Biscay. Its crew of fifteen—including its commander, Thames Valley Legitimist Club Vice-Chairman and Royal Navy Lieutenant Vincent English—were arrested, and its cargo of 3,664 Chassepot rifles confiscated.[42] According to Lowenna, not only were Jenner and Duncombe-Jewell involved in this foiled plot, but Crowley himself appears on the *Firefly* crew pay list for August 26, 1899, as "C. Alexander."[43] Although Crowley's involvement in these activities appears, like many of his romantic fancies, to be short-lived, he did receive a knighthood from one of Don Carlos's lieutenants.[44]

This, however, would not be Crowley's only contact with Legitimism. Mathers was also a Jacobite, and was translating magical texts at the British Library during the time that Jenner was Keeper of Manuscripts. Indeed, Lowenna contends that it was Mathers's preoccupation with Legitimist politics in France that took his focus away from the GD and ultimately led to the London temple uprising.[45] Lowenna reports that Crowley's friend, writer Herbert Vivian, was also connected to Lord Ashburnham.

After the *Firefly* debacle, Duncombe-Jewell served as *Morning Post* war correspondent with the 3rd South African Field Company from 1899 to 1900, receiving the queen's South Africa medal.[46] However, love of his birthplace, Cornwall, dictated the majority of his activities at this time. As early as April 1901 he appears in *Celtia* magazine as a contributor to the Pan-Celtic Congress;[47] by the August issue, he announced, "I shall attempt to found a Cornish Language Society a part of whose programme will be the revival of the Miracle Plays in the language."[48] He founded the Celtic-Cornish Society (or Cowethas Kelto-Kernuak) on August 15, 1901, with Henry Jenner as one of its vice presidents and himself as honorary secretary.[49] At the Pan-Celtic Congress that month, he proposed the recognition of Cornwall as a Celtic nation,[50] and in October published the first sonnet in Cornish.[51]

Alas, misfortune soon surrounded Duncombe-Jewell. His "disastrous personal financial situation led to his dismissal in the summer of 1902" from a projected *Victoria History of Cornwall*.[52] That November, a clearly preoccupied

Duncombe-Jewell visited W. B. Yeats and asked Annie Horniman to read his tarot cards concerning "a certain matter which he could not describe in any way." Mollified by the divination, he privately confided to Yeats,

> I came back from Ireland on Wednesday. I have not slept since then, with the exception of a few hours today. I have been in great trouble. My conscience has been going here and there like a weather cock. I could not find out what I had to do—I wanted to do right. She has held my conscience still. I know now where it is pointing. But there may be no miracle play now. This may be social extinction for me.[53]

Ludovic Cameron, a.k.a. Louis Charles Richard Duncombe-Jewell (1866–1947).

A few months later, on April 28, 1903, his son Anthony Michael Duncombe-Jewell was born at 11 St. James Terrace, Plymouth;[54] however, this child was not with him at Boleskine, nor is he mentioned in Duncombe-Jewell's biographies.[55] A year and a day later, on April 29, 1904, his wife Mary, aged thirty-four, died of shock from on operation for double salpingitis (inflammation of both fallopian tubes); her sister Frances H. Slaughter was present at the time of death.[56] It is unclear whether Duncombe-Jewell was present at either of these events; he is not the informant for the certified record of either the birth or the death. At this time, he changed his name by deed poll to Ludovic Cameron; Lowenna suggests this may have been a tactic to dodge creditors.[57] Whether the subject of his divination was financial, paternal, matrimonial, or other, his old friend's house Boleskine provided the perfect opportunity for Ludovic Cameron to lay low.[58]

In June, Crowley moved his bed into the temple, and five days later began practicing meditation for the Abramelin working. His introspection lasted nearly a month until, during a July 13 trip to Edinburgh to restock on wine, he hired a "red-haired Arabella" as his mistress and housekeeper. Endowed with wine and woman, Crowley moved on to song, writing "The God Eater."

Shortly after returning, he received a letter from Gerald Kelly. His mother was undergoing a medical cure in nearby Strathpeffer, and Gerald invited Crowley to join him there. Bored with the placidness of his Scottish estate, and with Arabella still packing in Edinburgh, he made the trip twenty miles north of Foyers and met the Kelly entourage: Gerald's mother was a typical Victorian lady who "worthily preserved the conditions of Tennysonian dignity."[59] His sister Rose Edith Skerrett (1874–1932), who accompanied Mrs. Kelly on the trip, was beautiful but uneducated, charming yet nervous. Rose's fiancé, a solicitor named Hill, was also present.

On August 11, while Gerald and Hill played golf, Crowley found himself and Rose walking along, watching and talking. "Your brother is a daring young man," he told Rose. "Playing golf is not the sort of thing one brags of to friends in London."

Rose laughed politely and smiled gracefully. Crowley was unsure what else to say to her: Her education was social and domestic in focus, leaving her ignorant of art and literature. Fearing Gerald's friend would continue looking at her dumbly, she said the first thing that came to mind: "'Bright Star, would I were steadfast as thou art.'"[60]

He smiled. "You like Keats?"

"Yes," she answered, eyes glittering, then averted her gaze. "Well, truth to tell, it's the only line I know. I keep a book of poems in my dressing case so I can impress Gerald's college chums by asking them to fetch it for me. I've never even read the book."

"I must applaud your brilliant device. It certainly served to find a suitor in Mr. Hill."

"Yes," she muttered with downcast eyes which suddenly rose to meet his gaze. "Can I confide in you?"

"'In quietness and confidence shall be your strength.'"[61]

She regarded him blankly. "Excuse me?"

"Mademoiselle," he clarified, "nothing would please me more."

Rose nodded in understanding, and explained her predicament. At age twenty-one—on August 31, 1897—she had married a man more than twenty years her senior, Major Frederick Thomas Skerrett (c. 1859–1899) of the Royal Army Medical Service.[62] He had received his medical license in 1879 through the King and Queens College of Physicians in Ireland, and became a fellow of the Royal College of Surgeons in Ireland in 1880.[63] Rose lived with him in South Africa until he died two years later, then returned home and enjoyed numerous lovers, two of whom even proposed. Not having the heart to turn either of them down, Rose accepted both offers. Suitor number 1, Hill, returned to South Africa to earn some money for their future, while Suitor number 2, Howell, a Cambridge chum of Gerald's, returned to America to ask permission of his father. Unfortunately, she did not love either man. No, she was in love with a married man named Frank Summers, who wanted to put Rose up in her own flat. As if this scandal wasn't enough, Rose convinced her parents to give her £40 for an abortion when in fact she merely wanted dinner and some new clothes. This pushed them to the limit, and when Hill and Howell both cabled that they were coming to marry her, her parents insisted she wed one of them. Her predicament was that her parents were pressuring her into a loveless marriage, while her true love, Summers, was already taken.

The tale brought out Crowley's "Shelleyan indignation," and he felt it incumbent upon himself to intervene. They sat down under a tree to ponder the circumstances. After contemplation, Crowley broke the silence by suggesting that she marry him. Afterward, he would return to his poetry, mountains and magick, and she would be free to do as she pleased.

Rose pondered the idea and did the thing that got her into trouble in the first place: she said yes. Counting her first husband, it was the fourth time Rose had accepted a proposal of marriage. For Crowley, it was the third time he had become engaged. Rose, despite AC's reservations, told her brother the news once he rejoined them from his game. Gerald laughed heartily, dismissed the announcement as a prank, and finished the course two under par. The future groom looked at his bride-to-be and shrugged. "And I was afraid the news would put him off his game."

Crowley went into town that day to arrange his hasty marriage to Rose Kelly. Although the parish sexton insisted that licensing took three weeks— one if rushed—he learned the sheriff could marry them on the spot.

The dawn was still dim when Crowley greeted Rose the next morning with a quote from *Macbeth*: "Wake Duncan with thy knocking! I would thou couldst!"[64] They sneaked off furtively so as not to wake Gerald, and caught the next train to Dingwall. Since she knew no literature, and Crowley couldn't guess what might interest her, they passed the ride in silence. "I don't have to live with her," he assured himself. "All I have to do is emancipate her. There's no reason to talk to her."

Dingwall was cold, damp, and asleep. So was the sheriff, whose maid said he would be unavailable until 8 o'clock … or 9, or 10. This was unacceptable, so they found a lawyer who said he could see them at eight. The couple nervously passed the time at breakfast, then meeting the lawyer, simply expressed their intention to marry and declared themselves husband and wife. On August

12, 1903, Alexander Ross declared Aleister Crowley MacGregor, landed proprietor and bachelor, and Rose Skerrett, widow, married. Aside from registering the marriage with the sheriff, that was all the law required.

Rose Edith Kelly (1874–1932).

Crowley, seeking to interject drama into the otherwise prosaic proceedings, pulled out his dirk and kissed it with a pledge of faith. The kiss was more than the bride herself received, for Gerald burst into the room at that moment, hell bent on stopping the marriage. When he learned he was too late, he threw a punch at Crowley. It missed completely, leaving Crowley smirking at his feeble gesture. When tempers cooled, they agreed it would be best if Crowley returned to Boleskine while Gerald took his sister home. Aleister was happy to comply: it was what he intended all along.

A furor erupted over the elopement. Rejected Mr. Hill insisted the marriage be annulled. Duncombe-Jewell assured the Kellys that their daughter's marriage was in fact legal. Meanwhile, Rose, "the game little bitch she was,"[65] stood by her decision. After the initial shock wore off, Crowley fetched Rose and registered their marriage with Dingwall's sheriff. Then, to silence local scandal, they took a train to the west coast of Scotland under the pretense of a honeymoon.

Giddy at having pulled this off, Crowley considered his work done, but felt uncomfortable—even embarrassed—continuing the charade. He sat opposite Rose in the empty car and, at an uncharacteristic loss of words, made small talk and jokes until their arrival early that evening. Sheepish about registering as a married man, he made up some excuse and sent Rose to the desk clerk. He was both disappointed and relieved that she booked a room with two beds.

They drank a lot of champagne over dinner that night. When Rose finished and retired to bed, Crowley went to the smoking room and drank a lot more. He was nervous about returning to the room with his "wife." Finding a sympathetic stranger, Crowley babbled about his troubles until he scared the man off. Then, remembering he was, after all, a romantic young poet on his honeymoon, he grabbed a scrap of paper and dashed off a rondel to his bride:

> Rose on the breast of the world of spring,
>   I press my breast against thy bloom;
> My subtle life drawn out to thee: to thee
>   its moods and meanings cling.[66]

Having discovered his poetic voice, Crowley found empathy with Rose. He finished the composition, went upstairs and pondered the possibility that Rose was in love with him. He also wondered if he was in love with her.

By the time the couple returned to Boleskine, Crowley's detached willingness to "propitiate physiology" on their honeymoon transformed into loving sentiments of "uninterrupted beatitude." They were in love with each other.

Gerald's initial fury about the wedding was slow to fade. Laird Boleskine was an entertaining and desirable friend while he was jaunting around the world writing sensual poetry and sending chummy letters detailing his latest conquests. But as a brother-in-law, he was a womanizing degenerate. These harsh sentiments gradually mellowed, and the friends again exchanged amusing letters. By the end of the summer, the Crowleys traveled to Paris to visit brother Gerald.

Crowley took Rose walking on the streets of Paris, showing her his old haunts and trying to impress her with stories of the local celebrities he had befriended during his last stay. While walking over the Pont Alexandre III, they encountered an even older luminary: Moïna Mathers. He chatted animatedly with Soror VNR, whom Rose assumed was a model. Only when later years left him with bitter and disillusioned memories of Mathers would he viciously claim he encountered her at a time when Mathers was pimping her on the streets of Paris. For now, they were simply fond friends.

In fall of 1903 he published *Ahab* as a companion volume to *Jezebel*. This edition consisted of twelve copies on vellum and 150 on handmade paper. Because it was set in Caxton type, the book was difficult to read and garnered little comment at all from the press. In November, Crowley dashed off a hasty note to Blackett, his agent at Kegan Paul: "Called suddenly away to distant lands,"[67] he wrote. He was going on his honeymoon.

Rose of the World deserved a better honeymoon than the obscure inn of some small Scottish town. Man of the world that he was, Crowley planned a cosmopolitan getaway, taking them to Bertolini's at Naples, on to Cairo for a short visit, to Ceylon to meet Allan Bennett, then to China.

In Cairo, as elsewhere, Crowley went to great trouble to impress his beloved, whom he now embraced with characteristic passion. A night in the King's Chamber of the Great Pyramid of Giza struck him as romantic, so he arranged it. They marched to the pyramid and had dinner; then Crowley dismissed the servants and took the dinner candles with them down into the chamber. Surrounded by mysteries as old as civilization itself, Crowley demonstrated for Rose his magical skills: He took out the *Goetia* and, crouched over the dim candlelight, straining to make out the words, he recited:

> Thee, I invoke, the bornless one.
> Thee, that didst create the Earth and the Heavens:
> Thee, that didst create the Night and the day.
> Thee, that didst create the darkness and the Light.

As he became enraptured in the reading, he stood upright and recited with feverish drama. Pausing only to catch his breath, he noticed something odd: He no longer crouched over the candle, straining to read. The chamber glowed with astral light, and he could now read without difficulty.

While the results encouraged him, he reminded himself he was now a married man. Extinguishing the candle, he blackened the room again and sought his bride in the darkness.

Crowley next wrote for this wife the poem "Rosa Mundi," which he would publish in 1905. To accompany it, Kelly offered Crowley an illustration dubbed "The Blood Lotus" after the poem of the same title in *White Stains* (later reprinted in *Oracles*). Fearing his reputation might suffer by association with Crowley, Kelly later reconsidered and asked him not to use it.[68]

In December, as the newlyweds headed toward Ceylon, Rose announced she thought she was pregnant. Overjoyed, Crowley canceled their visit and prepared to return to Europe, where she would receive proper care. However, since they had come this far, Crowley suggested, "Let's go and kill something for a month or two, and if you're right, we'll get back to nurses and doctors." So they headed south of Ceylon to Galle so he could show Rose what a great big game hunter her husband was. Pitching camp in a lakeside bungalow, Crowley kept busy stalking leopards, cheetahs, elephants, buffalo, and wild boars. Then, studying the low trees that grew along the shore, their branches jutting over the water, Crowley noticed new game. The bats that covered these branches while sleeping had red fur and white breasts. They looked like small foxes, and would make a fine toque for Rose and waistcoat for himself.

They took a boat onto the lake and floated silently under the sleeping bats. Crowley readied his gun, took aim, and fired. The gunshot echoed through the forests as the sky turned black with startled bats. He shot hastily at the escaping mammals until a scream pierced his ears. Rose! he thought, and spun around to find a wounded bat caught in her hair, thrashing about as wildly as she.

Even after AC managed to extract the bat from her hair and determined his wife was unharmed, Rose had difficulty calming down. He took her back to dry land, drew the mosquito netting around their bed, and climbed in beside her, soothing her and convincing her to rest until he too drifted off. In sleep, he heard the sound of a squealing bat. It persisted until, half conscious, he realized it was no dream. "Rose?" he whispered, prepared to ask, "Do you hear that?" He called her once, twice; but no reply came. He lit a candle and in its flickering light found Rose clinging naked to the mosquito netting frame, squealing wildly like a bat. She failed to respond to his voice, and resisted his efforts to help her down. When at last he got her back onto the bed, she scratched, spat, and bit at him like the creature that had taken a bullet.

In the morning, Rose was fine again. Crowley was unsure whether to attribute the spectacle to pregnancy or, as he later described it, "the finest case of obsession that I ever had the good fortune to observe."[69]

Leaving the wilderness, they stopped in Kandy, where Crowley wrote *Why Jesus Wept*. On January 28, 1904, they left for Suez, reaching Port Said by February 8. They continued back toward Cairo the next day, where they opted to rest. Crowley registered them into a hotel as "Prince Chioa Khan, and his Princess, Ouarda." The names were Arabic for Master Beast and Rose.

Because Scotland got so cold and damp in the winter, they decided to remain in Cairo until spring. So, on March 14, Prince Chioa Khan and Ouarda took a flat in a corner house near Cairo's museum in the fashionable European quarter. Two days later, in another demonstration of magical prowess, Crowley attempted to show Rose the sylphs, elemental spirits of the air. Entering the north room of the flat, which he had converted into his temple, he began to conjure the mystical creatures for his wife.

Crowley didn't notice Rose's vacant stare until she began to mutter, "They are waiting for you." At first, he paid no attention. When it happened again the next day during a repeat of his conjuration, he grew annoyed. "They are waiting for you," she hazily insisted. "It is all about the child; all Osiris." Crowley attributed it to morning sickness or alcohol, and proceeded to invoke. Finally, on the third day in a row when Crowley performed the conjuration, Rose's eyes glazed over, and she muttered, "He who waits is Horus," Crowley raised an eyebrow. Rose didn't read mythology, let alone study it. How did she come up with that name? Was she actually in contact with the god? Her comment piqued his interest, and he seized the opportunity to cross-examine her.

"How do you know Horus is telling you all this?" he asked her. "Can you identify him?" She said she could, and he proceeded to test her about the god: his appearance and corresponding color, weapon, planet, and numbers; his moral qualities; his enemy. To Crowley's astonishment, she answered every question correctly. The odds of her doing this by chance was infinitesimal.

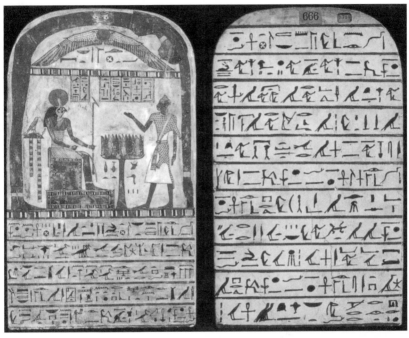

The twenty-sixth dynasty funerary stele of Theban priest Ankh-f-n-Khonsu, referred to in *The Book of the Law* as the Stele of Revealing.

As a final test, Crowley took Rose to the museum and asked her to point to the image of Horus. As she walked among the many steles and statues, passing various images of Horus along the way, Crowley smiled knowingly. Rose headed upstairs and pointed to a glass case across the room. "There he is."

Crowley squinted at the case, unable to make it out from this distance, and walked toward it. He found a wooden funerary stele from Egypt's twenty-sixth dynasty (c. 725 BC) that the Theban priest Ankhefenkhons I (or Ankh-f-n-Khonsu, in Crowley's era), had designed for himself. It depicted Ra-Hoor-Khuit or Ra-Herakhty, the composite deity of the sun god, Ra, with his son, Horus. Glancing at the exhibit, Crowley's heart leapt as he noticed it bore catalog number 666.

Having passed her test, Rose advised Crowley how to properly invoke Horus. He protested about form and style, but she insisted he perform the ritual as given. If he followed instructions, she promised, he would have results on Saturday or Sunday. Since the next day was Saturday, he followed the absurd directions and met with no success.

On Sunday, March 20, at 10 p.m., he again conducted the ceremony. This time, he learned this was the time of the Equinox of the Gods. While the GD celebrated the astronomical equinox that marked the first day of spring or autumn, in this case it referred to the beginning of the first day of a new age. According to this view, religious thought followed regular patterns: the world's oldest religions worshiped nature and the earth mother and are identified (arbitrarily) with the Egyptian mother-goddess Isis. In more recent history, religions were patriarchal and ultimately cast with suffering or dying figureheads such as Jesus, Adonis, and Attis; thus this phase of history was identified with the Egyptian slain and resurrected patriarch Osiris. The viewpoint that would become dominant in the next phase of humankind was typified by Horus, the son of Isis and Osiris. Adherence to this view of cosmic cycles betrays Crowley's Brethren upbringing, for dispensationalism, the belief that history proceeds in a series of stages or dispensations, is a common fundamentalist doctrine.[70]

Crowley also learned that the speaker of these messages was not Horus himself but a messenger named Aiwass or Aiwaz. Crowley regarded the name with suspicion, thinking Rose manufactured it from the Arabic word "aiwa" (yes) which she had heard in Cairo. Years would pass before Crowley accepted Aiwass as the actual name of his holy guardian angel. Even in his last years, however, Crowley remained uncertain about the nature of Aiwass:

> The only point undetermined is whether He is a discarnate Being, or ... a human being, presumably Assyrian, of that name. And that I simply do not know, and cannot reasonably surmise, because I do not know the limits of the powers of such an One.[71]

For the next two weeks, Crowley busied himself with stele 666. He dined with the museum's curator and expressed an interest in the artifact. Named by Crowley as Brugsch Bey, this curator was actually German Egyptologist Émile Brugsch (1842–1930); "Bey" along with "Pasha" were titles awarded him by the Egyptian government for his service to the Cairo and Boulak Museums.[72]

Brugsch arranged for his French assistant to translate and reproduce the stele. The inscriptions, it turned out, were adaptations from the Egyptian *Book of the Dead.* Once Crowley received the French translation, he set it to verse.

On April 7, Rose went into a trance and gave new instructions to her husband: for the next three days, he was to enter the temple in their flat precisely at noon and write down what he heard. He would stop again precisely at 1 o'clock. By this time, he believed Rose's instructions and followed them.

The next day, Crowley stepped into his temple at noon and sat at his desk, pen and paper ready. He waited for something to happen. Anticipation clenched him. *What if nothing happened?* he wondered. Then he reconsidered: *What if something did?*

Then it did: from behind his left shoulder, a voice spoke to him: "Had! The manifestation of Nuit. The unveiling of the company of heaven." Crowley described the experience in these words:

> The Voice of Aiwass came apparently from over my left shoulder, from the furthest corner of the room. It seemed to echo itself in my physical heart in a very strange manner, hard to describe.... The voice was of deep timbre, musical and expressive, its tones solemn, voluptuous, tender, fierce or aught else as suited the moods of the message. Not bass—perhaps a rich tenor or baritone.
>
> The English was free of either native or foreign accent, perfectly pure of local or caste mannerisms, thus startling and even uncanny at first hearing.
>
> I had a strong impression that the speaker was actually in the corner where he seemed to be, in a body of "fine matter," transparent as a veil of gauze, or a cloud of incense-smoke. He seemed to be a tall, dark man in his thirties, well-knit, active and strong, with the face of a savage king, and eyes veiled lest their gaze should destroy what they saw. The dress was not Arab; it suggested Assyria or Persia, but very vaguely.[73]

He scribbled down the words frantically as Aiwass proceeded. "Every man and every woman is a star. Every number is infinite; there is no difference. Help me, o warrior lord of Thebes, in my unveiling before the Children of men!"[74]

Aiwass described the Egyptian sky goddess Nuit, who represented the universe, infinite and complete. Although all things were part of her, she willingly separated into distinct elements, identities, and objects so that all the universe could experience the joy of union. Her message was clear enough: "For I am divided for love's sake, for the chance of union[75] ... Take your fill and will of love as ye will, when, where, and with whom ye will! But always unto me[76] ... Love is the law, love under will."[77] She called not for gratuitous sex, but for love as a transcendent experience, as the divine union of male and female principles. In exchange for this adoration, "I give unimaginable joys on earth."[78]

The point of this disquisition became clear with the words, "This that thou writest is the threefold book of Law."[79] Its verses contained the basic tenets of Thelemic philosophy: "The word of the law is $\Theta\epsilon\lambda\eta\mu a$.[80] ... Do what thou wilt shall be the whole of the Law ... thou hast no right but to do thy will. Do that and no other shall say nay. For pure will, unassuaged of purpose, delivered from the lust of result, is every way perfect."[81] The crux of this philosophy was the notion of True Will, expressed by the Greek word for "will," $\Theta\epsilon\lambda\eta\mu a$ or *thelema*. As part of the cosmic scheme, every being was imbued with a purpose to which it must devote itself. One's Will should be pursued to the exclusion of all else, barring activities—such as resting, eating, and working—that make the pursuit possible. In this view, if everyone were to do one's Will, there would be no conflict in the world. Magic was the means of discovering one's Will.

The phrase "Do what thou wilt shall be the whole of the Law"[82] was not entirely original with this book. St. Augustine himself had declared, "Love and do what you will."[83] An angel told John Dee, "Do that which most pleaseth you ... wherefore do even as you list." Satirist Francois Rabelais (c. 1494–1553) wrote *"Faictz ce que vouldras,"*[84] and described an *Abbaye de Thélème*. And Sir Walter Besant (1836–1901) and James Rice's (1843–1882) novel *The Monks of Thelema* describes a church similar to Rabelais's Abbey.[85] However, *The Book of the Law* was original in its interpretation of those eleven words.[86]

After an hour elapsed, the voice vanished with the statement, "The Manifestation of Nuit is at an end."[87]

Over the next two days, Crowley recorded two more chapters of what would become *The Book of the Law,* the cornerstone of his magical philosophy of Thelema. His life would never again be the same.

Chapter two is a small drama, a clash between the author and the scribe. Whereas Nuit represented infinity, the "speaker" of chapter two, Hadit, represented the finite point, or Nuit made manifest. When he announced, "Remember all ye that existence is pure joy,"[88] Crowley objected. The First Noble Truth of Buddhism taught that existence was sorrow. Aiwass responded, "O prophet! thou hast ill will to learn this writing. I see thee hate the hand & the pen, but I am stronger."[89] As the dictation continued, Crowley surrendered to the rapture of the words. After dictating magical ciphers and formulae, Aiwass observed, "Thou art exhaust in the voluptuous fullness of the inspiration."[90] Indeed, the experience swept him away in ecstasy and exhausted him.

Notions of existence being enjoyable appeared long before *The Book of the Law*. Tantra, for instance, imbued itself with similar life-positive viewpoints. However, such philosophies were generally driven underground by those who preferred to think of mankind dangling over the abyss of hell like a loathsome spider. Thus civilization had been shaped by asceticism, austerity, abstinence, sorrow, suffering, and sin. *The Book of the Law* marked a break with that perspective, proclaiming "The word of Sin is Restriction."[91] Original or not, such was the message Crowley received on that second day.

The final chapter was a disturbing and apocalyptic speech by the war god Ra-Hoor-Khuit. Amidst practical instructions and identification of Crowley as the Great Beast also fall its most repugnant statements: "With my Hawk's head I peck at the eyes of Jesus as he hangs upon the cross. I flap my wings in the face of Mohammed & blind him. With my claws I tear out the flesh of the Indian and the Buddhist, Mongol and Din. Bahlasti! Ompehda! I spit on your crapulous creeds."[92] The scribe was shocked by these declarations, and this initial reaction prevented him for some time from accepting the book. Only later would he understand these passages to symbolize the abrogation of old creeds.

Three days, three hours, and *The Book of the Law* was recorded. The process was not without problems: When, writing page 6 of the manuscript, he heard the words "the unfragmentary non-atomic fact of my universality," he failed to understand: "Write this in whiter words, but go on," Aiwass instructed. So, after the fact, Crowley changed the words to "The omnipresence of my body."

Similarly, when writing verse sixty of chapter one, Crowley missed a sentence. Rose herself later added the words, "The Five Pointed Star with a Circle in the Middle, & the circle is Red." Rose also corrected chapter three, verse seventy-two, where Crowley misheard the phrase, "Force of Coph Nia."

Throughout the manuscript, Aiwass left space for Crowley to add his poetic translations of the stele. This he did, also adding missing punctuation and verse numbers. With that, *The Book of the Law* was completed.

Crowley always maintained that this book originated from outside his own intelligence. As he wrote to a student in 1936,

> *The Book of the Law* is not in any way my work.... It is not inspired. It was dictated, and the only duty of a scribe is to take down accurately what is said. In this particular case, the scribe disagreed heartily with a very great deal of the material. This frequently happens in business offices. But I should not recommend you listen to the financial opinion of a girl who is transcribing the letters of J.P. Morgan at eighteen dollars a week.[93]

Nevertheless, one may reasonably ask whether *The Book of the Law* represented a startling revelation, or whether Crowley had prefigured some of its contents in his own work. Certainly, the notion of Will as has been described previously had crept into Crowley's thinking, even appearing in his letters to Gerald Kelly. He had already identified himself with the Great Beast in *The Sword of Song*. Adumbrations of "Do what thou wilt" occur in numerous earlier sources. And the corrupted magical formula "abracadabra," as restored in *The Book of the Law,* turns up three years earlier in Crowley's 1901 diary, where he "Designed Abrahadabra for a pantacle."[94] Nevertheless, subsequent events would convince Crowley that *The Book of the Law* was dictated by a being possessed of knowledge far greater than his own. "It is the only known document which carries in itself proof that its author belongs to a totally different Order of Being; he sees things from a point beyond our conception."[95]

Crowley was dumbfounded about what to do with *The Book of the Law.* Receiving it, he was certain, meant he was a great magician, but he had no desire to progress. Although Aiwass gave specific instructions for him to follow—for example, he was to take the stele from the museum, obtain an island and fortify it with weapons, and translate the book into all languages—none of these did he find realistic. Instead of publishing an elaborate edition of the book with a comment, as Aiwass told him, he merely sent typescripts of the work with a "careless manifesto,"[96] announcing the dawn of a new era. Then he put aside the book with relief.

The Crowleys set sail for Europe in April. Onboard, Aleister found Theosophist Annie Besant (1847–1933), future head of the TS; although they discussed many mystical subjects, he never mentioned his remarkable experience in Cairo. By April 26, he and Rose were back in Paris, lunching with Arnold Bennett. Crowley, dressed in a jeweled waistcoat and the largest ring Bennett had ever seen, proceeded to explain how he had registered as Prince Chioa Khan in Egypt. When the topic turned to the supernatural, Bennett recounted the tale of Beardsley being seen in London after his death. Bennett's accent was strong, and Crowley, although he understood the story, did so with difficulty.

"That's nothing," Crowley quipped when Bennett finished. "I know a man who saw Oscar Wilde in the Pyrenees and spoke to him while the man was supposedly imprisoned in England."

"Really?" Bennett bit. "Who's that?"

After a pause, he answered in a low voice, "Me."[97]

In all, Bennett enjoyed discussing the supernatural and the nature of intelligence with Crowley. AC had just written the essay "Time," and Bennett offered to introduce him to his friend, science fiction author H. G. Wells (1866–1946), that evening at the Metropole for comments on his essay. Bennett, in his difficult voice, offered only one bit of advice about Wells: "He speaks English with an accent."[98]

Despite the letter of introduction, Crowley never appeared at the Metropole to meet H. G. Wells. The next day he returned to London and ultimately Boleskine. The estate on Loch Ness became a watering hole for Crowley's friends: Doctor Percival Bott came in to watch over the course of Rose's pregnancy. Gerald arrived for a stay, as did their mutual friend, the London surgeon Ivor Back. Finally, Crowley's Aunt Annie came to help keep house.

The Crowleys practiced at magic on their return home, Rose retaining her powers of seership. Crowley followed a recipe from *The Book of the Law* for incense and cakes made of honey, wine, olive oil, and menstrual blood. If set out, the book claimed, the cakes would attract beetles. Were he to name an enemy and kill a beetle, that enemy would die; similarly, were he to eat a beetle, he would become strong and lusty. Crowley tested the claim by leaving cakes out, and as promised beetles appeared. Crowley neither named enemies nor ate the insects, but he sent samples to London's Natural History Museum, whose entomologists, he claims, had never seen this particular type before.

When Mathers failed to reply to receipt of *The Book of the Law* and a letter declaring that the Secret Chiefs had appointed Perdurabo as visible head of the order, Crowley assumed trouble was brewing. When his hunting dogs mysteriously died and a servant assaulted Rose, he concluded it was magical attack by a jealous Mathers. So, using a talisman from Abramelin, Crowley evoked Beelzebub against him while Rose, "arse high in the air," described the demon's forty-nine servitors.[99] When word of Crowley's deprecations reached him, Mathers cried slander and contacted his solicitor. He demanded a formal apology, and expelled Crowley from the order.

CHAPTER SIX

The Five Peaks

Kegan Paul disappointed Crowley with slow sales and price reductions on his overstocked titles. Since 1902, only ten copies of *Tannhäuser* had sold, five of *Carmen Sæculare,* seven of *Soul of Osiris,* and two of *Jephthah. Appeal to the American Republic, The Mother's Tragedy, Tale of Archais,* and *Songs of the Spirit* had not sold at all. In May 1904, Crowley closed his account with the publisher[1] and called on Charles Watts of London to do his printing. To combat what he considered mismanagement of his stock of books, Crowley decided to distribute his works himself. He named his publishing house the Society for the Propagation of Religious Truth (SPRT), a parody of the Church of England's venerable Society for Promoting Christian Knowledge. Much speculation has surrounded Crowley's decision to move his book publishing activities from London to Foyers, with some erroneously suggesting he was avoiding criminal charges for strangling a woman. As he rebutted,

> My dealings with Kegan Paul had nothing at all to do with the strangling of any woman. The unsold copies of my books were taken over by the Society for the Propagation of Religious Truth, because Kegan Paul were making no efforts to sell them.... So please loosen the rope round the poor lady's neck.[2]

A glut of new releases appeared in privately published editions as he prepared the transition to SPRT.

Alice: An Adultery, commemorating his Pacific affair in one hundred copies on China paper, met with cold press reactions. *The Star and the Garter* appeared in a companion edition of fifty on handmade paper and two on Roman vellum; although Crowley thought the book contained "some of my best lyrics,"[3] reviewers deemed it unintelligible. *The God Eater* followed the camel hair wraps format of these previous titles; it was a short play (thirty-two pages) that Crowley would later call "singularly unsatisfactory."[4]

Business stopped at Boleskine on July 28 when Dr. Percival Bott[5] (1877–1953) delivered the Crowleys' healthy daughter, whom the proud father named Nuit Ma Ahathoor Hecate Sappho Jezebel Lilith. For days afterward, Crowley celebrated with Bott, Back, Kelly, Rose, Duncombe-Jewell, and Aunt Annie. Rose wanted something to read while recuperating, but found her husband's collection of literature, philosophy, and mysticism far too cerebral. She wanted a simple romance. Having none at his disposal, Crowley decided to write his own brand of romance novel for the entertainment of his convalescing wife and their house guests. Thus, house party activities daily involved a reading of the chapter Crowley had written that day for "The Nameless Novel."

> "Good, by Jesus!" cried the Countess, as, with her fat arse poised warily over the ascetic face of the Archbishop, she lolloped a great gob of greasy spend from the throat of her bulging cunt into the gaping mouth of the half-choked ecclesiastic.[6]

So begins the chronicle of a sexually demented archbishop, a novel purposely vulgar and shocking to parody what Crowley considered the only type of book Rose would enjoy. Throughout the writing of this piece, Crowley kept Farmer and Henley's *Slang and its Analogues* nearby. The results so entertained his guests that Kelly and Back helped assemble Crowley's early attempts at vulgar verse and puerile parody into a package titled *Snowdrops from a Curate's Garden*. It included such gems as "To pe or not to pe," "All the world's a brothel," "Bugger me gently, Bertie!" and "Girls together." Of course, there wasn't an English press that would touch it.

After the household cleared, the Crowleys adjusted to their roles as parents. AC put aside magic to be a husband and father. In a letter to her brother, Rose captured the mood of these times:

> All goes well here. The kid—Nuit Ma Ahathoor Hecate Sappho Jezebel Lilith—to be called by the last name—flourishes. She's a good little maid tho' she does squawk occasionally which drives Aleister out rabbit shooting. We've such a stock to consume in the house![7]

Despite the time that fatherhood took from his magic, Crowley the poet continued to thrive: *The Sword of Song, called by Christians The Book of the Beast,* dedicated to Allan Bennett, appeared to the astonishment of the press. Stephensen (1930) correctly called it a complex work, and it is the most important of his early books. The edition of one hundred copies, at ten shillings, was one of his most expensive books to date, but, at 194 pages, it was also among his longest. Its navy blue cover, printed in gold, bore mysterious emblems: a three-by-three set of squares depicting the number 666 thrice, and the author's name rendered in Hebrew such that its numerical value added up to this same number. Within is the autobiographical passage:

> Yet by-and-by I hope to weave
> A song of Anti-Christmas Eve
> And First- and Second-Beast-er Day.

> There's one who loves me dearly (vrai!)
> Who yet believes me sprung from Tophet,
> Either the Beast or the False Prophet;
> And by all sorts of monkey tricks
> Adds up my name to Six Six Six …
> Ho! I adopt the number. Look
> At the quaint wrapper of this book!
> I will deserve it if I can:
> It is the number of a Man.[8]

In this poem, the one who loves him dearly is his mother; Tophet is the abyss of hell, and the last line refers to Revelation 13:18: "Let him that hath understanding count the number of the beast; for it is the number of a man; and his number is 666." This poem is significant because it corrects the common assertion that Crowley identified himself with the Great Beast when he assumed the mantle of prophet of the New Aeon of Horus: this poem was written before *The Book of the Law*. Similarly, Crowley registered himself in Egypt as "Chioa Khan," Master Beast, before writing his Holy Book. Thus, his identification with the Great Beast 666 predated *The Book of the Law*, and most certainly originated with Crowley's mother, who so often referred to him as such. In this and various other ways, *The Sword of Song* documents Crowley's intellectual and philosophical developments that adumbrate *The Book of the Law*.

Aside from poetry, *The Sword of Song* also contained the essays "Berashith," "Science and Buddhism," and "Ambrosii Magi Hortus Rosarum," a work that would come back to haunt him in later years. The entire package is an odd and entertaining mix of mystic poetry and essays on Buddhist thought. Its notes and contents are snide, cynical, and often amusing. While the *Literary Guide* praised the book as "a masterpiece of learning and satire" and its author as "one of the most brilliant of contemporary writers,"[9] reviewers generally reacted with perplexity. Following up on his review of *Soul of Osiris,* G. K. Chesterton titled his reactions to AC's latest work "Mr. Crowley and the Creeds," calling him a good poet but expressing reservations about his Buddhist faith and obvious hatred of Christianity.[10] Crowley reacted defensively, and issued a pamphlet titled "A Child of Ephraim." It merely signaled the beginning of Crowley's crusade against Chesterton.

In October, Crowley traveled to the resort town of Saint Moritz, Switzerland, for a holiday of skating and skiing. En route, the bard stopped in Paris around the 28th to arrange with Philippe Renouard the publication of *Snowdrops from a Curate's Garden* for his friends. The edition of one hundred copies was bound in green wrappers, bearing the false imprint place of "Cosmopoli" (taken from the homosexual novel *Teleny,* attributed to Oscar Wilde and printed by Smithers). Equally false was the imprint date of 1881 (the publication year of the homosexual novel *Sins of the Cities of the Plain*).[11] Rose, wishing a vacation from mothering, left Lilith with her parents and their nurse, and joined Aleister in November. They stayed at the fashionable Kulm Hotel. The other guests were stunned and amused by AC's ermine-lapelled velvet coat, silk knee-breeches, and enormous meerschaum pipe. He likewise sneered at the bourgeois patrons. They soon learned that he was not only an accomplished mountaineer, scholar, and poet, but the finest skater there.

Another guest at the hotel was author Clifford Bax (1886-1962), then just eighteen years old. He had come with his two cousins to regain his health, and spent his spare time reading *A History of the Rosicrucians*.[12] The book prompted a discussion when he and Crowley met. "What do you know of the Great Science?" AC asked eagerly. "Or of Cornelius Agrippa? Perhaps you would find this helpful." He handed the young man a vellum book. Looking it over, he discovered it was by Crowley. "It is a treatise on ceremonial magic."

"Thank you," Bax replied, looking around to see if anyone was watching.

Crowley dismissed his concern. "What do you think the morons in this hotel would make of your interest in the Rosicrucians?"

Before he knew what was going on, Bax found Crowley offering to instruct him in magic. "Most good of you," Bax replied sheepishly, "but … maybe I'm not ready. I think I should read some more."

"Nonsense! Reading is for children; men must do. Experiment! Seize the gift the gods offer. If you reject me, you will be indistinguishable from the idiots around us. If you accept my offer, you can help me found a new world religion." Suddenly, he shifted gears and asked, "What is the date?"

"January 25." Bloody Sunday, the massacre at St. Petersburg, had just occurred three days before.

"And the year, according to the Christian calendar?"

"1905."

Crowley nodded. "Exactly. And in a hundred years, the world will be sitting in the dawn of a New Aeon."[13]

When the frost yielded, the Crowleys returned to the British Isles. AC journeyed to London to tend to publishing business. Returning to Strathpeffer to fetch his wife, who was staying with her parents, he found Rose ill. She was also evasive about discussing her condition. Crowley pressed, and Rose finally explained: since Lilith was born, her periods had been irregular and she feared she was again pregnant. Her parents' nurse, to whom she confided, gave her ergot to induce an abortion. When the prescription failed, a double dose followed. Then she became ill.

Crowley's head swam with powerful emotions. He was furious that Rose should attempt to snuff a life and jeopardize her health through abortion. He was also suspicious of just what substance the nurse had been giving his wife to make her so ill. Bundling Rose and Lilith, he took his family to the Imperial Hotel and wired Bott and Back, the only physicians he trusted, to meet him at London's Savoy Hotel. Then he wired Gerald to get Roses's medicine under the pretense of sending it to her in London, and have a chemist analyze it. Then the Crowleys began a return trip to London. Bott and Back heard the case and, in the end, agreed on the diagnosis: Rose was not pregnant, but she was suffering from the worst case of ergot poisoning they had ever seen.

Having heard enough, he returned to Boleskine. Here he wrote "Rosa Inferni," a sequel to "Rosa Mundi," thus continuing what would become a cycle of four poems chronicling the phases of his relationship with Rose. He also wrapped up work on the manuscripts of *Orpheus* and *Gargoyles*.

Crowley's works appeared under the SPRT imprint faster than they'd come out before, with ten new works and various reissues appearing at this time.

The first of these was *The Argonauts* (1904), influenced by Crowley's exposure to Hinduism. Reviewers generally liked the writing in this five-act verse play, but considered it uneven. This comment underscores the disadvantage to Crowley's method of publication: unable to criticize his own works, he published books as he wrote them without an editor to identify their weaknesses. Furthermore, the limited print runs—generally one hundred to two hundred copies—left little opportunity for his name to become known.

The Book of the Goetia of Solomon the King (1904) was Mathers's translation of the *Key of Solomon*, which Crowley had acquired during his raid of the GD's Second Order headquarters in April 1900. Although Crowley was responsible for emendations, introduction, and notes, Mathers is credited only on the title page as "A Dead Hand."

One hundred copies of his next work, *Why Jesus Wept: A Study of Society* (1904), sold to subscribers at two guineas through a tacky advertisement:

WHY JESUS WEPT

by

Aleister Crowley
Who has now ceased to weep

With the original Dedication;
With the advertisement which has brought Peace and Joy to so many a sad heart!!
With the slip containing the solution of the difficulty on pages 75–76!!!
With the improper joke on page 38!!!!
With the beetle-crushing retort to Mr. G.K. Chesterton's aborted attack upon the Sword of Song!!!!!
With the specially contributed Appeal from the Poet's Mamma!!!!!!
Look slippy, boys! Christ may come at any moment. He won't like it if you haven't read the book about His melt.
...I say: Buy! Buy Now! Quick! Quick!
My Unborn Child screams "Buy!"

The poetic play, its title from John 11:35, is a religious satire explaining why Jesus wept. It reprints a letter from Crowley's mother, wherein she begs her strayed son to give up his evil ways. Crowley signed the dedication in Hebrew

such that the name "Aleister E. Crowley" added up to 666, as it did on the
cover of *The Sword of Song;* he dedicated the book to Jesus, Lady Scott (a portion of whose anatomy he compared to a piece of wet chamois), his Buddhist
friends, his unborn child, and, particularly, G. K. Chesterton, to whom Crowley wrote, "Alone among the puerile apologists of your detestable religion you
hold a reasonably mystic head above the tides of criticism." Inserted into the
book was an eight-page pamphlet reprinting Chesterton's "Mr. Crowley and
the Creeds," along with Crowley's rebuttals: "The Creed of Mr. Chesterton"
and "A Child of Ephraim." Chesterton appears in the book, along with "The
Marquis of Glenstrae" and a Horny-Handed Plymouth Brother.

   In Residence: The Don's Guide to Cambridge (1904), dedicated to Ivor Back,
reprinted Crowley's undergraduate verse; *The Granta,* Cambridge University's
undergraduate magazine, replied:

> Oh, Crowley, name for future fame!
>   (Do you pronounce it Croully?)
> Whate'er the worth of this your mirth
>   It reads a trifle foully.
> Cast before swine these pearls of thine,
>   O, great Aleister Crolley
>   "Granta" to-day, not strange to say,
> Repudiates them wholly.[14]

   Several of these books included the SPRT catalog and an entry form for a
contest: Crowley was offering £100 as grand prize for the best essay written on
his works. He designed the scheme to promote sales of his "Collected Works"
(see below) and the overstock of his previous works. The flier is every bit as
silly as that for *Why Jesus Wept:*

THE CHANCE OF THE YEAR!

THE CHANCE OF THE CENTURY!!

THE CHANCE OF THE GEOLOGIC PERIOD!!!

A CAREER FOR AN ESSAY[15]

By this time, SPRT's booklist numbered nineteen titles, with volume one of
the collected works offered at cost to any competitor, who was free to write
either a hostile or appreciative essay. His first editions were also for sale, priced
from twenty-one shillings *(Aceldama, Jezebel, Alice, Goetia,* and *Why Jesus Wept)*
to one shilling *(Appeal to the American Republic, The Star and the Garter).*

   The Works of Aleister Crowley, volume 1, covered his books from *Aceldama*
to *Tannhäuser* (omitting the anonymous publication *White Stains*), edited and
footnoted by Ivor Back. The uneven quality of his writing notwithstanding,
Crowley's accomplishment, at age twenty-nine, of a three-volume collection of
his published works remains remarkable.

   Five hundred copies of *Oracles: The Autobiography of an Art* (1905) were also
available, with the SPRT catalog bound in at the end. This book was a collec-

tion of poetic odds and ends, including his early work and selections from the unpublished *Green Alps*. The author described this book as "a hodgepodge of dejecta membra … [containing] beastlinesses too foul to cumber up my manuscript case any more."[16]

Crowley, ever searching for new ways to make his works rare and desirable, issued the two-volume *Orpheus: A Lyrical Legend* (1905) in five editions distinguished by the covers' elemental colors (either white, yellow, red, blue, or olive green). A one-volume edition was also available on India paper. Of this work, Crowley later wrote, "They had never satisfied me."[17]

Rosa Mundi: A Poem (1905), published by Philippe Renouard, featured the fifteen-page title piece and a lithograph of one of the sketches Rodin had given him. *Gargoyles: Being Strangely Wrought Images of Life and Death* (1906) marked what AC considered a new phase of his work. Finally, in addition to publishing new works, Crowley reissued some of his older books in inexpensive editions, including *The Star and the Garter, Songs of the Spirit,* and *Alice: An Adultery.*

Although the effort would not make Crowley famous, this publishing and publicity spree would soon mean more to Crowley than he ever dreamed.

Jacot-Guillarmod arrived at Boleskine on April 27 and presented the lord of the manor with a copy of his book about their climb on K2, *Six Mois dans l'Himalaya*.[18] Crowley recalled how Guillarmod spent his hours on the glacier keeping a journal—it was probably the only thing that kept him from snapping like the others—and gladly accepted the gift. He reciprocated with a copy of *Snowdrops from a Curate's Garden.*

During his visit, Guillarmod and Crowley discussed their respective adventures. When Guillarmod began to boast of his big game hunting, it piqued Crowley's interest. "Have you ever seen a haggis?" he asked.

"Haggis? What's that?" the Swiss asked.

Haggis was a Highland dish of minced sheep's heart, liver, and kidneys boiled with oatmeal in the animal's stomach. Drawing a dramatic breath, Crowley explained: "I am one of the only people who would dare answer that question. A haggis is a wild rogue ram." Guillarmod knew of Burma's wild buffaloes, and of elephants that were thrown out of their herds. Although he had never heard of a haggis, he equated it with these creatures. Crowley continued, "Just as rogue elephants are taboo, so is the haggis sacred in Scotland. They are rare, and, when found, must only be touched by the chief of the clan. They are also very dangerous."

Guillarmod nodded gravely, suitably impressed. It gave Crowley a wonderful idea.

Two days later, Crowley and Guillarmod rested in the billiard room after breakfast. Their idyll was interrupted when Crowley's servant, Hugh Gillies, burst breathlessly into the room, panic and urgency in his eyes. "My lord," he blurted out, "there is a haggis on the hill."

Guillarmod's gaze shot from Crowley to the servant and back again. AC, doing his best to keep a straight face, nodded in acknowledgment. "Good man," he muttered as he walked over to his gun case. "The best servant I've had." He grabbed his .577 Double Express and handed Guillarmod a 10–bore Paradox with steel-core bullets. "That gun," he told Guillarmod, "will bring down an elephant with a shot. You may need it. Now fall to. We haven't a moment to lose."

Crowley led Gillies, Guillarmod and Rose on a low-crouching, tiptoed course through icy rain that chilled them by the time they reached the artificial trout lake on his estate. Playing his part to the hilt, Crowley insisted, "We must wade through the lake to throw the haggis off our scent." So, with guns held high overhead, they marched through the neck-high water. Emerging on the other side, they climbed the hill on all fours. Stealthy and cautious, they finally reached the hilltop ninety minutes after leaving the house. Crowley looked over to the servant. "Where is it?"

Gillies pointed a trembling finger through the mist. "Th-there."

By this time, Guillarmod was so tightly wound that he advanced and fired at the beast in the mist. As the explosion of gunfire echoed through the hills, Crowley grabbed Guillarmod's arm to restrain him. "If you value your life, stay where you are." Lord Boleskine stepped into the gray haze. There, he found the ram he had purchased in town from Farmer McNab and tethered on the hill. Both bullets from the rifle had struck and expanded, completely blowing away the ram's rear section. Crowley arranged to have the ram cooked and served for dinner the next evening. Guillarmod, none the wiser, had the animal's head mounted on a plaque as a trophy.[19]

As great an adventure as the haggis was, Guillarmod did not come to Boleskine to hunt rogue rams. He had come to discuss mountains. *Six Mois dans l'Himalaya* chronicled their attempt on K2, and he again desired that type of experience. He suggested to Crowley that they climb Kangchenjunga, the third highest mountain in the world.

Located twelve miles south of the main Himalayan chain, it was only forty-five miles north of Darjeeling, eighty miles east of Mount Everest. Its name literally meant "Five Peaks" for its pentad of summits ranging in height from 25,925 to 28,169 feet. These pinnacles were buttressed by huge ridges with several lesser though nevertheless spectacular peaks of their own; running east-west and north-south, they formed a giant X around the range. At 28,169 feet, Kangchenjunga was less than one hundred feet smaller than K2.

Climbers considered it the most treacherous mountain in the world. Receiving more precipitation than virtually any other mountain, hundreds of feet of snow and ice plastered its face and slowly plowed down the mountain in the form of glaciers, and its millions of tons of debris could easily tumble down as an avalanche. Its history testified to its inhospitability: in January 1849— when mountaineering was still in its infancy—Antarctic explorer Sir Joseph

Dalton Hooker (1817-1911) attempted Kangchenjunga, but snow turned him back. Returning three months later, difficult conditions cut his climb short. Three years later, in 1852, an earthquake brought thousands of square yards of debris down the mountain, preempting Captain J. L. Sherwill's attempt.[20] W. W. Graham claimed to have circumnavigated the mountain in 1882 and to have climbed two of its lesser peaks in October 1883, but the account was controversial. Douglas Freshfield's 1899 tour around the base of Kangchenjunga was cut short when a storm dumped twenty-seven inches of rain on Darjeeling in twenty-eight hours. In 1905, Kangchenjunga remained unclimbed.[21]

The challenge appealed to Crowley. Disappointed by his abortive attempt on K2, he saw an opportunity to get it right. He insisted on leading the expedition, and he and Guillarmod both put five thousand francs into expenses. Crowley, realizing what little time they had if they wished to attempt the mountain that summer, devised a plan: Guillarmod would go to London and round up provisions while Crowley proceeded to Darjeeling to arrange transport, hire porters, and coordinate details with the local government.

When Crowley set off for London on May 6 to get his affairs in order, he was prepared to die. He left written instructions for his body to be embalmed, dressed in magical garb, and sealed in a vault on ground chosen and consecrated by his GD mentor, George Cecil Jones. In London, he sought Eckenstein, who considered the adventure foolhardy and declined to participate. Undaunted, Crowley gathered provisions and proceeded to Darjeeling. On May 12, Crowley sailed for India, where a month earlier a severe earthquake had killed over 19,000 people in its northern territory. He arrived in Bombay on June 9 and headed for Darjeeling the same day. From there he could have seen Kangchenjunga—and even the Himalayas—if not for the rain: it never stopped, and left everything damp and musty. Moving into the Drum Druid Hotel, he concluded he simply didn't like Darjeeling.

While in India, Crowley kept up on business by mail. His contest for the best essay on the works of Aleister Crowley had drawn a contestant in the form of J. F. C. Fuller (1876-1966), a young army captain stationed at Lucknow. He had ordered a copy of *Why Jesus Wept* based on a review in *The Literary Guide;* the book impressed him and, finding the contest entry form, he decided to try his luck. Since he had none of the poet's other works, Crowley sent along copies of everything. This included volume two of the *Works of Aleister Crowley,* which was still in press.

To prepare for the expedition, Crowley sent four tons of food to be taken as close as possible to the Yalung Glacier, where they would begin their ascent; this was conveyed by 130 porters provided by the Indian government. On the last day of July—having weathered a monsoon and mechanical difficulties— Jacot-Guillarmod arrived with two other Swiss climbers.[22] Crowley and a servant met them at the train station to help bring their bags to the hotel, where the manager had reserved for them his best rooms.

The team that Jacot-Guillarmod had assembled was solid. Charles Adolphe Reymond (1875–1914) of Fontaine, Val de Ruz, was a Swiss Army officer with Alpine experience, quiet and dour. He called himself a *Lebenskünstler,* or connoisseur of the art of living. His small pension afforded him a pleasant and simple lifestyle; for instance, he once spent an entire winter at Sainte-Croix, Switzerland, skiing and lazing in the sun. He was a natural and skilled climber, having worked with a guide primarily in the Valais and Mont Blanc chains. Until being enlisted for this climb, he worked as an editor at the Swiss telegraphic agency in Geneva.[23] Reymond quipped that the primary purpose of the expedition was to have a good time; beating the world altitude record was secondary.[24] AC liked him: he had good sense and seemed stable.

Charles Adolphe Reymond (1875–1914) of the Kangchenjunga expedition.

Crowley also liked Reymond's companion, Alexis Pache (c. 1874–1905) of Morges, Switzerland, whom he found to be an unaffected and unassuming gentleman. Aged thirty-one, he was the only son among the four children of Charles Louis Frederick Pache and Henriette Emma (née Cart); his sisters were Helene Marie Suzanne, Marguerite, and Marie.[25] Like Reymond, Pache was a Swiss army officer, having become a dragoon lieutenant in 1894.[26] Between 1899 and 1901, he spent twenty months in the Boer War at Natal, fighting the British on behalf of the Boer government. He returned home to some celebrity: A three-part interview concerning his observations on the war and the respect he found for his indefatigable and chivalrous opponents ran in the *Gazette de Lausanne,* and was picked up from the London *Times* to the New Zealand *Star.*[27] Although lacking in climbing experience, he was energetic and adventure-loving, joining the expedition mainly for the opportunity to hunt in the Himalayas.[28] Indeed, Jacot-Guillarmod noted how excited he got seeing monkeys and other animals from the train to Darjeeling.[29] Pache also brought along several glass specimen vials to collect indigenous ants for Professor Auguste-Henri Forel (1848–1931), a distinguished Swiss psychiatrist and neuroanatamist who retired to devote himself to myrmecology.[30]

AC also invited along Alcesti C. Rigo de Righi, the Italian manager of the Drum Druid Hotel on the Mall and proprietor of the Woodlands Hotel adjacent to the railway station.[31] The latter was Darjeeling's leading inn when American humorist Mark Twain (1835–1910) visited in 1896,[32] and Baroness Mary Victoria Curzon of Kedleston (1870–1906), after nine days' stay in 1900, raved about how "M. Righi took the greatest pains to see that everything was nice."[33] Climber Charles Granville Bruce (1866–1939) noted that de Righi was "always ready to assist any traveller to the upper ranges,"[34] while English illustrator Walter Crane (1845–1915), visiting in 1906, remarked, "He occasionally entertained his guests by a lecture in the evenings, illustrated by photographic slides taken on the expedition."[35] Although de Righi was a novice climber, he spoke Hindustani and Tibetan, which Crowley considered invaluable. Plus, "he spoke English like a native."[36] Thus, de Righi became the expedition's transport manager. Much like Guillarmod, de Righi also brought along his camera to document their historic climb. These five—Crowley, Guillarmod, Reymond, Pache, and de Righi—made up the party.

Drum Druid Hotel manager Alcesti C. Rigo de Righi.

It was raining so incessantly that Darjeeling's average annual rainfall of 120 inches was already reached in July, and the downpour continued throughout the party's nine days there. The rain was so persistent that they only caught fleeting glimpses of the famous view of Kangchenjunga.[37] On Tuesday, August 8, 1905, at 10:16 a.m., they marched in the pouring rain on their winding path through the countryside toward Kangchenjunga, with several thousand pounds of food, luggage, and camping equipment carried by an additional hundred porters. Even at this early stage, the expedition was plagued by problematic porters: because of the thin atmosphere at this altitude, it was a difficult haul. Several porters snuck off daily, taking with them days' worth of rations, requiring one of the team to be designated to bring up the rear. The explorers also resorted to tactics like offering a pack of cigarettes to the first ten porters to reach the next day's destination. To top it off, they discovered that the 130 porters they'd sent ahead had still not arrived; thus, de Righi went ahead to search for them. It was a sharp contrast to the dependable help they had on K2.[38]

At the last possible moment, word arrived that they had received official permission to cross into Nepal, which was normally prohibited to Europeans;[39] this allowed them to take the most direct route to the mountain, marching north from the Singalila Range to the Yalung Valley. On arrival, the 130 porters supplied by the government dropped their supplies at the foot of the glacier and left, refusing to go any further. To the Tibetans, mountains were strongholds of the gods, and these porters feared offending them. Between this and the other defectors, this left them with eighty porters.

On August 21, Crowley left Pache in charge of Camp 1 while he ventured up the glacier and set up Camp 2 at 14,000–15,000 feet, about two miles from Kangchenjunga's peak. Here, two pinnacles were visible, although clouds obscured the main peak, Kangchenjunga itself. The sight of their goal filled Crowley with excitement: He was in top shape, the weather was good, and the path looked easy. He was sure this ascent would make his adventure on K2 seem like a bad dream.

Guillarmod was not so optimistic. The sight of the glacier discouraged him: he had never seen one so tangled and torn, and the west ridge looked like it was constantly rained with avalanches. He declared this approach unclimbable, and objected to attempting it. That Crowley preferred this approach added more tension to what was shaping up to be a stressful expedition.

Crowley had good reason to choose this course: in 1899, Freshfield, based on his reconnaissance of the mountain, recommended the nearby ridge as a means of overcoming the steep glacier. In the view of the team that later surveyed the mountain in 1954, Guillarmod overreacted while Crowley formulated a reasonable, albeit optimistic, plan.[40]

By the next day, Crowley had already picked out the site for Camp 3 with his binoculars. Heading west up the steep slopes, he set up camp in the heart of

Kangchenjunga's basin. From here, he could survey the surrounding landscape. The route to the summit appeared to be clear.

Later that day, from Camp 3 he could also see as Guillarmod and his men came up the ridge and set up their own camp. AC harangued Guillarmod for his failure to follow orders, while Guillarmod claimed Crowley had marked the path poorly and left him no choice but to take control of his own men. Such miscommunications typified the expedition.

Guillarmod and Crowley clashed again over the march to Camp 4.[41] Crowley wished to start early to take advantage of the clear weather; so he rose at 3 a.m. and prepared his men by six. Guillarmod, however, insisted he wait until eleven so the men could warm in the sunlight. "That's absurd," Crowley retorted, and set forth. He found the route steep and slick, more difficult than he expected. In a series of short sprints, the team reached the flat ridge at the top of the slope, the site for Camp 4. Crowley thought the spot was a little narrow. Looking up the hill, the only other likely campsite was another three hours' climb. He noticed Reymond and Guillarmod were exhausted, and opted to set up camp where they were.

After putting a rope down the slope for the porters to retrieve supplies from below, he sent word to Pache: Camp 4 is established, move from Camp 2 to Camp 3. Crowley was surprised when Pache climbed up to Camp 4, reporting that de Righi was not sending up necessary supplies, and they were now low on petroleum and food. Owing to these conditions, some of the porters deserted; one of them, going off alone, had disappeared. Jacot-Guillarmod went down the next day to investigate, and discovered the missing man's badly mutilated corpse where he slipped and fell on the rocks 1,500 feet below. Examining the remaining porters, Guillarmod noticed some of them exhibiting altitude sickness and ophthalmia, their eyes bloodshot and painful.[42]

Leaving Guillarmod in charge of Camp 4, Crowley, Reymond and Pache advanced to Camp 5 at an elevation of 20,343 feet. Waiting for supplies that never arrived, a frustrated Crowley again observed how failure to follow orders stalled their progress. Finally, on August 31, the team pressed on. At this point, Crowley realized ascent would be more difficult than he initially estimated: the mountain was steep at this point, and sported many granite precipices.

With porters cutting steps out of the ice, they climbed quickly to a height of 21,000 feet. Crowley paused, watching small hunks of broken ice scuttle down the hillside as the workers hacked away. He noticed a few bits of snow also skimming along the surface. When a hiss like hot water coming to a boil reached his ears, he knew an avalanche was beginning. AC ordered the men to brace themselves on the steps, knowing they'd be safe there. They did as the sahib instructed. One porter, however, panicked and began untying his rope in order to sprint across the sliding snow. Crowley again instructed him to stay put. When he ignored the command, AC used the only swift and sure solution: He knocked the porter upside the head with the flat of his ax.[43]

Panic far outstripped the size of the avalanche, and the snowslide passed them without incident. Nevertheless, the party called it a day and returned to Camp 5. There, gossip among the porters changed the snowslide into a cataclysm and the blow to the porter's head into a violent assault. That night, several frightened men deserted, complaining to Guillarmod that Crowley was beating them. Crowley would later claim that the porters were exaggerating the incident during the avalanche. But Jacot-Guillarmod, despite the porters having been unruly and very difficult to keep in line, believed them.[44] Indeed, Reymond recorded in his diary that he and Pache had observed Crowley at Camp 5 beating old Penduck, alternately kicking him and hitting him with his alpenstock as the porter laid in the snow, howled, and pleaded with him to stop.[45] The doctor decided matters had gone far enough.

Photo of Kangchenjunga by Jacot-Guillarmod, showing the party's route up the mountain and the location of several of its camps. The camp numbers differ from Crowley's: VII is Crowley's Camp 5, and VI is Camp 4.

The next morning, as Crowley and his remaining company prepared another attempt on the slope, Guillarmod unexpectedly ascended to Camp 5 with de Righi and his party behind him. *What the hell are they doing here?* Crowley wondered, dumbfounded. He thought they had supplies but, learning they had none, AC once again pondered: *What the hell are they doing here?*

The answer was simple: mutiny.

Jacot-Guillarmod had had enough. The unfollowed orders, fleeing porters, and hazardous ascent convinced him to hold a meeting of the expedition's principals. The climbers voted to oust AC and make Jacot-Guillarmod leader. "You may be a good climber," the doctor told Crowley, "but you're a bad general."[46] The doctor even convinced de Righi, who ascended with him, into backing this plan. Although hurt, Crowley merely scoffed, "There is no provision for this stupidity in our contract."

"It is only a piece of paper," Jacot-Guillarmod replied coolly; it was his right as initiator of the expedition.[47] Assuming command at 5 p.m. on September 1, 1905, the doctor declared the expedition over, effective immediately. Crowley watched helplessly as Jacot-Guillarmod wrested the expedition from his hands; watched as all the porters, with insufficient room for all of them at Camp 5, descended to take shelter behind the rocks at Camp 4; watched as Pache, his campmate, sided with Guillarmod. Only Reymond (at Jacot-Guillarmod's request) remained with Crowley.

They're fools, AC thought. *None of them know the first thing about Himalayan climbing.* And there they were, preparing to climb down even though night would fall before they finished. As his friends left, Crowley implored—to Pache in particular—to wait until morning, when it would be safer. "If you go now, you'll be dead within ten minutes."

Deaf ears turned away and started down the mountain. Crowley retired to his tent, Reymond thought, with the injured air of a deposed monarch.

Connected by one hundred feet of rope, Jacot-Guillarmod, de Righi, Pache, and three porters with crampons—Bahadur Lama, Thenduck, and Phubu[48]—began their descent, with Jacot-Guillarmod and de Righi in the lead. As they turned a sharp corner of the slope, a porter slipped. "No," Pache cursed to himself in split seconds, "the descent has barely started." He watched helplessly as the porter fell over the edge, taking the next porter in line with him. "No," Pache lamented: "Seventeen porters just passed through here without a hitch." By the time Pache realized he was tied to the same rope as the two falling porters, he was also plummeting down the slope, taking another porter with him.

Below, Guillarmod and de Righi saw their four comrades plunging toward them. Preparing to intercept their sprawling friends, they spread their legs, planted themselves on the path, and braced themselves. As the four falling bodies slid by, they caught one of them. The rope which encircled the waists of the other three snapped tight. For a moment, they stopped.

Then the snow beneath them slid.

A fifty-yard-wide avalanche of snow started down the hill, and de Righi slipped. Guillarmod held him with one arm while his other gripped his ax— the only thing keeping them in place. He held with all his strength, but the five men were just too heavy. Guillarmod's fingers slid off the ax handle despite themselves, and the avalanche swept all six men down the mountain. Guillar-mod tried to grab an ax in his path, but everything was happening too quickly; all he could do was paddle to keep on top of the sliding snow.

In five seconds, it was over: they fell into a crevice, and Guillarmod watched his friends vanish under the falling snow. Then darkness and debris engulfed him as well.

Breathing was difficult at first. He couldn't move, and he wasn't even fully conscious. Gasping for air, he realized he was cold, and then he realized what had just happened. Guillarmod pulled himself free by his rope and found de Righi at the other end, on top of the crevice. He was pinned down by Guillar-mod on the one side of his rope and by their buried comrades on the other. Had Guillarmod died, he would have been trapped there and frozen to death. As it was, after Guillarmod freed him, he was so shaken he was unable to stand.

Guillarmod attempted to rescue the others alone. He tugged on the rope which ran vertically into the snow-filled crevice below, knowing four men were on the other end somewhere. With no tools with which to dig, he used his bare hands. Soon, de Righi joined in, but it was just too slow. The doctor cried out in desperation, "Help! Reymond, help! Bring ice picks!"

"What's that?" Reymond asked.

"What?" Crowley asked with sour disinterest.

"It sounds like de Righi and Guillarmod yelling."

He shrugged. "So? They've been yelling all day."

Reymond still had his boots on. "I think I should go and look."

"Well, send word back if you need help." Crowley obviously didn't mean it. He figured Reymond was deserting, too. He remained in his tent, drinking tea. When he received no word from Reymond, AC rolled over in his sleeping bag and fell asleep, alone at Camp 5.

So Crowley describes this incident. The account in Reymond's diary dif-fers: Hearing the cry for help, Reymond, who still had his boots on, ran out of their tent, looked over the edge, and saw Jacot-Guillarmod and de Righi pull-ing at a rope that disappeared into the snow at their feet.

"Where's Pache?" Reymond shouted.

"Buried in the snow with three porters," Jacot-Guillarmod replied. Rey-mond could hear the deep anguish in his voice. "Come on, hurry!"

Reymond ran back to the tent and reported to Crowley, "Pache and three porters have run into an avalanche." Crowley didn't move, but remarked that the stupidity of people could fill an entire avalanche. Not waiting for orders, Reymond packed food into a backpack, put on his crampons, and headed down the path. To his great surprise, Crowley did not follow.[49]

Reymond looked like an angel at the top of the crevice, looking down on the doomed party and asking, "Do you need help?" After he rounded up axes and joined them in the pit, they dug at the tons of snow and ice that covered Pache and the others. They worked in turns, individually digging with an ax in the ever-deepening pit and hacking out more snow until white powder coated their bodies and their fingers felt like they were aflame. When darkness came with no sign of their comrades in the snow, they knew the truth:

Pache and the porters were already dead.

Crowley awoke the next morning and climbed down to Camp 4 to look around. He thought he heard voices, but saw no one. When he reached Camp 3, he found Guillarmod badly bruised and his back hurt; de Righi's ribs were also bruised, and he complained of other injuries. Then he found out: Pache and his three best porters were dead at the bottom of an avalanche.

Anguish and anger mixed within Crowley: his rash comrades had died as the result of their ill-conceived coup. "The conduct of the mountaineers amounted to manslaughter. By breaking their agreement, they had assumed full responsibility," he wrote bitterly.[50] Reymond recorded in his journal that Crowley, to the surprise of the others, explained that he thought the victims had been thrown on the rocks like the last porter, which is why he didn't come to help the night before.[51] That evening, Crowley took Reymond's place in de Righi's tent (forcing Reymond into Jacot-Guillarmod's), and the next morning, around 11 o'clock on September 3, AC left for Darjeeling. He wired his accounts to *The Pioneer* and *Daily Mail,* and awaited the rest of the party.

The others, meanwhile, stayed behind to recover the dead. Three days of digging finally uncovered the deceased climbers. A lama in the group said prayers over the bodies. and the porters lowered their three dead companions, arms crossed, into a crevasse and covered them with snow. "The god of Kangchenjunga took them," they declared fatalistically, "and they will spend eternity near him." They carried Pache to Camp 3, where fifty porters helped erect a memorial cairn. Reymond spent three days engraving Pache's name and the date of his death onto a slab of granite. The moraine hillock where he died to this day is known as Pache's Grave.

The tension on the mountain that led to Jacot-Guillarmod assuming control of the expedition spilled into the world's newspapers at what the Alpine Club called "lamentable length."[52] Initial news of Pache's death was reported widely, including in the *Manchester Guardian, Journal de Genève, Science,* and the *Alpine Journal.*[53] Because Crowley returned to Darjeeling ahead of the rest of the party, his were the first press releases to reach print. He had been documenting the climb's progress in a series of articles for *The Pioneer* titled "On the Kinchin Lay."[54] His latest installment described the tragedy and placed the blame squarely on his teammates, saying that the accident occurred in the course of his team abandoning him on the mountain; they proceeded "ignorant or careless of the commonest precautions for securing the safety of the men."[55] Crowley described sending Reymond to investigate the ensuing avalanche, and even admitted that he remained in his tent:

> Reymond hastily set out to render what help he could, though it was perfectly out of the question to render effective aid. Had the doctor possessed the common humanity or commonsense to leave me a proper complement of men at Camp V, instead of doing his utmost to destroy my influence, I should have been in a position to send help. As it was I could do nothing more than send out Reymond on the forlorn hope. Not that I was over anxious in the circumstances to render help. A mountain 'accident of this sort is one of the things for which I have no sympathy whatever[56]

Alexis Pache's grave on Kangchenjunga.

This sparked a war of words between the expedition's principals, beginning with a detailed rejoinder by de Righi, countersigned by Jacot-Guillarmod and Reymond, in the September 29 edition of *The Pioneer*. Regarding the most serious charges, de Righi wrote:

> Mr. Crowley further says that we left him without men. Every coolie with him, owing I suppose to fear of the mountain and of Mr. Crowley, had bolted the night before, so that he only had with him Thenduck senior, who, after his treatment at Mr. Crowley's hands and feet, begged of us to be taken down. This was the only man we deprived Mr. Crowley of; as of

> Mr. Pache deciding to come down with us (he was not persuaded by the Doctor), his servant, Bahadur Lama, came down with him, making thus our party up to six men. We, of course, could not refuse them, so the charge that we left him without effective help, our answer is, we only took one man who was sick and bruised. He further states that had the Doctor possessed the common humanity and common sense to leave him men he could have sent an effective rescue party. This Doctor Guillarmod was unable to do as no coolie then would stop with such a Sahib, who convinced his coolies to march with the business end of his ice-axe or the toe of his well shod boot.[57]

In his final installment (penned the day after the accident but allegedly not edited in response to de Righi's letter), Crowley conceded that his last report was written on the heels of the accident while in a charged emotional state and without all the facts. "I was under the (false) impression that the Doctor and Righi were on one rope, and the rest … on another. What I supposed to be the matter was that these five had been seen to fall over the cliffs on to the lower glacier." So far, so good. However, his list of reasons for not rendering help after the avalanche shockingly concluded, "The doctor is old enough to rescue himself and nobody would want to rescue Righi." The article ended with the following dig at de Righi: "It is only fair to add that on my return I found (in spite of the absence of the brilliant young manager) that the food and attendance at this hotel had very much improved, even to excellence."[58]

This drama replayed itself in Switzerland, when these stories were picked up and run by the *Journal de Genève* and *Gazette de Lausanne et Journal Suisse*. These include de Righi's account, a detailed series on the climb by Jacot-Guillarmod, and conclude with Reymond's account of the climb in the February 5, 1906, *Journal de Genève*.[59] These accounts maintained that Crowley lacked the skills necessary to lead the expedition effectively. The clash ended quietly, however, when Guillarmod threatened, if Crowley did not desist, to accuse him of fraud, sending a copy of *Snowdrops* along with the complaint. Crowley relented. In the months to follow, Jacot-Guillarmod would go on to report the tale of their expedition to the French Alpine Club, the Swiss Alpine Club, and the Geographical Society of Geneva.[60]

In the end, the image that stuck not only with his peers in the climbing community but also with the general public was an unflattering portrait of Crowley painted by his own words, as quoted above. If his flippancy did not seem cold enough, his later letters commented that although it would have taken him only ten minutes to dress, he did not do so because there was no word from Reymond. Writing in the *Daily Mail,* Crowley added, "I am not altogether disappointed with the present results. I know enough to make certain of success of another year with a properly equipped and disciplined expedition."[61] Furthermore, the attacks on the Alpine Club couched within his narrative further drew the ire of fellow climbers. As one person wrote of Crowley's first article for *The Pioneer:*

> From the tone of it, I judge him to be a disappointed candidate for membership of the Alpine Club, to which I may add, I have not the privilege of belonging. The sport of mountaineering will certainly suffer no loss if Kinchenjunga permanently effaces this polished individual.[62]

In the end, Crowley painted himself as a detached and uncaring leader who simply did not want to rescue his comrades.

Kangchenjunga was history. The crushing, embittering experience scarred Crowley: he would never again make a climb of any consequence, and Kangchenjunga phobia would haunt him even in his last days.

Long after this tragic attempt, the Five Peaks remained elusive: Raeburn and Crawford's 1920 attempt was cut short because they were inadequately equipped. In 1929, snowstorms at 24,272 feet turned back Bauer's expedition. The following year, Dyhrenfurth lost a porter in an avalanche and abandoned the peak in favor of a smaller mountain. Bauer tried again in 1931 but gave up at 25,500 feet when he encountered an unclimbable slope. Cooke's 1937 expedition failed similarly, while Frey died in his 1951 attempt with Lewis.

Not until 1954 did John Kempe's expedition successfully conduct reconnaissance of Kangchenjunga's southwest approach, paving the way for the British expedition that conquered the mountain in 1955.[63]

And not until the twenty-first century—a century after this fateful climb—have Crowley's mountaineering accomplishments been seriously reevaluated. Colin Wells, author of *A Brief History of British Mountaineering* (2001), called him in 2002, "one of the most accomplished and talented climbers in his era," and quoted Mick Fowler, who repeated many of Crowley's Beachy Head climbs eighty-five years later, as saying admiringly,

> Crowley was outrageous! He was obviously good; something of a star rock climber, in fact.... He was light years ahead of his time in his attitude to tackling vertical chalk cliffs. The ground he covered was without doubt amongst the most technically difficult in Britain, but his achievements were never really appreciated in his lifetime.[64]

Similarly, Isserman, Weaver, and Molenaar conceded in *Fallen Giants,*

> From far outside the privileged purlieus of the Alpine Club and the Royal Geographical Society (who between them did in fact conspire to diminish or even erase Crowley's achievement), he found his way to the world's second- and third-highest mountains and somehow discerned and reconnoitered the routes by which they would first be climbed.[65]

Finally, *Canadian Alpine Journal* editor Geoff Powter noted in *Strange and Dangerous Dreams,* "Crowley's rehabilitation in climbing circles has been as dramatic as it has been elsewhere,"[66] due in no small part to the fact that the sport's vanguard and rock stars of today, living on the edge, share more in common with Crowley than they do with his staid and proper peers.

Life looked pretty grim. Crowley was a man who had climbed among the highest mountains in the world, only to have his first leadership snatched from him and his men buried in ice. As a poet, he had published so many books that his collected *Works* were available, even though the originals never sold. He had traveled around the world, and was now halfway around it again and finding it stale. And he was a master of magic who chose to forget his experience in Cairo. Now on the verge of his thirtieth birthday, life stared him in the face.

What next?

Empty and lost, he cabled Rose to join him in India and wrote soul-searching letters to his brother-in-law. Everything had soured, seemed stale. Even his poetry, which he had all but forgotten lately, was doubtful:

> I have thought of trying serious writing again, but I am 30 and a proud Papa. Shelley and Keats never touched 30—that day is over for me. I think some small bits of work are classical with theirs, I must leave it at that. Anyway, I hope I shan't simply go bad. At least I am certain to avoid the blunder of making a good thing and copying it forever.[67]

The only thing remaining was the truth that he had realized back at Cambridge, when he grasped for something in the world that could stir him: magic. He realized he had to change the world. Thus, *The Sword of Song* became his manifesto, and he wrote eagerly to Kelly:

> This book has been boycotted by English publishers and printers. I am in arms against a world, but after five years of folly and weakness, miscalled politeness, tact, discretion, care for the feeling of others, I am weary of it. Did Christ mince his words with the Pharisees? I say today to hell with Christianity, rationalism, Buddhism, all the lumber of the centuries. I bring you a positive and primaeval fact, magic by name; and with this I will build me a new Heaven and a new Earth. I want none of your faint approval or faint dispraise; I want blasphemy, murder, rape, revolution, anything, bad or good, but strong. I want men behind me, or before me if they can surpass me, but men, men not gentlemen. Bring me your personal vigour; all of it, not your spare vigour. Bring me all the money you have or can force from others. If I can get but seven such men, the world is at my feet. If ten, Heaven will fall at the sound of one trumpet to arms.[68]

By these words he would lead the rest of his life.

Crowley kept himself busy waiting for Rose and Lilith to arrive on October 29. He studied Persian, stayed with a maharaja in Moharbhanj, sacrificed a goat to Kali, visited his friend Edward Thornton, and went big-game hunting. Traveling to Calcutta, he also went to the infamous Culinga Bazar on October 28 during a boisterous holiday festival. At 10 o'clock in the evening, Crowley paused on the dark streets of the Bazar to revel in the fireworks and celebration until, despite himself, he stopped enjoying it. Amidst the noise and excitement, he felt uncomfortable.

He was being followed.

In an effort to shake his pursuer, Crowley ducked into an alley. Trouble followed him in the form of six figures. AC pressed into the shadows and held his breath, hoping his mountain tan and his dark clothes would conceal him until the throng passed. Just in case, he placed a tense hand on the Webley revolver in his coat. The first three walked right by him and, for a moment, he thought they hadn't noticed him.

Then they closed in. Strong hands pinned Crowley's arms to his sides while others searched his pockets. "Unhand me!" he barked, hoping an authoritative Englishman's voice would frighten them off. In the glimmer of a distant flare, he caught the glint of a blade and realized his life was worthless in this back alley. His hand, still on the Webley, automatically drew the gun from his pocket and tightened around its trigger. The flash captured the sight of four white-clad figures dropping back and running. Then he found himself in silent darkness.[69]

In the pulse-pounding moments that followed, it never occurred to him that a gunshot could pass unnoticed among noisy fireworks. Instead, he frantically imagined the worst: crowds would soon gather to investigate the commotion. The police would frown upon an Englishman—a foreigner—shooting someone in an alley. He pictured himself in prison somewhere, never to be seen again, and desperately sought a solution.

Recalling how he passed unnoticed on the streets of Mexico City, he thought to use that magic to get him out of this fix. Closing his eyes and calling on his holy guardian angel for protection, he cast a spell of invisibility upon himself and slipped down the alley, past the crowds, out of sight.

"Go to your room," Edward Thornton, groggy with sleep, told him that night. "Go to bed. Come around in the morning and I'll take you to the right man." The right man was a solicitor named Garth, who officially advised Crowley to go to the police with his story. "You'd be acquitted, of course. But you'd be kept hanging about Calcutta indefinitely. An unscrupulous man might hold his tongue and clear out of British India p.d.q."[70] Crowley waited two days before deciding to take action. He didn't even know if the gunshot had struck anyone.

Rose arrived that day with their child, and Thornton threw them a dinner party that night. Throughout the meal, Thornton caught Crowley's eye, gesticulated, and held up two fingers. Crowley simply looked back blankly. Thornton finally took him aside and explained: the bullet had struck two of his assailants, who confessed to the crime. *The Standard* carried the story the next morning; a reward was offered for the apprehension of the gunman. Ironically, the same issue featured an interview with AC as leader of the Kangchenjunga expedition. "Get out," Thornton advised, "and get out quick."

Heeding Thornton's advice, Crowley looked at Rose and asked her, "Which will it be: Persia or China?"

"I'm tired of Omar Khayyam," she remarked. "Let's go to China."

Rangoon began their journey. Crowley checked Rose and Lilith into a hotel while he visited Ananda Metteya, formerly known as Allan Bennett. They discussed the need for a common language if magic were ever to be studied scientifically, concluding that the system most accessible to Westerners was the kabbalah. It convinced Crowley of the importance of tabulating all systems of mysticism and religion according to the ten spheres and twenty-two paths of the Hebrew Tree of Life. Three days later, on November 6, Bennett had to return to the monastery per its rules. Following Allan's advice on writer's block, Crowley wrote "The Eyes of the Pharaoh" and what would form chapters I through XX of *The High History of Good Sir Palamedes the Saracen Knight*, a versified account of the path of initiation. The effort to write even this much, however, was stupendous.

On November 15, the Crowleys boarded the steamship *Java* for Mandalay. An artistic and intellectual vacuum within, Crowley spent the voyage leaning over the railing, watching the crests the boat cut into the water, watching the flying fish dancing along the surface, and trying to wrench some poetry out of himself. Finally, in his journal, he recorded, "the misery of this is simply sickening;—I can write no more."[71]

By November 29 they reached Bhamo, forty miles from the Chinese border. It marked a new phase in his life. Over the next months, his mundane existence became a series of bizarre adventures while his spiritual life became a simple and stellar affair, yielding to no interference from the mundane world no matter how crippling.

From Bhamo, the three Crowleys, their porters, and Lilith's nurse began a leisurely journey toward Tengyueh (now called Tengchung), China. All the while AC brooded about the anomie and purposelessness he felt ever since Kangchenjunga. Then, on their fourth day from Bhamo, something happened to snap AC out of his existential crisis.

Having crossed the river that marked the Chinese frontier, they climbed out of a ravine with Crowley bringing up the rear to discourage the porters from straggling. At one point, Crowley dismounted his Burmese pony to walk and stretch his legs. Once adequately limbered, he tried to mount the pony. The beast, however, reared and sent them both down a forty foot cliff. Laying on the ground, looking up at the length of their fall, Crowley waited for the pain of his broken body to kick in. When it never did, he realized he was unharmed and marveled that both he and the horse escaped without a scratch. In that moment, he recalled all his narrow brushes with death: from the bomb he made at age fourteen to the muggers in Calcutta, he concluded his charmed life was being preserved for a greater purpose. It resolved his existential crisis.

At that moment, Aleister Crowley achieved the rank of Exempt Adept (7°=4□), the highest grade of the Second Order. With this illumination came a resolve to resume magical work. Daunted by his perceived role as the world's greatest magus, Crowley confided in Clifford Bax:

> It is very easy to get all the keys, invisible and otherwise, into the King-
> dom, but the keys are devilish stiff, some of them dampered. I am myself at
> the end of a little excursion of nearly seven years in Hell, and the illusion
> of reason, which I thought I had stamped out in '98, was bossing me. It
> has now got the boot. But let this tell you that it is one thing to devote
> your life to magic at 20 years old, and another to find at 30 that you are
> bound to stay a Magus. The first is the folly of a child; the second, the
> Gate of the Sanctuary.[72]

On February 11, Crowley pledged to conduct a magical retirement even as
they marched across China. He devoted the next three days to studying the
Goetia for inspiration, then decided once and for all to contact his holy guardian angel. To this end, he decided to recite the Goetia's Preliminary Invocation
every day. Of paramount importance was to perform the invocation daily,
unfailingly. Rain or shine, tired or rested, good or bad, he had to do it.

He began on February 16, typically doing the invocation, which he called
Augoeides, after Bulwer Lytton's term for the holy guardian angel, on the astral
plane, performing the rite in his imagination as he rode across the countryside
on his pony. He maintained his resolve, performing the ritual every day until
June 7, when he could continue no longer.

China's Boxer rebellion was well underway when, at the beginning of January
1906, the Crowleys stayed at Tengyueh. On January 23 they reached
Yungchang (what is now Paoshan), where the mandarin Tao Tai treated them
to a twelve-hour banquet. Chinese New Year followed two days later.

After crossing the Mekong river on January 26, Crowley noticed that all his
porters smoked opium in their free time. Although his previous exposure to
the drug through Bennett had been fruitless, Crowley bought an opium pipe to
learn about the fashionable drug that wealthy and intellectual Europeans
flocked to the far and middle east to sample. After five hours and twenty-five
pipes, AC experienced neither euphoria nor tranquility. Regardless, his muse
returned, and he wrote "The King Ghost" and "The Opium Smoker."

From there, the next two months' journey took them to Yunnan, Mengtsz,
Manhao, Hokow, Laokay (now part of northern Vietnam), Yen Bay, and the
capital, Hanoi, "but only stayed for lunch."[73]

Toward the end of March, AC decided they would return home by two
separate routes. Crowley wished to stop in America and seek out backers for
another Kangchenjunga expedition while Rose retrieved their hastily abandoned luggage from Calcutta, returning to England via the continent. Rose
was very annoyed about being cast off in China with their young daughter to
return home alone. Crowley reasoned that, being wanted in Calcutta, he
couldn't return there with her. She finally agreed, with the intent of staying
with her father when she arrived in Scotland. She needed his help because she
was three months pregnant.

Meanwhile, her husband, unknown to her, was on his way to Shanghai to look up Elaine Simpson, the former Soror Fidelis. He arrived on April 6. There, he read tarot cards for Elaine and her friends. In private moments, Crowley and Elaine discussed *The Book of the Law*. She read it and, much to Crowley's chagrin, believed it to be a prophetic book; he was hoping she would denounce it and thus relieve him of the role of prophet, a burden that the book called for him to assume.

Crowley asked her to help him invoke Aiwass and speak to him. She agreed, and two days later they conducted the ceremony. In what would become Crowley's preferred method, he summoned Aiwass while Elaine looked for him on the astral plane. Aiwass appeared to her as brilliant blue with a wand in hand. "He has followed you all along," Elaine explained her impressions of him. "He wants you to follow his cult." Crowley instructed her to take his wand. When she did, Aiwass turned into brilliant light and dissipated. "He seems to be tangled in a mesh of light, trying to escape."

"Tell him that if he goes away, he cannot return," Crowley instructed.

"He has a message: 'Return to Egypt, with same surroundings. There I will give thee signs. Go with the Scarlet Woman, this is essential; thus you shall get real power, that of God, the only one worth having. Illumination shall come by means of power, pari passu … Live in Egypt as you did before. Do not do a Great Retirement. Go at once to Egypt: money troubles will be settled more easily than you think now. I will give you no guarantee of my truth.' Then he turns black-blue, and says, 'I am loath to part from you. Do not take Fidelis. I do not like the relations between you; break them off! If not, you must follow other Gods … Yet I would wish you to love physically, to make perfect the circle of your union. Fidelis will not do so, therefore she is useless.' "[74]

Satisfied with the ritual and the messages they received, they purified the area and finished. Despite Aiwass's suggestion that Elaine make love to Crowley, she lived up to her magical motto and remained faithful to her husband. On April 21, Crowley left Soror Fidelis and sailed for America on the *Empress of India*. While they would remain in touch—in 1929, Crowley would note "My old and dear friend Fidelis wants me to go to Frankfurt"[75]—their bond would never be as strong as during their alliance in the GD years.

On April 24, while his ship docked at the Japanese port of Kobe, Crowley dutifully performed his invocation on the astral plane. This time, a vision appeared to him. In it, he entered a room in which a naked man was nailed to a cruciform table. About this table sat a group of venerable sages, busily eating the flesh and drinking the blood of the naked man. A voice told Crowley that these sages were the adepts he would someday join. As the vision continued, Crowley entered a filigreed ivory hall, a square altar in the center its only contents. "What wouldst thou sacrifice upon the altar?" the voice asked.

Crowley replied, "I offer all save my will to know Augoeides." Knowledge and conversation of one's holy guardian angel, after all, was the goal of all magic. At least as far as he knew. Looking about, Crowley realized he stood before the Egyptian gods, their forms so immense he could only see up to their knees.

"Would not knowledge of the gods suffice?"

Crowley was adamant. "No."

"Thou art critical and rationalistic."

The magician apologized for his blindness, kneeling at the altar and placing both hands upon it, right over left. A luminous figure clad in white appeared before Crowley, placing his hands upon the magician's, then spoke, "I receive thee into the Order of the Silver Star."

With that, Crowley returned to earth in a cradle of flame. The Secret Chiefs had accepted him as one of them, a member of the Third Order—those grades that awaited beyond the highest ones in the GD; those reserved for the Secret Chiefs. He worried whether he was ready for the demands of the job. On April 30 he wrote in his journal:

> It has struck me—in connection with reading Blake—that Aiwass, etc. "Force and Fire" is the very thing I lack. My "conscience" is really an obstacle and a delusion, being a survival of heredity and education. Certainly to rely on it as an abiding principle in itself is wrong. The one really important thing is the fundamental hypothesis: I am the Chosen One. All methods will do, if I only *invoke often* and stick to it.[76]

No matter what else might happen, he had to prove himself by invoking often; otherwise, he would lose everything. Such was his understanding. What he didn't know at the time was that, if he did stick to it, he would have to lose everything anyway.

As he sailed, Crowley's muse moved him again, and he wrote "The True Greater Ritual of the Pentagram" and worked on commentary to *The Book of the Law*. The thought of returning to his wife and family also inspired him to compose "Rosa Coeli," the third in his cycle of poems to Rose.

The *Empress of India* reached Vancouver, British Columbia, in twelve days; he had just missed the earthquake and fires that gutted San Francisco on April 18. From Vancouver, Crowley traveled east across the continent, passing through Calgary, Winnipeg, and Toronto. Across the border in the United States, Niagara Falls impressed him. On May 15 he reached New York City, fatigued by travel. After ten days of restaurants and theaters, he found no one willing to invest in a Himalayan climb and sailed for England on May 26.

Arriving at Liverpool on June 2, Crowley picked up his mail, read the telegram, and his life fell apart.

His daughter Lilith was dead.

CHAPTER SEVEN

The Great White Brotherhood

Staring at the letters from his mother and Uncle Tom, Crowley was stunned. Lilith dead? Unbelievable, yet the facts were all there: she didn't even live long enough to reach London. Lilith Crowley had died of typhoid in Rangoon. Jewell, in one of his callous moments, remarked that Nuit Ma Ahathoor Hecate Sappho Jezebel Lilith Crowley actually died of acute nomenclature.

Despite the heartache, Crowley struggled to recite the preliminary invocation, which he had sustained for the past four months. A sad robot, he reaffirmed his oath to persevere no matter what, offering everything that remained of his life. He wandered the streets of London, emptily running through the words in his head. June 7, on the train to Plymouth where Rose awaited, was the last time he was able to complete the conjuration. When at last he saw his wife, they fell sobbing into each others' arms. The couple stumbled around— nervous, weak, and weeping—for the next two days.

In the midst of this misery, Crowley discovered that Rose had become an alcoholic. Desperate for something on which to blame his misfortune, he convinced himself that Lilith died because Rose, too drunk to properly sterilize a baby bottle, fed her with a contaminated nipple. But how could he blame his Rose of Heaven? The fault was not hers but the alcohol's. And the alcoholism he blamed on her family. Tellingly, he never pointed the finger at himself for leaving his pregnant wife and infant to make their own way home from the Far East while he returned in literally the opposite direction.

Crowley's health declined into a series of illnesses: after doctors removed an infected gland from his groin, his right eye required a series of operations, all unsuccessful. Neuralgia and an ulcerated throat then set in and remained with him most of the year. Life's miseries left him stunned and numb, sleeping much of the time.

Then, like an angel come to put his life back on track, George Cecil Jones, Exempt Adept (7°=4□) of the Second Order, arrived on June 23 to discuss Crowley's work. They did so for the next two days, after which Jones advised

Crowley to go on a Great Magical Retirement, albeit close to home so he could be reached by telegraph if necessary. The visit eased some of Crowley's sorrow, and helped him concentrate again on the Great Work. On July 11, three days after he entered a nursing home for an operation, Crowley resumed daily recitation of the Augoeides invocation.

Crowley left the nursing home on July 25 and, the day after, went to stay with Jones. They continued to discuss and compare their magical experiences, and the following day, Jones used a modified version of the GD's Adeptus Minor (5°=6□) ritual to initiate Crowley: Bound upon the Cross of Suffering, AC once again spoke the words, "I, Perdurabo, a member of the Corpus Christi, do hereby solemnly obligate myself to lead a pure and unselfish life …" as he had done before Mathers in Paris six years ago. However, the ritual was more than mere repetition. It was a potent synthesis of their independent magical work, taking the ceremony to undreamed levels and inspiring him like never before. Thus began a remarkable phase of Crowley's work, two ex-GD members collaborating on mysteries their parent order scarcely imagined.

On July 29 they started to think about founding a new magical order.

John Frederick Charles Fuller (1878–1966) shared much with Crowley. He was the son of an Anglican cleric—Rev. Alfred Fuller (1832–1927), formerly the Rector of Itchenor[1]—and, having a dreamy and introspective childhood, grew up later than most. He also attended Malvern and, like Crowley, learned to loathe it. In 1897, when Crowley began his third year at Cambridge, Fuller's parents sent their son to the Royal Military College at Sandhurst. The college nearly turned the boy down because he was too skinny, but accepted him on probation on August 30. He graduated a year later and joined the 43rd Infantry.

He spent the Boer War (1899) immersed in two hundred books on religion, philosophy, and other subjects and, while stationed in India in 1903, studied Hinduism, yoga, the *Vedas,* and the *Upanishads.* After reading Havelock Ellis's *Studies in the Psychology of Sex* (1903) and E. N. Huston's *A Plea for Polygamy* (1869), sexual freedom became one of his causes. Fuller believed that mankind needed to tear off the "mystic fig leaf … and stand naked and sublime in all the glory and consummation of perfect Nature."[2] In 1905 he begged his mother not to tell his father, the cleric, that he had just contributed the first of what would be many articles to the *Agnostic Journal;*[3] it was his first overt statement of apostasy from the creed of his upbringing. The second was his essay on Crowley's works, which he wrote during the hot summer of 1905. *The Star in the West* (1907) would prove to be the first and only entry into Crowley's contest for the best essay on his works. Throughout, it shamelessly praised the poet: "It has taken 100,000,000 years to produce Aleister Crowley. The world has indeed laboured, and has at last brought forth a man."[4] The praise, however, was not shallow. Fuller considered Crowley to be England's greatest living poet, and believed it all his life.

John Frederick Charles Fuller (1878–1966), Frater Non Sine Fulmina.

In October 1905, Fuller developed a record case of typhoid that lasted seventy days. On February 14, 1906, a medical board recommended an eight-month leave of absence. That April, he was discharged and sent home for a year's sick leave. He wrote to Crowley about these events, and AC responded with his first letter to Fuller in nearly a year. Arriving August 8, 1906, it read:

> I am sorry to hear of your enteric fever, but fate has treated me even worse; for after a most successful trip through China without a day's illness for any of us, our baby girl died of that very disease on the way home.[5]

By mid-August they arranged their first face-to-face meeting at the Hotel Cecil. Under Crowley's influence, his interest in the occult blossomed into fascination, and he plunged into its study. Likewise, Fuller's knowledge of Hinduism impressed AC, spurring him on to study as well. Despite his daughter's death, his pregnant wife's alcoholism, and his own illness, Crowley devoted himself to magic.

At this point, not one but two individuals answering to the name "Lola" entered Crowley's life. The first was a nickname for Vera Snepp, whom Crowley, frustrated by Rose's alcoholism, took as a mistress during visits with Jones in Coulsdon, Surrey. She acted under the name Vera Neville,[6] and was one of the most beautiful English women he had ever met. AC chronicled their affair in poems which would later become part of *Clouds without Water* (1909):

> Lola! now look me straight between the eyes.
> Our fate is come upon us. Tell me now
> Love still shall arbitrate our destinies,
> And joy inform the swart Plutonic brow.[7]

She would also become the dedicatee of *Gargoyles* (1906) and the model for the Virgin of the World in "The Wake World."[8]

The other Lola appeared in September when Rose gave birth to Crowley's second daughter, whom he named Lola Zaza, presumably after his mistress. The occasion was hardly glad. The infant was sickly and, for her first three days of life, so inactive that they often feared she was dead. At three weeks of age, bronchitis nearly killed her. Given what modern medicine knows about the deleterious effects of maternal alcohol consumption on a fetus, frailty and low birth weight are unsurprising; but in the Edwardian age the Crowleys could only marvel at their continued misfortune.

With Rose and the baby recovering in Chiselhurst, Crowley returned to Coulsdon to study with Jones and recuperate from his own ailments. Under these conditions, his health returned "suddenly and completely." As with his health, Crowley also recovered his magical impetus. On September 21, he marked thirty-two weeks' performance of Augoeides, with only a brief break during his crisis in June.

The following day, Jones and Crowley celebrated the autumnal equinox. For the occasion, Jones adapted the GD Neophyte ($0°=0^\square$) ritual, retaining and streamlining its potencies while eschewing unnecessary details. The result was a powerful formula of initiation for their proposed mystic society. Into the typical ceremony of testing and purifying a candidate they introduced spiral dancing and ritual scourging; and rather than binding the candidate to a cross as in the Adeptus Minor ($5°=6^\square$) ceremony, the candidate was pinned down and a cross cut on his chest. Jones asked Crowley to write the ceremony in verse form; the result was "Liber 671," later dubbed "Liber Pyramidos."[9]

After slight alterations by both magicians, they tested the revised ritual on October 9. Crowley considered the result among the greatest events of his career: he attained the knowledge and conversation of his holy guardian angel. He experienced *Shivadarshana,* the vision of Shiva. He entered the trance of *samadhi,* union with godhead. After six years of false starts, he succeeded at the Abramelin operation. In response, Crowley "thanked gods and sacrificed for Lola"[10]—his lover, not his child.

While his spiritual life soared with its victories, his personal life crumbled under the stress of its burdens: Lilith's death, Rose's alcoholism, and Lola Zaza's frail grip on life. On November 4 he wrote in his diary, "Dog-faced demons all day. Descent into Hell." In magical terms, he had plumbed the depths of the

Ordeal of the Abyss, a magical rite of passage designed to obliterate the magician's ego by destroying all he held dear: those physical attachments that Buddha blamed for reincarnation; one's selfishness, or sense of self. The magical text "Liber Cheth" later described this spiritual desert:

> Then shall thy brain be dumb, and thy heart beat no more, and all thy life shall go from thee; and thou shalt be cast out upon the midden, and the birds of the air shall feast upon thy flesh, and thy bones shall whiten in the sun.
>
> Then shall the winds gather themselves together, and bear thee up as it were a little heap of dust in a sheet that hath four corners, and they shall give it unto the guardians of the Abyss.
>
> And because there is no life therein, the guardians of the abyss shall bid the angels of the winds pass by. And the angels shall lay thy dust in the City of the Pyramids ...
>
> And behold! if by stealth thou keep unto thyself one thought of thine, then shalt thou be cast out into the abyss for ever; and thou shalt be the lonely one, the eater of dung, the afflicted in the Day of Be-with-Us.[11]

Mathers had never warned him about it, and he couldn't have, because he never advanced this far along the spiritual path. But Crowley now realized the truth: only one who released everything was light enough to cross the desiccated yaw of the Abyss, to surpass the Second Order's highest grade of Exempt Adept (7°=4□) and follow the path of the Secret Chiefs and their Great White Brotherhood. By contrast, those who clung to some vestige of their former lives were mired forever in the Abyss, doomed as one of the Black Brothers who elevated their egos to the godhead. "I cannot even say that I crossed the Abyss deliberately," Crowley wrote, illustrating that, although few ever advanced this far, the terrible ordeal was an eventuality for all magicians, a consequence of one's earliest oaths. "I was hurled into it by the momentum of the forces which I had called up."[12]

Thus Crowley surrendered all he valued, knowing that if he did not, the gods would wrench it from his feeble hands. When British Customs seized Philippe Renouard's shipment of AC's latest *(Alexandra)*, deemed it obscene, and destroyed all copies, it seemed like a test of his resolve.

This illumination also recalled the warning written in the repugnant third chapter of *The Book of the Law:*

> Let the Scarlet Woman beware! If pity and compassion and tenderness visit her heart; if she leave my work to toy with old sweetnesses; then shall my vengeance be known. I will slay me her child: I will alienate her heart: I will cast her out from men: as a shrinking and despised harlot shall she crawl through dusk wet streets, and die cold and an-hungered.[13]

And he understood. The gods had killed Lilith because his attachment to her was impeding his progress in the Great Work. The gods killed her because Rose had failed in her role as Crowley's magical partner. The gods killed her as a warning. In that moment, Crowley realized the cosmos played by very tough rules.

On the eighth anniversary of his initiation into the GD—his spiritual birthday—Crowley dedicated the epilogue of his collected *Works* to Jones, who had acted as Kerux at his admission to that group:

> Eight years ago this day you, Hermes, led me blindfold to awake a chosen runner of the course. "In all my wanderings in darkness your light shone before me though I knew it not." To-day (one may almost hope, turning into the straight) you and I are alone. Terrible and joyous! We shall find companions at the End, at the banquet, lissome and cool and garlanded; companions with a Silver Star or maybe a Jewelled Eye mobile and uncertain—as if alive—on their foreheads. We shall be bidden to sit, and they will wreathe us with immortal flowers, and give us to drink of the seemly wine of Iacchus—well! but until then, unless my heart deceives me, no third shall appear to join us. Indeed, may two attain? It seems a thing impossible in nature....[14]

The Silver Star and Jeweled Eye in the triangle were symbols of the Third Order, the A∴A∴, the Great White Brotherhood of Secret Chiefs. Crowley considered himself and Jones to be alone among the most advanced adepts in the world. However, lacking a third initiate to complete their founding triad (à la Westcott-Woodman-Mathers), they could not begin their new order.

On December 10, Jones served as harbinger for the Secret Chiefs, who again invited Crowley to join their ranks in the Third Order. No longer was he Frater OY MH, as he was known as an Exempt Adept ($7°=4□$), the seventh in the magical hierarchy and fourth from the pinnacle. He had crossed the Abyss and had advanced to the eighth level, previously considered unattainable by corporeal beings. Or, as Jones put it, "OY MH is $8°=3□$."

"And Mollie Lee rhymes with both," he replied flippantly. Nevertheless, Jones insisted that, as $8°=3□$, Crowley had not only attained the grade of Master of the Temple but had become *the* Master: the next Buddha, the logos, the prophet of a new age. He thereupon performed a ritual to consecrate Crowley a Master of the Temple. Although Crowley still considered himself unfit for the honor, the ritual made him feel like a genuine master.

The next day—when Crowley went to Bournemouth and placed himself under a doctor's care for throat trouble—he received a letter from Jones, reiterating the topic of their meeting:

> How long have you been in the Great Order, and why did I not know? Is the invisibility of the A∴A∴ to lower grades so complete?[15]

Crowley found his attainment increasingly difficult to deny.

As he recuperated, he recalled his conversation with Allan Bennett about the value and necessity of the kabbalah as a universal language for magic. Crowley sat down on December 15 with the table of correspondences that

Bennett had left him prior to his move to Ceylon and began to expand the entries. For the first four days, he devoted only eight hours to the project, but soon began to work on it in larger doses. On Christmas, for example, he spent all day and night working. Only a heated discussion between Crowley and Jones on the nature of truth and magical attainment, as discussed in Crowley's new essay "Amath"[16] (Hebrew for "truth"), diverted him. The completed work tabulated all the information taught by the GD, plus the knowledge Crowley had acquired in his trips to the world's sacred sites; it would be published as 777 in 1909.

On January 29, 1907, Crowley left Bournemouth and returned home.

Lola Zaza Crowley took a downturn on Friday, February 15. Since her first frail days, she had developed respiratory complications that required a nurse to watch over her. She was on oxygen, and the doctor ordered that only one person be permitted in the room with her at a time.

Rose's mother, Blanche Kelly, came in to visit the baby that Saturday. Crowley disliked his mother-in-law, and when she broke the rules about Lola's care, a row erupted. In the end, Crowley threw her out of the flat and, in his mind, saved the baby's life. Alas, combined with Rose's drinking and his own affair, the incident only contributed to marital discord.

The evening started out like any other: Crowley walked down to Stafford Street to his favorite haunt, chemist E. Whineray, who supplied unusual ingredients for his ceremonial perfumes and incenses. Whineray's bald head and large eyes—shining alike with laughter and cynicism—reminded Crowley of an owl. "He knew all the secrets of London. People of all ranks, from the courtier and the cabinet minister, to the coachman and the courtesan, made him their father confessor," Crowley wrote. "He understood human frailty in every detail and not only forgave it, but loved men for their weaknesses."[17] Like Eckenstein, he could see through Crowley and understood him—a trait on which Crowley depended.

Edward Whineray (1861–1924) was born in Ulverston, Lancashire, about a year after saddler William Whineray wed Betsy Hodgson.[18] He became an apprentice of the Pharmaceutical Society of Great Britain in 1875 and helped found the Chemists' Assistants' Union in 1898, after which he became managing director at pharmaceutical chemists W. E. Lowe Co. Ltd. on 8 Stafford Street, building a distinguished clientele.[19] Crowley claims that Whineray's shop appears in novelist Robert Smythe Hichens's *Felix* (1902), although Crowley fails to provide any details. In fact, Hichens's unnamed fictional chemist on Wigmore Street discreetly dispenses morphine to society ladies, even in the dead of night.[20] In his only review published in *The Equinox*, Whineray wrote of *Chronicles of Pharmacy*, "To the student of the occult it ought to appeal strongly, as the author gives a long list of drugs used in religious ceremonies in different ages."[21]

This day, Whineray had something new for him. The Right Honourable George Montagu Bennet (1852–1931), 7th Earl of Tankerville and Lord Ossulston, sought an introduction.[22] A thirteenth-generation descendent of princess of England Mary Tudor (1496–1533), Bennet was the second son of Charles Augustus Bennet (1810–1899) and Lady Olivia Montagu (1830–1922). He lived a colorful life, beginning as a Royal Navy midshipman in 1865, until severe sea-sickness compelled him to resign. From there, he won the Ottley prize for drawing at Radley College, was a member of the Rifle Brigade from 1872, and aide-de-camp to the Lord-Lieutenant of Ireland. His older brother Charles's death in 1879 of cholera in Pahawur, India, left him heir to the peerage, so he assumed the title of Lord Bennet and left the army. Next, he went ranching in the western United States, where he was friendly with Teddy Roosevelt (1858–1919). In 1892 he met and befriended American Methodist gospel singer and evangelist Ira D. Sankey (1840–1908), accompanying him on many revivals and conducting some of his own.[23] At one revival, he met Leonora Sophia van Marter, a music teacher of Tacoma, Washington, whom he married on October 23, 1895.[24] The earldom passed to Bennet upon his father's death in late December 1899.[25] Although one of the richest earldoms in England, with 31,500 acres of land and its chief seat Chillingham Castle in Northumberland (famous for its herd of white wild cattle), it also had the highest rent. Consequently, Bennet was constantly in financial straits, residing in the family's much more modest Thornington House in Northumberland.[26] Known as "The Singing Earl," he studied under Giovanni Sbriglia (1832–1916), was first president of the Newcastle Symphonium Society, sang at revivals, and participated in concerts until his death. He was also painted miniatures, some of which won awards[27] and were hung in the Royal Academy.[28]

No sooner did Crowley agree to a meeting than Bennet entered from the next room. Taking Crowley aside, the Earl spoke to him like a lifelong friend, disclosing intimate details and discussing family secrets with embarrassing frankness. But most remarkable was his claim that his mother and her friend were trying to kill him with magic. He wanted Crowley to protect him. AC viewed him as suffering from "persecution mania." His predilections for "his old habit of brandy tippling and his newly acquired one of sniffing a solution of cocaine" not only accentuated his concerns—leading Crowley to nickname him the "Earl of Coke and Crankum"[29]—but also explained his presence at Whineray's shop.

AC saw him as a religious man with a mystical bent, and although he doubted the accuracy of his story, he knew Bennet himself believed it. Therefore, Crowley suggested they take a retirement that spring so the master could teach him magical self defense. The Earl of Tankerville delightedly agreed, and Crowley gained a new student.

George Montagu Bennet (1852–1931), 7th Earl of Tankerville.

The magicians were coming out of the woodwork: Jones and Fuller, now the Earl of Tankerville. Crowley pondered what could possibly happen next. Then he met Victor Neuburg.

Victor Benjamin Neuburg (1883–1940) was a Jewish poet and native Londoner, born in Islington to Bohemian merchant Carl Neuburg and his wife Jeannette (née Jacobs).[30] Carl left the country shortly after Victor was born, so Jeannette moved in with her mother, Rebecca, where the Jacobs family helped raise Victor.[31] His first published poem, "Vale Jehovah!," appeared in the October 25, 1903, issue of the *Freethinker,* which encouraged him to continue publishing regularly, including in *The Agnostic Journal.*[32] He was a young mystic who believed in reincarnation, vegetarianism, and the existence of a greater reality. Thinking Judeo-Christian religions a sham and finding spiritualism unsatisfying, he was searching for a genuine master.

When he met J. F. C. Fuller in 1906, Neuburg explained that he was studying medieval and modern languages at Trinity College. Fuller remarked on two coincidences: first, he too was a regular contributor to the *Agnostic Journal* and had admired Neuburg's writing. Second, his friend—poet and mystic Aleister Crowley—had also attended Trinity. Neuburg was very interested in meeting this friend, and Fuller happily supplied Crowley's address. Thus he wrote and arranged a meeting.

Crowley stepped into Neuburg's room and introduced himself. Neuburg was a small man, with a head much too large for his slight body. His lips, Crowley thought, were three times too thick for his face, and he later characterized Neuburg as a "sausage-lipped songster of Steyning."[33] Despite this, his brown hair and distinguished features made him handsome. Crowley explained that he had read Neuburg's poetry and was very interested in it because it showed evidence of astral projection. No reply was necessary: Crowley could tell just by looking at him that Neuburg had a terrific capacity for magic. Neuburg confirmed this by stating he had practiced spiritualism and clairvoyance. As the two got to know each other that weekend, they became entranced with each other: Crowley with the apprentice poet and magician, and Neuburg with the older master.

Victor Benjamin Neuburg (1883–1940).

Despite the dons' objections, Neuburg invited Crowley to speak at Cambridge on Thursday, February 28, 1907. This "First Missionary Mission," as AC dubbed it, was one of many visits he would make to Neuburg's poetry club, the Pan Society, to read poetry, discuss magic, and recruit students into his fold. Neuburg in turn devoted himself to the study of magic.

A formative episode in Crowley's work occurred when he wrote to Jones on March 7, asking permission to take a vow of silence. Jones discouraged Crowley from using this fourth power of the Sphinx, and suggested an alternative: Crowley ought to vow to answer no questions for a week, punishing each violation of this oath with a razor-cut on the forearm. Crowley picked up the gauntlet. On the first day of his oath, he slipped twenty-four times, but with an equal number of gashes on his arm, he quickly learned. The next day, he slipped only twelve times, the total dwindling down to around seven for the following days. In all, he slipped seventy-two times in a week. The exercise taught Crowley an important lesson in vigilance: not only did it make him carefully measure his words and responses, but it raised his consciousness of the world around him. He was so impressed that he incorporated the lesson into his cannon of magical instructions as "Liber Jugorum."

Rose, seeing her husband's forearms covered with scabs and slices, hated the exercise. This friction further eroded their conjugal life and made him fear that she was interfering with the Great Work. With precious little in common, and Rose's drinking poisoning even that, Crowley moved into rooms on the fourth floor of 60 Jermyn Street, London, on the weekend of March 23–24.

Relieved to be alone, he worked to a peak at the end of May, when he took the oath of a Magister Templi (8°=3□) in the presence of "Tankerville." In so doing, Crowley vowed to emerge from the Ordeal of the Abyss and stand in the entrance hall to the Third Order as a purely magical entity, selfless and unattached. His task as a Master of the Temple was twofold: First, he had to found a temple (which was just the work he and Jones were doing). In addition, he vowed to interpret every event in his life as a particular dealing of God with his soul. While any person could theoretically take this oath to find the significance behind everything, the consequences for one unprepared for the grade of Magister Templi were terrible indeed; at the very least, it swept an inexperienced soul inexorably toward the Abyss.

The next day, Crowley and Tankerville arranged to take the magical retirement they'd planned since their first meeting. It was the perfect opportunity for both to study and learn. They planned to sail to Marseilles, Morocco, Mongolia, Gibraltar, and Spain, and began the voyage that June. Although Crowley attributed Montagu's claims of magical attack to paranoia, he taught him a protection technique to alleviate his worries. As Crowley wrote:

> Whenever he noticed his mother flying past the moon on her broomstick, he would perform a banishing ritual, and sail out in his astral body onto the word and chop the broomstick like Sigfried with the lance of Wotan, and down she would fall into the Straits of Gibraltar, plop, plop.[34]

As they journeyed, Crowley also wrote many of the pieces that would appear in *Konx Om Pax:* "The Mask of Gilt" (July 12), "There is No Other God than He" (July 13), "Return of Messalina" (July 22), and the piece considered by many to be his best poem, "La Gitana" (July 21). The last is about a Spanish gypsy who made Crowley forget his domestic troubles:

> Your hair was full of roses in the dewfall as we danced,
> The sorceress enchanting and the paladin entranced,
> In the starlight as we wove us in a web of silk and steel
> Immemorial as the marble in the halls of Boabdil,
> In the pleasaunce of the roses with the fountains and the yews
> Where the snowy Sierra soothed us with the breezes and the dews!

Crowley agreed with the critics, noting, "The Morocco poems seem to me about the best I have ever done."[35]

Before long, however, both men got on each other's nerves. Crowley tired of the Earl's incessant delusions, writing sarcastically in his journal for July 11, "I don't know about the Power of *Samadhi;* but I can tolerate Tankerville, and I want a new grade specially for *that.*" He summed up his feelings about Bennet in "The Suspicious Earl":

> There was a poor bedevilled Earl
> Who saw a Witch in every girl,
> A Wehr-Wolf every time one smiled,
> A budding Vampire in a child,
> A Sorcerer in every man,
> A deep-laid Necromantic plan
> In every casual word; withal
> Cloaked in its black horrific pall
> A Vehmgericht obscenely grim,
> And all designed—to ruin him![36]

Meanwhile, the earl tired of the master's constant lessons, telling Crowley, "I'm sick of your teaching, teaching, teaching as if you were God Almighty and I were a poor bloody shit in the street!" Shortly after they returned to Gibraltar on July 20, they had a row and parted. On July 25, they arrived in Southampton aboard the *Scharnhorst.*[37]

Throughout these adventures, Crowley continued to produce poetry. He had already completed in February the poems that made up *Clouds without Water.* Additional 1907 releases from SPRT included *Rosa Coeli, Rosa Inferni,* and *Rodin in Rime,* all of which featured color lithographs of Rodin's watercolors. The last book was a bold gesture on Crowley's part because it was fashionable to criticize Rodin at this time; but Crowley chose to defend and praise him instead. SPRT also reissued *Tannhäuser* and *The Mother's Tragedy.*

Finally, the winning essay on the works of Aleister Crowley appeared: *The Star in the West,* by J. F. C. Fuller, appeared as a prodigious, 328-page volume with white buckram covers gilt-stamped with Crowley's Magister Templi (8°=3□) emblem, or lamen. A vesica enclosed the lamen, which consisted of a crown with a sword's blade extending through and far above it, balancing on its tip a scale whose pans held the Greek letters alpha and omega; it also sported five V's, which represented Crowley's Magister Templi motto, *Vi Veri Vniversum Vivus Vici* ("By the power of truth, I have conquered the universe").

Although Crowley and Fuller released only one hundred copies of this signed and numbered edition,[38] it was significant in marking the appearance of Frater V.V.V.V.V., the Magister Templi.

Although Crowley professed not to accept this grade until 1909, he clearly claimed it much sooner: on May 30, 1907, five months after Jones declared him 8°=3□, he took his 8°=3□ oath with Montagu as a witness; he published *The Star in the West* with his Magister Templi lamen on the cover; and his diary from this period contains many references to the attainment, such as "I think this stamps me clearly as an 8°=3□ elect."[39] After returning to London from his trip with Montagu, Crowley mailed out cards which bore the lamen of V.V.V.V.V.; this mailing puzzled at least one recipient, who wrote to the *Daily Mirror:*

HOW THE MYSTIC SYMBOL AFFECTED OUR ARTIST. (*See Editorial*).

Contemporary cartoon about Crowley's Magister Templi lamen.

Two days ago I received the enclosed card anonymously, and just glancing at it briefly, thinking it an advertisement of some sort, I placed it on the mantlepiece.

Within a few minutes, disasters of a minor kind began to happen in my little home.

> First, one of my most valuable vases fell to the ground and was
> smashed to pieces. My little clock stopped—the clock was near the card—
> and then I discovered to my amazement that my dear little canary lay dead
> at the bottom of its cage![40]

Although the letter is unsigned, Crowley is likely the author.

Alas, *The Star in the West* turned out to be the name of a children's book
published in London the previous year.[41] This mix-up caused a chagrined
Fuller to publish an apologia that summer in the *Athenaeum:*

> I exceedingly regret that through an unfortunate coincidence my recently
> published volume *The Star in the West,* a critical essay upon the writings of
> Aleister Crowley, bears the same title as a Welsh story for children by Miss
> Mary Debenham, already published by the National Society. But for the
> fact that my work was already printed and bound before my attention was
> drawn to this point, I would willingly have changed the title. However,
> with the courteous consent of both publishers, the title is retained; and I
> trust this letter will save booksellers any inconvenience that might have
> arisen from this similarity of the titles.[42]

Unlike Crowley's postcard, no mishaps were reported with Fuller's book.

By this time, Crowley was living in London at Coram Street, and new
works continued to flow from his busy pen: he followed his poetic adaptation
of Poe's "The Tell-Tale Heart" and hymns to the Virgin Mary with "The Hermit," and "Empty-headed Athenians." Next, he worked on *Konx Om Pax,*
writing its prologue and dedication and designing its cover. That fall, Crowley
wrote the novella "Ercildoune" and the short story "The Wizard Way."[43]

Volume three of his collected *Works* was also in press at the time. Although
The Book of the Law had been typeset and slated to appear as an appendix with
a brief commentary,[44] Crowley scrapped the plan. Instead, the appendix
became a bibliography of Crowley's published works up through 1906, compiled by Duncombe-Jewell. Despite intentional omissions—notably, *White
Stains* and *Snowdrops from a Curate's Garden*—the bibliography was excellent
and progressive;[45] information on print runs, paper type, and binding clarified
to all how fine and collectible Crowley's first editions were.

Familial tension finally erupted at the end of October, when Crowley received
a grocer's bill for the 120 bottles of liquor that Rose had purchased over the
past five months. Pondering where the devil Rose could have stashed a bottle
of liquor a day, Crowley searched the house but found no trace of alcohol anywhere. He had to assume she drank it all. Armed with the evidence he needed,
Crowley confronted his wife with the facts. She admitted to drinking heavily,
and Crowley sent her to Leicester to dry out for two months.

When he first read *Sri Brahma Dhàra* ("Shower from the Highest") by yogi Mahatma Sri Agamya Guru Paramahamsa (born c. 1841),[46] Crowley had heard that the fierce author was nicknamed the Tiger Mahatma and that he referred to seekers who were too meek for his tastes as "sheep." A retired judge, he devoted himself to religion and was described by German philologist and orientalist Max Müller (1823–1900) as the only Indian saint he had ever known. His temper was both fierce and legendary, which seemed to attract—and ultimately repel—his followers.[47] Back on November 13, when the guru was on his second trip to London, Crowley had sent him a cryptic letter. "If you are the one I seek," the note read, "this will suffice." He had enclosed his name and address and awaited a reply. A response had come the next day, and several days later Crowley had begun meeting the guru for instructions on yoga.

The "Tiger Mahatma," Sri Agamya Guru Paramahamsa.

That was last fall. Now that Agamya had returned to London, Crowley rejoined him and his "tiger cubs" at 60 South Audley. Before long, however, Crowley and Agamya had "a devil of a row"[48] at a meeting of students. In response, AC asked Fuller—who, he knew, was well versed in both yoga and Agamya's writings (of which he thought little)—to attend a meeting the following Sunday. Fuller went, and his disdain for the proceedings was evident. After ninety minutes' talk, the yogi grew upset with Fuller, crying out, "You pig-faced man! You dirty fellow, you come here to take away my disciples …

Crowley send this pig-one, eh?" At that, Fuller politely took his hat and cane and walked to the door. Before closing it behind himself, Fuller poked his head back in and, in Hindi, replied, "Shut up, you son of a sow!"[49] Fuller could hear the yogi's characteristic fit of anger as he closed the door and walked away.

Agamya's concerns may have been well-founded. Crowley, trying to found an order with Jones, sought students, and the same purposefulness that caused Tankerville to exclaim "I'm sick of your teaching, teaching, teaching" may have made Agamya uneasy: the Tiger Mahatma's claim that AC took away his students may reflect either a concern or the truth.

Crowley's results with magic began to resemble those he obtained in Cairo in 1904. Crossing the Abyss required that he release everything dear to him: his wife, daughter, and that one item for which he had fought so hard—his holy guardian angel. The lesson, he learned, was not to lose these things but to be able to release them and act without attachment; for, that fall, Crowley realized his holy guardian angel was still with him. "I can, I know, get into touch with Adonai at will," he recorded in his diary.[50] *Adonai* was the Hebrew word for "lord," and was used as a title of the holy guardian angel.

On October 30, Crowley got it in writing. That evening, the automatic writing "Liber VII" was penned, the first of a series of "Holy Books" that Crowley claimed were dictated by his holy guardian angel, Aiwass. In one sitting of two and a half hours, Crowley took down its seven chapters, one for each of the traditional astrological planets; although longer than *The Book of the Law,* it took thirty fewer minutes to write. "Liber VII," Crowley explained, was an account of "the voluntary emancipation of a certain Exempt Adept from his Adeptship. These are the birth-words of a Master of the Temple."[51]

Immediately after finishing VII, he began another. Throughout this writing, Crowley basked in the trance of *samadhi,* his own identity dissolved into the cosmic dance, recording passively the dictation of his inner voice.[52] These writings continued intermittently until November 3, when he finished "Liber Cordis Cincti Serpente," or "The Book of the Heart Girt about by the Serpent," the longest of the Thelemic Holy Books. Each of its five chapters (one for each element) contains sixty-five verses describing the relationship of an Adeptus Minor (5°=6□) with his holy guardian angel.

Ever since Kangchenjunga, Crowley and Jones met regularly to discuss, compare and practice magic. They knew they held the key to a newer and more potent formula of initiation than that of old, and this led Crowley to write:

> O restless rats that gnaw the bones
> Of Aristophanes and Paul!
> Come up to me and Mr. Jones
> And see the rapture of it all![53]

For the past year, however, their lack of a third member to form a governing triad had stalled their formation of a magical order.

On November 15, Crowley visited Jones with a solution: his bright friend, Frater Per Ardua ad Astra ("To the stars through great effort"), also known as Frater Non Sine Fulmine ("Not without a thunderbolt"), known among mundane men as Captain J. F. C. Fuller, would be the third. Jones considered the proposition and consented to forming the triad.

The A∴A∴, commonly known as the Argenteum Astrum or Silver Star, successor to the GD, was born.

Through the remainder of that year, automatic writings continued to pour from Crowley's pen. On November 25 he wrote "Liber LXVI," or "Stellae Rubae." Its contents are cryptically described as "a secret ritual of Apep, the Heart of IAO-OAI, delivered unto V.V.V.V.V. for his use in a certain matter of Liber Legis."[54] The veiled passages of this writing become clear when they are understood to describe a sexual ritual with his current mistress, a golden-haired, green-eyed woman by the name of Ada Leverson. Her name appears as an acronym of the first two lines:

> Apep deifieth Asar.
> Let excellent virgins evoke rejoicing, son of Night! ...
> There shall be a fair altar in the midst, extended upon a black stone.
> At the head of the altar gold, and twin images in green of the Master. In the midst a cup of green wine. At the foot the Star of Ruby. The altar shall be entirely bare.

And so on. She is also "the gilded lily with geranium lips" in Crowley's short story, "Illusion d'Amoureux," which opens with the description:

> Kindlier than the moon, her body glowed with more than harvest gold. Fierier than the portent of a double Venus, her green eyes shot forth utmost flames. From the golden chalice of love arose a perfume terrible and beautiful, a perfume strong and deadly to overcome the subtler fragrance of her whole being with its dominant, unshamed appeal.[55]

Ada Esther Leverson, née Beddington (1862–1933), a dozen and one years older than Crowley, was an attractive author whose first novel, *The Twelfth Hour*, Grant Richards had published that year (1907). Although she had known all the important literary people since the 1880s, she made no attempt to write until Oscar Wilde—who dubbed her "The Sphinx" for her "strange, enigmatic expression"—suggested in 1892 that she contribute to the magazines *Black and White* and *Punch*. She did and by 1903 had a regular column, "White and Gold," in the *Referee*. She had married young and hastily—at age nineteen, she married Ernest David Leverson (c. 1851–1921), an East Indian merchant eleven years her senior, at Marylebone.[56] She had a daughter, Violet, around 1890, but nevertheless found marriage dissatisfying.[57] Finding divorce too scandalous, she simply split with her husband and carried on affairs with William

Ulick O'Connor Cuffe the fourth Earl of Desart, Prince Henri d'Orléans, and George Moore. "To marry at Hastings would be to repent at St. Leonard's," she often joked, and Crowley had to agree with another of Wilde's characterizations: she was the wittiest person he had ever met.[58] Reviewing her works, Crowley called her "easily the daintiest and wittiest of our younger feminine writers."[59] However, neither left much record of the affair; it appears to have been a brief and convenient tryst for them both.[60] Crowley followed Wilde in carrying on her nickname, dedicating to her the sensuous poem "The Sphinx" in *The Winged Beetle* (1910).

Ada Leverson (1862–1933).

On December 3, Crowley scribbled down a series of sigils representing the genii of the twenty-two paths of the reverse side of the Tree of Life—the World of Shells known as the Qlippoth—and the genii of the twenty-two paths of the kabbalah, corresponding to the twenty-two major cards of the tarot. This continued to December 5 and 6, when he received twenty-two verses describing "the cosmic process so far as it is indicated by the Tarot Trumps."[61] He also received the names of the genii whose sigils he recorded several days previously. This constituted "Liber Arcanorum," one of the more puzzling and inaccessible of the Holy Books, which, some believe, holds the key to a grimoire of magic dealing with the reverse side of the Tree of Life.

On December 8, Crowley took a break from being Aiwass's scribe and returned to Cambridge despite official protestations. This time he met Norman Mudd (1889–1934) of Manchester, the bright son of a poor certified school-master, William Dale Mudd (b. 1861) and his wife Emma (born c. 1860).[62] Born in Prestwich, Lancashire, Norman was the middle of three children, his other siblings being older sister Nellie (b. 1887) and younger sister Era (born c. 1894).[63] Norman attended Ducie Avenue Schools,[64] earned a mathematics scholarship to Cambridge, and had just entered Trinity that July. Physically short and unattractive, he introduced himself with his meek trademark state-ment, "You won't remember me. My name's Mudd." His intellect, however, was as virile as any: a Freethinker, he was a friend of Neuburg's and belonged to his Pan Society. He and Crowley spent hours talking. As Mudd recalled, "I then understood for the first time what life was or might be; and the spark of that understanding has been in me ever since, apparently unquenchable, always working."[65] Captivated by the magician, Mudd felt that magic was the only thing he had encountered that gave his life any meaning or value, and he gladly agreed to distribute Crowley's books on campus.

The automatic writing "Liber Porta Lucis, Sub Figura X" ("The Book of the Gate of Light") followed on December 11 and 12. Its brief text described how the Masters sent forth Frater V.V.V.V.V. as their messenger, giving their message and exhorting men to take up the Great Work. In short, it was an invitation to the A∴A∴. The number of this book, ten, was that of Malkuth, the sphere on the Tree of Life where the initiate symbolically begins.

"Liber Tau" followed the next day. The book divided the Hebrew alphabet into seven triads that represented "ideas relating respectively to the Three Orders comprised in the A∴A∴."[66] Its number, four hundred, is that of the Hebrew letter Tau, under which the remaining twenty-one letters are sub-sumed.

Later that day, he penned "Liber Trigrammaton" (XXVII). This book syn-thesized the Chinese duality of yin-yang (represented by the solid and broken lines of the I Ching) with the Tao (represented in this system by a dot). The result was twenty-seven trigrams and their corresponding text. Crowley equated this book with the Stanzas of Dzyan, upon which *The Secret Doctrine,* the cornerstone of Blavatsky's Theosophical movement, was a comment.

Finally that winter, Crowley received "Liber DCCCXIII vel Ararita." Its seven chapters described "a very secret process of initiation"[67] whereby any idea is reduced to unity by synthesis, then drawn beyond by the method itself.

The significance of these texts—from Stellae Rubae to Ararita—is that Crowley would ultimately place them in the same category as *The Book of the Law:* immutable revealed texts transmitted through him by a higher intelli-gence. Crowley would eventually devote time to explaining the contents of some of these books;[68] however, the meaning of others remains unclear to this day. Regardless, they represented an important spiritual advancement. On December 15, he wrote in his diary, "not since my attainment in October has there been any falling away whatever. I am able to do automatic writing at will … I cannot doubt that I am an 8°=3□ … At last I've got to a stage where desire has utterly failed; I want nothing."

The time to advertise the A.'.A.'. came at the beginning of 1908. To this end, Crowley commissioned Walter Scott to print five hundred copies of *Konx Om Pax* for SPRT. The book was one of Crowley's more enigmatic offerings, ranking up there with *The Sword of Song* for its stupefication value. Its title derived from a phrase used in Greek mystery religions; heated debate has long surrounded its meaning, but the GD equated it with the Egyptian *Khabs Am Pekht,* "light in extension." Illumination. Hence, Crowley subtitled the book "Essays in Light." Adding even more mystery, the black cover sported a curious design that careful investigation revealed was the title, stretched long and thin across the entire front cover so that it was nearly illegible. The book opened with quotes—in their original languages—from various religious and philosophical sources, including the Qur'an, Gnostic texts, Tao Teh King (Tao Te Ching), and the Stele of Ankh-f-n-Khonsu. The dedication left no doubt that Crowley was writing for a mystical society:

> To all and every person in the whole world who is without the Pale of the Order; and even to Initiates who are not in possession of the Password for the time being …[69]

The text itself was a mixed bag of essays: "The Wake World" was an allegorical account of initiation, using the symbolism of kabbalah and the tarot. The skit "Ali Sloper, or the 40 Liars" parodied several GD members, himself, and a yuletide argument between Bowley and Bones (Crowley and Jones) on the nature of truth. The philosophical essay "Thien Tao" followed, and "The Stone of the Philosophers," a collection of poems written during his association with Tankerville, concluded the volume.

Although the book is truly clever and witty, it bombed like a joke that needed explaining. *The Scotsman* considered it "more tolerable in its verse than its prose, for a poet is not expected to be sensible." Ironically, a reviewer for *John Bull*—which would make Crowley's destruction its personal crusade only three years later—was among the few to see its humor: "I was moved to so much laughter that I barely escaped a convulsion."[70] Perhaps the most critical review came from Mathers, who, objecting to its description of him as a thief, sicced his solicitors, Messrs. Nussey and Fellowes, on the author. Crowley replied simply, "I care as little for your threats of legal action as for your client's threats of assassination … I am surprised that a firm of your standing should consent to act for a scoundrel."[71]

CHAPTER EIGHT

Singer of Strange
and Obscene Gods

In February, 1908, Rose completed two months of treatment for alcoholism. The Crowleys marked the occasion with a visit to Eastbourne, where he had set records thirteen years ago for scaling Beachy Head. Just as climbing had brought young Alec from the brink of death as a youngster, they now went on some easy climbs for Rose's health. She seemed happy and cured of her drinking. During the visit, Crowley took five days to write *The World's Tragedy*, his autobiographical indictment of Victorian England. In terms of imagination, expression, and meter, Crowley ranked it among his best works. Both his wife and his muse had returned.

After a fortnight of vacationing, the Crowleys moved into a new residence at 21 Warwick Road. It was let in Rose's name, because Crowley, finding his fortune dwindling, feared he might not be able to assume responsibility for the rent. Within days of the move, Rose began drinking more than ever. Alcohol made her irritable, and the couple constantly bickered. Powerless to stop her yet unable to watch her abuse herself, Crowley went to stay with Monsieur and Madame Bourcier at the Hotel de Bois, 50 rue Vavin, Paris. It was a popular destination for expatriate writers and artists through the 1920s and 1930s, such as American journalist and anarchist Louise Bryant, British novelist Ford Maddox Ford, American critic and essayist Harold Edmund Stearns, Czech-American artist Jan Matulka, and Budapest photojournalist Robert Capa;[1] American diplomat Howard R. Simpson had lived there while an art student, and recalled it as a *hôtel de passe,* or house of prostitution.[2] Disillusioned by the unfulfilled promise of his wife's recovery, Crowley would have stayed in Paris indefinitely, had not his father-in-law, Reverend Kelly, written a few weeks later that the coast was clear. Rose's family and friends had pressured her into moderation.

He returned to London and resumed business as usual, looking up Alfred Richard Orage (1873-1934), publisher of *The New Age* magazine and secretary of the Society for Psychical Research. They had first met two years ago at the Society's meetings, where Crowley reportedly asked him, "By the way, what number are you?" Orage, unsure what the hell he meant, gave the first number that popped into his head: twelve. Crowley's eyes had widened in response. "Good God, are you really? I'm only seven."[3] Since that peculiar introduction, Crowley became "Orage's intimate friend."[4] *The New Age* reviewed both *The Star in the West* and *Konx Om Pax,* and ran his poem "The Pentagram."[5] Likewise, at the present meeting with Orage, Crowley arranged to publish "The Suffragette: A Farce" in the May 30 issue. The piece appeared under the pseudonym Lavinia King, a name Crowley would later use as a character in *Moonchild* (1929).[6] He intended to contribute more, but Orage's lover, Beatrice Hastings, claims she blocked Crowley from filling the journal's pages with what she considered his "turgid out-pourings."[7]

Crowley also met with Irish author and journalist Frank Harris (1856–1931), currently editor of London's *Vanity Fair* magazine. Harris was well known in his time for his irascible personality and friendships with the famous, and he is remembered for his many sexual exploits, detailed in his multivolume (and at one time banned) memoirs, *My Life and Loves* (1922).[8] Over the next year, Crowley would publish many of his cosmopolitan exploits in this magazine, ranging from serialized pieces such as "The Expedition to Chogo Ri" and "On a Burmese River" to short articles like "With a Madman on the Alps."[9]

Although London offered business, it could not return his wife. True, no one had seen Rose drinking. But Crowley knew something was wrong, and soon discovered she was sneaking drinks when she thought nobody was watching. Moreover, in her drunken rages, she locked him out of the house, insulted his guests, and generally became hysterical.[10] Sad and disappointed, he sent her back to the doctor. "I wonder why you didn't put your foot down a year ago," was all his brother-in-law Gerald could say when he visited at the end of April.

Gerald was right. His gesture was too little too late. Rose's drinking had exacerbated so much that her doctor visits were futile. Crowley packed his bags and told her, "When you fall down the stairs in a drunken stupor and kill yourself, I don't want anyone to say I hit you with a crowbar. I cannot live in the same house with a dipsomaniac, and I shall not return until you are cured." Given her past relapses, Crowley held out little hope for recovery. On May 23, he wrote to Fuller, perhaps a little too eagerly:

> I don't think we should shut our eyes to the fact that I am now a bachelor
> to all intents and purposes; and what is better, one in the glorious and
> unassailable position of not being able to marry if I want to![11]

Thus, he returned to Paris to look up some friends and take model Nina Olivier—a dedicatee in *The Star and the Garter,* "The Ordeal of Ida Pendragon," and *Rodin in Rime*—as a lover.

He also met artist's model Euphemia Lamb (c. 1889–1957), of Greenheys, Manchester. Born Nina Forrest, she was nicknamed Euphemia by artist Henry Lamb (1883-1960), who would later become an established war artist and portrait painter. She met him in 1905, married him in 1906 after becoming pregnant, and moved with him to Paris in 1907, where she sat for artists like Augustus John, James Dickson Innes, Ambrose McEvoy, and Edward Gore. Her best-known likeness is a Jacob Epstein bust, which he completed in 1908.[12] Euphemia had many liaisons in both England and France, leading Vanessa Stephen to observe how "interesting impure women are to the pure.... I see her as someone in mid ocean, struggling, diving, while I pace my bank."[13] This resulted in a jealous and tempestuous marriage, and when she met Crowley, she had recently separated from her husband. "A virgin always does the wrong thing at the right time," she told AC,[14] and became his lover. "She was incomparably beautiful," Crowley wrote, "capable of stimulating the greatest extravagances of passion."[15] Happy, witty, and bright, she could have become Crowley's *grande passion,* but he wasn't looking for anything so complicated as a relationship. Crowley wrote "After Judgement" for her—dedicating it, none too obliquely, to "Ophelia L."—and declared it one of the most passionate poems in the English language. "Telepathy" he dedicated even more overtly to "Euphemia L." Other poems in her honor included "The Wings," "The Eyes of Dorothy," "The Silence of Columbine," and "Belladonna," all bearing the discrete dedication to "Dot" or "Dot L." All of these would appear in *The Winged Beetle* (1910).

Victor Neuburg soon joined them in Paris to continue his magical training. At this time, Crowley learned that Neuburg was a gifted materializing medium, which is to say he had an uncanny ability to cause the spirits that they evoked to take on a definite, visible form. While Neuburg lacked the discipline to do it alone, he experienced spectacular results with Crowley's help. In one incident, a figure appeared in a locked room with them for nearly an hour, vanishing only when the magicians became exhausted. This ability made him an ideal partner: whereas Crowley previously relied upon faith or, at best, a form half-visible through clouds of Dittany of Crete, there was no doubt with Neuburg: entities appeared visibly at his bidding.

On July 31, they left Paris for Bordeaux, thus beginning a walking trip through Spain. In a letter to Fuller, Crowley wrote, "We've done 140 miles of hot, dusty mountain-road in a week, which isn't bad."[16] It was on this trip that Crowley analyzed his drug experiences in "The Psychology of Hashish."[17]

While swimming at a Spanish waterfall, Crowley noticed Victor had a varicocele and sent him to a physician. The result, Crowley reported, cured his sexual neurosis and unleashed his poetic talent. It seems strange that Crowley could notice a varicose vein on Neuburg's penis. Indeed, this incident may point to the beginning of their homosexual relationship. Edward Carpenter's (1844-1929) controversial book *The Intermediate Sex*[18]—which influenced Neuburg's opinions toward sexuality—appeared at this time. Carpenter was a lecturer, pacifist, political activist, and advocate of sexual freedom; *The Intermediate Sex* argued that homosexuality was biologically determined and, therefore, not a sin. Neuburg's poetry from this period depicts his struggle with both magic and sin as he and his mentor trekked through the Spanish countryside:

> Sweet wizard, in whose footsteps I have trod
> Unto the shrine of the most obscene god ...
> Let me once more feel thy strong hand to be
> Making the magic signs upon me! Stand,
> Stand in the light, and let mine eyes drink in
> The glorious vision of the death of sin.[19]

On August 28, 1908, they abandoned the idea of walking to Gibraltar, continuing instead to Granada and Rondon, where they caught a boat to Gibraltar. On September 13, Neuburg left to visit his relatives. At a loss, Crowley wrote his marvelous essay on questions and assertions, "The Soldier and the Hunchback ! & ?"[20]

Two days later, he sailed back to London and checked Rose's progress. Her drinking, he discovered, was worse than ever, so he returned to Paris, taking their daughter, Lola, with him. At best, the act might induce Rose to comply with her treatment; at the very least, it would keep the child out of harm's way.

On October 1, Crowley began a magical retirement dubbed "John St. John,"[21] whereby he hoped to demonstrate how any person could conduct a magical retirement for a fortnight while still living a mundane work a day life. Each day, he practiced *hatha yoga* and his rewritten, solitary version of "Liber Pyramidos" in order to demonstrate how any person could attain to the knowledge and conversation of their holy guardian angel.

The same evening he began his retirement, Nina Olivier introduced Crowley to Parisian model Mary Waska, whom he described as a redheaded bundle of mischief. He bought her dinner, then brought her to his room to make love. Naked, she reminded Crowley of Corregio's (1489?–1534) portrayal of Antiope.[22] Under this inspiration, he penned "The Two Secrets," which would later appear in *The Winged Beetle* (1910).

In November, Crowley purchased Maugham's newest novel, *The Magician*. It was the story of blubbery, debased magician Oliver Haddo and his victimization of an innocent couple. As he read, something about the book struck him as vaguely familiar. Then it dawned on him that many of Haddo's words were his own, uttered in conversations with Maugham at Le Chat Blanc. In fact, Haddo's entire character was modeled on him. Crowley was flattered.

Nevertheless, something else about the book seemed familiar. On closer inspection, it appeared that Maugham had inserted long unacknowledged quotes from magical texts that Crowley had recommended to him. As he read, Crowley recognized passages lifted wholesale from Mathers's *The Kabbalah Unveiled* (1887), Franz Hartmann's *The Life and Doctrines of Paracelsus* (1891), and A. E. Waite's translation of Éliphas Lévi's *Rituel et Dogme de la Haute Magie* (1896). He also noted portions that paralleled books by Mabel Collins and H. G. Wells.

Crowley wrote up an exposé and submitted it to *Vanity Fair*. Editor Frank Harris was incredulous until Crowley brought a stack of books into his office and proved his point. However, the piece was too long to use in its full form, so an edited version appeared in the December 30, 1908, issue as "How to Write a Novel! After W.S. Maugham."[23] As a final ironic twist, Crowley published it under the pseudonym Oliver Haddo.

When Crowley and Maugham met a few weeks after the article appeared, Maugham was good-humored about it all. He laughingly admitted that his book contained even more unacknowledged quotes than the article mentioned. Crowley replied, "Harris cut my article by two-thirds for lack of space. You know, I almost wish that you were an important writer." Crowley's statement is tinged with jealousy, since Maugham, after ten years of failure as a playwright, now had four plays running in London's West End and was the talk of the town. Crowley's own works, meanwhile, remained unsuccessful: book sales were slow, and he had released nothing since *Konx Om Pax* at the beginning of the year.

That changed around New Year's Day, when his next book, a collection of devotional poems to the Virgin Mary, appeared. The title came from the "password" Crowley had chosen randomly at the autumnal equinox of 1907 when the book was written: *Amphora*. The book was anonymous, "Privately printed for the Authoress and her intimates" by the Arden Press. Its epilogue contained one of Crowley's classic acrostics:

> Transcend, O Mage, thy soul redeemed!
> Her mercy shone where sorrow steamed.
> Exalted in the skies of even
> Virtue hath cleared thy way to Heaven.
> In darkness hides the glittering ore.
> Revealed thy Light, O mystic lore
> Given by God, lest I should err
> In dexter or in sinister.
> Now Mary Virgin to my speech
> Married Her fire that all and each
> At last should gather to the Tryst
> Ripe suns arisen above the mist!
> Yea! Thou hast given me favour! Yea!
> In utmost love and awe we pray;
> Devoted to Thy reverence
> Enkindle I the sweet incense.
> Secure from all the fears that chill
> In peace from them that rage and kill;
> Receive, O Queen, the glad Oration
> Even from a lost and pagan nation.
> But Thou will make us wholly fit
> Unto Thy grace and care of it.
> Till all the Elixir do receive
> (Amen) to heal the hurt of Eve.

Reading the first letter of the first word of each line then the first letter of the last word of each line reveals a phrase certain to thrill schoolboys and shock pontiffs: "The Virgin Mary I desire, but arseholes set my prick on fire." A simpler acrostic appears in the initial letters of the prologue:

> Those Pagans gazing on the Heavenly Host
> Were blest of Father, Son, and Holy Ghost;
> And me, though I be as an heathen mage,
> Thou wilt accept in this my pious page.

Both hidden messages went unnoticed by readers, and it is just as well, as Crowley's intent was not to blaspheme. The book originated with the realization that several of his poems in praise of non-Christian goddesses (and, often, gods) became perfectly acceptable hymns by merely changing the name to Mary and perhaps changing a key word or two. He thought this significant, and set about to write a set of hymns to the Virgin Mary from the mind set of a pious Christian. As Crowley explained, "I do not see why I should be confined to one life. How can one hope to understand the world if one persists in regarding it from the conning tower of one's own personality?"[24] The acrostics were merely a sign not to take the work *too* seriously.

When Catholic circles responded enthusiastically to the book, Crowley removed the epilogue and submitted it to the firm of Burns & Oates for republication. Crowley did nothing to dispel rumors that its author was a leading London actress. Some time later, Wilfrid Meynell (1852–1948), who ran the company, discovered who the "authoress" really was. In response, his wife passed out, and he pulled the book, returning the unsold sheets to Crowley.

The New Age, reviewing Crowley's reissue of the book two years later under the title *Hail Mary,* found the poems "all marked by that facility and freedom of diction and metrical fluency that are such striking features of the author's profaner works," but concluded, "Personally, I find Mr. Crowley the devotee of Mary considerably less interesting and much less amusing than Mr. Crowley the singer of strange and obscene gods, Abracadabras, and things one doesn't mention."[25]

The doctors gave up on Rose at the beginning of 1909. She was uncooperative with her regimen, refusing to stop drinking, and her only hope was institutionalization for two years. Only then could doctors control and monitor her behavior. Rose refused.

Hearing this news, Crowley too gave up. He claimed he still loved her, but could no longer bear to watch her kill herself. He demanded a divorce. So that the proceedings would not reflect poorly on her, Crowley agreed for Rose to divorce him for infidelity. Although Crowley says he manufactured the necessary evidence, he didn't have to look too far, given his recent trysts. Despite this wrinkle, Rose and Aleister still lived together and saw each other daily.

His friendship with Gerald Kelly, however, became strained, and they eventually parted. Gerald's bitterness would never fade; when Crowley called on him in the 1930s, an immediate altercation broke out, leaving Gerald too furious to speak for five minutes afterward. Although Crowley resentfully characterized him as a "quack painter," Kelly would be commissioned to do the state portraits of King George VI and Queen Elizabeth in 1938, knighted in 1945, and elected president of the Royal Academy in 1949, among other honors. He is remembered as "the most reliable portrait painter of his time."[26]

The order known as A∴A∴ came into its own in the first months of 1909. Although commonly referred to as the Argenteum Astrum (Latin for "Silver Star") or some variation thereon, the true name of the order was never publicly disclosed. As a preliminary stroke, Crowley anonymously released the tables of correspondences under the title *777* (1909), a number which refers to the flashing sword of creation superimposed on the Tree of Life. Walter Scott published the slim fifty-four–page volume. While the *Occult Review* praised its comprehensiveness in publishing what "has been jealously and foolishly kept secret in the past,"[27] Allan Bennett's *Buddhist Review* curiously found it obscure and undignified. In his personal copy of the book, GD member F. Leigh Gardner called it "Borrowed Plumes" from the Golden Dawn.[28] Indeed, the book expanded on the original tables of correspondence compiled by MacGregor Mathers, Allan Bennett, and George Cecil Jones.

Crowley had no time to worry about reactions to his newest book. Now that the A∴A∴ was taking on students, it was time to go public with the order's official organ. He had already laid the groundwork by December, 1908, and on the spring equinox of 1909—March 20—Crowley unveiled to the unsuspecting public his biannual journal, *The Equinox*.

But, he thought, how would it look for a great teacher to make vast sums of money on his occult knowledge? He would look like a con man, peddling "Secret Knowledge" to the man on the street while he himself lived like a king. No, it had to look like the rewards of initiation were so great that material reward was meaningless. He decided to make no money on this venture; his books on magic had to sell at or below cost. Thus no one could accuse him of profiting from his learning.

The Equinox was his most ambitious project to date. A ponderous, hardover journal, its first number was 255 pages long plus a 139-page supplement. It featured pieces by Crowley, Neuburg, and Fuller, plus contributions from *Vanity Fair* editor Frank Harris, Lord Dunsany, and chemist Edward Whineray. The title page said it all:

THE EQUINOX
The Official Organ of the A∴A∴
The Review of Scientific Illuminism
"The Method of Science—The Aim of Religion"

The editorial announced the existence of the A∴A∴, calling on students to contact the chancellor at their business address. The chancellor was Frater NSF (None Sine Fulmine, "Not without a thunderbolt"), which was Fuller's motto as Adeptus Minor (5°=6□), the first grade in the Second Order.

The contents, almost entirely by Crowley, ranged widely. "An Account of A∴A∴" digested Eckhartshausen's *Cloud upon the Sanctuary,* borrowing freely from Madame de Steiger's translation. "Liber Librae" was an instruction on equilibrium, a lightly edited version of the GD's Practicus 3°=8□ paper on ethics.[29] "Liber E," aimed at the beginning student, gave basic instructions in journal-keeping, clairvoyance, and yoga, plus a recommended course of reading. Other pieces included "The Chymical Jousting of Brother Perardua" (an allegorical look at initiation), "At the Fork in the Roads" (a dramatization of Crowley's encounter with Althea Gyles), "The Soldier and the Hunchback: ! and ?," and Crowley's serialized biography by Fuller, "The Temple of Solomon the King." The special supplement featured Crowley's "John St. John" diary.

Even though Crowley priced *The Equinox* at cost, the production by Simpkin Marshall was nevertheless expensive. Fifty subscription copies sold at one guinea, while another thousand, issued in boards, went for five shillings. Nevertheless, the book sold like hotcakes and would have made money if Crowley's overhead wasn't so high.[30]

Reactions to the journal varied as widely as its contents. Reviewers from small journals like *Light* and the *Literary Guide* considered it "expensively printed lunacy ... in oriental-occidental jargon," but the big guns praised it: Frank Harris, who had a stake as an *Equinox* contributor, considered it permanent in both production and value in his *Vanity Fair* review. *The New Age* offered a mixed review, calling it "finely unpopular," but acknowledging it as "large and luxurious"; they recommended that readers to pick it up if only for Frank Harris's "The Magic Glasses," warning Crowley that "If *The Equinox* can live up to this standard it will be bought by the profane."[31] Meanwhile, the *Morning Leader* wrote:

> It is a sort of thing no fellow can understand. One gathers vaguely out of the confusion that it deals with such things as Magic, wizardry, mysticism and so on ... From frequent references to some people called The Brothers of the A∴A∴ one gathers that they have a lot to do with this weird venture; but a grim perusal of an article purporting to explain the Order ... leaves one without any real clue as to their identity.[32]

The *Review of Reviews* put it more succinctly: "A strange, weird, incomprehensible magazine is the *Equinox,* whose publication is a curious sign of the times."[33] These last reviews are probably how the typical reader took it: with confusion and consternation. Its message was clear enough to those who mattered, however, and with this publication the A∴A∴ began to enroll students. Its first member was Victor Neuburg, who signed his Probationer's Oath on April 8, taking the motto "Omnia Vincam" (I will conquer all):

I, Victor B. Neuburg, being of sound mind and body, on this 5th day of April 1909 ... do hereby resolve: in the Presence of Perdurabo a neophyte of the A∴A∴. To prosecute the Great Work: which is, to obtain a scientific knowledge of the nature and powers of my own being.

May the A∴A∴ crown the work, lend me of Its wisdom in the work, enable me to understand the work!

Reverence, duty, sympathy, devotion, assiduity, trust do I bring to the A∴A∴ and in one year from this date may I be admitted to the knowledge and conversation of the A∴A∴![34]

Other students signing Probationer's oaths included Richard Warren, Austin O. Spare, H. Sheridan Bickers, George Raffalovich, Everard Feilding, Herbert Inman, Charles Stansfeld Jones, and Kenneth Ward.

Richard Noel Warren (1882–1912) wrote the A∴A∴ on May 16,[35] enquiring about occult books, and within a month signed his Probationer's oath. The first of Charles and Edith Warren's three children, he was born in Heybridge, Surrey, during the winter of 1882, and as a young adult attended Bradfield College.[36] On October 28 and 29, 1907, he took and passed his final examinations for the Law Society, becoming a solicitor in London.[37] He also joined the Society for Psychical Research in 1908.[38] As with many of the A∴A∴'s promising first crop of students, Neuburg dedicated a poem, "The Poet's Song," to him in *The Triumph of Pan* (1910). Although Warren contributed a review to the third issue of *The Equinox,* he finally quit on October 14, 1910—shortly after his one-year probationary period. He instead applied for membership in A. E. Waite's version of the GD, the Independent and Rectified Order R.R. et A.C., on October 24 with the motto "Amor et Veritas."[39] He died on September 19, 1912, after ten days' struggle with acute lobar pneumonia that developed into pericarditis.[40]

Austin Osman Spare (1886–1956) was a handsome London artist with black curly hair and striking Mediterranean features. The fifth of six children born to London constable Philip Spare and his wife Eliza, his proclivity for drawing was encouraged by evening classes at the Lambeth Art School and later the Royal College of Art. At age seventeen, he sent two black-and-white drawings to the Royal Academy; both were accepted and one hung, making Spare the youngest exhibitor ever to be shown at the Royal Academy.[41] The following year, 1905, the academy accepted a work titled "The Resurrection of Zoroaster," which the press described as "a strange example of fantastic symbolism, gloomy, tragic and very original."[42] In 1905 he put out his first book, *Earth Inferno,* followed by *Book of Satyrs* (1907).[43] By October 1907, at age twenty, his first exhibition—at the Brunton Gallery in London's West End—caused quite a stir, causing *The Art Journal,* in its February 1908 issue, to proclaim, "There must be few people in London interested in art who do not know the name of Austin Osman Spare."[44] When Crowley apparently sought him out[45] in 1909, he was working on his masterwork, *The Book of Pleasure,*[46] which Freud would call "one of the most significant revelations of subcon-

scious mechanisms that had appeared in modern times."[47] Spare joined the
A∴A∴ on July 10, 1909, as Yihoveaum, a motto that merged the great
Hebrew and Sanskrit holy words *Jehovah* and *om*. Although Crowley, for a time,
called Spare his favorite student,[48] Spare stayed with the A∴A∴ but briefly,
contributing two drawings to the second issue of *The Equinox*. Disappointed,
Crowley felt Spare could not understand the system; however, Spare probably
left because his own philosophy of magic—involving automatic drawing, sig-
ilization, and the dual concepts of Zos (the body considered as a whole) and
Kia (the atmospheric "I")—was already fully developed and at variance with
Crowley's ideas at the time. As Ansell has suggested, Spare's artistic ethos of
blurring and defying categories was not well suited to Crowley's highly structured system.[49]

Horace Algernon Sheridan-Bickers (1883–1957)[50] signed up on July 23,
choosing the motto "Superabo" (I will excel). He was recently divorced from
his first wife, Hermione Henrietta Margaret, and remarried to Minnie Elizabeth Hefford (b. 1880), who went by the name Betty.[51] While a student, Sheridan-Bickers was president of the Cambridge University Sociological Society
and, as a doctor of laws,[52] a frequent lecturer at the Eighty Club, a group
within Britain's Liberal Party that promoted political education and organization during the years 1880 to 1978.[53] In November 1909, Sheridan-Bickers
also lectured for *The Equinox* at Cambridge University, where he became
acquainted with Crowley's lifelong friend, Louis Umfreville Wilkinson.[54] He
was also announced as lecturing on behalf of *The Equinox* throughout 1910.[55]
From there, Sheridan-Bickers would travel to British Columbia, lecturing,
working as a journalist, editing *The Spokesman* magazine, and helping establish
Crowley's magical organizations.[56] He would soon resettle in Los Angeles,
working as a journalist for the *Los Angeles Examiner*,[57] continuing lecturing,[58]
and writing the story and screenplay for the motion picture *Her Body in Bond*
(1918).[59] The latter is about "a show girl (of course she is poor but honest)
who, in her efforts to save the life of her consumptive husband, is subjected to
the insults of those who want to force money upon her—for a reason."[60]
Working from Los Angeles, he would become established as a drama critic for
the *London Daily Express* and, under the pen-name "Yorick," edited *Theatre
World and Illustrated Stage Review* in the 1920s.[61] For a time, he was also managing editor of *Hollywood Life: An International Journal of Motion Pictures*.[62] While
in Los Angeles, he and Betty served as Crowley's representatives in Hollywood,
playing an important role in promoting Crowley's works. H. Sheridan-Bickers
appears in the *Confessions* as "Gnaggs" in a long and obscure story about jealousy and herpes.[63] He died in San Mateo, California, on August 2, 1957.

Author George Raffalovich (1880–1958) joined the A∴A∴ on August 11
as Frater Audeo et Gaudeo (I dare and I rejoice). Born in Cannes to Ukranian
Jewish banker Gregor Raffalovich, his father died in Paris in 1881 shortly after
George's birth.[64] His mother was reputedly a countess descended from one of

Napoleon's ministers of finance, and George squandered his fortune on wild extravagances like buying a circus. Fortunately, his family had set money aside for him, and they pulled him out of the hole and set him back on his feet.[65] He had a *Bachelier ès Lettres* from Nancy-Université,[66] and when Crowley met him in London, Raffalovich was living in Putney and associated with *Vanity Fair* magazine.[67] He had recently published *Planetary Journeys and Earthly Sketches* (1908)—of which British novelist and political activist Israel Zangwill (1864–1926) wrote "Your trips to a Planet betray, if I may say so, a very modern feeling of the plasticity of the universe, together with a sense of the comparative values which to my mind is the highest manifestation of the human reason"[68]—followed by "Nadia," a short story of the Russian Revolution, in *The Idler*.[69] AC found him a gentleman with "a remarkable imagination and a brilliant ability to use the bizarre."[70] Seeing some of himself in Raffalovich—he had also spent his fortune and quarreled with his family, and now professed great interest and knowledge in magic—Crowley helped him to become naturalized in 1910. Raffalovich repaid the money AC lent him in cash, and immortalized him in his stories as Elphenor Pistouillat de la Ratisboisière.[71] He contributed regularly to *The Equinox*,[72] and participated in its London activities. Neuburg dedicated two pieces in *The Triumph of Pan*[73] to him as well.

George Raffalovich (1880–1958) in 1921.

Hon. Francis Henry Everard Joseph Feilding (1867–1936, commonly misspelled "Fielding") was an eleventh-generation descendant of King Henry VIII and Catherine of Aragon. The second son of the 8th Earl of Denbigh Rudolph

William Basil Feilding (1823–1892) and Mary Berkeley (d. 1901), he was brother to the current 9th Earl of Denbigh, Rudolph Robert Basil Aloysius Augustine Feilding. Everard Feilding had served as a midshipman in the Royal Navy and fought in the Egypt Campaign in 1882. Educated at Oscott, he was admitted to Trinity College in 1887, earned his bachelors of law degree in 1890, and was called to the bar in 1894.[74] Friends recalled him as "full of humour, possessed of very unusual abilities, well read, fond of argument in conversation, and with a fund of information on all the varied things in life he had come across."[75] He was also a gifted musician, able to sight-read the most difficult selections. He was also active as Secretary of the Society for Psychical Research from 1903 to 1920. After his brother Basil died in a boating accident in August 1906, Feilding's interest heightened, and he obtained "a reasonably extensive experience in the investigation of psychical phenomena and the advantage of a fairly complete education at the hands of fraudulent mediums."[76] He is well known as one of the investigators of Italian spiritualist medium Eusapia Palladino (1854–1918) in Naples; although initially convinced of her abilities, Feilding returned for another investigation in 1910 and concluded that she was a fraud.[77] As the character Lord Anthony Bowling in *Moonchild,* Crowley calls Feilding a familiar friend.

> He was a stout and strong man of nearly fifty years of age, with a gaze both intrepid and acute.… Haughtiness was here, and great good-nature; the intellect was evidently developed to the highest possible pitch of which man is capable; and one could read the judicial habit on his deep wide brows. Against this one could see the huge force of the man's soul, the passionate desire for knowledge which burnt in that great brain.…
>
> This man was the mainstay of the Society for Psychical Research. He was the only absolutely competent man in it.[78]

He joined the A∴A∴ on August 21, selecting as his motto "Ut Deum Inveniam" (That I will meet with God). With the onset of World War I, Feilding— as a barrister, a member of the Committee of Naval Censors' Press Bureau, and a Lieutenant in the Special Intelligence Department—would prove a valuable contact for Crowley.

Herbert Edward Inman was an engineer who had been elected to the Liverpool Engineering Society on November 29, 1905; he would go on to serve as a private with the Royal Engineers during World War I, receiving the Allied Victory and British War medals.[79] Inman joined the A∴A∴ on October 22, 1909, as Frater Amor Clavis Vitae (Love is the Key to Life). Although he recruited one other member, he soon faded from the A∴A∴'s ranks. Although Inman reportedly broke with Crowley over a bad debt,[80] the two remained in touch even in the 1940s.[81]

Charles Robert John Stansfeld Jones (1886–1950) became a probationer on December 24, taking the motto Unus in Omnibus (One in all), or VIO, in Fuller's presence. Jones was born in London on April 2, 1886, and baptized on June 1 at Saint Luke's in Chelsea, the youngest of seven children to iron merchant William John Jones and his wife Eliza.[82] In the summer of 1907 he married Prudence R. Wratton (born c. 1888), and several years later adopted a daughter, Deirdre, and son, Anthony.[83] Although he had sung in a choir, at age twenty he decided to disprove the tenets of mysticism; instead, the systems he sought to discredit fascinated him. In 1909 he bought *The Equinox* and joined the A∴A∴. He met Crowley at this time, but his primary instructor was Fuller. In May 1910, he moved to British Columbia, where he worked as an accountant and quickly became one of Crowley's most devoted followers; in later years, when a friend discovered Jones at the roadside staring sadly at his broken-down Ford, this acquaintance snidely suggested reading AC's erotic verse to the car. Jones replied, "I've already tried that, but she just drips oil."

Finally, there was Kenneth Martin Ward (1887–1927), whom Crowley had previously met at Wastdale Head during the winter of 1908. Friends described him as "Amazingly clever and full of the weirdest conglomeration of beliefs."[84] Born in 1887 in Cambridge to James and Mary Jane Ward,[85] he stood over six feet tall and dressed unconventionally. He was a well-rounded scholar and sportsman from Emmanuel who entered Cambridge in October 1906 on a physics and chemistry scholarship and got first class marks in his mathematics tripos. Besides intellectual pursuits, Ward was also an avid gymnast, boxer, and swimmer. Taking up sea-cliff climbing as an undergraduate, he made several historical ascents and, during a visit to the chalk cliffs of Wastdale Head that winter, met Crowley. Returning to school to find math and physics spiritually unsatisfying, he ventured instead into literature, philosophy, and art. This ultimately led him to pursue, through Crowley, an introduction to the Pan Society. He became one of the A∴A∴'s earliest members on May 25, 1909, actively recruiting three more probationers and helping to found the Cambridge Freethought Association to host Crowley's talks. (Ward himself was the president, and Pinsent and Neuburg the committee.) Neuburg dedicated "The Thinker" in his *The Triumph of Pan* to Ward.

Ward visited Crowley at Boleskine the summer of 1909 to discuss both business and pleasure. With the second issue of *The Equinox* in the works, AC turned his mind toward the third, fourth, and fifth issues, with plans to explain John Dee's Enochian magic. Since they were both climbers, conversation soon turned to sports. Ward mentioned he would like to learn to ski, and Crowley, who'd learned to skate and ski during his winters in St. Moritz, promised Ward one of his spare pairs of skis.

Unfortunately, he couldn't remember where he had placed either his Enochian tablets or his skis.

Rummaging through his attic on June 28, Crowley found more than he bargained for. Yes, he located the Enochian tablets. He even ran across his skis. Moreover, among the other items in storage, he found a nearly forgotten, long-lost relic: the original manuscript of *The Book of the Law.*

Kenneth Martin Ward (1887–1927).

An eerie feeling settled over Crowley as he looked at the pages. Up to that point, he had been working off a typescript of the book, assuming the original had been lost. But now...

As a Magister Templi, he was sworn to interpret every event as a dealing of God with his life. So what of this? Crowley reasoned that, just as the masters made sure he became interested in mountaineering so he could discover the GD, they now ensured that Ward would enter the picture and lead to the rediscovery of *The Book of the Law*. This event was designed, and it was of the utmost significance. It forced Crowley to take a more serious look at the book than he ever had before. He realized this was more than his destiny: it was his True Will.

CHAPTER NINE

The Vision and the Voice

His faith in the Secret Chiefs and their message renewed, Crowley returned to London with his students and took a flat at 124 Victoria Street as the offices of *The Equinox*. He decorated the rooms with red curtains, a stuffed crocodile, and several Buddhas, then began work on the second issue. It appeared on the autumnal equinox, September 20, 1909, with a colorful assortment of articles: Crowley contributed an essay on the psychology of hashish as "Oliver Haddo," his fictitious counterpart in Maugham's *The Magician*. Lord Dunsany (1878–1957) offered the short story "A Sphinx at Gizeh,"[1] Neuburg "The Lost Shepherd," Crowley's Cambridge follower G. H. S. Pinsent[2] "The Organ in King's Chapel, Cambridge," Allan Bennett "A Note on Genesis," and George Raffalovich "The Man-Cover." Spare provided illustrations for the article "A Handbook of Geomancy." Most significantly, Fuller, under Crowley's supervision, contributed the second installment of "The Temple of Solomon the King." This chapter recounted Crowley's initiation into the GD, reproducing every one of its First Order rituals. Crowley believed the Secret Chiefs had released him from his vow of secrecy; as *The Book of the Law* put it: "Behold! the rituals of the old time are black."[3] By publishing these secrets, he dissipated their power in favor of the new order.

The Veil of Isis was lifted, and the whole world looked on the undergarments of the GD. Crowley promised to remove even these in the next issue, which would contain the remainder of the GD corpus.

Meanwhile, *Clouds without Water* appeared under the pseudonym of Reverend C. Verey. The book is a farce, supposedly edited from a private manuscript to reveal the horrors to which Satan can drive lost sheep. Its preface contains the odd semibiographical lines, "the wife of the man, driven to drink and prostitution by the inhuman cruelty of his mistress," paralleling Crowley's personal problems. Poetry formed the bulk of the text, with ridiculously pious end notes on its content ("only a Latin dictionary can unveil the loathsome horror" of the word "fellatrix"). It closes with a prayer for redemption.

While many of the poems grew out of his affair with Lola (Vera Bentrovata), Crowley loses sight of her part way through and recalls Rodin's student, sculptress Kathleen Bruce. Poems V, VI, and VII are for her, and her name even appears as an acrostic in the opening "Terzain":

> King of myself, I labour to espouse
> An equal soul. Alas! how frail I find
> The golden light within the gilded house.
> Helpless and passionate, and weak of mind!
> Lechers and lepers!—all as ivy cling,
> Emasculate the healthy bole they haunt.
> Eternity is pregnant; I shall sing
> Now—by my power—a spirit grave and gaunt
> Brilliant and selfish, hard and hot, to flaunt
> Reared like a flame across the lampless west,
> Until by love or laughter we enchaunt,
> Compel ye to Kithairon's thorny crest—
> Evoe! Iacche! consummatum est.

Her new husband, explorer Robert Scott, was reportedly furious to find his wife's name in this bizarre book.

The sharp division between Crowley's private and magical lives was more pronounced than ever. Although magic proceeded well, he nevertheless spent much of that summer in the Thames valley, brooding over his forthcoming divorce. As he put it, "My soul was badly bruised by the ruin of my romance."[4]

Seeking solace in his childhood nostalgia for weirs, Crowley spent time late that summer in a canoe on Boulter's Lock, Maidenhead, on the Thames thirty miles west of London. There, in a sixty-hour marathon session, he wrote his classic mystic poem, "Aha!" In the form of a dialogue between the teacher Marsyas (Crowley) and his pupil Olympas (any seeker), it describes the many mystical states he had experienced along the path to becoming a Master of the Temple, including the subjects of equilibrium, the veil of matter *(paroketh),* the knowledge and conversation of the holy guardian angel, the vision of the universal peacock *(atmadarshana),* the ordeal of the Abyss, the vanity of speech, the destruction of the ego, and the bliss of transcendence *(ananda).* In particular, his discussion of the ordeal of the Abyss poignantly mirrors the heartache he was feeling as he penned these verses:

> MARSYAS. Easy to say. To abandon all,
>   All must be first loved and possessed.
>   Nor thou nor I have burst the thrall.
>   All—as I offered half in jest,
>   Sceptic—was torn away from me.
>   Not without pain! THEY slew my child,

> Dragged my wife down to infamy
> Loathlier than death, drove to the wild
> My tortured body, stripped me of
> Wealth, health, youth, beauty, ardour, love.
> Thou hast abandoned all? Then try
> A speck of dust within the !eye!

With his divorce pending, Crowley was vividly aware of the demands of the path he had chosen: he had thrown away his family and fortune to lead the life of a magician. "Aha!" stands not only as autobiography, but as a manual of spiritual attainment.

As the date of his divorce approached, Crowley grew increasingly miserable. If the event itself wasn't bad enough, Rose was now seeking forgiveness and a second chance. He had managed to refuse so far, but knew he would eventually break down if she persisted. Thus he left town until the whole unpleasant business was over.

On November 10, 1909, Crowley and Neuburg left London for a walking vacation in Algeria. They arrived in Algiers a week later, purchased provisions, and headed south with no plan other than to rough it a few days in a new place. They camped in the open for two nights and slept in a primitive hotel a third before arriving at Aumale, about sixty miles southeast of Algiers, on November 21. The place felt right, so they bought notebooks and settled in.

Going through his rucksack, Crowley examined the papers he had brought on Enochian magic. He planned to publish them in a future *Equinox,* but they now held a greater usefulness for him. Recalling his abortive attempts at doing the Thirty Calls during his visit to Mexico nine years ago, he realized a lot had changed since 1900. He was a Master of the Temple now. Perhaps the barriers that once blocked the 28th Aethyr from him would now yield.

After dinner on November 23, Crowley and Neuburg found a secluded place in the desert. AC removed his scarlet calvary cross inset with a huge topaz. He gazed into the stone while concentrating on his third eye, the *ajna chakra,* and when he felt prepared to receive a vision, he began the 28th Call in the Angelic Language: *"Madariatza das perifa BAG cahisa micaolazoda saanire caosago od fifisa balzodizodarasa Iaida."* In English, it meant, "The heavens that dwell in the 28th Aire are mighty in the Parts of the Earth, and execute the judgement of the Highest!" Completing the conjuration, he gazed into the topaz and described what he saw and the words that came to him. Neuburg, with pen and notebook, recorded what followed:

> There cometh an Angel into the stone with opalescent shining garments like a wheel of fire on every side of him, and in his hand is a long flail of scarlet lightning; his face is black, and his eyes white without any pupil or iris. The face is very terrible indeed to look upon. Now in front of him is a wheel, with many spokes, and many tyres; it is like a fence in front of him.

>   And he cries: O man, who art thou that wouldst penetrate the Mystery? for it is hidden unto the End of Time.[5]

And so it began. The entire vision lasted an hour.

The Edinburgh courtroom came to order on November 24 to hear the uncontested complaint of Rose Edith Crowley (formerly Skerrett, née Kelly) against her husband, Edward Alexander Crowley, a.k.a. Lord Boleskine and Count MacGregor. Lord Edward Theodore Salvesen (1857–1942)[6] listened carefully from the bench as the thirty-five-year-old pursuer gave her testimony, from her 1897 marriage, her elopement six years later, the birth of their first daughter, her abandonment in China, and the death of their child. Mr. Jameson, who questioned Rose, asked, "When you met the defendant, was he then calling himself Aleister Crowley?"

She shook her head. "No, he was then Count Svareff. I knew, however, his real name was Edward Alexander Crowley. Later he called himself MacGregor in order to identify himself with Scotland. That's the name he used on our marriage certificate, although he gave his father's name as Edward Crowley. Shortly after we were wed, he began using the name Lord Boleskine. He said it was because Scots took the names of their property."

"I take it he is a little eccentric?"

"Oh, yes!"

The damning evidence came when she described her complaint against Crowley. That summer, on July 21, she left him and took a house on Warwick Road because he had been beating her. Two weeks later, according to testimony from Mrs. Dauby the charwoman (whom Crowley had called a drunken ex-prostitute), Master Crowley had a woman with him: he had asked Dauby to bring them tea in the library that evening, and again in the morning. Throughout the night, she heard laughter coming from the room. If that weren't scandalous enough, the chauffeur, Charles Randle, testified that Crowley had fathered a child by a friend of his. When Gerald Kelly took the stand, he confessed that, although he was Crowley's friend, he knew little about his background. AC, he said, purchased Boleskine for far more than its worth; the manor had a lot of land, but most of it was perpendicular. Crowley, he said, was very stupid about money.

"You said he is a writer," Salvesen posited. "Does he make anything by it?"

Gerald snorted. "Certainly not."

Salvesen considered the case, granted Rose her divorce, and awarded her custody of Lola Zaza, with £1 a week as alimony. Since Crowley had spent his fortune on publishing and mountaineering adventures, he had no money to offer as a settlement, but with the help of Dennes & Co., he set up a trust fund into which would be deposited the £4,000 he would receive when his mother died; these funds would be divided between Crowley and Lola at the discretion of the trustees, Jones and Eckenstein.

Looking at Crowley's photograph, the judge sat back and mused. "He looks as if he belonged to the stage."

Jameson said, "He is a literary character, sir. He rather affects the artistic."[7]

The Crowley family—Rose, Lola Zaza, and Aleister—taken shortly after the divorce.

In retrospect, their marriage was flawed even before alcohol became an issue. Admittedly, Rose's love inspired passionate songs from the poet, just as Lilith's death devastated him and the collapse of their marriage depressed him. And although comparatively uneducated and undisciplined, she was a valuable magical partner, leading AC to *The Book of the Law,* participating in his rituals, and scrying for his friends. Nevertheless, AC placed her third in his life, after books and magic. They shared little in common: he was a writer, she uninterested in literature. Moreover, they spent little time together: shortly after their marriage, he went on his expedition to Kangchenjunga; left her again in China to travel to America; went on a cruise with Tankerville; and maintained separate residences in London and Paris. In the end, theirs appears to have been a marriage held together by little more than the romance of their elopement.

While the divorce unfolded, Crowley and Neuburg headed out of Aumale into the heart of Algeria. Crowley wore a robe and turban and read from the Qur'an as they marched across the desert. Neuburg's head was shaved except for two tufts of hair that he twisted into horns. Thus Crowley led his familiar djinn about on a chain, to the amazement of the locals.

That evening, they reached Sidi Aissa and, at 8 p.m., performed the 27th Call. From there, they proceeded to Bou Sâada, where they spent most of their trip. It was a quaint little town with houses gathered upon a hill in the middle of the desert. A stream ran through the land below, framed with palms, cacti, orchards, and gardens.

As they regressed through the Thirty Aethyrs over the course of the next month, Crowley and Neuburg recorded the visions—apocalyptic, passionate, and inspired—which they experienced. AC encountered angels, streams of fire, dragons, ringing bells, and a landscape of knives. When they evoked the 21st Aethyr on November 29, Crowley faced an invisible entity that spoke by rapidly placing tastes into Crowley's mouth: salt, honey, sugar, asafoetida, bitumen, honey. As they progressed, Crowley understood the images to unify every system of magical attainment.

The Calls also initiated him into greater and greater mysteries. In the 15th Aethyr (December 3), a group of Adepts examined Frater Perdurabo at their Sabbath. The first one thrust a dagger into Crowley's heart, tasted his blood, and spoke the Greek word *katharos,* thus deeming him at least an Adeptus Minor (5°=6□); indeed, he had received this initiation in 1900 from Mathers himself in Paris. The second, testing the muscles of his right shoulder and arm, pronounced the Latin word *fortis,* signifying he was an Adeptus Major (6°=5□). The third, examining his skin and tasting the sweat of his left arm, uttered the Enochian word *TAN,* declaring him Adeptus Exemptus (7°=4□), an exempt adept at the top of the Second Order's hierarchy. The fourth, examining his neck, said nothing, then opened the right half of his brain and pronounced the Sanskrit *samajh.* He had crossed the abyss and was a Magister Templi (8°=3□).

A fifth Adept approached, examined the left half of Crowley's brain, pondered his evidence, and stiffened. He raised his hand in protest and, in his language, declared Crowley was not yet a Magus, 9°=2□: "In the thick of darkness the seed awaiteth spring." AC still belonged to the first of the three grades of the third and highest order, the Silver Star.

This vision occurred between 9:15 and 11:10 in the morning. Later that afternoon, the magicians climbed the mountain Dáleh Addin in the desert and, at 2:50, attempted to obtain a vision of the 14th Aethyr, named *UTI* in Enochian. As he proceeded, Crowley encountered thick veils of darkness. Tearing his way through the veils, trying to penetrate their mystery, the darkness was endless. Finally, a voice instructed him, "Depart! For thou must invoke me only in the darkness. Therein will I appear, and reveal unto thee the Mystery of

UTI. For the Mystery thereof is great and terrible. And it shall not be spoken in sight of the sun."

At 3:15, Crowley abandoned the vision.

Descending the mountain, inspiration seized Crowley. He suggested they gather rocks and build a stone circle around a rough stone altar dedicated to Pan. This they did, and wrote magical words of power in the sand. With the temple established, they now needed to worship the deity. A sacrifice was customary, but Crowley had no animal with him. He knew, however, that sacrifices often symbolized the sex act, the spilling of the seed of life. So upon the makeshift altar, beneath the desert sun, Victor assumed the active role in an act of anal sex with his master.

Crowley staggered back to Bou Sâada in a drunken state of spiritual ecstasy and collapsed on his bed, feeling insights he had never known before. In his own words, the ritual "produced a great wonder," for he realized for the first time what power could be wielded by using sex in ritual. He also accepted the homosexual component of his sexuality; this stood in sharp contrast to his college relationship with Pollitt, which ended with bitterness and recriminations. The indulgence and transcendence of the last taboo that Victorian-Christian mores had programmed into him completely obliterated "Aleister Crowley" and erased his ego. As he wrote:

> It was a repetition of my experience of 1905, but far more actual. I did not merely admit that I did not exist, and that all my ideas were illusions, inane and insane. I felt these facts as facts. It was the difference between book knowledge and experience.... All things were alike as shadows sweeping across the still surface of a lake—their images had no meaning for the water, no power to stir its silence.[8]

Through the Enochian Calls, Crowley was reliving all the initiations he had experienced: up to this point, he had had sporadic enlightenments that gave him claim to the exalted grades of the A∴A∴, but now he was systematically and formally going through his initiations.

For Victor, that day marked the consummation of a love that had grown steadily within him, and which would never in his life find equal.

At 9:50 that evening, they again tried the Call of the 14th Aethyr. This time the consciousness that had been Crowley penetrated the veil, encountered the angel, and by 11:15 was confirmed as one of the masters.

The remaining visions instructed him in what lay ahead. The 13th Aethyr described the work undertaken by a Master of the Temple (8°=3□). The 12th described the City of the Pyramids, the allegorical name for the third *sephira, Binah,* on the Tree of Life, which represents the 8°=3□ grade. Having been fully instructed on the Grade of the Magister Templi and having had his lease in the City of Pyramids approved, he could now move in. All he had to do was ritually recross the Abyss. Staring into the dark wind-swept void, Crowley beseeched his holy guardian angel, "Is there not one appointed as a warden?"

Aiwass replied with the torment-spawned last words of Jesus, "Eloi, Eloi, lama sabacthani."[9]

Returning from the 11th Aethyr, Crowley knew he was alone. Just as he had trodden upon mountains where no one had previously set foot, there was no other person living in the areas he now ventured.

"Accursed" was John Dee's word for the 10th Aethyr. Its path crossed the Abyss, but Choronzon, the demon of dispersion, guarded the higher grades from those unprepared. Edward Kelly called him "that mighty devil," the first and deadliest of all evil powers. Crowley and Neuburg knew they needed to be prepared to encounter this infernal entity.

On December 6, the magicians wandered until they found a suitable spot in a desert valley filled with white sand. Sparing no precaution, they gathered stones and arranged them in a huge circle. Around it they traced the protective kabbalistic names of God in the sand: *Yahweh, Shaddai El Chai,* and *ARAR-ITA*. Due east of the circle, they inscribed a triangle which enclosed the name Choronzon. To fortify it, they wrote on each of its sides a sacred name as advised in the *Goetia*: ANAPHAXETON, ANAPHANETON, and PRIMEUMATON. At its vertices they put a pair of letters from the name of MI-CA-EL, the archangel bearing the fiery sword. Into this space they would summon the demon. And in this same space Crowley, robed in black, would scry. Neuburg sat in the fortified circle; his duties were to use his consecrated dagger to command and contain Choronzon in the Triangle of the Art, and to record the content of the vision in his notebook. So grave and serious was this responsibility that he swore an oath:

> I, Omnia Vincam, a Probationer of A∴A∴, hereby solemnly promise upon my magical honour, and swear by Adonai the angel that guardeth me, that I will defend this magic circle of Art with thoughts and words and deeds. I promise to threaten with the Dagger to command back into the triangle the spirit incontinent, if he should strive to escape from it; and to strike with a Dagger at anything that may seek to enter this Circle, were it in appearance the body of the Seer himself. And I will be exceeding wary, armed against force and cunning; and I will preserve with my life the inviolability of this circle, Amen. And I summon mine Holy Guardian Angel to witness this mine oath, the which if I break, may I perish, forsaken of Him. Amen and Amen.[10]

Crowley performed banishing rituals of both the pentagram and hexagram, purging their workplace of both elemental and planetary forces. Then, calling on the sacred names of God, he recited the exorcism of Honorius:

> O Lord, deliver me from hell's great fear and gloom!
> Loose thou my spirit from the larvae of the tomb!
> I seek them in their dread abodes without affright:
> On them will I impose my will, the law of light....

> Their faces and their shapes are terrible and strange.
> These devils by my might to angels I will change.
> These nameless horrors I address without affright:
> On them will I impose my will, the law of light.
>
> These are the phantoms pale of mine astonished view,
> Yet none but I their blasted beauty can renew:
> For to the abyss of hell I plunge without affright:
> On them will I impose my will, the law of light.[11]

Traditionally, blood sacrifices helped provide the life essence a spirit needed to materialize. In order to assure a clear encounter with the guardian of the Abyss, he slit the throat of a pigeon at each vertex of the triangle and allowed its blood to drain out, all the while being careful that every drop stayed *within* the triangle lest its barriers be breached. Sacrifice was a practice as old as the Hindu, Jewish, and Greek religions, and this one represented one of the few he would make in his lifetime.[12] Once the blood soaked completely into the sand, Crowley squatted in the thunderbolt *asana* and recited the Call of the 10th Aethyr, called ZAX.

The vision began with a deep, chilling voice crying aloud, "Zazas, Zazas, Nasatanada Zazas." According to tradition, Adam once opened the gates of hell with these words. This time, Choronzon entered their midst.

"I am the Master of Form," the demon declared, "and from me all forms proceed. I am I. I have shut myself up from the spendthrifts, my gold is safe in my treasure-chamber, and I have made every living thing my concubine, and none shall touch them, save only I. From me come leprosy and pox and plague and cancer and cholera and the falling sickness. Ah! I will reach up to the knees of the Most High, and tear his phallus with my teeth, and I will bray his testicles in a mortar, and make poison thereof, to slay the sons of men."

Next, Neuburg heard Crowley say, "I don't think I can get any more; I think that's all there is." He was not fooled. Choronzon was mimicking his master's voice.

Suddenly, Euphemia Lamb appeared before him, tempting and inviting him to make love to her. Neuburg shook his head, attempting to dispel the hallucination. This was another of Choronzon's tricks, an attempt to lure him out of the protective circle. Neuburg refused to comply. In the face of hideous, loud laughter that echoed wildly about the valley, Neuburg commanded him to proceed with the vision.

"They have called me the God of laughter, and I laugh when I will slay. And they have thought that I could not smile, but I smile upon whom I would seduce, O inviolable one, that canst not be tempted." With that, Choronzon slipped in an appeal to Neuburg's pride and vanity: "I bow myself humbly before the great and terrible names whereby thou hast conjured and constrained me. Let me come and put my head beneath thy feet, that I may serve thee. For if thou commandest me to obedience in the Holy names, I cannot swerve therefrom. Bid me therefore come unto thee upon my hands and knees that I may adore thee, and partake of thy forgiveness."

"Back, demon!" Neuburg commanded. "And continue with the vision!"

He did. "Choronzon hath no form, because he is the maker of all form; and so rapidly he changeth from one to the other as he may best think fit to seduce those whom he hateth, the servants of the Most High. Thus taketh he the form of a beautiful woman." And so he did. "Or of a wise and holy man." He did so again. "Or of a serpent that writheth upon the earth ready to sting." And again. Then, shifting gears, Choronzon interrupted his dialogue with a request: "The sun burns him as he writhes naked upon the sands of hell so that he is sore athirst. Give unto me, I pray thee, one drop of water from the pure springs of Paradise, that I may quench my thirst."

Neuburg held his post and offered no water. "Continue with the vision!"

Next, Crowley's voice came from the triangle. "Sprinkle water on my head. I can hardly go on!"

Again calling upon the names of god, Neuburg commanded the uncooperative spirit to continue. He hedged, and Victor cursed him with the names and the pentagram. Undaunted, Choronzon simply roared back at the Neophyte. "I *feed* upon the names of the Most High. I *churn* them in my jaws, and I void them from my fundament. I fear not the power of the Pentagram, for I am the Master of the Triangle. Be vigilant, therefore, for I warn thee that I am about to deceive thee. I shall say words that thou wilt take to be the cry of the Aethyr, and thou wilt write them down, thinking them to be great secrets of Magick power, and they will be only my jesting with thee."

His was an unsettling declaration, as one of the basic assumptions of magic was that the true names of God compelled all spirits. But this chaotic entity that they had called forth openly defied these laws. Shaken, Victor commanded, "In the name of Aiwass, continue!"

The demon quickly shot back, "I know the name of the Angel of thee and thy brother Perdurabo. All thy dealings with him are but a cloak for thy filthy sorceries."

Neuburg replied indignantly to that remark, "I know more than you, foul demon, and I do not fear you. I command you to proceed."

"Thou canst tell me naught that I know not, for in me is all Knowledge: Knowledge is my name."

"I tell you, proceed!"

"Know thou that there is no Cry in the tenth Aethyr like unto the other Cries, for Choronzon is Dispersion, and cannot fix his mind upon any one thing for any length of time. Thou canst master him in argument, O talkative one; thou wast commanded, wast thou, not to talk to Choronzon? He sought not to enter the circle, or to leave the triangle, yet thou didst prate of all these things. Woe, woe, woe, threefold to him that is led away by talk, O talkative One."

"I warn you, you anger me. Unless you wish to feel the pain of hell, continue."

Again Choronzon retorted, "Thinkest thou, O fool, that there is any anger and any pain that I am not, or any hell but this my spirit?" Next, he sprang into a dialogue about Crowley's stupidity. "O thou that hast written two-and-thirty books of Wisdom, and art more stupid than an owl, by thine own talk is thy vigilance wearied, and by my talk art thou befooled and tricked, O thou that sayest that thou shalt endure. Knowest thou how nigh thou art to destruction? I heard it said that Perdurabo could both will and know, and might learn at length to dare, but that to keep silence he should never learn."

His words came quicker and quicker. Neuburg, concentrating on his note book, scribbled frantically to keep up. With the magician suitably distracted, Choronzon tossed sand on the circle, trying to fill it in as he rambled. Then, running out of things to say, the demon began reciting "Tom o' Bedlam."

Neuburg may have realized in that moment that Choronzon was up to no good, but it was far too late. The demon sprang over the hole in the circle and threw Neuburg hard to the ground. They struggled and rolled in the sand. Choronzon, in the form of a naked savage, tried to tear out Neuburg's throat and bite through the bones of his neck with his frothing fangs. Neuburg, meanwhile, reached desperately for his dagger. Fingers closing around the hilt of the magical weapon, Neuburg struck with the blade and called on the holy four-lettered name of God, commanding Choronzon back to the triangle.

And he obeyed.

Neuburg repaired the breech in the circle, and the demon continued, "All is dispersion. These are the qualities of things. The tenth Aethyr is the world of adjectives, and there is no substance therein."

The demon resumed the form of Lamb and again tempted Neuburg to no avail. Then he complained he was cold and asked permission to leave the triangle in order to find something to cover his nakedness. Neuburg refused, and again threatened Choronzon with retribution if he did not proceed.

So he did. "I am commanded, why I know not, by him that speaketh. Were it thou, thou little fool, I would tear thee limb from limb. I would bite off thine ears and nose before I began with thee. I would take thy guts for fiddle-strings at the Black Sabbath." Then, taunting, "Thou didst make a great fight there in the circle; thou art a goodly warrior!"

"You cannot harm one hair of my head," Victor stood firm.*

He roared, "I will pull out every hair of thy head! Every hair of thy body, every hair of thy soul, one by one."

"You have no power."

"Yea, verily, I have power over thee, for thou hast taken the Oath, and art bound unto the White Brothers, and therefore have I the power to torture thee so long as thou shalt be."

"You lie."

"Ask of thy brother Perdurabo, and he shall tell thee if I lie!"

"No. It is no concern of yours."

At that, Choronzon taunted Neuburg, trying to convince him that magic was all gibberish, that the names of power were, in fact, powerless. Realizing that all would be lost if he doubted for even an instant, Neuburg kept the demon at bay.

Choronzon continued, "In this Aethyr is neither beginning nor end, for it is all hotch-potch, because it is of the wicked on earth, and the damned in hell. And so long as it be hotch-potch, it mattereth little what may be written by the sea-green incorruptible Scribe. The horror of it will be given in another place and time, and through another Seer, and that Seer shall be slain as a result of his revealing."[13]

With that prophecy, the demon disappeared. Crowley knew he was gone. He removed his magical ring and, with it, wrote the name BABALON in the sand. Two hours after beginning, the vision was over. Together, Crowley and Neuburg destroyed the circle and triangle, scattering the rocks about. They lit a bonfire to purify the valley of the unholy power they had called to earth, and counted themselves lucky to be alive.

The next day, the Ninth Aethyr described Crowley's ascent from the Abyss and his arrival in the City of the Pyramids as a Magister Templi. Per its instructions, Crowley prostrated himself on the sand 1,001 times during the day's march, reciting from the Qur'an:, *Qul: Huwa Allâhu ahad; Allâhu alssamad; Lam yalid walam yûlad; Walam yakul lahu kufuwan ahad.*[14]

On December 8 they continued south, out of Bou-Sâada and toward the winter resort town of Biskra, over one hundred miles away. When one of Victor's relatives arrived, worried for his safety, Crowley determined to let nothing interfere with their plans. "Where's Victor?" Crowley was asked.

"There," he replied, gesturing toward a dromedary. "I've turned him into a camel." At that, he dismissed the chaperone and returned to his business.

Crowley and Neuburg followed the southbound road out of Bou-Sâada only to find it ran out after only a few miles. The rest of the day they walked through the Sahara, and that evening proceeded with the Eighth Aethyr.

The visions proceeded regularly throughout their march, describing the grade of Magus ($9°=2\square$)—ninth in the hierarchy of ten grades and second from last—and Crowley's final ascent as a Magister Templi into the Great White Brotherhood.

On December 16 they finally reached Biskra, a resort town full of palm trees and camels. They checked into the Royal Hotel, and Crowley dictated a thirteen-page letter to Fuller. In it, he dealt with *Equinox* business and complained incidentally about his difficulty in keeping Victor away from the bottoms of Arabic boys. While much has been made of this latter comment, it stands simply to reason that Crowley was dictating to none other than Neuburg, and that the comment was a joke; possibly one between Crowley and Neuburg, alluding to their own physical involvement. The poem "At Bordj-an-Nus," which Crowley wrote at this time, sheds some light on this matter. When Crowley published it in *The Equinox,* he signed it as "Hilda Norfolk" to disguise its homosexual undertones:

> The moon is down; we are alone;
> May not our mouths meet, madden, mix, melt in the
>   starlight of a kiss?
> El Arabi!
>
> There by the palms, the desert's edge, I drew thee to my
>   heart and held
> Thy shy slim beauty for a splendid second; and fell
>   moaning back,
> Smitten by Love's forked flashing rod—as if the
>   uprooted mandrake yelled!
> …
>
> Great is the love of God and man
> While I am trembling in thine arms, wild wanderer of
>   wilderness!
> El Arabi![15]

They called the Fourth Aethyr that evening at nine, learning more details about the Grade of Magus. The third, second, and first Aethyrs followed in rapid succession, wrapping up on December 19 at 3:30 in the afternoon.

With the conclusion of these visions, Crowley came to an understanding of the Great White Brotherhood and its three highest grades. He fathomed the sacrifices of the Abyss; understood how, as a Master of the Temple living in the City of the Pyramids under the Dark Night of Pan, he must interpret every event as a particular dealing of God with his soul; knew that as a Magus, he would become the Logos, the embodiment of the Word of the Aeon *(Thelema),* but be cursed to have his speech interpreted as a lie; and learned about Babalon, who as a guardian of the Abyss gathered into her chalice the life blood of the Exempt Adept before he crossed the Abyss and, as the priestess or sacred prostitute of the Thelemic system, was the epitome of love under will. Reliving his ordeal of the Abyss and initiation into the Third Order, Crowley completely accepted *The Book of the Law* and felt genuinely secure in his chosen role as its prophet. Even though he had claimed the grade previously, he now fully understood the tasks of a Magister Templi and knew like never before that he had reached that grade.

Returning to Southampton in January 1910, Crowley kicked into high gear. Although he published various booklets for members of the A∴A∴— including *Thelema* (the Holy Books in three volumes), "Liber Causae" (an account of the collapse of the GD and the A∴A∴'s emergence therefrom, included in *Thelema*), and *Liber Collegii Sancti* (a booklet in which to record the progress of students)—his most personal production was *Rosa Decidua,* the fallen rose, the last in his series of poems about his ex-wife. The piece is a mournful dirge, a romantic lament over lost love:

> This is no tragedy of little tears.
> My brain is hard and cold; there is no beat
> Of its blood; there is no heat
> Of sacred fire upon my lips to sing.
>
> ...
>
> I have no memory of the rose-red hours.
> No fragrance of those days amid the flowers
> Lingers; all's drowned in the accursèd stench
> Of this damned present ...
>
> See! I reel back beneath the blow of her breath
> As she comes smiling to me: that disgust
> Changes her drunken lust
> Into a shriek of hate—half conscious still
> (Beneath the obsession of the will)
> Of all she was—before her death, her death!
>
> ...
>
> Who asks me for my tears?
> She flings the body of our sweet dead child
> Into my face with hell's own epitaph
>
> ...
>
> And all my being is one throb
> Of anguish, and one inarticulate sob
> Catches my throat. All these vain voices die,
> And all these thunders venomously hurled
> Stop. My head strikes the floor; one cry, the old cry,
> Strikes at the sky its exquisite agony:
> Rose! Rose o' th' World.

Crowley printed only twenty copies of the eleven-page poem to commemorate the divorce. It sported a green cover, with a friendly photograph of the poet with his wife and daughter, taken shortly before the court date, tipped in. Crowley dedicated the piece to Lord Salvesen, who presided over the trial. With *Rosa Decidua,* Crowley closed the door on a tragic phase of his life and bid farewell to his Rose of the World and her brother, Gerald of the Festuses.

Business at the *Equinox* offices proceeded as usual toward publication of the next issue, set to contain a wide assortment of contributions: a description of the tasks for students in the A∴A∴; Crowley's "Aha!"; "The Shadowy Dill-Waters," a spoof on Yeats; Baudelaire's "The Poem of Hashish," translated by Crowley; poems by Neuburg and Arthur F. Grimble; a story by Raffalovich; and two installments by Fuller—"The Treasure-House of Images" and the contentious "Temple of Solomon the King."

On March 11, solicitor George Rose Cran[16] appeared and served Crowley with a writ: Mathers was seeking an injunction to keep *The Equinox* from publishing the remaining GD ritual, its 5°=6□ R.R. et A.C.[17] Or, in legalese, he was

> restraining the defendant, his servants, and agents from publishing, or causing to be printed or published in the third number of the book or magazine known as *The Equinox* or otherwise disclosing any matter relating to the secrets, forms, rituals, or transactions of a certain order known as the Rosicrucian Order, of which the plaintiff was the Chief or Head.[18]

"Balls," Crowley cursed. The books were already printed and ready to be released in ten days. "Prophetically," they offered a £10 reward for the source of a fictitious clipping sent to him:

> Cox, Box, Equinox,
> McGregors are coming to Town;
> Some in rag, and some on jags,
> And the Swami upside down.
>
> Cran, Cran, MacGregor's man
> Served a writ, and away he ran.[19]

This suggests he knew the writ was coming.

On March 14, Mathers applied for an *ex parte* interim injunction, which Justice Bucknill granted on March 18. One day after the spring equinox, March 21, Crowley's appeal came before the court. Hearing the case were appeals judges Vaughan Williams, Fletcher Moulton, and Farwell.[20] The plaintiff, the Comte Liddell MacGregor, appeared with long white hair brushed straight back to reveal the withered features of his aging face. He was represented by Frederick Low and P. Rose-Innes. It was an impressive team: Sir Frederick Low (1856–1917) was admitted to the Middle Temple in 1890, invested as king's counsel in 1902, and knighted in 1906; he would later serve as a member of Parliament for Norwich from 1910 to 1915, and as high court judge of the King's Bench in 1915.[21] Sir Patrick Rose-Innes (1853–1924) was called to the bar in 1878, established a reputation as a Unionist lawyer and tariff reformer, and in 1905 was appointed recorder of Sandwich and Ramsgate; he would go on to be knighted in 1918. While this might seem an odd fit for the case, the hook may have originated with Rose-Innes's role as provincial Masonic Grand Master for Aberdeenshire, which he would hold from 1905 to 1920: He may have been helping a fellow brother Mason, especially against someone breaking their oath of secrecy.[22]

Crowley's men were W. Whately and A. Neilson for the firm of Messrs. Steadman, Van Praagh, and Gaylor. William Whately (1858–1937) was a London-born Barrister-at-Law of the Inner Temple who would go on to be a Master of the Supreme Court.[23] Alexander Neilson (1868–1929) was educated at Fettes College and received his MA from Edinburgh University, passing his exam for the Middle Temple in 1891 and being called to the Bar in 1893; with

a general practice in the Midland Circuit, "his kindly nature and pleasant manner made him many attached friends."[24]

The courtroom was packed. The last trial with this much interest occurred
in 1905, when Mrs. Eliza Dinah Sheffield brought a breach of promise case
against the Marquis Townshend; she claimed to be High Priestess of the Rosicrucian Order, but as of late she was known only as a West End hostess. The
present trial promised to be just as colorful.

It began with Crowley's man, Whately, reading Mathers's affidavit:

> I am the chief of the Rosicrucian Order. It is an order instituted in its
> modern form in 1888 for the study of mystical philosophy and the myster-
> ies of antiquity. The order is upon the lines of the well-known institutions
> of Freemasonry.
>
> The exclusive copyright of the rituals, ceremonies, and manuscripts of
> the order is vested in me, I being founder and compiler of them, and I
> claim such an interest in the same as will entitle me to restrain any
> infringement of my rights therein.
>
> On November 18, 1898, Aleister Crowley, having duly qualified him-
> self, signed the preliminary pledge form, to which it is requisite intending
> candidates for membership should subscribe their signatures. After compli-
> ance with the necessary formalities he became a member, and thereupon
> ratified the obligation of his signed pledge form by a solemn obligation in
> open Temple of the Order.

Throughout the reading, the justices smirked and sneered at the sworn testimony. Their response visibly displeased Mathers.

Whately handed a copy of the pledge form up to the bench, and continued
to summarize the complaint. "The plaintiff claims the grossest possible breach
of the defendant's obligations and a serious infringement of the plaintiff's right
by publishing the order's secrets in the second *Equinox* under the title 'The
Temple of Solomon the King.' The article in question referred to the meetings
of the Rosicrucian Order, and gave notice to the effect that the publication
would continue in the March number."

At that, Justice Williams chimed in, "Is it a romance?"

"I do not know, my lord. I cannot describe it." After the laughter in the
courtroom died down, Whately continued with his summary. "The plaintiff
charges the matter to be printed in numbers three and four would continue the
infringement." Crowley, however, argued that Mathers was certainly not the
head of the Rosicrucians, did not write the rituals, had not established any
rights with respect to the material being published, and was not entitled to an
injunction. "If there is any obligation to anybody it is to the society, and that
cannot be a legal obligation, because they are a voluntary association and are
not the plaintiffs."

Williams asked Mathers's counsel pointedly, "May I take it there *is* such a
society as the Rosicrucians?"

"Yes," Low replied, "there is."

"And does the society have rules?"

"No, there are no rules of the society in fact, but there is a pledge of secrecy, which the defendant signed." He indicated the copy of the pledge form which had been submitted to the bench.

"I see the plaintiff says he is 'the earthly chief' of the order, and subject to the guidance of the 'spiritual' order."

Justice Farwell interrupted the questioning to ask, "What is the 'spiritual order'?" The courtroom giggled in response.

"I cannot go into it, my lord," Low apologized, "but it is clear the spiritual head would not be answerable for costs." Laughter erupted from the observers.

Justice Moulton asked to see a copy of the second *Equinox,* and the thick tome was handed up to him. Low also asked the judges to read "The Pillar of Cloud," a Rosicrucian piece by Mathers. As he read, Moulton's lips curled into a delighted smile. The other judges similarly enjoyed Mathers's article.

"The article is simply material which Comte Macgregor obtained from old books," Whately complained for Crowley. "He can have no copyright in such material. Moreover, if publication of the next number of *The Equinox* is stopped, the publication will practically be stopped altogether, because the subscribers will be scattered. Although the plaintiff knew all about the subject matter of his complaint since November 11, he did not issue his writ until March 11, after the magazine had already been printed."

"That is a question of pounds, shillings, and pence," Justice Williams stressed, trying to return to the legal question of infringement.

"It is a very serious matter to my client."

Low interrupted, "The plaintiff waited until the eve of publication because he was unable to locate Mr. Crowley's address before then. Our complaint is that wherever our ritual was got from, it was a gross breach of faith for the defendant, after being admitted and allowed to attend the meetings—and then being expelled from the order—to start publishing this matter."

"He has as much right to publish what is in the old books about the Rosicrucians as anybody else," Justice Moulton argued.

"But he is *not* entitled to publish a ritual ceremony which he had pledged himself to secrecy about, even if it was got from the Bible."

"Anybody who knows anything about these societies knows that the rituals of most of them have been published."

"Your lordship must not ask me to admit that."

Justice Williams, trying a different approach, interceded. "I have not observed any indication that you are, either of you, Masons." The courtroom broke into laughter.

"I don't propose to give your lordship any, either," Low replied, generating even more laughter. "This society is in no way a Masonic society."

Farwell selected several "strange and unpronounceable" words from the second *Equinox* and with a smile asked Mathers what they meant. Arouerist,

Onnophris, Jokam. He could not—or would not—answer. Farwell shook his head in response. "I can understand the publication of a trade secret doing a person irreparable injury, but I cannot see how any damage, irreparable or otherwise, could be done by the publication in question."

"If the initiation ritual is published in the March number, as Mr. Crowley proposes, the damage *will* be irreparable," Low argued. "The cat would be out of the bag."

Justice Williams replied, "But so much of the cat came out of the bag in September."

Farwell added, "And I think it is a dead cat." By this time, the courtroom roiled with laughter.

"Perhaps there is a second cat in the bag, my lord," Low feebly tried to continue his argument. "If they have let out one, they may let out another. If you cannot stop this sort of thing by an injunction, there is practically no remedy at all. The defendant has been turned out of the order, and is publishing the article as an act of revenge for having been expelled."

In the end, the Justices ruled that Mathers had waited too long to file an injunction: he could have done it a month or six weeks ago, before Crowley had gone to the expense of printing *The Equinox*. Based on the content of the second issue, they ruled the third issue would do the plaintiff no harm. Therefore, Mathers was not entitled to restrain the publication in question. Crowley was allowed to publish *The Equinox* and was awarded costs as well.

Response to the trial was overwhelming. Virtually every London newspaper sported headlines like "Secret Society: Amusing Comedy in Appeal Court," "Rosicrucian Rites: The Dread Secrets of the Order Revealed," "Secrets of a Mystic Society: Rosicrucian Ritual to Be Revealed," and "Secrets of the 'Golden Dawn': Quaint Rites of the Modern Rosicrucians."[25] Everybody knew about the magician Aleister Crowley, who was publishing the Rosicrucians' secrets. Many papers even excerpted rituals from the victorious *Equinox*.

Most significantly, as the *Evening News* reported, "The revelations of Mr. Crowley have created utter consternation in the ranks of the Rosicrucians."[26] Crowley's publication of the rituals, however, upset far fewer than did Mathers's claim to leadership of the Rosicrucian Order. As a result, Crowley was "invaded by 333 sole and supreme Grand Masters of the Rosicrucians,"[27] all of whom conferred upon him membership in their organizations. One of these was Theodor Reuss (1855–1923), head of the German organization Ordo Templi Orientis, which Crowley would come to embrace and direct in later years. At the time, however, he simply "booted [Reuss] with the other 332."[28]

Crowley also became acquainted at this time with John Yarker (1833–1913), a collector of patents to operate various clandestine and pseudo-Masonic lodges, all of which he believed to predate the Ancient and Accepted Rite (i.e., "legitimate" Freemasonry), or at the very least to be just as legitimate. Foremost amongst these was the Ancient and Primitive Rite of Masonry, or of Memphis-Mizraim, which was an amalgamation of two older rites of ninety-six and ninety degrees, respectively, over which Yarker was Supreme Grand Master General. Despite being embattled within and ultimately expelled from the Ancient and Accepted Rite because of his fringe interests,[29] he continued to be an active Masonic scholar, contributing regularly to Masonic publications, including the prestigious journal *Ars Quatuor Coronatorum*.[30] Many of his ideas in the journal, however, fell on deaf ears. It was in fact Crowley's positive review of Yarker's *The Arcane Schools* (1909) that initially prompted Yarker to contact Crowley and thus initiate correspondence with an appreciative listener.[31] Yarker, as did so many other groups, bestowed on Crowley high rank in various orders. As a result of these deluges of dignities, the list of honors conferred on Crowley at this time filled four dense pages.[32]

Illustrious Brother John Yarker (1833–1913) in his later years.

The publicity resulted in a boom year for the A∴A∴. Whereas sixteen probationers signed up in 1909, twenty-six joined in 1910. Among these were G. M. Marston, Frank Bennett, J. G. Bayley, Herbert Close, and J. T. Windram.

Commander Guy Montagu Marston (1871–1928) served in the Royal Navy as "one of the highest officials of the Admiralty."[33] He was born at Rempstone Hall, Dorset, to Rev. Charles D. Marston and Katharine Calcraft. Enlisting in the Royal Navy, he advanced to sublieutenant in 1892, and shortly thereafter served under Rear-Admiral Bedford on three punitive expeditions to the Gambia (February 1894), the Republic of Benin (September 1894), and Niger (February 1895). In 1901, Marston succeeded his uncle, William Montagu Calcraft, at Rempstone. The same year, he was made a full lieutenant, and in 1905 was promoted to commander, serving with the Hydrographic Department of the Admiralty. He was a friend of English poet Rupert Brook, whom W. B. Yeats had called "the handsomest young man in England"; Brook was also a friend of *Equinox* contributor G. H. S. Pinsent, which may provide the connection to Crowley. Marston was an avid reader, and his library reveals an interest in the sexual researches of Freud, Krafft-Ebing, and Havelock Ellis. Marston's own experiments on the psychology of married Englishwomen demonstrated—he believed conclusively—that shamanic drumming made them restless, intensifying until it resulted in "shameless masturbation or indecent advances."[34] His interest in ritual magic led him to join the A∴A∴ on February 22, 1910, with the motto "All for knowledge." On November 12, 1910, he would take command of the *Blanche* cruiser and leave for Devonport.[35]

Frank Bennett (1868–1930) was a Lancashire bricklayer who, due to personal hardships, worked with his hands since age nine. Magic and Theosophy had interested him for a long time, and he wrote Crowley in the winter of 1910 to ask his advice on a practical course of study. Crowley recommended the Abramelin operation, adding, "I am glad to hear that you are really at work. So many people now-a-days just prattle about magic, and never do any."[36] To help him along, Crowley sent him a copy of *The Book of the Sacred Magic of Abramelin the Mage*.

Bennett did as instructed but soon sent an alarmed letter to Crowley because he was hearing voices in his head. Crowley wrote back, reassuring:

> What you report is rather good in a way, because it shows you are getting some results. But of course it implies also that your sphere is not closed. I should use the banishing Rituals of Hexagrams and Pentagrams to begin and end each meditation and also assumption of the God-form of Harpocrates. I think I should do less reading and more gardening; and in particular I should go to a doctor and make sure that the symptoms are removed so far as they are physical.[37]

Here is Crowley at his best as a teacher: rule out medical problems; barring this, work in a more controlled environment and, most importantly, don't try too hard. The advice must have worked, as the problem did not come up again.

Bennett joined the A∴A∴ as "Sapienta Amor Potentia" (Love of wisdom is power) on March 12, 1910. In order to check on this potential student, Crowley sent his student Herbert Inman to call on him. Inman learned that Bennett shared his interest in Co-Masonry, a new movement in Freemasonry that admitted women alongside men in its ranks. The nature of their conversation is unknown, but shortly afterwards Inman left for Rio and set up a TS lodge. Despite threat of expulsion, Bennett pursued Theosophy instead of the A∴A∴ and moved to Australia in 1911.[38]

James Gilbert Bayley joined the A∴A∴ on March 22, 1910, taking the motto "Perfectio et Ministerium" (Perfection and service). Although Crowley initially considered him a doubtful member, having been brought in under Inman, he would stand by Crowley throughout his life, serving as his British liaison while he was out of the country in the 1920s and staying in close touch through his final years.[39]

Herbert H. Close (1890–1971) was an old friend of Fuller's, born to a well-to-do family of land owners. Under the pen name Meredith Starr, he was a writer and poet interested in mysticism, aromatherapy, and homeopathy, and described himself as a "constructive psychologist." He was also a contributor to *The Occult Review*.[40] Shortly after joining on June 6, 1910, Frater Superna Sequor (I follow the gods) began experiments with Crowley's drug of choice, the hallucinogen *Anhalonium lewinii,* commonly known as peyote.[41] After an astral journey convinced Close that he had attained a high grade, Crowley tested his claimed ability to stave off the effects of any drug by giving him ten grains of calomel. A note from Crowley to Fuller sheds light on this meeting: "I saw Starr & slew him. I hope he'll be all right soon. I've given him a week to study Kant and a fortnight to get Kunt."[42] Close's poem "Memory of Love" appeared in *The Equinox* I(7), but he eventually parted with AC, most likely when Fuller did, and later briefly became a follower of Indian guru Meher Baba (1894–1969), helping bring him to the West in the early 1930s. Crowley bitterly assessed the student: "Went out of his mind and never came back."[43]

James Thomas Windram (1877–1939) was a South African accountant who joined the A∴A∴ on August 11, 1910. He chose the magical name of "Servabo Fidem" (I serve the faith), and was one of only eight students who Crowley passed to Neophyte. Like Bayley, he stuck by Crowley for many years, taking on the A∴A∴ motto "Semper Paratus" (Always ready) and eventually becoming OTO National Grand Master for South Africa under the title of Mercurius X°.

On April 1, Crowley also admitted into the A∴A∴ Australian violinist Leila Ida Nerissa Bathurst Waddell (1880–1932). who would become one of his most important magical partners. Leila Waddell was the daughter of David Waddell and Ivy Lea Bathurst of Randwick, New South Wales. She was born in Bathurst, New South Wales, a city whose largely aboriginal population was transformed by the 1851 discovery of gold and the 1876 completion of a railway from Sydney. She took violin lessons from age seven, quickly mastering her instrument. However, when her tutor died, it became clear that she was playing by memorizing her teacher's performance, without either reading music or understanding theory. So she got a new tutor and started over.[44] She was trained by Henri Stael, principal violinist with the Pleyel Concert Company, and in the 1898 annual examinations at the Sydney College of Music she was first runner-up for a medal in advanced honors in violin.[45] She began teaching in suburban Sydney: at Presbyterian Ladies' College, a day and boarding school in the western suburb of Croydon, where she taught Junior Violin from 1901 to 1905; at Ascham, a nondenominational girls boarding school in the eastern suburb of Edgecliff, until March 1907; and at Kambala, an Anglican day and boarding school for girls in the eastern suburb of Rose Bay.[46]

With the press dubbing her "a very clever violiniste,"[47] she—along with a pianist, contralto, and bass—played a Grand Concert on January 21, 1904, under the management Walter E. Taylor. Selections included Grieg's Sonata No. 3 in C Minor (Opus 45) and Wieniawski's "Cappricio-Valse" in E major (Opus 7), both for violin and piano. This latter piece she played "with great delicacy and brilliancy, exciting prolonged applause." After two recalls, "her virtuosity being amply demonstrated," "the talented young lady" returned with "Le Cygne," the thirteenth movement of Saint-Saëns's *Carnival of Animals;* the "Romance" from Wieniawski's Violin Concerto No. 2; and Bohm's "Papillons."[48] In August 1905, she debuted as a soloist at a Sydney Town Hall concert recital given by Arthur Mason, dubbed "one of our busiest musicians" for his jobs as City Organist, organist at St. James' Church, and director of the Sydney Choristers.[49] A 1906 concert was held to honor the celebrated violinist's charitable works.[50] This attracted the attention of Henry Hawayrd, who hired her for the Brescians, a group of Anglo-Italian instrumentalists and vocalists who served as the movie-theater orchestra for T. J. West's West Pictures in New Zealand. Works performed by Waddell at this time included Charles Flavell Hayward's "Grand Concert Duet (Olde Englande) on English Airs, for Two Violins" (with Auelina Martinego) and Francesco Paolo Tosti's song "Beauty's Eyes," with violin accompaniment and obligato.[51]

Waddell played with the Brescians from 1906 to 1908, when she left for England to hone her craft. This is likely when she studied with world-class violin teacher Émile Sauret (1852–1920), who was teaching in England at this time; several years later, she would also study with Leopold Auer (1845–1930) in New York.[52] Success followed her, as the *Sydney Mail* reported in June 1909, that "the well-known Sydney violinist has been meeting with marked success at Bournemouth."[53] Soon she was performing as part of the Ladies' Orchestra in George Edwardes's revival of Oscar Straus's *A Waltz Dream,* which opened at Daly's Theater in Leicester Square on January 17, 1911. While the *Times* reviewer was admittedly jaded by having seen previous productions and thus gave the show a lukewarm reception, *The Play Pictorial* raved.[54] The show ran for 106 performances through the end of April 1911.[55]

Part Maori, Leila Waddell had square brusque features and thick eyebrows, nose, and lips. Her straight dark hair reached down to her waist. She was slender, attractive, and exotic, and Crowley fell madly in love with her. He dubbed her "the Mother of Heaven"—often referring to her simply as "Mother"— and through her the "purely human side of his life reached a proper climax."[56]

She became one of the most intriguing and important figures in Crowley's life. Within a week of her acquaintance, he was inspired to write "The Vixen" and "The Violinist." The first is an occult-horror short story about an heiress who uses black magic against her lover. The latter belongs to the same genre, about a woman who evokes a demon from one of the watchtowers though her music. In these pieces he portrayed Leila as happy, honest, shrewd, and huntress lithe. During a May trip to Venice, Crowley wrote *The Household Gods,* also dedicated to her. Penned at Hôtel Pallanza in Lago Maggiore, he called it "a charming little play showing how heaven confused a domestic quarrel between husband and wife."[57] In his *Confessions,* Crowley admitted a secret affection for this piece, and the writer Louis Wilkinson claimed it contained one of the funniest exclamations in literature.[58]

The Ladies' Orchestra for George Edwardes's revival of *A Waltz Dream,* 1911.

Crowley noted that since the Mathers trial, "For the first time, I found myself famous and my work in demand."[59] His poem about the Sahara, "The Tent," appeared in the March 1910 *Occult Review,*[60] followed in the May issue by a long discussion of the court case.

His next book was *The Scented Garden.* Purportedly translated from a rare Indian manuscript by the late Major Lutiy and another, it was fully titled *The Scented Garden of Abdullah the Satirist of Shiraz.* It appeared early in the year, was printed anonymously, and was issued privately in an edition of two hundred copies. Written during Crowley's Asian wanderings, it was his parody of the

Iranian poets and their texts on mysticism and homosexual love. It was also a tribute to his hero, Sir Richard Burton, whose scholarly books on sexual customs of the near and far east had caused a moralistic stir. "The *Scented Garden* deals entirely with pederasty, of which the author saw much evidence in India," Crowley wrote of his book. "It is an attempt to understand the mind of the Persian, while the preliminary essay does the same for the English clergyman."[61] When he wrote these words in 1913, most copies of the book had been seized and destroyed.

In the preface to his next book, Crowley wrote "In response to a widely-spread lack of interest in my writings, I have consented to publish a small and unrepresentative selection from the same." This anthology was *Ambergris,* published by Elkin Matthews. In typical manner, Crowley ran up £6 worth of proof corrections. He found the charges astronomical, and attacked the printer during his review of the book in the fourth *Equinox*. The investment was worthwhile, however, as the *Evening Post* declared it "the most interesting volume of new English verse seen this year."[62] The *Nation* found Crowley "as passionately possessed by his theme as any poet has ever been.[63] *The New Age* similarly declared that any lack of interest was attributable to the high price of his lavish editions, adding "Mr. Crowley is one of the principal poets now writing."[64] D. H. Lawrence (1885–1930)—his *The White Peacock* (1911) not yet published and his famous *Lady Chatterley's Lover* (1928) nearly two decades off—disliked the book, remarking, "If *Ambergris* smells like 'Crowley,' it is pretty bad. Civet cats and sperm whales—ugh!"[65] Ironically, Crowley and Lawrence would both be underdogs of the Mandrake Press stable some twenty years later.

The Winged Beetle collected many of Crowley's newer works, some reprinted from previous works[66] and others appearing for the first time. He dedicated its poems to various people in his life, including G. C. Jones, Euphemia Lamb, Austin Spare, Lord Salvesen, Raymond Radclyffe, Kathleen Bruce, Rose Crowley, Commander Marston, Elaine Simpson, J. F. C. Fuller, Victor Neuburg, Frank Harris, Norman Mudd, H, Sheridan-Bickers, Allan Bennett, Mary Waska, George Raffalovich, and his mother. Yielding to his publisher's concern that verse three of the dedication was too indelicate, Crowley consented to pen a less offensive substitute. However, the book's "Glossary of Obscure Terms" allowed readers to translate it back to read:

> Yea! God himself upon his throne
> Cringed at thy torrid truculence;
> Tottered and crashed, a crumbled crone,
> at thy contemptuous 'slave Get hence!'
> Out flickered the Ghost's marish tongue,
> And Jesus wallowed in his dung.

It also featured a poem called "The Convert (A Hundred Years Hence)," which took a tongue-in-cheek view of his current popularity:

There met one eve in a sylvan glade
A horrible Man and a beautiful maid.
"Where are you going, so meek and holy?"
"I'm going to temple to worship Crowley."
"Crowley is God, then? How did you know?"
"Why, it's Captain Fuller that told us so."

Fuller also had the honor of designing the book cover and having the volume as a whole dedicated to him. It remains one of the best anthologies of Crowley's works, and the press received it enthusiastically. A critic with the *Occult Review* wrote:

> I declare that Aleister Crowley is among the first of living English poets. It will not be many years before this fact is generally recognized and duly appreciated.... The range of his subjects is almost infinite ... his poems are ablaze with the white heat of ecstasy, the passionate desire of the Overman towards his ultimate consummation, reunion with God.[67]

Alas, Crowley was about to learn the press was quite fickle.

Leila Waddell (1880–1932).

CHAPTER TEN

Aleister Through the Looking Glass

The pungent smell of burning tobacco filled the Dorset home of Commander Marston on May 9, 1910, as he hosted an A∴A∴ ritual based on the lessons learnt in Algiers. The ceremony was designed to summon Bartzabel, spirit of Mars, and the burning of his incense, tobacco, was intended to make the residence more conducive to his appearance. Just as Crowley had sat in the Triangle of the Art during the call of the Tenth Aethyr, so Neuburg now sat in the space reserved for the spirit, ready to act as its conduit. As the ceremony proceeded, Neuburg entered a trance, rose to his feet, and to everyone's surprise, danced an unscheduled dervish. When the dance ended and Victor began to speak as the god of war, they realized that Bartzabel was among them.

Marston asked the obvious question: "Will nation rise up against nation?" Bartzabel, through Neuburg, warned them that two wars would break out within the next five years. The first would center on Turkey, the second in Germany. The conflicts would destroy both nations. (The prediction would prove to be correct, with the Balkan War in 1912 and World War I in 1914.)

Although the ritual was an unqualified success—it was the most startling and concrete magical result Crowley had known so far—its significance comes from neither Neuburg's channeling nor the accurate prediction. The ritual is important because Marston, impressed with the ceremony, half-jokingly suggested they charge admission and perform it publicly. Crowley's eyes lit up, and he replied, "I think you may be on to something."

While the spirit of Mars foretold war, a smaller battle brewed at Trinity College. Dean Reginald St. John Parry (1858–1935)[1] received a letter claiming Crowley was a pederast and was being followed by the police (the recent publication of AC's homosexual *Bagh-i-Muattar* doubtlessly prompted the rumor). Hearing claims that police were following him, Crowley responded with a flip "Good, I shan't be burgled."

Parry, gravely concerned about the moral character of this frequent campus visitor, summoned Norman Mudd to his office. Mudd, aside from being a Crowley devotee, was also secretary of the Cambridge Freethought Association, which Ward had formed under AC's direction to host his talks on campus. Dean Parry—explaining that he objected not to Crowley's talks but to his morality—instructed Mudd to cancel the Freethought Association's invitation and cease distributing copies of *The Star in the West*. Given that AC had just won a popular court case, Parry chose his words carefully to avoid slander.

Outraged, Mudd summoned the Freethought Association's other members, who sent their rebellious reply to the Dean:

> The Association having taken into consideration the request made to it by the Dean of Trinity regrets that it finds itself unable to comply with the request. It regards the right to invite down any person it thinks fit as essential to its principles and wishes to point out that its attitude towards any opinions advocated before it is purely critical.[2]

Crowley, meanwhile, fumed that someone—a "Parry-lytic Liar," as Crowley dubbed him[3]—should accuse him behind his back: shades of Champney! So he wrote Mudd's father, claiming his son's tutors were "indulging in things so abominable that among decent people they have not even a name,"[4] and recommended he place his son in the charge of more probitous tutors. That summer, Crowley came to Cambridge as scheduled.

Having failed to control the Freethought Association, Parry had no recourse but to single out one of them and issue an ultimatum. Indeed, Parry has been criticized "for a certain peremptoriness and a tendency to override opposition."[5] The ax fell on Mudd: he was to resign as secretary of the Freethought Association, write the dean a letter of apology, and promise on his honor as a gentleman never again to contact Aleister Crowley. If he refused, Parry would cancel his scholarship.

Mudd crumbled. As he later recounted, "I will not go into details as to the fight I put up. It was stubborn but unskillful and I was compelled ultimately to give in. You must understand that at this time I was quite poor, having gone up to Cambridge only with the help of scholarships."[6] That scholarship was his only means of staying in college, and his parents were already hundreds of pounds in debt over his other educational expenses. Set on an academic career, he had no choice but to comply: to resign and apologize. However, he secretly maintained his correspondence with Crowley.

Cambridge banned Crowley, and the battle was over for now. The incident would prompt AC's poetic critique "Athanasius Contra Decanum," eventually published in *The Equinox*.

On an idle evening with idle guests, Crowley posed a challenge to Leila Waddell, the Mother of Heaven: he would read a poem, and ask her to play a composition that reflected its mood. It became a call-response, with Crowley rifling through his library and Leila running through her repertoire to find responses to the other's statements. The evening turned into an artistic dialogue, with even the observers intrigued, entertained, and excited.

In the silent moments following the conversation, Crowley was spiritually charged and uplifted. So, he learned, were his friends. It felt as though they'd just done some powerful, primal ritual. Notions from this performance and the ritual at Marston's house met and joined: Neuburg's dance, Leila's music, and Crowley's poetry were all powerful adjuncts to dramatic ritual. Based on this sketchy theme, AC wrote two poems to the Mother of Heaven: "The Interpreter" and "Pan to Artemis." Both are frenetic and infectious invocations:

> Uncharmable charmer
>   Of Bacchus and Mars
> In the sounding rebounding
>   Abyss of the stars!
> O virgin in armour,
>   Thine arrows unsling
> In the brilliant resilient
>   First rays of the spring!
>
> By the force of the fashion
>   Of love, when I broke
> Through the shroud, through the cloud,
>   Through the storm, through the smoke,
> To the mountain of passion
>   Volcanic that woke—
> By the rage of the mage
>   I invoke, I invoke![7]

On August 23 these elements coalesced into the Rite of Artemis, performed at the *Equinox* offices for the press and public. Its name and form were more than a passing nod to the Matherses' "Rite of Isis" in Paris a decade before.

With lights dimmed, incense burning, and all clad in their magical robes, the rite began with the banishing ritual of the pentagram and purifications of the temple with water and fire. With the space duly cleared and consecrated, Crowley led the others in a circumambulation around the altar. One brother passed the Cup of Libation around the room while another recited poetry. After invoking Artemis via the Greater Ritual of the Hexagram, another libation celebrated the deity. A third libation followed AC's reading of "Song of Orpheus" from *Argonauts*.

Speculation surrounds the contents of this libation: although reporter Raymond Radclyffe described the concoction as pleasant smelling, attendee Ethel Wieland said it tasted like rotten apples and made her intoxicated for a week. The liquid clearly contained some active ingredient, for Neuburg wrote to the Wielands after the performance, "I am glad the effects of the drug have passed off from Mrs. Wieland and yourself."[8] Neuburg's biographer Jean Overton Fuller claimed the drug was opium, although Crowley himself gave the best explanation: to generate a bacchic exuberance without intoxicating patrons with wine, he opted instead for "the elixir introduced by me to Europe"— *Anhalonium lewinii* or mescal buttons infused with herbs, fruit juices, and alcohol—with instructions to skip anyone who showed signs of drunkenness. At this time, no laws prohibited the use of such substances.

Following the preliminaries, the brethren led in and enthroned on a high seat the Mother of Heaven. Solemn and reverent, Crowley recited Swinburne's first chorus from "Atalanta."[9] Another libation, an invocation to Artemis, and further ceremonies followed. The rite took on a greater energy when Crowley commanded Neuburg to dance "the dance of Syrinx and Pan in honour of our lady Artemis." Neuburg danced with beauty and grace until he collapsed from exhaustion in the middle of the room, staying there for the remainder of the rite. Crowley recited another poem to Artemis, and after a deathly silence, the Mother of Heaven took her Guarnerius violin and played. Her performance was sensual, subtle, masterful. The stunned audience was wafted away by the very ecstasy Crowley had hoped to produce.

The long, intense silence ended when Crowley announced, "By the Power in me vested I declare the Temple closed."

Raymond Radclyffe reviewed the ceremony for the August 24 edition of *The Sketch,* calling it "beautifully conceived and beautifully carried out. If there is any higher form of artistic expression than great verse and great music, I have yet to learn it."[10] Radclyffe hailed from an old and distinguished family, beginning as a financial journalist and editor at *St. Stepehen's Review,* where his partner, William Allison, called him "a singularly able man."[11] As a signatory on the paper's parent company, Radclyffe was named in a libel suit against *St. Stephen's Review;* although protesting innocence, the lawsuit and other financial troubles doomed the paper.[12] He personally suffered financially, appearing in court to account for over £5,000 in unpaid debt.[13] He recovered and continued to write, contributing to London's *Financial Times* and publishing his memoir, *Wealth and Cats,* in 1898.[14] During the 1910s he would go on to be financial editor for the *New Witness,* regular financial commentator for *The English Review,* and author of *The War and Finance;*[15] he beame so influential that his word could bolster how the public perceived the integrity of any new company or undertaking.[16]

According to AC, Radclyffe, "though utterly indifferent to Magick, was passionately fond of poetry and thought mine first-class, and unrivalled in my generation."[17] Theirs was a deep friendship, Crowley writing appreciatively of him, "he was one of the very best that ever lived; a City Editor straight as Euclid before Einstein attacked him, and one of the best literary critics and friends in the world."[18] This explained his presence at the Rite of Artemis, and AC appreciated the good review, inscribing a copy of *Clouds without Water* to "Raymond Radclyffe from his grateful friend Aleister Crowley."[19]

Financial writer and editor Raymond Radclyffe, c. 1898.

Radclyffe's positive review encouraged Crowley to compose and perform an entire series of rites. Although Fuller and his friends urged Crowley to leave well enough alone, Crowley stubbornly rented a room at Westminster's Caxton Hall. To this respectable venue accustomed to whist drives, subscription dances, and meetings of the fledgling suffragettes, Crowley planned to introduce incense, music, chanting, and dancing for the ritual of all rituals.

As the A∴A∴ geared up for a new issue of *The Equinox* and its forthcoming engagement at Caxton Hall, several new faces entered the picture that summer.

Ethel Archer, an aspiring poet in her early twenties, came aboard early enough to attend the Rite of Artemis. Ethel Florence E. Archer (b. 1885) was the fourth of five children, born in Slougham, Sussex, to Ormond A. Archer, curate of Whitbourne, and his wife, Emily.[20] Although she had written *The Book of Plain Cooking*,[21] she sought creative outlets through fiction and poetry. In 1908 she married artist Eugene John Wieland (c. 1880–1915), son of Thomas Thatcher and Eugenie Wieland of Sunnyfield House, Guisborough, Yorkshire;[22] she nicknamed him "Bunco." They were passionate lovers, as anonymously documented in a popular article written by a neighbor who watched their unselfconscious behavior through the open window of their "shabby old garret," which was furnished with little more than an easel, two chairs, and a mirror.[23] Both Ethel and Eugene became heavily involved with both OTO and A∴A∴ at this time, and Crowley would encourage Eugene to set up the publishing imprint Wieland & Co., which over the next couple of years would bring out subsequent issues of *The Equinox,* and several of Crowley's other works.[24] Archer's contributions to *The Equinox* were limited to love poems, and Neuburg, noting that these addressed women, teasingly dubbed her Sappho; meanwhile, she was surprised that someone as fey as Neuburg would point the finger. Although she explained to everybody's satisfaction that her poems described how she imagined a man might see her, she nevertheless adopted Sappho as her colorful moniker. Both Neuburg and Crowley intrigued her, and she spent long hours at the *Equinox* offices. Both she and Wieland would eventually part with Crowley, and Wieland would go on to serve with the 19th Battalion in the Great War, reaching the rank of sergeant. He would die in a Canadian hospital on October 5, 1915, as a result of injuries sustained at Loos, and be buried at Le Treport Military Cemetery.[25] Archer would continue to publish occasional books, poetry, and essays throughout her life.[26]

As one of Chelsea's great hostesses, Elizabeth Gwendolen Otter (1876–1958)[27] considered herself unshockable. Her Sunday luncheons attracted all manner of actors, painters, and writers; she even took in her fair share of them. A friend introduced her to Crowley because of her fascination with the odd and unconventional. AC was an admirable addition to her collection of personalities, and the magician became good friends with this plain-looking woman who claimed descent from Pocahontas. She contributed her opinions to the book review section of *The Equinox,*[28] while he in turn dedicated "The Ghouls"[29] to her and portrayed her in *Moonchild* (1929) as Mrs. Badger.

Vittoria Cremers could have been a storybook figure: she was born Vittoria Cassini around 1859 in Pisa to the Italian Manrico Vittorio Cassini and his British wife, Elizabeth Rutherford. Vittoria made her way to New York, where she was proprietor and editor of the *Stage Gazette.* Around February 1886 she married Russia's Baron Louis Cremers, who was the son of a famous St. Petersburg banking family, the Rothschilds, with a net worth of $40 million. A couple of weeks after the wedding, she reportedly told her husband that she "could not possibly love any man."[30] It was at this time that he learned of her habit of going out on the town dressed as a man, and Crowley later reports that "She boasted of her virginity and of the intimacy of her relations with Mabel Collins, with whom she lived a long time."[31] The Baron and Cremers soon separated, then divorced; Vittoria got a butch haircut and began answering simply to "Cremers." Mabel Collins (1851–1927) was a Theosophist and novelist whose novel *The Blossom and the Fruit* (1890) Crowley admired enough to include in the A∴A∴ reading list; he considered it "the best existing account of the Theosophic theories presented in dramatic form."[32] While Collins and Crowley never met, their mutual acquaintance Cremers doubtlessly saw parallels: Just as Crowley was editor of *The Equinox,* Collins was H. P. Blavatsky's coeditor of the Theosophical periodical *Lucifer.* And just as Crowley claimed to scribe various "Holy Books" dictated by the Secret Chiefs, so too did Collins claim that her books *Idyll of the White Lotus* (1884), *Light on the Path* (1885), and *Through the Gates of Gold* (1887) were dictated by Koot Hoomi, one of the Masters or Mahatmas who guided Blavatsky.[33] Cremers often repeated Collins's claim to know the identity of Jack the Ripper, and Crowley preserved the claim in "Jack the Ripper."[34]

Cremers was a sincere but penniless seeker, transcribing 777 in New York's Astor Library because she could not afford to purchase a copy. She wished to help "put the Order over," as Crowley called it, so AC paid her passage to England and introduced her to his circle. Aged in her fifties, she had white hair and unhappy eyes. Her stern, square face, yellow and hard, reminded Crowley of wrinkled parchment. When she boasted of her undercover work against New York's drug and prostitution rings, Crowley could more readily believe that she *directed* drug and prostitution traffic than fought it. "Crowley is one of three things," she once said of her mentor. "He is either mad, or he is a blackguard, or he is the greatest adept."[35]

Crowley also got to know W. E. Hayter Preston (b. 1891), a close friend of the Neuburg family, who acted as Victor's watchdog. Like Victor, he was a Freethinker and poet. Although he worked as a freelance journalist, he soon became literary editor at the *Sunday Referee.* Preston, who studied Lévi and the French magicians before he ever met Neuburg, took a dim view of Crowley. A dinner with AC and his mother helped solidify this opinion: according to Preston, Crowley snatched the menu out of his mother's hands and, closing it, told her, "Mother, you may have boiled toads. Or fried Jesu."[36]

Jeanne Eugenie Heyse (1890–1912) was a young actress and dancer at the Royal Academy of Dramatic Art, her tuition paid by a local businessman. She was the oldest of three sisters, born in Edmonton, Middlesex, to Holland-born wholesale merchant Ferdinand Francis E. Heyse and his Irish wife, Margaret.[37] Under her stage name Ione de Forest, her major previous experience was playing *The Blue Bird* (1909) by Belgian playwright and winner of the 1911 Nobel Prize for Literature Maurice Maeterlinck (1862–1949). Joan, as she preferred to be called, had no interest in the occult, but she entered Crowley's circle when she answered an ad in *Stage* seeking dancers for a performance at Caxton Hall. Her body was as gaunt and cadaverous, and the pale powders she wore made her anemic skin even more pallid. Black hair dangled to her slight waist, and golden eyes beamed vacantly from her oval face. Beautiful and sweet, she could be manic one moment, melancholic the next. Indeed, two years later her newlywed husband would describe her: "She was in poor health, highly strung, and occasionally suffered from hysteria."[38] Although considered a wooden and untalented dancer by some, her lover, American expatriate modernist poet Ezra Pound (1885–1972), offered the following portrait in his "Dance Figure":

Dark-eyed,
O woman of my dreams,
Ivory sandalled,
There is none like thee among the dancers,
None with swift feet.[39]

This tragic doll of a woman appealed to both AC and Neuburg, and she got the job.

With Leila, Ethel, Gwen, Joan, and Vittoria always around, these students became known as "the Harem." Crowley would work hard at his desk—on another issue of *The Equinox* or one of his students' books, such as *The History of a Soul* and *The Deuce and All* by Raffalovich, *The Whirlpool* by Archer, or *The Triumph of Pan* by Neuburg—while Joan stood behind him, running her fingers through his hair and calling him "Aleister," even though everybody referred to him as AC. Except for the Mother of Heaven: with her accent, it sounded like "IC." Her speech invariably prompted Crowley to declare, "Oh, Mother, I do wish you'd lose that accent. It sounds so bad in the Rites!" Although said in jest, it prompted Leila to ask Gwen for help with her dialect: "Will you tell me when I sy anything in Austreyelian?"[40]

Occasionally the Vickybird, as Neuburg was dubbed, would look up from his desk and make some offhand pun about Archer's sapphic tendencies, excusing himself with "If you'll pardon the ostroloboguosity." No week passed without Victor using this, his favorite word. Having had his say, he would return to business, reading page proofs or tossing coal onto the fire with his fingers. Both activities kept his fingers blackened, and when things got slow, Crowley would march over to his desk and paternally demand, "Victor, let me see your fingers." In response, Neuburg would adopt a childlike posture, hiding his hands behind his back and replying, "Shan't."

And, when Neuburg commented how lucky Otter was to know Crowley as long as she had without being hurt, she shot back, "How could he hurt me? *I'm* not in love with him, and I've never lent him money."

The fourth *Equinox* appeared that September, with its usual selection of fiction, poetry, and magic. Regarding *Mathers v. Crowley*, the editorial claimed "Mathers has run away too—without paying our costs." And, as prophetically as the clipping in the last issue, Crowley wrote, "I restrict my remarks; there may be some more fun coming."[41]

"We are the Greeks! and to us the rites of Eleusis should open the doors of Heaven." So read the artsy brochure, its gray cover stamped with a black swastika, issued at the end of September to promote the Rites of Eleusis. It described their goal simply:

> In order to induce religious ecstasy in its highest form Crowley proposes
> to hold a series of religious services; seven in number will be conducted by
> Aleister Crowley himself, assisted by other Neophytes of the A∴A∴, the

mystical society, one of whose Mahatmas is responsible for the foundation of THE EQUINOX.[42]

The seven rituals, one for each of the planets in traditional astrology, would occur on consecutive Wednesdays from October 19 to November 30, 1910, at Caxton Hall. The doors would open at 8:30 and lock promptly at 9 o'clock, when the rites began. They would run for one and a half to two and a half hours. Attendees were encouraged to wear colors appropriate to the evening's performance: black for Saturn, dark blue for Jupiter, red for Mars, and so on. One reporter complained that the rites "proscribe colours which are not in my wardrobe, although a few might be met by the choice of one of those ties which lie unworn at the back of every man's chest of drawers."[43] Admission to the entire series cost a hefty £5 5s., and only one hundred tickets were for sale.

Although the price of admission was high—about $200 by today's standards—Crowley urged Probationers to attend in their robes and assist in the ceremonies. He also sent a complimentary ticket to H. G. Wells,[44] but there is no record of his attendance. Regardless, spectators packed Caxton Hall for the debut. Fuller even brought his mother.

All the participants—Crowley, Waddell, Raffalovich, Ward, Neuburg, and Hayes—were nervous because they had never rehearsed the rituals all together. Nevertheless, when they began by the dim glow of candles and colored lights, the rites came together. They explored and described the metaphysical aspects of the planets as magic and myth understood them. Dance, music, and poetry (mostly Crowley's own) dressed up the ceremonial formalities.

Leila played from her violin repertoire, featuring numerous selections by the flamboyant Polish virtuoso Henryk Wieniawski (1835–1880). Her selections also included technically demanding works such as Paganini's "Witches' Dance," Bach's "Aria for G String," and a polonaise by Vieuxtemps. The remaining pieces were romances and other popular salon music by Beethoven, Brahms, Mendelssohn, Schumann, Tchaikovsky, Saint-Saëns, and Wagner. She even salted a few original compositions among the classics.

The Rites of Eleusis generated considerable interest in the press, the *Washington Post* reporting, "Meetings of the Rosicrucians for the purpose of conjuration and of invoking 'forbidden knowledge' have been secret until last week. Then the Eleusinian rites were performed openly in a London hall."[45] However, reviewers widely panned the first performance—a grim portrayal of death and darkness—as everything from innocuous eccentricity to blasphemy. The *Hawera and Normanby Star* (New Zealand) reported:

> An atmosphere heavily charged with incense, some cheap stage effects, an infinity of poor reciting of good poetry, and some violin playing and dancing are the ingredients of the rite.... Positively the only relief in a dreary performance was afforded by a neophyte falling off his stool, which caused mild hilarity among a bored and uncomfortable audience.[46]

The *New York Times* wrote, "the hall was so dark that one might well call the Rites of Eleusis elusive."[47] Closer to home, A *Morning Leader* reviewer warned, "Unless a more cheerful tone is imparted ... the people who have paid five guineas for the whole lot will have committed suicide before they reach Luna."

The *Penny Illustrated Paper,* however, articulated the fears of a staid and conservative society about Crowley:

> There always has been about his writings and preachings an atmosphere of strange perfume, as if he was swaying a censer before the altar of some heathen goddess.
>
> Not having been initiated, we cannot tell but Mr. Crowley's Eleusinian rites do suggest an elusive form of Phallicism or sex worship....
>
> Unfortunately, this Eleusis business is not new. It has been done in Paris, entitled the Black Mass, on several occasions.
>
> Far be it from us to suggest that the large-footed gentlemen from New Scotland Yard should visit Mr. Crowley's little act ... but the idea undermining the whole business is not healthy.[48]

By the second rite, the yellow press attacked. The *Looking Glass* ran "An Amazing Sect" on October 29; a cruel critique of the rites, it described the adepts' robes as Turkish bath costumes and explained how the Mother of Heaven attempted acrobatics or jujitsu while standing on Crowley's chest. *John Bull* entered the fray on November 5 with its own attack. Not to be outdone, the *Looking Glass* followed with "An Amazing Sect—No. 2," which pried luridly into Crowley's shadowy past, printing misinformation about him such as his years as an art student, his mirror-covered temple in Boleskine, and his pseudonym Count Skerrett.[49]

The attacks outraged Crowley's circle, whose members urged him to sue. Unwilling to defend his lifestyle to a middle-class Edwardian jury, AC, much to his friends' consternation, offered various excuses. "Suffer any wrong that may be done to you rather than seek redress at law," he would say on one occasion. On another, he would quote a friend of his in city journalism (Radclyffe), who advised, "AC, let the fellow alone! If you touch pitch, you'll be defiled." Sometimes he didn't want to stoop to his opponents' level by acknowledging the attacks. Other times, he heard the *Looking Glass* was in financial straits and could pay no damages. Or he was running out of money himself and couldn't afford to sue. And there were always the vague "mystical reasons." To defuse the situation, AC published a statement in two articles in the *Bystander.* "On Blasphemy in General and the Rites of Eleusis in Particular" appeared the third week of November, defending himself against accusations leveled by the press. The autobiographical "My Wanderings in Search of the Absolute" followed, clarifying accounts of his past. Finally, he planned to publish the Rites in the sixth *Equinox* for the public to judge for themselves.

Newspaper photos of the Rite of Saturn (above) and the Rite of Jupiter (below).

The Bystander, October 12, 1910   73

Nine O'clock Ecstasies!
NOCTURNAL PLANETARY RITES A FEATURE OF THE LONDON AUTUMN SEASON

Mr. Aleister Crowley
Editor of *The Equinox*, who devised the ceremonies

The Rite of Saturn
Suicide of the Atheist!

Jupiter, the inmost soul, enthroned in the ever-revolving wheel of the three great principles—and so forth

THE first of a series of seven rites, each dedicated to one of the planets, is to be held at the Caxton Hall, Westminster, on Wednesday, the 19th (Saturn night), at nine sharp. You are requested to attend in black or very dark blue for Saturn, and similarly appropriate colour-schemes in turn for other planets. The general object is to produce in the subject a carefully selected "ecstasy." In the case of Saturn, you should become, as you watch the rites, austere and melancholic; in Mars, of course forceful and fiery; with Venus —but why labour the obvious? Sufficient has been said to indicate that nine o'clock ecstasies will be an unusual and exciting experience. To obtain admission, one must communicate with the "Guardian of the Flame" himself, in the flesh, Mr. Aleister Crowley, the poet (compared with Coleridge, Shelley, Keats, etc.), and Editor of "The Equinox," 142, Victoria Street.

A Scene from the Rite of Luna
Artemis is being invoked by Pan. The former is the mysterious Virgin Mother of Eternity, and Pan is the Holy Spirit of Matter, from which union springs Humanity, the crown child of the future—and all that

Coverage from *The Bystander*.

John Bull contended that AC missed the point: at issue was not freedom of thought and expression but whether so notorious a person as he could espouse wholesome doctrines, and whether "young girls and married women should be allowed to go [to him] for 'comfort' and 'meditation.'"[50] A third "Amazing Sect" installment followed in the November 26 *Looking Glass*. As sensational and inaccurate as its predecessors, it extended its attack to Crowley's friends. A section titled "By Their Friends Ye Shall Know Them" claimed:

> Two of Crowley's friends and introducers are still associated with him; one, the rascally sham Buddhist monk, Allan Bennett, whose imposture was shown up in "Truth" some years ago; the other a person of the name of George Cecil Jones, who was for some time employed at Basingstoke in metallurgy, but of late has had some sort of small merchant's business in the City. Crowley and Bennett lived together, and there were rumours of unmentionable immoralities which were carried on under their roof.[51]

Unlike Crowley, Jones contacted his solicitor, who wrote the publisher to demand a retraction and damages. The retraction appeared in the next issue, announcing that Jones was no longer associated with Crowley and congratulating him for breaking off with so disreputable a man. The paper felt no damage had been done, but offered him £5 for his trouble. The gesture insulted Jones, and he brought the matter to court.

Four days after this inflammatory passage appeared, the seventh and final rite, of Luna, closed the series at Caxton Hall. Coming full circle, it derived from the Rite of Artemis that started it all. Overall, the Rites were a theatrical landmark, anticipating by fifty years the experimental theater of the 1960s and 1970s.[52] The Rites' first appreciation in academic writing on theater appeared in the 1975 article "Aleister Crowley's Rites of Eleusis." In it, Brown points out how innovative Crowley was in attempting to use theater's sensory possibilities to alter consciousness.[53] Tupman's 2003 dissertation argues that "Crowley's *Rites* were not merely a unique event with neither precedent nor subsequent influence." Indeed, despite the fact that they are overlooked in every major Symbolist or avant-garde study, "the *Rites* are a classic example of Symbolist theatre," and were simultaneously forward-looking:

> to include the audience as a part of the production foreshadowed the later work of theatre anthropologists and theorists such as Richard Schechner, and serves to illustrate one of the first attempts in the twentieth century to consciously create a psychological connection between theatrical and religious practice within the western hegemonic society.[54]

Lingan's survey of the theater in New Religious Movements also recognized *The Rites of Eleusis* as an example of Symbolist theater.[55]

Nevertheless, Crowley reflected on the event with disappointment: "I throw myself no bouquets about these Rites of Eleusis. I should have given more weeks to their preparation than I did minutes."[56] Subscriptions barely covered costs, and the bad press caused attendance to dwindle so much that he had to sell tickets to individual performances. Rather than draw flocks of recruits to the A∴A∴, it drove away members and alienated its cofounders.

Fuller, fearing his name would surface in the papers next, refused to risk his military career by contributing to *The Equinox,* and began to distance himself from Crowley. His decision would prove prescient, as a quarter century later the Imperial Fascist League's paper, *The Fascist,* would dig into Fuller's past and run the headline: "Amazing Exposures of Mosley's Lieutenant: General Fuller Initiated into Aleister Crowley's (Beast 666) Occult Group."[57] Fuller was outraged: during their association, Crowley was no more than a little erratic, and the "notorious" exploits of Crowley that *The Fascist* described occurred after they'd parted ways. Fuller instructed his solicitor to prepare a writ for libel. While the publisher, Arnold Spencer Leese, maintains that the writ was dropped because "I had so much ammunition concerning him,"[58] the real reason was simple: upon reviewing Crowley's more objectionable publications from 1907 to 1910, Fuller's solicitor advised against the lawsuit. If *The Fascist* continued its attacks, he reasoned, they could pursue a criminal, rather than civil, suit.[59] However, the headline did not have traction, and the subject matter quickly faded from sight.

Jones was even more displeased. He counted on Crowley's support in his suit against the *Looking Glass.* Instead, AC placed Archer and her husband in charge of *The Equinox* and returned to Algiers with Neuburg for new Enochian workings. The disgruntled Jones wrote to Fuller, "Crowley goes to Algeria tomorrow. Some of his friends will say he ran away." So too did his enemies. Crowley's quiet departure signaled a victory for the tabloids, which proudly announced:

> We understand that Mr. Aleister Crowley has left London for Russia. This should do much to mitigate the rigour of the St. Petersburg winter. We have to congratulate ourselves on having temporarily extinguished one of the most blasphemous and cold-blooded villains of modern times.[60]

While waiting in Marseilles for his boat on December 9, 1910, Crowley wrote the fifth installment of "Temple of Solomon the King" himself to show Fuller that he was expendable. It was an essay on the practical kabbalah. Although Crowley claims to have written it all from memory, it has the feel of several shorter essays concatenated into a long article.

Crowley and Neuburg motored from Algiers to Bou-Sâada, then advanced with their interpreter, Mohammed ibn Rahman, on the 15th, trekking farther into the desert than on their last visit. Southeast of Ain Rich, despite the proverb "it never rains south of Sidi Aissa," a torrential rainstorm caught and drenched them and their tents. Their guide refused to continue, so Crowley and Neuburg continued alone into the rain. When the rain let up on the third day, they attempted to pick up where their Enochian work left off: having scried into the thirty Aethyrs, they wished to continue with visions for the

eighteen Keys (another set of conjurations in Dee's system). At the moment
they began, however, Neuburg became ill, and they had to abandon the working. Crowley returned to London to conduct business, leaving Neuburg in
Biskra to recuperate, feeling like Rose abandoned in China.

Crowley journeyed home with a fresh crop of ideas in his notebook, most
of them inspired by desire for Leila Waddell. While still in Algiers, he wrote
"On the Edge of the Desert," "Return," and "Prayer at Sunset."[61] As he sailed,
he finished "The Scorpion,"[62] a tragedy based on the 30th degree of Freemasonry; although it reflected Crowley's idea to reformulate the Masonic rituals
(as he would eventually do with OTO), Agatha—Leila's A∴A∴ motto—was
one of its dedicatees. He also wrote "The Pilgrim"[63] for her and, during a layover in Paris's Pantheon Tavern, penned "The Ordeal of Ida Pendragon,"[64] a
short story whose title character combines traits of Leila Waddell, Kathleen
Bruce, and a new acquaintance, Jane Chéron; hence the dedication "To I, J,
and K," i.e., I = Ida (Leila's second name), J = Jane, and K = Kathleen.

During a layover in France, Crowley met Jane Chéron. Despite a French
name, her features suggested Egyptian extraction. She was "a devotee of that
great and terrible God" opium. Haidée Lamoureaux, *The Diary of a Drug
Fiend*'s heroin heroine, was based on her:

> [She] was a brilliant brunette with a flashing smile and eyes with pupils like
> pin-points. She was a mass of charming contradictions. The nose and
> mouth suggested more than a trace of Semitic blood, but the wedge-
> shaped contour of her face betokened some very opposite strain....
> Though her hair was luxuriant, the eyebrows were almost non-existent....
> Her hands were deathly thin. There was something obscene in the crook-
> edness of her fingers, which were covered with enormous rings of sap-
> phires and diamonds.[65]

She would also make a cameo in *Moonchild,* when the narrator spends a Paris
evening smoking opium with her. Although she had no interest in the occult,
Chéron became Crowley's mistress at odd intervals over the next sixteen years.
Alas, while her "opium soul" inspired Crowley to write, her weakness meant
years of addiction for her.

When Crowley finally reached Eastbourne, an expected cable from Leila
did not arrive, so he wrote "The Electric Silence,"[66] a summary of his career;
"The Earth,"[67] a short essay about Leila; and "Snowstorm," a three-act play in
which Leila, as the lead character Nerissa, expresses her lines through violin
solos. Despite the disappointment of the cable, his love for Leila burned strong.

Finally reaching his London offices, Crowley was displeased with progress
on the fifth *Equinox*. In addition, Raffalovich had assumed leadership during
AC's absence, endorsing and cashing checks made out to Crowley and altering
the content of advertisements. Reading the advertisement for 777 that incorrectly stated that less than one hundred copies remained for sale and that the
price would soon rise to one guinea, AC was so furious that he forced Raffalovich to purchase enough copies of the book to reduce the stock to ninety.

Afterward, the pupil broke off relations with Crowley. Raffalovich would go on to write *The History of a Soul* (1911), *Hearts Adrift* (1912), and *The Ukraine* (1914) and contribute to various magazines including the *British Review, Vanity Fair,* and *New Age.* In 1915 he would emigrate to the United States and work as a lecturer in French. From there, he lived in Italy for five years during the fascist regime as correspondent for British and American newspapers like the *New York Times* and *Chicago Tribune.*[68] This also gave him the opportunity to write Mussolini's biography.[69] With a doctorate from the Ukrainian University in Prague, he would become professor of French and international politics, and French and Slavic history; in this capacity, he would serve on the faculties of Harvard, Dartmouth, and Emory. Dying in New Orleans in 1958 at age seventy-seven, he would leave five children and seven grandchildren.[70]

Despite these setbacks, the fifth *Equinox* appeared as scheduled in March 1911. To meet costs, its price increased from five to six shillings while its length decreased. Nevertheless, the magazine contained its usual rich variety. In addition to Crowley's poems and essays, it also featured "The Training of the Mind" by Ananda Metteya (Allan Bennett),[71] "A Nocturne" by Neuburg, "The Vampire" by Ethel Archer, and as a special supplement, the record of Crowley and Neuburg's Enochian vision quest, "The Vision and the Voice."

His next book, *The World's Tragedy* (1910), also appeared around this time. Bearing the notice "Privately printed for circulation in free countries: Copies must not be imported into England or America," the book is another swipe at convention. The text is an indictment of Christianity and its morals, while the preface provides an autobiographical sketch of AC's Brethren upbringing. Pages XXVII and XXVIII of the preface—an unusual defense of sodomy that contained scandalous accusations about the morals of cabinet members and others in high power—were removed from all copies but those in the hands of his friends. Crowley, as usual, considered it his best work.[72]

Finally, the April issue of the *Occult Review* carried Crowley's essay, "The Camel: A Discussion of the Value of 'Interior Certainty.'"[73]

On April 26, 1911, *Jones v. The Looking Glass Publishing Company Ltd. et al.*[74] appeared before Lord Justice Scrutton of the King's Bench Division and a common jury. The suit sought damages for an alleged libel in the November 26, 1910, issue of the *Looking Glass.* Harold Simmons, instructed by Bullock and Co., represented Jones. For the defense, Mr. Schiller represented the publisher while West de Wend Fenton (the editor) represented himself, and Mr. Rowlands appeared for the printer.

Crowley sat in the courtroom, amused that neither side planned to call for his testimony. Fenton, he knew, was afraid of being exposed. Jones, meanwhile, he believed, feared what the notorious AC might say on the stand. To Fuller, however, Jones explained, "If, as my friend, he hasn't the decency to come forward willingly, it would be an insult to myself had I compelled him to do so."[75]

The case opened with Simmons, for Jones, summarizing the charges, stating that the *Looking Glass* printed so serious a libel about Jones "that if a tithe of it were true, my client was unfit to associate with human beings." Because of his friendship with AC, he was linked to Crowley's rumored immoralities. As a professional with a family to support, such statements were very damaging.

The proceedings were indeed unusual: although Jones and his past were briefly discussed—including his membership in the GD and his trusteeship on behalf of AC and Lola Zaza—the case quickly became a trial of Crowley's morality. While AC's failure to file suit with the *Looking Glass* was considered telling, the most damning evidence came from Crowley's own published works. Presented as evidence was "Ambrosii Magi Hortus Rosarum" from the collected *Works*. Schiller had marked several of the Latin marginal notes: "Quid Umbratur In Mari." "Adest Rosa Secreta Eros." "Terrae Ultor Anima Terrae." "Femina Rapta Inspirat Gaudium." "Puella Urget Sophiam Sodalibus." "Culpa Urbium Nota Terrae." "Pater Iubet Scientiam Scribe." The words formed by their initials—quim, arse, tuat (twat), and so on—were Crowleyan mischief that none of his associates had discovered up to that point.

Despite objections from Jones's counsel that Crowley's writings were irrelevant to the question of Jones's character, the defense revolved around a simple premise: the *Looking Glass* did nothing more than say Jones was an associate of Crowley. Any libelous meaning coming from such a statement was due to Crowley's notoriously evil character and not anything written by the paper.

Next was the subject of Allan Bennett recently being attacked in the paper *Truth,* and his failure—like Crowley—to file suit. The fact that Bennett, as a monk, had no possessions and was living five thousand miles away didn't seem to matter. Nor did Bennett's medicinal use of drugs help matters. In the end, the legal inaction of Crowley and Bennett was seen as admission of guilt.

Finally, Schiller introduced surprise witnesses for the defense: Mathers, the wizened patriarch of the GD, was introduced to the court as Mr. Samuel Sidney Liddell MacGregor, ready to return the favor to Crowley for his defeat in court. The other was Mathers loyalist Dr. Berridge. Mathers fielded questions about the secret Rosicrucian Order, Crowley's expulsion from the GD, previous incarnations and various pseudonyms attributed to either him or Crowley, and other mystical traditions. At one point, Justice Scrutton interjected, "This trial is getting very much like the trial in *Alice in Wonderland*." Berridge, meanwhile, recounted the rumors of "unnatural vice" that had circulated about Crowley during his GD years.

Fuller was the only witness called in Jones's defense and could do little to undo the damage done by the previous testimony. The court transcript—while an interesting read—is too extensive to reproduce here.[76] Schiller's closing comments to the jury, however, captures its gist:

> You have heard from Dr. Berridge the type of man Aleister Crowley is. Confessedly Crowley stands as a man about whom no words of condem-

nation can be strong enough. That is the man of whose friendship Captain Fuller is proud; that is the man whose associate Mr. Jones is. I submit I have proved to you up to the hilt both by his writing and his own confessions that Crowley is a man of notoriously evil character. If that be so, gentlemen, I have discharged the chief burden on my shoulders, and it only remains for you to say whether I have gone beyond the bounds of fair comment.

Gentlemen, was not the paper justified in showing up this amazing sect of Crowley's and were not they right in saying and fully justified in the comment they made about Mr. Jones's association with Aleister Crowley? Though he knew these rumours were flying about, rumours which Crowley did not dare to deny, he still associated with Crowley and would have you believe that he is a man of perfectly unblemished character, a man whom he would not hesitate to introduce to his own wife. If a man values his own reputation so cheaply that he does not mind associating with that kind of creature, he must not complain if comment is made about it and he must not come to you and ask you to give him exemplary damages. When he can associate with a creature of Aleister Crowley's description and can come here and be proud of it, and to corroborate him, call a friend who is proud of the friendship of a man who writes the kind of stuff you have seen, a man who does not hesitate to advertise his pernicious literature of a gross type by appealing to the worst instincts of degenerates amongst mankind, by appealing to their sense of the morbid, a man who himself publishes the criticisms of his books in order to attract purchasers for his wretched books, books that have been criticized in a well-known publication of one of the two leading universities as dealing with a revolting subject revoltingly handled, and who advertises the whole thing under the hypocritical guise of a society for the propagation of religious truth— what are you to say of a man who boasts of his associations with such a creature?

I ask you to say as twelve healthy-minded men that there is no comment strong enough which a paper is not entitled to make in criticizing the conduct of a man like the plaintiff in this case. It serves him right if he meets with strong criticism under such circumstances. Were we not justified in saying that you must judge this man's character by his association with this creature? Gentlemen, I ask you to say, and I ask you with confidence to say, that I have not and that I was amply justified in making the comment I did make, that it was a fair and proper comment to make under the circumstances, and I ask you therefore to give a verdict for my clients.

Scrutton posed four questions to the jury: 1. Were the words complained of defamatory of the plaintiff? 2. If so, were the defamatory statements of fact substantially true? 3. Were the defamatory statements so far as they consisted of opinion fair comment on facts? 4. What damage has the publication caused the plaintiff? After thirty-two minutes of deliberation, the jury returned its verdict. They answered the first three questions "Yes," and the last "None." In essence, the statements and their unsavory implications were accurate and fair comment on a friend of Crowley's, and Jones thereby suffered no damages. They entered judgment for the defendants. The *Looking Glass* had won.

Jones's defeat unleashed a new wave of gossip about the notoriously evil Aleister Crowley. When American art patron and book collector John Quinn (1870–1924) visited publisher Elkin Matthews at this time, the subject of Crowley inevitably came up. Matthews had published *Ambergris,* and told Quinn, "We had a very 'ard time getting him to cut things out of it. Right now, Crowley's out of England because of something he's done."

"What was the trouble?" Quinn asked.

"We don't know, sir, only he has got himself dreadfully talked about."[77]

The worst ramifications, however, were personal. Because Crowley offered no assistance, Jones ended their friendship. Although he would continue to oversee Lola Zaza's trust for decades, he maintained distance from Crowley. He would retire in 1939 because of wartime restrictions on trade; his planning would prove insightful, as an air raid would destroy his lab in 1941.

Fuller, whom Crowley considered his best friend, sent his last letter ever to Crowley on May 2. He thought Crowley a coward for not defending himself and broke with him on the same grounds as Jones. Fuller would go on to attain the rank of major-general and invent the blitzkrieg, which England would disregard and Germany would adopt. He would be the only Englishman invited to Hitler's birthday party in 1939. Throughout the years, however, his interest in magic would never fade: he would write books like *Yoga* (1925) and *Secret Wisdom of the Qabalah* (1937), and contribute articles to journals like *Form* and the *Occult Review.*[78] Even in his last days, Fuller maintained that Crowley was one of England's greatest lyric poets.[79]

At this time, Ward also became disillusioned with the A∴A∴. He not only doubted Crowley's honesty and character but also grew weary and critical of magic. Feeling a need to break away, he welcomed the opportunity to become professor of mathematics and physics at Rangoon College, where he would study Buddhism. His thoughts on the subject remained remarkably close to Crowley's: "Properly speaking, the 'theory' is philosophy, the 'practice' is science; and both together are religion," he would say. In the end, he would become a Christian Scientist.

Thus, in very short order, Crowley lost two of his oldest friends and, with Ward and Raffalovich, two of his best students. Two-thirds of the founding triad of the A∴A∴ had seceded, leaving him, like Mathers, sole authority of his occult organization, and bad press caused A∴A∴ enrollment to dwindle to only three applicants for the year 1911.

The Secret Chiefs were testing him, he decided, and help would soon be on its way.

The evening was dark, and seven poplars near the Vanne Rouge Inn looked the like vigilant spirits of God. Standing at the weir, Crowley felt an emptiness as if the dark current of the Loing had swept away his life's work. Not even his nostalgia for weirs staved off the pain he felt from having friends and students leave him, of having his work attacked, of having the order suffer. When he needed her most, Leila was off playing in the English Ladies' Orchestra in *A Waltz Dream*.

A lone star shone overhead, the moon set behind a tower, and he thought, *I am alone in the Abyss*. It felt as if he were again experiencing that soul-crushing ordeal. Crowley returned to his room and wrote "The Sevenfold Sacrament,"[80] a pendant to "Aha!" describing that evening's Abyss reprise.

Adversity, however, always inspired Crowley; this time, he entered an *annum mirabilis*. With Fuller gone, Crowley prepared to fill *The Equinox* with his own works, writing feverishly throughout his stay in Paris and Montigny-sur-Loing. The *English Review*'s June publication of "On the Edge of the Desert" served as the starting gun for his marathon.

On August 10, spending Leila's birthday separated from his love, Crowley dwelt all night on their year together. "A Birthday" resulted, recalling their meeting, her last birthday, the Rites of Eleusis, a tentative parting and reunion, their arrival in Paris. On their present separation, he wrote:

> Do not then dream this night has been a loss!
> All night I have hung, a god, upon the cross;
> All night I have offered incense at the shrine;
> All night you have been unutterably mine ...

Crowley wrote many other pieces at this time, including two short stories: "The Woodcutter," about a man with a one-track mind, and "His Secret Sin," about sexual hypocrisy. *Mortadello*,[81] his five-act play of Venice, also came out of this period. *Rhythm* gave it a decidedly mixed review, calling it

> a dull, stupid, dreary affair. The stale situations, the childish "comedy," and the peurile grossness, are incredibly school-boyish; though the verse in which the play is written is damnably accomplished. Mr. Crowley manipulates his medium with a deadly dexterity. He works the Alexandrine for all it is worth; and gets unexpected amusement out of it by the skillful surprise of unexpected internal rhymes. He is a master of metrical artifice.[82]

Nevertheless, *Mortadello* would remain one of his favorite pieces, which he would try throughout his life to produce on the stage.

He got the idea for his play "Adonis" next, and stopped at the Café Dôme in Montparnasse for a *citron pressé* before commencing. New inspiration struck unexpectedly when, to his bemusement, he saw Nina Olivier with her latest attachment, Scottish pianist and raconteur James Hener Skene (born c. 1878).[83] Accompanying them was Fenella Lovell, a consumptive-looking Parisian model of 203 Boulevard Raspail. Of Romany descent, she wrote Gypsy songs in English and Romany, and was involved in the Gypsy Lore Society.[84] In the summer of 1908 she gave Romany language lessons to British poet Arthur Symons (1865–1945), who offered her hospitality and found her to be an accomplished teacher.[85] She also modeled for many, including aspiring Welsh painter Gwen John (1876–1939), whose younger brother Augustus John (1878–1961) would become better known. Of Lovell, Gwen John wrote, "no one will want to buy her portrait do you think so? ... it is a great strain doing Fenella. It is a pretty little face but she is *dreadful*."[86] Her beauty and dress struck Crowley, who mentally cast her as the heroine of some yet-unwritten play. Eyeing her, he wrote in his head:

> By the window stands Fenella, fantastically dressed in red, yellow, and blue, her black hair wreathed with flowers. She is slight, thin, with very short skirts, her spider legs encased in pale blue stockings. Her golden shoes with their exaggerated heels have paste puckles. In her pale face her round black eyes blaze. She is rouged and powdered; her thin lips are painted heavily. Her shoulder-bones stare from her low-necked dress, and a diamond dog-collar clasps her shining throat. She is about seventeen years old.[87]

Yes, he mused, and left minutes later. Returning to his room at 50 rue Vavin, he wrote "The Ghouls," then proceeded immediately on to "Adonis." He completed both in a single forty-three-hour sitting.

Fenella Lovell.

While most of these stories appeared in the next two issues of *The Equinox*,[88] the bulk of his work that summer involved the magical papers of the A∴A∴, which he wrote in abundance. These documents he divided into four classes: Class A documents were Holy Books, "inspired" or "channeled" works not to be altered in any way; Class B documents were scholarship; Class C were inspirational or suggestive; and Class D were practical instructions.

While most of the Thelemic Holy Books were channeled at the end of 1907, the remaining ones came to Crowley this summer. These Class A documents included: "Liber B vel Magi" (The Book of the Magus), which describes the grade of Magus 9°=2□; "Liber Tzaddi vel Hamus Hermeticus" (The Book of the Hermetic Fish Hook), which calls mankind to initiation; "Liber Cheth vel Vallum Abiegni" (The Book of the Wall of Abiegnus, the great Rosicrucian mountain), which describes crossing the Abyss; and "Liber A'ash vel Capricorni Pneumatici" (The Book of Creation, or the Goat of the Spirit), an instruction in sexual magic in veiled language.[89]

Class B documents written at this time include "Liber Israfel," an invocation of the Egyptian god Thoth written by Allan Bennett and revised by Crowley; "Liber Viarum Viae" (The Way of Ways) on the tarot; "Liber Viae Memoriae vel ThIShARB" (The Way of Memory), a method for thinking backwards to understand the causes acting in one's life; and a tentative work on the Greek kabbalah.[90]

Class C, or suggestive, works include "Across the Gulf," an allegorical account of a past life in Egypt; and "Liber Os Abysmi vel Daath" (The Book of the Mouth of the Abyss), which describes a method of entering the Abyss based upon logical skepticism. "Adonis" he also classed in this category.

The Class D, or official instructions, included the following: "Liber NV" and "Liber HAD" describe, based on the *Book of the Law,* how to attain the states of consciousness associated with these Egyptian deities. Practical instructions in yoga were summed up in books on meditation ("Liber Turris vel Domus Dei"), devotion ("Liber Astarte vel Liber Berylli"), and pranayama ("Liber RV vel Spiritus"). "Liber IOD" (The Book of Vesta) contains instructions on thought reduction, while "Liber Resh vel Helios" (The Book of the Sun) contains adorations of the sun for dawn, noon, sunset and midnight.[91] This last exercise Crowley considered most important for reminding students of the Great Work, and Crowley practiced it regularly throughout his life.

On the autumnal equinox, the sixth issue of *The Equinox* appeared. Owing to difficulties with Fuller and Raffalovich, it was the slimmest volume to date, and notably missing was the next installment of "The Temple of Solomon the King." To compensate, Crowley printed "The Rites of Eleusis" as a supplement for the public to judge its contents. Besides several A∴A∴ *libri,* this issue also featured contributions from Archer and Neuburg as well as book reviews courtesy of two of his friends, chemist Edward Whineray and Freemason John Yarker. Yarker was a new acquaintance who would go on to influence Crowley's magick heavily. Yarker had previously awarded Crowley with various Masonic and pseudo-Masonic distinctions after his victory in court against Mathers over the GD rituals reproduced in *The Equinox.* AC had since reviewed Yarker's *The Arcane Schools* in the fourth *Equinox,* writing "The reader of this treatise is at first overwhelmed by the immensity of Brother Yarker's erudition," to which the author replied with a letter of thanks for "your kindly review."[92]

Sweet classical melodies issued from the piano; facile fingers deftly executed the performance; and silence greeted its conclusion. Hener Skene turned from the piano to face the man who had requested a lesson in music appreciation. "*That* was Chopin."

"I don't know," Crowley remarked, desperately hiding a smile. "I think it a trifle boring."

"Oh?" Skene lifted an eyebrow. "Then how about this?" He returned to the piano and played another piece. It was a selection from *Cavalleria Rusticana* (1890), the one-act opera by Pietro Mascagni (1863–1945) about a love triangle ending in bloodshed. Skene considered it a clearly inferior work.

Crowley applauded. "Much better! *This* music moves me."

The music stopped. Skene again turned to face Crowley, who quickly replaced the smirk on his face with an inquisitive expression. "No, no," the pianist objected. "You should prefer Chopin. Let's try again." He returned to the piano and began another piece by the Pole.

A smile returned to Crowley's lips, and he began thinking he had judged Skene too hastily. When Crowley's fiancée, Eileen Gray, first introduced them in Paris in 1902, Skene came off so witless and conceited that Crowley parodied him in the appendix to *The Star and the Garter*.[93] Meeting him at the Dôme for only the second time, he found Skene so unpleasant and cadaverous that he helped inspire "The Ghouls."[94] When Skene shifted his affections from Nina to dancer Isadora Duncan, to whom he was accompanist, he had "the manners of an undertaker gone mad, the morals of a stool-pigeon, and imagining himself a bishop."[95] Despite all that, Crowley saw Skene as a potential source of fun.

Chopin's piece ended, and Skene looked again at Crowley, who wore a pensive, almost pained, scowl. "I—I *think* I understand," AC stammered.

"Again!" Skene declared, and returned to the ivories for more Mascagni.

Crowley was so delighted he was loathe to release the moment. Then he devised a way to milk the game even further. When Skene again finished, Crowley feigned rapture. "Yes, yes, I see! If you would be so kind, I'd like you to repeat this lesson for my good friend, Princess Bathurst." Princess Leila Ida Nerissa Bathurst Waddell.

When Crowley bumped into Skene in London on October 11, 1911, it was another of their many subsequent encounters. This time Skene was on his way to the Savoy, where Isadora Duncan was throwing a wild fortieth birthday party for her best friend, Mary Desti. Since Crowley had no particular plans, the pianist brought him along. At this twenty-three-hour party, Crowley met Isadora Duncan (1878–1927), whom he admired as the greatest dancer of his generation; she is preserved in *Moonchild* as Lavinia King, while her brother Raymond appears as "a lantern-jawed American with blue cheeks."[96] The guest of honor, however, impressed him most.

Standing at five-foot-five, Mary Desti (1871–1931) was a voluptuous, big-boned woman with curly black hair and attractive—even magnificent—Irish-Italian features. Born in Quebec and raised in Chicago, she moved to Paris and adopted Duncan's penchant for wearing only sandals and a Greek tunic held together by a pin at her shoulder; indeed, Desti gained some notoriety when her landlord attempted to evict her for dressing too scantily.[97] She was a passionate, worldly woman, and her personality and magnetism attracted Crowley straight off. She felt the same profound emotion toward him. He spent the evening sitting cross-legged on the floor, "exchanging electricity with her."[98]

Mary Desti (1871–1931) in 1916, by E. O. Hoppé.

Mary Dempsey, to use her legal name,[99] had been married four times. Little is known of her first marriage. Her second husband, Edmund P. Biden, was a heavy-drinking traveling salesman whose banjo playing taught her to despise the instrument. The birth of their son Edmund Preston on August 29, 1898, came as a complete surprise; both were apparently naive about the facts of life. Up to the last minute, Biden believed his wife had a tumor. Their marriage ended in January when Mary, fed up with Biden's drunken rages, escaped with her infant to France. Reflecting on two wasted years, she detested her ex so much that she could not speak his name. Named after his father, her boy thereby went by his middle name, Preston.

While apartment-hunting in Paris, Mary met Mrs. Duncan, who took her home to meet her daughter, Isadora. The two became close friends, and Mary moved into Isadora's Paris studio while Mrs. Duncan took charge of Preston. Mary idolized Isadora, seeing in her the person she wanted to be.

Mary wed for a third time in Memphis, Tennessee, on October 2, 1901. Her new husband was childhood sweetheart Solomon Sturges, grandson of the pioneering financier who founded Solomon Sturges and Sons, later known as the Continental Illinois National Bank and Trust Company of Chicago. Sturges adopted Mary's son, and the new family was close and happy. Mary wrote a play called "The Freedom of the Soul," which had a single performance at Chicago's Ravina Park; of his wife's penchant for writing, Sturges remarked "it was infinitely to be preferred to bridge whist playing, and it wasn't so hard on a man's pocketbook."[100] After Paris, however, Chicago stifled Mary, and not even the wishes of her husband would keep her from Isadora. The marriage became strained when Mary followed the notorious dancer across Europe. Tolerant at first, Sturges eventually tired of his wife's dress and constant flitting across the Atlantic. After a terrible argument in 1907, they separated, and Mary later returned to Europe. Sending Preston to a Parisian boarding school, she was free to live an unconventional, liberated life. Solomon Sturges was eventually granted a divorce for desertion in January 1911.

Her fourth and unfortunate marriage would occur in London the following year—on February 12, 1912—to Turkish fortune hunter Vely Bey.[101] They had met years ago in Chicago, where Bey had been trying (ultimately unsuccessfully) to launch a Turkish tobacco import company. This husband liked how she dressed, and as a bonus his father was Ilias Pasha, court physician to the sultan of Turkey.[102] Both mistakenly thought the other was wealthy, and only after the wedding did the economic truth come out. This, combined with Bey's dislike of Preston, doomed the marriage from the start. Before things blew up, Mary learned the formula for the lotion her father-in-law had concocted to cure a rash on her face; it was supposedly common throughout the harems of Turkey, and it not only cleared up her rash but also smoothed away wrinkles. Seeing a lucrative opportunity, Mary marketed it as "Le Secret du Harem," and founded at 4 rue de la Paix her renowned perfumery "Maison d'Este." This name derived from Mary's dislike of her given surname, Dempsey; some amateur genealogy linked Dempsey to Desmond and d'Este, which she adopted. However, the d'Este family in Paris threatened to sue if she did not change the name of her salon and remove the garish neon sign out front. Hence the salon became "Maison Desti."

Encountering the free spirit of future entrepreneur Mary d'Este or Mary Desti, Crowley couldn't help feel she was a perfect match for him. Suddenly he found himself torn between his unshakable affection for Leila and the inexplicable feeling he got from this stranger.

"Preliminary skirmishing" characterized the following months as Crowley tried to make her acquaintance. Two days after the party, he met her for tea and tried to explain the feeling he got when they met. Unsurprisingly, she knew nothing of magic, but having written some plays, shared his literary aspirations. They dined the next evening, and after a snack of chocolate and rolls, Crowley left for northern England.

He must have come on too strongly, for she answered none of the letters he sent over the next two weeks.

Scottish art editor George MacNie Cowie (1861–1948) was deaf as a result of scarlet fever; he often felt alienated from others because of his handicap, and in 1885, he served as president of the Edinburgh Deaf and Dumb Benevolent Society.[103] Born in St. Ninians, Stirlingshire, to shoemaker William Cowie and Margaret King MacNie, he had an older half-sister, Christian (a dressmaker born in Ireland), and a younger sister, Isabella.[104] He worked as a lithographic artist and designer, and the 1901 Scottish census lists him as married to Eliza-beth Cowie, who was born around 1851 in Coatbridge, Lanarkshire.[105] Cowie was in his forties when, reading the commentary on creation in *The Perfect Way* (1890) by Anna Kingsford (1846–1888) and Edward Maitland (1824–1897), he converted to vegetarianism. He was in his fifties when, on November 1, he became one of only three probationers to join the A∴A∴ in 1911, choosing "Quarens Serenitatem" (I will seek serenity) as his motto. Employed as art edi-tor for Edinburgh publisher Nelson's, this new student prompted Crowley to note, "His character was unselfish and noble, his aspiration intense and sin-cere."[106] He would prove to be one of AC's more valuable students, advancing to Neophyte as Frater Fiat Pax (Let there be peace), and, in OTO, reaching the VIII° and serving as Grand Treasurer General.

While Crowley had been away, Rose, after years of heavy drinking, was com-mitted to an asylum on September 27. She suffered alcoholic dementia "in its most hopeless form."[107] Crowley hardly felt remorse over the tragedy: *Rosa Decidua* was his heart's final outpouring for her. As he saw it, the Secret Chiefs had chosen her; failing in her divine mission, she suffered the penalties described in *The Book of the Law*. Now, he suspected, the Chiefs had lined him up with a new candidate.

Out with the old, in with the new.

On October 29, Crowley sought Mary Desti at the Savoy, prepared to bury her in barbed words the way only a great poet could. How dare she ignore his letters! But his armor melted at the first sight of her, and he forgave all.

In November—even though he was hard at work on the next *Equinox,* which would include *The Book of the Law* and an account of its reception—AC and Mary set out on a vacation to one of his favorite spots: St. Moritz. They spent November 18 at Montparnasse, leaving Paris the next evening. As they traveled, Crowley studied his 1904 notebooks, *The Equinox* page proofs, and the manuscript of *The Book of the Law*. On the night of November 20, Mary dreamed she saw the heads of five old men called the White Brothers telling her, "It's all right." She didn't know what it meant, and, when she told AC, he showed no interest. It wasn't her mind that he wanted to get inside.

Weary from travel, they spent the night of November 21 at Zurich's National Hotel. "This town is so hideous and depressing that we felt our only chance of living through the night was to get superbly drunk,"[108] Crowley wrote. More drinks followed; then they had sex. As a lover, Crowley was magnetic and experienced; Mary was no less so, carrying on like an amorous but infuriated lioness.

As they rested in bed, exhausted but unsatiated, Mary slipped into a calm, relaxed state and began talking about the old white-bearded man from her dream. She said he held a wand in his hand, and on his hand was a ring with a feather in its glass. A large claw was on his breast.

Overstimulated, Crowley surmised. The combination of alcohol and sex was too much for her. As she continued, however, Crowley realized she was not recounting her dream of the previous night but was describing this old man as she saw him right now. It reminded him of Rose's strange, dazed condition when she contacted the Chiefs.

He sat upright and instructed her, "Make yourself perfectly passive. Let him communicate freely. What do you see?"

The five white brethren turned red, she said, and spoke: "Here is a book to be given to Frater P." Crowley nearly fell over with surprise: Mary did not know his magical name. "The name of the book is *Aba*," she continued, "and its number is four."

Crowley computed the values of the letters *a, b,* and *a* and came up with four. This was more knowledge she did not possess. So far, so good. Mary went on to describe a swarthy man named Jezel, who was hunting for the book. However, the elder commented, Frater P. would get it.

Suddenly, the vision became unclear, and Mary grew frightened. She didn't understand what this was all about. Crowley encouraged her to continue. "What's his name?" he asked.

Abuldiz, she replied.

"What about seventy-eight?" AC asked, giving a number of Aiwass.

"He says he *is* seventy-eight."

"What is sixty-five?" he tested again, giving the number of *Adonai,* the general godname for the holy guardian angel.

"Frater P is sixty-five, and his age is 1,400." Pure gibberish, he thought.

"What of Krasota?" he asked about the Word of the Equinox. Abuldiz the wizard only frowned in reply. Crowley was dissatisfied, and remained skeptical even though Abuldiz insisted Crowley show faith. Through Mary, Abuldiz promised to clear everything up in a week, at precisely 11 p.m. He instructed Crowley, at that time, to invoke as he did in Cairo in 1904.

An odd coincidence, he mused, as the rituals he used with Rose in 1904 were again in his possession as he prepared to publish *The Book of the Law*. Furthermore, he just happened to have with him all the necessary ritual implements, including the robe he wore at the Cairo Working in 1904. Mary had even packed a blue and gold abbai like Rose's. Arriving at St. Moritz the next day, their suite at the Palace Hotel contained a tall mirror very much like the one in his honeymoon suite in Cairo. This impending publication of *The Book of the Law,* he assumed, was causing a magical stir.

In the following days, Crowley told Mary everything he knew about magic. This way, he ensured that Abuldiz could only convince him of his authenticity by revealing something neither of them knew; it would have to be big. "Anything she said three times she believed fervently," her son attested to Mary's imagination. "Often twice was enough."[109] Coming from an intellect like Crowley's, the words opened a new dimension of reality that she accepted wholeheartedly. She found this business of magic fascinating.

On November 28 they prepared for the ceremony as instructed. They stowed all unnecessary furniture. Five chairs sat out for the five brethren. An octagonal table served as the altar, holding the magical weapons, invocations, and incense. Mary, wearing her abbai with rich jewels as described in *The Book of the Law,*[110] sat on the floor facing the mirror in the east. Dressed in his usual robes, Crowley kindled the incense and performed the Lesser Banishing Ritual of the Pentagram at 10:38 p.m. By 10:45, he began reciting the Augoeides vigorously. At the stroke of eleven, he uttered, *"Cujus nomen est Nemo, Frater A∴A∴, adest."* (I am he whose name is Nemo, a Brother of the A∴A∴.)

"He's here," Mary replied solemnly. "He wants to know what you want."

"Nothing!" he snapped. "Did I call him, or he me?"

"He called you…but there is seventy-seven."

That was Leila's number, and Crowley momentarily remembered his lover in London. Then, returning to the present, he asked, "Why did you call me?"

"He says, 'To give you this book.'"

"How will it be given?"

"He says, 'By the seer.' But I don't have any book!"

"Do you claim to be a Brother of the A∴A∴?"

"He has A∴A∴ in black letters on his breast."

"What does A∴A∴ mean?"

With this test, the vision became garbled. She saw images and symbols, numbers that meant little to either of them.

"Ask him to be slower and simpler," Crowley finally insisted. "Give further signs of your identity: Are you Sapiens Dominabitur Astris?" This was the motto of the GD's German contact, Fraulein Sprengel.

"I see nothing but a skull," Mary replied.

Good, Crowley thought to himself: *Sprengel is dead.* "Is Deo Duce Comite Ferro one of you?" He dragged Mathers into it.

"No. No longer," she replied as Abuldiz. After a few more questions, Mary began to complain of someone beside her, breathing on her. Looking about, Crowley could see small elementals bounding about the room.

"Ask who breathes," he instructed.

"The black man," she replied. "He has now a white turban." Using a technique Crowley had taught her, she banished the figure away. More garbled communication followed, with Abuldiz finally stating, "Ask me about nine."

Crowley raised an eyebrow. "Consider yourself asked."

"Nine is the number of a page in a book."

"We have none in stock. What book?"

"A book of fools." Only in later years would this make sense to Crowley, referring to his authorship of *The Book of Wisdom of Folly* after he assumed the grade of Magus (9°=2□). The communication went off on another apparent tangent. After a futile exchange, Mary announced, "He shows another book with a blazing sun, and covers in gold. He says, 'The Book IV. Your instruction to the Brothers.'"

"Then I'm not to publish it?"

"Abuldiz gives the sign of silence."

He nodded. "I understand by that that I am not to publish it."

"Never. But you are to find it."

When more gibberish followed, Crowley lost his patience. "Does he wish to go on with this very unsatisfactory conversation?"

Mary, as Abuldiz, replied, "Go to London, find Book IV, and return it to the Brothers."

"Where is Book IV?"

"In London. When you get Book IV, you'll know what the white feather means. Obey and return Book IV to the Brothers." By this time, after over nearly an hour, Mary complained she was tired.

Crowley agreed. "Ask for another appointment."

Abuldiz replied, "The fourth of December, between 7 and 9 p.m."

Fine. "Good-bye!"

The communication of December 4 was very much like the last. Contacting Abuldiz at 9 p.m., Mary announced they had better get to London quickly and find Book IV, even though neither one of them had any idea what book this was, or how to go about locating it. When Crowley asked Mary's magical name, Abuldiz responded VIRAKAM; convinced of the importance of this work, she became Soror Virakam.

Further communications with Abuldiz occurred on December 10, 11, 13, and 19. In all but the last instance, the communication began with champagne, sex, and incantations. They gradually came to the understanding that they needed to go on a retirement and write Book IV themselves. During the last communication, at Milan, Crowley received the final details.

By this time, Crowley asked questions in acronym form to further test the wizard. "N.w.a.t.V.?" Now what about the villa?

Abuldiz replied, "What you will. Patience; there is danger of health."

"H.o.f.?" Here or further?

"No. You asked wrongly."

"H?" Here?

"W?" Where?

"R?" Rome?

"No."

"N?" Naples?

"Yes."

"Is Virakam to work herself, or only to help Perdurabo?"

"Virakam is to work, to serve." This was appropriate, as Abuldiz had previously told them the word meant "I serve the light." "Tomorrow you will find what you seek; you will know, for he will be with you and give you the sign. Don't hesitate and don't worry, bring forth the fruit. Till tomorrow."

"Good-bye!"

"There is no good-bye. There's work to be done; I'm always ready. Don't struggle. Accept and believe." He held a finger to his eye, and was gone.

Crowley now understood: he and Mary were to travel past Rome and rent a villa. When Abuldiz told Crowley how to recognize the Villa—"You will recognize it beyond the possibility of doubt or error"—he had a vision of a villa on a hillside, with a garden and two Persian nut trees in the yard. There they would write Book IV, a text of practical magic.

They left for Rome the next day.[111]

Bickering tarnished the first few days in Rome. Actually, bickering was an understatement. It seemed that when they weren't engaged in drunken lovemaking, AC and Mary could only fight. This maelstrom of passion—and their faith in Abuldiz—was what kept them together.

As instructed, they moved past Rome after two or three days, combing the Naples countryside for a place matching Abuldiz's description. They expected to find dozens of suitable villas, but were sadly disappointed: after days motoring through the city and suburbs, they failed to find a single match. The villa became an obsession. They discussed it while driving and eating, and one night Mary even dreamed of it.

The day after her dream, Mary's son, Preston, was joining them for Christmas. The arrival of his train at four that afternoon cut short an idle search in Posilippo, a promontory southwest of Naples. After a futile cursory tour, Mary became anxious about Preston's arrival, and insisted they head for the station. As they drove down the road, however, Mary suddenly cried out. "Turn! Turn down that road." The "road" was a trail leading off the main thoroughfare, so slight as to be virtually indistinguishable.

Crowley regarded her blankly. A minute ago, she was in a hellfire hurry.

"Damn it," she urged the chauffeur, "turn off! The villa is down that road. I'm sure of it."

Once the car detoured onto the path as she demanded, they found themselves on a narrow washboard road that deposited them on a low stone parapet, a slope dropping down to their right. "There!" Mary chirped excitedly. "It's the villa I saw in my dream."

Crowley and the chauffeur craned their necks about. AC looked quizzical, then tried to speak rationally to her. "Mary, there's no villa here."

She huffed. "You're right. But I know it's here. Chauffeur, drive on." As they continued, they encountered a tiny piazza and church. It was the square she had seen in her dream. "Keep going," she urged the driver. After one hundred yards, the road became even more rugged, steep and narrow, rock piles blocking parts of the road. The chauffeur slowed and complained he could go no further. Turning around or backing up to the square were impossible. "Do as I say, you bastard," Mary hollered. She was livid, and violence was a distinct possibility. "Keep driving."

The chauffeur glanced at Crowley, who merely shrugged his shoulders. They continued a few more yards, after which the chauffeur stopped and flatly refused to proceed.

Mary cursed and punched the seat. Looking out the window, she saw an open gate to the left. Within, workmen were repairing a dilapidated villa. She burst out of the car and approached the foreman, asking in broken Italian if the building was for rent. Even though it wasn't, she was undeterred, and forced him to show her the place.

Amused, Crowley opened the door, sat in the car and watched the fiasco. *Disgusting,* he mused. Eventually, his gaze followed the grounds of the villa out to its garden. At its end he spotted two Persian nut trees, corresponding exactly to his vision. His amusement turned to astonishment.

Looking at the name on the gate, he computed its numerical value. Villa Kaldarazzo added up to 418. This was the number of Ra Hoor, Abrahadabra, and other key terms in *The Book of the Law.* Excitement finally infected him. They *had* found the villa that Abuldiz indicated.

AC leapt out of the car and hurried into the house, catching up to Mary and the foreman in the main room. Looking about, the walls decorated with crude frescoes, he believed this building had the atmosphere and emanation necessary for the Great Work. Learning the villa was not for rent, Crowley demanded the name and address of its owner. In the midst of their excitement, a practical thought intruded: Preston. On the verge of another panic, Mary grabbed AC's elbow and urged them to the train station.

Crowley disliked Preston, and the feeling was mutual. To AC, the brat was a godforsaken lout. This, however, was a compliment compared to what Preston called the "phonus bolonus" her mother had taken up with. He loathed Crowley and in later years remarked, "I realize my mother and I were lucky to escape with our lives. If I had been a little older he might not have escaped with his."[112] To the thirteen-year-old youth, far from home and missing his adoptive father, Crowley seemed like a monster.

The next morning, they found the owner of the villa and convinced him to rent it to them. Wasting no time, they moved in the following day, consecrated the temple, and began work on *Book Four*. Simplicity was their goal: Crowley dictated, and anywhere he was unclear, Virakam stopped him for clarification. Thus they planned an exposition that people from any walk of life could understand. Crowley envisioned *Book Four* in four parts: part one would deal with yoga, part two with magical implements, part three with Crowley's theory of "Magick," and part four with his commentary on *The Book of the Law*.

As they worked, the world saw many changes: New Mexico and Arizona became the 47th and 48th states; the Manchu Dynasty was overthrown, and China became a republic; coal miners went on strike in Britain; and on April 15, the *Titanic* sank along with 1,513 passengers.

At one point in the dictation, after working feverishly until midnight, Crowley sat back, dissatisfied with his words. "If I could only dictate a book like the Tao Teh King," he lamented. Mary watched as his face changed. His pupils dilated into large, dark discs. She wasn't even sure if he was still the same person. *He's meditating,* she thought when he closed his eyes, but then a yellow light bathed the room. She looked around but found no source for the light. Then the stranger and his chair rose, the chair looking like a throne and the master appearing asleep or dead. She looked desperately about the room, then, alone and overwhelmed, passed out.

Whether a vision or a dream, the experience betrayed Mary's sense of alienation: although they got through writing part two, their relationship deteriorated into hostility. After another major argument, Mary left and returned to Paris. Shortly thereafter, she telegraphed AC, apologizing for her rashness and inviting him to join her in Paris. This he did, but when they returned to London, the Turk in Abuldiz's vision appeared in the form of Veli Bey, the future husband who Crowley believed spoiled the Great Work. The story, however, was more complicated than that. To Crowley's disappointment, Mary had begun showing signs of alcoholism. *Just like Rose,* he mused; and this certainly contributed to their separation. In the end, he attributed their break to "my own great default of faith in her, more than her quite justified distrust of me."[113] Neither one was likely despondent over their separation: Mary had Isadora, Crowley had Leila, and all was well with the world.

As for *Book Four,* a decade would pass before Crowley finished part three, and nearly two decades before it would be published. The fourth part, published in 1936 as *The Equinox of the Gods,* would be promoted more as another installment of *The Equinox* than the final part of *Book Four.*

Mary Desti's name nevertheless graced the next four numbers of *The Equinox,* replacing Crowley as editor (doubtlessly to silence the yellow press). She also contributed a few pieces to the journal: the play "Doctor Bob," which she coauthored with Crowley,[114] her poem "On—On—Poet,"[115] and the play "The Tango," another Desti-Crowley collaboration.[116]

After they parted, Mary became wealthy with her Maison Desti, her products so popular that the Cody Corporation offered to buy her out. Her son, Preston Sturges, eventually returned to America and became a successful scriptwriter and movie director in the 1930s, 1940s and 1950s; while his first screenplay made a star out of actor Spencer Tracy (1900–1967), Sturges is best known for the comedies he directed. Looking back on Crowley, Mary would always recall him fondly as a model of charm and good manners, possessing one of the greatest minds she had encountered in her entire life.[117]

CHAPTER ELEVEN

Ordo Templi Orientis

The spring 1912 *Equinox* is arguably the most important issue of the set. For the first time, Crowley's name vanished from the masthead, which instead listed Mary d'Este Sturges as editor and Victor Neuburg as subeditor. Although Crowley, as the issue reported, was away on a magical retirement, the issue bore his unmistakable stamp. In addition to contributions from Ethel Archer, Herbert Close, and John Yarker, it featured many A∴A∴ *libri* as well as the next "Temple of Solomon the King," which recounted how Crowley received *The Book of the Law* in Cairo in 1904. The article featured extracts from his 1903–1904 diaries, a facsimile reproduction of the manuscript, and full-color plates of the stele. For this first publication of *The Book of the Law,* Crowley wrote a short comment on its verses; he considered it inadequate, but it was the best he could do at the time.

The price for this issue went up, partly to cover the cost of engraving its plates. Besides the stele reproductions, the issue also included several photographs. Some dubbed them pornographic; in them, with genitalia carefully painted out, a naked and overweight Crowley demonstrated yogic postures. The corresponding text read:

> Some of the weaker brethren having found the postures in Liber E too difficult, the pitiful heart of the Praemonstrator of A∴A∴ has been moved to authorise the publication of additional postures, which will be found facing this page. An elderly, corpulent gentleman of sedentary habit has been good enough to pose, so that none need feel debarred from devoting himself to the Great Work on the ground of physical infirmity.

Crowley, as always, had his tongue planted in cheek.

A lithograph of a sketch of Crowley commissioned from Welsh artist Augustus John (1878–1961) also appeared in this issue. The *Equinox* offices offered thirty copies for sale for a guinea apiece. The quality of reproduction pleased John when he saw the issue; however, as Crowley never paid him for the original sketch and was now selling lithos without permission, John wrote

him a perturbed letter. "Would you mind explaining your idea in this? Are *you*
going to make £30 out of the drawing instead of me? If so, you will indeed be
a great magician!"[1] As AC owned neither the sketch nor the prints,[2] he halted
sale of the prints. Despite this dispute, John and Crowley became good friends.

Augustus John (1878–1961) and his sketch of Crowley.

Crowley spent that spring working on *Book Four,* dictating part three—the
portion on practical magic—to Leila. He was unhappy with it, and felt completely unprepared for part four, which would be the full commentary on *The
Book of the Law.* Instead, he busied himself with other productions. He wrote
"Energized Enthusiasm," an essay on ecstasy and magick, and "The Testament
of Magdalen Blair." This latter work, dealing with the types of thoughts
accompanying sickness and death, he considered to be his best short story,
based on an idea Allan Bennett had given him back in 1898.

   Book Four, Part One by Frater Perdurabo and Soror Virakam came out at
this time, selling for four groats (one shilling). *Mortadello, or the Angel of Venice:
A Comedy,* followed. Like most of his books at this time, *The High History of
Good Sir Palamedes the Saracen Knight and of His Following of the Questing Beast*
was published by the publishing firm operated by Ethel Archer's husband,
Wieland & Company. Selling at five shillings, it bore the snide imprint date of
Anno Pseudo Christi 1912. Of this reprint from *The Equinox,* reviewers from
the *English Review* wrote "it makes the heart bleed to reflect that he might have
learnt more in three minutes' conversation with Mr. Crowley than in all those
wanderings."[3] Also appearing were Crowley's reissue of *Amphora,* retitled *Hail
Mary!,* and his critically acclaimed *Household Gods: A Comedy.* Finally, the May

26, 1914, issue of the *New York Times* printed Crowley's poem "Titanic Disaster" in comemoration of the ship's sinking the prior month; Crowley would reprint the article in *The Equinox* for spring 1913.[4]

By far, the most important book in this crop was *Liber CCCXXXIII: The Book of Lies, Which Is Also Falsely Called Breaks, the Wanderings or Falsifications of the One Thought of Frater Perdurabo, Which Thought Is Itself Untrue*. Known simply as *The Book of Lies*, this book is a little masterpiece of wit and wisdom as rewarding as it is demanding. Its ninety-one pithy chapters sometimes contain love poems to Leila ("Laylah" here), sometimes tangled kabbalistic puzzles, and often some clever and subtle pun. For instance, its chapter eighty-three is titled "The Blind Pig" because the two letters that add up to eighty-three, *p* and *g*, are "pig" without an *i*. Even its errata slip bears the playful comment, "It seems absurd, as the whole book is a misprint." The subtitle "Breaks" refers to thoughts that intrude upon meditation; hence the *Occult Review* correctly assessed the book:

> I am not at all sure what is the meaning (assuming there to be one) of this fantastic book by Mr. Aleister Crowley. Some of its chapters seem entire nonsense, but in others I can discern something of a philosophy which is a negation of philosophy; which regards thought as the excrement of mind, and reason as foolishness.... Certainly such philosophy as this is a lie, if that is the meaning of the title.
>
> But indeed, I am inclined to regard the book rather as a fantastic and elaborate joke; and I can imagine its author laughing at the thought of its readers striving to extract a profound meaning out of words which have no meaning.[5]

Most significant of all is Crowley's comment, "There is no joke or subtle meaning in the publisher's imprint."[6] This, of course, is a tip-off that the imprint is incorrect: although the book advertises a 1913 date, it was in fact published in 1912; an ad for the book even appears in the September 1912 *Equinox* as "Now Ready." This wasn't the first time AC used a false imprint date; *Snowdrops from a Curate's Garden* several years earlier was dated 1881. Regardless, Crowley tried all his life to conceal the pun, insisting that his dispute over the book with Theodor Reuss that summer was so sublime as to somehow defy the course of time.

Crowley answered the door to his flat at 124 Victoria Street to find Herr Reuss peering at him through pince-nez, his handlebar mustache curling up at the edges of his face while his mouth curled down in a dour expression. "You have published the secret of the IX°," he claimed, referring to the innermost secret of Ordo Templi Orientis, "and you must take the corresponding oaths." Nonplussed, Crowley admitted into his flat the head of OTO.

Reuss feared Crowley would advertise their secret the way he had published the GD's rituals in *The Equinox*, so he insisted Crowley take the appropriate oaths of secrecy. AC had no idea what this man was ranting about: after *Mathers v. Crowley,* Reuss had made him VII°, an honor corresponding to the 33° of Freemasonry (the highest honor conferred in the Scottish Rite). Of the grades beyond VII° and their instructions, which were peculiar to OTO., Crowley knew nothing. He protested, "I have done nothing of the sort. I don't know the secret, and I don't want to know the secret."

"The magical secret of sex? But of course you do." Reuss stepped across the room to Crowley's bookcases and retrieved a copy of the newly printed *Book of Lies.* Opening to page forty-six, he handed the little volume over. Crowley remembered the chapter, titled "The Star Sapphire." It was a ritual he wrote in an exalted state of mind, similar to that of the Holy Books, and he included it because he was uncomfortable altering or deleting the ritual. Reading the words "Let the Adept be armed with his Magick Rood [and provided with his Mystic Rose]," the sexual symbolism of magic struck Crowley. The Rosicrucian symbols of the rood, cross, and rose were codes for the male and female genitalia. In that awakening, he recognized the same hints in the writings of alchemy and mysticism the world over. In Crowley's own words, it was "one of the greatest shocks of my life."[7] Although the idea of connecting sex with ritual was not new to him—he had learned its usefulness with Virakam in contacting Abuldiz, with his work *The Scented Garden,* with Neuburg in the thirty Aethyrs, with his Holy Book *Stellae Rubeae,* and possibly even from the GD's informal instructions on Thomas Lake Harris—the idea that it had been spelled out for ages, veiled by the simplest symbols, was staggering.

For the next two hours the magicians discussed this mystery. Reuss explained to him the sacredness of OTO's secret and asked Crowley never improperly to reveal it. By the time the conversation was over, Reuss conferred upon Crowley and Leila the IX°, authorized the foundation of a British chapter of OTO, and asked Crowley to revise and flesh out the order's sketchy ceremonies. In exchange, Crowley agreed to allow *The Equinox* to serve as the OTO's official organ in England.

Albert Karl Theodor Reuss (1855–1923) was known in the order as Frater Merlin Peregrinus and was the author of works like *What Is Occultism?* and *What Should I Know about Freemasonry?*[8] He was born in Augsburg to the German innkeeper Franz Xavier Reuss and the Brit Eva Barbara Margaret Wagner. In 1876, at age twenty-one, he found himself in the United Kingdom, taking his Masonic initiation at London's German-speaking Pilgrim Lodge No. 238,[9] and marrying Delphina Garbois of Dublin, a woman ten years his senior, in Ireland. They returned to Munich two years later and had a son, the eccentric and prolific amateur herpetologist Albert Franz Theodor Reuss (1879–1958);[10] the marriage, however, was soon annulled by the German courts because Garbois was already married.[11] Reuss soon began working as a singer at the Royal Theater (Munich), the German Opera (Amsterdam), and the Richard Wagner

Festival (Bayreuth), where he sang in the first performance of *Parsifal* in 1882. In June 1885 he debuted in London at St. James's Hall, singing "Qui sdegno non s'accende" ("Within These Sacred Walls") from Mozart's *The Magic Flute*.[12] Before long, Reuss moved on to concert promotion.[13] Whether performing or promoting concerts, Reuss was simultaneously working as a journalist and a spy: he had joined the Socialist League, working secretly as an informer for the Prussian political police and denouncing the anarchist Victor Dave until Reuss was exposed and expelled in 1886.[14]

Outer Head of Ordo Templi Orientis, Theodor Reuss (1855–1923).

Parallel with these activities, Reuss also had an abiding interest in the occult. He states that he joined the TS in London in 1885, knew H. P. Blavatsky, and was at Avenue Road in May 1891 when her ashes were put into a casket.[15] In 1894, Reuss published the article "Pranatherapie" in the German Theosophical journal *Sphinx*.[16] In 1895 he joined Leopold Engel's (1858–1931) attempt to revive the Bavarian Illuminati.[17] Significantly, around 1898 he met Austrian industrial chemist Carl Kellner (1851–1905), who sought to establish an *Academia Masonica* within which the various degrees of high-grade Freemasonry could be conferred in German-speaking nations. While the Blue Lodge or first three degrees of Freemasonry—Entered Apprentice (1°), Fellow Craft (2°), and Master Mason (3°)—are universal, a number of optional, pendant rites proliferated at this time, claiming to provide greater insight into the three Blue Lodge degrees and offering numbered degrees beyond the third. These attracted many Master Masons (a requirement of admission to any of the higher degrees) who sincerely desired greater insight into the craft. Over the years, these rites were juggled and combined until a few standards emerged, such as the Royal Arch, Cryptic Rite, Knights Templar, and Scottish Rite. Many other systems—including those cultivated by Kellner and his colleagues—were eventually regarded as something between quaintly outdated to patently fraudulent (the vehemence of denunciation corresponding to how closely the rite in question resembled the legitimate degrees).

"Kellner was, of course, the reconstructor of the O.T.O.," Crowley wrote. "Reuss always spoke of him as quite a *hors ligne*."[18] However, because Kellner disapproved of the Illuminati, the idea lay dormant until Reuss apparently broke with Engel. Thereupon, Kellner and Reuss began collaborating with like-minded people like Franz Hartmann and Henry Klein.

Dr. Franz Hartmann (1838–1912) was a German physician, Theosophist, and Rosicrucian who, like Reuss, was a contributor to *Sphinx*. He had been at Adyar in 1885 doing damage control when the controversial Hodgson Report to the Society for Psychical Research proclaimed Blavatsky a fraud, and he later published his own Theosophical journal, *Lotusblüten* (1893–1900). Hartmann was prolific with articles and books like *Magic, White and Black* and *Secret Symbols of the Rosicrucians*.[19] Hartmann knew Kellner professionally.[20]

Henry Klein (c. 1843–1913) was a Bavarian-born naturalized British subject.[21] Although initiated into Freemasonry at the same German-English Pilgrim Lodge No. 238 as Reuss, he resigned two years before Reuss joined.[22] Despite being partially deaf, he worked as a composer, arranger, publisher, and distributor of popular sheet music through his business, Henry Klein & Co. Significantly, he was secretary to the New Philharmonic Society and later to the Popular Wagner Concerts Society, for whom Reuss sang early in his career;[23] this may have been the vehicle through which Klein and Reuss first met. Klein became a concert manager and impresario in 1885,[24] some two years before Reuss followed suit, and one wonders if Klein may have mentored him. By the time Reuss met Kellner, Klein had branched out into importing and wholesaling pianos, organs, polyphons, phonographs, and other musical devices. He retired in 1906; his business was acquired by the New Polyphon Supply Company, and Klein and Co. continued to operate through 1909.[25]

Together, Kellner, Reuss, Hartmann, and Klein acquired authority to operate various esoteric rites, such as the Swedenborgian Rite (from William Wynn Westcott), the Ancient and Primitive Rite of Memphis-Mizraim (from John Yarker), the Martinist Order (from Gérard Encausse),[26] and a form of the Scottish Rite deriving from the controversial Joseph Cerneau. Many Masons considered these rites to be clandestine or spurious; however, they were popular amongst the esoterically minded Masonic fringe. Reuss began publishing the *Oriflamme* in 1902[27] as the official organ of these collected rites.[28]

At some point after Kellner's death in 1905, Reuss combined the various rites into one system that would become Ordo Templi Orientis, establishing ten grades or degrees numbered O to IX.[29] Degrees O–VII reputedly concentrated all the teachings of Freemasonry; indeed, the similarity was so great that OTO at one time allowed Freemasons to affiliate as members up to the corresponding OTO degree. Beyond the VII° awaited what was called, under Kellner's tenure, the "Inner Triangle." This was where members learned esoteric teachings originating outside Freemasonry. Because few of Kellner's writings survive, the nature of these teachings has been the source of some controversy: some have argued that it involved yoga, in which Kellner was clearly knowledgable. Others claim that it taught sacred sexuality, since this became the central secret of OTO under Reuss. Because both sexes were necessary to practice this great secret, OTO also differed significantly from traditional Masonry in admitting both men and women as members.

Kellner reputedly had discovered this great secret from three teachers while traveling in the East. Certainly, Kellner learned yoga from three teachers commonly identified with him—yogi Sri Agamya Paramahamsa (with whom Crowley was acquainted) and fakirs Soliman ben Aissa and Bheema Sena Pratapa originally hailed from the Middle East and Far East and knew Kellner in Europe—but there is no evidence that any of them practiced sexual mysticism.[30] Indeed, the system ultimately promoted by Reuss appears to draw on American mystic Paschal Beverly Randolph (1825–1875), who introduced sex magic to America and Europe through his societies Fraternitas Rosae Crucis (the first Rosicrucian order in America) and the Fellowship of Eulis, as well as books from *The Grand Secret* to *Eulis*.[31] Randolph was arrested and tried in 1872 for publishing explicitly sexual materials, but his teachings were incorporated by other groups. One of these was the Hermetic Brotherhood of Luxor (or of Light), another school whose mysteries OTO claimed to assimilate.[32]

Under Reuss, the order soon claimed several hundred members, although a series of dissensions and controversies effectively decimated that number. Some have suggested that OTO existed only on paper prior to Reuss joining forces with Crowley; prior to that time, Reuss primarily operated the individual rites in which he had authority. A case in point is the membership of Austrian esotericist Rudolf Steiner (1861–1925), later founder of the Anthroposophical Society and on whose philosophy the Waldorf Schools are based. Because of the uncertainty over precisely when the *Academia Masonica* of Kellner became the Ordo Templi Orientis of Reuss, Steiner has been erroneously called a member of OTO; indeed, even Crowley quipped that "Rudolf Steiner discovered what the secret of the IX° did actually mean and took flight."[33] The truth is that Reuss chartered Steiner to operate a Memphis-Mizraim lodge called Mystica Aeterna. This he did from 1906 to 1914, but he ultimately decided to devote his attention to his own Anthroposophical Society.[34]

Reuss brought Crowley into his circle while preparing for the tenth anniversary or "jubilee" issue of *The Oriflamme*. The exact date is uncertain, as records do not survive and Crowley refers to two installation ceremonies, one taking place in Berlin and another in London. Crowley's charter from Reuss is dated April 21, 1912, and is issued from Berlin and London. However, Crowley's Constitution of Mysteria Mystica Maxima (MMM, the British section of OTO) gives the date of its foundation as June 1 in London.[35] Crowley presumably received his charter in Berlin, but a formal installation ceremony later took place in London. In any case, AC received the X° title of "Supreme and Holy King of Ireland, Iona and all the Britains within the Sanctuary of the Gnosis"—or, in plain English, administrative head of OTO for the United Kingdom. In this capacity, Crowley adopted the motto of "Baphomet" after the horned god the Templars were accused of worshiping when persecuted by the Catholic Church in 1307–1314.

Returning to London, Crowley worked on setting up MMM, printing up membership certificates, opening offices at 93 Regent Street—and later at 33 Avenue Studios and 76 Fulham Road in South Kensington—and recruiting initiates. Among the first members was Eugene "Bunco" Wieland, whose certificate from Reuss is dated August 18, 1912. George M. Cowie and Vittoria Cremers followed as the order's secretary and treasurer, respectively. On February 15, 1913, Crowley approved and signed the constitution of the MMM He also made good on his agreement to rewrite the OTO rituals; as he wrote:

> John Yarker saw in 1911 and 1912 that his 33 degrees were themselves unworkable. He gave me a printed copy of the 30 rituals—4° to 33°—the first three, of course, the Craft degrees of Masonry. This devastating volume I took with me on one of my journeys across the Sahara desert, and from it extracted anything that seemed useful to preserve, and very little there was. The desert was left dry.
> All of it, such as it is, is incorporated in the rituals of the O.T.O.[36]

Rites of Eleusis actress Ione de Forest (Jeanne Heyse) had become an art student and had gotten involved in the social circle of the *New Freewoman*,[37] a feminist journal run by Dora Marsden (1882–1960) and Rebecca West (1892–1983), to which both Ezra Pound and Richard Aldington (1892–1962) were literary editors.[38] In December 1911 she also married engraver Wilfred Merton (1888–1957), a Trinity College graduate and avid book collector credited with rescuing "the once-famous Chiswick Press," who had printed Crowley's early works.[39] She nevertheless carried on an affair with Victor Neuburg; this resulted in Wilfred naming both Jeanne and Victor as respondents in a divorce complaint.[40] Separating around early June pending their court date, her husband provided her with a £300 annual allowance, and she moved into a flat at Rosetti Studios, Flood Street, Chelsea. This, combined with the death of her father earlier in the year,[41] made for a stressful situation.

During these events, Heyse's art school peer Nina Hamnett (1890–1956) grew fascinated with Jeanne and Victor's talk of the Rites. Despite rumors that Crowley was so clever and wicked that no young girl was safe alone with him,

Nina, still a virgin, wanted to meet him. So they took her to his Victoria Street flat. "Extremely intelligent," she noted after that first visit, "and not very bad."

Crowley asked her to paint four panels for him, one for each element. This she did, noticing that the day she painted the fire panel, three blazes mysteriously broke out in the studio. On another occasion, while she painted, the secretary left on business. She was alone with Crowley, who was asleep on the rug by the fireplace. Nina pondered anew the rumors about AC, and feared for her safety. When the magician stirred, she held her breath. He sat up and stared at her. "Are you alone?"

Meekly, she replied, "Yes."

At that, he lay back down and returned to sleep.[42]

On Thursday, August 1, Jeanne announced to Nina that she was leaving in the morning for a long time, possibly not returning. She offered Nina her clothes if she were to come by; an underfunded art student, Nina gratefully accepted. Arriving the next morning, she found pinned to the door an envelope containing the keys to the flat. Nina let herself in. She looked and called for her friend but received no reply. Then, drawing aside a long red curtain, she discovered her friend's dead body.

Jeanne had shot herself through the heart with a pearl-handled revolver.

On a nearby table was a copy of her wedding certificate, her gun license, and a note addressed to the Coroner:

> The last statement of Jeanne Merton, living under the professional name of Jeanne de Forest, being an art student. I hereby state that, although of sound mind, I intend to commit suicide to-night because of the intolerable position in which my extremely rash and unfortunate marriage has placed me. It is my wish that my body be cremated.

In retrospect, she had threatened suicide over the months to both her husband and her solicitor, E. S. P. Haynes, but no one had taken her seriously. The day she died, her solicitor received a letter saying "I cannot endure things any longer." Her husband, meanwhile, received the note, "You have killed me." An inquest ruled her death as "suicide during temporary insanity."[43] Grief-stricken, Ezra Pound waited a year to write—and even longer to publish—the obituary poem, "Dead Iönè:"

> Empty are the ways,
> Empty are the ways of this land
> And the flowers
>   Bend over with heavy heads.
> They bend in vain.
> Empty are the ways of this land
>   Where Ione
> Walked once, and now does not walk
> But seems like a person just gone.[44]

The eighth *Equinox* appeared that September as the joint organ of the A∴A∴ and MMM. Fiction, poetry, and drama dominated the issue, which featured a violin piece by Leila titled "Thelema: A Tone-Testament," "Three Poems" by Neuburg, and the play "Doctor Bob," jointly penned by Desti and Crowley. AC's vicious streak ran wild in attacks on A. E. Waite ("Waite's Wet or the Backslider's Return") and his uncle Tom Bishop ("My Crapulous Contemporaries No. VI: An Obituary" … except he wasn't dead). The supplement contained the issue's only magical text, and it was a work of tremendous value: "Sepher Sephiroth" was a numerological dictionary of kabbalistic terms. The work, begun by Allan Bennett, benefitted from contributions by Crowley, Jones, Neuburg, and Gerald G. Rae Fraser (who joined the A∴A∴ in 1910).[45] This reference work represents one of Crowley's most important contributions to occult literature.

Nevertheless, A∴A∴ recruitment continued to wind down, with only three new members joining since 1911: Vittoria Cremers, Olivia Haddon, and painter Leon Engers Kennedy. That December, Crowley reviewed the status of his A∴A∴ probationers. Of some eighty-five students, only eight had advanced to Neophyte, with seven more "on the path." Compared with the GD and OTO, these figures were disappointing. Clearly, his energy was better directed toward the MMM.

Author Katherine Mansfield (1888–1923) first heard of Crowley through her friend, John Middleton Murry (1889–1957), who in turn had met AC around 1910 through his Oxford friend Frederick Goodyear (1887–1917).[46] Little is known of Goodyear's association with Crowley; however, Goodyear's lead article "The New Thelema" for the first issue of *Rhythm* proclaimed:

> Thelema lies in the future, not the never-never land of the theologian, but the ordinary human future that is perpetually transmuting itself into the past. These familiar to-morrows that keep breaking on the shore of the world throw up every time some priceless jetsam for its strengthening or decoration. No magic, no divine interference will affect the rise of Thelema. It will be independent of petty dynastic incidents such as the fall of Saturn, or the accession of Jove. The wrath of the Lord of Hosts is powerless to blast it. Men shall built it; this planet is its chosen site.[47]

While Goodyear may be alluding to Rabelais, his words also resonate with Crowley's Thelema. Since the exact date of Goodyear's meeting Crowley is unknown, this article may reflect their new acquaintance, or it may have captured Crowley's notice and prompted their meeting. Regardless, Goodyear went on to introduce the editor of *Rhythm*, Murry, who in December 1911 sent Mansfield a copy of Neuburg's *The Triumph of Pan* to review. Her review was far from glowing: while acknowledging that "He has something of the poet's vision, delighting in simplicity and sensuality which is born of passionate admiration," she dislikes his mysticism:

Mysticism is perverted sensuality; it is "passionate admiration" for that which has no reality at all. It leads to the annhilation of any true artistic effort. It is a paraphernalia of clichés. It is a mask through which the true expression of the poet can never be discerned. If he rejects this mask Mr. Neuburg may become a poet.[48]

Despite this review, she asked Murry for more information about the poet. Neuburg, he explained, was Crowley's lover, but they'd quarreled and parted, and Crowley was now with some other fellow named Kennedy; Murry also referred to Crowley's notorious works, *The Daisy Chain* and *Snowdrops from a Curate's Garden* as "the ne plus ultra of dirt."[49] While the facts were wrong— Crowley and Neuburg had not parted, and the first "notorious work" was *White Stains*—Mansfield's interest was piqued.

In 1913 she and Gwen Otter cowrote a sketch called "Mimi and the Major," the title characters played by Katherine and Gwen, respectively. After a performance at the Passmore Settlement, Gwen threw one of her legendary parties, which Crowley and Leila attended. Katherine soon found herself and the group exploring their inner selves while under the influence (accounts vary as to whether it was hashish or Crowley's favorite hallucinogen, *Anhalonium lewinii*). Accounts also vary as to what happened next. James Laver's account is closest to firsthand, and it is the least fantastic:

> "The stuff is beginning to work," [Crowley] said. "She's not going to be interesting; she's only going to sleep."
>
> Katherine lay on the sofa and lit a cigarette. She threw the match on the floor and it lay crookedly on the carpet. This caused her such acute distress that Gwen put it straight. "That's much better," said K. M. "Pity that stuff had no effect."[50]

According to Laver, she babbled a bit, remarked that she could do up the buttons on her nightgown "if we talk to them very gently," and munched some biscuits, repeating at intervals her refrain, "Pity that stuff had no effect."

Other versions say that, while her spirit rose to a "pink and paradisiacal" level, she passed the evening "arranging and rearranging with the greatest exactitude the matches from a box which she had in her hand, making patterns on the floor."[51] Then, as she came down, she saw "hundreds of parcels on shelves identically marked *Jesus Wept*."[52] Mansfield shortly thereafter encountered the writings of Gurdjieff and Alfred Orage, preferring them to Crowley, whom she considered "a pretentious and very dirty fellow."[53]

Obscure bits of Crowleyana trickled onto the market in this interim. The poem "Villon's Apology" appeared in the *Poetry Review* at the end of 1912.[54] *The "Rosicrucian" Scandal,* a hilarious parody of Mathers's testimony in *Jones v. The Looking Glass,* appeared under the pseudonym of Leo Vincey. The "M.M.M. Manifesto" also appeared, adorned with photographs of Boleskine. Gwen Otter's privately published *The Writing on the Ground* included Crowley's essay on Lord Alfred Douglas and his poem "A Slim Gilt Soul" from *The Winged Beetle*. Finally, part two of *Book Four* appeared as a blue paperback, selling for four tanners, the equivalent of two shillings.

On the first day of spring 1913, issue nine of *The Equinox* appeared. Although the names of Mary d'Este Sturges and Victor Neuburg still appeared on the masthead, the only contributions not by Crowley were a couple of one-page poems, book reviews, and a sketch cowritten with Mary Desti. At 313 pages, the issue contained no supplement and bore little magical matter: "The Temple of Solomon the King" was brief, and the evocation of Bartzabel mostly of didactic and historical value. The issue's only important magical essay was "Energized Enthusiasm."

Crowley dedicated plenty of space to attacking his enemies: he gleefully noted that *Looking Glass* publisher de Wend Fenton was fined over £91 on six charges of sending obscene matter through the mail; Mathers, he said, was "reduced to beggary, his only remaining capital, his brain, in a state of hopeless decay"; and he warned students to accept no instructions from Fuller, who never advanced beyond the grade of Probationer[55] and had no authority to represent the A∴A∴. This last warning was prompted by Crowley's discovery that Fuller, two years after their split, was still instructing Canadian disciple C. S. Jones. Meanwhile Raffalovich, who requested a printed statement that he was no longer associated with Crowley, received this mention:

> Mr. George Raffalovich is in no way connected with *The Equinox*.
> Mr. George Raffalovich has never been connected with *The Equinox* in any way but as an occasional contributor.
> It cannot be too clearly understood that *The Equinox* has no connection with Mr. George Raffalovich.
> We have much pleasure in stating that Mr. George Raffalovich is in no way connected with *The Equinox*.
> We have no reason to anticipate that *The Equinox* will in any way be connected with Mr. George Raffalovich.
> We trust that Mr. George Raffalovich will be satisfied with these statements of fact, to which we are prepared to testify on oath.

The poem "Athanasius Contra Decanum" attacked Reverend R. St. John Parry, who had banned Crowley from Trinity's campus, showing "that a Dean may be damned without being a liar and slanderer." The paper "How I Became a Famous Mountaineer" was a swipe at the Alpine Club, and "A Quack Painter" berated his former brother-in-law Gerald Kelly.

He also took pleasure in publishing pieces rejected by the *English Review*, including "Lines to a Young Lady Violinist," an amorous poem for Leila; the humorous book review "A Literatooralooral Treasure-Trove"; the poems "At Sea" and "Dumb!"; his novella "Ercildoune"; and the short story "The Testament of Magdalen Blair."

Music dominated the first months of 1913. Following her superb playing in 1910's Rites of Eleusis, Leila appeared, as noted previously, in the Ladies' Orchestra for *A Waltz Dream*. Next, she left from Liverpool on the *Mauretania*, arriving in New York on March 30, 1912,[56] for a stint of several weeks with the musical comedy *Two Little Brides*. The *New York Times* panned the show, saying that it "entirely lacks distinction" and that "faith and the best intentions in the world cannot help very much."[57] Nevertheless, it had sixty-three performances at the Casino Theater and Lyric Theater between April 23 and June 15, 1912. However, women rarely played in orchestras in 1913, and Leila, despite her skills, had trouble finding work. Crowley—no doubt inspired by his recent friendship with music impresario Theodor Reuss—responded by assembling a troupe of seven fiddlers (three dipsomaniacs and four nymphomaniacs, by his reckoning) and dubbing them the Ragged Ragtime Girls. Leila, the only one of the group with her head on straight, was first violinist. Contrary to their name, the musicians were lithe, dressing in diaphonous gowns and playing ethereal music while dancing. Crowley described them as

> seven beautiful and graceful maidens who dance and play the violins simultaneously. The strange, exotic beauty of the leader, Miss Leila Bathurst, as she weaves her dances in the labyrinthe of her attendant nymphs, thrills every heart with the sense alike of the rococo and the bizarre.... The weirdly fascinating appearance of the leader, Miss Leila Bathurst, first stupefied the house and then roused it to a frenzy. As exotic and bizarre as her beauty is, it is yet of that royal kind which goes straight to every heart. Her paces suggest the tiger and the snake, and her violin contains in itself all the music alike of nature and of art. The house could not wait for the fall of the curtain to rise to its feet in surging enthusiasm, and the last bars were drowned in the roars of applause that greeted the march past through the stalls. Women shrieked, and strange men wept. Babes at the press fainted with emotion, the very unborn emulated the execution of John the Baptist recorded in the first chapter of the Gospel according to St. Mark.[58]

Crowley acted as impresario. "It was a sickening business," he recalled.[59]

As early as February 1913, Crowley wrote to George M. Cowie that Leila "is going wildly with the girls into Abyssinia, and intends to abide and rejoice."[60] The Ragged Ragtime Girls played that March as part of the Easter program at the Old Tivoli, with nightly performances and Saturday matinees.[61] The *New York Times* noted the program "is practically American,"[62] specifically mentioning the Ragged Ragtime Girls even though they were American-sounding in name only. George M. Cowie attended a show in Edinburgh later that year, noting,

> I went with a friend to see [Leila's] performance on Friday and was greatly delighted with it—the only artistic thing in (to me) rather a dismal programme. It struck me what a very effective thing she and these girls might make out of a Witches Sabbath dance and an Act that would probably fetch her at least double the money.[63]

In April 1913, Crowley distributed photographs and press cuttings to announce that the Ragged Ragtime Girls were available for banquets, private engagements, and society functions. They knew immediate success, playing the London Opera House that month. In May, Crowley consulted Russian guidebooks and wrote to Moscow hotels for accommodations. Before long, he booked them for a summer theater engagement in Moscow.[64]

Before departing for Russia, AC took a break from the Ragged Ragtime Girls and OTO to relax at Eastbourne and Fontainebleau. When he returned to London, he found everything in turmoil: John Yarker had died. This was important because Yarker was the leading light of the Ancient and Primitive Rite of Memphis and Mizraim. It was he who had authorized Reuss to operate a lodge in Germany and who gave Crowley the 33° in his rite. Yarker's rise to power among the various flavors of Masonry is an interesting tale best left in Crowley's own words:

> Yarker was always bothering over these questions of jurisdiction. Wishing to contract an alliance with the Scottish Rite of France, he found that they quite naturally objected to him having degrees beyond their own 33rd. He, therefore, agreed to reduce the Memphis Rite to 33 degrees. It was, however, rather sharp practice on his part, because in the course of reduction the Scottish 33rd was made equal to the 20th of the reduced Rite. The alliance was concluded, and Yarker conferred the 33° on about 100 British Masons. He obtained toleration from the Grand Lodge of England; toleration, not recognition, by agreeing not to admit to the Rite any man who was not a Master Mason in good standing under the Grand Lodge of England or some body in alliance with it.
>
> You will understand from the above that the effect of Yarker's action was to put an end, once and for all, to the Rites of Memphis and Mizraim in their original form, though whether it had been worked any time within historical periods I cannot say. I strongly doubt it.[65]

At the June 28 meeting to elect Yarker's successor, Crowley objected to the presence of James Ingall Wedgwood, Supreme Secretary to Annie Besant's Co-Masonic Order. Although Yarker had made him an honorary Master Mason, Crowley—who opposed Besant's TS and its "world teacher," Krishnamurti—feared Wedgwood was there to co-opt the rite for the TS and its Co-Masonic Order. Crowley's opposition to Co-Masonry was so great that when the French Grand Lodge he had joined recognized Co-Masonry, AC resigned. Thus Crowley, the sole person in Ireland authorized to teach the rites of Memphis and Mizraim,[66] appeared and argued that the meeting was illegal.

Two days later, another meeting of members of the Sovereign Sanctuary—namely Crowley, Reuss, Kennedy, and other Masons—elected Henry Meyer, Yarker's own nominee, as Grand Master General. Over the next decade, a number of people would succeed him. As Crowley recorded, Meyer,

> whom nobody had heard of for years, appeared in the Sovereign Sanctuary to get elected, and has never been heard of. He did not answer any subse-

quent summons, and his death was presumed, whereupon we elected
Papus, and on the death of Papus, the Grand Master of Spain whose name
I have forgotten, and after him, Reuss, who died in '22 and I succeeded
him.[67]

Although lineage and jurisdiction were serious matters to British Masonry,
Crowley regarded such matters with disdain. "It's all what Roosevelt would
have described as blah, baloney, bullshit and bunk."[68] Noncoincidentally, newly
elected Grand Hierophant Meyer named Crowley's address at 33 Avenue Studios, 76 Fulham Road in South Kensington, as headquarters of the Rite.

This address was also headquarters of MMM. It foreshadowed Crowley's
plans for OTO: having approved the MMM constitution (which he wrote) on
February 15, he added to the order's Golden Book a note:

> In all lodges of O.T.O. and M.M.M. in Great Britain and Ireland the Vol-
> ume of the Sacred Law shall be the book of Thelema, or a facsimile copy
> of *Liber Legis* (CCXX), and no initiations upon any other document will
> be recognised by the Grand Lodge.[69]

Liber Legis was the Latin title of *The Book of the Law,* and CCXX its corresponding number. Crowley was preparing to make his philosophy of Thelema
or True Will the official doctrine of OTO.

On July 7, after paying for one thousand Ragged Ragtime Girls postcards and
sending the tenth *Equinox* proofs to Richard Clay for printing, Crowley and
the Ragtime Girls caught the 2:20 for Russia. The train ride seemed intermi-
nable, proceeding day after day through endless dull pines, dun earth, and
remorseless rain. The sky was "leaden, flat, featureless," made worse by the surrounding land's "monotony of grievous green and grey." Nobody on the train
spoke English, French, or even German.

Then, one morning, he awoke as the train entered Moscow. The colors of
this wonderful city sparked him to life, and he smiled to himself. "Our hashish
dream come true."[70]

Minor complications ensued: they could locate nobody to help them find
their hotel, and they eventually managed alone. Then, late that night, Crowley
and Leila received a frantic call from the other musicians: he had neglected to
warn them that in Russia, the bedbug "is as inseparable from the bed as the
snail is from his shell."[71] After a day or two of such minor problems, the country finally enchanted them.

Standing in the capital recalled for Crowley the passion he felt for Russia
over a decade earlier: back when he wanted to be an ambassador, back when he
took the name Count Vladimir Svareff. As he eagerly walked the streets, he
met a prostitute whom he dubbed "Olya of the broken nose." In a café he also
met a Hungarian girl named Anny Ringler,

tall, tense, lean as a starving leopardess, with wild, insatiable eyes and a
long straight thin mouth, a scarlet scar which seemed to ache with the
anguish of hunger for some satisfaction beyond earth's power to supply.[72]

She spoke only broken German and he faltering Russian. Despite the language
barrier, they became passionate lovers, meeting daily. He assuaged her masoch-
istic tendencies, and she inspired him to write about Russia's tortured world.

It was typical of Crowley that he should travel to Russia on so mundane a
premise as being impresario to a musical troupe, yet achieve profound inspiration
and enlightenment. "During my six weeks in Moscow in 1913, I had what I can
only call almost continuous illumination and wrote quite a number of my very
best poems and essays there."[73] New works flowed effortlessly from his pen as he
relaxed in the Aquarium Hotel or the nearby Hermitage: "The City of God,"[74]
a poem describing his train ride to Moscow; "The Heart of Holy Russia,"[75] a
prose description of Russia; "The Fun of the Fair"[76] (which he dedicated to
Anny Ringler and Olya), a description of the famous fair at Nizhni Novgorod;
"Morphia," a poem about drug addiction that features a description of Olya;[77]
"The Lost Continent," a humorous story/essay on Atlantis;[78] "To Laylah—
Eight-and-Twenty," a poem for the August 10 birthday of the Mother of
Heaven;[79] and "The Ship," a poetic adaptation of the mysteries of Masonry. This
last piece was one of Crowley's favorites, containing what he called the "Quia
Patris," a sublime poem to the Higher Self beginning with the words, "Thou
who art I …"[80] He also wrote "Hymn to Pan," his most potent invocation:

> Thrill with lissome lust of the light,
> O man! My man!
> Come careering out of the night
> Of Pan! Io Pan!
> Io Pan! Io Pan! Come over the sea
> From Sicily and from Arcady!
> Roaming as Bacchus, with fauns and pards
> And nymphs and satyrs for thy guards,
> On a milk-white ass, come over the sea
> To me, to me …[81]

Moved by the liturgy of St. Basil, Crowley also wrote his Gnostic Catholic
Mass.[82] That Crowley should write such a ritual is not as unusual as it may
sound, as one branch of Ecclesia Gnostica Catholica, or the Gnostic Catholic
Church, was connected to OTO. Gerard Encausse, as one of the church's bishops, was the link between the EGC and OTO; according to one theory, Crowley was consecrated a bishop by Reuss, who was consecrated by Encausse. It is
an important ritual because Crowley, busy writing OTO instructions, incorporated its Great Secret openly into the Gnostic Mass, much to the ire of his fellow OTO members. He wrote, "my idea was to write a Mass which would, in
once sense, carry on the old tradition yet not come into conflict with science.
The whole thing, as is almost invariably the case with my work, was written
straight off in white heat and never underwent revision."[83]

Although it more closely resembled the Tridentine rather than the Russian Orthodox mass, Crowley adapted the basic structure to the trappings of Thelema; hence the altar bears *The Book of the Law*. Its officers are the priest, priestess, deacon, and two "children." The main focus of the rite involves reanimation of the symbolically dead priest by the priestess, his invocation upon the priestess, and their symbolic sexual union: the priest, with his lance, advances and approaches the priestess, who is seated behind a veil; after much ceremony, the lance parts the veil, and they celebrate the mystic marriage by depressing the lance into the grail. The deacon begins the Mass by proclaiming the Law of Thelema, and at other points during the ceremony recites a Thelemic profession of faith and a list of Thelemic saints, including Roger Bacon, Sir Edward Kelly, Éliphas Lévi, Goethe, Wagner, Nietzsche, Carl Kellner, Sir Richard Burton, Theodor Reuss and, of course, Crowley. Despite its pretensions, the ceremony itself is beautiful and moving.

By the time he left Russia, AC had written about 150,000 words.

Crowley returned to London early in September, a fortnight later than he had planned. The six hundred pages of *Equinox* 10 snowed him under; Leila and the troupe had just gone to Glasgow for a two-month stint at the Theater Royale, and Spare declined to provide an illustration for the last issue. Facing these complications, he invited Neuburg to help pull it together.

Meanwhile, organizational upheaval rocked the MMM. Its financial records were in chaos, with several members behind in their dues. He accused the treasurer, Cremers, of misappropriating funds by using the signed checks he had left in her care. That October, Crowley demoted her to VI° and canceled her posts as Grand Secretary General and Trustee of MMM property. Furthermore, he called her to account for her actions. When Cremers refused to answer the charges, a Grand Tribunal met in Paris and expelled her. At this same hearing, they charged Nina Hamnett with being seriously behind in her dues, R. L. Felkin for absenteeism,[84] and W. C. Minchin for attempting to seduce the wife of a brother. Another member was expelled for swindling. Leila succeeded Cremers as Grand Secretary General, and George Cowie became Grand Treasurer General; both became cotrustees, along with Crowley, of MMM.

On the positive side, Crowley had encouraging news about his South African student, James Thomas Windram. Although his clairvoyance was so poor as to prevent his advancement to the grade of Zelator, he nevertheless excelled in other areas. When Crowley instructed him to use the Enochian system to evoke the fiery power of air, which was plentiful in his part of the world, he conjured up a storm that tore the roof from his home and struck his temple with lightning. Duly impressed, Crowley appointed him OTO's representative for South Africa.

In between crises, AC was as charming as ever, telling riveting stories of his travels to Russia. When someone asked him how one could sleep in Russia without being bothered by bedbugs, Crowley wryly replied, "Shift the frontier." And he sent his mother a spoon with "Christ is Risen" on it to help remind her guests to say grace. He also resumed his Sunday performances of the Mass of the Phoenix, a ritual from *The Book of Lies* that culminated in the Adept cutting his chest and blotting the blood with bread; socialites thought of these performances as nothing more than séances.[85]

The tenth and final issue of *The Equinox,* volume one, appeared that fall. If the previous issues had been slim, this one more than compensated, featuring 223 pages of material in the main body and an additional 244 in the supplement. It contained "In Memoriam: John Yarker," which Crowley had previously printed and distributed separately. It also featured the first typeset edition of *The Book of the Law,* a syllabus of official A∴A∴ instructions, "The Ship," and a biting obituary of the still-living occult scholar A. E. Waite. The supplement—AC's translation of Éliphas Lévi's *The Key of the Mysteries*—was supposedly superior to Waite's translations of other works by Lévi. Having spent his inheritance on publishing, Crowley announced that volume two of *The Equinox* would represent five years of silence to balance the five years of speech that the first volume consumed. Publications would commence with the third volume, due in 1919. In closing, he humorously added,

> It is of course common knowledge that the A∴A∴ and *The Equinox* and all the rest of it are a stupid joke of Aleister Crowley's. He merely wished to see if any one were fool enough to take him seriously. Several have done so, and he does not regret the few thousand pounds it has cost him.

When Jacob Epstein's (1880-1959) sculpture for the tomb of Oscar Wilde caused a sensation in France that fall, Crowley found himself embroiled in the controversy. The Père Lachaise guardian declared the statue obscene and ordered it covered with a tarp. In response, Crowley issued a manifesto to state his outrage and broadcast his plans to unveil the monument:

> Sir,
>
> I noticed that, in obedience to the order of the prefect of Seine the Oscar Wilde Memorial in Pére-la-chaise has been mutilated by the placing of an enormous black butterfly over the criticized parts, thus rendering Jacob Epstein's masterpiece as ridiculous and obscene as its critics themselves. And still the aforesaid prefect of the Seine keeps the tarpaulin on the statue.
>
> At noon on the fifth of November, Guy Fawkes' Day, it is my intention to proceed to Pére-la-chaise and, armed with an instrument adapted for the purpose of cutting the cords which hold the tarpaulin in position and to cut the same.
>
> I am yours, sir,
> Faithfully,
>
> Aleister Crowley.[86]

On the eve of this confrontation, Crowley and an accomplice attached a thin, nearly invisible wire to the tarp. On November 5 his accomplice hid out of sight, holding the end of the wire and awaiting his cue. Crowley gave a speech and, as he spoke, gesticulated toward the sculpture. As if by magic, the tarp flew off the sculpture.

Following his protest, as only he could, Crowley removed the butterfly and hid it beneath his waistcoat, slipping from the cemetery portlier than when he entered. Reaching London, Crowley put on his evening suit and strolled into the Café Royal wearing the butterfly as a codpiece.

The end of 1913 favored Crowley with a small spate of recognition: his critique of United States culture, "Art in America," appeared in the November *English Review*. Its premise was that Americans, despite the inspiring qualities of their nation, are uninspired; with few exceptions, America has spawned no great artists, poets, writers, actresses, dancers, musicians, or scientists. The London *Times* called it "An entirely preposterous, but quite enjoyable, tirade," while the *Academy* predicted it would "set all Americans … hot on his trail with loaded revolvers." The article garnered attention in the American press such as the *Chicago Daily Tribune* and *The State,* the latter conceding that "its author reveals a wider reading of American literature than most natives can claim."[87] Ten years later in the *English Review,* American poet Robert Haven Schauffler (1879–1964) reflected on Crowley, "His article is most readable. It bristles with wit and wisdom—and the wildest unsportsmanship."[88] The *Yorkshire Herald* put the debate into perspective by asking who had ever heard of Aleister Crowley.

Meanwhile, the anthology *Cambridge Poets, 1900–13* reproduced the following selections from Crowley's works: "In Neville's Court," "On Garrett Hostel Bridge," "The Goad," "The Rosicrucian," "Song," "In Memoriam A. J. B." [Ada Jane Bishop], "The Challenge," "Two Hymns on the Feast of the Nativity," "The Palace of the World," and "Perdurabo." It also included seven pieces by Victor Neuburg and G. H. S. Pinsent's "The Organ in King's Chapel, Cambridge" from *The Equinox*.[89] The collection was well received, although J. DeLancey Ferguson complained in his review for *The Dial* that

> Only rarely—notably in Aleister Crowley's "The Quest," every stanza of which requires at least one footnote to explain its symbolic meaning—do we feel that the poet is overdoing the thing. The true mystic can make his vision plain without footnotes.[90]

The volume's editor, Aelfrida Catherine Wetenhall Tillyard (1883–1959), was the daughter of the former mayor of Cambridge, Alfred Isaac Tillyard; a former Sunday School teacher; an aspiring writer of poetry and children's works; and wife of King's College undergraduate Constantine Graham. She had become interested in comparative mysticism before age twenty and by 1904 referred to her "thirst for mysticism," which was heightened by the experiences of being

nursed at a convent in 1905 and having a stillbirth in 1912.[91] She discovered
Crowley while researching her anthology, writing in her diary for April 26,

> I have discovered one genius for my book—Aleister Crowley, Victor Neu-
> burg's "master." There are odd legends about him ... But his poetry is *mar-
> velous*, great floods of it, mystic or sensual or singing or majestic—and
> once in a way downright beastly.[92]

Thus, she became a student, reading part one of *Book Four;* Crowley soon sent
her part two, the first nine issues of *The Equinox* and *777,* and began addressing
her in letters as "Soror Sarasvati."[93] She considered him "a great religious
genius"[94] and referred to him as her "guru." However, the relationship ended
that November after her husband, Constantine, met "Count and Countess
MacGregor" at the consulate in Paris and received an earful about his wife's
spiritual master; a controlling and physically abusive husband, he insisted that
Tillyard break off communications with "the devil incarnate"[95] because he was
having too much of an influence on her.

Another Crowley publication, "The City of God," was slated to appear as
the lead piece in the January 1914 *English Review*. Of this poem, the *Manchester
Guardian* would write, "Mr. Crowley is an expert in the portentous, a collector
of clanging, menacing phrases; we are a little doubtful about it all and disposed
to seek for relief in Anthony Trollope or Jane Austen."[96]

The MMM was back on its feet, his works were recognized, and he was in
Paris with Neuburg: these circumstances again inspired Crowley. His Canadian
student, Charles Stansfeld Jones—who had advanced to Neophyte earlier that
year and taken the motto of Achad (One, unity)—passed to the grade of Zelator on New Year's Eve and was eager to set up the A∴A∴ in Vancouver. All
were good portents.

Realizing they were on the verge of the six hundredth anniversary of the
immolation of Knights Templar Grand Master Jacques de Molay, AC decided it
was his duty to experiment with the secret of the IX°.

Walter Duranty (1884–1957) had just become a foreign correspondent for the
New York Times. An understated five-foot-six in height, what he lacked in
comeliness he made up for in brilliant wit and raconteur's skill. Duranty hailed
from an affluent British family and was educated at the prestigious Harrow and
Eaton schools, graduating in 1903 near the top of his class. His forte lay in
translating into other languages, particularly French, and he routinely astonished his fellow correspondents by taking any local newspaper and reciting a
perfect French, Latin, or Greek translation on the fly.

Years would pass before he would be acclaimed for his coverage of both
World War I and the rise of Joseph Stalin. Over a decade would pass before a
train crash claimed his leg, and nearly a score before his poem "Red Square"
appeared with the famous words, "you can't make an omelette without breaking eggs." In December 1913, Wally, as AC called him, was still a green jour-

nalist, sharing with Crowley the affections and opium of their mutual lover, Jane Chéron.

Crowley had devised a ritual amalgamating "Liber Pyramidos," the *Goetia,* "The Ship," and IX° sex magick to invoke the gods Mercury and Jupiter. It began with Crowley invoking Thoth, the Egyptian Mercury, as he had in Cairo. He proceeded with constructing the pyramid à la "Liber Pyramidos" and reciting conjurations from the *Goetia* and his own works. Then, at the stroke of midnight, Crowley and Neuburg rang in the new year with sex intended to invoke Mercury. Crowley assumed the passive role, and both chanted the versicle which Duranty had translated into Latin:

> Jungitur in vati vates: rex inclyte rabdou
> Hermes tu venias, verba nefanda ferens.

("Seer is joined with seer: Renowned king of the wand, come thou, Hermes, bearing the ineffable word.") As they proceeded, the room, in Crowley's eyes, filled with thousands of golden caducei, their entwined serpents writhing animatedly. Victor, manifesting the god, became giddy and childish. It reminded Crowley of the description in the Thelemic Holy Book "Liber Ararita": "Thou hast appeared to me as a young boy mischievous and lovely, with Thy winged globe and its serpents set upon a staff."

In the end, either the mischievous, childlike nature of young Hermes or the silly giddiness of Brother Lampada Tradam (Neuburg) prevented the active partner from reaching orgasm. The god could not take control and be questioned, and the first working ended at 1:40 a.m., disappointing yet promising.

Such began Crowley's first systematic experiments in sex magick, encompassing twenty-four workings over the next six weeks.

Crowley spent New Year's Day 1914 forming a phallic figure of Hermes out of yellow wax. Erecting it in the east that evening, the second working began at 11:20 p.m. Owing to poor performance in the first working, the magicians agreed to avoid distraction during sex by eschewing the Latin versicle. Just before midnight, after Neuburg climaxed, they commenced the chant, and Hermes took possession. The god appeared in this working not as a child but as a messenger, robust in body with caduceus and talaria. Although Victor initially lost control and began scrawling in the record, Crowley eventually initiated a proper dialogue. "Are we working right?" he asked the god.

"No," Hermes informed him.

"What's wrong?"

"The time, and, to a lesser extent, the place."

"What is the right time?"

"Three hours before dawn."

"Does this apply to Mercury alone, or to all the gods?"

"To Mercury alone."

"Are we to invoke Mercury again?"

"Yes."

"Tomorrow?"

"No."

"When, then?"

"On the day of the full moon."

"What god shall we invoke tomorrow?"

"Thoth."

"But Thoth *is* Mercury!"

"You will get another aspect."

"Shall we not use the same versicle?"

"It does not matter."

"Shall I make statues of all the gods?"

"No."

"Shall I make tablets of all the gods?"

"Yes."

"What tablets?"

"Tablets with the names only."

"In what order shall we invoke the gods?"

"The proper order is Venus, Mercury, Jupiter, Luna, Sol."

"Will he help in geomancy?"

"Yes." As a god of magic, Mercury should help in divination.

"And also in the conduct of affairs?"

"In some, not in all."

"In business?"

"In some business." Again, appropriate for the god of commerce.

"What?"

"Books, money, love." This prediction, Crowley noted at the conclusion of the workings, definitely came true.

"How can we invoke Mercury better?"

"Use a golden pentagram, placing the same in a prominent position; drink yellow wine and eat fish before the ceremony. Let the clock be removed."

"Can you suggest any improvements in the ceremonies, especially that of Jupiter?"

"Scarlet and silver should be worn, and the crown OSV. LT is to wear the scarlet robe, violets are to be strewn and trodden with bare feet." OSV was Crowley's Adeptus Major motto, while LT referred to Neuburg as Zelator.

At this point, Victor asked, "Shall I let him take full possession now?" Satisfied that the entity they had conjured was, in fact, the god Hermes, and that it was safe to allow him to take control of Neuburg's body, Crowley agreed. "I am going." Victor paused, handing himself over to Hermes, who took over the conversation. "What do you want to know now? There are other things I can tell you, or else ask me questions."

"Tell," Crowley replied curtly.

"You will receive good news in respect of money on the eleventh of January, in the forenoon. Frater LT will be concerned with it; it will be quite unexpected. Money will be given by someone to whom LT introduced OSV. A change in OSV's affairs in February." These predictions all came true by the end of the working, when Crowley, whose fortune was depleted by this point, saw his finances improve.

"I am going to ask a very important question. Concentrate hard. N.C.G.M.H.D." Crowley was asking in code when he would attain the grade of Magus (9°=2□), in the A∴A∴.

The god computed. "L is 50, and P is 6."

"Fifty-six what?"

"I don't know … Wait … Hours? I am not quite sure, but it is connected with time." It was remarkable enough that Neuburg, or whatever was answering, knew the question concerned time. Even more startling is the fact that the time between Crowley's formal induction as a Magister Templi (8°=3□) on December 3, 1909, and his reaching the grade of Magus on October 12, 1915, would be six years less fifty days.

The magicians next switched roles, with Crowley channeling Hermes and Neuburg asking the questions. Crowley launched into a discourse on the nature of Mercury and a comment on the Gospel of John, chapter one, which begins "In the beginning was the Word, and the Word was with God, and the Word was God." Crowley, as Hermes, spoke, "In the Beginning was the Word, the Logos, who is Mercury, and is therefore to be identified with Christ. Both are messengers; their birth-mysteries are similar; the pranks of their childhood are similar. In the Vision of the Universal Mercury, Hermes is seen descending upon the sea, which refers to Mary. The Crucifixion represents the Caduceus; the two thieves, the two serpents; the cliff in the vision of the Universal Mercury is Golgotha; Maria is simply Maia with the solar R in her womb." This discussion and vision went on until they closed the temple at 2 a.m.

The third working commenced on January 3. Crowley and Neuburg began the ceremony around midnight, but could not be sure since, per Hermes's instructions, the clock was gone. Around 1 a.m., they completed the "Quia Patris" and Hermes appeared. In this manifestation, Neuburg saw him as essentially phallic, bearing in his hand the Book II, subtitled BIA, whose 106 pages referred to the grade of Adeptus Exemptus (7°=4□). BIA, in Greek, meant force, might, or strength.

"Every drop of semen which Hermes sheds is a world," Neuburg explained. "The technical term for this semen is KRATOS." This Greek word, also meaning force, differed from BIA in that the former corresponded to the kabbalistic Boaz while KRATOS equated with Jachin: opposite pillars in Solomon's temple. Numerically, both words added up to be prime numbers,

BIA 13 and KRATOS 691; together they were 704, an important number in the Christian gematria of Bond and Lea.[97]

The discourse proceeded at length, finally providing instructions on the workings. "He wants us not to invoke the other forms of Mercury," Neuburg spoke. "He says that we have more knowledge than we know what to do with."

Regarding the rite of Jupiter, they learned banquets were not only in order for the ceremony, but that results depended on them. Therefore, they should be prepared carefully. In addition, Neuburg added, "He wants us to overcome shame generally, and says, 'There is no shame about me, is there?' He suggests an obvious method which I blush to repeat."

At 2:15 a.m., the third working ended.

Since the gods insisted on overcoming shame, they followed their suggestion: Crowley and Neuburg called on Jane Chéron and there engaged Duranty in an act of public sodomy. As Crowley noted, "W.D. was the victim"—i.e., he played the passive role—but AC neglected to record the aggressor's identity. It was more likely the shy Neuburg, who had more shame to overcome, than Crowley, who preferred the passive role.

Crowley had a cold and Neuburg a temper when they did the fourth working on January 5. Because of this, Crowley described the rites as "maimed." Nevertheless, he became oracular and interacted in the guise of Hermes with Neuburg. After closing the temple, however, Neuburg became possessed by something else and began to speak. The entity warned that they were unleashing an enormous magical force that would result in international complications. This would prove significant as World War I began only months afterward. "Those who adopt this rite will either succeed completely or fail utterly. There is no middle path for it is impossible to escape the ring of Divine Karma created."

The entity next described what it considered a most potent ritual: "The supreme Rite would be to bring about a climax in the death of the victim." The victim had to be willing, and was ideally a young girl. Hearing details on the rape, sacrifice, and vivisection of the "offering," Crowley was horrified. Both he and Neuburg agreed the directions involved black magic and should be ignored.

The entity went on to make predictions about the magicians. Neuburg, he said, would travel east, marry in June, and return to the Great Work in September; none of these predictions came to pass. For Crowley, he saw a long journey to the east, during which he would leave Neuburg in charge of his affairs. In retrospect, this erroneous prediction would amuse Crowley as, shortly after this Paris Working, he and Neuburg would split and Crowley would journey west, not east, to America for the duration of the war.

Unimpressed, Crowley closed the temple on the fourth working.

At about this time, Wally and Jane appeared with the remedy to Crowley's cold: an opium pipe. While the drug would prove harmfully habit-forming for his friends, Crowley recognized opium as sacred to Jupiter, the deity he was trying to contact. Taking this as a sign, he partook. Afterward, he took a nap.

Upon awakening, not only had his cold cleared up, but he was also inspired to write a story. Crowley's "Kubla Kahn," "The Stratagem," came to him in full form as a "subtle exposure of English stupidity."[98] The *English Review* would accept it straight off, and Joseph Conrad would reputedly consider it the best short story he had read in ten years.

From January 6 through 11, four more workings occurred, the first three of Jupiter and the fourth of Hermes. Then Neuburg took a week off to go to the forest and recuperate from an illness. The Paris Working resumed on January 19. Six more workings occurred up to the 27th, all invoking Jupiter. In these rites, they recalled past lives, including one as a priestess named Asteria or Astarte, recalling the great sacrifice of spring, wherein a bull was cut open and a virgin, laid inside the hot carcass, was violated by the High Priest as she choked on blood in orgasm.

Crowley and Neuburg shared an incarnation, they learned: as Mardocles, an aspirant for initiation, Neuburg's ordeal was to watch the temple dancer Aia (Crowley) without becoming aroused; if he did, he was to rape her or face castration. Mardocles, aroused by the dance, was moved by tenderness not to violate her. Favoring the candidate, the high priest spared him castration but expelled both him and Aia from the temple. The saga of Crowley and Neuburg as lovers in a past life unfolds from there. Taken as a spate of fantasy or wish-fulfillment, it illustrates their love for each other; accepted as truth, it explains why they were drawn together in this life with such compatible sexual styles.

When the temple opened at 10:20 on January 29 for the sixteenth working, Jupiter demanded blood. Crowley compliantly cut a four (the number of Jupiter) on Neuburg's breast. Afterward, AC sat in the yogic posture *Shivasana* while Victor danced. Crowley experienced a most complete possession of his person by the god, wrapping his consciousness into the godhead so intensely that the only appropriate expression he could arrive at was "Sanguis and Semen": Jupiter's energy flowed through the staple fluids of life, "blood and semen." Further workings followed on February 2, 4, 5, 9, 10, 11, and 12.

After twenty-four operations, the Paris Working finished with Neuburg's bibliomancy, "I am Thou, and the Pillar is established in the Void." Hermes had promised money: long-overdue checks arrived in the mail, and a Brother donated £500 of his recent inheritance to the order. Hermes promised to help with books: and Crowley's newest, *Chicago May,* was back from the printers; while in Tunisia on May 14, he would be inspired to write "The Soul of the Desert."[99] Jupiter promised health and hospitality: Crowley found his bronchitis cured, and friends offering him opium, the drug sacred to Jupiter, while Neuburg found himself flooded with dinner guests and hosts. Crowley and Neuburg considered the rituals an unqualified success.[100]

Another important result of these workings was their effect on Crowley's conceptualization of the OTO mysteries. While the VIII° dealt with masturbatory magick and IX° with vaginal intercourse, he saw no room for homosexual workings. Crowley found that his "researches into the mysteries of the IX° have compelled me to add an XI°."[101] Although it remains an obscure part of Crowley's system, the XI° represented a symbolic reversal of IX°: Just as the digits were reversed, so were the energies inverted.

Duranty, meanwhile, remained close with the opium-wracked Chéron, taking her as his wife for many years. However, after Crowley and Neuburg returned to Paris, he found he no longer believed in anything. On Crowley, he commented, "I don't believe in magic, but I'm not sure that I disbelieve it. But wouldn't it be funny if all the magicians went to heaven?"[102]

Finding his finances more and more overextended, Crowley protected himself from creditors by selling Boleskine and its thirty-four-acre parcel to the trustees of MMM (namely, himself, Leila, and Cowie). On May 5, the MMM paid £500 to Crowley and assumed £900 in debts and bills on the property. In order to protect his intellectual property, Crowley transferred the copyrights of all his works to OTO as well. In theory (but not, as it turns out, in practice), all of Crowley's possessions and works were now owned by OTO, and hence inaccessible to creditors.[103]

The *English Review*'s August publication of Crowley's "Chants Before Battle" was particularly well-timed, coinciding with the start of World War I. The piece, leading off the issue, integrates into classic selections of poetry the gist of the lines

> We don't want to fight, but, by Jingo, if we do,
> We've got the ships, we've got the men, we've got the money, too.

Some of the authors subjected to this clever and humorous mutation are Geoffrey Chaucer, Alfred Lord Tennyson, Robert Browning, Percy Bysshe Shelly, Francis Thompson, and D. G. Rosetti. It remains one of Crowley's greatest bits of literary parody.

Also contributing to Crowley's high public profile at this time was his introduction, through Frank Harris, to the "tramp poet" Harry Kemp (1883–1960). Attending one of Crowley's performances of the Mass of the Phoenix (or "séances" as they were popularly dubbed), Kemp wrote an article—which Crowley considered rubbish and Kemp himself called "a turgid bit of sensational journalism"[104]—for the *New York World*'s Sunday magazine of August 2, 1914. The title said it all: "Weird Rites of Devil Worshippers Revealed by an Eye Witness." Despite whatever virtues the piece may have lacked, it did stir up interest in the United States. As Crowley noted, "we have had a lot of letters from America on account of a lunatic's article in the *New York World*."

"Tramp Poet" Harry Kemp (1883–1960), who helped introduce Crowley to America.

Early in September, Crowley renewed his experiments in the IX° with Leila. Although he penned official OTO instructions on sex magick—"De Arte Magica," "De Nuptiis Secretis Deorum Cum Hominibus," and "De Homunculo Epistola"—they were obsolete even as they appeared. As Crowley wrote at this time, "My knowledge of the technique has largely increased since I wrote my Commentary on the IX°."[105]

While Crowley busied himself with writings and "séances," Neuburg began to maintain his distance. Although business kept them apart, Neuburg also tired of the fits of anger to which he, as AC's lover, had become subject. After a violent row between Crowley and Hayter Preston that past May, Neuburg took Preston's advice and went away for the summer to a cottage in Branscombe, South Devon. There, his close friends were Crowley's former students Olivia Haddon and Vittoria Cremers; to them, Crowley was an impostor and charlatan, and they made Victor see him in a new light. Unfortunately, they also led Neuburg to the far-fetched belief that Crowley had jealously caused Jeanne Heyse's suicide. A passage he would read years later in *Magick in Theory and Practice* would only confirm Victor's suspicions:

> An adept known to The Master Therion once found it necessary to slay a
> Circe who was bewitching brethren. He merely walked to the door of her

room, and drew an Astral T ("traditore," and the symbol of Saturn) with an astral dagger. Within 48 hours she shot herself.[106]

This passage was likely a case of Crowley, having heard the allegations against him, recounting the story in a way that bolstered his magical image.

When Neuburg faced Crowley that fall, tendering his resignation and renouncing all his oaths, the master ritually cursed him on the spot. Neuburg was too stunned to do anything but stand there. Three years previously, almost prophetically, Neuburg had written to Crowley in *The Triumph of Pan:*

> Because the fulfilment of dreams is itself but a dream,
> There is no end save the song, and song is the end;
> And here with a sheaf of songs barehanded I stand,
> And the light is fled from mine eyes, and the sword from my hand
> Is fallen; the years have left me a fool, and the gleam
> Is vanished from life, and the swift years sear me and rend.[107]

Neuburg would never again write poetry as moving as that he wrote under Crowley's influence, although he would go on to run the Vine Press and edit "The Poet's Corner" for the *Sunday Referee*. Through this column, which awarded weekly prizes to promising new talents, Neuburg would discover Welsh poet Dylan Thomas (1914–1953).[108] Up until his death from tuberculosis in 1940, Neuburg would recall his days with Crowley with a combination of tenderness and pain. It was the end of an era for both of them.

CHAPTER TWELVE

Chokmah Days

Crowley's life began to progress in episodic cycles lasting seventy-three days. These he dubbed Chokmah days, after the Tree of Life's second sphere, numerically valued seventy-three and representing the grade of Magus to which he aspired.

Day one.

News of the Great War arrived while Crowley was climbing in Switzerland to prepare for a £40,000 rematch with Kangchenjunga. As he wrote:

> I came down from a mountain to find the Swiss had mobilized and all the railways held up, but on the first day possible I went to Berne, where the British minister informed me it was impossible to get back, that the line had been torn up for 13 miles beyond the frontier, and that he could not get his own men through. Reduced to desperation, I consequently took the train and came home without any difficulty.[1]

The world had never seen fighting on so a large scale. While Neuburg—prior to his parting with Crowley—suggested it was a sign of the Reign of Horus, Crowley was "hoping it will be over in two or three months."[2] Nevertheless he dutifully offered to help with the war effort; but his assistance was unwanted. Whether due to age (thirty-nine), health, or notoriety, Crowley does not say.

However, we do know that a severe attack of phlebitis in his left leg incapacitated Crowley from September to mid-October. As he recuperated, he visited Boleskine one last time. His spent fortune required him to liquidate even this: since going over to MMM, Boleskine was mortgaged to raise funds for the Great Work and rented to Dr. Murray Leslie for £250 a year in order to pay the bank. In his final visit to his former home, Crowley worried about the war. He confided in C. S. Jones that, if the end of civilization was coming, he should share the secret of the IX° with several persons to ensure its survival. In a separate letter to MMM's treasurer, he wrote, "Unfortunately this Secret is in possession of very few, and it is quite conceivable that all the holders might perish within the next year or two. A part of the instruction of the IX° is in these words: "Trust not a stranger; fail not an heir."[3] The task of finding competent and capable people to carry on the mysteries would worry and motivate Crowley even in his last days.

Everywhere he looked, it seemed the propaganda of Lord Northcliffe (Alfred Harmsworth, 1865–1922) presented itself. A newspaper magnate and politician, Northcliffe is remembered as England's William Randolph Hearst. For years he had been publishing articles in his newspapers such as the *Daily Mail,* warning about the threats to Britain's sovereignty posed by the airplane and by Germany's politics. When the war finally broke out, the *Star* wrote, "Next to the Kaiser, Lord Northcliffe has done more than any living man to bring about the war."[4] Northcliffe's propaganda disgusted Crowley. To smash Wagner records and ban Father Christmas because of their German roots simply made England look ridiculous. Seeing England's own efforts reflect poorly on itself, it occurred to him that an unprincipled or clever man could easily use a nation's propaganda as a weapon against itself. The idea fascinated him.

This jumble of ideas played in Crowley's mind: finances; preservation of the IX° secret; rejection by a homeland that was embarrassing itself with its awkward propaganda. In the midst of the crisis, everything pointed to America.

Kemp's article in the *New York World* magazine helped pave the way, followed by the republication of "Appeal to the American Republic" in the October *English Review* as "To America." New York lawyer and patron of the arts John Quinn (1870–1924) had collected most of Crowley's books (but read none of them). He knew "some of them seemed to be the limit, both erotic and blasphemous. I can forgive the blasphemy."[5] He wished to buy Crowley's rare editions, and the desperate author shipped two trunks of rariora—special bindings, manuscripts, and the like—to the States. Valued at $20,000, Crowley hoped to sell at least $5,000.

In addition, C. S. Jones had collected signatures in Vancouver that October to found an OTO lodge. Reuss granted him a charter, and Crowley took him under his wing. Thus another pupil and friend stepped into the space vacated by Neuburg, Fuller, the other Jones, and Eckenstein.

On October 24 Crowley sailed for America on the *Lusitania,* six months before German U-boats would sink it and 1,198 passengers, drawing the United States into the war.

For the third time in fourteen years, Crowley set foot on American soil. He arrived in New York on October 31 with $200 in his pocket and his wax-paper charter as Honorary Magus of the Societas Rosicruciana. On his fingers were various magical rings, and in his vest hung a pocket watch bearing the emblem of a 33° Freemason. Henry Hall, a reporter from the *New York World* Sunday magazine, met him at the dock, following up the account of London "devil-worshippers" with a description of Aleister Crowley's arrival (it appeared in the December 13 issue, and was syndicated nationally):

Aleister Crowley, who recently arrived in New York, is the strangest man I ever met. He is a man about whom men quarrel. Intensely magnetic, he attracts people or repels them with equal violence. His personality seems to breed rumors. Everywhere they follow him.

One man to whom I spoke of him lauded Crowley as a poet of rare delicacy, the author of "Hail Mary," a garland of verses in honor of the Mother of God. Another alluded to him as an unsparing critic of American literature. Another knew him as the holder of some world records for mountain-climbing. Still another warned me against him as a thoroughly bad man, a Satanist or devil-worshiper steeped in black magic, the high priest of Beelzebub. An actor knew of him only as a theatrical producer and as the designer of extraordinary stage costumes. A publisher told me that Crowley was an essayist and philosopher whose books, nearly all privately issued, were masterpieces of modern printing.... By others he was variously pictured to me as a big game hunter, as a gambler, as an editor, as an explorer. Some said that he was a man of real attainments, others that he was a faker. All agreed that he was extraordinary.[6]

The account was far more accurate than Kemp's sensationalism.

Seizing on the publicity, Crowley issued a pamphlet announcing "The Master will remain in New York until the end of January." During his stay, he was offering a series of classes on world religions, divination, and magic. The latter curriculum is most interesting: although he hadn't yet adopted his idiosyncratic spelling of magick, the outline is virtually identical with the table of contents to *Magick in Theory and Practice* (1929), which at this point only existed as the first draft of *Book Four,* Part Three. This shows how little the structure of the book changed between its original draft, completed with Leila Waddell in Fontainebleau in 1912; its revision with Mary Butts in Cefalù in 1921–1922; and its final revision and publication with Gerald Yorke in 1929.

The class series was at one stage connected to George Winslow Plummer (1876–1944), Supreme Magus of the Societas Rosicruciana in America.[7] Plummer was born in Boston but moved to New York City to work as an artist; there, his encounter with Freemasonry prompted him, together with Sylvester C. Gould (1840–1909), to form the Societas Rosicruciana in America, which would be open to Masons and non-Masons alike. Gould's death in 1909 left Plummer the sole executive of the order while it was still in its formative stages. As early as 1912, Plummer had been in touch with Crowley's circle through *The Equinox.* By early 1913, both men had reciprocated recognition of each other, Crowley inscribing Plummer's name in MMM's Golden Book as a 32° Scottish Rite Mason, and Plummer forwarding Crowley an SRIA IX° diploma in *Honoris Causa.* On arriving in New York on November 1, one of the first things Crowley did was to write Plummer in order to meet and personally present him with a certificate recognizing him as an honorary Prince of the Royal Secret in OTO. The SRIA minute book for November 13, 1914, records that Plummer had a "satisfactory interview" with Crowley.[8] A four-page card produced at this time, advertising a series of talks very similar in structure to the one described above, listed a New York City address for G. W. Plummer. The level of Plummer's involvement, however, is unclear; he may simply have been providing a mailing address or a classroom.

AC found America unrecognizable, with its skyscrapers, capitalists, and bustle more distasteful than ever. Although he found accommodations at the Hotel Wolcott on 4 West 31st Street (today known as one of New York's great bargain hotels), he wound up at 40 West 36th Street. From there, he looked up friends and acquaintances: Frank Harris recalled how Crowley arrived at his St. Regis Hotel room looking "more like an Egyptian than ever"[9] and still suffering from phlebitis. Harris had worked with Crowley in the past, through both *Vanity Fair* and *The Equinox;* he was now editor for *Pearson's* magazine. Angered that the world treated poets like stray dogs, Harris treated Crowley kindly and provided him with introductions to many New Yorkers, including journalist William Buehler Seabrook (1886–1945)[10] and the man who would become Crowley's lifelong friend, writer and biographer Louis Umfreville Wilkinson (1881–1966), better known by his pen name Louis Marlow.

When Crowley called, John Quinn invited him to dinner. Crowley asked permission to reproduce the Augustus John pencil sketch of him that Quinn owned; since John himself had asked Quinn for copies, he agreed to have prints made for both John and Crowley. AC also helped Quinn select Crowleyana to purchase for his library. These included one of ten Japanese vellum copies of *Jezebel and Other Tragic Poems,* fine bindings of *The Sword of Song* and *Konx Om Pax* in blue crushed levant morocco by the master bookbinder Zaehnsdorf,[11] and the original manuscripts of *The Soul of Osiris, The Mother's Tragedy,* and *Alice: An Adultery,* all bound by Zaehnsdorf. The latter book contained a verse in "White Poppy" that the published edition omitted. In the end—on November 14—Crowley, hoping to exchange his cache of books for cash in hand, was sadly disappointed. Quinn bought only $700 worth of books. It hardly justified the transatlantic journey.

Crowley repeatedly offered dinner to Quinn, who always declined. Realizing that Crowley was hard up, and feeling charitable with the holiday season approaching, Quinn finally invited Crowley to his apartment for a mid-December Christmas dinner. He arrived in good spirits and presented Quinn with a gift of a manuscript. It was "The King of Terrors," published in *The Equinox* as "The Testament of Magdalen Blair." Its ninety pages were bound in limp crimson morocco with a cloth solander case. Crowley inscribed it, "To John Quinn the MS of my best story (so far). Christmas 1914, a tiny tribute from Aleister Crowley."[12]

Ironically, another of Quinn's dinner guests was John Butler Yeats (1839–1922), the talented father of Crowley's GD rival, W. B. Yeats. The elder Yeats, who was giving lectures in America, also brought former school teacher Dorothy Coates, his tall brunette mistress. Formerly Quinn's lover, she came between Quinn and Yeats, and only her recent affliction with tuberculosis prompted the two men to reconcile. Also attending was Frederic James Gregg (1865-1928), Quinn's good friend who left his journalistic job at the *Sun* to become one of *Vanity Fair's* main contributors.

A skilled and witty raconteur, Crowley dominated the conversation, recounting the history of the manuscript he had just given Quinn: he wrote the short story "The Testament of Magdalen Blair," originally titled "The King of Terrors," in November 1912. Having read it at a party one Christmas Eve, he shocked the guests so that, the next morning, he learned they all now disliked him. He submitted it pseudonymously to the *English Review* and to his astonishment, editor Austin Harrison (1873–1928), believing the story to be true, demanded authentication.

Then Crowley entertained everyone with his best party stunt: guessing, with remarkable accuracy, the birth date, hour, and rising sign of those present. When the conversation turned to the GD, an organization dear to W. B. Yeats, John Butler Yeats and Dorothy Coates questioned him: yes, he opposed Mathers, and was indignant about his alleged mistreatment of Moïna. All the while, he was courteous and well spoken. "Of course," Yeats recalled, "being an Englishman, he was throughout the hero of his own tales."[13] Yeats liked Crowley, and described the evening favorably in a letter to his son, "Willie":

> Do you know a man named Crowley?—a strange man and witty. Miss Coates and I met him at Quinn's at dinner; his conversation not witty but that of a witty man.... Have you noticed that any man possessing the gift of expression but absolutely without sympathy is inevitably a wit and a man of humour? A complete detachment from the people about him—this complete and perfectly natural estrangement puts him in easy possession of all that makes for humor and wit. It also makes him seem *formidable*. The combination is that of the *formidable stranger*, so that you pay attention to every word he lets fall from his lips. And if he makes you laugh, you hear him with a sense of relief and are almost grateful, this effect enhanced in this case by his bullet head and strong clumsy figure—his fingers thick but tapering.... Have you noticed that one is always inclined to like a formidable man? It is our way of getting back our courage.[14]

Quinn, however, decided the poet was simply not his type. Magick bored him, and their conversation left him thinking Crowley a dull, uninteresting speaker. Despite Crowley's reputation, Quinn found nothing objectionable about him except, perhaps, for his "strong appetite for strong drink." Quinn had supplied vintage Chartreuse and cigars to his guests, and Crowley consumed a good amount, although never becoming drunk. "I am not interested in his morals or lack of morals," he wrote. "He may or may not be a good or profound or crooked student or practitioner of magic. To me, he is only a third—or fourth—rate poet."[15]

Gregg's opinion of Crowley is unknown, but he appears to have played a role in introducing Crowley to *Vanity Fair,* for Crowley's works soon began to appear regularly in the New York edition just as they did in the London edition. These events, however, did not unfold until Crowley's fifth Chokmah day.

When W. B. Yeats learned that his father and Quinn had entertained Crowley for Christmas, he sent warnings to both. To his father, Yeats wrote:

> Crowley is not a man I appreciate. I am amused to find that he now praises Mrs. MacGregor, he slandered her in a very cruel way in one of his books but I suppose Bergson's sister is now worth considering. I am sorry Quinn has taken up with Crowley.[16]

Yeats was even more blunt with Quinn:

> He is I think mad, but has written about six lines, amid much bad rhetoric, of real poetry. I asked about him at Cambridge, and a man described him being dragged out of the dining hall by a porter, thrown out, struggling, because of the indecency of his conversation. He is an English and French type. You I think have nothing like him. He used to be a handsome fellow.[17]

Quinn assured the younger Yeats that he was no friend of Crowley's and had seen him only three or four times in all. Unknown to Crowley, a ghost from his past kept him out of Quinn's graces.

Another moneymaking scheme was meanwhile in the works. Crowley contacted lawyer Theodore Schroeder (1864–1953), whose writings on sex and religion attracted AC's attention. Crowley sent him a copy of the *Bagh-i-Muattar,* emphasizing,

> When you're done with it, you can walk straight down to Brentano's [Book Store] and get your money back. It's very very rare: Only 200 copies printed, many of these destroyed, and the bulk of the stock probably lost....[18]

The book, however, was merely bait. Crowley offered to send Schroeder OTO's secret documents at a deal too good to pass up: without the ceremonies, he could take a vow of secrecy and receive the instructions as an honorary VII° at two-thirds the price.

Such were Crowley's first days in America, financially depleted and disappointed. As he generated spare funds, he spent them on continued experiments in sex magick. Although Leila was with him around this time, Crowley confined his work to cheap prostitutes and masturbation.

Day two.

Despite the war, financial hardship, and distance from England, the Great Work proceeded. Cowie was doing his best as Grand Treasurer General of MMM to send Crowley £50–100 at regular intervals. Furthermore, Frank Bennett, the A∴A∴ student who left for Australia and the TS around 1911, recontacted MMM after three years of running a Theosophical lodge; he wanted to work the OTO rituals in Australia. Windram, Crowley's man in

South Africa, worked with Bennett and Ernest W. T. Dunn, 33°, to set up an OTO lodge down under, with Bennett as National Grand Secretary General and Dunn the reluctant Grand Master General. This arrangement placed Crowley in a comfortable political position in OTO, with supporters operating lodges on three continents beside Europe: Jones in Canada, Windram in South Africa, and Bennett in Australia.

Looking out on New York on New Year's Day, 1915, Crowley concluded that Mercury was lord of the city. The god of commerce was clearly with him, for opportunities waited at his door.

The omnibus headed up 5th Avenue. Inside, Crowley read the latest press clippings on himself that his London cutting service had sent him. A tap on his shoulder interrupted his leisure. "Excuse me," a man spoke as Crowley turned to face him. "Do you favor a square deal for Germany and Austria?"

Crowley considered the man and his question, and decided to play along. "I want a square deal for everybody," he replied noncommittally, much to the other man's interest. Their ensuing discussion of politics continued until they reached his stop. "I have to get off at 37th Street," the man explained and handed Crowley his card. Only after he left did Crowley examine the name on the card: O'Brien.

When Crowley's curiosity led him to call on O'Brien a few days later, the Irishman was nowhere to be found. Instead, he confronted a children's poet by the name of Joseph Bernard Rethy[19] at the offices of German propaganda rag *The Fatherland*. Subtitled "Fair Play for Germany and Austria-Hungary," its goal was to keep the United States neutral and out of the war. Rethy responded to Crowley's visit by fetching a higher authority.

He soon returned with poet George Sylvester Viereck (1884– 1962), *The Fatherland's* publisher. Wide-eyed and smiling, Viereck stepped forward, shook Crowley's hand, and remarked how nice it was to see him again.

Again? he thought.

Viereck reminded him: back in 1911, when Austin Harrison introduced them at the offices of the *English Review*. He remembered AC as an eccentric mix of poet, pornographer, adventurer, and devil worshiper. As he wrote:

> I knew nothing against him. I do not object to devil worship and I think that a man's personal life is his own. Hence, any rumors against him which may have reached me had no effect.[20]

Viereck was in a friendly mood, and engaged the poet in conversation.

Crowley found Viereck an intelligent and worldly man, particularly in matters of ideology and politics. Viereck's approach was a relief from Northcliffe's rabid propaganda. Turning on his charm, Crowley explained to Viereck that he was an Irishman looking for a job. In response, Viereck ran AC's "Honesty is the Best Policy" in the January 13 and 20 issues of *The Fatherland;* Reuss included a German translation in the March *Oriflamme*. It marked Crowley's

first foray into what his detractors would call treason. Shortly thereafter, a political letter that he circulated among his friends, "An Orgy of Cant," was printed
in *The Continental Times,* a European pro-German newspaper;[21] according to
Spence, its New York bureau was operated by Theodor Reuss out of 40 West
36th Street, which was also the address of Crowley's flat.[22] Crowley's politically
charged writings would continue to appear in subsequent issues of both *The
Fatherland* and *The Continental Times* over the next two and a quarter years.[23]

George Sylvester Viereck (1884–1962), editor of *The Fatherland.*

Crowley's motives with these pro-German writings have long been contested. While critics suggest Crowley was an unprincipled opportunist who
sold out his country for a paycheck, his friends believed the explanation that
Crowley gave: he was working with the knowledge of the British government
to infiltrate Viereck's circle and publish propaganda so ridiculous as to destroy
Germany's credibility, and to help bring the United States into the war. This
was done with the help of John O'Hara Cosgrave (1864–1947), editor of the
New York World's Sunday magazine (which had recently published two articles
about Crowley by Harry Kemp and Henry Hall). Cosgrave allegedly introduced Crowley to the U.S. Department of Justice.[24] Indeed, when the United
States terminated diplomatic ties with Germany just prior to entering the fray,
Crowley noted in his diary for February 2, 1917, "My 2¼ years' work crowned
with success; U.S.A. breaks off relations with Germany." This is significant as
some have argued that Crowley invented his secret-agent story years later in
order to return to England without being arrested. Indeed, this diary entry
shows that counterespionage was his intent all along.

Consistency, in fact, is a hallmark of Crowley's interviews with the Bureau of Investigation and the attorney general of New York about his apparent pro-German activities. The account he gave them is corroborated by a memorandum and affidavit that he prepared at that time, seeking intelligence work from the British authorities, and is also consistent with the essay "The Last Straw," which was included in his *Confessions*. This militates against the theory that Crowley changed his story later, and is thus worth summarizing here.

Crowley's September 1914 attack of phlebitis rendered him ineligible for active military service, although he did apply. As Crowley explained, "I asked my friend, the Hon. Everard Feilding, Lieut. R.N.V.R., of the Press Bureau, to get me a job. Nothing doing."[25] Several years had passed since Feilding was secretary for the Society for Psychical Research and joined the A∴A∴. Since then, he had been appointed a Naval Censor for the Official Press Bureau.[26] His reply to AC was not encouraging: whereas Feilding had a history of Naval service and a college degree, Crowley possessed neither of these. Feilding told him,

> You wear a short blue gown and an extremely battered mortarboard. You have an extraordinary personality—a reputation for having committed every crime from murder, barratry and arson to *quaternio terminorum*.... I cannot hold out any hopes that any way can be found whereby you might serve your country.[27]

Finding himself in America, Crowley got the idea to win the Germans' confidence and infiltrate their circle. Reading the press accounts of Crowley's declaration of Irish independence at the Statue of Liberty (described below), Feilding wrote Crowley a pained letter asking what he was up to. Knowing Feilding to be a reasonable man, Crowley explained that he had penetrated Viereck's propaganda ring and was doing his best to discredit the Germans. Although understanding and approving of Crowley's strategy, Feilding "could not authorize me to go ahead without appealing to his superiors. He put the case before them.... The result was that the negotiations came to very little, though I turned in reports from time to time."[28]

Although he could not obtain official authorization, Crowley proceeded on his own recognizance in hopes that the authorities would reconsider. "I got the idea of keeping up that illusion, so as to qualify for a post in the Secret Service of England.... I told Lieut. Feilding of the plan, which he thought a good one."[29] Thus, Crowley continued writing for *The Fatherland* to discredit the Germans and sway American public opinion. AC summarized his strategy to Joseph W. Norwood (c. 1878–1955), a former lawyer turned editor of the newspaper *Light* in Louisville, Kentucky, and founder in 1919 of the International Magian Society dedicated to the practical application of Masonic principles:[30] "I was employed by the Secret Service, my main object being to bring America into the War, my main method to get the Germans to make asses of themselves by increasing their frightfulness until even the Americans kicked."[31]

Then the May 24, 1916, issue of *The Fatherland* attacked Captain Guy
Gaunt for allegedly bribing an office boy at the magazine for information on
Viereck.[32] Sir Guy Reginald Archer Gaunt (1869–1953) was England's Naval
Intelligence attaché in Washington. According to his autobiography, *The Yield
of the Years* (1940), he came to the United States in May 1914, where he
reported to Ambassador Sir Cecil Spring-Rice; when the embassy learned of
German plots in America, "Permission came from London for me to take up
Intelligence work, but to work with the greatest caution."[33] At that, he moved
into the Biltmore Hotel in New York and took a couple of small offices at 43–
44 Whitehall Street. In light of the *Fatherland*'s attacks, Crowley wrote a supportive letter to Gaunt, offering his services. According to Crowley, "He
replied very nicely though in a rather off-hand way, in which he said that he
only knew of Viereck 'as one of the lesser jackals around von Papen'"[34] and not
worth his notice.

Shortly thereafter, Crowley had a conversation with investment banker and
patron of the arts Otto Herman Kahn (1867–1934), who was a German-born
naturalized British citizen who moved to New York in 1893 to work for
Speyer and Company. Spence suggests that he was also an intelligence agent.[35]
Indeed, after talking with him Crowley applied formally to Gaunt for work,
reporting that "I have ever since kept him informed of my address, so as to be
ready if called."[36] This is corroborated by Crowley's interviews with American
authorities, who wrote "Crowley then described his endeavors to become associated with the British Secret Service, detailing his dealings with Commodore
Gaunt of the British Intelligence Office but admitted that he had never succeeded in obtaining any official recognition."[37]

Many officials, both American and British, viewed Crowley's claims as
absurd, and were under the assumption that "the British authorities have conveyed to Crowley an intimation that if he returns to England, his reception will
be rather more warm than cordial and that it would probably be safer for him
to remain on this side for the present."[38] When questioned about this allegation, "Crowley denied that there was any action pending against him in London that would prevent him from returning to England at any time he
wished."[39] Indeed, when Crowley returned to England after the war in 1919
and talk of treason was rife, Gaunt contacted British Secretary for Foreign
Affairs Sir Edward Grey (1862–1933) and Basil Thompson (1861–1939), chief
of Scotland Yard's Criminal Investigation Department and head of MI5's Special Branch,[40] wherein he achieved renown as one of the great spy catchers.
Gaunt told these men, "Let him alone. I have got a complete line on him and
also *The Fatherland*."[41] However, as Crowley commented on a later attempt to
corroborate all this, "I am a little doubtful as to whether Gaunt will reply to
your letter. I think the obligation of professional secrecy may prevent him."[42]

However, not all officials were so skeptical of Crowley's explanation. When
the assistant to New York's attorney general questioned Crowley in 1918 about

his wartime activities, he satisfied them that he was truly serving the war effort.[43] Crowley provided the Bureau of Investigation with information about a man whose name is censored from the public record. This is almost certainly Viereck, who, as a paid German agent, received $140,000 to finance his propaganda prior to the entry of the United States into the war. Viereck came to regard Crowley as a spy, writing that AC "Came to me during the War. Worked for me, wrote about me. Tried to sell me out to the English."[44] Years later, when planning a trip back to the United States, AC noted in his diary,

> George Sylvester Viereck will sign an affidavit that I had no trouble with authorities in U.S.A. He said also that after the war he made friends with our N.I.D. [Naval Intelligence] chiefs, who told him that I had been working for them during the war.[45]

Another of Crowley's acquaintances in America, Albert Ryerson, recounted: "Crowley really was a secret service man for Great Britain, in the war ... German spies were continuously after him. He played a slick trick on the Germans by having himself, a British spy, on their publication. He practically destroyed the *Fatherland*."[46] While tales of German spies dogging Crowley suggests either Ryerson or AC was exaggerating, this further demonstrates that counterespionage was Crowley's original intent, not an afterthought.

Crowley's so-called propaganda actually supports this contention. He purportedly strove to write material so absurd as to discredit the Germans, and in this he seems to have succeeded. His essay "The New Parsifal" immodestly compared Kaiser Wilhelm to the knight Parsifal, searching for the Holy Graal. Meanwhile, in *The Fatherland,* Crowley made equally absurd statements:

> A great deal of damage was done at Croydon, especially at its suburb Addiscombe, where my aunt lives. Unfortunately her house was not hit; otherwise I should not have to trouble to write this article. Count Zeppelin is respectfully requested to try again. The exact address is Eton Lodge, Outram Road.[47]

Responding to this article, the *Chicago Daily Tribune* characterized Crowley as "an Irishman who will not be accused of sympathy for England."[48] This absurd humor permeates all of his propaganda writings.

Crowley also pointed out in his defense that he had never been to Germany except passing through, does not speak German, and had no German friends ("save one with whom I correspond on religious matters,"[49] i.e. Reuss). Also, he had published poems in *The English Review* encouraging England's alliance with America, namely "Chants before Battle" and "To America."

All this has prompted some of Crowley's biographers to search for evidence of an official cover-up of Crowley's full intelligence involvement for reasons of national security. For instance, Booth's *A Magick Life* points out that, during his 1913 trip to Moscow with the Ragged Ragtime Girls, Crowley had befriended Moscow Art Theater secretary Michael Lykiardopoulos, who in turn introduced Crowley to British secret agent Sir Robert Hamilton Bruce Lockhart

(1887–1970); Lockhart made Lykiardopoulos head of Britain's propaganda department in Moscow, and Booth suggests he was also in a position to facilitate Crowley's espionage activities. However, there is no evidence to suggest Lockhart ever gave Crowley such an appointment.[50] Similarly Spence, in *Secret Agent 666,* dedicates his entire book to exploring the clandestine political activities of Crowley and his numerous acquaintances, and speculating about possible connections with others in the intelligence community. Although the book claims a larger espionage role than Crowley himself reports—sometimes based on tenuous connections—Spence treats this topic with more thoroughness than is possible here; indeed, he has uncovered surprising new information and caused many to reevaluate Crowley's intelligence claims in a new light. For this, the book deserves a critical read.[51]

At the end of the day, the most compelling piece of evidence is that, during World War II, Crowley would work for Britain's secret service, MI5 and MI6: no traitor would have gotten such a job.

Day three.

Turbulent times rocked the world that May: German U-boats sank the *Lusitania* and killed 1,198. German Zeppelins began their first air raids on London. And German physicist Albert Einstein (1879–1955) published his *General Theory of Relativity.* For Crowley, however, all was stagnation. He was far from home, far from friends, and far from his business. He had left behind *The Equinox* and the circle of students that had filled his life for five years. Now alone in America, he felt adrift. His introduction to Viereck was no help in selling literary works, and his efforts at giving lectures or publishing the odd poem or political essay invariably ended in failure. For instance, he enlisted bookman Mitchell Kennerley (1878–1950) to publish *The Giant's Thumb,* a collection of poetry that he had had typeset by the Ballantyne Press in England but which was never released owing to the war; however, the project with Kennerley never advanced beyond page proofs. It was a miserable, despondent time.

When dawn broke on day four, oppression and obscurity lifted like morning fog burned off by the sun; and the world lolled its head languorously in Crowley's palm. The article "Aleister Crowley: Mystic and Mountain Climber" appeared in *Vanity Fair;* it was attributed to Arthur Loring Bruce, pen-name of *Vanity Fair* editor Frank Crowninshield (1872–1947).[52] One Chokmah-day later, this association would provide Crowley with a valuable literary outlet.

Then, on the evening of June 10, 1915, Crowley met two beautiful women through *Fatherland* journalist James Keating. The first was actress Helen Westley[53] (1879–1942), who reminded him of a snake that glittered

with the loveliness of lust; but she was worn and weary with the disappointment of insatiable desire. Her intellect was brilliant but cynical. She
had lost faith in the universe.[54]

A Brooklyn native, Westley studied at the Sargent Dramatic School, debuted at
the Star Theater in 1897, and acted in vaudeville and stock roles until 1915,
when she helped found the first company of the Washington Square Players.
She began playing the Oyster in *Another Interior,* and went on to many other
productions. Theresa Helburn provides a striking description of her: "She had
a theatrical appearance and manner, and dressed rather like a femme fatale—
coal-black hair and black, slinky dresses, a little like Charles Addams' young
witch."[55] Although she would later leave her mark on Hollywood as a "fine
character actress who played eagle-eyed grandmas,"[56] Crowley knew her while
she was still in her "Morticia Addams" phase.

The Snake (actress Helen Westley, 1879–1942, left) and the Cat (poet Jeanne Robert
Foster, 1879–1970, right).

The other woman, poet Jeanne Robert Foster (1879–1970), radiated
"sweetness long drawn out."[57] The *Chicago Daily Tribune* had proclaimed that
she had "the prettiest chin in the world,"[58] John Butler Yeats called her the
"loveliest woman ever,"[59] and Crowley agreed. An occultist and Theosophist
herself, starry spirituality studded her speech. She wore her brunette hair gathered on top of her head, and her dark eyes and full lips gave the impression of

a cat, domesticated but wild at heart. The following year, she would release two books, *Wild Apples* and *Neighbors of Yesterday*.[60]

Crowley considered the two women who had become rivals for his affections and mused which he preferred as his "Scarlet Woman": The Snake, Helen Westley? Or the feline Jeanne Foster? The Snake was already attached to Keating, but Crowley learned from Duranty and Chéron that journalists and their women could be accommodating. Staring across the dinner table at the most beautiful woman he had ever known, his course was clear. He chose the Cat.

As Crowley admired this golden rose of loveliness, his ideal, Jeanne looked back and saw a master of magick, a British poet, and the subject of a *Vanity Fair* article: her own ideal. She told Crowley that she worked for Shaw's *American Review of Reviews;* he asked if she might critique his recent writings and help him improve his prose. She suggested they meet for tea at her club the next afternoon. Although the Snake eagerly tried to work her wiles on Crowley, he was far away in a mutual falling-in-love.

By the end of their teatime conversation, Crowley felt he knew Jeanne intimately: she was born in the Adirondacks, the first child of French-Canadian lumberjack Frank Oliver and his English schoolteacher wife, Lizzy. Jeanne's mother encouraged her, "Use your mind; new avenues are opening up for women." In 1896, lumberjack jobs became scarce and her impoverished family moved to Glens Falls. That summer she married Matlock, a family friend who, at age forty-two, was older than her own father. She was seventeen and, within a year, pregnant with a child that would ultimately be stillborn. In the following years, she dabbled in various careers: taking the stage name Jean Elspeth, she acted with the American Stock Company; working for the *New York Sunday American,* she helped design the fashion pages; becoming a model herself, Jeanne's likeness appeared in newspapers, magazines, and books, including *Vanity Fair*'s covers and Harrison Fisher's art. In 1907 she attended Harvard, taking philosophy classes from psychologist William James. Finishing school in 1910, she quickly gained a reputation as a writer and in 1911 moved to New York City to edit the *Review of Reviews*. Thus, she became entrenched in New York's literary and artistic circles, counting John Butler Yeats among her distinguished friends. By this time, her husband was a sixty-one-year-old invalid, frequenting hospitals and spas in a desperate effort to preserve his health. She learned to live without sex since he was incapable and she was infertile.[61]

"So," Crowley attempted a synopsis as he stood in her doorway and bade her farewell, "you are tied to this old satyr who snatched you from the cradle. And where does that leave me?"

Crowley, to her, had a virility and charm that made her head swim. "I loved you at first sight," she admitted. "As a spiritual brother." She kissed him, and tea ended.

That night, Crowley found himself obsessed with Jeanne. He performed a VIII° ritual of thanksgiving for meeting her. Masturbating to the thought of "Babalon imagined as Jeanne," the image was poor as even now her face faded in his memory.

It was July 3, scarcely a month since the *Lusitania* had been sunk off the coast of Ireland. The sun had barely risen when a small motorboat with ten passengers left the recreation pier near West 50th Street and drifted down the Hudson River. Crowley manned the prow, accompanied by Leila, editor J. Dorr, and political agitator Patrick Gilley. Their plan was simple: sail to the Statue of Liberty and proclaim the independence of the Irish Republic. Crowley determined the most astrologically auspicious time to be 4:32 a.m.

As they approached the docks of Bedloe's Island, a wrinkle appeared in their plan. The watchman appeared and informed them that, without government permission, they could neither dock nor set foot upon the island of liberty. At first, Crowley and his compatriots shot lost looks at each other. Unable to dock, they floated about the perimeter of the island and awaited 4:32.

Then, at the appointed time, Crowley began:

> I have not asked any great human audience to listen to these words; I had rather address them to the unconquerable dream that surrounds the world, and to the free four winds of heaven. Facing the sunrise, I lift up my hands and my soul herewith to this giant figure of Liberty, the ethical counterpart of the Light, Life, and Love which are our spiritual heritage. In this symbolism and most awful act of religion I invoke the one true God of whom the Sun himself is but a shadow that he may strengthen me in heart and hand to uphold that freedom for the land of my sires, which I am come hither to proclaim.
>
> In this dark moment, before the father orb of our system kindles with his kiss the sea, I swear the great oath of the Revolution. I tear with my hands this token of slavery, this safe conduct from the enslaver of my people, and I renounce forever all allegiance to every alien tyrant. I swear to fight to the last drop of my blood to liberate the men and women of Ireland, and I call upon the free people of this country, on whose hospitable shores I stand as exile, to give me countenance and assistance in my task of breaking those bonds which they broke for themselves 138 years ago.

Crowley lifted a roll of fabric and declared, "I unfurl the Irish flag. I proclaim the Irish Republic. *Erin go Bragh*. God save Ireland." As he tossed the shreds of his passport into the bay and read the Declaration of Independence of Ireland, a flag with a gold harp on a green field flapped in the wind off the prow mast. They concluded with Leila playing "The Wearing of the Green." In his diary, Crowley noted that he had first been inspired to do this demonstration on July 3, when he went to "work at 6 as inspired and vigorous as possible, and never stopped until at 4:32 a.m. of the next day I had publicly proclaimed the Irish Republic. Never in history (I imagine) has a political movement of the first importance been conceived, prepared, and executed at such short notice."[62]

Although Crowley sent an anonymous account of the stunt to the press, describing himself as an Irishman and a close friend of Irish poet W. B. Yeats, only the *New York Times* picked up the story, devoting three long columns to it.[63] Thereafter, he sent the *Times* another letter, signed "Alex C. Crowley,"[64] clarifying that the Irish flag was not green with a gold harp and that Ireland, like Egypt, was colonized by ancient Atlanteans. (The theory was popular among occult "scholars" like Godfrey Higgins, 1773–1833.)[65]

This display of political activism has puzzled many biographers. Crowley the chameleon could be fiercely British one moment; then, caught up in the Celtic revival, change his surname to MacGregor; then, at times like these, trace his lineage to the O'Crowleys; at other times, his family tree had roots in France. Those who consider him an opportunist and turncoat see this as Crowley ingratiating himself to the political enemies of England. However, Crowley's sympathy for Ireland wasn't taken up suddenly or whimsically. Back in 1913, he wrote a revealing letter with tongue somewhat in cheek:

> I am going to hear Larking to-night. Of course, as a man I am an Irish rebel of the most virulent type, and I want to see every Englishman killed before my eyes. I would ship the English women to Germany, as I don't like Germans either. But, of course, speaking as a man of the world, I am a reactionary Tory of the most bigoted type, although a Pro-Boer; that is to say, my objection to the Boer war was the deprecation of property which it caused.[66]

The bait cast, Crowley tried to snare a job with *The Open Court,* a monistic Chicago periodical edited by Paul Carus (1852–1919). While the company had dedicated itself to the "Religion of Science and the Science of Religion" since its 1887 inception, Carus was eager to promote the German views of his ancestry. AC delineated his own war views in a letter to Carus:

> It seems to me that Germany stands for everything worth keeping— science, foresight, order, and so on. I am intensely sorry for France; I regard her as having been dragged into it by her rotten statesmen. To put it in a word, I hate England, I love France, I admire Germany, I fear Russia. My hate for England is now being replaced by contempt. But I have always taken care to write as an English Isaiah.

He submitted several articles and proposals—"Cocaine," "Perhaps Germany Should Take Poland?" "The Darlings of the Gods," and an article on the occult brotherhoods—but Carus rejected them all. He did, however, pay $10 for Crowley's "The New Parsifal"; likewise, he hoped to reprint Crowley's "gem of satire," "An Orgy of Cant."[67]

"The New Parsifal" appeared in the August 1915 issue of *The Open Court.* Crowley, looking at the world's rulers, declared Wilhelm II to be the knight Parsifal questing for the Holy Grail.

> In the present crisis there are more pigmies than men. Obscure dwarfs like George V, pot-bellied *bourgeois* like Poincaré, could only become

heroic by virtue of some Rabelais magic-wand. Joffre and Kitchener are quiet business-like subordinates with no qualities that can seize the reins of the horses of Apollo. The Czar is a nobody.

But there is no necessity to seek so far. The lavish gods have matched their prophets well with their hero this time. Wilhelm II has always been to a certain extent conscious of himself as an incarnation of Lohengrin, Siegfried, Parsifal.[68]

Crowley predicted he would become as legendary and famous a humanitarian as Jesus, Mohammed, Arthur, and Napoleon, calling Wilhelm savior of the world out of the twisted corner of his mouth.

Shortly after the issue appeared, Carus's book agent in England, Bryce, was arrested for carrying *The Open Court*. The authorities, taking exception to AC's statements about Edward VII, declared it propaganda, and the distributor, who had never so much as read the issue, spent three months in jail. Britain's traitorous black sheep—the greatest metrical genius in the English language, as Frank Harris called him—again shocked the nation. Subsequently, Crowley's mail at the Open Court offices began arriving opened. Paul Carus, having spoken with his British literary representative Mr. Jourdain, ultimately wrote Crowley, "as soon as you step on English soil you will be arrested."[69]

While AC's latest PR spectacle unfolded, Foster wrestled with her heart. Crowley, as a notorious poet and leader of a magical cult, emanated the forbidden. For years she had avoided John Quinn because she had heard young women were not safe around him; but now Crowley attracted her for the same reasons Quinn repulsed her. She was unable to forget him even in her poetry; her latest, "Wife to a Husband," expressed her distress over AC's first marriage. Desperate for advice, she wrote to John Butler Yeats, asking his opinion on her poem, offhandedly remarking that she wanted to learn magic from Crowley, and requesting Yeats's opinion of the man. Yeats detected the personal nature of the poem and, at least pretending not to connect it to AC, replied:

> I have met Crowley and enjoyed his conversation very very much, principally, I think, because of my profound distrust of the talker. I think he is a man to beware of. No one seems to think well of him. He has an ambiguous history—queer happenings, which probably rumour has further distorted. Learn magic by all means, but be careful of the magician. They that sup with the devil must have a long spoon.[70]

Despite Yeats's discouraging words, Jeanne returned from a business trip on July 8, promptly taking Crowley to bed. Although she claimed to dislike the physical aspects of love, they made love frequently for the next week.

She left town again just as suddenly. Hurt and infuriated, Crowley confessedly chose the typically male strategy of striking back: he took her rival, Helen Westley, to bed.

Day five.

"My God," Crowley had thought when Frank Crowninshield (1872–1947) first offered him work writing for *Vanity Fair,* "a New Yorker is treating me like a human being." Since then, Crowninshield read and accepted many of Crowley's submissions. Even when he rejected a manuscript, he explained why and suggested improvements. Looking back on his American period, Crowley saw working for the *Fatherland* and *Vanity Fair* as oases in a desolate search for work. And Crowninshield he recalled as a charming, intelligent businessman. As *Vanity Fair's* first editor (from 1914 to 1935), he was fearlessly avant-garde, a dilettante, and patron of the arts. These qualities forged *Vanity Fair* into the top literary magazine of its time. "I can never be sufficiently grateful to Frank Crowninshield for his kindness and patience. My association with him is the one uniformly pleasant experience of dealing with editors that I can quote."[71]

Left, Irish poet Aleister Crowley, from *The Fatherland;* right, Chinese poet Kwaw Li Ya.

And why shouldn't Crowninshield have treated him well? Ever since Crowley left him speechless by correctly guessing the birth date of every guest at a party, he knew there was something special about this Englishman. Crowley did not disappoint him with his contributions. His first publication with *Vanity Fair* was a clever interpretation of baseball from the devout Hindu's point of view: "A Hindu at the Polo Grounds: A Letter from Mahatma Sri Paramananda Guru Swamiji (Great Soul Saint Supreme-Bliss Teacher Learned Person) to His Brother in India."[72] Crowley appeared in the same issue as the Peking professor Kwaw Li Ya; in the August 1915 issue, Kwaw Li described the haiku and offered $10 for the best contribution from readers on the subject of the Manhattan skyline. It began a regular stream of *Vanity Fair* contributions from Crowley.

Around this time, Crowley decided he wanted a son. Thus Jeanne's early September return to New York overjoyed him. Calling her, at her request, by the magical name "Hilarion," they conducted several acts of sex magick with the intent of begetting a child. On the autumnal equinox, they received the word NEBULAE as an oracle for the next six months. As Jeanne seduced him, Crowley succumbed while concentrating on this password.

When Jeanne next left New York on October 6, it was with Crowley, heading for the West Coast on a "honeymoon." While Jeanne and her invalid husband went straight to California, Crowley took various side trips, planning to catch up and sneak off with her as circumstance permitted. Thus, Crowley traveled to Detroit to tour the Parke-Davis pharmaceutical plant, which prepared for him a tincture of *Anhalonium lewinii*. Proceeding to Chicago, Paul Carus gave him a tour of the Windy City. By October 12, Crowley arrived in Vancouver, where he helped establish Agape Lodge as OTO's foundling North American headquarters. He also performed a ceremony to advance Jones to the A∴A∴ grade of Babe of the Abyss, on his way to Magister Templi (8°=3□).

According to A∴A∴ rules, Crowley's finding a successor as Magister Templi entitled him to advance to the grade of Magus. The Magus was a special attainment, as only seven others in the past had ever attained the grade and founded a religion: Lao Tzu's Taoism; Thoth's Egyptian mysteries; Krishna's Vedanta; Gautama's Buddhism; Moses' Judaism; the suffering and slain pattern of Adonis, Attis, Osiris, Jesus, and Dionysus; and the Islamic religion of Mohammed. Crowley joined this elevated company as the eighth Magus in the history of humankind. As a Magus, Crowley's task was to speak a magical word representing the core of his teaching, thus symbolically destroying the world in fire. Just as Lao Tzu's word was *tao,* and Buddha's word was *dukkha,* Crowley's was *Thelema.*

As a Magus, residing in the House of the Juggler, Crowley chose for himself the magical identity that shaped so much of his life: *To Mega Therion,* the Great Beast, 666. According to magical and kabbalistic tradition, the number 666 is a sacred number attributed to the sun. Traditionally, the sun's basic number is six. Thus, 36, which is 6 x 6, is an extension of the sun, while 666, the sum of all the numbers from 1 to 36, provides the number derived from the magical square of the sun. The Great Beast, he believed, was no evil force. Years of study showed him that Revelation was written in gnostic and kabbalistic symbols, and that its text described Christianity's succession by a new religion whose prophet was the Great Beast.

This creature was a necessary part of magical tradition: Christianity reigned in the Age of Pisces the fish; this, along with its complementary zodiacal sign, Virgo the virgin, described the exoteric and esoteric aspects of the religion, respectively. Jesus fed the masses with a fish, and the Greek word for fish, $\iota\chi\theta\tilde{\upsilon}\varsigma$, is an acronym for the phrase $I\epsilon\sigma o\upsilon\varsigma\ X\rho\iota\sigma\tau o\varsigma\ \Theta\epsilon o\upsilon\ \Upsilon\iota o\varsigma\ \Sigma o\tau\eta\rho$ ("Jesus Christ, Son of God, Savior"). Meanwhile, more mystically inclined Christians observed the cult of the Virgin Mary. In a similar way, Crowley saw himself ringing in the Age of Aquarius, whose complementary zodiacal sign is Leo, the lion. In the zodiac, Aquarius is a man, just as Revelation states 666 is the number of a man. This man, nevertheless, is a Great Beast, just as the esoteric aspect of this man is Leo, the lion, whose astrological ruler is the sun. So strong was this connection that Crowley came to believe that Leo, not Aquarius, dominated the present cosmic cycle.

The prophecy was fulfilled. His mother was right all along. Aleister Crowley was the Great Beast 666.

Day six.

Crowley regretfully left Vancouver and proceeded to San Francisco via Seattle. The last time he had been in California, the earthquake and fire of 1906 had devastated San Francisco. As he toured the city with dissatisfaction, he mused, "The phoenix has perished and from the cinders arose a turkey buzzard."[73] He nevertheless welcomed the opportunity to give an impromptu speech on the Law of Thelema. Then, traveling south, Crowley looked up Katherine Tingley (1847–1929), former head of the TS in America, in Point Loma; although he proposed an alliance between her society and his organizations, she refused to see him. Thence he proceeded to the Grand Canyon, which he thought was the best part of the United States. By December, he returned to New York.

Throughout the journey, Jeanne and Crowley met at odd intervals. He was madly in love with her, and wrote a series of poems, *The Golden Rose,* about his passion.[74] One of these, "Dawn," recounts awakening with her one morning in Santa Cruz:

> Sleep, with a last long kiss,
> Smiles tenderly and vanishes.
> Mine eyelids open to the gold.
> Hilarion's hair in ripples rolled.
> (O gilded morning clouds of Greece!)
> Like the sun's self amid the fleece,
> Her face glows. All the dreams of youth,
> Lighted by love and thrilled by truth,
> Flicker upon the calm wide brow,
> Now playmates of the eyelids, now
> Dancing coquettes the mouth that move
> In all overtures to love.
> The Atlantic twinkles in the sun—
> Awake, awake, Hilarion!

Jeanne, however, was torn between her love for this strange wanderer and her commitment to her husband. Somewhere after Los Angeles, she broke down. Unable to bear the strain of sneaking about and getting away from her husband, Jeanne left Crowley and returned home.

Back in New York, Crowley took up a new residence at 25 West 44th Street in the name of Cyril Grey. (Crowley used this name for himself in the novel *Moonchild*, which was still being worked on at this time.) He resumed his acquaintance with John Quinn, found more of his work in *Vanity Fair*, and on New Year's Eve wrote his first official proclamation of the Law of Thelema as a Magus: "The Message of the Master Therion."[75]

As far as his feline lover, Jeanne, went, Crowley did his best to get her back. Nevertheless, she refused his advances. Her deceitful mask of innocence outraged him: she who had left her husband and slept with another man who filled her with ecstasy now hid behind propriety when Crowley, the other man, knew it was a lie. He noted that he had been "enlightened as to the falseness of the Cat; it therefore became my duty to slay her."[76]

On day seven, Matlock Foster began to receive letters that claimed his wife was living with a wealthy lawyer and was planning to poison him. Although unsigned, the letters were undoubtedly Crowley's. Now that his true colors were showing, Jeanne was grateful that she escaped his clutches unharmed. "He's probably a cocaine fiend," she told herself. "Thank God I never sent him anything with my name on it." A visit by a shivering and weeping woman, claiming "I have a message for you," puzzled Jeanne until she heard its content: Crowley warned that if she did not return and help him with the Great Work, she would be destroyed. Although he most likely meant that the Secret Chiefs would drive her to the same sort of infamy that they had with Rose, Jeanne took it as a threat. Stiffening, she told the messenger, "You and Mr. Crowley can both go to the devil."

When Crowley finally accepted that Hilarion would not return to him, he decided to magically sever his ties with her, as he had done with Neuburg before leaving for America. Thus, he waited outside her Manhattan office until she appeared on the street at closing time. He confronted her, drawing from his coat his dagger, yellow and inscribed with Hebrew names and sigils. She gasped, thinking he was about to kill her. As he conducted the banishing ritual, a crowd gathered to watch. In the confusion, Jeanne vanished into the mob, believing she had escaped a clumsy murder attempt. The incident disturbed her, and she believed that Crowley astrally visited her one night in her bedroom until she banished him.[77] Their encounter on the street, however, satisfied AC: The ritual was complete, and she was gone from his life. Along with Crowley's *The Golden Rose,* only Jeanne's poems "Wife to a Husband" and "The Answer" remained to commemorate their relationship and its passing.

When Leila returned to New York that February 1916, Crowley, impoverished in money and affection, sought consolation in her arms, only to realize
how far apart they'd grown. They no longer had anything in common, and she
could console him no more than Elaine Simpson had after his break with
"Alice." Like the Cat, Laylah was history. All that remained of her was a poem
commemorating their seven years:

> Seven times has Saturn swung his scythe;
>   Seven sheaves stand in the field of Time.
> And every sheaf's as bright and blithe
>   As the sharp shifts of our sublime
> Father the Sun. I leap so lithe
>   For love to-day,
>   My love. I may
>   Not tell the tithe...
>
> We know to-day what once we guessed,
>   our love no dream of idle youth;
> A world-egg, with the stars for nest.
>   Is this arch-testament of truth.
> Laylah, beloved, to my breast!
>   Our period
>   Is fixed in God—
>   Eternal rest.[78]

Waddell would remain in the United States for several more years, taking violin
work as opportunity presented and writing occasional short stories and music
articles for the Los Angeles press. These latter activities would lead to her contributing the article "Two Anzacs Meet in London"—recounting her acquaintance with Katherine Mansfield—to New York's *Shadowland* magazine in
1923.[79] She would continue to travel between Sydney, America, and England
through 1926.[80] Ultimately, news of her father's illness would cause her to
return to his side in suburban Sydney,[81] where she'd teach at Convent of the
Sacred Heart in Elizabeth Bay[82] and make concert appearances with the Conservatorium Orchestra under Dr. William Arundel Orchard (1867–1961) and
the Royal Philharmonic Society of Sydney under Gerald Peachell,[83] who
served as director from 1928 to 1931.[84] On September 14, 1932, at age fifty-
one, Leila Waddell would die of uterine cancer.[85]

For Crowley, day seven was a time of emotional desolation.[86]

Day eight.

Deja vu swept over Crowley that April as once again he considered which
of two women would be his next scarlet concubine. On the one hand, there
was Alice Ethel Coomaraswamy, née Richardson (1885–1958), the second wife
of art critic and historian Ananda Kentish Coomaraswamy (1877–1947), who
was the cousin of Ponnambalam Rámanáthan. She was a Yorkshire musician
who, under the stage name of Ratan Devi ("jewelled goddess"), donned tradi-

tional garb and sang Indian melodies while accompanying herself on the tamboura. Crowley considered her a great artist, but likened her "insensate passion, volubility, and vanity"[87] to that of a monkey. Alternately, there was Gerda Maria von Kothek, "a girl with a fancy for weird adventures,"[88] whom Crowley described in some places as a prostitute and elsewhere as "that brilliant young 'Angel of the Revolution.'"[89] While coarse and base, she was also pleasant, sensible, and unaffected: a pleasant break from Alice. Like his other lovers at this time, he theriomorphically compared her to an owl. This tendency to compare lovers to animals was not derogatory. Traditionally, animals, familiars, and spirit guides assisted great initiations, and Crowley viewed his American period as his initiation into the grade of Magus. Thus his lovers became officers of his initiation, taking on the attributes of some sacred beast and helping him learn important magical lessons.

> The Owl offered all the delights of carefree ease and placid pleasure; but there was nothing to be gained. The Monkey represented a life of turmoil and anxiety, with few magnificent moments amid the hours of fretfulness; but progress was possible. It was as if the Secret Chiefs had asked me, 'Are you content to enjoy the fruit of your attainment and live at peace with the world, surrounded by affectation, respect and comfort, or will you devote yourself to mastering and fertilizing mankind, despite the prospect of continual disquietude and almost certain disappointment?' I chose the Monkey.[90]

While in her twenties, Alice had moved to India, taken up study of its modern and ancient languages, and found an instructor in its music.[91] In the summer of 1911 she was living in a houseboat in Srinagar with Ananda Coomaraswamy; her pregnancy and confrontation with Coomaraswamy's wife caused the breakup of his first marriage and the beginning of his second. According to Crowley, she was all the while having an affair with Coomaraswamy's best friend. By 1912, after the birth of her son, Narada, her performances in England became quite popular; she had what might be called perfect pitch, the ability to distinguish—and reproduce—the microtonal notes that characterize Indian music. W. B. Yeats wrote, "Mrs. Coomaraswamy's singing delighted me. It was as though a moment of life had caught fire, an emotion had come to a sudden casual perfection."[92] George Bernard Saw also praised her work. In 1913 she published the book *Thirty Songs from the Pentop and Cashmere*.[93] By 1916 the Coomaraswamys had come to New York with their two children (a daughter, Rhino, had been born in 1914) for Ratan Devi's U.S. concert debut. In advance of her debut, she was interviewed in the *New York Times,* where she lamented, "It seems to be that intensity is the chief thing which distinguishes the poetry of the East from the poetry of the West. I find very seldom in English poetry the poignancy that is common in Oriental poetry."[94] Coomaraswamy called on Crowley to help with his wife's publicity; AC responded by providing introductions and writing about her in *Vanity Fair* under the guise of "the celebrated Recut singer, Sri Paramananda Tat."[95] By mid-April, the Beast became another in her supposed string of lovers.

Alice Ethel Coomaraswamy, née Richardson (1885–1958), a.k.a. Ratan Devi.

It was also in mid April—the 13th—that Ratan Devi debuted at the Princess Theater on 39th Street off of 6th Avenue in Manhattan.[96] A reporter for *Outlook* described the performance:

> the audience, which filled all the seats, saw on the stage in the foreground two vases of red flowers, and between them, lying on the floor, a long-necked stringed instrument. The background consisted simply of dark curtains. In a moment the curtains parted and a woman stepped out. She wore Oriental garments, of warm and harmonious colors. Seating herself on the floor, she raised the instrument and held it vertically before her.
>
> Then began a recital of music such as most of the audience had never heard before.... The ragas that Ratan Devi sang sounded very strange, of course, to Western hearers; but, strange as they were, they were most enticing in their beauty.[97]

She quickly became a sensation in New York.

Crowley's affair with Ratan Devi was a bizarre romp in which he was as much a pawn as an instigator. As Crowley tells it, Ananda Coomaraswamy, dubious about her musical career and appalled by New York's high cost of living, was relieved that someone took on the financial burden of caring for her. "All he asked," Crowley says, "was that I should introduce him to a girl who would be his mistress while costing him nothing."[98] Crowley obliged, introducing Coomaraswamy to the Owl; soon, the two began living together. "The cost of a double room being slightly less than that of two singles," Crowley described Coomaraswamy's frugal ways, "he effected a prudent economy by putting this girl in the same bed with his wife when he was out of town."[99]

Just as expenses drove Coomaraswamy to accept this arrangement, Crowley suggests, Ratan Devi's success brought him back. By the time he demanded her return, however, she was pregnant by Crowley. The encounter turned into a screaming match between husband and wife while Crowley, to their annoyance, watched with placid indifference, refusing to participate in this distasteful game. "You are welcome to stay," he told her, "but the door is also open."

His position clear, Crowley left on business for Washington, D.C. It was perhaps the *Washington Post*'s four-column story on Crowley[100] that first brought him to the attention of eccentric and colorful "Stuart X" (Henry Clifford Stuart, 1865–1952) whose letters Crowley was hired to edit and introduce for the book *A Prophet in His Own Country*. As Crowley described Stuart:

> Imagine to yourself a big man, a really big man, six foot three in height, broad and well-proportioned. The entire impression is bigness. And, as should always be the case with homo sapiens, the most important part of the impression is given by the head. Such a brow is only seen in the world's greatest thinkers.... When he speaks he is transfigured before you. The placid power of the man gives place to elemental energy.[101]

Born in New York in 1865, he was ten years Crowley's senior. He began working for his father at age fourteen, and by twenty-one had become freight traffic manager for Central America's most important railroad. From there, he went on to sundry other jobs, including in real estate, as a mining engineer, and as U.S. Consul-General to Guatemala City.[102] He spent fifteen years in Spanish America building railroads,[103] and Crowley identified him as the land commissioner of the Panama Railroad.[104] A successful businessman, he was "one of the big boomers in Guatemala industries" and had financial investments in New Orleans.[105] He married Grace Ingersoll Patchin in New York on December 11, 1894,[106] and eventually settled in Washington, D.C., where in 1915 he was voted a member of the Washington Board of Trade.[107]

Stuart was an avid letter-writer, sending his quirky, almost free verse, observations about life and politics to hundreds of newspapers and other correspondents across the country. One recipient, the White House, responded to the first few letters, but the vast majority he sent thereafter went unanswered; the Secret Service, investigating, found him "harmless and 'light.'"[108] Another recipient was John R. Rathon, editor of the *Providence Journal,* who forwarded the letter to the Bureau of Investigation suggesting, "You might give this lunatic the once over."[109] Crowley collected, edited, and commented on 191 of these letters, which appeared as *A Prophet in His Own Country* that summer. Ever the entrepreneur, AC even tried selling a copy to Theodore Roosevelt.[110] He also pitched a new edition—equally unsuccessfully—to Henry Holt & Co.:

"Its complete originality, both of thought and of style, marks this book as unique. Nothing, since Nietzsche in Germany and Carlyle in England, is at all comparable to it."[111] The book's marketing, however, hit a snag when advertisements instructed that orders be sent to the Fifth Avenue Bank, Crowley's bank in New York; the volume of mail became so bothersome that they forced Crowley to close his account with them.[112] To promote the book, Stuart was also wont to leave copies in various hotels during his travels.[113]

Stuart X: Henry Clifford Stuart (1865–1952).

Despite the book being by Stuart, its editor also received attention in press reviews. *The New Age* quipped, "To be introduced and annotated by Mr. Aleister Crowley is a distinction that most prophets have been unable to obtain.... Either prophets are rare in America, or they avoid introductions by, perhaps even to, Mr. Crowley."[114] Meanwhile, the *Indianapolis Sunday Star,* observed, "With Mr. Crowley's tremendous introduction in mind (nobody introduces Crowley) the reader will no doubt approach the lucubrations of Mr. Stuart with keen expectation."[115]

The August 1916 *Vanity Fair* featured an article about Stuart. Although unsigned, it is doubtlessly by Crowley, who damns the book and author with faint praise: "His point of view may be rudely described as that of an inspired baby," his writing style "destroys the peace of mind of editors," and "it will not be his fault if he does not sell at least one copy."[116] Two months later, Crowley published a letter in the *Washington Post* insisting that the European press had mistakenly claimed that he and Stuart X were the same person, and that Crowley had only written the "imbecile introduction";[117] since the *Washington Post* is not a European newspaper, the letter appears to be a publicity stunt. Stuart eventually relocated to Northern California, and after his wife died in 1929,[118] he legally changed his name to Stuart X,[119] giving himself (arguably) the world's shortest last name. He died on May 21, 1952, in Alameda California.[120]

While preparing *A Prophet in His Own Country* for press that spring, Crowley encountered a curious array of distractions in Washington, D.C. One of these involved a missing jade statue of Kuan-yin, a title of Avalokitesvara, the Bodhissattva of compassion in Buddhism. On May 28, 1916, the following ad ran in the *Chicago Daily Tribune* and papers in fifty other cities from Washington to St. Louis:

> JADE KWANNON—STOLEN—$10,000 WILL be paid for information leading to the recovery intact of the jade kwannon stolen from Dr. S. Y. S. on Aug. 29, 1914. Stuart X., 2619 Woodley-pl., Washington, D.C.[121]

"Dr. S. Y. S." is Sun Yat Sen (1866–1925), the Chinese revolutionary and father of modern China, who served in 1912 as the first provisional president of the newly formed Republic of China. The ad sparked interest in the press, causing Stuart to say "This is a very delicate matter. I prefer to think over it until tomorrow morning, and if you will telephone me then I may be able to say something about it."[122] Upon the statue's recovery a few days later, Crowley, on Stuart's behalf, announced to the press that its recovery "will, through its powerful influence over the minds of superstitious Chinese, mean a return to power of Dr. Sun Yat Sen."[123] At this same time, an article appeared in *The Washington Post* on "The Oriental Mind"; an elaboration of the previous statement attributed to Crowley, the article, although unsigned, is likely by AC: "Once more in hand, a wonderful influence is promised over the minds of the superstitious Chinese, with the by no means remote possibility that through its beneficent presence Sun Yat Sen will again be placed in the full tide of prosperity as regards himself and the future of his beloved nation."[124]

Other less prominent activities also landed Crowley in the D.C. press. He gave a lengthy interview for the April 30 *Washington Post* about good and evil spirits and nature of possession, after poisoner Dr. Arthur Warren Waite claimed in his defense that he was possessed by an evil spirit called the "Man from Egypt" who drove him to murder his in-laws.[125] In a May 12 letter to the *Washington Post,* Crowley—recalling his Statue of Liberty stunt—nominated Ireland as arbiters of universal peace.[126] On Friday, May 26, Crowley played four games of chess at the National Press Club against twenty-five-year-old chess champion Norman Tweed Whittaker (1890–1975); despite excellent playing on both sides, Whittaker won all four games.[127] Later that summer, he posed as a physician to condemn the cruel way in which anesthesia was administered, because psychological stress was the cause of nine out of ten deaths in surgery; Crowley advocated allowing patients to self-medicate, to slowly savor the ether intoxication so that when the surgeon arrives, the patient goes under easily and willingly:

> The nurse should be instructed to lead the thoughts of the patient into pleasant channels; she should describe as vividly as she can the glories and joys of ether…. The surgeon should arrive at from 2 to 3 hours after the beginning. If things have been done properly, the patient should feel just about as much interest in his arrival as the theatergoer does when the curtain rises.[128]

Crowley advocated this medical practice in a letter to the editor of the *Washington Post,* signing himself "Aleister Crowley, St. George's Hospital, London."

While he was away, Alice and Ananda Coomaraswamy resolved their dilemma. Although Alice loved Crowley and wanted to be with him, her husband convinced her to return with him to England for her confinement. Crowley, with a detached "Do what thou wilt," offered no resistance with her choice. By the end of May she was on a boat for England. Even though she was heading east, for Crowley she was sailing off into the sunset.

On the morning of day nine, Crowley left the consoling arms of the Owl and his forthcoming work in *Vanity Fair* and Viereck's other magazine, the general interest *The International,* for a Great Magical Retirement. Although he had formally accepted the grade of Magus in October, Crowley felt, in June of 1916, his understanding to be imperfect, his initiation incomplete, and his providence uncertain. In short, he was stuck in a magical rut.

Crowley took a meditative vacation at Adams Cottage, located on Lake Pasquaney near Bristol, Hebron, and Alexandria, New Hampshire. Known today as Newfound Lake, Pasquaney was seven miles long and two and a half miles wide, the third-largest lake in the state and perhaps its most beautiful.

> Lake Pasquaney lies among the mountains of New Hampshire. It is about 17 miles in circumference. Bristol, the nearest railway station, a town of 1200 inhabitants, is some three miles from the lower end. The lake contains several islands, and its shores are dotted with summer villas, mostly of the log hut type, though here and there is a more pretentious structure, or a cluster of boarding-houses. Bristol is about three hours from Boston, so the Lake is a favorite summer resort, even for week-enders. The scenery is said by Europeans who know both to compare with Scotland or Switzerland without too serious disadvantage.[129]

Adams Cottage was wooden with a brick fireplace and chimney. Its main room faced Newfound Lake with the bedroom and kitchen behind the fireplace.

Owned by astrologer Evangeline Smith Adams (1868–1932), it was "not her principal cottage which she called the Zodiac, but a sort of spare cottage."[130] He had met Adams in 1915 and agreed to coauthor a book on astrology. The pairing seemed ideal, as a few months earlier he had complained, "I do not think there is any book on Astrology of any value whatever."[131] Collaboration was not in the stars, however, and the authors ultimately split, Crowley believing Adams tried to cheat him. In the November 1918 *International,* Crowley, writing as Cor Scorpionis, published "How Horoscopes Are Faked," a scathing critique of Adams and her methods.

> She is grotesquely ignorant of the first principles of astronomy. She has no conception, for example, of the Solar System as a Disk, but imagines that the planets are all over the place, like the raisins in a plum pudding. She calls her country house the Zodiac—and doesn't know what the Zodiac is![132]

In the end, Crowley's manuscript would be published fourteen years later in Adams's name.[133]

In his first days there, he wrote the essay "De Thaumaturgia."[134] The following day, Independence Day, he mused about his adventures in America and the attainment to the grade of Magus (9°=2□). This was the first time that he recognized the seventy-three-day cycles that characterized his initiatory journey toward becoming a Magus. Crowley speculated that thirty-one of these "Chokmah days" would encompass his initiation, since thirty-one was the number of AL, the formal title of *The Book of the Law,* whose message it was his job as Magus to promulgate. His first three Chokmah days in America— through June 9, 1915—were miserable, lonely, stagnant times. These ended on the dawn of the fourth day, when, like clockwork, he met Jeanne Robert Foster. On the fifth day, he formally accepted the grade of Magus. Crowley and Foster parted by the sixth day, while Ratan Devi appeared and vanished on the eighth. Now, on the ninth Chokmah day, he pondered the meaning of his ordeal.

Despite the illumination, Crowley remained uninspired. His diary records his frustration with this creative and spiritual block:

> I am tempted for example to crucify a toad or copulate with a duck or sheep or goat or set a house on fire or murder some one with the idea—a perfectly good magical idea, of course—that some supreme violation of all the laws of my being would break my Karma or dissolve the spell which seems to bind me.[135]

Horrible as it may strike some, the idea was one of great antiquity. For instance, the Hindus who participated in the holy tantric ritual of the *panchatattva*— popularly known as the five elements—would drink wine, eat meat, and have casual sex (regardless of caste or relationship); any one of these was antithetical to the Hindu lifestyle, but in its proper context this ceremonial violation of convention constituted a powerful magical act.

This technique gave Crowley an idea to banish the dying god of the old aeon (Jesus/Osiris/Adonis) and pave the way for the new aeon of Thelema. Early one morning in mid-July he caught a frog and ensconced it in a chest. After presenting it with gold, frankincense, and myrrh, he released it and baptized it with the name Jesus. Throughout the day, Crowley sincerely identified both the frog and himself with the old aeon, worshiping this Jesus and asking it to perform miracles. That night, he again captured the toad, saying to it,

> All my life thou hast plagued me and affronted me. In thy name—with all other free souls in Christendom—I have been tortured in my boyhood; all delights have been forbidden unto me; all that I had has been taken from me, and that which is owed to me they pay not—in thy name.

He next condemned and crucified the frog, then ended the magical passion play by blessing it, vowing to assimilate its character, and stabbing it in the side. He ritually ate its legs to incorporate the familiar, and the remains he burned to symbolically consume the old aeon in fire.

"The result was immediately apparent,"[136] he noted when a young woman from Bristol asked Crowley for a job as his secretary. He considered it and, believing she bore a striking resemblance to the toad, recognized her as the next animal guide or officer of his initiation. He hadn't planned on writing, but the gods apparently wished him to; so he hired the Toad and went to work.

On July 12, 1916, at about 4 p.m., a sudden cloudburst dumped torrents of rain and lightning on Lake Pasquaney. Dashing out of his cabin and up to shore, Crowley rescued his canoe from the water, then dashed back indoors. When he stepped inside, rain dripping onto the floor from his soaked clothes, he encountered a drenched man and his equally waterlogged wife and child smiling sheepishly back at him. They too sought shelter from the storm. Crowley smiled in welcome, then excused himself to change into dry clothes.

A weary sigh escaped his lips as he stepped into his bedroom and out of his garments. He was in no mood for uninvited guests. More than withdrawn, Crowley felt downright despondent, wondering if he was deluded to think himself a Magus. What if he had strayed in some way, and the Secret Chiefs had abandoned him just as they'd abandoned Mathers? While he could surely continue to write, what would be the point in living? And how could he be sure he was really any good at it?

As he pulled on a dry shirt, a his thoughts were interrupted by a "tremendous bang, like the bursting of a bomb, not like thunder."[137] A fireball a foot in diameter appeared in the cabin, striking the floor inches from his feet and projecting an electric spark, bright as an arc light, up to his left middle finger. It was gone as suddenly as it came. After the initial shock wore off, he scanned the room and found no sign of damage to the building. Like a true Magister Templi, he pondered the significance of this event. The left middle finger was particularly sacred, and this coupled with the appearance of the Toad Officer and the unusual presence of those taking shelter in his abode constituted a clear omen to Crowley, assuring him that his ongoing initiation was genuine.

He reported the event in a letter to the *New York Times*,[138] generating some interest in the scientific community. One of those interested was Doctor William Sturgis Bigelow (1850–1926), a retired Boston physician who had studied anatomy and pathology in Strasbourg and bacteriology with Louis Pasteur in Paris, then returned as a lecturer to Harvard Medical School. A "gay blade who never married,"[139] Sturgis had converted to Buddhism, delivered the Ingersoll Lecture on "Buddhism and Immortality" at Harvard in 1908, and in 1911 gave to the Boston Museum of Fine Arts his collection of 25,000 pieces of Chinese and Japanese art.[140] At his request, Crowley provided him a detailed description, with diagrams, of his electrical experience, e.g., "The colour was violet and ultra-violet, like an arc light, but with much crimson in it," and "It did not oscillate, but remained steady for a period which I dare hardly estimate, and then burst."[141] For two of Crowley's qeustions, however, Bigelow referred him to Professor Thompson.

Professor Elihu Thomson (1853–1937)—inventor of the dynamo and founder of General Electric—confirmed Crowley's encounter as that anomaly of electricity, ball lightning. He also entertained Crowley's theories about the phenomenon.[142] Writing privately to Thomson, Bigelow remarked "His letter seems clear, all but the first and last lines, which, with the odd red stamp on the first page, suggest that he may possibly be some kind of a crank."[143]

Also convincing AC of the validity of his initiation was a state of consciousness he dubbed the Star-Sponge Vision. It began gradually rather than full-blown, with Crowley losing his sense of all substance in the universe. Aware only of infinite space—the kabbalistic *Ain Soph*—this void soon filled with countless pinpoints of light. He understood this to represent the basic structure of the universe. Concentrating on the vision, the black void receded into the background while all of space bathed in light, the kabbalistic *Ain Soph Aur* (limitless light). Despite the field of light against which they shone, all the pinpoints of light remained visibly distinct. *Nothingness with twinkles,* he thought. *But what twinkles!* In time, Crowley associated these points with stars, souls, and thoughts. And he saw all the points interconnected through a network of luminescent rays, just as the universe's contents were all related. He would never again see the world in the same way.

On day ten, Ratan Devi began sending letters to Crowley, begging him to take her back: on the boat to England, she had gotten sick and miscarried. She had reconsidered and wanted to be with him. Crowley minced no words in his reply. She had made her decision, and the only way he would take her back was if she made a clean break with her past and left her husband. Despite daily letters to him, she was unable to take what Crowley considered to be the necessary steps. Unfortunately, in 1917, after Crowley was well out of the picture,

her husband left her for Stella Bloch, a seventeen-year-old dancer from one of
her rehearsals, thus ending their troubled marriage.

Meanwhile, Crowley was oblivious to the wheels turning in Vancouver.
While AC was at Adams Cottage, Frater Achad passed through the Abyss and
took the oath of a Magister Templi, filling the grade so his Master could proceed to that of Magus. Unfortunately, Jones soon concluded that he had leap-
frogged over Crowley to the ultimate grade of Ipsissimus ($1°=10^{\square}$) at the top of
the Tree of Life; but, unable to manage so great an attainment, he plunged
down the tree's central shaft back to its base as a Neophyte ($10°=1^{\square}$). To match
the reversal of his grade from $1°=10^{\square}$ to $10°=1^{\square}$, Jones expanded his new motto
from OIV (Omnia in Unum, "All in one") to OIVVIO (Omnia in Unum,
Unus in Omnia).

Hearing the news on August 21, 1916, Crowley was, as might be expected,
surprised. The logical holes in Achad's claim notwithstanding, Crowley considered his star pupil's attainment to the grade of Magister Templi (the only claim
he accepted) to be a remarkable fulfillment of prophecy. Exactly nine months
after his rituals to have a child by Jeanne Foster culminated on the September
1915 equinox, Crowley had not a physical child but a metaphysical one: Frater
Achad emerged from the Abyss and assumed the mantle of a Magister Templi.
He was furthermore the child prophesied in *The Book of the Law:*

> The child of thy bowels, *he* shall behold them.
>   Expect him not from the East, nor from the West; for from no
> expected house cometh that child.[144]

Crowley always expected a biological child, and OIVVIO came from no
expected place. AC was overjoyed to have not only a son, but his first successor
since the days of Jones, Fuller, and Neuburg.

With the Toad Officer goading him to write, Crowley took inspiration from
his leisure reading at the cottage. These included Shaw's *Androcles and the Lion*
(1913) with its long preface on Christianity; anthropologist Sir James G.
Frazer's (1854–1941) classic and elephantine tome on ancient myth and magic,
The Golden Bough (1890, 1900, 1911–1915); and psychoanalyst Carl G. Jung's
(1875–1961) *Psychology of the Unconscious: A Study of the Transformations and
Symbolisms of the Libido* (1916), whose chief argument, Crowley thought, was
that sex is an outgrowth of the Will, not the converse, as Freud argued.

Shaw was his first catalyst. Plymouth upbringing left Crowley well versed
with the Bible, and reading Shaw's disquisition on Jesus, he concluded the playwright knew neither the Bible, the East, nor mysticism. So he critiqued it in
The Gospel According to St. Bernard Shaw, which weighed in at roughly 55,000
words. He claimed that it "establishes the outline of an entirely final theory on
the construction of Christianity."[145] Introducing his edition of the book, Francis King called it

a treasury of Crowley's wit, wisdom and criticism which, even if it was the only book its author had written, would suffice to rebut the slander that Crowley was a pleasure-seeking fraud whose occultism was no more than "making a religion out of his weakness."[146]

After finishing this work, Crowley penned a set of eight short stories based on *The Golden Bough*. The first, written on August 30, was "The Priest of Nemi" (eventually retitled "The King of the Wood"), which took its title directly from Frazer. In the two weeks that followed, he finished "The Mass of Saint-Sécaire," "The Burning of Melcarth," "The Oracle of the Corycian Cave," "The Stone of Cybele," "The God of Ibreez," "The Old Man of the Peepul-Tree," and "The Hearth."[147]

Finally, Jung's book inspired Crowley's synopsis, "An Improvement on Psycho-analysis: The Psychology of the Unconscious—for Dinner-Table Consumption," which would appear in *Vanity Fair*.[148]

Meanwhile, his Thelemic pamphlet "The Law of Liberty" was out in England, with another 250 copies for Australian distribution by Frank Bennett.

Despite this prodigious output, Crowley nevertheless found time for his sex magick research, commencing on the fall equinox with Gerda von Kothek, the Owl. This working resulted in Gerda having a vision wherein "Monks in brown robes and hoods go up a green hill, with misty top, in an endless line. They wear rings with red cross within a gold triangle."[149] These visions continued for four days, and inspired Crowley to paint "Four Red Monks Carrying a Black Goat across the Snows to Nowhere." It marked an early stage of his foray into art.

On day eleven, Crowley wrapped up business at Lake Pasquaney and departed for New Orleans. He arrived on December 9, 1916, still despairing over the state of his life and determined to continue his Great Magical Retirement. Promptly on arrival, his depression lifted in his experience of the Beatific Vision. Harmony and calm overwhelmed him, healing his spiritual woes. Finally convinced the gods were with him, Crowley decided to test them. After a decade of struggle and poverty, he tired of it. The Logos, the prophet of the New Aeon, was going on strike until he received better pay and benefits:

> I therefore down tools until I have (1) a competent stenographer (2) money enough in hand to see me comfortable through until the Equinox of Spring.... (3) a guarantee—by some signal, sign or in some more practical manner—that all will be well in the future.... (4) means of publishing immediately all MSS except those destined for *Equinox* Volume III.[150]

He would do nothing. And if he starved, then the gods could damn well pull his fat out of the fire.

The strike continued for two weeks before Crowley realized matters had not improved. Finally succumbing to pressure, he noted in his diary:

> 27 December. I am now going to start work again, with absolutely no
> resources. I have not even proper paper or money to buy it. Total cash in
> hand, 70 cents.

Day twelve.

Simon Iff was a mathematician, chess master, Freemason, and mystic. He
solved crimes using the principles of psychology and the Law of Thelema. As
Crowley described him,

> He had a habit of disappearing for long periods, and it was rumoured that
> he had the secret of the Elixir of Life. For although he was known to be
> over eighty years of age, his brightness and activity would have done credit
> to a man of forty; and the vitality of his whole being, the fire of his eyes,
> the quick conciseness of his mind, bore witness to an interior energy
> almost more than human.
>
> He was a small man, dressed carelessly in a blue serge suit with a nar-
> row dark red tie. His iron-grey hair was curly and irrepressible; his com-
> plexion, although wrinkled, was clear and healthy; his small mouth was a
> moving wreath of smiles; and his whole being radiated an intense and con-
> tagious happiness.[151]

Crowley's newest literary creation, Simon Iff was his idealized self-portrait. The
gods willing, Iff would also pull him out of the economic pit into which he had
fallen. This foray into the popular genre of crime fiction nevertheless permitted
him to advertise Thelema. The key was to make the stories accessible—a task
at which Crowley had failed with his books of poetry and magick.

Remarkably, he successfully produced well-written and entertaining popular fiction; in short order, he wrote six Simon Iff short stories: "Big Game,"
"The Artistic Temperament," "Outside the Bank's Routine," "The Conduct of
John Briggs," "Not Good Enough," and "Ineligible." These, like his Frazer-
inspired pieces, appeared in *The International*.[152] Crowley went on to write
another eighteen Simon Iff short stories based on his experiences in America,
but these were never published in his lifetime.

He based the story "Not Good Enough" on his relationship with Ratan
Devi, who, even as he wrote it, was still begging Crowley to visit her for
Christmas and take her back. By this time, Crowley blamed Ananda Coomar-
aswamy for sending Ratan Devi on the boat trip that killed their child; in his
diary, AC would remember him as a "bastard, thief, coward and murderer."[153]
Thus, he modeled his story's villain, Haranzada (Hindi for "bastard"), after
Coomaraswamy, who was reportedly shocked to read it.

Finishing the short stories, Crowley wrote his novel *The Butterfly Net*.[154]
Although Simon Iff figured into this one as well, the main character of the
story was Lisa Guiffria (based on Mary Desti), who became involved in the creation of a homunculus. This difficult and convoluted story remains of interest
largely because it lampoons his notable acquaintances, including A. E. Waite,
Gwen Otter, Annie Besant, Everard Feilding, W. B. Yeats and Isadora Duncan.

While staying at Adams Cottage, Crowley had entertained himself by dealing and playing through several hands of card games like skat, piquet, and bridge. In the process, he developed a variation on auction bridge that was such an improvement that he convinced Frank Crowninshield to share it with the readers of *Vanity Fair*. Crowley's innovation was this: rather than partners being preselected, players paired up *after* the cards are dealt using a bidding process. Thus players with a strong combined hand could team up. Crowninshield dubbed the game "pirate bridge" and convened private play-testing sessions to flesh out the rules and strategies.[155]

Crowley was delighted when they enlisted the help of New York surveyor and noted card-game authority Richard Frederick Foster (1853–1945), "a man who, twenty years before, had been the inaccessible godhead of the universe of card games to my undergraduate enthusiasm!"[156] He began writing in 1890 with a manual on whist and over his career penned some sixty-eight books on card games, including the encyclopedic tour de force *Foster's Hoyle*.[157] Initial play-testing took place on November 3, 1916, at New York's Knickerbocker Whist Club, with Crowley and Crowninshield observing. Over the following weeks, it was tried in various settings and, according to Foster, "everywhere met with an enthusiastic reception."[158] Foster believed that pirate bridge would supplant auction bridge to become America's favorite card game, and at the end of December 1916 issued a press release that was picked up by papers from Boston to Chicago to Kansas City.[159] He prepared a thirty-six-page booklet on *The Official Laws of Pirate Bridge,* which sold for twenty-five cents, to promote the game.[160] He also wrote a series of seven articles on the game that ran in *Vanity Fair* from January through July 1917,[161] another fifteen weekly articles for the *Philadelphia Inquirer* that ran from January through April,[162] and very quickly prepared *Foster's Pirate Bridge,* which appeared in February 1917.[163]

Not everyone shared Foster's high hopes for pirate bridge. American bridge authority Milton Cooper Work (1864–1934) complained, "Its play compared with auction in two-thirds of the hands is a joke. Whenever the partners sit next to each other all finessing and much of the beauty of the play is lost."[164] Nevertheless, the game became trendy in the last years of the 1910s. According to the *Lincoln Sunday Star,* "people in the east are quite mad about the new game of bridge and ... pirate bridge parties are the *dernier cries*."[165] Indeed, excitement spread, and pirate bridge games, clubs, and demonstrations soon popped up across the United States.[166] Pirate bridge products appeared to meet the demand, and soon the trend even hit London and Paris: *Foster's Pirate Bridge* was released in London, and the free "War Issue" of *Brain Power,* distributed to 100,000 readers, included an article on the game.[167] French-language books on the game also appeared at this time.[168]

Although he says that Foster misunderstood one of the rules—thus spoiling the game—Crowley nevertheless enjoyed his newfound celebrity. He was featured as the creator of pirate bridge in an illustrated article for *The Washington Post,* with his "Appeal to the American Republic" excerpted as an example of his poetic work.[169] As Crowley recalled this period, "I had only to wander into the appropriate circles to make myself the darling of the community."[170]

As with all pop culture trends, this one soon faded. Contract bridge came along in the 1920s and became the next big thing in the bridge world; it has since become virtually synonymous with the term *bridge.*

On January 22, 1917, Reuss released a revised OTO constitution and a manifesto for an Anational Grand Lodge, whose headquarters was at Monte Verità, a utopian commune located near Ascona, Switzerland. He planned an Anational Congress on August 15–25, its announcement proclaiming, "There are two centres of the OTO, both in neutral countries, where enquiries can be lodged by those interested in the aim of this congress. One is at New York (U.S. of America), the other at Ascona (Italian Switzerland)." During the congress, readings were conducted of Crowley's poetry and of the Gnostic Mass. On August 18 and 19 there was also a twelve-hour open-air performance of a *Sonnenfest*—a Sun Festival or "choral play"—by modern dance pioneers and IX° members Rudolf Laban (1879–1958) and Mary Wigman (1886–1973), along with their female troupe. According to Wigman biographer Mary Anne Santos Newhall, "Under Reuss's influence, Laban founded his own women's lodge and inducted his dancers, creating some local outrage and escalating speculation about the 'sexual magic' practiced by the Order."[171]

Back home, MMM experienced its share of growing pains: financially, things were tight. With creditors presenting bills and threatening legal action, the MMM lodge at 33 Avenue Studios was shut down and moved to 93 Regent Street, and much of its contents warehoused. Some items were even pawned to pay bills.

Destitute, Crowley left New Orleans to stay with his cousin, Lawrence Bishop (1872–1961), and his wife, Birdie. A father of three, Bishop was born in Kentucky and had been a merchant and farmer, but in the 1910s he became a citrus grower in Titusville, Florida.[172] When Bishop came to Streatham around 1894, Crowley's family had put him up; they reciprocated when Emily Crowley visited them in Kentucky in 1904.[173] AC now counted on similar hospitality. It was hardly an imposition, as Bishop had plenty of money in the bank, and his orange and grapefruit plantation was so large that his nearest neighbor was ten miles away. On February 9, 1917, Crowley arrived.

Although the Bishops did their best to accommodate Crowley, the fundamentalist beliefs of his cousin, now fiftyish, sickened AC so that he recalled him as "spiritually stunted and corrupted in every way by savage superstition"; for instance, he believed God sank the *Titanic* as punishment for its builders' pride. His wife, Alma, was no better. Although under thirty, she appeared a "wrinkled hag of sixty, with no idea of life beyond the gnawing fear of the hereaf-ter."[174] A tyrannical mother, her children constantly cried, "I don't want to grow up to be like Mother!" Although she and Crowley did not get along, she inspired the Simon Iff story "Suffer the Children," which Crowley considered one of his best.

Despite these public sentiments from his *Confessions* some thirteen years after the fact, at the time Crowley offered a grateful gesture, certainly anony-mously. On March 6, 1917, his diary records:

> Threatened severe frost. I averted same, to repay my cousin for his hospi-tality. The Op[us] was very remarkable. I went out at noon, in bitter cold and high wind; and I willed. I then slept very deeply for three hours, and woke in still, warm weather, with the sun shining. The forecasts had given several days of cold; and forecasts in America are very different to those in England; the rarely go wrong.

Crowley's misguided confidence in American meteorology notwithstanding, he believed he saved his cousin's orchards.

Still miserable, Crowley concluded that the Secret Chiefs were punishing him for being so cocksure as to go on strike. When he left Titusville that spring, Crowley sang softly to himself,

> What though the spicy breezes
> Blow soft o'er Titusville,
> Though every prospect pleases,
> The people make me ill.[175]

Day thirteen.

Although Crowley left the South far behind when he returned to New York, poverty followed him. "I really don't quite remember what I did about eating," he recalled.[176] His friend and pupil, Leon Engers Kennedy (1891–1970),[177] let Crowley sleep on the sofa in his Manhattan studio for "quite a long time."[178] He first entered Crowley's circle when he joined the A∴A∴ on September 23, 1912; and when John Yarker died in 1913, it was he, as newly appointed Patriarch Grand Secretary General of the Sovereign Sanctuary of the Ancient and Primitive Rite of Masonry in and for Great Britain and Ireland, who announced Henry Meyer's election to the membership.[179] In the last *Equinox,* Crowley dedicated the poem "The Disciples" to him.[180]

Leon Engers (he later dropped his last name altogether) was born in Antw-erp, Belgium, on February 22, 1891, but he described himself as a Dutch citi-zen.[181] This may be explained by Crowley's comments that Engers was "the adopted son of a multi-millionaire" and "was in receipt of an ample allowance from his family."[182] Studying art at the Sorbonne and Académie Julian in Paris, Engers's drive to paint something deeper than the physical appearance of his subjects eventually led him to occultism. The result was the "psychochrome," or painting of his sitter's aura.[183]

In exchange for the hospitality, Crowley encouraged Engers's artistic endeavors by arranging a November, 1917, exhibition of his art and reviewing it in *The International,* where he enthused: "These pictures must be seen to be appreciated at their full value. But it is certainly possible to predict a great vogue for these portraits. Everyone must naturally wish a representation in permanent form of their inner as well as their outer body."[184] In an unpublished essay, Crowley similarly praised his paintings,

> Psychochromes represent a duplex advance: one column attacking aesthetic, the other vision. Mr. Engers Kennedy has happily combined the forms of penetration into soul, and character with the art, of *decoratrice* and in his psychochromes he expresses in some cases the individuality of the sitter, in others a temporary mind in such a way that truth varies with beauty.[185]

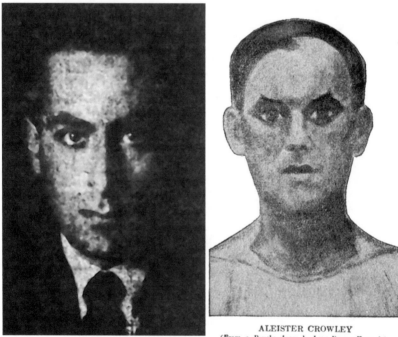

ALEISTER CROWLEY
(*From a Psycho chrom by Leon Engers-Kennedy*)

Soul-painter Leon Engers Kennedy (1891–1970), and one of his portraits of Crowley.

In January 1919 the *Atlanta Constitution* ran a full-page story on Engers and his "soul-paintings"; a month later he exhibited his psychochromes at the Paint Box Galleries in Washington Square South.[186] Engers would go on to study art under Lyonel Feininger (1871–1956) at the Bauhaus.[187] When he married Catherine Elizabeth Reilly of New York,[188] Crowley lamented:

> I failed, however, to keep him out of the clutches of a very beautiful red-headed Irish typist, hysterical from sexual suppression. She finally per-

suaded him to marry her, and I am afraid his last chance of a career is among the dusty documents in the files of the marriage bureau at City Hall. At least, I have heard no more of him since his return to Holland.[189]

Despite this direful judgement, Engers went on not only to teach painting and drawing at Bradley University's School of Art from 1949 to 1958 but also to serve as its director.[190] Even late in life, he held several exhibitions, including at Bradley's Gallery 20 in 1964 and New York's Fulton Gallery in 1965.[191] These exhibits included, among his portraits and studies in light, paintings from his Transcendental Series. As he then explained them, "Here I attempt to depict, to give form to a subjective, spiritual experience, one relating to the destiny of man in his cosmic evolution." His definition of an artist, although not original, nevertheless resonates with Thelemic philosophy: "The true artist must paint. He finds his painting an inescapable necessity—he has an inner drive that demands that his ideas, philosophies, feelings, and his soul be put on canvas. This is the distinction between a master and a talented amateur."[192]

When Crowley met slice-of-life author Theodore Dreiser (1871–1945), his classic *An American Tragedy* was still a decade off. In 1917 he nevertheless had a reputation with his books *Sister Carrie* (1900), *The Financier* (1912), and *The Titan* (1914). Viereck had offered to publish his newly completed *The "Genius"* in *The International,* but Dreiser, loyal American that he was, refused; shortly after publication this same novel would be banned by the New York Society for the Suppression of Vice. For his part, Crowley sold Dreiser copies of *The Works of Aleister Crowley* and *The World's Tragedy* and borrowed $15.

Dreiser, whom Crowley considered to be one of the few people in New York worth speaking to, reluctantly attended one of AC's *Anhalonium* parties at the insistence of their mutual friend, Louis Wilkinson. When they arrived, Crowley sized up the author and declared, "It will take treble the usual dose to move Dreiser." He disliked Crowley's antics and resented the dare implicit in the statement. When Crowley presented him with a hallucinogenic drink, Dreiser snatched it from his hand and boldly knocked it back.

Unfamiliar with the drug, however, Dreiser soon questioned the wisdom of his action. What if the drug made him sick? What if he had a bad reaction? What if it was poisonous? "Uh, Crowley," he approached his host sheepishly, "is there a good doctor in the neighborhood ... in case anything goes wrong?"

Crowley responded reassuringly, "I don't know about a doctor ... but there's a first-class undertaker on the corner of 33rd and Sixth Avenue."

Dreiser sat in stunned silence. After a time, he finally said, "I don't like that kind of joke, Crowley." However, after the colorful visions began, he described in detail his hallucinations while a small English actor lay beside him, moaning and vomiting into the bedside basin. It was a toss-up which was worse, Dreiser's narration or the actor's retching.

On May 4, 1917, Crowley—oblivious to the trouble that was about to explode at Regent Street—dreamed that his mother had died. The quality of this dream differed markedly from his usual dreams, causing him to ponder its significance. The answer arrived two days later: he learned that Emily Crowley was indeed dead at age seventy.[193] Ironically, Crowley was on the wrong side of the Atlantic to collect his £3,000 inheritance (equivalent to roughly $125,000 today).

By the end the month, Crowley's health returned. He sought out a prostitute to perform his first act of sex magick in a month—only his fifth this year—with the goal of completely restoring his health. He proceeded with operations to energize his will and spread the Law of Thelema. It signaled the end of Crowley's dry spell and the beginning of renewed prosperity.

At its new location at 93 Regent Street, MMM thrived under the direction of medium Mary Davies, V°. Mary Davies (née Brick) was born in 1867 on Portsea Island, Hampshire, to Elizabeth and Edward Brick, the latter a Civil Guard sergeant at the Portsea Convict Prison.[194] She was the oldest of five children.[195] According to Davies,

> My name, Mary, was given to me in Baptism in the hope that I should be blessed by the Virgin Mother, so I was brought up and confirmed in the Faith soon after the age of seven, made my first Confession and Communion, and was enrolled in the order of the Scapular of our "Lady of Mount Carmel" at the age of twelve.[196]

While a girl of seven, she awoke to a spiritual visitation from her patron, Saint Theresa. From that point, her childhood was filled with clairvoyant and other psychic experiences; this gradually led to her leaving Catholicism and devoting herself to study, public speaking, and holding classes. In February 1886 she married William Robert Davies, a friend of the family and a petty officer in the Royal Navy.[197] She had two children, William Clemance (b. 1888), who died in 1893 from a childhood illness, and Theophilus Stewart (b. 1892).[198] Relocating to London,[199] the Davieses encountered a Spiritualists' Society, of which Mary would become president; they also formed a circle of fourteen to sixteen people, holding meetings at their home twice a week and launching her career as a medium; her career up to 1912 is detailed in her memoir, *My Psychic Recollections* (1912). Although reviewed in *The Theosophist* and *Atheneaum,* it is Crowley's 1912 review in *The Equinox* that is of most interest:

> Mrs. Davies is a "professional medium"; of such I have said things which only my incapacity for invective prevented from being severe. But though (no doubt) the phenomena recorded in this book are 'non-evidential,' I do feel the sincerity of the writer. I am confident of her good faith.[200]

Indeed, Davies had been aware of Crowley and his circle as early as 1910, when she met George Raffalovich at one of the rites (whether one of the lesser rituals like the Rite of the Phoenix or the grand Rites of Eleusis is unclear). Both

Crowley and Cowie privately disparaged her interests in clairvoyance and spiritualism but quietly tolerated them in light of her other strengths. By the summer of 1913, she took her III° initiation, and by 1916 the Lodge, with her help, moved into its space on Regent Street.

MMM members were unanimous in her praise. Organist William Steff Langston described her as "one of the most lovable of her charming sex, she has sweetness, tact, power and ability in profusion … she is just the one to attract the people we need."[201] Cowie concurred. "She's a good soul and a good sort altogether, and her gift, which appears to amount to ability to knock about on the plane next to material, is quite genuine."[202] That April, Davies reported, "we had 3 Initiations and an affiliation of a Master from Rugby—we now have only 2 First Degree all the others are raised, as a L[odge] we number 21 (9 M[inerval] & 11 F[irst]) with 3 waiting Initiation."[203] As G. M. Cowie recounted: "We owe much to Mary Davies. Practically every new member has been brought in by her. Besides, the membership is steadily growing."[204]

Alas, during this fecund period MMM came under police scrutiny. Cowie was shadowed by an investigator, his reputation the subject of official inquiry. Late in the winter of 1917 he was finally questioned about what MMM was, and the nature of his involvement. It soon became clear that this inquiry was connected to AC's political writings. As Cowie wrote to Crowley:

> I learn that it is only my known probity of character, which unknown to me, has been closely inquired into, that has satisfied the authorities that the Lodge is exactly what is set forth in the Manifesto and that we have no political motive…. The authorities say that so long as I am in control in England and so long as we are not helping you, they are satisfied and we may continue. Otherwise, I have no doubt we should have been closed down…. I must make it clear that everyone who has joined us did so in complete ignorance of your 'views'—and is guiltless of any political motive.[205]

The authorities' assurances, however, proved fleeting.

A couple of months later—on Monday, May 14, 1917—Detective-Inspector John Curry of New Scotland Yard went with another officer to 93 Regent Street. The glass panel of the door bore the letters "MMM," which he knew stood for Mysteria Mystica Maxima. Inside, they found additional signage that read MARY DAVIES, SITTINGS 11 TO 5 and CLAIRVOYANCE. Entering a front room on the third floor, they found five men and five women dressed in Master Masons' uniforms, and Davies herself dressed as a Worshipful Master, or head of the Lodge. The police presented a warrant for Davies's arrest. Protesting that she had done nothing wrong, she was told, "I understand you call this the 'Order of the Temple of the Orient,' and your founder is Aleister Crowley, a man of evil reputation and a traitor to this country." The arrest warrant, however, simply charged her under the Vagrancy Act for telling fortunes. She was taken into custody, and the police seized furniture, regalia, books, and papers for examination (never to return them). The arrest garnered headlines, like the *Times's* "'M.M.M.' Mysteries: Order of the Temple of the Orient Raided."[206]

Witnesses for the prosecution recounted visits to her under false pretenses. Bertha Brondle consulted Davies about a fictitious sick child and received instructions on how to affect a spiritual cure. Similarly, Blanche Daisley consulted her about a similarly fictitious brother in the Flying Corps, to be told that he had died but that he was now being guarded by two spirits. For this advice, the women paid 10 shillings 6 pence. Davies protested that she did not profess to tell fortunes; she described herself as an author and preacher. Nevertheless, she was found guilty and fined £40, plus 10 guineas costs.[207]

Crowley initially believed the raid was arranged by Feilding as a publicity stunt to maintain his cover, but soon realized it was an official response to his wartime activities. This hampered fund-raising efforts to pay his passage back to England. As Cowie informed Crowley, "We could not even think of raising funds to bring you back, desirable as it is, when we are told you will certainly be arrested if you return."[208] As a solution, AC resigned as head of MMM and appointed Frater Achad as nominal Grand Master. In subsequent letters, Cowie wrote to Crowley, "It's just 'care frater' [dear brother] now, as in happier days of old"[209] and "As you are no longer G[rand] M[aster] but my guru as of old."[210] Nevertheless, efforts to continue operating were difficult. Other than membership dues, MMM's only revenue came from sales of Crowley's books … and even this had to be discontinued. "I've not been able to supply one of the rare orders for books lately," Cowie explained to Crowley at the end of 1917. "The real and vital reason however, and here you force my hand, is that the police were trying to trace your property in this country."[211]

In response to the bad publicity resulting from both her arrest and her connection to the "evil" and "traitorous" Crowley, Davies ran the following letter in *The Occult Review*:

> On May 15 last, the Press generally stated in connexion with the prosecution against me, Mary Davies, of 93 Regent Street, that I was the protégée of a man of evil reputation and a traitor to this country. I desire emphatically to disavow any such association. I have no knowledge whatsoever, nor ever had, of the views and actions—political, social or private—of the person referred to. The only link I had with this person was on Masonic grounds, in the mysteries which no one could be more profound. It is scarcely necessary to stress my own patriotism, as my public know since the beginning of the war my Intercessory Services at Kensington have been solely such as to encourage and to fortify every patriotic effort, and I deliberately repudiate the stigma implied by the quotation given above.[212]

Davies appealed the ruling but, on October 26, 1917, the decision was upheld.[213] The legal bill for her defense topped £250, and Cowie—indignant that this sweet and sincere fifty-year-old woman had suffered publicly and financially because of Crowley's politics—adopted an increasingly bitter tone in his correspondence: "In one way and another, the Lodge has cost me more than the total contributions of the members; and all lost uselessly thanks to your politics."[214] Bitterness quickly became resentment:

> I told you long ago that the continental origin of the O.T.O. would make it impossible to work it in England and that is now evident. It now will *not* be allowed....
>
> A little tact on your part and the assumption of the vice of sympathy even if you have it not would have helped things along better.
>
> I hope M.O.H. [Mother of Heaven, Crowley's nickname for Leila Waddell] is flourishing, and yourself better in health. It beats me to explain to people why the Sole Proprietor and Patentee of the Universal Medicine should be always fatally, even seriously, sick.[215]

And finally, "Come on! be a sporting Beast, not the kind of animal who gets out of pits by inviting some confiding creature to come in & taste the waters of Liberty—how good they are!—and climbs out over his shoulders."[216] By the end of the year, the stress fractures became fissures and Cowie closed the Lodge. On April 30, 1918, a classified ad ran in the *Times* reading "Regenta Tea Rooms, 93 Regent-street, newly decorated. Apartments furnished; also one floor as office; part attendance. Can be viewed 11–5."[217]

Davies, with the help of another member, Mrs. Scott, ultimately sold Boleskine for £2,500 to Dorothy C. Brook on July 12, 1918. This final act was a relief to Cowie, who sank much of his own money, including his retirement fund, into keeping the mortgage afloat.[218] Cowie's last tie to Crowley had been cut.

On August 6, Crowley opened an account in the name Ordo Templi Orientis with the Title Guarantee and Trust Company, wherein the proceeds from the sale were deposited from England through the law firm of Lord, Day and Lord. Although this was technically OTO's money, Crowley felt entitled to it "inasmuch as he was personally responsible for having supplied about nine tenths of the total amount of money on deposit."[219] It allowed him to support himself through the remainder of his time in America.

CHAPTER THIRTEEN

Amalantrah

Although Chokmah days ticked by, Crowley, enjoying one boon after another through the summer of 1917, knew the worst of his trials had passed. Editors Daniel Howard Sinclair Nicholson (1883–1923) and Reverend Arthur Hugh Evelyn Lee (1875–1941)[1] included his poems "The Quest," "The Neophyte," and "The Rose and the Cross" in *The Oxford Book of English Mystical Verse*.[2] Louis Wilkinson offered his comments on the newly completed *Butterfly Net* manuscript. And Viereck appointed Crowley editor of *The International* with a $20-per-week salary. He first appeared on the masthead as "contributing editor" with the August issue. In the tradition of *The Equinox,* Crowley wrote most of the magazine's contents under various pseudonyms, publishing his Simon Iff and *Golden Twigs* stories along with practical articles on magick, such as "The Revival of Magick," "Cocaine," "The Ouija Board," "The Message of the Master Therion," "Geomancy," and "Ecclesiae Gnosticae Catholicae Canon Missae" (the Gnostic Mass).[3]

For a short time, Crowley lived with a Pennsylvania Dutch woman named Anna Catherine Miller. He met her at a Singalese restaurant on 8th Avenue and likened her to the Egyptian god Anubis, the dog-headed underworld guide. He and the Dog, as AC dubbed her, took a furnished Central Park West apartment near 110th Street. Miller was "the only member of her family not actually insane,"[4] but she drank heavily, and when she proved unable to quit, Crowley left her. The last thing he wanted was another Rose Kelly or Mary Desti.

Crowley promptly took up with Miller's friend Roddie Minor (1884–1979). Standing five-foot-eight with gray eyes and brown hair, she was "physically a magnificent animal"[5] with broad muscular shoulders and masculine features. She was born in Lawrenceville, Georgia, on April 9, 1884, the third of four daughters to farmer William Jackson Minor and Lide Hawthorne Minor.[6] While a student at Columbia University, she became active in winter 1908 in New York's suffrage movement, where she was described as a lieutenant to radical feminist activist Bettina Borrman Wells. When police refused to grant a parade permit for a Sunday demonstration, Minor told reporters, "If necessary to avoid the molestation of the police, we shall get a corpse and a coffin, or one of us will pretend she is dead, so that the procession will be a funeral march."[7] To avoid arrest, she was one of eight who held a "silent march" up Broadway from Union Square to the Manhattan Trade School, their numbers swelling to two thousand along the way. Encountering a crowd surrounding a Salvation Army band, Minor complained "Fine justice this. Here are persons in uniform, carrying banners and with a brass band. If they can parade, why can't we?"[8] The march resulted in Minor's photograph appearing in the papers under the headline "She Wants to Vote," and when Borrman Wells and several of her people left New York to spread their message elsewhere, Minor was placed in charge of the Progressive Woman Suffrage Union headquarters.[9]

Roddie Minor, the Camel (1884–1979).

She graduated in 1911 from Columbia University's New York College of Pharmacy with a Doctor of Pharmacy degree.[10] The following year, she began working as a chemist for druggists and importers W. H. Schieffelin & Co., joined the American Pharmaceutical Association as a corresponding member, and helped found the American Women's Pharmaceutical Association, serving as its vice president.[11] She would soon leave her medical pathology laboratory job to become managing chemist for a large perfume manufacturer.

Because Crowley saw her carrying him out of a dry and desiccated period of his life and into a comfortable phase, he dubbed her the Camel, although she went by the nickname Eve. By early October, he was living with her in a West 9th Street studio. In these new surroundings, Crowley returned to the work of promulgating the Law of Thelema. Thus, 1918 began on a productive note: Crowley wrote "De Lege Libellum" ("The Law of Liberty"), revised his "Message of the Master Therion," and quickly published both tracts.

It looked like it would be a typical Saturday night. It was past midnight—technically now Sunday, January 14. Eve lay on a mattress on the floor, smoking opium and muttering about this thing and that. Crowley, meanwhile, blocked out the distraction of her babbling as he worked at his desk writing *Liber Aleph*. Alternately known as *The Book of Wisdom or Folly, Liber Aleph* was a series of epistles of a magician (the Magus To Mega Therion) to his magical son (the Magister Templi OIVVIO) covering a broad array of spiritual and magical topics. Its style was that of prose poetry. Each one-page epistle bore a Latin title, with every noun in the book capitalized. Beginning as a challenge to Freud, it became one of his most elevated and sublime works.[12]

He set down his pen when the Camel muttered that she saw herself as a candlestick with thirteen candles. Crowley expounded on the number ninety-three (the value of the words *thelema,* will, and *agape,* love, among others), explaining how adepts had sent messages for him through his Scarlet Women and how he tested these adepts and their messages. Then he returned to work.

Eve interrupted again to explain that she was now thirteen naked women being caressed simultaneously. The image did nothing to distract him, nor did the recurrence of the number thirteen interest him. As he scribbled away, Crowley offhandedly suggested she try to obtain a message.

Asking for a message, she heard gurgling water. A dark farmhouse appeared to her, transforming into an equally dark vagina, and then into a group of soldiers with guns surrounding an enthroned king. Roddie Minor asked for a clearer message. In response, she saw a flesh-like egg with intricate convolutions, encircled with clouds, trees, mountains, and water—the four elements. A camel then stepped into the foreground.

Hearing her mention an egg, Crowley perked up, recalling it was an important image in the Abuldiz Working with Mary Desti. The camel, of course, was Roddie.

She asked the king's name, and the word *Ham* appeared. This Crowley interpreted as Khem, the ancient name of Egypt. When the king stood and walked off, a gray-bearded wizard in a long black gown appeared. Looking back at Roddie, he took the king's arm and led him into a cave. She followed.

"Tell them you're Eve," Crowley suggested. When she did, everything vanished. Roddie now found the king sitting in a canopy-covered niche in the mountainside. The wizard sat beneath a tree and fanned himself. Crowley urged her again to ask the king's name. Despite her fear, Roddie asked. The king smiled, and she understood she had to build a fire before he would speak. So the king and the wizard taught her the fire-building ritual. Once lit, she saw a beautiful lion beside the blaze. The wizard, still holding a pair of sticks, smiled at her and said, "child." A naked boy danced in the woods before them.

Contented, the wizard sat and extended his hand toward her. Roddie accepted the invitation, sitting at his left hand and watching the dancing boy. Tenderly putting his arm around her, he rested her head on his shoulder and said, "It's all in the egg."

The Beast and the Camel repeated their experiment of January 14 over the next few months, generally on weekends. It became Crowley's longest, most detailed working. The king, they learned, was Eosophon, and the boy was Augustus Fionchare. The most important actor, however, proved to be the old wizard. "There was what I may call a permanent background to the vision," Crowley said of the workings,[13] adding that the wizard "lived in a place as definite as an address in New York, and in this place were a number of symbolic images representing myself and several other adepts." His name was Amalantrah, and he proved himself to Crowley by providing the elusive spelling of Baphomet (a thorny problem, since its etymology is unknown and its orthography suspect): As BAFOMETHR, it added up to Amalantrah's own number, 729, and suggested the meaning "Father Mithras."

On January 25, Amalantrah showed the Camel a green multiarmed deity seated by a door bearing the inscription "Gate of Abdullah" in strange characters. Beyond this gate was the Marrakesh oasis of Oseika, where Roddie met the tall Moor Athanan.

"What is my true number?" the Camel finally asked.

"103," Athanan answered.

"What is my magical name?"

"In my language, it is Ahitha." This Crowley quickly tallied to 417. Both 103 and 417 were one digit shy of being magically significant: 104 being the Hebrew letter Tzaddi, the fish hook, while 418 was the number of Abrahadabra, Aiwass, Heru-Ra-Ha, Ankh-f-n-Khonsu, and Nuit's cry of "To me!"[14] The lacking digit, Crowley deduced, symbolized the phallus.

During the discussion, Crowley began to ask about his plan to solicit support from his friends to unify all occult groups. "Tell me if Annie Besant will live long in her present body?"

"Yes."

Damn. "Is a political campaign among existing occult societies with a view to unification under 666 a good plan?"

"Yes."

"Should I approach Bert Reese?" Reese (1851–1926) was an American spiritualist whom Crowley had met in London before the war. Aged in his sixties, he earned a lucrative income consulting for wealthy businessmen.

"Yes."

"Should I approach another person?" He was thinking of Ada Leverson.

"No."

"Should I approach Gouraud?" This was Aimée Crocker Gouraud (1871–1941), daughter of Pacific Coast millionaire E. B. Crocker, who had helped finance the Union Pacific Railroad. Born in Sacramento, she lived a colorful life wherever she went, whether it was New York, France, England, or India. Author of *Moon-Madness and Other Fantasies*,[15] the *Philadelphia Inquirer* described the Queen of Bohemia thus: "Call her a millionairess, an aesthete, a genius at bizarre and extravagant entertainment, a citizeness of many lands, a dabbler in art and the occult, a seeker after weird adventure and you have not begun to say it all."[16] Her passport application listed her occupation simply as "capitalist."[17] She had married four times: her first two marriages ended in divorce, she was a widow to her third husband Jackson Gouraud, and in 1914 she married Prince Alexandre Miskinoff of Russia.[18] Her interests in mysticism and the occult caused her to embrace many religious traditions. Indeed, Crowley had enrolled her into OTO prior to the war; she was one of the dedicatees of the poem "The Disciples" in the last *Equinox*.[19] Crowley unsuccessfully wooed her (and would continue to do so over the years). As her friend Leah Hirsig recalled,

> He has proposed marriage to her nearly every time he has seen or written her for the last ten years.
>
> She adores him; she realizes that he is far beyond any of her Russian counts and other suckers that fill her drawing-room; but she fears him. Some fortune teller told her that her fifth marriage—if she contracted a fifth marriage—would be the death of her.[20]

Ironically, Crowley's main hindrance was that he always presented an air of wealth while she preferred her men penniless.

"Yes," he agreed, AC should approach Gouraud.

"Is there anyone else to approach?"

"Some woman." Athanan described an attractive, middle-aged American, stout and large-breasted, with chestnut hair and fair skin. Married but without children, she was educated, worked as a singer or musician, and knew Aimée Gouraud. She lived near 5th Avenue. and her name was Elsie Gray Parker.

Given enough information to search for this mysterious ally, Crowley asked about practical matters. "When may Therion expect fulfillment of *Liber Legis* chapter three, verse thirty-one?" This passage read, "There cometh a rich man from the West who shall pour his gold upon thee."

"September."

"What year?"

"1918." Athanan would be wrong on this point.

"What nationality is the man referred to in that verse?"

"Austrian." The rich man Crowley would eventually discover was German. He was not, however, a man of leisure as Athanan described. It was one of several dead ends given by Amalantrah. Although Crowley would search for the mysterious Elsie Gray Parker, he would never find her. And, despite Crowley's soliciting the help of Bert Reese, a union of magical orders did not occur.

As the workings progressed, Crowley increasingly incorporated the IX°, anal sex, *Anhalonium lewinii,* and hashish in order to improve the connection. At this time, Amalantrah assured Crowley that he could transliterate his motto, To Mega Therion, into Hebrew without losing its numerical value. (Try though Crowley might, the wizard's solution only added up to 740, not 666.)

That very day, however, one reader of *The International* responded to Crowley's essay, "The Revival of Magick," which had run in the September and October, 1917, issues. The inciteful passage read:

> "Herein is Wisdom; let him that hath understanding count the number of the Beast; for it is the number of a man; and his number is 600 & 3 score & 6." [TO MEGA THERION], the Great Wild Beast, has the value, according to the Greek system, of 666. It is, of course, the title of the Master Therion.

The letter (dated February 24, 1918) came to Viereck at *The International* offices, and read,

> Please inform your readers that I, Shmuel bar Aiwaz bie Yackou de Shirabad, have counted the number of a man.
>
> Tau+ 400 + Resh + 300 + Yod + 10 + Vau + 6 + Nin + 50. Read from right to left.

N	V	I	R	Th
50	6	10	200	400

666

A reader had sent in the solution to Amalantrah's puzzle! Then he noticed the correspondent's name: Samuel bar *Aiwaz.* All these years, Crowley thought the name of his holy guardian angel was artificial; in reality, it was a Hebrew name! Without hesitation, he dashed off a letter to the man, Shmuel bar Aiwaz bie Yackou de Shirabad, who had Anglicized his name to Samuel A. Jacobs (c. 1891–1971). Born in Persia, he came to America as a youth, and in 1909 became a printer for the *Persian Courier* in New York, then designed and revised unusual typefaces for the Mergenthaler Linotype Company. In future years, he would operate the Golden Eagle Press in Mount Vernon, New York, and design books for Covici Friede, New Directions, Oxford University Press, and Dutton; his design for Covici Friede's 1930 edition of *The Canterbury Tales* was named one of the "Fifty Books of the Year" by the American Institute of Graphic Arts. However, his claim to fame may well be as designer of poetry books for e. e. cummings (1894–1962).[21] When Crowley responded to his letter, he supplied Crowley with the spelling of Aiwaz: OIVZ. This Crowley anxiously tallied to the number ninety-three.

The coincidence floored him: from a single man he received the Hebrew orthography of Therion plus the traditional and numerically significant spelling of Aiwass as Aiwaz. Significantly, these were solutions that had eluded Crowley, the scribe of *The Book of the Law*. The importance of this event caused him to write of Samuel A. Jacobs, "He is one of the most important links in the chain of evidence that superhuman intelligences really exist."[22]

Samuel Aiwaz Jacobs (c. 1891–1971).

Through February and March, several "sisters of the order" helped with the operations; these individuals Crowley likened to three scorpions of the desert through which the Camel was leading him. The first of these, Eva Tanguay (1878–1947), was the highest-paid vaudeville star of her time (at the time of the 1929 stock-market crash, she lost over $2 million). A "hoydenish, frizzy-haired blonde, celebrated for her animated delivery and her outlandish, often wildly feathered costumes,"[23] she had been a performer since childhood, when she toured for five years portraying Cedric Errol in *Little Lord Fauntleroy*. Her voice was ordinary—Percy Hammond described it as "the wail of the prehistoric diplodocus"[24]—but her energetic performances more than made up for it, inviting comparison to "a human dynamo."[25] Admittedly egotistical (her songs included "T-A-N-G-U-A-Y" and "The Tanguay Rag"), she nevertheless parodied herself in her hit "Egotistical Eva." Her trademark song, however, mirrored her lifestyle and earned her the title of the "I Don't Care" girl.[26] And she truly didn't care what others thought: she sang risqué songs (e.g. "It's Been Done Before but Never the Way I Do It") and had very public love affairs (she was linked to African American heavyweight champion Jack Johnson). When

Crowley met her she was at the top of her game, having just produced and starred in *Energetic Eva* (1916) and *The Wild Girl* (1917).[27] AC considered her a supreme artist, writing, "I have no words to hymn her glory, nay, not if I were Shelley and Swinburne and myself in one."[28] His appreciation of her, "Drama be Damned," appears in the April 1918 *International*.

Singer Eva Tanguay (1878–1947, left) and lecturer Marie Roehling (b. 1891, right).

Second was Marie Lavrov, née Roehling (b. 1891). A Russian immigrant from Odessa, she became a U.S. citizen upon her April 17, 1913, marriage in Chicago to Herman Roehling.[29] Although she made her home in Chicago, at the time she met Crowley she was traveling as a lecturer on Russia. On May 23, 1917, she had addressed representatives of 125 women's organizations at a meeting of the League of Cook Country Clubs in Chicago, speaking on the condition of Russia before and after prohibition, remarking, "The revolution never would have succeeded without prohibition. Our peasants had been encouraged to stupefy themselves with drink. When that was taken away they could think better. The Russians have been forty years starting a real revolution, but when it came it was good."[30] From there, she lectured at Milwaukee-Downer College on Russian women, and on March 10, 1918, the Ethical Culture Society in Philadelphia.[31] Standing five feet, six and a half inches tall with gray eyes, dark brown hair, and a fair complexion, her magical name was Olun, after Plato's *Timaeus*. Meaning "the whole of wholes" or "Absolute Whole," Crowley connected it to Nuit, Our Lady of the Stars. Shortly after meeting her, Crowley took her as his new Scarlet Woman, noting that Olun and Marie both added to 156, the number of Babalon. Her name appears throughout *Liber Aleph*. Although by March 22 Crowley had her and Roddie Minor together in bed with him doing magick to cure Marie's "sin complex" and

Roddie's jealousy, Olun "soon abandoned the unequal contest."[32] When reprinting his Russian memoir *The Fun of the Fair* nearly three decades later, Crowley would name her among the dedicatees.

Completing the triad was Dorothy A. Troxel (1896–1986), a musician who held an associate of music degree from Dana School in her native Warren, Ohio. AC cultivated her as a magical partner at the request of Amalantrah, who dubbed her Wesrun; depending on the spelling, her name was either 333 (dispersion) or 888 (redemption), making Crowley feel obligated to save her. Thirty years later, as a geographic names specialist with the Army Map Service, she would begin the five-year project of compiling the first modern Mongolian-English dictionary.[33]

Besides this trinity of scorpions, a fourth woman figured into the Amalantrah Working: Mrs. Elsa Lowensohn Lincke (b. 1864),[34] who reputedly introduced the cabaret to America.[35] A German musician who had lived in New York since 1904, she was described by Crowley as "antique, but sprightly" and as having "abandoned worldly pleasures for spiritual joys." She had been interested in H. Spencer Lewis[36] and his Rosicrucian group, Ancient and Mystical Order Rosæ Crucis (AMORC), "merrily disdainful of criticism based on his elementary blunders in Latin and his total ignorance of the history of the Order which he claimed to rule. The old lady was simple-minded, sincere and earnest."[37] She helped the order by giving AC money for the Great Work. Amalantrah dubbed her Bazedon, calling her totem a toad and her numeral 444 (significantly, 444 was the number of the frog-headed god of the earth).

On March 30, 1918, Frater Achad, having sold all his possessions to be by his master's side, arrived from Vancouver. He assumed the magical name Arcteon, which Amalantrah had given earlier as the name of an unborn prophet of the Law. Besides helping Crowley interrogate the wizard, he also helped prepare the new *Equinox,* and participated in a series of experiments with ether.

Disaster struck in April, when Viereck transferred ownership of *The International* to Dr. Lindley Miller Keasbey (1867–1946), the former chair of the University of Texas Department of Economics and Political Science and an authority on international law. The previous summer, he had been dismissed for his pro-German pacifist activism in forming the People's Council for Democracy and Terms of Peace and lecturing across the country on its behalf.[38] Although Crowley dedicated "Concerning the Law of Thelema"[39] to him, Keasbey refused to include his work in future issues. This caused Crowley to accuse Keasbey of mismanagement; any trouble at the paper, however, Viereck attributed to Crowley's tendency to publish his own writings in favor of contributions by talented new writers.

The Amalantrah Working nevertheless proceeded, with new assistants arriving in May. Operations continued until June 16, when Crowley, satisfied that he and Roddie had built the Temple of Jupiter, ended the Amalantrah Working.

That July, another pilgrim sought Crowley in New York. Cecil Frederick Russell (1897–1987) was a "surly, mulish and bitterly rebellious"[40] attendant at an Annapolis naval hospital who, having saved his earnings to purchase *The Equinox* for $100, was memorizing the Holy Books. Russell was born in Greenwood, Massachusetts, on June 9, 1897.[41] His family later moved to Orlando, Florida, and two months short of his twentieth birthday, Russell enlisted in the U.S. Navy. Serving from April 22, 1917, to December 12, 1918, Russell began as a Hospital Apprentice stationed at the U.S. Naval Academy Hospital in Annapolis, Maryland, and also aboard the USS *Reina Mercedes*. By 1918 he had advanced to the office of Pharmacist Mate.[42] He wrote Crowley at *The International,* arranging a visit where he and Crowley ate lunch and took an astral journey; that evening, Crowley and his local OTO officers initiated him to the III°. His amazing ability and exceptional energy, Crowley thought, were well-suited to the Great Work, and he was likewise anxious to help the cause. Alas, duty called him back to Annapolis for the time being.

Cecil Frederick Russell (1897–1987).

The following month, AC's relationship with Roddie Minor ended. Although Crowley claimed to treat her as an equal in all respects, she nevertheless felt inferior. He attributed the resulting friction and resentment to the Vision of the Demon Crowley, a phrase he used to describe the phenomenon where every student at one point or another saw him as a horrible monster; those who endured would see beyond the illusion and know him as a great teacher, while those frightened off by this smoke screen recalled him superficially as a beast. In Roddie Minor's case, she and Crowley talked the matter out, agreeing calmly and amicably to part.

August's dog days found Crowley feeling lost without *The International,* Roddie Minor, and Amalantrah. So he stood at the dock, surrounded by friends, waiting for a morning Albany boat to carry him to his latest Great Magical Retirement on Esopus Island, near the Catskills Mountains on the Hudson River. According to reporter William Seabrook, his only baggage was the tent and canoe that Seabrook had donated to him, plus provisions purchased with a monetary gift from Seabrook. The reporter, however, was disgruntled to discover AC's curious-looking luggage containing not food but brushes, rope, and fifty gallons of paint. Crowley had only $2.25 left to his name. "For crying out loud," Seabrook reportedly sniped, contemplating shoving AC into the river, "what are you going to eat?" With a grand, pontifical gesture, Crowley affected the embodiment of his father. "My children, I will be fed as Elijah by the ravens." Crowley, reading Seabrook's account twenty-five years later, clarified,

> the story about going up the Hudson in a canoe loaded with red paint. It was loaded with camping apparatus and supplies, of course. What else would an explorer do? The paint (I think about four pots of it) was bought at a local shop after I had been living on the island for a month.[43]

Crowley arrived at the island, pitching his tent and sitting in his *asana.* Realizing that since coming to America his emphasis on sex magick was a detriment to his other disciplines, he took this opportunity to refine his skills in meditation and concentration. He often sat for hours before realizing someone had left food for him. The milk, eggs, and sweet corn came not from ravens but local farmers who, though uncertain whether Crowley was a sage or a psycho, decided he needed to eat.

Combining yoga and drugs produced an intense series of trances that he believed recalled his past lives. Working back from his last incarnation as French occultist Éliphas Lévi (1810–1875), who died six months before Crowley's birth, he relived memories as Count Cagliostro, Edward Kelly, and Pope Alexander VI. Among his less illustrious incarnations were a suicide, a Polish scholar, and the monk Father Ivan. In one dismal life he was a deformed hermaphrodite who, conquering tuberculosis and scoliosis, died from syphilis after a German knight raped him. In Mohammedan times, he served on a council of Secret Chiefs who, despite the skepticism of older masters, revealed the Mysteries to mankind through Mohammed, Luther, Adam Weishaupt, Christian Rosenkreuz, and similar teachers. In a much earlier incarnation, he was Ko Hsuen, a disciple of Lao Tzu, author of the King Khang King. While basking in the illumination of these memories, Crowley prepared "translations" of the Chinese classics Tao Teh King and King Khang King—actually enlightened paraphrases of James Legge.

Subjected to empirical rigors, these memories are unconvincing. In the case of well-known figures, his "recollections" contain obscure or unverifiable details; sometimes they even conflict with known facts. For example, Crowley recalled Cagliostro being born not in Palermo but in a Tunisian brothel, and dying not as a prisoner of the Inquisition at San Leo but in a mountain forest with a gaily dressed youth. Despite their empirical failings, Crowley attached great significance to these memories and claimed to benefit from them.

Even greater illumination came on September 5 when, at 5 p.m., he recorded in his diary,

> The meditation of this afternoon resulted in an initiation so stupendous that I dare not hint at its Word. It is the supreme secret of a Magus, and it is so awful that I tremble even now—two hours later and more...as I write concerning it. In a single instant I had the Key to the whole of the Chinese wisdom. In the light—momentary glimpse as it was—of this truth, all systems of religion and philosophy became absolutely puerile. Even the Law [of Thelema] appears no more than a curious incident. I remain absolutely bewildered, blinded, knowing what blasting image lies in this shrine.[44]

Following this vision, he used the rope he had brought to make rigging by which to dangle from the cliffs facing the Hudson. Upon these cliffs, plainly visible to passing steamers, Crowley painted in large red letters:

DO WHAT THOU WILT SHALL BE THE WHOLE OF THE LAW
EVERY MAN AND EVERY WOMAN IS A STAR

By the time he left Esopus Island, Crowley realized that the magical current that had fueled his American period had depleted itself. The time had come to wrap up business and move on.

Tan and trim, Crowley returned to New York early that September and took a one-room studio at 1 University Place on the corner of Washington Square, hiding his bed behind a triptych screen whose panels he painted as sun, moon, and fire. Boasting to Seabrook of his newfound magical skills, he encountered only skepticism and so arranged a demonstration: walking down 5th Avenue, he assumed the slouched posture of a well-to-do gentleman and fell into step behind him. As an example of sympathetic magic, AC adapted the man's mannerisms so strongly that when Crowley dropped briefly to a squat, the gentleman in front of him fell to the ground. Seabrook and Crowley helped the puzzled fellow to his feet as he searched vainly for a banana peel or something slick on the soles of his shoes.

Also at this time, Crowley made the stunning announcement that he was now a painter. "My familiar spirit visited me in the night and commanded me to paint," he told Willie. "I have been under the misapprehension that I was a great poet. I was clearly mistaken. Paint is my real medium, and I am destined to become one of the outstanding artists of my age."[45] Alas, his skill remained poor despite diligent work. He eventually confided in Seabrook, "I am certain Aiwass has something important to express through paint, but he doesn't know a thing about technique!" So Willie took him to the Metropolitan Museum of Art, where Crowley spent the day studying Rembrandt's "Old Woman." Then he understood painting.

While this tale of Crowley's artistic awakening is courtesy of Seabrook, Crowley himself gives an explanation that sheds more light on the origins of this interest:

> I probably would never have taken up painting if it hadn't been for the *International,* of which I became editor. I couldn't find artists who would draw the covers I wanted, so, finally I became disgusted about fifteen months ago and decided to draw my own covers. I had never studied art and had never drawn or painted a picture in my life. When I tried to draw those covers I became so interested in the work that I gave up the editor-ship of the magazine and went in for art.[46]

None of Crowley's concepts, however, ever covered the magazine.

To locate models for his unusual and often grotesque pictures, Crowley ran the following ad in the newspaper:

WANTED

> DWARFS, HUNCHBACKS, Tattooed Women, Harrison Fisher Girls, Freaks of All Sorts, Coloured Women only if exceptionally ugly or deformed, to pose for artist. Apply by letter with photograph.

He drew preliminary sketches of his subjects, mixed pigments, and "began to paint the amazing pictures that have come to be the despair of art critics here and abroad."[47] Though an unskilled draughtsman, the haunting quality of his pictures nevertheless attracted acclaim from New York's ultramodernists.

While S. L. Mathers died that November in the worldwide Spanish flu epidemic, Crowley nurtured two ambitions, as described in a letter to author James Branch Cabell (1879–1962):

> I am just off to Detroit to give three lectures—Labour, Religion, and Death—and thence by the Beard of the Prophet to a Free Country. I am trying to find an Abbey of Thelema for free men.[48]

The latter ambition involved starting a utopian society based upon Thelemic principles, inspired by Rabelais's Abbey of Thélème for his own law of "Do what thou wilt." Its first tentative steps, however, remained more than a year away. More pressing was Crowley's visit to Detroit, which would figure promi-nently in his plans during 1918–1919, both for publication and establishment of OTO's U.S. headquarters.

His link to Detroit was Albert Winslow Ryerson (1872–1931), general manager of Universal Book Stores Inc. Born in Hollis, New Hampshire, to John and Evelyn Ryerson, who traced their family back to the *Mayflower,*

Ryerson was raised in Concord, where he drove a dog cart for his neighbor, transcendentalist philosopher Ralph Waldo Emerson (1803–1882). From Emerson and his distinguished visitors,[49] he acquired a keen interest in philosophy and the ancients' worship of sex. As he explained obliquely:

> Why it was my father who took the wild grape and the Isabella together, the male and the female and they formed the present Concord grape. Father introduced them there was no engagement, they were married, he married them, and I assume the Concord grape must have been a love grape. This school of philosophy is the same that Thoreau and all those people believed in where they delved into the finest things of nature. It was in that atmosphere that I was reared and that atmosphere surrounded me and which in a measure determined or directed my life. And many of these fine people, because of the libelous press, have to go into hiding to think and talk about these finer things, which give great truths to the world. Of course in such an atmosphere there were so-called "love cults," but in this school there were people of high ideals.[50]

He later moved to Boston, where in 1893 he married Vida E. F. Marsh, with whom he had three children: Martin Albert, Grace Louise, and Winslow George. In 1896 he moved to Detroit and introduced there the ninety-nine-year lease. He worked as a representative for an eastern rubber company; while traveling for work, he spent years building up an inventory of unusual books in order to start a bookstore.

Albert Winslow Ryerson (1872–1931), proprietor of the Universal Book Stores.

He was an active Mason, claiming membership at Detroit's Free and
Accepted Masonic Lodge No. 2. He was also a knight of the Detroit Commandery No. 1 and held the 32° with the Michigan Sovereign Consistory of
the Ancient and Accepted Scottish Rite.[51] Through his Masonic Lodge, Ryerson met two men who were interested in partnering in his bookstore: Gordon
Hill and Hugh Jack. Gordon W. Hill (1883–1971) was a dental surgery student
from Windsor, Ontario, who took his Craft degrees at Detroit's Lotus Lodge
No. 549 in 1909 and shared Ryerson's esoteric interests.[52] Reverend Hugh Jack
(1864–1949) took his Craft degrees at Dearborn Lodge No. 172 in May 1906;
he was the Irish-born pastor of Central Presbyterian Church, and would
receive an honorary doctor of laws degree from Dubuque College in June
1918.[53] As Ryerson recalled his December 1917 purchase of Homer W. Adair's
bookstore at 131 Grand River Avenue:

> The Universal Book Store was formed for the purpose of handling all kinds
> of religious literature, all over the country, or the world, with everything
> that was odd or out of the way. We did not specialize in any one thing, to
> make it sacred, but bought anything that had to it any great amount of reli-
> gion, consequently the stores became phenomenally successful.[54]

Hill was president, Jack vice president, and Ryerson general manager.

Before long they opened two other branches in the city and a third in
Toledo, Ohio. In July 1918, Maryland native William A. Gibson (born c.
1874), an educator with the auto industry,[55] came onboard as their treasurer.
The following month, Ryerson took Gibson on a book-buying trip through
New York, Boston, Philadelphia, and Baltimore to stock up their new store
and show him the ropes. It was on this trip that they met Crowley.[56]

Ryerson was already familiar with Crowley's works and quite eager to meet
him when their travels brought them to New York in early October 1918.
Arranging a meeting, however, proved challenging. They arrived at what they
thought was Crowley's address only to discover that he had moved; although
the staff knew his new whereabouts, they were unwilling to say. Ultimately the
janitor directed them to Crowley's regular lunch spot at the Brevoort Hotel on
5th Avenue. There they left a note and, a couple of days later, received an invitation to meet with Crowley's intermediary, Jones, who would determine if
they could talk to Crowley. After meeting Jones, he took them downtown to
see Crowley face-to-face. These cloak-and-dagger activities, coupled with
Jones's attitude, convinced Gibson that Crowley "was under police surveillance;
he could not go out in the open because of the police."[57] Ryerson, however,
understood things differently:

> Mr. Crowley was the accredited agent of the British Government in the
> employ of their Secret Service Department. That was one of the reasons
> why it was always so difficult to get in touch with him. German spies were
> continually after him, and he would never allow anyone to see him, unless
> he first knew who they were.[58]

In addition to Crowley, Jones, Ryerson, and Gibson, two women also attended the meeting. One was "some sort of lecturer in connection with some Russian movement or propaganda,"[59] i.e. Marie Roehling. The other was English, the wife of a British vice consul.[60] Although unidentified, she would appear to be Helen Hall, wife of Frederick Hall: both arrived in New York on September 1, 1917.[61] According to Spence, Mr. Hall was posing as a journalist as a cover for his intelligence work out of Guy Gaunt's offices at 44 Whitehall.[62] As Crowley reported with respect to his own intelligence work, "There was a Temporary Gentleman named H...l in the British Military Mission with whom I had such dealings as is possible with the half-witted."[63] Completing the puzzle is a note attached to Crowley's painting from this period, *La Femme de Chez Moi:* "This cannot be described for fear of a consular scandal. For particulars, apply to Mr. Hall of the British Mission."[64]

Crowley's recollections indicate that more than bookselling was on the agenda; his OTO work had generated interest amongst Detroit Freemasons:

> The accounts of the new Rite made a great impression; and in particular, attracted the attention of the Supreme Grand Council, Sovereign Grand Inspectors General of the 33rd and Last Degree of the Scottish Rite in the Valley of Detroit, Mich. This Council deputed two Princes of the Royal Secret from the Consistory dependent from their jurisdiction to interview me in New York.[65]

Crowley "offered to reorganize freemasonry, to replace the pomposities and banalities of their ragbag of rituals by a simple, lucid and coherent system,"[66] and Ryerson believed his fellow Masons back in Detroit would be equally excited. Crowley, however, was uninterested in discussing the particulars of OTO with anyone but the highest-ranking Freemasons of his coterie, remarking, "It was of course impossible for me to deal with subordinates, and I refused to discuss the matter except with Sovereign Grand Inspectors General [33°]."[67]

In all, Ryerson had three meetings with Crowley early that October. The result was an agreement to market the next volume of *The Equinox,* an informal agreement to accept on consignment the Crowley rariora that John Quinn hadn't purchased, and an invitation for Crowley to come to Detroit. Ryerson embraced Thelema … evidently to the detriment of his marriage, as his wife, Vida, filed for divorce shortly thereafter, writing in her complaint:

> The defendant by his acts and declarations appears to be possessed of a religious conviction that he is not bound longer to recognize any of the conventions or formalities of society, but insists that he is free to conduct himself according to the dictates of his own conscience.[68]

Ryerson soon found a lover in Bertha Almira Bruce, a feisty and independent woman who shared his perspective on sexual freedom. Born in Kansas around 1889, she was proprietor of a rooming house on 381 West Grand Boulevard.[69] She was also the "financial angel" of the publishing venture, loaning money to both him and the Universal Book Stores to help with their projects.

While Ryerson returned to Detroit, Crowley made arrangements to print *The Equinox*. In November 1918 he received a quote from New York's DeVinne Press to typeset, print, and bind the volume for $4,050 with a promised delivery date of March 21, 1919: the vernal equinox, perfectly concluding the publication's "five years of silence." Crowley gave the printer the contents to set, and he had a cover design in mind. By January he was working out details of the inserts, which included color plates, black and white photographs, and line drawings. Since he was so busy with the printers, Crowley sent his Deputy Grand Master General (Jones) to Detroit to generate interest in *The Equinox* and prepare to establish OTO in Detroit.

The timing couldn't have been better. In early November, Gibson resigned as treasurer-accountant for the bookstore. Although he later pointed to his disapproval of Crowley and the way Ryerson "toadied" up to him,[70] the real reason, according to Ryerson, was that his demand for a half interest in the bookstore was denied. In response, Gibson emptied their bank accounts, took some of the merchandise, and started his own mail-order business.[71] Fortunately, Jones had just arrived in Detroit, representing the public accounting firm of A. E. Duncan. Ryerson hired him as their new accountant.

Jones wasted no time in getting to work. Arriving early on Sunday morning, February 16, 1919, he just made a 10:30 a.m. meeting with Ryerson at the store. Later that day, he took a furnished apartment at 108-75 Sibley Street. He began work the next morning, and after work met at the law offices of Frank T. Lodge (1859–1930). Born in Indiana, Lodge relocated to Michigan, where he became Past Grand Master of Michigan's Grand Lodge of Freemasonry, a Sovereign Grand Inspector General (33°) in the Scottish Rite, and was now the presumptive leader of the embryonic OTO group in Michigan. He was the author of *Why Weepest Thou?*,[72] which he wrote and published in 1913 in his grief over the loss of his wife, Gemma, twenty-seven years his junior. In terms reserved for those who angered or disappointed him, Crowley wrote, "Their leader, for all his fine talk, had only one real desire—to communicate with his dead wife, a silly smirking society waxwork, a pink-tea princess!"[73] Whatever Lodge's motives, Jones emerged from the office with a signed contract from the Universal Book Stores for two thousand copies of latest *Equinox*.

Ryerson initially planned to order five hundred copies of *The Equinox*. When Jones produced two hundred orders from OTO members as far away as Europe, Canada, and Mexico, this convinced Ryerson that they could sell more. Plus, the larger order would mean a bigger wholesale discount. He later scaled his offer to take the entire two-thousand-copy print down to a more reasonable one thousand copies. In exchange, the book would show "Universal Publishing Company" on the title page. The name was merely a pseudonym for the Universal Book Stores to facilitate mail-order sales.[74]

Jones's meeting with Lodge also concerned the establishment of a Supreme Grand Council of OTO. Discussions of this undertaking had begun with

Crowley as early as November 1918. Because OTO had its origins in high degree Freemasonry, however, the similarity of its rituals made the Detroit Masons uncomfortable. As Crowley recounted,

> However, when it came to the considerations of the practical details of the rituals to be worked, the general Council of the Scottish Rite could not see its way to tolerate them, on the ground that the symbolism in some places touched too nearly that of the orthodox Masonry of the Lodges.... In order to meet these views, it was suggested that I should re-write the rituals in an entirely new symbolism, which would in no way be considered as in competition with the accepted ritual of the Craft.[75]

Thus, on November 23, 1918, Jones had written to W. T. Smith, "There is a possibility that the rituals may be revised, and the Words of the first Two Degrees correctly given, and the Masonic connection made less in evidence."[76] In a letter to Jones that February, Crowley himself wrote, "I am then determined to revise the rituals of the OTO in such a sense that they will not conflict in any way with the Masonic ideals."[77]

After a while, Universal Book Stores' stockholders, initially enthusiastic about the deal, developed reservations because they didn't understand *The Equinox*'s contents; Ryerson assured them that, as an occult book, it would have a ready market. Just over two weeks before the release date, he reported to Crowley on March 4, 1919, "Our work is stirring up the opposition of the churches."[78] Crowley's light-hearted reply offered little solace:

> Cheer up little book store, don't you cry;
> You will be a barroom bye and bye,
> Where the Right Wine of Iacchus will be dispensed.[79]

Ryerson's mistress, Bertha Bruce, whom Crowley shared during his visits to Detroit, became his next Scarlet Woman. She was the presumptive priestess of the Detroiters' Gnostic Mass, and known locally as "Bruce of the OTO." To her, Crowley wrote the following lines:

Almira
To Bertha Almira Bruce

> Strong poison of thy mouth, my love, faint amber of thy breath,
> A fierce red wine that sucks me down a drunkard into death.
> Snake of my soul, thou leapest up to feed upon my brain
> That thrills and sobs wild music to the murder-lust refrain!
> Come, there's a tent pitched on the sand; the camel-bells ring clear;
> The stars are violent like young suns—I will to have thee here.
> Why linger in the moody north? There's welcome in the south.
> Strong poison of thy mouth, my love, strong poison of thy mouth.

Detroit, 1918[80]

Two summers later, while living in Cefalù, Crowley was still thinking of this "sexual and magical partner," counting her as the fifth of his five Scarlet

Women to date, writing "Almira, whose vocation I cannot doubt, seems to have failed altogether, unless she gave me that very non-attachment I so needed. But I cannot make out whether she is still in office."[81] That office would next be filled by Leah Hirsig (1883–1975).

On their first meeting, Hirsig was simply tagging along with her older sister, Marian Dockerill,[82] who had previously met AC at one of his lectures. As he described the lecture, "Among my hearers was only one bearing even a remote resemblance to the human species, an old lady painted to resemble the cover of a popular magazine."[83] This "old lady" was actually three years younger than Crowley and had previously been involved in several of what she would call "love cults." Her sister Leah was a thin woman with a boyish figure, standing five-foot-eight in height. Crowley felt an irresistible urge to draw close and kiss her on the lips. To his surprise, she offered no resistance. In fact, she liked it. While Crowley did his best to participate in a conversation with her sibling, he found himself unable to do much more than rain kisses upon Leah. Her sister nearly had to pry them apart when the time came to leave.

Brooklyn schoolteacher Leah Hirsig (1883–1975).

That was in the spring of 1918. Hirsig called on Crowley a second time three seasons later, on January 11, 1919. She was attending law classes at New York University and wanted Crowley's advice on Greenwich Village accommodations. This time they spoke, and Crowley learned she was thirty-six years old, born on April 9, 1883, at Trachselwald in Berne, Switzerland. She was the youngest of ten children born to Magdalena Lüginbühl (1845–1923) and Gottlieb Hirsig (1844–1933).[84] Her father was a drunkard and her mother fled with her children to New York City in April 1885 when Leah was age two. Her siblings now lived in places as remote as Switzerland, New York, Florida, and Argentina. At age twenty-one she became an elementary school teacher of music. When Crowley met her, she was teaching at Public School No. 40, located in the Bronx at Prospect Avenue and Jennings Street.[85] On November 13, 1917, she gave birth in Florida to Hans Hammond (1917–1985), whom Leah named after her brother. Hans Hammond was purportedly the son of Edward Jack Hammond, whom Leah said died around the same time.[86] Crowley, however, reports that the boy's father was actually someone named Edward Carter;[87] if so, then this person may well be related to Samuel S. Carter (1864–1951) of St. Petersburg, Florida, who shortly thereafter married Leah's sister, Fanny.[88] Whatever the story, Leah's son lived in Florida with his aunt and uncle while his mother sent what she could from her earnings to support him.

When they finished talking, Crowley walked up to Leah and undressed her. As when he first kissed her, she offered no resistance. "Let her be shameless before men," Crowley recalled Aiwass's description of the Scarlet Woman from *The Book of the Law*. He looked at her naked body: a lean-hipped, small-breasted, and slender form surmounted by a wedge-shaped face adorned with large warm eyes and supple lips. They made love, and afterward Crowley, feeling awkward with his forward approach, took up his sketchbook. "What shall I paint you as?" he asked.

"Paint me as a dead soul."

The night offered Crowley no repose. Images of Leah as a dead soul filled his restless mind. Sleepless, he left bed to examine his sketch and discovered that, standing the dead soul vertically, he saw it in a new light. In a spasm of inspiration, he worked till dawn to paint his *Dead Souls* on a trifold screen. The center panel depicted Leah, ghastly, emaciated, and green; a gross, admiring woman flanked her left and a huddled, agonized woman her right. Disfigured heads littered the bottom of all three screens. It pleased him.

In an interview with an Atlanta-area newspaper, Crowley gave a different account of this painting's genesis, doubtlessly tailored to make better copy:

> I walked up to a blank canvas one day and, standing very close to it, I placed the wet brush before it and shut my eyes. I had no preconceived idea of what I was going to paint. My hand simply moved automatically over the canvas.
>
> I don't know how long I worked in that subconscious way, but you can imagine my astonishment when I found that I had painted a likeness of a friend whom I hadn't seen in many years. It was that person's dead soul I had painted.[89]

Although lacking veracity (for example, Crowley hadn't yet known Leah for years), this version sheds new light on the *Dead Soul's* oft-repeated origin.

When Leah visited later that day, Crowley kissed and stripped her again, powerless to repress the attraction between them. He did a banishing ritual and consecrated her as his Scarlet Woman. Shortly thereafter, he and Leah moved into larger accommodations on the third floor of 63 Washington Square South, overlooking 5th Avenue.[90]

In February the press interviewed Crowley in his studio to promote an exhibition of his art at Greenwich Village's Liberal Club, the epicenter of New York's bohemian scene and dubbed "A Meeting Place for Those Interested in New Ideas." The *Fort Wayne Journal-Gazette* called him "The newest sensation in Greenwich Village." Neatly dressed and groomed, however, Crowley did not look like a stereotypical artist; and his art was anything but conventional. The *Syracuse Herald* captured the effect of first entering the room:

> The walls of this studio are covered with the wildest maelstrom of untamed and unrelated colors ever confined under one roof. They look like a collision between a Scandinavian sunset and a paint-as-you-please exhibit of the Independent Artists association.
>
> The effect is riotous, blinding—but not distressing, after one gets used to it. Mr. Crowley helps one to do that, with a dash of cognac, an imported cigarette and a delightful personality.

"Study art?" he told the reporter. "Never have and never intend to. What sort of artist am I? Oh, I don't know just what to call myself. I'd say, off-hand, that I was an old master, because I'm a painter mostly of dead souls." Although Crowley does not acknowledge the influence, his concept of painting "dead souls" is clearly influenced by the psychochromes or soul-paintings of Leon Engers Kennedy; Crowley's approach, however, was decidedly different.

His method involved approaching the canvas with his eyes closed; next, as he explained to the *Wilkes-Barre Times,* his hand, moving automatically, "wanders into the realm of dead souls and very frequently the result is the likeness of some living person." Elaborating, Crowley remarked, "But please, whatever you do, don't call me a cubist or a futurist or anything queer like that. I guess you might call me a subconscious impressionist, or something on that order. My art really is subconscious and automatic." When the *Evening World* magazine asked about the *Vanity Fair* biography that praised him as a great poet and explorer, Crowley lamented, "Alas, he had me all wrong. My only claim to distinction is as a painter."

Significantly, these interviews included descriptions of, and Crowley's comments on, several pieces from this period: *A Day Dream of Dead Hats* depicted "a lady asleep on a veranda, while the spirits of bygone bonnets pass over a mystic bridge on the heads of a dozen undressed ladies." Crowley explained, "Most women dream of dead bonnets when they take a nap." Of his watercolor *The Burmese Lady,* he remarked, "If you look at it closely you will discover that it is none other than our old friend, Bennett." Pointing to another, he said, "That fluffy one dancing on one toe is supposed to be the dead spirit of Eva Tanguay." Of his large three-paneled *Screen of the Dead Souls.* Crowley said,

> All those figures you see on it are dead souls in various stages of decomposition. That central figure in the middle panel is the queen of the dead souls. Of course you recognized the head looking over her shoulder. That's Hearst. Over her other shoulder is Oscar Wilde. I don't know how he got in there, because I really hate him. The parrot sitting on the head of the dead lady's soul in the third panel is one that belongs to Bob Chanler.[91]

He also had a story for his painting of French actress Madame Yorska[92] with her head thrown backward, a jeweled dagger in her throat:

> I got that impression at some affair given in Greenwich Village at which a certain violinist played. Madame Yorska was there. The violinist, in rendering one striking piece, asked that the lights be turned low. While he was playing I saw Madame Yorska throw her head back and close her eyes. I carried the impression of that long white throat home with me. I tried to sleep but couldn't. During the night I got up and going to the canvas closed my eyes and that picture was the result.

Asked about the dagger, Crowley explained "Oh, that long sweeping white line of throat had to be cut somewhere, and I couldn't think of any better way to cut a throat than with a dagger. So I stuck the knife into it. Rather good effect, I think." Other works on display for the press included *Ella Wheeler Wilcox and the Swami* ("One of my best works, that"), *Is This the Face That Launched a Thousand Ships?* ("something I did in rather a hurry"),[93] and *Young Bolshevik Girl with Wart Looking at Trotsky.* "My pictures look more beautiful," Crowley instructed, "if you look at them with your eyes closed."[94]

Limousines carried uptown passengers to the premiere of Crowley's parade of grotesque figures and landscapes in the salon. Here, they found the smiling artist decked out in a lemon waistcoat with knickers. While viewers remarked ambiguously, "Oh, how symbolic!" even the conservative members of the club, wary of hosting someone as notorious as Crowley, could find nothing immoral or offensive in the twenty-three pencil and chalk drawings, forty-eight watercolors, and twenty oils.

"Dear Mr. Crowley," an older woman asked about the piece titled *May Morn*, "won't you please explain the meaning of this picture?" Set in a large field, the painting depicted an ecstatic woman dancer, a corpse hanging by a noose from a dead tree, and a bearded figure peeking from behind the tree. It was Crowley's interpretation of the demise of Christianity.

"Certainly, madam. The painting represents the dawn of a day following a witches' celebration as described in *Faust*. The witch is hanged, as she deserves, and the satyr looks out from behind a tree. In the background, all is a beautiful spring and a nymph dances joyously to the piping of a shepherd."

Satisfied, she smiled and replied, "How very charming!"[95]

Back at the Universal Book Stores, Jones was in charge of sales and marketing
for *The Equinox*. He did his best to stir up interest in Thelema and the works of
the Master Therion, giving lectures for sympathetic audiences. The Friday after
his arrival in February, Jones gave a talk on kabbalah to the TS. He soon started
a Sunday afternoon study group on the then-unpublished *Liber Aleph*. He also
began a series of weekly Monday lectures at the Universal Book Stores, beginning with a lesson on astral journeys. He promoted these talks with a flyer
whose flipside advertised *The Equinox*.[96] In addition, he began holding private
meetings at his apartment on other weeknights. Before long he was teaching
four days out of the week. On one Friday night, he lectured on "Eastern and
Western Methods of Attainment" to a crowd of 150 at the Rosebud Club.[97]
Another speaker at the store's Woodward Avenue location was a man named
Russell;[98] this may well have been C. F. Russell, who is recorded in the 1920
census as living at the same address as Jones.

The official organ of the A∴A∴ proclaimed the Law of Thelema at the
price of $6.66 per copy when Volume III, Number 1 of *The Equinox* went on
sale that spring. Nicknamed the "blue *Equinox*" for the color of its cover, the
book contained, according to Crowley, "a complete programme of my proposed Operation to initiate, emancipate and relieve mankind,"[99] including a
syllabus of A∴A∴ instructions, various tracts on Thelema, and many organizational and historical documents of OTO. Among these was "Liber LII," the
revised OTO Manifesto, which Crowley considered singularly important.

> Liber LII was difficult to compose, but I was so sick of the stacks of diplo-
> mas that people sent me from all parts of the world it was plainly unprac-
> tical. So I did what the Alexandria crowd did with all the confused and
> confusing religions of the period: lumped them anyhow and called it
> Christianity.[100]

The issue also contained "Hymn to Pan," "The Sevenfold Sacrament," "The
Book of the Heart Girt with the Serpent," and the Gnostic Mass. Corresponding to "The Temple of Solomon the King" from the first volume of *The Equinox* was "A Master of the Temple," the first installment of an account of Frater
Achad's magical career up to the grade of Magister Templi (8°=3□). Achad also
contributed the essay, "Stepping out of the Old Aeon into the New." Finally,
the supplement contained H. P. Blavatsky's *The Voice of the Silence,* with Crowley's commentary. As he wrote about this important book:

> *The Voice of the Silence* is the only Theosophical publication of the slightest
> literary distinction or even of occult merit. This new edition is far more
> valuable to students than any previously published because the meaning of
> the treatise is for the first time made plain by the commentary of Frater
> O.M. No Theosophist can afford to miss buying a copy.[101]

Crowley hoped—in vain—to issue a sixty-cent version through E. P. Dutton.

The issue also contained two color plates: one was a portrait of Crowley in his robes, painted by Leon Engers Kennedy. The *New York Times Book Review* described it as follows:

> It [*The Equinox*] starts with a portrait of the most occult of all the occult, the innermost of all the Inwards, the Master Therion, otherwise known as To Mega Therion, which is to say The Big Brute.... The Big Brute is not very formidable looking: he sits half way in and half way out of a scarlet kimono before a blaze of yellow light, contemplating something firmly clutched between thumb and finger which seems most plausibly to be a hair from a head fast growing bald.[102]

Portrait of Aleister Crowley by Leon Engers Kennedy from *The Equinox* III(1).

The other was Crowley's "May Morn." Contrary to the sanitized description that the artist had offered at his exhibit, *The Equinox* described it thus:

> The picture is symbolical of the New Æon. From the blasted stump of dogma, the poison oak of 'original sin,' is hanged the hag with dyed and bloody hair, Christianity.... The satyr [is] a portrait of Frater D.D.S., one of the Teachers of The Master Therion.... The Shepherd and the Nymph in the background represent the spontaneous outburst of the music of

sound and motion caused by the release of the Children of the New Æon
from the curse of the dogma of Original Sin, and other priestly bogies.

After reading this description, the members of the Liberal Club were horrified,
excitedly contemplating the appropriate response. Although one piped in,
"Burn them," cooler heads prevailed. They stripped Crowley's paintings from
the walls and phoned him with instructions to retrieve his pictures immediately.

Optimism ran high on the heels of the book's release. Ryerson reported
that "Brentano's in New York gave *The Equinox* a very nice display and they
sent us some money for the sale of it afterwards."[103] Jones also celebrated the
book's release by dining with eleven others at the Fellow Crafter's Club.[104]
After psychical researcher Hereward Carrington (1880–1958) called the first
volume of *The Equinox* "a veritable mine of occult lore, and real knowledge" in
an article on "What Is the Best 'Psychical' Literature?" Crowley presented a
copy of the new issue to the American Society for Psychical Research.[105]

Crowley, in fact, got to know Carrington when he first arrived in America.
As Carrington recounts,

> It was soon after World War I started that I received a visit from the most
> remarkable man I have ever known.… My visitor brought with him a let-
> ter of introduction from the Hon. Everard Feilding, then Secretary of the
> Society for Psychical Research. It read:
>> *This will introduce to you Aleister Crowley, poet, sage, mountain climber and
>> general lunatic. I am sure you will have much in common.*[106]

They indeed had much in common: both Feilding and Carrington had tested
Italian spiritualist medium Eusapia Palladino, and Crowley—based on Feilding's
report—had had a sitting with her when he and Mary Desti were in Naples.
Crowley was furthermore interested in Carrington's scientific approach to psychic science, noting he "boasts that he has explained every single 'sealed letter
reading' that has come under his notice."[107] Through Carrington, Crowley lectured under the auspices of "a particularly transparent charlatan named [Chris-
tian P.] Christensen, who worked the sealed letter swindle with a crudity that
paid a very poor compliment to his audience";[108] significantly, this was the lecture at which he met Leah Hirsig's sister. Finally, Carrington saw Crowley to
the port when he left America:

> I saw Crowley off on the boat when he sailed. He had not been a "suc-
> cess" in this country, as he had in Europe, and, while expressing my regret
> at this, I also reminded him that this was largely his own fault. His parting
> words—his last shot as he went down the gang-plank—were "Well, what
> can you expect of a country which accepts Ella Wheeler Wilcox as its
> greatest poet!"[109]

Around this time, Jones met with Lodge at the house of Dr. Frank E. Bowman (1873–1947), another of the prospective Detroit Thelemic circle who had
taken his Craft degrees a dozen years earlier at Oriental Lodge No. 240.[110] A

Canadian-born naturalized citizen, he was a physician and surgeon with offices on Kenilworth in Detroit.[111] Of him, Crowley wrote:

> The best of the crowd was a young doctor who had sufficient sense to see how stupid the rest were, to disdain the bluff of the advertising adepts, and to realize that genuine magicians were necessarily gentlemen and scholars. He felt himself utterly lost in the darkness of Detroit, but despaired of mending the matter by setting forth to seek the Graal without guidance.... Pluck would have pulled him through in the long run; as Blake said, "if the fool would persist in his folly he would become wise."[112]

Anxious to proceed with establishing a Supreme Grand Council for the Lake Section of the United States, as well as the Great Lakes Council VII° of OTO, Lodge and Bowman paid Crowley's $100 fare to Detroit. To prepare, Crowley sent revised initiation rituals to Jones, who in turn instructed Lodge that "a Meeting of the Grand Council be called at an early date to discuss the details of the establishment of an Oasis in this City of Detroit and arrange for the production of this Degree as soon as possible." [113]

After Crowley's arrival, according to Ryerson, "a Supreme Grand Council got together at the D[etroit] A[thletic] C[lub], and I think then it was formed, tentatively, if the ritual be re-written and if drafted and accepted." This meeting took place on April 13, 1919. Of these negotiations, Crowley later reflected, "Even their compact group was torn by bitter jealousies."[114] Neither Ryerson nor Hill were invited, causing considerable rancor. As Ryerson noted,

> This is what started the rupture between Dr. Hill and Mr. Crowley.... Because of the book store's officers [not] being a part of it, Dr. Hill took great exception and thought that inasmuch as we were going to market the literature of the Order, someone of us ought to be represented, and he made some very terse comments about it and Crowley in the store here. And the result of it all was that Dr. Hill said, "Well, we won't handle your books" and he then tried to cancel the order, and made a mess of it generally, and that started the fuss between them.[115]

Hill would ultimately resign in January 1920 as president of Universal Book Stores and burn his copy of *The Equinox*.[116]

During this visit, Crowley also affiliated eight Detroit Masons to OTO. "Affiliation" indicated that no initiation was performed, but the members were formally accorded a rank in OTO commensurate with their degree in Freemasonry. In addition to Lodge, Ryerson, and Bowman, the other men signing on at this time included Dr. C. P. Sibley, C. Y. Smith, W. H. Bogrand, George Jarvis, and Albert A. Stibbard.[117] U.S. District Attorney Frank Murphy would later comment, "They are big men. The mention of their names would immediately bring on a scandal."[118]

Dr. Cedric Putnam Sibley (b. 1886)[119] was the second of five children born in Bennington, Vermont, to Edward L. Sibley and Delia A. Putnam. A surgeon in Cleveland, Ohio, who moved to a private practice in Detroit's Kresge Building until he left for Vienna in June 1914—the same month that

Archduke Franz Ferdinand's assassination triggered the start of the Great War—on a mission to help Austria's wounded.[120] He currently worked for Parke-Davis Pharmaceuticals, whose facility on the Detroit River Crowley had visited:

> Parke Davis were charming and showed me over their wonderful chemical works. They had installed countless and ingenious devices for conduction the processes involved in manufacture by machinery. Many of these produced effects of exquisite beauty of a land till then dreamed of in my philosophy. A great mass of pills in a highly polished and rapidly revolving receiver was infinitely fascinating to watch. The spheres tumbled over each other with a rhythmical rise and fall in a rhythm which sang to the soul.
>
> They were kind enough to interest themselves in my researches in Anhalonium Lewinii and made me some special preparations on the lines indicated by my experience which proved greatly superior to previous preparations.[121]

If Sibley prepared the peyote, Crowley did not recall him kindly:

> Their second string was a doctor, who spent sleepless nights sweating with shame and sentimentality in an agony of anxiety as to whether it was his duty to get divorced in order to marry a white-haired spinster, half-crazy with the pain of cancer, with whom he had no sexual relation at all, but an overwhelming obsession that she was his sister-soul, his mystic mate, his psychic partner and his Ouija Wife.[122]

Insurance salesman Charles Yale Smith was born in Algonac, Michigan, in 1862 to Thomas and Rowena Smith. His mother was descended from Yale University founder Elihu Yale, whence Smith's middle name. Schooled in Alpena, Michigan, he married Eugenia Wilson of Detroit in 1901 and settled on a career in insurance, in whose circles he became well known. He was also a prominent Mason, with memberships in Damascus Commandery of the Knights Templar (York Rite), the Michigan Sovereign Consistory (Scottish Rite), and the Moslem Temple of the Mystic Shrine.[123]

William Henry Bogrand (1873–1949) was born in Munsing, Michigan, to Elias Bogrand and Harriet Harris. At age nineteen, he married Angeline Frost in neighboring Windsor, Ontario; the marriage did not last, as the 1900 census shows him married to a woman six years his senior named Hattie. He worked as a house painter, and as an electrician's helper with the Electrical Construction Co. on Grand River Avenue. He took his Masonic initiations at Friendship-Lincoln Lodge No. 417 in September and October 1903.[124]

Albert Alexander Stibbard was born in York, Ontario, to farmer John Sheldrake Stibbard and Mary Collings in 1875, making him Crowley's age. He was a builder with the Reliable Construction Co., applied for U.S. citizenship in 1918, and his wife's name was Elisabeth.[125]

Finally, George Jarvis was born in Ovid, Michigan, on July 15, 1873, taking his three Masonic Craft initiations at Ovid Lodge No. 127 in April, May, and October 1909.[126]

As Crowley's relationship with Leah entered rough waters that May, he culti-vated other paramours. He wrote to Helen Westley, the Snake, proposing mar-riage; she had scarcely received the letter when she declined and Crowley reconsidered. He grew more interested in American actress Sarah Jane Wolfe (1875–1958), a St. Petersburg, Pennsylvania, native who, after ten years as a college-trained stenographer, changed careers after an attack of neuritis in her right arm. She moved to Hollywood in 1910 and became an actress, playing supporting roles—mostly mothers—in more than forty early silent movies, primarily with the Pioneer Picture Company, including some with Mary Pick-ford.[127] Coincidentally, Wolfe played in the 1917 version of *Rebecca of Sunny-brook Farm,* while Westley would go on to appear in the 1938 remake.

Wolfe became interested in the occult in 1913 when she received a copy of Franz Hartmann's *Magic, White and Black* (1889). In 1917, she turned from her Ouija board to *The Equinox* and *Book Four* on the advice of Sheridan Bickers, an early A∴A∴ student who had relocated to California and become Crowley's West Coast representative. Achieving success in *pranayama* and astral visions—which included one of the Master himself—she contacted Crowley through *The International.* He responded by putting her back in touch with Bickers; but she wrote again and began corresponding directly with AC about her visions.[128]

In June, Leah learned she was pregnant with Crowley's child. This was happy news to AC, as the Secret Chiefs had taken his first child and Rose his second, and neither Jeanne Foster nor Ratan Devi bore him an heir. They rec-onciled promptly.

When Crowley interrupted a Magical Retirement on Montauk Point at the eastern extremity of Long Island and returned to New York to prepare the sec-ond new issue of *The Equinox,* a manuscript by Frater Achad was awaiting him. *Liber 31* stunned him with its revelation of a major key to *The Book of the Law* that Jones had discovered in the winter of 1917. His exegesis, briefly, was this: the Hebrew word for God, *El,* numbered thrity-one, and a trinity of thirty-ones, referring to the supernal triad of the kabbalistic Tree of Life, totaled ninety-three, the value of Thelema. *The Book of the Law* itself implied this triad with references to "the threefold book of Law" and "Three Grades." Even the numbers of the tarot cards attributed to these three grades—IX (The Hermit), VI (The Lovers), and XVI (The Tower)—added to thirty-one.

The important twist came from noting that *El,* spelled backward, meant "not." This notion of reversibility was paramount in religious and magical prac-tice. When Hadit asked, "Is God to live in a dog?"[129] he alluded to the princi-ple; so too did Achad when altering his motto from V.I.O. to O.I.V.V.I.O. As synchronicity would have it, Achad, the Hebrew word for "one," had a numer-ical value of thirteen, which was the reverse of thirty-one. Crowley had also applied this idea to derive the XI° by a "reversal" of OTO's IX° formula of sex magick, and Austin Spare used it in his practice of "atavistic resurgence." Even the god name Allah, or AL-LA, incorporated it.

In Crowley's mind, Achad's thesis was further proof that *The Book of the Law* originated from an intelligence possessing knowledge greater than the instrument of its writing. Both Samuel Jacobs and Frater Achad found important keys and solutions that Crowley failed to see. In response to Achad's paper, Crowley changed the official name of *The Book of the Law* from *Liber L vel Legis* to *Liber AL vel Legis*.

Frater Achad, Charles Stansfeld Jones (1886–1950).

The Equinox proved to be a white elephant. It did not, as claimed, find a ready market. When a distributor in Louisville, Kentucky, reconsidered carrying it, Ryerson complained that "Norwood appears to have become concerned in the evil reports, apparently circulated by our enemies."[130] This was Joseph Norwood of the International Magian Society, who at this time also reported Crowley to the Bureau of Investigation as a possible spy. Things worsened when Crowley threatened to sue Universal Book Stores for payment on the rariora he had on consignment with them. On June 16, 1919, Ryerson pleaded with Crowley, stating that publication of *The Equinox* had alienated his family, friends, and business associates, and that a lawsuit would bankrupt his company. They reached an understanding, and work proceeded on the second issue, which would contain the continuation of "A Master of the Temple," a reprint of the Holy Book "Liber Liberi vel Lapidis Lazuli," "Liber XXI," and, as a special supplement, *The Gospel According to St. Bernard Shaw*.[131] Alas, this volume would never get beyond page proofs.[132]

When September 23 came and went without a new issue, Crowley resigned himself to a delay in the next *Equinox*. Despite this setback, the Great Work proceeded. Thus that same day, Crowley—together with Leah and Roddie Minor, the new and old Scarlet Women—received a Double Word: Ahitha-Alostrael, the combination of both women's magical names. For Leah, this established a succession between Crowley's magical and sexual partners. Thereafter the priest and whore, Beast and Babalon, swore to promulgate the Law of Thelema and establish somewhere an Abbey of Thelema.

Both prepared to pull up stakes. On October 2, Leah resigned from New York's public schools; a month later, she went to stay with her ailing sister in Switzerland. Meanwhile, that October Crowley traveled to Decatur, Georgia, to bid farewell to the Seabrooks. One evening, as he stayed on their farm, AC decided with Willie to try a variation on the Trappist monk vow of silence. For a week they agreed to confine their speech to a single nonsense syllable: wow. Although visitors thought them mad and Shep, the servant, was bewildered, they soon learned the importance of intonation, speaking several rudimentary things in "wow." The experiment culminated when Shep produced a gallon of moonshine; becoming very drunk, they conducted a sublime philosophical conversation in "wow," interrupted only when Kate, who had tolerated their eccentricity, insisted in the early morning hours that they go to bed. Although Seabrook thought the experience sublime, she believed they simply got drunk and barked at each other all night.[133]

During this time, Crowley wrote increasingly passionate letters to Jane Wolfe, addressing her as "Best beloved," "My darling child," and "Janet o' mine." He begged her to meet him in England before he joined Leah in Switzerland, but the best she could do was promise to visit him in June.

From Georgia, Crowley took a side trip to the Mammoth Caves of Kentucky, then returned to business. "I once went from Louisville to Detroit," he recalled, "I think, on a train called the Big Four, car number four, berth number four. It started at 4:44 p.m. from platform number four, and my ticket was numbered 44444. Meant nothing. Why should it be otherwise?"[134]

In November 1919, Crowley had another meeting with several Detroit-area Masons. Things did not go smoothly. It included only four of the original charter members, and "a certain prominent attorney was elected its head."[135] This was undoubtedly Frank T. Lodge. In response to this tentative organization of OTO, Crowley and Jones sponsored Ryerson's application for initiation (rather than mere affiliation) into OTO's preliminary degree on November 24,

1919. The Detroiters rehearsed "the ritual" of OTO one night in November, but it is unclear which ritual was rehearsed. In one place it was described as involving kneeling before a priestess,[136] suggesting the Gnostic Mass.

Regardless, trouble brewed. According to Ryerson, there was an argument about who should be the "Supreme Grand Cheese," with the result that OTO was never organized, no one was initiated, and no dues were paid. Nevertheless, Crowley entrusted *The Equinox* with "the bug house" in Detroit, who promised to bring out the next issue once funds became available; Achad became his business manager in absentia. Thus, in mid-December, Crowley left the United States, his book business in the hands of Achad and Ryerson, to chase even bigger dreams back to England. As he recalled, "When I returned to England at Christmas 1919, all my plans had gone to pieces owing to the dishonesty and treachery of a gang which was bullying into insanity my publisher in Detroit."[137] Unknown to Crowley, he had left a scandal brewing behind him.

The summer, fall, and winter months of 1920–1921 saw a great deal of shuffling amongst the Detroit Thelemites. On April 13, 1920, W. T. Smith was fired from his job, so he left Vancouver and joined Jones in Detroit to help with the Great Work. He soon found a job at the Detroit City Gas Company,[138] and remained there with Jones until they both moved to Chicago the following June. Russell, who had been in Detroit since May 1919, left that fall to join Crowley at the Abbey of Thelema in Sicily, arriving on November 21, 1920. Shortly after Russell left town, another Thelemite arrived in the person of Norman Mudd. He had taken a sabbatical from his professorial position in South Africa's Grey University College to seek out Crowley, whom he hadn't seen since his undergraduate days at Cambridge. Having purchased the latest *Equinox,* he went to Detroit but found only Jones and Smith. They treated their visiting Brother well, and Jones admitted him as a Neophyte into the A∴A∴[139] before he continued on to Cefalù finally to reunite with Crowley.

When, in September 1920, six tons of books arrived unexpectedly from Crowley, Jones was dumbstruck. He had to beg and borrow money to pay the substantial duty on these books, which he then placed in storage with Detroit's Leonard Warehouse. He sold them on the side through Universal Book Stores in an effort to recoup his money. When he moved to Chicago, he somehow lost track of these crates—this would become an irreconcilable bone of contention between him and Crowley—and they remained forgotten in Detroit until rediscovered in 1958. The bulk of this collection wound up in the Harry Ransom Humanities Research Center in Austin, Texas.

Jones and Smith left Detroit on March 26, 1921, for Chicago. There, on April 2, Jones opened a post office box under the name Collegium ad Spiritum Sanctum to sell Crowley's books and for putting out his own writing. Their decision to leave Detroit was well timed. Poor sales of *The Equinox* and the postponed (and ultimately abandoned) second issue prompted Ryerson to write to Crowley in January 1921 offering to exchange some unsold blue *Equinoxes* for older issues. In May 1921 the beleaguered Universal Book Stores were in bankruptcy court. Their creditors and trustees alleged that Ryerson single-handedly ruined the business by misappropriating as much as $35,000 for the publication of Crowley's book (a falsehood, as the actual printing costs were far less). As Grover L. Morden, counsel for the creditors and trustees, put it, "A business man should have known that the frontispiece of *The Equinox,* representing the hanging of Christianity on a gibbet, alone would have resulted in the failure of the publishing house."[140] Although Universal Book Stores was adjudicated bankrupt on September 6, 1921,[141] a series of hearings followed concerning these allegations.

These bankruptcy proceedings drew the attention of the press, and soon the tale of Ryerson, Crowley and OTO filled the front pages of the January and February 1922 newspapers in a series of exposés that Ryerson called "the mess in the press." The first of these articles exposed the existence of Detroit's "love cult," as the papers dubbed OTO. *The Equinox*'s naked priestess and Christianity hanged on a gibbet shocked casual readers. Dr. James W. Inches, Detroit police commissioner, remarked, "The sort of conduct described in *The Equinox* is common in Europe, but it will not do for Detroit."[142] Federal prosecutor Paul W. Voorheis was even more vocal:

> I consider this book the most remarkable and most degenerate book I have ever seen. I am going to stop the sale of it, and will instruct the police to seize every copy found in bookstores in this city. Furthermore, if a chapter of this organization exists in Detroit, we are going to wipe it out. The rites described in *The Equinox* calls for a sort of conduct we are not going to tolerate in Detroit, if we can prevent it.[143]

U.S. District Attorney Frank Murphy concurred, calling *The Equinox* "the most lascivious and libidinous book that has ever been published in the United States"[144] and "the most indecent and obscene book I ever have seen."[145] A divorcée soon recounted to Murphy under conditions of anonymity how *The Equinox* ruined her marriage:

> As a result of my husband's studying this book, my home is wrecked and I am forced to face the world alone and make my own living. Before this book was given to my husband, he was a good man, true, devoted and industrious. Night after night he studied this book. He wanted me to read it, but I soon saw that it was not fit even for beasts. I pleaded with him to give it up, but he refused to do so. Finally he began to go to meetings. He said the book gave him the right to go where he pleased, to do what he pleased and to love whom he pleased. As a result of my experiences, my health is so broken that, while I want to stamp out this book, my physician tells me that if I go into court that I will die, as my heart has been affected.[146]

In mere days, the news coverage snowballed from uncovering the existence of a secret society in the city of Detroit. On January 12, 1922, Voorheis received a search and seizure warrant, sealing all books in the basement storage facility of Universal Book Stores until they were either turned over to creditors or destroyed. Furthermore, Voorheis pointed out than anyone "publishing, causing to be published, printing, selling, exposing for sale, distributing, exhibiting or even having in his possession any book found to be hurtful to the public morals"[147] was subject to a $1,000 fine.

Four private investigators claimed they had been bribed to keep quiet, and "a prominent Detroit attorney" (presumably the same one who had earlier supplied Murphy with details regarding OTO's activities) found $700 on his desk with a note asking him to shut up. Upon inventorying the book stock, an even more troubling finding emerged: of 2,000 copies of *The Equinox* printed, only 1,100 became the property of Universal Book Stores. The whereabouts of the 900 other copies then became a concern.

When bankruptcy lawyer Morden showed Voorheis mail order records for *The Equinox,* the stakes got even higher. If the book was obscene, then sending or receiving it by mail was a federal offense. Postal inspector E. E. Fraser was brought in to determine whether postal laws had been violated, with Voorheis promising, if so, to convene a grand jury to subpoena and prosecute every single person who either produced or purchased the book.

The yellow press believed the answer came with the murder of motion picture director William Desmond Taylor (1872–1922). Investigators of this still-unsolved homicide discovered love letters from nineteen-year-old actress Mary Miles Minter (1902–1984) in Taylor's copy of *White Stains*. Furthermore, actresses Mabel Normand (1892–1930), questioned by police as the last person to see Taylor alive, admitted she was a recipient of *The Equinox*. Indeed, copies of *The Equinox* had circulated among many Hollywood luminaries (thanks, no doubt, to Crowley's Hollywood connections Sheridan Bickers and Jane Wolfe). This drove Grover Morden to wild conjecture:

> It is possible that the order has obtained a foothold in the picture colony and color is lent this theory by the frequent occurrence of alleged drug orgies among the movie stars.... Some drug crazed maniac or jealous woman of the O.T.O. may have been Taylor's mysterious assailant.... There are nearly 900 copies [of *The Equinox*] unaccounted for and there is every reason to believe that the most of these reached the Pacific coast.[148]

Credence was lent to this theory by the back inside cover of *The Equinox*. Just as the previous issue contained "Dead Waite," Crowley's premature obituary of occult author A. E. Waite, the latest issue contained yet another love note from Crowley to Waite. Titled "Arthur Back From Avalon," it described Waite's latest purported exploits by reproducing newspaper headlines about Grand Rapids, Michigan, dentist and murderer coincidentally named Arthur Waite:

> Waite Confesses; Gave Poison that Killed Millionaire Peck.
>
> Waite Confesses to Two Murders.
>
> Waite Grins in Telling How He Killed Victims.

To Michiganders for whom the Grand Rapids Waite was far more familiar, Crowley's send-up of the British writer was mistaken as sympathizing with the killer and advocating murder.

Because Ryerson, as the manager of the Universal Book Stores, was the only name the press could attach to the scandal, he was cast as the love cult's ringleader. As Crowley recounted,

> In Detroit, months after my return to Europe, they repeatedly raided poor half-crazed Ryerson's house in search of some evidence of the "Devil Worshipper's Mystic Love Cult" and of course found nothing; from which they concluded not my innocence, but that my pact with the devil contained a clause guaranteeing me against the discovery of my crimes. If any of those obstinate asses had possessed sufficient intelligence to study a single page of my writings, he would have seen at once what ridiculous rubbish were the accusations made against me by foul-minded and illiterate cheats whom I had never so much as met.[149]

The other members of the Great Lakes Council were understandably nervous about being subjected to the same treatment and having their names dragged through the mud. Thus a deal was worked out between Universal Book Stores' main stockholder: he would not sue (and, as a Mason, was forbidden from doing so anyway) provided Ryerson would not name any of the other members. He agreed, and in the end, bankruptcy referee George A. Marston ruled the questioning out of order.

At the end of 1922, Ryerson's name again filled headlines in a divorce case that served as a final cautionary tale regarding Detroit's love cult. Having parted from Bertha Bruce (they had filled out a marriage license but never filed it with the city), Ryerson, at age forty, wed eighteen-year-old model Mazie Mitchell on a thirty-day trial basis. When she sued for divorce twenty-nine days after their wedding, Ryerson's role in the scandal—and his ongoing interest in the ancients' worship of sex—returned to the headlines. She accused him of beating her. He accused her of being previously married.

Ryerson's last public statement about the OTO controversy in which he became embroiled is both succinct and tragic:

> I was not a part of the official organization nor never was invited, neither was I its head.... When trouble came and unsavory notoriety, I was made the "goat".... I have in my silence practically laid down my life for my friends, who have not shown any disposition to help me in this awful trouble, allowing me to stand the brunt of it all alone when they know I am entirely innocent of any complicity in the matter.
>
> My home has been completely ransacked at various intervals, my papers and books seized, my servants bribed, my library robbed, and I have been persecuted beyond endurance by people seeking evidence concerning the O.T.O. which has been in error dubbed a love cult and which never had any active existence in Detroit.[150]

He then moved to Georgia, remarried, and disappeared from public life until his 1931 death in Florida.[151] The drama in Detroit, however, was a prelude to an unprecedented "mess in the press" that would soon confront Crowley.

When James Branch Cabell expanded his short tale "Some Ladies and Jurgen" into the critically acclaimed libertine fantasy *Jurgen*—the most ambitious prose saga since Byron's *Don Juan*—Crowley and the blue *Equinox* became the center of another American scandal. After the book went through three printings, the public began crying out against the phallic symbolism of the hero's lance, staff, and sword. Outrage swelled until January 14, 1920, when John Sumner of the New York Society for the Suppression of Vice marched into Robert M. McBride and Co., seized the plates and all copies of *Jurgen,* and presented book department manager Guy Holt with a summons on charges of violating Section 1141 of New York's penal code.

Much of the controversy, it turned out, involved Chapter XXII, "As to a Veil He Broke," which Cabell based upon the Gnostic Mass. In this part of the book, Jurgen travels to the land of Cocaigne, whose pagan philosophy was "Do that which seems good to you." Here, Jurgen encounters Queen Anaitis and conducts what is essentially a Gnostic Mass:

> Then Jurgen raised Queen Anaitis so that she sat upon the altar, and that which was there before tumbled to the ground. Anaitis placed together the tips of her thumbs and other fingers, so that her hands made an open triangle....
>
> Then Anaitis said: "Yea, for I speak with the tongue of every woman, and I shine in the eyes of every woman, when the lance is lifted. To serve me is better than all else. When you invoke me with a heart wherein is kindled the serpent flame, if but for a moment, you will understand the delights of my garden, what joy unwordable pulsates therein, and how potent is the sole desire which uses all of a man. To serve me you will then be eager to surrender whatever else is in your life: and other pleasures you will take with your left hand, not thinking of them entirely: for I am the desire which uses all of a man, and so wastes nothing. And I accept you, I yearn toward you, I who am daughter and somewhat more than daughter to the Sun. I who am all pleasure, all ruin, and a drunkenness of the inmost sense, desire you."
>
> Now Jurgen held his lance erect before Anaitis....[152]

Crowley, duly flattered, called Cabell's work "the best book that has yet to come out of U.S.A." and "an incomparable splendour, a star of the first magnitude blazing in the firmament."[153] Cabell stood trial on October 16, 1922. Although John Quinn believed the case hopeless, Cabell successfully argued that the lance ceremony in his book had a real model, one that was already in print in the blue *Equinox.* Cabell was acquitted on October 19, and the resulting popularity transformed him into a literary giant.

CHAPTER FOURTEEN

The Abbey of Thelema

Crowley returned to his war-ravaged homeland just before Christmas, finding merrie olde England much like he remembered it: cold, damp and dreary. It was only the first misery he would find awaiting him. Having no place to live, he stayed with his aunt at the same Eton Lodge abode that he, in *The Fatherland,* had challenged Count Zeppelin to level. As he wrote at the time, "Not only has the war changed nothing in this house of my aunt's where I have roosted, but they haven't altered the position of a piece of furniture since Queen Victoria came to the throne."[1]

When the weather flared his chronic bronchitis into asthma, Crowley turned to his physician since 1898, Harold Batty Shaw (1866–1936), a specialist in consumption and chest diseases. A man of abnormal energy and strong opinions, Shaw was educated at Yorkshire College, Leeds, and University College, London. He gave the 1896 Goulstonian Lectures before the Royal College of Physicians a year before earning his MD degree and two years before joining the Royal College's ranks. His students at University College and Brompton Hospital found a dogmatic and precise teacher in him. His most famous patient was arguably Indian mathematical genius Srinivasa Ramanujan (1887–1920).[2] For Crowley, Shaw prescribed a common analgesic: heroin.[3] Despite his physician's credentials, Crowley became dependent on what was then a legal if not efficacious drug. Alas, passage of the British Dangerous Drug Act in 1921 would leave Crowley in a predicament, as will be seen later.

For now, he was destitute. The money and possessions he had put into storage before the war had vanished: doubtlessly, he believed, at the hands of Cowie and Waddell. Although Crowley inherited £3,000 on his mother's death, the provisions of his divorce settlement earmarked the money for a trust fund to be split between himself and his daughter, Lola Zaza.

When Crowley checked to see how his old friend Oscar Eckenstein had fared since the war had interrupted their planned attempt on Kangchenjunga, he found him a stodgy married man, and never saw him again. While AC's dis-

355

appointment is thinly veiled, the inescapable truth is that Eckenstein was sixty-one years old at this point, to Crowley's forty-four. Furthermore, in the years since their 1902 expedition, Eckenstein had remained far more active in the sport than Crowley: he continued climbing until at least 1912, when he was fifty-three. In 1908 he redesigned the crampon into the prototype from which modern designs derive; he invented an innovative short ice-ax; and he published technical articles on knot-tying and on the use of nails on climbing boots.[4] Eckenstein died of consumption shortly thereafter in 1921.

The final straw was the yellow press rolling out the welcome mat in its inimitable style. *John Bull* greeted Crowley with the headline:

Another Traitor Trounced
Career and Condemnation of the Notorious Aleister Crowley

The article read, "We await an assurance from the Home Office or the Foreign Office that steps are being taken to arrest the renegade or to prevent his infamous feet ever again polluting our shores."[5] Although the attack upset Crowley, he followed the I Ching's advice to do nothing. Fortunately, Commodore Gaunt interceded to advise authorities against taking action. Thus, while public opinion of Crowley remained low, nothing came of the outcry.

Knowing there had to be something better than this, feeling himself caught up in a new magical current, he wired Leah to meet him in Paris. She arrived eight months pregnant and with Hansi in tow. On January 11, a year after Leah first became the Scarlet Woman, they swore to build an Abbey of Thelema.

At this time, Leah described to AC how, on the boat from America, she befriended a French woman, Augustine Louise Hélène Fraux Shumway, nicknamed Ninette (1894–1990). Born in Decazeville, France, on June 9, 1894, she had lived in the United States since 1911, marrying American Howard C. Shumway in 1915, who died in an automobile accident before their son, Howard, was born in Boston on July 17, 1916. Ninette found work as a nursery governess, but with no family to help support her, she decided to leave Concord, Massachuestts, and return to her homeland, where she could leave Howard in the care of her parents, get a governess job, and possibly help with the reconstruction of France.[6] Crowley could practically read Leah's mind and agreed that they would need a governess for their new child. Besides, Howard would be an ideal playmate for Hansi. Recognizing another kismet in the Great Work, he arranged to meet Mrs. Shumway in Paris and offer her a position.

A pallid, wilted woman of twenty-five, she stood five feet, two inches tall with gray eyes and brown hair, listlessly holding her child's hand. Ninette Shumway reminded him of Ratan Devi. The boy was as white and lifeless as her, clinging tightly to his mother and crying incessantly. "They gave me the shock of my life," Crowley recalled.[7] Offered a job, Ninette, in well-spoken but imperfect English, accepted. She returned with Crowley to Fontainebleau, where they and Leah stayed in a rented house at 11-bis rue de Neuville. Here, Crowley pondered potential locations for his Abbey of Thelema.

Ninette Shumway (1894–1990) and her son, Howard.

On January 30, Crowley called on his old mistress, Jane Chéron, hoping to make love, smoke opium, and catch up with Walter Duranty. He struck out on all three counts: Duranty was still on assignment in Russia for the *New York Times,* and Chéron was disinclined to both sex and drugs. However, when Crowley prepared to leave empty-handed, Jane insisted, "Shut your eyes!" Then she unfurled a piece of cloth and told him he could look.

His stunned eyes beheld a four-foot silk appliqué reproduction of the Stele of Revealing. She explained that in February 1917 she and her "young man"—almost certainly Duranty—searched the south of France for a cure for opium addiction. Suffering from insomnia, she awoke one day after dozing off to realize she had drawn, in her sleep, a reproduction of the Stele. This so impressed her that she spent the next three months reproducing it in silk. Such a labor from a woman uninterested in magick also impressed Crowley. That this encounter should come at such a crucial time in his life was, to Crowley, an unmistakable sign that he was on the right course with this Abbey business.

AC's priapic tendencies did not end with Chéron. He continued writing passionate letters to the distant and faceless Jane Wolfe: "Now I see you before me shining in the dark—I turn out the lights for a little—I hold you closely—our light kindles—."[8] Impatient for her to visit, he arranged a meeting in Bou-Sâada on June 25, the place and date of his Magister Templi initiation.

Eventually, however, his desires found a more practical object: Ninette Shumway. It began innocently enough, the two taking long walks in the country while Leah convalesced. Crowley soon dubbed her "Beauty," and Shummy, as she was otherwise known, found him increasingly attractive. Then, one afternoon after lunch at the Barbison, Beauty and the Beast walked in the Fontainebleau forest. The vernal weather made them feel young, the wine made them giddy, and the danger made her irresistible. They chased each other through the glade and finally fell into each other's arms with a passionate clasp. Crowley and Shummy soon began doing sex magick to locate a suitable Abbey.

Curiously enough, Leah did not object. She knew that, as the Scarlet Woman, she was number one in Crowley's book. Furthermore, she understood the promiscuous interpretation of "Love under will" and found it was one Crowley encouraged without double standards. Ninette, however, brooded jealously and insecurely about sharing her man.

At 5 o'clock on the morning of Thursday, January 26, Leah's water broke. She went to the hospital in Fontainebleau and, after an easy labor, gave birth to a daughter at 12:05 that afternoon. She looked like her mother except for the mouth, which was unmistakably Crowley's. On March 8, Leah returned home from the hospital.

Ever the magician, AC named the baby Anne Lea—after the goddess of summer and the Scarlet Woman, respectively—thus giving her the monogram AL, the Hebrew name of God and the key to *The Book of the Law*. However, when little Howard declared during a walk in the forest, "I shall call her Poupée," the name (French for "doll") was so spontaneous and appropriate that they unanimously adopted it as her nickname.

Shortly after Poupée's birth, Ninette herself became pregnant.

Although the I Ching directed them to locate the Abbey in Cefalù, Italy, they lacked the money to do so. Thus, on March 21, Crowley took Leah and Poupée to London, where Leah stayed with AC's aunt and arranged finances with his lawyer; evidently, Crowley had £700 coming in another inheritance. He then fetched Shummy and "the brats" from France and proceeded toward Cefalù. He thought it a good omen that his train seat was number 31, a key value in *The Book of the Law*. The money arrived for them in Naples on March 30, allowing them to continue to their destination.

Cefalù was a small seaport with only one main street, located northwest of Sicily and thirty-seven miles from Palermo. In ancient times, when known as Cephaloedium, it allied with Carthage in 396 BC and was taken by the Moors in 858 AD. More recently, it was known for its marble quarries and the cathedral built by the great Norman hero Count Roger. Here, one night in a dingy hotel changed their lives. When Crowley swore not to stay another day in such despicable lodgings, Giordana Giosus overheard and told them he had a villa for rent. Crowley, again seeing fate's hand, agreed to view the place.

A sinuous path just beyond town wound up the mountainside to an eighteenth-century villa known as the Villa Santa Barbara. Located south of the rock of Cephaloedium and just beyond a Capuchin monastery, it faced the sea amid a field of grass, trees, and a garden. It was a single-story stone structure, encased in plaster and painted all white except for the red-tiled floor. Five rooms and a shelf-lined pantry flanked its large central room, which Crowley immediately saw as a temple.[9]

Crowley assessed the place rapidly. Despite a complete lack of plumbing, gas, and electricity, it had everything he needed: a temple, access to water, and rocks to climb. The size was ample. And near the building, Crowley noted two Persian nut trees; just as they were a sign for the Villa Caldarazzo in 1911, so in Crowley's mind were they good omens for Cefalù. He struck a deal on the spot to rent the Villa Santa Barbara as the Abbey of Thelema.

They moved in immediately and that evening blessed the grounds with an act of sex magick. "Salutation to the Gods and Goddesses of this place! May they grant us abundance of all good things, and inspire me to the creation of beauty,"[10] he wrote in his journal. And so the Inglesi, Signor Caroli, began to prepare the Abbey of Thelema. He dubbed the main building the "Whore's Cell," and turned the main room into a temple: he painted a circle on the floor and placed in its center an altar, a copy of the stele, *The Book of the Law*, numerous candles, and other implements. The Throne of the Beast sat in the east, facing the altar in the center of the room. The Scarlet Woman's throne sat across from this, in the west. Statues of various gods were placed around the room. The temple, according to Crowley's design, would be open to all students at the Abbey.

The children soon quit sniveling and became active, healthy boys, Hansi taking to swimming and Howie to chess. Crowley would approach the boys in the morning and point to the sky. "Up there is the sun. When it gets over *there*, you may come back." Thus he sent them off to play, and they would invariably return with fruits stolen from local farms or Sicilian bread given to them by the farmers. Equally often, one or both lost their clothes. And they were always full of stories of the day's adventures.

For Crowley, this was paradise.

The question "Why Cefalù?" naturally arises, and the answer lies in a confluence of several influences. One was the migration to Italy of the literati he admired. Much as he was an individualist, Crowley nevertheless emulated those he esteemed, and validated himself by comparison to them. Thus he modeled not only his poetic style but even the byline of *Aceldama* (1898) after Shelley; when he left Cambridge without a degree, he followed the footsteps of Byron, Shelley, Swinburne, and Tennyson; after introductions by Gerald Kelly, he became a fixture at Le Chat Blanc in Paris; and he followed Allan Bennett and Oscar Eckenstein to India. Years later, when commenting on being expelled from Italy, Crowley would remark tellingly, "Like Mr. H. G. Wells and many other distinguished Englishmen, my presence was not desired by Mussolini."[11]

Another impetus stemmed from his newfound love of art and the model presented by postimpressionist painter Paul Gauguin (1848–1903). Gauguin was a successful stockbroker whose pursuit of painting led him to abandon his career, wife, and children. In 1891, at age forty-three, he moved to Tahiti and married a native girl. He moved into a cottage that he called the "House of Carnal Pleasure" and filled it with his paintings. Similarly, Crowley, having himself squandered his fortune and divorced his wife, had, at age forty-four, moved to a remote villa he dubbed the "Whore's Cell" to pursue art. The influence of Gauguin is unmistakable; Crowley paid the painter a high honor by adding his name to the list of saints in his Gnostic Mass in 1921.[11] The versions published in *The International* (1918) and the blue *Equinox* (1919) do not contain his name, although subsequent editions do. Clearly, Crowley regarded Gauguin as a kindred spirit.

Crowley's works are relatively silent on the topic of Paul Gauguin; so what prompted this interest in the painter nearly twenty years after his death? Crowley did not say, although one possibility exists in W. Somerset Maugham's fictionalization of Gauguin's life, *The Moon and Sixpence* (1919), which had just come out. It is easy to imagine Crowley identifying with protagonist Charles Strickland, a man whose single-minded devotion to art ruined his finances and family and even drove his wife to suicide. Strickland's comment,

> "I don't want love.... I am a man, and sometimes I want a woman. When I've satisfied my passion I'm ready for other things. I can't overcome my desire, but I hate it; it imprisons my spirit; I look forward to the time when I shall be free from all desire and can give myself without hindrance to my work."[12]

is echoed epigrammatically by Crowley: "The stupidity of having had to waste uncounted priceless hours in chasing what ought to have been brought to the back door every evening with the milk!"[13] Crowley and Strickland even shared a passion for chess. Maugham's description of the artist's mural-covered walls in Tahiti is especially evocative:

> From floor to ceiling the walls were covered with a strange and elaborate composition. It was indescribably wonderful and mysterious. It took his breath away. It filled him with an emotion which he could not understand or analyse. He felt the awe and the delight which a man might feel who watched the beginning of a world. It was tremendous, sensual, passionate; and yet there was something horrible there, too, something which made him afraid. It was the work of a man who had delved into the hidden depths of nature and had discovered secrets which were beautiful and fearful too. It was the work of a man who knew things which it is unholy for men to know. There was something primeval there and terrible. It was not

human. It brought to his mind vague recollections of black magic. It was beautiful and obscene.[14]

Indeed, the 1921 diary entry which canonizes Gauguin reads, "It is easy enough to paint a wall to look like a jungle; but what about the furniture in the foreground? [...] So much for the description in *The Moon and Sixpence* of P[aul] G[auguin]'s house." There is an appealing symmetry in the author who modeled Oliver Haddo after Crowley later influencing Crowley to model himself after another of his characters: art imitating life, and life imitating art.

On April 14, Leah and Poupée arrived at the Abbey to complete the family. She and Crowley signed the lease to the villa as Sir Alastor de Kerval and Contessa Léa Harcourt. In this spiritual haven, they donned new names: Crowley became Beast; Leah was Alostrael, Virgin Guardian of the Sangraal; Ninette was Cypris; Howie and Hansi became Hermes and Dionysus. And Poupée, who arrived ill from England, drank goat's milk, which nourished Jupiter.

They quickly developed a schedule for work at the Abbey: every morning, Leah would rise, strike a gong, and proclaim the Law of Thelema. Everyone present, even the children, would respond with "Love is the law, love under will." Everyone would follow with the solar salutations of "Liber Resh" (to be practiced morning, noon, sunset, and midnight). Sitting down to a breakfast prepared by Ninette, they would "Say Will," which was Crowley's answer to grace. He would begin meals by rapping on the table to call all to attention. "Do what thou wilt shall be the whole of the Law," the diners would say. Crowley, in response, would ask, "What is thy will?"

"It is my will to eat and drink," came the reply.

"To what end?"

"That my body may be fortified thereby," came the reply.

"To what end?" he pressed on.

"That I may accomplish the Great Work."

With that, Crowley would declare, "Love is the law, love under will." This ritual—or some variation thereon—began the meal. They would then eat in contemplative silence. These progressive questions betrayed his father's influence, recalling Edward "Get-Right-with-God" Crowley's repeated use of the question "And then what?" to lead up to his own trademark statement.

Aside from these regimented tasks, the rules permitted individual work and study. Climbing, swimming, studying, and writing filled most days; Ninette, after finishing her housework, took long walks. And in keeping with his philosophy, Beast bought drugs from a Palermo pusher named Amatore and made them available to all residents of the Abbey; his goal was not to encourage drugs, but to make them so readily accessible that he removed all temptation.

With routine at the Abbey established, all that remained was to send invitations to his students.

Leah's arrival on April 14 left Ninette intensely bitter and jealous. In her experience, Leah had always been a convalescing and nonthreatening other woman, and even though she knew better, Ninette felt on top of the situation. She enjoyed having Beast all to herself while Leah was in England, but now the master bedroom belonged to Leah. The Virgin Guardian of the Sangraal commanded Beast's attention and affection, and Ninette felt rejected.

On April 20, less than a week after Leah's arrival, their ménage à trois slipped into an emotional morass. That night, all three got intoxicated and aroused; Beast, following an intense sexual performance, jokingly remarked, "You girls would wear out any man's tool, were it steel or stone. Would God that you were Lesbians and I could sleep alone!" Leah, taking the jibe good-heartedly, made mock overtures toward Ninette, who grabbed a thin cloak to cover her nakedness and dashed into the rain. Crowley cursed and pursued her, fearing what mischief she might discover in her recklessness. Meanwhile Leah fumed, seeing through Shummy's attention-getting ploy and knocking back some more liquor. Eventually she persuaded Howard to call for his mother.

An hour of searching finally uncovered Beauty, whom Beast convinced to return home. Ushering her into the Whore's Cell—past Leah, who cursed drunkenly at her—and into bed, Beast emerged to find Leah vomiting. He soothed her next. Finally, he produced his manuscript of the Tao Teh King and recited from it to return their minds to a higher plane. As he read, he smirked inwardly. "Next please! Let's all live up to 'Never dull where Crowley is.'"[15]

The following day, Poupée's health worsened visibly. Unable to absorb food, she was literally wasting away. This was precisely the augury which the I Ching had given for Poupée's birth: Hexagram XLI, Diminution. Beast consulted her progressed astrological chart and found Saturn and the sun both opposing Mars: this was bad, and he feared she might not live through the week. "I have been howling like a mad creature nearly all day," he recorded in his journal. "I want my epitaph to be, 'Half a woman made with half a god.'"[16]

To take his mind off his troubles, Beast immersed himself in writing and painting. If he was lucky, he slept at odd times, but in the main he suffered chronic insomnia. And, even though Poupée survived the next week without incident, Crowley's symptoms continued. This was because the insomnia was not due to stress but to his continuing abuse of heroin and cocaine.

Crowley soon found himself with two expectant "wives" when Leah became pregnant again that May.

On June 21, Leah was with Beast on a train to meet Jane Wolfe. However, he left her in Palermo and continued alone to his rendezvous in Tunis. Beast had become obsessed with the mystery of Jane Wolfe. Having reconsidered summoning Jane to a summer clime as inhospitable as Bou-Sâada's, he had wired her to meet him in Tunis instead. "I adore her name," he anticipated her arrival. "I hope she is hungry and cruel as a wolf." In his diary, he wrote,

I am hers.... I die that She may live.... I drown in delight at the thought that I who have been Master of the Universe should lie beneath Her feet, Her slave, Her victim, eager to be abased.[17]

His health failed in Tunis, and he recorded in his diary, "A most unpleasant day of severe illness. I think I may have been poisoned by reading Conan Doyle."[18] More likely, his illness stemmed from the same sanitary conditions at Cefalù that had given Leah dysentery a month earlier.

When the appointed day came and went without Jane Wolfe's arrival, Crowley filled himself with cocaine and wrote "Leah Sublime," a poem dedicated to his Scarlet Woman. While not as subtle or artistic as the poems he wrote for Rose, it certainly holds a unique place in Crowley's corpus, collecting all his filth into one poem. Its most memorable (and polite) lines were:

> Stab your demoniac
> Smile to my brain!
> Soak me in cognac
> Cunt and cocaine ...[19]

By July 3, Crowley impatiently scribbled in his diary, "I shall certainly not wait for more than two weeks for her, one only has to wait three for Syphilis herself." After a few more fruitless days, he gave up. Crowley returned to Cefalù on July 10.

At this time, Crowley was undergoing what Norman Mudd would later describe as the "mystery of filth," and Leah happily indulged his wishes. Thus, on July 22, Crowley experimented with masochism in a bedroom game wherein Leah became a dominant, menacing tyrant, exclaiming at Crowley:

> So low art thou—crawl to my floor-blackened feet, and call them snow-pure marble.... You dog! to your slaves' task! to your mock Love, you dog! You dirty dog! Do it, you dirty dog! To my soiled feet, lap them ...[20]

While the actions of consenting adults are a private matter, this incident is of biographical interest because it sheds light on his perspective. As Gerald Yorke stated about AC's sexuality: "Crowley didn't *enjoy* his perversions! He performed them to overcome his horror of them."[21] Thus he followed the path of thesis, antithesis, and synthesis to deprogram his mind of Victorian mores.[22]

Sitting in her Bou-Sâada hotel room, Jane Wolfe cursed Crowley's name. Having left home a month ago, she had still to reach her destination. Complicating matters was a cryptic cable from Palermo:

COMME CEFALU

Nobody could shed light on the missive. She had always said Los Angeles was the modern Athens, and it seemed preferable to the Mediterranean. An actor with the Pathé Motion Picture Company, a French company filming on loca-

tion in Bou-Sâada, finally provided the translation. "It is in English," he
remarked to her surprise. "It says 'Come Cefalù.'" Thus Jane made her way via
Algiers, Tunis, and Sicily to the Hotel des Palmes in Palermo. Directed to a
second-floor waiting room, she relaxed with a heavy sigh, closing her eyes and
resting her head in her palm. Forty days of delays and itinerary changes since
leaving Los Angeles left her exhausted.

Actress Jane Wolfe (1875–1958).

A man's high, thin voice pierced the silence. "Do what thou wilt shall be
the whole of the Law." She opened her eyes to find AC and Leah in the room
with her. In that instant, all their romantic illusions shattered.

Jane's first thought was "filth personified." Leah was unwashed and
ungroomed, with charcoal-blackened fingers. Crowley, with a striped suit,
walking stick, and hat, presented a more wholesome picture, but her clairvoyant sight presented her with a terrifying vision of a bird trapped in mud. Likewise, the actress made a disappointing first impression on Crowley. After
months of anticipating the arrival of his "movie star," he discovered she was
older than he anticipated; she was also more masculine, haggard, and unattractive than he had hoped. As he wrote in his diary, "I am like the girl who was to
meet a 'dark distinguished gentleman' and did, he was a nigger with one eye."[23]

Proceeding to the Abbey the next morning, Jane encountered more rude
surprises. It was as filthy as its inhabitants. Finding Ninette five months along in
her pregnancy with only one man in the Abbey, Jane deduced Crowley was the
father. Having come to Cefalù expecting to be Crowley's lover, she found the
job filled twice over … not that she *wanted* to be his lover, on closer inspection.

As a newcomer to the Abbey, Jane had three days to adjust to the schedule. She stayed for a time in the Whore's Cell, but ultimately ended up in the Abbey's second building. Called the Umbilicus, it was the nursery where Ninette stayed, babysitting and cooking. After three days, Crowley put Jane on a rigorous schedule of yogic exercises and had her typing his manuscripts. Despite his constantly belittling her previous visions—particularly her Persian Master named Schmidt—Jane finally understood that Beast was merely breaking down her preconceptions. After a week or so, she relaxed enough for a new task: to help paint the Chamber of Nightmares.

La Chambre des Cauchemars was Crowley's name for the main ritual room after decorating it with three grotesque and disturbing murals. Its north wall, dubbed *La Nature Malade,* depicted hell as "false intellectual and moral consciousness"; it bore scenes such as "Japanese Devil-Boy Insulting Visitors," "Faithful on the Gallows" and "The Long-Legged Lesbians." The wall depicting heaven, subtitled "The Equinox of the Gods," encapsulated the A∴A∴ teachings and Holy Books with the theme "Aiwass gave Will as a Law to Mankind through the mind of The Beast 666." The mural of earth, finally, depicted love in terms of the base desires it spawned. "The purpose of these pictures is to enable people, by contemplation, to purify their minds,"[24] Crowley wrote. Once unaffected by this lurid sensuality, Crowley believed, the mind was clear of the life-negative taboos and mores of Judeo-Christian culture.

"There, in the corner, are Lesbians as large as life," Crowley would tell visitors. "Why do you feel shocked and turn away: or perhaps overtly turn to look again? Because, though you may have thought of such things, you have been afraid to face them. Drag all such thoughts into the light … 'tis only your mind that feels any wrong.… Freud endeavors to break down such complexes in order to put the subconscious mind into a bourgeois respectability. That is wrong—the complexes should be broken down to give the sub-conscious will a chance to express itself freely.…"[25]

Poupée became so sick that Leah took her to the doctor in Palermo on October 8. Although the parents desperately attempted sex magick to cure her, Beast was so grief-stricken that he broke off the operation. On October 11, Poupée went into the hospital. The following day, Crowley passed what he considered his saddest birthday. Waiting and worrying, he returned to Cefalù and tried to lose himself in poetry and painting. It was useless.

On October 14, Leah came home alone. Her heavy sobs said everything. Shattered by grief, Crowley led her into the main temple and pronounced a blessing on Poupée's soul. In her diary, Leah recorded the tragedy:

> A Thelemite doesn't need to die with a doctor poking at him. He finishes up what he has to do and then dies. That's what Poupée did. She didn't

pay attention to anything or anybody. Her eyes grew filmy and she died with a grin on her face. Such a wise grin.[26]

Leah was inconsolable, her grief impenetrable. She would not heed Beast's advice to rest and began suffering nocturnal pains, followed on October 18 by heavy spotting. Although Beast sent Ninette after a midwife, it was too late. Besides losing her daughter, Leah had miscarried. She was so far along in her pregnancy that they had to call in a surgeon. "I stood as if petrified in the studio while in the next room the surgeon drew forth the dead from the living," Crowley wrote. Learning that the unborn child would have been a boy, he added, "My brain was benumbed. It was dead except in one part where slowly revolved a senseless wheel of pain."[27] In the end it was Leah, suffering physical and psychological loss, who mustered her remarkable inner strength to urge Beast to persevere in the Great Work despite the tragedy.

When Leah noticed that Ninette, who'd always envied her place beside Beast, experienced an uncomplicated pregnancy, she convinced herself that Ninette had caused her misfortune. On November 3, after another of Leah's tirades, Beast humored her and skimmed through Ninette's diary. (At the Abbey, all residents made their magical records available to Beast for perusal and comment.) What he read made him feel physically ill. Her diary's hostility and jealousy convinced him that Ninette's negativity had indeed claimed the lives of both infants. He entered the temple and exorcized the shadow. Banishment was the only solution, so he left a note for Beauty:

Do what thou wilt shall be the whole of the Law.

> Initiation purges. There is excreted a stench and a pestilence. In your case two have been killed outright, and the rest made ill. There are signs that the process may lead to purification and things made safe within a short time. But we cannot risk further damage; if the hate is still in course, it had better coil back on its source. Keep your diary going carefully. Go and live in Cefalù alone; go to the hospital alone; the day before you come out send up your diary, and I will reconsider things. I shall hope to see the ulcers healing. Do not answer this; simply do as I say.

Love is the law, love under will.

666[28]

On November 5, Ninette left the Abbey and went into Palermo to have her baby. She gave birth on Friday, November 26, to a daughter, whom Crowley named Astarte Lulu Panthea; he readmitted Shummy to the Abbey.

C. F. Russell arrived at the Abbey on November 21, full of stories of his exploits of the last two years: how, as a Pharmacist Mate First Class aboard the USS *Reina Mercedes* in Annapolis, he injected forty grains of cocaine on November 24, 1918, as a magical experiment, resulting in his December 12 discharge;[29] how he made his way to Detroit in May 1919 and helped with the

Great Work there; and how he applied for a passport on October 11, 1920—with Ryerson vouching for him—so he could come to Italy for study.[30] His sailor's coarseness estranged him from the residents, prompting Beast to describe him as "a husk of 100% American vulgarity which conceals a Great Adept."[31] Jane Wolfe was not so kind:

> From the way Russell has done the odd jobs around here, I am bound to say he either lacks intelligence, lives in another world entirely … or does not care especially how a thing is done.[32]

Crowley nevertheless saw his potential. Shortly after arriving at the Abbey, he became a Probationer in the A∴A∴ as Frater Genesthai, and Beast prepared to conduct, with him and Leah, the first major magical operation since 1918's Amalantrah Working.

The Cephaloedium Working had three goals: to inspire Crowley to finish writing a commentary on *The Book of the Law;* to invoke Hermes and Apollo; and to obtain true understanding of the tarot trump "The Tower." The participants included Leah, who ceremonially wore a scarlet Abbai girt with a sword; Russell, who wore a black robe with a gold lining; and Crowley, who wore orange and bore a Janus-headed wand entwined with four serpents. They began with a banquet of fish and yellow wine, then, after appropriate banishings, purifications and consecrations, took an oath:

> Hear all that we, *To Mega Therion* 9°=2□ A∴A∴ The Beast; Alostrael, The Scarlet Woman; and *Genesthai* 0°=0□ A∴A∴ do now in The Presence of TAHUTI most solemnly swear to devote ourselves to the Establishment of *The Book of the Law* as authored by Aiwaz 93 to 666 by the Way of the Cephaloedium Working as in the record thereof it hath been written.

After invoking the gods by song and dance in the tradition of the Paris Working, AC and Leah disrobed and got Russell high on ether. Their intent was to coax him to make love to Crowley, who would thereafter make love to Leah; scryings and prophecies would follow thereafter. Unfortunately, the plan failed. As Russell recalled,

> Your Circean enchantment didn't give me a bone-on—add that Ethyl Ether is no aphrodisiac—you were in bed between me and the Virgin (sic) Guardian of the Sangraal who had to lean over you to do what she did and you played down in the Record—in fact more than merely to shake the hand of a stranger *faire gonfler son andouille.*[33]

The working ultimately ended on a sour note, Beast deeming it a failure on January 20, 1921.

With the unhappy end of the Cephaloedium Working, Beast and Leah traveled to Palermo. With a vow to "give the body to whoever should desire it,"[34] the lovers parted, AC heading to Paris to recruit new students while Leah stayed in town with their landlord, Baron Carlo la Calce. Monsieur Bourcier again let

Crowley stay on credit in his Hôtel de Blois at 50 rue Vavin. Nina Hamnett, who saw Crowley regularly at this time, found him despondent and miserable, shattered by Poupée's death. After passing the hospital where Poupée had been born, he retreated to the forest of Fontainebleau, a place that had always been special to him, and broke down sobbing.

Hamnett introduced Crowley to budding writer and poet Mary Francis Butts (1890–1937), who contributed to *The Little Review* and *The Transatlantic Review*. One might call her literary and artistic interests hereditary: her grandfather, Thomas Butts, had been a patron of poet, artist, and Gnostic Catholic Saint William Blake (1757–1827).[35] Her father, likewise, befriended several pre-Raphaelite artists. Butts and Crowley shared a lot in common: Mary was very close to her father, who died in 1904 when she was thirteen. Like Crowley, she lived on a small annuity from her inheritance but tended to over-spend. Also like Crowley, she attended college (from 1909 to 1912) without completing a degree. After a string of lesbian relationships during the war years, Butts married Jewish writer and publisher John Rodker (1894–1955) in 1918, and had a child in November 1920. She had a serious and long-standing interest in the occult and had even spent time the previous year studying Éliphas Lévi's works at the British Museum. Fair and winnowy, her beaming blue eyes, fiery red hair, and boundless energy nevertheless made her seem immense. Of her, Crowley later wrote, "My relations with her were never very intimate. We enjoyed exchanging views."[36]

When she met Crowley in 1921 she was in the process of separating from her husband and forging an emotional and spiritual bond with writer James Alexander Cecil Maitland (d. 1926). Maitland was "a lovable but dilapidated Scotch 'aristocrat'"[37] whose grandfather worked on the Revised Version of the Bible, and whose father was a Catholic clergyman. Interested in magic and the occult from an early age, he was known to draw chalk circles on the floor of his Belsize Park apartment and attempt various conjurations. Butts and Maitland had, the previous year, ritually bonded by cutting crosses on each other's wrists, sucking and kissing the other's wound.

Crowley instructed them both in basic techniques of magic, meditation, and yoga, and conducted several experiments with them in astral projection. Butts excelled at the latter, referring to herself as a "secular Isis." Butts's journals from this period include long entries detailing her magical practices, astral visions, and spiritual meditations. On March 11 she took her I° initiation into OTO,[38] and on the 18th Crowley taught her the "gnostic cross."[39] She approached Crowley with caution, noting "Aleister is an assistance, not a good or an evil. It is a good practice to notice a phenomena and its antithesis.... In that case it depended which way you looked."[40] However, she would later write of Crowley, "I believe the Beast to be a technical expert of the highest order."[41] Her impressions of Thelema were likewise favorable, noting in her diary, "I believe in 'Do what thou wilt' etc."[42]

When Crowley invited the couple to stay at the Abbey, they hesitated at first. As Butts noted in her journal, "Aleister Crowley must know by now that we are playing for time with regard to Cefalù, i.e., that we won't come to him unless driven there by poverty or are reassured as to his intentions."[43] Whatever their reservations, they were evidently assuaged, as Butts and Maitland would arrive that summer for a stay at the Abbey.

Hamnett also introduced Crowley to John Wilson Navin Sullivan (1886–1937), former mathematical and scientific reviewer for the London *Times* and *Athenaeum*. His friend Aldous Huxley described him as having "a very clear, hard, acute intelligence, and a very considerable knowledge, not merely on his own subjects—mathematics, physics and astronomy—but on literature and music. A stimulating companion."[44] Educated at University College, London, he had broad interests in science, mathematics, literature, and music, and contributed articles to newspapers and periodicals. He even wrote a novel, *An Attempt at Life.*[45] In the years to follow, Sullivan would establish himself as one of the foremost popularizers of science, combining his love of mathematics, physics, philosophy, and music into classic books like *Aspects of Science*, *Beethoven: His Spiritual Development,* and *The Limitations of Science.*[46] He was one of the few people in Britain to understand the theory of relativity when it was first introduced, and when Einstein visited the University of London, Sullivan was the only journalist able to discuss it in Einstein's native German.[47] His interest in the intersection of science and aesthetics made him a natural foil for Crowley's thinking; the following quote from *Aspects of Science* easily could have flowed from AC's own pen:

> Mathematics, as much as music or any other art, is one of the means by which we rise to a complete self-consciousness. The significance of mathematics resides precisely in the fact that it is an art; by informing us of the nature of our own minds it informs us of much that depends on our minds.[48]

They spent long nights playing chess and discussing mathematics. Sullivan had no interest in the occult[49] but, when he responded to Beast's discussions of *The Book of the Law* by seeing numerical theorems in its passages, Crowley excitedly invited him to the Abbey to write a mathematical proof of *Liber AL.*

Sullivan's wife, (Violet) Sylvia Mannooch (b. 1896),[50] was a beautiful, tragic figure trapped in an unhappy marriage. They shared only a love of music, and Sullivan's preoccupation with mathematics much eroded even this. Both realized their relationship was pointless. When Sullivan vowed to AC to find his true will, Sylvia became a greater hindrance. Crowley recalled, "He asked me point-blank to take her off his hands for a time."[51] Crowley agreed and told him, "You can have her back whenever you like by whistling for her." It was a replay of his affair with Ratan Devi at the behest of her husband.

As in the original liaison, Sylvia became pregnant. She and Beast planned to return to Cefalù, where Sullivan would meet them and write his precis on

Liber AL. Sullivan, however, met them at the dock during lunch and demanded, "I want Sylvia back."

"Righto!" Crowley nodded his head, stuffing food in his mouth and swallowing. "I'll have to get the cabin changed and take a few of Sylvia's things out of my trunk."[52] The scene was a perfect picture of irony, with Crowley agreeable, Sylvia enraged, and Sullivan flabbergasted. In the end, Crowley returned to Cefalù alone. Sylvia would die of typhoid shortly thereafter.[53]

Over the years, the relationship between Fratres Merlin Peregrinus and Baphomet had grown strained: Crowley had lost respect for the head of OTO, finding Reuss's experience in the IX° to be unsatisfactory and nearly nonexistent. As AC wrote of Reuss, "He told me that he had applied it with success but twice in his whole life."[54] Likewise, Reuss's own doubts about Crowley resulted in bitter correspondence wherein he denounced *The Book of the Law;* however, when he visited Beast in Palermo, it was on civil terms. No record survives of this summit. However, when Reuss suffered a stroke shortly thereafter, Crowley claimed to have been named his successor as Outer Head of the Order, pending election by all the world heads. Four years would pass before the appointment was ratified.

Beast returned to the Abbey on April 6, where the following two months passed in miserable dullness. Although he concluded this signified the end of a magical cycle—and the I Ching confirmed this—he was unsure what to do next. Everyone, it seemed, was poor, depressed, and ill. Around May 20, as the sun entered the sign of Gemini, he and Leah conducted an operation of sex magick designed to release within her the power of Babalon. Although, in Leah's mind, the ritual transformed her from simply being a Scarlet Woman, consort to the Beast, into Babalon herself, for Crowley the lull continued.

Then, on May 23, another inspiration seized Crowley. Sitting at his desk, he knew it was time to take the most awful obligation possible. He scribbled in his diary, "I am mortally afraid to do so. I fear I might be called upon to do some insane act to prove my power to act without attachment." Then, at 9:34 p.m., his mind became calm. "As God goes, I go," he told himself. Discarding his clothes, he entered the temple with Leah at his side. There, before his Scarlet Woman and all the powers of the universe as his witness, Crowley took the Oath of an Ipsissimus, (10°=1□), the final grade in the A∴A∴ hierarchy. The oath began his final and greatest initiation, one that would not see its conclusion until 1924. In his diary, he wrote:

> I am by insight and initiation an Ipsissimus; I'll face the phantom of myself, and tell it so to its teeth. I will invoke Insanity itself, but having thought the Truth, I will not flinch from fixing it in word and deed, whatever come of it.

Along with the grade came the obligation never to advertise its attainment. This vow Crowley kept his entire life, the only hint of his attainment appearing in *Magick in Theory and Practice* (1929), where, among a catalog of his attainments up to the grade of Magus, he wrote that his holy guardian angel "wrought also in me a Work of Wonder beyond this, but in this matter I am sworn to hold my peace."[55]

By 10:05 p.m., Crowley was back at his desk.

Having had enough of Jane's obstinate preconceptions and asinine visions, Beast decided she needed a magical retirement. It would span a month and involve six daily meditations: in the first week, these would each last thirty minutes; in the second week, the meditations would be an hour long; by the fourth week, she would be meditating twelve hours a day. Wolfe reacted poorly, however, when Crowley instructed her to go to the top of the rock of Cephaloedium for a month. "You're crazy," she told him.

"A boat leaves for Palermo in the morning," he replied calmly but firmly, pointing to the open door of the Whore's Cell. "There's the door."

When she grudgingly agreed to the retirement and Crowley told her she could take nothing with her—no books, games, visitors or other distractions—she objected again. "What am I supposed to do?"

Beast smiled sagaciously. "You will have the sun, moon, stars, sky, sea, and universe to read and play with."

Unconvinced, she nevertheless began her retirement on June 13 on a secluded part of the beach designated by Crowley. Russell transported and pitched AC's Himalayan tent, which she regarded disparagingly because the wardrobe trunk she brought to Cefalù was nearly the same size. Beginning the retirement, she vowed not to speak, except to reply "Love is the law, love under will" when Russell brought her meals—typically grapes, a loaf of bread, and a jug of water. Emotions washed over her that first day: she was nervous lest nothing happen. She missed the niceties of her Hollywood life and resented the rocks beneath her that made her bed and floor uncomfortable. Although angry at Crowley, she nevertheless determined to succeed.

Jane awoke the next morning feeling as if the ground beneath her was rocking and swaying. Looking out the door, she found the tent surrounded by the water of the high tide. Fortunately, Crowley and Russell had appeared to check on her and moved the tent back to dry ground. After that, her retirement proceeded as scheduled. Although she grew calm, boredom persisted. To amuse herself between meditations, she exercised and swam naked in the water. Finally, after nineteen days of solitude, her thoughts dissolved into "perfect calm, deep joy, renewal of strength of courage."[56] Looking about, she understood what Crowley meant about the world being her toy. She had found both herself and a fulfilling spirituality.

At the end of the retirement, Jane returned to the Abbey looking better than ever. Not only had her disposition changed, but the exercise and diet trimmed off sixteen pounds.

Mary Butts and Cecil Maitland arrived at the Abbey on July 5, 1921, and were enchanted by the summer weather and setting. Butts arrived having recently outlined her objectives in studying magick:

I.   I want to study and enjoy, and to enter if I can into the fairy world, the mythological world, and the world of the good ghost story.

II.   I want by various mystical practices and studies to produce my true nature, and enlarge my perceptions.

III.   I don't only want to find my true will. I want to do it. So I want to learn how to form a magical link between myself and the phenomena I am interested in. I want power.

IV.   I want to find out what is the essence of religion, study the various ideas of God under their images.

V.   I want to make this world into material for the art of writing.

VI.   I want to observe the pairs of opposites, remembering that which is below is as that which is above. From this I wish to formulate clearly, the hitherto incommunicable idea of a third perception. This is a perception of the nature of the universe as yet unknown to man, except by intuitions which cannot be retained, and by symbols whose meaning cannot be retained also. I want to fix it in man's mind.

VII.   I want to write a book not about an early theocracy and fall of man, … but a book written about the subject, historically, under terms of human fallibility without deification of Pythagoras or the writers of the Kabala.… A book to show the relation of art to magic, and shew the artist as the true, because the oblique adept.[57]

In Thelemic parlance, it was her Will to be a writer, and she looked to magick to give her both discipline and subject matter for writing. Thus, while staying at the Abbey, she worked on editing her novel *Ashe of Rings* (1925).[58] However, writing was but one of her activities. There were, of course, the Abbey's mandated activities and lectures. But she also continued her experiments with astral projection and studied Crowley's unpublished works. These included *Liber Aleph,* his commentary on *The Book of the Law,* and the third part of *Book Four* which would later become *Magick in Theory and Practice.* As she read *Magick,* Butts made a number of recommendations on the content and additional topics for the Master Therion to cover. In his *Confessions,* Crowley acknowledged his debt to her:

I practically re-wrote the third part of *Book Four.* I showed the manuscripts to Soror Rhodon (Mary Butts) and asked her to criticize it thoroughly. I am extremely grateful to her for her help, especially in indicating a large number of subjects which I had not discussed. At her suggestion, I wrote essay upon essay to cover every phase of the subject. The result has been the expansion of the manuscript into a vast volume, a complete treatise upon the theory and practice of Magick, without any omissions.[59]

Judging from her Cefalù diaries, Butts struggled with many aspects of life at the Abbey, her record punctuated by flashes of anger, disappointment, and doubt. She complained about the rationing of cigarettes, infrequent structured teaching, uninhibited sexuality (even in the presence of children), and the fact that "both [Hirsig and Crowley] dope out of all reasonable proportion." Privately, she also speculated that Poupée had died because Leah had neglected her.[60] Even while helping with *Magick in Theory and Practice,* she records a remark by Cecil Maitland regarding the high esteem in which the Thelemites regarded Crowley: "it makes AC tragic, because he is a kind, wise, honourable, gentle man crucified by his utter belief in his own teaching."[61] Nevertheless, she continued her magical work throughout, and offered suggestions on how to make the Abbey more inviting to other visitors.[62]

Reading Herodotus' account of an Egyptian priestess copulating with a goat in the course of a religious ceremony, Crowley pondered the occult significance of these "prodigies." The unions of humans and animals was certainly sacred to ancient cultures: the Egyptians venerated gods who had human bodies and animals' heads. Similar ideas appeared in Greek mythology, with the bull-headed Minotaur and the story of Leda and the swan. Other ancient religions around the world told similar tales. Thus Crowley suggested such a working. Leah agreed to act as priestess. They got a goat, and the Scarlet Woman knelt naked on the ground, presenting herself to the indifferent beast. Crowley tried coaxing the goat to mount Leah, but the animal failed to respond to a human female. To save the ritual from utter failure, Crowley took the goat's place with Leah, as he recorded in his diary: "I atoned for the young He-goat at considerable length."[63]

On September 14, as their visit drew to a close, both Butts and Maitland signed A∴A∴ Probationers' oaths. Oddly enough, they left for Paris two days later. Back in London, Butts continued her magical work and struggled with her ambivalence, writing, "'Do what thou wilt shall be the whole of the Law.' That is all right. But people are to be made aware of this by fear, coercion, bribery, etc., a religious movement re-enacted. The founder is to be Crowley and his gulled, doped women."[64] In the end, she concluded the Abbey was a sham. "I'd sooner be the writer I am capable of becoming than an illuminated adept, magician, magus, master of this temple or another."[65]

When Jane returned to the Abbey from her retirement, all were abuzz anticipating the arrival of Frank Bennett, VII°, Beast's man from Australia. He was a senior member in Crowley's circle, both in terms of his fifty-five years of age and his eleven years in the A∴A∴, and his visit posed a logistic puzzle: there was no room for him in the Whore's Cell, and the Umbilicus, as a nursery, was inappropriate for such an August Brother. Crowley asked Russell to give up his room for Bennett. The student refused, complaining that he needed to study and meditate. Jane, seeing Crowley bristle, quickly offered her room. At this point, however, the matter of a room was no longer the point. So the student sulked and the master stewed, until Beast grabbed a towel and told Russell sharply, "Your work doesn't matter a tinker's cuss. You'd better be out by the time I finish my bath." However, he returned from the beach to find Russell still entrenched in the room. AC ultimately confronted him with the tack that had been so successful with Jane: he said he worried that Russell was working too hard and suggested he take a holiday from the Abbey for his own health.

The student feared this meant banishment, so on July 18, the day after Bennett arrived, he climbed the rock of Cephaloedium and began a magical retirement. Cleaning his makeshift hut, he kept his mind active by counting the 273 handfuls of dirt and 219 small stones that he threw out. Then he brought in a stone slab to serve as an altar for the Thelemic Holy Books, a copy of the Stele of Revealing, his magical knife, and the Greek Zodiacal cross that Frater Achad had made for him. Then, at 8 p.m., he did the Lesser Banishing Ritual and resolved not to descend the rock for food or water for eight days. Less than an hour later, he began acting like a Master of the Temple, interpreting every event as a particular dealing of God with his soul. Waking early the next morning, he proceeded with solar adorations and recitations of the Holy Books.

Ninette, who considered Russell a child requiring gentle treatment, begged Beast to intervene. He simply shrugged his shoulders, "Let him come down. He's up there by no will of *mine*." Crowley thought Russell had lost his mind. "He has no sense of proportion, and so mixes the planes that he attaches real importance to the number of handfuls of dirt he finds in his hovel."[66] Ninette, however, carried a rucksack of food and water up the rock. While Russell would neither talk nor eat, he was grateful for the water. On July 24, after a week on the rock, Russell descended shortly after noon and slept on the nursery's living room floor.[67]

As Crowley told the end of the story, the sound of his name being shouted hoarsely awakened Beast from his lunchtime nap. He opened his eyes just in time to see Russell, unshaven and bedraggled, drop a rucksack at his feet and run off whooping. He had supposedly visited the barber for a shave but, after being lathered, remembered his oath not to descend the rock for water and dashed out of the shop, shaving cream flying in all directions. When Crowley opened Russell's rucksack, he found it full of incoherent diaries and concluded Russell *had* lost his mind.

Frank Bennett's spiritual awakening occurred during a walk on the beach with Leah and Beast. The morning was cloudless and still, the sea a clear indigo. Although a poor swimmer, Bennett joined the other two in the water and afterward sat naked with them in the shade, admiring the scenery. "Progradior,"

Beast launched into a lecture, "I want to explain to you fully, and in a few words, what initiation means, what is meant when we talk of the Real Self, and what the Real Self is." In speaking, he equated the holy guardian angel with the subconscious mind: illumination began when one let it work without interference from the conscious mind, for the conscious mind repressed impulses of the subconscious, resulting in restriction and evil. "There is no sin but Restriction," *The Book of the Law* said, and it applied here. The most ubiquitous urge, which was constantly repressed to the detriment to our mental and physical health—and Freud concurred with this—was sex. Rather than treat it as an unfortunate and shameful accident of nature, AC saw it as a basic part of himself, not only physically but as a symbol of God's ability to create.

This was news to Bennett, who thought the holy guardian angel was superconscious. If Crowley was right, then all he had to do was listen to his subconscious. That was one meaning of "Do what thou wilt shall be the whole of the Law." The revelation made his head reel. He next had a wild impulse. Rather than ignore it, he gave in. Bennett ran down the beach and jumped into the water, joined shortly thereafter by Leah and Crowley. After the swim, Bennett excitedly asked Beast, "Please tell me again what you said just now."

"How the devil should I remember?" he asked, but with Bennett's reminders, he reconstructed the discussion as best he could. Bennett smiled with satisfaction. "You have given me the key to the inmost treasury of my soul."

Returning to the Abbey, he pondered his illumination, musing, "I wish I knew this before. It would have saved me a lot of misery." Going to bed at eleven that night, the churning in his mind kept him awake, and his head throbbed painfully with a pressure within, threatening to split. Suffering for four hours, suffocating, he rose from his sweat-soaked bed, threw open his window, and pressed his hands to his head to ease the pain. Then, palms to temples, Bennett dashed out into the night, gasping for air like a drowning man. Finally, a voice deep within instructed, "Breathe deep." When he did, his body relaxed. He felt the sweat coating his skin, the stones and thorns pressing into his feet. The pain dissolved, and the pressure folded upon itself. Bennett returned to the Abbey thirty minutes after leaving and quickly fell asleep. "Absolute blackness pervaded my whole being," he recorded in his journal.

Bennett stayed in his room the next day and went to bed early. His claustrophobia returned that evening, but one thought penetrated the chaos in his brain. Bennett grabbed a piece of paper and desperately scribbled it down.

> What fools we men are! We make for ourselves a prison, and erect mirrors that cover all the four walls of this prison; and not being satisfied with this, we cover the ceiling with a mirror as well. And these are our five senses which reflect themselves in hundreds of forms until we are so befogged that we believe that these reflections of ourselves—of man as Man and Bull— are all that is. But there are a few who have examined these mirrors and polished them, and discovered that the more the mirrors are polished the less

reflection they give. Then a time has come when they have found that they are not mirrors at all, but only veils, and that one can see through the veils.[68]

Thus he understood that one could find one's holy guardian angel.

On the third night of his trance, Bennett's mind remained placid. He felt no pain or discomfort, and he understood Thelema better. In his diary he recorded what, in his mind, was conclusive proof of the Law's importance: "Our Father, which art in Heaven, Hallowed be Thy Name. Thy Kingdom Come, Thy WILL be done ..." Frank Bennett understood.

Frater Progradior, Frank Bennett (1868–1930).

As 1921 drew to a close, the Abbey's visitors returned to their homes. Butts and Maitland's appearance reputedly shocked their Parisian friends, with Nina Hamnett describing them looking "like two ghosts and were hardly recognizable."[69] Goldring's description of them in 1925, from *South Lodge,* shows no sign of the health-wrecked drug fiends he claimed the Abbey made of them; Butts would live on for another fifteen years, while Maitland would commit suicide in 1926, the year after he and Butts parted company.

Frank Bennett, meanwhile, advanced to the A∴A∴ grade of Adeptus Major (6°=5°) and the OTO grade of IX° during his stay. Beast gave him a X° charter as head of the Australian OTO on October 5, and, in November, Bennett returned to Australia to set up branches of OTO and A∴A∴.

The year 1922 began with a visit from Ninette's two sisters. Her twin, Mimi, thought Crowley impressive, while Helen Fraux found him loathsome. When Beast threw out the latter sister for trying to poison the children's minds, she went to the Palermo police with all sorts of wild stories. A resulting visit and search of the Abbey by the *sotto-prefetto* turned up nothing to validate her complaints. Shortly thereafter, Russell married Mimi and prepared to leave. Beast asked if he would visit Australia and help Bennett set up the order there. This he did, the cocky sailor finding Bennett "puffed up like a frog with the importance of his recently gained grade of Adeptus Major in the A∴A∴ and IX° in the OTO."[70] Without a meeting of the minds, they simply traded copies of Crowley manuscripts and parted. Russell arrived back in the United States on January 28, 1922;[71] years later, he would found his own Crowley-derived magical organizations, the Choronzon Club and GBG.

Winter rolled in damp and cold, and brought with it the first snow in Cefalù's history. The unheated villa was miserable, driving Crowley and Leah, dispirited and impoverished, back to Paris that February while Jane, back at the Abbey, sold Crowley's liquor for spare change. AC again called on the Bourciers at 50 rue Vavin, where they stayed on credit. Unable to muster any enthusiasm, his attempts to recruit new students found no takers. "For the first time in my life, Paris disappointed me," Crowley wrote.[72]

On February 14, Crowley left Paris and returned to Fontainebleau (while Leah returned to London). Here he stayed at Au Cadran Bleu, near the hospital where Poupée had been born, and again confronted the painful memories of his recent losses:

> I was so happy and hopeful here two years ago; and now my little Poupée has been dead over a year and her little brother never came to birth; and my manhood is in part crushed.[73]

Two years before, he had first been searching for an Abbey. Now he was broken in spirit and wallet. Furthermore, he was facing the ugly truth about himself: despite his philosophy about drug use, he had become addicted to heroin.

Crowley decided to break his drug habit, setting up a progressive method of weaning himself: each day there was a time he called "Open Season," when he could take as much heroin or cocaine as he wanted. "Closed Season" was the remaining part of the day when drug use was prohibited. His goal was to reduce gradually the length of Open Season until Closed Season was twenty-four hours. He also planned to reduce his heroin intake during Open Season. He began on February 15. He had taken no drug since 8 the previous evening, and only one dose that morning. By 4 o'clock that afternoon, he encountered the Storm Fiend, his name for withdrawal: "The acute symptoms arise suddenly, usually on waking up from a nap. They remind me of the 'For God's sake turn it off' feeling of having an electric current passing through one."[74] Despite taking a 2 milligram dose of strychnine to help fight withdrawal and eating to reduce his craving, his withdrawal ran the classic course: mucous lined his throat, and the bronchitis that first drove him to heroin use reappeared. He felt emotionally blunt and indifferent. Throughout, Crowley recorded his rationalizations for taking the drug: "A small dose—to show my indifference to these

considerations"; "Simply because I feel rotten"; "I felt no craving today, but …
I had so much expectation that I took 3 small doses."[75]

While cocaine proved easier to quit, his heroin need persisted. And
although he failed to stop heroin altogether, he did substantially reduce his
intake. On March 20 he recorded his "triumph over temporal trials."[76] He was
kidding himself in the way any addict rationalizes his or her behavior. Drug
addiction would continue to weigh heavily on Crowley's mind. Over two years
later, he would write to Norman Mudd,

> I have thought the matter over very thoroughly in the last few weeks, and
> can give you (at last) a considered judgement.
> 1   I have never maintained that any man could stop at any time under
>   any condition.
> 2   Favorable conditions are that a man should a) will to stop, b) know
>   his True Will, c) be able to take steps to carry it out, d) be free
>   from physically depressing stress.
> 3   I'm all right for a and b. For c I should be all right if I were all
>   right as to d.
> 4   Given, therefore, that I am safely entrenched at Hardelot or some
>   such place, I think there should be little or no trouble in stopping
>   either suddenly or gradually, as may seem desirable.[77]

Yet the same letter contains more rationalization: "a little solid heroin (the first
in that form for two months—immediate violent activity) have made me better than my normal good form. I have certainly recovered my drug-virginity;
which is clear proof that I can stop at will, the moment physical conditions permit of my throwing a little temporary strain on my constitution." In the end, it
would be the summer of 1924 before his drug addiction was broken.

Back at the Abbey, Jane received instructions from Beast to spend two weeks in
a brothel to get a healthy idea about sex. Interpreting this as a great spiritual
ordeal, she applied to the local brothel to find the madam only interested in
career whores. Undaunted, Jane propositioned la Calce; the landlord, however,
had his eye on Ninette and promised to bring by some friends who might be
willing. Although he did bring one or two men to meet her, none returned for
her favors. Thus Jane, unwilling to walk the streets, resigned herself to failure.

In May, Crowley joined Leah, who was waiting for him in London. Having
nothing but £10 and some Highland garb he had put into storage before the
war, he pawned his watch and tried to raise money. His first thought was to sell
his stock of unsold books. Since Jacobi had published them, however, Chiswick
Press had changed owners, and the new company refused to release the books
because they found their imprint irregular. Try as he may, Crowley could not
convince them to release his books.

He next called on *English Review* editor Austin Harrison (1873-1928), hoping to get back in touch with London's editors and sell some manuscripts. Harrison was the same man who had introduced Crowley to Viereck in London before the war and who had rejected Crowley's "King of Terrors," thinking it was an unsubstantiated factual account.[78] Although Crowley was now unpopular in London, Harrison agreed to buy some pieces out of friendship and publish them pseudonymously. Some of them—the centennial article on "Percy Bysshe Shelley," "The Jewish Problem Re-Stated," and "The Crisis in Freemasonry"—showed Crowley up on some soapbox or another, but failed to impress. As Michael Fairfax, he offered the poems "Moon-Wane," "The Rock," and "To a New-Born Child."[79] More interesting were two pieces he wrote on his newly enlightened view of drug addiction. "The Drug Panic," by a London Physician, was Crowley's attack on the recent Dangerous Drugs Act, which made illegal the sale of drugs to which Crowley was accustomed to purchasing from his local chemist. In a telling autobiographical passage, Crowley complained, "The public is ignorant of the existence of 'a large class of very poor men' who would die or go insane if morphine were withheld from them. Bronchitis and asthma, in particular, are extremely common among the lower classes...."[80] Crowley had but little experience with morphine; in a 1932 letter he wrote, "I have not touched morphine in any form bar about a dozen minute doses by the mouth in 1917."[81] He claimed that ignorance inspired the Dangerous Drugs Act and called instead for compulsory education.

Crowley's article "The Great Drug Delusion" (written under the pseudonym "a New York Specialist") described his own drug delusion: "Though I obtained definitely toxic results, I was always able to abandon the drug without a pang."[82] He again advocated legalization of drugs, claiming it would eliminate underground traffic. Toward the end of the article appeared the germ of a new idea brewing in Crowley's mind:

> In the author's private clinic, patients are not treated for their 'habit' at all. They are subjected to a process of moral reconstruction; as soon as this is accomplished, the drug is automatically forgotten. Cures of this sort are naturally permanent, whereas the possible suppression of the drug fails to remove the original causes of the habit, so that relapse is the rule.[83]

Of course, AC had no private clinic, and he treated no patients. But he had a theory: that drug use guided by morality and Will was harmless, and addiction occurred from casual or indiscriminate use. While this was not his own experience, it was his interpretation of *The Book of the Law*'s "To worship me take wine and strange drugs whereof I will tell my prophet, & be drunk thereof! They shall not harm ye at all."[84] It worked on paper; he just needed to test it.

On May 24 he met with book publisher Grant Richards (1897–1948) and tried to sell him on a book idea. Richards's firm had published books by Crowley's old Le Chat Blanc acquaintance Arnold Bennett, as well as G. K. Chesterton and George Bernard Shaw. Offered Crowley's autobiography, however, Richards demurred, doubting its marketability. Offered a shocker about drug addiction, Richards again declined, referring him to Hutchinson or Collins. On his way home, Crowley therefore moved on to the firm William Collins. There, science fiction novelist, essayist, and literary advisor John Davys Beresford (1873–1947) liked the idea of a drug shocker. Beresford, who started as an advertising writer, knew Crowley from his days as the editor of *What's On:*

> We had one remarkable contributor during my editorship, I may add, none other than Aleister Crowley, who was supplying a serial narrative something in the manner of Tom Hood, speckled with problems and puzzles, for the best solution of which a money-prize was offered.[85]

Beresford had recently written articles on metaphysical topics for *Harper's* magazine.[86] His recommendation, and Crowley's forthcoming articles in the *English Review,* convinced Collins to take the book. On June 1, 1922, AC received a £60 advance on the manuscript. He later admitted that, aside from a few chapter titles, "I had in fact no detailed idea of how the story would develop."[87]

Crowley summoned Leah to his side and began dictating immediately. In twenty-seven days, twelve hours, and forty-five minutes, Crowley dictated the entire 121,000-word text of *The Diary of a Drug Fiend,* a story of wretched pharmacological excess and the redemption of its drug-crazed protagonists by the philosophical code of Thelema. The book is inelegant and unimpressive; but, written in under a month, it was never intended as more than a potboiler. Throughout it appear thinly veiled caricatures of acquaintances and Abbey residents. For instance, Crowley modeled the hero of the story, Pendragon, after Cecil Maitland, who supposedly became an addict at the Abbey. Crowley himself was Mr. King Lamus. Most interesting was the book's note to Part II:

> The Abbey of Thelema at "Telepylus" is a real place. It and its customs and members, with the surrounding scenery, are accurately described. The training there given is suited to all conditions of spiritual distress, and for the discovery and development of the "True Will" of any person. Those interested are invited to communicate with the author of this book.[88]

When he wrote "The Great Drug Delusion," his drug treatment clinic was just a theory. With this manuscript, Crowley prepared to make it a reality.

When Crowley appeared in Collins's office with the manuscript, the publisher couldn't believe anyone could have written an entire novel since they last spoke. But there it was on his desk. Impressive. When Crowley asked about his autobiography, Collins considered the offer and paid him a £120 advance on the manuscript. They also offered to publish Crowley's Simon Iff stories, promising an advance by November 9, but this compilation never materialized.

With the novel completed, Leah returned to the Abbey to recover from illness and to help Ninette, who was pregnant by their landlord. Crowley remained in Paris, visiting friends like writer Jane Burr (b. 1882–1958)[89] and banker-patron of the arts Otto Kahn, hoping to find new students.

CHAPTER FIFTEEN

Adonis

"I shall kill myself and I shall kill you, too, if you don't marry me," Raoul Love-day insisted, thus becoming Betty May's third husband in the summer of 1922.[1] They were wed at the registry office in Oxford, where the groom was a student. Raoul was nervous, fumbled the wedding band, and dropped it on the floor. A photo of the newlyweds, taken in the gardens of St. John's College, featured above Raoul's head the apparition of a young man lying horizontally in slumber or death. All in all, it was an ominous affair.

Born Charles Frederick Loveday (1900–1923)—he would adopt the name "Raoul" while a student at Oxford—he was a frail youth with an unhealthy pallor. Born in Rangoon on July 3, 1900, he was one of two children to Royal Navy officer George Loveday (born c. 1859) and his wife, Amelia Ann Lewendon (b. 1859).[2] Sickly since birth, malaria struck Raoul as a child while still living in Rangoon. They later moved to South London, raising their family at 112 Barry Road in East Dulwich.[3]

On Aug. 2, 1918, at age eighteen, he enlisted in the Inns of Court Officers Training Corps. Nicknamed "The Devil's Own," the Inns of Court were a volunteer battalion, part of the London Territorial Force based in Berkhamsted, Hertfordshire, from September 1914 to June 1919.[4] From there, Loveday attended St. John's College, Oxford, where he studied history, played football (Raymond Greene said "he was very good"), wrote poetry, and became interested in the occult.[5] Betty May reported that his poetry had attracted critical attention, but Greene deemed it "remarkably bad."[6] One example appears in the journal *Oxford Poetry*:

> Sing now of London
> At fall of dusk;
> A summer dragonfly—
> Crept from the husk.
> Dragonfly, on whose wing
> Run golden wires;

So, down a street pavement,
Lamps throw their fires.
Dragonfly, whose wing is pricked
By many a spark;
Electric eyes of taxis
Bright through the dark.
Dragonfly, whose life is
Cold and brief as dew,
Drone now for London dusk,
Soon dead too.[7]

Loveday was also an early member of Oxford's Hypocrites Club, whose later members included writers Evelyn Waugh (1903–1966), Anthony Powell (1905–2000), and Terence Lucy Greenidge (1902–1970). Originally the least fashionable of Oxford's clubs—devoted to the discussion of philosophy—it soon developed a raucous reputation. According to Evelyn Waugh, it was "notorious not only for drunkenness but for flamboyance of dress and manner which was in some cases patently homosexual."[8] Loveday was in fact the club's secretary;[9] after one late night of drinking, he returned to Oxford after hours and tried to climb back into the college, managing only to impale himself on the gate railing, where he hung upside down by his thigh and nearly bled to death before help arrived. His extracurricular activities distracted the youth from his studies so much that he was nearly sent down from St. John's; to everyone's surprise, he managed a first class in history, graduating in 1922.[10]

Raoul Loveday and Betty May.

Betty May has been described by her friends as "A bad girl with a beautiful face and a good heart."[11] Crowley uncharitably called her "a half-crazy whore, who had been twice married and once divorced."[12] Born in Limehouse as Betty Marlow Golding,[13] she grew up in poverty. She worked as an artist's model for a time, sitting for Augustus John, Jacob Kramer, and Jacob Epstein.[14] Enjoying some celebrity, she moved to Paris, became a heavy drug user, and claims to have been known among Apache robbers as the "Tiger Woman," a name that stuck when she returned to England. Her first husband, an addict, left her a widow, and the second divorced her over her own cocaine addiction before she was able to cure herself.[15] Although she reports that she met Raoul at the Harlequin, a Soho pub where she sang, Raoul's sister gave a less romantic account: he attended an undergraduate's party where all the men present placed their names in a hat to decide by lottery who would marry Betty May. "Unlucky Raoul was the one," she lamented.[16] In any event, they married three weeks later, in September.

Loveday had discovered Crowley through reading *The Oxford Book of Mystical Verse* and struck up a correspondence with the poet.[17] That fall, in 1922, he met Betty Bickers, wife of Sheridan Bickers, at the Harlequin. When she learned that Raoul had been studying *The Equinox* for two years, she told him Crowley was staying with her at 31 Wellington Square, teaching her magick and giving lectures on Thelema. To Raoul's delight, she arranged a meeting. Betty May, who had been unimpressed with Crowley when she met him at the Café Royal in 1914, refused to accompany Raoul on the visit. So he went alone, and never came home that night. Nor the next.

A scraping at her third-story bedroom window woke Betty May out of a sound sleep. Switching on her light, she walked to the window, pulled aside the curtain, and nearly cried out when she saw a face pressed up against the glass. Then she recognized the eyes that pleaded to her. They were Raoul's. Betty threw open the window to find her husband, covered with soot and stinking of ether, hanging from a drainpipe thirty feet off the ground. She grabbed his arms, pulled him inside, and undressed him. Although he passed out before he could answer any of her questions, answers were unnecessary. Raoul had obviously spent three days with Crowley, who had exposed her husband to the vices that had wrecked her previous marriages. Seduced by the romance of Betty's bohemian days, Raoul was eager to experience the wild life that she now shunned. Crowley pointed the way for him. Raoul became devoted to mysticism and, even though he had a £1,000 a year job lined up, lost his ambition for anything but magick. Betty's fears came true when she answered her door one day to a portly, middle-aged bald man with a bottle of wine. "Do what thou wilt shall be the whole of the Law," he said.

Raoul rushed up behind her and replied, "Love is the law, love under will."

The Beast smiled and politely kissed Betty's stiff hand. He offered her the bottle and explained, "I've come to dinner."

She turned around to find Raoul simultaneously beaming at the Master and looking sheepishly at his wife. Fury boiled over her face in the form of a furrowed brow and tautly pressed lips. She grabbed her hat and coat and, passing AC in the doorway, fired off one last shot. "I shan't cook any meal for *you*."

She was scarcely two steps away when Crowley replied, "The day will come when you will cook *all* my meals for me."

Contrary to the preceding account of drain-climbing and menacing meals—drawn from Betty May's memoirs[18]—Crowley paints a strikingly different picture of the couple. From his perspective, Betty wasn't living the clean life that her memoirs claim she was, and the indulgent lifestyle to which she was exposing Raoul appalled Crowley. Recognizing the youth's capacity for magick, AC wished to groom him as his successor, and so he invited the Lovedays to Cefalù:

> I hope you will come p.d.q. and bring Betty. I honestly tell you that the best hope for your married life is to get out of the sordid atmosphere of 'Bohemian' London....
>
> Does it surprise you that the notoriously wicked A.C. should write thus? If so, you have not understood that he is a man of brutal commonsense and a loyal friend. So come and live in the open air amid the beauty of Nature.... Beak Street and Fitzroy Street are horrors unthinkable even in Rome; and Rome is a cesspool compared with Cefalù.
>
> The society of Scholars, of free women and of delightful children will indeed be a great change for Betty; but it is what she needs most. There is in her not only a charming woman, but a good one; and she will develop unsuspected glories, given a proper environment. In London she has not one single decent influence, except your own; and however deeply and truly she may love you, she won't be able to resist "la nostalgie de la boue" for ever.[19]

Raoul accepted enthusiastically, promising to join him later that month, and Crowley returned to the Abbey on November 4.

In November, *The Diary of a Drug Fiend* appeared in bookstores. The press responded cooly to the book, the *Times Literary Supplement* calling it "a phantasmagoria of ecstasies, despairs, and above all verbiage," and the *New York Times Book Review* deeming it nothing more than a tract on Thelema.[20] Few copies sold, and the book would ordinarily have vanished into obscurity had James Douglas of the *Sunday Express* not seen it. A proponent of the suppression of James Joyce's *Ulysses,* he dubbed Crowley's novel "A Book for Burning" in his November 19 article.

> I have therefore determined ... to do my best to secure the immediate extirpation of *The Diary of a Drug Fiend* (Collins, 7/6 net) by Aleister Crowley. It is a novel describing the orgies of vice practised by a group of

moral degenerates who stimulate their degraded lusts by doses of cocaine and heroin. Although there is an attempt to pretend that the book is merely a study of the depravation caused by cocaine, in reality it is an ecstatic eulogy of the drug and of its effects upon the body and the mind. A cocaine trafficker would welcome it as a recruiting agent which would bring him thousands of new victims.

He called for the immediate suppression of this repulsive, blasphemous, obscene book.

The *Sunday Express* followed with a sensational front-page exposé:

Black Record of Aleister Crowley
Preying on the Debased
His Abbey
Profligacy and Vice in Sicily

The article reviewed the controversial aspects of his past: the suggestive titles of books (such as *The Honourable Adulterers*), his Rites of Eleusis, and his pro-German propaganda. It summed up Crowley's literary record as "blasphemy, filth, and nonsense," calling his books "either incomprehensible or disgusting—generally both. His language is the language of a pervert, and his ideas are negligible." Adding to the controversy was that a portrait of Crowley, by Ukrainian expatriate artist Jacob Kramer (1892–1962), was currently on display at the Goupil Galleries. At the request of a Chelsea hostess, he agreed to do Crowley's portrait; but after meeting his subject, Kramer avoided working on it until, after much prodding, he produced it in a single sitting.

The Beast 666 by Jacob Kramer (1892–1962).

The article also gave "details" of Crowley's orgies, which they claim involved smelly cakes made with goat's blood. "Suffice it to say that they are horrible beyond the misgivings of decent people." The article then described the inhabitants of the Abbey:

> Three women he keeps there permanently for his orgies. All of them he brought from America two or three years ago. One is a French-American governess, one an ex-schoolmistress, and one a cinema actress from Los Angeles.
>
> Whenever he needs money, and cannot get it from fresh victims, he sends them on the streets of Palermo or Naples to earn it for him. He served once a prison sentence in America for procuring young girls for a similar purpose.
>
> The French-American governess has two children (of which he is the father), who live in the midst of the debauchery. The children of the schoolmistress by him are dead.[21]

The source of these exaggerations and untruths was Mary Butts.

Butts, seeing her lover and herself painted unflatteringly as the protagonists of *The Diary of a Drug Fiend,* provided anonymous information to the *Sunday Express* as a means of striking back at Crowley. Butts also fictionalized details of Crowley's abortive ritual with Leah and the goat: in her version, Leah and the goat did copulate, and Crowley, at the moment the goat climaxed, slit its throat, spilling blood over Leah's back. When the Scarlet Woman stood and looked helpless, asking "What should I do now?," Butts, cool and collected, reputedly lit a cigarette and jibed, "If I were you, I'd take a bath." Aside from an uncharacteristic portrait of Leah as a lost sheep, it also raised the question of how an observer knows when a goat is climaxing. According to Butts's journal, she was not even present for the ritual;[22] she repeated it to the *Sunday Express* as hearsay and injected herself into the story as an observer to deliver the punch line. Regardless, the story circulated widely and passed unchallenged as fact.[23] Ironically, before the controversy over *The Diary of a Drug Fiend* finally died down, Butts's first book, *Speed the Plough and Other Stories* (1923), would be listed alongside Crowley's in *John Bull's* article "Books We'd Like to Burn."[24]

Crowley chalked up James Douglas's initial review to the inanity peculiar to the *Sunday Express,* but the November 26 attack was pure libel. Alas, he was now so broke that he managed to return to Cefalù only through a £20 advance from Austin Harrison; initiating libel proceedings was financially impossible, particularly as defending the infamous Aleister Crowley would require a great barrister indeed. However, he planned to send Jane Wolfe, accused of being a prostitute, to London, thinking she would stand a better chance of winning damages. Even a small settlement would allow Crowley to prepare his own large and expensive lawsuit.

By the time the book was released in America the following summer, the press there remarked "Aleister Crowley has written a new book which is said to have made a bigger sensation in London than *Jurgen* did in America."[25]

An ad for the American edition of *The Diary of a Drug Fiend*.

Despite—or perhaps because of—the controversy, Éditions Kemplen of Paris wrote to Crowley on April 2, 1924, proposing a French translation. The press, however, was short-lived, and this edition never appeared.[26]

En route to the Abbey, the Lovedays broke camp in Paris to visit Nina Hamnett. When the artist learned that Raoul was heading for Cefalù to be Crowley's secretary, she became concerned. Raoul had been very ill, his handsome face still corpse-like, and she believed the Mediterranean heat, mosquitoes, and food would delay his recovery. "If you go to Cefalù now, you'll die," she insisted, urging him to recuperate first. But Raoul pressed on, determined to find his destiny at the Abbey of Thelema.

On Sunday night, November 26—the day the *Sunday Express* launched its front-page assault on Crowley—the Lovedays arrived at the Abbey. Their first act as visitors was to read and sign the Oath of Affiliates, stating that they agreed to live by the Abbey's rules:

> I, willing to abide within the Abbey of Thelema, make Oath and sign: that I do utterly deny, abjure and condemn all allegiance soever to all gods and men, accepting the Law of Thelema as my sole Law:
> that I affirm *The Book of the Law* to be the Word of Truth and the Rule of Life:
> that I dedicate myself utterly and without stint my body and soul to the Great Work which is to proclaim and execute the Law of Thelema:
> that I will accept unquestionably and irrevocably the conditions of life in the Abbey of Thelema, and uphold its ordinances and customs (as declared in the Books LII, CI, CXCIV) and maintain the authority of the Scarlet Woman and of her Lord the Beast 666.[27]

With the waiver signed, Beast formally accepted them as visitors to the Abbey. Given the *Sunday Express* articles, Raoul sent a reassuring note home:

Dear Mum and Dad,

Another line just to let you know how happy and comfortable we both are. Also to let you know that the articles in the *Sunday Express,* about the man in an annexe of whose house we are staying, are absolute lies, and

written by an enemy. He was in the Secret Service in America; and had to
pretend to be pro-German: hence they have a good opportunity to attack.
An answer has been sent showing that every word is untrue. He has been
as nice to us as anyone could be; and Robinson Smith is his friend. I
thought I'd just send you this so that you could contradict it and needn't
worry. Best wishes.

Your loving son,

Fred[28]

Betty also sent a letter confirming what their son had written:

> All the things you have read in the *Sunday Express* are absolutely untrue.
> Crowley is quite nice and this house is well conducted. I give you my
> word of honour and we are very happy and we are looking much better
> and feeling it. We get up at 7.30 and go to bed at 8 o'clock so you see
> what a healthy life we are really leading but when we come back you will
> see for yourself how well we look. I hope you are all well and not worry-
> ing a little bit.[29]

In all, they sent eight letters to Raoul's parents, assuring them over and again
that the *Sunday Express* was lying about Crowley.

Raoul loved the Abbey from the first morning he awoke to the sound of
tom-toms and praises to the rising sun. "I cannot express my feeling of exalta-
tion as I stood there inhaling the sweet morning air."[30] He climbed rocks and
performed the rituals he had been studying, now under the tutelage of the
Master. According to Betty May,

> Raoul spent most of the days playing chess with the 'Beast' in his study, or
> poring over books on magic. There were various magical incantations,
> including the killing of a cat because it was an 'evil spirit,' and the 'Beast'
> would, on state occasions, appear for some ceremony clad in gorgeous
> robes and wielding a word or colored wand.[31]

He soon became an A∴A∴ Probationer, taking the magical name of Frater
Aud (the magical light, whence the term *odic force*). Raoul quickly ascended to
the position of being Crowley's favorite pupil ever. Neuburg, for all his manifesting mediumship, and Achad, despite discovering the Key, had both strayed
from the Path; but Raoul was a brilliant and devoted student, and AC felt they
had a powerful magical current in full swing.

Betty, however, reacted unfavorably to life at the Abbey, and made life miserable for everyone by refusing to cooperate with the rules. At one point, she
got so fed up with holding a basin for Crowley as he ate that she dumped the
water over his head; amidst the breathless silence that followed, Beast simply
continued his meal nonchalantly. In another incident, Betty pulled a gun on
him. Crowley admired her pluck and spirit, and he responded as the insidious
jester that was so much a part of him: one day at dinner, he announced that
they would sacrifice Betty at dawn. After the color drained from her face, she
saw Raoul chuckling at the comment. She was so frightened that she sneaked

away from the Abbey that night, and Raoul had to find her and assure her it was just a joke. In time, Betty warmed up to Beast. Particularly memorable was the day they both climbed the Rock of Cephaloedium. Betty was surprised at the deftness and agility of this fat forty-seven-year-old man, and comforted by his gentle reassurance: "Remember, it is I who will get hurt first."

One day, he suggested the Lovedays take a break from the Abbey's rigors and get some fresh air and exercise. Thus he sent them hiking to the monastery thirteen miles away. On the return trip, they stopped by a spring to rest. Parched, Raoul dipped his hand into the water. "Raoul," his wife interrupted, "remember what Beast said about drinking the water?" He had advised against it. Frater Aud shrugged his shoulders, cupped water in his hands, and drank. He sighed deeply and, seeing Betty's surprise at his disregard for his Master's directions, explained, "If I didn't have a drink, I should have died."

Winter hit the Abbey hard in January 1923. The air was cool, the sky constantly overcast, and the concrete walls and floor of the Abbey were icy slabs. No sooner had Leah recovered than the "Cefalù plague" struck Crowley down with emphysema, asthma, and bronchitis. Shortly thereafter, Raoul suffered a recurrence of his childhood malaria, but nevertheless continued the Great Work, going on astral journeys and reporting his visions.

When February came around and neither Crowley nor Raoul improved, they called Dr. Maggio, president of the district hospital. He diagnosed Raoul with a liver infection. Although the doctor represented the best possible care, Crowley, not placing his faith entirely in the hands of Aesculapians, calculated Raoul's horoscope and its progressions; his face turned grim as he looked at the aspects. "It looks as if you might die on the 16th of February at 4:00."

On February 10, matters at the Abbey became tense, and a fight broke out between Betty and Ninette. The Tiger Woman had called Shummy a slob and refused to work with her. The others appeared, Crowley siding with Betty, Leah defending Ninette, and Jane listening silently. In the end, Crowley suggested that, with everyone sick lately, discipline had slipped and that they must all try harder to live together and pursue higher goals.

Things erupted again the next day. Although Beast had banned newspapers from the Abbey—encouraging students to read literature, philosophy, and magic in the Abbey library instead—he agreed to rethink his policy and discuss it with Betty. When she failed to meet him as scheduled, he came to Raoul's room and, in order to get her attention, snatched the London paper from her hands. Betty reacted violently, first screaming and cursing, then grabbing anything that wasn't nailed down and throwing it at the Master Therion. His suggestions that they step outside of the sick room and speak civilly only met with more flying crockery. When Crowley resorted to restraining her, she swung and kicked at him defiantly. Finally Raoul, barely strong enough to stand, staggered between them and persuaded Betty to calm down.

That evening, Betty packed her bags and left the Abbey, dropping into the mail a note that Raoul had written to his parents earlier that day:

> Forgive me for not having written before but I have had a very sharp bout of malaria which has left behind it a persistent diarrhoea. I have had this for about ten days now and it has left me as weak as water. As you see I have had to get Betty to write this letter for me. The doctor here is giving me various things but I do not seem to be making much headway. I trust, however, that by the time you get this letter I shall be quite well. Betty, herself, has been unable to keep anything in her stomach for the last week but I think she is just on the turn now. I believe that the air or the water or something here, perhaps the place, does not agree with me. If I can earn enough without having to spend it on the doctor or on the other million extras which surround one in a foreign country if one wants any comfort, if I can do this I think I shall come back.

On the back of this letter, Betty had appended her own note:

> Dear Mrs. Loveday,
>
> Raoul doesn't know I am writing and I hope you will not tell him anything I have written on this page to you. I really think Raoul is very very ill and if he doesn't come home soon he will be too weak to be moved.[32]

Betty went to Palermo, where she lodged a complaint against Crowley with the British consul. As it turns out, His Majesty's Consul for the Compartimento of Sicily and the Sicilian Islands was Reginald Gambier MacBean (1859–1942),[33] a Theosophist and Co-Mason who became the Italian Grand Master of the Ancient and Primitive Rite of Memphis-Mizraim in July 1921. Although Spence suggests that this fact may have worked in Crowley's favor,[34] it may actually have done quite the opposite: after John Yarker died in 1913, Crowley opposed the participation of Theosophist and Co-Mason James Ingall Wedgwood in the election of Yarker's successor as Sovereign Grand Master General of the Rite,[35] an act that would not have endeared Crowley to those closely allied camps. Furthermore—given AC's claim to have distilled the Memphis-Mizraim ceremonies into its rituals—OTO would have been viewed as spurious by the Ancient and Primitive Rite. Indeed, in his history of the Rite, MacBean wrote that he revived Memphis-Mizraim in Italy in order "to prevent a spurious revival of the Memphis Rite with political aims in Italy, which would have compromised the regular Obedience of the Memphis Rite in Palermo."[36] Thus, Betty's complaint could have set into motion, or contributed to, a disastrous chain of events for AC

The next day, February 12, Leah found Betty and gave her a romantic note from Raoul, wherein he begged his wife to return to his side. As she read the note, her anger dissolved. She dropped the charges and returned with Leah.

They summoned Dr. Maggio again when Raoul took a turn for the worse on February 14. This time, he revised his diagnosis as acute enteritis, an intestinal illness common in the Mediterranean: in 1905 this disease killed Crowley's first daughter, Lilith, and incapacitated and nearly killed J. F. C. Fuller; at the Abbey, everyone suffered intestinal distress almost constantly. The diagnosis caused the Lovedays to recall the day they stopped at the spring where Raoul drank the water despite Crowley's warnings.

Raoul's condition worsened, so on February 16, Beast and Betty went into town to fetch Dr. Maggio. Returning to the Abbey up the mountain path, Betty fainted from exhaustion. Crowley knelt and gently revived her. When she was able to stand, he helped her to her feet and announced, "We will make adoration." She nodded quietly, and Crowley turned to face the sunset.

> Hail unto Thee who art Tum in Thy setting, even unto Thee who art Tum in Thy joy, who travellest over the Heavens in Thy bark at the Down-going of the Sun.
> Tahuti standeth in His splendour at the prow, and Ra-Hoor abideth at the helm.
> Hail unto thee from the Abodes of Day!

As he spoke the passage from "Liber Resh," Betty noticed tears streaming down his cheeks, and she understood the words were also a prayer for Raoul.

They marched solemnly back toward the Abbey until Leah met them on the path, as grim-faced as they. Betty grew concerned. "Is he worse?"

Leah answered bluntly. "He's dead."

Betty fainted again.

Raoul had died at 4 o'clock, just as Crowley had predicted. Betty found him in bed, laying with his head canted on his arms, just like the deathly apparition in their wedding picture. Dr. Maggio ascribed the cause of death to paralysis of the heart, and assured everyone that, even if they'd called him when Raoul first got sick, he was so weak that the outcome would not have changed.

Within an hour of death, Raoul's body was placed in a coffin; local law required that the body be disposed of within twenty-four hours. So Crowley spent the night reciting over the clay and rapping with his wand on the side of the box to prepare for his hasty burial. In the morning, Crowley donned his long white silk robe and the star sapphire ring he had worn in Bou-Sâada with Neuburg. On his breast hung a topaz Rosy Cross, and on his head was a cornet inscribed with the name of the northern archangel Uriel. For Crowley, this was the only funeral over which he had ever presided, and the first funeral he had attended since his father died back in 1887.

A mule-driven cart carried the coffin to the local Catholic cemetery as the local monks watched the solemn procession of the Master Therion and his acolytes. Howard, dressed in a blue silk robe and crowned with a wreath of flowers, ran ahead excitedly. The mourners found him at the cemetery, running in circles and announcing, "We're going to bury Raoul!" AC, Leah, Ninette, Jane, and Betty, all robed, gathered round the bier. Crowley struck his Tibetan bell and conducted a Thelemic service, reciting the "Quia Patris" from his play

The Ship; it had always been a poem of great import to Crowley, and he worked it into many rituals, including the Gnostic Mass and the Paris Working. Today, it was for Raoul's funeral:

> Thou, who art I, beyond all I am,
> Who hast no nature and no name,
> Who art, when all but thou are gone,
> Thou, centre and secret of the Sun ...[37]

In the end, the words that best summed up the tragedy of Raoul's premature death were from Dr. Faustus: "'Tis magic, magic that hath ravished me."[38]

Since Raoul was not a Catholic, he could not be interred in the cemetery; however, a piece of unconsecrated ground outside was made available. The Lovedays would later have their son's body exhumed and shipped to England.

The funeral concluded, Crowley staggered back to the Abbey, exhausted and sick. He collapsed in bed, where he remained for three weeks with a fever of 102 degrees. Betty, meanwhile, returned to Palermo and awaited funds from London for her passage home. From Palermo, Betty sent Crowley a friendly note, beginning and ending with the Thelemic salutations, referring to him as "Beast," and promising to visit again if possible.[39]

"I don't charge Crowley with causing Raoul's death," she would reflect. "That would be silly."[40] However, by the time Betty reached London and met reporters at the dock, venom replaced her amity. The *Sunday Express* paid her £80 for a story, and Betty May gave them a good one. A cat, she said, had wandered into the Abbey and Crowley caught it. During one of his rituals, he instructed Raoul to slit its throat, but the acolyte slipped and sliced its neck without killing it. The cat escaped and ran about the room, spitting blood everywhere and breaking the protective magic circle around them. Crowley finally caught and anesthetized the cat, permitting Raoul to finish the job. Leah, meanwhile, caught the blood in a chalice and gave it to Raoul to drink. He did, and it is from this rite, overseen by Crowley, that her husband died. Although Crowley denied this story, his friend Gerald Yorke conceded in later years that the sacrifice had indeed occurred, but emphasized that it was unrelated to Loveday's cause of death.[41]

P. R. Stephensen, who would later become Crowley's friend and publisher, called the stories that filled newspapers for the next two months a campaign of vilification unparalleled in the history of journalism. It began in the February 25, 1923, *Sunday Express* with a headline splashed across the front page:

> New Sinister Revelations of Aleister Crowley.
> Varsity Lad's Death.
> Enticed to "Abbey"
> Deradful Ordeal of a Young Wife.
> Crowley's Plans.

The article described Raoul, without naming him, as "a boy of twenty-two." His wife—the thrice married, cocaine-addicted pub singer whose bandit friends named her the "Tiger Woman"—became a naive and defenseless maiden whose idyllic marriage was destroyed by the manipulations of the depraved Aleister Crowley at his Abbey of iniquity. The abominations published in the *Sunday Express,* she said, only hinted at the real horrors that occurred at the Abbey. Betty's warning that Crowley planned to sue the *Sunday Express* for £5,000 over the libels printed in their attack on *The Diary of a Drug Fiend*—met with cocksureness:

> The "Sunday Express" promises Crowley that it intends to pursue its investigations with the utmost ruthlessness, and that next Sunday it will endeavour to supply him with considerable further material on which to base any action which he may care to bring.

An artist's conception of Betty May's account of a cat being sacrificed at the Abbey.

While the *Sunday Express* followed the article with an interview with Betty May on March 4, *John Bull* commandeered the bandwagon. In the following weeks, its lurid stories featured headlines that would be at home on any tabloid:

A Wizard of Wickedness (March 17).
The Wickedest Man in the World (March 24).
King of Depravity Arrives (April 11).
A Man We'd Like to Hang (May 19).

The paper claimed Crowley was actually in London and called for his arrest. It reported that as a mountaineer, Crowley had at one time run low on provisions and chopped up two of his coolies for food. It called him "one of the most shameless degenerates who ever boasted of his British birth."[42] These attacks generated so much interest that even American newspapers picked up the story of Raoul's death.

When the onslaught began, Crowley was still too sick to care. Jane, however, arrived in London on February 28. Seeking legal counsel to sue the *Sunday Express,* she learned that she could not sue for defamation because the article did not mention her name. Before long, an undercover reporter from *John Bull* tracked down this "unscrupulous harpy" and interviewed "the elusive and dangerous Jane Wolfe." The result was "We Trap the Temptress,"[43] an article disclosing how Jane was seeking new students for the Abbey, along with other equally horrible truths.

Among those shocked by the news of Raoul's death was dramatist and producer Lance Sieveking (1896–1972). He had just written his novel *The Psychology of Flying* and was in his second year at Cambridge. Like other students, he and his friends absorbed themselves in the newspaper accounts, trying to name Crowley's "nameless rites" and imagine his "unimaginable horrors." Ultimately, all they managed was to revolt each other with images far more twisted than any Crowley or the press could suggest. Then, around Easter, students and perfect strangers began asking him, "I say, *do* tell me about Aleister Crowley. Is he really as bad as they say?" Sieveking denied knowing Crowley, to the disbelief of his interrogators. This mystified him until he discovered *The Diary of a Drug Fiend* contained the line, "I suppose every one has read *The Psychology of Flying* by L. de Giberne Sieveking" on page 24. Although the passage explained the connection, he found the remaining text incomprehensible. It would be years before he thought of Crowley again.

Raoul's death robbed Crowley of a friend, student, magical son, and secretary. While there was no replacing him, he still needed a secretary. Thus he summoned Norman Mudd, one of his most devoted and stalwart students.

Mudd had changed a great deal since Crowley last saw him on Trinity's campus in 1910. After finishing his master's degree, Mudd received two job offers, one at the National Physical Laboratory and another as a professor at Grey University College in Bloemfontein, South Africa. He chose the latter, hoping to leave the country, forget his college dealings with Crowley, and make a fresh start. He ran the Department of Applied Mathematics from 1911 to 1912, all the while experiencing fits of depression. In 1915 he lost an eye due to a gonorrheal infection. From 1916 to 1917 he ran the Department of Pure Mathematics and wrote a criticism of Einstein's theory of relativity. He nevertheless remained unhappy. In 1920, a decade after he last saw AC, Mudd went on sabbatical to seek the only man who'd ever made him feel he had a purpose in life: Aleister Crowley. Sailing from South Africa, he arrived in Southampton on December 13, 1920,[44] and began his quest. Finding the blue *Equinox,* he traveled to America, arriving aboard the *Imperator* on January 18, 1921.[45] On reaching Detroit, he learned from the Thelemites there that, to his disappointment, AC had already returned to England, where Mudd thus returned on February 7, 1921.[46] A letter to his colleague, Leo Marquard, reveals Mudd's state of mind at this time. Beginning and ending his letter with the standard Thelemic salutations, Mudd wrote about the path of initiation:

> The taking up of this Path is what is referred to variously as the Second Birth, or being Born of the Water of the Spirit, or (by Dante) the Vita Nuova, or (by the Egyptians) the Entrance on Light, or (by the Buddhists) The Noble Aryan Path, or (by the Alchemists) the Great Work, and so on. Also each of these groups possesses and communicates to aspirants a body of wisdom and a set of disciplines which guide and protect the beginner and prevent his task from being harder and more dangerous than is, in the nature of the case, unavoidable. *Also, it is possible to investigate this Path in a purely scientific manner and to pursue the Work without committing oneself to any definite creed or philosophy.*[47]

When he finally got hold of Crowley, he received an invitation to Cefalù. This coincided with an invitation to organize the school of astronomy for the University of South Africa. He turned down the job to visit the Abbey.[48]

Mudd would become Crowley's biggest challenge: as an academician, he was accustomed to the logical rigors and proofs of mathematics, and refused to engage in any activity or initiation that compromised his objectivity. Nevertheless, he was Christian-reared and caught up in the passion of Crowley's convictions, eager to understand and spread the Word of Thelema. He longed to dissect *The Book of the Law* and argue its philosophical and historical elements with AC. All Crowley wanted was a secretary.

Frater Omnia Pro Veritate (All for Truth), as Mudd was known in the A∴A∴, arrived the third week of April 1923. At the same time, two of Raoul's friends, John Pigney and Claud Bosanquet, also came to the Abbey to determine for themselves the circumstances of their classmate's death. The pair only stayed long enough to discover the facts and return home satisfied, if not disappointed, with the truth.

Raymond Greene (1901–1982) also came to Cefalù at this time. An acquaintance of Raoul's, Greene and two of his schoolmates had devised a plan for Greene to go to Cefalù, assassinate Crowley, and flee to the south coast, where his friends would pick him up in a sailboat and take him to Morocco; from there, he would return home via Spain. Greene, however, doubted the stories about Crowley, and refused to participate in such a plan. What finally convinced him was a letter that he received from Crowley just before Easter:

> Dear Sir,
>
> > Do what thou wilt shall be the whole of the Law.
>
> Forgive me if I suggest, from the little experience that I have in such matters, that when one is establishing a spy system it is rather important to prevent one's principal plan coming directly into the hands of the person whom you want watched.
>
> > Love is the law, love under will.
>
> > > Yours truly,
> > >
> > > Aleister Crowley
> > > Knight Guardian of the Sangraal[49]

Greene visited Italy that Easter, where Crowley met him in Naples to discuss drugs, sex, and libel. "Did Shelley bring libel actions?" AC asked. Before Greene could respond, he continued. "No. He came to Italy. Did Byron bring libel actions? No. He came to Italy. Did I bring libel actions?" By this time, Greene was able to follow the answer in his mind. Crowley received Greene warmly, and a visit to Cefalù left him reporting to Raoul's mother that Crowley was well-liked in the community, the children seemed clean and healthy, and that he saw nothing suspicious about Raoul's death.

Then, just as Crowley prepared to get back to business, the Office of the Commisario summoned him. Accompanied by Mudd and Leah, Crowley learned that he had one week to settle his affairs and leave the country.[50]

CHAPTER SIXTEEN

Eccentrics in Exile

Poor and downtrodden, accused of murdering his best friend and favorite pupil, Crowley faced expulsion from his Abbey of Thelema at the Villa Santa Barbara. A petition signed by local villagers sorry to see Crowley go did nothing to undo the expulsion order. He wrote his will on April 30, leaving his possessions to Mudd, then pondered what to do tomorrow, when his deadline came to leave the country. Unsure where to go or what to do, he knew only that the Great Work had to continue. So, on May 1, he consulted the I Ching. It advised that he go to Tunis.

Leah, convinced that a detective was following them, accompanied Crowley while Norman, Ninette, and the children stayed behind, maintaining the Abbey until matters were rectified. They reached Tunis on May 2, and shortly thereafter ended up twenty-five miles northeast in Au Souffle du Zéphyr, the cheapest hotel in La Marsa. Crowley's journal at this time records:

> Another bad night: this time because a mouse ran across Leah's face at 1:15 a.m. She started screaming and became violently hysterical. I copied her as faithfully as I could.[1]

The image of Crowley shrieking hysterically with Leah is both funny and sad. They soon found themselves under a doctor's care as their health suffered from stress. Meanwhile, the *Sunday Express* triumphantly proclaimed:

The Beast Told Go:
Move by Fascisti against Crowley:
Week's Notice.[2]

Back at the Abbey, the remaining Thelemites fared their best. On May 19, at 7:26 a.m., Ninette gave birth to la Calce's daughter; the father contributed nothing to the child's support and complained when Ninette was unable to pay the rent. "Carlo is a piece of shit," Leah wrote Ninette in a supportive note. "I wish O.P.V. [Mudd] would tell him so." Crowley, however, gladly took on the paternal role. He named the child Isabella Isis Selene Hecate Artemis Diana Hera Jane, although Ninette would come to call her simply Mimi after her twin sister. Casting the child's horoscope, he observed:

> Mars, rising above Luna, is rather threatening, but there are no close bad aspects either to the Sun or Moon, so probably there is not much to worry about. There is no big complex to make the child distinguished. She is likely to develop into a fairly ordinary little whore.[3]

To the Thelemite who venerated the whore Babalon, this last sentence was not intended as derogatory. As Crowley stressed in closing the letter: "Ever yours with lots of love, Beast." Elsewhere, he asked Mudd to "Tell Ninette that I love her very dearly and enjoyed her letter immensely."[4]

In another letter, Leah tried to keep morale up and family ties tight by adding, "Please tell Miss Lulette that Big Lion and Lala talk about her more than about anyone else." Ninette similarly did her best to keep "Mama Lala" abreast of developments at the Abbey: Hansi had stripped someone's tree of green apricots; Isabella had bedbugs in her crib; Lulette asked Beast to bring her back some chocolates; and Howard's sagacity grew by leaps and bounds. In matters of the Great Work, she took on Salvatore, their drug connection, as a Probationer. Regarding her own practice of *pranayama,* Ninette wrote, "I was doing it the other day outdoors whence Hansi came up. Lulette called to him, 'shh, Hansi! Shummy's doing polyoner.' I had to stop and have a beneficial laugh."[5]

Crowley spent the spring writing. After a series of drug experiments in May, he dictated the essay "Ethyl Oxide" to Leah. He also worked on his life story, which he cynically dubbed the Hag, or 'autohagiography,' i.e., the autobiography of a saint. Even at this early stage, Crowley's vision—projected at 600,000 words long—was quite ambitious:

> The MS though lively is censor proof. It can be represented artfully in prosepctuses as the Confessions of A.C. A great fuss can be made about mailing copies to subscribers in a plain wrapper and otherwise ensuring their delivery.... There should be no difficulty in selling outright 2000 at $10 a copy. Surplus subscriptions can be absorbed in a second Edition which can be in some way different from the first—either abridged or edited or in some way sufficiently altered. During the issuing of the prospectuses the Author will undertake some feat which will bring him great extra publicity.[6]

Work also progressed at this time on a commentary to *The Book of the Law.* Regarding this comment, Crowley wrote in 1946:

> Remember always that Commentary was written 25 years ago, and in a peculiarly exalted state of mind which I can never regain; which is why I never dared touch it. Afraid even to read it![7]

On June 17 he began his commentary on "Liber LXV, or the Book of the Heart Girt with the Serpent." Also at this time, he wrote "Eruption of Aetna":

> Have not I spoken, even I, Benito,
> The big, the brave, the mighty Mussolini,
> The ultra-modern Cæsar, with my 'Veni
> Vidi, Vici'?—let all the world agree, too!
> Does a mere mountain think that it is free to
> Stir up sedition? Shall such teeny-weeny
> Volcanoes venture to display their spleeny
> And socialist cant?—Subside, mosquito![8]

It was the first in a series of anti-Mussolini poems Crowley wrote in response to his expulsion, published later that year as *Songs for Italy*.

Mudd had come to Tunis as early as June 20 to be closer to Crowley and help with the Great Work. Unable to afford separate lodgings, they shared a room, giving them ample time to talk. Mudd was so devoted a student and so dedicated an academician that he took reams of notes on everything they discussed. Among these were Crowley's plans: he would summon Frank Bennett back to the Abbey, and he planned to contact Trotsky "to suggest that I be put in charge of a world-wide campaign to eradicate Christianity";[9] neither Bennett nor Trotsky would come through.

On July 22, Mudd's mathematician friend joined them. Edmund Hugo Saayman (1897–1971) was born at Orange Free State in southern Africa, attending Boys High School in Riversdale and Grey University College in Bloemfontein, where he earned his BS degree.[10] He arrived in the United Kingdom in October 1921[11] as a Rhodes Scholar attending New College, Oxford. Here, he was supervised by prominent English mathematician and number theorist G. H. Hardy (1877–1947).[12] After his summer holiday with Mudd, he would return to Oxford to marry Janet Stokes in 1924, receive his BA with a third class in maths in 1925 and his MA in 1927.[13] As a physics master at High Pavement School, Nottingham, and a part-time lecturer at Leicester University College, he would publish several influential papers in physics.[14]

A few days later, Crowley moved into the luxurious Tunisia Palace on a Lesser Magical Retirement.

In July, Crowley's article on "The Genius of Mr. James Joyce" appeared in *The New Pearson's*.[15] Frater Achad, meanwhile, was publishing his own books in Chicago: the first, *QBL: The Bride's Reception* (1923), was a boiled-down Thelemic version of Crowley's own kabbalistic essays from *The Equinox*. Although this was acceptable, his next book, *Crystal Vision through Crystal Gazing* (1923) angered Crowley because of its unacknowledged extracts from *The Vision and the Voice*. On April 14, 1923, Jones completed the manuscript for his next book, *The Egyptian Revival*. In it, he claimed to restore the order of the paths on the Tree of Life by inverting their conventional arrangement. After finishing this book, he had a vision that inspired the pinnacle of his kabbalistic work, *The Anatomy of the Body of God*. On Achad's output, Crowley wrote:

> The books—even apart from the absurd new attribution proposed for the
> Paths—are so hopelessly bad in almost every way—English, style, sense,
> point of view, oh everything!—yet they may do good to the people they
> are written for.[16]

August and September became a flurry of activity, Crowley finishing his comment on "Liber LXV"' proceeding with the Hag, fuming about Achad's *Egyptian Revival,* and wooing Aimée Gouraud. On August 16 he wrote "Tyrol,"
another anti-Mussolini poem. By August 25 he was planning a Golf Course
Hotel that would never materialize. When he learned at the end of the month
that his South African pupil Adam Gray Murray was in town, Crowley summoned him to his side in London. Like Bennett, Murray failed to show.

September began on a sour note for Crowley, who wrote in his diary for
the 2nd:

> This a.m. read of the Bombardment of Corfu, killing some dozen or more
> Armenian children—refugees—in revenge for the murder of some Wop
> fools by some persons unknown some 1,500 miles away! What utter
> fools—as well as blackguards—statesmen are!
>   Spent all day writing 6 sonnets (& some other verse) on the atrocity.

On September 17, Crowley updated the Hag to include a chapter covering the
Abbey and his expulsion.

The Thelemites' situation became even more tumultuous when Norman
Mudd realized he was in love with Leah. It was, in AC's opinion, a breakdown
in reason and discipline, and he responded by devising an Act of Truth by
which Mudd could regain his grip on reality. This "Act of Truth" concept was
so important to Crowley's magick that he would later devote a section to it in
his *Magick without Tears;* it is Mudd, however, who gives the best explanation:

> All initiation must begin with an Act of Truth, a definite commitment
> which affirms and seals the faith of the Aspirant that success in the Great
> Work is of a higher value than any other conceivable good.... It is there-
> fore an absolute rule in this work of establishing among men the kingdom
> of the Aeon of Heru-Ra-Ha, that every aspirant is required, right at the
> start, to make a crucial decision, to take an irrevocable step without receiv-
> ing full information as to its significance and without security. The cling-
> ing to safety in one form or another is the mark of a Slave. To break it
> quite simply and completely is the only mode open to the aspirant of
> asserting the Kingly nature. This is the first necessity and the first ordeal is
> designed to accomplish it.[17]

Crowley, Saayman, and Leah witnessed Mudd's written Act of Truth:

> Do what thou wilt shall be the whole of the Law.
>
>   I, Omnia Pro Veritate, a Probationer of A∴A∴ hereby call the Lords
> of Initiation to witness this mine Oath, which I subscribe in the presence

of The Beast 666, 9°=2□, A∴A∴ and of the Scarlet Woman Alostrael 8°=3□, A∴A∴.

I call upon them by the Power of the Act of Truth done by me shortly after the Winter Solstice of the Eighteenth Year of the Aeon, when I renounced my career and my material possessions without reservation, that I might devote my energies wholly to the Great Work, that is, to the Establishment of the Law of Thelema as given by Aiwass through The Beast 666 (the man Aleister Crowley) in the *Book of the Law* (Liber Al s[ub] f[igura] XXXI) as in the MS which I have seen, and which I here declare to command by allegiance, in loyal cooperation with The Beast its Prophet.

I hereby acknowledge that most if not all men when in the condition known as 'being in love' become temporarily unable to use their normal judgment.

The Beast and Alostrael have told me that I, being by my own admission 'in love' with Alostrael, have become, and am now unable to reason correctly, and to devote my energies to the Great Work.

The Beast furthermore officially lays it upon me as a Probationer of A∴A∴ to take this present Oath, by virtue of the clause in my Obligation pertinent to the matter.

Albeit unable to admit the justice of their view, I am resolved to adhere to the letter of my Oath, and to trust their statement that I am at present incapable of deciding rightly for myself in this matter.

I hereby solemnly pledge myself to extirpate once and for all the consciousness of the tendency to perceive the sensation of my being 'in love' with Alostrael.

And I conjure the Lords of Initiation by the Password of the present Equinox, the Word [IHI AUD] that this Oath be of power to establish in me the Magical Light and to make me wholly master of my animal and emotional impulses.

Wherein if I fail, may the light of my body be darkened, and the virtue of manhood abide no more with me.

Love is the law, love under will.[18]

Mudd signed the form, and the witnesses endorsed it. While Crowley had originally planned to send Mudd away on a soul-searching retirement, he noted improvement in Mudd's disposition later that same day: "I am much less anxious as to the issue than I was when I wrote the Act of Truth for him."[19] Mudd nevertheless decided to take eight days to meditate and learn by example from Crowley's autobiography. "Well," Mudd, with downcast eyes, said to Leah, "goodbye. Look after yourself and the Beast, won't you?"

She nodded. "Love is the law …"

"Love under will."

Leah clenched Mudd tightly, pressed her lips against his, and said, "I love you." She repeated it twice.

Mudd was a wretchedly frozen clod, feeling more awkward and unattractive than ever. Deep inside, his soul cried out, *You're a damned good comrade, and that's all that matters.* But tongue-tied, he only repeated himself lamely like a stuck record. "Love under will."

"You *will* come back to us, won't you, and work together again?"

He hoped so, but was unsure. "Well, anyhow, we *will* work." With that, he left.[20] Contemplating his love for Leah, his oath to forget her, and their parting words that could have been so much more, he wept. Rather than clear his mind of the Scarlet Woman, it made him love her more than ever.

Portrait of Norman Mudd by Aleister Crowley.

Applying logic to the problem, he produced a solution: *The Book of the Law,* their moral guidebook, demanded that the Scarlet Woman be loud and adulterous. This meant Leah had to be married: not to Beast, her lover, but to Mudd. Thus, having sex with Beast would make her an adulteress. Crowley, of course, rejected the idea, responding, "Adultery does not imply marriage, no more than whoredom implies commerce."[21]

By the end of October, Mudd's fixation moved from Leah to *The Book of the Law,* and he and Beast corresponded freely on the subject. He viewed AC's role as Beast logically, asking what he should have done upon receiving the book. What were its instructions? How were the tenets of Thelema to be disseminated? Mudd believed *The Book of the Law* was never intended for the masses, Aiwass calling it the law of princes and kings: "Therefore the kings of the earth shall be Kings for ever: the slaves shall serve."[22] Thus, Crowley had erred in publishing *The Book of the Law,* Mudd telling him, "You have assumed that you were free to 'broadcast' CCXX [*The Book of the Law*] even to force it on the attention of the General Public."[23] Crowley's real task, Mudd believed, was to put *The Book of the Law* into the hands of politicians, to train world leaders in Thelema and magick, and to amass the wealth necessary to put over the

Great Work. Furthermore, Mudd noted that after nearly twenty years, many explicit instructions in the text had not been carried out: writing the comment, abstructing the Stele, and selecting an island. Thus, Crowley had so seriously fumbled *The Book of the Law*'s clear instructions that the Secret Chiefs were now punishing him with misfortune.

Although Crowley seriously considered Mudd's observations, agreeing with most and encouraging further comment, he disagreed on several points. According to *The Book of the Law,* for instance, anyone could be a king. It referred to one's spiritual, not political, nobility. In order to control Mudd's excited exegeses, Crowley recorded, "I should warn Fra∴ O.P.V. once and for all that he is dangerously excited mentally and will become definitely insane (legally speaking) unless he can control and slow down his *chittam* [Sanskrit, mind, mental activities]."[24] During this contentious exchange, Crowley penned what has become known as the "Short Comment":

> The study of this Book is forbidden. It is wise to destroy this copy after the first reading.
> Whosoever disregards this does so at his own risk and peril. These are most dire.
> Those who discuss the contents of this Book are to be shunned by all, as centres of pestilence.
> All questions of the Law are to be decided only by appeal to my writings, each for himself.
> There is no law beyond Do what thou wilt.

Crowley ascribed so much importance to this brief text that he included it in subsequent editions of *The Book of the Law*. Regardless of whether one interprets it as a tool of convenience or an inspired text, it silenced Mudd.[25]

In late October, AC and Leah hired a boy named Mohammed and drove to Nefta, where they rented a camel and set off into the desert. They were on a magical retirement, seeking new inspiration or direction. They walked at night and slept through the day, planning on a month of it. However, all three took ill and returned to a Nefta hotel. Waiting for them they found Mudd, who had pawned the ring Crowley had given him in order to get to Tunis.

Setbacks aside, the trip proved valuable. While staying at the Hotel du Djerid, Crowley wrote the Djeridensis Comment, or Commentary D, to *The Book of the Law;* it was one of his major analyses of the text. Meanwhile, Leah experienced a series of visions that Crowley believed demonstrated direct communication with the Secret Chiefs. Her first vision began at 10:30 p.m. after taking laudanum. Without prompting from Crowley, she saw a street lined with houses, and the geomantic symbol *Via* (the way or path) appeared in a white cresence. Crowley reached for his ephemeris, noting the moon's rising in Cancer. Via, he recalled, corresponded to water, Cancer, and the moon. The day, Monday, was even named for the moon. "Repeat *Gayatri*[26] while I write this up," he instructed, and reached for his diary to scribble these observations.

Aleister Crowley in Tunisia, 1923.

"Okay, shoot!" he prompted when ready, and she continued to describe a horseman wearing jeweled armor and riding a white steed. Crowley equated him with the Knight of Cups, one of the watery tarot cards. Next, she saw two turtles drawing a boat, which reminded her of Lohengrin. Invoking the moon, she saw a woman hidden behind a lyre and fountain. The fountain, Crowley noted, represented the Two of Cups—the aspect of Venus in Cancer—but the woman's countenance was too bright to describe. When he asked, "What is her name?" the woman opened her hand—actually a bird's claw—and dropped a crystal ball. Although unspoken, the word implied by her was *NiLZA.* Using the Hebrew Nun, English i, Latin L, Arabic Z, and Greek A, Crowley tallied the word to ninety, for the watery Queen of Cups tarot card.

Leah finally vibrated the magical word *Thelema* to get a clearer image, but the image went up in sparks and flame like a sun. Unintelligible images flooded her vision until she insisted, "I want to hear, not see!" Into her mind popped the response from *Liber AL* ii.9, "but there is that which remains." She descended a valley into an elaborate chapel wherein a peacock, a symbol of the Knight of Cups, was worshiped. Its name was *PIRA.* Crowley tallied the name to 291 (denoting a torrent of water, and the Angel of Aquarius, the water bearer). Leah, who was quick on her feet at gematria, suggested the spelling APIRA, which yielded 292, a number of the moon.

Finally, Leah encountered a white man, cast in blue light, and knew she had reached the ruler of this vision. "Do what thou wilt shall be the whole of the Law," she greeted. He responded by slaying Pira with a *dorge,* and the temple burst into an uproar. His name, in Greek, was FAB, and his number, 503, was that of the chalice; appropriate since the chapel reminded Leah of the Sangraal. After he proved his knowledge and attainment, Crowley instructed her, "Enough for now. Return."

Planted firmly in this reality, Leah and Crowley analyzed the recurrent watery images of her vision, in harmony with the planetary position of the Moon (itself a symbol of water) in the aqueous sign of Cancer the crab. As they spoke, the clouds opened and dumped torrents of rain on Nefta.

The visions continued, but they desperately needed financial and spiritual support. Crowley instructed Mudd to send a summons to all his students:

> Do what thou wilt shall be the whole of the Law.
>
> These letters: to summon the Aspirant _____ to present himself in person without delay or excuse before my Acting Chancellor Frater Omnia Pro Veritate Prof. Norman Mudd, M.A. Camb. from him to receive my further Instructions as to his Training as a Kingly Man that he may discover and do his True Will and fulfill his proper function in the Aeon of Heru-Ra-Ha.
>
> Witness my hand: TO MEGA THERION 666 9°=2□ A∴A∴
> LOGOS AIONOS THELEMA 93[27]

Alas, the summons scared off everyone but Windram's student Adam Gray Murray. He arrived at the Abbey on November 20 with a donation of two hundred lire. "Hip-hip-hoorah," lonely Ninette wrote excitedly to Mudd. "Murray has arrived from South Africa. He is a dear. He meets all requirements for being the most enjoyable companion I could wish for. I hope he remains right here with me and you never get a glimpse of him."[28]

Meanwhile, Crowley described his financial dilemma to American book collector and patron of the arts Montgomery Evans II (1901–1954):

> I have been living literally from hand to mouth for I don't know how long. This fact is well known to my enemies who do not scruple to attack my honour and my property in every base way, knowing that I cannot take the proper legal action. If we had a business partner with a few thousand dollars, I and my secretary could put everything on a sound basis very quickly, and incidentally vindicate my reputation against the creatures who have been vile enough to publish all sorts of idiotic falsehoods about me.[29]

Thus the Thelemites, congregating at the end of 1923, parted ways in an attempt to salvage their life's work.

Crowley sailed to Marseilles, where he stayed at the Hotel de Blois and, on January 2, 1924, met Frank Harris—the business partner alluded to above—for lunch in Nice. Harris was happy to see Crowley, and together they planned to purchase the *Paris Evening Telegram*. Both saw it as a handy means to a profit, and Crowley hoped that owning his own press would empower him to clear his name. Alas, neither one could amass their half of the necessary capital.

When Leah recovered from another illness and arrived in Cefalù, she finally met Mimi, who was now "shamelessly fat."[30] Another new, but slightly older, resident of the Abbey was Arturo Sabatini, a poor boy who hated his home and hung around at the Abbey, hoping to join them. His eyes were damaged during the war, and he had spent his pension of two hundred lire a month to buy sweet wine and cigarettes for Ninette. He was pleasing company, and when she was lonely, Ninette would let him stay the night. Leah soon began instructing him, while Ninette practiced sex magick with him.

Finally, there was Murray, the Abbey's newest arrival and oldest member. His attitudes clashed with Leah's, prompting him to say, "She said she was divinely appointed by the Gods to teach me, but a woman cannot teach a man." At long last, however, Leah felt optimistic, glad to be back at Cefalù:

> There is no 'back home.' Though I had furniture, cut-glass, a salary, and a very good housekeeper in the form of my mother, I never knew about home till I came here. I have no personal possessions here—not even a lock on my door—and all sorts of people blow in and stay a while, people with whom I seem to have nothing in common—no privacy in the ordinary sense of the word—yet I am free as a bird and not a libertine!…
>
> Even if I had been deserted, neglected, abused, doped, etc. ad infinitum, in this awful 'Hell Hole of Devil Worshippers' I should have started a pennant stand in Paris rather than to have gone back to my raised (?) salary as a music supervisor![31]

Mudd remained in Tunis, trying unsuccessfully to raise money for passage to London, where he hoped to resolve the problem with Chiswick Press's stock of Crowley books and to publish "positive truth" in response to the *Sunday Express* libels. Feeling hopeless about his situation, he found a stamped postcard and wrote to Crowley, "Beloved Father, I haven't eaten in thirty-six hours, and I am completely indifferent whether I eat again." Crowley reported he was "in bed with a bitch," causing Mudd to shudder at the irony of his unrequited love for Leah. Faced with overwhelming monetary problems, his crusade in England to clear Crowley's name went on indefinite hold.

Crowley was but one of several mystics drawn to the sylvan glades of his beloved Fontainebleau, including influential Greek-Armenian mystic George Ivanovich Gurdjieff (c. 1866–1949) and his disciple Pyotr Demianovich Ouspensky (1878–1947). Gurdjieff called his teachings the Fourth Way, developing the body, mind, and emotions in tandem in order to achieve spiritual awakening. Believing group work superior to solitary work, he established Schools of the Fourth Way, founding the Institute for the Harmonious Development of Man at the Château Le Prieuré in Fontainebleau-Avon in October 1922. After Katherine Mansfield died of tuberculosis during a visit there, Gurdjieff was unfairly called "the man who killed Katherine Mansfield,"[32] thus giving him something in common with Crowley's own tragedy with Loveday.

Crowley called on Gurdjieff on February 10, 1924, but the master was out; so he settled for a stimulating dinner with his right-hand man, former British Intelligence officer Major Frank Pinder. Crowley considered Pinder "a hell of a fine fellow" and recorded the visit in his diary:

> Gurdjieff, their prophet, seems a tip-top man. Heard more sense and insight than I've done for years. Pinder dines at 7:30. Oracle for my visit was "There are few men: there are enough." Later, a really wonderful evening with Pinder. Gurdjieff clearly a very advanced adept. My chief quarrels are over sex (I doubt whether Pinder understands G's true position) and their punishments, e.g., depriving the offender of a meal or making him stand half an hour with his arms out. Childish and morally valueless.[33]

Years later, Crowley would meet Gurdjieff disciple C. Stanley Nott (1887–1978) and, through this connection, come to meet the mystic. In his account, Nott reported that Crowley arrived and told the boys stories of how he was teaching his own son to be a devil, while Gurdjieff kept a close eye on him.[34] In Yorke's version, "they sniffed around one another like dogs."[35] A more colorful conclusion is relayed by Webb: as Crowley prepared to leave that Sunday evening, Gurdjieff ascended the staircase to the second floor halfway, turned, and asked, "Mister, now you go?" The Beast, heading toward the door, stopped, faced him, and replied that he was, in fact, leaving. "You have been a guest? And now you are no longer guest?" Crowley agreed with both statements. Gurdjieff, released from the constraints of hospitality, grew red with the rage he had kept pent inside the entire weekend. "You filthy!" he spat. "You dirty inside! Never again you set foot in my house." Gurdjieff's histrionic tirade rambled on as a puzzled Crowley continued on his way.[36] None of Crowley's diaries or letters, however, mention this incident; neither do Gurdjieff's.

Separation proved hard on Crowley's extended family. Ninette and Beast missed each other, prompting the second concubine to write, "My well-loved Beast, 93. I write to you tonight because I feel I must tell you I love you and long to be with you."[37] Meanwhile, his daughter wrote separately:

> Dear Beast,
>
> My first tooth has come out. I am sending it to you. It is Lulette who is writing it. Thank you for my box of candies.
> Beast, I love you. Soon I will come to you. Love to you, A.
>
> Lulu P.[38]

Although he had taken the oath of an Ipsissimus two years earlier (on May 23, 1921), Crowley's final initiation into the ultimate grade of the A∴A∴ did not begin until the winter solstice (December 21, 1923); it climaxed in February 1924 and concluded that March. A fox, an Eastern symbol of wisdom, served as his spirit familiar in this initiation; on February 21, it escorted Crowley into the upper realms of Air, through unimaginably huge caverns of ice, and into the lowest Spheres of Fire. As he recorded:

> At one period it was necessary for me to ascend from the most tenuous regions of pure air through a series of vast caverns so devised that nothing human could possibly pass through them into the regions of pure fire. To accomplish this it was necessary that I should be exhausted physically to the utmost point compatible with continued life.[39]

While he left few details on the nature of his ordeal, his letters show that Crowley was sick from nervous prostration and recovering from two operations. He was so ill that, back at the Abbey, Ninette and Arturo performed a sex magick ritual to hasten his recovery. He was also having dark moments of self-doubt. At one point, he asked Mudd, "Have I ever done anything of any value, or am I a mere trifler, existing by a series of shifts of one kind or another. A wastrel, a coward, man of straw?" Amused by the question, Mudd answered by quoting *The Book of the Law*—"thou hast no right but to do thy will. Do that, and no other shall say nay"—to which Crowley responded, "You have probably saved my life."[40] At this time, he also pondered his continuing drug use. "Was the whole of my trouble really due to withdrawal of heroin, and my rapid recovery to cautious restocking?"[41] Recognizing that he required the drug medically because of his asthma, he conceded there was also a psychosomatic component to his condition. "My general conclusion on this part of the problem is that drugs are fundamentally useless—and treacherous, the Lord knows! They are just Emergency Rations.... the Asthmatic is in fact a *Malade Imaginaire* [imaginary invalid] in a certain sense."[42]

Regardless, Crowley described his initiation:

> At this time he lay sick unto death. He was entirely alone; for They [i.e. the Secret Chiefs] would not even permit the presence of those few whom They had themselves appointed to aid him in this final initiation [Leah, Ninette, Mudd]. In this last ordeal the earthly part of him was dissolved in water; the water was vaporized into air; the air was rarefied utterly, until he was free to make the last effort, and to pass into the vast caverns of the Threshold which guards the Realm of Fire. Now naught human may come through those immensities. So in that Fire he was consumed wholly, and as pure Spirit alone did he return, little by little, during the months that followed, into the body and mind that had perished in that great ordeal of which he can say no more than: I died.[43]

While the manner in which he was rarefied and destroyed by each of the four elements is indescribable, Crowley recorded its result in his diary:

> I am beginning to realize faintly of how many and gross deceits I have been cleansed in my ascent into the Sphere of Fire. In particular, the 'invincible Love' which Frater O.P.V. discovered in me is now quite 'unassuaged of purpose' and 'delivered from the lust of result' flowing forth freely 'under will' as it should; now therefore on its waters there shall

bloom deathless the Lotus of Purity whereupon Hoor-paar-kraat may
stand and glow with Silence....
  Now am I wholly entered within the Sphere of Fire, the Empyrean;
and no other shall say nay.
  It has been a terrible ordeal.[44]

But Crowley, in his estimation, survived to become his very own self, the Ipsissimus, looking on the world from the Crown of the Tree of Life.

When Leah and Norman went to attend to their ailing master, she was nervous about meeting Crowley. If his initiation was genuine, the man she loved was no more: as a Magus, he had been the logos, the word Thelema, incorporated in human form as the Beast. As an Ipsissimus, he was now a being of pure spirit, and she was unsure how to approach him. Back in Cefalù, she had done a ritual to prepare herself for this meeting. As she described the rite, "All thoughts fled leaving me with, 'My whole being calls out to you to see us thro' this crisis.' I used this as my opening speech and then the ideas flowed."[45] Gone were her fears of dire consequences for failing the Great Work; gone were her feelings of inferiority, for she was, after all, the Scarlet Woman. For the first time in ages, Leah felt confident and happy.

However, she also brought news that they risked losing the Abbey unless they paid the rent. Thus Crowley called in debts and friendships, even going so far as to contact George Cecil Jones's representative about obtaining an advance against future payments of the trust fund from his mother's death. Meanwhile, Leah wrote instructions for Frank Bennett to cable whatever money he had saved for his voyage to the Abbey per Crowley's earlier summons.

Meanwhile, Crowley, in his mission to rehabilitate his name, wrote *An Open Letter to Lord Beaverbrook*. It was the desperate gesture of a man who was now too impecunious to travel to London, let alone hire a solicitor. As he remarked bitterly to Holman Hunt—who worked for Crowley's solicitors Parker, Garrett & Co[46]—"The *Sunday Express* made sure that I was penniless before printing its lies."[47] He sent Mudd to take the essay to the *Sunday Express* and circulate it to London's literati. Although Mudd was poor and dressed in rags, Crowley felt the apparent ruin of a good man by the *Sunday Express* would only help their case. Mudd soon wound up living in Chelsea. His room at 27 Redburn Street was uncomfortable, "a poor sort of affair."[48] He was working with Jane Wolfe, who'd been in London since March 1923, and for a time became her lover. When Murray joined them, they sold their clothes to raise money for food and rent.

With money coming in from various sources and the I Ching promising a great change, Crowley and Leah anticipated the end of April. Over the years, May was always a big month: they conceived Poupée in 1919; Crowley's unborn son was conceived a year later; in 1921, Crowley took his Ipsissimus oath; Collins contracted *The Diary of a Drug Fiend* in 1922; and in 1923, Italy expelled Crowley. Just as things were looking up, they received a notice of eviction from 50 rue Vavin.

Although in the past Bourcier had allowed Crowley to stay at 50 rue Vavin on credit, he had sold the establishment. The new owner honored no such arrangement; on May 1, he ejected Crowley and Leah from the hotel and kept their luggage in lieu of payment. Crowley angrily cursed the hotel for interfering with the Great Work. Holed up at 6 rue Jolia, they spoke to police and lawyers for several days. By May 8, they had retrieved most of their luggage, and the cursed hotel at 50 rue Vavin soon went bankrupt.

Soon afterward, Crowley met Argentinian artist Xul Solar (1887–1963). Oscar Agustín Alejandro Schulz Solari was a painter, poet, and visionary known for weaving mystical elements from kabbalah, astrology, tarot, I Ching, and Crowley into his works. His close friend, Argentinian writer Jorgé Luis Borges, called him "our William Blake."[49] Having spent the last dozen years studying modernist art in Europe, Solar was still early in his career when he arrived in Paris on April 29, 1924, to exhibit three pieces at the Musée Galliera as part of a show organized by La Maison de l'Amérique Latine and the Académie Internationale des Beaux-Arts. He also used this opportunity to track down Crowley, whom he had been seeking as a teacher for some time. Solar found him in Chelles on May 14, and the following day Crowley accepted him as a student, noting in his diary, "Xul Solar Signed Oath in Silence Diary."[50] Playing chess with AC later that evening, Solar remarked that "his True Will is to unify South America on Spiritual lines."[51] Solar had read *The Equinox* and translated *Book Four,* so Crowley had high hopes that he would produce translations of the Holy Books and help to establish OTO in Argentina. Having tested his astral visions and liked what he saw, AC tasked his new student with recording astral visions for each of the sixty-four I Ching hexagrams. In a letter to Solar five years later, Crowley reminded him, "By the way, you owe me a complete set of visions for the 64 Yi symbols. Your record as the best seer I ever tested still stands today, and I should like to have a set of visions as a model."[52] Solar eventually did produce these visions as *San Signos* (Holy Signs), written in his invented language of Neo-criollo; only a few of these visions have ever been published. Solar returned to Buenos Aires shortly after meeting Crowley, becoming prominent among the South American avant garde in the 1920s.[53]

Early that June, when Crowley apprised Frank Harris of his plans with the *Open Letter,* Harris advised Crowley to hire a good solicitor. If he agreed to split the profit with his counsel, Harris claimed, Crowley could sue Lord Beaverbrook for libel and receive $20,000 in damages. More than ever, AC felt the need to retaliate.

He hired Herbert Clarke of rue St. Honoré to print three thousand copies of the fifteen-page *An Open Letter to Lord Beaverbrook,* a document that called for full public investigation of the outrageous attack on one of England's most prolific contemporary poets. With Jane's help, Mudd sent copies with cover letters to friends and important people, including members of the House of Lords, Scotland Yard, the British press, George Bernard Shaw, Arnold Bennett, writer Miguel de Unamuno (1864–1936), and anarchist Emma Goldman (1869–1940). In his naive enthusiasm, Mudd even asked the Bureau of Investigation for a letter of recommendation for Crowley's espionage work during the Great War; the U.S. government, of course, sent no such document.[54]

Responses to the *Open Letter* were mixed. Augustus John promised his support, and philosopher Bertrand Russell wrote:

> I received your letter and one from Dr. Crowley. The latter seems to show that he is in a position to establish the falsehood of the libel ... If you can put any wide-read newspaper to print a letter ... asserting that the *Sunday Express* lied on this occasion, it would bring an action against the editor of the newspaper in question. Probably this is strategically the best way to goad the *Sunday Express* into action. For this purpose, you must find the right editor ... I know nothing about Dr. Crowley, but should be glad to see the Beaverbrook press shown up.

Bernard Shaw, knowing nothing of the matter, would not support Crowley. "I replied that no such proposition was ever made," AC wrote. "He was asked to fight for the decency of public controversy." Emma Goldman wrote helplessly:

> I regret I am too poor to be a help to anybody just now. Neither can I lend my name as support to any undertaking until I myself am on my feet.

Similarly, Philip Heseltine (a.k.a. Peter Warlock, 1894–1930) wrote to Mudd, "I am very sorry to hear that Crowley is at present in such straitened circumstances. I very much regret that, financially at any rate, I can do nothing to help him, being in perhaps as bad a case myself." Even those with money proved unsupportive. Otto Kahn, for instance, responded simply: "I regret to learn of the situation which Mr. Crowley describes, but as I leave for New York tomorrow morning, I am sorry that it will be impossible for me to see you during my present stay in Europe." Austin Harrison simply dismissed Crowley as a "moral wreck from the abuse of heroin." Most discouraging was the reply Mudd received from his father:

> Your letter and enclosure reached us last evening and both mother and I are deeply concerned and very despondent about the whole affair. We hope you are quite sure of your facts, for the events referred to seem to relate to the period of your absence from this country when you were thousands of miles away from your hero and therefore not fully cognizant of his doings. If you are relying mainly on his word, I am afraid you are trusting on a very broken reed. You know we never liked him and have not the slightest sympathy with his cause. We have always looked on him as your evil genius right from your Cambridge days, and are terribly afraid that he will blight your whole life.[55]

In the end, the lukewarm response to the letter and Mudd's own poverty rendered impotent this plan to salvage Crowley's name. It was the beginning of the collapse of everything the Thelemites held dear.

Back at Cefalù, Ninette's sex magick with Arturo resulted in her pregnancy. Announcing it to Leah, she wrote, "I am the prospective mother of a kicking healthy bastard, who should show its sex barring accident during the month of March. I hope this will be a painful shock to no one, in spite of the warning I received once of not to indulge in my natural pastime; I promise to let up a bit after this one."[56]

Meanwhile, fearing the Baron would make good on his threats to evict the Thelemites from the Abbey, she and Murray pawned the Abbey's furniture. They placed Crowley's books, manuscripts, paintings, and diaries in the care of a Palermo gentleman named Aguel, who began shipping them to Mudd via the American Express Company. After the first box reached London safely, Mudd eagerly requested shipment of the remaining dozen cases, postage due. These Aguel sent aboard the SS *Suein Jarl*. Alas, His Majesty's Customs inspected the cases and found some questionable Crowley pieces, including the patently obscene "Leah Sublime," his "A Book of Photographs," and thirty-three copies of the homosexual *Bagh-i-Muattar*. On July 8, Customs sent Mudd a "Notice of seizure of goods prohibited to be imported under Section 42 of the Customs Consolidation Act 1876." They confiscated all twelve boxes. Mudd received the bad news on July 17 and went into a panic: what would Beast do when he found out? On July 24, his nerves frazzled, Mudd took a rest cure from the Great Work.

When Crowley finally found out, he noted with displeasure, "Some lunatic directly inspired by the High Gods sent all my private papers and books to England! The Customs House has had a continuous spasm of Priapism ever since."[57] Writing to Inspector Draper of Scotland Yard, he claimed his research was clinical, intended for mental pathologists. Customs disagreed. When Leah headed for London to help, she experienced considerable difficulty:

> I was refused entrance to England (though I was already seated in the train for London, having passed Customs and Immigrations inspections) for a rat-faced person stage-whispered "Aleister Crowley" to a tall sandy Immigration clerk who asked me to descend myself and accompany him. Not finding A.C. or even C. on my person or in my baggage they announced after 3 hours or more … that they had received telephone orders to send me back.[58]

In the end—March 1926—Customs would destroy the crates containing Crowley's confiscated Cefalù diaries, manuscripts, and rare books. This at least is what has been reported in a number of sources. However, the story does not end there. Two years hence Crowley would write to his new disciple, Gerald Yorke, "The trouble about the Cefalù diaries—and all other MSS —is that any day now there may be nothing to edit!… There are 3 cases still unopened and 10 or 11 more still to come from Italy." And, three weeks thereafter, he would write to this same pupil, "The cases have come (from Italy)." Finally, on Christmas Day of 1928, he wrote to Yorke,

My marginal note was not intended to affirm that any given manuscripts have not been seized. It is in fact probable that duplicates of these diaries were in the cases, but I don't care in the least about this. What I meant by my note was that these particular manuscripts had not been destroyed.... I am delighted with your report about the Customs. It is deliciously characteristic that they should preserve just those portions which they suppose to be obscene, and destroy the rest. What other portion would they understand?[59]

While an early shipment of Crowley's material was seized and destroyed in 1925, it appears a substantial amount survived.

Leah returned to Crowley in Paris after her abortive London trip, and Mudd and Murray soon joined the ailing couple. Finances forced them all to share a room at the Hotel du Maine, with Murray sleeping on the floor. "We are in desperate straits," Leah reported to Montgomery Evans.[60] A day later, Crowley collapsed. "My legs assumed independent control of the situation," he noted. "I had a very amusing time watching them try to kick the bedstand to pieces."[61] Poverty had placed Crowley in a state of involuntary heroin withdrawal, breaking the habit that his Will merely curtailed.

Mudd and Murray fared no better on their return to London: they often went hungry, and Jane was evicted for not paying her rent. In order to get by, Murray soon began pocketing A∴A∴ donations sent from American disciples Frater Achad and Max Schneider (of whom more will follow).

One last crisis completed the tragedy: after Leah's sister Alma visited her and her eccentric lover that August, she proceeded to Cefalù, planning to take Hansi into her custody. Alma Hirsig Bliss (b. 1875) was an artist specializing in miniatures. Loving art from a young age, she attended the Peter-Cooper Institute and spent a year at the Art League. While studying in Paris, she discovered her medium—miniatures—for which she became well known.[62] Examples of her works are kept at the Metropolitan Museum of Art in New York and the Smithsonian American Art Museum.[63] Sometime after 1920 she married New Yorker Louis E. Bliss, who died shortly thereafter in June 1923.[64] In July 1924 she sailed aboard the SS *Minnekahda,* arriving in Plymouth, England, on the 12th,[65] proceeding from there to visit her sister and the Abbey.

Forewarned, Crowley instructed Ninette, "Should Alma come to Cefalù, she is not to be admitted to the Abbey, or allowed to talk to the children. Don't parley with her: throw her out quick!" Alma arrived the same day as the letter, but Ninette nevertheless let Alma in. By September 13 she had snuck off with Hansi. She returned to New York via Southampton, arriving with Hansi in October;[66] the next year, an illustrated feature on Alma pictured "her adopted child" beside one of him "as he appeared when his home was in Italy."[67]

Seeing himself surrounded by misfortune, Crowley, much to Leah's displeasure, sought a fresh magical current in Dorothy Olsen, a thirty-two-year-old American who had joined the A∴A∴ that summer in Chelles. Born in Chicago on September 6, 1892, she'd been summering in France, Belgium, England, Spain, Norway, and Italy the last few years.[68] When Beast announced that the Secret Chiefs were sending him and "Soror Astrid," his new Scarlet Woman, on a magical retirement in Tunis—possibly for several months—Leah collapsed. Reluctant to surrender the rank of Scarlet Woman yet powerless to prevent the retirement, Leah convinced herself that she was Babalon incarnate and that Dorothy was her magical child. Two days before the autumnal equinox, Leah entered on one of the scraps of paper that constituted her diary at this time, "I hereby renounce the title the Scarlet Woman and pass it on to the 'scarlet Concubine of his Desire,' the daughter of Babalon."[69] Together, they received the equinoctial password "Om."

Dorothy Olsen (b. 1892).

That day, Crowley and Dorothy sailed for the Majestic Hotel, Tunis. There they began "a magical operation of the very highest class"[70] in which Crowley wrote "To Man," otherwise known as "The Mediterranean Manifesto":

TO MAN

Do what thou wilt shall be the whole of the Law.

My Term of Office upon the Earth being come in the year of the foundation of the Theosophical Society, I took upon myself, in my turn, the sin of the whole World, that the Prophecies might be fulfilled, so that Mankind may take the Next Step from the Magical Formula of Osiris to that of Horus.

And mine Hour being now upon me, I proclaim my Law.

The Word of the Law is ΘΕΛΗΜΑ. [*Thelema*]

Given in the midst of the Mediterranean Sea
An XX Sol in 3 Libra die Jovis
by me TO ΜΕΓΑ ΘΗΡΙΟΝ [*To Mega Therion*]
ΛΟΓΟΣ ΑΙΟΝΟΣ ΘΕΛΗΜΑ [Logos of the Aeon of Thelema]

Crowley printed this broadsheet to distribute as the new World Teacher, hoping to use the TS's announcement of a coming messiah to fuel his own work.

Back in Paris, the day after Crowley left with Dorothy, Leah prepared to die. Her Big Lion had run off with another woman. She had given up her crown as Scarlet Woman. She was sick, and, furthermore, she was sick of being sick. As a Thelemite, she not only awaited death but felt it was her *Will* to die. Like Poupée, she had finished her job and desired to move on.

On September 24, she wrote her will, leaving her possessions to Mudd, with a few exceptions: to Jane, the bravest woman she knew, Leah left her blue cape; to Ninette, she left custody of Hansi; and her little red purse went to Lulette. She also left instructions for Mudd "to prosecute the swine who are responsible for my death," namely Lord Beaverbrook, Alma Bliss, and H. Roy (the latest landlord to seize Crowley's things for nonpayment of rent). The next day she telegrammed news of her impending death to her good friend Aimée Gouraud, who rushed to her side with food and reassurances. Despite her despair, Leah stressed, particularly to Aimée, that she did not blame Crowley:

> Understand that you are not to think that A.C. deserted me. He did not. He liberated me. I die, not as you imagine through neglect by him but in service to the Work which we united to do. He and I are One, nay are None.
> When you see him you will understand.[71]

On September 26, still convinced she was dying, Leah wrote a tender *au revoir* to the man to whom she was hopelessly devoted:

> My beloved Beast,
>
> 93.
>
> I am going to die tonight. There is very little I can say for now that the conspiracy of Silence is at an end, your monkey takes on the silence.
> I have always loved you, as you have me. That is why you have never failed me as I have never failed you. We have both misunderstood often but we always found that misunderstanding did not matter for it lead to understanding in our case, always at the right time. Only gods know what time means.
> You will not grieve over my death. You will rejoice, God that you are. Remember that Alostrael, Babalon ... the Scarlet Woman, lives forever.
> Leah Hirsig died but then I never knew her ...
>
> I am yours, you are mine
> 93 93/93
> Babalon[72]

Her only regret was that the Beast was so far away while she was on her death bed. On September 28, she wrote in her diary:

> I should have liked, as a human creature, to have died in the arms of The Beast 666, who, as will be noted in my very first diary (commencing Mar 21, 1919) was and is my lover, my mate, my father, my child and every-thing else that Woman needs in Man.[73]

Unable to pay rent, she lost her room, wandering rain-drenched Paris and finally collapsing in the hallway of her hotel as onlookers speculated whether she was ill or merely drugged; a jeering crowd gathered until the police arrived.

Death was all that remained for her. She felt she had fulfilled the prophecy of *The Book of the Law,* which warned that the Scarlet Woman would be "cast out from men: as a shrinking and despised harlot shall she crawl through dusk wet streets, and die cold and an-hungered."[74] She hoped to die on a Monday because in that same scripture, it is written "he is ever a sun, and she a moon."[75] When Monday, September 29, came, she did not die; however, a telegram from Ninette devastated her with news that Alma Bliss, with help from the American consul in Palermo, had fled to America with Hansi. "Alma Bliss," Leah complained, "has communicated with both the governess and myself as though she had done a wonderful deed. She is quite crazy."[76]

The next day, Mudd, having given up in his campaign with the *Open Letter,* joined her in Paris. *Good old Mudd,* she thought: *he's always there when you need him.* On October 3, she placed the Seal of Babalon on his penis; two days later, they celebrated their informal Thelemic wedding, feasting on tea, bread, ham, grapes, and figs. They consummated the marriage on October 7 with an act of sex magick.

"Who is your best girl?" Leah asked as they made love.

"You," he replied.

"What is thy will?"

He recalled the purpose of this act. "To help establish the Law of Thelema."

"Who are you?" she asked pointedly.

"Omnia Pro Veritate." This answer disappointed Leah. When next they made love, Leah described it in her diary: "With a man who does not know who he is but is commonly called Norman Mudd."[77]

Mudd soon returned to London, unable to scrounge up any further money or arrive at any other means of support. On November 19 he signed himself into the Metropolitan Asylums Board home for the homeless poor. He gave his age as thirty-five and his occupation as literary agent.

Leah, meanwhile, remained in France, finding temporary work washing dishes, peeling potatoes, and carrying coals in a Montparnasse restaurant for thirteen hours a day, waiting for Beast and Astrid to pay her passage to Tunis.

By now, the Abbey was practically empty, Ninette having given all but two large cases to Aguel. Only Ninette, Arturo, and the children remained; and the four young ones—with a fifth on the way—kept her busy. Mimi was eighteen months old, and when she wasn't wandering off and making her mother look for her, her upset stomach kept her constantly screeching as if she was being skinned alive. This racket put the other kids on edge, Lulu often hiding in the Umbilicus for peace.

Although Crowley constantly sent as much money as he could to the Abbey, finances were worse than ever. They had neither coffee nor red meat, and only the kind heart of the milkman kept milk coming. She was again behind on the rent, and la Calce threatened to evict her January 1. Desperate, she tried selling Raoul's shoes to raise money for the milkman or to buy coal.

Arturo, who had by now left home and moved into the Abbey, did his best to help; however, his pension came irregularly, and boils on his thumb and foot made it difficult for him to work. At one point they quarreled so bitterly about money that Ninette finally threw him out.

After ten days, Arturo returned penitently with fresh bread, kerosene, coffee, tea, and sugar. He had played his last six cents on a lottery, won, and spent it on her. "Santa Claus never was so thoughtful," she bubbled to Leah:

> God, what good these little things did me. That was a change, and my spirits bounced up like a balloon, and the boy did enjoy our delight.... Dear me, Lala, do you know what that coffee and French bread tasted like? Months without coffee. This insipid bread and milk has become intolerable. I drank it with as reverent a feeling as if it had been ambrosia sent down by the Gods.... Perhaps I am crazy, Lala, but I feel happy.[78]

The man she loved, and the woman she once loathed as her fiercest competitor, she missed dearly. "I need but one satisfaction," she wrote again, "i.e., a little Lala to laugh out loud with, and to swap stories about the last eight months. When will we see you again?... Don't write such beautifully neat, good-looking pages next time you write, Lala, but be sociable and fill every bit of your paper with nonsense. Chat if you have no special anxiety on your mind."[79]

Crowley returned to Tunis from his desert trek with Dorothy Olsen late in December 1924, three months after it began, finding his business in limbo. Jane had stopped typing the Hag while she took a rest cure for colitis, placing Crowley's autobiography on indefinite hold. AC wrote to Mudd emphasizing practicality: "We are now doing our best to pick up the pieces. You must not expect everything at once and you must forget about Magick altogether."[80]

Shortly thereafter, an intense trance engulfed Crowley, who recorded his vision, incorporating "To Man," in *The Heart of the Master*.[81]

When Dorothy became pregnant, Crowley summoned Leah to assist in her convalescence. The former Scarlet Woman—herself pregnant by a new student named George Barron—dutifully bought a third-class ticket and hurried to their side, much to Dorothy's displeasure. Crowley recorded one late-night episode in his diary:

> A single drink of rum (on top of a good deal of mental worry during the day) was enough to induce in Dorothy Olsen an attack of acute mania. Lying in bed, close cuddled, I nearly asleep, she suddenly started to scratch my face without the least warning, with a spat of the filthiest incoherent abuse of me and everyone connected with me.[82]

Leah's services became unnecessary, however, for Dorothy miscarried, and they all returned to Paris.

Leah found herself alone again, but friends like Gérard Aumont, Aimée Gouraud, and George Barron helped her keep her head together. Her will to die subsided in favor of a new vitality as she came to terms with life with and without Crowley. Giving herself over to anger, she wrote to Sir Aleister Crowley, "The Sir means as little to me as 'Lord' Beaverbrook—Aleister is a mere wish phantasm.... You are no more a Magus than you are a cunt. You seem to disregard all Holy Books etc. in your sexual stupidity."[83] In the end, she discovered the detachment to distinguish between Crowley the prophet—a vehicle of the divine word that she most fervently accepted—and Crowley the man, who was capable of inexplicable coldness. "I do in the main consider him merely a Word, but it's damn hard when one has to have 'human' dealings with what appears to be the rottenest kind of creature, to think of it as an Idea."[84]

Meanwhile at Cefalù, Ninette's next child, Richard, was born; while la Calce did not evict her on January 1 as threatened, the possibility loomed constantly. As Leah wrote, "Ninette is threatened with expatriation: where that is to I am sure I don't know. Is she American or French? Evidently her birth certificate and passport are among the Customs' spoils. Great collection, that!"[85]

The Thelemites gathered again in June 1925, more motley and desperate than ever. Drab Leah had learned simultaneously to admire and dislike Crowley. Dorothy—who, like so many of Crowley's lovers, drank heavily—was suspicious and jealous of the former Scarlet Woman. And Mudd, who'd been homeless and hungry in London, believed Crowley to be straying farther and farther from the obligation given him by the Secret Chiefs in *The Book of the Law*. All they had in common was their mission to spread the word.

Bringing them together was the Conference of Grand Masters being held in the secluded twelfth-century German city of Weida, Thuringia. Heinrich Tränker (1880–1956), head of OTO's German branch as Frater Recnartus and founder of his own organization the Collegium Pansophicum (or Pansophical Lodge), was hosting this convocation of chiefs of major occult organizations for the summer solstice. The only snag in the plan was that OTO currently had no leader: Reuss, the Outer Head of the Order, had died in 1923, and the remaining administrative heads (X°) needed to elect a new Frater Superior. Crowley reasonably expected the honor would fall to him: not only had he students acting as X° in America, Africa, and Australia, but Tränker had a vision of Crowley leading OTO, which convinced him that Baphomet was the intended successor. In response to Tränker's vision, Crowley had American student Max Schneider translate *The Book of the Law* into German and send it ahead. When Tränker read the manuscript, he concluded it was demonically inspired; yet before he could condemn it too strongly, another vision cleared up everything and restored his faith. In a letter to Tränker, Crowley wrote, "Frater Peregrinus [Reuss] in the last letters that we exchanged definitely designated me to succeed him."[86] Similarly, he wrote to C. S. Jones:

> I now feel at liberty to inform you that in the O.H.O.'s [Outer Head of the Order] last letter to me he invited me to become his successor as O.H.O. and Frater Superior of the Order and my reply definitely accepted. I cannot give the exact dates of these letters, and cannot be sure that he died before receiving my reply.[87]

No records survive to document Reuss's nomination of Crowley, but one observer noted, "The only fact that we know is that Reuss died and the above two elected AC as O.H.O."[88]

On June 21, Crowley arrived at the home of the man who paid their fares to Germany. Frater Saturnus, known in the mundane world as Karl Germer (1885–1962), was Tränker's personal secretary. University educated, he received first- and second-class Iron Crosses during the Great War for "special services," probably spying. Germer and Tränker were both members of the Pansophical Society. In 1923, Germer sold his Vienna property and founded the publishing house Pansophia Verlag in Munich. Tränker was general editor, Pansophist Otto Wilhelm Barth[89] oversaw sales, and Germer did translations and put up the capital. By the end of 1924, Germer began thinking about publishing Crowley translations exclusively, although he had never met him.

Soon thereafter, Crowley met the remaining Grand Masters. Albin Grau (1884–1942), known by the magical name Pacitus, had been Master of the Chair in Tränker's Pansophical Lodge, the first Grand Master of Fraternitas Saturni, and a member of Crowley's A∴A∴. A painter, he worked as a set designer, art director, and costume designer on UFA Studios silent films such as Friedrich Wilhelm Murnau's (1888–1931) classic unauthorized Dracula adaptation, *Nosferatu—Eine Symphonie des Grauens* (*Nosferatu—A Symphony of Horror,* 1922).[90] Other films utilizing Grau's talents included *The Cabinet of Dr. Caligari* (1919), *Dr. Mabuse the Gambler* (1922), *Warning Shadows* (1922), and *The Nibelungs* (1924).

Eugen Grosche (1888–1964) ran an antiquarian and occult bookstore in Berlin. Grosche's mother had been housekeeper of Berlin's TS, and when Tränker supplanted Rudolf Steiner as secretary in 1921, he also tapped Grosche to establish a Berlin lodge of the Pansophical Society. This he did under the magical name Gregor A. Gregorius.

Dr. Henri Clemens Birven (1883–1969), despite an apparently French ancestry, was born in Aachen, Germany. Although he studied philosophy in Berlin—even writing a dissertation on Kant—professionally he lectured on electrical engineering. Finding himself a prisoner of Russia during the Great War, he escaped through China and ultimately returned to Berlin, where he taught at the Humboldtschule Tegel, one of Berlin's top secondary schools. By 1927 he would begin publishing the occult journal *Hain der Isis* (Veil of Isis), which would include some of Crowley's writings.

Martha Küntzel (1857–1941), occultist and devoted student of Thelema, was known affectionately to Crowley as "Little Sister." Küntzel and her lover, Pansophical Lodge and OTO member Otto Gebhardi, had been involved in the TS. However, the Law of Thelema proved to be Küntzel's path, which she followed with the utmost devotion.

Germer's friend Oskar Hopfer was a Thuringian publisher and technical artist who helped Crowley devise a new 777, which placed correspondences on the appropriate sphere or path of a drawing of the Tree of Life in favor of a tabular listing. He was probably also the one to publish *Ein Zeugnis der Suchenden,* or "The Testament of a Seeker." Penned by Crowley with help from Mudd and Tränker, it was another anti-Theosophical broadsheet that proclaimed the Master Therion to be the new World Teacher.

These eight—Tränker, Germer, Grau, Grosche, Birven, Küntzel, Hopfer, and Crowley—made up the conference, which ironically took place in the nation from which, a year previously, anthroposophist and former OTO member Rudolph Steiner was driven by Nazi persecution. The conference's unfolding revolved around the Masters' mixed feelings about Crowley. While Germer, Tränker, Küntzel, and Grosche hailed him eagerly, his irresponsible references to the IX° in his writings angered the others; Grau disliked *The Book of the Law* and renounced *Ein Zeugnis*. A debate split the Masters on this issue, and a heated and bitter argument between Crowley and Tränker drove the wedge deeper. In the end, Grau, Hopfer, and Birven sided with Tränker, who, as cosignatory of *Ein Zeugnis,* repudiated the document. Mudd appealed to Grau's A∴A∴ membership in an effort to win his support, but the politics proved terminal. The Masters split into three camps: those who sided with Tränker in rejecting Crowley's teachings; moderates like Grosche, who regarded Crowley a teacher and incorporated Thelema into his philosophy but nevertheless rejected him as OHO; and finally, Karl Germer and the others, who accepted Crowley as Frater Superior.

The schism destroyed the Pansophical Lodge, which would ritually close and dissolve on Maundy Thursday 1926; neither Tränker nor Grau were heard from again. On May 8, 1926, Grosche founded the Fraternitas Saturni, a magical brotherhood that accepted Thelema but remained independent of the Master Therion. A third of the Pansophists flocked to this new organization, which in 1928 began publishing its own magical papers and the journal *Saturn Gnosis*. With the subsequent collapse of Pansophia Verlag, in 1927 Germer would establish a press devoted to Crowley's writings: Thelema Verlag.

The differences of opinion that split OTO into different factions that summer soon split apart the magical family Crowley had built around himself.

That August of 1925, the subtle conflict between Crowley and C. S. Jones came to a head. Although Jones had endorsed Crowley as OHO, Crowley found his increasingly unorthodox books on the kabbalah intolerable. When Jones was unable to account for book sales in Detroit, Crowley grew suspicious, suspended Jones's officer status in OTO, and placed Max Schneider in charge of his personal stock. Schneider arrived in Detroit to find two trunks of Crowley's rariora gone. The difference between them—Jones protesting his innocence, and Crowley believing himself robbed—would never be resolved. Not until the 1950s would it be discovered that the books were not stolen by Achad but lost track of in a Detroit warehouse.

Jones continued on his own eccentric path. Around 1930 he became Mahaguru (head) of an organization called the Universal Brotherhood, which he had joined after moving to Chicago. Around this same time, he converted to Catholicism in an effort to introduce English papists to Thelema. Finally, in his paper *The Teachings of the New Aeon,* he attacked Crowley and Thelema:

> The Beast may be considered as his own worst enemy, but Aiwaz is quite evidently the enemy of mankind, and should be recognized as such, if this new system, deliberately calculated to bring about the self-destruction of the human race, is to be rightly evaluated.[91]

His expulsion from OTO followed shortly thereafter.

Leah and Mudd left Weida to live with Martha Küntzel and Otto Gebhardi in their small abode. On December 4, 1925, Leah gave birth to Barron's son. Although the father had left her high and dry, she was indifferent, naming the baby Al after the god name that was the key to *The Book of the Law.* His nickname was Bubby. Although Alostrael lived up to Thelemic principles, Crowley grew distrustful of her and her self-determined title of Babalon. He finally eliminated her by instructing all OTO members to shun her as a "center of pestilence" per the Short Comment to *Liber AL.* Disgusted, Leah renounced both the Beast and her title on December 26, 1929. She returned to America to be with Alma and Hansi and to resume her job as a schoolteacher. She died at Meringen, Switzerland, on February 22, 1975.

Mudd's story is even more bizarre. Late in 1925 he concluded Crowley had completely failed his commission from the Secret Chiefs and was no better than a false prophet. Mudd declared himself, as the only person to understand *The Book of the Law,* the World Teacher. Küntzel called him a saboteur and threw him out of her house. Crowley would eventually banish him from the order. Mudd returned to his father on the Isle of Man and on February 24, 1926, formally withdrew his signature from *Ein Zeugnis der Suchenden.* In a 1927 letter to Jane Wolfe, he wrote, "I have dropped all interest in anything that calls itself magick and any kind of work that insists on a capital W."[92] On September 6, 1930, he and Leah sent Crowley a letter renouncing their magical oaths; then he faded from the scene altogether. On May 6, 1934, at about age forty-five, he took a room at 220 Arling Road in Guernsey, an English Channel Island. A month later, he bicycle-clipped his pant-cuffs, filled his trousers and pockets with stones, and waded into the English Channel. The hotel proprietor reported Mudd missing on June 16, and the police recovered his body from Portlet Bay around noon that same day. "I feel sure that he must have left a long, elaborate mathematical proof as to why he had to do this," Crowley later remarked.[93] One of the greatest and eeriest ironies of Crowley's corpus is that *The Winged Beetle* (1910), published just after Mudd first entered Crowley's circle, contains a poem dedicated to him; it is titled "The Swimmer."

CHAPTER SEVENTEEN

The French Connection

Around November 1925, Crowley left Weida and began working on his incisive and inspirational *Little Essays Toward Truth*. After a bout of ptomaine laid him up in Marseilles, he attended a party and met Ernest Hemingway, who described him simply as "a tall, gray, lantern-jawed man."[1] In January 1926, Crowley settled into a villa at La Marsa, Tunis. Jane Wolfe joined him for five months at the beginning of February. At this time, Crowley was also corresponding with a young Tom Driberg (1905–1976), who, at age twenty, was more concerned about finding an artificial stimulant to help him pass his exams than about the Labour Party for which he would later become a member of Parliament.[2] Crowley invited him to Tunis and later to Paris, but their acquaintance was largely confined to correspondence.

While Crowley was in Tunis, Karl Germer took his wife, Maria, on a trip to the Abbey of Thelema. On January 10, 1926, Ninette received them in the empty shell that was once the stronghold of Thelema. Dirty and dilapidated, just about everything had been sold off. The living conditions appalled Germer. Although he stayed at the Abbey until at least February, he joined Crowley in Tunis that April, describing bluntly and exactly the conditions at the Abbey. Although this convinced AC that Lulu, now five years old, should come to Tunis for proper care and education, repeated complications and miscommunications prevented it.

The positive reception of the Mediterranean Manifesto, coupled with the realization that publicity was the key to putting over the Great Work, encouraged Crowley to spend much of 1926 absorbed in his "World Teacher" campaign. "The Only way of getting proper publicity is to arrange for the World Teacher campaign," Crowley wrote, hoping Evans or someone else with journalistic connections would pick it up. This World Teacher campaign sought to use as its springboard the publicity that Annie Besant and Charles Leadbeater of the TS prepared to introduce the world to Jiddu Krishnamurti (1895-1986), the boy they had groomed to be the next messiah. Theosophy based its concept

423

of the World Teacher on the Buddhist Maitreya, a future bodhisattva or enlightened being, which Leadbeater equated with Christ. Leadbeater discovered Krishnamurti as a young teenager on the beach of the TS headquarters at Adyar in 1909. Declaring him the vessel for the expected World Teacher, Leadbeater and Besant adopted him and began preparing him for this role. In 1911 the Theosophists founded the Order of the Star in the East to prepare for the World Teacher's arrival, and in 1926, Krishnamurti began a lecture tour of the United States as this World Teacher. Crowley planned to use the TS's propaganda to declare himself, not Krishnamurti, the World Teacher. "If this is done as it should be, there is bound to be a big scrap with unlimited stories of excellent news value."[3] Thus, AC wrote defiantly to Montgomery Evans, "The World Teacher informs the public that Doctor Annie Besant is in error when she states that He will manifest through Mr. Krishnamurti in December, or at any other time."[4] Characteristically, Crowley was full of unkind opinions:

> About Krishnamurti: There is no objection on my part to pæderasty as such. This is a totally different matter. It is the question of the following practice, which I class as black magical because it is unnecessary, uneconomical from the magical standpoint, and likely to arouse highly undesirable forces as being in opposition to the Law of Thelema.[5]

On H. P. Blavatsky's successor, Crowley called Besant "totally devoid of all spiritual greatness, as of moral decency."[6]

The TS was naturally on Crowley's radar as it influenced every occultist contemporary with Crowley, from Westcott and the rest of the GD to his own students, like Frank Bennett. As strongly as Crowley admired its founder, H. P. Blavatsky, he disliked just as strongly, if not more so, her successors. When Annie Besant introduced Co-Masonry to England in connection with the TS in 1902, Crowley was outraged. This reaction was only exacerbated when Yarker, in his last years, befriended not only Crowley (and thereby OTO) but also Co-Masonry, contributing to its journal and receiving an extensive obituary;[7] likewise when Co-Mason J. I. Wedgwood attended the first meeting to elect Yarker's successor.[8] When Crowley prepared his commented edition of Blavatsky's *Voice of the Silence* as the supplement to the blue *Equinox,* he expected it not only to send tremors through the TS, but to "have the San Francisco earthquake looking like 30¢."[9] Indeed, at that time Crowley went so far as to draft a manifesto to the TS, declaring himself Blavatsky's successor; seeking to turn weakness into strength, Crowley even argued (unconvincingly) in his document, "The fact that he has never compromised himself with any branch of the T.S. is highly significant."[10] Thus Crowley's current campaign was an expression of his long-standing ideas regarding Theosophy.

Mudd, who was still collaborating with Crowley at this time, would sneak into London's TS headquarters and pin the Mediterranean Manifesto to their bulletin board. Crowley followed it up with several other broadsheets swiping at the TS. "The World Teacher to the Theosophical Society" read:

The World-Teacher sayeth:
Find, each of you, your own true Way in the Universe, and follow it with eager joy!
There is no law beyond Do what thou wilt!
Do that, and no other shall say nay.

Greeting and Peace!

ANKH-F-N-KHONSU,
the Priest of the Princes.

Next, "The Avenger to the Theosophical Society" was more to the point:

You have done well to protest against the grotesque mummeries of the bottle-fed Messiah; you will still do wisely to beware of its Jesuitical wire-pullers. The attempted usurpation is most sinister Black Magic of the Brothers of the Left-hand Path.

I need not remind you of the shameless and nauseating fraud by which the Grand Old Procuress worked herself into the presidency of your Society, of her blatant attempts to capture various rites of Freemasonry, and her imbecile parodies of the Romish heresy, of the obscene manusturpations practised by Leadbeater on the wretched Krishnamurti, with a view of making him a docile imbecile, in imitation of the traditions of the Dalai Lamas, or of a thousand other duplicities, tergiversations, and crimes. It is your daily shame to remember.

April 1926 saw Driberg distributing these broadsheets for Crowley.

If, as Dorothy Olsen reported, "At last this World Teacher business seems to have caught fire everywhere and we are being interviewed by newspapers and the newspapers seem to be taking it up as quite important news,"[11] they must have been incidental presses since no articles survive among Crowley's papers. In the end, the campaign fizzled like many of AC's other grand schemes. Likewise Krishnamurti, it turns out, was uninterested in his spiritual calling, declaring he was *not* the World Teacher and precipitating an embarrassing crisis for the TS.

Crowley published a most rare edition of *The Book of the Law* on April 9, the twenty-second anniversary of the writing of its second chapter. It consisted of photographic reproductions of the original sixty-five handwritten pages, housed as loose sheets in a maroon leather box; the title leaf was printed in red and black ink on handmade paper. He printed only eleven copies of this work, the first eight being presentation copies for Crowley, Dorothy, Leah, Jane, Karl, C. S. Jones, Otto Gebhardi, and student Dorothea Walker. Only three copies were for sale, one for each of three countries at £93, $418, and 2,542 reichsmarks.[12] Leah returned her copy of the book along with a scathing letter:

I therefore return Copy No. 2 of your Book, signifying thereby that I revoke all my recognition of you heretofore as Beast, or Priest of the Princes, or as having any authority whatsoever in respect of the Law of Thelema.[13]

Karl Germer, who received the unenviable job of selling the American edition of the book, emigrated to the United States with his wife, Maria, on June 12. He checked Crowley's book stock in Detroit, confirming it was missing. Achad had taken a larger trunk of books to sell in Chicago, but the whereabouts of the second remained unknown. "Achad never handed over the storage checks for us to go seriously into the matter," Germer recalled.[14] So he got a job, cut back expenses, and sent Crowley the better part of his income to keep the Great Work going: of his $190 monthly salary, he sent Crowley $100.

Although Crowley bought a magical dagger to banish malignant forces and impediments, turmoil nevertheless dogged him. Six days after joining Dorothy and Jane in France that August, he had a major row with Dorothy. As Jane described it in her diary, "Dorothy went on a mad ranting, raving explosion last night which continued until 2:00 a.m."[15] Two days later, Crowley left for Bordeaux, realizing that Dorothy wasn't his ideal Scarlet Woman after all. Although she remained his lover for a time, she left England on Crowley's fifty-second birthday to continue the Great Work in Chicago.

Once again, Beast went on the prowl for a suitable sex-magical partner. He found many candidates, including one Louis Eugene de Cayenne. Crowley's January 2, 1927, diary entry describes the extent of his quest: "Eugene and all his tribe disappeared, leaving me with nine mistresses in Paris.... I am now eliminating these one by one."[16] Alas, none of Crowley's subsequent Scarlet Women would live up to the precedents set by seers like Rose Kelly, Mary Desti, and Roddie Minor, let alone the pillars of strength represented by Leila Waddell and Leah Hirsig.

The most promising contender for the role of Scarlet Woman at this time was K. Margaret Binetti. Crowley met her at the end of August, and despite his promiscuous sex magick couplings, they soon became engaged. Margaret lacked interest in magic and the philosophical rationale behind his infidelity, and this strained their relationship. Crowley soon reconsidered spending his life with the woman to whom he wrote "Lines on being seduced by Madame Binetti."[17] On February 6, 1927, he burned the talisman of Jupiter he had consecrated for her. "Her callous heartlessness and hypocritical falsity doom her to dire ends,"[18] he recorded in his diary, then cast out his net once again.

In March 1927, Germer, now living in Boston, founded Thelema-Verlags-Gesellschaft to publish German translations of Crowley's complete works as quickly as possible. Its cofounders included Gebhardi, Hopfer, and Küntzel. In quick succession, they published *Book Four, The Heart of the Master,* "The Three Schools of Magick," and "The Message of the Master Therion."

Despite the press's promise, this was otherwise a time of failure for Crowley. Hopfer's color, diagrammatic revision of 777 was a great idea but would cost an unreasonable $100 per copy. Similarly, plans for a book on the oracle of geomancy, to sell with a box painted in flashing colors and filled with holy sand from Mecca or Jerusalem, remained just an idea.

Finally, on March 9, a final nail sealed the coffin on Crowley's Cefalù period. Ninette wrote a letter complaining of her seven years in Cefalù, "Thinking too much, making resolutions and taking oaths, keeping none, violating my better impulses, have worn my nerves to shreds." Then she bid Jane and Beast "an eternal Adieu."[19] The Abbey's financial situation was dire, and although he wired Ninette £500, Crowley realized his dream of a Thelemic community was a lost cause. The best plan was to get Ninette and the children back to France and cut their losses.

Mrs. Kasimira Bass learned of Crowley from Thelemite Wilfred T. Smith while living in California. She was born on February 10, 1887, in Lemberg, Austria (modern-day Lviv in western Ukraine), a historically Polish city that became part of Austria in 1772. With an eight-year-old daughter, Marian, from her previous marriage in Vienna, Kasimira de Helleparth emigrated to the United States aboard the SS *Majestic,* arriving in New York on December 12, 1922. Three days later she married John F. Bass Jr. in Cleveland, Ohio. The fact that she settled in Glendale, California, in December 1923 while her husband lived in Chicago suggests that the marriage may have been arranged to help her obtain citizenship.[20] While living in Southern California she met Smith, and while traveling in Europe she stopped in France to meet Crowley.

AC took her to dinner and, to her surprise, proposed. Four times. He wanted to marry her in Paris the next day. She was too stunned to answer. The next day, having met her daughter Marian, he proposed again. This time, she explained she had to return to Poland (her birthplace had reverted from Austrian back to Polish rule from 1918 to 1939), but promised to return. Crowley wrote to Smith, "I thank you for the galleon of treasure which came under full sail into port here last week. Unfortunately, she has chartered to make more distant shores."[21] Nevertheless, he hoped to take her to Egypt, where he had had such stunning magical success with Rose.

On October 1, Jane Wolfe, the last remaining member of the Cefalù community, sailed for New York. Crowley was sad to see her go, but she would carry on the Great Work in America with Dorothy and Karl, and supervise students Max and Leota Schneider and W. T. Smith in California. She hoped to return to acting, but would soon find herself blacklisted for her connection to the notorious Aleister Crowley; after returning to Hollywood, she would have a role in only one other film, *Under Strange Flags* (1937).

Gerald Joseph Yorke (1901–1983) stood in the Paris airport on New Year's Eve 1927, waiting to meet Aleister Crowley. He was born two months prematurely

in 1901, the second of three sons to landowner and industrialist Vincent Wodehouse Yorke (1869–1957) and Hon. Maud Evelyn Wyndham (1874–1963),
daughter of Henry Wyndham, the second Baron Leconfield.[22] Attending Eton
and graduating with distinction from Cambridge, he had played cricket for
Gloucestershire in 1925, making a first-class appearance in a game that season
against Glamorgan.[23] His youngest brother, Henry Vincent (1905–1973), was
an aspiring writer, his first novel *Blindness* (1926) having appeared the previous
year; he would go on to renown under the pen name Henry Green, his sixth
book *Loving* (1945) making *Time* magazine's list of the "100 Best English-Language Novels from 1923 to 2005."[24]

After graduation, Gerald began to study *The Equinox* and Crowley's other
magical writings. He was bright enough to distrust the rumors circulating
about Crowley and judge the man for himself, so he contacted Crowley
through J. G. Bayley and received an invitation to meet the Master in Paris.
What he encountered impressed him immensely: Crowley struck Yorke as a
brilliant and talented man with tremendous unrealized potential. His unpublished manuscripts testified to the many important lessons Crowley still had to
teach the world … he only lacked a business manager to make a success of his
work. Crowley took Yorke's enthusiasm as an offer and accepted. While *The
Book of the Law* prophesied a rich man from the west, he found instead a benefactor from Germany and a rich boy from Gloucestershire.

In January 1928 Yorke took the name Volo Intellegere (I will to understand) upon joining the A∴A∴, and he devoted his spare time to managing
Crowley's finances. He sold his Chinese paintings and ivories to raise money
and, that spring, put £400 into a publication account to rehabilitate Crowley's
name and publish his works. From this fund, Yorke paid Crowley a weekly
allowance of £10. He also wrote the eight remaining A∴A∴ members—
including Jacobi, Wolfe, Olsen, and Smith—to regularize their membership
subscriptions and permit Crowley to continue writing without monetary concerns; of these, only Jacobi regularly contributed $20 a month to the cause,
forcing Crowley to rely on the Germers for much of his support. Nevertheless,
this permitted Crowley a furnished flat at 55 Avenue de Suffren in Paris.

Yorke also paid a typist to copy Crowley's manuscripts for publication. One
of these new projects was AC's magnum opus, part three of Book Four, *Magick
in Theory and Practice*. Of this manuscript, Crowley wrote to Yorke:

> Montague Summers appears to know what he is talking about. People
> generally do want a book on Magick. There never has been an attempt at
> one, anyhow since the Middle Ages, except Lévi's.[25]

Alphonsus Joseph-Mary Augustus Montague Summers (1880–1948),
occult scholar, offered a curious contrast to AC. Whereas the latter identified
with the infernal trappings of the Great Beast while explicating the holy quest
for one's divine nature, the former was an ordained deacon of the Church of
England who specialized in demonology and black magic. Nevertheless the

two men shared a mutual respect. Éliphas Lévi, also cited in the above quote, Crowley claimed as his previous incarnation, and a translation of his book, *The Key of the Mysteries,* appeared as a supplement to *The Equinox* I(10). Crowley correctly states the literary primacy of his book: whereas Montague Summers, A. E. Waite, and even Francis Barrett (*The Magus,* 1801) were primarily purveyors of medieval traditions, *Magick in Theory and Practice* was the first modern textbook on the subject in English. How big a market existed for such a book was another matter entirely.

Alas, managing Crowley's old stock of books was more complicated than Yorke had imagined. While he hoped to inventory these books, Yorke found them scattered around the world: in Chicago with Achad and Olsen, in Naples with Aguel (presumably), in Leipzig with Küntzel, and in London with Pickford's storage. The latter stock (early works of poetry), he discovered, had been damaged when Pickford's storage facilities flooded; although Crowley valued these books at thousands of pounds, professional booksellers hired by Yorke estimated that even a good salesperson would be lucky to realize £200 on them. Yorke settled with Pickford's for the balance of past charges and £40 damages. He then paid the American Express Company to ship Crowley's remaining works from Naples to Crowley's Paris address.

Finally, Yorke kept AC's pipe dreams in perspective: one such scheme involved Metro-Goldwyn's film adaptation of Maugham's *The Magician,* which was opening on the Grand Boulevard March 23. Since Crowley received no compensation as the model of Oliver Haddo, he filed an injunction against showing the film. However, when representatives from the film company offered to pay Crowley, he refused. "The lawsuit is a pretext for a business deal," he explained to Yorke. "I'm holding out for publicity and power."[26] Crowley wanted a contract to produce a series of educational films on magick. Yorke was pessimistic about the scheme.

> I cannot say that I think you will get any damages from Metro-Goldwyn over *The Magician* film. Your reputation is too bad to be damaged by that. Nor do I think there is any hope for rehabilitation of character. To my mind, part of your "mission," if I may use a word I mistrust, is to show that the code of morals of what a Thelemite calls the Old Aeon has been superseded, and that now any act is right provided it is done in the right way, as in interpretation of True Will. It must have been your Will to be the Beast, and a whitewashed Beast is an useless commercial article.[27]

He was right: when Crowley could have taken a quick financial settlement, he pushed too hard and got nothing at all from the film company.

Promotional leaflet for Metro-Goldwyn Pictures' adaptation of *The Magician*.

Kasimira Bass returned to Crowley that spring. While they didn't run off and marry, they did find bliss together. "She is the one possible magical partner for me, and she is perfect," Crowley enthused. "Already, despite the greatest difficulties, we have succeeded beyond all my hopes in awakening a current of creative energy of enormously high potential."[28] Although she began signing her letters to W. T. Smith as 156,[29] she complained that her standard of living fell below the expectations Crowley had given her. While he was used to living hand to mouth with faith that the gods would provide for his needs, Kasimira had no such conviction. "This is her first experience of living under magical laws," he commented on their finances, "so that the funny little ways of the Gods rather get on her nerves."[30] They soon began quarreling over money and other petty matters. By June 6, Crowley's glowing praise of her magical talent declined to "Kasimira is that same cauliflower Ego which destroyed Achad."[31]

During the summer of 1928, Ninette's daughter Mimi was in the hospital for twenty-four days with a fever, measles. and bronchitis. Public assistance was in sorry shape there, and, penniless, Ninette could obtain no better care for her child. She wrote desperately to Crowley and Kasimira, begging for help, but to Crowley's frustration forgot to include her address. He had no way to respond.

That season, Crowley met Lance Sieveking, whose book he cited in *The Diary of a Drug Fiend*. The young author was in St. Tropez recovering from his wife's leaving him for another man. Crowley walked the beach with Sieveking, consoling and conversing; he later did Sieveking's horoscope and put him in touch with Yorke to work on *Magick*. Both Yorke and Sieveking agreed that no English publisher would touch the manuscript; and even if one did, they believed Scotland Yard and the Home Office would object and the Beaverbrook press would suppress it. Although Yorke could have printed it privately, he feared the consequences and encouraged Crowley to seek a U.S. printer.

With £190 left in the publication fund, Yorke was now pulling out—from his trusteeship and from his editorship. His change of heart stemmed from personal difficulties with *The Book of the Law:*

> The crux of the matter is a) I have tried to accept the Law of Thelema and the New Aeon with you as Σοτηρ Κοσμου [Savior of the Universe], *Liber Legis [The Book of the Law]* as the book, and Thelema as the logos. I cannot accept it. *Liber Legis* and its claims have bothered me throughout, as it bothered you until it beat you, and I suspect still does.... I cannot therefore support a movement whose sole aim is to spread the teaching contained in *Liber Legis* and the commentaries thereon.... Owing to my convictions, therefore, I cannot honestly assist in the practical handling of a publication fund or the raising of money for that purpose.[32]

So Crowley hired Carl de Vidal Hunt (b. 1869) to prepare the public for his book. After becoming a naturalized U.S. citizen in 1895, Hunt settled in Los Angeles,[33] where he became part of the nascent motion picture industry, appearing in such early films as *Roaring Camp* (1916), *The Marriage of Arthur* (1916), and *Jeremias* (1922).[34] While in his mid-fifties, he became a journalist, writing racy human interest stories that were syndicated across America.[35] In Crowley's employ, he published a story about Hollywood "film mother" Jane Wolfe's stay at Cefalù as a resident of the "mystery house" run by "Sir Aleister Crowley, high priest of Thelema (oriental philosophy)":

> Sir Aleister, known among his disciples as the "Beast," is a Britisher, who spent his patrimony in search of the stoic philosophies of the East. He had lived with the Yogis in the silent wastes of India and had published books on the subject. Now he is a wanderer, barred even from his own country—but his friends declare him a genius.[36]

When publishers Turnbull became interested in taking *Magick,* Crowley gave them a £200 deposit; however, they returned his deposit at the end of October after he refused to let them edit problematic passages.

About this time, Kasimira announced she was getting £3,000 for Beast's publication fund. Yorke loaned her £200 against a promissory note, but it soon became clear that Kasimira was skimming money off the publication account. Yorke suggested Crowley dump her. AC concurred, writing in his diary,

K. has been acting outrageously for some days. She is stupidly jealous of
my talking to Yorke. She sulks and rages without sense. She complains of
everything in the most idiotic way. She interferes with every act one does.
It is intolerable, save for the Magical Necessity.

I definitely appeal to the Gods to let this Cup pass from me.[37]

Young Philadelphian art student Francis Israel Regardie (1907–1985) was born
Israel Regudy in London on November 17, 1907, to a pair of poor Orthodox
Jewish immigrants from Russia: cigarette maker Barnet Regudy and his wife,
Phoebe Perry. The family name, Regudy, was mistakenly recorded as
"Regardie" when Israel's older brother joined the army, and the family adopted
this spelling when it emigrated to Washington, D.C., in August 1921, where
young Regardie studied art. At age fifteen he also began studying H. P. Blavatsky, Eastern scriptures, and yoga. When, at age eighteen, a lawyer friend read
him Crowley's writings on yoga from *Book Four,* their simplicity and clarity
stunned him. As a result, his yoga interests quickly extended to magick. He
read every Crowley title he could find, and he contacted the author in 1926.
Crowley put him in touch with Germer, whom he met in New York and
thereby acquired a set of *The Equinox.* Around this same time, he also received
special dispensation as a minor to join the Washington College of the Societas
Rosicruciana in America, taking his 0=0 degree in March 1926 and his Zelator
initiation in June 1927.[38]

When Crowley sought a new secretary during the summer of 1928, he
wrote Regardie and offered him the job. He dearly wanted it but, as a minor,
needed parental permission to obtain a passport. Knowing his parents would
never let him study mysticism in France with Aleister Crowley, he told his
father he had been invited to study with an artist in England.

He sailed from New York, arriving at the noisy Gare St. Lazare station on
the morning of October 12. Through the backdrop of French conversation he
heard a distinctly British voice say, "Do what thou wilt shall be the whole of
the Law." Regardie turned to face Crowley, tall and pudgy, dressed in blue-gray
plus fours. They shook hands—firm, Regardie noticed—then gathered his
luggage. They took a taxi to Crowley's flat, where AC made them coffee in a
glass apparatus heated by an alcohol lamp. Thus Regardie, henceforth known as
Frater NChSh (Serpent) or Frater Scorpio, became Crowley's new secretary.
He was not yet twenty-one.

In person, Crowley proved to be venerable. He played chess frequently
because his phlebitis often kept him homebound. On weekends when Yorke
visited, he would set each of them up at a chessboard; then, seated in his favorite chair, smoking a pipe of perique tobacco and warming a snifter of brandy,
he would sit with his back to them and call out his moves, playing them both
simultaneously. Most amazing was that he usually won.

Crowley spent much of his energy teasing timid Regardie, trying to persuade him to be a bit more outgoing. At one point he suggested Regardie forget about magick altogether and first hit the streets of Paris in order to become acquainted with every human vice. One evening he and Kasimira went out to see the sights of Paris and watch a movie. There, away from Beast's watchful eye, she confided in him: she was leaving Crowley and wanted Regardie to deliver the message.

Hearing the news, Crowley shrugged and calmly responded, "The Lord giveth, and the Lord taketh away." On November 3 he recorded in his diary simply, "Kasimira bolted." In a candid note to Yorke, he wrote:

> Relieved from the strain of Kasimira, I have been able to start serious magick with ritual precautions. The Climax of the first ceremony was marked, as it should be, by the sudden arising of a violent wind; and subsequent ceremonies have been equally notable.[39]

Shortly thereafter, the mage was furious to learn that his ex-fiancée had previously been the lover of W. T. Smith, to whom he wrote:

> You send me a letter in which you tell me as plainly as anything can possibly do that she has been your mistress. She presents me this letter and imagines that I will not understand anything by it and dismiss the whole thing for weeks and months until, in a burst of confidence, the cat comes out of the bag. I am now looking like Diogenes with a lantern of much greater power to find somebody whose mistress she has not been.[40]

A year later, Kasimira Bass would be safe and happy, conducting business in South America, eventually finding her way back to the United States.

Crowley was now paying Hunt £20 a month for his services. Besides preparing the British public for the appearance of *Magick in Theory and Practice* and editing his *Confessions,* Hunt was responsible for arranging Crowley's marriage to a wealthy woman who would support his work. One potential wife, Cora Eaton, did not work out but, on January 15, 1929, she married Karl Germer in Jersey City. Since Germer was supporting Crowley, the result was almost as if Crowley had married her himself. Cora, however, was not as willing as Germer to hand over her money to the Master.

By November 8, 1928, Crowley found a new mistress in Nicaraguan-born Maria Teresa Ferrari de Miramar. A dark, short divorcée, she was charmingly convivial despite her poor grasp of English. Crowley called her "marvellous beyond words,"[41] and she certainly made an impression: Jack Lindsay described her as "a fairly well-blown woman, oozing a helpless sexuality from every seam of her smartly cut suit, with shapely legs crossed and uncrossed."[42] Regardie's first dinner with the new Scarlet Woman was likewise memorable: while he was busy pondering which utensil was proper to use for which portion of the meal, Crowley fell upon Marie and began humping her right on the floor.

Her magical talents were also remarkable. She claimed to have conjured the devil on four occasions while dancing around bonfires in Nicaragua, and Crowley attested to her abilities shortly after their meeting, "She has absolutely the right ideas of Magick and knows some Voudou.... We did proper ritual consecrations, and arranged for the next Work."[43] Soon thereafter, AC noted in his diary the consequences of their magical workings:

> The Magical Phenomena in this apartment are now acute. Lights and shadows, dancing sparks, noises as of people walking about, a large dark ghost in the bedroom lobby, short attacks of rheumatism (to 3 of us) and a Nameless Fear which seized Regardie.[44]

The following day, he also wrote about these manifestations to Yorke:

> The phenomena that have taken place in this apartment since the High Priestess of Voodoo [Marie de Miramar] displaced the woman from Samaria [Kasimira Bass] would be quite interesting to the Psychical Research Society, if any of them are not in a coma.[45]

Visiting Paris in December 1928, Yorke recounts in his diary an impromptu magical working with Crowley, de Miramar, and Regardie. While Crowley banished and recited the Bornless One invocation, Marie saw visions and did a dance to evoke a fire spirit.

Maria Theresa Ferrari de Mirimar and Aleister Crowley.

By this point, relations between Hunt and Crowley deteriorated. Hunt, realizing he had his work cut out for him, complained to Yorke of Crowley's "dormant, inarticulate, wheezy way of speaking what little he has to say."[46] Crowley, meanwhile, opined

> Hunt's limitation is that he sees everything in terms of journalism. He is apparently unaware of the existence of the serious occult public. The trouble with him is that he is a cynic. If he could only believe in people and look for noble motives instead of base ones.[47]

In Crowley's mind, Hunt, with his irons in too many fires, was unable to devote enough time to any.

Their business dealings came to a head when Hunt asked Crowley to "fix" the horoscopes of a couple to show them as perfectly compatible. "Hunt was bribed by the Infanta Eulalia, the mother of Don Louis, to arrange a marriage by which her son should get about £24,000 a year settled on him for life," Crowley recorded;[48] to Hunt's displeasure, he refused to sell the Great Work. Before long, Crowley stopped paying him altogether.

Hunt promised dire consequences if AC did not pay his salary. "It is a type of blackmail well known in France," Crowley scoffed,[49] and his friend Gérard Aumont concurred. Yorke also noted, "Hunt had written me what AC interpreted as a blackmail letter. It probably was the first step towards blackmail."[50] Nevertheless, Hunt took a stack of Crowley's news cuttings and the manuscript of *Mortadello* to the Prefecture. He also told the official that Crowley had been questioned regarding rumors that he had strangled three women in Sicily, and asked the authorities to look into the matter.

In response, Crowley alleged that Hunt had stolen his employer's personal property, i.e. the manuscripts. Furthermore, AC argued, Hunt showed bad faith by going to the police with papers entrusted to him as Crowley's agent. "His first capital was the pennies he stole off his dead mother's eyes," Crowley said.[51] As with his Metro-Goldwyn stunt, Crowley wasn't out to ruin Hunt as much as he hoped to drum up publicity for *Magick*.

Learning of this conflict, Yorke was furious. He had planned to sink a fortune into printing *Magick,* and now AC threatened to ruin it with a spate of bad publicity. He fired off a virulent criticism:

> you are a bloody, not a divine, fool in attacking Hunt. To start with, he was not in our employ when he sent those papers to the Prefecture. He told me at the time, and wrote to me afterwards, that he honestly thought it was impossible to help you, as you would not play up to the necessary parlour tricks, and that your past reputation was too much of a good thing. He could not, therefore, continue to take your money. He introduced you to good people, and can make a good showing that he worked for you. It was my honest opinion at the time that he was doing his best, and I wrote and told him so at the time.[52]

Such blunt exchanges typified the Crowley-Yorke correspondence from this period. Referring to *The Book of the Law* ii.59–60, Yorke said their dealings should "Strike hard and low" when they disagree; if they were kingly men, brutally honest words would not hurt them.

When, on December 14, 1928—nearly a year after he first met Crowley—Yorke became trustee of the fund set up for Lola Zaza, he wrote AC's oldest daughter and suggested that she, now a woman of twenty-two making seventeen shillings a week as a showroom assistant for a West End dressmaker, meet her father. She replied:

> I wrote to my uncle, and he said that I am old enough to choose for myself. I will give you certain books to read, he said, and they will help you think. So I read parts of them. After all, an author's work is a part of himself. So I have judged him by his own works and what could be fairer? But the answer is no. I really have no time to spend on a man so rude or conceited. His works are a part of him and I am very sorry for the other part. What a hash he has made of it.[53]

Her polite refusal must have been a disappointment for Crowley, who so desperately wanted a family. A few years later, on June 9, 1934, she would marry boot and shoe operative Frank Hill; she would outlive her husband, dying of a myocardial infarction at Battle Hospital, Reading, on March 9, 1990.[54] She would never reconcile with her father.

At age twenty-seven, Yorke became director of both Mexican Railways and H. Pontifex & Sons. He offered £800 toward the publication of *Magick in Theory and Practice* with a promise of another £1,000. By the end of December, Lecram Press of Paris agreed to take the job. Crowley soon had an estimate in hand and a prospectus in press. He also decided on the book's format: "By issuing *Magick* in four parts," he told Yorke, "we save 12% buying tax."[55]

AC believed this publication had set a powerful magical current into motion. Looking at the turmoil in his life—Kasimira leaving, Hunt threatening, plus minor events like Regardie getting sick and Marie becoming paranoid—he saw himself under magical attack. His most important works always met with difficulty going to press.

On January 9, 1929, Kasimira and Marie encountered each other on a bus. Exactly what transpired between them is unclear, as Marie seemed prone to paranoia and exaggeration. Based on Marie's report, Crowley described the incident as follows:

> Having departed for Fontainebleau on Friday afternoon, Mdme de Miramar went forth for her own base purposes ... I think to the cinema ... on Saturday afternoon. She was followed, I understand, more or less from the house or its vicinity by Mrs. Bass. At any rate, Kasimira took her seat beside Mdme de Miramar on the omnibus, accosted her, and began a sort of cinema Roman conversation. She was evidently quite furious at having lost her last chance in life.[56]

Fearing Kasimira might throw sulfuric acid on her, Marie ran. It convinced Crowley that Kasimira was plotting against him with Hunt.

Domestic worries continued as an ailing Regardie entered the hospital. On January 13, 1929, he was back home again, but would soon thereafter contract gonorrhea from a prostitute.

On the afternoon of January 17, an inspector from the *Sûreté Générale* called at Crowley's flat to question Paris's celebrated visitor. When Crowley opened his door, the man walked right in and plopped down on a chair. "May I offer you a seat?" Crowley asked with mock politeness. He was immediately suspicious.

The inspector rattled off a series of disconnected questions for Crowley to answer: why did Regardie lack a *carte d'identité* (identification card)? Why did people refer to Crowley as the King of Depravity? Taking keen interest in Crowley's Bunsen-powered coffee machine, he asked if it was a drug distillery. Did he take drugs? Was he ever expelled from the United States? Did he write pro-German propaganda during the war? Was he the head of a German occult organization? Was he actually a German spy?

Crowley did his best to set the inspector straight. This wasn't the first time the authorities got him wrong. As he recounted at this time,

> We have a very valuable witness in Aumont.... I once gave a little tea-party at the Tunisia Palace Hotel, and somebody brought him along as interested in literature. Within a few hours the police called upon him, and asked him if he knew who he had been having tea with, because it was a man who had strangled three women in Sicily.[57]

The nature of these questions, however, demonstrated that Crowley's colorful reputation was finally catching up with him.

Where had he lived for the past year?

"I have a friend here in France," Crowley answered, "Dr. Henri Birven, who calls me the Patriarch of Montparnasse. I first went to Montparnasse in 1899 and settled down there in 1902. Since that date, I have lived constantly there." Crowley paused and looked at the inspector askance; "the only exceptions being when I was elsewhere."[58] Referring to his diary, Crowley gave the Inspector the address of every hotel he had stayed at for the last year, plus the date and hour of his every move.

Wearied by details, the inspector moved on. "People come to consult you. And what do you advise them to do?"

"That depends entirely upon the questions. My sheet anchor is common sense. In any case, I should not advise them to do anything against the law, which I honestly respect as far as it will allow me to do so."

"And how much are you paid for your advice?"

"I take no money for consultations."

He was incredulous. "None?"

"None."

"Do you tell fortunes?"

"No."

Stumped, he moved on to the kabbalah.

"It takes seven years of uninterrupted study to even begin to know about it," Crowley answered. To the bewilderment of the Inspector, he launched into a long disquisition on the kabbalah.

After a while, the inspector commented, "For the first time in my life, I don't understand at all what is being said to me."

Crowley smiled. "This is very natural: I have been spending over fifty years trying to make myself clear, but nobody seems to benefit by my endeavors."[59]

At that, the inspector became polite. When he concluded the interview, he seemed satisfied that Crowley was a decent man.

But on February 15, Crowley learned that the authorities had declined to renew his identity card, issuing a *refus de séjour* despite his frequent visits since 1920. The news came as a shock, and Crowley searched for a reason: that idiot inspector thought his coffee machine a cocaine distillery; or that miscreant Hunt cried to his government contacts because Crowley refused to falsify those horoscopes to cement an arranged marriage; or perhaps Regardie's sister, worried about her brother's welfare, had asked the authorities to intervene. Perhaps all of these played a role. When *Paris Midi* reported Crowley had been expelled—not merely having his identity card renewal denied—for being a German spy using OTO as his cover, matters only became worse.

Crowley wrote to the British Embassy, but they would not intercede on his behalf.[60] He then wired Yorke to come over and help clear up the mess. Yorke, reluctant to have himself or his family dragged into the incident, declined. Instead, he urged AC not to start any trouble.

Crowley called Yorke a coward, unwilling to stand up for truth and decency. He was also foolish to think he could hide from the press. If he didn't rise up indignant, he would only look guilty. No, Crowley decided, he would rather defy the order, stay in Paris, and wind up in prison rather than buckle under and leave. If the government was going to arrest him, they'd have to press charges and *prove* he had done something wrong, which he hadn't. It was a Mexican standoff. The story and its newspaper coverage made Crowley a sensation in Paris … just the thing to generate brisk sales for *Magick*.

At the time this bombshell fell in Crowley's lap, he was sick with a cold. Paris's winter of 1929 was damp, shrouding the countryside with rain, snow, and frost. A week after the *refus de séjour*, Crowley was so ill he spent the next five days in bed. Owing to illness, authorities allowed him to stay in France until he recuperated—which, Crowley planned, would not happen until he saw *Magick* through its publication.

Meanwhile Regardie, fingered as an associate of Crowley's, and Marie, also lacking a valid *carte d'identité,* were asked to leave the country. The police told Marie they were doing her a service by separating her from Crowley. On

March 9 Regardie and Marie left for England, only to be refused entry because Marie was neither a citizen nor possessed of a visa. Turned back, France denied them entry, forcing them to go to Belgium. They arrived in Brussels on March 11. Holed up in a foreign nation, Marie took advantage of the naive Frater Scorpio and seduced him.

While Regardie spent the next weeks worrying what Crowley would do when he found out, Beast was performing sex magick with a woman named Lina "to help deM[iramar] out of her trouble."[61] He spent his remaining time correcting proofs of *Magick;* on April 12 he held an advance copy of the book, his first major publication since the blue *Equinox* a decade earlier. Crowley spent his last day in Paris speaking to reporters and being photographed. He left France on April 17 satisfied *Magick* would appear as scheduled.

Aleister Crowley at the time he left France in 1929.

Paris Midi had company in taking up his story. As he recorded in his diary, "Articles going on by the dozen. Hear that U.S.A. has already had lots of wild fables."[62] On April 17 the *New York Times* ran the headline "Paris to Expel A. Crowley." On April 21, *Reynolds Illustrated Newspaper* published an interview with Crowley, who expressed bewilderment at his treatment. "There is no accusation against me," he told the reporter:

> My sweetheart was expelled…. When she demanded what it was the French authorities had against me they suggested that I was a trafficker in cocaine. This is ridiculous. Afterwards, they said: "It is not that. Perhaps that is not true. It is something else. The real reason is too terrible."[63]

Meanwhile, back in England, *John Bull* gloated:

> Soon Hell will be the only place which will have you. You were driven
> out of England, America deported you and so did Sicily. Now France has
> given you marching orders. Since I exposed you for the seducer, devil
> doctor and debauched dope fiend that you are, not a decent country will
> tolerate either you or your sinister satellites.[64]

If Marie could not enter England because she was not a citizen, then the solution was to make her a citizen. Thus Crowley proposed to marry her. It was
simply a matter of practicality: neither romance nor passion influenced the
decision. He even ignored the I Ching's May 13 description of his proposed
marriage as "a rash act" (Kwan, hexagram XX), huffing to himself, "I knew
that." Delays crept in, however, as Crowley learned that, to marry in Brussels,
he needed a copy of his divorce papers from Scotland and a translator to render
them into French. Realizing the requisite papers would take months to collect,
Crowley applied, in vain, to the British Consul for permission to bring Marie
to England on grounds of public morality. Reflecting on his persistent misfor-
tunes, he remarked, "It is like sitting on the Baltoro Glacier waiting for two
consecutive fine days which never turned up."[65]

The publicity over Crowley's "expulsion" incited people to deluge Scotland
Yard, insisting they arrest Crowley for all the women he killed in France. Lieu-
tenant-Colonel John Filis Carré Carter (1882–1944) of Scotland Yard's Special
Branch[66] politely questioned young Yorke, knowing his involvement with AC.
Yorke insisted Crowley was not as bad as people made him out to be, and sug-
gested, "Why not bring AC over and put these questions to him yourself?"
Carter handed him £10 and said "Bring Crowley to London."

Crowley arrived on June 11 for dinner with Colonel Carter. They apparently got along well, for Crowley noted in his diary, "All clear" and thereafter
referred to him as "ol' Nick" and "Saint Nicholas." Thereafter the two met
occasionally for dinner.

While in London, Crowley visited some of his acquaintances, including
Gwen Otter, Montgomery Evans II, and linguist Charles Kay Ogden (1889–
1957). *Observer* art critic Paul George Konody (1872–1933) expressed interest
in Crowley's work, encouraging him to paint. Thus when James Cleugh, literary director of the Aquila Press, mentioned that the press was for sale, Crowley
planned to buy it, turn it into a gallery, and charge artists to exhibit their works.
Major Robert Thompson Thynne, whom he met at this time, promised to
help with the scheme. And although he still planned to sue *John Bull,* a publishing contract and £50 advance from the Mandrake Press distracted him.

The Mandrake Press was a small publishing house run by Edward Goldston
(1892–1953) and Percy Reginald Stephensen (1901–1965). Goldston was an
enterprising businessman who went from working in the Oriental department
of Kegan Paul, Trench, Trübner and Company to running his own rare book-

store and publishing house on Museum Street. Both his clients and his books were rich—in 1925, for instance, he bought and sold the vellum Melk monastery copy of the Gutenberg Bible—and Goldston shrewdly reinvested his profits into other private presses. Jack Lindsay (1900–1990), who sought a publisher for D. H. Lawrence's artwork, united Goldston with Stephensen to form the Mandrake Press. Stephensen, an Australian nicknamed Inky, was

> a thin and immensely energetic young man, with a sandy moustache, fierce, keen eyes and a quick, nervous manner. He was a Rhodes scholar at Oxford, where his views were rarely exactly coincident with those of the university authorities.[67]

In his school days, he had been a staunch defender of Communism. He later married but continued to spearhead various causes. In his native Australia he operated for a time the Fanfrolico Press, and this background made him an ideal business partner for Goldston.

Mandrake made a big splash by publishing and exhibiting Lawrence's paintings at their 41 Museum Street offices: the authorities had already suppressed his *Lady Chatterley's Lover,* and after newspapers attacked the exhibition, the police raided the show and seized any artworks that showed pubic hair or genitalia—about half the pieces. The final trial, held on August 8, ended with Mandrake returning the paintings, stopping the exhibition, and destroying the books; however, no charges were pressed. Although losing Lawrence's book struck the small press hard, it also gave Mandrake a sensational launch. Through the publicity, Mandrake signed twenty new titles between June and August.

Stephensen, in the midst of a battle against censorship, was eager to take on a dark horse like Crowley. A controversial figure whose theories of sexual liberation were sure to outrage the prudes who attacked the Lawrence exhibit was just what he wanted. The press offered to publish *The Stratagem and Other Stories* and talked of exhibiting his paintings. On June 28, AC signed a contract and received his £50 advance. He would use it to rent a cottage in Knockholt, Kent, which he would occupy that fall. Stephensen had found it for him; it was thirty miles south of London and separated from Stephensen's own weekend place by a household of elderly spinsters.

Telegrams were usually bad news, and the July 19 cable from Marie was no exception: she and Regardie were forced to leave Brussels. Crowley called on the Germers, who had returned to Berlin on July 4, and they met Marie the next day, taking her to Leipzig, where Sister Martha Küntzel put her up. Realizing the situation had become untenable, Crowley on July 24 signed a power of attorney allowing Yorke to conduct business for him. He also signed another contract with Mandrake to bring out *Moonchild, Golden Twigs,* his autobiography, and a critical treatment of Crowley's work. Then he left for Leipzig, fetched Marie, and made wedding plans. Crowley hoped that as a married person he could bring Lulu to England and legally adopt her. On August 16,

1929, at 11:20 a.m., Marie Teresa de Miramar became Mrs. Aleister Crowley in a ceremony before the British consul in Germany. That evening they left for London, arriving the following night. "No one to meet us," AC lamented.

Returning to work brought new problems. One of them emerged from Crowley's visit to Germany, where he permitted Birven, who was publishing the magical magazine *Hain der Isis,* to serialize a German translation of parts of *Magick,* as well the entirety of his article "The Psychology of Hashish" … in violation of his Mandrake contract. Meanwhile, Yorke, Goldston, and Stephensen all agreed that Crowley needed to change the names of *Moonchild's* characters, which AC had modeled after real-world people such as Yeats, Mathers, and Desti, before they could publish it. Finally, on August 29, Crowley instructed Lecram Press to send the copies of *Magick* to Mandrake for distribution; however, December would arrive before the books.

Nevertheless, Mandrake soon released new Crowley titles. *The Stratagem and Other Stories* came out September 10, followed on September 25 by *Moonchild,* which boasted a dust jacket by artist Beresford Egan (1905–1984). Mandrake also released another book of lesser interest to the Crowley corpus: not only did *Merry Go Down* by Rab Noolas contain poetry by Victor Neuburg but Noolas was a pseudonym for Philip Heseltine, better known as Peter Warlock (1894–1930). He was one of Stephensen's drinking buddies who had helped with the Fanfrolico Press.

The public eye also beheld Crowley in Betty May's biography, *Tiger Woman: My Story.* Published by Duckworth in 1929, it identified Crowley only as "The Mystic," painting a kind picture of him. Most significantly, the book stated that Raoul died not from drinking cat's blood during a ritual but from contaminated water. When he lunched with Duckworth's representative Anthony Powell (1905–2000) one afternoon, Crowley complained just a bit about *Tiger Woman,* his main gripe being the hard life of a magician. Powell would model Dr. Trelawney of his acclaimed twelve-volume novel sequence *Dance to the Music of Time* (1951–1975) after Crowley.

On October 9, Crowley moved to Ivy Cottage in Knockholt, Kent. He quickly became popular among the locals and could be seen walking down the streets in his winter jacket and scarf, bellowing old sailor's songs. Stephensen visited often, playing chess and rummaging through Crowley's room full of books, manuscripts, and press cuttings. It was here that Stephensen put aside his autobiographical novel *Clean Earth* to write a defense of the Beast, *The Legend of Aleister Crowley.* He hoped such a book, issued cheaply to sell, would promote sales of forthcoming books by Mandrake's star author.

Marie, meanwhile, became difficult. The new Mrs. Crowley drank heavily, and her suspicious nature blossomed into rabid paranoia. The day before their move to Knockholt, she had made a scene; then, the day after they moved, Crowley recorded in his diary that Marie "had several bad attacks of delusion."

Two days later, during Crowley's fifty-fourth birthday party with the Germers and Stephensens, "Marie relapsed badly in P.M. & there was a most nerve-wracking scene."[68] When, shortly thereafter, Marie worsened and began having fainting spells, Crowley sent her to a nursing home. "Seven hours' rest worked wonders," he noted.[69] Crowley's luck with women was again showing.

Regardless, that October was important as the press got hold of Crowley's newest books. While the *Birmingham Post* panned *The Stratagem and Other Stories, Moonchild* met with mixed reviews. The *Aberdeen Press and Journal* called it "one of the most extraordinarily fantastic yet attractive novels we have read,"[70] while the *New Statesman* expressed perplexity, writing, "Possibly the author may know what this nonsense is all about."[71] Finally, the *New Age* slammed its sensational jacket blurb:

> I had no idea that Mr. Crowley was one of the "most mysterious" of living writers, or even that he was mysterious. What does it mean, anyway? That he writes mystery novels? That it is a mystery why he writes novels? That no one knows who he is? Or what?[72]

Mandrake also released Crowley's autobiography. Although the author titled it *The Spirit of Solitude,* Stephensen "re-antichristened" it *The Confessions of Aleister Crowley* after St. Augustine's autohagiography. It was so long that Mandrake planned to issue it in six volumes. The October 1929 invoice for volume one cited printing costs of £167. The book was handsome, bound in oversize white buckram, and sold for two guineas.

Unfortunately, October 1929 was the worst possible month to release expensive, privately printed books, for the stock market crash on Black Friday, October 28, meant slow book sales. Furthermore, the Germers lost a lot of money on the stock market, making support of Crowley more difficult.

Stephensen attributed the difficulty in selling Crowley's books to his anonymity, which exceeded his notoriety. Since Mandrake had such success with its D. H. Lawrence exhibition, he planned to show Crowley's artworks. When Goldston skeptically refused to fund the exhibit, Crowley's people paid to ship and frame his paintings with reimbursement from Mandrake pending a successful show. On Friday, November 1, starting at 10 a.m., the public could pay £1 to see AC's artwork at the Mandrake offices. With many of Crowley's works remaining soiled and unframed, it was disappointing and, unlike the Lawrence exhibit, generated no interest.

Goldston, convinced of Stephensen's folly, finally closed the Mandrake offices for the winter. Among Mandrake's last official actions that December were releasing Volume Two of the *Confessions,* working on Volume Three, and transferring three thousand unbound copies of *Magick in Theory and Practice* to England for distribution. This last book was supposed to bear a talisman on its cover, but no engraver would take on so ignominious a task; but the four paperbound volumes did include a color plate reproducing the talisman.

CHAPTER EIGHTEEN

Beast Bites Back

When the Oxford University Poetry Society invited Crowley to speak at the university, AC hesitated at first. Nearly two decades earlier, the dons had banned his lectures at Cambridge; since then, his name had fallen into such disrepute that public opinion made him into a devil-worshiping madman, in much the same way that wealthy French baron Gilles de Rais (1404–1440) had been accused, tried, and executed on the extraordinary charges of satanism, kidnapping, and killing and eating six hundred children. Whether he was a serial killer or victim of witchcraft hysteria is debated to this day. Identifying with the idea of a falsely accused magician, AC accepted the invitation, telling club secretary (and future novelist) Arthur Calder-Marshall (1908–1992) that he would be lecturing on Gilles de Rais.

Alas, history repeated itself. When Oxford's chaplain, Father Ronald Arbuthnott Knox (1888–1957),[1] learned of the impending lecture by that notorious black magician Aleister Crowley—at whose debased Abbey Oxford student Raoul Loveday had died—he canceled the talk. The Poetry Society defiantly rented an off-campus room, planning to shuttle students to and from the lecture by bus, but Knox threatened to expel any students who attended the talk. Poetry Society secretary Hugh Speaight, remembered as very sophisticated and well-schooled in contemporary arts,[2] hoped to become a Dominican monk and was thus beaten just as Mudd had been twenty years earlier. He sent a rueful cancellation to Crowley on January 30, 1930:

> Dear Mr. Crowley:
>
> I am writing to tell you that we have been unfortunately forced to cancel next Monday's meeting of the Poetry Society. It has come to our knowledge that if your proposed paper is delivered disciplinary action will be taken involving not only myself but the rest of the Committee of the Society. In these circumstances you will, I trust, understand why we have had to cancel the meeting. I feel I must apologize to you for the trouble I have caused you. I must confess that I had credited the University with more tolerance—or at any rate with a greater sense of humour.[3]

This must have been a bitter pill for Speaight, who, in his book of Catholic meditations published the previous year, wrote, "censorship provides the sinner with one of his rare chances of winning a dream of martyrdom."[4]

Oxford University Poetry Society secretary Hugh Speaight.

Crowley refused to give in this time, and decided to make his lecture available to Oxford students even if he *was* forbidden to speak it. On February 1 he wrote to Stephensen:

> I authorize you to take whatever steps you consider advisable to secure the publication of "The Banned Lecture" on the 3rd of February of the present year.[5]

Stephensen—a notorious Oxford alumnus because of his Communist views— rallied behind Crowley and arranged to typeset and print Crowley's lecture on the date of his proposed talk.

Tremendous hype greeted February 3. In the pages of local papers like the *Oxford Mail, Daily Sketch, Birmingham Post, Birmingham Gazette, Manchester Evening Chronicle, Manchester Guardian, Daily News,* and *Darlington Northern Echo,* Crowley fumed to reporters, "I challenge anyone to show why I should not lecture in Oxford today. There is some underhand business behind this"; after an exasperated pause, he smiled. "The authorities are afraid that I may kill and eat eight hundred Oxford undergraduates."[6] Students with sandwich boards marched along Oxford's High Street, announcing that copies of Crowley's forbidden speech would go on sale tomorrow. Consequently, various rumors spread around the campus: that Calder-Marshall and Speaight were trying to form a coven; or that Father Knox had refused Speaight Communion in church for inviting Crowley.[7] Thus *The Banned Lecture* enjoyed brisk sales, with curious students who would otherwise never have attended the talk paying sixpence to see what all the fuss was about.

Believing the current economy could not support a small press, and with Goldston getting cold feet, Stephensen began seeking a prospective buyer for Mandrake. He suggested that Yorke and Germer begin a financial syndicate to produce and sell Crowley's books. The proposal was ambitious: Germer and Yorke would acquire Mandrake and rename it the Thelema Bookshop and Publishing Co. Ltd. They planned to release *The Vision and the Voice, Liber Aleph,* the comment on *The Book of the Law, 100 Short Poems, Simple Simon* (his Simon Iff short stories in two volumes), *Golden Twigs* (his Frazer-inspired short stories), *The Legend of Aleister Crowley, Collected Short Stories,* and the Hopfer color edition of 777. Alas, they lacked the capital for so large a venture.

Thus they chose the cheaper option, to take over the press as a limited liability company. Germer and Yorke negotiated a loan from Cora Germer, for which Yorke agreed to take out a life insurance policy should he die before repaying her.[8] Then Yorke contributed £1,000, Major Thynne £1,000, and Germer £500, to form Mandrake Press Ltd. Painter, surgeon, and psychoanalyst Grace Winifred Pailthorpe (1883–1971) also put in £200 to £300 in exchange for publication of her Freudian book, *What We Put in Prison.*[9] Goldston happily relinquished the floundering press on March 28. Yorke, Stephensen, Thynne, and Thynne's associate, Major J. C. S. McAllan, formed the board of directors, and Regardie became bookkeeper.

While Yorke and the others organized business that April, Crowley visited Germany. He planned a fall exhibit of his paintings in Berlin; met with several OTO members, including Henri Birven, whose *Hain der Isis* had debuted that January;[10] and befriended Hanni Larissa Jaeger, a nineteen-year-old spitfire who shared Crowley's interest in painting.[11]

When Germer got his license at the end of the month, he took Crowley for a drive, only to overturn the car into a ditch. In his diary, Crowley humorously recorded the incident:

> What I said during yesterday's accident. (1) "Ease her up!" He didn't: so (2) "Are you mad?" He was: so (3) "Take care of the glass." (4) "Let me lower myself, so that you can get out."[12]

When Maria joined him in Berlin, he took her shopping for birthday presents; when she treated him to another drunken row that evening, Crowley sent her back to Leipzig and, on May 5, returned himself to London.

That May, the Mandrake Press Ltd. put out its first and only catalog. It included Mandrake's backlist along with some twenty proposed titles, only a few of which ever appeared. In the following months, however, they did publish a broad range of titles: a translation of Gustave Flaubert's *Salammbô;* D. H. Lawrence's posthumous *A Propos of Lady Chatterley's Lover;* and Liam O'Flaherty's (1896–1984) *The Ecstasy of Angus.* Although finely produced, the books generated little interest.

On top of slow sales, Crowley's constant presence in the office was a nuisance. He was suing Goldston for the promised but unpaid reimbursement for the cost of shipping his paintings to London for the Mandrake exhibit (an act that severed Goldston entirely from the press and ensured that the third and future volumes of *The Confessions* would never appear). He was also attempting to ply another £500 from Cora Germer to purchase the Aquila Press, a venture he eventually abandoned. Plus, his many comments on the ongoing typesetting of volume three of *The Confessions* and the upcoming *Legend of Aleister Crowley* made Stephensen believe Crowley was trying to *prevent* the books from appearing. Stephensen finally insisted that Crowley keep out of the offices and to cease extorting money out of his supporters.

> I want absolute *carte blanche* for Mandrake Press Ltd. to go ahead publishing, as and how I think fit, in consultation with Thynne & Yorke. I want you to regard Mandrake Press Ltd. solely as your publishers, and not to prejudice the purely commercial side of that purely publishing concern with any of your fits and starts, Thelemite politics, earthquakes, and the other distracting phenomena of art and nature, such as pin pricks, dogmatism, human chess, brawls, faux pas, bravado and braggadocio, pure bluff, brainwaves, and dementia precox, which tend to accompany your too personal intrusion into the world of practical affairs.[13]

Despite his joking tone, Stephensen was firm.

So Crowley kicked back with a copy of the finished proofs to volume three of his autobiography, enjoying the £500 he decided not to spend on the Aquila Press. When Yorke encouraged him to economize, Crowley made a diary entry in his inimitable manner:

> Yorke niggling again, that one must cut one's coat in accordance with one's cloth; whereas the meanest tailor knows that one must cut one's cloth in accordance with the size of the man.[14]

Crowley was doubtless full of himself because Mandrake was finally releasing *The Legend of Aleister Crowley.*

Although it was ready as early as October, Goldston delayed its publication. When the blue paperback finally appeared, the printer suppressed the "Epistle Dedicatory to James Douglas (editor of the *Sunday Express*)" for fear of libel; its tone was most unfriendly:

> Investigation reveals that you had neither a sense of responsibility nor a sense of shame nor any substantial reason for attacking Crowley except your own squamous vanity. You had called for the suppression of his book in accents which are more familiar now days than they then were. You followed up

this clamour with a campaign of personal vilification more severe than anything of its kind which has yet disgraced even modern gutter journalism.[15]

Interestingly enough, Crowley's old *chela* Victor Neuburg reviewed the book
and defended Crowley in the August 24 *Freethinker:*

> although in some respects he was perhaps "not quite nice to know," as the
> slang phrase goes, we do not think that it is quite fair to charge him with
> murder, cannibalism, black magical practices, moral aberrations, treachery,
> druggery; as is the custom amongst the cunninger and more degraded
> jackals of Fleet Street ... Crowley is at least as important a figure as the late
> D. H. Lawrence and Mr. James Joyce, both unquestionably men of genius;
> and when we remember the kind of thing said about these artists in our
> cheaper prints, we hesitate to acquiesce in the Sunday Newspaper verdict
> on Aleister Crowley.[16]

Crowley had been trying to exhibit his paintings in London; a jobber named
Hanchant tried to arrange an exhibit at Aquila, but that fell through with the
purchase deal. When Crowley turned his hotel room into a gallery, his landlord
evicted him. Thus Crowley packed 160 of his paintings and drawings for Berlin, where he hoped for a better reception. "Miss Jaeger fucks every one farewells," Crowley recorded on his departure from London on August 1. His bon
voyage party was quite an affair, with "Marie drunk and vomiting all day."[17]

He arrived in Berlin on August 2 and relegated his alcoholic wife to history, writing to Maria that he wanted nothing to do with her until she stopped
drinking. (Yorke meanwhile sent her off to Hampstead.) AC renamed luscious
Fräulein Jaeger as the Monster (he also gave her the magical name Anu) and
began practicing sex magick with her. Germer, in his reckless manner, motored
them about Germany, including a visit to his therapist, Austrian psychoanalyst
Alfred Adler (1870–1937), whom Crowley claimed to have helped with his
patients. Regarding psychology, Crowley wrote,

> There are only three authors on the subject worth reading, the original
> Freud, Adler and Jung. Freud is completely obsessed with the nonsense
> about infantile sexual theories. There may possibly be children in Ger-
> many or Austria sufficiently morbid, but nothing of the sort ever crossed
> my own mind when I was a child—nor have I ever met a child so morbid.
> Jung appears to me to have gone off the rails by his innate incurable
> romanticism. To my mind, the best of the three is Adler, whom, of course,
> I know personally; with him I did actually work when I was in Berlin. He
> could only come up from Vienna for a fortnight every year, and I handled
> some of his patients in his absence.[18]

Crowley took a manuscript from Adler for Mandrake to publish, thinking it
would be a boon for the troubled press whose greatest asset, D. H. Lawrence,
had just died; alas, Mandrake never managed to publish it.

Another notable contact at this time was with writer and critic Aldous
Huxley (1894–1963). Although best known for *Brave New World* (1932), his

The Doors of Perception (1954) would serve almost as a manifesto for the psychedelic revolution of the 1960s. He was already an established writer when he and Crowley met. One can only imagine what they discussed, although on the heels of their meeting Crowley wrote to Regardie,

> Please send a copy of *Clouds without Water* to Aldous Huxley Esq., Athenaeum Club, Pall Mall (with prospectuses etc.) with my compliments— we had a gorgeous 3 days with him in Berlin. Also please set up a figure [astrological chart] for him. Godalming, 4 A.M., July 26 '94.[19]

Mandrake had fallen on bad times, and Crowley's absence brought proof correction and other business to a standstill. Owing £2,000 and sitting on £4,000 worth of unsold stock, Mandrake was in no position to repay its creditors. Stephensen, convinced that Thynne and Crowley were both diverting funds into their own pockets, left the business: Packing up the page proofs for *The Confessions* Volume Three and *Golden Twigs,* he retreated to his little village in Kent and left Mandrake to its fate. He soon returned to Australia and set up the Endeavor Press with Norman Lindsay.

Mandrake would go into voluntary liquidation that winter, and ultimately collapse from lack of capital a year after Stephensen's departure. Although Grace Pailthorpe lost her investment in the press, she harbored no hard feelings; when *What We Put in Prison and in Preventive and Rescue Homes* debuted in 1932, she mentioned Mandrake in the dedication. This book gained her worldwide acclaim and prompted the psychological treatment of criminals.

In the midst of Mandrake's struggle, Crowley was, as Yorke put it, "up to some stunt in Portugal."[20] His scheme was to travel round the world with Fraulein Jaeger on a shoestring budget, writing a travelogue. AC detailed the plans in a letter to biographer and poet Herbert Gorman (1893–1954):

> The Monster & I have started to go round the world on £14.10.10. The question has arisen as to whether we shall not need some more between Lisbon, Madera, Rio Monte Video, Buenos Aries, Volparaiso, the Galapagos Isl (where the turtles come from), the South Seas, China, India, &c, &c, &c & London.
>
> Style: as *Confessions,* but more cynical & romantic.
>
> So cable me a contract from one of your millionaire papers to write it all up.[21]

The steamship *Alcantara* carried them to Lisbon, where poet Fernando Pessoa (1888–1935) greeted them at the dock on September 2, 1930. Like Crowley, Pessoa found inspiration for his poems—like "Nirvana" (1906) and "The Circle" (1907)—in mediums, kabbalah, Rosicrucians, Theosophy, magic, and mysticism. He had ordered a copy of 777 from a London book dealer in 1917, and in November 1929 contacted Mandrake Press to purchase the *Confessions.* When Pessoa identified an error in the *Confessions* in Crowley's natal chart and notified the press in a letter dated December 4, 1929, it prompted a personal reply from Crowley. Thus began their correspondence. Pessoa would even translate "Hymn to Pan" into Portuguese to include in his *Presença 33* (1931). Crowley called him "a really good poet, the only man who has ever written Shakespearean Sonnets in the manner of Shakespeare. It is about the most remarkable literary phenomena in my experience."[22]

The wayfarers took a room at the Hotel de l'Europe. They bathed in the sea at Estoril beach, walked along the shore, and enjoyed the sights. One of these was the Boca de Inferno, or Mouth of Hell, in Cascaes, twenty-three miles from Lisbon. The fantastic rocks of this ravine leading out to sea, jutting straight up from the mouth of the Tagus, had been hollowed out by the waves. It so impressed Crowley that he wrote in his diary, "I wish the west coast of Scotland could see it."

As they traveled, Crowley also trained the Monster to become his next Scarlet Woman. Although she easily saw astral visions with the help of drugs, they disturbed and frightened her. On September 16 she used alcohol during a ritual for success in some moneymaking scheme: when she saw visions, she began sobbing and became hysterical; then said she was sick of magick and wanted to kill herself. In the end, the manager interrupted the incident and ordered them to leave the hotel.

Moving to Estoril the next day, Hanni seemed better; however, as Crowley booked a room for them, she vanished. He searched the area, recording in his diary, "There is no news of her yet—6 p.m." The next day, with still no word, he noted: "Worrying like the devil." The next day, September 19, he resolved: "I am not going to get over this—unless she comes back." He found her later that day in Lisbon, where the American Consul advised her to go home. Crowley—seeing both his romance and travelogue crumbling—asked her to reconsider. Although she returned with him that evening, she sailed for Germany early the next morning.

Finding himself alone, Crowley vented his frustration in a letter to Maria, who complained that he did not visit during his last trip to London.

> Dear Maria,
>
> I did not ring you up when I passed through London because you answered my very serious letter with the most trivial everyday nonsense.
>
> Also you have been trying to seduce Israel Regardie and I know not who else. It is galling to my pride that some say you failed!
>
> Anyhow, you had better get a man who will stand for your secret drinking and your scandalous behavior. I gave you a great chance in life, and you threw it away. *Tant pis!*[23]
>
> You should get a divorce. I admit what some dithering nincompoops are still imbecile enough to call "misconduct" on 47 occasions since August 3rd—the fatigue of constant travel must excuse the smallness of the figure—with Hanni Jaeger of Berlin.
>
> It will be no good asking for alimony because we are all in the soup together with the Rt. Hon. Lord Beaverbrook and the British Empire. Best of all to you![24]

Crowley stuffed the letter into an envelope and set out on a walk. Passing the astonishing Mouth of Hell, inspiration struck.

On September 23 at 6:36 p.m., the moment of the autumnal equinox, he left a cryptic note at Boca de Inferno, weighted down by his cigarette case:

L.G.P.

I cannot live without you. The other "Boca de Inferno" will get me—it will not be so hot as yours!

Hjsos!

Tu
Li
Yu

The signature was a joke on Crowley's part: toodle-oo. (Pessoa would explain to the press that this was one of Crowley's previous incarnations, a Chinese sage who lived some three thousand years before Christ; but he may well have been perpetuating the joke.) The next day, Crowley received a note from Hanni. It contained only one sentence, yet said everything: "Love is the law, love under will." Crowley quietly left Portugal on September 24 to rendezvous with his lover in Germany.

Meanwhile, Pessoa (according to plan) told the press that his friend Aleister Crowley had disappeared. When journalist Ferreira Gomes found the note at Hell's Mouth the next day, the *Diario de Noticias* and *Noticias Illustrado* carried the story of Crowley's mysterious disappearance. Papers throughout Europe quickly picked it up, including the French magazine *Détective,* which ran a large article titled "L'énigme de la Bouche d'Enfer" ["The Mystery of the Mouth of Hell"]. The *New York Herald, Paris* ran a photo of two silhouettes looking out at the sea from Boca de Inferno; although the figures are unidentified, they are Crowley and Hanni, photographed by the Beast's friend, writer Herbert Gorman (1893–1954). However, British censors delayed the stories pending further information. Many papers nevertheless carried the news as it broke, helping spread rumors that Crowley had been murdered, perhaps by a fanatic Catholic priest.

The case became even more mysterious when Portuguese officials stated that, according to their records, Crowley had left the country on September 23. Pessoa, however, insisted that he saw Aleister Crowley on the 23rd and twice on the 24th. Thus, either Crowley left Portugal on the 23rd and returned the next day, or there were *two* Crowleys, one who left Portugal and another who committed suicide. "Famous Mystic or His?" ran a headline in the *Empire News.* The plot thickened when rumor had it that police raided Crowley's posh Berlin headquarters, finding information on a Soviet plan for world domination, suggesting Crowley was a wealthy secret agent who had run afoul.

AC, who kept a low profile in Germany as the drama of his disappearance unfolded, instructed Thynne and Yorke to milk this for all it was worth. Hanni had Regardie set up a bogus seance with Alfred Vout Peters (1867–1934), the well-known London clairvoyant and trance medium who had attempted to contact the recently departed Sir Arthur Conan Doyle (1859–1930). "Students of magick should avoid all spiritualists as they should avoid syphilis," Crowley warned Regardie; it was a double entendre, referring not only to mediums but also to the Serpent's bout with venereal disease. On October 14, the *Oxford Mail* announced the seance to reach Crowley's spirit. The Doyle Medium Jest, as Crowley called it, began with a slow description of Crowley's visit to Lisbon; eventually, Peters described Crowley's walk in the countryside, where he stopped by Boca de Inferno. Suddenly, he was pushed from behind. By whom? His enemies: either Roman Catholics or Freemasons. The body, Peters claimed, would never be found. Regardie's management of the stunt and its ensuing publicity so pleased Hanni that she told Crowley, "Wait till I get to London. I'll fuck that bastard silly."[25]

In order to milk money out of the publicity, Crowley pseudonymously sent the following letter to Anthony Powell at Duckworth:

> My dear Powell,
>
> I am the beautiful German girl for whose love the infamous Aleister Crowley committed suicide.

Posing as Hanni, AC offered to sell the manuscript of *My Hymen,* the eighty-thousand-word story of their elopement, for a £500 advance on a fifteen percent royalty. Although this was the same deal they gave Betty May for her biography *Tiger Woman,* they declined the offer.

While Crowley traipsed across the continent with Hanni Jaeger, Yorke fumed in London. He thought Crowley irresponsible for leaving Marie penniless and begging Yorke for help. "If that woman starves, you can be sent to prison for not keeping her since you married her," Yorke threatened him at one time;[26] later, he wrote with exasperation, "You are a callous old sinner at times."[27] The two argued passionately about Marie, Yorke insisting that Crowley live up to his responsibility and AC accusing Yorke of sleeping with his wife. 'Twas to no avail.

Yorke ultimately resigned himself to accepting Crowley's vagaries and to maintaining a distance from him. In a note to himself, he wrote:

> It is a curious world. I cannot stand for A.C.'s behaviour in leaving Marie without a bean and refusing to support her. I cannot stand for his wasting other people's money the way he does, or for his taking money for one purpose and using it for another. In his own mind of course he so associates himself with the work that he thinks money spent on himself as money spent on the work. Possible theoretically, but won't go down in practice. I cannot sincerely pull with him in that side of his work. Yet I am heart and soul in the movement. I see his actions as endangering the movement. Practically he has still to prove his point. Up till now his method has only led from one mess to another. It is up to him to prove his way. Meanwhile my best way to help the world is quietly to do my best to prepare what I consider a decent solid foundation … But I cannot work with A.C. in the way he would like as I sincerely disapprove of his method.[28]

Yorke ultimately became a distant but staunch advocate of Crowley, supporting his work without becoming involved in it. Developing an interest in Buddhism, much of his attention would go to the Dalai Lama, serving as his spokesman and publishing his books.

Thinking it was better for Marie to receive a token amount than for Crowley to face charges of not supporting her, Yorke paid her an allowance from the publication fund, over which Crowley had given him power of attorney. Yorke paid her £60 by the time he received a telegram from Crowley, asking for the publication fund money to help with his stunt. In response, Yorke wired back, "Tell 666 there are two of them. They both bounce." Or, in vernacular, "Balls." Incensed, Crowley revoked Yorke's power of attorney and placed Regardie in charge. Thus, AC cast off the rich boy from Gloucestershire.

Knowing only £30 remained in the account, Yorke advised the bank to accept Regardie's signature but warned that he would not be responsible for overdrawn checks. He contends Regardie used the money on himself.[29] Per Crowley's instructions, Yorke then gave the diaries, books, photos, and other materials he had been storing to Crowley's solicitor, Isidore Kerman (1905–1998).[30] The only thing keeping Yorke from resigning his trusteeship was the fact that legal costs would come from the fund; as much as he wanted to sever business ties with Beast, he knew Crowley needed the money.

AC seemed to be owning up to his responsibility when he offered Marie a portion of his trust payment. Since the law required Crowley to send the money to her himself, Yorke sent him the balance of their storage settlement on October 25, assuming this money would go to Marie. However, Crowley spent it all. Yorke could bear no more. In frustration, he suspended his financial dealings with Crowley. "You are funny when you propose disassociating yourself from matters out of which you have been chucked," AC responded. "You will do more wisely to ask rehabilitation in a chastened spirit."[31]

Life with Hanni Jaeger continued to be as stormy and intense as ever. When harmonious, it left Crowley in emotional and sexual bliss. But when they clashed, it was fierce: she often moved out for the night, only to return the next day. Further complicating things were her profound mood swings, bizarre behavior, and physical symptoms that always subsided long enough for her to seduce him. Thus, when Hanni complained of abdominal pains after Halloween, Crowley found it difficult to take her seriously. When a man called to say Hanni was in the hospital and would not be home that night, Crowley assumed she had simply found someone else with whom to sleep. He was alarmed to discover she was truly in the hospital with kidney trouble. Despite her illness, constant seductions of Crowley—and just as many rows—studded Hanni's return home. Some of Crowley's diary entries from this period are illuminating:

> *November 22, 1930.* She is violently excited all day—sexually & otherwise. Severe melancholic & erotic outbursts. There is absolutely no reason

for any nervous upset of any kind; but she changes from mood to mood in the most sudden way. This attack is more prolonged & severe than any I have observed so far. And it is more than usually causeless. She ended by wanting to go out; when I objected, pretended to ring up the police—a too familiar trick. She then calmed down, & at last woke up into an infantile state. I undressed her, & put her to bed in my pyjamas. In short, every possible phase—She has now called me in, to listen to hallucinations, real or no; e.g. "I don't want you to go away behind the tree."

December 16, 1930. One of her sadistic tricks is to make herself suffer physically from starvation, cold etc. in order to make me suffer from sympathy. E.g. she will ask for something she obviously needs (& could take without asking) & when supplied (as of course) she refuses it with violent rage, & then moans & screams because she hasn't got it.

Crowley summed up their antipathy by writing: "I love her. I've thought of nothing else all day. I've even abused her to have an excuse to talk about her!"[32]

They fought again two days before Christmas, and she again moved out. Depressed, Crowley dreamed of her on Christmas Eve and went home early from Christmas dinner with the Germers, hoping she might call. She did not. When, on boxing day, he found her at Romanisches Café (one of Berlin's great coffeehouses), she claimed she had purchased a gift for him, but the waiter had lost or stolen it. Then she told Crowley of her plans "to stop eating, prostitute herself to get money for cigarettes & brandy & to hire a room with gas & a hot bath to open her veins in."[33] Two days later she was again herself, but the magic was gone. Their rituals soon trailed off, she moved out, and they both moved on. When Crowley became sick in January 1931, he likened his intestinal difficulties to his soul's purging of Hanni Larissa Jaeger.

Crowley later heard that the Monster had killed herself shortly after they parted.[34] However, a twenty-one-year-old Hanni Jaeger arrived in New York from Hamburg in late 1931.[35] It is entirely possible that Crowley (along with his biographers) was tricked by her own version of the suicide stunt.

Yorke continued urging Crowley to deal honorably with his wife by writing:

I gave Maria dinner the other night, and found her in a very bad way. Rent is paid up to the end of the month, but she is very short of food, and in a bad nervous condition, talking to everyone of suicide. Her genuine attempts to find work have met with very little success. She got one regular job, but lost it through being your wife when *John Bull* attacked you and the Mandrake Press early in January.... I tell her that from your letters to me you appear to want to treat her decently and to make some allowance—you know she is not extravagant. But in practice she receives nothing, and one cannot blame her for suspecting you of prevarication.[36]

Given Crowley's continued inaction, Marie finally sued for support in Marelybone Police Court. Crowley responded by advising his solicitor of Marie's drunken scenes and paranoid outbursts. But as Regardie made brutally clear:

> Monster's note about it being much better for the Great Work if you were plaintiff is perfectly true. It is too bad that that wasn't thought of several months ago when Maria received your letter stating that you had committed adultery umpteen times and that only the rigours of travelling prevented the number being greater. The letter must have caused you a great deal of pleasure when written, but, alas, it prevents you even thinking of being plaintiff for divorce now. One can't have things both ways.[37]

Before the case ever came to court, Marie lost her resolve and wrote to Yorke:

> Alas everything is cruel to me. When you get this letter, I am died. I leave this world without regret, because I know that now I go for ever take a dear rest. Please write after to Crowley that in my last moment I could not forgive him. Farewell.[38]

On February 28, 1931, Marie also wrote to Colonel Carter, "Nobody is responsible of my suicide only Aleister Crowley."[39] Carter had previously advised Crowley, "I suggest that you had better cease knocking around the continent and come back to your wife at once or you will be getting yourself into serious trouble...."[40] Now he warned Yorke that Crowley could get two years in prison for wife desertion.

Marie soon disappeared. She drifted to the Embankment, eventually winding up in a workhouse where she was certified insane and committed to Colney Hatch Asylum near Southgate—the same place, ironically, that Rose went with alcoholic dementia. Because she was certified, Crowley could not sue for divorce. Maria became case number 23112, suffering from delusions that she was married to the Great Beast 666, was the daughter of the King and Queen of England, and that she married her brother, the Prince of Wales. When Yorke visited Marie later in 1931, he showed her doctor, to his great surprise, one of Crowley's calling cards, which identified him as the Great Beast 666.

The Great Work of 1931 revolved around planning an exhibit of Crowley's paintings. Crowley was in touch with Karl Nierendorf (1889–1947), a German dealer and promoter of modern art.[41] Nierendorf claimed only three other painters could be classed with Crowley, and believed the public would pay twenty-five thousand reichsmarks per painting. He offered to show the paintings at his Porza Gallery in Berlin. As Yorke and Hanchant shipped the paintings for a planned February showing, Crowley wrote excitedly, "The great Nierendorf is showing my pictures (Time will show whether this is a practical joke on Europe or on me)."[42]

The joke, it turns out, was on Crowley. On February 11 the exhibit was postponed. Undaunted, Crowley spent the next months painting hard and organizing the framing and storage of his works until the rescheduled exhibit. Many of those whom he sampled as potential Scarlet Women that spring and summer served as models, but none of them fit the bill as Whore of Babalon.

Despite continued bouts with cold, asthma, and other ailments, Crowley's search for a sexual partner continued.

On August 1, feeling sidetracked by his recent romances and painting, Crowley did a ritual to get back on track with his prophetic mission. His partner in this act of sex magick was Pola Henckels; of all his lovers at this time, Crowley noted she "may possibly be the one."[43] The ritual felt potent, and convinced him that they'd generated a new current.

Two days later, he met Bertha Busch.

Crowley went walking on Monday, August 3. He saw Adlon and Bristol that morning and, at half-past noon, paused at the window of a travel agency on Unter den Linden. The woman who'd been watching him seized the opportunity to step forward and speak. "Where are you going for your next trip?" He turned and faced the beautiful thirty-six-year-old redhead who was trying to pick him up. Although her name was Bertha Busch, she preferred "Billie." And although Crowley was twenty years older, age did not dissuade her.

Within three days, Crowley performed his first sex magical ritual with her. "I love Billie passionately & truly—& I must avoid her," he soon wrote in his diary. "She might return my love."[44] His words were prophetic, for he was soon bedridden with bronchial asthma; Billie came to his side, dubbed him her "Darling Boy," and nursed him to health. On August 29, Crowley introduced Billie to the Germers over dinner. Karl, who had been growing more eccentric with each passing month, explained "everything about Danish Butter to the amazed admiration of all parties."[45] Although they passed a pleasant time, Germer disliked Billie: he found her coarse and unworthy of the Beast. Despite this friction, Germer grudgingly agreed to pay the rent on their flat. They moved in September 15 and, at the end of the month, conducted a sex magick ritual to consecrate Billie as Crowley's new Scarlet Woman.

That October—despite Germany's economic catastrophe and Germer's own financial distress—the art exhibit was on the verge of opening. Tension was high as Germer paid for framing seventy-three paintings and drawings (ultimately fifty-one were shown) and Crowley brought his copies of *The Equinox, Konx Om Pax, The Legend of Aleister Crowley, Moonchild, The Diary of a Drug Fiend,* and other books to display. The exhibit opened at the Gallery Neumann-Nierendorf on October 11 with many newspapers, the *New York Times* included, photographing and interviewing Crowley about the show. In the exhibition's catalog, Nierendorf—comparing him to Dix, Nolde, Beckmann, Mueller, Schmidt-Rottluff, and Scholz—praised Crowley's works:

> there can be no doubt that the arranged exhibition is stimulating and more impressive than a lot of the English artwork we might otherwise have shown. The paintings are by the intensity of their desire and the primitive-

ness of their execution more closely related to German artists than to the rehash of customary French recipes commonly knocked together on the other side of the Channel today.[46]

Crowley's diary for the day notes "Show about normal." Despite the warm response, whether anything sold is unknown.[47] In the end, Crowley packed his paintings and stored them with Martha Küntzel.

One good thing resulted from the show, however. On its first day, Crowley received a phone call from Gerald Hamilton (c. 1888–1970), who identified himself as Berlin correspondent for the London *Times*. He wanted to interview Crowley. Hamilton has been described as a strange wanderer: born in China, he was a world traveler and a connoisseur of fine food, and described Crowley as a "bon bourgeois" sharing his fondness for good talk and good food. They had so much in common that—despite Hamilton's lack of interest in magick— they hit it off well. By the time Germer discovered Hamilton was not really a press correspondent, it no longer mattered: the two men were close friends. Compared to Germer's antics, Hamilton was a godsend. Crowley filled his days "pentagramming off the Germers"[48] until, that fall, "Karl ... ditched Cora with his family and got a charming girl of thirty-one."[49]

During the art exhibit, an associate of Martha Küntzel's had a vision of the Scarlet Woman pregnant. When, on October 22, Billie suffered again from what Crowley dubbed the Nameless Fear—menstruation marked by heavy bleeding and painful cramps—the prophecy seemed wrong. AC was nevertheless nervous. When the pain became worse on October 26, he called a physician, who diagnosed her complaint as a miscarriage. "I was utterly crushed by sorrow and anxiety all day," Crowley recorded.[50]

Billie recovered by the end of the month, and that November their sex lives assumed wildly orgiastic dimensions, driven by an intense, violent passion that brought out the beast in both of them. Crowley's diary entries make this clear:

Monday, November 2. We went crazy. Instantly we got home I got down on S[carlet] W[oman]. She pissed gallons—we tore off our clothes & fucked & fucked & fucked. She tore my lips & my tongue—the blood streamed all over her face. We fucked. And suddenly she got a jealous fit about 3 cheap whores at Brunnigs & I strangled her—

Tuesday, November 3. Woke early & finished the fuck. Opus 59 very gently: both exhausted.

Tuesday November 10. S[carlet] W[oman] again rather upset at night—for no reason unless too much Korn & cunnilingus before dinner.

Wednesday November 11. A general orgie—including every possible device—from 3 to 6.30.

Thursday November 12. Recuperating—making vows of chastity—U.S.W. And while I was telephoning after lunch, she went into the study & waited for me with her bare bottom in the air ... Opus 66.

On December 6, Billie got drunk again on corn alcohol, and she and Crowley began humping on the sofa. When their landlady walked in, Billie sheepishly hid in the kitchen while Crowley retreated to his study. Billie surprised AC when she walked into the study and drove a carving knife into him, just below the shoulder blade. "She then became violent," he recalled.[51] "I had to hold her down. So I bled till Marie [the landlady] got a doctor, about 2 hrs. later." Most interesting about this incident is Crowley's reaction. When Hamilton heard about the stabbing, he felt ill; and when Crowley wrote matter-of-factly that had the wound been a quarter inch lower it would have been fatal, Yorke was alarmed. Yet Crowley responded, "I wish you would read my letters carefully. The wound was not dangerous though I lost quarts of blood, but it just missed being fatal, which is different."[52] Rather than making it a bone of contention, he took it in stride as a facet of their relationship. The day after the stabbing, he noted with relief in his diary, "Bill started to menstruate, thus explaining everything neatly."[53]

Crowley shared Christmas dinner of 1931 with Karl, his mistress Hedy, and Hamilton, along with novelist Christopher Isherwood (1904–1986) and poet Stephen Spender (1909–1995). Throughout the meal, Billie threatened Crowley with the silverware for misbehaving, and afterward slunk over and said,

> Nach dem Essen sollst Du rauchen
> oder deine Frau gebrauchen.[54]

("After dinner you should smoke, or use your wife.") Crowley laughed and asked her to fetch his pipe.

Hamilton and Isherwood were both homosexual and became close friends after Crowley introduced them. That evening they took AC to the Cosy Corner, a small blue-collar gay bar. Finding masculine and vain young men driven to prostitution by the economic collapse of the Weimar republic, Crowley giggled, "I haven't done anything like this since I was in Port Said." He bellied up to the bar and fixed his gaze on a bare-chested, sinewy man there. Beast, accustomed to Billie's wild appetites, walked up and scratched him deeply on the chest. The man prepared to pulverize Crowley, and only a large gift of money saved Crowley from a pummeling. On the last day of 1931, AC again found himself in the company of his gay friends at a ball of homosexuals. Crowley called it "Frightfully dull, pretentious, & grotesque. Left at 11:30."[55]

Crowley's friendship with Hamilton intensified when, on January 22, 1932, the strange wanderer became a boarder in the spare room of Crowley's flat. The arrangement also gave Crowley another opportunity to earn money: since Hamilton's politics leaned leftward, and he had introduced Crowley to German communist leaders such as Ernst Thaelmann (1886–1944), Beast worked as a British agent, submitting regular reports on Hamilton to Colonel Carter in Scotland Yard. In a letter to Yorke, Crowley cautioned,

Hamilton leaves for London to-morrow night, and may probably call on you. If he should learn that I am as I was born, my usefulness would be over; and if he should even suspect that I have any relations with N[icholas Carter] beyond pulling his leg, there would be work for you within a week or two with that embalmer. So please avoid discussing my politics, or, if forced to do so, say that you regard me as at least 80 per cent Bolshevik. Do please take this most seriously and be as cautious as you know how.[56]

Hamilton was good-humored about the arrangement; as Deacon suggests,[57] he was probably spying on Crowley for the Germans.

Living with Crowley, Hamilton witnessed the constant and frequently violent relationship between Beast and Frau Busch. Early one afternoon, Hamilton came home to find Billie trussed up like a chicken, with a note beside her warning that under no circumstances should he untie her. On another occasion, Hamilton came home late one night to find broken crockery strewn all over and Billie sleeping, stark naked, in front of the long-extinguished hearth. Although the room was freezing in the dead of winter, Hamilton left her undisturbed. He went to Crowley's room, where the master was sleeping fully clothed, shook him, and asked, "Is Billie sick?" Crowley sighed angrily. "Hasn't that bitch gone to bed yet?" To Hamilton's surprise, Crowley rolled out of bed, stomped into the living room, and gave Billie a stern kick. She leapt to her feet, and their obvious struggle began anew. Hamilton watched, dumbfounded, as Crowley tried to hold her down and reach for the rope simultaneously. "Don't just stand there looking like a bloody gentleman," Crowley cried. "Help me bind her!" Hamilton ignored both their pleas for assistance and left the flat, returning later with a doctor, who gave her morphine (the usual cure when she got this way). Crowley's diary entry for this evening is indeed cryptic: "Bill— whew! the best show yet. Started to fuck—she got sadistic—then savage— poor Hamilton!—(I had got her quiet when he came in & woke her) doctor—morphia—hell till 6:30."[58]

Finances picked up again that May 1, 1932, when Crowley heard the sad news that Rose had died in February; Lola Zaza was now receiving £232 annually from her mother's estate, entitling Crowley to the full £165 annually from their joint trust fund. However, this only guaranteed £3 a week for himself and Bill, and Crowley insisted he needed at least fifty a month to carry on his business. Before long, Crowley would petition Yorke that

the trustees have it in their discretion to pay none, or any part, or the whole, of the income to any one of the beneficiaries. I made my application to you and Frater D.D.S. [George Cecil Jones] to let me have the whole amount while things remain in their exceedingly critical situation.... Lola is the only child of her mother who has quite an adequate income of at least £500 a year; and Gerald Kelly is making very large sums out of his outrages upon the art which he professes and prostitutes.

Yorke's terse recollection of this matter: "We continued to pay Lola some or all or none in accordance with her needs."[59]

At this time, Crowley's literary career was looking up. A producer in Berlin named Ribbons wished to put on *Mortadello* if Crowley could get it translated into German; publisher Hans Weber hoped to issue translations of Crowley's works; and a filmmaker named Offuls wanted to make occult films based on Crowley's work. AC was notorious for misspelling names, and "Offuls" is almost certainly German—and later Hollywood—movie director Max Ophüls (1902–1957), who was just beginning to gain international acclaim with his *Liebelei* ("Love Affair," 1932). To capitalize on these opportunities, AC planned a German publication syndicate with Yorke and other backers. He hoped to publish full and condensed versions of his *Confessions,* the plays *Mortadello* and *Three Wishes,* and several leftovers from the Mandrake plan, including a short story collection, *Liber Aleph,* and *Little Essays Toward Truth.* He wrote eagerly, "The plan is to put me over in Germany as they did for Bernard Shaw, Frank Harris and Oscar Wilde. Then and only then will the English follow."[60]

Once again he counted on Yorke to produce the capital necessary to pull off the deal; but, stung by Mandrake's collapse, Yorke was reluctant to place himself—or any of his acquaintances—at Crowley's mercy. Although he contacted potential financiers, none wished to invest in the Great Beast. When a much-anticipated loan to Yorke fell through, Crowley was so disappointed and furious that he accused Yorke of sabotaging the deal. He fired off several acrid letters to Yorke, including the following:

> Every word you write is in an attempt to avoid your own responsibility. The £30, not yet here, means a reprieve until the end of the month, no more, and does not in the least remove the feeling that we are standing on the drop. You are treating us as Boston treated Sacco & Vanzetti,[61] and you apparently expect compliments and gratitude.
>
> Now here is another ethical point, and one so deadly serious that I must copy your words and rub it in: "If we start talking of the cat, I would suggest you qualify for its reception by involving a sick woman in your affairs when you are not in a position to look after her properly." You really wrote that base and vile sentence. It is before my eyes or I should find it hard to believe that any man, however low, could ever admit. But I'm afraid that's you all over. "What? He's sick? He's poor? He's likely to die? His work is in danger? Hurrah. That lets me out."
>
> Your one thought is to abandon the ship. "Alright, I'll take the MSS and you can die in the gutter."... Never mind. Go on with your little dinners and dances with people who don't count and who are doomed anyway to perish in their own stupidity..."[62]

That was just the beginning. Although Frater Volo Intellegere passed from Probationer to Neophyte in November 1931, he failed, in AC's estimation, to accept the work of the order. Crowley expected him to sacrifice everything— his family, fortune, and reputation—for the Great Work: namely helping the chosen Prophet of Thelema do his job. His reluctance to do so, in Crowley's mind, was cowardly, the sort of materialistic clinging that doomed the Babe of the Abyss. In an effort to return Yorke to his senses, Crowley wrote a series of insulting letters questioning Yorke's motives, loyalty, and manhood.

Yorke, however, was not about to throw away his life the way that Leah, Norman, Ninette, and others before him had. Perhaps he was materialistic, but he had a lot to lose; at this point he was contemplating marriage and an extended trip to Shanghai. While he admired Crowley as a great writer and teacher, Yorke had no intention of ruining himself to put over the Great Work.

Yorke recalled the episode ending unresolved when "I told him to come to London and raise the money himself."[63] On May 29, Crowley instead sent Billie to London to negotiate loans with Yorke. She arrived in old clothes and stayed in a cheap Fitzrovia hotel, with Yorke feeding and supporting her. "Without your presence, it is hopeless for her to raise money," Yorke said, trying to convince him to come to London himself. "Do try and get it into your head that, however willing, I have not got the cash to support Bill."[64] Crowley maintained he could not make the trip without £200 to buy new clothes.

Frustrated by Crowley's refusal to tend to his own business, Bill spent much of her time in suicidal tears. Yorke was aghast, thinking he was seeing Crowley destroy Bill the way he did Marie. To complicate things, Crowley had written a £10 check without funds to cover it: an offense punishable by imprisonment. "I cannot see how sitting tight will help you," he wrote again. "You will merely mope, play chess, drink, and develop toothache, asthma and other nervous complaints."[65] However, Crowley soon found himself evicted from his flat on June 17 for nonpayment, and he set off five days later for London. It was the last time Crowley would reside outside England.

Crowley traveled north of London to the Colney Hatch asylum on July 5. Checking on Marie, he spoke with her doctor, Alexander Cannon (1896–1963), a figure as odd as Crowley.

> Square and stout with a very large head, entirely bald except for patches of greying hair above the ears, he reminds you a little of an outsize Pickwick. His round clean-shaven face is pink but a trifle blotchy; his mouth pursed.... Black coat, striped trousers, spats, and the scarlet ribbon of one of the foreign orders of which his is a member—he prefers to be known as "His Excellency Doctor Sir Alexander Cannon"—complete one of the most striking ensembles in Medicine.[66]

He earned both an MD and PhD from his schooling in Leeds, London, Vienna, and Hong Kong, and wrote several texts for his profession. He also traveled in the Orient, studying under yogis and learning secrets of mediumship, teleportation, and magic. His book *The Invisible Influence* (1933) would contain an account of him levitating himself, his porters, and his luggage across a chasm in Tibet.[67] Crowley noted he had "rather a bug in his brain over hypnosis," which he felt could be used to tap mankind's hidden powers.

Cannon would go on to publish his eccentric theories in *The Invisible Influence,* with the result that, in December 1933, he would be asked to resign from Colney Hatch. Although he would find another post at Bexley Heath Mental Hospital, he would devote much energy to teatime lectures and demonstrations of magic at the Mayfair Hotel.

For now, he said Mrs. Crowley's case was hopeless, and he requested AC "to leave Marie severely alone."[68] Despite differences of opinion between the man who claimed to have levitated himself across a fifty-foot river and the man who claimed to be the World Teacher as prophesied in the Book of Revelation, Crowley respected Cannon's request to leave Marie alone. Colney Hatch was her home for the next twenty years, where she died during the 1950s.

A series of disappointments marked the second half of the summer of 1932. Yorke's plans to travel to Shanghai left Crowley financially high and dry. When AC's landlord evicted him, seizing his possessions in lieu of unpaid rent, Yorke paid £50 for the manuscripts and added them to his growing collection. Crowley's plan to put on a performance of *Mortadello* fell through when his collaborator, Ribbons, backed out. The metaphorical backbreaker came on September 7 when Crowley read Nina Hamnett's autobiography, *Laughing Torso* (1932). It had come out while he was in Berlin, and this was his first chance to peruse it. Nina mentioned AC throughout, painting him in a kind light, and imagined her former guru would be delighted. However, Crowley reacted with acrimony when he read the following passage:

> Crowley had a temple in Cefalù in Sicily. He was supposed to practise Black Magic there, and one day a baby was said to have disappeared mysteriously. There was also a goat there. This all pointed to Black Magic, so people said, and the inhabitants of the village were frightened of him.[69]

"Abominable libels," he wrote in his diary,[70] and took the book to his solicitor. He demanded an injunction and planned to sue. While he was at it, he also sued Ribbons and Yorke for good measure.

On September 7, Crowley filed for £40,000 in damages against Yorke, the sum he *would* have made if Yorke hadn't mismanaged his finances. Stunned, Yorke figured this could only be a ploy to keep him from leaving for Shanghai. It clarified to Yorke that Crowley would stop at nothing to extract contributions from his students. Thus Yorke resigned from the A∴A∴. He gave Kerman the diaries of two probationers he had been supervising—Mrs. French (Soror Maximus) and Mr. Vilette (Volo Vincere)—along with the remaining stock of Crowley's books. He provided his own solicitors with a written account of his dealings with Crowley, then left for China in the middle of September. The case never came to court.

Despite the harsh words between them, Yorke and Crowley corresponded and visited after his return from Shanghai. Because Yorke was no longer a student, Crowley made no further financial demands of him. Because he was free to support Crowley when and how he saw fit, Yorke continued to help both morally and financially. He saw something remarkably brilliant in Crowley and, despite their differing ideologies, vowed to preserve Crowley's legacy. Nevertheless, their past was an invisible wall between them. It would be eleven years before they made peace. On June 6, 1944, Crowley would write to Yorke:

1. It is dangerous to judge a man unless you have been able to put yourself in his place. I want you to understand me first of all; to look through my eyes at what happened between us.

2. I have always taken myself and my mission with absolute seriousness. I believed in the chiefs and in my authority; also that those who opposed me were asking for trouble. I was, if you like, 80% crazy in the same sense that Mohammed was, and I have often regretted that my common sense and my sense of humour prevented me from going over the line. But I was never $\frac{1}{10}$th of 1% dishonest. Use your imagination. Suppose I had been a Spencer Lewis. What a garden path I could have led you down, and nothing would ever have persuaded you that it wasn't the path of the wise.

3. When we first met, I was having my Indian Summer. No. 1 with Kasimira and Hanni.... Plus I interpreted your motto as 'I will to become a Master of the Temple' in just that sense of the words that was true to me. I see now that you had not really bound yourself by this oath, but I thought you had done so. The crux of this initiation, as you know, is to surrender—or, rather, to annihilate—"all that I have and all that I am." When, therefore, it seemed to me that you were not taking your fences cleanly, I concluded that you were becoming divided against yourself—whence, of course, Black Brothers and all the rest of it—and jumped. What you read as abuse I had written as the Archbishop's most fatherly of rebukes....

4. About money ... Do please try once more to put it on my boots. Remember that I had spent over £100,000 of my own money, directly or indirectly, on the Great Work. This purchase of the egg without haggling was completely in my blood, so that I simply could not understand how any serious aspirant could even think of doing otherwise ... I am still utterly sure that this is a condition Number 1 of full attainment, but I realize that there are people who don't see, and can't be made to see, the necessity.[71]

On August 17, 1932, in the midst of frustrations and litigations, AC met with London's largest and most famous bookseller, William Alfred Foyle (1885–1963), and his daughter, Christina (1911–1999). Crowley's was a familiar face to the Foyles, and they arranged to buy half the four hundred remaining copies of *Magick in Theory and Practice* that Hanchant had remaindered, trimmed in size, and bound in a red hardcover sans the color plate. Foyle paid five shillings apiece for the books, and scheduled AC to speak at its September 15 literary luncheon.

Miss Foyle began organizing her literary luncheons in 1930 when she was just nineteen. She hosted not only prominent writers like Shaw and Wells but also painters, actors, prime ministers, and other celebrities. They proved wildly successful, not only providing great publicity but also keeping the business afloat during the lean 1930s.[72] Although people told her that she should be ashamed of herself for hosting a man of Crowley's reputation, she knew him as a frequent patron of her father's bookstore. Having spent many enjoyable hours visiting him in his Earls Court flat, she knew him to be harmless. Her attitude was more in line with Rose Macaulay, who said of the luncheon, "I don't mind what he does, as long as he doesn't turn himself into a goat."

Five hundred guests, including London's social and literary elite, attended Foyle's Twenty-third Literary Luncheon at Grosvenor House. Crowley's talk on "The Philosophy of Magick" was one of his most lucid.

> I am sorry if I am not as frivolous as might be required by the exigencies of the occasion, but Magick is a very serious subject, and I have a very serious message to bring to you. It is very little understood what Magick is. It is connected in the minds of some people with conjuring. In the minds of others it is connected with charlatanism. I want to tell you that Magick has been since the very earliest ages of humanity the tradition of the wise men. I want to tell you what the essential doctrine of the magician is with regard to man's place in the universe and that it is given in *The Book of the Law* that "every man and every woman is a star." What is a star? Philosophers have always agreed about one thing—that is that the Universe to be intelligible at all must be considered as one and homogeneous. Therefore you can understand the position of the mystic who says that each of us is a member of the body of God. You can understand what is written in the Bible, "Your bodies are the temples of the Holy Ghost." It is upon these postulates that the general theory of Magick is founded.[73]

After the luncheon, women with autograph books lined up for an introduction to the Wickedest Man in the World. He was elated with the outcome, writing in his diary, "Made a good speech!!!!!!"[74] With the book released to the public, rather than subscribers, for the first time, the *Occult Review* finally reviewed it. Neuburg also gave it a positive treatment in *The Referee;* in fact, he was so impressed that he briefly contacted Crowley again.

After he became the *Referee's* poetry editor in April 1933 Neuburg discovered Dylan Thomas and eventually passed on his tales of AC. Shortly thereafter, Thomas formed a second connection to Crowley when he took Betty May as a lover; her involvement in AC's lawsuit against Nina Hamnett would soon follow. Unsurprisingly, several apocryphal tales have circulated wherein Dylan Thomas meets the Beast. As one legendary account goes, some time later, in 1941 or 1942, Thomas would find himself in pubs, retelling the stories he had heard from Neuburg, such as the time Crowley turned him into a camel in the Sahara Desert. One evening, Thomas and his companion, Theodora, were waiting to meet someone when the patrons began discussing ghosts. "Dullan," one finally called out, "tell us: have ye ever seen a ghost?"

Thomas, who was normally very uneasy about paranormal events, replied jovially, "No, but Aleister Crowley appeared in my bathwater once."

The room fell silent. Only then did he realize that the Wickedest Man in the World himself was sitting at the end of the bar. Thomas dropped his head and absorbed himself in doodling, as he often did when moody or uncomfortable. Eventually, Crowley walked up and presented Thomas with a scrap of paper. Upon it was a duplicate of his doodle. In response, Dylan grabbed Theodora's hand and, even though they hadn't met their friend, whisked her out of the pub. Certainly more fiction than fact, it remains a popular "Crowley story."

On September 20, 1932, Isidore Kerman served a writ on Hamnett's publisher, Constable and Co., to immediately cease production of *Laughing Torso* until the courts heard Crowley's libel complaint. Two days later in Vacation Court, Chancery, AC argued that Hamnett's collection of anecdotes about him were indecent, vulgar, and ignorant. They were entirely untrue, and he couldn't understand how the book came to be written. Justice Lawrence ruled that the injunction against Constable and Co. should stand until the October 5 hearing.

Crowley claimed he, Kerman, Hamnett, and her publisher met thereafter and agreed to an out-of-court settlement of £1,000 and a published apology, but that "Nina got a crook lawyer to start a fuss."[75] Lawyer Martin O'Connor convinced Nina to defend herself. On October 5, the injunction *Crowley v. Constable and Co., Limited and Others* came to court. After four hours' testimony and fifteen minutes' consideration, the injunction was defeated pending the outcome of the libel suit. "Considering that he had by law to decide against us," Crowley commented, "he made it damned hot for O'Connor."[76] Even though the injunction was settled, the libel case itself had only begun.

AC moved into 20 Leicester Square on September 26 and began preparing a talk on psychic rejuvenation. Harry Price (1881–1948) of the National Laboratory of Psychical Research for the Scientific Investigation of Alleged Abnormal Phenomena had invited Crowley to give the lecture before the Society for Psychical Research on October 5. Admission was ten guineas a head, and the lecture, titled "Amrita," was Crowley's ploy to advertise OTO's secret "tonic of rejuvenation." The basis of his claims rested in the youthful bursts of energy Crowley experienced during his retirement at Lake Pasquaney in 1916, when he was experimenting heavily with sex magick. While sworn not to reveal the sexual components of this elixir, he accepted a few "patients" to receive the miracle drug at the rate of twenty-five guineas weekly.

As Frau Busch increasingly frequented London's pubs—including one named Cheerio, where a drugged prostitute reputedly bit her—her relationship with Crowley became less intimate. She faded from the picture at this time. Shortly after New Year's Day 1933, she entered Grosvenor Hospital for Women; shortly thereafter, Crowley noted in his diary that he was "Arranging Bill's marriage."[77] She finally ran off with a former middle-weight boxing champion, who supposedly beat her and forced her to walk the streets; because "it does not improve a woman's allure … if her face is a purplish pulp,"[78] she fared poorly, for which her husband would beat her and send her back out again. These claims about fallen friends were typical of Crowley, going back to the first time he claimed an impecunious Mathers was pimping his wife.

On Saturday, January 7, 1933—after seeing Billie off to Brighton—Crowley walked the Paddington streets. Passing the Modern Book Co. at 23 Praed Street, he spied a copy of *Moonchild* in the window, along with a card reading "Aleister Crowley's first novel, *The Diary of a Drug Fiend,* was withdrawn from circulation after an attack in the sensational press." He was furious at the implication that his first novel had been suppressed. Despite his efforts with the "Open Letter to Lord Beaverbrook" and *The Legend of Aleister Crowley,* the public still considered him a degenerate. "Libel!" he muttered to himself.

That Tuesday, Crowley visited his solicitor and began a suit charging the bookseller, Mr. Gray, with libel. The case came to court on May 10, when Justice Bennett ruled in favor of Crowley, who received £50 and costs:

> There was not the smallest ground for suggesting that any book Mr. Crowley had written was indecent or improper. Mr. Gray wanted the public to believe that the book to which the label was attached was an indecent book.[79]

In order to produce documentation for his elixir of rejuvenation, Crowley began recording his physical state when taking this elixir. On January 23, 1933, he began the experiment, noting the condition of his asthma, weight, stricture, sex drive, and other matters. After the first week, Crowley noted marginal improvement in his asthma and his stricture "quite miraculously less," although he still suffered from broken sleep and a distended abdomen. On February 8, he had sex for the first time in months, noting "These were difficult to perform and quite unsatisfactory in result."[80]

When he completed the experiment after five weeks, he decided that his active sex life and absence of stricture indicated success. "Thoughts all robust & juvenile e.g. I think naturally of ski if it snows; I want to walk rather than ride etc., etc. Irritated (7 a.m.) because I can't go & take exercise!"[81] Although Crowley judged his experiment a success, his diaries suggest otherwise: he was still unable to sleep, his asthma constantly left him coughing badly, and he spent February 19 sick in bed all day.

Another scheme at this time was to market Crowley's distinctive sex attraction ointment. Called "IT," the perfume gave AC an unusual—but not unpleasant—scent. As with Amrita, the active ingredient of IT was Crowley's sexual fluids. On June 9, Crowley recorded in his diary, "IT worked wonders—all women after me!" Like the previous scheme, IT never took off.

That June, Crowley sold a series of articles to the *Sunday Dispatch* for £40. In them, he defended himself against accusations made about him in the press, and sought to educate readers on matters of the occult:

> I have been accused of being a 'black magician.' No more foolish state-ment was ever made about me. I despise the thing to such an extent that I can hardly believe in the existence of people so debased and idiotic as to practice it....
>
> The "Black Mass" is a totally different matter. I could not celebrate it if I wanted to, for I am not a consecrated priest of the Christian Church.[82]

These articles were evidently ghost-written by *Dispatch* feature writer Ian Coster (b. 1903), who translated AC's florid words into journalistic prose. Hop-ing to attract readers with a series of articles "by" the wickedest man in the world, Coster was disappointed to find Crowley less wicked than expected, complaining, "He makes black magic as tame as a kids' party" and "The only black things I discovered about him were his pipe and tobacco."[83]

The *Sunday Dispatch* pieces were among several articles that ran in London papers in 1933, including the *Referee* and *Empire News,* to rehabilitate his repu-tation.[84] Although Crowley could not undo the damage done by the *Sunday Express* and *John Bull,* he hoped to regain some credibility.

Crowley around the time of his 1933 lawsuit with Ethel Mannin.

At this time, Crowley read novelist and travel writer Ethel Mannin's (1900–1984) memoirs, *Confessions and Impressions* (1930), where she described Crowley as "that high priest of black magic who likes nothing better than to be regarded as His Satanic Majesty the Prince of Darkness, and who would take it as a compliment to be called an arch-devil."[85] This and similar passages sent Crowley into Kerman's office, filing an injunction against the publisher and printer. When the case appeared before Justice Farwell on July 25, 1933, Mannin's solicitor, John W. Morris, argued that the book came out in 1930, and Crowley had voiced no objection to its contents. Constantine Gallop argued on Crowley's behalf that he knew nothing at all about the book when it appeared, and that the passages about him were entirely untrue. Alas, Justice Farwell declined to grant the injunction.

Meanwhile, AC's students thrived in the United States. As early as May 1929, Jane Wolfe had begun preparing for an OTO lodge in Hollywood. Her circle included her voice teacher Regina Kahl, Max and Leota Schneider, and Wilfred Talbot Smith (1885–1957), with whom Wolfe had had a brief affair. Smith was a pale and short man who had signed Jones's 1914 petition for a Vancouver OTO charter from Reuss. In 1921 Crowley appointed him Grand Treasurer General of British Columbia, honorary VII°, and Sovereign Grand Inspector General. When in 1932 Crowley appointed Smith as his successor, he and Kahl (now his lover) took a large house at 1746 Winona Boulevard in Los Angeles as their headquarters. Loving simple things in life—nature, literature, conversation, and handiwork—Smith eagerly converted the attic into a temple.[86]

Crowley encouraged their public performances of the Gnostic Mass every Sunday, with the ambitious hope that the California group could find a priestess with lots of sex appeal and film the mass with Crowley as priest. The masses in Smith's attic temple attracted a dozen or so observers, largely from a curious group of science fiction writers. When the group began to recycle its profits into improving the temple, the perpetually penniless Crowley objected to having his contributions cut. Smith, meanwhile, insisted they needed a properly equipped temple to attract people and money with a spectacular Gnostic Mass. Ultimately, their correspondence became petty, Crowley ridiculing Smith's grammar and accusing him of mismanaging the Great Work. Smith, who worked for a pittance as a bookkeeper for the California Gas Company since 1922, objected to the accusations:

> Christ, you are like a child.... Listen, I may write rotten letters as far as spelling and literary style, but I don't misrepresent or exaggerate. I never said or intimated that 80 or 100 people attended the Mass. I merely said we had two social affairs which that number attended.
>
> My attic temple is 36 by 16 feet, and at the most, if the floor would stand it, could not contain more than 30 people. I don't sit on my arse all day, but leave the house at 8 in the morning and return at 5:30 pm if I

don't stay at the office until 10:00 pm as I did twice last week. In my spare time, when not too worn out, I endeavor to make social contacts in the hope that they may be of use to Us....

Three times I have built a temple on this continent. There is nothing to it, I know, for any dumb carpenter could have done the same if we had had the money to pay him. The point is we did not have it....

You have not made much money out of your talent with a pen and paper. I have not made money out of my talent with a hammer and nails. Perhaps together we may yet become bloated capitalists for the world's good.[87]

Regina Agnes Kahl (1891–1945) came to Smith's defense. Kahl was a mezzo-soprano opera singer and music teacher who gave concerts in Los Angeles in the early 1930s. In subsequent years, she would be civically active as a member of the Los Feliz Women's Club and the Hollywood branch of the National League of American Pen Women (serving as its corresponding secretary before becoming its president), and even direct the Los Angeless Evening College Players' production of the Gertrude Tonkonog Broadway comedy *Three Cornered Moon*.[88] As Smith's lover, she was defensive; and as someone described as as "60% male,"[89] she responded aggressively to Crowley:

Dear 666,

I don't know how you judge devotion to a cause, but by your letter to [Jacobi], I take it it's by a dollar and cent basis. If there's one thing I hate about this age of commercialism and ballyhoo, it is that gilt complex and I don't give a damn who manifests it, it's still the shits! If there is no other thing bred in the brethren of the house of Thelema in Los Angeles there is loyalty to our head here and devotion to the Master Therion—but when he gets the big idea that we are all sitting on our arses doing nothing he is mistaken and in my very best American slang "And how!"

You can jolly well bet we are not doing a Christly lot of ballyhooing. We are leaving that to Amy [sic] McPherson[90] and her kind. Being born in this country of hot air and big noise, bluff and bullshit, I prefer to have no part in that sort of propaganda.

Personally for Leota, Jake and Wilfred especially, and the others as well as they can, all are doing what can be done to put what we all consider the greatest work of the age by the greatest genius to a mass of people who are suffering for the need of a new ethics, true morality, sane values and spiritual outlook. This is not to be done overnight by a publicity campaign a la Bob Scheuller method. The whole country is fed up to the gills with this crap now. We can only hope to succeed by loyalty and tenacity....

Now kick me out of the Order if you like, but you will still find me hanging on the tail of the A∴A∴ kite.[91]

Crowley responded evasively to this onslaught, dismissing most of what was flung at him. To Smith he wrote, "The letter from Regina is misspelt and overloaded with filthy words. I cannot take any notice of such things."[92]

IT wafted from Crowley on July 3 when he met Evelyn Pearl Brooksmith, née Driver (1899–1967). A thirty-four-year-old widow, Pearl, as she was known, lived at 40 Cumberland Terrace with her son, John. She shared AC's appreciation for strong drink. She didn't know him as Aleister Crowley until their second meeting on August 9. "She was staggered when I told her my name," he wrote in his diary. Within a week they began practicing sex magick; he moved in with her mere days later, and they soon became engaged. On September 1, Crowley consecrated her as his Scarlet Woman. "I feel the flame of fornication creeping up my body," she told him, and he took it as a perfect magical phrase; however, the events to follow overshadowed this.

On the autumnal equinox, after a ritual to obtain the word of the equinox, Pearl had a vision of an Adept in the Himalayas. Several days later, Crowley recorded in his diary:

> Wednesday, September 27. Opus 24. Invoking the Essence of Godhead within the Scarlet Woman. She became One with the Infinite White Light. Then, minor visions.
>
> Opus 25 natural. S.W.'s Vision of Παν [Pan].
>
> Thursday, September 28. Vision of Rosy Light in room. (Only other case I had was in Nefta).

Brooksmith had a gift for visions, and she and the Beast enjoyed a terrific psychic rapport. On one occasion, Crowley had a clairvoyant vision of her cottage and various people she knew; two days later, Pearl heard a voice tell her she was Kali. "The Goddess of lust and murder," Crowley replied. "Yes, yes!"[93] Despite her talents, AC commented little on her visions and even tired of them. After thirty years of clairvoyant alcoholics, he had become jaded.

On October 25, as Pearl's menstruation completed its cycle, Crowley insisted they curtail their constant sex "unless she was prepared to play up to her body." Although he desired no unwanted pregnancies, Pearl was unconcerned. "All great Saviours have been bastards," she replied, and their intimacy continued unabated. In fact, they actively sought to have a child. On November 2, during one sex magical act, Pearl had a vision of icy peaks jutting out of a sandy plain where a dark-haired, white-skinned woman offered Pearl a baby boy on a white dish. A good omen, they concluded. On November 18, however, Crowley noted with disappointment that Pearl began her period on schedule. "Alas! Yet it is better for all three to wait a little while."

When Pearl's visions became more intense that December, Crowley distanced himself:

> Tuesday, December 5. Opus 68 ... S.W. goes on prolonged wild visions, very uncontrolled, & is near the borderline. I don't like it too well.

He was too preoccupied to pay attention to hallucinations. His libel case over Laughing Torso was coming up, and frankly he was worried. His sex magick rituals with Pearl were frequently for victory in his forthcoming legal battle, and he spent the autumn of 1933 repeatedly consulting the I Ching about the outcome of the trial. Seeking three character witnesses, he contacted his most respectable acquaintances: J. W. N. Sullivan, J. F. C. Fuller and J. D. Beresford. All three declined. Beresford, in fact, urged Crowley to drop the case. "I haven't the least doubt that some very extraordinary and damaging charges will be made against you if you come into court."[94]

Kerman agreed with Beresford. When he saw a copy of *White Stains,* he said the case was as good as lost if the defense had it, as such a book had no justification. Crowley, knowing most copies of the book had been destroyed, wasn't worried. Thus Kerman, with Germer as Crowley's only character witness, worked diligently to prepare the libel case against Constable and Co.

Then, on December 18, Crowley heard from a man named Eddie Cruze, who offered to produce damning evidence for the trial.

CHAPTER NINETEEN

The Black Magic Libel Case

On April 10, 1934—the thirtieth anniversary of writing chapter three of *The Book of the Law*—Justice Swift and a special jury heard the case of *Crowley v. Constable and Co., Limited and Others,* informally known as the "Black Magic Libel Case."[1] J. P. Eddy and Constantine Gallop represented Aleister Crowley; Malcolm Hilbery represented the publishers, Constable and Co.; and Martin O'Connor, one of the bar's most famous personalities, represented author Nina Hamnett. For what promised to be the most sensational trial in recent memory, droves of reporters and curiosity seekers turned out, ranging from a nineteen-year-old girl named Deirdre MacAlpine to editor and author Anthony Powell, who worried that if Crowley won he would next sue Duckworth over *Tiger Woman.*

This trial did not disappoint, with newspapers devoting pages to its coverage over the ensuing four days. While the full transcript cannot be reproduced here, some gems of testimony passed Crowley's lips in response to questions from both the prosecution and the defense; selected highlights are reproduced.

John Percy Eddy (1881–1975) was a former *Daily Chronicle* reporter who was called to the bar in 1911. Serving as Judge of the High Court of Judicature in Madras in 1929, he returned to the bar in England the following year. He published *The Law of Distress* the same year as this trial. Although not a brilliant orator, he was known for his calm manner, his deliberate walk, and his plodding and persistent advocacy.[2] His opening statement summarized Crowley's complaint: "The *Laughing Torso* purports to be an account of the author's own life, with intimate studies of her friends and acquaintances. Mr. Crowley complains that in the book he is charged with having practiced that loathsome thing known as Black Magic. There is White Magic, which is on the side of the angels, and rests on faith in the order and uniformity of Nature. Black Magic is a degrading thing, associated with the degradation of religion, the invocation of devils, evil in its blackest forms, and even the sacrifices of children." Crowley, Eddy explained, had fought black magic for years, stressing the importance of the Will. He was so serious, in fact, that he started a community in an old farmhouse at Cefalù, Sicily, in 1920 to study this principle. Hamnett's depiction of the Abbey, however, was damaging. Eddy insisted, "No child disappeared mysteriously, and the only goat on the premises was kept for its milk."

"Are you familiar with the words 'Do what thou wilt shall be the whole of the Law'?" Eddy asked at one point.

A smile crossed Crowley's face in spite of himself. "I am."

"Did they have any reference to this house?"

"They are the general principles on which I maintain all mankind should base its conduct."

"What do they mean?"

"The study of those words has occupied the last thirty years of my life," Crowley explained proudly. "There is no end to what they mean, but the simplest application to practical conduct is this: That no man has a right to waste his time on doing things which are mere wishes or desires, but that he should devote himself wholly to his true work in this world."

"Have those words anything to do with black magic?"

"Only indirectly. They would forbid it, because black magic is suicidal." Asked about the difference between black and white magic, Crowley continued, "In boxing you can fight according to the Queensberry rules or you can do the other thing."

Malcolm Hilbery, for the defense, interjected, "Does that mean that his definition of Black Magic is the same as all-in wrestling?" Laughter filled the courtroom.

"I approve some forms of magic and disapprove others," AC elaborated.

Eddy continued with his questions. "What is the form you disbelieve?"

"That which is commonly known as black magic, which is not only foul and abominable, but, for the most part, criminal. To begin with, the basis of all black magic is that utter stupidity of selfishness which cares nothing for the rights of others. People so constituted are naturally quite unscrupulous. In many cases, black magic is an attempt to commit crime without incurring the penalties of the law. The almost main instrument of black magic is murder, either for inheritance or for some other purpose, or in some way to gain personally out of it."

Malcolm Hilbery, hands in his pockets, questioned Crowley about his identification with *To Mega Therion,* the beast in the Book of Revelation. "Did you take to yourself the designation of 'The Beast 666'?"

"Yes."

"Do you call yourself the 'Master Therion'?"

"Yes."

He nodded. "What does 'Therion' mean?"

"Great wild beast."

"Do these titles convey a fair impression of your practice and outlook on life?"

"It depends on what they mean."

"The Great Wild Beat and Beast 666 are out of the Apocalypse?"

"It only means sunlight; 666 is the number of the sun," he dismissed, then cracked a smile. "You can call me 'Little Sunshine.'"

At one point, Hilbery produced a book, to Crowley's great surprise. He only knew of one or two other surviving copies. "Is *White Stains* a book of indescribable filth?"

Crowley remembered his lawyer's warning that, if the defense had that book, he would lose the case. In fact, Crowley identified himself as its author in his *Confessions,* thus tipping off the defense.[3] Early on in preparing their case, Constable & Co.'s lawyers had tracked down a copy of *White Stains,* apparently borrowed from Scottish novelist Compton Mackenzie (1883–1972).[4] When they finally read the book, they declared, "I regard *White Stains* as an important find, especially as it is admitted by Crowley to have been written by him."[5]

Crowley quickly tried to explain. "The book is a serious study of the progress of a man to the abyss of madness, disease and murder. There are moments when he does go down into all those abominations, and it is a warning to people against going over."

"Have you made sonnets about unspeakable things?"

"Yes. I have described in sonnet form certain pathological aberrations."

"*White Stains* is described as 'Being the Literary Remains of George Archibald Bishop, a Neuropath of the Second Empire.'"

"Yes," he agreed. "I think only one hundred copies were printed and handed to some expert on the subject in Vienna."

"Was that done because you feared there might be a prosecution if they were published in this country?"

"It was not," he denied flatly. "It was a refutation of the doctrine that sexual perverts had no sense of moral responsibility and should not be punished. I maintained that they had, and showed the way they got from bad to worse." Crowley had argued the same point twenty years earlier when explaining to John Quinn that *White Stains* was written as a response to Krafft-Ebing.

"You *know* it is an obscene book."

"I don't know it. Until it got into your hands, it never got into any improper hands at all."

On April 11, the second day of the trial, Crowley's cross-examination continued. Hilbery quoted Crowley's articles in the *Sunday Dispatch*. "'I have been shot at with broad arrows. They have called me the worst man in the world. They have accused me of doing everything from murdering women and throwing their bodies into the Seine to drug peddling.' Is that true?"

"I hear a new canard about me every week. Any man of any distinction has rumors about him."

"Does any man of any distinction necessarily have it said about him that he is the worst man in the world?"

"Not necessarily: he has to be *very* distinguished for that." Observers chuckled, and Crowley smiled.

Hilbery asked pointedly, "Do you believe in the practice of bloody sacrifice?"

"I believe in its efficacy."

"If you believe in its efficacy, you would believe in its being practiced?"

Crowley scowled. "I do not approve of it at all."

"Do not approve it?" Referring to page 96 of Crowley's *Magick in Theory and Practice*, he read:

> Those magicians who object to the use of blood have endeavoured to replace it with incense. For such a purpose the incense of Abramelin may be burnt in large quantities. Dittany of Crete is also a valuable medium.... But the bloody sacrifice, though more dangerous, is most efficacious; and for nearly all purposes human sacrifice is the best.

From page 95 of the same book, Hilbery read:

> For the highest spiritual working one must accordingly choose that victim which contains the greatest and purest force. A male child of perfect innocence and high intelligence is the most satisfactory and suitable victim.

A footnote that accompanied this text read, "It appears from the Magical Records of Frater Perdurabo that he made this particular sacrifice on an average about 150 times every year between 1912 and 1928."

Crowley argued that the passages were statements about ancient practices, and not meant seriously. What he did not explain was that his words were entirely allegorical. "Sacrifice" meant to "make sacred," and, to him, symbolized the most sacred act of all: sex. He referred not to the sacrifice of a life, but to making the sacred "elixir," or combined sexual fluids of man and woman.

Hilbery went on. "In March, 1923, did a Sunday newspaper publish about you an article headed, 'Black Record of Aleister Crowley. Preying on the Debased. Profligacy and Vice in Sicily.'"

Crowley agreed.

"Have you taken any action about that?"

"I have not." When that article appeared, Crowley explained, he did not have enough money to begin proceedings; he considered it a compliment to be "blackguarded in such an obviously filthy way."

Swift interposed at this point. "When you read, 'it is hard to say with certainty whether Crowley is man or beast,' did you take any action?"

"It was asked of Shelley whether he was a man or someone sent from Hell," he answered vaguely.

"I am not trying Shelley. Did you take any steps to clear your character?"

"I was 1,500 miles away," Crowley replied. "I was ill. I was penniless."

Swift's patience wore thin. "I didn't ask about the state of your health. Did you take any steps to clear your character?"

"Yes." Crowley said his solicitor advised that the action would last fourteen days and cost £10,000; thus, he could do nothing.

"Now you see how absurd that advice was, because this case won't take anything like fourteen days. It has now taken two whole days, and it will probably take the whole of tomorrow. It may go into Friday, though I am not sure about that. It won't last more than four days. I imagine you have not found £10,000, have you?"

"You said yesterday that as a result of early experiments you invoked certain forces with the result that some people were attacked by unseen assailants," Martin O'Connor asked Crowley on the morning of Thursday, April 12, when the third day of the black magic libel case opened. "That is right, is it not?"

"Yes."

"Will you try your magic now on my learned friend?" He pointed to Hilbery.

Tempting though the prospect must have seemed, Crowley replied promptly, "I would not attack anybody."

"Is that because you are too considerate or because you are an impostor?" He chuckled at his debunking of the magician.

"I have never done willful harm to any human being."

"Try your magic now," he taunted. "I am sure my learned friend will consent to you doing so."

"I absolutely refuse."

Justice Swift intervened, stating, "We cannot turn this court into a temple, Mr. O'Connor."

O'Connor nodded. "There is one other question. You said, Mr. Crowley, 'On a later occasion I succeeded in rendering myself invisible.' Would you like to try *that* on? You appreciate that if you do not I shall denounce you as an impostor."

"You can denounce me as anything you like," Crowley replied. "It will not alter the truth."

"Have you at any time practiced black magic?" J. P. Eddy asked of his client for clarification.

"No. I have always written in condemnation of black magic."

"What is the object of the magic in which you believe?"

"My particular branch is the raising of humanity to higher spiritual development."

When Crowley prepared to leave the stand, Justice Swift asked one last question. "I would like to ask if Mr. Crowley could give the court the shortest and, at the same time, most comprehensive definition of magic which he knows."

He happily obliged, quoting his own work on the subject. "Magick is the science and art of causing change to occur in conformation with the Will. It is white magic if the Will is righteous and black magic if the Will is perverse."

"Does it involve the invocation of spirits?" Swift asked.

"It *may* do so. It does involve the invocation of the Holy Guardian Angel, who is appointed by Almighty God to watch over each of us."

"Then it does involve invocation of the spirits?"

"Of one spirit. God is a spirit, and they that worship Him must worship Him in spirit and in truth."

"Is magic, in your view, the art of controlling spirits to affect the course of events?"

"That is part of magic, one small branch."

"If the object of the control is good then it is white magic?"

"Yes."

"And if the object of the control is bad, it is black magic?"

"Yes."

"When the object of the control is bad, what spirits do you invoke?"

This was becoming technical, and Crowley tried to be clear. "You cannot invoke evil spirits; you must *evoke* them or call them out."

"When the object is bad, you evoke evil spirits?"

"You put yourself in their power. In that case, it is possible to control, or bind, evil spirits for a good purpose, as we might if we use the dangerous elements of fire and electricity for heating and lighting, and so on."

"Thank you."

After two days of testimony, Crowley stepped down from the witness stand.

Karl Germer appeared on the stand as a character witness for Crowley. When Martin O'Connor cross-examined Germer, he asked incredulously, "Have you ever *seen* Mr. Crowley invoke spirits?"

"Yes."

"What spirits?"

He answered proudly, "The spirit of magnanimity."

"How do you *know* it was the spirit of magnanimity?"

"I suppose you have got to be sensitive in order to perceive."

Justice Swift asked Germer, "Can you point to any difference between the spirit of magnanimity and the spirit of hospitality?"

Karl mused and answered, "I think that is very easy."

O'Connor pressed him, "You are *sure* it was the spirit of magnanimity which came, and not the spirit of hospitality?"

The highlight of this ridiculous bit of testimony, according to an observer, was "the unforgettable scene of an Irish barrister requesting a German witness to read an alleged obscene poem that Crowley had written in French."[6]

Images from the trial (left to right): Aleister Crowley giving the sign of silence; Betty May; and Karl Germer.

It was Friday the 13th. As Justice Swift predicted, the trial entered its fourth day. Betty May had been called by the defense, and J. P. Eddy attempted unsuccessfully to discredit her the same way the defense had discredited Crowley. An unexpected incident, especially damaging to Crowley, came out of this questioning. "In regard to your position in this case," Eddy proposed, "I put it to you plainly that you are here as a 'bought' witness."

"I am here to help the jury," Betty May replied.

"I am suggesting, without making any imputation against the solicitors, that you were obviously unwilling to come unless you were paid to come."

"No." She said she received £20 at most from the defendants' solicitors.

"What was it for?"

"It was for my expenses."

"What expenses?"

"I lived in the country and they wanted me in London, and they had to pay my expenses."

"In reply," Eddy addressed the court, "she received a letter stating, 'I am afraid I cannot send you as much as another £5. I am grateful for your help, but

I thought previous remittances covered a good deal.'" The reading of that letter staggered everyone—the witness and the defense included. Betty May admitted she received £5 from Messrs. Waterhouse, the solicitors. Without missing a beat, he handed another letter to the witness and asked, "Are you known as 'Bumble Toff'?"

"Lots of people call me by that name."

"Do you know anyone by the name of 'Poddle Diff'?"

"Yes, he is an old friend of mine."

"Is that letter signed by an old friend of yours?"

"I don't know, I have not seen him for so long."

"Do you swear you have not received that letter addressed to 'dear Bumble Toff'?"

Before she could answer, Hilbery voiced an objection, which Swift sustained. "The witness says she does not remember receiving the letter," the Justice ruled. "There the matter must stop." Betty returned the letter to Eddy.

"Did you not discuss with 'Poddle Diff' the question of your giving evidence in this case?" Eddy asked.

"No," she answered. "He had enough troubles of his own without troubling about mine."

With that, Eddy rested his unusual cross-examination.

Hilbery reexamined Betty, who stated she hadn't seen the letters produced by Eddy for a long time: they'd been removed from a small box of her personal papers. "Did you ever authorize anyone to extract those documents from your box of private papers and give them to Mr. Crowley?" Hilbery asked.

"Certainly not."

Justice Swift asked, "Are these the ones produced by Mr. Crowley?"

"Yes," she answered.

"Do you know how Mr. Crowley got possession of your letters?" Swift probed.

"I cannot imagine how he got them."

"Were there other letters in the case?" Hilbery asked her.

"Yes. Everything was taken from the case but the case was left. The contents were all stolen."

Martin O'Connor opened the case for Nina Hamnett's defense with an attack not only of Crowley's credibility but his very beliefs. "It is appalling that, in this enlightened age a court should be investigating magic which is arch-humbug practiced by arch-rogues to rob weak-minded people. I hope this action will end for all time the activities of this hypocritical rascal. As to his reputation, there is no one in fact or in fiction against whom so much inquity has been alleged. I suggest the jury stop this case, say they have heard enough of Mr. Crowley, and return a verdict for the defendants."

Noticing two jurors talking, Swift interrupted O'Connor's statement. The two jurors looked up at Swift inquisitively. "Members of the jury," he explained to them, "I thought that you were speaking to each other." After a few sheepish looks, he added, "There is no reason why you should not whisper to him."

The foreman asked, "May I be given an opportunity to do so?"

"I have stopped learned counsel so that you might speak to each other, if you want to do so."

The jurors conferred; the foreman addressed the bench. "It is unanimous amongst the jury to know whether this is a correct time for us to intervene."

"You cannot stop the case as against the defendants. You may stop it against the plaintiff when Mr. Eddy has said everything he wants to say."

Feeling success imminent, O'Connor added nothing more and called no evidence, passing the trial back to Eddy to close. He did his best to argue Crowley's case. Sticking to strictly legal ground, he pointed out that no evidence supported the allegation that a baby had disappeared from the Abbey, or that local peasants were afraid of Crowley. Moreover, Mrs. Sedgwick's testimony on the events at Cefalù was wholly unreliable. "No reasonable jury can do other than find a verdict in favor of Mr. Crowley. The defendants' views notwithstanding, the law of libel is available to everybody, whether he is of good or bad character."

When Eddy finished, Swift addressed the jury. "Thirty minutes ago you intimated to me that you had made up your minds about this case and that you did not want to hear any more about it. I pointed out to you that before you could stop it, Mr. Eddy was entitled to address you. I also pointed out that before I could take your verdict I must be satisfied that you understand the issues you are trying.

"I have nothing to say about the facts except this: I have been over forty years engaged in the administration of the law in one capacity or another. I thought I knew of every conceivable form of wickedness. I thought that everything which was vicious and bad had been produced at one time or another before me. I have learnt in this case that we can always learn something if we live long enough. I have never heard such dreadful, horrible, blasphemous, and abominable stuff as that which has been produced by the man who describes himself to you as the greatest living poet.

"If you think that the plaintiff fails on the ground that he was never libeled, or that his reputation was never damaged, or if you think the defendants have justified what was written, then your verdict should be for the defendants. Are you still of the same mind or do you want the case to go on? If there is any doubt about the matter, the case must go on."

They returned a unanimous verdict for the defendants with costs. Crowley had lost.

In retrospect, *Crowley v Constable and Co.* was a truly bizarre case. It is difficult today to imagine the events of this trial: the notorious self-styled Great Beast— who explained to the court that this name simply meant "Little Sunshine"— testifying on the differences between white and black magic; the prosecution challenging Crowley either to magically attack Malcolm Hilbery or to render himself invisible in the courtroom; poor Karl Germer being chided about the differences between the spirit of magnanimity and the spirit of hospitality; and a stupefied Betty May being asked on the stand to admit to irrelevant pet names like "Poodle Diff" and "Bumble Toff" from stolen letters. In the end, the trial was much like *Jones v. The Looking Glass* over two decades earlier: Crowley was a person of such notoriously bad character that he had no basis for claiming damage from what, to the jury, appeared to be factual statements. In this case, Crowley's past failures to take legal action to protect his reputation worked against him. Ultimately, Hamnett's book did not accuse Crowley of black magic but reported what villagers near the Abbey purportedly believed.

"Case violated by collapse of Swift & Nina. General joy—the consternation of Constable & Co. & co.," Crowley mysteriously recorded in his diary for Friday the 13th of April—a decidedly unlucky day. He filed out of the courtroom past the reporters who would plaster his name and face all over their papers. His only remark, to the puzzlement of the paparazzi, was a quote from Rudyard Kipling's "If":

> If you can meet Triumph and Disaster
> And treat those two impostors just the same.

After the trial, Robin Thynne introduced Crowley to his nineteen-year-old mistress, Deirdre Patricia Maureen Doherty (b. 1915).[7] Granddaughter and legal ward of Newlyn painter of children Thomas Cooper Gotch (1854-1931; Royal Society of British Artists, Royal Institute of Painters in Watercolour), she had been sent to London to stay with a relative, Lord Justice Slesser. For her amusement, Slesser suggested she watch a trial in progress: *Crowley v. Constable and Co.* While they were, for the time being, casual acquaintances, "the girl Pat," as Crowley would come to know her, would give AC the thing which neither Bill nor Pearl nor any other Scarlet Woman could: an heir.

CHAPTER TWENTY

The War of the Roses (and the Battle of the Book)

Even as his solicitors lodged a notice of appeal for the so-called "Black Magic Libel" case, Crowley felt repercussions from the trial. Arraigned on charges of feloniously receiving stolen letters—four originals and one copy—he pleaded not guilty and was released from the Marylebone police station on £10 bail until his trial. Although Kerman announced, "Mr. Crowley has a complete answer to this charge," Captain Eddie Cruze, from whom Crowley had purchased the letters to use against the Tiger Woman in court, was nowhere to be found despite a warrant for his arrest.

Judge Whiteley tried the case at the Old Bailey on July 24 and 25. Although Betty (May) Sedgwick testified that Cruze had stolen the letters from her Seymour Street residence, Constantine Gallop (c. 1893–1967)[1] argued on Crowley's behalf that she had given Cruze the letters as a guarantee of money she had promised him; and, since they were therefore his letters, he was free to pass them along to Crowley.

"Is this the first time there has been any charge against you in any place in the world?" Gallop asked Crowley.

"Yes," he agreed.

"Apart from the criticism justly or unjustly leveled against you for your book, has anything ever been leveled against your character in any court?"

"Not in any court."

"Were you plaintiff in the action *Constable and Another?*"

"I was and I am," Crowley answered, alluding to his appeal.

"In the course of that action, did you hear that Mrs. Sedgwick would probably be called as a witness against you?"

"Yes." He testified that in December 1933 he learned that Cruze knew all about her plans. "Betty May was preparing to commit perjury. That I already knew from several sources.... I wanted to know whether these letters did prove the plans of Mrs. Sedgwick." He paid £5 for the letters.

"Did you at any time suspect that these letters had been stolen?"

"No."

The jury deliberated half an hour before reaching a verdict. Believing Betty May's letters to be valueless, and hence useless as a security, they disbelieved Crowley's story and found him guilty. Because of his clean record, Judge Whiteley let him off lightly. "These letters ought not to have been used, ought never have been in your possession, or handed to your solicitor at all. However, they *were* used, and no harm had in fact been done; therefore I am not going to send you to prison." Whitely put AC on probation for two years and ordered him to pay fifty guineas toward costs for the prosecution.[2]

"Thank you, my Lord," Crowley replied. In the back of his mind, however, he was screaming: "Idiots! Even a scapegoat is liable to butt." He planned an appeal, but advised against it by both his lawyer and the I Ching, he dropped it.

On November 8, however, Crowley's appeal of the "Black Magic Trial" made it to court. After three days of testimony, Lord Justices Greer, Slesser, and Roche decided that, although the case was well argued, it was unfair to take the objectionable passages out of context, where they were clearly not libelous. They sustained Swift's judgment and dismissed the case.[3]

The day after losing his appeal, Crowley, sick with pneumonia, was evicted from his room in Grosvenor Square. All told, 1934 had been a bad year.

Another unfortunate upshot of Crowley's popularity in the daily law reports was that his creditors now knew where to find him. On February 14, 1935, Crowley faced the Official Receiver as case number 38 in bankruptcy court, with liabilities from thirty-eight unsecured loans and ten partly secured loans totaling £4,695. AC described himself as an author and psychiatrist. When asked why, during the years in which he was affluent, he never paid income tax, Crowley replied that he never received any forms, nor was he ever asked to pay taxes. Questioned about his lifestyle, he remarked that he always bought the most expensive clothing and paid £25 per pound for tobacco. Although he valued his stock of books at £20,000 and his life story at £2,000, he claimed to be unable to sell them because of a boycott of his works in England and the damage done to his reputation by recent lawsuits. For these reasons, he had earned only £78 in book sales and £135 from articles since January 1932; loans and his family trust covered his remaining expenses. He also blamed his insolvency on mismanagement by Yorke. "The assets comprised a large claim in a pending action against a person now said to be in Shanghai," Crowley reported, claiming that once the suit was settled he would again be solvent.

At that, Yorke's representatives, who attended the trial in case Yorke was dragged into this, informed the Receiver that the claim to which Crowley referred was two years old and that he had made no attempts in that time to pursue it. The receiver invited Crowley's creditors to help him bring his case to court and thereby reclaim their money. None took up the gauntlet.

It was settled: Crowley was bankrupt. Finding he had no household furniture, creditors seized his manuscripts and diaries. (Fortunately, his trust fund
payments were not subject to this ruling.) Not until 1939 did he pay dividends
on his debts, amounting to two pence on the pound.[4]

The last time Hayter Preston saw Aleister Crowley—in May 1914—they were
arguing over Victor Neuburg. He never expected to hear from AC again, so his
invitation to dine at the Old Ship in Brighton was too curious to pass up.
Crowley's motives, however, became clear once he pitched an article to Preston
for the *Referee*. Nevertheless, he accepted and, after considerable editing, "My
Wanderings in Search of the Absolute" appeared in the March 10, 1935, edition. It was a digest of Crowley's early life, focusing on travel and mysticism.[5]

The next working day, AC strolled into the *Referee* offices wearing his black
Homburg hat. "These," he said, depositing a stack of manuscripts on the editor's desk, "are the future installments of my article." Crowley became livid
when told that the *Referee* wanted no other articles. He claimed Preston had
contracted a series of articles, and if that agreement was broken, he would sue
for breach of contract.

And sue he did. As with his other lawsuits at this time, Crowley lost.

Martha Küntzel had been overjoyed when Adolf Hitler became Führer on
August 19, 1933. She had considered Hitler her Magical Son, and intended to
convert him to Thelema because *The Book of the Law* claimed that the first
nation to accept it would rule the world. Although she attempted to get a copy
of *The Book of the Law* to Hitler in the 1920s—and Crowley heavily annotated
a copy of *Hitler Speaks*,[6] claiming references to Thelema were interspersed
throughout its pages—this was certainly not the case. Hitler's ideology was
formed long before Küntzel entered the picture. The Nazis began gunning for
magicians in 1933, first banning fortune-telling, next confiscating occult books
and outlawing secret societies, and finally imprisoning high-ranking occultists,
including those from Freemasonry to the Fraternitas Saturni. Eventually, Küntzel's own papers—including the stock of Crowley paintings stored with her
after the Berlin exhibit—were seized and destroyed. Although AC initially supported the idea of converting a political leader to Thelema, his support of Hitler quickly dissipated when the chancellor showed his true colors.

When the British Home Office refused to extend Karl Germer's temporary
visa, it forced him to return to Germany on February 2, 1935. He was arrested
at a relative's house in Leipzig on February 13, charged with having illegal
Masonic connections. He was taken first to Berlin, then to Esterwegen, a camp
on the Dutch frontier.

Cora sought help from the American consul, but when she sent him a telegram from the States, the Nazis intercepted it and placed Karl in solitary confinement. He maintained his sanity by reciting the Thelemic Holy Books from

memory and aspiring to his holy guardian angel. Cora's constant inquiries to the American consul finally resulted in Germer's release on August 1. That he was a German and had served as a major during the Great War helped.

A condition of his release forbade Germer to leave Germany and required him to report his residence and movements regularly. Thus Karl took an apartment near Belgium and reported it as per his parole, but also took another residence under an assumed name. One October night, he sneaked across the border to Belgium. Although he returned to England on a Belgian refugee passport, Germer was ultimately forced back to Belgium, where he stored his belongings and worked for an exporter of farm machinery in Brussels.

On April 14, 1934—the day after Crowley lost his court case against Constable and Company—W. T. Smith incorporated the Church of Thelema. This act was a bone of contention because Crowley wanted his American students to incorporate OTO, while Smith and Jacobi both argued that a church would net them tax-exempt status.

In June 1935, Smith wrote to Crowley about an influx of students to their group. C. F. Russell had set up his own OTO spin-off groups, "The Choronzon Club" and "G∴B∴G∴," which advertised a shortcut to initiation. "It appears that, in a few short weeks, one may become 7°=4□ or more," Smith wrote.[7] It had started five years previously—in spring 1930—when Russell wrote a series of articles for Chicago's *The Occult Digest*.[8] Coinciding with his first article, "Viens," in May 1930, he began running a banner ad that read:

SPECIAL NOTICE TO ADVANCED STUDENTS

We will disclose a short cut to INITIATION to ALL those who are willing to perform THE GREAT WORK! Here is the TEST. Can you do exactly as you are told, just one simple easy thing and KEEP SILENT FOREVER about your success? Then send your name and address with one dollar to C. F. Russell, Secretary.

CHORONZON CLUB, P. O. Box 181, Chicago
MAKE SURE YOU KNOW YOUR OWN MIND BEFORE YOU ANSWER!

This ad ran for twenty-six months, from May 1930 to June 1932. The following month he switched to a new banner ad which ran until February 1933:

THERE IS A SHORTCUT TO INITIATION

The ANCIENT WAY to the Adeptship and beyond the ULTIMATE ATTAINMENT is now opened to Members of the CHORONZON CLUB by a scientific technic based on the Supreme Secret of all PRACTICAL MAGICK. The enrollment fee is one dollar. The final fee is six dollars. There are absolutely no further fees, dues or alms of any kind. Our business is to Initiate, not to make money. If you are willing to do exactly as you are told and can keep silence, apply today to any Member in your own town or send your application with the enrollment fee directly to:

MR. C. F. RUSSELL, Secretary, P. O. Box 181, Chicago.

After that, he ran a series of shorter classified ads that ran until December 1933.

THE SHORT CUT TO INITIATION *Write for Premonstrance* **CHORONZON CLUB** P. O. Box 181 CHICAGO	WANTED: Advanced students to take and teach the short cut to initiation and qualify for executive positions. **CHORONZON CLUB** C. F. RUSSELL, Secretary P. O. Box 181, CHICAGO
IF YOU CAN READ THIS you need not play a losing game with Fate. Write for the PREMONSTRANCE **CHORONZON CLUB** C. F. RUSSELL, Sec'y P. O. Box 181 CHICAGO	**FOR YOU—** there is a message from your **HOLY GUARDIAN ANGEL in the PREMONSTRANCE** If you want to be an Initiate ask for it. **CHORONZON CLUB** C. F. Russell, Secy. P. O. Box 181 CHICAGO

C. F. Russell's later advertisements in *The Occult Digest* for the Choronzon Club (clockwise from upper left: June, September, October, and November/December, 1933).

From what Smith had gathered, the system provided financial incentives for people to initiate more members and set up more lodges: while membership cost $1, the Lodgemasters split the $6 Neophyte initiation fee with Russell in Chicago. The group boasted five hundred members in Denver alone. However, Russell announced the beginning of the order's five years of silence that summer: no more initiations would take place, and all typescript instructions were to be returned or destroyed. In response, members flocked to Crowley's group.

Appalled by the details of Russell's activities, Crowley asked Jane Wolfe to talk sense into him. When Russell refused to cooperate, Crowley expelled him from OTO and circulated the following encyclical:

> To those whom it may concern,
>
> The Master Therion warns all aspirants to the Sacred Wisdom and the Magick of Light that initiation cannot be bought or even conferred. It must be won by personal endeavour. Members of the true Order of the A∴A∴ are pledged to zeal and service to those whom they supervise, and to accept no reward of any kind for such service. Nor does the Order receive any fees whatsoever when degrees of initiation are conferred by its authority.
>
> He especially warns all persons against C.F. Russell of Chicago, Illinois, and his agents. He is a thief, swindler, and blackmailer. He has stolen the property of the Order, and used it to enable him to pose as its representative and so to carry on his swindles upon would-be initiates. Russell is a man of no education; he cannot even spell correctly. Steps have already been taken to prosecute him for his frauds.
>
>   Therion.
>   Aleister Crowley.[9]

That fall, far from the depredations of the German war machine, OTO took its first steps in California. On September 21 at 7 p.m., Jane Wolfe escorted seven aspirants into the desert. Here, Smith, Schneider, Jacobi, and Kahl conducted the 0° initiation, admitting the seven seekers into the OTO grade of Minerval. Afterwards, Smith announced the name of their lodge: *Agape.* It was the Greek word for "love," and, like *thelema,* added to 93.

At this time, a war that had nothing to do with Hitler or Europe raged. The battlefield was the United States, but the combatants never faced each other, and no casualties resulted. Sounding like the 1910 *Mathers v. Crowley* case, both sides of the skirmish—the Fraternitas Rosae Crucis (FRC) and the Ancient and Mystical Order Rosæ Crucis (AMORC)—deemed themselves the "true" Rosicrucian Order and their opponents "Black Magicians."

The Pennsylvania-based FRC was descended from Paschal Beverly Randolph (1825–1875), whose psychosexual doctrines in *Eulis!*[10] and other books influenced OTO system of sex magic. Randolph had received a charter from the Societas Rosicruciana, and over the years the mantle of leadership passed to Freeman B. Dowd then to R. Swinburne Clymer (1878–1966). Now Clymer was slugging it out with a Mr. Lewis.

Before H. Spencer Lewis (1883–1939) founded AMORC in 1915, he was simply Harvey Lewis, illustrator for a New York mystery magazine. He was initiated into a French Rosicrucian tradition in 1909, then founded his own branch in the United States. As mentioned previously, he met Crowley in New York in 1918, shortly before moving the AMORC headquarters to California, where it has flourished ever since. Crowley had recognized Lewis as an honorary VII° and in 1921 Theodor Reuss issued a "Gauge of Amity" stating that OTO and AMORC worked along cooperative lines. Since his degree was honorary, Lewis took no initiation or instruction; it was simply Crowley's (and, later, Reuss's) recognition of Lewis's other accomplishments to which the VII° corresponded. Lewis admittedly drew on Crowley, Eckartshausen and Franz Hartmann as sources of information, and even borrowed the GD's Rosy Cross and the Thelemic motto "Love is the law, love under will." In his *Militia* (1933), Lewis claimed his authority derived from OTO.

Clymer, having read and thoroughly misunderstood Crowley, accused Lewis of following the tenets of a black sex magician. Ironically, Clymer's organization, descended from Randolph—who was, in turn, one source of OTO's sex magical teachings—denied and shunned Randolph's doctrines and branded them evil. To discredit Lewis as head of a competing Rosicrucian organization, Clymer issued a two-volume diatribe titled *The Rosicrucian Fraternity in America.*[11] Its sole purpose was to expose Lewis and the people connected to him. Lewis responded to these attacks by publishing *Audi Alteram Partem*—also known as *White Book "D"*—sending copies to various libraries and adding another stack of paper to the fire.[12] Next, Crowley added gasoline.

In Crowley's opinion, Lewis's sole authority stemmed from OTO. Reuss had given Lewis a diploma and, now that Crowley was OHO, Lewis was acting "entirely without my knowledge and approval, in complete disregard of, and in opposition to, my principles."[13] The solution was simple: Since Lewis owed everything he had to OTO, Crowley proposed that he give it all back to OTO. The entirety of AMORC and its property was valued at £150,000 (about $7 million by contemporary standards). Crowley thereby hoped to run AMORC honestly and to dispense authentic teachings. To get his way, he was prepared to go to the Federal Trade Commission and if necessary to go to California himself.

Correspondence proved fruitless. Lewis argued that even if Crowley did control OTO and the Rites of Memphis and Mizraim, AMORC was Rosicrucian, not Masonic. Furthermore, American Masons recognized neither OTO nor Memphis-Mizraim. In the end, Lewis saw Crowley making claims without documentation of his authority, running a spurious British order—and he claimed to have correspondence with Reuss and Krumm-Heller to prove it. Crowley, however, was also in contact with Krumm-Heller, writing:

> Spencer Louis [sic] was never a disciple, either of Reuss or myself in any sense of the term. He had been knocking about for years trying to run a fake Rosicrucian Order. He cast about everywhere for authority and when I first met him in New York in 1918 E.V., he was showing a charter supposed to be from the French Rosicrucians in Toulouse. He devoted so much time to the conquest of the innermost secrets of nature that he had not been able to spend any to learn French. Now even in New York there are a few people who know French and this ridiculous forgery made him a general laughing stock so that he withdrew it.
>
> Now in the last 2 or 3 years of his life Peregrinus Reuss was sick, impoverished and desperate. He was anxious at any cost to find people to carry on his work. He, accordingly, handed out honorary diplomas up to the 95th degree and sometimes very foolishly the 96th. That is how people like Spencer Lewis and Tränker get their standing....
>
> It is amusing to notice that my own personal seal is on the documents quoted by Lewis as his authority and the words 'Ordo Templi Orientis' are sprawled all over the document...Either he had no authority at all or he had mine. If he had none he can be prosecuted, if he had mine he must account for the 900,000 dollars odd which he had amassed in the last few years.[14]

To get the wheels moving, Crowley circulated this document:

MEMORANDUM

> Aleister Crowley is the head of the O.T.O. (Ordo Templi Orientis).
> His authority is sole and supreme, and the property of the Order is vested in himself and his Grand Officers, who are his nominees.
> The Order is international in scope.
> A Mr. H. Lewis Spencer has been in control of an Order with headquarters in California under the title of AMORC. His authority is, however, derived from the O.T.O.

> The property of the AMORC is, therefore, by the Constitution of the Order, legally the property of Mr. Aleister Crowley.
>
> The real and personal property of the AMORC is estimated at $900,000 by his ex-Grand Treasurer, and its annual income is said to amount to about $350,000.
>
> Mr. Crowley proposes to go to California and claim the property....
>
> There should be no difficulty in getting lawyers in San Francisco or Los Angeles to undertake the prosecution of the claim on a contingent basis....
>
> [Mr. Crowley's] ultimate aim is to establish the Order on a large scale in the U.S.A. and elsewhere, on a basis of the most scrupulous honesty.
>
> We require $5,000 to finance Mr. Crowley's journey.
>
> The details of this proposition, with documentary corroboration, will be shown to interested parties on application, and if a satisfactory basis of action can be agreed, the terms of the loan will be discussed by us on his behalf.[15]

When Lewis suffered a stroke around this time, Crowley wrote to Smith, "This is where you jump in and file a claim on my behalf to the whole property of the AMORC."[16] Alas, like so many of AC's schemes, this never transpired.

Over the past two years, Crowley and Pearl tried desperately to conceive a child together. Yet AC's diary notes with disappointment the start of her every period. Then, on January 14, 1936, Pearl went into the hospital. The following day, doctors removed her uterus and fallopians. While Crowley loved her and stood by her, he realized she could never be the mother of his child.

As fate would have it, Patricia Doherty reentered the picture. Her relationship with the much older Thynne ended with his death in 1935. She mournfully traveled abroad, returning to England in spring 1936. She looked up Crowley and resumed a platonic friendship with him ... until that summer when out of the blue he asked her to bear his child. She agreed, and on May 2, 1937, Deirdre produced an heir.[17]

Crowley inaugurated 1936 with yet another pastime: cooking. Though he had been a bit of a chef in the past, this time he was serious. He planned to start "The Exotic Restaurant"—another pipe dream. Nevertheless, he delighted the palates of his many friends, with Louis Wilkinson ranking him among the best cooks in the world and Clifford Bax reporting AC's to be "the most delicious curry which I have tasted."[18] This same curry was reputedly so spicy that decades ago it sent Eckenstein headlong into a snowbank in search of relief.

His first dinner for Charles Richard Cammell—remembered today as a poet of both children's verse and of World War I—was a gastronomic spectacle. They'd met at a luncheon with their mutual friend Gwen Otter where Crowley impressed Cammell by correctly guessing his sun sign. "How did you guess?" the dumbfounded poet asked.

"I didn't guess," Crowley replied blankly. "I knew."

Shortly thereafter, AC called him with a dinner invitation. Asked if he liked curry, the poet, a connoisseur of spicy food, taunted Crowley with the response, "Yes, but very mild please." Crowley, of course, conjured his most infernal curry, which to his surprise Cammell devoured with impunity. Astonished that his liquid fire had failed to burn a hole in Cammell's tender tongue, he finally asked, "Did you like it?"

"It was delicious," Cammell remarked.

"Not too hot?"

"No, not at all. In fact, it was rather mild."

Mild? "Would you like more?"

"Please, and make it plenty."

This was all too much. "I suppose you'd like some vodka after your wine."

"Yes," he nodded, "I would."[19]

With that, Cammell passed into the ranks of Crowley's closest friends.

The Great Beast seemed to be vanishing into a purely mythical status. His last book had appeared in 1930 when Mandrake Press was still a going concern. Since then he had published almost nothing. Only the newspapers kept him in the public eye. Thus Crowley began working in the spring of 1936 on a republication of *The Book of the Law* that would do the book justice. He wanted to publish the text along with a complete account of its receipt and a thorough commentary on its contents—just as Aiwass had instructed him to do thirty-two years ago. A facsimile of the original pages, again according to Aiwass's instructions, would be included. However, such a tome was more than just *The Book of the Law,* and only one title fit this sweeping collection of papers. Crowley prepared to publish it as *The Equinox,* Volume III Number 3, otherwise known as *The Equinox of the Gods.*

This new *Equinox* was a different breed from its predecessor. It had no contributions from other authors; neither poetry, plays, nor short stories; no serialized features; no book reviews; and most significantly, no plan of regular publication. He had no idea how often he could bring issues out. Thus *The Equinox* became an irregular publication, each issue a self-contained book with its own title and format. Crowley designed a prospectus and subscription form for the book in June. On the 25th, after minor difficulties with his printer, the four-page flyer was completed.

On April 8, 9 and 10, 1904 e.v.[20] this book was dictated to 666 (Aleister Crowley) by Aiwass, a Being whose nature he does not fully understand, but who described Himself as "the Minister of Hoor-Paar-Kraat" (the Lord of Silence)

The contents of the book prove to strict scientific demonstration that He possesses knowledge and power quite beyond anything that has been hitherto associated with human faculties.

The circumstances of the dictation are described in *The Equinox,* Vol I, No. vii: but a fuller account, with an outline of the proof of the character of the book, is now here to be issued.

The book announces a New Law for mankind.

It replaces the moral and religious sanctions of the past, which have everywhere broken down, by a principle valid for each man and woman in the world, and self-evidently indefeasible.

The spiritual Revolution announced by the book has already taken place: hardly a country where it is not openly manifest.

Ignorance of the true meaning of this new Law has led to gross anarchy. Its conscious adoption in its proper sense is the sole cure for the political, social and racial unrest which have brought about the World War, the catastrophe of Europe and America, and the threatening attitude of China, India and Islam.

Its solution of the fundamental problems of mathematics and philosophy will establish a new epoch in history.

But it must not be supposed that so potent an instrument of energy can be used without danger.

I summon, therefore, by the power and authority entrusted to me, every great spirit and mind now on this planet incarnate to take effective hold of this transcendent force, and apply it to the advancement of the welfare of the human race.

For as the experience of these two and thirty years has shown too terribly, the book cannot be ignored. It has leavened Mankind unaware: and Man must make thereof the Bread of Life. Its ferment has begun to work on the grape of thought: Man must obtain therefrom the Wine of Ecstasy.

Come then, all ye, in the Name of the Lord of the Aeon, the Crowned and Conquering Child, Heru-Ra-Ha: I call ye to partake this Sacrament.

Know—will—dare—and be silent!

The book was priced at eleven shillings (eleven being a key number in Crowley's magick), with an autumnal equinox publication date.

Within two days of receiving the prospectuses, he sent out nearly three hundred copies. He sold twenty-five books to poet and occultist Michael Juste, who, under his given name Michael Houghton (died. c. 1956), was the proprietor of London's Atlantis Bookshop, which he, an Eastern European refugee, founded in 1922. By June 29 subscription checks began coming. On July 9, Simpkin Marshall agreed to distribute the book. Things were going his way.

While Crowley got his destiny firmly in hand, Pearl was quickly losing her grip. Her uncontrollable visions from the early part of their relationship became what Crowley called "almost constant hallucinations." On May 12 he recorded in his diary that she was "showing serious symptoms of insanity." Granted that after three years of trying to conceive a child with Crowley, she'd just had a hysterectomy and was experiencing tremendous hormonal and psychological changes. Then, on June 14, a woman she had never seen before—Elsie Morris—came by and insisted Crowley had gotten her pregnant that January;

while Crowley nonchalantly replied, "Possible, but I paid 5 shillings at the time,"[21] it rubbed Pearl's nose in her perceived biological inadequacy. Then there was Pat (Deirdre MacAlpine), who was out to have the baby she could never have. Pearl was more than jealous: she resented and loathed Pat for being able to give Crowley the one precious thing she could not.

A firm kick awakened AC on June 25. Another soon followed before he realized that Pearl was thrashing about in her sleep, bedeviled by a nightmare. Having worked late that night, he was too exhausted to do anything but wait for the episode to subside; but after forty-five minutes, he crawled out of bed and into his sitting room. Then Pearl burst in, gesticulating and shouting, "You shan't sleep all night unless you come back to bed!" Crowley was speechless. When she started crying and apologizing, he thought it was just as bad. When he finally slipped into sleep at 4 o'clock, he told himself, "This won't do."

Alas the violent dreams continued, infrequent at first but growing more common as the weeks passed. By August they occurred regularly:

> *August 1, 1936.* A hellish night. Kicked out—much harder kicking than before—slept in chair? No! She started screaming & rushed in.
>
> *August 2.* To sleep. More violence.
>
> *August 3.* Pat to lunch. Foul remarks by Pearl.
>
> *August 4.* Kicked more violently than ever: much of it awake and deliberate.
>
> *August 7.* New nightmare of Pearl's.
>
> *August 19.* 3rd Anniversary of Pearl … Pearl gave adequate demonstration of the kicking, moaning & muttering. Perhaps people will believe me in future.
>
> *August 21.* Pearl till 3 a.m. wakened by sudden & violent physical attack. She remembers nothing before finding herself in the room remaking the bed.

Pearl had snapped, and Crowley felt he might also.

On August 30 he moved out of what he called the "Doomed Bastion" and into Room 6 on 56 Welbeck Street. His new landlord was Allan Burnett-Rae, whom Crowley had met a few years previously at the Mayfair Hotel during one of Dr. Cannon's teas. Crowley wore the same knickerbocker suit he had worn then—it, his books, asthma machine, and incense burner were his only remaining worldly possessions.

Alas, trouble followed. "Pearl started her Macbeth act," Crowley wrote in his diary for September 3. "Had to throw her out. She fought like a tiger-cat. Hell to pay in house." Tenants' complaints resulted in Burnett-Rae storming upstairs and pounding on the door; judging from the noise, he assumed Beast was beating her. "Crowley!" he demanded. "Open this door!" When Pearl opened the door and apologetically explained that Mr. Crowley was having a nightmare, he believed none of it and insisted they see him in the morning.

Crowley and Pearl rose early the next day and ordered tea in their room. When the waiter arrived, Pearl screamed at him, "Go and shit yourself!" Crowley did his best to calm her before meeting their landlord. Burnett-Rae hadn't even dressed when they called on him. Taking the rap for Pearl, Crowley explained to him that he had, in fact, had a nightmare. They were rare, and he promised it would never happen again. Convinced Crowley had been beating her, Burnett-Rae insisted they pay their rent immediately or be expelled. Crowley spoke vaguely of money from American supporters and a family trust, and Burnett-Rae prepared for the unpleasant business of eviction.

After the meeting, AC sent Pearl away for a bit so he could continue his magical work. Then he met again with his landlord, paid him cash for the rent, and cleared things up about Pearl. Burnett-Rae told Crowley he could stay—he would even tolerate his incense—if Crowley promised to stop sending his helper Adolphe out for pigs' trotters in the dead of night. Crowley agreed.

This, combined with failing health, marked the beginning of Pearl's inexorable passing out of Crowley's life.

As the autumnal equinox approached that September, Crowley was quite busy. Despite previous failures in both Berlin and London, Crowley sought a play or film deal for *Mortadello.* Asked to produce the play, athlete, actor, scholar, and civil rights activist Paul Robeson (1898–1976) smiled and politely shook his head; he later confided in Cammell, "There are certain lines and gestures which the British public would not care to see enacted between a Negro and a white woman. As for the American stage, why, if I were to produce it there, somebody in the audience would stand up and shoot me with a revolver."[22]

By September 18, despite difficulties with papermakers and printers, Crowley held an advance copy of *The Equinox of the Gods,* his first book in six years. Germer, visiting from Brussels, bought dinner for the celebration. On September 23, 1936, the book was officially released. Selling at one guinea, it was an opulent volume: the pages were large—quarto in size—on handmade Japanese paper. The white buckram cover was stamped with gilt lettering. In a pocket in the back of the book was a facsimile reproduction of the manuscript of *The Book of the Law.* Its contents included an extract from "Aha!," the text of *The Book of the Law,* a brief account of Crowley's life, and the comment that emerged from the Cephaloedium Working. Although some typos marred this edition, one has become legendary: The plate of the Stele of Revealing was ironically mislabeled "The Stele of Revelling." The book sold well, and Crowley contemplated the need for a second printing.

The autumnal equinox was indeed a special day for Crowley. His new book was out. That morning, he had a vision of four adepts representing four races of man presenting him with the Word of the Equinox. Then, celebrating with Pat that day, he first learned that she was pregnant.

Internal strife wracked Agape Lodge in California. Regina had entered an asylum late in 1935, shortly after Smith tried to seduce her. Schneider, who never seemed to be around anymore, blamed the Lodgemaster for her fate. Then, in August 1936, Jacobi flipped. It began on Thursday night, August 13, when Smith received an anonymous phone tip: Jacobi was under investigation by his employers, the gas company, for living openly with a woman and for belonging to an immoral order wherein candidates for initiation were stripped naked. He was certain to lose his job.[23] Smith, of course, immediately phoned Jacobi (Jake) with the information.

The next night, members of Agape Lodge anxiously awaited Jacobi's arrival. A letter arrived special delivery in his stead, stating he had severed his relations with his friends and OTO. Although Smith contacted Jacobi, urging him to stick to his principles and speak to his boss, they heard nothing from him until August 20. "Regina saw him last night, and he would hardly open the car window to talk to her," Smith reported. "In almost a frantic way, he told her he was through with us all, and did not want to see any of us again, that he would send all of the books of the order to you, a copy of O° and I°."[24]

Outraged by this news and by Schneider's lurid reports about Smith, Crowley promptly sent a vicious letter to the Agape Lodgemaster, accusing him of running OTO as a racket to sell sex. He declared the Lodge at Winona Boulevard off-limits until matters were cleared up and said, "If you have a defense, you better cable me."[25] Although Smith promptly cabled Crowley that he was astounded beyond measure—denying the charges, professing his loyalty, and promising to write fully—AC simply rebuked him for sending such a long and costly telegram. Regarding charges of trafficking in sex, Smith wrote to Crowley, "in the last 20 years, up to last Sunday as a matter of fact, I have defended so many of the same and other attacks on yourself that I got quite hardened and merely considered the source."[26]

When Jane Wolfe sided with Smith and repudiated Max's report, Schneider broke off from the Lodge, taking most of the students with him. Before long, other members—presumably warned off by Schneider—began avoiding the Lodge. On November 7, Smith wrote to Crowley that he was suspending the Lodge until they had a better core of initiates to work with.

Back in 1934, Crowley's former secretary Israel Regardie had joined the Stella Matutina branch of the GD with Crowley's blessing. His introduction came from occultist Dion Fortune (1890–1946), who had long admired Regardie's first two books, writing glowing appraisals of them in the *Occult Review*. Although Waite had considerably revised, polished, and Christianized the rituals from their original Isis-Urania form, they deeply impressed Regardie.

In the following years he published GD influenced books like *My Rosicrucian Adventure* (1936) and *The Golden Dawn* (1936). The latter four-volume set contained the complete rituals and instructions of the Outer Order of the GD, and it quickly became a classic. Crowley, however, considered the book "pure theft"—particularly ironic since Crowley pirated much of "The Temple of Solomon the King" from Mathers.

Crowley, noting Regardie's pen name "Francis," wrote a glib letter to "Frank," chiding his former pupil about his Jewish faith and inferiority complex. Regardie took criticism poorly, and the jeering struck his insecurities like a sledgehammer. He rifled off a nasty retort, beginning with "Darling Alice, You really are a contemptible bitch!"[27] It infuriated the Beast; perhaps, as Crowley's letter triggered Regardie's insecurities, something about this struck a nerve in him. In response, AC circulated a cruel letter about Regardie:

> Israel Regudy was born in the neighborhood of Mile End Road, in one of the vilest slums in London.
> Of this fact he was morbidly conscious, and his racial and social shame embittered his life from the start.
> "Regardie" is the blunder of a recruiting sergeant in Washington on the occasion of his brother enlisting in the United States Army. Regudy adopted this error as sounding less Jewish. "Francis" which he has now taken appears to be a pure invention.
> About the year 1924 he began to study the work of, and corresponded with, Mr. Aleister Crowley. He put up so plausible an appeal that the latter gentleman paid his passage from America and accepted him as a regular student of Magic.
> Apart from his inferiority complex, he was found to be suffering from severe chronic constipation, and measures were taken to cure him of this and also his ingrained habit of onanism.
> The cure in the latter case was successful, but Regudy abused his freedom by going under some railway arches and acquiring an intractable gonorrhoea.[28]

This incident so embittered Regardie that he never again communicated with Crowley. Thirty years would pass before he overcame his resentment and regained his appreciation for Crowley.

With the popularity of the phonograph, Crowley spent that autumn cutting some wax 78 rpm records of himself reciting poetry and invocations. On November 18 and 19 he did the first and second Enochian Calls, followed on the 23rd by the "Anthem" from "The Ship" and "Hymn to Pan." On December 1 he recorded "Hymn for July 4" and some other pieces. "I did make a record of the 'Hymn to Pan,'" Crowley reported, "5 minutes all, but for 2 or 3 seconds continuous roaring and raging, so my lungs are not quite done for. The magical effect of that recording will soon be seen in London."[29]

That winter he returned to the more familiar role of teacher, appearing at the Eiffel Tower on Wednesday, January 13, 1937, to give his first of four lectures on "Yoga for Yellowbellies." Crowley thought the talk went well, but it was an uncharacteristic understatement. His talks on yoga, given twenty-seven years after he wrote about it in *Book Four,* rank among the best available expositions: lucid, direct, and good-humored.

The remaining talks followed on January 20, January 25, and February 3. So favorable was the response that Crowley ran a second series of four lectures, "Yoga for Yahoos." Beginning at the Eiffel Tower on February 17, the talks were every bit as sublime and witty as their predecessors—perhaps too clever. During his second lecture on February 24, Crowley found his audience staring blankly at him; Cammell thought they couldn't distinguish his learned words from deadpan one-liners. To remedy this, Crowley paused at odd intervals and blurted out, "To hell with the Archbishop of Canterbury!" Instead of waking the audience, he only confused them more. The third and fourth lectures followed on successive Wednesdays. Crowley offered the lectures to *Daily Express* reporter Tom Driberg, but the paper passed on the opportunity to print them. Someday, he thought, he would have to publish them himself.

Although May 2, 1937, was one of the happiest days in Crowley's life, his diaries are curiously silent on the matter. With no miscarriages or complications, Pat MacAlpine gave birth to a healthy baby boy at Newcastle-on-Tyne. Crowley had the heir he had sought. Contrary to popular rumor, he did not name the boy Mustapha because on seeing the mother for the first time he said, "I must 'ave 'er." The mother named him Randall Gair Doherty, although Crowley would carry on the tradition that left AC with his father's name, nicknaming the boy Aleister Ataturk.[30] A celebration followed the next day.

Since the start of 1937, Crowley was absorbed in the study of the Chinese oracle of I Ching, making some incisive observations and arriving at new theories. On June 7 Crowley recovered his I Ching sticks—a set of six turtle shell rectangles with a solid line on one side and a broken line on the other. This apparatus, which diverged from the traditional method of using fifty-one yarrow wands to produce a series of six broken, unbroken, and moving lines, provided a quick and dirty way of casting a hexagram. From this point on, Crowley consulted the I Ching daily for a general hexagram, and deferred to the Chinese oracle for many other decisions.

On June 9, Crowley met Clifford Bax for lunch at the Royal Automobile Club. Although over thirty years had passed since he and Bax first met at St. Moritz, when Crowley was a newlywed and Bax but a boy, they were still good friends. "What has happened to the Queen of Heaven?" Bax would ask Crowley, who dryly requested, "Year and name, please."

That afternoon, three ladies escorted Bax to lunch. The first, artist Leslie Blanche,[31] Bax introduced as "la Comtesse de Roussy de Sales," but Crowley knew Bax was merely attempting to titillate him. Next was Meum Stewart,[32] who spent much of the lunch asking for details about Raoul Loveday's death. The last of these women, older and more staid, was Lady Harris.

Marguerite Frieda Harris, née Bloxham (1877–1962), was the daughter of Charing Cross Hospital's consulting surgeon John Astley Bloxham (1843–1926) and wife of Sir Percy Harris (1876–1952), a member of Parliament. It was only a few years ago, in 1932, that Percy Harris was created a baronet, thus making his wife "Lady Harris" (although she preferred to eschew the formal title). She was also an artist, having illustrated her book *Winchelsea: A Legend* (1926) and having exhibited at the New English Art Club in 1929 under the name Jesus Chutney.[33] Lady Harris also professed an interest in magick: having at one time been an adherent of Mary Baker Eddy's Christian Science, she would, at other points in her life, study Anthroposophy, Co-Masonry, Thelema, and Indian mysticism.[34] As her friend, sculptor Edward Bainbridge Copnall (1903–1973), described her, "She had an alive and virile brain, though she was inclined to be very absent-minded, and a most amusing sense of humour and a love of the bizarre."[35] Bax had invited her at the last minute as an afterthought, and she failed to impress AC, who recorded their meeting only scantily in his diary. Nobody imagined that she would play a role in Crowley's life every bit as important as Allan Bennett, George Cecil Jones, J. F. C. Fuller, Victor Neuburg, Leah Hirsig, Gerald Yorke, or Karl Germer.

For the next few weeks, the I Ching was right on the money for Crowley. When, on June 25, he met Bobby Barefoot, he asked for a symbol for their relationship. *Kwai,* hexagram forty-three, came the response. Crowley interpreted this correctly as "Plain fucking and no more." She became one of several women Crowley bounced between in his sixty-second year. On August 9, AC got the first hexagram, and Frieda Harris contacted him again through Leslie Blanche. When Crowley received the second hexagram the next day, he noted in his diary, "I think I and II coming like this should announce a totally new current prepared, without my will or knowledge, by the Gods."[36]

That fall found Crowley in a publishing frenzy. He not only corrected page proofs for his next book, *The Heart of the Master,* but was also preparing a second printing of *The Equinox of the Gods.* When Simpkin Marshall threatened to renege on their agreement to distribute the reissue, on December 10 AC changed his personal British Monomark Corporation box BM JPKH to the commercial address BCM/ANKH through which to sell this and future books. The second printing of *The Equinox of the Gods* would appear in two formats: a standard issue uniform in paper and binding with the first edition; and a less elaborate subscriber's edition of 250 copies on machine-made paper with cloth-backed boards, priced at eleven shillings. The production cost of both editions was roughly £400; those expenses not covered by subscriptions were paid by Pearl and OTO donations from California.

Crowley's publication announcement for this edition of *The Equinox of the Gods* was more dramatic than that for the first printing:

THE FIRST PUBLICATION

nine months before the outbreak of the Balkan War, which broke up the Near East,

When this was done, it was done without proper perfection. Its commands as to how the work ought to be done were not wholly obeyed.... Yet, even so, the intrinsic power of the truth of the Law and the impact of publication were sufficient to shake the world, so that a critical war broke out, and the minds of men were moved in a mysterious manner.

THE SECOND PUBLICATION

nine months before the outbreak of the World War, which broke up the West.

The second blow was struck by the re-publication of the Book in September, 1913, and this time ... caused a catastrophe to civilisation. At this hour, the Master Therion is concealed, collecting his forces for a final blow. When the Book of the Law and its Comment is published ... in perfect obedience to the instructions ... the result will be incalculably effective. The event will establish the kingdom of the Crowned and Conquering Child over the whole earth, and all men shall bow to the Law, which is love under will."

Magick, pp 112–113, written in 1922 published in 1929.

THE THIRD PUBLICATION

nine months before the outbreak of the Sino-Japanese War which is breaking up the Far East.

THE FOURTH PUBLICATION

6:22 a.m., December 22, 1937 e.v.

Do what thou wilt shall be the whole of the Law.

The world is stricken to-day by an epidemic of madness.... On every side we are confronted by evidence of insanity which is sweeping across the earth like a pestilence.

Murder and terror in Soviet Russia; Concentration Camps and persecution in Germany; war fever and blood lust in Italy and Japan; civil war in Spain; economic crisis in U.S.A.; recurrent strikes and labour discontent in France—there is no corner of the Globe untouched!

What is the cause?

The old standards of human conduct, the ancient religions which have served humanity for thousands of years, have broken down....

The old order has broken down, and mankind is searching frantically for a formula which will take its place—a standard of human conduct independent of tradition and dogma which will stand up to the stress of modern conditions, and create a new engine for the further progress of mankind.

The *Bible,* the *Koran* and other codes are proving incapable of resisting the shattering effect of modern thought; humanity is drifting rudderless through a stormy sea of doubt and despair. Belief is bewildered. Conviction is shaken. But there is a way out!

A universal law for all nations, classes and races is here. It is the Charter of Universal Freedom.

"The Law of Thelema," revealed in Cairo in 1904, has come to replace the outworn creeds, the local codes; to help the peoples of the world to march on to a new era of peace and happiness.

Its power has been made evident time after time. On three occasions its publication has been followed by disaster—catastrophes to awaken mankind to its message. For the fourth time the Law of Thelema has been published....

The prospectus following gives particulars of the book "The Equinox of the Gods" which contains in facsimile the manuscript of the "Book of the Law" of Thelema, and an account of how it came into existence.

You cannot afford to neglect the powerful message which it propounds, and the guidance it gives for your future and the future of the world.

Crowley was proud of this book as he believed its proper publication would cause such social and political upheaval that the Law of Thelema would sweep the world. On December 13 he presented an advance copy of the book to his seven-month-old son.

On December 21, he prepared to make a dream come true. The first time he published *The Equinox of the Gods,* he had a vision of adepts representing the earth's different races presenting him with the Word of the Equinox. Crowley wanted to return the favor by presenting a representative for each race with his own word.

A representative for the white race was easy enough to find: Crowley chose Yorke. That evening, the two of them dined and embarked on a pub-crawl and gin-soak, accompanied by *Daily Express* reporter Tom Driberg. On their bizarre trek, they added a black dancing girl, a Bengali Muslim, a Jew, and a Malayan to their party along the way. The challenge, according to Yorke, was to keep the party going until 6 o'clock the next morning; this, presumably, they did by crashing a party at the Erskine. Crowley called it "a terribly dull party, brightening when we got rid of most of 'em and started whiskey."

At 6:22 a.m., Crowley and Yorke took the group of puzzled strangers to Cleopatra's Needle on the Embankment. There, as the sun entered Capricorn, Crowley made a brief speech: "Do what thou wilt shall be the whole of the Law. I, Ankh-f-n-Khonsu, the Priest of the Princes, present you, as representatives of your race, with *The Book of the Law.* It is the charter of universal freedom for every man and woman in the world. Love is the law, love under will." He presented each of them with a copy of the book, officially marking its publication. After the confused recipients staggered back to their homes, Crowley went to bed. "It was one of the craziest evenings I have ever spent," Yorke remarked. The next morning, Crowley's diary noted "Hangover very bad."

CHAPTER TWENTY-ONE

The Book of Thoth

"An Englishman, a Jew, an Indian, a Negro, a Malayan—no, it's not one of those saloon-bar jokes—assembled on the Embankment by Cleopatra's Needle soon after 6 a.m. yesterday...." Thus Tom Driberg, using the pen name William Hickey, began his *Daily Express* article on the bizarre republication of *The Equinox of the Gods*. It ran in the December 23 edition of the newspaper. Despite the free publicity, this reissue sold poorly. Crowley reports that only forty copies of the book got out;[1] after Crowley's death, the unbound sheets sold in editions by Samuel Weiser and Thelema Publications.[2]

He was now aged sixty-two—"Old Crow," as Gerald Yorke affectionately called him—and his asthma grew increasingly worse. More so than in his youth, Crowley realized the time limits to publishing his backlog of writing. Ditto for his opportunities to have children and train pupils. Thus he began a frenzied schedule of publishing, procreation, and searching for a successor. These activities would dominate the rest of his life.

Crowley's next project was a one-shilling edition of *The Book of the Law*. Early in February 1938 he checked proofs of the prospectus; a month later, proofs of the book itself. Many preorders came in, and on March 19 Crowley distributed advance copies. It officially appeared on March 21, the vernal equinox of 1938. It was a small paperback with white wrappers, later reprinted in America with blue wrappers. Despite brisk sales, Crowley had an ample stock to circulate until his death.

One copy, warmly inscribed with thanks for support and friendship in the publication of his most important work, went to Cammell. The poet curiously read this book until he reached the dreaded chapter three and could read no further. He confronted Crowley for printing such inexcusable blasphemy. Shaken and lamentful, Old Crow pleaded that he was simply the book's stenographer, not its author, and that he had acted on orders to publish the book in unaltered form. Cammell found Crowley's excuses lame. Despite his love of books, he was compelled to burn the volume—per the commentary's instructions—and felt great relief when he did.[3] In later years another recipient, Madame Wellington Koo, would write, "Instead of destroying your *Book of the Law,* I venture to return it to you in case you might be short of copies."[4]

Back in February, Crowley had written of Frieda Harris, "She is seriously on the Path."[5] His May 3 diary added, "She is now quite definitely a pupil." Within a week she affiliated to OTO for £10[6] and joined the A∴A∴ with the motto TzBA (which in Hebrew meant "Host" and added up to ninety-three). Later that summer, she bought a copy of *The Equinox* I(8) from Crowley for £1. It contained Crowley's description of the tarot cards, which prompted discussions on the subject. That August, Crowley suggested that Soror Tzaba design a deck. "I don't know anything about tarot cards," she pleaded. He assured her, "It will be easy." They'd start with an existing deck of cards and simply embellish the designs based on descriptions in *The Equinox.* He estimated six months' work, and she readily agreed.

Looking back over forty years of study, Crowley found the descriptions in *The Equinox* woefully inadequate. Frieda suggested he redesign the deck and write a book on the subject while she painted the cards to his specifications. AC averred:

> You are under a complete misapprehension about this tarot business. My original idea was simply to get hold of the best available old pack and have them re-drawn with occasional corrections and emendations. I expected to stick very closely to the *Equinox* description. As you will remember very well, I thought the whole thing could have been finished easily by Christmas.... it is entirely due to your genius that things are otherwise. It is you who have goaded me into getting the heart out of the whole business and taking each card separately as an individual masterpiece. The result is that any given card is something immensely beyond anything that I have ever contemplated.[7]

As a final carrot, Harris offered Crowley a stipend in exchange for lessons in magick. This, she reasoned, would better enable her to execute the new cards. That August they began the task, originally projected for an optimistic six months but which kept them both hard at work for five years. Crowley and Harris were both perfectionists: He with a very specific vision of what he wanted each card to look like, and she determined to meet his high standards.[8] In a lighthearted mood, Frieda wrote AC, "All day yesterday I wore three pair of glasses and squinted at a small map and at my design.... My eyes fell out and my hair went white and today I can't see at all and I've had to go to bed and am now writing with my eyes tied up in hot tea...."[9] In a more serious letter about card XX, "The Aeon," however, she revealed that her humor did not greatly exaggerate the truth:

> My Guardian Angel shouts to do it the best you can and not second best in
> a hurry and you must hit a perfect structure to build the pictures on. The

elemental Cherubims are quite jolly but the Little Lady has twisted and turned 'till I am insane with wiggling lines and I've done about forty drawings of her.[10]

Aside from Frieda Harris, several others became involved in Thelema in 1938. California's Agape Lodge admitted several new members that January, including twenty-year-old Phyllis Evelina Pratt (1917–2004), who would become involved not only in OTO, but also in A∴A∴ as Soror Meral; she would eventually advance to IX° in OTO and remain a fixture on the scene for the rest of her life, being one of those instrumental in carrying Crowley's teachings on to a new generation.[11] Joining with her was her sweetheart (and future husband), twenty-two-year-old Paul Seckler, who could go on to officiate at initiations, act in Regina Kahl's production of "Petrified Forest" for the Adult Evening College, and serve three years in San Quentin State Prison from 1940 to 1943 after he was convicted of grand theft auto.[12] Luther L. Carroll, who took over as Deacon in the Gnostic Mass, also acted in Kahl's productions and became an A∴A∴ Probationer on March 18, 1939.[13] Finally, American disciple Louis Turley Culling (1894–1973), a member of both OTO and A∴A∴, helped Crowley seek lawyers to denounce AMORC.[14]

Meanwhile, Crowley admitted Arthur Day to the grade of Minerval on August 24; he became a frequent visitor and promised to affiliate to the V° for £17 15s. AC also contacted psychologist and Co-Mason and Martinist Grunddal Sjallung (1895–1976), recognizing him as Frater Galahad, Grand Master X° of the Danish OTO; this was one of the rare occasions Crowley took interest in OTO in other countries.[15]

Another new student was John Bland Jameson (born c. 1915) of the Theatre Arts Club. From all accounts he was a dilettante, unemployed and living a wild life of dining, parties, and travel. Struggling with natural sciences at Cambridge, he became stage struck and dropped out to pursue theater. He was interested in magick, having long collected Crowley's works, and wrote AC on May 11, 1938, to invite him to lunch. As a result, Jameson became his student. Furthermore, as the actor was away during July and August—playing in the Cornish Shakespearean Festival—he sublet his large flat on 6 Hasker Street to Crowley. After his return in August, Jameson became a Probationer with the agreement that, if Crowley was satisfied with his progress in a year, Jameson would become his successor.

Around August 16, Jameson paid a £100 founders' share in Crowley's newest scheme: a clinic that, for a minimum fee of £50, would provide rejuvenation through massage, ultraviolet radiation, and OTO's elixir of life. The clinic was but one of many tricks filling Crowley's sleeves: If he could raise £2,000, he would go to America and seize control of AMORC, guaranteeing an annual income of £80,000. He also sought producers for *Mortadello* and *The Three Wishes,* and pursued other magical plans aside from the tarot. "The orchard has many apples," he told Jameson, "though one cannot tell which tree shall ripen first."[16]

As the autumnal equinox approached, Crowley prepared to publish *The Heart of the Master*. Written in 1924, it was originally published in the 1925 German periodical *Pansophia,* which was not distributed much outside of the small membership of the Collegium Pansophicum.[17] AC devoted September to reviewing its proofs and binding and on the 21st received eleven special copies of the book. Two days later the OTO publication officially appeared in its flashing colors of yellow and purple.

September also marked nine months since publication of *The Equinox of the Gods*. As expected, the news from Europe looked worse and worse:

September 11. Grave news on BBC. Will there be immediate war?

September 21. WAR.

September 26. Hitler's speech. War seems certain.

September 27. I.W.E. [Küntzel] raving against Czechs: these people are really insane.

Then, on September 29, the bottom fell through at the Munich Conference, and Britain and France yielded to Nazi demands. In disgust, Crowley jotted in red ink on a copy of *The Equinox of the Gods's* prospectus that publication occurred "Nine months before the Betrayal, which stripped Britain of the last rags of honour, prestige and security, and will break up civilization."

Crowley's various romantic forays stabilized for a time with a runner named Peggy Wetton. On October 7 and 8 they began a series of sex magick workings to beget another son for Crowley. "She claims that this worked right away," Crowley noted in his diary,[18] but at the end of December, Crowley recorded her miscarriage. After a kitchen fire burned Peggy's hand and sent her into the hospital, Crowley conducted sex magick workings with someone named Josephine Blackley to heal her arm. Peggy Wetton faded from the scene shortly thereafter.

Crowley spent autumn of 1938 working on more books. He busily dictated descriptions of the tarot cards, beginning with their traditional designs and building on or revising them in accordance with forty years' study of magick and mysticism. Frieda, meanwhile, continued the arduous task of painting the cards. Since she lived in the country and communicated with Crowley by mail, work proceeded slowly. Crowley was a hard task-master, supplying very specific descriptions (and sometimes sketches) of the cards, rejecting even the slightest deviation from his ideal. The artist on some occasions went through as many as seven revisions before an acceptable card was produced, much to her frustration. Fortunately her dedication and patience won out. She respected Crowley's learning, and he admired her ability to interpret and render his descriptions in her own style.

Meanwhile his secretary, Nora Knott, prepared typescripts of "Yoga for Yellowbellies" and "Yoga for Yahoos." He had long considered these prime candidates for publication, and now planned their release as *Eight Lectures on Yoga.* On December 15 he began dictating a manuscript on the I Ching.

Little Essays toward Truth, a collection of Crowley's philosophical writings, became his next book to go to press. He took it and a £10 deposit to the printer on November 4. The prospectus was ready by the 18th, and Crowley was soon taking orders for the book. He designed the dust jacket on December 3, and two days later Soror Tzaba rendered it to his specifications. OTO published the five-shilling book on December 22, 1938, at 12:13 p.m. as the sun entered the sign of Capricorn: precisely the winter solstice.

At the end of 1938, Jameson dashed in to appoint Crowley power of attorney, then dashed out again for business in Switzerland. Various ailments laid AC out for the first two months of 1939 despite frequent treatments for his asthma. When Jameson returned from Switzerland on January 17 they began petty and open bickering. The conflict came to a head in mid-February when Crowley moved out and Jameson entered a nursing home for surgery.

Spring of 1939 saw Old Crow as busy as ever. On the evening of Wednesday, March 17 (two days after Germany occupied Czechoslovakia), he gave a talk and demonstration titled "Travelling on the Astral Plane" at 32 Fairhazel Gardens. He also designed the cover for his yoga book and began correcting its page proofs. By April 3, Crowley had a sample copy of *Eight Lectures on Yoga,* by the Mahatma Guru Sri Paramahansa Shivaji. Of his pseudonym, Crowley wrote, "The name is, of course, a little slap of mine at the swinish scoundrels who confer high-sounding titles on themselves, and write books about a subject which they do not understand at all."[19] He was referring to His Holiness Mahatma Sri Agamya Guru Paramahamsa, with whom he was associated at the dawn of his *Equinox* period in London. *Eight Lectures on Yoga* was a large-sized book, constituting the next issue of *The Equinox:* Volume 3, Number 4.[20]

That May, Crowley had another manuscript and prospectus ready for the printer: his interpretation of the Chinese classic King Khang King. It resulted in a slim edition, with Crowley inscribing each of the specially bound copies with a different drawing, rendering each one unique.

In June, Crowley continued working on the tarot. When he found himself without a secretary, Lady Harris herself visited AC and took dictation so the Great Work could proceed. She continued until mid-July, when he finished the forty numbered and sixteen court cards of the tarot's minor arcana. That August, AC began making headway on the twenty-two major arcana cards.

In America, Agape Lodge continued to grow. New members included Brother Floyd E. Wade and Sister Margaret Arnold. The senior members busied themselves with their new property: Roy Leffingwell's Rancho Royal, on fifty desert acres in California's Rainbow Valley. Roy Edward Leffingwell (1886–1952) was a professional composer who, during the 1930s, had hosted morning radio shows on Los Angeles stations KECA, KPAC, KFI, and KIEV.[21] Born November 30, 1886, in Grand Rapids, Michigan, he had worked in various cities before settling in the Los Angeles area in the early 1920s.[22] He took his Minerval initiation into OTO on February 24, 1938, became an A∴A∴ probationer on September 23, 1938,[23] and would in Crowley's lifetime ultimately advance to the IX° in OTO. His wife, Reea, would join OTO some eighteen months after him.

Smith, Kahl, and the Leffingwells—Roy, Reea, and their son—took a two-day pilgrimage at the end of August to the property, which they renamed Agape Valley. Although Smith wanted to consecrate the land to the Great Work, the only ritual he knew was the Gnostic Mass. So, with no paraphernalia, they improvised: a circle of small stones constituted the temple, and a large rock became the altar. An old army overcoat that they found on the land became Smith's robe; a wreath of leaves became his crown, and a stick his lance. Leffingwell acted as Deacon, using a water glass for the chalice and a cracked dinner plate for the paten. Kahl was Priestess. They lit some dry leaves for incense and did the ritual, Smith adding his benediction, "Be this valley and the hills, the earth thereof and the water, the air and the fire, consecrated to the Great Work and the establishment of the Law of Thelema."[24] The ceremony was especially potent for the small group. As Leffingwell recalled,

> Wilfred so intense, so reverent, so impressed with the solemnity of the ritual that it literally tore him apart. Regina couldn't go through her love chant due to emotional choke up. Wilfred, in an old army overcoat and some ridiculous leaves on his bald head, looking, acting, feeling every inch the Priest. The finest rendition of the Mass I ever saw.[25]

Life in Britain changed drastically as the Nazis continued their invasions and persecutions. The British prepared for the worst by blacking out their windows at night with screens and blankets to make houses difficult for bombers to spot. Tension ran high, and Crowley wrote Küntzel disparagingly about Germany:

> Over there you have no idea of what the world is thinking. As for the ravings about the Jews, they are simply unintelligible. Almost the whole of life in Germany above brutality, stupidity and cruelty, servility, and bloodthirst was Jewish. Germans are far below Jews, generally speaking, as monkeys below men; but I have always been fond of monkeys and don't want to offend them by comparing any German to one.[26]

Britain, he warned, would "knock Hitler for a six." He never heard from her again; Küntzel reportedly died of old age in Germany in December 1941.[27]

On August 31 women and children evacuated London; it would be nearly three weeks before he learned that Deirdre and Ataturk were safe in Yugoslavia. The day after the evacuation, September 1, Germany invaded Poland with the result that Britain and France declared war. The next day, Crowley noted in his diary, "First air raid (perhaps). No noises here."

In a flurry of patriotism, Crowley composed a poem in honor of his homeland and sent it to the printer. The four-page card *England, Stand Fast!* appeared, courtesy of OTO, at 10:50 p.m. on September 23, the autumnal equinox. On October 8, the day the Third Reich annexed western Poland, Crowley sent copies of his poem to the BBC and others to whip up patriotism.

Three days after the declaration of war, AC contacted England's Naval Intelligence Division (NID) offering to serve his war-torn homeland:

> Sir,
>
> I have the honour to apply for employment. At the end of 1914, being incapable of active service owing to phlebitis, I went to New York, where I saw Captain (later Commodore) Gaunt, R.N., to whom I reported directly or indirectly until the Armistice. My work was to get in touch with the most important leaders of German opinion in the United States, especially George Sylvester Viereck, Professor Hugo Münsterberg, and Graf von Vernstorff, to supply them with false information and to wreck their propaganda by inducing them to commit psychological blunders: all with the object of inducing the United States to enter the war on our side. As soon as they did so, I was able to report directly for their Department of Justice, principally in discovering spy activities.
>
> In 1927, I began work for the Special Branch, this time to watch and report on Communist activities, especially in Berlin, where I lived almost continuously for three years.
>
> With regard to my qualifications, I speak several languages, though none of them very well except French. But I have spent many years in the study of psychology, especially morbid psychology. In particular, I have a sympathetic understanding of Americans, so that they do not feel for me that distrust and aversion which is the lot of so many English. My reputation as a writer in America is very considerable, and I have maintained for the last 25 years close connection with several of the most important leaders of thought in that country.
>
> I have also great sympathetic understanding of Eastern modes of thought, whether of the Mohammedean, Hindu or Chinese type; it was in fact at one time proposed that I should be detailed to counteract the influence of Gandhi over his co-religionists; but this came to nothing, as the situation was cleared up otherwise.
>
> Your obedient servant,
>
> Aleister Crowley[28]

The mention of Gandhi is most interesting, as reference to this proposed activity turns up nowhere else. Two days later, Crowley completed an NID application. When they declined to hire him, Crowley attributed it to his advanced age of sixty-four.[29] Nevertheless, AC passed several bits of information to the

NID, which gratefully thanked him. He claimed to have met with the NID and suggested a magical gesture that opposed the Nazi swastika: V for Victory (more on this will follow). He also suggested air-dropping magical English propaganda to demoralize the Germans.

Over the years he had met several agents of Britain's counterintelligence. Guy Knowles, who'd accompanied him on the K2 expedition, was an MI6 agent. Tom Driberg, who was also an agent, had introduced Crowley to two others: horror writer Dennis Wheatley (1897–1977),[30] to whom Crowley inscribed a copy of *Mortadello* in May 1934 and who would join MI5 in 1943; and his wife, Joan, whom Crowley remembered from Foyle luncheons as wearing silly hats. Dennis Wheatley was close friends with Maxwell Knight, who met Crowley at the Wheatley's and described him as "a well-dressed, middle-aged eccentric with the manner of an Oxford don."

James Bond creator Ian Fleming (1908–1964) was also an MI5 agent acquainted with Crowley—probably through Knight, who was the model of the Bond character M. Fleming tried unsuccessfully to convince his superiors to use the Enochian alphabet as a code for planting bogus information. And when England planned to capture Hitler's deputy, Rudolf Hess (1894–1987), by setting him up with a bogus British astrologer, Fleming and Knight both cast Crowley in the role; unfortunately, AC was too familiar to the Germans, so they used an unknown. After Hess was captured, Fleming urged his superiors to let Crowley interview him, convinced that the Nazis based their activities on occult knowledge that only a master would know how to extract. Unfortunately, Fleming's superiors nixed the plan.

Another agent of Crowley's acquaintance was Second Viscount and Fourth Baron Tredegar, Lord Evan Frederick Morgan (1893–1949), an eccentric Welsh dilettante: a poet, painter, musician, occultist, and collector of objects d'art.[31] As part of MI8, the Radio Security Service,[32] he and Wing-Commander (later Right Honourable Sir) George Stanley Waller (b. 1911) launched a disastrous response to Nazi spy pigeons. Their plan—for the Royal Air Force to drop hundreds of pigeons along the south coast of England to confuse the enemy—bombed when the jets' slipstreams sucked up the birds and defeathered them. Tredegar was ultimately arrested and imprisoned in the Tower of London for treason because he took his date to his office and divulged details of his work; ultimately MI5 intervened to arrange his release.

Tredegar's arrest typified MI5 security. All agents took oaths of secrecy and were expected to describe their jobs as "work in a rather dull department in the war office." Even today MI5 is secretive of its World War II activities. Thus, although he assisted MI5 agents, little is known about the exact services Crowley provided the government.

On December 7, Crowley returned to his literary pursuits and prepared another manuscript. On the 11th, he sent *Temperance: A Tract for the Times*, a collection of five poems, to Apex Printing Service. One hundred copies of the book were officially released on December 22 at 6:06 p.m., with copies sold, as with his other recent titles, through BCM/ANKH.

New hardships marked the beginning of 1940. On January 8, England began rationing bacon, butter, and sugar. Deirdre, meanwhile, was still in Yugoslavia, seriously ill with septicemia, while Ataturk recovered from the flu; after their recovery they would leave Europe altogether and seek solace with Pat's grandmother in Jerusalem. When Germany invaded the Netherlands, Belgium, Luxembourg, and France in May, Germer wrote to Crowley that he expected immediate arrest. This is, in fact, what happened: he was apprehended in Belgium, where he was reputedly trying to revive magick, and sent to a French concentration camp.

Crowley himself hardly fared better. Late that spring, AC began suffering debilitating attacks of asthma that kept him up at night and forced him to cancel and postpone work. His usual medications were no longer helping to relieve the symptoms. As his diaries record:

Wednesday June 12. Really bad attack of asthma.

Friday June 14. Inflamed throat still bad. Asthma much worse.

Saturday June 15. Throat—shade better. Asthma very bad indeed.

Sunday June 16. Throat better: asthma very much worse. Almost continuous.

Monday June 17. Throat still improves: asthma still bad.

Wednesday June 19. Asthma all day.

Thursday June 20. Asthma still v bad.

And so it continued until July 19, when his doctor, C. H. Cranshaw, prescribed heroin. The dosage, between a sixth and a quarter of a grain (a standard medical dosage), was Crowley's first since he kicked the habit in the mid-1920s. Hence, he recorded in his diary, "I'm quite dopy!" It is worth noting that, contrary to popular belief that Crowley was a lifelong addict, his first use of heroin was in 1919 at age forty-four. At that time, the drug was legal and his physician had prescribed it for asthma. An addiction naturally developed, but Crowley tried repeatedly—and ultimately successfully—to cure himself. His 1925 diary is the last time he mentions heroin; and P. R. Stephensen attested that, between 1929 and 1930, Crowley took no drugs at all.[33] Now, at age sixty-four, he received another heroin prescription for his asthma. It was twenty years since his first prescription and was again for purely medical reasons.

Beginning with this 1940 reintroduction to the drug, Crowley took his first step toward renewed heroin dependency. Given his age and the state of his health, it was simpler for Crowley to register himself with the government and medicate himself as his asthma warranted. On July 23, 1940, his diary expressed his caution: "Another very bad night. Used 2 tablets heroin: but oh! such lots of Asthmosana."[34]

The Battle of Britain began in July, with ninety German bombers shot down over England. Although outnumbered and overpowered, the British air force scored a major victory in this air battle. Germany responded with the Blitz. Air-raid and all-clear sirens filled Crowley's days that August, and explosions vigorously shook his home in Richmond. Initially infrequent, the raids soon escalated to multiple daily occurrences. Crowley first tried to intellectualize the raids rather than feel threatened, writing to Montgomery Evans:

> The raids last summer were exciting, not alarming. There was nothing one could do about it, so I slept quietly through everything. But they were so interesting—guessing what any particular noise might mean and (sometimes) spectacular that they made it difficult to concentrate on Work, and I just *had* to finish the tarot book.[35]

After a full day of air raids on September 18, however, Crowley wrote in his diary, "11:35. Great air fuss, but not much fun! Too near here." Five minutes later, an explosion went off nearby, its echoes resounding for a full minute. At this time, Crowley wrote Evans, "Had a certain bomb fallen 20 yards further west, I should have not got your letter of Sept. 25, but London would have been a more wholesome place...."[36]

The strain of worsening asthma and bombings wracked Crowley's body. One night, AC's landlord phoned Cammell, stammering, "Mr. Crowley is very ill, and I'm worried. With his breathing the way it is, I don't think his heart will hold out through the night. He's asking for you; could you come?" What Cammell found shocked him: illness had withered Crowley's stout and portly frame into to a wiry skeleton; that night, sleeplessly straining for air, he looked jaundiced and mummified. His eyes were like embers, bloodshot from hours of congestion. And when occasional words of gratitude or humor wheezed from his weary lungs, Cammell cringed. Meanwhile, a stream of German bombers flew overhead. Although England had only a few antiaircraft guns, a huge one at the nearby railway fired continuously. As explosions shook Crowley's home, Cammell pondered how simply death could snatch these two old men.

A brilliant explosion filled the sky with a light visible even through the blackout curtains. A screeching sound followed, and Cammell, his vigil interrupted, knew a bomber had been hit. Dashing down the rickety stairs and out the front door, he watched its flaming wreckage strike the Twickenham bank, until the cheer "Hooray!" startled him. Cammell turned to see that Old Crow had dashed down the stairs two at a time behind him. The Crowley who hovered on the brink of death now hopped about, waving his arms in the air. The friends watched day break over the wreck's yellow and mauve flames, then went inside and drank a toast.[37]

His doctor put it simply: get out of London or die of heart failure. With the I Ching's advice, Crowley decided to stay in Torquay until the stressful bombings stopped. Setting out on the fall equinox, he arrived September 25. Crowley

called the town "my ancestral temple,"[38] for it was here, fifty years ago, that his
tutor Archibald Douglas taught him the facts of life, and here that Alec discovered the awful mysteries of love and sex in the open country air. "Torquay is
anything but gray and shapeless," he enthused upon arrival. "It is astonishingly
beautiful. Flowers bloom afresh daily in my garden, and the woods, the hills,
the harbour and the sea are just a constant benediction. This morning, one of
the loveliest dawns I have seen anywhere in the world."[39] Ironically, Crowley's
nurse here was a Plymouth sister.

Yorke sent Crowley a secretary named Mrs. Martin so he could continue
his work, and by October 23 he finished his descriptions of the twenty-two
major tarot cards. "Polished off the last bit of the blasted tarot book and took it
to be typed," he wrote in his diary. "Later, discovered that I still have to do the
other fifty-six cards. SHIT." It would be a year and a half before Crowley was
finished, writing to Yorke:

> Anyway, nearly killing myself in the process I finished the Court and small
> cards. They needed what was practically rewriting in parts, as I have found
> identities between certain cards and (a) the Yi (b) the Geomantic figures.
> This is exceedingly important from the point of view of official science, as
> it demonstrates beyond doubt that these independent systems reach the
> same conclusions, and therefore that they all represent a reality in Nature,
> not an arbitrary set of artificial conventions. I assure you that one day this
> will be the corner-stone of the scientific acceptance of the fact of Magick.[40]

While science and magick are no nearer an intersection today than they were
then, Crowley rightly assesses the importance of his work. Just as *Magick in Theory and Practice* was the first modern textbook on magick—standing today as
the definitive text of its kind—so would the *Book of Thoth* (as it would be
named, after the Egyptian god of magic) be a quantum leap in the tarot's conceptualization. It would be the crystallization of everything Crowley had
learned over the course of an entire lifetime's study and practice of magick.

For the moment, however, Crowley became sick for three months with
acute lobar pneumonia. His asthma machine, which gave him little relief nowadays, broke down, and he received an injection of atropine to dry up his bronchial secretions. Then, on December 14, he swallowed a tooth; this was the
beginning of dental problems for him.

As he recovered, Crowley resurrected his interest in chess. He had recently
attended London's chess club, facing seasoned players like M. A. Sutherland;[41]
but in Torquay's chess clubs he easily beat all comers. One incident epitomized
for Crowley the club's mentality: they had been discussing Lord Haw-Haw, the
Anglo-American who broadcast anti-British propaganda from within Germany
(and who would be tried and executed for treason after the war) when one person responded, "Isn't that the fellow in the Tower?" Crowley wrote in his
diary,[42] "When I told the ignorant bastards that he was William Joyce, one said
'Isn't that the fellow that wrote the dirty book?'"[43] Ironically, within the year,
AC would find himself the subject of one of Haw-Haw's attacks.

Miscellaneous difficulties haunted Crowley for the first couple of months of 1941. Lawyers contacted him demanding past rent; a difficult new secretary, Sophia Burt, appeared on the scene. Tooth decay threatened to turn into an abscess and improved only temporarily with tincture of iodine. Insomnia forced him to take Luminal, and the police fined him for turning on his lights on sleepless nights during the blackout.

Around this time, Crowley contributed his expertise in magick to the war effort. If the Nazis could wield crushing power through the ancient symbol of the swastika, then England could certainly use more powerful magick to win the war. Hence a magical antidote to the swastika became his quest. Crowley's first suggestion was the poem "Thumbs Up!" The corresponding gesture, popular among pilots, was phallic, and Crowley wished to publish the poem with an equally phallic pantacle on the cover. However, he desired a more potent symbol. "How can I put it over pictorially or graphically?" he pondered. "I want positive ritual affirmation, like Liber Resh, 'saying will,' and so on."[44]

Soon afterward, he found this even more potent formula "to bring victory ... [and] a way to put it across."[45] Crowley decided on the letter V: in Hebrew, *vav* is phallic in both image and meaning; it literally meant "nail," and Crowley thought this symbolized the nails in Hitler's coffin. Furthermore, V suggested AC's Magister Templi motto, V.V.V.V.V. And, according to the GD formula of LVX, V also designated the Egyptian deities of Apophis and Typhon; these deities suggested the tarot card "The Devil," appropriate since the V also symbolizes a pair of horns. The V for Apophis sign occurred in the Adeptus Minor (5°=6□) ritual, which is appropriate since V is the number five in the Roman numeral system but six in gematria. It also suggested the famous "Veni, vidi, vici" ("I came, I saw, I conquered"). But most importantly, Crowley recognized "V for Victory." "Seabrook should be thrilled," he wrote, "in view of his story about 'Wow!'"[46]

Although "V for Victory" has been attributed to BBC broadcasts by Victor de Lavaleye or David Ritchie, Crowley maintained he invented the gesture as a magical counterattack to the Nazi swastika; then, using his MI5 connections, he suggested it to NID and had it accepted by Churchill. As he wrote to Yorke,

> The V sign. My object is to disclaim connection with my B.B.C. friend. The plate in Eqx I 3 and to face p 374 of Magick is entitled "The Signs of the Grades," caption to photographs "The L.V.X. signs." Each photo is marked L - Isis mourning, the Swastika. V - Apophis, the Trident. X - Osiris risen - the Pentagram. Dates at least from the '80s G.∴D.∴, but I have "Squatter's Right" as first to publish it.[47]

Since Crowley demonstrates his primacy in publishing the V-sign, the second part of his claim—his intelligence connections—are of interest. He was on casual and friendly terms with high-ranking naval officers, and the Director of Naval Intelligence had personally requested Crowley to apply to him. Shortly after developing this scheme, AC began meeting with Major Penny of the Air Ministry, presumably about putting it over. In various letters at this time he refers to anonymously "sneaking" his idea past the BBC.[48]

On March 14, Crowley cast a general hexagram for the day as he usually did. "Ta Yu," the fourteenth hexagram, was his oracle. It denoted "great happenings." When his mail arrived, Crowley sorted through the day's parcels and came upon one that made him stop cold. The handwriting was distinctly familiar. The corners of his face curled up into a tremendous smile. Karl had written. "Great Happenings/Havings indeed," he wrote in his diary. "A letter from Germer, who is safe after all. The happiest evening of my life! Even the birth of little Ataturk is not in the same class, for that I expected. *This* is a stirring/stunning joy!" Germer had been liberated from a French concentration camp on February 18 when Cora obtained a nonquota visa for him through the President's Committee for Refugees. Germer sailed for America on March 31, and applied for his U.S. citizenship papers the following month.

Although he escaped physically unscathed, Germer carried the psychological scars of persecution in the form of paranoia. "Since 1942," he wrote, "every one of my telephones is tapped. The house in which we lived in New York was wired. Microphones had been installed in the walls. We left NY. But in this house it is the same."[49] His suspicions became so intense that the Germers never spoke in their own home.

Crowley was nevertheless overjoyed that his dear friend was alive. On May 5 he appointed Germer Grand Secretary General of OTO, and on July 19 appointed him as Crowley's representative in the United States. Germer was also Crowley's chosen successor.

A new magical current was sweeping into AC's life. Ideas formed in his mind, and the I Ching encouraged him to pursue them; so on March 16 he announced to Louis Wilkinson, "I'm starting an Abbey of Thelema."[50] After twenty years, Crowley's desire for a Thelemic community endured. The next day he looked at accommodations in Barton Brow, just outside Torquay and thirty miles from Plymouth; on the 18th, he rented a house as his new Abbey.

Once settled in, Crowley resumed work on his war poetry, completing "Thumbs Up!," his national anthem of free England, on April 9. He kept long hours, one time working twenty hours in one day and giving himself an asthma attack. He began taking digitalis for his overworked heart.

The Abbey maintained but a vague existence, with Crowley and Grace M. Horner (whom Crowley dubbed Charis, Greek for "grace") signing the following proclamation on April 20:

> We, the undersigned members of the Abbey of Thelema at Barton Brow Barton Cross, declare ourselves completely satisfied with the conduct & conditions thereof during the passage of the Sun through Aries.[51]

Despite his satisfaction, Crowley wanted more. He wrote to Wilkinson, "The Abbey is a bit stagnant: I do wish you would find a couple of suitable people, or a single man, to join."[52]

In the same letter, written two days after air raids destroyed Britain's House of Commons, Crowley described the wartime conditions at Barton Brow:

> Raids over here almost every night; this house is constantly shaken.... They went for it last night, there was also a dogfight, complete with crash, right over these moors. There is more accident than most people suppose. Twice, close to me, people have been killed by bombs jettisoned in despair from limping 'planes.

In the end, however, lack of finances doomed the Abbey.

A new current of growth also infused the Agape Lodge in California, with new members including rocket scientist Jack Parsons and, most recently, college student Grady McMurtry.

John Whiteside Parsons (1914–1952) was born with the forename Marvel but known as "Jack" to his friends. Standing six-foot-two, he was an eccentric and handsome young scientist developing explosives at the California Institute of Technology under a government contract. Born in Los Angeles to a wealthy and well-connected family, Parsons had grown up in a Pasadena mansion and was captivated from an early age by images of rockets in science fiction pulp magazines like *Amazing Stories*. He began launching homemade rockets from his back yard in the 1920s and later worked for the Hercules Powder Company, manufacturers of various explosives. By the 1930s he was part of a rag-tag group of people performing rocketry experiments at Caltech. Parsons— together with his colleagues, who were disparagingly nicknamed the "Suicide Squad"—effectively established rocketry as a science, founded the Jet Propulsion Laboratory (JPL),[53] developed solid rocket fuels, and invented jet-assisted takeoff (JATO). Parsons also had a long-standing interest in the occult. He attended events at Agape Lodge as early as 1939, and with his wife, Helen (1910–2003),[54] was initiated on February 15, 1941. Taking the motto "Thelema Obtentum Procedero Amoris Nuptiae," his devotion to the Great Work made W. T. Smith remark to Crowley, "I think I have at long last a really excellent man."[55]

Grady Louis McMurtry (1918–1985) met Parsons at a meeting of the Los Angeles Science Fantasy Society,[56] where Parsons struck up a conversation with him on science fiction, poetry, and magick. McMurtry was initiated into Agape Lodge shortly thereafter on June 13, 1941. Born in Big Cabin, Oklahoma, to an alcoholic mother and a father who was repeatedly imprisoned for bank robbery, McMurtry was raised by his maternal grandfather and other relatives, relocating frequently throughout childhood to various parts of Oklahoma and the Midwest. He attended Valley Center High School in Kansas, graduating in 1937. He enrolled in the ROTC and began studying engineering at Pasadena Junior College. Months before joining Agape Lodge, he had quit school without taking a degree. Although he lacked a plan for what to do next, he shared Parsons's enthusiasm for poetry and Thelema.[57]

With the Lodge now burgeoning, the members planned fund-raising to bring Crowley to America, where he could live out his last years in southern California's comfortable climate, surrounded by students and supporters. On May 6, Smith went to the U.S. Department of Immigration and Naturalization to sponsor Crowley's visit.

Amidst frequent air raids, Lady Harris planned an exhibition of the tarot paintings at the Nicholson and Venn galleries in Oxford. That May, inspecting her budget and proposed show catalog, Crowley objected vehemently:

> I never saw such horror. No title, no lay-out, no word of what the show was about. Utterly obscure, full of bad grammar & misspelling, ill-typed, single-spaced, full of italics a full meal for 6 hungry printers! Pages & pages (20 typescript—over 6,000 words!!) of complete obfuscation. No hint of what terms like Tetragrammaton, *Sephiroth* & their kind may mean. She had also sent The Juggler—the one trump that must be done again, & in any case very unsuitable indeed for wrapper—to be reproduced very expensively so that printing & paper must be cheap!!! I have no memory of so black a rage as has consumed me for the last 5 hours. All this though I had long ago prepared a proper catalogue, approved by Louis Wilkinson & other sensible people who understand such things; clear, modest, cheap to produce.[58]

Frieda responded with a letter asking Crowley to avoid Oxford during the exhibition, lest his reputation prejudice and frighten off potential supporters, and allow her to pass off the cards as her own work:

> The opposition against you in Oxford is very strong. My business is to get money to publish those cards if possible and this is nearly impossible in the present war conditions. I have been successful through using what influence I possess in getting at people with money to come and see the Exhibition. This is using my social position fully. If they suspected that the cards were inspired by the Arch Magician of Black Magic (what do they mean?) they would withdraw their patronage. I have had this conveyed to me politely and impolitely. Therefore if you come to the Private View or show up in any prominence this attempt to launch the cards is doomed and all the work and money lost. Can you be so large-minded and detached as to keep away until the thing is launched?[59]

Oxford was, after all, the campus that banned his Gilles de Rais lecture a decade earlier. The day of the exhibition, Crowley telegrammed a wry answer: HEARTIEST ACQUIESCENCE APPROVAL THERION.

It was just as well, because a quick series of moves—seven in two weeks— had upset his life. As an undischarged bankrupt and the "Wickedest Man in the World," Crowley had difficulty locating a landlord. He remained philosophical about it all, anticipating his move to California. He simply put his things into storage. "Burnt my boats magically," he wrote in his diary, "by deciding to discard anything not wanted for Rainbow Valley in the Palomar Mountains."[60]

By June 7, in the middle of the tarot exhibition, he grew agitated. He had received no word from Frieda whether the show was a success or failure, and finally wired her two days later. While awaiting her reply, he happened by Michael Houghton's Atlantis Bookshop. There in the window was a postcard from Frieda Harris noting that the show was "Cancelled owing to war." The postmark, Crowley noted indignantly, was June 3. Yet she never informed him. Crowley went to Oxford himself to get to the bottom of this, but found nothing more than "a scared and hostile youth in dull desolation" who "refused all information."[61] Returning empty-handed, Crowley found Frieda's reply telegram awaiting him. It offered little by way of information, but a June 16 visit from her clarified everything: when Crowley's involvement in the tarot project became known, Nicholson and Venn canceled the show with no warning. Harris quickly rented the largest room at the Randolph Hotel down the street, exhibiting the cards there and attracting "so many people that I had to leave the gallery open at night in Oxford to allow the undergraduates to look at them."[62]

That June, Crowley went to Whiteley's, his storage company, and instructed them to sell all his possessions except for his books and papers. "Why?" he explained, "Because I must either die or get to California.... In neither case shall I need furniture and other perishable goods."[63] Shortly thereafter, in new accommodations at 14 Lassall Gardens, he prepared his next book—the anti-Nazi pentagram—for the printer. On June 22, the fateful day Germany invaded Russia, he officially named it *Thumbs Up!* The next day, he took it to Apex Printing for publication.

When the proofs of *Thumbs Up!* arrived on July 1, Crowley was busy seeking a new home and courting the press with "England, Stand Fast!" "I think the poem by Aleister Crowley is vigorous and certainly patriotic," wrote Beverly Baxter of Allied Newspapers Ltd. "At the same time, there is very little space in newspapers, and there is practically no chance of a poem being printed."[64] It was the same all around. Driberg, whom AC considered a shoo-in with the *Daily Express,* replied, "But how do I know if the government *wants* England to stand fast?" And H. L. Mencken told Crowley, "I daren't show it to an American editor. He'd die of laughing."[65] Nevertheless, Crowley also wrote of *Thumbs Up!* at this time, "So far, good and enthusiastic response; e.g., C. E. M. Joad, John Cooper Powys, Louis Wilkinson, Harold Mortlake, and other more or less prominent people. Navy quite thrilled!" and later "*Thumbs Up!* has extracted praise and thanksgiving from U.S. Embassy, Naval blokes, Joad, John Cooper Powys, Ralph Straus and so on. Joad specially nice about it. I'm encouraged."[66] Thus AC took on other projects: having Sun Engraving make blocks of Frieda's tarot cards; looking for a composer to render his songs into French; and meeting with the U.S. consul about obtaining a passport for his pilgrimage to California.

On July 28, Crowley received an irate letter from Cammell. A month earlier his wife, Ionia, had sent samples of her handmade tweeds to AC, who promptly sold them to his various acquaintances and kept the money. Ionia sought remuneration, and although Crowley laughed it off at first, the matter became a bone of contention that tore a rift in their friendship. Although Cammell continued to admire Crowley's talent as a poet, his unfriendly behavior mystified him. Standing by his wife, Cammell decided honor prohibited their friendship. They would never speak again.

The notorious fascist and Nazi propaganda broadcaster William Joyce (1906–1946),[67] known as Lord Haw-Haw, attacked Crowley during one of his broadcasts, chiding that England ought to replace its prayer intercessions with Crowley conducting a Black Mass at Westminster Abbey. AC, who felt his character had been tarnished enough, worried that the attack would undermine his V-Sign campaign. "Thanks to Lord Haw-Haw, it is now quite generally known that I invented this campaign," Crowley bemoaned. "Of course, I am denying strenuously that I ever had anything to do about it, as the bloke who slipped it over on the idiots at the BBC would get into the most hellish trouble if it were found out that he knows me."[68]

On August 17, Crowley sent his newly revised *Thumbs Up!* manuscript to Chiswick Press. He had asked Frieda to draw the cover, but notes in his diary: "FH wouldn't draw any V cover, sent me a nice tie instead."[69] She ultimately relented and provided the artwork of Crowley's "Mark of the Beast" magical sigil. Although Chiswick Press turned out an advance copy of *Thumbs Up!* within three days, it also demanded advance payment before delivering the completed job. Crowley fumed, "I told them they could sell the edition for waste paper and I would get another printer."[70] They allowed him to pick up the finished product a day later.

Crowley's "Mark of the Beast" from *Thumbs Up!*

Even as the book appeared, he was designing its reprint. As Yorke suggested, he dropped the magical "mumbo-jumbo" and his name; its eight pages would have no cover, its title page simply reading "Thumbs Up! Five poems by the author of the V-Sign for free distribution among the soldiers and workers of the soldiers of freedom."[71] This edition would arrive on September 19.

Response to the book was apparently positive, for Crowley wrote ebulliently to Yorke, "Navy quite thrilled. If I can get really big success, it will put me in a position to ask for an interview with Winston to put up to him the 2nd half of my V plan. This might be the war engine in AL iii.7–8."[72] The interview never came to pass, leaving us to ponder what Crowley had in mind.

At the end of August, AC and Yorke took a brief foray into the past to the poet's forty-year-old haunts at Cambridge. Visiting Trinity Chapel—something he never did as a student—he exorcized one of his ghosts by mounting the high altar and proclaiming, "Do what thou wilt shall be the whole of the Law." The visit was wonderful and Yorke's company delightful.

Reminiscing concluded, Crowley returned to work. When his lover, Alice Upham, suggested he send a copy of *Thumbs Up!* to Charles de Gaulle, AC, although he liked the idea, remarked, "OK, but I had better write a poem in French for Free France."[73] This he wrote the following day.

Crowley turned sixty-six that October. Since sixty-six was the sum of the numbers from one to eleven, and eleven was such a significant number in his magick, he wanted something more special than the presents and letters he received from Pearl, Frieda, Alice, Karl. and former student J. G. Bayley. So, taking *The Book of the Law* in hand, he rededicated his life to the Great Work. Sliding the book back onto the shelf, Frieda's rejected tarot card for the Aeon slipped down from the shelf overhead. Picturing the Stele of Revealing, the card symbolized the beginning of the Aeon of Horus and was as good an omen as Crowley had ever seen.

Shortly thereafter, he decided that the war-torn world needed a concise statement of the Law of Thelema: an epigrammatic explanation of "Do what thou wilt shall be the whole of the Law"; a proclamation of the basic rights of every human being as given in *The Book of the Law*. Declaring that the enemy was depriving people of their basic rights, AC gave this project the working title of "War Aims."

"Oh for a title for my War Aims!" he lamented. "Can't use 'Rights of Man.' I want to keep monosyllabic ... 'Words of the Way of the Will'?" He brainstormed on possible terms: "Watch-Words Law Plan Sketch Step Strict Path Clue Key Rule Guard Bawe Curve Straight Line Snake." Finally on November 6 he came up with the name: Oz. The word was Hebrew for goat—an animal renowned for its independence and perseverence—and added up to seventy-seven (denoting strength and the influence of Kether, the highest emanation on the Tree of Life). Thus the War Aims became *Liber Oz,* and its summary of human rights required 220 words (220 being the number of verses in *The Book of the Law*). Ultimately, he drew on the language of one of the OTO rituals he had revised in 1918–1919:

OZ: LIBER LXXVII

"the law of the strong:
this is our law
and the joy of the world."
—AL. II.21

"Do what thou wilt shall be the whole of the Law." —AL. I. 40.

"thou hast no right but to do thy will.

Do that, and no other shall say nay." —AL. I. 42–3.

"Every man and every woman is a star." —AL. I. 3

THERE IS NO GOD BUT MAN

1. Man has the right to live by his own law.
   to live in the way that he wills to do:
   to work as he will:
   to play as he will:
   to rest as he will:
   to die when and how he will.
2. Man has the right to eat what he will:
   to drink what he will:
   to dwell where he will:
   to move as he will on the face of the earth.
3. Man has the right to think what he will:
   to speak what he will:
   to write what he will:
   to draw, paint, carve, etch, mould, build as he will:
   to dress as he will.
4. Man has the right to love as he will: —
   "take your fill and will of love as ye will,
   when, where, and with whom ye will." —AL. I. 51.
5. Man has the right to kill those who would thwart these rights.

"the slaves shall serve." —AL. II. 58.

"Love is the law, love under will." —AL. I. 57.

That evening he made up a dummy for a postcard bearing this message. His printer estimated two hundred copies at £3 3s.

This project troubled his friends. Frieda Harris and Ethel Archer both sent letters discouraging Crowley from publishing the statement; despite the insistence of patriots on defending to the death people's rights, point five of *Liber Oz* gave them pause. He nevertheless determined to see the project through because it was more than just a postcard: it was a powerful magical act. Only Bayley, an A∴A∴ student from thirty years ago and now returned to the fold, offered to help pay the costs. Appropriately, the proofs were completed on Crowley's magical birthday: the anniversary of his initiation into the GD. In the end, fifty copies bore Frieda's artwork for "The Devil" (the fifteenth tarot trump) on one side and the proclamation on the other, while 250 had "The Aeon" (the twentieth trump). To magically affirm the publication, AC sent cards to everyone he could think of, including figureheads of various walks of life: H. G. Wells for literature; journalist Lord Edward Donegall (1903–1975), the Sixth Marquis of Chichester, for the press; Ivor Back for medicine; Gerald Kelly for art; J. F. C. Fuller for the army; Admiral Sir Roger John Brownlow Keyes (1872–1945), Conservative member of Parliament, for the navy; F. W. Hylton for agriculture; and Frederic Maugham (1866–1958), Lord Chancellor and First Viscount Maugham, for law. To Louis Wilkinson he wrote, "I think this publication may turn out to be a Magical Gesture; you may therefore look out for a Revolution (in one form or another) at the Autumnal Equinox."[74]

On that fall equinox of 1942, the top-secret Manhattan Project commenced under Brigadier General Leslie R. Groves.

As 1941 came to a close, winter came in cold and snowy. Crowley succumbed to illness and depression for the remainder of the season. On top of a pleurisy-inflamed chest, worsening asthma, and a fibrillating heart, he was now taking heroin regularly, as prescribed by his physician, Cranshaw. As the winter wore on and the *Sunday Dispatch* ran a premature obituary on Crowley, he remarked, "I want a vast empty heaven to laugh into for several eternities."[75] Nevertheless, he wrote his will and sent Germer a letter naming him his legatee and successor as OHO.

In January of 1942 a creative spasm inspired Crowley to write about "'our inbred fucked-out families' who are strangling us,"[76] resulting in the humorous political poem "Landed Gentry." He celebrated the January 30 completion of his first draft with a recital for his friends, who responded with laughter and cheers. As an encore, Crowley read an old favorite, "The City of God." When he finished, he smiled sentimentally and wept. After all these years the poem had lost none of its power.

On February 12 he found two more rhymes for "acity," added them to "Landed Gentry," and officially completed it. The next month, he met Mr. Green of the Chiswick Press to print it in waistcoat pocket–size format. Green, fearing trouble from the censor, would not take the job; nor would any other printer. Green did, however, estimate the tarot book, set in twelve-point type, quarto format, at £239 for one hundred copies or £281 for two hundred. That much money was unavailable, and Crowley knew he would have to set the book up in stages once funds became available.

With the tarot book slowly working its way to press, Crowley forged ahead with another book of poetry: his "greatest hits" with additional new material. He was decidedly cagey about the title, *Olla*. While it was Latin for "vase," he told Ethel Archer, "The meaning of Olla is, roughly, 'stew,' a Spanish dish."[77] Yet to Wilkinson, he attributed the name to Catullus's "particularly foul" epigram: *Ipsa olera olla legit* ("the pot gathers its own herbs").[78] In this instance, "Olla" referred to the vagina. Knowing Crowley, this last meaning is likely the correct one. Regardless, much of his energy went into composing new poems.

As spring warmed things up, Crowley's spirits lightened accordingly. He awoke Easter Sunday, stretched, and said, "Hail Eastre—goddess of Spring!"[79] At about that time, Gerald Hamilton, who was again sharing his flat, passed his open door. "Is that you, Gerald?" he called out. "Where are you going?"

"To mass and communion at St. James's," Ham answered.

"Well, I hope your god tastes nice; you're such a bloody gourmet."[80]

Circumstances incessantly delayed AC's California move: first, he could not afford passage; then the visa procedure for British citizens changed. The kicker came when Crowley cabled Germer that he was collecting together the order's archives. The message arrived as COLLECTING ARCHIES FRATERNITY. The Germers puzzled long and hard over this one, until one day Cora discovered that *archies* was slang for antiaircraft guns. Karl sat back, pondered this a while, and declared, "So, *that* makes it clear in a way, does it not?"[81]

Crowley sent Germer the following retraction on April 2: EQUINOX WORD KUSIS MEANING GREAT MOTHER GODDESS STOP ARCHIVES NOT ARCHIES STOP PERIQUE EARLIEST STOP HUNDRED RECEIVED STOP LOVE CROWLEY. The message contained the equinox word, the spelling correction, a request for more perique tobacco, and an acknowledgment of Germer's latest contribution to the Great Work. British censors, however, questioned Crowley about the cryptic telegram at least twice before sending it; then, on April 12, the American censor refused the telegram outright. Forced to submit another, Crowley responded with an ever more ridiculous telegram on July 18:

MEDICAL METEOROLOGICAL MIX-UP MORTALLY MENACES MAGNANI-
MOUS MORIBUND MAGUS MUSTN'T MARCH MAIDENHEAD. MAY MAR-
RIAGE MOVE MARY MOTHER MAIDEN MULTIPLY MELLIFLUOUS
MUNIFICENCES. MACGREGOR.

To his surprise, they accepted it.

By then, however, the damage was done. With the war waging in Europe and American citizens of Japanese descent being interred, official paranoia raged. The FBI was investigating persons visiting the U.S. from enemy nations, and on March 3 began a file on Germer. Karl was guilty of buying Crowley's books; his occult bookseller told the FBI that Germer admired Hitler's ideology and that Crowley was Hitler's advisor on black magic. These ridiculous claims confirmed the FBI's assessment of AC as "a notorious moral pervert."[82] Thus Germer's efforts to obtain a visa for Crowley looked suspicious. When that "cryptic" telegram arrived, the FBI repressed it and sealed their fates: despite supporting documentation from his doctor, C. H. Cranshaw, Crowley would never receive an American visa, and Germer would remain under investigation until July 1944.

The only bright spot for the order was Roy Leffingwell's plans to turn his property—Rancho Royal off Route 1 in Barstow, California—into a turkey farm and donate all profits to the tarot publication fund. Crowley's only complaint was over the ranch's logo: Roy preferred to replace the *A* with a stylized Western star, to which Crowley took exception:

> "Call yourself a cabalist? Bah! Poo! Here you are, with the Word in all its beauty and perfection, handed to you on a golden plate, the Key Word, the Word of Words, the Heart of the whole system of Thelema, and you deliberately mutilate it, deform it, make the title look like a fad, all for the sake of a measly two-penny ha'-penny mouldy, mangy Judeo-Christian two-bit pentagram. How artificial and how incomplete it looks, your Rancho Roy★l. No, no, no. In future, please, it's Rancho RoyAL."[83]

Crowley spent the next weeks moving from residence to residence, seeking a more or less permanent home. This inconvenience, however, was trivial compared to his tension with Frieda over the tarot. Although rationing inflated the cost of printing either the book or the cards, they remained committed to seeing the work through, often at cross purposes.

For instance, when he received a £15 contribution for printing the cards, AC sent it to Sun Engraving with instructions to add one more trump to the plates they were making. When he learned that two plates cost £20, he sent an additional £5 of his own money to get two cards done. All this was news to Frieda, who preferred the savings in printing four cards at a time. When she learned that Crowley had ordered two more plates set up, she feared she was losing control of the project and took all her originals back from Sun Engraving. She informed Crowley that she would permit nothing lest her business manager approved.

On May 18, with the approval of Frieda's manager, AC gave Green the tarot book manuscript with instructions to set up Part One.

That summer, Agape Lodge moved into a Victorian-style mansion at 1003 South Orange Grove in Pasadena, California, to their neighbors' dismay. This, Parsons's inheritance, was timely, as the owner of their former abode planned to demolish the building and erect a hotel. The mansion had three floors, sixteen rooms, five baths, and a cellar: just the place for the burgeoning lodge. Coinciding with the move, Smith left his job at the gas company, donating the $1,200 that he received from his employers to the household's general fund.

If Crowley's sources are to be trusted, they celebrated the move in grand style. "Have had to listen to things that really appalled me," Crowley complained. "That the Lodge was actually termed a whorehouse is the least. But what a low class of a whorehouse!"[84] To Crowley's dismay, the Agape Lodge also appeared to have stopped initiations and performances of the Gnostic Mass. Despite Crowley's inquiries about the status of the group, he received only conflicting reports—one rumor had Smith claiming the exalted A∴A∴ grades of Magister Templi and Magus. Another had Smith using his influence to induce women initiates into bed with him. Upon learning that Smith was sleeping with Soror Grimaud—Parsons's wife—and had gotten her pregnant, Crowley decided it was time for a shakedown. Smith had to go.

Crowley had sent a copy of *La Gauloise* ("The Gallic One")—his "England, Stand Fast!" for the French—to Charles de Gaulle and received a flattering letter from de Gaulle's aide that May. Encouraged, he revised the poem and gave it to Chiswick Press at the end of June for a print run of one thousand copies. These he distributed all over London. He wanted it broadcast on the BBC, but they insisted it first be put to music. Fortunately, Roy Leffingwell offered his arranging talents. Minor revisions followed when, on July 10, Germer pointed out two grammatical errors. "And after 5 Frenchmen had OK'd me, a German spots it!" Crowley laughed. "Symbolic? I fear so."[85] Next, he changed the name "from 'Free' to 'Fighting' French," and thus finished "La Gauloise."

Later in 1942 he received the music for "La Gauloise" from Leffingwell and arranged for a French baritone to record it. He retitled the song "L'Etincelle" ("The Spark") and anonymously sent the recording to the BBC, which played it on December 10. Later, AC would report even greater success with the song to Leffingwell: "McMurtry took your tune to Normandy, and there is a great premiere of La Gauloise in a town and on a date unnamed for security's sake."[86]

While Crowley worked on war poetry, Frieda rallied support for the tarot by appearing on radio talk shows and at lectures. On July 1 the Berkeley Galleries in London exhibited the cards. Despite their agreement to present the work anonymously, the exhibition credited her as the artist … with no mention of Crowley. In addition, a new catalog for the show was put together, containing a number of serious errors that AC considered amateurish and feared would disrcredit the work. "No word of credit to the Order," he complained. "She has no self-respect." He nevertheless found comfort in knowing the deck was unmistakably his design: the XX (The Aeon) card he identified as the Crowley coat of arms, and the Ace of Disks, which traditionally bore the artist's signature, was inscribed with the name TO MEGA THERION.[87]

An August 4 exhibit at the Royal Society of Painters in Water Colours on Conduit Street followed the Berkeley Galleries exhibition. Learning of this show, Crowley remarked, "Again, she didn't tell me."[88] He feared Frieda was stealing all the credit for their work, and his friends encouraged this perception. Thus Crowley appeared unexpectedly at the exhibit's opening on August 4, confronting a stupefied Frieda Harris, who stammered something about how she had just sent him a letter about the show. Coolly, he replied, "I knew about it on Saturday morning." It was difficult to stay angry at her, however. Aside from the "abominable Mercury" on the program's cover, Crowley thought the show was perfect. Aside from printing, the tarot project was essentially done (barring minor details). When Crowley moved into 93 Jermyn Street, just off London's Piccadilly Circus, that November, Frieda began weaning Crowley off his £2 weekly stipend; since Germer had sent Crowley around £800 in 1942 alone, he managed.

On November 4 Old Crow dug out his poem "The Fun of the Fair." Lamenting that it never appeared as scheduled in the October 1914 *English Review,* he decided to publish it for Christmas. Dedicating it to Karl's new wife, Sascha—whom he married on September 23, about two months after Cora's death—he sent the manuscript to Louis Wilkinson for an introduction, then to Chiswick Press for printing. He tried to sneak "Landed Gentry" into *Fun of the Fair,* but Chiswick still rejected it. He finally made copies at a local duplicating place and would insert them loose into the booklet himself.

Toward the end of the month he wrote a prospectus for the poem, claiming "This book will be as expensive and nice as this prospectus is cheap and nasty." He also had a photographer named Churchill take his portrait for the booklet. By November 30 the proofs and the photographs were ready. Three weeks later, on December 22, 1942, at 11:31 a.m.—the winter solstice—Crowley ceremonially published *The Fun of the Fair.* It was published by OTO, whose address was given as "Rancho RoyAL, Route I, Barstow, Cal., USA and at 93 Jermyn Street, London SW1."

Crowley's portrait from *Fun of the Fair* (1942).

CHAPTER TWENTY-TWO

The Great Turkey Tragedy: Or Heirs Apparent

The year 1943 brought support from Agape Lodge in an American edition of *The Book of the Law,* a proposed resuscitation of *The Oriflamme* magazine, and "parcels of food and not-so-food,"[1] a problem that Crowley eased with the following telegram to Regina Kahl: "ORDER DISAPPROVES CHEMICAL TREATMENT FOODSTUFFS DISAPPROVES SEALED CANS INSISTS CLOSEST APPROXIMATION NATURAL STATE."[2] Meanwhile, he anxiously awaited the news of Leffingwell's turkey ranch, the proceeds of which were earmarked for Crowley's trip to America and OTO's publication fund. "I keep on hanging around day after day in the hope of hearing something about these unfortunate turkeys," Crowley wrote in February of 1943.[3] Alas, the Thelemic turkeys suffered some catastrophe that required their immediate slaughter or sale. With this tragedy, Crowley's American publication fund vanished.

In other order business, Crowley entrusted Jane Wolfe, his disciple of twenty-three years, to carry out orders to depose Smith. Although she had defended the lodge master in the past, she obediently complied with AC's wishes, writing Smith on January 13:

> Pursuant to instructions from Baphomet, it is my duty to inform you that, for the time being, you will be relieved from your function in the Lodge, and that you will retire from the Community House at 1003 South Orange Grove Avenue, Pasadena. Your full reinstatement will follow the achievement of some definite personal action conceived and executed by yourself alone to the advancement of the work of the Order.[4]

The other lodge members, as loyal to Smith as they were to Crowley, objected. Parsons begged Baphomet to reconsider, stressing that the lodge was coming along well and that this division of authority would upset everything. Even Smith began a vitriolic exchange with Crowley on his own behalf:

> In 1936 I was a whoremonger, dishonest, a black magician.... Now I am a clown, vile, and have a swelled head. Personally, I cannot take these criticisms too seriously because I do not take myself too seriously because the

accusations are so positively stupid and false.... You seem so often to be responsible for the continual disturbances. Just as we are trying our hardest to get out a small monthly publication of dignity and quality which we hope will please you, got a quotation on it, figured how we can squeeze it into our expenses, you let fly another charge of buckshot or tell somebody else to. I say, "Hell, what's the use!", write a few strongly worded letters, throw them in the fire, clench my teeth, and make another effort. Oh, yes, feeble if you will: We are not all A.C.s.[5]

Crowley responded by criticizing Smith for sending lodge reports irregularly and for lacking the proper stature to act as priest in the Gnostic Mass. AC, who sought a Hollywood production of the rite, imagined someone with more stage presence. "I do not think that in 20 years or more you contributed more than £150 at the very outside."[6] This accusation was completely false, and ignited an angry spate of hostility between them. "Wherever Smith was," Crowley complained, "there was a ferment about A objecting to B sleeping with C because D wanted E to sleep with F and so on through the alphabet about six times round. In the early days in California, the only letters I ever got were asking me to settle all sorts of rather dirty complications."[7]

Yet another problem arose that spring when the FBI scrutinized Jack Parsons's OTO membership. Because he worked on classified projects for the government, his ties to a group "alleged to have been involved in immoral activities"[8] concerned them. Parsons explained that the Church of Thelema, which he had joined three years previously, was a small fraternity modeled after England's Order of Oriental Templars. Their ideologies, he assured them, opposed communism and fascism, and agreed entirely with the war effort. "We are entirely tolerant and concerned with the brotherhood of all mankind, and dedicated to individual freedom and liberty." The investigators searched the lodge with Smith's permission, including his correspondence with AC, and found nothing subversive.

Crowley pushed on with *Olla* for the first months of 1943, hoping for its ceremonial publication on the spring equinox. When informed in February that Chiswick couldn't possibly have an entire book ready by then, AC decided, "Fine, we'll do *The City of God* instead. It will save me a lot of immediate cash."[9] It would also make a nice companion to "The Fun of the Fair." So, Churchill prepared a new set of photo proofs, and on March 13, Crowley finished the dedication and preface. By then, however, it was too late to set up and print *The City of God* by the equinox; they were already quite busy with the tarot book. Anxious to release the book on an auspicious date, Crowley took the delays ungraciously. "Chiswick Press calmly announces 'City' not ready 'till Wednesday next!" he noted in his journal for April 15, 1943. "What bastards of bastards!"[10] The book finally appeared on April 20, in a format uniform with the gray paper covers of *Fun of the Fair* and in a limited edition of two hundred. From there, he continued with other book projects.

Crowley from *The City of God* (1943).

While revising his text for the small tarot cards that summer, the solution to his problems with Smith occurred to him: it was, in a word, apotheosis. W. T. Smith was not a man but a god. AC decided that Smith's astrological chart indicated a latent deity within him, and that realizing his divinity would require a protracted Great Magical Retirement, during which time he could have contact with nobody but Germer. While Smith retired to the desert to live in a shack, meditating until the god within him spoke, Parsons would take charge of Agape Lodge. Crowley sent these instructions to Smith as "Liber Apotheosis" and telegrammed instructions to Agape Lodge that Smith was off limits under threat of expulsion. Proud of his scheme to dump Smith and appoint young Jack Parsons as the new lodge master, Crowley bragged to Max Schneider, "I had Machiavelli under my pillow and dreamed it."[11]

Smith recognized "Apotheosis" as an inelegant plan to depose him yet had no choice but to comply. Frater 132 withdrew to the desert on June 3, bringing the letters Crowley had sent him over the years. At age fifty-eight—having devoted the last thirty-seven years of his life to seeking occult wisdom, twenty-nine years after helping Achad found the original Agape Lodge in Vancouver—he finally gave up. On August 13, Wilfred T. Smith left the desert for the mundane world.[12]

Having moved to Piccadilly Circus under the assumption that the bombings in London had stopped, Old Crow was dismayed when they resumed that spring. By summer they got so bad that Hamilton left the city. Lord Evan Tredegar, an MI5 acquaintance and student of magick who was pouring his wealth into properly outfitting a temple, invited AC to stay with him. On June 17, 1943, having sent "Apotheosis" to California, he left for Tredegar Park. The lord was working on his own tarot book, and the occultists passed time comparing notes. Of his host, Crowley wrote, "He's one of the very few people I know who *can* throw a party," and "Tredegar owns 121,000 acres in S. Wales (mostly coal) and whole streets in London (mostly bombed)."[13] During his stay, AC also befriended Cordelia Sutherland (1894–1980). Born Emily Cordelia Landers, she married John J. Sutherland at Middlesex in 1926 and worked for the past fourteen years as Tredegar's housekeeper, secretary, and manager.[14] Being released when Tredegar sold his country home, she began a long correspondence with AC, occasionally sending powdered chocolate and plover's eggs his way. After staying for two weeks in Tredegar's best room, Crowley returned to London to continue his tarot work.

At the end of October a gray and withered Crowley answered a knock on the door of his 93 Jermyn Street apartment. Standing before him was a young American army captain with round glasses, a mustache, and a smirk. "News from the front indeed!" Crowley remarked.[15] Grady McMurtry—along with the rest of his ROTC class—had been called to active duty in February 1942. Since the Italian government had surrendered to the Allies on September 3, 1943, McMurtry was on leave from the 1803rd and decided to visit the master. During his visits in the following weeks—when he and AC generally talked late into the night—he met Yorke, Harris, and Wilkinson. Although his visits only numbered about six in all, he endeared himself greatly to AC, loaning him £50 and buying copies of his books. He was young yet level-headed, a breath of reason amidst the California madness. Crowley seized the opportunity to advance him to the IX°, skipping the II° through the VIII°. As a IX° member, Grady needed a magical motto but uncertain about a fitting one, he deferred to AC. Agonizing over the matter, Crowley came up with the Greek motto "Hymenaeus Alpha," which added up to the mystical number 777.

At this time, Crowley offered McMurtry a fifty percent share of the tarot book in exchange for a $200 investment. AC figured he could defray the prohibitive cost of publishing *Olla* by having Chiswick buy an extra-large stock of paper for the tarot book at a better discount and use the surplus to print *Olla*. By the end of March 1944, McMurtry accepted the offer.

Grady Louis McMurtry (1918–1985).

As 1943 drew to a close, AC's projects became even more ambitious and consuming. Besides *Olla* and the tarot he encouraged his friends to ask him for letters of instruction on remedial points of magick; these he hoped to collect and publish under the working title of *Aleister Explains Everything*. Questions posed to Crowley ranged from "Do angels cut themselves shaving?" to "Why accept so revolting a book as *Liber AL?*" Its writing filled most of the months to follow and would take years to complete.

Early in 1944 some metaphysical literature distributed by Dr. William Bernard Crow (1895–1976) caught his attention. Crow was a lecturer in biology for several colleges, the latest being South West Essex Technical College. Educated at the University of London, he was a fellow of the Royal Society of Medicine, Linnean Society, and Zoological Society of London.[16] He wrote extensively not only on biology but also on many occult topics[17] and was a contributor to the *Occult Review*.[18] He was also connected with various spiritual groups like the Institute for Cosmic Studies and the Ancient Orthodox Catholic Church; on June 13, 1943, he was consecrated bishop as Mar Basilius Abdullah III, enabling him to act as autocephalous head of his own church, the Order of the Holy Wisdom or *Ekklesia Agiae Sophiae*. The purpose of this church was to teach the "Orthodox Catholic Faith" to occultists in their own vernacular. According to one of his fliers, the church incorporated the traditions of the Hindus, kabbalists, gnostics, Zoroastrians, Rosicrucians, Druids, Buddhists and Sufis.

When Crowley sent him comments in early February, a correspondence ensued. Crow was a serious and knowledgeable student of the occult, was curious about Crowley's Memphis-Mizraim lineage, and wished to work the Gnostic Mass. Before long, Crow's advisor, Hugh George de Willmott Newman (b. 1905), also known as the Archbishop Mar Georgius I, Metropolitan of Glastonbury in the Catholicate of the West,[19] contacted Crowley to negotiate an authorization. The EGC and Gnostic Mass were particularly sacred to Crowley, and he felt Crow out carefully before granting anything. Crowley was amused by these *episcopi vagantes,* or wandering bishops: Crow reportedly kept a statue of Buddha that he called St. Jehosaphat.[20] Newman, meanwhile, signed his name with numerous titles and initials.

The Beast yawned elaborately. Mottoes and titles had long since failed to impress him, ever since he filled pages of *The Equinox* with all the titles conferred upon him after the Mathers lawsuit. Masonic authority and succession, another of their concerns, were subjects that bored Crowley even more. He nevertheless strived to set them on the right path. About the EGC, Crowley said, "I never wrote any rituals of ordination and such things, and I am certainly not going to start at my time of life. The people in America go on perfectly well without anything of the sort."[21] Regarding the Mass, he advised, "Keep one eye fixed firm on Hollywood. You mustn't have a Priest with a squeak or a drone or a drawling, and you mustn't cast some frightful hag as the Virgin Harlot. The furniture, robes, etc. may at first be severely plain, but as pestilence is the pretentious, the theatrical or the tawdry."[22]

Crow pursued this for a while, distributing flyers to drum up interest in the Mass, but he and Newman eventually parted. In Crowley's mind the doctor had a ways to go. "You are quite wrong in thinking that *The Wizard of Oz* has anything to do with me," he told Crow. "That was the title of a film which I did not see, but I could not change the title of my book because … Hollywood chose to pinch the word."[23] To be fair, L. Frank Baum's (1856–1919) *The Wonderful Wizard of Oz,* on which the movie is based, came out in 1900, the year of the GD revolt against Mathers and over forty years before Crowley penned *Liber Oz.* Ironically, a few years later the film came to Hastings while Crowley was living at Netherwood House; AC very much wanted to see it, only to be told by the proprietress, "It wouldn't interest you at all, it's a children's thing."[24]

The year 1944 started off with a bang as intense air raids frequently shook Crowley's abode. As he wrote to Louis Wilkinson, "My nerves just went with a bang."[25] His diaries record many episodes, including the following:

> Blast knocked house about quite a little. Other tenants behaved very well (i.e., they go to the kitchen & huddle, & 'make cheerful talk': They cannot bear to be alone: it comforts them to hold each others' hands! They depressed me almost more than the company of such people normally does).[26]

Shortly after he received an eviction notice on February 16, a bomb landed 250 yards southwest of 93 Jermyn, leveling most of King and Duke streets. Ducking outside to look, Crowley stepped into a hailstorm of rubble and shrapnel. When he sought shelter indoors and started upstairs, an explosion blew the lock off the door and knocked him over.

Although Crowley tried fairly successfully to maintain a normal lifestyle, the constant raids took their toll. Driven north of London on April 8, he took a room at the famous Bell Inn at Aston Clinton, Buckinghamshire. It was a stately seventeenth century country hotel with twenty rooms, huge bathtubs, a large open fire, and a talented cook; Crowley however felt far from his friends, bored, and lonely.

That spring he prepared an eight-page prospectus for the tarot book, officially dubbed *The Book of Thoth,* and began selling subscriptions in May. He enthusiastically claimed "These cards, with the explanatory Essay, are destined to be the Atlas and Practical manual of all Magick for the next 2,000 years."[27] He found takers in McMurtry, Sutherland, Tredegar, and Bayley as well as E. N. Fitzgerald, Dion Fortune, and others. Yorke even contributed £100 toward publication costs. These prospectuses were the source of some concern after they were mailed, owing to wartime rationing. As AC wrote:

> it seems that I may have technically infringed one of those fool regulations about sending out prospectuses free of charge, but luckily *The Book of Thoth* is No 5 of Vol III of *The Equinox,* which constitutes it a periodical and therefore not subject to the paper control at all. Of course it is very trivial and technical: but considering how I have been framed up in the past, and how many wolves are out after my blood, I must confess to more than a little apprehension.[28]

Crowley needn't have worried, as his publication appeared without incident.

Although *The Book of Thoth* gives a publication date on the spring equinox of 1944, Crowley was still signing the unbound sheets that August; indeed, he arranged with legendary bookbinders Sangorski and Sutcliffe to bind the books as orders arrived; hence not all copies were bound at the same time. Nevertheless, the signed and numbered edition did appear that year. In November, Crowley expressed delight at the initial sales of the book: "To my amazement I have sold over fifty copies of *The Book of Thoth.* If you had told me six months ago I would have said, in my most optimistic mood, that I could get rid of a dozen."[29] It was a spectacular book, with eleven copies bound in half morocco leather and the rest in quarter-leather, gilt-samped with the OTO logo and seal of Ankh-f-n-Khonsu on the spine. It was printed on mold-made paper, which was not only elegant but also exempt from wartime paper restrictions. The book contained nine color plates of the cards, technical appendices, and a bibliographic note (by Crowley but attributed to Martha Küntzel). Authorship was attributed to "The Master Therion," with Frieda Harris listed as artist executant. Crowley inscribed her copy,

To my dearest Sister TzBA 93,

> My admired accomplice in the perpetration of this atrocity....

To Mega Therion 666[30]

The book has since become the definitive work on the tarot and has enjoyed many reprintings. Although test printings of several cards were made at this time, the deck was was not printed in either collaborator's lifetime despite repeated attempts. The first color edition was produced by Llewellyn in 1971.[31]

The fall of 1944 was also notable not for anything that Crowley accomplished but for a fascinating glimpse of what could have been. The American OTO members were still hoping to import Old Crow to California, and a new twist developed: Jean Schneider was working as a housekeeper for film director Orson Welles (1915–1985). She sent AC the book for *Citizen Kane;* although the 1941 film—which Welles wrote, directed, and performed in—is considered by many the best movie ever made, it was a financial failure in its theatrical release. Schneider hinted that Welles was interested in magick. In December she sent the telegram GAVE ORSON WELLES MORTADELLO. Crowley must have been excited, as this was the play he had been shopping around to producers for years. He also asked her to give him "Across the Gulf" and *The Three Wishes* to consider for screenplays.[32] Alas, no movie deals were forthcoming.

During his last visit, McMurtry accompanied Crowley on a drive along the Seine up to the cathedral town of Chartres. AC had already called him "the most serious and intelligent of the younger lot.... This singles you out as the proper man to take charge of affairs when the time is ripe. It is supremely important that you should understand fully the 9th degree...."[33] Now—having participated in the Invasion of Normandy and the liberation of France and Belgium—McMurtry was again visiting. As they drove, they discussed the future of OTO, Crowley spoke for the first time of the office of Caliph. Denoting the successor to a prophet in Islam, such a position exists in none of the official OTO documents, its charter, the blue *Equinox,* or anywhere else. Thus, when Crowley later referred to the Caliphate in an October 16 letter to McMurtry, the puzzled serviceman replied, "As for the Caliphate, I remember no concrete proposal—just a vague reference once."[34] Crowley responded at length:

> "The Caliphate." You must realize that no matter how closely we may see eye-to-eye on any objective subject, I have to think on totally different premises where the Order is concerned. One of the (startlingly few) commands given to me was this: "Trust not a stranger: fail not of an heir." This has been the very devil for me. Frater Saturnus is of course the natural Caliph; but there are many details concerning the actual policy or working which hit his blind spots. In any case, he can only be a stopgap, because of his age; I have to look for *his* successor. It has been hell; so many have come up with amazing promise, only to go on the rocks....

But—now here is where you have missed my point altogether—I do not think of you as lying on a grassy hillside with a lot of dear sweet lovely woolly lambs, capering to your flute! On the contrary. Your actual life, or "blooding," is the sort of initiation which I regard as the first essential for a Caliph. For—say 20 years hence—the Outer Head of the Order must, among other things, have had the experience of war as it is an actual fact to-day.[35]

Just as Crowley left behind a son and a publishing program, he also planned a line of succession. He gave McMurtry "more solid instruction in IX° than I ever gave before to any one."[36] He was grooming McMurtry for bigger things.

"It is infinitely dark, dull, damp, depressing, dirty, drear, dead and decomposing in this hideous hell-hole," he wrote of the Bell Inn when the bombings and loneliness became too much,[37] and he asked Louis Wilkinson to help him find a new home. It turned out that his son, Oliver, knew E. C. Vernon Symonds through the Hastings Court Players. Symonds was an ex-alcoholic, actor, and playwright who in 1930 wrote *The Legend of Abd-El-Krim*.[38] He and his wife Kathleen, who went by the name "Johnny," had turned a gloomy Victorian mansion into an "intellectual guest house" named Netherwood. They tempted various luminaries to come for a visit and offer a talk to the other guests in exchange for a free room and meals. Some of their speakers included philosopher and broadcaster C. E. M. Joad (1891–1953), geneticist and evolutionary biologist J. B. S. Haldane (1892–1964), aristocrat and communist Edith Hajós Bone (1889–1975), and mathematician and biologist Jacob Bronowski (1908–1974). In addition, a young Julian Bream (b. 1933) occasionally played classical guitar for the guests.[39]

Surrounded by four wooded acres and located on the Ridge, the highest point of Hastings at an elevation of five hundred feet, it offered panoramic views of the town, the sea, and Crowley's childhood haunt, Beachy Head. It was the perfect place for an aging magician to retire, with Symonds's house rules reading:

> Guests are requested not to tease the Ghosts.
> Guests are requested to be as quiet as possible while dying of fright.
> Breakfast will be served at 9 a.m. to the survivors of the Night.
> The Hastings Borough Cemetery is five minutes walk away (ten minutes if carrying body), but it is only one minute as the Ghost flies.
> Guests are requested not to dig graves on lawns, but to make full use of newly filled graves under trees.
> Guests are requested not to remove corpses from graves or to cut down bodies from trees.
> The Office has a certain amount of used clothing for sale, the property of guests who have no longer any use for earthly raiment.[40]

Also staying at Netherwood House was world-famed chess champion Edward Mackenzie Jackson (1867–1959), eleven-time winner of the Hastings Chess Club Championship.[41] There was also another skilled player named Kirk.

In advance of his arrival, Crowley reputedly telegrammed Netherwood House to expect a consignment of frozen meat. This rather perplexed the Symondses, who had placed no such order. All became clear when Crowley arrived on the appointed day in an ambulance. bearing his belongings, He insisted on having room number 13.[42] He moved in on January 17, 1945, lining his small room with his books and paintings. In gratitude, he sent a box of cigars to Oliver. When Oliver smoked them all before realizing they were the world's most expensive cigars, Crowley sent him a second box.

Netherwood House, The Ridge, Hastings, where Crowley spent his last years.

Kenneth Grant (b. 1924) had a dream in 1939 of a powerful magical symbol and its associated name, spelled variously A'ashik, Oshik, or Aossic. Becoming a young student of magick three years later, he adopted the emblem and nomen. He had tried in vain to reach Crowley through the address given in *Magick,* which was over a decade old at the time. Then, when *The Book of Thoth* appeared in 1944, Michael Houghton refused to give him AC's current address, fearing young Grant to be "mentally unstable";[43] Grant presumed that Houghton merely wanted to recruit him into his own Society of Hidden Masters.[44] He persevered and finally tracked down Crowley at the Bell Inn, where he first visited and met the master in late 1944. During these years, Grant had, volunteered for the army at age eighteen and by age twenty was invalided from service for an unspecified medical condition.[45]

Through the winter of 1945, Grant sent letters and books to Crowley. Thus when Crowley decided at the end of February that he needed a secretary, this eager young student, as Regardie before him, seemed the logical choice.

What Grant lacked in secretarial skills he made up for in exuberance. "I made a bargain with Symonds," Crowley wrote. "It's supposed to cost me £1.0.0 a week to have him here."[46] Accepting the offer, Grant arranged to join Crowley on March 9. On the appointed day he wired Crowley that he had been delayed and would arrive on Sunday, March 11. He finally appeared on March 12.

Using ether as an aid, Crowley taught Grant astral projection until he could obtain similar, although less spectacular, results without drugs.[47] He was a good student, and Crowley saw great promise in him. "I am trying to get him to look after me and my work," he wrote to Louis Wilkinson. "A definite gift from the Gods."[48] Grant, however, was far from home and pining for his lady love; in addition, as he recalls, "I was unable ever to acquire a practical approach to mundane affairs … which so exasperated Crowley."[49] Thus, AC's patience for Grant wore thin. When Grant disingenuously tried convincing his employer to return to London, Crowley mused, "The murderer's puzzle, how to get rid of the body, has been on my nerves for the last two days."[50] Two weeks later, Crowley's tongue sharpened and, during an argument with Grant, he blurted, "You are the most consummate BORE that the world has yet known. And this at 20!"[51] Later, however, Crowley reflected, "I feel that I may have treated him too severely."[52]

On April 11, Crowley certified McMurtry a IX° member of OTO and owner of twenty-five percent of the copyright of "Aleister Explains Everything," now officially *Magick without Tears*. A greater honor fell on him when Crowley expressed his umbrage over the situation in California and the contradictory accounts he received by mail. "I may be the world's greatest magician, but I need *some* facts to go on!"

"Well," Grady suggested, "you know me, and I know them. When I get home, I'll survey the situation and write you a report." Crowley thereupon appointed him Sovereign Grand Inspector General of the Order.[53]

The months that followed were tumultuous: President Roosevelt died on April 12 during his fourth term in office, Russian troops entered Berlin eight days later, Mussolini was assassinated on April 28, and Hitler committed suicide shortly thereafter. The Allies announced victory in Europe on May 8.

Days after Hitler was announced dead, AC gave Grant the sketch that had accompanied his commentary on "The Voice of the Silence" in the blue *Equinox*. Then, on May 14, Grant announced that he was returning to London. This angered Crowley, but also came as a bit of a relief.

> In London he had been A1; here he broke down altogether. Memory went west; you couldn't trust him to do anything; he would leave me with the impression that he had done it when he had shelved it or forgotten altogether. Then, silly things like signing & posting letters that should have come to me fair-copied for revision & signature. He got worse every week.[54]

After returning to London, Grant helped AC oversee business there. May 16, the day of Grant's departure, would be the last time he would see Crowley alive. That June, AC complained to Wilkinson that he was still "dog-tired try-ing to clean up after Grant!"[55]

It was difficult for Crowley to fault him for wanting to be with his love. Looking back over his own romantic conquests, Crowley listed eighty names he could recall and saw how devoid of true love most of them were. "Hence-forth," he solemnly vowed, "I, Perdurabo, whose benign bum now permits him to stroll the streets of Hastings, shall never fail to tip my hat to every court-ing couple I encounter."[56]

During the goings-on with Grant and McMurtry, the *Occult Review* published a six-page appreciation of AC titled "Aleister Crowley, Poet and Occultist." Its author, Frederick Henry Amphlett Micklewright (1908–1992), was an Angli-can priest (1935) and fellow of the Royal Historical Society who had been educated at Oxford and the Anglican theological college Ripon Hall. Inter-ested in unusual forms of religion, he contributed a series of articles to the *Occult Review* during the 1940s; his article on Crowley was quite laudatory:

> It is not always the case that the poems of occultists are essential to an understanding of their work. But Aleister Crowley is fundamentally an art-ist. He is a creative personality, expressing his individuality in terms of rhythm. His sense of the rhythmic, which ultimately implies the sense of a fundamental beauty, is aptly expressed whether in prose or in verse; his art is a necessary entrance to an understanding of his occultism.[57]

Crowley might have missed the article had W. B. Crow not asked if he'd seen the latest issue. Crowley responded, "I have not seen a copy of the *Occult Review,* unless by accident, since [Ralph] Shirley left it [in 1925]. I did not know that it printed anything serious at all nowadays."[58] Even so, it appears from his diary that AC did not see the article until 1946. He was very pleased, writing to Crow that Amphlett Micklewright "has done a *supreme* thing; he has shown a coherent and consistent *pattern* in my work from first to last.... He has shown me what I didn't know about myself."[59] He told his student Frederick Mellinger that it was the "best thing that's happened to me in 100 years!"[60]

The world would never be the same after July 16, 1945. That day, the first atomic bomb test occurred in New Mexico; weeks later on August 6, the United States dropped an atomic bomb on Hiroshima. Crowley pondered if this was the war engine mentioned in *The Book of the Law,* writing to Louis Wilkinson, "The 'Atomic Bomb' is interesting, not only because of *Liber AL* III.7–8, but because one of the men who were working on it was for some time at the Abbey in Cefalù."[61] After the second bomb fell on Nagasaki, AC left a cryptic entry in his diary:

> O.T.O. Ophidian vibrations. Non-filterable virus. X-ray dermatitis. "Gal-loping cancer." Amrita. NUITh Nitrogen Uranium Iodine (& sea-life) The-riumm = New Atom 666. Atomic No.: 93. H A D 6 plus 5 A D = He.[62]

A cold, black sky scowled at the world on New Year's Day 1946. Professor E. M. Butler looked out her train window at the turbulent sea, too nervous to prepare to interview Aleister Crowley for her book *The Myth of the Magus*. Crowley's reputation was as enormous as it was sinister, and she feared the inclement weather was somehow wound up with his evil.

Eliza Marian Butler (1885–1959) was the third of seven Anglo-Irish children to Theobald Fitzwalter Butler (1845–1914) and Catherine Elizabeth Barraclough (d. 1946). Educated at Newnham College (Cambridge) and Bonn University, she became a lecturer at her alma mater in 1914, where she would remain for much of her career, writing books on language and literature, especially German. From 1936 she was professor of German at Manchester University, but returned to Cambridge in 1945, where she remained until her 1951 retirement. She would be Professor Emeritus at Cambridge and receive an honorary doctorate in literature from Oxford in 1958.[63]

She was surprised to arrive at Hastings to find not the Prince of Darkness but a polite and friendly scarecrow of a septuagenarian. "Do what thou wilt shall be the whole of the Law," he greeted her. "And a Happy New Year to you, Miss Butler." After Crowley's lunchtime discussion of Thelema failed to impress her, they retired to his room for cognac and the interview. She did it in two sessions: from lunch until high tea, then again that evening.

Butler had a structuralist model of the myth of the magus, much as Claude Lévi-Strauss (1908–2009) had developed the traditional pattern of the hero myth. According to her research, great magi usually claimed a supernatural birth, with a childhood surrounded by portents and perils, and so on. Crowley denied these traits but admitted having undergone initiations. He cited the GD and his contact with Aiwass as instances of these. When Butler asked about a period of questing to distant lands for occult knowledge, Crowley listed his voyages to Mexico, India, Ceylon, Burma, Egypt, and China.

"Have you had a contest with a rival magician?" she asked him.

"Never," he answered proudly. "I have no rival."

When asked about having blinding visions of beauty, glory, and truth, Crowley readily agreed. He took up *The Book of the Law* and read:

> Behold! the rituals of the old time are black. Let the evil ones be cast away; let the good be purged by the prophet! Then shall this Knowledge go aright. I am the flame that burns in every heart of man, and in the core of every star. I am Life and the giver of Life, yet therefore is the knowledge of me the knowledge of death. I am the Magician and the Exorcist.

When Butler looked up from her note-taking, she saw him crying. Wiping his eyes with his hand, he whispered, "It was a revelation of love."

Crowley was a gentleman, escorting her back to her hotel and paying for her meals at Netherwood; he would later send her Frieda Harris's "Punch and Judy" sketches as a gift. Butler nevertheless sneaked away from Netherwood early the next morning, shuddering as if she had just vacated a shunned house; she later confessed to Yorke that the Beast had frightened her. His statement "Magic is not *a* way of life, it is *the* way of life" echoed menacingly in her head, and she wrote only a couple of sentences about him in *The Myth of the Magus.*

Ironically, AC described their meeting in an entirely different light: "Professor Butler of Newnham came ... and talked *(and made me talk)* with such sympathy, consideration, and understanding that the day was a dream of joy!"[64] It was a pleasant change from his incessant sickness and chronic depression.

He spent the next months correcting *Olla,* sending the finished proofs to Guys on March 25. When he wrote his old friend Augustus John to request a sketch for the book, the artist gladly obliged and planned to visit that summer. "So glad to hear you keep signing 'do what thou wilt,'" he wrote. "How right you are."[65] With that settled, Crowley took up one other project: prodding Wilkinson to edit a popular edition of *The Book of the Law* and its comment.

After Helen jilted him in 1945, Jack Parsons transferred his affections to her sister, Sara Elizabeth Northrup (1924–1997). Known as Betty, she was a student at the University of Southern California, although she soon dropped out and moved in with Jack, becoming his partner in sex magick rituals.

In August of 1945, L. Ron Hubbard appeared on the scene. He had not yet written on Scientology, for which he is best known; at this time he was known simply as a science fiction writer and naval lieutenant. Lafayette Ronald Hubbard (1911–1986) was born in Tilden, Nebraska, to a military family and moved around a lot as a child. He attended George Washington University but, more interested in contributing to the school newspaper and literary journals, he left after two years without taking a degree. During the 1930s he published several novels and dozens of short stories in pulp magazines like *Astounding Science Fiction* and *Unknown Worlds,* becoming well-known in the science fiction and fantasy communities. He had entered the navy in 1941 and served for four years. When science fiction illustrator Lou Goldstone, a frequent visitor to the mansion on Orange Grove, introduced him to Agape Lodge, Parsons, a fan of science fiction, befriended Hubbard. Together with Betty, they soon founded the company "Allied Enterprises" to buy yachts on the east coast and sail them to California, where they could be resold at a profit.[66]

Their friendship became strained, however, when Hubbard, although married, began sleeping with Betty. As Parsons described:

> About three months ago I met Ron ... a writer and explorer of whom I had known for some time.... He is a gentleman; he has red hair, green eyes, is honest and intelligent, and we have become great friends. He moved in with me about two months ago, and although Betty and I are still friendly, she has transferred her sexual affections to Ron.

> Although Ron has no formal training in magick, he has an extraordinary amount of experience and understanding in the field. From some of his experiences I deduce that he is in direct touch with some higher intelligence, possibly his guardian angel. Ron appears to have some sort of highly developed astral vision. He described his angel as a beautiful winged woman with red hair, whom he calls the Empress, and who has guided him through his life, and saved him many times.[67]

Twice jilted, Parsons began on January 4, 1946, a series of rituals known as the Babalon Working. He wished to summon an air elemental and thereby cause Babalon to be born in this world. The workings involved a variety of systems, including the Enochian tablet of air, the invoking ritual of the pentagram and the Augoeides. In the Mojave Desert on January 18, while conducting another of the rituals with Hubbard, Parsons watched the setting sun and declared flatly, "It is done." Returning to Agape Lodge, Parsons found a new visitor there: Marjorie Cameron. He concluded his ritual had been a success.

Marjorie Cameron Parsons Kimmel (1922–1995) was born on April 22, 1922, in Belle Plaine, Iowa.[68] She was the first of four children to a churchgoing family whose father, Hill L. Cameron (1902–1962), was a railroad worker.[69] After graduating from Davenport High School in 1940—finding her artistic and mystical bent at odds with her small-town community—she enlisted in the Navy, where she worked in a photographic unit and drew maps. During the war she learned that her brother James, a tail-gunner, had been injured in action and rushed back home to Iowa to be by his side; declared AWOL, she was confined to base from the time of her return until her honorable discharge in 1945. From there she, along with her family, resettled in Pasadena. No longer a map-drawer, she began working as a fashion illustrator. Shortly thereafter she met Jack Parsons.[70]

For the next nine days, Parsons performed a series of invocations of Babalon, for which Hubbard acted as scribe. Shortly thereafter, on February 28, Parsons was back in the Mojave Desert, where he received *The Book of Babalon,* ostensibly the fourth chapter to *The Book of the Law.* When Cameron became pregnant, Parsons concluded she would give birth to Babalon.

Describing his success to Crowley, Parsons attributed his devastating success to "the IX° working with the girl who answered my elemental summons.... I have been in direct touch with One who is most Holy and Beautiful, mentioned in *The Book of the Law*."[71] AC's reply was lukewarm:

> I am particularly interested in what you have written to me about the elemental, because for some little time past I have been endeavoring to intervene *personally* in this matter on your behalf. I would however have you recall Lévi's aphorism: 'The love of the Magus for such things is insensate and destroys him.'[72]

With Germer, he was more candid: "Apparently he ... is producing a Moonchild. I get fairly frantic when I contemplate the idiocy of these louts."[73] In the midst of escalating problems with Agape Lodge, Crowley gave McMurtry the following document:

> This is to authorize Frater Hymenaeus Alpha (Capt. Grady L. McMurtry) to take charge of the whole work of the Order in California to reform the Organization in pursuance of his report of January 25, '46 e.v. subject to the approval of Frater Saturnus (Karl J. Germer). This authorization is to be used only in emergency.[74]

He followed this letter with another stating, "These presents are to appoint Frater Hymenaeus Alpha, Grady Louis McMurtry IX° O.T.O., as Our representative in the United States of America and his authority is to be considered as Ours, subject to the approval, revision, or veto of Our Viceroy, Karl Johannes Germer IX° O.T.O."[75] These documents assured Crowley that if everything in Pasadena crashed, McMurtry was empowered to step in and put it back together. "I think it is best to leave as much in your hands as possible," Crowley told him, "as you are more or less on the spot and appear to be full of youth and energy as ever."[76]

The time soon arrived for Allied Enterprises to purchase its first yacht, and Jack agreed that Ron and Betty would take $10,000 of his money to the East Coast, buy the boat, and sail it back to California. Unbeknownst to Parsons, Hubbard had asked the Chief of Naval Personnel for permission to sail to South America and China; he had no intention of returning. After a couple of weeks passed with no word from his partners, Parsons deduced this for himself. Not to be taken in, Jack took a train to Miami and discovered that Allied Enterprises had purchased three boats in all: a yacht plus two schooners that they bought on mortgages exceeding $12,000. He tracked down the schooners but could find no trace of Ron or Betty.

Several days later, a phone call from Howard Bond's Yacht Harbor informed Parsons that Ron and Betty's yacht had sailed at 5 o'clock earlier that afternoon. It was now 8 p.m. and he could do little about the situation. So he evoked Bartzabel, the spirit of Mars, to stop his dishonest partners. As if in response, a squall struck the yacht off the coast, tearing off its sails and forcing it back to port, where Parsons had them arrested. The Circuit Court of Dade County, Florida, slapped them with a restraining order that prevented their selling the boats or leaving Miami until the courts settled the charges. At this time, Jack wrote despondently to his "Dear Father" at Netherwood:

> Here I am in Miami pursuing the children of my folly. I have them well tied up. They cannot move without going to jail. However, most of the money has already been dissipated. I will be lucky to salvage $3,000 to $5,000.[77]

On July 11, Hubbard and Northrup agreed to a deal drawn up by Parsons's lawyer: Jack got the yacht and one of the schooners. Ron and Betty kept the other schooner, split his legal costs, and signed a promissory note of $2,900. Parsons returned to Pasadena, feeling fleeced but having salvaged as much as he possibly could. Hubbard would later claim that he was working undercover for the FBI to break up an immoral secret society.

Jack Parsons (1914–1952).

Lilliput magazine wanted Aleister Crowley to contribute an article to their June issue and sent their assistant editor, John Symonds (1914–2006), to meet with him on Friday, May 3. Symonds was born on March 12, 1914, in Battersea, London, to a single mother, Lithuanian Jewish immigrant Lily Sapzells, who ran a boarding house in Margate. He was estranged from his father, architect and antiques expert Robert Wemyss Symonds, who had married and refused to acknowledge John as his son. Spending his spare time in the British Museum reading room, Symonds's first job was as a journalist for the *Picture Post,* where he befriended Dylan Thomas and poet-novelist Stephen Spender, whom Crowley had met back in 1931. During the war he was exempted from military service and edited *Lilliput* magazine; in 1946 he completed his first novel, the gothic fantasy *William Waste.*[78] Clifford Bax had encouraged him to visit Crowley, saying, "He will die soon and then you would have lost your chance." Symonds—living at 84 Boundary Road, Hampstead, the very house where Victor Neuburg had died in 1940—already had an interest in AC. So he and astrologer Rupert Gleadow (1909–1974) journeyed to Netherwood. Crowley greeted them in the drawing room with his customary "Do what thou wilt shall be the whole of the Law." As Symonds and Gleadow checked him out,

AC incited them by stating his disbelief in astrology. At one point, he examined his small, bony arm and explained that he needed an injection of heroin. "Do you mind?" he asked.

"Not at all," Symonds answered. "Can I help?"

Smirking, Crowley related the squeamish reaction of a visiting army officer—most likely either McMurtry or Mellinger—when he went to the bathroom to inject himself. "I left the bedroom door open, and from behind the bathroom door I bent down to the keyhole and began to squeal like a stuck pig. When I came out, I found my poor friend had almost fainted."[79]

Their visit ended with Crowley asking him, "Do you play chess?"

"No," answered Symonds. "I don't, but I know how to."

"I wish *I* did," he deadpanned. "I've been trying to learn for the last sixty years," then presented each of them with a copy of the blue paper-covered *Book of the Law* published by the Church of Thelema.

Shortly thereafter, *Lilliput* received his story "The Young Man and the Post Office" (printed as "How to Tell an Englishman from an American").[80]

His publication plans forged ahead, with Lady Harris designing a cover for *Olla,* which was due out that summer. Crowley realized this plan was optimistic and, receiving the proofs on June 6, knew its publication date would be later than anticipated. He nevertheless proceeded with other projects. "My main object in this revived burst of activity is to get my principal works published somehow—anyhow—so as to have them in a definite form while I still encumber this planet," Crowley explained to John Symonds,[81] who had offered to help however he could. Although Symonds preferred *Magick without Tears,* AC wanted the long-completed *Liber Aleph* to be his next book in print, with a Christmas release date every bit as tentative as that for *Olla.*[82]

His worsening eyesight, however, interrupted the Great Work. As far back as April, he had complained to McMurtry, "My eyes are really bothering me so much that I feel totally unable to deal with your letter as I should like."[83] Glasses did not help. A London optician, Dr. McGowan, diagnosed him with amblyopia or "lazy eye," and insisted Crowley quit smoking "immediately and forever" in order to save his vision. That noon, Crowley ceremonially renounced tobacco. Although optical and dental problems continued to plague Crowley, his vision had improved so much by July 20 that he "Decided to risk half a pipe at 6 p.m. chiefly to make sure that this did not bring about an immediate relapse."[84] By September, Crowley happily noted, "Eyes quite o.k. so far, despite moderate resumption of smoking."[85]

When Augustus John did Crowley's portrait that summer, it was the first time he had seen the mage in decades. Frankly, the sight of his shrunken friend, with vacant eyes staring out of his wrinkled, gray head, frightened John; only his sharp mind retained its youthful vigor. "A glorious sketch!" Crowley congratulated the artist, who offered to help Crowley by arranging for collotyping by Chiswick Press himself.

He gave the *Olla* proofs a final inspection, setting its publication date for December 22. He printed fifty prospectuses and on December 11 sold the first copy. On December 22, 1946, at 10:54 a.m., the moment of the winter solstice, *Olla: An Anthology of Sixty Years of Song* was officially published in an edition of five hundred copies. The book listed Symonds's 121 Adelaide Road address as OTO's place of publication. "I think of it as a unique publication," Crowley remarked. "I doubt whether anyone else can boast—if it is a boast—of 60 years of song."[86] The *Occult Review* concurred, devoting four pages to reviewing what would be the last book he would publish. In his review, Nicholas Sylvester introduced Crowley as "one of the foremost, as well as one of the most logical, investigators in the field" of magic, and said of *Olla,* "This collection of poems is the work of a great occultist and a great poet," predicting "it may well prove that he will be remembered in the future as a poet of outstanding genius and ability."[87]

Crowley continued making regular payments to his Hastings printer, who promised to have page proofs of *Liber Aleph* ready by the end of May.

When James Laver (1899–1975)—art historian, museum curator, and author of books on many subjects, including a recent one on the prophet Nostradamus[88]—accepted Crowley's invitation and visited him at Netherwood on March 27, he found the Mage sickly. He was on a special diet and left his boiled egg uneaten in favor of brandy and perique. Blood dotted his shirt sleeves, and only an injection of heroin cleared his dull eyes and perked him up. During their conversations on magick, Crowley made the insightful comment, "Ah, you realize that magick is something we do to ourselves. But it is more convenient to assume the objective existence of an angel who gives us new knowledge than to allege that our invocation has awakened a supernormal power in ourselves."[89] In his diary, Crowley recorded the day, "Most delightful interview, A.C. at his best."[90]

Arnold Crowther (1909–1974) was another in the carnival of visitors who—in the tradition of Symonds, Butler, and Laver—came to Netherwood to see the quickly decaying mage, Aleister Crowley. Crowther was neither a disciple nor detractor; and, although he was a magician, it was not in the same manner as the Beast. His magic was sleight of hand, and he only knew of Crowley through the media and a discarded copy of *Magick in Theory and Practice* that had been given to him during one of his World War II performances for the army. He was also a ventriloquist, puppeteer, and puppet-maker who entertained the like of Princess Elizabeth and Princess Margaret at Buckingham Palace.[91] When, after one of his shows, someone asked him, "Are you that awful man?," he realized the similarity between the names Arnold Crowther and Aleister Crowley. His curiosity piqued, he arranged to visit on May 1. He brought with him his friend Gerald Brousseau Gardner (1884–1964), a retired civil servant fascinated by magic and witchcraft. In later years, Crowther would become inolved in Gardner's revival of paganism.

Gardner was born near Liverpool to a middle-class family, proprietors of the United Kingdom's oldest hardwood importers, Joseph Gardner & Sons. He spent much of his life living abroad in exotic locations like the Canary Islands, Ceylon, Borneo, and Malaya. The cultures to which he was exposed—particularly their magical practices and their weaponry—fascinated him. Becoming an amateur anthropologist, he published a book on *Keris and Other Malay Weapons* in 1936.[92] That same year, at age fifty-two, he retired and settled back in England. Here, he joined the Folkore Society and contributed to its journal, and also became involved in groups based on Rosicrucianism and witchcraft.[93]

May 1, 1947, was the first of four visits for Gardner, who got along well with Crowley. Beast admitted him into OTO as Brother Scire ("To know"), advancing him to VII° and authorizing him to get OTO going again in England. "We are getting a Camp of Minerval started during the summer if plans go as at present arranged," Crowley reported excitedly to Germer.[94] Alas, Gardner never used his charter, explaining, "I tried to start an order, but I got ill and had to leave the country."[95]

Two years later, Gardner would publish the novel *High Magic's Aid* through Atlantis Bookshop. Since the eighteenth-century Witchcraft Act made the practice of witchcraft illegal, the title page bore as a pseudonym a garbled version of Gardner's OTO motto: Scire O.T.O. 4°=7°. Although it was a novel, its description of a witch cult intrigued his readers. "A.C. read part of the MS, and highly approved," Gardner reported. "He wanted me to put the witch part in full."[96] The book was, in fact, a springboard for introducing witchcraft to the world. Gardner, according to apocryphal reports, had paid Crowley $1,500, or £300, to write a pagan grimoire—the *Book of Shadows*—for his witchcraft revival;[97] however, no record of such an arrangement exists in Crowley's letters or diaries. The truth, according to long-time friend and student Doreen Valiente, is that Gardner borrowed liberally from various works, including Leland's *Gospel of the Witches*[98] and the works of his friend AC.[99]

Gardnerian witchcraft, particularly its early forms, clearly draws heavily from Crowley. The symbolic great rite comes from OTO's VI° ritual; the pagan catchphrase "Perfect love and perfect trust" is drawn from "The Revival of Magick," and the Wiccan III° initiation—the highest in the Craft—is essentially a Gnostic Mass. And, for all its evocative beauty, the Charge of the Goddess is largely a paraphrase of *The Book of the Law*. Even Gardner himself, in a cagey way, admits the lineage of his witchcraft movement: in his second book, *Witchcraft Today*, he writes:

> The great question which people ask is: "How do you know the cult is
> old?" ... The only man I can think of who could have invented the rites was
> the late Aleister Crowley. When I met him he was most interested to hear
> that I was a member, and said he had been inside when he was very young,
> but would not say whether he had rewritten anything or not.... There are
> indeed certain expressions and certain words which smack of Crowley.[100]

Gardner's relationship with Crowley has become quite a fish story over the
years, but the simplest account is still the accepted truth: Gardner met Crowley
through Arnold Crowther; they met four times in all; Crowley gave Gardner
authority, which he valued but never used, to operate an OTO body; and
Gardner was so impressed with Crowley's writings that he borrowed sections
when developing the rituals for his coven.[101]

"A miracle has just happened," AC wrote excitedly to E. N. Fitzgerald. "The
girl Pat and Aleister Ataturk, who I had long since given up for dead, are in
London. She phoned me last night. I am delirious with joy. They come here
Thursday."[102] Pat and Aleister Ataturk, who just turned ten on May 2, came
out from Cornwall to visit Crowley for three days in the middle of May. The
visit pleased AC, who, old and lonely, missed his family. He was so happy to see
them that on May 22 Crowley instructed members of OTO to ensure Ataturk's
care and education after his father died. He also seized the opportunity to write
his son a fatherly letter while he still had the chance. His advice provides great
insight into Crowley's mind, and is quoted in full:

> Do what thou wilt shall be the whole of the Law.
>
> My dear son,
>
> This is the first letter that your father has ever written to you, so you
> can imagine that it will be very important, and you should keep it and lay
> it by your heart.
>
> First of all let me tell you how intensely happy your reappearance has
> made me; I feel that I must devote a great deal of my time to watching
> over your career.
>
> I was very pleased to hear that you had decided to learn to read, and
> that, of course, means learning to write. A word of warning about this! In
> these last years children have been taught to write "script" as they call it,
> which is a very bad thing: you must write in such a way that it impresses
> your personality on the reader.
>
> On top of that, I wanted to tell you something about yourself. One of
> your Ancestors was Duke of a place called La Querouaille in Brittany, and
> he came over to England with the Duke of Richmond, who was the orig-
> inal heir to the English throne, to help him turn out the usurper known to
> history as Richard III: since then our family has made its mark on the
> world on several occasions, though never anything very brilliant.
>
> Now I want you to take this very seriously: I want you to be very
> proud of yourself for belonging to such a family. Owing to the French
> Revolution, and various other catastrophes, the Dukedom is no longer in

existence legally, but morally it is so, and I want you to learn to behave as a Duke would behave. You must be high-minded, generous, noble, and, above all, without fear. For that last reason, you must never tell a lie, for to do so shows that you are afraid of the person to whom you tell it, and I want you to be afraid of nobody.

I think that is all about that. Now with regard to your education. I want you particularly to insist on learning Latin, and I will give you my reasons. Firstly, anyone who knows Latin gains a greater command of, and understanding of, the English language than he would otherwise possess. He will be able to reason out for himself the meanings of words with which he is unfamiliar. Secondly, if you are well-grounded in Latin, you are half way to a knowledge of French, Spanish, Italian and Portuguese, for all these languages, as well as English, are derived from Latin. Thirdly, and most important of all, much of the unconscious part of your mind has been formed by the writing of Latin and Greek authors (this implies that you should also learn a certain amount of Greek). One of the wisest men of olden time gave this instruction to his pupils—"Know thyself"—and learning Latin helps you to do this for the reason I have already explained above.

I regard this as very important indeed! There are a great many people going about today who tell you that Latin is no use to you in the ordinary affairs of life, and that is quite true if you are going to be some commonplace person like a tradesman or a bank clerk, but you are a gentleman, and if you want to be an educated gentleman, you must know Latin.

There is another matter that I want to put before you. It will be a very good plan if you learn to play chess: for one thing it is a very good training for the mind, and for another it is the only game of all the games worth playing, which lasts you throughout your life. You can get as much pleasure out of it when you are 60 as when you are 20.

I think that is all I have to say to you today, and I shall expect you to manage somehow to write me an answer. You see, much of the time we shall not be able to communicate face to face, and there will be a good many questions that you will want to ask me which you cannot do unless you write good English. That reminds me, there is one more point that I want to impress on you! The best models of English writing are Shakespeare and the Old Testament, especially the Book of Job, the Psalms, the Proverbs, Ecclesiastes, and the Song of Solomon. It will be a very good thing for you to commit as much as you can, both of these books and of the best plays of Shakespeare to memory, so that they form the foundation of your style; and in writing English, the most important quality that you can acquire is style. It makes all the difference to anyone who reads what you write, whether you use the best phrases in the best way. You will have to devote some time to grammar and syntax, and also to logic. Logic is the science and the art of using words, and it teaches you to think correctly without making blunders in reasoning, which nowadays everyone is liable to do just because they have not got the training which I am proposing to give you.

Now my dear son, I will close this long letter in the eager hope that you will follow my advice in all respects.

Love is the law, love under will.

Your affectionate father.[103]

Also visiting that summer was Harvard scholar Richard David Ellmann (1918–1987), who had a grant from the Rockefeller Foundation to write a biography of Yeats. Born in Highland Park, Michigan, to Jewish Romanian immigrant James Isaac Ellmann and Ukrainian immigrant Jeantte Barsook, Ellman graduated from Yale University with exceptional distinction in English and received his MA in 1941. His position as an instructor at Harvard was interrupted by the United States's entry into the war and his army enlistment. In 1945 he found himself in London with the Office of Strategic Services, where that September he met W. B. Yeats's widow. Impressed with Ellmann's knowledge of Yeats, she granted him access to her archive. Thus he began writing what would be Yale University's first doctoral dissertation on a twentieth-century writer.[104] Clifford Bax had passed AC's address along to Ellmann, who wished to interview Crowley about his "magical war" with Yeats in the GD days. The result of this interview was a colorful article titled, "Black Magic against White: Aleister Crowley versus W. B. Yeats."[105]

As his health deteriorated, AC had difficulty making more than an occasional diary entry or remembering names and dates. Reuss's advice echoed in his mind, "Trust not a stranger: fail not of an heir." He had already hastily awarded IX° honors to several students, ensuring the secret would survive his death. Now he wrote to McMurtry:

> It seems a long time since I heard from you. This is a great mistake: I will tell you why *in strict confidence*. In the event of my death Frater Saturnus is of course my successor, but after *his* death the terrible burden of responsibility might very easily fall upon your shoulders; for this reason I should like you to keep closely in touch with me.
>
> I am sending you a bound copy of "Olla" to remind you of me....[106]

Shortly thereafter, he wrote similarly to Frederick Mellinger (1890–1970):

> Any time you can spare a moment think of me, and remember that you can bring no greater happiness into my life than by dropping me a brief note: never mind whether there is anything to say or not.
>
> I am very anxious indeed that you should keep in close touch with me, if only because I think it quite possible that after Frater Saturnus and myself have moved on into the next stage, you *may* find yourself saddled with the whole responsibility of carrying on the work of the Order. It is most important that you should have paid the greatest attention to practiced experience of every side of the work, because whenever you become the supreme head of everything you will find that people write to you from everywhere and anywhere asking all sorts of the most impossible questions, and you have to answer them not merely with tact and discretion, but with detailed knowledge.
>
> Please remember this above all things ... you never know at what moment you may find yourself in a position of supreme responsibility, and you must not shirk it or dodge it....[107]

Mellinger was an actor in both his German homeland and in the United States, to which he emigrated as a Jewish refugee. He had a long-standing interest in the occult, publishing in 1933 while still in Germany *Zeichen und Wunder: Ein Führer durch die Welt der Magie (Signs and Wonders: A Guide to the World of Magic)*.[108] He became a U.S. citizen in the mid-to-late 1930s and traveled to Europe on occasional military assignments. Living in Los Angeles he had various bit parts in Hollywood films[109] and in 1940 met W. T. Smith. They became instant friends, and Mellinger joined both OTO and the A∴A∴ under Smith's sponsorship. In 1945, with Germer's financial help, he returned to Germany and visited Crowley at Hastings. Judging from the above-quoted letter, he certainly made an impression. However, in the years following Crowley's death, he would remain on the periphery of the Thelemic circle.

Although it may appear that Crowley was willing to give the IX° to anyone, he had a definite plan in mind. He described it to Germer:

> You seem in doubt too about the succession. There has never been any question about this. Since your re-appearance you are the only successor of whom I have ever thought since that moment. I have, however, had the idea that in view of the dispersion of so many members, you might find it useful to appoint a triumvirate to work under you. My idea was Mellinger, MacMurtrie [sic] and, I suppose, Roy.... I shall leave it entirely to you to decide about your triumvirate after my death.[110]

After writing his letter to McMurtry, Crowley prepared his last will and testament. Then, before he even finished correcting the proofs of *Liber Aleph* that August, he added *Golden Twigs* to the print queue.

Karl Johannes Germer (1885–1962), Crowley's successor in OTO.

As AC grew progressively ill that summer, the Netherwood housekeepers prayed for his own sake that he would die soon. Karl planned to come to Hastings that autumn to care for Crowley, but British authorities denied him a visa. Thus, when Lady Harris found Crowley dirty and neglected, she asked him if he had any money for a trained nurse. "I have over £400 in banknotes in the strongbox under my bed," he explained, "but that's not for my personal use. It's money from America, earmarked for the order." Especially now, when publishing his works was so important, Crowley refused to dip into his publication fund. So, that September, Frieda hired a nurse herself. In addition, Mr. H. Watson of the Ridge Stores also helped look after him.

When Crowley turned seventy-two in October, his grip on life was slipping. "I have myself been very ill, confined to bed for six months or more," he wrote.[111] Wilkinson noticed the light fading in his eyes. Laying pathetically helpless in bed, he reflected despondently on his life and realized he hadn't obtained the recognition he felt he deserved; he hadn't completed the Great Work he had set out to accomplish. He was only a front-page sensation for the newspapers to trot out whenever circulation slipped. Even now, he insisted that reporters were hiding in the bushes, waiting for him to die. With a sigh, he remarked, "This is a good world to leave."

Louis replied, "Don't talk that way."

"You are my greatest friend, Louis." Crowley smiled sadly. "I'm sorry you have wasted your time visiting a log." Those were his last words to his oldest friend.

On the anniversary of his GD initiation, Crowley sent a cable to Karl:

GERMER:

> PERDURABO BORN 49 YEARS AGO. THERION SENDS DEEPEST LOVE
> HIGHEST BLESSING YOURSELVES AND THELEMITES, THE UNIVERSE.

To Frieda, Louis, and Karl—the ones who really mattered—Crowley had said his piece and given his farewells.

His condition became so severe that Pat and her children, including Ataturk, came to his side on the last day of November. Frederick Mellinger and his wife also made the journey, finding Crowley disoriented and unsure of where he was. When he finally passed, the stillness of the day was interrupted by a peal of thunder and a gust of wind that blew the curtains across the room. "It was the gods greeting him," recalled Deirdre.

On Monday, December 1, 1947, at 11 a.m., Aleister Crowley died of myocardial degeneration and chronic bronchitis. In his pocket was an Abramelin talisman "for a great treasure" and an old letter, tattered from repeated unfoldings and foldings. Dated September 10, 1939, it read: "The Director of Naval Intelligence presents his compliments and would be glad if you could find it convenient to call at the Admiralty for an interview."

Wilkinson took the phone call at Netherwood, where he was staying to arrange Crowley's funeral. Lifting the receiver to his ear, he greeted, "Hello," then firmly replied, "I'm sorry, but the funeral is a private affair." Since his death, everyone was calling for details of the evil Aleister Crowley's demise; Wilkinson grew intolerant of the reporters, remembering how his friend, shortly before death, believed they were waiting outside his window for him to die. How right he was. The newspapers said it all in their headlines:

Black Magician Crowley Dies: "Wickedest Man in Britain."

World's Worst Man Dies.

Awful Aleister.

Rascal's Regress.

Aleister Crowley Dies; Once the "Invisible" Man.

Mystic's Potion to Prolong Life Fails.

"Worst Man in the World" Dies, Leaves Weird Pictures.[112]

Crowley gained no respect while living and received even less in death. When it was discoverd that his attending physician, William Brown Thomson (c. 1889–1947), of 12 Park Way in Greenford, died within twenty-four hours of his patient,[113] rumors of a curse fueled further headlines, like "Crowley's Doctor Dies: 'Curse Put on Him.'"[114] The fact that Thomson was fifty-eight years old did nothing to deflect conspiracy theories of postmortem revenge.

Crowley's will named Frieda Harris, Louis Wilkinson, and Karl Germer as his executors, charged with settling his debts. Revoking all previous bequests, he left his copyrights to OTO, which was to ensure Pat and Ataturk's care. He named Wilkinson and Symonds his literary executors, charging them to collect his literary remains and ship them to Germer in New York. He asked that no religious service be performed at his funeral, wishing instead for Yorke or Wilkinson to read selections from his works.

Friday afternoon of December 5 was cold and dank. Mourners and spectators gathered inside the chapel at the Brighton cemetery where, at 2:45, Crowley's flower-covered coffin was solemnly brought.

Carrying a copy of *The Book of the Law* and *Magick,* Louis Wilkinson took the rostrum and looked out at the group of fifteen mourners, including, according to the press, "five well-dressed women and six youths in need of haircuts."[115] Among those he recognized were Gerald Yorke, Frieda Harris, John Symonds, J. G. Bayley, Pat and Aleister MacAlpine, and Kenneth Grant and his wife, Steffi. Yorke counted three reporters.

Wilkinson, tall and dignified, began without hesitation. "Do what thou wilt shall be the whole of the Law." Deep and articulate, his voice filled the chapel as he read "Hymn to Pan," excerpts from *The Book of the Law,* the Col-

lects from the Gnostic Mass, and the "Quia Patris" from "The Ship," which
Crowley had read at Raoul Loveday's funeral:

> Thou who art I, beyond all I am,
> Who has no nature, and no name,
> Who art, when all but thou are gone,
> Thou, centre and secret of the Sun,
> Thou, hidden spring of all things known
> And unknown, Thou aloof, alone,
> Thou, the true fire within the reed
> Brooding and breeding, source and seed
> Of life, love, liberty and light,
> Thou beyond speech and beyond sight,
> Thee I invoke, my faint fresh fire
> Kindling as mine intents aspire.
> Thee I invoke, abiding one,
> Thee, centre and secret of the Sun,
> And that most holy mystery
> Of which the vehicle am I!
> Appear, most awful and most mild,
> As it is lawful, to thy child!
> For of the Father and the Son
> The Holy Spirit is the norm:
> Male-female, quintessential, one,
> Man-being veiled in Woman-form.
> Glory and worship in the Highest,
> Thou Dove, mankind that deifiest,
> Being that race—most royally run
> To spring sunshine through winter storm!
> Glory and worship be to Thee,
> Sap of the world-ash, wonder tree!
> Glory to Thee from gilded tomb!
> Glory to Thee from waiting womb!
> Glory to thee from virgin vowed!
> Glory to Thee from Earth unploughed!
> Glory to Thee, true Unity
> Of the eternal Trinity!
> Glory to Thee, thou sire and dam
> And Self of I am that I am.
> Glory to Thee, beyond all term,
> Thy spring of sperm, thy seed and germ!
> Glory to Thee, eternal Sun,
> Thou One in Three, Thou Three in One!
> Glory and worship be to Thee,
> Sap of the world-ash, wonder-tree!

Mourners' ecstatic or tearful interjections of "Io Pan!" and "Do what thou wilt
shall be the whole of the Law" punctuated the recital. The reporters just
looked at each other, nonplussed.

Wilkinson closed the book and solemnly ended with "Love is the law, love under will." He sat down, and Pat threw a spray of roses on the coffin. Rollers turned, and the coffin entered the furnace.[116]

Reporters formed a gauntlet around mourners as they left the chapel, barking out questions and jotting down quotes to include in the next edition of their tabloids. "Beware what you write," Symonds said, locking eyes with one reporter. "Crowley may strike at you from wherever he is." The heavens released a downpour, and Wilkinson, riding back to Hastings, remarked of the weather, "Just what Crowley would have liked."

Unable to fathom the meaning of the funeral, reporters described Crowley's last rites as a Black Mass, running headlines like

Cremating "Great Beast"
Desecrated by Black Magic

The scandalized Brighton Town Council met to discuss this spectacle and assured the public that such a thing would never happen again.

They were right.

Epilogue

He was wasted in England. In Persia or India or Japan, millions would have followed him.

—Andrew Green[1]

His poetry undoubtedly ranks among the finest ever written.

—Hereward Carrington[2]

Crowley's story after death was as colorful as it was in life.

Karl Germer accepted Crowley's nomination as Outer Head of the Order and took over OTO business. With the help of Yorke and Harris he sought high-ranking British members to identify the new X° for Ireland, Iona, and all the Britains. Symonds, whose address appeared in *Olla* as the order's, acted as an administrative assistant to Germer but was not actually an OTO member. E. N. Fitzgerald had received the IX° from Crowley, but according to Germer, "He does not however know what it is about."[3] Therefore the nod went—briefly—to Gerald Gardner, who had been chartered by Crowley to operate an OTO camp. But Gardner reported, "owing to ill health I so far haven't been able to get anything going. I've had some people interested, but some of them were sent to Germany with the army of occupation, and others lived far away, and so nothing happened."[4] And nothing ever would. Agape Lodge remained the only active OTO body under Germer. Since he never performed nor liked rituals, and discouraged the lodges from initiating new members, Agape struggled to endure. Germer instead focused on seeing *Liber Aleph* and *Golden Twigs,* which were in press at the time of Crowley's death, to publication. The difficulty of conducting transatlantic business forced him to abandon the projects by November 1948.

Yorke pleaded with Germer, "Please do *not* send me Power of Attorney to act on your behalf.... It would not be honest for me having refused to have official business relations with him [Crowley] since at least 1932 to take them up after his death."[5] Yorke, however, did spend his life keeping his vow to preserve Crowley's papers, often purchasing them from creditors, forgotten storage facilities, solicitors, auction houses, and acquaintances. These materials he readily shared with Germer, who, possessing the bulk of Crowley's papers, lent material to Yorke to copy. Both men believed that only a later generation would understand and appreciate Crowley's literary legacy, and they hoped someday to store archival copies of all his papers on each continent. Yorke's collection is currently kept at the Warburg Institute, part of the postgraduate School for Advanced Studies at the University of London, and is the world's largest public archive of Crowleyana.

Frieda Harris, meanwhile, published a booklet commemorating Crowley's funeral. Titled *The Last Ritual,* it contained the text of his funeral and boasted an original cover by Harris; she asked for a contribution of $1 per copy to defray printing costs. One year after his death she carried out another of Crowley's last wishes by arranging a curry party in his honor. Held at 7:30 p.m. on December 1, the dinner party attracted about fourteen of AC's acquaintances, who retired afterward to Yorke's home for the evening.

Not all of Crowley's acquaintances remained so loyal, however.

"Now that Crowley is safely dead, do you think his story can be told?" John Symonds voiced the question which typified the unfortunately common reaction to Crowley's death. Symonds went on to write *The Great Beast* (1951), a sensational and critical portrayal of Crowley's life. At least one publisher turned the book down for fear of libel, but London publishers Rider eventually bought it. Those loyal to AC saw it as a betrayal of trust, and Yorke's catalog of the book's inaccuracies is a lengthy and damning document. Nevertheless, the book remained the primary source of information on Crowley throughout the second half of the twentieth century; ironically, its sensational tone may well have contributed to Crowley's enduring popularity.

Longtime student and friend J. G. Bayley pulled an equally remarkable about-face. Although he had joined the A∴A∴ in 1910, visited Crowley regularly in his last years, and paid his respects at the funeral, he wrote Germer a surprising letter two years after Crowley's death:

> Do what thou wilt shall be the whole of the Law.

> Thanks for your letter of the 13th ulto. I don't want to engage in any long rigmarole about Crowley.... I could go on reeling off dozens of other people who had despicable, abominable, criminal tricks played on them by that scoundrel.

> Love is the law, love under will.

> Yours Fraternally,

> L.O.V.[6]

Particularly ironic is the bracketing of his condemnation with Thelemic salutations and his A∴A∴ motto.

In 1942, C. S. Jones—the once-beloved Frater Achad—was teaching kabbalah and magick to *Under the Volcano* (1947) author Malcolm Lowry (1909–1957). Jones sought to mend his fences with Crowley, who saw no way his erstwhile magical son could compensate for what he regarded as twenty years of egoism and insanity. Thus Jones sought to build his own magical universe on the ashes of his former master. On April 8, 1948—four months after Crowley's death, and forty-four years to the day after Crowley received *The Book of the Law*—"An Open Letter from Frater Achad" announced that the 2,160-year reign of the Aeon of Horus had ended prematurely, replaced by the Aeon of Maat, the daughter, of which Achad was the chosen prophet.[7] Despite his life-long love of Thelema and ceremonial magic, Jones reportedly embraced Catholicism on his deathbed.[8]

As Agape Lodge fell into abeyance, Jack Parsons sold his mansion to a developer, took the Oath of the Abyss in 1949, and wrote to Germer in mid-1952:

> No doubt you will be delighted to hear from an adept who has undertaken the operation of his H.G.A. in accord with our traditions.
>
> The operation began auspiciously with a chromatic display of psychosomatic symptoms, and progressed rapidly to acute psychosis. The operator has alternated satisfactorily between manic hysteria and depressing melancholy stupor on approximately 40 cycles, and satisfactory progress has been maintained in social ostracism, economic collapses and mental disassociation.[9]

On Friday, June 20, 1952, Parsons was working alone in his coach-house laboratory when, at 5:08 p.m., an explosion blew out the doors and walls of the stable, reducing the building to rubble. The police soon found Ruth Virginia Parsons at the home of an invalid friend, notifying her of her son's death. After the officers left, Mrs. Parsons sat down and swallowed a bottle of sleeping pills, her handicapped friend helpless to do anything but watch while Mrs. Parsons slipped into death.

An inquest later determined that, as experienced as Parsons was in handling explosives, it was an accident. The press later reported evidence to the contrary, but authorities never followed up; thus it is the belief of many, his widow Cameron included, that he was murdered.[10] Given the way Parsons died, a passage from his *Book of Babalon* sounds eerily prophetic:

> And in that day my work will be accomplished, and I shall be blown away upon the Breath of the Father, even as it is prophesied. And thus I labour lonely and outcast and abominable, an he-goat upon the muck heaps of the world....

Meanwhile in England, Kenneth Grant had continued to study Crowley's doctrines, and applied for a charter to operate the first three degrees of OTO. Germer granted this until 1955, when Grant announced the formation of the New Isis Lodge of OTO. He claimed to have contacted an intelligence from a trans-Plutonian planet and received secret instructions to reorganize OTO; instructions that were secret, Grant claimed, even to the OHO. Germer repudiated the manifesto and, when Grant persisted in this direction, expelled him on July 20, 1955:

NOTIFICATION OF EXPULSION

Do what thou wilt shall be the whole of the Law.

You are notified that the very small and limited authority I gave you at one time to establish a Camp of O.T.O. in the valley of London is withdrawn, and I formally expel you from membership in the Ordo Templi Orientis...

Love is the law, love under will.

Saturnus

Karl Germer X° and Frater
Superior of O.T.O.[11]

Undeterred, Grant continued working his version of magick, drawing not only from Crowley but also from Eastern tantra and the work of his friend, artist Austin Spare.[12] He also published a series of articles, monographs, and books on these subjects from the 1950s until the present day.[13]

Germer had one other student worth mentioning, the Brazilian Marcelo Ramos Motta (1931–1987). Germer admitted him into OTO and A∴A∴, and together they published Crowley's *Liber Aleph* (1961). Although Germer had released *Magick without Tears* in mimeographed form seven years earlier, *Liber Aleph* represented a fine typeset edition of one of Crowley's masterpieces. Germer died shortly thereafter in 1962. He named no successor, and his widow notified few of his passing, leaving OTO leaderless.

Fortunately, the late 1960s era of flower power, psychedelics, free love and Transcendental Meditation made Crowley fashionable. He appeared on the Beatles' *Sergeant Pepper's Lonely Hearts Club Band* (1967) album cover and in the pages of Robert Heinlein's science fiction classic *Stranger in a Strange Land* (1961), and quickly became a pop-culture icon. Regrettably, Crowley's popularity also attracted the attention of some ignoble peers. When Anton LaVey founded his Church of Satan in 1966, he cited Crowley as an influence; thus, even though AC rejected Satanists and black magicians, the media again categorized him as both. Similarly, after a group of admirers known as the Solar Lodge locked one of their boys, Anthony Gibbons, in a wooden box in the Southern California desert—his punishment for playing with matches and burning down their compound—the press linked Crowley's name to the incident.[14]

McMurtry had been out of touch with his fellow Agape Lodge members, but when he learned of Germer's death and the sad state of OTO, he knew something needed to be done. Remembering that Crowley had named him Caliph and had given him authority to assume control or restart OTO in an emergency, McMurtry declared the situation an emergency and resuscitated the order. He gathered the surviving members of Agape Lodge to legally incorporate OTO in the 1970s and quickly established initiations, lodges, and camps worldwide.[15]

Because of the unresolved issue of Germer's OTO successor, two other people claimed the mantle of OHO. Kenneth Grant, despite his expulsion from OTO in 1955, began calling himself the OHO when he and Symonds coedited *The Confessions of Aleister Crowley* (1969). He argued control not by succession but by virtue of having that magical spark of inspiration that he believed Germer lacked. Much as Crowley had claimed that Mathers had lost contact with the Secret Chiefs, so did Grant claim that heirship of Thelema had passed over Germer to him. Of all OHO contenders, he made the greatest effort to expand and build upon Crowley's work rather than confine himself to the letter of the law. During the 1970s he was one of a handful of people editing material by Crowley and Austin Spare, and he was practically alone in offering new contributions to the literature of magick. While his system differs considerably from Crowley's, he gets high marks for originality. Indeed, Henrik Bogdan called him "the perhaps most original and prolific author of the post-modern occultist genre," while Martin P. Starr described Grant's work as "fashioned out of the stuff of dreams."[16] However, his manner of exegesis—relying on complex numerologies, webs of symbolism, and coded language—is difficult for the beginner, and his later books are progressively more bizarre.[17] His works nevertheless remain in demand.

Motta, learning of Germer's death, believed it appropriate to single-handedly organize a convocation of IX° members to elect a new OHO. His dedication to the task came off as belligerence, however, and he quickly alienated the American OTO members who were closest to Germer. When this happened, Motta proclaimed *himself* OHO, convinced he was entitled to a percentage of Crowley's book sales. He began publishing volume five of *The Equinox,* in its pages attacking everyone who ever published or wrote anything about Crowley. His position became increasingly extreme and his opinions so vehement that he alienated most of his followers, and his organization, the Society Ordo Templi Orientis, dwindled in size by 1984 to four members.

A 1985 lawsuit between McMurtry and Motta resulted in the OTO headed by McMurtry—descended from the only chartered organization in operation at Crowley's death and throughout Germer's reign—being recognized as owner of Crowley's copyrights. (A similar ruling was made in the United Kingdom in 2002.) McMurtry died shortly before the 1985 ruling—and Motta shortly thereafter—and the remaining members of OTO met to elect the next Caliph and OHO, per McMurtry's wishes. Over the years, OTO has made great strides in preserving and publishing authoritative versions of Crowley's existing works, many of which have been out of print or unpublished, and have amassed a sizable archive based on Germer's surviving papers. It has also won several libel cases, demonstrating that it would not tolerate the abuse that typified Crowley's life. Today the organization claims over three thousand members worldwide.

Aleister Crowley stands as one of the most remarkable and innovative figures of his century: a man of fervent belief, he devoted his life and squandered his fortune seeking a glimpse of spiritual truth and sharing that vision with anyone willing to listen. Tragically, he spent his last years discredited, impoverished, and far from his family and friends in London. Yet he was ultimately successful in a way few people are: despite adverse or indifferent responses to his message, Crowley never doubted the correctness of his vision or his role as its advocate. Thus he lived every moment of his life based on his convictions regardless of their personal cost, whether to his fortune, friendships, or reputation. The best summation of the man may be by Crowley himself:

> I wish therefore that you would realize that my universe is very much larger than yours.... Some time ago I thought of writing a book on internationally famous people with whom I had been intimate. The number ran to over 80. Am I wrong to suppose that you never met such people?
>
> Take another point: have you visited the monuments of antiquity; have you seen the majority of the great paintings and sculptures? Have you discussed all sorts of intimate matters with natives of every civilized quarter of the globe? Perhaps more than any of the above in importance, have you made your way alone in parts of the earth never before trodden by any human foot—perhaps in hostile and nearly always inhospitable country? You may think it pompous of me to mention these matters, but the fact is that they don't matter unless you think they don't matter.
>
> The point that I am trying to get you to realize is that any statement or action of mine is enormously modified by my having had these experiences.[18]

Perhaps immodest, the contentions in this letter are nevertheless accurate.

Crowley's substantive merit bears explanation, as much of what made him innovative actually anticipated many things that are commonplace today. The emphasis here will be on magick for two reasons: first, Crowley's other accomplishments have been discussed earlier in this text. Also, magick is the avenue through which most people first encounter Crowley.

As a practical system, magick introduced many innovations to the Masonic and Rosicrucian traditions from which Crowley borrowed. Most notable is its syncretic quality. While magical traditions have often been eclectic (see Pike's *Morals and Dogma* [1871] or Blavatsky's *Isis Unveiled* [1877] for examples),[19] Crowley was much broader and more systematic.

Consider the Eastern mystical traditions of Hinduism, Buddhism, and Confucianism. Crowley's magical alma mater, the GD, offered only minor nods toward these paths: its technique of moon breathing was borrowed from the *hatha yoga* practice of *pranayama* and the belief in the body's subtle energy channels, or *nadis*. Likewise, the system of *tattva* visions is adapted from the Hindu system of five elements *(tattvas)*. The likely source for both teachings is Prasad's book *Nature's Finer Forces*,[20] which was very influential on the GD founders. After the 1900 disintegration of the London temple, Crowley's own travels to the East gave him a far better grasp of the indigenous spiritual traditions of India and China. By the time *The Equinox* I(4) (1910) and the first part of *Book Four* (1911) appeared, Crowley had seamlessly integrated a broad range of yogic, divinatory, and meditative techniques into his teachings. To appreciate how innovative this was, note that Legge's translation of the I Ching first appeared in 1882,[21] and when Allan Bennett returned to London in 1908 as the Buddhist monk Ananda Metteya, he was considered the first Buddhist missionary to England.

Crowley's syncretism didn't end with Eastern mysticism. A glance at the recommended reading list from "One Star in Sight" reveals the extent to which he integrated disparate perspectives. It covers classics of Hinduism (Upanishads, Bhagavad-Gita, Hathayoga Pradipika), Buddhism (Dhammapada), Taoism (Tao Teh King), gnosticism *(Pistis Sophia, The Divine Pymander)*, Zoroastrianism *(The Oracles of Zoroaster)*, Pythagoreanism *(The Golden Verses of Pythagoras)*, Christian mysticism *(The Spiritual Guide of Molinos)*, Jewish mysticism *(Kabbala Denudata)*, alchemy *(Scrutinium Chymicum)*, mythology *(The Golden Ass)*, psychology *(Varieties of Religious Experience)*, and anthropology *(The Golden Bough)*. Nor did he shun the rationalism of the great philosophers, encouraging students to study the likes of George Bishop Berkeley (1685–1753), David Hume (1711–1776), and Immanuel Kant (1724–1804).

The crowning achievement of this cross-cultural approach is the correspondences collected in 777 (1909). Although built on the notes of his GD mentors Mathers and Bennett, Crowley expanded the contents considerably. Similarly, Crowley's summation of his lifelong study in a new interpretation of the tarot resulted in a deck that remains unchallenged as the deepest ever produced. In laying out the parallels between all systems of symbolism, Crowley prefigured the structuralism of Claude Lévi-Strauss (1908–2009)[22] and Joseph Campbell's (1904–1987) elaboration of the myth cycle of the hero.[23] He also anticipated the eclecticism that is part and parcel of the so-called New Age or alternative religion movement, in which as much as ten percent of the population participates.[24]

Given the quantity of information available today on the world's esoteric traditions, Crowley's reading list does show its age. At its time, however, it was so innovative as to invite ridicule—which the yellow press obligingly supplied. Indeed, subsequent secret societies (such as Dion Fortune's Fraternity of the Inner Light and W. E. Butler's Servants of the Light) are overshadowed by the enormity of Crowley's intellectual achievement in crafting an all-inclusive system of attainment.

While these syncretistic tendencies provided an inviting field day for intellectuals, Crowley's approach was also notable for its pragmatism. As Yeats discovered to his dismay, the synthesis promised by the TS was purely intellectual; its extreme discomfort with practical work (i.e. magic) was what ultimately drove Yeats to switch his allegiance to the GD. Crowley likewise stripped away the window dressing to get at the heart of various teachings, extracting the practical tools for enlightenment. Crowley and George Cecil Jones's distillation of the GD initiation rituals into "Liber Pyramidos" is but one example of this approach. Refreshingly, Crowley—unlike most gurus—challenged his students to disbelieve him, to experiment and discover for themselves those formulae and practices that worked best for them.

Another innovation was Crowley's attempt to apply the rigors of the scientific method to a decidedly nonscientific pursuit. From the beginning, *The Equinox* described its contents as "The method of science, the aim of religion." As scientists kept lab notes, Crowley advocated keeping a magical record to facilitate tracking the success of magical rituals and the conditions under which they were conducted. Likewise, replication was emphasized in order to establish which methods were most successful. The structured practices and curriculum of the A∴A∴ also provided uniformity among his students' experiments, facilitating replication among different practitioners. Finally, in 1929, his magnum opus provided an operational definition of magick as "the Science and Art of causing Change to occur in conformity with Will."[25] What he proposed didn't completely incorporate the methods of empirical science, but it was a bold step in that direction.

So far, this discussion has focused on Crowley's innovations as the proponent of a method of spiritual attainment—a method applicable to the practices of any faith. But Crowley was also the prophet of the belief system he called Thelema. While the presence of a revealed holy text gives Thelema the outward appearance of a religion, its principles are more like a philosophy or spiritual perspective that, like Buddhism, can overlay any particular creed. Indeed, the central principle of Thelema—which directs each person to discover the specific role he or she plays in the cosmic scheme—is compatible with any religious belief (although other portions of *Liber AL* admittedly could be a more challenging fit).

An inviting trait of Thelema is its nonconformity. The epigram "Do what thou wilt shall be the whole of the Law" is a statement of moral relativism. Depending on one's True Will, what's right for one person may not be right for another. It exhorts Thelemites to celebrate their individuality (and the individuality of others). At its core, it rejects the orthodoxy and schism that dominated young Crowley's childhood.[26] Partly because its roots lie in secret societies, and partly because it presupposes a motive for enlightenment among its adherents, Thelema does not engage in the distasteful strong-arm proselytizing that is the bane of faiths that encourage testifying and conversion.

Given all his merits and innovations, the natural question is, why wasn't Crowley more successful than his contemporaries? Crowley's life story is peppered with the names of mystics and spiritual philosophers who achieved greater renown both during their lifetimes and since their deaths: the TS (H. P. Blavatsky, Annie Besant, Charles W. Leadbeater), Anthroposophy (Rudolf Steiner), the Fourth Way (G. I. Gurdjieff, A. R. Orage), AMORC (H. Spencer Lewis), and Scientology (L. Ron Hubbard). Why, then, was Crowley so obscure, so misunderstood? There are several reasons.

First, Crowley's books were expensive productions printed in small quantities with limited distribution. Even though he priced his works at cost to enhance their affordability, his choice of lavish papers and bindings kept them out of reach for most. Indeed, his audience was largely limited to the affluent (who could afford the books) and the persistent (who would go to the trouble of finding his works).

In addition, most of Crowley's books are written for what may be termed "hard-core" students. Like any specialist literature, Crowley's was difficult for the layperson to approach. His most widely available book, *Magick in Theory and Practice,* refers so often to *The Equinox* or even to unpublished works that it is a daunting read to anyone who isn't familiar with his entire corpus. It's not that Crowley was incapable of writing for a wider audience—see *The Revival of Magick and Other Essays* for proof—but that his books of magick were written for a specialized audience.

Finally, Crowley was the victim of his own unfortunate choice of terminology. However justifiable his reason for adopting terms like "magick," "the Great Beast," and "Thelema," the effect was to put people off. The word "magic" suffered from such negative connotations and confusion with stage magic and trickery that Crowley adopted the spelling "magick" to distinguish what he was talking about. But even with the k, "magick" produced a knee-jerk association with medieval demonology. Consider the times: séances and spiritualists were all the rage, and Harry Houdini was busy exposing frauds and charlatans.[27] In this climate, Crowley's rituals were popularly perceived as spiritualism. They were, in fact, often mistakenly called séances, and thereby classed alongside the fakes and pretenders against which he railed.

Calling himself "the Great Beast" didn't help. Despite what AC believed this figure from Revelation represented—a solar icon for the Magus of a New Aeon—most people connected it with the devil. The situation is akin to the similarly unfortunate choice among modern Pagans and Wiccans to reclaim the terms *witch* and *witchcraft*. Argue as they may (like Crowley) that the terms mean something other than the popular or consensual definitions, centuries of preconceptions are not easily overturned. Thus today's witches perpetually complain about the portrayal of witchcraft in books, movies and television just as Thelemites face a similar uphill battle in convincing the man on the street that the Great Beast Aleister Crowley was not a devil-worshipper.

In a similar way, Crowley's very message invited misunderstanding. By naming his philosophy after the Greek word for will, *thelema,* Crowley (or

Aiwass, if you prefer) guaranteed the term would be received with confusion by a good number of people. This could be clarified by referencing the primary principle of Thelema: "Do what thou wilt shall be the whole of the Law." This same confused person could understandably conclude Thelema to be a libertarian creed, and would become only more confused to be told "'Do what thou wilt' doesn't mean 'Do what you like.'" Indeed, so much of *The Book of the Law*'s meaning lies not in its literal interpretation but in the highly codified meaning of its words that one is tempted to call it a stylistic forebear of James Joyce's *Finnegans Wake* (1939)—although Joyce never met or read AC.[28]

Combined, these factors—small and expensive print runs, high expectations for his audience's reading level, and the adoption of unsettling or confusing terminology—helped guarantee his circle was confined to a small but devoted group of admirers.

Crowley's admirers have grown steadily in number since the 1970s, and it's easy to see why. He was a fascinating mix of audacity and titillation, mystery and discovery, eccentricity and substance; a misfit in his own time but a forebear of social changes that would not occur until well after his death. Half a century before Timothy Leary told the flower children to "Tune in, turn on, drop out," AC had experimented with drugs as an adjunct to consciousness expansion. By the time the Beatles had discovered meditation as a consciousness-altering alternative to drugs, Frater Perdurabo had already been there too. When the birth control pill sexually liberated a generation, they found Beast had kept a light on in the window. And before the 1980s were dubbed the "Me Generation," the prophet To Mega Therion had made a religion out of individuality. Rock music offers a prime example of AC's persistent presence in our culture, as he has been embraced by psychedelic rock in the 1960s, hard rock in the 1970s, heavy metal in the 1980s, goth and industrial music in the 1990s, and progressive metal in the twenty-first century. In our jaded modern age, magick offers an opportunity for adventure and discovery in the only uncharted domain that doesn't require a space shuttle: the spirit. Crowley may be gone, but look around: the spirit of Frater Perdurabo endures.

Notes

Throughout, *Confessions* refers to Aleister Crowley's *The Confessions of Aleister Crowley* (edited by John Symonds and Kenneth Grant, London: Jonathan Cape, 1969); the unexpurgated *Confessions* refers to the full work prepared and edited by Hymenaeus Beta. *World's Tragedy* is Aleister Crowley's *The World's Tragedy* (Foyers: Society for the Propagation of Religious Truth, 1910; reprinted in 1985 by Falcon Press). *AL* refers to *The Book of the Law*, to which Crowley gave the Latin title *Liber AL vel Legis;* citations are given *chapter:verse*. *Works* refers to *The Collected Works of Aleister Crowley* (1905–1907, Foyers: SPRT).

Acknowledgments

1   61 in Anthony DeCurtis, "Paul McCartney," *Rolling Stone*, 3–17 May 2007, 1025/ 1026: 60–62.

2   Benjamin Svetkey, "Robert Downey Jr.: Entertainer of the Year," *Entertainment Weekly*, 14 Nov 2008, http://www.ew.com/ew/article/0,,20240193,00.html (accessed Jan 20 2010). A recent *Rolling Stone* interview sheds further light on this "ritual": "Downey prepared himself for the next stage ... by doing artistic flexibility exercises augmented by ceremonial white magic.... So he did some astral-plane conjuring. Before his *Iron Man* screen test, he built, for real, an 'altar to the possibility of self' out of 'some intuitively gathered objects' that included a picture of the superhero and—it gets spooky here—'a sunstone wand'" (Walter Kirn, "Robert Downey Jr.: Hardass, Flake, Superstar. He's Anything You Want Him to Be, and an Iron Man, Too," *Rolling Stone,* 13 May 2010, 1104: 44–6).

3   Donna Zuckerbrot, *Aleister Crowley: The Beast 666* (Reel Time Images, 2007).

4   http://www.abebooks.com/books/authors-corner/ (accessed Jan 19 2010).

5   Rosalie Parker, "Aleister Crowley," *Book and Magazine Collector,* Aug 2008, 297: 26– 35. Blair MacKenzie Blake, *The Wickedest Books in the World: Confessions of an Aleister Crowley Bibliophile* (n.p., 2009).

6   Egil Asprem, "Magic Naturalized? Negotiating Science and Occult Experience in Aleister Crowley's Scientific Illuminism," *Aries* 2008, 8(2): 139–65. Henrik Bogdan, "Challenging the Morals of Western Society: The Use of Ritualized Sex in Contemporary Occultism," *The Pomegranate* 2006, 8(2): 211–46. Nick Freeman, "Wilde's Edwardian Afterlife: Somerset Maugham, Aleister Crowley, and The Magician," *Literature and History* 2007, 16(2): 16–29. Richard Kaczynski, "The Crowley-

Harris Thoth Tarot: Collaboration and Innovation" in Emily E. Auger (ed.), *Tarot in Culture* (under review). Marco Pasi, "The Influence of Aleister Crowley on Fernando Pessoa's Esoteric Writings," *Gnostics 3: Ésotérisme, Gnoses & Imaginaire Symbolique* (Leuven, Belgium: Peeters, 2001), 693–711. Marco Pasi, "The Never-endingly Told Story: Recent Biographies of Aleister Crowley," *Aries* 2003, 3(2): 224–45. Hugh Urban, "The Beast with Two Backs: Aleister Crowley, Sex Magic and the Exhaustion of Modernity," *Nova Religio*, Mar 2004, 7(3): 7–25. Hugh Urban, "Unleashing the Beast: Aleister Crowley, Tantra, and Sex Magic in Late Victorian England," *Esoterica* 2003, 5: 138–92.

7   Marco Pasi, *Aleister Crowley und die Versuchung der Politik* (Ares Verlag, 2006). Richard B. Spence, *Secret Agent 666: Aleister Crowley, British Intelligence and the Occult* (Los Angeles: Feral House, 2008).

8   Mark S. Morrison, *Modern Alchemy: Occultism and the Emergence of Atomic Theory* (Oxford Univ. Press: Oxford, 2007)

9   Marcus Boon, *The Road of Excess: A History of Writers on Drugs* (Cambridge: Harvard Univ. Press, 2002).

Chapter One • Birthday

1   Crowley discusses his initiation into the GD in *Confessions*, 176–177; "The Temple of Solomon the King," *The Equinox* 1909, 1(2): 217–334; and AC to N. Mudd, 18 Nov 1923, Old D1, Yorke Collection. The GD Neophyte Ceremony, presented here in abridged form, can be found in R. G. Torrens, *The Secret Rituals of the Golden Dawn* (New York: Samuel Weiser, 1973); Israel Regardie, *The Complete Golden Dawn System of Magick* (Phoenix, AZ: Falcon Press, 1984); Israel Regardie, *The Golden Dawn: An Account of the Teachings, Rites and Ceremonies of the Order of the Golden Dawn* (Saint Paul, MN: Llewellyn Publications, 1978); Crowley, "The Temple of Solomon the King," *op. cit.* GD scholar R. A. Gilbert (personal communication) contends that November 18, 1898, was not the day of Crowley's initiation, but rather the date he signed his application; whether correct or not, Crowley observed November 18 as his magical birthday.

2   Neil L. York, "Crowley, Thomas (c.1713–1787)," *Oxford Dictionary of National Biography* (Oxford Univ. Press, 2004).

3   Joseph Smith, *A Descriptive Catalogue of Friends' Books, or Books Written by Members of the Society of Friends, Commonly Called Quakers: From Their First Rise to the Present Time: Interspersed with Critical Remarks, and Occasional Biographical Notices, and Including All Writings by Authors before Joining, and by Those after Having Left the Society, Whether Adverse or Not, as Far as Known* (London: Joseph Smith, 1867), 496.

4   *Oxford Dictionary of National Biography, op. cit.*

5   Ann Crowley and Thomas Crowley, *Some Expressions of Ann Crowley, Daughter of Thomas and Mary Crowley, of London, during Her Last Illness, from the 23d of the First Month 1773, to the 12th of the Second Month 1774: With an Introductory Testimony Concerning Her, from the Family* (London: Mary Hinde, 1774). This collection saw British printings in 1774 and 1784 (London: James Phillips), and American printings in 1775 (Burlington, NJ: Isaac Collins) and 1776 (Norwich, CT: Henry Spencer). Ann Crowley's tale was also recounted in Thomas Wagstaffe, *Piety Promoted In Brief Memorials, and Dying Expressions, of Some of the People Called Quakers. The Ninth Part*, 2nd ed. (London: James Phillips and Son, 1798), 50–3.

6   *Oxford Dictionary of National Biography, op. cit.*

7   Smith, *Descriptive Catalogue*, 496–500. Royal Commission on Historical Manuscripts and William Legge Dartmouth, *The Manuscripts of the Earl of Dartmouth*, v. 2 (London: Eyre and Spottiswoode, 1895), 38, describes a letter from Thomas Crowley signed "Amor Patriæ." See also the letter (possibly to Lord Bute) signed "Amor Patriæ" dated 1 Feb 1766, MS 2007.5, Colonial Williamsburg Foundation, John D. Rockefeller Jr. Library, Williamsburg, VA.

8   Franklin's October 21, 1768, letter to Crowley is reprinted in Albert Henry Smyth
      (ed.), *The Writings of Benjamin Franklin,* v. 5, 1767–1772 (London: Macmillan,
      1906), 166–8. Thomas Crowley's letters, signed "Amor Patriæ," to Benjamin Frank-
      lin on November 17 and December 10, 1770, are in the Benjamin Franklin Papers,
      Hays Calendar Part 12 Section 1640–1778 B F85, items 53: 5 and 69: 92–3, Amer-
      ican Philosophical Society, Philadelphia, PA. For Crowley's political writing, see
      Neil York, "Federalism and the Failure of Imperial Reform, 1774–1775," *History*
      2001, 86: 155–79.

9   Works of Thomas Crowley (alphabetically arranged): *By a Professor of the True Chris-*
      tian Religion, without any mixture of Superstition, who proposeth to build a Meeting-house,
      at or near Walworth, for the use of sober, rational Christians, unless the Society of Quakers
      should be wise and honest enough, to establish a just Liberty of Conscience…. [anonymous
      handbill] (n.p,, [1784]); *A Plan of Union, by Admitting Representatives from the American*
      Colonies, and from Ireland into the British Parliament (London: 1770); *Account of a plan*
      for civilizing the North American Indians, 2nd ed. (n.p., [1766?]); *The Controversy*
      between Great-Britain and Her Colonies Briefly Analysed (n.p., 1766); *Copies of Eight Let-*
      ters from T. Crowley to the Quakers and Others (London: the author, 1782); *Copies of*
      Thomas Crowley's Letters and Dissertations on Society Concerns since the 7th Month, 1773
      (n.p., [1774?]); *Copies of Thomas Crowley's Letters to the Quakers, Not Printed Before,*
      May 1, 1776…. (n.p., [1776?]); *Copies of Thomas Crowley's Letters to the Quakers,*
      Printed Since May I, 1776…. (n.p., [1779?]); *Copy of a Letter to the Chairman of a Meet-*
      ing of the Clergy, and Also Inserted in the Public Ledger (n.p., [1779?]); *Copy of a Letter*
      to Thomas Corbyn—dated, Walworth, 8th Nov. 1784, with "A System of Religion" (n.p.,
      n.d.); *Copy of a Letter wrote and sent, or delivered, to the late Lord Archbishop of Canter-*
      bury…. (n.p., n.d.); *Desultory observations on the Education and Manners of the fair sex—*
      dated, August 10,1785 (n.p., n.d.); *Dissertations on the Peculiarities of the Quakers, in a*
      letter to Dr. F. and D. B.—Walworth—20th April, 1776 (n.p., n.d.); *Dissertations on*
      the Pecuniary Testimonies of the People Called Quakers…. (n.p., 1773); *Dissertations, on*
      the Grand Dispute between Great-Britain and America (n.p., 1774); *The Divine Authorities*
      of the Prophet Malachi, our Saviour, and the Apostles Paul and Peter, relative to Tithes and
      Submission…. (n.p., n.d.); *Fourteen Letters of T. Crowley's to the Quakers* (London: the
      author, 1782); *General Rules with Their Exceptions, Calculated for Such as Are Curious*
      to Know the Grounds, & Delicate Turns of the French Language…. (London: n.p., 1748);
      Letters and Dissertations on Various Subjects (London: the author, [1776?]); *Letters and*
      Queries, together with Quotations from the Holy Scriptures, Intended to Demonstrate the
      Necessity and Utility of Allowing Liberty of Conscience among Ourselves…. (London: n.p.,
      1769); *Letters Inserted in the Public Ledger* (n.p., n.d.); *Letters to the King, from an Old*
      Patriotic Quaker, Lately Deceased, ed. Thomas Crowley (London: R. Baldwin, 1778);
      The Life and Adventures of Mademoiselle De La Sarre: Containing a Great Many Indidents
      [Sic] Presumed to Be New…. (Rotterdam: Stephen Hebert, 1751); *Observations and*
      Propositions for an Accommodation between Great Britain and Her Colonies (London: n.p.,
      1768); *Poetical Essays on Various Subjects. Originally Wrote Agreeable to the Date….*
      (London: the author, 1784); *Reasons for Liberty of Conscience, Respecting the Payment*
      of Tythes, or Complying with Other Pecuniary Laws, Enacted by the Legislature (London:
      the author, 1771); *Thomas Crowley's Dissertations on Liberty of Conscience … Together*
      with The Proceedings of the Society of Quakers against Him Thereon, and His Subsequent
      Letters on that Occasion (London: the author, [1775?]); *To the Chief Priests or Preachers,*
      Scribes or Clerks, and Elders, Who as Tools Do Rule (Walworth, 3 Oct 1782); *To the*
      Superstitious Priests, Lovers of their own Power, and to Their Silly Tools of Priestcraft,
      Quacks and Money-Mongers, among the Misled People called Quakers (n.p., n.d.); *To the*
      Unhappily Misled—Dated, Walworth, 6th March, 1776 (n.p., 1776).

10 J. R. Grey, *Crowley's Brewery, 1763–1963: A Brief History* (London: Watneys, 1963),
      11.

11 Records of the Sun Fire Office, MS 11936/423/727667, Guildhall Library, Alder-
      manbury, London. Thomas Crowley appears in numerous London business directo-
      ries between 1777–1790, e.g., *Kent's Directory for the Year 1777* (London: Richard
      and Henry Causton, 1777). For Thomas Crowley's bankruptcy, see "Bankrupts,"

Literary Magazine and British Review, Dec 1788, 480; "Dividends," *Times* (London), 17 Aug 1789, (1232): 1; William Smith and Co., *A List of Bankrupts, with Their Dividends, Certificates, &C. &C. for the Last Twenty Years and Six Months, Viz. from Jan. 1, 1786, to June 24, 1806, Inclusive* (London: The Proprietor, 1806).

12   The children, in order, were Maria, Alfred (1786–1786), Edward, Elizabeth, Alfred Driver (c. 1790–1809), Henry, Abraham, and Charles Sedgefield. Thus, Thomas Crowley had another son, Alfred, who died in infancy prior to Edward's birth. "Crowley family tree," http://www.manicai.net/genealogy/crowley/crowley_tree.pdf (accessed Apr 23 2010). Alfred Driver Crowley's 22 Jan 1809, obituary appears in *Gentlemen's Magazine,* Feb 1809, 94, where he is described as "Aged 19, Alfred, second son of Mr. Thomas Crowley of Camomile-street."

13   For Henry Crowley's death, see *Weekly Reporter,* 11 Jul 1863, XI: 861; William Hugh Curtis, *A Quaker Doctor and Naturalist in the 19th Century: The Story of William Curtis* (London: Bannisdale Press, 1961), 114–5.

14   The Quakers were generally pioneers in opposing slavery in the eighteenth and early nineteenth centuries. Abraham, Charles, and Henry Crowley were delegates to the General Anti-Slavery Convention [*The British and Foreign Anti-Slavery Reporter* 28 Jun 1843, 4(14): 113]; Abraham also appears as a supporter in *The Anti-Slavery Reporter and Aborigines' Friend,* 1 Dec 1865, 167 and elsewhere. Similarly, his father Thomas Crowley of 35 Camomile Street, and his grandfather, Thomas Crowley of 73 Gracechurch Street, were subscribers in the *Fifth Report of the Committee of the African Institution* (London: African Institution, 1811), 127. *Life of William Allen, with Selections from His Correspondence* (Philadelphia: Henry Longstreth, 1847) contains a February 4, 1791, note after the House of Commons moved to appoint a Committee on the Slave Trade: "as the Slave Merchants' party in the House had given notice that they would oppose it, I had a great inclination to hear the debate, and accordingly, Thomas Crowley and I went" (p. 10). Likewise on April 19, 1791, he noted, "I could not with any degree of convenience, go to hear the debates on the Slave Trade to-day, but my friend Thomas Crowley went" (p. 12).

15   Crowley family tree, *op. cit.* See the marriage announcement of C. S. Crowley and Emma Curtis in "Births, Marriages, and Deaths," *Observer* (London), 29 Jul 1838, 1; the death announcement of Emma Crowley in "Births, Marriages, and Deaths," *Observer* (London), 4 Jan 1846, 8 and "Died," *Times* (London), 30 Dec 1845, 19120: 9. For the Crowley and Curtis families, see Curtis, *Quaker Doctor.*

16   William Curtis, *A Short History and Description of the Town of Alton in the County of Southampton* (London: Simpkin & Co.), 154–5. James Baverstock, *Hydrometrical Observations and Experiments in the Brewery* (London: the author, 1785). Michael T. Davis, "Baverstock, James B. (1741–1815)," *Oxford Dictionary of National Biography* (Oxford: Oxford Univ. Press, 2004).

17   Peter Mathias, *The Brewing Industry in England, 1700–1830* (Cambridge: Univ. Press, 1959), 298–9.

18   Grey, *Crowley's Brewery,* 10.

19   John Hollingshead, *According to My Lights* (London: Chatto & Windus, 1900), 48–9.

20   Grey, *Crowley's Brewery,* 13.

21   291 in Charles Dickens, "An Unsettled Neighborhood," *Household Words,* 11 Nov 1854, 10(242): 289–92.

22   544 in An Ex-Official, "Tales out of School," *London Society: An Illustrated Magazine of Light and Amusing Literature for the Hours of Relaxation,* May 1883, 43(257): 544–56.

23   Edmund Hodgson Yates, *Edmund Yates: His Recollections and Experiences,* vol. 1(London: R. Bentley & Son, 1884), 121.

24   Hollingshead, *According to My Lights,* 50.

25   Hollingshead, *According to My Lights,* 48–9.

26   E.g., *Times* (London), 24 Jun 1843 and 1 Jul 1843.

27   Classified ads in *Times* (London) for 25 May 1844, 22 Jan 1853, 25 Feb 1854, and

21 Nov 1863. Henry Downes Miles, *The London and Suburban Licensed Victuallers', Hotel and Tavern Keepers' Directory together with a List of the Brewers, Maltsters, Hop Factors, Distillers, and Rectifiers of the United Kingdom* (London: the author, 1874). *Kelly's Directory of the Wine and Spirit Trades, with Which Are Included Brewers and Maltsters, and Other Trades connected Therewith, of England, Scotland and Wales, and Also the Principal Wine Merchants, etc., on the Continent* (London: Kelly and Co., 1884).

28   "Abridged Police Intelligence," *Observer* (London), 12 Oct 1846, 7; a photo of Crowley's Alton Ale Wharf (c. 1915), referred to in the *Times* article, can be seen at http://www.lashtal.com/nuke/module-pnCPG-view-soort-1-album-10-pos-2024 .phtml (accessed Jul 26 2009). W. T. Marchant, *In Praise of Ale; or, Songs, Ballads, Epigrams, & Anecdotes Relating to Beer, Malt, and Hops; with Some Curious Particulars Concerning Ale-wives and Brewers, Drinking-Clubs and Customs* (London: George Redway, 1888), 462.

29   "Money Market and City Intelligence," *Spirit of the Times: A Chronicle of the Turf, Agriculture, Field Sports, Life,* 24 Aug 1950, 20(27): 315.

30   GRO, Class HO107; Piece 1679; Folio 151; Page 37; GSU roll: 193587.

31   GRO RG9/704, Folio 116, page 5.

32   Grey, *Crowley's Brewery,* 11. Much as they did with the Curtis family, the Crowleys also married into the Ashby family: Abraham's sister Elizabeth (1789–1879) married Thomas Ashby Jr. (c. 1787–1866) in 1819; his sister Maria (1785–1854) married Ashby's other son, William (1788–1850), in 1811; his son Abraham Curtis married Ann Ashby (1827–1909) in 1850; his son Alfred married Catherine Sophia Ashby (1826–1854) in 1850; and his daughter Elizabeth (1828–1912) married Charles Ashby (1828–1914) in 1853. Crowley family tree, *op cit.,* and the Ashby family genealogy at http://captionsfordisplay.blogspot.com/2008/09/c.html. Elizabeth "Bella" Crowley's marriage notice appears in the 4 Mar 1819 *Times* (London), 10613: 3, and her death date of November 25, 1879, is given in *The Annual Monitor for 1881, or Obituary of the Members of the Society of Friends in Great Britain and Ireland, for the Year 1880* (London, 1880), 13. Elizabeth Crowley's notice of marriage to Charles Ashby on September 14 appears in the *Observer* (London), 18 Sep 1853, 8. The marriage and death dates of Catherine Sophia Ashby are found, respectively, in GRO Croydon, Surrey, Q1, 1850, 4: 77, and GRO Croydon, Surrey, Q1, 1854, 2: 85; her January 13, 1854, death is also reported in *The Annual Monitor for 1855, or Obituary of the Members of the Society of Friends in Great Britain and Ireland, for the Year 1854* (London, 1854), 24.

33   Counterpart lease of the Barley Mow Public House, 39M89, Knight Archive, Hampshire Record Office. This partnership continued through 1824; see http://www.manicai.net/genealogy/crowley/letter_to_ashbys.pdf for letters dated 1926 between the Crowley and Ashby families regarding dissolution of their partnership.

34   Paul Hudson, "English Emigration to New Zealand, 1839–1850: Information Diffusion and Marketing a New World." *Economic History Review* 2001, 64(4): 680–98. Abraham Crowley was the sixth of seventy-four agents employed by the company (p. 696).

35   "Obituary," *Gentleman's Magazine,* Jul 1864, 2: 123.

36   Grey, *Crowley's Brewery,* 13–4.

37   See, for instance, the agreement signed in 1867 by Abraham Curtis, Alfred, Frederick, and Philip Crowley: "Counterpart lease, 31 Dec 1867," 34M91W/472/8, St. John's Winchester Charity, Hampshire Record Office.

38   W. H. Jacob, *Hampshire at the Opening of the Twentieth Century* (Brighton: W. T. Pike & Co., 1905), 62M91/1, Hampshire Archives and Local Studies, Hampshire Record Office; William White, *History, Gazetteer and Directory of the County of Hampshire, Including the Isle of Wight...* (Sheffield: W. White, 1878), 104–5. Curtis, *Short History,* 132–4.

39   *Journal of the Society of Arts* 16 Oct 1857, 643; "Obituary," *Gardeners' Chronicle,* Dec 29, 1900, 481; "The Late Mr. Philip Crowley," *Gardeners' Magazine* 1900 (43): 847;

Proceedings of the Linnean Society of London 1901, 113: 42–3; "Obituary," *Entomologist's Monthly Magazine* 1901, 49; "Obituary," *Ibis: A Quarterly Journal of Ornithology* 1901 1: 352–3, 521–2; Croydon Natural History and Scientific Society, *Proceedings and Transactions* 1903, 5: xlvii–iii.

40   Harry Percy Burrell married Abraham Crowley's daughter Gertrude Evelyn (1858–1939) in 1878, a year after taking over the brewery; Crowley family genealogy, *op cit.;* "Deaths," *Times* (London), 25 May 1938, 48003: 1; "Deaths," *Times* (London), 12 Jul 1939.

41   "Married," *Times* (London), 22 Aug 1823, 11957: 3. Mary Crowley's date of death (29 May 1868) is given in "Births, Marriages, and Deaths," *Observer* (London), 7 Jun 1868, 8 and is recorded in GRO, London, Surrey, Q2, 1d: 321. Sarah Maria Crowley's birth is announced in "Births, Marriages and Deaths," *Observer* (London), 23 Aug 1829, 4.

42   For Sarah Maria Crowley's birth, see "Births, Marriages and Deaths," *Observer* (London), 23 Aug 1828, 4. Re. Edward Crowley: Aleister Crowley's August 17, 1943, diary reads "My father's 109th birthday—had he lived" (Yorke Collection, Warburg Institute, University of London), implying an 1834 birthdate. However, Edward Crowley's March 5, 1887, death certificate gives his age as fifty-seven years (GRO, Millbrook, Southampton), as does his death notice in the *Times* (8 Mar 1887), suggesting he was born around 1830. This latter year is more consistent with his age in the British Census from 1841 to 1881. If Aleister is correct about the date (August 17), then Edward Crowley would have to have been born in 1829 to be fifty-seven years old at the time of his death.

43   *Reports from Committees: Sixteen Volumes. 14 Part II, Railway Subscription Lists 407, Bath and Weymouth Railway Subscription List, Session 31 January–17 July 1837* vol. 18, part 2 (London: House of Commons, 1837).

44   Henry Tuck, *Railway Directory for 1845: Containing the Names of the Directors and Principal Officers of the Railways in Great Britain* (London: Railway Times Office, 1845). Henry Glynn, *Reference Book to the Incorporated Railway Companies of England and Wales* (London: John Weale, 1847). Henry Glynn, *A Reference Book to the Incorporated Railway Companies of Ireland, Alphabetically Arranged* (London: John Weale, 1847). Charles Barker & Sons, *The Joint Stock Companies' Directory for 1876* (London: John King & Co., 1867). "Court Circular," *Times* (London), 13 Nov 1844, 18767: 5. "Railway Intelligence," *Observer* (London), 29 Sep 1845, 2. The London *Times* reported on the elections of directors in its "Railway Intelligence" section, with the Crowley brothers appearing in the following issues: 17 Dec 1851, 20987: 8; 24 Jan 1852, 21020: 8; 18 Jul 1853, 21483: 8; 31 Jan 1855, 21965: 7; 30 Jan 1856, 22277: 6; 7 Feb 1856, 22284: 5; 9 Feb 1863, 24477: 6. Additionally, various British railways announced the results of their directors' meetings, or printed prospecti for new railways, in the classified sections of the London *Times*; the Crowley brothers appear as directors in classified ads in the following issues: 21 Jun 1843, 3; 7 Sep 1844, 3; 5 Jul 1845, 1; 15 Jul 1845, 2; 31 Jul 1845, 11; 8 Aug 1845, 2; 21 Oct 1845, 13; 19 Apr 1848, 3; 26 Jan 1849, 8; 1 Jan 1851, 2; 3 Nov 1852, 9; 27 Jan 1854, 4.

45   Meeting notice in classified ad section, *Times* (London), 6 Aug 1852, 21187: 2.

46   "Railway Speculation," *Times* (London), 13 Aug 1846, 19314: 3.

47   The June 16, 1843, elections of the London and Brighton Railway were announced in the June 21 issue, while the Alton Ales notice ran on the 24th.

48   Henry O'Neil, *Two Thousand Years Hence* (London: Chapman & Hall, 1867), 113.

49   "Select Committees on Bills," *Times* (London), 31 Mar 1846, 19198: 7 and "Select Committees on Bills," *Times* (London), 29 Apr 1846, 19223: 7, respectively.

50   "London and South Western Railway," *Observer* (London), 27 Oct 1850, 2.

51   "Branch Railway to Alton," *Hampshire and Southampton County Paper,* 31 Jul 1852, 4. Curtis Museum of Alton 4M51/212.

52   Edward Crowley, *The Age We Live In: High Art No Evidence of a High State of Civilization* (Clapham: Clapham Athenæum, 1854).

53 "Deaths," *Times* (London), 19 Feb 1856, 22294: 1. Edward Crowley, Last will and testament, prob 11/2228, Public Record Office, National Archives.

54 *The Law Times: The Journal of the Law and the Lawyers,* 16 May 1868, 45: 56; Classified ad, *Times* (London), 25 Apr 1868, 26108: 15.

55 GRO Wandsworth, Surrey. "Births, Marriages, and Deaths," *Observer* (London), 7 Jun 1868, 8.

56 His occupation is listed as "civil engineer" as early as the 1851 census (HO107, piece 2137, folio 34, page 10, GSU roll 87767) and on his 1853 marriage certificate (GRO, Marylebone, London, 1a: 796). Although his occupation is listed as "head of household and householder" in 1861, he appears as a civil engineer in the 1867 *Surrey Post Office Directory* (p. 1671), 1871 census, and the 1878 *Surrey Post Office Directory* (p. 2174); in the 1881 census, he appears as a retired civil engineer.

57 For the railway crash, see "Dreadful Collision on the Brighton Railway," *Times* (London), 2 Nov 1852, 21262: 5 and "The Collision on the Brighton Railway," *Times* (London), 3 Nov 1852, 21263: 8. Provisional protection for the patent is noted in "Notices of Intentions to Proceed," *Mechanics' Magazine, Museum Journal, and Gazette,* 2 Nov 1852, 57(1529): 439; "Provisional Protections Granted," *London Journal of Arts, Sciences, and manufactures, and Repository of Patent Inventions* 1852, 41(252): 473. Details of the invention are in Charles Dickens, "Self-Acting Railway Signals," *Household Words* 1853, 7(155): 43–5; Anonymous, "Crowley's Safety Switch and Self-Acting Railway Signals," *Mechanics' Magazine,* 22 Jan 1853, 58(1537): 66–7.

58 He was balloted for and elected as an associate on January 13, 1863, see *Minutes of the Proceedings of the Institution of Civil Engineers* 1863, 22: 167; his election was also reported in "Learned Societies," *The Reader* 1863, 4: 103.

59 He became a fellow of the Geographical Society on November 11, 1861 (see *Proceedings of the Royal Geographical Society of London* 1861, 6: 1; *Journal of the Royal Geographical Society of London* 1862, 32: xxviii) and of the Ethnological Society on January 14, 1862 (see *Transactions of the Ethnological Society of London* 1863, 2: 34).

60 GRO, Marylebone, London, 1a: 796; their wedding was also announced in "Marriages," *Times* (London), 17 May 1853, 21430: 9, and "Births, Marriages, and Deaths," *Observer* (London), 23 May 1853, 8.

61 "Deaths." *Times* (London), 15 Aug 1854, 21820: 1 and "Births, Marriages, and Deaths," *Observer* (London), 21 Aug 1854, 8. For Agnes and Claude Crowley, see the biographical supplement (vol. 7) to the unexpurgated edition of *The Confessions of Aleister Crowley,* ed. Hymenaeus Beta.

62 Certified record of death, 23 Aug 1869, GRO: Marylebone, Middlesex.

63 Her surname is given as "Higginbotham" on her April 2, 1840, birth certificate (GRO, Colesville, Warwick); as "Heginbottom" on her April 4, 1872, marriage certificate (GRO Coventry, 6d: 590); and variously as "Higgenbotham," "Heginbotham," and "Higginbotham" on the 1841, 1861, and 1871 censuses, respectively. Similarly, her forename was "Ann" on the registration of her birth, "Anne" on her marriage certificate, and all censuses from 1841 until 1891, where she appears as "Anna." On the 1901 census, she is listed as "Annie." For additional details, see the biographical appendix to the unabridged *Confessions, op. cit.*

64 Certified record of marriage, 12 Sep 1869, GRO: Warwick, Warwickshire, 6d: 609; certified record of death, 15 Dec 1880 GRO: Warwick, Warwickshire, 6d: 328; certified record of death, Q4, 1890, GRO: Warwick, Warwickshire, 6d: 377. "Deaths," *Times* (London), 23 Dec 1880, 30072: 1 .

65 Crowley, *Confessions,* unexpurgated edition, biographical index.

66 Certified record of marriage, GRO Lambeth, Surrey 1d: 605. "Births, Marriages, and Deaths," *Observer* (London), 24 Sep 1854, 1.

67 "Deaths," *Daily News* (London), 19 Feb 1856, 7.

68 "Obituary," *Solicitors' Journal and Reporter,* 29 Jan 1870, 283. "Legal Obituary," *Law*

Times, 19 Feb 1870, 325. Thrupp and Dixon are listed as "petitioners' solicitors" for the Crowleys in a classified announcement in *Times* (London), 8 Jun 1865, 25206: 3. For John Thrupp's writing, see: *Historical Law Tracts* (London: O. Richards), 1843. *The Anglo-Saxon Home: A History of the Domestic Institutions and Customs of England, from the Fifth to the Eleventh Century* (London: Longman, Green, Longman & Roberts, 1862) and *On the Domestication of Certain Animals in England between the Seventh and Eleventh Centuries* (np, 1865?).

69   *Confessions,* 35.

70   1851 census, Battersea, Surrey, HO107, piece 1577, 165: 19. 1861 census, Clapham, Surrey, RG9, piece 368, 230: 5. 1881 census, Leamington Priors, Warwickshire, RG11, piece 3093, 48: 39. Around this time, while living in Wandsworth, Edward Crowley also ran a classified ad offering a £1 reward for the return of his lost black dog, Pilot; *Times* (London), 22 Sep 1864, 24984: 1.

71   Classified ad, *Times* (London), 26 Nov 1853, 21596: 3. Additional ads for the company ran regularly for nearly two years.

72   "From the London Gazette of Tuesday, April 24," *Observer* (London), 29 Apr 1855, 8. See also the ad by Crowley, White, and Crowley in *Pope's Yearly Journal of Trade Advertiser* 1854, 90.

73   Aleister Crowley, *The Law is for All: The Authorized Popular Commentary on Liber AL vel Legis sub figura CCXX The Book of the Law,* ed. Louis Wilkinson and Hymenaeus Beta (Tempe, AZ: New Falcon, 1996), 90.

74   The 1841 census of the Crowley household lists a female servant named Ann Lewis, aged thirty-five (GRO, Battersea, Surrey, HO107, piece 1046, district 8, 57: 14); Edward was eleven years old at the time. She may be the namesake of Edward Crowley's card "Poor Anne's Last Words," described in *Confessions,* 39. A card by this title, however, is not in Anthony R. Naylor, *Notes towards a Bibliography of Edward Crowley, tegether with Library Resources and Catalogue Information* (Thame: I-H-O Books, 2004).

75   Napoleon Noel and William Franklin Knapp, *The History of the Brethren* (Denver: W. F. Knapp, 1936), 140. See also Grayson Carter, *Anglican Evangelicals: Protestant Secessions from the Via Media, C. 1800–1850,* Oxford theological monographs (Oxford: Oxford Univ. Press, 2001), 400, where Edward Crowley appears in the appendix of "Evangelical Seceders from the Church of England, c. 1730–1900."

76   Members of this group eschew any labels which smack of denominationalism, preferring simply to call themselves "Christians." Thus, Edward Crowley's 1865 pamphlet on the sect is titled "The Plymouth Brethren, so-called." I nevertheless use the term "Brethren" for the sake of clarity.

77   Dr. James H. Brooks, quoted in H. A. Ironside, *A Historical Sketch of the Brethren Movement* (Neptune, NJ: Loizeaux Brothers, 1985).

78   See Ironside, *Historical Sketch*; Miles J. Stanford, "The Plymouth Brethren: A Brief History," http://withchrist.org/MJS/pbs.htm; Napoleon and Knapp, *History of the Brethren;* Peter Blackwell, "The Plymouth Brethren," http://www.victorianweb.org/religion/plymouth.html; Shawn Abigail's "Plymouth Brethren FAQ," http://www.brethrenonline.org/faqs/Brethren.htm (all sites accessed on Apr 23 2010).

79   This evangelical sophism is interesting in light of Crowley's later instruction for his followers to "say Will" before every meal. While variants exist, its general form is illustrated on page 361.

80   Crowley, *World's Tragedy,* xiii.

81   *Confessions,* 46.

82   GRO Q1 1848 births, Farnborough, Hampshire. "Deaths," *Times* (London), 25 Apr 1917. GRO 26 Nov 1854 deaths, Taunton, Somerest. GRO 1871 Census, Kensingon, London, RG10, piece 34, 7: 7. GRO 18 Nov 1874, Kensington, London. Unexpurgated *Confessions,* biographical supplement. Note the marriage record incorrectly gives Emily's age as twenty.

83   *Times* (London), 11–13 Oct 1875.

84 *Confessions,* 54.

85 *Confessions,* 37. While Crowley only gives surnames for Miss Arkell and Miss Carey, evidence from the 1881 Warwickshire census identifies them. For instance, Mary Arkell of 31 Campion Terrace, Leamington, is listed as a "daily governess" living with three of her sisters (RG11, piece 3093, 122: 8; her birth and death records are also in Warwickshire). Mary A. Carey is listed as a "lady" born in Warwick and visiting the widow Frances M. Ferguson of 25 Dale Street, Leamington (RG11, piece 3092, 94: 27). Emma and Susan Copwer are listed as "annuitants" at 67 Rugby Road, Leamington, with the former recorded as head of household (RG11, piece 3094, 106: 2).

86 Again, the parallels to Crowley's later spirituality leap out. In *AL* ii.28–33, we read "Now a curse upon Because and his kin! May Because be accursèd for ever!... Enough of because! Be he damned for a dog!"

87 *World's Tragedy,* xx.

88 Krsitine Hughes, *The Writer's Guide to Everyday Life in Regency and Victorian England* (Cincinnati: Writer's Digest Books, 1998).

89 GRO, 1881 Census, Leamington Priors, Warwickshire, RG11, piece 3093, 48: 39.

90 Crowley's *Confessions,* 42, says she lived five hours; her record of death gives four hours and includes the cause of death (GRO Warwick, Warwickshire, 6d: 374).

91 This response is typical, as death is generally not understood by young children. Worden, Davies & McCowan (1999) note that, among boys, sibling loss has much less impact than parent death. For children experiencing the death of a sibling, the greatest response is frequently not to the death itself, but to their parents' coping behaviors (Schwab, 1997). J. William Worden, Betty Davies,& Darlene McCown, "Comparing Parent Loss with Sibling Loss," *Death-Studies* 1999, 23(1): 1-15. Reiko Schwab, "Parental Mourning and Children's Development," *Journal of Counseling and Development* 1997, 75(4): 258–65.

92 Aleister Crowley, *The Diary of a Drug Fiend* (London: William Collins, 1922), 4. Crowley's annotated copy in the Yorke Collection notes on this passage, "I idealized from The Grange, Redhill, Surrey, where I lived from 1881 to 1886 E.V."

93 *Confessions,* 46.

94 Advertisement, *The Lancet,* 14 Aug 1886, 42. Death records, Q4 1885, GRO, Hastings, Sussex. British census, 1891 GRO, RG12, piece 765, 48: 41. Birth records, Q3 1861, Gravesend, Kent. Birth records, Q3 1864, North Aylesford, Kent.

95 See *Confessions,* 48–9, for Crowley's recollections surrounding Habershon's death.

96 Aleister Crowley, *Crowley on Christ,* ed. Francis King (London: Daniel, 1974), 187 (first published in 1953 in a limited edition of two-hundred spiral bound, mimeographed copies as *The Gospel according to St. Bernard Shaw.* Barstow, CA).

97 "Memories of the 1880's and 1890's," Bateman Street newsletter c. 1999, courtesy of Ian Glover.

98 Aleister Crowley, *The Works of Aleister Crowley* (Foyers: SPRT, 1906), 2: 11 (originally published in 1905 in *Oracles: The Autobiography of an Art.* Foyers: SPRT). The last line quotes Proverbs 20: 1.

99 For English-language editions of his works, see: Cesare Mattei, *Electro Homeopathy: New Vade-Mecum: New and True Guide for All Who Wish to Cure Themselves by Electro Homeopathy* (London: Modern Press, 1883). Cesare Mattei, *Electro-Homoeopathic Medicine; A New Medical System, Being a Popular and Domestic Guide Founded on Experience* (London: Stott, 1888). Kennedy's book is announced in the *Times* (London), 13 May 1886, 31758: 12. By July 14, 1886 (31811: 12), the text "for Cancer and Kindred Diseases" is added.

100 *Directory of Southampton, and Neighbourhood* (London: George Stevens, 1884), 188, lists a house called Glenburnie on 27 Hill Lane.

101 This estimate is based on several Consumer Price Indices which indicate that a dollar today is equivalent to roughly $0.04 in 1887. (A dollar was equivalent to exactly

$0.06 in 1913, but conversions to earlier years require extrapolations which are, at best, approximate.) Thus, £150,000/.04 = £3,750,000. However, since £1 is equal to approximately $1.70, we must multiply £3,750,000 x 1.7, yielding a net worth of $6,375,000.

102 Ironically, Crowley's schoolmaster, H. d'Arcy Champney, wrote *A Letter to the Saints Gathred in the Name of Jesus Christ* (Cambridge, 1890) in defense of Raven's ministry and in 1903 would write the poem "The Battle Fought" in memory of Raven's 1903 passing. See http://mybrethren.org/bios/frambios.htm (accessed Apr 23 2010).

103 *Confessions*, 36.

104 *World's Tragedy*, xx.

105 GRO birth records, Q1 1838, Strand, London. GRO death records, 26 Nov 1854, Taunton, Somerest. Percy Sitters, *TBB of the CSSM: A Memoir of Tom Bond Bishop* (London: Children's Special Service Mission, 1923). "Archives Edwin Roberts: Biographies, Books, Branches, Churches and Organisations," http://studymore.org.uk/arcedbbb.htm (accessed Apr 23 1910).

106 *Confessions*, 55.

107 A. Quiller Jr. [Aleister Crowley]. "My Crapulous Contemporaries No. VI: An Obituary," *The Equinox* 1912, 1(8): 243–49.

108 Thomas B. Bishop, *Evolution Criticised* (Edinburgh: Oliphants, 1918). Aleister Crowley, "The Tank," *The Equinox* 1919, 3(1): 284–6. In his critique, Crowley vents about his mother's death in 1917 and Bishop's response thereto.

109 David C. Clark, Robert Pynoos, & Ann E. Goebel, "Mechanisms and Processes of Adolescent Bereavement," in Robert J. Haggerty, Lonnie R. Sherrod, et al. (eds). *Stress, Risk, and Resilience in Children and Asolescents. Processes, Mechanisms, and Interventions.* (New York: Cambridge Univ. Press, 1996), 100–46. Steven Fleming & Leslie Balmer, "Bereavement in Adolescence," in Charles A. Corr and David E. Balk, et al. (eds), *Handbook of Adolescent Death and Bereavement* (New York: Springer, 1996), 139–54.

110 *World's Tragedy*, xviii.

111 *Confessions*, 69.

112 *World's Tragedy*, xvii.

113 The fate of Champney and his school is open to some debate. While Crowley reports the man's downfall shortly after this incident, subsequent research has produced conflicting results. Martin Booth says that Champney came under official observation, the school closed shortly thereafter, and, impoverished, he applied for aid under the Clerical Disabilities Act in 1899 (*A Magick Life: The Biography of Aleister Crowley,* London: Hodder & Stoughton, 2000, p. 23). Conversely, Lawrence Sutin's *Do What Thou Wilt* (2000) contends that Champney remained headmaster for another twelve years, after which the still-thriving school relocated to Bexhill (*Do What Thou Wilt: A Life of Aleister Crowley,* New York: St. Martin's Press, 2000, p. 30). Available evidence suggests that the truth may lie somewhere inbetween: The school did not close but was taken over, renamed and ultimately relocated. A. G. Brown, who knew Champney, says Champney "ran the brethren's school at Cambridge which my father [A. J. H. Brown] subsequently took over and transferred to Bexhill about 1898" (http://mybrethren.org/bios/frambios.htm, accessed Apr 23 2010). Indeed, Arthur John Henry Brown (1866–1934) is associated wtih the Ebor School in Bexhill-on-Sea (College of Preceptors, *The Calendar, for the Year 1900,* London: Francis Hodgson, p. 200), which was located in Bexhill as early as 1897 (see *Education Outlook* 1897, v. 50), and possibly earlier.

114 Certifed record of death, 13 Sep 1888, GRO, Croydon, Surrey.

115 Line 285.

116 *Confessions*, 73.

117 The bicycle had only been invented some twenty-nine years earlier, in 1862, and quickly became a popular alternative to the horse drawn carriage or train.

118 1891 census, GRO, RG12, piece 1703, 70: 33. Birth record, GRO, Q2 1866, Ecclesall Bierlow, Yorkshire. 1881 census, GRO, RG11, piece 4634, 61: 14. James A. Douglas was the second of Robert Douglas's three sons.

119 *World's Tragedy*, xx.

120 The 1851 census of England and Wales indicated that 40 percent of female servants were under age nineteen; frequently, they were in the thirteen- to fourteen-year-old range. A parlour maid—the "junior" staff position in the household—was more likely to be young, so one may assume that this parlour maid was roughly contemporary with Alec's fifteen years.

121 *Confessions*, 80.

122 AC to John B. Jameson, 5 Jan 1939, Yorke Collection.

123 Unabridged *Confessions*, v. 3 (with thanks to Hymenaeus Beta).

124 *World's Tragedy*, xxi.

125 Crowley's *Confessions* recount that he actually began climbing as an amateur prior to this time, out of sheer enjoyment of his recovering health. For instance, his application to the Scottish Mountaineering Club records ascents as early as summer, 1890, for Ben Vane (3,002 feet), Ben Cruachan (3,694 feet) and the highest mountain in the British Isles, Ben Nevis (4,409 feet). Likewise, in August, the month prior to meeting Lister at Skye, Crowley had also climbed the following Scottish peaks: Ben Ledi (2,884 feet), Ben A'an (1,488 feet), Ben Vorlich (Loch Earn, 3,232 feet), Ben More (Crianlarich, 3,852 feet), Ben Lawers (3,983 feet), Ben Lui (3,707 feet), Ben Oss (3,376 feet) and Beinn Dubhchraig (3,209 feet). But it was his experience with Lister that opened his eyes to climbing as a competitive sport. (Thanks to Clint Warren, Scottish Mountaineering Club archivist Robin Campbell, and William Breeze for Crowley's SMC application.)

126 Nick Greenslade, "Tonbridge and the Beast," *Tonbridgian*, date unknown, 18–9 (courtesy of Ian Glover). Nearly forty years later, Crowley would take a cottage in Knockholt, Kent, near his literary partner and editor, P. R. Stephensen.

127 *World's Tragedy*, xxi.

128 Crowley's *Eastbourne Gazette* contributions included "A Welcome to Jabez," reprinted in *Oracles* (1905). His contribution to *The Christian* is quoted in the *Confessions*, 73.

129 Crowley's *Eastbourne Gazette* column ran every Wednesday beginning on January 31, 1894, and ran for thirteen weeks (through April 25). For copies of the articles, see http://www.lashtal.com/nuke/Downloads-req-viewdownloaddetails-lid-52.phtml.

130 Crowley's application to the Scottish Mountaineering Club records his April/May 1893 climbs in Snowdonia as including Tryfan (3,002 feet), Glyder Fach (3,261 feet), Glyder Fawr (3,278 feet), Y Garn (Glyderau) (3,107 feet), Foel Grach (3,202 feet), the Craig Yr Ysfa ridge, Carnedd Dafydd (3,425 feet), Carnedd Llewelyn (3,491 feet), Yr Elen (3,156 feet), Pen yr Helgi Du (2,733 feet), Y Lliwedd (2,946 feet), the Twill Ddu cliff of Cloqwen y Geifr, and the highest mountain in Wales, Snowdon (3,560 feet). That June (and later that September) 1893 he visited the Lake District for the following Cumbrian ascents: Helvellyn (3,117 feet), Dollywaggon Pike (2,815 feet), Harrison Stickle (2,415 feet), Stickle Pike (1,230 feet), Thunacar Knott (2,372 feet), High White Stones (High Raise, Langdale)(2,500 feet), Sergeant Man (2,415 feet), Skiddaw (3,054), Helvellyn Lower Man (3,035 feet), Bowfell (2,959 feet), Great End (2,986 feet), Ill Crag (3,068 feet), Broad Crag (3,064 feet), Scafell Pike (3,209 feet), Sca Fell (3,163 feet), Pillar (2,927 feet), Great Gable (2,949 feet), Pike o' Blisco (2,313 feet), Crinkle Crags (2,818 feet), Shelter Crags (2,673 feet), Bowfell (2,959 feet), Hanging Knott (2,828 feet), Rossett Crag (2,136 feet), and Pavey Art (2,288 feet). Thanks to Clint Warren, Scottish Mountaineering Club archivist Robin Campbell, and William Breeze for Crowley's SMC application.

131 Aleister Crowley, Essay on magic and yoga, Old E1, Yorke Collection.

132 Walter Parry Haskett Smith, *Climbing in the British Isles: England* (London: Long-

mans, Green, 1894).

133 P. 288 in E. A. Crowley, "Chalk Climbing on Beachy Head." *The Scottish Mountaineering Club Journal,* 3(17): 288–94.

134 In his article, Crowley said it was "called, I believe, after a lady who never walked there" (p. 289).

135 John Cleare and Robin Collomb, *Sea Cliff Climbing in Britain* (London: Constable, 1973), 20.

136 Crowley, "Chalk Climbing," 291.

137 Ibid., 293.

138 Unofficial UK Climbing home page, http://www.lbell.demon.co.uk/chalk/history.html.

139 Cleare and Collomb, *Sea Cliff Climbing,* 12. For additional details on the climb, see Edward Charles Pyatt, *Climbing and Walking in South-East England* (Newton Abbott: David & Charles, 1970).

140 "The SMC abroad in 1894," *Scottish Mountaineering Club Journal,* 3(16): 238. Of the Suldenspitzse, Crowley noted "My first snowslope. Got on to ice, slipped, and the guide failed to hold me but himself fell." Of the Königspitze, "Guides too drunk to start. Went a solitary climb up Eissespitze, reported facts, and they were struck off the list" (Aleister Crowley, "On the Kinchin Lay: V. Mountains or Metaphysics?" *The Pioneer,* 15 Oct 1905, 3–4).

141 "Proceedings of the Club," *Scottish Mountaineering Club Journal,* 3(16): 229. Crowley was one of seven members elected at this meeting.

142 *World's Tragedy,* xxi.

143 This is not only Crowley's own estimation but also that of T. S. Blakeney in a review of Symonds's *Great Beast* in the May 1952 *Alpine Journal.*

144 Aleister Crowley, "With a Madman on the Alps." *Vanity Fair,* 24 Jun 1908, 823.

145 Crowley, Essay on magic and yoga.

146 The club has certainly evolved over the years, and functions to this day. For the Alpine Club's early years, see Ronald Clark, *The Victorian Mountaineers* (London: BT Batsford, 1953). For its current activities, see http://www.alpine-club.org.uk/.

147 Christine Mill, *Norman Collie, A Life in Two Worlds: Mountain Explorer and Scientist, 1859–1942* (Aberdeen: Aberdeen Univ. Press, 1987), 94–9. For additional details on his scientific work, see E. C. C. Baly, "John Norman Collie 1859–1942," *Obituary Notices of Fellows of the Royal Society* 1943, 4(12): 329–56, and Ronald Bentley, "John Norman Collie: Chemist and Mountaineer," *Journal of Chemistry Education* 1999, 76(1): 41–7.

148 Aleister Crowley to Elihu Thomson, 23 Aug 1916, Elihu Thomson Papers, MS Coll. 74, #MS61-930, American Philosophical Society, Philadelphia, PA. Regarding Collie's abiding interest in alchemy, see also "Birth of Atom Stirs Scientists: Sir William ramway Points Out Momentous Possibilities of British Experiments: New Line in Nature's Book: Prof. Collie, a Fellow-Discoverer, Asserts that Transmutation of Elements Is Achieved," *New York Times,* 8 Feb 1913, 1. This "discovery" was also covered in Henry Smith Williams, "Science," *Hearts's Magazine* 1913, 23(5): 793–4. Mark S. Morrison, *Modern Alchemy: Occultism and the Emergence of Atomic Theory* (Oxford: Oxford Univ. Press, 2007) demonstrates how a resurgence of interest in alchemy among nineteenth and early twentieth century scientists influenced the discovery of radioactivity and atomic theory. In this light, the number of chemists and scientists that Crowley would meet over the coming years makes sense.

Chapter Two • A Place to Bury Strangers

1   *Confessions,* 107.

2   T. S. Blakeney prints it in the *Alpine Journal, op. cit.*

3   *Confessions,* 107.

4   In *The Equinox of the Gods* (London: OTO, 1936) Crowley describes H. E. Atkins as "The first man to beat him" (p. 43).

5   Nicholas Culpeper, private communication, 19 Feb 1991, paraphrasing the Oxford vs. Cambridge record of inter-university contests. See also *British Chess Magzine,* May 1896, 16: 196; "C. U. Chess Club v. City of London Chess Club," *Cambridge Review* supplement 25 Feb 1897, 18(452): xlviii; "Chess," *Cambridge Review* supplement, 29 Apr 1897, 18(455): lviii; "C. U. Chess Club," *Cambridge Review,* 25 Nov 1897, 19(467): 109; *British Chess Magazine,* Jan 1897, 17(19): 3; "Deaths," *Times* (London), 28 Jan 1941, 48835: 1; "Obituary," *British Chess Magazine,* Oct 1902, 22: 431–3. Fox and James (1987), *The Complete Chess Addict.*

6   University of Cambridge, John Venn, and John Archibald Venn. *Alumni Cant-abrigienses; A Biographical List of All Known Students, Graduates and Holders of Office at the University of Cambridge, from the Earliest Times to 1900* (Cambridge: Cambridge Univ. Press, 1922–1958).

7   John Ruskin (1819–1900) was an influential English writer and champion of the Gothic Revival in architecture.

8   *Confessions,* 113.

9   In 1922 he wrote the *English Review*'s centennial article on Shelley: Prometheus. [Aleister Crowley], "Percy Bysshe Shelley." *English Review,* Jul 1922, 16–21.

10   *Confessions,* 112.

11   These contributions were largely collected and reprinted in *In Residence: The Don's Guide to Cambridge* (Cambridge: Elijah Johnson, 1904). Bookseller Nicholas Culpeper kindly shared with me references he had collected to some of the original poems: "Of the Mutability of Human Affairs," *Granta,* 26 Feb 1898, 11: 223; "Ballade of Bad Verses," *Granta,* 30 Apr 1898, 11(233): 271; "A Sonnet of Spring Fashions," *Granta,* 21 May 1898, 11(236): 308; "Ballade of a Far Country," *Cambridge Magazine,* 27 Apr 1899, 1(1); "Ballade of Whist," *Cambridge Magazine,* 11 May 1899, 1(3); "Ballade of Criticism," *Cambridge Magazine,* 18 May 1899, 1(4); "Ballade of Summer Joys," *Cambridge Magazine,* 1 Jun 1899, 1(6). One notable omission to this compilation—pointed out in Culpeper's spring 2009 catalog—is "The Ballad of Burdens," which appeared in *Granta,* 3 Feb 1899 (vol. 13). It parodies Swinburne's poem of the same name—originally appearing in Algernon Charles Swinburne, *Poems and Ballads* (London: J. C. Hotten, 1866)—as a ballad for the Cambridge rowing team, as seen in a short excerpt (thanks to Mr. Culpeper):

> The burden of hard rowing. This is pain,
>> For days shall come upon thee, when to swing,
>> Yea, and to finish, shall be wholly vain
> Beyond thine uttermost imagining,
> While down thine eyelids slowly shuddering
>> The sharp salt sweat drips tremulous like fire,
> Till life seem hateful, and a hideous thing,
>> This is the end of every man's desire.

Although Crowley included "Suggested Additional Stanzas for A Ballad of Bur-dens" in *White Stains: The Literary Remains of George Archibald Bishop, a Neuropath of the Second Empire* (n.p., 1898), 72, he never reprinted the original poem.

12   *Confessions,* 119.

13   "The Easter Meet at Fort-William," *Scottish Mountaineering Club Journal* 1896, 4(2): 130–3.

14   W. P. Haskett-Smith, "In Memoriam: J. W. Robinson," *Climber's Club Journal,* 10(38): 56–9. W. P. H.-S., "In Memoriam: J. W. Robinson," *Alpine Journal* 1907, 23(178): 625.

15   From *Songs of the Spirit* (1898), reprinted in *Works,* 1: 43. Crowley discusses his visit to Wastdale in *Confessions,* 89.

16   *Mysteries: Lyrical and Dramatic* (1898), reprinted in *Works,* 1: 102.

17   *In Residence,* 56–8.

18   *Confessions,* 394. Crowley, *Equinox of the Gods,* 46.

19   "The S.M.C. abroad in 1896," *Scottish Mountaineering Club Journal* 1896, 4: 243.

20   "The S.M.C. abroad in 1897," *Scottish Mountaineering Club Journal* 1897, 5(1): 41.

21   *Confessions,* 124. References are scattered throughout Crowley's writings, including *Confessions* (124), *Equinox of the Gods* (48), and *The Equinox* 1913, 1(10): 13. Of this event, Crowley writes in his *Confessions,* "I had unconsciously discovered my true will and devoted myself to find the means of carrying it out" (514).

22   *Confessions,* 123. See also Crowley, *Equinox of the Gods,* 111.

23   *White Stains,* 41.

24   *Equinox of the Gods,* 112.

25   Manuscript book, "About 1898 or earlier," N1, Yorke Collection, Warburg Institute, University of London.

26   "Herbert Charles Pollitt" in *Alumni Cantabrigienses.* Registered record of marriage, Q4 1864, Kendal, Westmorland, 10b: 1023. 1871 British Census, Kendal, Westmorland, RG10, piece 5287, 54: 30. "Deaths," *Times* (London), 1 Jan 1892, 33523: 1. John F. Curwen, *Kirkbie-Kendall: Fragments Collected Relating to Its Ancient Streets and Yards; Church and Castle; Houses and Inns* (Kendal: T. Wilson,1900), 285. Sell's Advertising Agency, *Sell's Dictionary of the World's Press* (London: Sell's Advertising Agency, 1887), 265. Charles Pollitt and William Wordsworth, *De Quincey's Editorship of The Westmorland Gazette: With Selections from His Work on That Journal from July 1818, to November 1819* (Kendal: Atkinson and Pollitt, 1890).

27   "Herbert Charles Pollitt" in *Alumni Cantabrigienses.* Margaret F. MacDonald and James McNeill Whistler, *James McNeill Whistler: Drawings, Pastels, and Watercolours: A Catalogue Raisonné* (New Haven: Published for the Paul Mellon Centre for Studies in British Art by Yale Univ. Press, 1995). 1901 British Census, London, England, RG13, piece 106, 27: 4. Army Medical Office, WWI Medical Rolls Index Cards. See also Timothy d'Arch Smith, *The Books of the Beast: Essays on Aleister Crowley, Montague Summers, Francis Barrett and Others.* (London: Crucible, 1987).

28   Robert Hewison, *Footlights! A Hundred Years of Cambridge Comedy* (London: Methuen, 1983), 16.

29   The reviewer "Pittite" in *The Cam,* quoted in Hewison, *Footlights!,* 16.

30   Steven Hobbs, "Mr. Pollitt's Bookplate," *Book Collector* 1987, 36(4): 518–30.

31   John Robert Reed, *Decadent Style.* (Athens: Ohio Univ. Press, 1985). R. K. R. Thornton, *The Decadent Dilemma* (London: Edward Arnold, 1983).

32   Miriam J. Benkovitz, *Aubrey Beardsley: An Account of His Life* (New York: G. P. Putnam's Sons, 1981), 136. The bookplate is discussed in Philip Kaplan Vertical File Manuscript 222, Morris Library Special Collections, Southern Illinois University at Carbondale (hereafter cited as Kaplan Papers). Crowley's only reference to Beardsley is in *Aceldama* (1898), stanza XXVIII, rpt. *Works* 1: 5.

33   Beardsley to Pollitt, 11 Dec 1897, in Henry Maas, John Duncan, and W. G. Good (eds.), *The Letters of Aubrey Beardsley* (Rutherford: Fairleigh Dickinson Univ. Press, 1970), 405. While Maas and colleagues assume that this was for *White Stains* (1898), it may also have been for Crowley's first book *Aceldama* (1898); as discussed below, Crowley signed one of the two outsized copies of this book to Beardsley, who died before he could receive it.

34   Matthew Sturgis, *Aubrey Beardsley: A Biography* (Woodstock: Overlook Press, 1999).

35   David Low, *"With All Faults"* (Tehran: Amate Press, 1973), 102. Quoted in Hobbs, "Mr. Pollitt's Bookplate," 530.

36   Maas, et al., *Letters of Aubrey Beardsley,* 439.

37   MacDonald and Whistler, *Catalogue Raisonné,* 199. The *Catalogue Raisonné* reproduces one full–length lithograph, 1896, as Plate 433, "whereabouts unknown." The second, of Pollitt seated, is also from 1896 and housed at the Art Institute of Chicago,

http://www.artic.edu/aic/collections/artwork/20101 (accessed Apr 23 2010).

38   Edward F. Benson, *The Babe BA: Being the Uneventful History of a Young Gentleman at Cambridge University* (London: G. P. Putnam's Sons, 1897), 30–3.

39   Maas et al., *Letters of Aubrey Beardsley,* 254. "Dodo Benson" is a reference to Benson's earlier novel, *Dodo: A Detail of the Day* (London: Methuen, 1893).

40   Quoted in Hewison, *Footlights!,* 16.

41   *Confessions,* 142.

42   "The Goad," from *Songs of the Spirit* (1898), rpt. *Works* 1: 30.

43   *Oracles: The Autobiography of an Art* (1898), rpt. *Works* 2: 14–5.

44   Arthur Edward Waite, *The Book of Black Magic and of Pacts: Including the Rites and Mysteries of Goetic Theurgy, Sorcery, and Infernal Necromancy* (London: George Redway, 1898), vii–viii.

45   As with his Uncle Tom, Crowley published a premature obituary of the author in *The Equinox* 1913, titled "Dead Waite." 1(10): 211–23. See also "Waite's Wet" in *The Equinox* 1912, 1(8): 233–42.

46   Anna Bonus Kingsford (1846–1888) and Edward Maitland (1829–1897) founded Britain's Hermetic Society in 1884 and started Esoteric Christianity. Kingsford also introduced S. L. Mathers to H. P. Blavatsky and her Theosophical Society.

47   Helena Petrovna Blavatsky (1831–1891) founded the Theosophical Society in New York in 1875 (the year of Crowley's birth), and published her magnum opus, *The Secret Doctrine,* in 1888.

48   Crowley to Louis Wilkinson, 30 Dec 1944, Louis Umfreville Wilkinson Collection, 1916–1960, Harry Ransom Humanities Research Center, University of Texas at Austin.

49   *Confessions,* 148.

50   Carl von Eckartshausen, *The Cloud upon the Sanctuary,* trans. and notes by John William Brodie-Innes and Isabel de Steiger (G. Redway: London, 1896), 15 and 16.

51   Listed as "Gottlieb Eckenstein" in the 1861 census (RG9, piece 141, 91: 51), he appears in the 1856 *London Postal Directory* as "Frederick Gottlieb Eckenstein" of 17 St. George's Villa. He also appears in the 1881 census (RG11, piece 262, 82: 39). Certified record of death, Q2 1891, Islington, London, 1b: 303. Certified record of death, Q2 1891, Islington, London, 1b: 303. Jane Chance, *Women Medievalists and the Academy* (Madison: University of Wisconsin Press, 2005), 57. Although Oscar's mother Antonie, as she appears in the 1861 and 1881 census, is often identified as British, both these censuses record her being born in Germany.

52   T. S. Blakeney and D. F. O. Dangar, "Eckenstein: The Man," *Alpine Journal,* 65(300): 71.

53   *The Merchant Shippers of London, Liverpool, Manchester, Birmingham, Bristol, and Hull: A Comprehensive List of Merchant Shippers...* (London: S. Straker & Sons, 1868). A Custom House Employé, *The Export Merchant Shippers of London, Manchester, Liverpool, Birmingham, Wolverhampton, Walsall, Leeds...* (London: Dean And Son, 1882). In the 1881 census *(op. cit.),* Eckenstein reports employing six clerks.

54   Although often identified as one of three children, the 1861 census, *op. cit.,* lists the Eckenstein children as Anna (age nine), Ernst (age seven), Hermine (age six), Antonie (age five), Lina (age three), and Oscar (age one). The 1881 census lists another sister, Tony, born about ten years after Oscar. Islington birth records give his siblings' full names as Anna Lena Antonia Romana (b. 1851), Ernst Ferdinand Gottlieb (1853–1915), Hermine Lina Antonia Erica (1854–1863), Antonia Sina Dorina Sophie Viola (1856–1863), Lina Dorina Johanna (1857–1931), and Antonia J. S. T. Eckenstein (b. 1868). His brother Ernst appears to have continued the family business, as the 1881 census lists him as a "general merchant," and the 1901 census identifies him as a self-employed "seed merchant."

55   Around 1881 Eckenstein helped to develop a method of measuring the amount of

iron in Eaton's Syrup (a syrup of phosphates of iron, quinine and strychnine, marketed as a nerve tonic). See Robert H. Davies and Emil B. Schmitd, "The Composition of Eaton's Syrup," *Phramaceutical Journal and Transactions,* 24 Nov 1883, 14: 416. For his railway work, see: Oscar Eckenstein, "An International Technical Dictionary of Railway Terms," *Bulletin of the International Railway Congress,* Sep 1903, 17(9): 874–5, and W. Robinson, Karl Richard Oscar Bertling, and Oscar Eckenstein, *Modern Railway Practice: A Treatise on the Modern Methods of the Construction and Working of German Railways: Approved by the Prussian Minister of Public Works, the Bavarian Minister of Communications, and the Railway Authorities of Other German States* (London: R. Hobbing, 1914).

56   Quoted in Blakeney and Dangar, "Eckenstein the Man," 73.

57   See *Spirit of Solitude,* v. 1, stanza XVIII, 222–6; these passages are also restored in the unabridged edition of *Confessions,*

58   Blakeney and Dangar, "Eckenstein the Man," 75.

59   Oscar Eckenstein and August Lorria, *The Alpine Portfolio: The Pennine Alps, from the Simplon to the Great St. Bernard* (London: the editors, 1889) was issued in an edition of one hundred sixty copies, making it a rare and valuable title.

60   William Martin Conway and Lina Eckenstein, *Literary Remains of Albrecht Dürer: With Transcript from the British Museum Manuscripts and Notes Upon Them by Lina Eckenstein* (Cambridge: Univ. Press, 1889). Lina Eckenstein would go on to establish her own academic credentials with wide-ranging works such as *Woman under Monasticism: Chapters of Saint-Lore and the Convent Life between AD 500 and AD 1500* (Cambridge: Univ. Press, 1896) and *Moon-Cult in Sinai on the Egyptian Monuments* (London: Macmillan, 1914). For more on Lina Eckenstein see Sybil Oldfield, "Eckenstein, Lina Dorina Johanna (1857–1931)," *Oxford Dictionary of National Biography* (Oxford: Oxford Univ. Press, 2004) and Chance, *Women Medievalists, op. cit.*

61   "Projected Glacial Exploration in the Karakoram," *Proceedings of the Royal Geographical Society and Monthly Record of Geography* 1892, 14(3): 178.

62   In "Mr. Conway's Karakoram Expedition," *Proceedings of the Royal Geographical Society and Monthly Record of Geography* 1892, 14(11): 753–70, Conway reported that "Mr. Eckenstein's health compelled him to quit the party" (p. 754). In a follow-up article, W. M. Conway, "Exploration in the Mustagh Mountains," *The Geographical Journal* 1893, 2(4): 289–99, he reported that both Eckenstein and J. H. Roudebush "were prevented by ill-health or other hindrances from continuing with us" (p. 289). In his *Climbing and Exploration in the Karakoram Himalayas* (London: T. Fisher Unwin, 1894), Conway writes, "Eckenstein had never been well since leaving Gilgit. It was evidently useless for him to come further with us, so I decided that he had better return to England" (p. 293).

63   Oscar Eckenstein, *The Karakorams and Kashmir: An Account of a Journey* (London: T. Fisher Unwin, 1896). While the existence of friction between Conway and Eckenstein is well established, Conway's account in "The Crossing of the Hispar Pass," *The Geographical Journal* 1893, 1(2): 131–8, contains several mentions of Eckenstein, and even reproduces a lengthy extract from his jounal on p. 134–5.

64   E.g., Blakeney and Dangar, "Eckenstein the Man," 72, 74.

65   P. 70 in David Dean, "Oscar Eckenstein, 1859–1921," *Alpine Journal* 1960, 65(300): 62–71. For Guy Knowles's dates, see "Mr. Guy Knowles: Benefactor of the Fitzwilliam," *Times* (London), 8 May 1959, 54455: 15.

66   N. M. Penzer, *An Annotated Bibliography of Sir Richard Francis Burton, KCMG* (London: A. M. Philpot, 1923). "The Richard Burton Memorial: Gift of the Eckenstein Collection," *Times* (London), 1 Mar 1939, 48242: 14. Jon R. Godsall, *The Tangled Web: A Life of Sir Richard Burton* (Leicester: Matador, 2008). The archives of the Royal Asiatic Society contain not only Eckenstein's collection of Burtonania, but also the correspondence of Eckenstein, Penzer, Lloyd, and others (including Roger Ingpen, who wrote the foreword to a 1915 edition of Burton's *Kasidah of Haji Abdu El-Yezdi: A Lay of the Higher Law).*

67   Dean, "Oscar Eckenstein," 63.

68   Blakeney and Dangar, "Eckenstein the Man," 73.

69   *Confessions,* 166.

70   Crowley to J. H. Doughty, n.d. (c. 1920), Yorke Collection.

71   Issued in *Jezebel, and Other Tragic Poems* (1898).

72   *Aceldama* (1898).

73   *Works* 1: 115.

74   Aleister Crowley, *The Magical Record of the Beast 666: The Diaries of Aleister Crowley 1914–1920,* ed. John Symonds and Kenneth Grant. (Montreal: Next Step, 1972), 6.

75   This identification is by Yorke, Old E1, Yorke Collection.

76   *Confessions,* 149.

77   *Aceldama,* stanzas IX and X. Also in *Works* 1: 3.

78   Quoted in Percy Reginald Stephensen, *The Legend of Aleister Crowley: Being a Study of the Documentary Evidence Relating to a Campaign of Personal Vilification Unparalleled in Literary History* (London: Mandrake Press, 1930), 36.

79   *Confessions,* 138.

80   G. F. Sims Catalogue No. 12 (1951).

81   Bibliotheca Crowleyana, early draft c. 1965, J. F. C. Fuller Papers, Special Collections, Archibald Stevens Alexander Library, Rutgers University. Later seen at the Times Bookshop, London, 16 Jun 1966 (according to Smith, *Books of the Beast,* 33).

82   Oscar Wilde to Reginald Turner, Aug 1897, quoted in Benkovitz, *op cit,* and George Sims, *The Rare Book Game* (Philadelphia: Holmes Publishing Co., 1985), 47.

83   Although published anonymously, *Teleny* is sometimes attributed to Oscar Wilde, whose works Smithers also published.

84   Gerald's father was admitted to Trinity College on December 7, 1855, received his LLB in 1860, and LLM in 1863 *(Alumni Cantabrigienses).*

85   Gerald Kelly to John Symonds, 18 Jun 1968, author's collection. Dean, "Oscar Eckenstein," 66–7.

86   AC to John Quinn, 1 Sep 1913, New 12, Yorke Collection.

87   p. 28. See also Thomas R. Whissen, *The Devil's Advocates: Decadence in Modern Literature* (New York: Greenwood Press, 1989).

88   In *Oracles: The Autobiography of an Art* (1905), rpt. *Works* 2: 6–19.

89   "The S.M.C. abroad in 1898," *Scottish Mountaineering Club Journal* 1898, 5(4): 196.

90   See *Diary of a Drug Fiend,* 159–160.

91   J. P. Farrar, "Mountain Craft," in Geoffrey Winthrop Young (ed.), *Mountain Craft* (New York: Charles Scribner's Sons, 1920), 92.

92   *Confessions,* 293.

93   Oscar Eckenstein, "Hints to Young Climbers," *Sandow's Magazine of Physical Culture,* May 1900, 394–402.

94   Eckenstein, "Hints to Young Climbers," 399.

95   John Symonds, *King of the Shadow Realm* (London: Duckworth, 1989), 89.

96   Tom Longstaff, *This My Voyage* (New York: Charles Scribner's Sons, 1950), 24.

97   See, e.g., *Proceedings of the Chemical Society* 1895, 12: 3, and "Action of Distaste on Starch," *Journal of the Chemical Society, Abstracts* 1897, 72: B34. Their work is cited, for instance, in *Chemisches Zentralblatt* 1895, 2(1): 26.

98   "Proceedings of the Society of Public Analysts," *Analyst,* Apr 1899, 24: 85.

99   He is listed as FIC (Fellow of the Imperial College) and FCS (Fellow of the Chemical Society) in his 1905 book, *The Brewing Industry, vide infra.*

100 A year later, 1947, Watney, Combe, Reid and Co. Ltd. would buy Crowley & Co.

101 Society of Chemical Industry and Julian L. Baker, *Handbook of London and Provincial*

Excursions (London: The Society, 1905). For a related text, see International Congress of Applied Chemistry and Julian L. Baker, *Members' Handbook* (London: Jas. Truscott & Son, 1909).

102 Julian L. Baker, *The Brewing Industry* (London: Methuen, 1905). Julian L. Baker, "Malt and Malt Liquors," in Henry Leffman and W. A. Davis, *Allen's Commercial Organic Analysis: A Treatise on the Properties, Modes of Assaying, and Proximate Analytical Examination of the Various Organic Chemicals … Vol.1, Introduction to Alcohols, Yeast, Malt Liquors and Malt, Wines and Spirits* [...] (London: J. & A. Churchill, 1909), 133–64. "Fermentation," in Hugh Chisholm, *Encyclopædia Britannica*, 11th ed., 1911, v. 10, 275b.

103 *Transactions of the American Brewing Institute* 1907, 3: 243.

104 "The Chemist and the Fermentation Industries," *Nature*, 15 Nov 1924, 114: 735.

105 Ironically, it was Baker himself who in 1925 proposed establishing this award to recognize outstanding contributions to the science and technology of fermentation.

106 George Cecil Jones, "Obituary: Julian Levett Baker," *Analyst* 1958, 985: 187–8.

107 "Obituary," *Journal of the Royal Institute of Chemistry* 1958, 82: 367.

108 Julian L. Baker is listed in *Who Was Who in Literature, 1906-1934* (Detroit: Gale Research, 1979), 64. Obituaries are found in *Chemistry and Industry*, 15 Mar 1958, 11: 327; *Nature*, 22 Mar 1958, 181: 809; *Analyst* 1958, 985: 187–8 and *Journal of the Royal Institute of Chemistry* 1958, 82: 367.

109 *Confessions*, 172.

110 1901 British Census, GRO, RG13, piece 1108, 66: 10.

111 "Certificates of Candidates for Election at the Next Ballot, December 6, 1894," *Proceedings of the Chemical Society*, 14 Nov 1894, 142: 203.

112 Ibid., 195–210. *Proceedings of the Chemical Society*, 18 Dec 1894, 144: 221. "List of Members," *Journal of the Society of Chemical Industry* 1905, 24: xxviii.

113 City and Guilds of London Institute for Advancement of Technical Education, "Report to the Governors, March, 1896," *Chemical News and Journal of Industrial Science* 1896, 73: 279.

114 *Analyst* 1902, 27: 264. "Proceedings of the Society of Public Analysts and Other Analytical Chemists," *Analyst* 1908, 386: 160a. *Proceedings of the Institute of Chemistry of Great Britain and Ireland* 1917, 15.

115 G. C. Jones's papers include: "The Need for Greater Care in Introducing Gas-Firing into Small Gasworks," presented to the Society of Chemical Industry on 3 Jun 1901 (*Nature* 1901, 64: 120); "Standardisation of Malt Analysis," *Journal of the Institute of Brewing* 1905, 11: 264–87; Arthur R. Ling and G. Cecil Jones, "The Volumetric Determination of Reducing Sugars, Part II: The Limits of Accuracy of the Method under Standard Conditions," *Analyst* 1908, 33: 160b–7; "Note on the Determination of Extracts during Summer," *Journal of the Institute of Brewing* 1908, 14: 9; "The Determination of Diastic Power by Lintner's Method," *Journal of the Institute of Brewing* 1908, 14: 13; G. Cecil Jones and John H. Jeffery, "The Estimation of Iron by Permanganate in Presence of Hydrochloric Acid," *Analyst* 1909, 34: 306–16; "Purchase of Fuel under Specifications," *Journal of the Institute of Brewing* 1911, 17: 182–209; "Note on Ground Almonds" (see "Proceedings of the Society of Public Analysts and other Analytical Chemists," *Analyst* 1912, 430: 2–3; "Vinegar" in Georg Lunge and Charles Alexander Keane, *Technical Methods of Chemical Analysis*, v. 3 pt. 1 (London: Gurney and Jackson, 1914); "Estimation of Methyl Alcohol in Presence of Ethyl Alcohol," *Analyst* 1915, 470: 218–22. His book reviews appear in *Analyst* 1912, 437: 385–90; 1915, 470: 267–70; 1915, 471: 299–308; and 1915, 473: 374–8.

116 Jones's chapters in *Allen's Commercial Organic Analysis* (1909, *op. cit.*) are "Alcohols" (85–131) and "Wines and Potable Spirits" (165–203); in the 1913 edition, vol. 7, he also supplied the chapter "Non-Glucosidal Bitter Principles" (137–93).

117 G. Cecil Jones, "Analytical Chemistry" in *Annual Reports of the Progress of Chemistry for 1915* (London: Chemical Society, 1916). This book is listed in *Chemical Abstracts*

1916, 10: 1970, and reviewd in *Journal of the American Chemical Society* 1916, 38: 2576.

118 "Obituary," *Journal of the Royal Institute of Chemistry,* Mar 1961, 122. See also "Jones, George Cecil. Chemist," in Henry Hdder Stephenson (ed.), *Who's Who in Science (International)* (London: J. & A. Churchill, 1912–1914). Many preceding details of Jones's life are drawn from these sources, unless otherwise noted.

119 Dedication to Epilogue, *Works,* 219.

120 AC to RC Newman, 16 Aug 1944, New 24, Yorke Collection. See also AC to Gerald Yorke, 1 Feb 1928, New 115, Yorke Collection, where he writes, "Abramelin warns us about these family troubles.... In my own case, I simply disappeared and lived under an assumed name."

121 Based on vision 13 of Crowley's 1898 diary, Aleister Crowley Collection, 1889–1989, Harry Ransom Humanities Research Center, University of Texas at Austin (hereafter referred to as HRHRC). Five other visions from this diary were rewritten by Fuller and published in *The Equinox* 1909, 1(2).

Chapter Three • The Golden Dawn

1 "University Intelligence," *Times* (London), 6 Aug 1869, 26509: 10. "Apothecaries' Hall," *Times* (London), 16 Apr 1870, 26726: 10.

2 Eliza Westcott's death (from which her birth year is estimated) is reported in "Fatal Fall into a Courtyard," *Times* (London), 10 Aug 1921, 42795: 5. The 1891 census lists three of her children as Ida, Elsie, and George (RG12, piece 161, 182: 39).

3 Westcott is referrred to as deputy coroner for central Middlesex in the *Times'* reports of inquests as early as 28 Mar 1883, and as late as 2 Dec 1893; the first reference to him as coroner for north-east London appears in the 22 Dec 1894 issue.

4 25 in W. Wynn Westcott, "Twelve Years' Experiences as a London Coroner," *Transactions of the Medico-Legal Society* 1907, 4: 15–32.

5 W. Wynn Westcott, *A Social Science Treatise: Suicide, Its History, Literature, Jurisprudence, Causation, and Prevention* (London: H.K. Lewis, 1885). Westcott, "Twelve Years' Experiences," *op cit.* William Martindale and W. Wynn Westcott, *The Extra Pharmacopœia of Unofficial Drugs and Chemical and Pharmaceutical Preparations* (London: H. K. Lewis, 1883). Westcott contributed occasionally to the *British Medical Journal* and *The Lancet,* and his contributions there are: "Rupture of the Heart," *British Medical Journal* 1872, 1: 554; W. Wynn Westcott and Samule Lloyd, "A Medico-Legal Mystery," *The Lancet* 1883, 122(3142): 851–2; "Suicide," *The Lancet* 1885, 125(3211): 497; "Deaths from Alcoholic Excess in London," *The Lancet* 1888, 132 (3386): 132–3; "The Arsenio-Ferric Water of Levico," *The Lancet* 1890, 135(3475): 748; "The Mandrake," 1890, *British Medical Journal* 1: 620–4; "A Coroner's Notes on Sudden Deaths," *British Medical Journal* 1891, 2: 841–2; "An Address on the Coroner and his Relations with the Medical Practitioner and Death Certification: Delivered at a Meeting of the North London District of the Metropolitan Counties Branch of the British Medical Association," *British Medical Journal* 1902, 2: 1756–9; "The Overlaying of Infants," *British Medical Journal* 1903, 2: 1208–9; "On Suicide," *Transactions of the Medico-Legal Society* 1905 2: 85–98; "Twelve Years' Experiences," 1907, *op. cit.;* "An Address on Sudden and Unexpected Deaths: Delivered before the St. Pancras and Islington Division of the British Medical Association," *British Medical Journal* 1908, 1: 490–3; "Twins: A Curious Incident," *The Lancet* 1908, 171(4401): 49–50; "A Note upon Deodands," *Transactions of the Medico-Legal Society* 1910, 7: 91–7; "A Note on a Curious Result of Burning a New-born Child," *Transactions of the Medico-Legal Society* 1912, 9: 69–70; "Exhibition of Specimens," *Transactions of the Medico-Legal Society* 1918, 13: 48.

6 "2nd December, 1886," *Ars Quatuor Coronatorum* 1888, 1: 27–8. *Representative British Freemasons: A Series of Biographies and Portraits of Early Twentieth Century Freemasons* (London: Dod's Peerage, Ltd., 1915), 159–60.

7 "2nd December, 1886," *Ars Quatuor Coronatorum,* and the ballot result in *Ars Quat-*

uor Coronatorum 1893, 6: 168. See also "Friday, 5th October, 1894," *Ars Quatuor Coronatorum* 1894, 7, for the conclusion of his term.

8   For additional details on Westcott, see his obituary in *Ars Quatuor Coronatorum* 1925, 38: 224–5, and R. A. Gilbert, "William Wynn Westcott and the Esoteric School of Masonic Research," *Ars Quatuor Coronatorum* 1987, 100: 6–20. Westcott wrote around one hundred Masonic, Rosicrucian and other esoteric articles and reviews, too many to list here. Twenty-eight of these were collected as *The Magical Mason: Forgotten Hermetic Writings of William Wyn Westcott, Physician and Magus,* ed. R. A. Gilbert (Wellingborough: Aquarian, 1983). His books—as author, editor or translator—up to Crowley's 1898 introduction to the GD include: *Sepher Yetzirah: The Book of Formation and the Thirty-Two Paths of Wisdom, Translated from the Hebrew* (Bath: Robert H. Fryar, 1887); *Tabula Bembina sive Mensa Isiaca: The Isiac Tablet of Cardinal Bembo, Its History and Occult Significance* (Bath: Robert H. Fryar, 1887); *Nicholas Flammel: His Exposition of the Hieroglyphical Figures which He Caused to Be Painted upon an Arch in St. Innocents Church Yard in Paris: Concerning Both the Theory and Practice of the Philosophers Stone. Bath* (Bath: R. H. Fryar, 1890); *Numbers: Their Occult Power and Mystic Virtue, Being a Résumé of the Views of the Kabbalists, Pythagoreans, Adepts of India, Chaldean Magi and Mediæval Magicians* (London: Theosophical Pub. Society, 1890); *The Science of Alchymy, Spiritual and Material: An Essay* (London: Theosophical Pub. Society, 1893); *Collectanea Hermetica,* 10 vols. (London: Theosophical Pub. Society, 1893–1896); *The Magical Ritual of the Sanctum Regnum, Interpreted by the Tarot Trumps: Translated from the MSS of Eliphaz Levi, and Edited* (London: George Redway, 1896).

9   S. L. MacGregor Mathers, *The Kabbalah Unveiled, Containing the Following Books of the Zohar: The Book of Concealed Mystery. The Greater Holy Assembly. The Lesser Holy Assembly* (London: G. Redway, 1887). Anna Bonus Kingsford and Edward Maitland, *The Perfect Way: Or, the Finding of Christ* (London: Field & Tuer, 1882).

10   In 1927 Henri Bergson won the Nobel Prize in literature for *Creative Evolution,* trans. W. R. Victor Brade (Wilmslow: Stillings, 1911).

11   W. B. Yeats, *Autobiography* (New York: Macmillan, 1944), 115.

12   Maude Gonne MacBride, *A Servant of the Queen: Reminiscences* (London: Victor Gollancz, 1938), 248.

13   Ellic Howe, *Magicians of the Golden Dawn: A Documentary History of a Magical Order 1887–1923* (London: Routledge & Kegan Paul, 1972), 61fn.

14   From *Soul of Osiris,* rpt. *Works* 1: 196.

15   While Crowley and Fitzgerald place this book after *Jephthah,* Yorke places it after *The Tale of Archais.* Neither appears to be correct, as the Archives of Kegan Paul, Trench, Trübner & Henry S. King (Doheny Library, University of Southern California) show the date of *Songs of the Spirit*—the book traditionally believed to follow *The Tale of Archais*—as December 1898, while *Archais* is dated January, 1899. In either event, December, 1898, leaves little time for the remaining 1898–imprinted books to appear. *Jezebel* was probably published before Crowley's introduction to the GD, fresh with Gerald Kelly's praise for *Aceldama.* The correct order of publication then would be: *Aceldama* 1898; *White Stains* around May, 1898; *Jezebel* mid 1898; *Songs of the Spirit,* December, 1898; *Tale of Archais,* January, 1899; *Jephthah,* July, 1899.

16   Crowley and Svareff exchanged honors with Crowley's *Ahab and Other Poems* (1903), Svareff penning the introduction and epilogue. Svareff is also listed as the author of "Au Theatre du Grand Guignol" in *In Residence* (1904), 89–94.

17   Stephensen, *Legend of Aleister Crowley,* 36–7.

18   *Works* 1: 28 fn: "With the exception of this epilogue and one or two of the lyrics, Crowley wished to suppress the whole of *The Tale of Archais.*"

19   *Confessions,* 556.

20   Stephensen, *Legend of Aleister Crowley,* 37.

21   "A First Glance at New Books," *Outlook,* Dec 1898, 2(46): 640.

22   Aleister Crowley, "The Revival of Magick." in Hymenaeus Beta and Richard Kac-
      zynski (eds), *The Revival of Magick and Other Essays* (Tempe, AZ: New Falcon, 1998),
      23–4; orig. pub. in *International* 1917, 11(8): 247–8; 11(9): 280–2; 11(10): 302–4;
      11(11): 332–3.

23   Aleister Crowley, "Origins," unpublished MS quoted in Kenneth Grant, *The Magical
      Revival* (London: Muller, 1972), 84.

24   S. M. Mitra, *The Life and Letters of Sir John Hall* (London: Longmans, Green & Co.,
      1911), 535.

25   Beatrice Irwin appeared in Broadway productions of *There's Many a Slip* (Sep–Oct
      1902), *At the Telephone* (Oct 1902), *His Excellency the Governor* (Oct–Nov 1902), *The
      Unforseen* (Jan–Apr 1903), and *The Admirable Crichton* (Nov 1903–Mar 1904). For
      her poetry, see "Miss Irwin's 'Color Poems,' *New York Times* 25 Nov 1910, and
      "'Pagan' and Otherwise," *New York Times* 31 Mar 1912.

26   *Confessions*, 225.

27   W. B. Yeats to John Quinn, 21 Mar 1915, Quinn Memorial Collection.

28   For a comparison of Yeats's *The Resurrection* and *The Book of the Law*, see Kathleen
      Raine, *Yeats, the Tarot, and the Golden Dawn* (Dublin: Dolmen Press, 1972), 34.

29   Gerald Yorke to Virginia Moore, 22 Oct 1954, private collection.

30   Ithell Colquhoun, "Two Pupils and a Master," *Prediction*, Oct 1971, 12–4.

31   *Confessions*, 177.

32   Josephine Johnson, *Florence Farr: Bernard Shaw's "New Woman"* (Gerrards Cross,
      London: Colin Smythe, 1975), 84.

33   Reviews, good and bad, appear in Stephensen, *Legend of Aleister Crowley*, 38–40.

34   "A Mystery Man," *Outlook*, Jul 1899, 3(78): 840–1.

35   W. B. Yeats to Lady Gregory, 25 Apr 1900, in Allan Wade, *The Letters of W. B. Yeats*
      (New York: MacMillan, 1955).

36   W. B. Yeats to John Quinn, 21 Mar 1915, Quinn Memorial Collection.

37   Johnson, *Florence Farr*, 84.

38   *The Equinox* 1909, 1(1): 101–8. In his copy Crowley wrote, "This story is true in
      every detail. Date of occurrence 1899 E.V. May or June." (Equinox Notes, HRHRC:
      115). In the story, Will Bute=William Butler Yeats and Hypatia Gay=Althea Gyles.

39   Despite many claims to the contrary, there is no evidence that Gyles was a member
      of the GD. Crowley certainly would have mentioned it, and she does not appear in
      any membership rolls or histories of the GD. Indeed, Hyde writes of the covers she
      designed for Yeats,"While Gyles was not a member of the Hermetic Order of the
      Golden Dawn as Yeats was, she was clearly aware of some of its symbolism." Virginia
      Hyde, "Variant Covers of *The Secret Rose*" in Warwick Gould (ed.), *Yeats Annual No.
      13* (London: Macmillan, 1998).

40   William Butler Yeats, "A Symbolic Artist and the Coming of Symbolic Art," *Dome*,
      Dec 1898, 233–7.

41   "At the Fork in the Roads," 104.

42   Faith Compton Mackenzie, *Tatting: A Novel* (London: Jonathan Cape, 1957), 12.

43   *The Equinox* 1910, 1(3): 205. Although this essay was credited to J. F. C. Fuller,
      Crowley oversaw and edited the writing.

44   W. B. Yeats to Lady Gregory, 6 Jun 1900. In Wade, *Letters of W. B. Yeats*, 346.

45   By today's standards, Crowley paid about $85,000; in 1991, Boleskine went on sale
      for a minimum bid of £225,000 or roughly $400,000.

46   AC to Gerald Kelly, n.d., Old D6, Yorke Collection. Itallics mine.

47   Francis Toye, *For What We Have Received: An Autobiography* (New York: Alfred A.
      Knopf, 1948), 124. Toye was Gerald Kelly's cousin.

48   Johnson, *Florence Farr*, 81.

49   Lilian Horniblow née Horsford was also known as Laura Grahame; she married
     Frank Herbert Horniblow in 1895. See biographical appendix, unexpurgated *Con-
     fessions*. See also Crowley's "Sirenae" from *The Argonauts* (1904), for which Laura
     Graeme is a dedicatee.

50   *Confessions*, 181–2.

51   These papers included material on kabbalistic numerology *(gematria)* and correspon-
     dences that would form the basis of later Crowley works *Sepher Sephiroth* and 777.

52   "To Allan Bennett MacGregor," from *The Soul of Osiris* (1901), rpt. *Works* 1: 207.
     The phrase "Man of Sorrows," besides reflecting his physical state, also applies to the
     Buddhist trance of *dukkha*.

53   Abramelin Diary, 24 Feb 1900, HRHRC. These letters came from one of Crowley's
     lovers, Evelyn Hall, c.f. biographical appendix to the unexpurgated *Confessions*. Of
     Hall's warning, Crowley wrote in his diary, "her description of the 'college chum' is
     absurd and her whole attitude ridiculous. She knows one fact only—the name
     Crowley at Cambridge."

54   Abramelin Diary, HRHRC. Quoted in Howe, *Magicians of the Golden Dawn*, 223.
     Thomas Lake Harris (1823–1906) was a mystic whose theories about sex circulated
     informally among members of the GD's Second Order.

55   These points refer to the ten *sephiroth* of the Tree of Life. The oath is taken from *The
     Equinox* 1910, 1(3): 214; the ritual appears on pages 208–3. and in Regardie, *Golden
     Dawn* and *Complete Golden Dawn,* and Torrens, *Secret Rituals of the Golden Dawn*.

56   Regardie suspected AC's motto was very Christian and, given his later ventures into
     alternative forms of religion, embarassing in retrospect. His guess of "Heart of Jesus
     Girt About By a Serpent" is wrong. Skinner, in *Magical Diaries of Aleister Crowley,*
     incorrectly gives the name "Parzival." Crowley actually recorded his motto, Chris-
     teos Luciftias, in his notebook currently with Special Collections, Northwestern
     University Library. In Enochian, *Christeos* is "let there be," while *Luciftias* is "bright-
     ness" or "light." Its obvious Latin analogue *Lucifer* was not a name of the devil in
     mystic circles as it is in popular parlance. The name literally means "light bringer"
     and was an ancient name of Venus as the Morning Star. In its older, pre-Christian
     form, Lucifer was similar to Prometheus, the Greek god who brought fire and light
     to mankind. It is in this sense of the word that H. P. Blavatsky named the Theosoph-
     ical Society's magazine *Lucifer*.

57   Abramelin diary, HRHRC.

58   W. B. Yeats to George Russell, May 1900, in Wade, *Letters of W. B. Yeats,* 343–4. A
     1920s *Sunday Express* article corroborates this claim; it reported that, in 1900, Crow-
     ley stole £200 from a widow with whom he cohabited ("Aleister Crowley's Orgies
     in Sicily: Woman's Account of His Last Visit to London. 'The Beast 666.' Black
     Record of Aleister Crowley. Preying on the Debased. His Abbey. Profligacy and
     Vice in Sicily," *Sunday Express,* 26 Nov 1922).

59   Abramelin Diary, HRHRC. Also reprinted in *Confessions;* Howe, *Magicians of the
     Golden Dawn;* Regardie, *Eye in the Triangle;* and Charles Richard Cammell, *Aleister
     Crowley: The Man, the Mage, the Poet* (London: Richards Press, 1951).

60   Symonds describes many other incidents for which I can find no source, with one
     exception. He tells the story of how a local butcher cut himself and died after Crow-
     ley scribbled the names of two demons on the butcher's bill. Symonds is in error, as
     AC gives the following account in the *International:*

     > His student J. F. C. Fuller once marked his place in the Abramelin book with a
     > butcher's bill. A few days later, the butcher slipped, stabbed himself in the thigh,
     > and died. Fuller's reaction: "It may be only a coincidence, but it's just as bad for the
     > butcher!" (rpt. Crowley, *Revival of Magick,* 32).

61   This letter appears in full in Howe, *Magicians of the Golden Dawn,* 209–11 and is
     excerpted in *The Equinox* 1910, 1(3): 255–6. The relevant correspondence has also
     been collected in Darcy Küntz (ed.), *Sent from the Second Order: The Collected Letters*

of the Hermetic Order of the Golden Dawn (Austin, TX: Golden Dawn Trust, 2005).

62 186 in George Mills Harper, "'Meditations upon Unknown Thought': Yeats' Break with MacGregor Mathers," *Yeats Studies* 1971, 1: 175–202.

63 Howe, *Magicians of the Golden Dawn,* 213.

64 Harper, "Unknown Thought," 192; Howe, *Magicians of the Golden Dawn,* 216.

65 Howe, *Magicians of the Golden Dawn,* 207.

66 *Confessions,* 194–195.

67 *The Equinox* 1910, 1(3): 251.

68 *Confessions,* 196.

69 Crowley to Gerald Yorke, 27 Mar 1946, Yorke Collection.

70 Harper, "Unknown Thought," 194; Howe, *Magicians of the Golden Dawn,* 225.

71 This was not, as some suggest, melodrama on Crowley's part. The purpose of a mask for Crowley was to maintain anonymity: Mathers wanted his representative to act for him *in media res,* and not to be associated with any individual within the order. Further, the notion of masks is an adaptation of the GD instructional document Z1. As Mathers explained in a letter to M. W. Blackden on April 26, 1900: "to mark his impersonality in this matter, I distinguished him by a symbol, and not by a name, and advised him further to wear a mask of Osiris as laid down in Z, should the same be necessary; so as completely to separate and distinguish between his individuality and the office with which I had invested him. And I may remark that to term the Highland Dress a 'masquerade' is hardly even *English good taste…*"

72 Howe, *Magicians of the Golden Dawn,* 226–7.

73 Harper, "Unknown Thought," 180; Howe, *Magicians of the Golden Dawn,* 229.

74 W. B. Yeats to Lady Gregory, 25 Apr 1900, in Wade, *Letters of W.B. Yeats,* 340.

75 Howe, *Magicians of the Golden Dawn,* 230. Fuller states that Crowley, during his raid of the GD temple, absconded with a copy of the *Goetia,* translated by Mathers; this he published without Mathers's consent in 1904. See John Frederick Charles Fuller, *Bibliotheca Crowleyana* (Tenterden, Kent: Keith Hogg, 1966).

76 W. B. Yeats to Lady Gregory, 29 Apr 1900, in Wade, *Letters of W. B. Yeats,* 341.

77 This partnership is curious given the accusation Mathers made of Westcott.

78 *The Equinox* 1910, 1(3): 266.

79 W. B. Yeats to George Russell, May 1900, in Wade, *Letters of W. B. Yeats,* 344.

80 W. B. Yeats, 1983. [1920]. "All Soul's Night," in Richard J. Finneran (ed.), *The Collected Poems of W. B. Yeats* (New York: Collier Books, 1983 [1920]), 229.

Chapter Four • The Mountain Holds a Dagger

1 Frederic Lees, "Isis Worship in Paris: Conversations with the Hierophant Rameses and the High Priestess Anari," *The Humanitarian,* Feb 1900, 16(2): 82–7. Interestingly, Moïna used the publicity from these events to advance a feminist agenda, noting the centrality of priestesses in the ancient mysteries—something which has been neglected in recent history. "When a religion symbolises the universe by a Divine Being," she asked, "is it not illogical to omit woman, who is the principal half of it, since she is the principal creator of the other half—that is, man?" (p. 86).

2 "Obituary," *New York Times,* 10 Nov 1893, 4. "Demas Strong," *New York Tribune,* 10 Nov 1893, 7.

3 Theodore Baker and Alfred Remy, *Baker's Biographical Dictionary of Musicians* (New York: G. Schirmer, 1919), 924. César Saerchinger, *International Who's Who in Music and Musical Gazetteer: A Contemporary Biographical Dictionary and a Record of the World's Musical Activity* (New York: Current Literature Pub. Co, 1918), 626. *Critic* 1906 48(1): 12–3. "The World of Music," *Munsey's Magazine* 1896, 14(5): 575. "Production of 'The Valkyrie' in English," *Manchester Guardian,* 17 Oct 1895, 8.

"The Opera," *Musical News,* 19 Oct 1895, 9: 322. A. C. R. Carter, *The Year's Music: Being a Concise Record of All Matters Relating to Music and Music Institutions* (London: J. S. Virtue & Co., Ltd., 1896), 244–5.

4   *Academy,* 19 Oct 1895, 48(1224): 323.

5   "English Opera," *Times* (London), 17 Oct 1895, 34710: 6.

6   "The Opera Season," *Times* (London), 2 Aug 1897, 35271: 2. Hermann Klein, *Thirty Years of Musical Life in London, 1870–1900* (New York: Century Co., 1903), 437–8. "Royal Opera, Covent Garden," *Punch, or the London Charivari,* 22 May 1897, 244. *Opera Glass* 1897, 4(6): 86. "Royal Opera, Covent Garden," *Musical Times* 1897, 38 (1 Jul): 461–2, 384. A. C. R. Carter, *The Year's Music: Being a Concise Record of All Matters Relating to Music and Musical Institutions* (London: J. S. Virtue & Co., Ltd., 1898), 132–6. *Times* (London), 22 Apr 1899, 35810: 5. "Royal Opera," *Times* (London), 17 Jun 1899, 35858: 8. Frank Moore Colby, Edward Lathrop Engle, and Harry Thurston Peck, *The International Year Book: A Compendium of the World's Progress During the Year 1898* (New York: Dodd, Mead & Co., 1899), 561. "Editorial Bric-a-Brac," *Music: A Monthly Magazine Devoted to the Art Science, Technic and Literature of Music,* Dec 1899, 17: 183. "Operatic Notes," *Punch, or the London Charivari,* 23 May 1900, 364. "Royal Opera," *Times* (London), 18 Jun 1900, 36171: 9. "The Opera Season," *Bookman* 1900, 11: 220.

7   *Confessions,* 204. However, Strong's name does not appear on any GD membership rolls (Robert A. Gilbert, personal communication).

8   *Confessions,* 204.

9   All her press cuttings refer to her as "Miss Susan Strong," and I have not found any record of her marriage. Unless other information should come to light, it is possible that this was a convenient excuse on her part for putting off their marriage. Alternatively, the couple may have been so estranged that he never came up in the press.

10   Oscar Thompson, *The American Singer: A Hundred Years of Success in Opera* (New York: The Dial Press, 1937), 198–9. Francis Cowley Burnand, *The Catholic Who's Who and Year-Book* (London: Burns & Oates, 1908). 380–1.

11   Stanley Sadie, *The New Grove Dictionary of Opera* (London: Macmillan, 1992).

12   Published as the epilogue to *Carmen Sæculare* (1900).

13   See, e.g., "Heat's Holocaust in the Five Boroughs: 87 Deaths and 178 Prostrations Mark Hottest July 1 on Record," *New York Times,* 2 Jul 1901, 1. "Philadelphia's Hottest Day: 102 Degrees; Highest Ever Recorded—Thousands of Industrial Workers Compelled to Quit," *New York Times,* 2 Jul 1901, 2. "Whole Country Swelters: Weather Bureau Points Out High Temperature Records, but Promises No Immediate Relief," *New York Times,* 2 Jul 1901, 2. "Fierce Heat Lays Low Many: Deaths and Prostrations All Over the Country—No Relief in Sight; Terrible Suffering Here—Hospitals Rushed," *New York Tribune,* 2 Jul 1901, 1. "Highest Ever Recorded: Philadelphia Has 102 Degrees—Every Hospital Busy," *New York Tribune,* 2 Jul 1901, 2. "A Cool Wind Fans City: Northeast Breeze Drives Out the Heat; The Day Doubly a Celebration—Many Deaths Still Reported, but They Were of Those Who Had Long Suffered," *New York Tribune,* 5 Jul 1901, 1. "Heat Brings Death to Over 200 Persons; Several Hundred Others Collapse in Stifling Atmosphere; Stores and Offices Close," *New York Times,* 3 Jul 1901, 1. "Heat Keeps Up Work of Death," *New York Tribune,* 3 Jul 1901, 1. "Storm Breaks Heat Grip on Boston; Seventy Deaths, Due Directly to Intense Weather, the Record in New England," *New York Tribune,* 3 Jul 1901, 3. "New Jersey Deaths Again Reach 100," *New York Times,* 4 Jul 1901, 2.

14   593 in Aleister Crowley, "Art in America." *English Review,* Nov 1913, 578–95.

15   *The Mother's Tragedy,* rpt. *Works* 1: 178–9.

16   *Oracles,* rpt. *Works* 2: 29–30.

17   *The Vision and the Voice,* the Cry of the 29th Aethyr RII.

18   John Hamill, quoted in Martin P. Starr, "Aleister Crowley: Freemason!" *Ars Quatuor Coronatorum* 1995, 108: 150.

19   Crowley says that he both met Medina-Sidonia and received his 33° in "the City of Mexico" (*Confessions*, 202–3; *The Book of Lies*, commentary to Chapter 33). Elsewhere, he reports that he founded the LIL with Medina-Sidonia in Guanajuato (*The Equinox* 1910, 3(1): 269), about 230 miles northwest of Mexico City.

20   J. F. C. Fuller notes the Enochian parallel in "The Temple of Solomon the King," *The Equinox* 1910, I (4): 45fn. The timing of these events can be reconstructed from several sources: In his "Prologue" to *John St. John,* Crowley notes that he "received the mysteries of L.I.L. in October" [*The Equinox* I(1, supplement): 8]; however, this reception must have pre-dated Crowley's founding of the order with Don Jesus de Medina-Sidonia, as Crowley's Enochian visions were recorded on November 14 and 17; according to *Confessions* and "The Temple of Solomon the King," their meeting happened after these dates. The poem "Venus," *op. cit.,* has the note "Written in the temple of the L.I.L., No. 9, Central America." Finally, in *Temple of Solomon the King,* Crowley writes, "At the End of the Century: At the End of the Year: At the Hour of Midnight: Did I complete and bring to perfection the Work of L.I.L." (45).

21   Rough working notes of the rituals of LIL are pencilled into the back of Crowley's Jan–May 1901 diary in the Yorke Collection.

22   These experiments are described in part in *The Equinox* 1910, 1(4): 107 et seq.

23   See, e.g., Ezequiel Ordóñez, *Observaciones relativas a los volcanes de México* (México: Imprenta del Gobierno Federal, 1894). Ezequiel Ordóñez, "Notas acerca de los ventisqueros del Ixtaccihuatl. Mexico," *Memorias y revista de la Sociedad Científica* 1894, 8: 31–42. *Las rocas eruptivas del suroeste de la Cuenca de México* (México: Oficina Tip. de la Secretaría de Fomento, 1895). José G. Aguilera and Ezequiel Ordóñez, *Expedición Científica al Popocatapetl* (México: Oficina Tip. de la Secretaría de Fomento, 1895). Ezequiel Ordóñez, "Bosquejo Geológico de México," *Boletin del Institute Geológico de México* 1897, no. 4–6. Ezequiel Ordóñez, *Les volcans Colima et Ceboruco* (México, n.p., 1898). For his obituary, see "Ezequiel Ordóñez," *New York Times,* 10 Feb 1950, 22, and Everette Lee DeGolyer, "Memorial, Ezequiel Ordonez (1867–1950)," *AAPG Bulletin* 1950 34(5): 985–9.

24   Oscar Eckenstein, "Mountaineering in Mexico," *Climbers' Club Journal* 1903, 5(20): 159–67.

25   *Alpine Journal* 25: 268–72, quoted by Eckenstein, "Mountaineering in Mexico."

26   Eckenstein, "Mountaineering in Mexico," 161.

27   Oscar Eckenstein, quoted in "Editorial Notes." *Climbers' Club Journal* 1901, 3(12): 199–200 gives a detailed account of all these climbs, See also Crowley's *Confessions*.

28   Crowley, Unpublished essay on yoga and magic, Yorke Collection.

29   Eckenstein, "Mountaineering in Mexico," 161.

30   *Confessions,* 216.

31   Eckenstein, "Mountaineering in Mexico," 163.

32   "Metempsychosis," from *Oracles* (1905), rpt. *Works* 2: 33. "Night in the Valley," from the same collection, was also written at this time.

33   As Eckenstein wrote, "I was rather upset in my inner works. …We both had a good deal of trouble from our canned provisions on several occasions and we gained some valuable experience on the subject." Eckenstein, "Mountaineering in Mexico," 166.

34   "Poetry," *Westminster Review,* Jun 1908, 155(6): 715–6.

35   Quoted in Stephensen, *Legend of Aleister Crowley,* 44–6.

36   Eckenstein, "Mountaineering in Mexico," 167.

37   "Mr. Dooley Climbs Popo," *Mexican Herald,* 21 Apr 1901, 12(233): 13.

38   *Confessions,* 223.

39   Written on May 12, 1901, it appeared in *Oracles* (1905), rpt. *Works* 2: 33–4.

40   AC to Gerald Kelly, 26 Apr 1901, Old D6, Yorke Collection.

41   See biographical appendix, unexpurgated *Confessions*. See also Crowley's "Sirenae" from *The Argonauts* (1904), where Mary Beaton is one of the dedicatees.

42   Crowley, "Art in America," 580.

43   *Confessions*, 226.

44   Diary, 22 May 1901.

45   Diary, 26 May 1901.

46   "The Twenty-Second Day" from *Alice: An Adultery*, reprinted in *Works* 2: 74.

47   Diary, 1 Jun 1901.

48   AC to Gerald Kelly, n.d., 1901, New 4/Old D6, Yorke Collection.

49   "Triads of Despair," from *Oracles*, rpt. *Works* 2: 34–6.

50   AC to Gerald Kelley, n.d., New 4/Old D6, Yorke Collection.

51   From Stephensen, *Legend of Aleister Crowley*, 41–3.

52   "Poetry," *Westminster Review*, Oct 1901, 156(4): 476. "Above Average," *The Academy*, 26 Oct 1901, 1538: 379–80.

53   Register of marriages, Saint Savior, Paddington, P87/SAV, item 013. The groom—son of Ignatz and Julia Witkowski of Leipzig—was baptised as an adult the day of his wedding (Register of baptisms, Saint Saviour, Paddington, P87/SAV, item 004). Although *The Life and Letters of Sir John Hall* includes a photograph of Alice Simpson holding her grandchild in Hong Kong in 1901, the marriage would appear to have been short, although whether due to death or divorce is not stated; however, Witkowski is never mentioned, and the text states that Elaine "is married to Herr Wölker in the service of the Kaiser. Frau Wölker has inherited some of her grandfather's wonderful adaptability to new environments, which makes her so popular in German society" (p. 544).

54   Ponnambalam Rámanáthan's works are: *On Faith or Love of God: As a Fruit of Sound Teaching* (Farmer & Sons, 1897); *The Gospel of Jesus according to St. Matthew, as Interpreted to B.L. Harrison by the Light of the Godly Experience of Sri Parananda* (London: Kegan Paul, Trench, Trübner Co., 1898); *An Eastern Exposition of the Gospel of Jesus according to St. John, Being an Interpretation thereof by Sri Parananda by the Light of Jnana Yoga* (London: W. Hutchinson, 1902); *The Spirit of the East Contrasted with the Spirit of the West* (New York: the author, 1905); and *The Culture of the Soul among Western Nations* (London: G.P. Putnam's Sons, 1906).

55   M. Vythilingam, *The Life of Sir Ponnabalam Ramanathan*, 2 vol. (Colombo: Ramanathan Commemoration Society, 1971), 494–511.

56   Crowley, *Magick without Tears*, 157. He is quoting the introduction to his "translation" of the Tao Teh King, which remained unpublished until 1976.

57   *Oracles*, rpt. *Works* 2: 36–37.

58   AC to Gerald Kelly, n.d., Old D6, Yorke Collection.

59   AC to Gerald Kelly, n.d., Old D6, Yorke Collection.

60   *The Equinox* 1910, 1(4): 166.

61   *Book Four*, 32.

62   *Confessions*, 254.

63   *Oracles*, rpt. *Works* 2: 38–43.

64   *Oracles*, rpt. *Works* 2: 37–8.

65   *Confessions*, 261.

66   *Confessions*, 259.

67   *Proceedings of the Asiatic Society of Bengal, January to December 1902* (Calcutta: Asiatic Society, 1903).

68   *Oracles*, rpt. *Works*, 2: 43–4.

69   *Orpheus*, Book III, rpt. *Works* 3: 177.

70   Aleister Crowley, "On a Burmese River: From the Note Book of Aleister Crowley," *Vanity Fair* (UK), 24 Feb 1909, 232.

71   Appearing in *Oracles*, rpt. *Works* 2: 48.

72 "Guy John Fenton Knowles, 1879–1959." *Alpine Journal* 1959, 64(299): 288–9.

73 *Confessions,* 279.

74 In his *Confessions,* Crowley said that Knowles "knew practically nothing of mountains" (279). Similarly, the account in *Berge der Welt* likewise reports that Knowles was an inexperienced mountaineer who was enlisted primarily as a financier for the expedition. See "Im Jahre 1902 greift ein Schweizer den K2 (8611 m) an," *Berge der Welt* 1948, 1: 111–20.

75 "Mr. Guy Knowles, Benefactor of the Fitzwilliam," *Times* (London), 8 May 1959, 54455: 15. *Alumni Cantabrigienses.*

76 51 in Aleister Crowley, "The Expedition to Chogo Ri: Leaves from the Notebook of Aleister Crowley," *Vanity Fair* (UK), 8 Jul 1908, 51–52.

77 "Heinrich Pfannl, Wien," in Adolfo Hess, *Saggi sulla psicologia dell'alpinista: Raccolta di autobiografie psicologiche di alpinisti viventi* (Turin: S. Lattes & C., 1914), 435–47.

78 Peter Grimm, "Pfannl, Heinrich," in Bayerische Akademie der Wissenschaften. *Neue deutsche Biographie* (Berlin: Duncker & Humblot, 2000), 20: 300. "Aiguille du Géant," *Jahrbuch des Schweizer Alpenclub* 1990 36: 262. *Österreichische Alpenzeitung* 1900, 22: 344–5. Club alpino italiano, *Bollettino del Club alpino italiano* 1900, 34/35: 200. Club alpino italiano, "Cronaca Alpina: Nuove Ascensioni," *Rivista Mensile: Pubblicata per cura del consiglio direttivo* 1900, 19: 352–3. "Historical roots" at http://www.bergrettung-stmk.at/muerzzuschlag/geschichte_e.htm (accessed Apr 23 2010). He was a popular speaker, and a collection of his talks—incluidng his account of the K2 expedition—was published posthumously as Heinrich Pfannl, *Was bist du mir, Berg?* (Wien: Österreichischer Alpenklub, 1929).

79 *Confessions,* 51.

80 Sam Hield Hamer, *The Dolomites* (London: Methuen, 1910).

81 "Oesterreichische Alpen-Zeitung," *Rivista Mensile* 1899, 21/22: 153. *Zeitschrift des Deutschen und Österreichischen Alpenvereins* 1902, 33: 264.

82 Dr. Viktor Wessely, "Karakoram-Erinnerungen," *Österreichische Alpenzeitung: Organ des Österreichischen Alpenklub,* Sep 1934, 56(1149): 271–4.

83 Dr. H. Pfannl, "Eine Belagerung des Tschogo-Ri (K2) in der Mustaghkette des Hindukusch (8720m)," *Zeitschrift des Deutschen und Österreichischen Alpen-Vereines* 1904, 35: 88–104. Alternately, Jacot-Guillarmod summarized their goals as "a sporting ambition to break all former rcords in mountaineering, but scientific observations will also be made, and the flora and fauna of the Himalayas, of which scientists have so little knowledge, will not be neglected" ("A Great Climb: To Conquer the Himalayas and Mount Everest," *Daily Chronicle,* 13 May 1902; with thanks to Glyn Hughes, Hon. Archivist, Alpine Club.)

84 "Ascensions et passages en 1897 des membres des Sections romandes du C. A. S.," *l'Écho des Alpes* 1898, Supp. 1, 4.

85 "Jules Jacot-Guillarmod, 1868–1925," *Berge der Welt* 1948, 1: 191–8. "Dr. Jules Jacot-Guillarmod, 1868–1925," *Alpine Journal* 1925, 37(231): 348. Charles Biermann, "Nécrologie: Le Dr. Jules Jacot Guillarmod (24 décembre 1868–5 juin 1925)," *Bulletin de la Société Neuchâteloise de Géographie* 1926, 52–4. Eugène Pittard, "Nécrologies: Jules Jacot-Guillarmod," *Le Globe: Organe de la Société de Géographie de Genève* 1927, 23–4. Marcel Fleury and Mireille Stauffer, "Le Docteur Jules Jacot-Guillarmod," http://www.fondation.lignieres.org/download/050201_resume _dr_jules_jacot_guillarmod_par_g_ terrier.pdf (accessed Apr 23 2010).

86 *Confessions,* 51.

87 *Confessions,* 51.

88 Galen Rowell, *In the Throne Room of the Mountain Gods* (San Francisco: Sierra Club Books, 1977). On p. 38, Rowell reports an interview where Guy Knowles agrees that Conway put obstacles in Eckenstein's way to prevent him from climbing K2.

89 A, Ferrari, "La spedizione del 1902 mei monti del Karakorum (Himalaya)," *Rivista Mensile* 1902, 21(11): 397–9.

90   Pfannl, "Eine Belagerung des Tschogo-Ri," 90.

91   Paraphrased from *Confessions,* 303.

92   Although this sounds harsh by today's standards, it was some twenty years later that Gandhi began to stage his protests against British colonialism. Only then was light shone on Britain's brutal attitude toward the Indians. It was 1947—the year of Crowley's death—before India gained independence. This is not to excuse Crowley's behavior, but to place it in the context of his times.

93   Op cit.

94   247 in Aleister Crowley, "The Expedition to Chogo Ri, V: Leaves from the Notebook of Aleister Crowley," *Vanity Fair* (UK), 19 Aug 1908, 246–7.

95   Pfannl, "Eine Belagerung des Tschogo-Ri," 104.

96   Rowell, *Throne Room,* 90.

97   Ronald W. Clark, *Men, Myths and Mountains* (NY: Thomas Y. Crowell, 1976), 104.

98   Aleister Crowley, "On the Kinchin Lay: I. Prospect and Retrospect," *Pinoeer,* 10 Aug 1905, 3–4 (with thanks to Glyn Hughes, Hon. Archivist, Alpine Club).

99   "The Earl's Quest," from *Oracles,* rpt. *Works* 2: 49–51.

100 310 in Aleister Crowley, "The Expedition to Chogo Ri VI: Leaves from the Notebook of Aleister Crowley," *Vanity Fair* (UK), 2 Sep 1908, 310–1.

101 372 in Aleister Crowley, "The Expedition to Chogo Ri VII: Leaves from the Notebook of Aleister Crowley," *Vanity Fair* (UK), 16 Sep 1908, 372–3.

102 For Eckenstein's obscurity, see Dean, "Oscar Eckenstein," which notes the absence of an Eckenstein obituary in every climbing journal.

103 Francis Younghusband, *The Epic of Mount Everest* (London: E. Arnold, 1926).

104 Dr. J. Jacot Guillarmod, "Un record dans l'Himalaya," *Jahrbuch des Schweizer Alpenclub* 1903, 38: 212–27. "Séance du 20 Février 1903," *Société Neuchateloise des Sciences Naturelles Bulletin* 1903, 31: 373–8. "The Western Himalayas," *Geographical Journal* 1904, 23(1): 121–33. Jules Jacot-Guillarmod, *Six mois dans l'Himalaya, le Karakorum et l'Hindu-Kush; voyages et explorations aux plus hautes montagnes du monde* (Neuchâtel: W. Sandoz, 1904).

105 Rudolf Cyriax "A Conquest on K2," *Times* (London), 8 Aug 1938, 48067: 6.

Chapter Five • A Rose by Any Other Name

1   Born in Calcutta around 1877, Sybil Meugens was one of three children to Edith Meugens (1901 UK Census, St. Mary Magdalene, Sussex, RG13, piece 869, 103: 40). Of his later painting of her, Crowley wrote, "The lady is an Anglo-Indian of Dutch extraction—mistress of Bimby 'Hawkes,' Gerald Festus Kelly and anyone else she could get. Lived in wind-mills, Martello Tower, etc. and is now probably Red Cross, YMCA" (PH:LF Crowley, 63, Photographic Collection, Harry Ransom Humanities Research Center, University of Texas at Austin). She studied art with Stephen Haweis (1878–1969) and at the Académie Colarossi; returning to art after a four-year hiatus, she injected her "Oriental sympathies and her leaning to the occult" into her oil paintings. some of which were exhibited at the West End's prestigious Ryder Galleries in 1915. For more on Meugens, with examples of her artwork, see Arthur Reddie, "Still-Life Paintings by Sybil Meugens," *International Studio,* Apr 1915, 55(218): 130–4, and Malcolm C. Salaman, "The Art of Miss Sibyl Meugens," *International Studio,* Jun 1919, 67(268): 49–57.

2   Peter Adam, *Eileen Gray: Architect-Designer* (New York: Harry N. Abrams, 1987), 37.

3   AC to Gerald Kelly, 12 Aug 1903, Old D6, Yorke Collection.

4   "Small Brown Armchair Sells for £19 Million," *Telegraph* (London), 25 Feb 2009.

5   "A Tour of Eileen Gray's Hideaway," *Irish Times,* 6 Jul 2009.

6   *Confessions,* 676.

7   *Confessions,* 556.

8   *Confessions,* 556.

9   Quoted in Claire Harman, 1995. "Reluctant Widow," *Times Literary Supplement,* 11 Aug 1995, 4819: 24.

10 All three poems are from *Clouds without Water.* The quotation is from "The Black Mass," 70.

11 From Aleister Crowley, *The Winged Beetle* (Edinburgh: Turnbull & Spears, 1910).

12 *The Equinox* 1913, 1(9): 103–14.

13 *The Equinox* 1911, 1(6): 113–48. The author is given as "Martial Nay," no doubt a commentary on their relationship.

14 In Aleister Crowley, *Konx Om Pax: Essays in Light* (Foyers: SPRT, 1907), 79–82 and 95–8, respectively.

15 W. Somerset Maugham, *Of Human Bondage* (New York: Vintage Books, 1956 [1915]), 202.

16 Quoted in Anthony Curtis, *The Pattern of Maugham: A Critical Portrait* (London: Hamish Hamilton, 1974), 60.

17 See Richard A. Cordell, *Somerset Maugham: A Writer for All Seasons* (Bloomington: Indiana Univ. Press, 1969), 39.

18 Quotes from *Of Human Bondage,* 207, 207, and 210, respectively.

19 Symonds, *Shadow Realm,* 56–7.

20 *Confessions,* 344.

21 "W. E. Henley," in *Rodin in Rime* (1907), rpt. *Works* 3: 119.

22 Aleister Crowley, *Snowdrops from a Curate's Garden,* ed. Martin P. Starr (Chicago: Teitan Press, 1986 [Paris, 1904]), 9.

23 Frank Swinnerton, *Figures in the Foreground: Literary Reminiscences, 1917–40* (London: Hutchinson, 1963), 90.

24 "Obituary of Ivor Gordon Back," *The Lancet,* 23 Jun 1951, 260: 1371.

25 G. F. Newbold, "Ivor Back, FRCS," *British Medical Journal,* 21 Jul 1951, 2: 182. See also D'Arcy Power, *Lives of the Fellows of the Royal College of Surgeons of England, 1930–1951* (London: The College, 1953), 30–1; Ivor Back and A. Tudor Edward, *Surgery,* Student's Synopsis Series (London: Churchill, 1921). Other works include Ivor Back and John Haskell Kemble, *Round the World—and Back: An Account of the Journey of Ivor Black, A.K. Travelling Fellow, 1911–1912* (London: University of London Press, 1913), a record of his time as a 1911 recipient of an Albert Kahn Traveling Fellowship. See "'Albert Kahn Travelling Fellowships' in University of London," *The Historical Record (1836–1912), Being a Supplement to the Calendar* (London: University of London Press, 1912), 568 and *Nature,* 4 May 1911, 86(2166); 337. Back also wrote "Entries on Diseases and Affection of the Penis, Urethra, Scrotum, Testicle, and Tunica Vaginalis," in Arthur Latham and T. Crisp English (eds.), *A System of Treatment, vol. 2: General Medicine and Surgery* (New York: Macmillan, 1915). He also contributed essays on diseases of bone to vol. 1, and was cited as "a distinguished authority on rectal diseases" ["'Bubble' and 'Squeak': A Simple Story with a Moral," *American Journal of Clinical Medicine* 1916, 23(6): 479].

26 *Confessions,* 342.

27 *Confessions,* 349.

28 Crowley, *Snowdrops,* 8.

29 *Confessions,* 338.

30 "Balzac," from *Rodin in Rime* (1907), rpt. *Works* 3: 122.

31 A. Rodin to AC, 25 Feb 1903, box 1, file 1, C0195, Auguste Rodin Collection, Rare Books and Special Collections, Princeton University, NJ.

32 Frederic V. Grunfeld, *Rodin: A Biography* (New York: Henry Holt and Company, 1987), 455–6.

33 *Confessions,* 340. Schwob's translations of Crowley's "Rodin" and "Balzac" appear in *Les Maîtres Artistes: Revue mensuelle,* 15 Oct 1903, 8: 283.

34 Crowley's 1903 contributions to the *Weekly Critical Review* are: "Balzac: To Auguste Rodin," 5 Feb 1903, 1(3): 5; "The Triads of Despair," 12 Mar 1903, 1(8): 6; "The Hermit's Hymn to Solitude," 2 Apr 1903, 1(11): 3–4; "Rodin," 21 May 1903, 1(18): 8; "II. Rodin: Tête de Femme (Luxembourg)," 28 May 1903, 1(19): 6; "Rodin III: Syrinx and Pan," 4 Jun 1903, 1(20): 10; "Rodin IV: Illusion," 11 Jun 1903, 1(21): 3; "Rodin V: La Fortune," 18 Jun 1903, 1(22): 19; "Rodin VI: Paolo and Francesca," 25 Jun 1903, 1(23): 16–7; "Rodin VII: Les deux Génies," 2 Jul 1903, 1(24): 16; "Rodin VIII: La Vielle Heaulmière," 9 Jul 1903, 1(25): 18; "Rodin IX: La Tentation de Saint-Antoine," 16 Jul 1903, 1(26): 8; "Rodin X: La Main de Dieu," 30 Jul 1903, 2(28): 38; "Rodin XI: An Indicent (Rue de l'Université. 182)," 6 Aug 1903, 2(29): 56; "Le Bourgeois de Calais," 1903 v. 2; "Rodin I: Eve," 5 Nov 1903, 2(42): 374.

35 *Confessions,* 361.

36 For Richard Jewell and family, see the 1871 British Census for Cornwall, RG10, piece 2238, 57: 30. L. C. R. Duncombe-Jewell is listed as "Richard D. Jewell," age four, and his two younger siblings are given as Arthur (three), and Catherine (one). For the family's subsequent locations, see the censuses for 1881 (RG11, piece 730, 47: 14) and 1891 (RG12, piece 457, 116: 21). For Crowley at Streatham, see *Confessions,* where Crowley refers to "when my uncle moved to Streatham" (p. 59), furnishing "a laboratory in the house at Streatham" (p. 62), and a conversation with his uncle John "one day at Streatham" (p. 56). During this time, Emily Crowley lived at 7 Polworth Road in Streatham, while her brother Tom Bond Bishop lived literally down the road (see 1891 census, RG12, piece 456, 151: 64).

37 Captain L. C. R. Cameron to S. J. Looker of Constable & Co., 24 Sep 1932, Nina Hamnett Papers, Temple University, Philadelphia, PA.

38 400 in L. C. Duncombe-Jewell, "About Myself and the Celtic-Cornish Movement," *Candid Friend and the Traveller* 1902, 3(62): 399–400. He indicates that most copies were destroyed by a fire at the printer's.

39 W. P. W. Phillimore and Edward Alex Fry, *An Index to Changes of Name Under Authority of Act of Parliament or Royal License, and Including Irregular Changes from I George III to 64 Victoria, 1760 to 1901* (London: Phillimore & Co., 1905), 100. Marriage record, Honiton, Devon, 5b: 51. Birth record, Devon, 5b: 367. Death record, Plymouth, Devon, 5b: 158.

40 Sharon Lowenna, "Noscitur A Sociis: Jenner, Duncombe-Jewell and their Milieu," *Cornish Studies* 2004, 12: 61–87.

41 *Confessions,* 121.

42 "Seizure of a British Yacht," *Times* (London), 19 Jun 1899, 35859: 8. "Seizure of a British Yacht," *The Brisbane Courrier,* 20 Jun 1899, 5. "Spain," *Times* (London), 7 Aug 1899, 35901: 3.

43 *Firefly* crew pay list 26 Aug 1899, Ashburnham Carlist Papers, Lewes, quoted in Lowenna, "Noscitur A Socis," 68.

44 *Confessions,* 123. One wonders whether this "lieutenant" was a sly reference Lt. Duncombe-Jewell of the Royal Fuslilers, or to the *Firefly's* skipper, Lt. English.

45 Lowenna, "Noscitur A Socis," 69–70.

46 *Image of War* collects Duncombe-Jewell's memoirs and essays on this period. See also Duncombe Jewell, "The Boers Appear to Have the Best of the Fight," *Daily Picayune,* 25 Feb 1900, 10. "Dinner to Mr. E. F. Knight," *Observer* (London), 29 Jul 1900, 4. For his medal, see Lowenna, fn. 55, p. 84.

47 *Celtia,* Apr 1901, 53, lists his £1 contribution as from "Duncombe Jerrell, M.A."

48 Letter to *Celtia,* Aug 1901, 117.

49 *Celtia,* May 1902, 79. For more on the Celtic-Cornish Society, see Amy Hale, "Genesis of the Celto-Cornish revival? L.C.Duncombe-Jewell and the Cowethas Kelto-Kernuak," *Cornish Studies* 1997, 5: 100–11.

50　"Ireland," *Times* (London), 24 Aug 1901, 36542: 8. See also Duncombe-Jewell's "Cornwall: One of the Six Celtic Nations," *Celtia,* Oct 1901, 151–4, 159.

51　L. C. Duncombe-Jewell, "A Sonnet in Cornish," *Celtia,* Oct 1901, 161.

52　"About VCH Cornwall," http://www.victoriacountyhistory.ac.uk/Counties/ Cornwall/AboutVCH/About_VCH_Cornwall.

53　W. B. Yeats, John Kelly, Eric Domville, and Ronald Schuchard, *The Collected Letters of W. B. Yeats* (Oxford: Clarendon Press, 1986), 251–2.

54　Birth record, GRO, Plymouth, Devon, 5b: 239.

55　See Henry Robert Addison, Charles Henry Oakes, William John Lawson, and Douglas Brooke Wheelton Sladen, *Who's Who, An Annual Biographical Dictionary, with which Is Incorporated "Men and Women of the Time"* (London: A. and C. Black; 1906).

56　Death record, GRO, Plymouth, Devon, 5b: 158.

57　*Collected Letters of W. B. Yeats,* 215–2. Lowenna, 73.

58　Duncombe-Jewell would later remarry, taking as his second wife Janet Sarah Bruce, daughter of the late General Robert Bruce of Glendouglie; see Alexander Henry Higginson, *British and American Sporting Authors: Their Writings and Biograpics* (London: Hutchinson & Co., 1951), 167–8. Duncombe-Jewell was a prolific writer, and some of his works not previously cited include: *A Modern Resurrection, A Romance,* 1889; "The True Jacobitism: A Survival," *Albemarie* 1892, 2(1): 31–4; "The Present State of Politics in France," *Month: A Catholic Magazine and Review,* Oct 1896 88: 217; *The Handbook to British Military Stations Abroad* (London: S. Low, Marston & Co., 1898); L. Duncombe-Jewell, "Orders of Mercy," *Genealogical Magazine* 1899, 3(26): 43–5; L. Duncombe-Jewell, "The Arms, Seals, and Plate of Plymouth," *Genealogical Magazine* 1899, 3(31): 292–5; L. Duncombe-Jewell, *A Guide to Fowey and Its Neighbourhood* (Fowey: J.W. Denison, 1901); L. C. D. J. (trans), "A Christmas Song in the Cornish Language of the 17th Century," *Celtia,* Jun 1902, 90; L. C. Duncum-Joul, "Dr. Magnus Maclean and Cornish Literature," *Celtia,* Nov 1902, 173; "Mermaid of Zenor: Written for the Psaltery, 10 *Mis Merh* 1903," *Green Sheaf,* Oct 1903, 6: 3; "Kyn Vyttyn (Before Morning)," *Green Sheaf,* Dec 1903, 8: 10; Ludovick Charles Richard Duncombe-Jewell Cameron, *The Hunting Horn, What to Blow and How to Blow It* (London: Köhler & Sons, 1905); Ludovick Charles Richard Duncombe-Jewell Cameron, *The Book of the Caravan; A Complete Handbook to the Pastime of Caravaning, Illustrated from Photographs, and by Line-Plans and Drawings to Scale* (London: L. Upcott Gill, 1907); L. C. R. Cameron, "Superstitions Connected with Sport," *Occult Review* 1908, 7(6): 329–34; L. C. R. Cameron, "The Mystery of Lourdes," *Occult Review* 1908, 8(4): 203–7; Ludovick Charles Richard Duncombe-Jewell Cameron, *Otters and Otter-Hunting* (London: L. Upcott Gill, 1908); L. C. R. Cameron, "Otter Hounds," in Arthur W. Coaten (ed.), *British Hunting* (London: Sampson, Low, Marston & Co., 1909); Ludovick Charles Richard Duncombe-Jewell Cameron, *The Wild Foods of Great Britain, Where to Find Them and How to Cook Them* (London: G. Routledge & Sons Ltd, 1917); L. C. R. Cameron, "The Brahan Seer (Kenneth Dun (Coinneach Odhar Foisache)): An Appreciation," *Occult Review,* Jun 1918, 27: 318–25; Ludovick Charles Richard Duncombe Cameron, *Minor Field Sports* (n.p., 1921); Ludovick Charles Richard Duncombe Cameron, *Rhymes of Sport in Old French Verse Forms* (London: Benn, 1926); Ludovick Charles Richard Duncombe-Jewell Cameron, *Rod, Pole & Perch; Angling & Otter-Hunting Sketches* (London: M. Hopkinson & Co., 1928); Ludovick Charles Richard Duncombe Cameron, *Love Lies Bleeding: Lyrics in Old French Verse-Forms* (London: John Bale, Sons & Danielsson, 1929); Ludovick Charles Richard Duncombe-Jewell Cameron, *The Lady of the Leash: A Sporting Novel* (London: Lincoln Williams, 1935); Ena Adams and Ludovick Charles Richard Duncombe-Jewell Cameron, *Deer, Hare & Otter Hunting* (Philadelphia: J. B. Lippincott, 1936).

59　*Confessions,* 363.

60　This is the first line from John Keats's sonnet of the same title.

61　Isaiah 30: 15.

62 GRO, London Metropolitan Archives, Saint Giles, Camberwell, Register of marriages, P73/GIS, Item 048.

63 *The Medical Register* (London, 1899), 1455. *The Medical Register* (London, 1895), 1189.

64 William Shakespeare, *Macbeth,* Act 2, Scene 2, Line 71. The play takes place in Inverness, and the quote reflected his passion for Scotland.

65 *Confessions,* 367.

66 XIX from *Rosa Mundi, and Other Love Songs,* rpt. *Works* 3: 64.

67 RPKTT Archives.

68 AC to Gerald Kelly, Aug 1903, Old D6, Yorke Collection.

69 *Confessions,* 380.

70 J. Gordon Melton, "Thelemic Magick in America," in Joseph H. Fichter (ed.), *Alternatives to American Mainline Churches* (Barrytown, NY: Unification Theological Seminary, 1983), 68–9.

71 AC to Gerald Yorke, 9 Mar 1945, Yorke Collection.

72 For more on Brugsch, see *KMT: A Modern Journal of Ancient Egypt* 1996, 7(3): 14–8.

73 Crowley, *Equinox of the Gods,* 117–8. Crowley's identification of Aiwass's clothing as Assyrian is interesting, as Crowley later equated Aiwass with a Sumerian god. For more on this theory linking Aiwass to the Yezidi god, see Grant, *Magical Revival.*

74 *AL* i.3–5.

75 *AL* i.29.

76 *AL* i.51.

77 *AL* i.57.

78 *AL* i.58.

79 *AL* i.35.

80 *Thelema* is Greek for "will."

81 *AL* i.39–44.

82 *AL* i.40.

83 *"Dilige et quod vis fac,"* from *Homilies on the First Epistle of John,* VII, 8.

84 "Do what thou wilt."

85 Walter Besant and James Rice, *The Monks of Thelema: A Novel* (London: Chatto and Windus, 1878). Walter Besant was the brother-in-law of Annie Besant (1847–1933), who succeeded H. P. Blavatsky as head of the Theosophical Society.

86 For more on these parallels, see: Crowley's "Antecedents of Thelema" in *Revival of Magick,* 162–9.

87 *AL* i.66.

88 *AL* ii.9.

89 *AL* ii.10–1.

90 *AL* ii.63.

91 *AL* i.41.

92 *AL* iii.51–4.

93 AC to R. F. Holm, 8 Jul 1936, Yorke Collection.

94 Diary, 11 May 1901.

95 AC to Gerald Yorke, 10 Jul (1944?), Yorke Collection.

96 *The Equinox* 1912, 1(8): 7.

97 Arnold Bennett, *The Journals of Arnold Bennett 1896–1928* (New York: Viking Press, 1932), 169.

98 Harris Wilson, *Arnold Bennett and H. G. Wells: A Record of a Personal and a Literary Friendship* (Urbana: Univ. of Illinois Press, 1960), 107–8. Bennett based a portion of his *Paris Nights* on this luncheon with Crowley. See Arnold Bennett, *Paris Nights:*

And Other Impressions of Places and People (London: Hodder & Stroughton, 1913), 36.

99   Her descriptions are published in *Scented Garden,* also included in Marcelo Motta, *Sex and Religion.* (Nashville, TN: Thelema Publishing Co., 1981). In *Sexuality, Magick and Perversion* (Secaucus, NJ: Citadel, 1972), Francis King argues that this ritual, of which only fragments survive in Yorke MS27, employed sex magic, but there is little evidence to support it.

Chapter Six • The Five Peaks

1   Archives of Kegan Paul, Trench, Trübner & Henry S. King.

2   AC to Gerald Yorke, 4 Dec 1928, Yorke Collection.

3   *Confessions,* 335.

4   *Confessions,* 360.

5   Percival George Albert Bott (1877–1953) was born in Devises, Wiltshire, to John H. and Elizabeth M. Bott. Although a brother and three sisters appear as children in the 1881 Scottish Census, only his older brother John Cecil Latham Bott appears in subsequent census, marriage, or death records. The Bott family relocated from Wiltshire to Aberdeenshire, Scotland, around 1880. Percival attended Wellington College from 1889 to 1893, continuing at the University of London; he passed the intermediate examination in medicine, second division, on Feburary 9, and received his bachelors of medicine in June 1903. He became a licentiate of the Royal College of Physicians in April 1901 and the following month a fellow of the Royal College of Surgeons. At this time he also joined the London Medico-Chirurgical Society, the Obstetrical Society of London, and the Medical Society of London. During the Great War he served as a captain in the Royal Army Medical Corps in the Mesopotamia theatre of operations from 1917 to 1920. He married Stella Edith Robinson in Cheltenham, Gloucestershire, in the winter of 1907; she petitioned for divorce in 1925. In autumn of 1932, he married Gladys Blair in Paddington, London. See: Birth record, Q2 1877, GRO, Devises, Wiltshire, 100. *Wellington College Register: 1859–July 1905,* 37. "University Intelligence," *Times* (London), 10 Feb 1898, 35436: 10. "Royal College of Physicians of London," *Times* (London), 29 Apr 1901, 36441: 13. "Faculty of Medicine: Bachelors of Medicine," *The Historical Record (1836–1912) Being a Supplement to the Calendar* (London: University of London, 1912), 254. *Medical Register* (London, 1903), 227. "University Intelligence," *Times* (London), 9 Jun 1903, 37102: 11. "Royal College of Surgeons, Edinburgh," *Medical Press and Circular,* 12 Aug 1903, 127: 185. "Royal College of Surgeons, Edinburgh," *Dublin Journal of Medical Science* 1903, 116: 253. Membership list of the London Medico-Chirurgical Society, *West London Medical Journal* 1905, 9: 313. Membership list, *Transactions of the Obstetrical Society of London* 1907, 48: xvii. Membership list, *Transactions of the Medical Society of London* 1904, 27: xxvi. *Medical Register* (London, 1907), 241. Marriage record, Q1, 1907, GRO, Cheltenham, Gloucestershire, 6a: 677. Divorce Court File 8888, Subseries J77/2200, Court for Divorce and Matrimonial Causes, Records of the Supreme Court of Judicature and Related Courts, National Archives. Marriage record, Q3, 1932, GRO, Paddington, London, 1a: 173.

6   Crowley, *Snowdrops.* Most copies were destroyed in 1925, but the book was reprinted in 1986.

7   Rose Crowley to Gerald Kelly, n.d., Old D6, Yorke Collection.

8   "Ascension Day," lines 98–111, rpt. *Works* 2: 146–7.

9   Stephensen, *Legend of Aleister Crowley,* 56.

10   *Daily News,* Sep 1904, quoted in Stephensen, *Legend of Aleister Crowley,* 50–1.

11   See Martin Starr's "Prolegomenon" to the 1986 edition of *Snowdrops.*

12   Although Bax doesn't cite the author, he was most likely reading Arthur Edward Waite, *The Real History of the Rosicrucians: Founded on Their Own Manifestoes, and on Facts and Documents Collected from the Writings of Initiated Brethren* (London: G. Red-

way, 1887). It was written in response to Jennings's immensely popular—but not very historical—book, *The Rosicrucians: Their Rites and Mysteries; with Chapters on the Ancient Fire and Serpent-Worshipers, and Explanations of the Mystic Symbols Represented in the Monuments and Talismans of the Primeval Philosophers* (London: J.C. Hotten, 1870). There were the main Rosicrucian references at the time.

13   This conversation is drawn from two of Bax's books: *Some I Knew Well* (London: Phoenix House, 1951), 51–5, and *Inland Far: A Book of Thoughts and Impressions* (London: William Heinemann, 1925), 41–2. While Bax quotes Crowley as saying "the world will be sitting in the sunset of Crowleyanity," its accuracy is suspect: Either Bax misremembered or Crowley misspoke, for AC believed his impact was just beginning; in other words, dawning, not setting. Furthermore, the term "Crowleyanity" is attributed to J. F. C. Fuller, who coined the term later that year.

14   Stephensen, *Legend of Aleister Crowley*, 36.

15   Crowley's ploy worked, for the contest was reported in *Longman's Magazine*, Mar 1905, 45(269): 477–8.

16   AC to Gerald Kelly, n.d., Old D6, Yorke Collection.

17   *Confessions*, 416.

18   Jules Jacot-Guillarmod, *Six Mois Dans l'Himalaya, le Karakoram et l'Hindu-Kush- Voyages et Explorations aux Plus Hautes Montagnes du Monde.* (Sandoz: Neuchatel, 1904).

19   This tale has been told so often that it has become legendary: Crowley tells it in his *Confessions*, 417–9, but variations appear in biographies (Cammell, *Aleister Crowley,* 47, and Marlow, *Seven Friends,* 61–2), and newspapers (newsclippings file, 24 Nov 1929, Yorke Collection).

20   J. L. Sherwill, "Journal of a Trip Undertaken to Explore the Glaciers of Kanchanjungha Group in the Sikkim Himalayas, in November 1861," *Journal of the Asiatic Society of Bengal* 1862, 31: 33-5.

21   John Tucker, 1955. *Kanchenjunga* (New York: Abelard-Schuman Ltd., 1955).

22   Jules Jacot-Guillarmod, "Vers le Kangchinjunga (8585m): Himalaya népalais," *Jahrbuch des Schweizer Alpenclub: Einundvierzigster Jahrgang 1905 bis 1906* (Bern: Verlag der Expedition des Jahrbuches des S. A. C., 1906), 190–205, This account differs from Crowley's in both perception and details. I have attempted to incorporate both into my presentation; unless noted otherwise, the account originates with Crowley.

23   "Charles-Adolphe Reymond, 1875–1914," *Berge der Welt* 1948, 1: 198–208.

24   "Drei Schweizer, darunter Jacot-Guillarmod, griefen im Jahre 1905 den Kantsch an," *Berge der Welt* 1948, 120–7.

25   Genealogical information is from "The ORR family of Richmond-upon-Thames: Index of Individuals" and its sub-pages at http://familytreemaker.genealogy.com/users/o/r/r/Stephen-Orr/WEBSITE-0001 (accessed 23 Apr 2010).

26   "Fribourg," *Revue militaire suisse* 1894, 40(1): 50.

27   Pache's interview ran in the *Gazette de Lausanne* on June 1, 10 and 12 of 1901. Excerpts appeared in "Chronique Politique," *Bibliotheque Universelle et Revue Suisse,* July 1901, 23(67): 211–24. See also: "The War, the King and the South African Medal," *Times* (London), 17 Jun 1901, 36483: 12. "With the Boers," *The Star* (New Zealand), 12 Jul 1901, 7148: 2. "As Others See Us," *Bush Advocate* (New Zealand), 30 Sep 1901, 12(2076): 2. Pache recounted how the constant Boer retreats frustrated the British troops, who would fight and rush to the top of a hill only find no one there to engage; as he quoted one of them, "We don't car a hang if we get a bayonet through us at the top as long as there is someone there to do it!"

28   "Scaling Kinchinginga: Swiss Lieutenant Killed," *Manchester Guardian,* 11 Sep 1905, 7.

29   Jacot-Guillarmod, "Vers le Kangchinjunga," 191.

30   Auguste Forel, "Les Fourmis de l'Himalaya," *Bulletin de la Société Vaudoise des Sciences Naturelles* 1906, 42(155): 79–94. Although largely remembered for his groundbreaking study of ants, Forel was, prior to retiring in 1893, a highly accomplished psychi-

atrist and neuroanatomist. He was cofounder of neuron theory (for *Untersuchungen über die Haubenregion und ihre oberen verknüpfungen im Gehirne des Menschen und einiger Säugetiere, mit Beiträgen zu den Methoden der Gehirnuntersuchung ...*, 1877), director of Zürich's Burghölzli Asylum, founder of an alcoholism treatment center, professor of psychiatry at Munich, the first Swiss sexologist (for *Die sexuelle Frage: eine naturwissenschaftliche, psychologische, hygienische und soziologische Studie für Gebildete*, 1905), and an influence on Sigmund Freud.

31   The archives of the Royal Geographical Society identify de Righi as proprietor of the Woodlands Hotel, which Crowley refers to in his *Confessions*, 423. See "Tashi Lama in Darjeeling," *Hawera & Normanby Star*, 8 Feb 1906, 9013: 6, for a contemporary article on the Drum Druid Hotel that mentions de Righi.

32   Robert Leon Cooper, *Around the World with Mark Twain* (New York: Arcade Pub., 2000), 238–9.

33   Testimonial letter of Capt. Henry B. Wilkinson to the Woodlands Hotel, 24 Mar 1900, quoted in *Newman's Guide to Darjeeling and Its Surroundings: Historical & Descriptive, with Some Account of the Manners and Customs of the Neighbouring Hill Tribes, and a Chapter on Thibet and the Thibetans* (Calcutta: W. Newman and Co, 1900), 118.

34   Hon. Charles Granville Bruce and Hon. Mrs. Finetta Madelina Julia Campbell Bruce, *Twenty Years in the Himalaya* (London: E. Arnold, 1910), 31.

35   Walter Crane, *India Impressions, with Some Notes of Ceylon During a Winter Tour, 1906–7* (London: Methuen & Co, 1907). 227–8

36   Crane, *India Impressions*, 227–8.

37   Guests at the Woodlands Hotel were treated to a breathtaking view of Kangchenjunga, even though the mountain was forty-five miles away. For contemporary reactions to the sight by visitors, see: John James Aubertin, *Wanderings & Wonderings India, Burma, Kashmir, Ceylon, Singapore, Java, Siam, Japan, Manila, Formosa, Korea, China, Cambodia, Australia, New Zealand, Alaska, the States* (London: Kegan Paul, Trench, Trübner & Co., 1892), 25; Paul Eve Stevenson, "Up to the Hills in India," *Outing* 1899, 34(2): 117–23; and Crane, *India Impressions*, 232.

38   Jacot-Guillarmod, "Vers le Kangchinjunga," 196–7.

39   Jules Jacot Guillarmod, "Au Kangchinjunga (8585m): Voyage et explorations dans l'Himalaya du Sikhim et du Népal," *Le Globe: Journal Géographique* 1906, 45(2): 87–90.

40   Charles Evans, *Kangchenjunga: The Untrodden Peak* (New York: E.P Dutton & Co., 1957), 1–3, 29. Tucker, *Kanchenjunga*, 25, 45–50.

41   Crowley and Jacot-Guillarmod's numbering of the various camps diverge at this point, further underscoring the disconnect between how the two climbers viewed even major details of their ascent. For instance, what Crowley here calls Camp 4, Jacot-Guillarmod calls Camp V. Crowley's numbering will be followed here.

42   Jacot-Guillarmod, "Vers le Kangchinjunga," 201.

43   In *The Pioneer*, Crowley described this incident as follows: "These slopes proved excessively bad after a while, the snow lying thin on hard blue ice at an angle of 50 degrees or more. Easy enough for me with my claws: difficult or impossible for the men. The leader in fact fell who was unroped, but supporting him, I caught, and held him safely. But the shock of the fall shook his nerves, and he began to untie himself from the rope. A sharp tap brought him to his senses and probably saved his life.: the only occasion on which I have had to strike a man." Aleister Crowley, "On the Kinchin Lay: The March," *Pioneer*, 20 Sep 1905.

44   Jacot Guillarmod, "Au Kangchinjunga."

45   Reymond's diary entries are reproduced in "Charles-Adolphe Reymond," 200.

46   A. C. Rigo de Righi, Dr. J. Jacot-Guillarmod and Ch. Reymond, "The Kinchinjunga Expedition," *Pioneer*, 29 Sep 1905.

47   "Charles-Adolphe Reymond," 202.

48   The porters' names are given in "Drei Schweizer, darunter Jacot-Guillarmod."

49   "Charles-Adolphe Reymond," 202–3.

50   *Confessions*, 441.

51   "Charles-Adolphe Reymond," 204.

52   "The Disaster on Kangchenjunga," *Alpine Journal* 1906, 23(171): 51–4.

53   See, e.g., "Scaling Kinchinginga: Swiss Lieutenant Killed," *Manchester Guardian*, 11 Sep 1905, 7. "Expédition suisse dans l'Himalaya," *Journal de Genéve*, 11 Sep 1905, 3. "Other Accidents," *Alpine Journal*, 1905, 22(170): 615. *Science*, 20 Oct 1905, 22: 511. "Une expédition tragique à l'Himalaya," *La Revue scientifique*, 23 Sep 1905, Series 5, 4(13): 413.

54   Aleister Crowley's articles "On the Kinchin Lay" for *The Pioneer* are: "I. Prospect and Retrospect," 10 Aug 1905; "II. Bandoblast," 17 Aug 1905; "The March," 20 Sep 1905; and "V. Mountains or Metaphysics?" 15 Oct 1905.

55   Crowley "The March."

56   Crowley, "The March."

57   de Righi et al., "The Kinchinjunga Expedition."

58   Crowley, "V. Mountains or Metaphysics?"

59   See the following *Journal de Genéve* articles: "Expédition suisse dans l'Himalaya" (11 Sep 1905, 3); Crowley's version appeared in "L'Expédition Jacot-Guillarmod: Mort du lieutenant Pache" (12 Sep 1905, 1), "Confédération: La mort du lieutenant Pache" (14 Sep 1905, 2), "Confédération: L'expédition Jacot-Guillarmod" (6 Oct 1905, 2) and "L'expédition Jacot-Guillarmod" (10 Oct 1905, 2–3). de Righi's letter (countersigned by Jacot-Guillarmod and Reymond) ran as "L'expédition de l'Hima-laya" (20 Oct 1905, 2), while Reymond's account ran as "L'Expédition de l'Hima-laya" (5 Feb 1906, 2). See also the account in Jacot-Guillarmod, "Dans l'Himalaya," *Gazette de Lausanne et Journal Suisse*, 9 Nov 1905, 10 Nov 1905, 11 Nov 1905, 17 Nov 1905, and 1 Dec 1905.

60   See *La Montagne, Le Globe,* and *Jahrbuch des Schweizer Alpenclub,* respectively, as cited above. In later years, Jacot-Guillarmod also wrote "Au Kanchinjunga (8585 m.): Voyage et explorations dans l'Himalaya du Sikhim et du Népal," *l'Écho des Alpes* 1914, 8: 389–406 and 9: 425–44. Crowley, however, may have had the final word, as he wrote a response to the late Dr. Jacot Guillarmod's account; it is included as an appendix in the unexpurgated edition of *The Confessions*.

61   Aleister Crowley, "The Great Climb: Four Men Killed on Kinchinjunga: Expedition Abandoned at 21,000 Feet," *Daily Mail,* 11 Sep 1905.

62   A., "The Kinchenjunga Expedition: To the Editor," *Pioneer,* 24 Aug 1905.

63   Kangchenjunga is discussed in Evans, *Kanchenjunga,* and Tucker, *Kanchenjunga,* Guil-larmod, *Six mois,* and Crowley's *Confessions.* New 87, Yorke Collection, contains additional articles, e.g., *Times,* 3 Jan 1930 and *National Advertiser,* 18 Mar 1930.

64   Colin Wells, "Something Wicked This Way Comes," *Rock and Ice,* Sep 2004, 136: 58–61, 105–9. This article, although hostile toward Crowley, contains a great deal of technical information about his various climbs, and is highly recommended for those seeking a modern assessment.

65   Maurice Isserman, Stewart Angas Weaver, and Dee Molenaar, *Fallen Giants: A History of Himalayan Mountaineering from the Age of Empire to the Age of Extremes* (New Haven: Yale Univ. Press, 2008), 63. See also their discussion on page 461, where they note that Crowley's attitude about acclimatization "anticipated today's high-altitude mantra of 'get in, get up, get out.'"

66   Geoff Powter, *Strange and Dangerous Dreams: The Fine Line between Adventure and Madness* (Seattle: Mountaineers Books, 2006), 135.

67   AC to Gerald Kelly, n.d., Old D6, Yorke Collection.

68   AC to Gerald Kelly, 31 Oct 1905, Old D6, Yorke Collection.

69   This incident was reported as "Calcutta Shooting Affray: European wounds Bad-mashes," *Indian Daily News and Overland Summary,* 2 Nov 1905, 23. There are some

difference in these accounts: While Crowley says he attended Durga Puja, the article refers to the national holiday of *Diwali,* the Hindu festival of light (although it's possible these two festivals may have overlapped). AC describes firing once, but two of the six assailants were shot in the stomach and admitted in serious condition to the Chandney Hospital. While the newspaper account suggests that the unidentified European fired twice, Crowley writes in his *Collected Works,* "the apprehension that six savages will rob and murder you is immediately allayed by the passage of a leaden bullet [...] through the bodies of two of the ringleaders" (v. 3, 229). This may make sense of the report that the bullet passed through the stomach and back one of the men, Sheik Nanka, while the other had a bullet that entered his stomach and lodged in his back. (With thanks to the research acumen of Clint Warren.)

70   Based on *Confessions,* 453–8.

71   *Confessions,* 465.

72   AC to Clifford Bax, 28 Mar 1906, New 4, Yorke Collection.

73   *Confessions,* 498.

74   Diary, 1906. HRHRC. Reprinted in Motta, *Sex and Religion.*

75   AC to Gerald Yorke, 1 Jan 1929, Yorke Collection.

76   Diary, 1906.

Chapter Seven • *The Great White Brotherhood*

1   The only son of Richard and Maria Fuller of Chichester, Rev. Alfred Fuller (1832–1927) attended Brighton College and Pocklington as a youth and matriculated in 1852 to St. John's College, Cambridge; he received his BA in 1857 and MA in 1859. Inbetween, he was ordained deacon (1857) and priest (1858), and served Kirk-Hallam (1857–1860) and Stoughton (1860–1864) before becoming rector of Itchenor, a post he held from 1865 to 1879. He married Selma Marie Philippine de la Chevallerie (c. 1847–1940)—not Thelma, as is often reported—on August 16, 1875. After retiring as rector, he moved to Chichester, where his son John was born. See: *Alumni Cantabrigienses.* "Deaths," *Times* (London), 5 Jul 1927, 44625: 18. "Deaths," *Times* (London), 7 Dec 1940, 48793: 1. Family Papers of the Fuller Family of Sussex, Add Mss 28260–28316, West Sussex Record Office.

2   Fuller's own words, quoted in Brian Holden Reid, *J. F. C. Fuller: Military Thinker* (London: Macmillan Press, 1987), 13.

3   J.F.C.F., "From India," *Agnostic Journal,* 7 Jan 1905, 56(1): 7. For a complete list of Fuller's contributions to this journal, see Richard Kaczynski (ed.), *Two Agnostics: The Early Writings of Victor Neuburg and J.F.C. Fuller* (in preparation).

4   John Frederick Charles Fuller, *The Star in the West: A Critical Essay upon the Works of Aleister Crowley* (London: Walter Scott Publishing Co., 1907), 211.

5   AC to Fuller, 3 Aug 1906, IV/12/3, Papers of Maj. Gen. John Frederick Charles Fuller (1878–1966), GB99 KCLMA Fuller, Liddell Hart Centre for Military Archives, King's College Library (hereafter cited as "Fuller Papers").

6   See biographical appendix, unexpurgated *Confessions,* v. 7.

7   117. Note that her name appears as the first word of the first line, and as an acrostic. Other acrostics occur on pages 3, 19, 35, and 67.

8   Published in *Konx Om Pax.*

9   This early form of the ritual is from the Aleister Crowley Papers, George Arents Research Library, Syracuse University (hereafter cited as GARL).

10   Diary, 1906.

11   "Liber Cheth vel Vallum Abiegni sub figura CLVI," verses 4–6, 12.

12   *Confessions,* 513.

13   *AL* iii.43.

14   *Works* 3: 219.

15   *The Equinox* 1912, 1(8): 47.

16   Published in *Konx Om Pax.*

17   *Confessions,* 546.

18   Marriage record, Q2 1860, GRO, Bootie Cul, Cumberland, 10b: 813. Birth record, Q2 1861, GRO, Ulverston, Lancashire, 8e: 681. UK 1871 census, GRO, RG10, piece 4241, 31: 21.

19   "Registered Apprentices or Students of the Society," *Calendar of the Pharmaceutical Society of Great Britain* (London: Phrmaceutical Soceity of Great Britain, 1885), 207. "Transactions of the Pharmaceutical Society," *Pharmaceutical Journal and Transactions* 1880, third series, 10(10 Jan): 522. "Deaths," *Chemist and Druggist* 1924, 101 (11 Oct): 533. For Whineray's marriage record, see Q4 1888, GRO, Cardiff, Monmouthshire, 11a: 478.

20   *Confessions,* 546. Robert Smythe Hichens, *Felix: Three Years in a Life* (London: Methuen & Co, 1902). The chemist's shop appears on 162–4, and is subsequently referred to on 178, 237–42 and 860.

21   "The Big Stick," *The Equinox* 1911, I(6): 170. A. C. Wootton, *Chronicles of Pharmacy* (London: Macmillan and Co., 1910).

22   Birth record, Q2 1852, GRO, St. George Hanover Square, London, Middlesex, 1a: 148. Death record, 1931, GRO, Glendale, Northumberland, 10b: 468.

23   "Lord Bennet's Religious Work: The Son of an English Peer an Evangelist in a Pacific Town," *New York Times,* 2 Feb 1896, 12. "An Evangelist Earl: Lord Tankerville and His American Wife Now Over Here," *New York Tribune,* 22 Dec 1911, 7.

24   Together they had four children (Georgina, who died shortly after birth in 1896), Charles Augusts Ker (1897–1971), Ida Lovia Sophie (1898–1900), and George William Bennet (b. 1903).

25   "Earl of Tankerville Dead: An American Girl, Wife of His Son, Is Now a Countess," *New York Times,* 20 Dec 1899, 3. "New American Countess," *Los Angeles Times,* 24 Dec 1899, 3. "The New Earl of Tankerville," *Washington Post,* 24 Dec 1899, 10.

26   "Lord Tankerville: Talented, but Poor," *Washington Post,* 22 Dec 1911, 6. Marion Elliston, "English Ancestral Homes of American Women," *Appleton's (Booklovers) Magazine,* Jul 1905, 6(1): 41–55. Shortly after he died in 1931, his son announced that he would cell Chillingham Castle because of the hefty taxation and death duties. "Earl to Sell Castle," *Chicago Daily Tribune,* 2 Oct 1931, 7.

27   "Amateur Art Exhibition: Yorkshire Railway Porter a Prize-Winner," *Manchester Guardian,* 8 Mar 1910, 13.

28   "La Marquise de Fontenoy," *Chicago Daily Tribune,* 22 Dec 1911, 10. "Lord Tankerville The Chillingham Wild Cattle," *Times* (London), 10 Jul 1931; 45871: 16. "The Earl of Tankerville," *Manchester Guardian,* 10 Jul 1931, 8. "Lord Tankerville, 'Singing Earl,' Dies: Had Possessed a Fine Tenor Voice and Studied under Italian, Sbriglia: French King an Ancestor: Served as Sailor, Soldier, Cow-puncher and Evangelist— Enjoyed U.S. Ranch Experience," *New York Times,* 10 Jul 1931, 19.

29   *Confessions,* 547–8.

30   Birth record, Q2 1883, GRO, Islington, London, 1b: 390.

31   In the 1891 British Census, Victore (sic) Neuburg is listed with his mother Jeannette Jacobs (married, age thirty-one), residing at 123 Highbury New Park. Other residents include Jeannette's mother Rebecca (age fifty-nine, widowed head of household), and her six siblings Hannah (age thirty-four), Benjamin (age thirty-one), Sydney (age twenty-nine), Theresa (age twenty-seven), Edward (twenty-six) and Montague (twenty-one). See RG12, piece 173, 43: 23. The 1901 census for the same address still spells his name Victore, but this time Jeannette appears with the surname Neuburg; other siblings at the address were Benjamin, Theresa, and Edward. See RG13, piece 196, 38: 16.

32   Neuburg's signed contributions to the *Freethinker* were limited to "Vale, Jehovah!," 25 Oct 1903, 23(43): 684 and "The Pagan," 21 Aug 1904, 24(34): 541. His first of many contributions to the *Agnostic Journal* began with "Only," 10 Oct 1903, 53(15): 238. For a full list of his other contributions, see Richard Kaczynski (ed.), *Two Agnostics: The Early Writings of Victor Neuburg and J.F.C. Fuller* (in preparation). For additional biographical details, see Jean Overton Fuller, *The Magical Dilemma of Victor Neuburg* (London: W.H. Allen, 1965; rev. ed. Oxford: Mandrake, 1990).

33   Diary (limerick), 28 Jun 1930.

34   *Confessions*, 550.

35   Diary, 15 Dec 1907, HRHRC.

36   Written on July 16, 1907, it appears in *Konx Om Pax*, 101–5.

37   UK incoming passenger list, Scharnhorst, 25 Jul 1907, Southampton. The passenger list shows both G. M. Bennet and Aleister Crowley boarding the ship at Gibraltar.

38   *The Star in the West* was simultaneously released in both a white buckram limited edition signed by both Crowley and Fuller, and in a red buckram trade edition.

39   Diary, 11 Jul 1907, HRHRC. In fact, this diary is attributed to V.V.V.V.V.

40   *Daily Mirror*, 15 Aug 1907.

41   Mary H. Debenham, *The Star in the West* (London: National Society's Depository, 1906).

42   "Literary Gossip," *Athenaeum*, 13 Jul 1907, 4159: 44.

43   "The Hermit" appears in *Clouds without Water*, 33–48. "Empty Headed Athenians" in *Konx Om Pax*, xii, "Ercildoune" in *The Equinox* 1913, 1(9): 175–258, and "The Wizard Way" in both *The Equinox* 1909, 1(1) and *The Winged Beetle*. These dates are from marginal notes in Crowley's copy of *The Equinox*, Yorke Collection.

44   Page proofs, dated 24 Sep 1907, and numbered pages 231–48, are extant in Fuller's collection, which is now at HRHRC.

45   For comments on this work, see Smith, *Books of the Beast*.

46   Sri Agamya Guru Paramahamsa, *Sri Brahma Dhara: Shower from the Highest through the Favour of the Mahatma Sri Agamya Guru Paramahamsa* (London: Luzac, 1905).

47   For more on Paramahamsa, see Richard Kaczynski, "Carl Keller's Esoteric Roots: Sex and Sex Magic in the Victorian Age," *Beauty and Strength: Proceedings of the Sixth Biennial National Ordo Templi Orientis Conference* (Riverside, CA: OTO, 2009), 77–103.

48   AC to Fuller, Sep 1907, IV/12/11, Fuller Papers.

49   The story appears in "Half-hours with famous Mahatmas," *The Equinox* 1910, 1(4): 284–290. The phrase "Chup raho! Tum suar ke bachcha ho!" translates literally as "Shut up! you are the child of a pig." (Thanks to N. Bordia for the translation.)

50   7 Oct 1907.

51   From Aleister Crowley, "One Star in Sight," in *Magick in Theory and Practice* (Paris: Lecram Press, 1929), 215.

52   His diary from this period reads, "Again, no shadow of *Samadhi;* only a feeling that V.V.V.V.V. was in His *Samadhi,* and writing by my pen: i.e., the pen of the scribe, and that scribe is not OY MH, who reasons, etc., nor A.C., who is a poet & selects; but of some perfectly passive person."

53   *Konx Om Pax*, 82 ("Ovariotomy").

54   Printed in *The Equinox* 1912, I(7): "One Star in Sight," 29–36.

55   [Aleister Crowley], "Illusion d'Amoreux," *The Equinox* 1909. I(2): 187–90.

56   Marriage record, Q4 1881, GRO, 1: 1187. British Census, 1891, St. George Hanover Square, RG12, 33: 40. Death record for Ernest David Leverson, 25 Dec 1921, 1921-09-286116, Vancouver, British Columbia Vital Statistics Agency.

57   Violet H. Leverson appears in the 1891 census at one year of age (RG12, 33: 40), and also in the 1901 census (RG13, 151: 62). Violet L. H. Leverson married Guy P. Wyndham in spring, 1923 (GRO London, Middlesex, 1c: 23). Ada also had a son

who died in infancy; extant records show an infant, George Ernest Leverson, born in the summer of 1888 (GRO Kensington, London, 1a: 160) and who died that fall, 1888 (GRO Kensington, London, 1a: 133).

58   Charles Burkhart, *Ada Leverson.* (New York: Twayne Publishers, Inc., 1973).

59   See Crowley's reviews of Leverson's *The Limit* in *The Equinox* 1911, I(6): 169 and of her *Tenterhooks* in *The Equinox* 1912, I(8): 255; these are essentially the same review, with the latter adding an extra paragraph.

60   For more on Leverson, see Burkhart, *Ada Leverson.* Violet Wyndham, *The Sphinx and Her Circle: A Biographical Sketch of Ada Leverson, 1862–1933* (New York: Vanguard, 1963). Julie Speedie, *Wonderful Sphinx: The Biography of Ada Leverson* (London: Virago, 1993).

61   Aleister Crowley, "A Syllabus of the Official Instructions of A∴A∴ Hitherto Published," *The Equinox* 1913, 1(10): 43–7.

62   Birth record, Q3 1861, GRO, Manchester, Lancashire, 8d: 227. 1881 British census, RG11, piece 3559, 104: 20. 1891 British Census, RG12, piece 3200, 16: 26. William Dale Mudd wed in the fall of 1886 (marriage record, GRO, Prestwich, Lancashire, 8d: 571).

63   Birth record, Q1 1889, Prestwich, Lancashire, 8d: 403. Birth record, Q4 1887, GRO, Prestwich, Lancashire, 8d: 396. 1901 British Census, Chorlton, Hulme, RG13, piece 3709, 23: 37.

64   "Rehearsing for the Army Pageant at Fulham Palace," *Manchester Guardian,* 17 Jun 1910, 5.

65   Norman Mudd to C. S. Jones, 15 Jan 1923, Yorke Collection.

66   A∴A∴ Syllabus.

67   Aleister Crowley, "Praemonstrance of A∴A∴ and Curriculum of A∴A∴," *The Equinox* 1919, 3(1): 11–38.

68   For commentaries on the "Holy Books," see Aleister Crowley, *Commentaries on the Holy Books and Other Papers,* ed. Hymenaeus Beta (York Beach, ME: Samuel Weiser, 1996). Regardless, the interpretation of the more cryptic books such as Tau, XXVII, and 231 is unclear.

69   *Konx Om Pax,* xi.

70   From Stephensen, *Legend of Aleister Crowley,* 66–9.

71   Leo Vincey [Aleister Crowley]. *The "Rosicrucian" Scandal* (London: privately printed, 1912–1913).

Chapter Eight • Singer of Strange and Obscene Gods

1   Noel Riley Fitch, *Walks in Hemingway's Paris: A Guide to Paris for the Literary Traveler* (New York: St. Martin's Press, 1992), 129. Douglas Goldring, *The Last Pre-Raphaelite: The Life of Ford Madox Ford* (Searcy, AR: Harding Press, 2007), 221. Christian Derouet and Sophie Lévy, *A Transatlantic Avant-Garde: American Artists in Paris, 1918–1939* (Berkeley: University of California Press, 2003), 241. Richard Whelan, *Robert Capa: A Biography* (New York: Knopf, 1985), 80. Ruth Blackmore and James McConnachie, *The Rough Guide to Paris* (London: Rough Guides, 2008), 299.

2   Howard R. Simpson, *Bush Hat, Black Tie: Adventures of a Foreign Service Officer* (Washington: Brassey's, 1998), 5.

3   This conversation is reported in C. S. Nott, *Teachings of Gurdjieff: A Pupil's Journal. An Account of Some Years with G. I. Gurdjieff and A. R. Orage in New York and at Fontainebleau-Avon* (York Beach, ME: Samuel Weiser, 1978), 122. Details of this conversation have almost certainly changed in the recording: The numbers seven and twelve are not particularly relevant to Crowley's magical ideas. More likely, Crowley asked Orage his grade, and was given by chance a number higher than his own.

4   Beatrice Hastings, quoted in James Webb, *The Harmonious Circle* (London: Thames

and Hudson, 1980), 210.

5   "Garter and Star," *New Age,* 29 Aug 1907, New Series 1(18): 282–3. "The Beautiful What," *New Age,* 29 Feb 1908, 2(18): 352–3. Aleister Crowley, "The Pentagram," *New Age,* 21 Mar 1908, 2(21): 410.

6   Lavinia King, "The Suffragette: A Farce," *New Age,* 30 May 1908, 3(5): 91–2.

7   Beatrice Hastings, *The Old "New Age": Orage—and Others* (London: Blue Moon Press, 1936).

8   Frank Harris, *My Life and Loves* (Paris: the author, 1922). This multi-volume memoir may have inspired Crowley's multi-volume *Confessions.*

9   Following are some of Crowley's *Vanity Fair* contributions: "Jeremiah in the Quartier Montparnasse," 3 Jun 1908, 713. "With a Madman on the Alps," 24 Jun 1908, 823. "The Mystic," 22 Jul 1908, 105. "Ezekiel in the Quarter Montparnesse," 12 Aug 1908, 211. "How to Write a Novel! After W. S. Maugham," 30 Dec 1908, 838–40. "(On) A Burmese River," 3 Feb 1909, 135; 10 Feb 1909, 169; 17 Feb 1909, 201; 24 Feb 1909, 232; 3 Mar 1909, 269; 31 Mar 1909, 393. "Mantra Yogi," 3 Mar 1909. "The Art of Lord Dunsany: *The Sword of Welleran,*" 21 Apr 1909, 505. "The Expedition to Chogo Ri," 8 Jul 1909, 51–2; 15 Jul 1909, 71–2; 22 Jul 1909, 106–7; 5 Aug 1909, 179–80; 19 Aug 1909, 246–7; 2 Sep 1909, 310–1; and 16 Sep 1909, 372–3.

10   From a letter by Crowley to Rose's doctor, W. Murray Leslie. Given Crowley's unfaithfulness with Lola and Fenella Lovell, one may wonder if Rose locked him out and accused him with good reason.

11   IV/12/16, Fuller Papers.

12   See, for instance, mentions of the bust in Stephen Bone, "Artists of Fame and Promise: Leicester Galleries," *Manchester Guardian,* 22 Jul 1954, 5 and "A Sculpture Exhibition at Cirencester," *New York Times,* 5 Sep 1956, 53628: 16.

13   Jill Berk Jiminez and Joanna Banham, *Dictionary of Artists' Models* (London: Fitzroy Dearborn, 2001), 311–2.

14   Crowley, *Magical Record of the Beast 666,* 97.

15   *Confessions,* 575.

16   Crowley to Fuller, Aug 9, 1908, IV/12/25 Fuller Papers.

17   Published in *The Equinox* 1909, 1(2): 31–89, under the pseudonym "Oliver Haddo."

18   Edward Carpenter, *The Intermediate Sex: A Study of Some Transitional Types of Men and Women* (London: S. Sonnenschein, 1908).

19   Victor B. Neuburg, "The Romance of Olivia Vane" in *The Triumph of Pan.* (London: The Equinox, 1910), 139–70.

20   Published in *The Equinox* 1909, 1(1): 113–35.

21   Published as the supplement to *The Equinox* 1909, 1(1).

22   From his painting "Jupiter and Antiope", ca 1524–1525.

23   *Vanity Fair,* 30 Dec 1908, 838–40.

24   *Confessions,* 559.

25   Jack Collings Squire, "Recent Verse," *New Age,* 21 Dec 1912, 10(8): 184.

26   Kenneth Clark in Derek Hudson, *For Love of Painting: The Life of Sir Gerald Kelly, KCVO, PRA.* (London: Peter Davies, 1975), ix.

27   Stephensen, *Legend of Aleister Crowley,* 69–70.

28   Harrington Books listing. http://www.ilabdatabase.com/member/detail.php3 ?custnr =&lang=&membernr=804&booknr=340345812 (accessed Oct 19 2009).

29   Compare the text of "Liber Liberae" to "On the General Guidance and Purification of the Soul" (Regardie, *Complete Golden Dawn,* 3:19–21).

30   Fuller, *Bibliotheca Crowleyana,* 5.

31   "Books and Persons (An Occasional Causerie)," *New Age,* 25 Mar 1909, 4(22): 445.

32   Stephensen, *Legend of Aleister Crowley,* 70–2.

33   "The Equinox," *Review of Reviews,* Apr 1909, 39(232): 374.

34   Neuburg's Oath of a Probationer, Mortlake Collection of English Life and Letters, 1591-1963, Accession 1969-0024R, Rare Books and Manuscripts, Special Collections Library, University Libraries, Pennsylvania State University.

35   Warren to Fuller, IV/12/37, Fuller Papers.

36   Birth record, Q1 1882, GRO, Chertsey, Surrey, 2a: 35. 1891 British Census, GRO, Kingston, Surrey, RG12, piece 612, 68: 35. 1901 British Census, GRO, Bradfield, Berkshire, RG13, piece 1141, 178: 4.

37   "The Law Society: Final Examination," *Weekly Notes,* 23 Nov 1907, 42: 324.

38   "New Members and Associates," *Journal of the Society for Psychical Research,* Dec 1908, 13: 314.

39   Robert Gilbert, *The Golden Dawn Companion: A Guide to the History, Structure, and Workings of the Hermetic Order of the Golden Dawn* (Wellingborough, Northamptonshire: Aquarian Press, 1986), 173.

40   Death record, Q3 1912, GRO, Paddington, London, 1a: 20.

41   *Manchester Guardian,* 3 May 1904, 6.

42   "Policeman's Son is Painter of Mystics," *Duluth News Tribune,* 5 Jun 1905, 3.

43   Austin Osman Spare, *Earth Inferno* (London: Co-operative Printing Society, 1905). Austin Osman Spare and James Guthrie, *A Book of Satyrs* (London: Co-operative Printing Society, 1907).

44   R. E. D. Sketchley, "Austin Osman Spare," *Art Journal,* Feb 1908, 50.

45   Ian Law, "Austin Osman Spare," in *Austin Osman Spare 1886–1956: The Divine Draughtsman. An Appreciation of the Man, the Artist and the Magician* (London: Beskin Press, 1987).

46   Austin Osman Spare, *The Book of Pleasure (Self-Love): The Psychology of Ecstasy* (London: The Author, 1913).

47   From Kenneth Grant's introduction to Austin Osman Spare, *The Book of Pleasure (Self Love): The Psychology of Ecstasy.* (Montreal: 93 Publishing, 1975).

48   Bax, *Inland Far,* 293.

49   Robert Ansell, "Adventures in Limbo: Exploring the Creative Sorcery of Austin Osman Spare's Magico-Aesthetic." Presentation at the first annual Esoteric Book Conference, Seattle, September, 2009. For more on Spare, who has seen widespread appreciation in recent years, see Robert Ansell (ed.), *Borough Satyr: The Life and Art of Austin Osman Spare* (London: Fulgur, 2005) and A. R. Naylor (ed.), *Existence: Austin Spare, 1886–1956* (Thame: I.H.O., 2006).

50   World War I draft registration card, Los Angeles, draft board 17, FHL roll 1530898. Death record, 2 Aug 1957, San Mateo, CA.

51   Divorce Court File 8022, 1907, National Archives, KEW. Divorce Court File 8381, 1908, National Archives, KEW. Record of marriage, Q4 1908, GRO, Strand, London, 1b: 1030.

52   "Talkon Britain," *Los Angeles Times,* 10 Jun 1927, A8.

53   "Court Circular," *Times* (London), 29 Dec 1905, 37903: 8. "Court Circular," *Times* (London), 2 Jan 1906, 37906: 8. "Court Circular," *Times* (London), 5 Jan 1906, 37909: 8. "The General Election: Letters from Mr. Chamberlain," *Times* (London), 8 Jan 1906, 37911: 10. "Court Circular," *Times* (London), 27 Feb 1907, 38267: 10. "Court Circular," *Times* (London), 13 Mar 1907, 38279: 10.

54   AC to Louis Wilkinson, 9 Oct 1940, Wilkinson Collection.

55   "Editorial," *The Equinox* 1910, I(3): 2.

56   An example of Sheridan-Bickers's journalisic work is Horace Sheridan-Bickers, "The Treatment of the Insane: Farming as a Cure for madness—British Columbia's Novel Experiment," *Man to Man* 1910, 6(12): 1050–9. For editing the *Spokesman,* see "Talk on Britain," *Los Angeles Times,* 10 Jun 1927, A8. For his magical work, see

Martin P. Starr, *The Unknown God* (Bolingbrook, IL: Teitan Press,, 2003), 37.

57 World War I draft registration card, *op. cit.*

58 "Limns Horros of Red Russia: Journalist Tells Rotarians about Bolshevism: Declares Anarchy is a Real Menace to America: Extols Kolchak as True and Democratic Patriot," *Los Angeles Times,* 13 Sep 1919, II10. "Letters to 'The Times,'" *Los Angeles Times,* 15 Sep 1919, II2. Lady Jane, "Women's Work, Women's Clubs," *Los Angeles Times,* 16 Dec 1919, II2. "Japanese Balk U.S. in Siberia, Briton Warns: Military Party Seeking in Every Way to Alienate America from Sympathy of Allies, He Asserts: Stir Hatred of Russians: Sheridan-Bickers en Route Home to Make Private Report to Lloyd George," *New York Tribune,* 27 Dec 1919, 3.

59 *Her Body in Bond* was directed by Robert Z. Leonard, produced by Universal Films, and released on 16 Jun 1918. It starred Mae Murray, Kenneth Harlan, and Alan Roscoe, among others.

60 "Written on the Screen," *New York Times,* 16 Jun 1919, 36.

61 "Over-exploited Stars Scored: English Critis Brings News of Anti-American War: Favors Money for Stories rather than Players: Tactless Advertising Ruins Many Films Abroad," *Los Angeles Times,* 16 May 1926, C19.

62 "Hollywood Magazine Editor Resigns Post," *Los Angeles Times,* 21 Dec 1927, A1.

63 *Confessions,* 606–8.

64 United States passport application, 24 Mar 1921, National Archives, College Park, MD. George Raffalovich, United States Naturalization Records Indexes, petition no. 45566, certificate no. 1165685. George Raffalovich, United States draft registration card, no. 3444, Cambridge, MA. "Dr. Raffalovich Dead: Writer and Teacher of Slavic and French History, 77," *New York Times,* 22 May 1958, 29.

65 *Confessions,* 633.

66 Frederick G. Aflalo, Joseph Jacobs, H. A. Morrah, Basil Stewart, and Mark Meredith, *The Literary Yearbook* (London: G. Routledge and Sons, 1917), 247.

67 The 1911 London metropolitan phone book, p. 561, lists his address as 22 Church Road. For his association with *Vanity Fair,* see "Dr. Raffalovich Dead."

68 Ad for *Planetary Journeys and Earthly Sketches* (London: Arnold Fairbairns, 1908), *Observer* (London), 24 May 1908, 4.

69 George Raffalovich, "Nadia," *Idler: An Illustrated Monthly Magazine* 1908, 33(70): 399–402.

70 *Confessions,* 634.

71 See J. F. C. Fuller, and George Raffalovich, "The Eyes of St. Ljubov: De La Ratiboisière's Account of the Typhlosophists of South Russia," *The Equinox* 1910, 1(4): 293–309. Also featuring characters based on Crowley's circle is George Raffalovich, *The Deuce and All* (London: The Equinox, 1910).

72 In addition to "The Eyes of St. Ljubov," Raffalovich's contributions to *The Equinox* include "The Man Cover," 1(2): 353–84; "The Brighton Mystery," 1(3): 287–303; "My Lady of the Breeches," 1(4): 25–35; "Ehe," 1(4): 281–3.

73 *Op. cit.,* "An Origin," 29–32, and "The Sunflower," 66–70. "The Sunflower" is dated 21 Jun 1910.

74 Mosley, *Burke's Peerage and Baronetage,* 107th ed., 1: 1088. *Alumni Cantabrigienses.* "Calls to the Bar," *Times* (London), 20 Nov 1894, 34426: 7.

75 "The Hon. Everard Feilding," *Times* (London), 13 Feb 1936, 47297: 17.

76 *Proceedings of the Society for Psychical Research* 1909, 23: 320.

77 Everard Feilding, W. W. Baggally, and Hereward Carrington, *Report on a Series of Sittings with Eusapia Palladino* (London: Society for Psychical Research, 1909). Everard Feilding and W. Marriott, "Report on a Further Series of Sittings with Eusapia Palladino at Naples," *Proceedings of the Society for Psychical Research* 1910, 25: 57–69.

78 Aleister Crowley, *Moonchild: A Prologue* (London: Mandrake Press, 1929), 72–3.

79   *Transactions of the Liverpool Engineering Society* 1906, 27: 41. Regimental Number
      (T)2043, 448403, WWI Medal Rolls Index Cards, 1914–1920. British birth records
      show a Herbert Edward Inman born in Croydon, Surrey, in fall of 1880 (2a: 216),
      but I have been unable to positively identify this person.
80   J. G. Bayley to Karl Germer, 7 Jan 1950, Yorke Collection.
81   AC to Cordelia Sutherland, 22 Aug [Bell Inn period], GARL.
82   Birth record, Q2 1886, GRO, Fulham, Greater London, 1a: 272. Death record
      #1950-09-002876, 24 Feb 1950, North Vancouver, British Columbia Vital Statistics
      Agency. Register of Baptisms, London Metropolitan Archives, Saint Andrew, Park
      Walk, P74/AND. Jones's siblings (and birth years) are Florence M. (c. 1867),
      Herbert E. (1866), Edith J. (c. 1870), Eliza C. F. (c. 1878), Claud P. (c. 1880), and
      Annie G. (c. 1882), c.f. 1891 UK census, RG12, piece 1044, 86: 40. According to
      Jones's son (Anthony Stansfeld Jones, private communication), the family descended
      from Sir Chapman Marshall (c. 1787–1862), Lord Mayor of London from 1839 to
      1840, and his wife, Ann Stansfeld (1786–1848).
83   Marriage record, GRO, Wandsworth, Greater London, 1d: 1542. 1920 US Census,
      Detroit Ward 14, Wayne, MI, district 419, 2A. Tony Stansfeld Jones, private com-
      munication.
84   Anonymous, *Memoirs of Kenneth Martin Ward* (London: Simpkin Marshall, 1929).
85   Birth record, Q3 1887, GRO, Cambridge, Cambridgeshire, 3b: 507. 1901 British
      Census, GRO, Cambridge, Cambridgeshire, RG13, piece 1533, 15: 22.

Chapter Nine • The Vision and the Voice

1   For Lord Dunsany's letters to AC, see Vertical File Manuscript 349, Special Collec-
     tions, Morris Library, Southern Illinois University at Carbondale.
2   Gerald Hume Saverie Pinsent (1888–1976) was educated at King's School, Canter-
     bury, and Trinity College, Cambridge, with scholarships in mathematics to both
     institutions; his cousin David Pinsent was a friend of philosopher Ludwig Wittgen-
     stein (1889–1951). In 1909, Pinsent was secretary for the Cambridge University
     branch of the socialist reform movement, the Fabian Society. Entering the Treasury
     in 1910, he would go on to work as the Prime Minister's private secretary, receive
     his M.A. in 1914, serve as a second lieutenant in the Royal Garrison Artillery during
     the Great War, act as commercial attaché and financial adviser to His Majesty's
     embassy in Berlin in the late 1930s, and ultimately work as Comptroller General for
     the National Debt Office during World War II. See: "Mr. Gerald Pinsent," *Times*
     (London), 3 Mar 1976, 59643: 16. *Journal of Education: A Monthly Record and Review*,
     Aug 1903, New Series 25(409): 550. "University Intelligence" in *Times* (London)
     for 17 Dec 1906, 38205: 7; 23 Mar 1907, 38288: 14; 25 Mar 1908, 38603: 14; 27
     Jun 1908, 38684: 14; and 11 May 1914, 40520: 4. *Twenty-Sixth Annual Report of the
     Fabian Society*, 31 Mar 1909. Brian McGuinness, *Young Ludwig: Wittgenstein's Life,
     1889–1921* (Oxford: Clarendon Press, 2005), 95. "Mr. Asquith's New Secretary,"
     Times (London), 24 Nov 1914, 40706: 11. British Army WWI Medal Rolls, Royal
     Garrison Artillery. "The King's Birthday Honours List in Full, Commemoratio of
     the Jubilee," *Times* (London), 3 Jun 1935, 47080: 19. *The London Gazette* 15 Nov
     1946, 5632 and 19 Nov 1948, 6084. Hymenaeus Beta, "Notes on Contributors,"
     appendix to *The Equinox* (York Beach, ME: Weiser, 1998), 43–4.
3   *AL* ii.5.
4   *Confessions*, 606.
5   "Liber XXX Aerum vel Saeculi sub figura CCCCXVIII: (Being of the Angels of
     the 30 Aethyrs): The Vision and the Voice." *The Equinox* 1911, 1(5), special supple-
     ment, 11. This was later republished, with Crowley's commentaries, as Aleister
     Crowley, Victor Neuburg, and Mary Desti. *The Vision and the Voice with Commentary
     and Other Papers,* ed. Hymenaeus Beta (Yorke Beach, ME: Samuel Weiser, 1998).
6   Salvesen was judge of the Court of Session, Scotland, from 1905 to 1922, and is

recalled, amongst various accomplishments, for helping to reform Scottish divorce laws and for his presidency over the Zoological Society of Scotland. See "Obituaries," *Nature*, 14 Mar 1942, 149 (3776): 296–7. "Obituary," *Times* (London), 25 Feb 1942, 49169: 4.

7   Several newspapers covered the proceedings, e.g., "Scottish Divorce Suit: The MacGregor Tartan," *Daily Telegraph*, 25 Nov 1910, and "Scottish Romance: Entertaining Story of a Kilted 'Lord'" unidentified clipping. These articles are preserved in the Yorke, HRHRC and OTO collections.

8   *Confessions*, 621.

9   My Lord, my Lord, why have you forsaken me?

10 Crowley, *Vision and the Voice*, 93; all other quotes regarding this vision are likewise from this source.

11 Éliphas Lévi, "The Magician," trans. Aleister Crowley, *The Equinox* 1909, 1(1): 109. It was also later reprinted in Crowley, *The Winged Beetle*.

12 The others, incidentally, included a goat in honor of Bhavani during his tour of India; a toad during his World War I stay in the United States; and a cat, performed at the behest of his students. See Gerald J. Yorke, "Aleister Crowley: A Biographical Note," *Occult Observer* 1949, 1(2): 121–4.

13 The dialogue for this section is drawn from the text of the Tenth Aethyr; see Crowley et al., *The Vision and the Voice*.

14 Surah 112 of the Qur'an: "Say: He, God, is One. God is the Absolute Source. He does not beget and is not begotten. And nothing is like unto him." See also Crowley et al., *Vision and the Voice with Commentary*, 176.

15 1(4): 37–8.

16 Cran was the son of Dr. John Cran, London. He passed his Law Society preliminary exam in 1891, Intermediate Exam in 1895, and Final Exam in 1897, setting up shop at 5 King's Bench Walk, London. See *Scottish Notes and Queries* 1927, 141. "The Incorporated Law Society," *Times* (London), 18 Jul 1891, 33380: 14. *Law Notes* 1891, 10: 252–3. "The Law Society," *Times* (London), 6 Jul 1895, 34622: 17 and 6 Feb 1897, 35120: 5. *Weekly Notes*, 13 Feb 1897, 32: 59. *Royal Blue Book: Fashionable Directory and Parliamentary Guide* 1906, 756. *London Phone Book*, 1909, 160.

17 The Rosæ Rubeæ et Aureæ Crucis ("Ruby Rose and Golden Cross") was the first degree of the Inner Order of the GD, for which all the previous grades were merely preparatory.

18 Stephensen, *Legend of Aleister Crowley*, 72.

19 Editorial. *The Equinox* 1910, 1(4): 3–4.

20 Lord Justice Vaughan Williams was the uncle of composer Ralph Vaughan Williams (1872–1958), and is credited with suggesting that his nephew be provided with an organ at Leith Hill Place. Baron Moulton, John Fletcher Moulton (1844–1921), was educated at Kingswood and St. John's College, Cambridge, admitted to the Middle Temple in 1874 and to the Queen's Counsel in 1885. He served as an M.P. for the years 1885–1886 (Battersea, Clapham) and 1894–1895 (South Hackney), and held the office of Lord Justice of Appeal from 1906–1912. See Michael Kennedy, *The Works of Ralph Vaughan Williams* (London: Oxford Univ. Press, 1964), 1992. L. G. Pine, *The New Extinct Peerage 1884–1971: Containing Extinct, Abeyant, Dormant and Suspended Peerages With Genealogies and Arms* (London: Heraldry Today, 1972), 198.

21 Mosley, *Burke's Peerage and Baronetage*, 106th ed, 1: 57.

22 "Sir Patrick Rose-Innes," *Times* (London), 3 Oct 1924, 43773: 14. Henry Robert Addison, Charles Henry Oakes, William John Lawson, Douglas Brooke Wheelton Sladen, *Who's Who, An Annual Biographical Dictionary, with Which Is Incorporated "Men and Women of the Time"* (London: A. and C. Black), 1849–1919, 1456. *The Independent*, 11 Jul 1907, 63(3058): 62. *New Age Magazine* 1920, 28(12): 575.

23 Birth record, Q3 1858, GRO, Marylebone, London, 1a: 376. "Deaths," *Times* (London), 21 Dec 1937, 47873: 1. "Obituary," *The Solicitors' Journal* 1937, 81(pt. 2):

1042. *The Law Times* (London), 26 Apr 1884, 76: 465.

24   "Obituary: Mr. Neilson, K.C.: Successful Career at the Bar," *Times* (London), 11 Apr 1929, 45174: 11. "The Inns of Court," *Times* (London), 27 May 1891, 33335: 8. "Calls to the Bar," *Times* (London), 18 Nov 1893, 34112: 8. "Deaths," *Times* (London), 15 Apr 1929, 45177: 17.

25   The headlines are respectively from: *Morning Leader,* 22 Mar 1910; *Morning Leader,* 23 Mar 1910; *Daily Express,* 22 Mar 1910; and *Evening News,* 22 Mar 1910. In all, some seventeen clippings are preserved in various archives.

26   22 Mar 1910.

27   AC to Henri Birven, 8 Oct 1929, New 24, Yorke Collection.

28   AC to Birven, ibid.

29   See John Mandelberg, *Ancient and Accepted: A Chronicle of the Proceedings 1845–1945 of the Supreme Council Established in England in 1845* (London: Supreme Council 33°, 1995). Similarly, on March 17, 1878, J. M. P. Montagu, Grand Secretary General of the Ancient and Accepted Scottish Rite in the UK, wrote to the Illustrious Grand Secretary General of the Supreme Council for the Northern Jurisdiction of the United States that Yarker "was expelled by this Supreme Council for Unmasonic and other conduct" (Van Gorden-Williams Library & Archives, National Heritage Museum, Lexington, MA.)

30   Yarker was a prolific writer of articles and letters to various journals, and a complete bibliography of his works is beyond the scope of this book. I am working on a history of western esotericism that will take a closer look at Yarker's work.

31   John Yarker to AC, 4 Nov 1910, OTO Archives.

32   Aleister Crowley, "Waite's Wet," *The Equinox* 1912, 1(8): 233–42.

33   *Confessions,* 629.

34   Francis King, *The Magical World of Aleister Crowley* (New York: Coward, McCann & Geoghegan, Inc., 1978), 61–2.

35   "Captain G. M. Marston," *Times* (London), 5 May 1928, 44885: 14. Birth record, Q1 1872, GRO, Salford, Lancashire, 8d: 35. "From the London Gazette," *Times* (London), 12 Oct 1892, 33767: 11 and 1 Jul 1905, 37748: 14. "Naval and Military Intelligence," *Times* (London), 18 Jun 1901, 36484: 11; 27 Jul 1901, 36518: 13, and 11 Nov 1910, 39427: 7. "Trawlers and Submarine Cables," *Times* (London), 7 Jul 1908, 38692: 16. Richard D. Ryder, *The Calcrafts of Rempstone Hall: The Intriguing History of a Dorset Dynasty* (Devon: Halsgrove, 2005). Paul Newman, *Ancestral Voices Prophesying War: A Tale of Two Suicides* (St. Austell: Abraxas Editions, 2009).

36   AC to Frank Bennett, 9 Feb 1910, New 92, Yoke Collection.

37   AC to Frank Bennett, 26 Feb 1910, New 92, Yorke Collection.

38   For a biographical study of Bennett, see Keith Richmond, *Progradior and the Beast: Frank Bennett & Aleister Crowley* (London: Neptune Press, 2004). For Bennett's further correspondence with Crowley and members of his circle, see Aleister Crowley, Frank Bennett, Charles Stansfeld Jones, et al,. *The Progradior Correspondence, Letters by Aleister Crowley, Frank Bennett, C. Stansfeld Jones, & Others,* ed. Keith Richmond (York Beach, ME: Teitan Press, 2009).

39   A James Gilbert Bailey was born in Crewe, Cheshire, in 1885 to iron smith James-Bailey and his wife Mary. However, I have been unable to positively identify this as the same J. G. Bailey. Birth record, Q3 1885, GRO, Nantwich, Cheshire, 8a: 320. 1901 British Census, Kingston Upon Hull, Yorkshire, RG13, piece 4485, 91: 10.

40   Meredith Starr's 1910 contributions to the *Occult Review* include "Transformation," 11 (May): 241; "*The New Creation* by Mary Higgs" [review], 11 (Jun): 346; "*Maurice Maeterlink* by Gérard Harry" [review], 12 (Jul): 57; "*The Lost Valley and Other Stories* by Algernon Blackwood" [review], 12 (Aug): 121; "Reflections on Reincarnation," 12 (Sep): 158–162. "Maeterlinck's Symbolism; The Blue Bird; & Other Essays by Henry Rose" [review], 12 (Dec): 399. A complete list numbers over one hundred reviews and contributions, and is beyond the scope of this book.

41 In a marginal note to the Abbey of Thelema library's copy of *Diary of a Drug Fiend,* Crowley wrote, "*Anhalonium lewinii*...I made many experiments on people with this drug in 1910, and subsequent years" (p. 39, paragraph 3).

42 From notes written on the sheets of *The Equinox* 1910, 1(4). HRHRC.

43 Comment on Close's oath, Mortlake Collection. See also AC to Henri Birven, 13 Dec 1929, New 24, Yorke Collection.

44 *What's On,* 15 Oct 1910. Quoted in Keith Richmond, "Introduction," in Aleister Crowley, *The Rites of Eleusis,* ed. Anthony N. Naylor (Thame, Oxon: Mandrake Press Ltd., 1990).

45 "Sydney College of Music: Annual Examinations," *Sydney Mail,* 10 Dec 1898, 8.

46 H. J. Gibbney and Ann G. Smith, *A Biographical Register, 1788–1839: Notes from the Name Index of the Australian Dictionary of Biography.* (Canberra: Australian National University, 1987), vol. 2, 321. Debby Cramer, Archivist, Presbyterian Ladies' College, private communication, 28 Oct 2009. Margaret Gillezeau, Archivist, Ascham School, private communication, 9 Nov 2009.

47 "Bain's Gaiety Entertainers," *The Mercury* (Hobart, Tasmania), 18 Jan 1904, 5.

48 Quotes are from the concert's review, "Concert at Masonic Hall," *The Mercury* (Hobart, Tasmania), 22 Jan 1904, 3. Advertisements for the concerts appeared in *The Mercury* for 11 Jan 1904, 5; 18 Jan 1904, 5; 19 Jan 1904, 5; 20 Jan 1904, 5; 21 Jan 1904, 5. I have been unable to identify Bohm's "Papillons," although it is not likely to be a misprint as Crowley also lists Waddell playing this piece in *The Rites of Eleusis,* see *The Equinox* I(6): supp. 60. Around the time of this concert, the 1904 Sydney directory (p. 1166) lists a "Miss L. Waddell" living at 166 King Street.

49 *Sydney Mail,* 16 Aug 1905, 443. Given the information presented previously, this was not Waddell's debut, as is sometimes claimed.

50 *What's On, op. cit.*

51 *Evening Post* (New Zealand), 29 Dec 1906 72(154): 6. *Evening Post* (New Zealand), 5 Jan 1907. 73(4): 6. *The Colonist* 7 Mar 1908, 50(12185): 2. *Nelson Evening Mail* 7 Mar 1908, 42: 2.

52 For Waddell's studies under Sauret and Auer, see "Our Contributors," *Shadowland,* Oct 1923, 9(2): 69; [Leila Waddell], "Music," *The International,* Apr 1918, 12(4): 128; Leila Bathurst, "An Interview with Leopole Auer," *The International,* May 1918, 12(5): 156–7.
   French violinist-composer Émile Sauret was a child prodigy who began performing in Vienna before age eight. His *Gradus ad Parnassum du violiniste* (Leipzig, 1896) reports that he studied with Vieuxtemps and Wieniawski and played on several occasions to the court of Napoleon III. Although he toured the world, there is no record of him residing or teaching in Sydney; however, from 1908 he settled in London and taught at Trinity College of Music. See Roger J. V. Cotte, "Sauret, Emile," Grove Music Online, www.oxfordmusiconline.com (accessed Oct 23 2009).
   Hungarian violinist-teacher Leopold Auer studied at the Budapest and Vienna Conservatories from age eight, and went on to a successful career as a performer and orchestra leader. On Anton Rubinstein's recommendation, he succeeded Wieniawski in 1868 as violin teacher at the St. Petersburgh Conservatory, where he remained until 1917. As one of the most sought-after violin teachers in the world, he taught in London during the summers of 1906–1911, and in February 1918 sailed for New York, where he continued to teach and perform. One of his students, Clara Rockmore, famously went on to become the world's foremost theremin player. Leila Waddell had opportunity to study with Auer during his summers teaching in London, or possibly after he moved to New York. See Boris Schwarz, "Auer, Leopold," Grove Music Online, www.oxfordmusiconline.com (accessed Oct 23 2009).

53 "Music," *Sydney Times,* 23 Jun 1909, 47.

54 "Daly's Theatre: 'A Waltz Dream,'" *Times* (London), 9 Jan 1911, 39477: 10. *The Play Pictorial* 1910, 17(103): 74–96.

55   "Theatres, &c.," *Times* (London), 27 Apr 1911, 39570: 8.

56   Aleister Crowley, "The Temple of Solomon the King," *The Equinox* 1913, 1(10): 95.

57   Postcard from AC to Sybil Meugens, no date, HRHRC. [Her name is spelled "Meagens" in Crowley's notes to *The Equinox* 1910, I(4).]

58   Louis Marlow [Louis Wilkinson], *Seven Friends* (London: Richards Press, 1953), 60.

59   AC to Henri Birven, Oct 1929, New 24, Yorke Collection.

60   Aleister Crowley, "The Tent," *Occult Review*, Mar 1910, 11: 160.

61   AC to John Quinn, 1 Sep 1913, New 12, Yorke Collection.

62   A. G. Stephens, "The Bookfellow," *Evening Post*, 17 Dec 1910, 80(146): 17.

63   Stephensen, *Legend of Aleister Crowley*, 74.

64   Jacob Tonson, "Books and Persons," *New Age*, 13 Apr 1911, 8(24): 566.

65   D. H. Lawrence to Grace Crawford, 9 Jul 1910, in James T. Boulton, *The Letters of D. H. Lawrence, Volume 1: September 1901–May 1913* (Cambridge: Cambridge Univ. Press, 1979), 169. See also the letter dated July 24, 1910, where Lawrence simply remarks, "I return Crowley: didn't like it."

66   In addition to works previously identified as reprinted in *The Winged Beetle*, the volume also reproduced from *Vanity Fair* several poems—including "The Muse," "The Child," and "The Jew of Fez"—and poetic translations—including "Le Vin Des Amants," "Le Balcon," "L'amour et le Crane," "Woman," "Le Vampire," "Le Revenant," "Tout Entière," "En Sourdine."

67   Stephensen, *Legend of Aleister Crowley*, 74.

Chapter Ten • Aleister Through the Looking Glass

1   Born in Leamington, Warwickshire, in 1858, Reginald St. John Parry was the third son of Rev. Edward St. John Parry, headmaster of the famous private school at Stoke Popes. Parry attended Charterhouse, where he was a prize scholar, Talbot scholar, and medalist. Matriculating to Trinity College in 1876, Parry received his BA in 1880, MA in 1883, deacon ordination (Ely) in 1884, priest ordination in 1885, BD in 1903, and DD in 1913. Over the years, he filled various roles at Trinity: He was elected a fellow of Trinity in 1881, was a junior proctor from 1890–1891, a tutor from 1894–1908, and, when Professor Henry Jackson died, Parry succeeded him as vice master in 1919, a post which he held until his death in 1935, His published works include *A Discussion of the General Epistle of St. James* (London: C. J. Clay, 1903), *The Epistle of Paul the Apostle to the Romans* (Cambridge: Univ. Press, 1912; rev. ed. 1916),*Cambridge Essays on Adult Education* (London: Cambridge Univ. Press, 1920),*The Universities and Adult Education: Extramural Work* (London, n.p., 1920),*The Pastoral Epistles* (Cambridge: Univ. Press, 1920), *The Epistle of Paul the Apostle to the Romans* (Cambridge: Univ. Press, 1921), and *Henry Jackson, O.M., Vice-Master of Trinity College & Regius Professor of Greek in the University of Cambridge* (Cambridge: Univ. Press, 1926). See "Obituary," *Times* (London), 23 Feb 1935, 46996: 14. *Alumni Cantabrigienses*. "Ordinations," *Times* (London), 22 Sep 1885, 31558: 7. Sir Thomas Gery Cullum, *Register* (Cambridge: Univ. Press, 1898), 816.

2   John Symonds *The Great Beast: The Life of Aleister Crowley* (London: Rider & Co, 1952), 217.

3   See Aleister Crowley, "Reviews," *The Equinox* 1910, I(4): 239–40. In his personal notes to this issue, he identifies the Parry-lytic Liar as "Rev. R. St. J. Parry."

4   Symonds, *Great Beasti,* 217–8.

5   "Obituary," 23 Feb 1935, 14.

6   Norman Mudd to C. S. Jones, 15 Jan 1923, Yorke Collection.

7   Aleister Crowley, "Pan to Artemis," *The Equinox* 1910, 1(4): 197–8.

8   Jean Overton Fuller, *The Magical Dilemma of Victor Neuburg* (London: W. H. Allen, 1965), 163.

9   See, for instance: Algernon Charles Swinburne. 808. Chorus from "Atalanta," in Arthur Quiller-Couch (ed.), *The Oxford Book of English Verse: 1250–1900,* 1919.

10 Raymond Radclyffe, "Aleister Crowley's 'Rite of Artemis,'" *The Sketch,* 24 Aug 1910.

11 William Allison, *"My Kingdom for a Horse!": Yorkshire, Rugby, Balliol, the Bar, Bloodstock and Journalistic Recollections* (London: G. Richards, 1919), 319. "Mr. William Allison," *Times* (London), 16 Jul 1925, 44015: 20. Ada Elizabeth Jones Chesterton, *The Chestertons* (London: Chapman & Hall, 1941), 32.

12 "Reg. v. Allison and Others," *Law Times,* 23 Feb 1889, 59: 933–6. R. Cunningham Glen, *Reports of Cases in Criminal Law, Arbued and Determined in All the Courts in England and Ireland* (London: Horace Cox, 1890), 559–66.

13 "In Re Radcliffe," *Times* (London), 16 Jan 1892, 33536: 11.

14 Raymond Radclyffe, *Wealth and Wild Cats: Travels and Researches in the Gold-Fields of Western Australia and New Zealand* (London: Downey & Co, 1898).

15 Martha S. Vogeler, *Austin Harrison and the English Review* (Columbia: Univ. of Missouri Press, 2008), 210–1. Raymond Radclyffe, *The War and Finance: How to Save the Situation* (London: W. Dawson and Sons, 1914).

16 Chesterton, *The Chestertons,* 85.

17 *Confessions,* 639.

18 Crowley's inscription to a copy of his collected *Works,* originally belonging to Radclyffe but, after the journalist's death, was later signed over to Collin Brooks (from a catalog listing by Harrington Books, U.K.).

19 http://archive.rarebookreview.com/detail/437/149.0 (accessed Oct 24 2009).

20 Birth record, GRO, Q4 1885, Cuckfield, Sussex, 2b: 176. 1881 British Census, Whitbourne, Herefordshire, RG11, piece 2603, 100: 5. 1891 British Census, Oxford, Oxfordshire, RG12, piece 1164, 123: 8.

21 Ethel Archer, *The Book of Plain Cooking,* practical housewife series v. 2 (London: A. Treherne, 1904).

22 Record of marriage, GRO, Q4 1908, Strannd, London, 1b: 1028. British Commonwealth War Graves Registers, 1914–1918.

23 Elizabeth Robbins Pennell, "Les Amoureux," *Century Illustrated Monthly Magazine,* Jun 1911, 82(2): 217–23.

24 Wieland & Co. published issues 6–10 of *The Equinox* (1911–1913), and the following titles: *Book IV* parts I and II (1912–1913), *The Book of Lies* (1912), *Hail Mary* (1912), *The High History of Sir Palamedes* (1912), *Mortadello* (1912), and *The Tango Song* (1913). Given Wieland's impecuniousness, Clive Harper (personal communication, 2010) suggests that AC set up Wieland & Co. for strategic business reasons. Indeed, the company shared the address of *The Equinox* offices, and the only books it published were Crowley's.

25 Eugene's letters from the front to Ethel are collected in Elizabeth Robins Pennell, *The Lovers* (London: W. Heinemann, 1917).

26 Archer's work after parting with Crowley consists of: "An Idyll of Dawn," *English Review,* Apr 1914, 8–9; "Silence," *English Review,* Jul 1919, 7; "A Song," *English Review,* Jul 1919, 7; "A Ballad of Bedlam," *English Review,* Nov 1919, 392–3 (rept. from *The Equinox*); "Song," *English Review,* Jul 1921, 8; "Phantasy," *English Review,* Mar 1922, 204–6; "Vision," *English Review,* Sep 1924, 401; *Phantasy, and Other Poems* (Steyning: The Vine press, 1930); "The Golden Thread of Truth," *Occult Review,* Jan 1932, 47–9; *The Hieroglyph* (London: D. Archer, 1932).

27 Birth record, Q3 1876, GRO, Ecclesall Bierlow, Derbyshire, 9c: 398. Herbert van Thal, "Miss Gwendolen Otter," *Times* (London), 11 Jul 11958, 54200: 10.

28 Under her initials E. G. O., Otter reviewed Helen George's *The Clay's Revenge* and Sidney Place's *Les frequentations de Maurice* in the spring, 1913, issue I(9).

29 *The Equinox* 1912, 1(7): 159–78.

30   "A Fresh Young Russian: He Falls Victim to a Siren's Wiles: A Romantic Story—He Sues for Damages for Libel—A Shoemaker and His Daughter the Cause," *Dallas Morning News,* 20 Feb 1888, 6. "A Baron's Suit," *Wisconsin State Journal* 3 Feb 1888.

31   *Confessions,* 691.

32   Aleister Crowley, "Jack the Ripper." *Sothis* 1974, 1(4): 62.

33   Sylvia Cranston, *HPB: The Extraordinary Life and Influence of Helena Blavatsky, Founder of the Modern Theosophical Movement* (New York: Jeremy P. Tarcher, 1993), 371.

34   Available in various editions as pamphlets and chapbooks, and in *Sothis, op. cit.*

35   James Laver, "Some Impressions of Aleister Crowley," New 18, Yorke Collection.

36   Fuller, *Magical Dilemma,* 183.

37   Birth record, Q3 1890, GRO, Edmonton, Middlesex, 3a: 270. Death record, Q3 1912, GRO, Chelsea, London, 1a: 391. 1901 UK census, Walthamstow, Essex, RG13, piece 1630, 35: 3). Jeanne's two younger sisters were Eileen (b. 1892, according to the 1911 census) and Blanche Mildred (b. 1897). 1911 UK census. Birth record, Q3 1897, GRO, West Ham, Essex, 4a: 75.

38   Wilfred Merton, quoted in "Art Student's Suicide: 'Unfortunate Marriage,'" *Times* (London), 5 Aug 1912, 39969: 2.

39   Ezra Pound, "Dance Figure," *Poetry,* Apr 1913, 2(1): 1–12; also published in *New Freewoman,* 15 Aug 1913, 1(5): 87–8. Heyse was but one of Pound's retinue of lovers in 1910; see Maria Luisa Ardizzone, *Guido Cavalcanti tra i suoi lettori* (Fiesole, Firenze: Cadmo, 2003), 274. Although unnamed in the poem, Terrell identifies Heyse as the subject, named in an earlier draft. See Carroll F. Terrell, *A Companion to the Cantos of Ezra Pound* (Berkeley: University of California Press, 1980), 31–2. Felicia M. McCarren, *Dancing Machines: Choreographies of the Age of Mechanical Reproduction* (Stanford: Stanford Univ. Press, 2003), 79.

40   James Laver, *Museum Piece: or the Education of an Iconographer* (Cambridge: Riverside Press, 1964), 117.

41   "Editorial," *The Equinox* 1910, 1(4): 3–4.

42   Fuller, *Bibliotheca Crowleyana,* 6.

43   "To-night's gossip," *Evening News,* 28 Sep 1910.

44   Wilson, *Arnold Bennett and H. G. Wells,* 108 fn.

45   "'Teaching' Titled Beauties to Raise 'Evil Spirits': Diversion of English Society which is Conjuring 'Demons' and Practicing the 'Black Art': But Seems to Need a Lot More Practice," *Washington Post,* 27 Nov 1910, MT4.

46   "New 'Religion': Strange Rites Performed in Semi-Darkness," *Hawera & Normanby Star,* 15 Dec 1910, 60: 2.

47   "'Rites of Eleusis' in London," *New York Times,* 13 Nov 1910, C2.

48   "The Black Mass Idea: Mystic (?) Rites at a Guinea a Rite," *Penny Illustrated Paper,* 5 Oct 1910, 2580: 596.

49   Crowley was never an art student. He set up mirrors in one of his rooms in Chancery Lane. And Skerrett was one of Rose's married names, never used by Crowley … although he did reside at Chancery Lane under the name Count Svareff.

50   "The Amazing Sect Again—Crowley on His Defence," *John Bull,* 19 Nov 1910.

51   "An Amazing Sect—No. 3: Further Details of Mr. Aleister Crowley," *John Bull,* 26 Nov 1910, 268.

52   Richmond, "Introduction" to *Rites of Eleusis.*

53   J. F. Brown, "Aleister Crowley's Rites of Eleusis," *Drama Review,* Jun 1978, 22(2): 3–26.

54   Tracy W. Tupman, *Theatre Magick: Aleister Crowley and the Rites Eleusis,* doctoral dissertation, Ohio State University, 2003, 269, 269 and ii–iii, respectively.

55   Edmund B. Lingan, *The Theatre of the New Religious Movements of Europe and America from the Nineteenth Century to the Present,* doctoral dissertation, City Univ. of New

York, 2006.

56 *Confessions,* 636.

57 "Amazing Exposures of Moseley's Lieutenent: General Fuller Initiated into Aleister Crowley's (Beast 666) Occult Group: Control of Kosher Fascists," *The Fascist,* May 1935, 72: 1.

58 Arnold Spencer Leese, *Out of Step: Events in the Two Lives of an Anti-Jewish Camel Doctor* (Guildford: n.p., 1951).

59 Stanley Passmore to Sir Oswald Mosley, 27 May 1935, Oswald Mosley Papers, XOMN/B/7/4, Special Collections Department, Birmingham University.

60 *The Looking Glass* 17 Dec 1910.

61 From AC's desert notebook, auctioned by Sotheby's. "On the Edge of the Desert" appeared in the *English Review,* Jun 1911, 362–363. "Return" and "Prayer at Sunset" were slated for the ill-fated *The Giant's Thumb* (1915); although page proofs survived a fire at the printers, the book never appeared. "Prayer at Sunset" ultimately turned up in Crowley's last book, the poetry anthology *Olla* (1946), 30.

62 *The Equinox* 1911, 1(6): 67–107.

63 *The Equinox* 1911, 1(5): 130–2.

64 *The Equinox* 1911, 1(6): 113–48.

65 Crowley, *Diary of a Drug Fiend,* 65.

66 *The Equinox* 1911, 1(6): 53–65.

67 *The Equinox* 1911, 1(6): 108–11.

68 George Raffalovich, U. S. Passport Application, 24 Mar 1921, National Archives, College Park, MD. "Duce Biographer to Speak Monday on Emory Campus," *Atlanta Constitution,* 3 Nov 1929, 4.

69 George Raffalovich, *Benito Mussolini: A Preliminary Sketch* (Firenze: The Owl, 1923).

70 "Dr. Raffalovich Gives Lecture to Atlanta University Women," *Atlanta Constitution,* 24 Jan 1932, 6M. "Lecture Tomorrow by Dr. Raffalovich," *Atlanta Constitution,* 3 Mar 1932, 14. "Dr. Raffalovich Dead: Writer and Teacher of Slavic and French History, 77," *New York Times,* 22 May 1958, 29. His wife, Dorothy Dawson, would predecease him by eighteen years in 1940; see "Obituary," *Atlanta Constitution,* 3 Apr 1940, 12.

71 After his ordination, Bennett, now Ananda Metteya, established the International Buddhist Society in Rangoon. He also published its journal, *Buddhism: An Illustrated Quarterly Review* from 1903 to 1908 when he returned to London as its first Buddhist missionary. His visit generated worldwide press coverage; alas, this also included "exposures" in the magazine *Truth,* which would later be used against Crowley by *The Looking Glass.* By this point the spiritual paths of Crowley and Metteya had diverged and they continued to drift apart. In London Metteya announced plans to continue his mission in America, but ill health prevented him. For press examples, see: "Unusual Appearance in London of Buddhist," *Montgomery Advertiser,* 10 May 1908; "Priest Who Shuns the Women Coming to Convert America," *Atlanta Constitution,* 7 Jun 1908; "Will Teach Buddhism in the United States," *Baltimore American,* 7 Jun 1908; "New Buddhist in England: Cockney by Birth, Hopes to Convert His Countrymen," *The Sun* (New York), 16 Aug 1908, 6; "Has a New Religion: Englishman Picks up Buddhist Doctrine in India: Born of Scottish Parents," *Washington Herald,* 23 Aug 1908, 5.

72 AC to John Quinn, 1 Sep 1913, New 12, Yorke Collection.

73 Aleister Crowley, "The Camel: A Discussion of the Value of 'Interior Certainty,'" *Occult Review,* Apr 1911, 13: 208–13.

74 Accounts of this trial are based on copious newspaper coverage, including the official transcript printed in *The Looking Glass.* I am faithful to the reports, but delete or paraphrase sections which are too long, impertinent, or undocumented. Crowley's unspoken reactions are drawn from *The Rosicrucian Scandal.*

75   Fuller, *Bibliotheca Crowleyana*, 7.

76   This transcript was the basis of an unused chapter in *Perdurabo* (2002), which has since been printed separately with extensive documentary material from the press in Richard Kaczynski, *Perdurabo Outtakes* (Royal Oak, MI: Bue Equinox Oasis, 2005).

77   B. L. Reid, *The Man from New York: John Quinn and His Friends* (New York: Oxford Univ. Press, 1968), 101.

78   Fuller's subsequent occult-themed writings include "The Black Arts," *Form*, Nov/Dec 1921, 2(1): 57–62; *Yoga: A Study of the Mystical Philosophy of the Brahmins and Buddhists* (London: William Rider & Son, 1925); "A Study of Mystical Relativivy," *Occult Review* 1933, 57(5): 306–12, 57(6): 370–7, and 58(1): 14–20; *The Secret Wisdom of the Qabalah; A Study in Jewish Mystical Thought* (London: Rider & Co, 1937); "Magic and War," *Occult Review* 1942, 69(2): 53–4 "The Attack by Magic," *Occult Review* 1942, 69(4): 125–6; and "The City and the Bomb," *Occult Review* 1944, 71(1): 10–2; Two unpublished works also survive in his papers at King's College: *The Hidden Wisdom of the Illuminati* (1926, IV/14) and *Four Dimensional Man* (1930, IV/16).
      Interestingly, Gerald Gardner's occult novel *High Magic's Aid* (1954) apparently draws the chant "Eko! Eko! Azarak! Eko! Eko! Zomelak!" from Fuller's "Black Arts." See James W. Baker, "White Witches: Historic Fact and Romantic Fantasy," in James R. Lewis (ed.), *Magical Religion and Modern Witchcraft* (Albany: State Univ. of New York Press, 1996), 174–5.

79   John Frederick Charles Fuller, "Aleister Crowley 1898–1911: An Introductory Essay," in *Bibliotheca Crowleyana*, 8.

80   First published in the *English Review*, Nov 1911, and later in *The Equinox* 1919, 3(1): 187–94.

81   Aleister Crowley, *Mortadello, or the Angel of Venice: A Comedy* (London: Wieland & Co., 1912).

82   W. W. G. "Mortadello, or the Angel of Venice: A Comedy" [Review], *Rhythm*, Oct 1912, 9: 234.

83   Although born in England, Hener Skene self-identified as Scottish; c.f. the passenger list for the *La Provence*, which arrived in New York on February 11, 1911 (Passenger Lists of Vessels Arriving at New York, NY, National Archives, Washington, D.C.).

84   *Journal of the Gypsy Lore Society*, 1907, v. 1; 1908, v. 2, and the *Referee*, 12 May 1907. In the society's 1911 member list, she was member no. 130 out of over three hundred.

85   Roger Lhombreaud, *Arthur Symons, A Critical Biography* (Philadelphia: Dufour Editions, 1964), 17, 277.

86   Quoted in Simon Wilson, *Tate Gallery: An Illustrated Companion*, rev. ed. (Tate Gallery: London, 1991), 101. See also Emmanuel Cooper, *The Sexual Perspective: Homosexuality and Art in the Last 100 Years in the West* (London: Routledge, 1994), 104.

87   Aleister Crowley, "The Ghouls," *The Equinox* 1912, 1(7): 161.

88   *The Equinox* 1911, 1(7), included "Adonis" (117–57), "The Ghouls" (159–78) and "A Birthday" (419–24). *The Equinox* 1912, 1(8), ran "His Secret Sin" (49–60) and "The Woodcutter" (79–88).

89   As with all of the A∴A∴ documents, the names of the instructions are laced with symbolism. "The Book of the Magus" is titled "B vel Magi" because the Hebrew *B, Beth,* is attributed to the Magus or Magician in the tarot. Because *Beth* is the second letter, it also has associations with the grade of Magus in the A∴A∴, which is the second highest grade in the system. "Tzaddi vel Hamus Hermiticus" is the "Hermetic Fish-Hook" because the Hebrew letter *Tzaddi* literally means "fish hook." "A'ash vel Capricorni Pneumatici" is the "Goat of the Spirit" because the book's number, seventy, is that of the Hebrew letter *Ayin,* which, in turn, is attributed to the astrological sign of Capricorn the goat.

90   Unpublished (and probably unfinished) in his lifetime, two modern reconstructions of *The Greek Qabalah* have appeared: One as an article in *OTO Newsletter* 1979, 2(7–8): 9–44, and one as a booklet (Auckland, NZ: Kantharos Oasis OTO, 1984).

91   The *libri* appeared in the following *Equinox*es. In 1(6): "Turris" (8–15); "Tzaddi" (17–22); "Cheth" (23–7); "Resh" (29–32); and "A'ash" (33–9). In 1(7): "B" (5–9); "NV" (11–20); "Israfel" (21–7); "Astarte" (37–58); "RV" (59–67); "Os Abysmi" (77–81); "HAD" (83–91); "IOD," inaccurately called TAV (93–100); "Viarum Viae" (101–3); and "Across the Gulf" (239–54).

92   Aleister Crowley's review of *The Arcane Schools* appears in *The Equinox* 1910, 1(4): 240. Yarker's thanks comes from John Yarker to AC, 4 Nov 1910, OTO Archives.

93   Aleister Crowley, *The Star and the Garter* (London: Watts & Co., 1903).

94   *op. cit.*

95   Crowley, *Moonchild,* 13. For other impressions of Skene, see *Confessions* 356, 669, 676. Carl Van Vechten, *Sacred and Profane Memories* (London: Cassell, 1932), 110–2.

96   Crowley, *Moonchild,* 12.

97   "Hail! Spring She is Due in Newark Tonight," *Newark Daily Advocate,* 20 Mar 1912, 7.

98   *Confessions,* 676. Here, Crowley says he sat cross-legged like a Chinese god. Hence the fictionalized account of this party in *Moonchild* is titled "A Chinese God."

99   Her parents' names are curiously listed as Dominick d'Este and Catherine Campbell Dempsey (née Smyth) in Ebenezer Buckingham, *Solomon Sturges and His Descendants: A Memoir and a Genealogy* (New York: Grafton Press, 1907), 73.

100 "Met Here; Wed in London: Former Mrs. Sturges' Turkish Spouse Once Chicago Man: Cigaret Company failure: Pretty Divorcee and 'Soul Dancer' Renwed Acquaintance Abroad," *Chicago Daily Tribune,* 15 Mar 1912, 3.

101 Crowley reports that Mary Desti married Vely Bey *after* he met her, and the 15 Mar 1912 *Chicago Tribune* article on her wedding (ibid.) supports this. However, other sources give the date of her wedding and business as 1911 [c.f. James Curtis, *Between Flops: A Biography of Preston Sturges* (New York: Harcourt Brace Jovanovich, 1984), 9; Ray Cywinski, *Preston Sturges: A Guide to References and Resources* (Boston: G. K. Hall & Co., 1984), 3; Andrew Dickos, *Intrepid Laughter: Preston Sturges and the Movies* (Metuchen, NJ: Scarecrow Press, 1985), xi]. Most accounts give this husband's name as Vely Bey, although Dickos gives it as Vely Bey Denizli.

102 "Met Here; Wed in London," *Chicago Daily Tribune.* Noel F. Busch, "Preston Sturges: Brilliant Producer of Eccentric Movie Comedies Has Led an Eccentric, Implausible Life," *Life,* 7 Jan 1946, 89. Ean Wood, *Headlong through Life: The Story of Isadora Duncan* (Lewes: Book Guild, 2006), 236. Rob White and Edward Buscombe. *British Film Institute Film Classics* (London: Fitzroy Dearborn, 2003), 507.

103 "George McNie Cowie, a.k.a. George MacNie Cowie, Sir George McNie Cowie," http://www.nethop.net/~sandness/COWIE_Geo_M.htm (accessed Mar 3 2009).

104 1891 Scottish Census, GRO, Edinburgh St. Cuthberts, 102: 10.

105 1901 Scottish Census, GRO, Edinburgh Morningside, 113: 6.

106 *Confessions,* 856.

107 Abuldiz Working, OTO Archives.

108 *Confessions,* 676.

109 Curtis, *Between Flops,* 9.

110 *AL* i.61.

111 "Liber LX: The Abuldiz Working" appears in Crowley et al., *Vision and the Voice with Commentary.*

112 Dickos, *Intrepid Laughter,* 10–1.

113 Crowley, *Magical Record of the Beast 666,* 145.

114 *The Equinox* 1912, 1(8): 63–77.

115 *The Equinox* 1912, 1(8): 211–4.

116 *The Equinox* 1913, 1(9): 295–305.

117 Dickos, *Intrepid Laughter,* 11.

Chapter Eleven • Ordo Templi Orientis

1   Augustus John to AC, 9 May 1912, Augustus Edwin John Vertical File Manuscript 388, Morris Library Special Collections, Southern Illinois University at Carbondale.

2   AC to Augustus John, n.d., New 12, Yorke Collection.

3   *English Review,* Aug 1912, 163.

4   Aleister Crowley, "Titanic Disaster," *New York Times,* 26 May, 1912, SM4; reprinted as Aleister Crowley, "The 'Titanic,'" *The Equinox* 1913, I(9): 47–8. The first line of the last verse was changed from "No norm of nature shall withstand" to "No power of nature shall withstand."

5   Stephensen, *Legend of Aleister Crowley,* 99.

6   AC's opening comment to *The Book of Lies,* published in newer editions of the book.

7   AC to Henri Birven, Oct 1929, New 24, Yorke Collection.

8   Theodor Reuss's books include: Br. Pregrinus, *Wass muss mann von der Freimaurerei wissen? eine allgemeinverständliche Darstellung des Ordens der Freimaurer, der Illuminaten und Rosenkreuzer* (Berlin: H. Steinitz, 1901). Hans Merlin, *Das grosse Buch der Wahr-sage-Kunst: Eine kurze, allgemeinverständl. Darstellung d. Kleromantie, Chiromantie, Kar-tomantie, Onomantie, Kephalomantie nebst e. Anh. über d. kabbalistisch-math. Glücksrad* (Berlin: H. Steinitz, 1901). Hans Merlin, *Was ist Okkultismus und wie erlangt man okkulte Kräfte?: Einführung in den modernen Okkultismus und die Geheimwissenschaften der alten Kulturvölker* (Berlin: H. Steinitz, 1903). Hans Merlin, *Das große Buch der Träume und ihrer Deutung: Nach d. Aufzeichn. d. Artemidoros* (Berlin: H. Steinitz, 1904). Pendragon, *Lingam-Yoni* (Berlin, Verlag Willsson, 1906), actually a German translation of Hargrave Jennings, *Phallism: A Description of the Worship of Lingam-Yoni in Various Parts of the World, and in Different Ages, with an Account of Ancient & Modern Crosses, Particularly of the Crux Ansata (or Handled Cross) and Other Symbols Connected with the Mysteries of Sex Worship* (London: Privately printed, 1889).

9   Ellic Howe, "Theodor Reuss and the Theosophical Society," *Theosophical History* 1990, 3: 17–8.

10 László Krecsák and Daniel Bohle, "The Eccentric Adder Man: A Note on the Life and Works of Albert Franz Theodor Reuss (1879–1958)," *Herpetological Bulletin* 2008, 103: 1–10.

11 Bernd-Ulrich Hergemöller, *Mann für Mann: biographisches Lexikon zur Geschichte von Freundesliebe und mannmännlicher Sexualität im deutschen Sprachraum* (Hamburg: Män-nerschwarmSkript, 1998), 581–3.

12 "Concerts," *Orchestra Musical Review,* 13 Jun 1885, 159: 125.

13 At the Wagner Concerts Society, Reuss sang the aria "Schusterlied (Jerum! Jerum! Hallahallohe!)" from *Die Meistersinger von Nürnberg.* See "Musical Jottings," *Orchestra Musical Review,* 30 Jan 1886, 182: 521. By 1888, he was producing "A new and sen-sational operatic sketch, titled *Zanniel the Midnight Hunter,* founded on *Der Freischutz,* and in 1892 Reuss had sold to Sir Augustus Harris the exclusive English rights to Richard Wagner's *Die Feen* (The Fairies). See "Facts and Comments," *Musical World,* 11 Aug 1888, 67(32): 624. "By the Wayside," *Musical Opinion and Music Trade Review,* 1 Sep 1888, 132: 539. "Detached Notes," *Musical Standard,* 1 Sep 1888, 35(1257): 142. "Crochets," *Musical Standard,* 22 Oct 1892, 43(1473): 319. Wilhelm Richard Wagner, *The Fairies: Die Feen, A Romantic Opera in Three Acts, Translated from the German and Arranged for the English Stage by Theodor Reuss* (London, n.p., 1906). Theodore Reuss Papers, 1885–1907, #1979-0047R/A-S, Rare Books and Manu-scripts, University Libraries, Pennsylvania State University, University Park, PA.

14 "A Row Among the Anarchists: Theodore Reuss and Victor Daye Likely to be Expelled," *Boston Daily Globe,* 14 Oct 1886, 2.

15 Howe, "Theodor Reuss and the Theosophical Society."

16 Theodor Regens, "Pranatherapie," *Sphinx,* Jul 1894, 19(101): 14–6.

17 Leopold Engel, *Geschichte des Illuminaten-Ordens: Ein Beitrag zur Geschichte Bayerns.*

Vorgeschichte, Gründung (1776), Beziehung zur Freimaurerei, Verfolgung durch die Jesuiten, Fortentwicklung bis zur Jetztzeit, nach authentischen Dokumenten in den Geheimen Staats-Archiven zu München, Berlin, Dresden, Gotha, Paris, Wien, dem Geheimarchiv des Illuminaten-Ordens und verschiedenen Privat-Archiven (Berlin: Bergmühler, 1906).

18   AC to Henri Birven, 13 Dec 1929, New 24, Yorke Collection.

19   Franz Hartmann, *Magic, White and Black, or, The Science of Finite and Infinite Life: Containing Practical Hints for Students of Occultism* (London: George Redway, 1886). Franz Hartmann, Adrian von Mynsicht, Theophilus Neander, and Walter Arensberg, *Cosmology, or, Universal Science, Cabala, Alchemy: Containing the Mysteries of the Universe Regarding God, Nature, Man, the Macrocosm and Microcosm, Eternity and Time; Explained According to the Religion of Christ, by Means of the Secret Symbols of Rosicrucians of the Sixteenth and Seventeenth Centuries* (Boston: Occult Pub. Co, 1888).

20   Kaczynski, "Carl Kellner's Esoteric Roots."

21   1901 UK Census, Walton on Thames, Surrey, GRO, RG13, piece 587, 21: 33. Death record, Q2, 1913, Chertsey, Surey, GRO, 2a: 91.

22   Ellic Howe and Helmut Möller, "Theodor Reuss: Irregular Freemasonry in Germany, 1900–23," *Ars Quatuor Coronatorum* 1978, 91: 28–46. According to Robert Gold (quoted in the article), Klein joined in 1872 and resigned on 14 Oct 1874. Reuss was initiated in Nov 1876.

23   "Waifs," *Musical World*, 28 Feb 1874, 52(9): 134. *Musical Opinion and Music Trade Review*, 1 Feb 1886, 9(101): 230.

24   Around September, 1885, Klein signed young violinist Teresina Tua to an American concert tour, for which she was to be paid £10,000. In April and May of 1886 he turned up as an impresario in Berlin. "Waifs," *Musical World*, 26 Sep 1885, 63(39): 614. "Musical Gossip," *Athenaeum*, 31 Oct 1885, 3027: 579. "Foreign Musical Intelligence," *Musical Standard*, 14 Nov 1885, 29(1111): 306. *Lute*, Dec 1885, 3(12): 288. *Musikalisches Wochenblatt*, 22 Apr 1886, 17: 222–3. *Musikalisches Wochenblatt*, 27 May 1886, 17: 278.

25   "Trade Jottings," *Musical Opinion and Music Trade Review*, 1 May 1906, 29(344): 622. *London Telephone Directory*, years 1900–1909. The author is preparing a study of Klein, whose role in the formation of OTO has not been previously explored.

26   Docteur Gérard Encausse (1865-1916) was a French physician best known in western esotericism for the book he wrote under his magical name of Papus, *Le Tarot des Bohémiens* (1889), or *The Tarot of the Bohemians*. He was also involved in several important French secret societies: He was a cofounder of *l'Ordre Kabbalistique de la Rose+Croix* in 1888; founder in 1891 of *l'Ordre des Supérieurs Inconnus* (the Martinist Order); consecrated a bishop of *l'Église Gnostique de France* by Jules Doinel in 1893. He was also a member of the TS, GD, and HBL. He was also behind the occult magazine *l'Initiation* which ran from 1888 until 1914. He served in the French army medical corps during World War I, dying of tuberculosis in 1916. For more on Encausse, see http://www.hermetic.com/sabazius/papus.htm and Philippe Encausse, *Papus (Dr Gérard Encausse): sa vie. Son oeuvre. Documents inédits sur Philippe de Lyon, maître spirituel de Papus. Opinions et jugements. Portraits et illustrations* (Paris: Ed. Pythagore, 1932).

27   Issue "0" of *Oriflamme* appeared as four pages within the January 1902 issue of *Übersinnliche Welt;* the same month, *Oriflamme* appeared as a separate monthly journal.

28   For more on Reuss, see Ellic Howe and Helmut Möller, "Theodor Reuss: Irregular Freemasonry." Ellic Howe and Helmut Möller, *Merlin Peregrinus: vom Untergrund des Abendlandes* (Würzburg: Königshausen und Neumann, 1986).

29   The number of degrees varied somewhat, especially under Crowley; however, the main system consists of the degrees 0 through IX.

30   Kaczynski, "Carl Kellner's Esoteric Roots."

31   Paschal Beverly Randolph, *The Grand Secret; or, Physical Love in Health and Disease* (San Francisco: Pilkington & Randolph, 1861). Paschal Beverly Randolph, *Eulis! The History of Love: Its Wondrous Magic, Chemistry, Rules, Laws, Modes, Moods and*

Rationale (Toledo: Randolph Pub. Co, 1874). For more on Randolph, see John Patrick Deveney, *Paschal Beverly Randolph: A Nineteenth-Century Black American Spiritualist, Rosicrucian, and Sex Magician* (Albany: State Univ. of New York, 1997).

32   Joscelyn Godwin, Christian Chanel, and John-Patrick Deveney, *The Hermetic Brotherhood of Luxor: Initiatic and Historical Documents of an Order of Practical Occultism* (York Beach, ME: Samuel Weiser, 1995). Kaczynski, "Carl Kellner's Esoteric Roots."

33   AC to W. B. Crow, 16 Jul 1944, New 24, Yorke Collection.

34   Rudolf Steiner, *Freemasonry and Ritual Work: The Misraim Service* (Great Barrington, Mass: SteinerBooks, 2007). This volume includes Steiner's correspondence and rituals, clarifying a great deal about the topic.

35   Copies of both Crowley's charter and the MMM constitution are in the OTO Archives.

36   AC to RC Newman, 16 Aug 1944, New 24, Yorke Collection.

37   Terrell, *Companion to the Cantos*, 31–2.

38   The journal was a continuation of the *Freewoman*, which ran from November 1911 to October 1912. The *New Freewoman* ran for half a year, from June to December 1913 before changing its name to *Egoist* in January 1914; it ran until December 1919.

39   Marriage record, Q4 1911, GRO, St. George Hanover Square, London, 1a: 1083. "Bernard Breslauer: Bookdealer and Collector across Two Continents," *The Independent,* 25 Sep 2004. "Mr. Wilfred Merton: Book Production at Its Best," *Times* (London), 8 Nov 1957, 53993: 13. Graduating from Trinity, Merton became a partner in Sir Emery Walker's firm and became renowned for his top-quality book production.

40   Divorce Court File 2768. Appellant: Wilfred Merton. Respondent: Jeanne Merton. Co-respondent: Victor Benjamin Neuburg. J77/1080, National Archives, KEW, 1912.

41   Death record, Q1 1912, GRO, Lambeth, Surrey, 1d: 419.

42   Nina Hamnett, *Laughing Torso: Reminiscences of Nina Hamnett* (London: Constable & Co. Ltd, 1932).

43   "Young Wife's Suicide: 'My Rash and Unfortunate Marriage,'" *Observer* (London), 4 Aug 1912, 12. "Art Student's Suicide: 'Unfortunate Marriage,'" *Times* (London), 5 Aug 1912, 39969: 2.

44   Ezra Pound, "Dead Iönè," *Poetry and Drama,* Dec 1914, 2(8): 353. The poem was retitled "Ione, Dead the Long Year" in *Lustra of Ezra Pound, with Earlier Poems* (London: Elkin Matthews, 1916).

45   When he joined the A∴A∴ on October 1, 1910, G. G. Rae Fraser took the motto "Je suis prest" (I am ready). Crowley later noted on his application, "On the Path, and helping. Difficult to catch." With the publication of "Sepher Sephiroth," Crowley referred to him as Fra∴ Ψ, suggesting he had passed beyond Probationer, and acknowledged his contributions a specially-constructed typewriter and numerous mathematical additions. Hymenaeus Beta, "Notes on Contriubtors," in *The Equinox* (York Beach, ME: Weiser, 1998), 40, notes that Fraser was 3°=8□ in 1918.

     In *The Record of Old Westminsters,* George Gerald Rae-Fraser (1888–1974) is listed as the elder son of George Thomson Rae-Fraser and Catherine Monkhouse, of Belsize Park Gardens, Hampstead, Middlesex. He was admitted to the Westminster School in 1906, and graduated with a BA in 1901 as a chartered accountant. He would go on to join various professional societies, serve as a flight lieutenant in the Royal Air Force, and marry in 1918. See "Deaths," *Times* (London), 15 Jan 1974, 58988: 26. Westminster School (London, England), George Fisher Russell Barker, and Alan Herbert Stenning, *The Record of Old Westminsters: A Biographical List of All Those Who Are Known to Have Been Educated at Westminster School from the Earliest Times to 1927* (London: Chiswick Press, 1928), 350.

46   Frederick Goodyear was the oldest son of Frederick Goodyear of Fallow Corner, North Finchley. He attended Christ's College, Finchley, University College School, and Brasenose College, Oxford, from which he graduated in 1910 with a second

class in *Literae Humaniores* (classics). He worked as a journalist—contributing primarily to *The Field* and *Rhythm*—and later as assistant manager of the Oxford University Press in Bombay. He enlisted in the Artists Rifles in February 1915, was gazetted to the Essex Regiment in 1917, was injured on May 12, 1917, during an attack on Fampoux, France; after having his left leg amputated, he died on May 23 at the Canadian Casualty Clearing Station at Aubigny. Frederick Goodyear, *Letters and Remains, 1887–1917* (London: McBride, Nast & Co., 1920). "Fallen Officers: *The Times* List of Casualties," *Times* (London), 26 May 1917, 41488: 9. 1901 UK census, RG13, piece 1233, 73: 20. Angela Smith, "Katherine Mansfield and *Rhythm*," *Journal of New Zealand Literature* 2003, 21: 102–21.

47 1 in Frederick Goodyear, "The New Thelema," *Rhythm* 1911, 1(1): 1–3.

48 K. M., "The Triumph of Pan" [review], *Rhythm,* Jul 1912, 2(2): 70.

49 C. A. Hankin, *The Letters of John Middleton Murry to Katherine Mansfield* (New York: Franklin Watts, 1983), 16.

50 Laver, *Museum Piece*, 118–9.

51 LM, *Katherine Mansfield: The Memories of L.M.* (London: Michael Joseph, 1971), 86.

52 James Moore, *Gurdjieff and Mansfield* (London: Routledge & Kegan Paul, 1980), 18.

53 Moore, *Gurdjieff and Mansfield,* 18. See also *Memories of L. M.* and Claire Tomalin, *Katherine Mansfield: A Secret Life.* (New York: Viking, 1987), 98–100.

54 Aleister Crowley, "Villon's Apology (On Reading Stevenson's Essay)," *Poetry Review,* Dec 1912, 1(12): 540.

55 Fuller had indeed advanced beyond Probationer status: It will be remembered he acted as Chancellor of the A∴A∴, and his Adeptus Minor motto appeared in the imprimatur of the order's *libri.*

56 Passenger Lists of Vessels Arriving at New York, NY (National Archives, Washington, D.C.), roll T715_1830, 12.

57 "'Two Little Brides' Lacks Distinction: But James T. Powers Is Warmly Welcomed in New Musical Show at the Casino: Not Much To Commend; Comedian Has Been Seen to Far Better Advantage and the Show as a Whole Is Dull," *New York Times,* 24 Apr 1912.

58 Aleister Crowley, Draft of a puff for the Ragged Ragtime Girls, New 12, Yorke Collection.

59 *Confessions,* 690.

60 AC to G. M. Cowie, 24 Feb 1913, New 4, Yorke Collection.

61 Classified ad, *Times* (London), 25 Mar 1913, 40168: 1.

62 "London Vaudeville Owns Yankee Sway: English Variety Artists Are Bitter at the Prominence of American Performers: Stars at Leading Halls: Any One Can Get a Place if He Has a Strong Accent, Says the Leader of the Disgruntled Ones," *New York Times,* 9 Mar 1913, 40.

63 George M. Cowie to AC, n.d. (letter 13), Old D5, Yorke Collection. See also AC to Cowie, 6 Sep 1913, New 4, Yorke Collection, where he writes, "The Ragged Ragtime Girls will be in Edinburgh in 3 weeks. Mind you look up Mother [Waddell] that Monday night."

64 W. F. Ryan, "The Great Beast in Russia: Aleister Crowley's Theatrical Tour in 1913 and his Beastly Writings on Russia," in Arnold McMillin (ed.), *Symbolism and After: Essays on Russian Poetry in Honour of Georgette Donchin* (Bristol: Duckworth, 1992), 137–61.

65 AC to RC Newman, 16 Aug 1944, New 24, Yorke Collection.

66 AC to Societas Rosicruciana, n.d., 1913. New 12, Yorke Collection.

67 AC to RC Newman, 16 Aug 1944, New 24, Yorke Collection. Many of Crowley's letters in New 12 from 1913 also deal with these elections.

68 AC to W. B. Crow, 3 Jul 1944, New 24, Yorke Collection.

69   14 in R. A. Gilbert, "Baphomet and Son: A Little Known Chapter in the Life of 666," *Nuit-Isis* 1982, 1: 13–7.

70   Aleister Crowley, "The City of God (Moscow)," *The English Review,* Jan 1914, 161–6. Reissued in 1943 (London: The OTO).

71   *Confessions,* 712.

72   *Confessions,* 712.

73   AC to WB Crow, 2 Apr 1945, New 24, Yorke Collection.

74   "The city of God" first appeared in the *English Review,* see above.

75   Aleister Crowley, "The Heart of Holy Russia," *The International* 1918, 12(1): 10–4.

76   Originally slated for the October 1914 *English Review,* publication of "The Fun of the Fair" was canceled to make room for Crowley's "Appeal to the American Republic," renamed "To America." The former poem remained unpublished until reissued in a limited edition by OTO in 1942.

77   This poem is reproduced in Crowley's *Diary of a Drug Fiend.*

78   Unpublished in Crowley's lifetime.

79   "To Laylah—eight-and-twenty" is the colophon to *The Equinox* 1913, 1(10): 235–6.

80   Aleister Crowley, "The Ship," *The Equinox* 1913, 1(10): 57–79.

81   Slated for the ill-fated *The Giant's Thumb* (1915), it ultimately appeared in *The Equinox* 1919, 3(1): 5–7.

82   "Ecclesiae Gnosticae Catholicae Canon Missae." *The International* 1918, 12(3): 70–4. It later appeared in *The Equinox* 1919, 3(1): 247–70 with the numerical title "Liber XV."

83   AC to WB Crow, 2 Apr 1945, New 24, Yorke Collection.

84   Around this time, Dr. R. L. Felkin was busy organizing a branch of the GD. See R. A. Gilbert, *A. E. Waite: A Bibliography* (Wellingborough, Northamptonshire: Aquarian Press, 1983), 141.

85   The blurring of lines between spiritualism and other forms of occultism, including ceremonial magic, is explored in Richard Kaczynski, "Séances and Suffrage: The Victorian New Age and Equal Rites" (paper presented at the annual meeting of the Mid-Atlantic Popular Culture/American Culture Association, Baltimore, Oct 2006).

86   AC to the editor of an unknown newspaper, 1913, New 24, Yorke Collection.

87   "The Magazines," *Academy and Literature,* Nov 1913, 2169: 695. "Art in America," *Chicago Daily Tribune,* 23 Nov 1913, A4. "Private Censor Destroys Books: Shows Disapprobation of Eden Philpotts: Very Harsh Critic: Aleister Crowley Has Little Good to Say of American Art But Looks Ahead," *State* (Columbia, SC), 7 Dec 1913.

88   Robert Haven Schauffler, "American Poetry Comes of Age," *English Review,* Nov 1922, 388.

89   Aelfrida Tillyard, *Cambridge Poets, 1900–1913: An Anthology* (Cambridge: W. Heffer, 1913).

90   J. DeLancey Ferguson, "Lucid Mystics," *Dial,* 13 Sep 1917, 207–8.

91   Finding aid, "Personal Papers of Aelfrida Tillyard," GBR/0271/GCPP Tillyard, Girton College Archive, Cambridge.

92   Diary, 26 Apr 1913, GCPP Tillyard 1/18, Girton College Archive, Cambridge.

93   Assorted letters, New 12, Yorke Collection. Saraswati is the Hindu goddess of knowledge and of the arts; her name literally means "essence of the self."

94   Diary, 3 Jul 1913, GCPP Tillyard 1/19, Girton College Archive, Cambridge.

95   Diary, 5 Dec 1913, GCPP Tillyard 1/19.

96   "The Reviews," *Manchester Guardian,* 6 Jan 1914, 6.

97   F. B. Bond and T. S. Lea, *Gematria.* (Northamptonshire: Thorsons Publishers, 1977).

98   *Confessions,* 722.

99   Aleister Crowley, *The Soul of the Desert.* (Kings Beach, CA: Thelema Publications,

1974).

100 The Paris Working is documented in *Vision and The Voice with Commentary*. Other published accounts include Motta's *Sex and Religion* and John Symonds, *The Magic of Aleister Crowley* (London: Frederick Muller, 1958). Typescripts are preserved in the Crowley Papers at GARL, HRHRC, Yorke Collection, and the OTO Archives.

101 *Confessions,* 704 and fn 5.

102 Harrison E. Salisbury, *Without Fear or Favor: The New York Times and Its Times* (New York: Times Books, 1980), 459.

103 Disposition of Boleskine, Scottish Records Office. AC to Karl Germer, 6 Jun 1947, number 214, Collection AL3, OTO Archives.

104 For Crowley's opinion, see *Confessions,* 762. For Kemp's, see William Brevda, *Harry Kemp: The Last Bohemian* (Lewisburg: Bucknell Univ. Press, 1986), 94.

105 AC to Frater Achad, quoted in Grant, *Magical Revival,* 32–3.

106 *Magick in Theory and Practice,* 196.

107 *Triumph of Pan,* 175–6.

108 Coincidentally, Dylan Thomas was born on October 27, 1914; it was this same fall—if not the very same month—that Crowley and Neuburg had split.

Chapter Twelve • Chokmah Days

1 AC to GM Cowie, 19 Aug 1914, New 4, Yorke Collection.

2 AC to GM Cowie, 19 Aug 1914.

3 AC to GM Cowie, 7 Sep 1914.

4 J. Lee Thompson, *Politicians, the Press, & Propaganda: Lord Northcliffe and the Great War, 1914-1919* (Kent, OH: Kent State Univ. Press, 1999).

5 John Quinn to James Hunneker, 5 Nov 1914, Quinn Memorial Collection.

6 Henry N. Hall, "Master Magician Reveals Weird Supernatural Rites," *World Magazine,* 13 Dec 1914, 9, 17.

7 Two American groups descend from Societas Rosicruciana. The oldest of these, Societas Rosicruciana in Civitibaus Fœderatis (SRICF), dates from the formation of its High Grand Council 1880. During a period of apparent dormancy, Societas Rosicruciana in America (SRIA) was chartered in New York in 1909 with Plummer as its Supreme Magus. Both groups continue to operate today.

8 G. W. Plummer's correspondence with Crowley and his circle, the record book of the Metropolitan College, and Plummer's honorary OTO certificate are all preserved by the SRIA, who kindly granted me access to their archives.

9 Philippa Pullar, *Frank Harris* (Hamish Hamilton: London, 1975), 300.

10 As he described his first meeting with Crowley (W. B. Seabrook, "Astounding Secrets of the Devil Worshippers' Mystic Love Cult," *Sensation,* Nov 1939, 33, courtesy of the private collection of T. M. Caldwell):

> My first glimpse of this man who has been described as a "poet, mystic, mountain climber, big game hunter and general lunatic" came at a very social party a few years ago at the Metropolitan opera.
>
> Crowley appeared during the first entre-act intermission. He gave the impression of a punctiliously correct Britisher in conventional evening clothes–a big man of heavily athletic build, who looked as if he had spent most of his life outdoors. But the conventionality was only on the surface. On being presented to each member of the party, instead of murmuring the usual 'How do you do?' he said:
>
> "DO WHAT THOU WILT SHALL BE THE WHOLE OF THE LAW."
>
> And thereafter, for the entire evening, he sat like an incarnation of Buddha, staring straight before him, saying nothing at all. The women of the party, I noticed, seemed strangely fascinated by this man—a fascination mingled with a sort of repulsion and fear. Their eyes were on him more than on the stage.

11   The firm was founded by Hungarian-born Joseph Zaehnsdorf (1816-1886), and carried on by his son Joseph William Zaehensdorf, at which time it served as bookbinder to Edward VII. In 1920, Joseph William retired and the business was run by
his son, Ernest, until the end of World War II.

12   *Complete Catalogue of the Library of John Quinn Sold by Auction in Five Parts (With
Printed Prices). Volume One Abb-Mey (1–6498)* (New York: Anderson Galleries,
1924), 230. This book lists all the Crowley books in Quinn's library on p 226–32.

13   J. B. Yeats to W. B. Yeats, 18 Dec 1914, in Richard J. Finerman, George Mills
Harper and William M. Murphy, *Letters to W. B. Yeats. Vol 2* (New York: Columbia
Univ. Press, 1977), 309–10.

14   J. B. Yeats to W. B. Yeats, ibid.

15   John Quinn to W. B. Yeats, 25 Feb 1915, in Alan Himber, *The Letters of John Quinn
to William Butler Yeats* (Ann Arbor, MI: UMI Research Press, 1983).

16   W. B. Yeats to J. B. Yeats, 18 Jan 1915, in Wade, *Letters of W. B. Yeats.*

17   W. B. Yeats to John Quinn, 21 Mar 1915, Quinn Memorial Collection.

18   AC to Theodore Schroeder, 15 Dec 1914, Theodore Schroeder papers, 1842–1957,
1/1/MSS 017, Southern Illinois University Carbondale Special Collections.

19   Joseph Bernard Rethy, *The Song of the Scarlet Host and Other Poems* (Portland, ME:
Smile and Sale, 1915).

20   G. S. Viereck to Elmer Gertz, 2 Oct 1935, box 129, Elmer Gertz Papers, Manuscript
Division, Library of Congress, Washington, D.C. See also the letters dated 1 May
1935, and 16 Sep 1935, for more.

21   Aleister Crowley, "An Orgy of Cant: Aleister Crowley, the British Poet, Calls a
Spade a Spade," *Continental Times,* 24 Feb 1915, 21(23): supplement. Introducing
the piece was the following text: "Aleister Crowley, the well known English
reformer, has sent out to the educated classes in England a circular letter, in which
he tells his countrymen a few very unpleasant facts, tearing from their minds the veil
of hypocrisy through which they hitherto have looked at everything connected with
the war." Similarly, *The Open Court* wrote that "Early last year Mr. Crowley gave
expression to his view of the war in a short circular titled 'The Orgy of Cant' which
he sent out pretty widely in letter form among his friends. It was reprinted in *The
Continental Times,* an American paper published in Europe" (Paul Carus, "An Orgy
of Cant," *The Open Court,* Feb 1916, 30(2): 70–9).

22   Spence, *Secret Agent 666,* 74.

23   Crowley's contributions to the *Fatherland* include the following (note that the magazine underwent a name change in volume 6 (1917), to *New World: The American
Weekly* in issue 2, to *Viereck's The American Weekly* in issue 3, and finally to *Viereck's
American Weekly* with issue 3): "Honesty is the Best Policy," *Fatherland,* 13 Jan 1915,
1(23): 11–15; 20 Jan 1915, 1(24): 5–6; "England on the Brink of Revolution,"
Fatherland, 21 Jul 1915, 2(24): 3–5; congratulatory letter on the *Fatherland's* first year
in print, 11 Aug 1915, 3(1): 9; "The Future of the Submarine," *Fatherland,* 6 Oct
1915, 3(9): 152–3; An Englishman, "Skeletons in the Cabinet," *Fatherland,* 10 Nov
1915, 3(14): 245; "Behind the Front: Impressions of a Tourist in Western Europe,"
Fatherland, 29 Dec 1915, 3(21): 365; 5 Jan 1916, 3(22): 383–4; L. P. 33. Y., "Leaves
from a Lost Portfolio," *Fatherland,* 8 Mar 1916, 4(5): 67–9; "Lifting the Mask from
England," *Fatherland,* 15 Mar 1916, 4(6): 85–6; "Delenda Est Britannia: Being a Prologue and Epilogue to 'The Vampire of the Continent')," *Fatherland,* 3 Jan 1917,
5(22); "England's Blind Spot," *Viereck's The American Weekly,* 18 May 1917, 6(11):
182–3; and a joke attributed to Crowley in "The Latest Submarine Outrage," *Viereck's The American Weekly,* 16 May 1917, 6(13): 247. Ironically, Crowley's former
pupil, George Raffalovich, also contributed to the journal in 1917: "Rasputin: The
Sorcerer of Russia," *Fatherland,* 7 Feb 1917, 6(1): 3–4 and "Aristide Briand: Ex-
Leader of the Allies," *Viereck's The American Weekly,* 25 Apr 1917, 6(12): 198–200.
Crowley's subsequent contributions to the *Continental Times* included "End of
England," *Continental Times,* 26 Jul 1915, 22: n.p.; "A New Parsifal, Wilhelm II: The

Vision of an English Poet," *Continental Times,* 20 Aug 1915, 22(22): n.p..; "America's Attitude to the War: Hatred of the People for the Press," *Continental Times,* 6 Oct 1915, 22(42): n.p.; and "Aleister Crowley Explains," *Continental Times,* 11 Oct 1915, 22: n.p.

24   AC to Gerald Yorke, n.d., New 115, Yorke Collection.

25   "Memorandum," typescript addendum to Affidavit: Memorandum of My Political Attitude since August, 1914," Yorke Collection, op. cit., typescript in OS F2.17, Yorke Collection, Warburg. Hereafter cited as "Memorandum." As Crowley repeated in the aforementioned "Affidavit," "I hoped to get a commission through the good offices of my friend Lieut. the Hon. Everard Feilding, R. N. V."

26   "Personnel of the Press Bureau," *Manchester Guardian,* 9 Sep 1914, 10.

27   Aleister Crowley, "The Last Straw," OS C3.5, Yorke Collection, Warburg; reproduced in *Confessions.*

28   Crowley, "The Last Straw," quoted in *Confessions,* 753–4. Similarly, in his "Memorandum," Crowley wrote, "I pointed out the possibilities of this course to Feilding, and urged him to get me some work, officially. Still nothing doing, but I made him reports on the activities of von Riatlen, and some other matters." Years later, on June 20, 1929, Feilding would write to AC, "Although I am anxious to help as well as I can set right a matter in which I believe you have been unjustly criticized, I would prefer for reasons into which I don't wish to enter not to resume our personal acquaintanceship" (Old E21, Yorke Collection).

29   Crowley, "Affidavit: Memorandum of My Political Attitude since August, 1914," typescript in OS F2.17, Yorke Collection, Warburg. Hereafter cited as "Affidavit."

30   1910 U.S. Census, Lexington Ward 5, Fayette, Kentucky, page 8A, enumeration district 30, 708. 1920 U.S. Census, Louisville Ward 6, Page 1A, enumeration district 126, image 733. Kentucky, Kentucky Death Index, 18 Apr 1955, Jefferson, KY, 16: 7599. Alberg Gallatin Mackey, Robert Ingham Clegg and Harry LeRoy Haywood, *Encyclopedia of Freemasonry* (Chicago: Masonic History Company, 1946), 1: 489.

31   Quoted in J. W. Norwood to Chief of Intelligence Bureau, 9 Jun 1919, Case Number 365985, *Investigative Case Files of the Bureau of Investigation 1908–1922.* Crowley expounded his motives more fully in his "Affidavit" as follows: "My object was fourfold: (a) to discredit the German cause by committing the enemy to manifest absurdities and infamies, (b) to induce the Germans to give me their full confidence, (c) to arouse the indignation of the Americans, (d) to warn England of certain of her own weaknesses by exposing them."

32   "The Criminal Methods of Captain Guy Gaunt, C.M.G., Naval Attaché of the British Embassy: How the British Secret Service Rifles United States Mail," *The Fatherland,* 24 May 1916, 4(16): 243–6.

33   Guy Gaunt, *The Yield of the Years: A Story of Adventure Afloat and Ashore* (London: Hutchinson & Co, 1940), 139.

34   AC to Gerald Yorke, 20 Apr 1929, Yorke Collection. See also Crowley's similar statements: "I saw Capt. Gaunt, and suggested that I could be of great use in keeping track of the Irish-Americans, and so on; but I have not yet heard definitely from him" ("Memorandum"), and "I wrote to Capt. Guy Gaunt R. N. from Washington early in 1916, when *The Fatherland* was attacking him personally for briding the office boy etc., a letter of sympathy and an offer of help and service. Captain Gaunt replied cordially, but as if *The Fatherland* were not worth notice" ("Affidavit").
         Gaunt's reference to would-be saboteur Franz von Papen (1879–1969) is interesting, as Crowley claimed in his "Memorandum" that he reported to Gaunt on the activities of von Papen's rival, German spy Franz von Rintelen (1877–1949). Indeed, Crowley's later acquaintance, George Langelaan (1908–1972)—a British writer best known for science-fiction classic "The Fly" (1957)—reported that Crowley was indeed a spy, and that by winning the confidence of the Germans in America, he had access to members of their inner circle. See George Langelaan, "L'agent secret, fauteur de paix," *Janus: L'Homme, son Historie et son Avenir* 1964, 2: 49–53.

35 Spence, *Secret Agent 666*, 52.

36 Crowley, "Affidavit." Similarly, the "Memorandum for Mr. Hoover" reports that "he had attempted to join the [secret] service but never succeeded in obtaining an official position with them. He states throughout his communications for a position he dealt with Commodore Gaunt of the British Intelligence office." Memorandum for Mr. Hoover, 1 Aug 1924. FBI document 61–2069–4, p. 3.

37 Frank X. O'Donnell, "In RE: Aleister Crowley (Radical Activities), 30 Jul 1919, case number 365985, *Investigative Case Files of the Bureau of Investigation 1908–1922*.

38 Letter to Frank Burke, 30 Jan 1920, case number 365985, *Investigative Case Files of the Bureau of Investigation 1908–1922*.

39 Frank X. O'Donnell, "In RE: Aleister Crowley."

40 The British Secret Service Bureau was founded in 1909 to assess the threat of Germany's new navy, and to thwart the German Intelligence Service by arresting its spies. In January 1916 the Bureau was subsumed under a new directorate of Military Intelligence, the MI5.

41 Guy Gaunt to John Symonds, quoted in Symonds, *Shadow Realm,* 208.

42 AC to Gerald Yorke, 20 May 1929, Yorke Collection. As Spence explains in *Secret Agent 666,* "In 1911 Parliament approved a new Official Secrets Act (OSA), which remains, with various provisions in force. The heart of it was Section Two, which forbade anyone 'who holds or who has held' a position under His Majesty, or simply contracted in any way with the government, from disclosing information about his or her work without lawful authority. Its most important aim was to keep intelligence operatives quiet—permanently" (p. 42).

43 Memorandum for Mr. Hoover, 1 Aug 1924. FBI document 61–2069–4, p 2–3.

44 G. S. Viereck to Elmer Gertz, 1 May 1935, Box 129, Gertz Papers.

45 Diary, 30 Jul 1936.

46 Trouble Laid to O.T.O. Cult—Business Wrecked, Friends Lost, Ryerson Wrote to Compiler of "Equinox." *Detroit Times,* 10 Jan 1922.

47 Crowley, "Behind the Front," 383.

48 "German Resources," *Chicago Daily Tribune,* 4 Jan 1916, 6.

49 Crowley, "Affidavit."

50 See Booth, *A Magick Life,* 322–3. Also, 328–30 describes official documentation which, although inconsequential to the discussion here, is unavailable elsewhere.

51 See also his original article, Richard B. Spence, "Secret Agent 666: Aleister Crowley and British Intelligence, 1914–1918," *International Journal of Intelligence and Counter-Intelligence* 2000, 13: 359–71.

52 For a contemporary account of Crownenshield and his running of *Vanity Fair,* see Robert C. Benchley, "Mr. Vanity Fair," *Bookman: A Recview of Books and Life* 1919, 50(3–4): 429–33.

53 See the August, 1915, letter from Carl van Vechten to Edna Kenton (Kellner, p. 18), which says that Helen Westley's two lovers at the *Fatherland,* Crowley and his journalist friend James Keating, are in danger of being arrested. Previous biographers have conflated Westley, The Snake, with another of Crowley's lovers, Helen Hollis (b. 1899); for further information, see the biographical appendix to the unabridged *Confessions,* v. 7.

54 *Confessions,* 798.

55 Gerald Bordman, *The Oxford Companion to American Theatre* (New York: Oxford Univ. Press, 1984), 709.

56 David Ragan, *Who's Who in Hollywood. The Largest Cast of International Film Personalities Ever Assembled* (New York: Facts on File, 1992), 1797. See also "Regarding Helen Westley," *New York Times,* 16 Dec 1917, X7. Westley starred in the following films: *Anne of Green Gables* (1934), *Splendor* (1935), *Heidi* (1937), and *Sing and Be Happy* (1937). She also appeared in *The Age of Innocence* (1934), *Chasing Yesterday*

(1935), *Captain Hurricane* (1935), *Roberta* (1935), *Banjo on My Knee* (1936), *Stowaway* (1936), *Show Boat* (1936), *Dimples* (1936), *Cafe Metropole* (1937), *I'll Take Romance* (1937), *The Baroness and The Butler* (1938), *Rebecca of Sunnybrook Farm* (1938), *All This, And Heaven Too* (1940), *Million Dollar Baby* (1941) and *Lady From Louisiana* (1941). See http://www.imdb.com/name/nm0922818 for more information.

57 *Confessions*, 767.

58 "The Prettiest Chin in the World," *Chicago Daily Tribune*, 16 Apr 1905, H4.

59 William M. Murphy, *The Prodigal Father: the Life of John Butler Yeats (1839–1922)* (Ithaca: Cornell Univ. Press, 1978), 431.

60 Jeanne Robert Foster, *Wild Apples* (Boston: Sherman, 1916). Jeanne Robert Foster, *Neighbors of Yesterday* (Boston: Sherman, 1916).

61 Crowley commented on his attempt at having a child by Foster, "I did not know I was attempting a physical impossibility." (*Confessions*, 801).

62 Addendum to 2 Jul 1915 diary entry.

63 "Irish Republic Born in New York Harbor: Ten Patriots at Daybreak Renounce Allegiance to England near Statue of Liberty: Independence is Declared: Sympathy with Germany, They Say, a Matter of Expediency—Then They Breakfast at Jack's," *New York Times*, 13 Jul 1915, 7.

64 Alex C. Crowley, "The Irish Flag," *New York Times*, 21 Jul 1915, 10.

65 Godfrey Higgins, *Anacalypsis, an Attempt to Draw Aside the Veil of the Saitic Isis; or an Inquiry into the Origin of Languages, Nations and Religions* (London: Longman, Rees, Orme, Brown, Green & Longman, 1833, 1836).

66 AC to G. M. Cowie, 20 Nov 1913, Yorke Collection.

67 "An orgy of cant" had been published in *The Continental Times* in 1915, and Paul Carus published his response in The Editor, "An Orgy of Cant," *The Open Court*, Feb 1916, 30(2): 70–9. "Cocaine" appeared in *The International* 1917, 11(10): 291–4. For details on Crowley and Carus, see AC to Paul Carus, 15 Jun 1915, 15 Jul 1915, 10 Aug 1915; Paul Carus to AC, 17 Jun 1915, 25 Jun 1915, 12 Jul 1915, 29 Jul 1915, 20 Sep 1915. Open Court Publishing Company records, 1886-1953, 1/2/ MSS 027, Southern Illinois University Carbondale Special Collections.

68 Aleister Crowley, "The New Parsifal: A Study of Wilhelm II," *Open Court* 1915, 29 (8): 499–502; rpt. in Stephenson, *Legend of Aleister Crowley*, 113–6.

69 Paul Carus to AC, 22 Sep 1915, Open Court records. See also Carus to AC, 4 Nov 1915.

70 J. B. Yeats to J. R. Foster, 4 Jul 1915, no. 29, Jeanne R. Foster–William M. Murphy Collection, Manuscripts and Archives Division, New York Public Library.

71 *Confessions*, 767.

72 "A Hindu at the Polo Grounds: A Letter from Mahatma Sri Paramananda Guru Swamiji (Great Soul Saint Supreme-Bliss Teacher Learned Person) to His Brother in India," *Vanity Fair*, Aug 1915, 63. Reprinted in *Revival of Magick and Other Essays*.

73 *Confessions*, 770.

74 While this collection was never published in AC's lifetime, the following selections appeared in *The International:* "In the Red Room of Rose Croix," 11(10): 294 (Oct 1917); "Love is One," 11(10): 309 (Oct 1917); "Hymn" (from Baudelaire), 11(11): 333 (Nov 1917); "A Riddle," 11(12): 379 (Dec 1917); "Dawn," 12(1): 9 (Jan 1918); "A Vision of the Eucharist," 12(2) (Feb 1918); "Knight-errant," 12(3): 85 (Mar 1918); "Visions" 12(4): 117 (Apr 1918).

75 Published in *The International* 1918, 12(1): 25 and later in *The Equinox* 1919, 3(1): 39.

76 *Confessions*, 805.

77 Richard Londraville, private communication.

78 A septennial. *The International* 1917, 11 (12): 376.

79 Leila Waddell, "Two Anzacs Meet in London," *Shadowland: Expressing the Arts*, Oct

1923, 9(2): 51, 72.

80   Incoming passenger lists show that Leila Waddell arrived from Sydney in Vancouver/ Seattle on April 3, 1925, aboard the Aorangi, en route to England; she departed from New York aboard the Aquitania, arriving in Southampton on May 5, 1925. In 1926, she traveled from Sydney aboard the Jervis Bay, arriving in London on October 29, 1926.

81   David Waddell died at Randwick in 1929, age seventy-nine. Registry of Death 13559/1929, New South Wales.

82   Gibney and Smith, *A Biographical Register,* v. 2, 321. The Elizabeth Bay school, known as Kincoppal, was founded in 1909. In 1971, it merged its campus with that of its older sister, the first Convent of the Sacred Heart (which was founded in1882) and became known as Kincoppal-Rose Bay, School of the Sacred Heart.

83   "The Late Leila Waddell," *Sydney Mail,* 21 Sep 1932, 8.

84   Clare Thornley, *The Royal Philharmonic Society of Sydney: The Rise and Fall of a Musical Organisation,* master's thesis, Sydney Conservatorium of Music, University of Sydney, 2004.

85   Registry of death, 16225/1932, Woollahra, New South Wales.

86   Crowley's works continued to appear in the *International* and *Vanity Fair* on a regular basis. Likewise, *The Open Court* paid Crowley $10 for "Culture vs Kultur."

87   *Confessions,* 805.

88   *Confessions,* 774.

89   Aleister Crowley, *The Gospel According to George Bernard Shaw* (n.p., 1953), 101. I have been unable to trace a Gerda Maria von Kothek; however, the 17 Apr 1918 entry of Crowley's *Rex De Arte Regia* names her as Gerda von Kothek (Gebauer), suggesting that, sometime between 1916 and 1918, Gerda married. A Rudolph and Gerda Gebauer appear in the 1920 U.S. Census at St. Luke's Place in Manhattan; both were German-born, she (born c. 1897) immigrating in 1908 and he in 1913. Further research is required.

90   *Confessions,* 806.

91   "Peculiarity of Hindu Music Compared with the Occidental: Recent Recitals in Manhattan Give Opportunity for Analysis of Songs Peculiar to East India—Concerts and Recitals in Two Boroughs for the Week," *Brooklyn Daily Eagle,* 7 May 1916, 11.

92   Roger Lipsey, *Coomaraswamy. 3: His Life and Work* (Princeton: Princeton Univ. Press, 1977), 92–3.

93   *Thirty Songs from the Panjab and Kashmir: Recorded by Ratan Devi with Introduction and Translations by Ananda K. Coomaraswamy and a Foreword by Rabindranath Tagore* (London: The Authors, 1913).

94   Joyce Kilmer, "Oriental Poetry More Realistic than Ours: Not Result of Deliberate Effort, Says Hindu Philosopher; Part of Everyday Life of People, Says His Wife, Madame Devi," *New York Times,* 2 Apr 1916, SM12.

95   [Aleister Crowley], "Ratan Devi: Indian Singer," *Vanity Fair,* May 1916, 79. The same issue contains another article by Crowley, writing as Dionysus Carr, "On the Management of Blondes: Prolegomena to Any System of Philosophy Devoted to Their Treatment and Care," wherein he writes "And here lies, I think, the key to the solution of our difficulty. The natural enemy of the blonde is the brunette. The blonde knows it, and fears the brunette" (p. 85).

96   "A Concert of Indian Music: Ratan Devi Sings Classical ragas and Kashmiri Folk Songs," *New York Times,* 14 Apr 1916, 7. After several name changes over the decades, the Princess Theater was torn down in 1955.

97   "Music of Hindustan," *Outlook,* 26 Apr 1916, 941.

98   *Confessions,* 774.

99   *Confessions,* 774.

100 "Poet and Magus Explains Magic on a Basis of Scientific Facts; Defends Yoga and

Mystic Rites: Another Who Set London Literary World Agog by Verses and Occult Exploits Stirs American Students of Mysticism by Visit Here—Rosicrucian Mysteries Revived through His Facile Pen," *Washington Post,* 26 Dec 1915, R2.

101 Aleister Crowley, "Introduction," in Stuart X, *A Prophet in His Own Country: Being the Letters of Stuart X to Many Men on Many Occasions* (Washington, D.C.: the author, 1916), 11–27.

102 Crowley, "Introduction" to *Prophet,* 25. 1910 U.S. Census, precinct 8, Washington, District of Columbia, 5A. "Stuart X, The Great Unknown: An Unofficial Adviser to the Universe in General," *Vanity Fair,* Aug 1916, 35.

103 E. O. Irish, "In re: Henry Clifford Stuart: Alleged German Propaganda," 25 Jan 1919, case number 33537, publication no. M1085, *Investigative Case Files of the Bureau of Investigation 1909–1922.*

104 Crowley, "Introduction" to *Prophet,* 25.

105 "Gossip Gathered in Hotel Lobbies,"*Times Picayune,* 9 Apr 1896, 9.

106 "The Social World," *New York Times,* 7 Dec 1894, 16. "In Society," *Omaha World Herald,* 16 ec. 1894, 30(76): 6.

107 "City News in Brief," *Washington Post,* 13 Apr 1915, 13.

108 "Neutrality Matter," case number 8000–1514, publication number M1085, *Investigative Case Files of the Bureau of Investigation 1908–1922.*

109 "Neutrality Matter," ibid.

110 AC to Theodore Roosevelt, 12 Apr 1916, Theodore Roosevelt Papers, Manuscripts Division, Library of Congress.

111 AC to Henry Holt & Co., 3 Jun 1916, Henry Holt Collection (C0100), Box 26, Department of Rare Books and Manuscripts, Princeton University Library. The letter includes a copy of AC's circular promoting the book.

112 Frank X. O'Donnell, "In RE: Aleister Crowley." The Fifth Avenue Bank was acquired by the Bank of New York in 1948.

113 "Henry Clifford Stuart: Alleged German Propaganda," *op. cit.*

114 A. E. R., "Views and Reviews: Not without Humour," *New Age,* 10 Aug 1916, 19(15): 356.

115 "A Great Man's Opinions," *Indianapolis Sunday Star,* 19 Nov 1916, 19.

116 "Stuart X, The Great Unknown: An Unofficial Adviser to the Universe in General," *Vanity Fair,* Aug 1916, 35.

117 Aleister Crowley, "Protests He Is Not Author of Book by Stuart X," *Washington Post,* 2 Oct 1916, 9.

118 "Deaths," *New York Times,* 3 Feb 1929, 35.

119 "X," *Time,* 3 Mar 1930. "Strange as It Seems," *Brooklyn Daily Eagle,* 28 Apr 1931, 29.

120 Social Security death index, 21 May 1952, Alameda, CA.

121 Classified ad, *Chicago Daily Tribune,* 28 May 1916, H1.

122 "$10,000 for Lost Jade Idol: Offer of Reward Suggest Sun Yat Sen May Have Been Owner," *New York Times,* 29 May 1916, 11.

123 "Dr. Sun Yat Sen's Missing Idol Found: And It Means His Return to Power, His Secretary Declares," *Fort Wayne Daily News,* 1 Jun 1916, 2.

124 "The Oriental Mind," *Washington Post,* 2 Jun 1916, 6.

125 "Dr. Waite's 'Wicked Man from Egypt': A Modern Magician and Student of Occult Forces Explains His Belief that Evil Spirits Possess Us To-day just as They Did in in Old and New Testament Times," *Washington Post,* 30 Apr 1916, MT5.

126 Aleister Crowley, "Ireland as Peace Arbiter: Irish Poet Would Have Forgiveness, Not Revenge, Free Erin's Motto," *Washington Post,* 12 May 1916, 9.

127 "Chess: Local Tournament Is Arranged: Washington Clubs to See Some Interesting Matches This Week," *Washington Post,* 28 May 1916, ES2. In addition to being

acknowledged as an International Master of chess in 1965, Whittaker is also remembered for serving time for attempted extortion in connection with the Lindbergh kidnapping; while in prison, he befriended Al Capone.

128 Aleister Crowley, "Protests against Normal Way of Giving Anesthetics," *Washington Post,* 4 Sep 1916, 7.

129 From Crowley's Simon Iff story, "The Pasquaney Puzzle" (not to be confused with the article of the title cited above). Although the Simon Iff stories have not all been published, photocopies have circulated among collectors for many years.

130 AC to Karl Germer, 27 Jul 1945, Yorke Collection.

131 AC to CS Jones, 20 Aug 1914, Yorke Collection.

132 Cor Scorpionis [Aleister Crowley], "How Horoscopes Are Faked," *The International,* Nov 1917, 11(11): 345.

133 Compare Adams's *Astrology: Your Place in the Sun* (1928) and *Astrology: Your Place Among the Stars* (1930) to Crowley's *Complete Astrological Writings,* published posthumously. Not until 1936 would Crowley realize this, writing to Adams's publishers the following note:

> Gentlemen,
>   My attention has just been drawn to a book published by you in 1930 e.v., *Astrology: Your Place Among the Stars* by Evangeline Adams. Practically the whole of this book, except the hack work calculations, is taken from a manuscript of mine. It is quite probable that the rest of the manuscript has been printed in the other two books by my late friend and colleague. My arrangement with her was that we should divide the profits in equal moieties. I should be greatly obliged for information as to the other two books, and an accounting.
>   Yours sincerely,
>   Aleister Crowley

(AC to Messrs Dodd, Mead & Co, Publishers, 28 Dec 1936, New 117, Yorke Collection.) Unfortunately, this matter was never settled in Crowley's lifetime. The books sold out many print runs, and Crowley saw none of it. OTO now owns the rights to these works; a reconstruction of the Crowley-Adams collaboration was published as Aleister Crowley, Evangeline Adams, and Hymenaeus Beta, *The General Principles of Astrology. Liber DXXXVI* (Boston: Weiser Books, 2002). See also Karen Christino, *Foreseeing the Future: Evangeline Adams and Astrology in America* (Amherst, MA: One Reed Publications, 2002) for Adams's biography.

134 *The International* 1918, 12(2).

135 Diary, 12 Jul 1916.

136 *Confessions,* 808.

137 AC to Elihu Thomson, 31 Jul 1916, Box 11, Elihu Thomson Papers, MS Coll. 74, American Philosophical Library, Philadelphia, PA.

138 Aleister Crowley, "A Curious Kind of Lightning," *New York Times,* 16 Jul 1916, E2.

139 Douglass Shand-Tucci, *The Crimson Letter: Harvard, Homosexuality, and the Shaping of American Culture* (New York: St. Martin's Press, 2003), 49.

140 T. J. Jackson Lears, *No Place of Grace: Antimodernism and the Transformation of American Culture,* 1880–1920 (New York: Pantheon Books, 1981), 225–34. M. A. De Wolfe Howe, *Later Years of the Saturday Club, 1870–1920* (Boston: Houghton Mifflin, 1927), 265–8. M. W. Wiseman, "Buddhism and Immortality: The Ingersoll Lecture" [review], *American Journal of Psychology* 1909, 20(1): 140–1. Edmund H. Hollands, "Buddhism and Immortality" [review], *Philosophical Review* 1909, 18(3): 346–7. "Art Gift to Boston Museum: Dr. W. S. Bigelow Gives Chinese and Japanese Collection of 25,000 Pieces," *New York Times,* 10 Sep 1911, 13. "Dr. W. S. Bigelow, Noted Orientalist, Dies in 77th Year: Was Deep Student of Buddhism and Collector of Eastern Art Objects," *Hartford Courant,* 7 Oct 1926, 7. Arthur Fairbanks, "William Sturgis Bigelow (1850–1926)," *American Academy of Arts and Sciences* 1930, 64(12): 507–10. Constance J. S. Chen, "'The Esoteric Buddhist': William Sturgis Bigelow and the Culture of Dissent," *Amerasia Journal* 2008, 34(1): 31–51.

141 AC to William Sturgis Bigelow, 26 Jul 1916, Elihu Thomson Papers.

142 AC to Elihu Thomson, 31 Jul 1916, Elihu Thomson Papers. AC to Elihu Thomson, 23 Aug 1916, Elihu Thomson Papers.

143 W. S. Bigelow to E. Thomson, 7 Aug 1916, Elihu Thomson Papers. The "first and last lines" are, of course, "Do what thou wilt shall be the whole of the Law" and "Love is the law, love under will." As for the red stamp, Crowley explained, "the red seal is super-Masonic, pertaining to a degree–the ninth–in an order of which the seventh degree corresponds to the 33° A[ncient] & A[ccepted Scottish Rite]. I venture to enclose a pamphlet, as you appear interested" (AC to W. S. Bigelow, 8 Aug 1916, Elihu Thomson Papers).

144 *AL* i.55–56.

145 *Confessions*, 809.

146 Francis King, "Introduction," in *Crowley on Christ*, 16. The book (sans Mr. King's introduction) was originally published in 1953 by Thelema Publishing.

147 Most of these appeared in *The International* as follows: "The King of the Wood." 12(4): 99–102 (Apr 1918); "The Mass of Saint Secaire." 12(2): 42–6 (Feb 1918); "The Burning of Melcarth." 11(10): 310–2 (Oct 1917); "The Oracle of the Corycian Cave," never published in Crowley's lifetime; "The Stone of Cybele," never published in Crowley's lifetime; "The God of Ibreez," 12(1): 19–24 (Jan 1918); "The Old Man of the Peepul-tree," 12(4): 107–10 (Apr 1918); "The Hearth," 11(11): 334–8 (Nov 1917). All eight stories are collected in the volume *Golden Twigs*, ed. Martin P. Starr (Chicago: Teitan Press, 1988).

148 Dec 1916, 60, 137.

149 Diary, 9 Oct 1916.

150 Diary, 15 Dec 1916.

151 Crowley, *Moonchild*, 22–3.

152 "Big game," 11(9): 259–67 (Sep 1917); "The Artistic Temperament," 11(10): 295–301 (Oct 1917); "Outside the Bank's Routine," 11(11): 323–31 (Nov 1917); "The Conduct of John Briggs," 11(12): 323–31 (Dec 1917); "Not good enough," 12(1): 3–9 (Jan 1918); "Ineligible," 12(2): 35–40 (Feb 1918). All six stories have been collected in *The Scrutinies of Simon Iff*, ed. Martin P. Starr. (Chicago: Teitan Press, 1987).

153 Diary, 9 Apr 1920.

154 Published in 1929 by the Mandrake Press as *Moonchild*.

155 *Confessions*, 825. Aleister Crowley, "The Origin of the Game of Pirate Bridge," *Vanity Fair*, Jan 1917, 56.

156 *Confessions*, 825.

157 R. F. Foster, *Foster's Whist Manual: A Complete System of Instruction in the Game* (New York: Brentano's, 1890). R. F. Foster, *Foster's Complete Hoyle: An Encyclopedia of All the Indoor Games Played at the Present Day, with Suggestions for Good Play, a Full Code of Laws, Illustrative Hands, and a Brief Statement of the Doctrine of Chances as Applied to Games* (New York: Frederick A. Stokes, 1897).

158 R. F. Foster, *Foster's Pirate Bridge: The Latest Development of Auction Bridge, with the Full Code of the Official Laws* (New York: E.P. Dutton & Co, 1917), 5.

159 "'Pirate' Hits Hard at Auction Bridge" New Card Game takes Strong Hold, Gives Relief from Erratic Partners," *Grand Gorks Herald* (North Dakota), 30 Dec 1916, article location given as "Chicago, Dec 29." "Pirate Bridge: New Game Is Offered as a Rival to Auction: Object Is to Combine as Partners Holders of Two Best Hands," *Boston Daily Globe,* 31 Dec 1916. "Pirate Bridge: The Latest Improvement on Auction," *Kansas City Star,* 31 Dec 1916, 37(105): 1.

160 The book was advertised in each of Foster's *Vanity Fair* articles on pirate bridge (see below). It was also promoted in the press; see "Good Points of Pirate Bridge," *Kansas City Star*, 11 Jan 1917, 37(116): 18.

161 R. F. Foster, "The New Game of Pirate Bridge," was serialized in *Vanity Fair* as fol-

lows: Jan 1917, 57, 122, 124; Feb 1917, 73, 104; Mar 1917, 73, 114, 116; Apr 1917, 77, 126, 128; May 1917, 79, 124, 126; Jun 1917, 77, 97; Jul 1917, 61, 81.

162   R. F. Foster, "Pirate Bridge: The Latest Variety of Auction" was serialized in the following issues of the *Philadelphia Inquirer:* 7 Jan 1917, 176(7): 4; 14 Jan 1917, 176(14): 4; 21 Jan 1917, 176(21): 6; 28 Jan 1917, 176(28): 6; 4 Feb 1917, 176(35): 6; 11 Feb 1917, 176(42): 6; 18 Feb 1917, 176(49): 6; 25 Feb 1917, 176(56): 6; 4 Mar 1917, 176(63): 6; 11 Mar 1917, 176(70): 6; 18 Mar 1917, 176(77): 6; 25 Mar 1917, 176(84): 4; 1 Apr 1917, 176(91): 4; 8 Apr 1917, 176(98): 4; and 15 Apr 1917, 176(105): 4.

163   *Foster's Pirate Bridge* was announced in "Latest Publications: Books Received during the Week Ended Feb 15 Classified and Annotated According to Contents," *New York Times,* BR3, and "21,764 Books Given out at Library in 60 Days," *San Jose Mercury news,* 4 Mar 1917, 92(63): 6.

164   From a syndicated article that ran as Milton C. Work, "Will the New Pirate Bridge Displace Auction? Chairman of Card Committee of the Whist Club of New York Discusses the Question and Tells Why He Believes It Will Fail," *New York Times,* 14 Jan 1917, SM6. Or see "'Pirate' Analyzed by Milton C. Work: Expert Makes Examination of New Card Game and Declares Arguments for It Really Are in Favor of Auction," *Philadelphia Inquirer,* 14 Jan 1917, 176(15): 8.

165   "Society Finds New Substitute for Bridge," *Lincoln Sunday Star,* 21 Jan 1917, 1.

166   See, e.g., "Pirate Bridge Party at John A. Sinclair Home," *Duluth News-Tribune,* 28 Jan 1917, 48(267): 2B. "Second of Evening Bridges at Sinclair Home," *Duluth News-Tribune,* 30 Jan 1917, 48(269): 7. "Learn Pirate Bridge," *Idaho Daily Statesman,* 25 Mar 1917, 36: 12. "Pirate Bridge Party," *Idaho Daily Statesman,* 1 Apr 1917, 36: 12.

167   "Great Rush for New Magazine: Thousands of Applications for Free Copies: Remarkable Articles Everyone Should Read," *Observer* (London), 8 Apr 1917, 9 and *Times* (London), 17 Apr 1917.

168   *Pirate-Bridge d'après Aleister Crowley* (Paris: E. Cassegrain, 1918). *Traité du jeu de bridge* (n.p., 1918). With thanks to Clive Harper for details on these publications.

169   "Here's the Man Who Invented 'Pirate' Bridge: How Aleister Crowley, the Poet, Devised the Method by Which Players May Demonstrate Individual Skill and Judgment and Avoid Being Tied Up With Tiresome Partners," *The Washington Post,* 11 Mar 1917, 47.

170   *Confessions,* 825.

171   29 in Mary Anne Santos Newhall, "Uniform Bodies: Mass Movement and Modern Totalitarianism," *Dance Research Journal* 2002, 34(1): 27–50. This article contains a great deal of information on Laban and Wigman's portion of the program. See also Mary Anne Santos Newhall, *Mary Wigman: A Life in Dance* (London: Routledge, 2009). 25. For more on Monte Verità see Martin Burgess Green, *Mountain of Truth: The Counterculture Begins, Ascona, 1900–1920* (Hanover, NH: Tufts University, 1986). Information on Laban can be found in Suzanne Perrottet and Giorgio J. Wolfensberger, *Suzanne Perrottet, ein bewegtes Leben* (Bern: Benteli, 1989).

172   1920 United States Federal Census, Titusville, Brevard, Florida, 9A. 1930 United States Federal Census, Titusville, Brevard, Florida, 4B. Biographical Supplement, *Confessions,* unexpurgated ed., vol. 7.

173   New York passenger list, *Vaderland,* 23 Aug 1904, National Archives, Washington, D.C., lists the widow Emily Bertha Crowley visiting Joy, Kentucky.

174   *Confessions,* 824.

175   "Suffer the Children," unpublished.

176   *Confessions,* 826.

177   Social Security Death Index, 130-16-2933, New York.

178   Crowley described the studio as "a garret in an old half-decayed house on Fifth Avenue" (*Confessions,* 779); Engers's draft registration card gives his address as 900 West 70 Street (World War I Draft Registration Cards, Manhattan, NY, Draft Board 124).

179 "In Memoriam: John Yarker," *The Equinox* 1913, I(10): xxiii–vi.

180 Aleister Crowley, "The Disciples," *The Equinox* 1913, 1(10): 91–2.

181 Engers draft registration card, *op. cit.*

182 *Confessions*, 779.

183 "Have You Had Your Soul Painted Yet? The Newest After-the-War Art and Its Astonishing Translations of Life," *Atlanta Constitution*, 5 Jan 1919, D1. Fred Walter, "Dr. Engers, Ex Director, Views Art from Within," unidentified newspaper clipping c. Sep 1964, Special Collections Center, Bradley University Libraries (with thanks to William Breeze).

184 [Aleister Crowley], "Art and Clairvoyance," *International* 1917, 11(12): 379.

185 Article on Leon Engers-Kennedy, OS 5.a.4, Yorke Collection. See also Crowley's "Psychochromes," letter to Sigmund Freud, OS 5.b, Yorke Collection.

186 "Have you Had Your Soul Painted Yet?," *Atlanta Constitution*. "Random Impressions in Current Exhibitions," *New York Tribune*, 16 Feb 1919, A2.

187 Walter, "Dr. Engers, Ex Director," *op. cit.* This article does not date when Engers studied at the Bauhaus, but Feininger taught there between 1919–1932.

188 1930 U.S. Census, Manhattan, enumeration district 310, 1548: 12B. "Deaths," *New York Times*, 6 Feb 1959, 25.

189 *Confessions*, 779.

190 Walter, "Dr. Engers, Ex Director," *op. cit.*

191 "Gallery Shows, Museum Exhibits," *New York Times*, 8 Aug 1965, X11. "What's New in Art Shows," *New York Times*, 31 Oct 1965, X26.

192 Walter, "Dr. Engers, Ex Director," *op. cit.*

193 "Deaths," *Times* (London), 25 Apr 1917, 41461: 1.

194 Birth record, Q2 1867, GRO, Portsea Island, Hampshire: 2b: 408. 1871 UK Census, Portsea, Hampshire, RG10, piece 1127, 88: 7.

195 Her siblings' names and birth years are Joseph Patrick (1868), Elizabeth Catherine (1870), Martha Ann (1874) and Edward Charles (1877). 1881 UK Census, Portsea, Hampshire, RG11, piece 1130, 83: 4. Birth records, GRO, Portsea, Hampshire.

196 Mary Davies, *My Psychic Recollections* (London: the author, 1912), 12.

197 Marriage record, 22 Feb 1886, GRO, Parrish Registers, Portsea, Portsmouth and Southsea. 1881 UK Census, Portsea, Hampshire, RG11, piece 1146, 110: 47.

198 Birth records, GRO, Portsea, Hampshire. Death record, Q4 1892, GRO, Portsea, Hampshire, 2b: 296. Davies, *My Psychic Recollections*, 36–9.

199 1901 UK Census, Lewisham, London, RG13, piece 554, 125: 27.

200 Diogenes [Crowley], "Reviews," *The Equinox* 1912, I(8): 254. *The Theosophist*, Dec 1912, 470–1. *Atheneaum*, Apr 1912, 439.

201 W. Steff Langston to G. M. Cowie, 4 Sep 1916, Yorke Collection.

202 G. M. Cowie to AC, 18 Oct 1916, Yorke Collection.

203 Mary Davies to AC, 21 Apr 1917, Yorke Collection.

204 G. M. Cowie to AC, 20/22 Feb 1917, Yorke Collection.

205 G. M. Cowie to AC, 8 Mar 1917, New 4, Yorke Collection. See also: Cowie to Frank Bennett, 21 Nov 1917, New 92, Yorke Collection; newspaper articles in New 87, Yorke Collection; Warburg; Gilbert, "Baphomet and son"; and Inquire Within [Stoddart, C. M.] *Light Bearers of Darkness*. (Hawthorne, CA: Christian Book Club of America, 1930), 163.

206 "'M.M.M.' Mysteries: Order of the Temple of the Orient Raided," *Times* (London), 16 May 1917, 41479: 3. While this case was the only one where an underlying political motive was reported by the press, it was by no means the only arrest under the Vagrancy Act during this era. For other cases of arrests for fortune telling, see "Pretending to Tell Fortunes: Brisk Business in Chorlton-on-Medlock," *Manchester*

Guardian, 4 Jun 1915, 5. "'Fortune-Telling' in Ancoats: A Severe Sentence," *Manchester Guardian,* 31 Jan 1916, 12. "Fortune-Telling at Southport: Five Women Fined," *Manchester Guardian,* 20 Jul 1916, 10. "Fortune-Telling: An Indian's Plea for Leniency," *Manchester Guardian,* 19 Aug 1916, 9. "Fortune-Teller Fined: London Magistrate's Warning," *Manchester Guardian,* 30 Dec 1916, 4. "Asking the Spirits: Journalist and 'Psychic': Amusing Interview," *Observer* (London), 31 Dec 1916, 11. "More Fortune Telling," *Observer* (London), 4 Mar 1917, 8. "The General's Friend: Case against Alleged Fortune Teller Dismissed," *Observer* (London), 21 Apr 1918.

207 "Psychist fined: A Claim to Supernatural Qualities," *Times* (London), 23 May 1917, 41485: 3.

208 G. M. Cowie to AC, 28 Jul–2 Aug 1917, New 4, Yorke Collection.

209 G. M. Cowie to AC, 26 Jul (1917).

210 G. M. Cowie to AC, 28 Jul–2 Aug 1917.

211 G. M. Cowie to AC, 31 Dec 1917.

212 Mary Davies, "A Disavowal: To the Editor of the *Occult Review,*" *The Occult Review,* Sep 1917, 26: 176.

213 "King's Bench Division (Before Mr. Justice Darling, Mr. Justice Avory, and Mr. Justice Sankey): A Regent-Street Fortuneteller's Appeal: Davis v. Curry," *Times* (London), 26 Oct 1917, 41619: 2.

214 G. M. Cowie to AC, 22 Nov 1917. See also G. M. Cowie to AC, 31 Dec 1917.

215 G. M. Cowie to AC, 27 Dec 1917.

216 G. M. Cowie to AC, 6 Jan 1918.

217 Classified ad, *Times* (London), 30 Apr 1918, 41777: 14.

218 G. M. Cowie to AC, 25 Apr 1917. See also the letters dated 20 Feb 1917, and 12 Jul 1918, as well as Disposition of Boleskine, Foyers, Inverness shire, 5 May 1914. Scottish Records Office.

219 Frank X. O'Donnell, "In RE: Aleister Crowley."

Chapter Thirteen • Amalantrah

1   Nicholson and Lee were both, coincidentally, members of A. E. Waite's GD. See R. A. Gilbert, "The Masonic Career of A. E. Waite," *Ars Quatuor Coronatorum* 1986: 99; Gilbert, *Golden Dawn Companion,* 171, 173.

2   1917 (Oxford: Clarendon Press), 520–4.

3   The following articles appeared in the *International:* "The revival of magick" was serialized through the August through November, 1917, issues as follows: 11(8): 247–8 (Aug 1917), 11(9): 280–2 (Sep 1917), 11(10): 302–4 (Oct 1917) and 11(11): 332–3 (Nov 1917). "Cocaine," 11(10): 291–4 (Oct 1917). "The Ouija Board," 11(10): 319 (Oct 1917). "The Message of the Master Therion," 12(1): 26 (Jan 1918). "Geomancy," 12(1): 28–9 (Jan 1918). "Ecclesiae Gnosticae Catholicae Canon Missae," 12(3): 70–4 (Mar 1918).

4   *Confessions,* 781.

5   *Confessions,* 781.

6   1900 US Census, Oooee, Orange, Florida, registration disctrict 122, 10B. U.S. Passport Applications, 11 Apr 1921, National Archives, College Park, M.D. Roddie Minor's sisters were Waskie (b. 1880), Jessie (b. 1882) and Vee (b. 1890).

7   "Will Arrest Suffragettes: New York Police Officer Threatens and is Defied: Parade Will Be Formed into Funeral Procession, if Necessary, to Make It Legal," *Washington Post,* 16 Feb 1908, 12.

8   "Suffragists Did Not Parade: Only Six Women Marched up Broadway Sunday: Police Prohibited March: Crowd of Several Thousand Followed, Watching the Six Women, Who Are Clamoring for Woman's Rights," *Logansport Reporter,* 17 Feb 1908.

9 "She Wants to Vote," *Coshocton Daily Times,* 19 Feb 1908. "Alas! Poor Suffragettes: Feminine Clothes Threaten to Disrupt Their Ranks–A Row on for Monday," *New York Tribune,* 28 Mar 1908, 4.

10 Columbia University *Catalogue,* 1911, 403. *Catalogue of Officers and Graduates of Columbia University from the Foundation of King's College in 1754,* 16th ed. (New York: Columbia Univ., 1916), 884. Columbia University, *Catalogue and General Announcement 1911–1912,* series 12 (New York: Columbia Univ., Dec 1911) 2: 420.

11 Alumni Association of the College of Pharmacy of the City of New York, *Alumni Journal* (New York: Pharmaceutical Department of Columbia University), 19(1): 9. *Journal of the American Pharmaceutical Association* 1912, 1282. *Pacific Pharmacist* 1912, 134. Metta Lou Henderson, *American Woman Pharmacists: Contributions to the Profession,* 34. By 1926 she was president of the American Institute of Cosmetics and Chemistry, predicting that soon men and women alike would be wearing makeup. She remained in Manhattan for many years, living in the same apartment building as her sister Vee, who was working as a Registered Nurse. She eventually moved to Pocokoke, Maryland, where she married merchant marine engineer Robert Lee Warwick. Her husband predeceased her in 1963 and Roddie Minor Warwick died at age ninety-three at Bi-County Nursing Home on January 17, 1979. See "Is Day of Dandified Men Quietly Dawning? Half Million Males Now Use Cosmetics as Freely as Women and Claim They Are an Aid in Transacting Business," *Brooklyn Daily Eagle,* 1926. 1930 U.S. Census, Manhattan, New York, enumeration district 1188, page 1A. "Deaths and Funerals: Robert Lee Warwik," *Salisbury Times,* 28 Feb 1963. Obituary, *Accomac Eastern Shore News,* 25 Jan 1979 (with thanks to William Breeze).

12 Although he would try on several occasions to print the book, some setback or another always prevented him from seeing it in print. See Karl Germer to Philip Kaplan, 23 Jul 1961, Kaplan Papers.

13 *Confessions,* 833.

14 AL i.65.

15 Aimée Crocker Gouraud, *Moon-Madness and Other Fantasies* (New York: Broadway Pub. Co, 1910).

16 "Prepare To Be Startled—The Queen of Bohemia Is Here: But What New Sensation Can Mrs. Aimee Gouraud, the Woman of a Thousand Fads and Fancies, Possibly Have to Spring on a Public Which She Has Already Amazed in Such Countless Ways?" *Philadelphia Inquirer,* 4 Dec 1921.

17 Passport application, 10 Feb 1919, National Archives, College Park, MD.

18 Marriage record, Q2 1914, GRO, London, 1a: 1243.

19 *The Equinox* 1913, 1(10): 91–2.

20 Leah Hirsig to Norman Mudd, 12 Aug 1923, Yorke Collection.

21 "Samuel A. Jacobs, Designer of Books," *New York Times,* 17 Sep 1971, 46. "Fine American Bookmaking of 1930: The American Institute of Graphic Arts Holds its Ninth Annual Exhibiion," *New York Times,* 15 Feb 1931, 60.

22 AC to Montgomery Evans II, 22 Oct 1926, Evans Papers.

23 Gerald Bordman, *The Oxford Companion to American Theatre* (New York: Oxford Univ. Press, 1984), 656.

24 Bordman, *Oxford Companion,* 656.

25 David A. Jasen, *Tin Pan Alley: The Composers, The Songs, The Performers and Their Times: The Golden Age of American Popular Music from 1886 to 1956* (New York: D. I. Fine, 1989), 64.

26 Actress Mitzi Gaynor portrayed Eva Tanguay in *I Don't Care Girl* (1953).

27 Additional biographical information on Eva Tanguay came from: Ragan, *Who's Who in Hollywood, op cit.; Who Was Who in the Theatre: 1912-1976. A Biographical Dictionary of Actors,actresses, Directors, Playwrights, and Producers of the English-speaking Theatre* (Detroit: Gale Research, 1978); and Alice M. Robinson, *Notable Women in*

the American Theatre: A Biographical Dictionary (New York: Greenwood Press, 1989).

28   "Drama Be Damned," *International* 1918, 12(4): 127–8.

29   U.S. passport application, 6 Apr 1921, National Archives, College Park, MD. Passenger list, SS *Rochandeau*, 24 Sep 1921. Passenger list, SS *President Garfield*, 3 Oct 1923. The 1921 passenger list gives Roehling's marriage date as 17 Apr 1913, but the 1923 passenger list gives 17 Apr 1917. The latter is presumed to be a typo.

30   "Women Urge Wilson and Congress to Pass National Dry Law," *Chicago Daily Tribune,* 24 May 1917, 17.

31   "Ethical Culture," *Philadelphia Inquirer,* 9 Mar 1918, 178(68): 15. "News from Colleges," *Journal of the Association of Collegiate Alumnae,* Sep 1917–Jun 1918, 11: 536. In 1922, returning from a visit to Russia, she would address Le Cercle Français, and the Chicago Drama League on "The Russian Drama of Today." See "Women's Club Page," *Chicago Daily Tribune,* 5 Mar 1922, F5–6.

32   Diary, 20 Jun 1920.

33   According to Troxel, "The Map Service had started on an atlas of 14 maps of Central Asia. When we got to Inner and Outer Mongolia we had trouble even finding place names." She was already interested in Asian culture, had lived for a year in China, and had studied at the University of California and Harvard, so she worked nights at home to compile a ten-thousand-word dictionary that she presented to the Army. In those Cold War years, this was extremely valuable to the military, who printed the book and for her "scholarly achievement and unselfish patriotism" gave her the Exceptional Civilian Service Award, its highest civilian award. Asked how she managed to accomplish such a task, she remarked, "Really, it was simple." See "Army Gives Woman Top Civilian Award," *Washington Post,* 12 Jun 1953, 18. "Civilian Gets High Award for Mongolian Dictionary," *Schenectady New York Gazette,* 17 Jun 1953. Arthur Edson, "Mongolian Dictionary Given Army: Woman Employee of Map Service Wins Award for Her Work," *Hartford Courant,* 17 Jun 1953, 11C.

34   Elsa Lincke was born in Berlin on February 16, 1864, daughter of Carl Ernst Lincke. She married Samuel Lowensohn of Russia in New York City in 1886; he died in Chicago in 1901. She became a naturalized U.S. citizen on 18 Nov 1914. See New York County Supreme Court Naturaliation Petition, 18 Nov 1914, 169: 139. U.S. Passport Application, 14 Mar 1921, National Archives, College Park, MD. U.S. Passport Application, 9 Apr 1923, National Archives, College Park, MD.

35   *American Club Woman,* Oct 1916, 11: 58.

36   AC and Harvey Spencer Lewis (1883–1939) met in 1918. Prior to that point, Lewis had reviewed Crowley's edition of the *Goetia* in "Some Books NOT Recommended," *American Rosea Crucis,* Oct 1916, 22–4. In a letter dated July, 1918, Crowley offered Lewis recognition as a member of the Order of Illuminati, VII° in OTO, and a Magister Templi (letter sold at Sotheby's, 17 Dec 1996, catalogue LN6731, lot 344). Whether Lewis actually received this letter from Crowley has been the subject of debate. However, Crowley later wrote of Lewis, "I made him Honorary VII° O.T.O. in 1918 and he works under charters from Peregrinus [Reuss]." (AC to Roy Leffingwell, 19 Aug 1934, Yorke Collection.) Elsewhere, he refers to Lewis "whom I recognise as a member of the 95°, *not the 96°,* of the Rite of Mizraim; and VII°, *not X°,* of the O.T.O." as "an honorary member, not a full member" of OTO (AC to W.T. Smith, 3 Jan 1936, Yorke Collection).

37   *Confessions,* 791.

38   Asked during a pro-German lecture whether he supported Germany's invasion of Belgium and devastation of northern France, he shrugged and replied, "A lot of this talk about Belgium and France is Piffle." In dismissing Keasbey, the University of Texas board of regents stated, "for the best interests of the university Dr. Keasbey is removed from his position." See "Drop Peace Leader of Texas University: Dr. L. M. Keasbey Dismissed, Following Campaign Made along No Annexation Lines: Derided Belgian Charge: Organization of which He Is Moving Spirit Lays His Downfall to 'Financial Interests,'" *New York Times,* 21 Jul 1917, 11. "University of

Texas Discharges Pacifist: Removes Professor Keasbey, Who Organized Meeting Here," *New York Tribune,* 21 Jul 1917, 11.

39 *The Equinox* 1919: 3(1): 225–38.

40 *Confessions,* 871.

41 U.S. Passport Application, 11 Oct 1920, National Archives, College Park, MD. California Death Index, Los Angeles, 12 Jun 1987.

42 World War I service card, 1969052, Orlando, Florida.

43 AC to Roy Leffingwell, 11 Jul 1942, Yorke Collection.

44 *Confessions,* 840.

45 William Buehler Seabrook, from Chapter 4 of his serial for International Features Service, Inc, ca 1923. TS, New 18, Yorke Collection.

46 "Artist Paints Dead Souls but Refuses to be Classed with Futurists' School: Englishman Portrays Weird Spirits at His Studio in Greenwich Village," *Syracuse Herald,* 9 Mar 1910, 10.

47 Seabrook, ibid.

48 Mathers's obituary is in New 87, Yorke Collection. The letter is AC to James Branch Cabell, 17 Nov 1919, HRHRC.

49 As Ryerson recalled, "I remember that there were many times when I drove to the railroad station in a little cart, to get Julia Warde Howe from the station to take her to this school of philosophy." Howe (1819–1910) was an abolitionist and author of "The Battle Hymn of the Republic." See testimony of A. W. Ryerson, 9 Jan 1922, Universal Book Stores Bankruptcy, Case #4946, 8, National Archives, Chicago, IL.

50 Testimony of A. W. Ryerson, 9 Jan 1922, 8–9.

51 C. M. Burton, *The City of Detroit Michigan 1701–1922* (Detroit-Chicago: S.J. Clarke Publishing Company, 1922). U.S. passport application, 10 Oct 1892, National Archives, College Park, MD. Jefferson S. Conover, *Freemasonry in Michigan* (Coldwater, MI: Conover Engraving and Printing Co., 1897). Detroit Telephone Directory, 1919. Albert W. Ryerson, *The Ryerson Genealogy.* (Chicago: Privately printed for Edward C. Ryerson, 1916). "Weird 'O.T.O.' Cult Here Recalled by London Suit: Crowley, Its Sponsor, Fails in Libel Action: 'Love' Teachings Blazed into Prominence in 1923 in Young Mazie Ryerson's Case against Elderly Husband," *Detroit News,* 15 Apr 1934. "Black Magic once Detroit Cult: Lives Ruined Decades Ago by Sorcerer Aleister Crowley," *Detroit News,* 26 Jan 1958. "Aleister Crowley," *Detroit News,* 24 Oct 1967. *Confessions,* 842 et seq. Francis Dickie, "Aleister 'Black Magic' Crowley," *American Book Collector* 1961, 11(9): 34–7. Kaplan Papers. Robert Lund, private communication. Ken Spencer, private communication. C. S. Jones Papers catalogue, typewritten MS, private collection.

52 Membership record, Grand Lodge of Michigan. Testimony of Gordon W. Hill, 30 Dec 1921, 30–1. He appears as "dental student" in the 1920 U.S. Census, Detroit Ward 8, Wayne, MI, unumeration district 251, 4B.

53 Membership record, Grand Lodge of Michigan. Presbyterian Church in the U.S.A., *Minutes of the Synod of Michigan,* 1949, 11. 1920 U.S. Census, Detroit Ward 8, Wayne, MI, enumeration district 269: 8B.

54 Testimony of A. W. Ryerson, 23 Dec 1921, 4–5.

55 1920 U.S. Census, Detroit Ward 6, Wayne, MI, enumeration district 200, 10A.

56 Testimony of A. W. Ryerson, 23 Nov 1921, 12.

57 Testimony of W. A. Gibson, 30 Dec 1921, 5–7.

58 Testimony of A. W. Ryerson, 9 Jan 1922, 13.

59 Testimony of A. W. Ryerson, 9 Jan 1922, 1–2.

60 Testimony of W. A. Gibson, 30 Dec 1921, 17. Testimony of A. W. Ryerson, 9 Jan 1922, 1–2.

61 Passenger list, SS *Orduña,* 22 Aug 1917.

62 Spence, *Secret Agent 666,* 146.

63 *Confessions,* 754. Note that the lacuna given in the published version gives the name as H..d; however, the original manuscript has H..l.

64 PH:LF Crowley, Humanities Research Center. With thanks to William Breeze. However, another possibility is suggested by Crowley's marginalia to *Diary of a Drug Fiend,* where he identifies the "tall bronzed Englishman" (p. 128) as modeled "Mostly from Smart, English Vice-Consul in New York during the war."

65 AC to Arnold Krumm-Heller, 22 Jun 1930, Yorke Collection.

66 *Confessions,* 842.

67 AC to Krumm-Heller, *op. cit.*

68 "'Do Anything You Want to Do'—Their Religion," *New York American,* date unknown.

69 1920 U.S. Census, Detroit Ward 14, Wayne, MI, enumeration district 411, 3A.

70 Testimony of W. A. Gibson, 30 Dec 1921, 26–7.

71 Testimony of A. W. Ryerson, 9 Jan 1922, 3–4.

72 Frank T. Lodge, *Why Weepest Thou? Book to Offer Comfort to the Sorrowing, the author, a Physician and Attorney in Detroit, Was Inspired to Write* (Detroit: Frank T. Lodge, 1913).

73 *Confessions,* 842.

74 General examination of A.W. Ryerson, 8 Dec 1921, 10–1. General examination of A.W. Ryerson, 23 Dec 1921, 1, 8. Testimony of A.W. Ryerson, 9 Jan 1922, 9–10.

75 AC to Krumm-Heller, *op. cit.*

76 Quoted in Martin P. Starr, *The Unknown God: W. T. Smith and the Thelemites* (Chicago: Teitan Press, 2003), 92.

77 AC to C. S. Jones, 19 Feb 1919. CSJ Papers.

78 Quoted in *Detroit Times,* 10 Jan 1922.

79 AC to A. W. Ryerson, 6 Mar 1919, quoted in *Detroit Times,* 10 Jan 1922.

80 Aleister Crowley, *Olla: An Anthology of Sixty Years of Song* (London: OTO, 1946), 69.

81 Diary, 31 May and 2 Jun 1920.

82 Although it has been almost universally reported that "Marion (sic) Dockerill" is a pseudonym for Leah's sister Alma Hirsig Bliss, this is untrue: Anna Maria (Marian) Dockerill née Hirsig is a completely different person, *vide infra.*

83 *Confessions,* 791.

84 Leah Hirsig's siblings were Martha (1869–1950), Margaritha Rosa (1870–1961), Johannes (1872–1965), Friedrich (1873–1905), Gottlieb (1873–1922), Fanny Christina (b. 1874), Magdalena Alma (b. 1875), Andreas (1877–1877), and Anna Maria (or Marian) (b. 1878). [Familienregister der Gemeinde Amsoldingen, Zivilstandsamt Kreis Thun, Zivilstands- und Bürgerrechtsdienst des Kantons Bern, Amt für Migration und Personenstand. With thanks to Michela Megna.]

85 Passenger list, *St. Laurent,* Apr 1885. U.S. 1910 Census, Manhattan Ward 12, New York, New York, enumeration district 399, 1A. "Promotion Licenses Granted to Teachers in the Elementary Schools," *New York Times,* 12 May 1915, 19. U.S. Passport Application, 14 Oct 1919, National Archives, College Park, MD.

86 Although Leah Hirsig reportedly married Edward Jack Hammond in 1917, I have been unable to trace a record of this union. Indeed, Leah did not take his surname, her 1919 passport application lists her marital status as "single," and on that application she claims Hansi was her "nephew." Hans Hammond would go on to have four years of college, work as an actor, and enlist in the army during World War II. [U.S. World War II Army Enlistment Records 1938–1946, National Archives, College Park, MD. Social Security Death Index, 114-24-4532, New York.]

87 In *Equinox of the Gods,* Crowley refers to "Hans 'Carter' (or Hirsig)" (p. 127), and in his marginalia to *Diary of a Drug Fiend* notes that the "even smaller boy" on page

309 is based on "Hansi, natural son of Leah Hirsig and Edward Carter."

88 Samuel S. Carter married Fanny Cristina Hirsig in Pinellas, Florida, on 18 Mar 1918, four months after Hans was born.

89 "Poet-painter Who Studied Magic Visits Atlanta," unidentified newspaper clipping, Yorke Collection.

90 Marian Dockerill gives a different account of Leah's first meting with Crowley. One of Dockerill's former lovers wrote to her that she should not miss seeing Crowley, and arranged an invitation to one of Crowley's events. At this party, Leah and AC stared at each other for a while until Crowley came over and offered them wine. Dockerill, feeling unnerved, tried persuading her sister to leave; Hirsig, however, insisted on remaining, telling her sister to go home and that she would see her later. Although Dockerill left, Hirsig wound up staying the night along with several of Crowley's other lady friends. When Dockerill came the next morning to fetch her sister, Hirsig—knowing full well that Dockerill herself had engaged in quite a wild sex life—replied "Oh, don't protest, Marian! Have you thought your life a secret from *me?*" This and other details of Dockerill's account of their first meeting matches what Crowley described as their second meeting. See Marian Dockerill, *My Life in a Love Cult: A Warning to All Young Girls* (Dunellen, NJ: Better Publishing, 1928).

91 Robert Winthrop Chanler (1872–1930) was a New York painter, designer and muralist; Crowley's *Temperance: A Tract for the Times* (1939) contains the poem "Bob Chanler." For more, see "Bob Chanler," Biographical Notes, *Confessions* (unexpurgated edition), vol. 7.

92 French actress Madame Yorska was cofounder of the Theatre Français in New York; she appeared in America on Broadway (*All Star Gambol*, 1913, and *The Greatest Nation*, 1916) and in film (*Our Mutual Girl*, 1914, and *It Happened in Paris*, 1919). See "Who Is Madame Yorska?" *New York Tribune*, 3 Jun 1917, C3.

93 In hand-written notes on his artwork, Crowley wrote, "*Was This the Face That Launched a Thousand Ships?* No, but it kept me busy in Atlantic City and annoyed Helen Westley."

94 "Artist Paints Dead Souls but Refuses to be Classed with Futurists' School: Englishman Portrays Weird Spirits at His Studio in Greenwich Village," *Syracuse Herald*, 9 Mar 1910, 10. "You Agree with Artist, His Pictures Look Best with Your Eyes Closed: Aleister Crowley Paints Dead Souls as His Brush Wanders Undirected over Canvas," *Fort Wayne Journal-Gazette*, 10 Mar 1919, 5 and *Wilkes-Barre Times Leader*, 17 Mar 1919.

95 Seabrook, *op. cit.*

96 Jones's class flier and the *Equinox* prospectus are reproduced in Richard Kaczynski, *Panic in Detroit*, Blue Equinox Journal 2 (Troy, MI: Blue Equinox Oasis, 2006).

97 Charles S. Jones, "A Master of the Temple." *The Equinox* III(2). Forthcoming.

98 Testimony of Homer W. Adair, 20 Jan 1922, 3–4.

99 *Confessions*, 841.

100 AC to RC Newman, 24 Sep 1944, New 24, Yorke Collection.

101 AC to Mr. Ackland of EP Dutton & Co, n.d., New 4, Yorke Collection.

102 *New York Times Book Review*, 23 Nov 1919, 681–2. This portrait currently hangs in England's National Portrait Gallery.

103 Testimony of A. W. Ryerson, 9 Jan 1922, 15.

104 Kaczynski, *Panic in Detroit*, 12.

105 Hereward Carrington, "What Is the Best 'Psychical' Literature?" *Bookman: A Review of Books and Life*, Aug 1919, 49(6): 689. "Books Received," *Journal of the American Society for Psychical Research*, Jul 1919, 13(7): 384. Although Crowley and Carrington knew each other, the ASPR's journals and files contain no other references to Crowley (thanks to Jeff Twine, ASPR librarian, for checking). Since attendance at meetings was not logged, it is unknown what other association, if any, Crowley may have

had with the ASPR.

106 Hereward Carrington, "Men of Mystery: Aleister Crowley," *Fate,* Sep 1949, 2(3): 66–72.

107 *Confessions,* 683–4.

108 *Confessions,* 791. In the *Confessions,* Crowley mis-spells the name "Christiansen."

109 Carrington, "Men of Mystery," 72. Wilcox died on October 30, 1919, shortly before Crowley sailed for London.

110 Membership record, Grand Lodge of Michigan.

111 World War I draft registration card, National Archives, Washington, DC. 1910 and 1920 U.S. Census, Detroit Ward 1, Wayne, MI.

112 *Confessions,* 842–3.

113 C. S. Jones to F. T. Lodge, Apr 22, 1919, CSJ Papers.

114 *Confessions,* 842.

115 Testimony of A. W. Ryerson, 9 Jan 1922, 10.

116 *Detroit Free Press,* 21 Jan 1922.

117 Starr, *Unknown God,* 99.

118 *Detroit Free Press,* 14 Jan 1922.

119 His siblings were Tarrant (b. 1884), Edmond L. Jr. (b. 1891), Eleanor (b. 1893) and Edith (b. 1899). James Scarborough Sibley, *The Sibley Family in America 1629–1972.* (Midlothian, TX: privately printed, 1982). 1900 and 1910 U.S. Census, Bennington, VT. 1920 and 1930 US Census, Detroit, MI. Passport application, 20 May 1914, National Archives, College Park, MD. World War I draft registration card, Wayne County, MI, National Archives, Washington, D.C.

120 "Emperor Thanks American Surgeons," *New York Times,* 4 Oct 1914, 84.

121 *Confessions,* 768.

122 *Confessions,* 842–4.

123 Burton, *City of Detroit,* 4: 216–7.

124 World War I Draft Registration Card, National Archives, Washington, DC. Marriage record, Division Registrar Vital Statistics Records, Toronto, Canada. 1900, 1910, and 1920 U.S. Census, Detroit Ward 4, Wayne, MI. Membership record, Grand Lodge of Michigan.

125 Birth record, 5 Aug 1875, York, Ontario, Archives of Ontario, Toronto. 1910 and 1920 US Census, Detroit, Wayne, MI. World War I draft registration card, National Archives, Washington, D.C. U.S. Naturalization Indexes, 1794–1995.

126 Membership record, Grand Lodge of Michigan.

127 Pictures featuring Jane Wolfe (sometimes credited as Jane Wolf or Jane Wolff): *A Lad from Old Ireland* (1910); *The Stolen Invention* (1912); *Shannon of the Sixth* (1914); *The Invisible Power* (1914); *The Boer War* (1914); *The Majesty of the Law* (1915); *The Case of Becky* (1915); *Blackbirds* (1915); *The Immigrant* (1915); *Pudd'nhead Wilson* (1916); *The Blacklist* (1916); *The Thousand-Dollar Husband* (1916); *The Selfish Woman* (1916); *Each Pearl a Tear* (1916); *The Lash* (1916); *Unprotected* (1916); *The Plow Girl* (1916); *Castles for Two* (1917); *Unconquered* (1917); *The Crystal Gazer* (1917); *On the Level* (1917); *Rebecca of Sunnybrook Farm* (1917); *The Call of the East* (1917); *The Fair Barbarian* (1917); *A Petticoat Pilot* (1918); *Mile-a-Minute Kendall* (1918); *The Bravest Way* (1918); *The Firefly of France* (1918); *Less Than Kin* (1918); *The Cruise of the Make-Believes* (1918); *The Girl Who Came Back* (1918); *Under the Top* (1919); *The Poor Boob* (1919); *The Woman Next Door* (1919); *An Innocent Adventuress* (1919); *Men, Women, and Money* (1919); *A Very Good Young Man* (1919); *The Grim Game* (1919); *The Thirteenth Commandment* (1920); *The Six Best Cellars* (1920); *Why Change Your Wife?* (1920); *Thou Art the Man* (1920); *The Round-Up* (1920); *Behold My Wife* (1920); and *Under Strange Flags* (1937). See http://www.imdb.com/name/nm0938059.

128 Jane Wolfe's life is serialized in *In the Continuum,* a periodical published by the Col-

lege of Thelema. The biography was collected and published as volumes 10 and 11 of the journal *Red Flame* in 2003.

129 *AL* ii.19.

130 A. W. Ryerson to AC, 5 Jul 1919, quoted in *Detroit Free Press,* 21 Jan 1922.

131 In AC to Frank Bennett, 18 Dec 1920 (New 92, Yorke Collection), Crowley refers to Libri XII and DCCCLXXX. Neither of these correspond to known writings. DCCCLXXX is almost certainly DCCCLXXXVIII, *The Gospel According to St. Bernard Shaw,* for, in AC to Ben Stubbins, 13 Oct 1942 (Yorke Collection), Crowley writes "It is the bound set of proofs of Equinox Vol III No 2 which has a big supplement 'Jesus,' which has vanished."

132 The issue was actually printed by W. J. Hanson in New York, but the balance was never paid. Around 1928, the unbound sheets were finally destroyed. See Kaczynski, *Panic in Detroit,* 16.

133 William Seabrook, *Witchcraft: Its Power in the World Today* (New York: Harcourt, Brace & Co., 1940), 195–6.

134 AC to Roy Leffingwell, 23 Oct 1942, New 14, Yorke Collection.

135 *New York American,* 8 Jan 1923.

136 *Detroit Free Press,* 10 Jan 1922.

137 *Confessions,* 598.

138 Starr, *Unknown God,* 103.

139 Starr, *Unknown God,* 107.

140 *Detroit Free Press,* 10 Jan 1922.

141 Bankruptcy notice, *Detroit Legal News,* 26 Oct 1921.

142 *Detroit Free Press,* 13 Jan 1922.

143 Ibid.

144 "Do Anything You Want to Do" *op cit.*

145 *Detroit Free Press,* 14 Jan 1922.

146 *Detroit News,* 16 Jan 1922.

147 *Detroit News,* 13 Jan 1922.

148 "Cult Men Facing Arrest," *Detroit Times,* date unknown.

149 *Confessions,* 888.

150 *New York American,* 8 Jan 1923.

151 1930 U.S. Census, Militia District 1199, Brooks, GA, enumeration district 7: 17B. Death record, Orange, FL, Florida Department of Health Office of Vital Records. For additional details about Ryerson and the Universal Book Stores, see Kaczynski, *Panic in Detroit.*

152 James Branch Cabell, *Jurgen: A Comedy of Justice* (New York: R. M. McBride & Co, 1919), 154–6.

153 AC to James Cabell, undated telegram, item #7779–b, James Branch Cabell Papers, Collection M 214, James Branch Cabell Library, Virginia Commonwealth University. The second quote is from Crowley's review of *Jurgen* for *The Equinox* 1920, 3(3). Although this issue never appeared, the typescript survives as item #7779–b, Cabell Papers.

    Crowley had high hopes for Cabell, hoping to make a convert out of a great author. Crowley wrote to Cabell about the philosophy of Thelema and praised him in print, but, in the end, Cabell maintained his distance. Their extant correspondence includes: AC to Cabell, undated telegram, *op. cit.* AC to Cabell, 24 Oct 1919, Cabell Papers. Cabell to AC, 10 Nov 1919, Evans Papers. AC to Cabell, 17 Nov 1919, HRHRC. Cabell to AC, 26 Nov 1919, Evans Papers. AC to Cabell, 17 Sep 1922, HRHRC. "Memorandum re CCXX", ca 1923, HRHRC. AC to Cabell, 24 May 1942, HRHRC. Crowley's article in praise of Cabell, "Another note on Cabell" appeared in the *Reviewer* 1923, 3(11–12): 907–14. The relationship of these men is discussed in Roger Staples, "The Lance and the Veil," *Kalki* 1969, 4(1): 3–8.

Chapter Fourteen • The Abbey of Thelema

1   Quoted in Booth, *A Magick Life,* 355.

2   "Obituary: H. Batty Shaw, M.D., F.R.C.P., Consulting Physician, University Col-
      lege Hospital and the Brompton Hospital," *British Medical Journal,* 23 May 1936,
      1(3933): 1081. "Royal College of Physicians," *British Medical Journal,* 7 May 1898,
      1(1949): 1226. Bruce C. Berndt and Robert A. Rankin, *Ramanujan: Letters and
      Commentary* (Boston: American Mathematical Society, 1995), 154. R. A. Rankin,
      "Ramanujan as a Patient," *Proceedings of the Indian Academy of Science and Mathematical
      Sciences* 1984, 93(2–3): 79–100.

3   See, e.g., Robert H. Babcock, *Diseases of the Lungs; Designed to Be a Practical Presen-
      tation of the Subject for the Use of Students and Practitioners of Medicine* (London: D.
      Appleton and Co., 1907). "Heroin in Asthma," *Clinical Excerpts,* Mar 1905, 11(3):
      93. *Journal of the American Medical Association,* 15 Nov 1902.

4   John Shorter, "Humphrey Owen Jones, F.R.S. (1878–1912), Chemist and Moun-
      taineer," *Notes and Records of the Royal Society of London* 1979, 33(2): 261–77. Oscar
      Eckenstein, "Claws and Ice-Craft," *Climbers' Club Journal* 1912, 32–48. Oscar Eck-
      enstein, "The Tricouni Nail," *Climbers' Club Journal* 1914, 76–80. Geoffrey Win-
      throp Young (ed.), *Mountain Craft* (New York: Charles Scribner's Sons, 1920).

5   *John Bull,* 10 Jan 1920.

6   Passport application, 28 Feb 1919, National Archives, College Park, MD.

7   *Confessions,* 857.

8   AC to Jane Wolfe, 8 Jan 1920. Quoted in "Letters from Aleister Crowley to Jane
      Wolfe." *In the Continuum* 1981, 2(8): 28.

9   For a modern-day account of the villa with photos, see Richard T. Cole, *Thelema
      Revisited: In Search of Aleister Crowley* (n.p.: Orange Box Books, 2007).

10   Diary, 2 Apr 1920.

11   Quoted in many of the 11 Apr 1934 press reports of the so-called Black Magic Libel
      Case, such as the *Daily Telegraph* and *Yorkshire Post.* In 1921, Crowley's diary entry
      for this canonization reads:

> Gauguin literally torments me; I feel as if by my own choice of exile rather than
> toleration of the bourgeois, I am invoking him, and this painting of my house seems
> a sort of religious-magical rite, like the Egyptian embalmers', but of necromancy. I
> would he might come forth "his pleasure on the earth to do among the living."
>
> I gladly offer my body to his Manes, if he need a vehicle of flesh for new
> expression. I could never have done quite that for any other spirit—I have been
> faithful to my own Genius.
>
> It is maddening to think that I might have known him in the flesh; he died in
> 1903, May 8, eleven months before the First day of the Writing of the book of the
> Law. Just six months after I had met Rodin.
>
> I feel very specially that I should consecrate my house to him, not to Beardsley,
> a quite inferior type deriving from pifflers like Burne-Jones, and the over-elaborate
> school of Japanese, while he snivelled and recanted disgustingly when his health
> gave way.
>
> So, by the Power and Authority invested in Me, I Baphomet 729 ordain the
> insertion of the name of PAUL GAUGUIN among the More Memorable Saints in
> the Gnostic Mass.

12   W. Somerset Maugham, *The Moon and Sixpence* (New York: Vintage International,
      2000 [1919]), 185.

13   *Confessions,* 113.

14   Maugham, *Moon and Sixpence,* 267–8.

15   Diary, 20 Apr 1920.

16   Diary, 21 Apr 1920.

17   Diary, 18 Jun 1920.

18   Diary, 24 Jun 1920.

19   Aleister Crowley, *Leah Sublime*. (Montreal: 93 Publishing, 1976).

20   Diary, 22 Jun 1920.

21   Fuller, *Magical Dilemma*, 244.

22   For an examination of this approach of Crowley's to spirituality, see Richard Kaczynski, "Taboo and Transformation in the Works of Aleister Crowley" in Christopher Hyatt (ed.), *Rebels and Devils: The Psychology of Liberation* (Tempe, AZ: New Falcon, 1996).

23   Diary, 25 Jul 1920.

24   The paintings are described in an untitled essay on the Abbey of Thelema, p. 3, GARL. The quote is from "Paintings in the Chambre des Cauchemars," GARL.

25   Captain J. H. E. Townsend to J. F. C. Fuller, 19 Apr 1921, HRHRC.

26   Leah Hirsig's diary, 26 Sep 1924, Yorke Collection.

27   *Confessions*, 867.

28   Diary, 5 Nov 1920.

29   World War I recruitment card, National Archives, Washington, D.C. Magical record of C. F. Russell, courtesy of Martin P. Starr.

30   U.S. passport application, 11 Oct 1920, National Archives, College Park, MD.

31   Diary, 12 Dec 1920.

32   Jane Wolfe's diary, 31 Mar 1921, quoted in "Jane Wolfe: Hammer and anvil, Part II." *In the Continuum* 1981, 2(10): 38. A facsimile edition of Wolfe's Cefalù diaries has been published as Jane Wolfe, Aleister Crowley, and David Shoemaker, *Jane Wolfe: The Cefalu Diaries 1920–1923* (Sacramento: College of Thelema of Northern California, 2008).

33   Literally "to make his sausage inflate." C. F. Russell, *Znuz is Znees: Memoirs of a Magician* (privately printed, 1970), v. 2, 176.

34   "Jane Wolfe: Hammer and Anvil, Part II," *op. cit.*, 35.

35   The Butts family's collection of Blakes is now in the Tate Gallery, London.

36   AC to Gerald Yorke, 4 Dec 1928, Yorke Collection.

37   Douglas Goldring, *South Lodge: Reminiscences of Violet Hunt, Ford Madox Ford and the English Review Circle* (London: Constable & Co., 1943), 147.

38   Nathalie Blondel (ed.), *The Journals of Mary Butts* (New Haven: Yale Univ. Press, 2002), 179.

39   This was a variation on the kabbalistic cross—a GD formula where the sign of the cross is coupled with intoning the Hebrew words *Ateh Malkuth ve-Geburah ve-Gedulah le-Olam, Amen"* ("Thine is the kingdom, the power, and the glory unto the ages, amen"). Crowley instructed his students to insert the name of their holy guardian angel between the first two words. In Butts's case, he instructed her to use the word *Therion*. She evidently did not realize this was Crowley's magical name, although her diary notes that she recognized the word a deriving from the Greek θερῖοι (wild beast), and considered it interesting that she had pinned to her wall a post card reproduction of a Mycenaean vase depicting the ποτνια θεροϑ (mistress of the animals). See the diary of Mary Butts, 18 Mar 1921, Mary Butts Papers, Gen MSS 487, Box 2, folder 58, Beinecke Rare Book and Manuscript Library, Yale University, New Haven, CT.

40   Butts diary, 31 Mar 1921.

41   Nathalie Blondel, *Mary Butts: Scenes from the Life* (Kingston, NY: McPherson & Co., 1998), 99.

42   Butts diary, 14 Apr 1921.

43   18 May 1921 in Blondel, *Journals of Mary Butts*, 182.

44   Sybille Bedford, *Aldous Huxley: A Biography* (Alfred A. Knopf: New York, 1973),

147.

45 J. W. N. Sullivan, *An Attempt at Life* (London: G. Richards, 1917).

46 J. W. N. Sullivan's publications include: *Gallio, or the Tyranny of Science* (London: Kegan Paul, Trench, Trubner, 1920); *Atoms and Electrons* (London: Hodder and Stoughton Ltd, 1923); *Aspects of Science* (London: R. Cobden-Sanderson, 1923); *The History of Mathematics in Europe: From the Fall of Greek Science to the Rise of the Conception of Mathematical Rigour* (London: Oxford Univ. Press, 1925); *Three Men Discuss Relativity* (London: Collins, 1925); *Beethoven: His Spiritual Development* (London: J. Cape, 1927); *The Bases of Modern Science* (London: E. Benn, 1928); *Present-Day Astronomy* (London: G. Newnes, 1930); (and T. L. Poulton), *How Things Behave: A Child's Introduction to Physics* (London: Black, 1932); *The Physical Nature of the Universe* (London: V. Gollancz, ltd, 1932); *But for the Grace of God* (New York: A.A. Knopf, 1932); *The Limitations of Science* (London: Viking, 1933); *Contemporary Mind; Some Modern Answers* (London: H. Toulmin, 1934); (and Walter Grierson), *Outline of Modern Belief: Modern Science, Modern Thought, Religious Thought* (London: Newnes, 1935); *A Holiday Task* (London: Cape, 1936); *Science: A New Outline* (London: Nelson, 1937); (and Charles Singer), *Isaac Newton, 1642–1727* (London: Macmillan, 1938); and *Living Things* (Cambridge: Orthological Institute, 1938).

47 "J. W. N. Sullivan, 51, Writer on Science: British Essayist also Served as Book Reviewer—Interpreter of Relativity Dies in England," *New York Times,* 13 Aug 1937, 18. H. M. Tomlinson, "J. W. N. Sullivan: The Man and His Work," *Observer* (London), 15 Aug 1937, 9. "J. W. N. Sullivan," *Manchester Guardian,* 13 Aug 1937, 10. Crowley also penned an obituary of Sullivan, see "These Names Make News: Master of Maths," *Daily Express,* 14 Aug 1937, 6.

48 Sullivan, *Aspects of Science,* 94.

49 However, it should be pointed out that, during his time in Fontainbleau, he was also associated with Gurdjieff. See "Fontainbleau's High Priest and His Cult: They Have a Snug Retreat in the Famous Old French Forest, Where Dazzling Beauty and Oriental Luxuriousness Are Sharply in Contrast with Cloister-Like Cells, Coarse Food and Hard Labour with the Hands—Trying to Bridge the East and the West," *Atlanta Constitution,* 29 Apr 1923, H332.

50 Birth record, Q3 1896, GRO, East Preston, Sussex, 2b: 335.

51 *Confessions,* 869.

52 *Confessions,* 870.

53 Sullivan married Manooch in 1917. Sullivan depicts their relationship in his autobiographical novel, *But for the Grace of God,* calling himself "Julian" and her "Sybil." In his account, Sybil was an aspiring composer married to Greek scholar Richard Sauncers, who did not love her. They eventually divorced; although Julian desperately loved her, Sybil refused to marry him, preferring each of them to retain their "freedom." As Sullivan wrote, "I see now that this was a disastrous decision for both of us" (183). This may refer to her affair with Crowley and her subsequent affair with poet Vivian Locke-Ellis [see *1922–1923: The Collected Letters of Katherine Mansfield,* ed. Vincent O'Sullivan, Vol. 5. (Oxford: Oxford Univ. Press, 2008), 323]. After months of wandering about Paris, Florence, and the Riviera, Julian realized that her ex-husband was right: "Nothing could make Sybil happy. The central core of her was something I could never touch. I would never even be able to understand her" (193). She was later stricken with an unspecified illness and died.

54 AC to Heinrich Tränker, An. XX Sol 26° Capricorn (16–17 Jan 1924), Yorke Collection. See also AC to Henri Birven, 29 Dec 1929 and 3 Feb 1930, Yorke Collection.

55 Master Therion [Aleister Crowley], *Magick in Theory and Practice.* (Paris: Lecram Press, 1929), 301.

56 Seabrook, *Witchcraft,* 198. This retirement, with slightly different details, is also described in "Jane Wolfe: Hammer and anvil, Part III" *In the Continuum* 1981, 2(12): 18–29.

57 Blondel, *Mary Butts,* 100–1.

58 Mary Butts, *Ashe of Rings* (Paris: Three Mountain Press, 1925).

59 *Confessions,* 922.

60 Butts diary, 7 Aug 1921 and 16 Aug 1921.

61 Butts diary, 4 Aug 1921, Mary Butts Papers, box 3, volume 9.

62 Butts diary, 17 Aug 1921.

63 Diary quoted in John Symonds, "Introduction," in Aleister Crowley, *White Stains* (London: Duckworth, 1986), ix.

64 11 Jan 1922 in Blondel, *Journals of Mary Butts,* 193.

65 Blondel, *Mary Butts,* 106.

66 Russell, *Znuz is Znees,* 178–92. *Confessions,* 871–5.

67 Diary of C. F. Russell, courtesy of Martin P. Starr.

68 Frank Bennett, "Magical Record of Frater Progradior in a Retirement at Cefalue (sic) Sicily," Yorke Collection. An edition of this diary, with supplemental material and an introduction by Crowley scholar Keith Richmond, was published as Frank Bennett, *The Magical Record of Frater Progradior* (London: Neptune Press, 2004).

69 Nina Hamnett, *Laughing Torso.* (London: Constable & Co., 1932), 177.

70 Russell, *Znuz is Znees,* 192.

71 Passenger and crew list, RMS *Marama,* 28 Jan 1922.

72 Cefalùsions, GARL.

73 Liber Nike, 14 Feb 1922, Old A4, Yorke Collection.

74 Liber Nike, *op cit.*

75 Liber Nike Part II, Old A4, Yorke Collection.

76 Liber Nike Part III, Old A5, Yorke Collection.

77 AC to Norman Mudd, 18 Mar 1924, Yorke Collection.

78 For a recent biography, see Martha S. Vogeler, *Austin Harrison and the English Review* (Columbia: University of Missouri Press, 2008).

79 Crowley's 1922 contributions to the *English Review* from this period are: A New York Specialist, "The Great Drug Delusion," 163 (Jun): 571–6; A London Physician, "The Drug Panic," 164 (Jul): 65–70; A Gentile, "The Jewish Problem Re-Stated," 164 (Jul): 28–37; Prometheus, "Percy Bysshe Shelley," 164 (Jul): 16–21; A Past Grand Master, "The Crisis in Freemasonry," 165 (Aug): 127–34; Michael Fairfax, "Moon-Wane," 167 (Oct): 283–5; Michael Fairfax, "The Rock," 167 (Oct): 285–6; and Michael Fairfax, "To a New-Born Child," 167 (Oct): 287.

80 Crowley, "The Drug Panic," 65–6.

81 AC to Gerald Yorke, 1 Feb 1932, Yorke Collection.

82 Crowley, "Great Drug Delusion," 573.

83 Ibid., 576.

84 *AL* ii..22

85 115 in J. D. Beresford, "Fate: Confessions of an Author, Part IV," *Nash's and Pall Mall Magazine,* Jan 1926, 76(393): 37, 114–6.

86 J. D. Beresford, "A New Form of Matter," *Harper's,* May 1919. J. D. Beresford, "More New Facts in Psychical Research," *Harper's,* Mar 1922.

87 Marginalia from Crowley's personal copy of *Diary of a Drug Fiend,* Yorke Collection.

88 Crowley, *Diary of a Drug Fiend,* 246.

89 "Jane Burr" was the pen-name of Rosalind Mae Guggenheim Winslow, an American writer on women's rights, marriage, birth control and changing sexual attitudes. She was part of the Greenwich Village scene during the 1910s and 1920s. By this time, she had written *City Dust* (1917), *The Glorious Hope* (1918), *I Build My House* (1918), and *The Passionate Spectator* (1921).

Chapter Fifteen • *Adonis*

1   Marriage record, Q3 1922, GRO, Oxford, Oxfordshire, 3a: 2930.

2   See "More Lovedays in India," http://archiver.rootsweb.ancestry.com/th/read/
LOVEDAY/2003-03/1047503830 (accessed Feb 9 2009) and British army W.W.I
service record, regimental number 13732. Greene describes George Loveday as a
"very decent dependable fellow," a retired naval petty officer who ran messages for
Secretary of the Admiralty Sir Graham Greene [Raymond Greene, *Moments of Being:
The Random Recollections of Raymond Greene* (London: Heinemann, 1974), 20]. Ame-
lia Ann Lewendon was born on January 21, 1859, in Newington, Surrey; baptised
August 26, 1860, in Bermondsley; and married October 1, 1882, at St. Saviour,
Middlesex. (Birth record, GRO, Newington, Surrey, 1d: 197. Baptism record,
GRO, Saint Paul, Bermondsley, Register of Baptisms, P71/PAU. Marriage record,
1 Oct 1882, GRO Saint Saviour, Denmark Park, Middlesex, Southwark, P73/SAV.)

3   British army WWI service record. Amelia A. Loveday, UK incoming passenger list,
Caledonia, 2 Apr 1925.

4   British army WWI service record.

5   Greene, *Moments of Being,* 19–20. Anthony Powell, *To Keep the Ball Rolling: The
Memoirs of Anthony Powell* (London: Heinemann, 1976), 161. Andrew Jones, private
communication, 23 Apr 2008, and 24 Apr 2008.

6   W. B. Seabrook, "The Angel-Child Who 'Saw Hell' and Came Back: Heartfelt
Confessions of the London Art Model Who Turned Apache and Took Drugs, and
How a Genuine Vision Redeemed Her at the Brink," *Salt Lake City Tribune,* 19 Aug
1928, 3. Greene, *Moments of Being,* 19.

7   Raoul Loveday, "A Song of Town," *Oxford Poetry* 1922, 26.

8   Evelyn Waugh, *A Little Learning* (Chatham, Kent: W.J. Mackay & Co., 1964), 179.
See also Christine Berberich, *The Image of the English Gentleman in Twentieth Century
Literature: Englishness and Nostalgia* (Aldershot, Hampshire: Ashgate, 2007): "One of
the places where young men could openly live out their homoerotic fantasies was the
Hypocrites Club which achieved notoriety for its rowdy, drunken revels." (117).

In *Bright Young People: The Lost Generation of London's Jazz Age* (New York: Farrar, Straus and Giroux, 2009), D. J. Taylor quotes an early impression of the Hypocrites Club by the Oxford undergraduate magazine *Isis:* "The Hypocrites are perhaps
the most entertaining people in the University. They express their souls in terms of
shirts and gray flannel trousers and find outlet for their artistic ability on the walls of
their clubrooms. To talk to they are rather alarming. They have succeeded in picking
up the whole series of intellectual catch-phrases with which they proceed to dazzle
their friends and frighten their acquaintances: and they are the only people I have ever
met who have reduced rudeness to a fine art" (p. 30). However, according to Lebedoff, "The discussions of philosophy that had formerly made up the principal entertainment were supplanted by drunken and licentious revels" when Waugh and his
friends joined and transformed the club [David Lebedoff, *The Same Man: George
Orwell and Eveyln Waugh in Love and War* (New York: Random House, 2008), 29].

9   As Waugh noted upon his election to this post, "My predecessor in the office, Love-
day, had left the university suddenly to study black magic." Evelyn Waugh, *Brideshead
Revisited: The Sacred and Profane Memories of Captain Charles Ryder, a Novel* (Boston:
Little, Brown, 1945), 180.

10 Greene, *Moments of Being,* 20. Seabrook, "The Angel-Child Who 'Saw Hell.'"
Oxford University, *Oxford University Calendar* 1922, 469.

11 Seabrook, "The Angel-Child Who 'Saw Hell.'"

12 AC to Norman Mudd, 16 Mar 1923, Old D1, Yorke Collection.

13 In Seabrook, "The Angel-Child Who 'Saw Hell,' she gives her real name as Marlow
Golding. Her marriage certificates, however, give her name as "Betty M. Golding."

14 Seabrook, "The Angel-Child Who 'Saw Hell.'" Epstein's sculpture of Betty May
sold at Sotheby's on May 20, 2009.

15   According to U.K. marriage records, Betty M. Golding married Miles L. Atkinson
      at St. Marylebone in summer, 1914; George D. K. Waldron at St. Martin during
      autumn, 1916; and Frederick C. Loveday at Oxford in 1922. GRO, Q3 1914, St.
      Marylebone, London, 1a: 1623; Q4 1916, St. Martin, London, 1a: 1268; Q3 1922,
      Oxford, Oxfordshire, 3a: 2930.

16   Marie Attree to John Symonds, 12 Jan 1952, New 96, Yorke Collection.

17   Seabrook, "The Angel-Child Who 'Saw Hell.'"

18   Betty May, *Tiger-Woman: My Story* (London: Duckworth, 1929).

19   Stephensen, *Legend of Aleister Crowley,* 146–7.

20   *Times Literary Supplement* 1087: 749 (16 Nov 1922); *New York Times Book Review* 29
      Jul 1923, 18. Additional review clippings may be found in New 87, Yorke Collec-
      tion, and Stephensen, *Legend of Aleister Crowley,* 133 et seq.

21   *Sunday Express,* 26 Nov 1922, 1,7.

22   Her entry 7 Aug 1921 reads, "Leah—apparently—if the Beast's word is worth any-
      thing, had sexual union with the goat before he was killed." Butts papers, Yale.

23   Both John Symonds and Francis King present Butt's account as accurate, even
      though it is at variance with Crowley's diary as quoted above. Yorke maintained the
      story was untrue, and such was the view of biographer Susan Roberts (see *Magical
      Link* Vol 1 No. 8) and myself. While the ritual was certainly attempted, it did not
      unfold in the way that Butts describes.

24   Frank Vernon, "Books We'd Like to Burn," *John Bull* 28 Apr 1923, 18.

25   "Life in Wild Parts of Earth Pursued by British Writer," *Fresno Bee,* 14 Jul 1923, 2C.

26   A. Kemplen to AC, 2 Apr 1924, pasted into Crowley's 1924, diary. In its brief his-
      tory, Éditions Kemplen produced about a dozen titles, all between 1923 and 1924.

27   Symonds, *Shadow Realm,* 319.

28   Raoul Loveday to his parents, undated, New 92, Yorke Collection.

29   Betty May to Mr. and Mrs. Loveday, undated, New 92, Yorke Collection.

30   Raoul's description of the Abbey of Thelema, New 92, Yorke Collection.

31   Seabrook, "The Angel-Child Who 'Saw Hell.'"

32   Raoul Loveday to his parents, 11 Feb 1923, New 92, Yorke Collection.

33   "Foreign Office, January 1, 1912," *London Gazette,* 19 Jan 1912, 444. Great Britain
      Foreign Office, *The Foreign Office List and Diplomatic and Consular Year Book* (Lon-
      don, 1925), 483. Death record, GRO, Paddington, London, 1a: 27.

34   Spence, *Secret Agent 666,* 184.

35   Starr, "Aleister Crowley: Freemason!"

36   Reginald Gambier McBean (sic), *A Complete History of the Ancient and Primitive Rite
      from Its Establishment down to the Present Time, together with Translations of Original
      Manuscripts and Illustrated,* http://www.scribd.com/doc/7120414/McBean-Official
      -History-of-the-Ancient-and-Primitive-Rite (accessed Jan 3 2010), 40. Italy's polit-
      ical situation forced the Rite to go dormant again in 1925.

37   *The Equinox* 1913 1(10): 76–9.

38   Christopher Marlowe, *The Tragical History of Doctor Faustus,* act 1, scene 1, line 112.

39   Betty May to AC, Feb 1923, Old EE1, Yorke Collection.

40   Seabrook, "The Angel-Child Who 'Saw Hell.'"

41   Crowley conceded that a wild cat had caused some damage at the Abbey, but stressed
      that he certainly never sacrificed it. Neither was he a hater of cats, for Yorke states
      that, in later years, Crowley kept one as a pet. In a letter to Roger Staples dated Sep-
      tember 25, 1963, Yorke wrote, "Symonds is wholly incorrect about the death of
      Loveday and the sacrificed cat at Cefalù. He would follow the newspaper accounts
      of the day which were mostly fabrication by Betty May." However, on November
      3, 1963, Yorke conceded to Staples (private collection), "The cat was indeed sacri-
      ficed. It had been making a nuisance of itself by keeping the Cefalù inhabitants

awake at nights. So AC used it for a blood sacrifice—a thing he rarely did. I only know of it, one goat, two pigeons and a few sparrows … and once a toad ritually crucified. They chloroformed it, but did not use quite enough chloroform. Loveday made a bosh of cutting its throat and it crawled out of the consecrated circle. Technically this broke the circle and let undesirable elements in. But it had nothing to do with Raoul's death, which was due to typhoid or dysentery."

42 *John Bull,* 14 Apr 1923 and 17 Mar 1923.

43 *John Bull,* 28 Apr 1923.

44 UK incoming passenger list, *Balmoral Castle,* 13 Dec 1920.

45 New York passenger list, *Imperator,* 18 Jan 1921.

46 UK incoming passenger list, *Carmania,* 7 Feb 1921.

47 Norman Mudd to Leo Marquard, 10–12 Feb 1921, BC 587, Leo Marquard Papers, University of Cape Town.

48 Biographical information on Mudd is drawn from Ninette Shumway to Frank Bennett, Apr 26, 1923, New 92, Yorke Collection, and Mudd's own autobiographical statement in New 116, Yorke Collection.

49 Greene, *Moments of Being,* 21.

50 Spence, *Secret Agent 666,* 188, reports that Rome's Central State Archive has a dossier on Crowley, containing a 13 Apr 1923 expulsion order from the Ministry of Internal Affairs which cites Crowley's "obscene and perverted" sexual activities, including polygamy, as justification. He had until May 1 to leave; the other residents, however, were free to remain.

Chapter Sixteen • Eccentrics in Exile

1 Diary, 16 May 1923.

2 *Sunday Express,* 6 May 1923.

3 AC to Ninette Shumway, 27 May 1923, Old D1, Yorke Collection.

4 AC to Norman Mudd, 13 Jun 1923, Yorke Collection.

5 Ninette Shumway to Leah Hirsig, 15 Sep 1923, New 116, Yorke Collection.

6 Diary, 15 Apr 1924.

7 AC to Louis Wilkinson, 8 Jul 1946, Wilkinson Collection.

8 Aleister Crowley, *Songs for Italy: "Parturiunt Montes—Nascitur Ridiculus Mus"—Solini* (London: n.p., 1923).

9 AC to Norman Mudd, Sun 5° Leo (ca Jul 28), 1923, D1, Yorke Collection.

10 *Register of Rhodes Scholars, 1903–1945* (London: Oxford University, 1950), 54. Death record, GRO, Northampton, Northamptonshire, 3b: 46s.

11 UK Incoming Passenger List, *Kenilworth Castle,* 3 Oct 1921.

12 Millennial Conference on Number Theory and Michael A. Bennett, *Number Theory for the Millennium* (Natick, MA: A. K. Peters, 2002), v. 3, 197–9.

13 Marriage record, GRO, Oxford, Oxfordshire, 3a: 2475. *Register of Rhodes Scholars,* 54.

14 Saayman's publications include: Henry L. Brose and E. H. Saayman, "The Atomic Diameters of Hydrogen and the Inert Gases with respect to Electrons of Very Low Velocity," *Nature,* 13 Sep 1930, 400–1; H. L. Bröse and E. H. Saayman, "Über Querschnittsmessungen an Nichtedelgasmolekülen durch langsame Elektronen," *Annalen der Physik,* 5(7): 797–852; H. L. Brose and E. H. Saayman, "LXXXI. A note on Heisenberg's relation," *Philosophical Magazine* 1931, Series 7, 11 (72): 980–6; E. H. Saayman and T. L. MacDonald, "Notes on the Teaching of Science in Adult Classes," *Tutors' Bulletin of Adult Education,* Oct 1932.

15 Aleister Crowley, "The Genius of Mr. James Joyce," *New Pearson's,* Jul 1923, 52–3.

16 Diary, 9 Aug 1923. See also Norman Mudd to Leah Hirsig, 28 May 1923, New 116, Yorke Collection.

17 Norman Mudd to Marion Clark, n.d., Old DD6/New 116, Yorke Collection. For Crowley's description, see *Magick without Tears*, 95–6.

18 Diary, 27 Sep 1923.

19 Diary, 27 Oct 1923.

20 Details of this account are drawn from Leah Hirsig, *Three Chapters in My Life*, Aleister Crowley Papers, Syracuse.

21 Mudd's diary, Yorke Collection. See also Norman Mudd to AC, 11 Oct 1923, New 116, Yorke Collection..

22 *AL* ii.58

23 Norman Mudd to AC, 31 Oct 1923. New 116, Yorke Collection.

24 AC to Norman Mudd, 31 Oct 1923. New 116, Yorke Collection.

25 In addition to Crowley's debate with Mudd, another biographical trigger for this text is arguably Crowley's childhood experience of schisms within the Plymouth Brethren over differences in Biblical interpretation. This informs—but in no way invalidates—the short comment's spiritual significance in establishing *The Book of the Law* as a spiritual text that no one can interpret for another.

26 The *Gayatri Mantra,* one of the oldest Vedic hymns, is "Om bhur bhuvah svah tat savitur varenyam bhargo devasya dhimahi dhiyo yo nah prachodayat." This translates as "May the Supreme Divine Being stimulate our intellect so that we may realise the Supreme Truth."

27 18 Nov 1923. New 116, Yorke Collection.

28 Ninette Shumway to Norman Mudd, Sunday (n.d.), Nov 1923. New 116, Yorke Collection.

29 AC to Montgomery Evans II, 26 Dec 1923, Evans Papers.

30 Ninette Shumway to Norman Mudd, 2 Dec 1923, New 116, Yorke Collection.

31 Leah Hirsig to Blanche Conn, 17 Feb 1924, New 24, Yorke Collection.

32 James Moore, *Gurdjieff and Mansfield* (Routledge & Kegan Paul, 1980), 3.

33 Symonds, *Shadow Realm,* 288fn.

34 Nott, *Teachings of Gurdjieff,* 121–2.

35 Suster, *Legacy of the Beast,* 93.

36 Webb, *Harmonious Circle,* 314–5.

37 Ninette Shumway to AC, 15 Feb 1924, New 116, Yorke Collection

38 Ninette Shumway to AC, 22 Feb 1924, New 116, Yorke Collection

39 Memorandum on the Fox of the Balkans, from Crowley's 20 Oct 1924 diary. MON: 13, OTO Archives.

40 Diary, 4 Mar 1924. *Liber AL* I: 42–3.

41 AC to Norman Mudd, n.d. (ca Mar 1924), Yorke Collection.

42 Diary, 19 Mar 1924.

43 "The Master Therion: A Biographical Note," *The Equinox* 1986, 3(10): 16–7.

44 Diary, 24 Feb 1924. This quote references *Liber AL* i.44: "For pure will, unassuaged of purpose, delivered from the lust of result, is every way perfect."

45 Magical Record of the Scarlet Woman, 1 Apr 1924, Yorke Collection.

46 A long-established firm, they were located at 3 King William St. E.C., London.

47 Holograph note on a letter from Holman Hunt to AC, 7 Jan 1924, Yorke Collection.

48 Norman Mudd to Montgomery Evans II, 27 Jun 1924, Evans Papers.

49 Quoted in Larry Rohter, "Mystical Visions of Argentine Artist," *New York Times,* 27 Jul 2005.

50 Diary, 15 May 1924.

51 Diary, 16 May 1924.

52   Quoted in Álvaro Abós, *Xul Solar: Pintor del Misterio* (Buenos Aires: Sudamericana, 2004), 107.

53   For more on Solar, see: Abós, *Xul Solar*. Mario H. Gradowczyk, *Alejandro Xul Solar* (Buenos Aires: Ediciones ALBA, 1996). Fermín Fèvre, *Xul Solar: Tesoros de la pintura argentina* (Buenos Aires: Editorial El Ateneo, 2000). The first American exhibition of his works was held in 2006; see Patricia C. Johnson, "Xul Solar Exhibit Sheds Light on an Artist ahead of His Time," *Houston Chronicle,* 27 Jan 2006. In 1961, Solar would paint Crowley's portrait as *Muy mago Krowley Alistör*.

54   Reproduced in Crowley's FBI file, obtained under the Freedom of Information Act.

55   These extracts, in order of appearance, are from: Bertrand Russell to Norman Mudd, 29 May 1924, Old E21, Yorke Collection; AC to Montgomery Evans II, 13 Sep 1924, Evans Papers; Emma Goldman to Norman Mudd, quoted in Symonds, *Shadow Realm,* 367; Philip Heseltine to Norman Mudd, n.d. (1924), Old E21, Yorke Collection; Otto Kahn to Norman Mudd, 5 Aug 1924, Old E21, Yorke Collection; Norman Mudd to AC, 5 Apr 1924, New 5, Yorke Collection; Letter to Norman Mudd from his parents, quoted in Symonds, *Shadow Realm,* 375.

56   Ninette Shumway to Leah Hirsig, 15 Oct 1924. New 116, Yorke Collection.

57   AC to Montgomery Evans II, 19 Nov 1924, Evans Papers.

58   Leah Hirsig to Montgomery Evans II, 6 Aug 1924. Evans Papers. See also AC to Norman Mudd, 6 Aug 1924, New 116, Yorke Collection.

59   AC to Gerald Yorke, 16 Mar 1928, 4 Apr 1928, and 25 Dec 1928, Yorke Collection, respectively.

60   Leah Hirsig to Montgomery Evans II, 11–12 Sep 1924, Evans Papers, respectively.

61   AC to Montgomery Evans II, 12 Sep 1924, Evans Papers.

62   "Visitor is Noted Miniature Artist," *St. Petersburg Times,* 8 Aug 1925, 5: 3.

63   Her watercolor "The White Elephant" is at the Met, while her miniature of "Miss Georgette Bickley" is at the Smithsonian. See http://www.metmuseum.org/works_of_art/collection_database/all/objectview.aspx?OID=20016752 and http://americanart.si.edu/collections/search/artwork/?id=2187 (accessed Dec 14 2009).

64   1920 U.S. Census, Bronx Assembly District 4, Bronx, NY, district 237, 3B. U.S. passport application 28 Jun 1924, National Archives, College Park, MD.

65   UK incoming passenger list, *Minnekahda,* 12 Jul 1924.

66   New York passenger list, *Nieuw Amsterdam,* 4 Oct 1924.

67   "Visitor is Noted Miniature Artist."

68   There is some question about her exact date of birth. She has two passport applications, a supporting letter from her great aunt, and an entry on a 1925 passenger list giving 6 Sep 1892. Another passenger list has it 10 Sep 1892, while a third gives 6 Sep 1873. U.S. passport application, 29 Jul 1924, National Archives, College Park, MD. New York passenger list, SS *France,* 6 May 1922. New York passenger list, S S *France,* 19 May 1923. New York passenger list, S. S. Republic, 12 Oct 1925.

69   Leah Hirsig, Three Chapters of My Life, GARL.

70   AC to Montgomery Evans II, 29 Sep 1924, Evans Papers.

71   26 Sep 1924, Three Chapters of My Life. The line "He and I are One, nay are None" is a wordplay on *Liber AL* i.27, "O Nuit, continuous one of Heaven, let it be ever thus; that men speak not of Thee as One but as None; and let them speak not of thee at all, since thou art continuous!"

72   26 Sep 1924, Three Chapters of My Life.

73   28 Sep 1924, Three Chapters of My Life.

74   *AL* iii.43.

75   *AL* i.16

76   Leah Hirsig to Montgomery Evans II, 30 Nov 1924, Evans Papers.

77   10 Oct 1924, Three Chapters of My Life.

78 Ninette Shumway to Leah Hirsig, 9 Nov 1924, New 116, Yorke Collection.

79 Ninette Shumway to Leah Hirsig, 17 Nov 1924, New 116, Yorke Collection.

80 AC to Norman Mudd, 18 Feb 1925, Old D1, Yorke Collection.

81 Published in German in 1925, and in English in 1938.

82 Diary, 24 Apr 1925.

83 Leah Hirsig to Norman Mudd, 24 Oct 1924, Three Chapters of My Life.

84 Leah Hirsig's diary, Apr 1925, Yorke Collection.

85 Leah Hirsig to Norman Mudd, quoted in Symonds, *Shadow Realm,* 402.

86 AC to Heinrich Tränker, An. XX Sun 26° Capricorn (c. 19 Jan 1924), Yorke Collection.

87 AC to C. S. Jones, An. XXI, Sol in Capricorn (Jan 1924), Yorke Collection.

88 Germer to Heinrich Tränker, 6 Jan 1954, OTO Archives. As O.H.O., Crowley took the magical motto Phoenix. His pseudonym of Comte de Fénix for *The Scientific Solution to the Problem of Government* (London: privately printed, c. 1937) is likely an allusion to this motto.

89 Otto Barth had published an occult magazine called *Lotusblätter* ca 1923–1924, which served the Lotus Society he had founded with Heinrich Tränker to promote the teachings of Franz Hartmann. From 1927–1930, he would also produce the alchemical newspaper *Alchemistische Blätter.* He was also proprietor of the publishing house Otto Wilhelm Barth Verlag. During the first and second World Wars, Major General Otto Barth (1891–1963) served the German army, but I have been unable to confirm whether this is the same person.

90 Albin Grau is portrayed by Udo Kier in the 2001 release *Shadow of the Vampire* about the making of this classic horror film. The filmmakers were spooked to discover that Grau's group, Fraternitas Saturni, shared its name with their production company, Saturn Films.

91 Quoted in Grant, *Magical Revival,* 155.

92 Mudd to Jane Wolfe, 13 Sep 1927. Quoted in "Jane Wolfe: Tunis and France." *In the Continuum* 1983, 3(3): 38.

93 AC to Roy Leffingwell, n.d., New 14, Yorke Collection.

Chapter Seventeen • The French Connection

1 Arthur Mizener, *The Saddest Story: A Biography of Ford Madox Ford* (New York: World Publishing Co., 1971), 208. Carlos Baker, *Ernest Hemingway: A Life Story* (New York: Charles Scribner's Sons, 1969), 539–40. Jeffrey Meyers, *Hemingway: A Biography* (New York: Harper & Row, 1985), 131–2. Matthew J. Bruccoli and Margaret M. Duggan, *Correspondence of F. Scott Fitzgerald* (New York: Random House, 1980), 193–6. The circumstances of Crowley and Hemingway's meeting form the amusing story "Ford Madox Ford and the Devil's Disciple." Ernest Hemingway, *A Moveable Feast* (New York: Charles Scribner's Sons, 1964), 79–88.

2 Thomas Edward Neil Driberg was studying classics at Oxford at this time, but left in 1927 without taking a degree. In the ensuing years, he would join the Communist Party as an MI5 spy, write for the *Daily Express,* be elected to Parliament in 1941, become the Labour Party whip in 1945, and be made Baron Bradwell shortly before his death. Given his career choices, Driberg concealed from the public two facts about himself: his homosexuality, and his early association with Crowley.

3 AC to Montgomery Evans II, 6 Oct 1926 and 18 Oct 1926, Evans Papers, respectively.

4 AC to Montgomery Evans II, 18 Oct 1926, Evans Papers.

5 AC to Montgomery Evans II, 22 Oct 1926, Evans Papers. In 1906, Leadbeater was accused of pederasty after it was discovered that he had been encouraging young boys to masturbate. He resigned in a cloud of controversy to save the Theosophical Society from any embarrassment, but to Annie Besant, he explained that he had dis-

cussed masturbation, amongst many other topics, as something completely natural in order to help the boys avoid feelings of shame. Leadbeater was readmitted in 1908, shortly after Besant succeeded Henry Steel Olcott as president of the Theosophical Society. The charges resurfaced again with regard to Krishnamurti around 1912, resulting in further scandal. The matter is treated at length in King, *Sexuality, Magic and Perversion.*

6   AC to Unknown Recipient, 1 Mar 1926, HRHRC.

7   Yarker's contributions include "Guild Free Masonry and the Critics Criticised," *Co-Mason* 1910, 2: 62–3; "The System of the Worshipful Society of Free Masons," *Co-Mason* 1910, 2: 109–16; "The Relationship of Freemasonry to the Collegia of Rome," *Co-Mason* 1911, 3: 163–7; and "The Ancient York Rite," *Co-Mason* 1913, 5: 7–10. His obituary appeared as "In Memoriam: Very Illustrious Brother John Yarker, VII° (Guild); 33° S.R.; 97° A.A.P.R.," *Co-Mason* 1913, 5: 65–71.

8   See Starr, *Aleister Crowley: Freemason!*

9   AC to C. S. Jones, 19 Feb 1919, C.S. Jones Papers.

10   Kaczynski, *Panic in Detroit,* 7. Further details regarding Crowley's plans regarding *The Voice of the Silence* and the Theosophical Society are also presented there.

11   Dorothy Olsen to Montgomery Evans II, 27 Jan 1926, Evans Papers.

12   93 is the numerical value of *thelema* (will), *agape* (love), Aiwaz, etc. 418 is the value of Abrahadabra, Ra Hoor, the Hebrew letter *Cheth,* etc. Finally, 2,542 is the numerical value of *thelema* spelled "in full" i.e., the value of the words theta (*th*), epsilon (*e*), lambda (*l*), eta (*e*), mu (*m*) and alpha (*a*).

13   Leah Hirsig to AC, 22 Aug 1927, New 116, Yorke Collection.

14   Karl Germer to Philip Kaplan, 16 Mar 1958, Kaplan Papers.

15   Jane Wolfe's diary, 18 Aug 1926. Quoted in "Jane Wolfe: Tunis and France." *In the Continuum* 1983, 3(3): 33.

16   Diary, 2 Jan 1927.

17   Described in Crowley's 1926–1927 diary at HRHRC.

18   Diary, 6 Feb 1927.

19   Quoted in *In the Continuum* 1983, 3(3): 36.

20   New York passenger list, *Majestic,* 12 Dec 1922. Record 15381, 30 Oct 1925, Naturalization Records of the U.S. District Court for the Southern District of California, Central Division (Los Angeles), 1887–1940, National Archives, Washington, D.C.

21   AC to W. T. Smith, Sep 1927, New 15, Yorke Collection.

22   Charles Mosley, *Burke's Peerage, Baronetage & Knightage,* 107th ed. (Wilmington, DE: Burke's Peerage, 2003).

23   Cricket Page, http://cricketarchive.com/Archive/Players/34/34149/34149.html (accessed Dec 15 2009).

24   Henry Green, *Loving, A Novel* (London: Hogarth Press, 1945). "100 Best English-Language Novels from 1923 to 2005," http://www.time.com/time/2005/100books/0,24459,loving_living_party_going,00.html (accessed Dec 15 2009).

25   AC to Gerald Yorke, 20 Nov 1928, New 115, Yorke Collection.

26   AC to Gerald Yorke, 23 Mar 1928, New 115, Yorke Collection.

27   Gerald Yorke to AC, 20 Mar 1928, New 116, Yorke Collection.

28   AC to WT Smith, 4 May 1928, New 15, Yorke Collection.

29   The numerical value of Babalon. B (2) + A (1) + B (2) + A (1) + L (30) + O (70) + N (50).

30   AC to WT Smith, *op cit.*

31   AC to WT Smith, 6 Jun 1928, New 15, Yorke Collection.

32   Gerald Yorke to AC, 14 Aug 1928, New 116, Yorke Collection.

33   New York passenger list, *Chicago,* 7 Nov 1923. New York passenger list, *Europa,* 11

Dec 1931. UK passenger list, *Annie Johnson,* 7 Oct 1933.

34 Carl V. de Hundt, Internet Movie Database, http://www.imdb.com/name/ nm0212007/ (accessed Dec 15 2009). The last film, *Jeremias,* was produced in Germany and relased in the U.S. under the name *The Fall of Jerusalem.*

35 Examples of Hunt's journalistic output around the time Crowley hired him include: "Why America's Models Have had Enough of Paris," *Washington Post,* 4 Oct 1925, SM5. "The Penitent Burglar of the Beautiful French Actress," *Atlanta Constitution,* 18 Oct 1925, F10. "Not a Penny for Pretty 'Zeff': Paris Stage Star's Claim for a Fortune in Alimony from Her American Husband Thrown Out of Court when Judge and Jury Saw What a 'Walking Art Gallery' She Was," *Washington Post,* 1 Nov 1925, SM5. "Almost Killed by Duke Who Now Woos Her," *Atlanta Constitution,* 10 Jan 1926, E6. "Danced as Never Before to Save Her Lover's Life," *Atlanta Constitution,* 17 Jan 1926, E10. "What Really Happened at the Mysterious 'Assassins' Bar,'"*Atlanta Constitution,* 7 Mar 1926, E6. "Should Women Strive to Look Like Men?" *Washington Post,* 18 Apr 1926, SM1. "Latest Lovely Victim of Paris Dope Ring," *Atlanta Constitution,* 23 May 1926, F6. "How the Love Pirate Trapped His Silly Victims," *Atlanta Constitution,* 27 Jun 1926, F6. "Secrets of Life in a Persian Harem Revealed," *Washington Post,* 26 Dec 1926, SM1. "Paris Traps for the 'Easy Marks,'" *Washington Post,* 27 May 1928, SM4. "Reveals Rivaling Ancient Orgies," *Washington Post,* 30 Sep 1928, SM7.

36 Carl de Vidal Hunt, "Film Mother Stoned in House of Mystics Tells of Attack," *Charleston Gazette,* 3 Jun 1928.

37 Diary, 25 Jul 1928.

38 Birth record, GRO, Mile End Old Town London, Middlesex, 1c: 420. New York passenger list, S.S. Celtic, 15 Aug 1921. Gerald Suster, *Crowley's Apprentice: The Life and Ideas of Israel Regardie* (York Beach, ME: Weiser, 1990). Dr. Israel Regardie, http://www.sria.org/israelregardie.htm (accessed Dec 15 2009).

39 AC to Gerald Yorke, 18 Nov 1928, New 115, Yorke Collection.

40 AC to W. T. Smith, 16 Dec 1928, New 15, Yorke Collection.

41 Diary, 19 Nov 1928.

42 Lindsay, Jack. 1982. *Life Rarely Tells: An Autobiography in Three Volumes.* New York: Penguin Books, 672.

43 Diary, 14 Nov 1928.

44 Diary, 23 Nov 1928.

45 AC to Gerald Yorke, 28 Nov 1928, Yorke Collection.

46 C. de Vidal Hunt to Gerald Yorke, 26 Nov 1928, Yorke Collection.

47 AC to Gerald Yorke, 5 Nov 1928, New 115, Yorke Collection.

48 AC to Henri Birven, 8 Oct 1929, New 24, Warburg. This is confirmed in Marlow, *Seven Friends,* 48–9.

49 AC to Gerald Yorke, 21 or 22 Nov 1928, New 115, Yorke Collection.

50 Yorke's annotation on AC to Gerald Yorke, 20 Dec 1928, Yorke Collection.

51 AC to Gerald Yorke, 13 Jan 1929, New 115, Yorke Collection.

52 Gerald Yorke to AC, n.d., New 116, Yorke Collection.

53 Lola Zaza Crowley to Gerald Yorke, Yorke Collection.

54 Marriage record, 9 Jun 1934, GRO, Paddington, Middlesex. Death record, 9 Mar 1990, GRO, Reading, Berkshire.

55 AC to Gerald Yorke, 5 Feb 1929, New 115, Yorke Collection.

56 AC to Gerald Yorke, 13 Jan 1929, New 115, Yorke Collection.

57 AC to Gerald Yorke, 19 Jan 1929, Yorke Collection.

58 AC to Karl Germer, 9 Jan 1930, Old D8, Yorke Collection.

59 See AC to Gerald Yorke, 18 Jan 1929, New 115, Yorke Collection.

60   The registry index of the Foreign and Commonwealth Office summarizes the British Embassy's response to Crowley's request: "[T]he Embassy are unable to intervene with the French authorities on his behalf. Has ascertained that Mr. Crowley has been asked to leave French territory exclusively on moral grounds. Proposes therefore to take no action on his behalf." Quoted in Spence, *Secret Agent 666*, 198.

61   Diary, 16 Mar 1929.

62   Diary, 18 Apr 1929.

63   *Reynolds Illustrated Newspaper*, 21 Apr 1929.

64   *John Bull*, 27 Apr 1929.

65   AC to Gerald Yorke, 1 Jun 1929, New 115, Yorke Collection.

66   "Lieut-Col. J. F. C. Carter," *Times* (London), 17 Jul 1944, 49910: 6. Death record, GRO, Tavistock, Devonshire, 5b: 349.

67   *Daily Express*, 9 Jul 1929.

68   Diary, 10 and 12 Oct 1929.

69   AC to Karl Germer, 7 Nov 1929, Old D8, Yorke Collection.

70   *Aberdeen Press*, 28 Oct 1929.

71   *New Statesman*, 4 Nov 1929.

72   *New Age*, 7 Nov 1929.

Chapter Eighteen • Beast Bites Back

1   Knox was raised an Anglican and attended Eton and Balliol College, Oxford, on a classics scholarship. He became a fellow of Trinity College, Oxford, in 1910, and was ordained in 1912, taking the post of Trinity's chaplain. In 1917, he left the college when he converted to Roman Catholicism, being ordained into that church in 1918. He wrote several books about the issues that led to this spiritual journey, e.g., *Some Loose Stones* (1913), *Reunion All Round* (1914), *Apologia* (1917), *A Spiritual Aeneid* (1918), and *The Belief of Catholics* (1927). He was Roman Catholic chaplain at the University of Oxford from 1926 to 1939. He also wrote detective stories, compiling the rules for the genre in 1929 into a decalogue of ten commandments.

2   Hugh Speaight was the brother of actor and writer Robert Speaight (1904–1976), and puppeteer and theatre historian George Victor Speaight (1914–2005). For Hugh Speaight, see A. J. Ayer, *Part of My Life* (London: Collins, 1977), 95.

3   Hugh Speaight to AC, 30 Jan 1930, Box Y2143, Stephensen Papers.

4   Hugh Speaight, *Period: Being Seven Studies Followed by an Open Letter to the Author of "Bees from an Undergraduate Bonnet"* (Oxford: Basil Blackwell, 1929). Quoted in "Books of the Day," *Manchester Guardian*, 23 Dec 1929, 5.

5   AC to PR Stephensen, 1 Feb 1930, Box Y2143, Stephensen Papers.

6   *Birmingham Evening Dispatch* 3 Feb 1930.

7   *The New Statesman*, 19 Jul 1952, 8(379): 80. Anne Jackson Fremantle, *Three-Cornered Heart* (New York: Viking Press, 1971), 280.

8   As soon as he could, Yorke paid Cora £25 a quarter until her death, when he and Germer settled the matter; they probably wrote the balance off.

9   Grace Winifred Pailthorpe, *What We Put in Prison and in Preventive and Rescue Homes* (London: Williams & Norgate, 1932). Although Pailthrope studied medicine and served as a surgeon during World War I, she became a psychoanalyst and opened a practice in 1922. After publication of her book, she would establish the world's first institution for the treatment of delinquency, with vice presidents including luminaries like Freud, Jung, Adler. In 1935, she would also begin the study of automatic drawing and painting. See Penelope Rosemont, *Surrealist Women: An International Anthology* (Austin: University of Texas Press, 1998), 105–12.

10   Crowley's writings appeared in issues 2, 3, 4, 6 and 7 in 1930, and issues 1, 2, 5, 6

and 7 in 1931.

11 New York passenger lists from 1924–1931 show visits from Hanni Jaeger of Bernau, born c. 1910, coming into the United States as a student heading for Santa Barbara, CA. In 1924, she arrived with her mother Martha (age forty-one), and her sisters Kaethe (eighteen) and Else (fifteen). In 1928, she was a "returning resident alien," age eighteen, traveling alone. She departed Hamburg for America yet again on November 22, 1931, age twenty-one. New York passenger lists. SS *Deutschland,* 4 Aug 1924; SS *Cleveland,* 4 Dec 1928; SS *St. Louis,* 3 Dec 1931. While the travel dates fit, this is not a positive identification.

12 Diary, 29 Apr 1930.

13 P. R. Stephensen to AC, 3 May 1930, Box Y2143, Stephensen Papers..

14 Diary, 13 Jun 1930.

15 From a TS in the Stephensen Papers.

16 Victor Neuburg, "The Legend of Aleister Crowley: A Fair Plea for Fair Play," *Free-thinker,* 24 Aug 1930.

17 Diary, 31 Jul 1930.

18 AC to Max Schneider, 15 Feb 1943, Yorke Collection.

19 AC to Israel Regardie, n.d., Yorke Collection.

20 Gerald Yorke to Montgomery Evans II, n.d., Kaplan Papers.

21 AC to Herbert Gorman, 30 Aug 1930, MS 9040, Clifton Waller Barrett Library of American Literature, Special Collections, University of Virginia Library.

22 Quoted on p. 380 of Edouard Roditi, "Fernando Pessoa: Outsider among English Poets," *Literary Review* 1963, 6(3): 372–85.

23 French, "So much the worse."

24 AC to Marie Crowley, 20 Sep 1930, New 117, Yorke Collection.

25 AC to Francis Israel Regardie, 17 Oct 1930, New 117, Yorke Collection.

26 Gerald Yorke to AC, 21 Sep 1930, New 116, Yorke Collection.

27 Gerald Yorke to AC, 26 Sep 1930, New 116, Yorke Collection.

28 Gerald Yorke, draft (never sent), 1930, Yorke Collection.

29 Regardie closed the account with a £3 payment to himself in August, 1931, but it is unknown how he used the money.

30 After Crowley died, Yorke bought all these things back from Kerman for £100. Kerman was born in 1905 to poor Jewish immigrants from Odessa. He attended Cheltenham College and, while still in his twenties, set up a one-man law firm named "Forsyte and Kerman"—an homage to Nobel literature laureate John Galsworthy's "Forsyte Saga"— specializing in divorces. "Endowed with good looks and charm," he is remembered for his willingness "to turn his hand to anything," as attested to by his interests as a bridge player, horse racer, property speculator, and restaurant owner. Stephen Aris, "Obituary: Isidore Kerman," *The Independent,* 21 Aug 1998.

31 AC to Gerald Yorke, 3 Dec 1930, New 115, Yorke Collection.

32 Diary, 2 Nov 1930.

33 Diary, 26 Dec 1930.

34 Symonds, *Shadow Realm,* 505.

35 See note 11 above.

36 Gerald Yorke to AC, n.d., New 117, Yorke Collection.

37 Francis Israel Regardie to AC, n.d., New 117, Yorke Collection.

38 Marie Crowley to Gerald Yorke, 28 Feb 1931, New 117, Yorke Collection.

39 Colonel Carter to Gerald Yorke, 31 Mar 1931, New 117, Yorke Collection.

40 Col Carter to AC, 21 Oct 1930, Old EE2, Yorke Collection.

41 Originally a banker, Nierendorf started in the art trade in Cologne in 1920 and later

promoted the German Expressionists in Berlin. In 1936 he moved to America and opened another modern art gallery in New York, from which several pieces were acquired by the new Guggenheim Foundation. After World War II he returned to Germany to help the American military return works of art to their rightful owners. After his death, the Guggenheim Museum purchased his estate, acquiring not only his gallery's inventory but also his personal collection.

42 AC to Louis Wilkinson, 7 Feb 1931, Wilkincon Collection, Humanities Research Center.

43 Diary, 12 Jun 1931.

44 Diary, 12 Aug 1931.

45 Diary, 29 Aug 1931.

46 Karl Nierendorf, "Aleister Crowley: The Ultimate Outsider" in Hymenaeus Beta, Martin P. Starr and Karl Nierendrof, *An Old Master: The Art of Aleister Crowley* (London: October Gallery, Apr 7–18, 1998), 29–31.

47 However, the "Aleister Crowley Timeline" at LAShTAL.com asserts "He even sells one painting!" http://www.lashtal.com/wiki/Aleister_Crowley_Timeline (accessed Aug 24 2009).

48 Diary, 21 Oct 1931.

49 AC to Gerald Yorke, 24 Dec 1931, New 115, Yorke Collection.

50 Diary, 26 Oct 1931. See also AC to Gerald Yorke, 17 Nov 1931, New 115, Yorke Collection, wherein Crowley confirms she had a miscarriage.

51 Diary, 6 Dec 1931.

52 AC to Gerald Yorke, 24 Dec 1931, New 115, Yorke Collection. See also the letters of 12 Dec and n.d. for more.

53 Diary, 7 Dec 1931.

54 This comes from a popular bit of German erotic verse:

> *Nach dem Essen sollst Du rauchen,*
> *Oder eine Frau gebrauchen.*
> *Hast Du beides nicht zur Hand,*
> *Bohr ein Loch und fick die Wand!*
> ("After the meal, you should smoke
> Or use a woman.
> If you don't have both handy,
> Bore a hole and fuck the wall!")

A variant of the two lines Billie quotes replaces *"eine Frau gebrauchen"* (use a woman) with *"eine Frau missbrauchen"* (abuse a woman). Billie's version changes *"eine Frau"* ("a woman") to *"deine Frau"* ("your woman" or "your wife").

55 Diary, 31 Dec 1931.

56 AC to Gerald Yorke, 26 Jan 1932, Yorke Collection.

57 Roger Deacon, *A History of the British Secret Service.* (London: Frederick Muller, 1969). Also see AC to Gerald Yorke, 26 Jan 1932, New 115, Yorke Collection. Yorke's handwritten note identifies Colonel Carter as Crowley's employer, and states that the £50 Yorke asked Hamilton to give to Crowley that January was a loan— not payment from Colonel Carter, as Hamilton himself later came to believe. See Gerald Hamilton, *The Way It Was with Me* (London: Leslie Frewin, 1969), 56–7.

58 Diary, 27 Feb 1932.

59 AC to Gerald Yorke, 24 Aug 1931, Yorke Collection. Yorke's hand-written annotation to the same, Yorke Collection.

60 AC to Gerald Yorke, n.d., New 115, Yorke Collection.

61 Italian immigrants Nicola Sacco and Bartolomeo Vanzetti were arrested in 1920 and charged with a payroll robbery and murder. A controversial political trial ensued, where the men were convicted on circumstantial evidence and executed on August 23, 1927.

62 AC to Gerald Yorke, 20 May 1932, New 115, Yorke Collection.

63 Yorke's handwritten note to Crowley's diary, 27 May 1932.

64 Gerald Yorke to AC, n.d.. New 116, Yorke Collection.

65 Gerald Yorke to AC, 16 Jun 1932, New 116, Yorke Collection.

66 Richard Lane, "Portrait of a Yorkshire Yogi," *The Bedside Lilliput* (London: Hulton Press, 1950), 414–9.

67 Cannon's works include: *The Pathology of Beriberi* (London: Royal Society of Tropical Medicine and Hygiene, 1929); *Hypnotism* (London: Heinemann, 1932); (and Edmund Duncan Tranchell Hayes), *The Principles and Practice of Psychiatry* (London: W. Heinemann, 1932); *Hypnotism, Suggestion and Faith-Healing* (London: W. Heinemann, 1932); *The Invisible Influence; A Story of the Mystic Orient with Great Truths Which Can Never Die* (London: Rider & Co, 1934); *Powers that Be* (London: Mott, 1934); (and Edmund Duncan Tranchell Hayes and G. H. Monrad-Krohn), *The Principles and Practice of Neurology* (London: Heinemann, 1934); *Sleeping through Space, Revealing the Amazing Secrets of How to Get What You Want and Keep Well* (Woodthorpe: Nottingham, Walcot, 1938); and *The Shadow of Destiny* (London: Rider, 1947).

68 Diary, 5 Jul 1932.

69 Hamnett, *Laughing Torso*, 173–4.

70 Diary, 7 Sep 1932.

71 AC to Gerald Yorke, 6 Jun 1944, New 115, Yorke Collection.

72 At the time of her death, she had hosted over six hundred luncheons and attended most of them. "Obituary: Christina Foyle," *The Independent,* 11 Jun 1999.

73 "The Philosophy of Magick," Foyle's Archives.

74 Diary, 15 Sep 1932.

75 Diary, 22 Sep 1932.

76 Diary, 5 Oct 1932.

77 Diary, 24 Mar 1933.

78 AC to Gerald Yorke, 17 Jun 1935, New 115, Yorke Collection.

79 Law Report. *Daily Telegraph,* 11 May 1933.

80 These experiments are recounted in Aleister Crowley, *Amrita: Essays in Magical Rejuvenation,* ed. Martin P. Starr (King's Beach, CA: Thelema Publications, 1990). The quote is from Crowley's diary, 8 Feb 1933.

81 Diary, 27 Feb 1933.

82 Quoted in Grant, *Magical Revival,* 5. Similar entries also appear in Crowley's diary, on 4, 5, and 9 Jun 1933.

83 Quoted in Clive Harper, "'He Makes Black Magic as Tame as a Kids' Party': An Afterword to the *Sunday Dispatch* Articles." *Behutet,* spring 2009, 41: 4–5. Ian Coster was born in New Zealand and worked as a reporter for the Auckalnd *Sun*; after the paper went under he moved to England in April 1929. He was hired as a writer for *Nash's Magazine,* and would later marry its proprietor, Martha Harris. He evidently had an interest in the occult, having asked psychic researcher Harry Price to arrange a séance to contact the spirit of Arthur Conan Doyle and also having written for *Nash's* an article on "Black Magic as Practised in London at the Present Day." After two years with *Nash's*, he moved onto London's *Sunday Dispatch,* where he claims to have written his articles on Crowley's behalf. In later years, he would become a columnist for the *Daily Mail* and *Evening Standard* and author of the memoir *Friends in Aspic* (1939). See also UK Incoming Passenger List, 24 Apr 1929; *New Zealand Railways Magazine,* May 1933, 8(1): 19 (http://www.nzetc.org/tm/scholarly/tei-Gov08 _01Rail-t1-body-d19-d1.html, accessed Apr 20 2010); Margaret MacPherson, "New Zealanders in Fleet Street: Maoriland's Distinguished Sons and Daughters," *New Zealand Railways Magazine,* Apr 1935, 10(1): 27 (http://www.nzetc.org/tm/ scholarly/tei-Gov10_01Rail-t1-body-d7.html, accessed Apr 20 2010); "Nicolas Coster Soaps It Up," *Rome News-Tribune,* 7 Sep 1984, 28; "'Modern Prodigal Sun'

Flying Home," *Sydney Morning Herald,* 18 Aug 1947, 5; John Miles, "Feast of Friendship," *Sydney Morning Herald,* 3 Feb 1940, 12.

84 These are reprinted in P. R. Stephensen and Stephen J. King, *The Legend of Aleister Crowley,* 3rd. rev. and exp. ed. (Enmore, N.S.W.: Helios Books, 2007).

85 Ethel Mannin, *Confessions and Impressions* (London: Jarrolds, 1930), 203.

86 The story of W. T. Smith and the other California Thelemites is a story unto itself, and is recounted excellently in Starr, *The Unknown God.*

87 W. T. Smith to AC, 1933, New 15, Yorke Collection.

88 1930 U.S. Census, Los Angeles, CA, district 54, 29.0. Death record, 5 Jan 1945, State Vital Statistics Unit, Department of Heatlh, Harris County, TX. "Singer to Be Heard," *Los Angeles Times,* 25 Jan 1931). "Historic Shawls Attract Clubwomen," *Los Angeles Times,* 11 Feb 1935, A6. "Dancing 'neath Sycamores," *Los Angeles Times,* 11 Sep 1937, A6. "Pen Women Will Hear Author Talk," *Los Angeles Times,* 11 Oct 1940, A10. Katherine von Blon, "Little Theaters," *Los Angeles Times,* 16 Apr 1939, C4. "'Wuthering Heights' Due on Warner Screens Today," *Los Angeles Times,* 20 Apr 1939, A15.

89 Starr, *Unknown God,* 181; q.v. for more on Kahl's life and untimely death.

90 Aimee Semple McPherson (1890–1944) was a well-known Los Angeles evangelist whose popular radio program pioneered faith healing over the airwaves.

91 Regina Kahl to AC, 13 Aug 1933, New 15, Yorke Collection.

92 AC to W. T. Smith, n.d., New 15, Yorke Collection.

93 Diary, 3 Oct 1933.

94 Symonds, *Shadow Realm,* 491.

Chapter Nineteen • The Black Magic Libel Case

1 This trial is exhaustively documented in Kaczynski, *Perdurabo Outtakes,* which reproduces a much longer version of this chapter, along with transcriptions of dozens of newspaper articles on the case. The trial has also been documented in the following sources: Joseph Dean, *Hatred, Ridicule or Contempt: A Book of Libel Cases* (London: Constable & Co., 1953), 190–201; *Daily Herald,* 14 Apr 1934; *Daily Mail,* 14 Apr 1934; *Daily Mirror,* 13–14 Apr 1934; *Daily Telegraph,* 11–14 Apr 1934; *Evening News,* 13 Apr 1934; *Evening Standard,* 13 Apr 1934; *Evening Star,* 11 Apr 1934; *Times* (London), 11–14 Apr 1934; *Manchester Guardian,* 12–14 Apr 1934; *Sunday Express,* 14 Apr 1934; *Yorkshire Post,* 11 Apr 1934; and *Yorkshire Telegraph,* 13 Apr 1934, plus numerous unidentified news clippings from the Yorke Collection.

2 John Percy Eddy, *The Law of Distress: Being a Guide to the Law Relating to Distress for Rent, Distress for Rates, Distress for Tithe Rent Charge* (London: Sweet & Maxwell, 1934). "Obituary: Mr. J. P. Eddy: A Life Committed to the Law," *Times* (London), 15 Jul 1975, 59448: 16.

3 Crowley, *Spirit of Solitude,* 184–5.

4 Charles J. S. Harper to C. Somerford, 28 Sep 1932, Nina Hamnett Papers. Michael Sadleir to C. J. S. Harper, 3 Nov 1932, Nina Hamnett Papers.

5 C. J. S. Haper to Michael Sadleir, 1 Feb 1933, Nina Hamnett Papers.

6 Unidentified newsclipping, New 87, Yorke Collection.

7 Birth record, Q2 1915, GRO, Penzance, Cornwall, 5c: 365.

Chapter Twenty • The War of the Roses (and the Battle of the Book)

1 Gallop was born in Bermondsey around 1893, earned his LLB from London University, and was called to the bar at age twenty-one. He served in the Great War, after

which he recevied his B.C.L. from Balliol, Oxford University. He died in his residential chambers in Essex Court at age seventy-four. W. L., "Mr. Constantine Gallop," *Times* (London), 21 Apr 1967, 56921: 10. 1901 UK Census, Islington, Highbury, RG13, piece 203, 120: 26. Death record, 1967, GRO, London, 5d: 337.

2   "Aleister Crowley Sent for Trial: Mystery of Woman's Letters: Model in the Box," *News Chronicle,* 29 Jun 1934. "Aleister Crowley on His Trial: Counsel Questions 'Betty May': Book Issued As Her Story," *Morning Post,* 29 Jun 1934. "Mr. E. A. Crowley in Court on Charge of Receiving Letters," *Daily Mail,* 29 Jun 1934). "Charge of Receiving Letters: Mr. Aleister Crowley on Trial," *Times* (London), 25 Jul 1934). "Charge of Receiving Letters: Mr. Aleister Crowley Bound Over," *Times* (London), 26 Jul 1934.

3   "Law Report, Nov. 8, Court Of Appeals: Mr. E. A. Crowley's Appeal Fails: Crowley v. Constable and Co Limited, and Others before Lord Justice Greer, Lord Justice Slesser, and Lord Justice Roche," *Times* (London), 9 Nov 1934.

4   "An Author's Affairs," *Times* (London), 9 Feb 1935. See also the following unidentified press clippings from the Yorke Collection: "Aleister Crowley and 'Boycott of His Works': Complains that Public Cannot Get His Books" and "Puts £2,000 Value on His Life-Story." See also the 1935 correspondence of Charles J. S. Harper and Otto Kyllmann, Nina Hamnett Papers, especially Harper's notes on the bankruptcy hearing, included in C. J. S. Harper to O. Kyllmann, 1 May 1935.

5   This article is reprinted in Stephensen and King, *Legend of Aleister Crowley,* 3rd ed.

6   Hermann Rauschning, *Hitler Speaks: A Series of Political Conversations with Adolf Hitler on His Real Aims* (London : T. Butterworth, 1939).

7   W. T. Smith to AC, 3 Jun 1935, New 15, Yorke Collection, Warburg.

8   Russell's articles for *The Occult Digest* are: "Viens" (May 1930); "Mikrokosmogonia" (Jul 1930); "Black and White" (Jul 1930); "The Black Raven" (Aug 1930); "Cosmic Dawn" (Oct 1930); "The First Matter" (Oct 1930); "The Chymical Marriage" (Nov 1930); "The Mead of Odhraerir" (Dec 1930); "Silence: The Lightning Path" (May 1931); "The Universe Depends on You" (Nov 1931); "The Ritual of the Flaming Star..." (Nov 1932); "The Oracle of the Sun" (Sep 1933).

9   AC to W. T. Smith, 15 Aug 1935, New 15, Yorke Collection.

10   Paschal Beverly Randolph, *Eulis! The History of Love* (Toledo, OH: Randolph Publishing Co., 1874).

11   Reuben Swinburne Clymer, *The Rosicrucian Fraternity in America: Authentic and Spurious Organizations as Considered and Dealt with in Treatises Originally Published and Issued in Monograph Form* (Quakertown, PA: The Rosicrucian Foundation, 1935).

12   Ancient and Mystical Order Rosae Crucis, *White Book "D": Audi Alteram Partem (Hear the Other Side)* (San Jose, CA: Rosicrucian Press, 1935).

13   AC to F. M. Spann, 13 Jan 1936, Evans Papers.

14   AC to Arnold Krumm-Heller, 28 Dec 1936, New 117, Yorke Collection.

15   AC to Montgomery Evans II, 28 Jan 1936, Evans Papers. This text also appears in AC to Louis Wilkinson, 8 Aug 1939, Wilkinson Collection; and in AC to W. T. Smith, 28 Jan 1936, New 15, Yorke Collection.

16   AC to W. T. Smith, 23 Jan 1936, New 15, Yorke Collection.

17   She would later marry intelligence agent Captain James MacAlpine, who, alas, died during a mission in the Balkans (see Spence, *Secret Agent 666,* 232–3). Thus, she is often referred to in Thelemic circles by her married name, MacAlpine. She later married again, becoming Deirdre MacLellan.

18   Louis Marlow [Louis Wilkonson], *Forth, Beast!* (London: Faber and Faber, 1946), 190–1. Bax, *Some I Knew Well,* 54.

19   Adapted from Charles Richard Cammell, *Aleister Crowley: The Man, the Mage, the Poet* (London: Richards Press, 1951), 175–7.

20   Short for *era vulgari* or vulgar year, Crowley's designation for the "common era" or

years counting from the birth of Christ.

21   Diary, 14 Jun 1936.

22   C. R. Cammell's recollections of Crowley, New 18, Yorke Collection. See also AC to Gerald Yorke, 3 Sep 1936, New 115, Yorke Collection.

23   Oddly enough, Smith—who also worked for the California Gas Company, and was master of this "immoral" order—received no such threat.

24   W. T. Smith to AC, 21 Aug 1936, New 15, Yorke Collection.

25   AC to W. T. Smith, 16 Sep 1936, New 15, Yorke Collection.

26   W. T. Smith to AC, 4 Oct 1936, New 15, Yorke Collection.

27   Regardie, *Eye in the Triangle*, 8.

28   Regardie, *Eye in the Triangle*, 8–10.

29   AC to Edward Noel Fitzgerald 20 Oct 1942, New 117, Yorke Collection.

30   Over the years, he would go by Aleister Macalpine, Aleister Ataturk Crowley, Randall Gair Doherty, and Charles Edward d'Arquires. He died on November 20, 2002, at Chalfont St. Peter, Bucks. Death record, Nov 2002, GRO, Chiltern, Buckinghamshire, register L8D, district 3271D. See also http://www.lashtal.com/nuke/PNphpBB2-viewtopic-t-959.phtml (accessed Dec 18 2009).

31   She provided watercolor illustrations for *Songs and Poems of John Dryden*. London: Golden Cockerel Press, 1957.

32   She and Bax compiled the anthology of women's poetry, *The Distaff Muse*. London: Hollis & Carter, 1949.

33   Frieda Harris, *Winchelsea, a Legend* (London: Selwyn & Blount, 1926). J. Johnson and A. Greutzner, *The Dictionary of British Artists 1880–1940* (Woodbridge, Suffolk: Antique Collectors' Club, 1976), 107.

34   For a detailed biography of Frieda Harris, see Richard Kaczynski, "The Crowley-Harris *Thoth Tarot*: Collaboration and Innovation" in Emily A. Auger (ed.), *Tarot in Culture: An Anthology* (under review); Hymenaeus Beta, "Editor's Foreword" in Aleister Crowley and Frieda Harris, *The Thoth Tarot: A Descriptive Essay* (Neuhausen, Switzerland: AGMüller, 2007, German edition; English edition forthcoming).

35   Edward Bainbridge Copnall, *Cycles: The Life and Work of a Sculptor*. Box 6, Edward Bainbridge Copnall Papers, 2003.2, Henry Moore Institute, Leeds. With thanks to Claire Sawyer.

36   Diary, 10 Aug 1937.

Chapter Twenty-One • The Book of Thoth

1   AC to anonymous, GARL.

2   After Crowley died, Karl Germer was sent a large number of unbound sheets of the second standard printing and a small number of sheets—estimated at ten to twenty sets—of the subscriber's edition. He passed about five hundred sets of the standard issue to New York publishers Samuel Weiser, who cropped the margins and reissued the book in maroon cloth around 1956. The sheets from the subscriber's edition passed to Helen Parsons Smith, who bound them in a facsimile of the standard issue's white buckram boards and sold them through Thelema Publications in the 1980s.

3   Cammell, *Aleister Crowley*, 108–10.

4   Madame V. K. Wellington Koo to AC, 20 Nov1945, Old E21, Yorke Collection.

5   Diary, 18 Feb 1938.

6   As mentioned earlier, "affiliation" indicates administrative conferral of a degree, with no additional ceremonies, in recognition of an equivalent degree in another Masonic tradition. Harris held the VII° in OTO, which was equivalent to the highest degree, 33° or Sovereing Grand Inspector General, in the Scottish Rite. See http://weiserantiquarian.com/catalogfiftyseven/ (accessed May 12 2009) for Har-

ris's holograph copy of the VII° instructional paper, "De Natura Deorum."

7   Roberts, *Magician of the Golden Dawn*, 308–10.

8   See Kaczynski, "The Crowley-Harris *Thoth Tarot*" and Hymenaeus Beta, "Editors' Foreword" for a detailed account of this project's execution.

9   Roberts, *Magician of the Golden Dawn*, 308–10.

10 Ibid., 313.

11 Death record, 554-12-1613, California, Social Security Administration.

12 Starr, *Unknown God*, 247. "Plays: New Productions," *Los Angeles Times*, 4 Jun 1939, C4.

13 Starr, *Unknown God*, 247. "Plays: New Productions."

14 Death record, 572-12-4456, California, Social Security Administration. Starr, *Unknown God*, 274.

15 See http://grunddal_sjallung.totallyexplained.com/ (accessed Dec 19 2009). Starr, *Unknown God*, 375. Sjallung's works include Amélie André Gedalge, Mary Haller, and Grunddal Sjallung, *Haandbog i Frimureriets Symbolik* (København: Co-F. M. Forlag, 1926). Grunddal Sjallung, *Litteratur for Frimurere* (Kbh, 1934). Grunddal Sjallung, *De ældste Afsløringer af Frimurernes Hemmeligheder* (Kbh, 1941).

16 See J. B. Jameson to AC, 11 May 1938, Old E21, Yorke Collection, as well as the correspondence related to Jameson in the New 117, Yorke Collection.

17 Khaled Khan, "Das Herz des Meisters," *Pansophia* 1925, 1(7): 93–124. It was also issued as a separate offprint in wraps.

18 Diary, 7 Oct 1938.

19 AC to unknown, 11 Nov 1944, tipped into Crowley's *The Book of Thoth*, T198.b.1.15, Cambridge University.

20 Volume 3, number 1 was the so-called "blue" *Equinox*. Number 2 was printed but never bound, and ultimately destroyed by the printer for non-payment. Number 3 became *The Equinox of the Gods*.

21 For but a few examples, see the following *Los Angeles Times* program listings: "Notables will Talk on Radio," 19 Sep 1931, 14; "Football Goes on Radio Today," 26 Sep 1931, 16; "Much Music on Air Today," 29 Sep 1931, 20; "Jujitsu Menu for Breakfast," 21 Oct 1931, A15; "Moslem Voice to Span Seas," 22 Oct 1931, 12; "Melody, Bridge and Golf on Air," 9 Jan 1932, 12; "International Broadcast Set," 11 Jan 1932, 14; "Radio Brings Grand Opera," 16 Jan 1932, A5.

22 Leffingwell was the middle child of Wendel (b. 1849) and Mary (b. 1855) Leffingwell. He had an older sister Mabel (b. 1882) and a younger sister Mildred (b. 1896). See 1930 U.S. Census, Pasadena, Los Angeles, California, district 1120, 16A. World War I draft registration card, roll # 1411593, Cleveland, Cuyahoga, OH; National Archives, Washington, DC. 1900 US Census, Chicago Ward 19, Cook, Illinois, district 591. Los Angeles, California, voter's registration logs for 1924, 1928, 1930, 1936, 1940.

23 Starr, *Unknown God*, 251, 366.

24 W. T. Smith to AC, 1 Sep 1939, New 15, Yorke Collection.

25 Roy Leffingwell to AC, n.d., New 14, Yorke Collection.

26 Roberts, *Magician of the Golden Dawn*, 305

27 AC to Gerald Yorke, 27 Mar 1946, Yorke Collection.

28 AC to NID, 6 Sep 1939, New 117, Yorke Collection.

29 See Spence, *Secret Agent 666*, 248–9, which reports that Crowley was interviewed by Admiral Godfrey of the Naval Intelligence Division.

30 A biography of Wheatley was recently published as Phil Baker, *The Devil is a Gentleman: The Life and Times of Dennis Wheatley* (Sawtry, Cambs: Dedalus, 2009). See also Phil Barker, "Dennis and All His Works," *Fortean Times,* Jan 2010, 256: 38–43.

31 "Viscount Tredegar: A Modern Dilettante," *Times* (London), 28 Apr 1949, 51367: 7.

32 Spence, *Secret Agent 666,* 225.

33 P. R. Stephensen to J. K. Moir, 6 Jun 1952, Box Y2116, Stephensen Papers.

34 The Asthmosana was a German-made glass asthma inhaler, consisting of a hollow flat oval with three openings, used for filling the inhaler and atomizing its contents.

35 AC to Montgomery Evans II, 27 Jul 1940, Evans Papers.

36 AC to Montgomery Evans II, ibid.

37 Cammell, *Aleister Crowley,* 182–9.

38 Diary, 22 Sep 1940.

39 AC to Edward Noel Fitzgerald, 12 Dec 1940, New 117, Yorke Collection.

40 AC to Gerald Yorke, 28 May 1942, Yorke Collection.

41 In 1939, Sutherland and H. M. Lommer published *1234 Modern End-Game Studies: With Appendix Containing 24 Additional Studies* (Philadelphia, David McKay).

42 Diary, 16 Dec 1940.

43 The speaker had confused William Joyce for novelist James Joyce.

44 Diary, 12 Feb 1941.

45 Diary, 14 Feb 1941.

46 AC to Montgomery Evans II, *op. cit.*

47 AC to Gerald Yorke, 13 Sep 1941, Yorke Collection.

48 AC to Louis Wilkinson, 14 May 1941, Wilkinson Collection; AC to Montgomery Evans II, *op. cit.*

49 Germer to Frater FT, 6 Jan 1954, OTO Archives.

50 AC to Louis Wilkinson, 16 Mar 1941, Wilkinson Collection.

51 Diary, 20 Apr 1941.

52 AC to Louis Wilkinson, 12 May 1941, Wilkinson Collection.

53 Some in the aerospace community reputedly joke that JPL stands for "Jack Parsons' Laboratory."

54 Helen Parsons Smith was born Mary Helen Cowley in Chicago, the oldest of three daughters to Thomas Philip Cowley and his wife Olga Helena (née Nelson). After Thomas died of pneumonia in 1920, Olga met Burton Ashley Northrup, whom she married in 1922. The family soon moved to southern California, where two more daughters were born. When Burton Northrup was imprisoned in 1928 for fraud, Helen was forced to drop out of high school and work to help support her family. She later worked for her stepfather at Northrup Business Adjustments and graduated from Pasadena Junior College. She met Jack Parsons at a church social and married him in 1935, making her home in Pasadena. In later years, she would be instrumental in maintaining OTO and Thelema in the decades after Crowley died, editing, publishing and selling his works. U.S. 1930 census, Pasadena, Los Angeles, CA, district 1212, 4A. Jean Kentle, "Pasadenan Married in Church Rite," *Los Angeles Times,* 29 Apr 1935, A7. "Advancement in the Light [obituary]," *Thelema Lodge Calendar,* Oct 2003, http://www.billheidrick.com/tlc2003/tlc1003.htm (accessed 9 Jan 2010). Starr, *Unknown God.* George Pendle, *Strange Angel: The Otherworldly Life of Rocket Scientist John Whiteside Parsons* (Orlando: Harcourt, 2005).

55 W. T. Smith to AC, Mar 1941, New 15, Yorke Collection. For Parsons's biography, see Pendle, *Strange Angel* and John Carter, *Sex and Rockets: The Occult World of Jack Parsons* (Venice, CA: Feral House, 1999). For Parsons's writings, see John Whiteside Parsons, *Three Essays on Freedom,* ed. Hymenaeus Beta (York Beach, ME: Teitan Press, 2008) and John Whiteside Parsons, *Freedom is a Two-Edged Sword and Other Essays (The Oriflamme 1),* ed. Cameron and Hymenaeus Beta (Las Vegas and New York: New Falcon Publications in association with OTO, 1989).

56 The society was established by Forrest J. Ackerman (1916–2008), who coined the term "sci-fi" and served as editor and principal writer for *Famous Monsters of Film-land.* They frequently met at Clifton's Cafeteria in Los Angeles, and counted

amongst its members aspiring young writer Ray Bradbury and stop-motion animator Ray Harryhausen.

57 For a memoir of McMurtry, see J. Edward Cornelius, *In the Name of the Beast: A Biography of Grady Louis McMurtry, a Disciple of Aleister Crowley* (Red Flame #12 and 13 (Berkeley: Red Flame, 2005). For his poetry, see Grady Louis McMurtry, *Poems: The Angel & the Abyss, Dark Space & Bright Stars* (London and Bergen: OTO, 1986).

58 Diary, 13 May 1941.

59 Frieda Harris to AC, 26 May 1941, GARL.

60 Diary, 30 Apr 1941.

61 AC to C. R. Cammell, 14 Jun 1941, Yorke Collection.

62 Harris to Alexander Watt, 3 Aug 1954, OTO Archives.

63 AC to Gerald Yorke, 20 Jun 1941, New 115, Yorke Collection.

64 Beverly Baxter to AC, 1 Jul 1941, Old E21, Yorke Collection.

65 AC to Roy Leffingwell, n.d., New 14, Yorke Collection.

66 AC to Gerald Yorke, 6 Sep 1941 and 13 Sep 1941, Yorke Collection, respectively. The people mentioned include rationalist philosopher and University of London lecturer Cyril Edwin Mitchinson Joad (1891–1953); writer John Cooper Powys (1872–1963); bookseller Harold Mortlake and literary critic, novelist and Dickens biographer Ralph Straus (1882–1950).

67 After the war, Joyce was hanged for treason on January 3, 1946.

68 AC to E. N. Fitzgerald, 11 Aug 1941, New 117, Yorke Collection.

69 Diary, 20 Aug 1941.

70 Diary, 21 Aug 1941.

71 AC to Gerald Yorke, 30 Aug 1941, New 115, Yorke Collection.

72 AC to Gerald Yorke, n.d., New 115, Yorke Collection.

73 Diary, 6 Sep 1941.

74 AC to Louis Wilkinson, 8 Jan 1942, Wilkinson Collection.

75 Diary, 25 Feb 1942.

76 Diary, 12 Jan 1942.

77 AC to Ethel Archer, 26 Mar 1927, New 4, Yorke Collection.

78 AC to Louis Wilkinson, 30 Mar 1942, Wilkinson Collection. Crowley is referring to Catullus' epigram 94, addressed to Julius Caesar's lieutenant Mamurra:

> *Mentula moechatur. Moechatur mentula? Certe.*
> *Hoc est quod dicunt. Ipsa olera olla legit.*
> ("Mr. Prick is screwing around. Is Mr. Prick screwing around? Certainly.
> This is the proverb: The pot gathers its own herbs.")

The proverb may be taken as "the pot makes sure it gets what it needs."

79 Diary, 5 Apr 1942.

80 This incident appears in Hamilton, *The Way It Was with Me;* and in John Symonds, *Conversations with Gerald* (London: Duckworth, 1974).

81 AC to Roy Leffingwell, n.d., New 14, Yorke Collection.

82 FBI report on Karl Germer, 16 Apr 1942, FOIA file #100–18329.

83 AC to Roy Leffingwell, 12 Sep 1942, New 14, Yorke Collection. See also the letters dated 11 Jul 1942, and 8 Dec 1942.

84 AC to Karl Germer, 7 Aug 1946, OTO Archives.

85 Diary, 25 Jul 1942.

86 AC to Roy Leffingwell, 15 Sep 1944, New 14, Yorke Collection.

87 Diary, 8 Jul 1942.

88 Diary, 1 Aug 1942.

Chapter Twenty-Two • The Great Turkey Tragedy: Or Heirs Apparent

1   Diary, 19 Jan 1943. The American *Book of the Law* was issued in 1942.

2   Diary, 27 Jan 1943.

3   AC to Frater Viator, 15 Feb 1943, New 14, Yorke Collection. See also the letter of 3 Mar 1943.

4   Jane Wolfe to W. T. Smith, 13 Jan 1943, New 15, Yorke Collection.

5   W. T. Smith to AC, 3 Feb 1943, New 15, Yorke Collection.

6   AC to W. T. Smith, 1 Apr 1943, New 15, Yorke Collection.

7   AC to Viator, 15 Feb 1943, New 14, Yorke Collection.

8   FBI report on John Whiteside Parsons, 2 Nov 1950, p. 10, FOIA file # 65–59589.

9   Diary, 18 Feb 1943.

10   Diary, 15 Apr 1943.

11   AC to Max Schneider, 17 Aug 1943, New 14, Yorke Collection. A similar statement appears in AC to Roy Leffingwell, 10 Aug 1943, Yorke Collection.

12   For a detailed treatment of Smith's life and ordeals, see Starr, *Unknown God.*

13   AC to Grady McMurtry, 9 Dec 1943 and 15 Dec 1943, OTO Archives, respectively.

14   Death record, GRO, Bracknell, Berkshire, 19: 52. Marriage record, GRO, St. George Hanover Square, Middlesex, 1a: 1077.

15   Diary, 30 Oct 1943.

16   "William Bernard Crow," *Contemporary Authors Online,* http://galenet.galegroup .com/servlet/BioRC (accessed Dec 24 2009). "University and Educational Notes," *Science,* 18 May 1928, 67 (1742): 509. "Universities And Colleges," *British Medical Journal,* 30 Mar 1929, 1(3560): 626. Henry R. T. Brandreth, *Episcopi Vagantes and the Anglican Church* (London: Society for Promoting Christian Knowledge, 1947). Peter F. Anson, *Bishops at Large* (London: Faber and Faber, 1964).

17   W. B. Crow's professional publications include: "The Classification of Some Colonial Chlamydomonads," *New Phytologist,* Jul 1918, 17(7): 151–9; "A Critical Study of Certain Unicellular Cyanophyceae from the Point of View of Their Evolution," *New Phytologist,* 25 Apr 1922, 21(2): 81–102; "Dimorphococcus Fritschii: A New Colonial Protophyte from Ceylon," *Annals of Botany* 1923, 37(1): 141–5; "The Taxonomy and Variation of the Genus Microcystis in Ceylon," *New Phytologist,* 19 May 1923, 22(2): 59–68; *Freshwater Plankton Algae from Ceylon* (London: Taylor and Francis, 1923); "The Reproductive Differentiation of Colonies in Chlamydomonadales," *New Phytologist,* 28 May 1925, 24(2): 120–3; "Phylogeny and the Natural System," *Journal of Genetics,* 17(2): 85–155; "The Generic Characters of Arthrospira and Spirulina," *Transactions of the American Microscopical Society,* Apr 1927, 46(2): 139–48; "Symmetry in Organisms," *American Naturalist* 1928, 62(680): 207–27; *Contributions to the Principles of Morphology* (London: Kegan Paul, 1929); *Voice and the Vocal Apparatus* (Cambridge, 1930); "The Protista as the Primitive Forms of Life," *Scientia* 1933, 54: 93–102; "Nature Analogies," *Scientia* 1935, 58: 157–71; "Periodicity in Classification," *Scientia* 1938, 63: 133–43; "Periodicity, Analogy and Homology," *Scientia* 1947, 53: 19–23; and *A Synopsis of Biology,* (Baltimore, MD: Williams & Wilkins, 1960).

His esoteric writings include the "Mysteries of the Ancients" series published in London by Houghton as follows: 1. *Planets, Gods, and Anatomical Organs* (1941); 2. *The Astrological Correspondences of Animals, Herbs and Jewels* (1942); 3. *The Planetary Temples* (1942); 4. *Human Anatomy in Temple Architecture* (1942); 5. *Noah's Ark* (1942); 6. *Astronomical Religion* (1942); 7. *The Calendar* (1943); 8. *The Seven Wonders of the World* (1943); 9. *The Mysteries* (1943); 10. *The Cosmic Mystery Drama* (1943); 11. *The Historical Jesus, High Priest of the Mysteries* (1943); 12. *The Law of Correspondences* (1943); 13. *The Symbolism of Chess and Cards* (1944); 14. *Druids and the Mistletoe Sacrament* (1944); 15. *The Symbolism of the Coronation* (1944); 16. *Initiation* (1945); 17. *The*

Nature Mysteries (1945); and 18. *Appendices to the Series: The Human Body As a Solar System; The Human Body As a Colony of Animals; Symbolism of Colour and the Fire Bird* (1945). In addition, he wrote the following books: *Table of the Sovereigns of England: Historical, Legendary and Mythical ... in Inverse Chronological Order* (Leicester: Order of the Holy Wisdom, 1953); *Precious Stones: Their Occult Power and Hidden Significance* (London: Aquarian, 1968); *The Occult Properties of Herbs* (London: Aquarian Press, 1969); *A History of Magic, Witchcraft and Occultism* (London: Aquarian Press, 1969); and *The Arcana of Symbolism* (London: Aquarian Press, 1970).

18 E.g., Dr. W. B. Crow, "The Gnostics," *Occult Review* 1945, 72(1): 27–30.

19 Hugh George Newman was born in Essex during the winter of 1905 (Birth record, GRO, West Ham, Essex, Greater London, 4a: 225). He was involved in New Southgate politics in the early 1930s, and was the Conservative and Municipal Reform candidate as a councillor in 1933. Later in that decade, he became associated with the National Association of Cycle Traders (NACT), writing *The History of the Bicycle* (1938); compiling *The National Association of Cycle & Motor Cycle Traders: Its Aims, Objects and Benefits* (1938) and *Cycle Traders Unite!* (1939); and issuing on its behalf a *Joint Memorandum* (1942). He was also associated with the Incorporated Institute of Cycle Traders and Repairers (IICTR)—founded by Arthur Gillott in 1941—appearing as the publisher of its 1942 publications. For more on Newman's work in this field, see the 1944 *Incorporated Institute of Cycle Traders and Repairers Year Book, 1944* (London, 1944). See also Borough of Southgate, *Election of councillors, 1st November, 1933. South Ward* (London, 1933). H. G. de W. Newman, *The History of the Bicycle* (London, 1938). H. G. de W. Newman (comp.), *National Association of Cycle & Motor Cycle Traders: Its Aims, Objects and Benefits* (London: National Association of Cycle and Motor Cycle Traders, 1938). H. G. de W. Newman (comp.), *Cycle Traders Unite!* (London: National Association of Cycle and Motor Cycle Traders, 1939). Arthur S. Gillott and H. G. de Willmott Newman, *Joint Memorandum [...] on the Third Interim Report of the Retail Trade Committee of the Board of Trade, and on the Future of Private Enterprise in relation to the Retail Cycle Trade* (Watford: N. J. Publishing Co., 1942). IICTR, *Syllabus* (Watford: H. G. de Willmott Newman, 1942). IICTR and H. G. de Willmott Newman, *Report of Bidlake Memorial Dinner* (n.p.: H. G. de Willmott Newmann, 1942).

Crow consecrated Newman a bishop on April 10, 1944, right around the time Crowley made contact with Crow. Although in later years Newman was no longer "in communion" with Crow, in his travels he cross-consecrated numerous other *episcopi vagantes* (in other words, the two bishops consecrated each other), "with a view to 'combining the lines of succession' under the apparent misconception that a person is consecrated a bishop of a particular line of succession rather than a bishop of the Church of God" (Brandreth, *Episcopi Vagantes,* 51). Consequently, Newman's episcopal name, Mar Georgius I, is described as "ubiquitous" because it turns up in the line of apostolic succession of many modern day wandering bishops.

20 Some have argued that the name "Jehosaphat" derives from or is a transliteration error of the Sanskrit word *bodhisattva* (enlightened being), a title of the Buddha. See, e.g., E. A. Wallis Budge, *Baralâm and Yewâsef: Being the Ethlopic Version of a Christianized Recension of the Buddhist Legend of the Buddha and the Bodhisattva* (Cambridge: Univ. Press. 1923).

21 AC to Cardinal Newman, 24 Sep 1944, New 24, Yorke Collection.

22 AC to W. B. Crow, 11 Jun 1944, New 24, Yorke Collection. Copies of this correspondence are also found in the OTO Archives.

23 AC to W. B. Crow, 26 Oct 1944, New 24, Yorke Collection.

24 Dave Arnold, "What Rough Beast: The Last Days of Aleister Crowley, at Hastings," *Hastings Trawler*, Jan 2006, 2(1): 12–4. Rod Davies, "Crowley in Hastings: Last Days of the Great Beast," unidentified clipping, Yorke Collection.

25 AC to Louis Wilkinson, 28 Mar 1944, Wilkinson Collection.

26 Diary, 24 Feb 1944.

27 AC to Ben Stubbins, n.d., Yorke Collection.

28 AC to Gerald Yorke, 2 Nov 1944, Yorke Collection.

29 AC to Edward Noel Fitzgerald, 13 May 1947, Yorke Collection.

30 Frieda Harris Papers, 1923–1964, Rare Books and Manuscripts, University Libraries, Pennsylvania State University.

31 Attempts by Crowley and Harris to publish the deck, together or individually, are detailed in Kaczynski, "The Crowley-Harris Thoth Tarot." For the deck's printing history, see Hymenaeus Beta, "Editor's Foreword." A detailed comparison of the deck's various printings appears in R. Leo Gillis, "The (Printer's) Devil is in the Detail: A Printing History of the Book of Thoth Tarot Deck," *Tarosophist International* 2009, 1(4): 39–62.

32 AC to Jean Schneider, 19 Oct 1944, Yorke Collection. AC to Jean Schneider, 7 Dec 1944, Yorke Collection. AC to Jean Schneider, 22 Jun 1945, Yorke Collection.

33 AC to Grady McMurtry, 22 Aug 1944, OTO Archives.

34 Grady McMurtry to AC, 6 Nov 1944, OTO Archives.

35 AC to Grady McMurtry, 21 Nov 1944, OTO Archives.

36 Diary, 22 Dec 1944.

37 AC to Cordelia Sutherland, 23 Nov 1943, GARL.

38 Vernon Symonds, *The Legend of Abd-El-Krim: A Play in Three Acts* (London: Elzevier, 1930).

39 Arnold, "What Rough Beast,"; Davies, "Crowley in Hastings."

40 Hastings House Rules, Old EE2, Yorke Collection.

41 For more, see "Edward Mackenzie Jackson," http://www.hastingschessclub.co.uk/emjackson.html (accessed Dec 23 2009).

42 Arnold, "What Rough Beast"; Davies, "Crowley in Hastings."

43 Diary, 4 Apr 1945.

44 Kenneth Grant, *Remembering Aleister Crowley* (London: Skoob Books, 1991), 1.

45 Dave Evans, *The History of British Magic after Crowley: Kenneth Grant, Amado Crowley, Chaos Magic, Satanism, Lovecraft, the Left Hand Path, Blasphemy and Magical Morality* (n.p.: Hidden Publishing, 2007), 286. Grant is very private about his life and interactions with Crowley, so little biographical information is available outside of what is in various archives. That Grant's writings are "semi-autobiographical" only adds to the mystery, as has been thoroughly examined by Evans. See also Dave Evans, "Kenneth Grant: True Tales, Ancient Grimoires, and Magical Fiction," *Wormwood* 2008, 10: 48–58.

46 AC to Grady McMurtry, 8 Mar 1945, OTO Archives.

47 Grant, *Magical Revival,* 93. Kenneth Grant, *Outside the Cirles of Time* (London: Frederick Muller, 1980), 87.

48 AC to Louis Wilkinson, 27 Jan 1945, Wilkinson Collection.

49 Grant, *Remembering Aleister Crowley,* v.

50 Diary, 4 Apr 1945.

51 Diary, 19 Apr 1945.

52 AC to David Curwen, 22 Jan 1946, from Grant, *Remembering Aleister Crowley.*

53 AC to Grady McMurtry, 11 Apr 1945, OTO Archives, is where Crowley appoints McMurtry Sovereign Grand Inspector General. Additional details come from *Grady McMurtry et al., v. Society Ordo Templi Orientis,* official transcript, U.S. District Court for the Northern Jurisdiction of California, Civil Case No. C-83-5434, p. 32, 45.

54 AC to Grady McMurtry, 21 May 1945, OTO Archives.

55 AC to Louis Wilkinson, 24 May 1945, Wilkinson Collection.

56 Roberts, *Magician of the Golden Dawn,* 216.

57 F. H. Amphlett Micklewright, "Aleister Crowley, Poet and Occultist." *Occult Review*

1945, 72(2): 41–6.

58 AC to W. B. Crow, 2 Apr 1945, Yorke Collection.

59 AC to W.B. Crow, 14 May 1946, Yorke Collection.

60 AC to Frederick Mellinger, 7 May 1946, quoted in "Addenda," *F. H. Amphlett-Micklewright: Aleister Crowley, Poet & Occultist* (n.p.: Fine Madness Society, 2009).

61 AC to Louis Wilkinson, 7 Aug 1945, Wilkinson Collection. Three men of science had visited Cefalù: Norman Mudd, his colleague Oxford mathematics scholar Edmund Saayman, and J. W. N. Sullivan. Crowley is almost certainly referring to Sullivan, easily the most prominent of the three (and a physicist besides); however, I have been unable to connect him with the atom bomb.

62 Diary, 23 Aug 1945.

63 Hugh Montgomery-Massingberd, *Burke's Irish Family Records* (London, U.K.: Burkes Peerage Ltd, 1976), 195. "Dr. E. M. Butler: Learning And Letters," *Times* (London), 14 Nov 1959; 54618: 10. Butler's publications include: *The Tempestuous Prince, Hermann Pückler-Muskau* (London: Longmans Green and Co, 1929); *Sheridan, a Ghost Story* (London: Constable, 1931); *The Tyranny of Greece over Germany: A Study of the Influence Exercised by Greek Art and Poetry Over the Great German Writers* (Cambridge: Univ. Press, 1935); *The Direct Method in German Poetry; An Inaugural Lecture Delivered on January 25th, 1946* (Cambridge: Univ. Press, 1946); *The Myth of the Magus* (Cambridge: Univ. Press, 1948); *Ritual Magic* (Cambridge: Univ. Press, 1949); *Goethe and Byron: Byron Foundation Lecture, 1949–50* (University of Nottingham, 1950); *Daylight in a Dream* (London: Hogarth Press, 1951); *The Fortunes of Faust* (Cambridge: Univ. Press, 1952); *Silver Wings: A Novel* (London: Hogarth Press, 1952); Heinrich Heine: A Biography (London: Hogarth press, 1956); Antony Borrow and Eliza Marian Butler, *John Faust: A Drama in Three Acts* (Ashford: Hand & Flower Press, 1958); *The Faust Legend* (n.p.: The Royal Institution of Great Britain, 1958); *Paper Boats: An Autobiography* (London: Collins, 1959); *The Saint-Simonian Religion in Germany; A Study of the Young German Movement* (New York: H. Fertig, 1968).

64 Diary, 1 Jan 1946.

65 Augustus John to AC, n.d. 1946, Old E21, Yorke Collection.

66 Hubbard is a controversial figure, and his life story according to Church of Scientology literature has been contested by several Hubbard biographers. See, e.g., Bent Corydon and L. Ron Hubbard, Jr. *L. Ron Hubbard: Messiah Or Madman?* (New Jersey: Lyle Stuar, 1987) and Russell Miller, *Bare-faced Messiah: The True Story of L. Ron Hubbard* (New York: Henry Holt, 1988).

67 John W. Parsons to AC, Feb 1946, Yorke Collection.

68 Marjorie C. Kimmel, 483-16-5928, Social Security Death Index, Social Security Administration.

69 Marjorie Cameron's younger siblings were James R. (b. 1923), Mary L. (b. 1927), and Robert E. (b. 1929). Her mother, Carrie V. Ridenour, was born in Iowa and died in Los Angeles on September 2, 1970 (Death record, Los Angeles, California Death Index). See: Hill L. Cameron, death record, 22 Nov 1962, Los Angeles, California Death Index. 1925 Iowa State Census, Belle Plain Ward 2, Benton, Iowa. 1920 U.S. Census, Belle Plain Ward 1, Benton, IA, district 1, 11B. 1930 U.S. Census, Belle Plaine, Benton, IA, district 1, 10A.

70 Michael Duncan, *Cameron* (New York: Nicole Klagsbrun Gallery, 2007.

71 John W. Parsons to AC, Mar 1946, Yorke Collection.

72 AC to John W. Parsons, 15 Mar 1946, Yorke Collection.

73 In the December 1999 *Thelema Lodge Newsletter,* the word "louts" is read as "goats," suggesting that "louts" was a transcription error.

74 AC to Grady McMurtry, 22 Mar 1946, OTO Archives.

75 AC to Grady McMurtry, 11 Apr 1946, OTO Archives.

76 AC to Grady McMurtry, 10 Apr 1946, OTO Archives.

77   Jack Parsons to AC, 5 Jul 1946, Yorke Collection.

78   "John Symonds: Biographer of 'The Great Beast,'" *The Independent,* 11 Nov 2006. "John Symonds," *The Telegraph,* 11 Nov 2006. Christoopher Hawtree, "John Symonds: Teller of Charming Children's Tales Who Made a Devilish Friend," *Guardian,* 22 Nov 2006. John Symonds and André François, *William Waste* (London: Sampson Low, Marston, n.d.). Although the novel is undated, a publication date of 1946 or 1947 has been inferred from dated presentation copies.

79   Symonds, "Aleister Crowley: The Devil's Contemplative."

80   AC to Louis Wilkinson, 31 May 1946, Wilkinson Collection. Aleister Crowley, "How to Tell and Englishman from an American," *Liliput,* Aug 1946, 147.

81   AC to John Symonds, 15 Jun 1946, OTO Archives; also in Yorke Collection.

82   See, however, AC's letter of 2 Jul 1947, where he sought to place the manuscript of *Magick without Tears* with John Bunting, and asks him to forward it to John Symonds for placement with another publisher. Aleister Crowley fonds, SC181, McPherson Library Special Collections, University of Victoria, British Columbia.

83   AC to Grady McMurtry, 14 Apr 1946, OTO Archives.

84   Diary, 20 Jul 1946.

85   AC to John Symonds, 5 Sep 1946, OTO Archives; also in Yorke Collection.

86   AC to Gerald Yorke, 27 Mar 1946, New 115, Yorke Collection.

87   Nicholas Sylvester, "Sixty Years of Song: A Book Review," *Occult Review* 1947, 74(2): 115–8.

88   James Laver, *Nostradamus: or, the Future Foretold* (London: Collins, 1942).

89   This account is based on Laver, *Museum Piece,* and Laver's "Some Impressions of Aleister Crowley," New 18, Yorke Collection.

90   Diary, 27 Mar 1947.

91   Birth record, fall 1909, GRO, Medway, Kent, 2a: 692. Death record, 1974, GRO, Sheffield, Yorkshire West Riding, South Yorkshire, 3: 1534. Rosemary Guiley, *The Encyclopedia of Witches, Witchcraft and Wicca* (New York: Facts On File, 2008). Shelley Rabinovitch and James Lewis, *The Encyclopedia of Modern Witchcraft and Neo-Paganism* (New York, N.Y.: Citadel Press, 2002). Crowther's published works include *Let's Put on a Show* (London: Stanmore Press, 1964), *Yorkshire Customs: Traditions and Folklore of Old Yorkshire* (Clapham: Dalesman, 1974), and Arnold and Patricia Crowther, *The Secrets of Ancient Witchcraft with the Witches Tarot* (Secaucus, N.J.: Univ. Books, 1974).

92   G. B. Gardner, Keris and Other Malay Weapons, ed. B. Lumsden Milne (Singapore: Progressive Pub. Co, 1936).

93   For Gardner's life, see Jack L. Bracelin [Idries Shah], *Gerald Gardner: Witch* (London: Octagon Press, 1960). Ronald Hutton, *The Triumph of the Moon: A History of Modern Pagan Witchcraft* (Oxford: Oxford Univ. Press, 1999). Philip Heselton, *Wiccan Roots: Gerald Gardner and the Modern Witchcraft Revival* (Freshfields, Chieveley, Berks: Capall Bann Pub, 2000). Philip Heselton, *Gerald Gardner and the Cauldron of Inspiration: An Investigation into the Sources of Gardnerian Witchcraft* (Auton Farm, Milverton, Somerset: Capall Bann Publishing, 2003).

94   AC to Karl Germer, 30 Jun 1947, OTO Archives. He wrote a similar letter to Jean Schneider, 25 May 1947, Yorke Collection.

95   Gerald Gardner to John Symonds, Dec 1950, Old EE2, Yorke Collection.

96   Gardner to Symonds, ibid.

97   Francis King, *Ritual Magic in England: 1887 to the Present Day* (London: Neville Spearman, 1970), 140–3, recounts Gerald Yorke's claim that Gardner commissioned Crowley to write his *Book of Shadows.*

98   Charles Godfrey Leland, *Aradia: The Gospel of the Witches* (London: David Nutt, 1899).

99   Doreen Valiente, *The Rebirth of Witchcraft* (London: Robert Hale, 1989). See also Aidan Kelly, *Crafting the Art of Magic* (St Paul, MN: Llewellyn, 1991).

100 Gerald Gardner, *Witchcraft Today* (New York: Citadel Press, 1954), 46–7.

101 This subject is treated very thoroughly in: Valiente, *Rebirth of Witchcraft;* Kelly, *Crafting the Art of Magic;* Hutton, *Triumph of the Moon;* Roger Dearnaley, "The Influence of Aleister Crowley upon 'Ye Bok of ye Art Magical,'" http://www.lashtal.com/nuke/module-subjects-viewpage-pageid-141.phtml (accessed Dec 26 2009); Philip Heselton *Gerald Gardner and the Cauldron of Inspiration: An Investigation into the Sources of Gardnerian Witchcraft* (Auton Farm, Milverton, Somerset: Capall Bann Publishing, 2003); David Rankine and Sorita D'Este, *Wicca: Magickal Beginnings: A Study of the Possible Origins of This Tradition of Modern Pagan Witchcraft and Magick,* 2nd ed. (London: Avalonia, 2008); and Rodney Orpheus, "Gerald Gardner and Ordo Templi Orientis," *Pentacle* 2009, (30): 14–8.

102 AC to Edward Noel Fitzgerald, 13 May 1947, New 117, Yorke Collection.

103 AC to Aleister Ataturk MacAlpine, 30 May 1947, New 117, Yorke Collection.

104 John Kelly, "Ellmann, Richard David (1918–1987)" *Oxford Dictionary of National Biography* (Oxford: Oxford Univ. Press, 2004).

105 Richard Ellmann, "Black Magic against White: Aleister Crowley verus W. B. Yeats," *Partisan Review,* Sep 1948, 15(9): 1049–51. His Yeats book appeared the same year as Richard Ellmann, *Yeats, the Man and the Masks* (New-York: MacMillan, 1948).

106 AC to Grady McMurtry, 17 Jun 1947, OTO Archives.

107 AC to Frederick Mellinger, 15 Jul 1947, OTO Archives.

108 Friedrich Mellinger, *Zeichen und Wunder: ein Führer durch die Welt der Magie* (Berlin: Neufeld & Henius Verlag, 1933).

109 Mellinger's film work includes *Hitler: The Beast of Berlin* (dir. Sam Newfield: Sigmund Neufeld Productions, 1939). plus uncredited appearances in *The Hunchback of Notre Dame* (dir. William Dieterle: RKO Radio Pictures, 1939), *A Dispatch from Reuter's* (dir. William Dieterle: Warner Bros., 1940), and *Dr. Ehrlich's Magic Bullet* (dir. William Dieterle: Warner Bros., 1940).

110 AC to Karl Germer, 6 Jun 1947, OTO Archives.

111 AC to Max Schneider, 20 Oct 1947, Yorke Collection.

112 These are but a few headlines from news clippings found in New 87, Yorke Collection, and elsewhere. Respectively, they are: *Daily Express,* 2 Dec 1947; unidentified; *Newsweek,* 15 Dec 1947; *Time,* 15 Dec 1947; *Chicago Daily Tribune,* 3 Dec 1947; *Walla-Walla Union-Bulletin,* 2 Dec 1947; unidentified. On the sixtieth anniversary of Crowley's death, several of these obituaries were collected and issued as *Mystic's Potion to Prolong Life Fails: Aleister Crowley's Death in the Press* (n.p.: The Aleister Crowley Dependant Collective, 2007).

113 Death record, GRO, Westminster, London, 5c: 399. London phone books, 1939–1947. "Births, Marriages and Deaths," *British Medical Journal,* 13 Dec 1947, 2(4536): 984.

114 *Daily Express,* 4 Dec 1947.

115 Awful Aleister. *Newsweek,* 15 Dec 1947, 34–5.

116 The text of the funeral service was published by Frieda Harris as *Aleister Crowley, October 18th, 1875–December 1st, 1947: The Last Ritual, Read from His Own Works, according to His Wish, on December 5th, 1947, at Brighton. 1947* [n.p., 1948].

Epilogue

1   Andrew Green to John Symonds, 14 Jul 1949, New 96, Yorke Collection.

2   Hereward Carrington, *Psychic Oddities* (London: Rider, 1952).

3   Gerald Yorke to Karl Germer, 7 Mar 1948, OTO Archives.

4   Gerald Gardner to John Symonds, Dec 1950, Old EE2, Yorke Collection.

5   "Jane Wolfe: Hollywood," *In the Continuum* 1990, 4(7): 27–8.

6   J. G. Bayley to J. Symonds, 7 Jan 1950, New 96, Yorke Collection.
7   As of this writing, an edition of Jones's correspondence with Gerald Yorke is being prepared for a late 2010 release as *The Incoming of the Aeon of Maat* (London: Starfire).
8   Alexander Watt to John Symonds, 5 Apr 1952, New 96, Yorke Collection. Jones, in fact, had joined the Roman Catholic church decades earlier in 1928 and took confirmation in 1929. However, he saw this act to be in accordance with *Liber Legis*.
9   John W. Parsons to Karl Germer, 1952, OTO Archives.
10 Parsons, *Three Essays on Freedom*.
11 Karl Germer to Kenneth Grant, 20 Jul 1955, OTO Archives.
12 For Grant's association with Spare, see Kenneth Grant and Steffi Grant, *Zos Speaks!: Encounters with Austin Osman Spare* (London: Fulgur, 1998).
13 Henrik Bogdan, *Kenneth Grant: A Bibliography from 1948* (Gothenburg: Academia Esoterica Press, 2003).
14 For an insider's perspective, see Frater Shiva, *Inside the Solar Lodge, Outside the Law* (York Beach, ME: Teitan Press, 2007).
15 For OTO's history under McMurtry, see http://oto-usa.org/history.html#ohogrady (accessed Dec 26 2009).
16 Bogdan, *Kenneth Grant,* viii and vi, respectively.
17 Readers interested in Grant's perspective could try *The Magical Revival* (1972) for a general overview; *Aleister Crowley and the Hidden God* (1973) and *Remembering Aleister Crowley* (1991) for his take on Crowley; or *Images and Oracles of Austin Spare* (1975) and *Zos Speaks! Encounters with Austin Osman Spare* (1998) for Austin Spare. The last of his three "Typhonian Trilogies," *The Ninth Arch* (2002), is a return to form of his earlier works, and provides an *au courant* overview of Grant's magical worldview.
18 AC to John W. Parsons, 19 Oct 1943, Yorke Collection.
19 Albert Pike, *Morals and Dogma of the Ancient and Accepted Scottish Rite of Freemasonry.* (New York: Robert Macoy, 1871). Helena Petrovna Blavatsky, *Isis Unveiled: A Master-Key to the Mysteries of Ancient and Modern Science and Theology,* 2 vols. (New York: J. W. Bouton, 1877).
20 Rama Prasad, *The Science of Breath and the Philosophy of the Tattvas Translated from the Sanskrit. With Introductory and Explanatory Essays on Nature's Finer Forces Reprinted from "The Theosophist" with Modifications and Additions.* (London: Theosophical Publishing Society, 1890).
21 James Legge, "The Yi King," in *The Sacred Books of China: The Texts of Confucianism,* vol. 2 (Oxford: Clarendon Press, 1882).
22 Lévi-Strauss was an anthropologist who studied the parallels in world mythologies and concluded that the meaning of myth lies in its fundamental structure and not the minor cultural variations in content. His chief works include *Anthropologie Structurale* (Paris: Plon, 1958) and *Le Cru et le Cuit [The Raw and the Cooked]* (Paris: Plon, 1964).
23 Joseph Campbell, *The Hero with a Thousand Faces* (New York: Pantheon, 1949).
24 J. Naisbitt, and P. Aburdene, *Megatrends 2000* (New York: Avon, 1990). F. Bird and B. Reimer, "Participation Rates in New Religious and Para-religious Movements," *Journal for the Scientific Study of Religion* 1982, *21,* 1–14.
25 *Magick*, xvi.
26 Alas, Thelema in practice is no less immune to these evils than any other religious, political or social group.
27 Interestingly, Houdini owned a set of *The Equinox,* currently among the holdings of the Harry Ransom Humanities Research Center, University of Texas at Austin.
28 Crowley did, however, read Joyce. See Crowley, "The Genius of Mr. James Joyce."

References

Manuscript Collections

The following collections contain manuscripts or letters by Crowley.

Clifton Waller Barrett Library of American Literature, MS 9040, Special Collections, University of Virginia Library.

Clifford Bax's copy of *Little Essays Toward Truth* with tipped-in letter from AC, Department of Special Collections, University Research Library, UCLA.

Sylvia Beach Papers (C0108), Box 190, Department of Rare Books and Special Collections, Princeton University Library.

James Branch Cabell Papers, Collection M 214, James Branch Cabell Library, Virginia Commonwealth University, Richmond, VA.

James Branch Cabell Papers, 7779-b, Alderman Library Special Collections, University of Virginia.

Aleister Crowley Collection, 1889–1989, Harry Ransom Humanities Research Center, University of Texas at Austin.

Aleister Crowley, Comment on AL, Oasis of Nefta, al-Djerid, 1923. Rare Books Department, Z. Smith Reynolds Library, Wake Forest University.

Aleister Crowley fonds, SC181, McPherson Library Special Collections, University of Victoria, British Columbia.

Aleister Crowley notebook, Special Collections, Northwestern University Library.

Aleister Crowley Papers, George Arents Research Library, Syracuse University.

Aleister Crowley Papers, Rare Books and Manuscripts, University Libraries, Pennsylvania State University.

Astrology #11049-z, Southern Historical Collection, The Wilson Library, University of North Carolina at Chapel Hill.

Mary Desti Papers (Collection 2055). Department of Special Collections, University Research Library, UCLA.

Norman Douglas Collection. GEN MSS 88, series II, box 17, General Collection, Beinecke Rare Book and Manuscript Library.

Theodore Dreiser Papers, Special Collections, Van Pelt Library, University of Pennsylvania.

Tom Driberg Papers, Christ Church Library, Oxford.

Montgomery Evans MSS, 1918–1952, Lilly Library, Indiana University.

Foyle's Bookstore private archives, London, England.

Papers of Maj. Gen. John Frederick Charles Fuller (1878–1966), GB99 KCLMA Fuller, Liddell Hart Centre for Military Archives, King's College Library.

J. F. C. Fuller Papers, Special Collections, Archibald Stevens Alexander Library, Rutgers University.

Frieda Harris Papers, 1923–1964, Rare Books and Manuscripts, University Libraries, Pennsylvania State University.

Henry Holt Collection (C0100), Box 26, Department of Rare Books and Manuscripts, Princeton University Library.

Augustus John Papers, Department of Manuscripts, National Library of Wales.

Archives of Kegan Paul, Trench, Trübner & Henry S. King, 1858–1912, Doheny Library, University of Southern California.

Manuel Komroff Papers, 1890–1974, MS# 0723, Rare Book & Manuscript Library, Butler Library, Columbia University.

Mabel Dodge Luhan Papers. YCAL MSS 196, box 7, folder 209, Yale Collection of American Literature, Beinecke Rare Book and Manuscript Library.

H. L. Mencken Papers, 1905–1956, Manuscripts and Archives Division, New York Public Library.

H. L. Mencken Papers, Enoch Pratt Free Library, Baltimore, Maryland.

H. L. Mencken Papers, #6253–h and #9040, Alderman Library Special Collections, University of Virginia.

Harold Mortlake Collection of English Life and Letters, 1591–1963, Accession 1969–0024R, Rare Books and Manuscripts, Special Collections Library, University Libraries, Pennsylvania State University.

Open Court Publishing Company records, 1886–1953, 1/2/MSS 027, Southern Illinois University Carbondale Special Collections.

Ordo Templi Orientis Archives, New York, NY.

James B. Pinker and Sons records, Henry W. and Albert A. Berg Collection of English and American Literature, New York Public Library.

Katherine Susannah Prichard Papers, MS6201, National Library of Australia, Canberra.

John Quinn Memorial Collection, Rare Books and MSS Division, New York Public Library.

Burton Rascoe Papers, Van Pelt Library Special Collections, University of Pennsylvania.

Theodore Roosevelt Papers, Manuscripts Division, Library of Congress.

Theodore Schroeder Papers, 1842–1957, 1/1/MSS 017, Southern Illinois University Carbondale Special Collections.

P. R. Stephensen Papers, Collection ML1284, Mitchell Library, State Library of New South Wales.

Ralph Straus Papers, Special Collections Department, Northwestern University Library.

Elihu Thomson Papers, MS Coll. 74, #MS61-930, American Philosophical Society, Philadelphia, PA.

H. G. Wells Papers, WELLS-1, C-537, Rare Book and Manuscripts Library, University of Illinois at Urbana-Champaign.

Louis Umfreville Wilkinson Collection, 1916–1960, Harry Ransom Humanities Research Center, University of Texas at Austin.

Gerald Yorke Collection, Warburg Institute Archive, University of London.

Bibliographies of the Works of Aleister Crowley

Cornelius, J. Edward. 1997. *The Aleister Crowley Desk Reference.* (*Red Flame* #4). Berkeley, CA: J. Edward & Marlene Cornelius.

Crowley, Aleister, and Frater 137. 1981. *Source Book 93.* San Francisco: Stellar Visions.

Duncombe-Jewell, L. C. R. 1907. Towards an outline of a bibliography of the writings in prose and verse of Aleister Crowley. In Aleister Crowley, *The Works of Aleister Crowley* 3. Foyers: SPRT, 233–239.

Fitzgerald, Edward Noel. 1951. The works of Aleister Crowley published or privately printed: A bibliographical list. In Charles Richard Cammell, *Aleister Crowley: The Man, the Mage, the Poet.* London: Richards Press, 207–218.

Fuller, John Frederick Charles. 1966. *Bibliotheca Crowleyana: The Collection of J.F.C. Fuller.* Tenterden, Kent: Keith Hogg [rpt. 1989, Edmonds, WA: Sure Fire Press, with a preface by Richard Kaczynski].

Parfitt, Will, and A. Drylie. 1976. *A Crowley Cross-Index.* Faulkland, Avon: Zro.

Yorke, Gerald. 1951. Bibliography of the works of Aleister Crowley. In John Symonds, *The Great Beast: The Life of Aleister Crowley.* London: Rider & Co., 301–310.

Published Works by Aleister Crowley

Although Crowley's works have been reprinted over the years, the following bibliography cites the first publication—or reprints during Crowley's lifetime—of works cited in this book. All works identify Aleister Crowley as the author unless otherwise noted. "Society for the Propagation of Religious Truth" is abbreviated SPRT.

I. Books, Pamphlets and Broadsides

A Gentleman of the University of Cambridge. *Aceldama: A Place to Bury Strangers In.* London: privately printed, 1898.

Ahab and Other Poems. London: privately printed, 1903.

Alexandra. Edited by Anthony Naylor. Thame: Mandrake, 1991.

Anonymous. *Alice: An Adultery.* Privately printed, 1903 (rpt. SPRT, 1905).

Ambergris: A Selection from the Poems of Aleister Crowley. London: Elkin Matthews, 1910.

Anonymous. *Amphora.* London: privately printed, 1908 (rpt. London: Burns & Oates, 1909, and as *Hail Mary,* London: Wieland & Co., 1912).

Amrita: Essays in Magical Rejuvenation. King's Beach, CA: Thelema Publications, 1990.

An Appeal to the American Republic. London: Kegan Paul, Trench, Trübner & Co., 1899 (also appeared in *Cambridge Magazine,* 1899, and as "To America," *English Review,* November 1914, 273–9).

The Argonauts. Foyers: SPRT, 1904.

Atlantis. S.l: Dove Press, 1970.

Alastor. *The Avenger to the Theosophical Society.* Tunis: privately printed, 1925.

Anonymous. *Balzac: Hommage à Auguste Rodin.* Paris: privately printed, 1903.

The Banned Lecture: Gilles de Rais. Oxford: P. R. Stevenson, 1930.

Abhavananda. *Berashith: An Essay in Ontology, with Some Remarks on Ceremonial Magic.* Paris: privately printed, 1903.

Frater Perdurabo and Soror Virakam. *Book Four,* part 1. London: Wieland & Co., 1911.

Frater Perdurabo and Soror Virakam. *Book Four,* part 2. London: Wieland & Co., 1913.

Frater Perdurabo. *The Book of Lies: Which is also Falsely Called Breaks. The Wanderings or Falsifications of the One Thought of Frater Perdurabo, which Thought is in Itself Untrue.* London: Wieland & Co., 1913 [1912].

O. M. and the Master Therion. *The Book of the Law.* London: OTO, 1938 (rpt. Los Angeles: OTO, 1942; also see *Liber AL vel Legis*).

Master Therion. *The Book of Thoth: A Short Essay on the Tarot of the Egyptians.* London: OTO, 1944.

St. E. A. of M. and S. *Carmen Saeculare.* London: Kegan Paul, Trench, Trübner & Co., 1901.

Chicago May: A Love Poem. New York: privately printed, 1914.

The City of God: A Rhapsody. London: OTO, 1943.

Verey, Rev. C. *Clouds without Water.* London: privately printed, 1909.

Commentaries on the Holy Books and Other Papers. Edited by Hymenaeus Beta. Yorke Beach, ME: Samuel Weiser, 1996.

The Complete Astrological Writings. Edited by John Symonds and Kenneth Grant. London: Duckworth, 1974 (see *General Principles of Astrology*).

Dawn of a New Life, s.l., n.d.

The Diary of a Drug Fiend. London: William Collins & Sons, 1922.

Mahatma Guru Sri Paramahansa Shivaji. *Eight Lectures on Yoga.* London: OTO, 1939.

Anonymous. *Ein Zeugnis der Suchenden.* Leipzig: privately printed, 1925.

England, Stand Fast! A Poem. London: OTO, 1939.

The Equinox, volume I. London: Simpkin, Marshall, Hamilton Kent & Co./ Wieland & Co., 1909–1913.

The Equinox, volume III, number 1. Detroit: Universal Publishing Co., 1919.

Ankh-af-na-Khonsu. *The Equinox of the Gods*. London: OTO, 1936 (2nd printing, 1937).

The Fish. Edited by Anthony Naylor. Thame: Mandrake, 1992.

The Fun of the Fair. London: OTO, 1942.

Gargoyles: Being Strangely Wrought Images of Life and Death. Foyers: SPRT, 1906.

Crowley, Aleister, Evangeline Adams, and Beta Hymenaeus. *The General Principles of Astrology. Liber DXXXVI*. Boston, MA: Weiser Books, 2002.

The Giant's Thumb. Thame: First Impressions, 1992.

The God Eater: A Tragedy of Satire. London: Chas. Watts & Co., 1903.

A Dead Hand. *The Goetia: The Book of the Goetia of Solomon the King, Translated into the English Tongue by a Dead Hand and Adorned with Diverse Other Matters Germane, Delightful to the Wise*. Edited by Aleister Crowley. Foyers: SPRT, 1904.

Golden Twigs. Edited by Martin P. Starr. Chicago: Teitan Press, 1988.

The Gospel According to St. Bernard Shaw. Barstow, CA: privately printed, 1953 (rpt. *Crowley on Christ*, ed. Francis King, London: C. W. Daniel Company, 1974).

Khaled Khan. *The Heart of the Master*. London: OTO, 1938.

The High History of Good Sir Palamedes the Saracen Knight and of His Following of the Questing Beast. London: Wieland & Co., 1912.

A. E. C. *The Honourable Adulterers: A Tragedy*. London: privately printed, 1899.

Household Gods: A Comedy. Pallanza: privately printed, 1912.

Hymn to Pan. New York: Argus Bookshop, n.d. (c. 1917).

In Residence: The Don's Guide to Cambridge. Cambridge: Elijah Johnson, 1904.

A Gentleman of the University of Cambridge. *Jephthah: A Tragedy*. London: privately printed, 1898.

Jephthah and Other Mysteries, Lyrical and Dramatic. London: Kegan Paul, Trench, Trübner & Co., 1899.

Svareff, Count Vladimir. *Jezebel and Other Tragic Poems*. London: Chiswick Press, 1898.

Anonymous. *Kreis um Thelema*. Leipzig: privately printed, 1925.

Crowley, Aleister, Louis Wilkinson, and Hymenaeus Beta, 1983. *The Law is for All: The Authorized Popular Commentary on Liber AL vel Legis sub figura CCXX, The Book of the Law*. Phoenix, AZ: New Falcon Press, 1983.

Anonymous. *The Law of Liberty*. London: privately printed, n.d. (1917?).

Ankh-af-na-Khonsu. *Liber AL vel Legis sub figura XXXI*. Tunis: privately printed, 1926.

Anonymous. *Liber Collegii Sancti*. London: privately printed, 1910.

Ko Yuen. *Liber XXI: Khing Kang King, The Classic of Purity*. London: privately printed, 1939.

Konx Om Pax: Essays in Light. Foyers: SPRT, 1907.

La Gauloise (Song of the Free French). London: privately printed, 1942.

Leah Sublime. Montreal: 93 Publishing, 1976.

Liber Aleph vel CXI: The Book of Wisdom or Folly in the Form of an Epistle of 666 The Great Wild Beast to his Son 777. West Point, CA: Thelema Publishing Co., 1961

Liber Oz. London: OTO, 1942.

Liber XXX Aerum vel Saeculi sub figura CCCCXVIII: (Being of the Angels of the 30 Aethyrs): The Vision and the Voice. *The Equinox* 1911, 1(5), special supplement.

Little Essays Toward Truth. London: OTO, 1938.

Baudelaire, Charles. *Little Poems in Prose.* Translated by Aleister Crowley. Paris: Edward W. Titus, 1928.

Fra. H. I. Edinburgh. *Madame Tussaud-Besant.* Tunis: privately printed, 1925.

The Magical Diaries of Aleister Crowley: The Magical Diaries of Το Μεγα Θηριον, The Beast 666, Aleister Crowley, Λογος Αιωνος Θελημα 93. 1923. Edited by Stephen Skinner. New York: Samuel Weiser, 1979.

The Magical Record of the Beast 666: The Diaries of Aleister Crowley 1914–1920. Edited by John Symonds and Kenneth Grant. Montreal: Next Step Publications, 1972.

Master Therion. *Magick in Theory and Practice.* Paris: Lecram Press, 1929 [1930].

Magick without Tears. Hampton, NJ: Thelema Publishing Company, 1954 (edited rpt. St. Paul, MN: Llewellyn, 1973, ed. Israel Regardie; an unexpurgated edition is being prepared by Stephen J. King).

Anonymous. *Manifesto of the M∴M∴M∴.* Issued by order of L. Bathurst, Grand Secretary General. Privately printed, 1912.

Anonymous. *The Message of the Master Therion.* London: privately printed, n.d. (c. 1917).

Moonchild: A Prologue. London: Mandrake Press, 1929.

Mortadello, or the Angel of Venice: A Comedy. London: Wieland & Co., 1912.

The Mother's Tragedy and Other Poems. London: privately printed, 1901 (rpt. SPRT, 1907).

New Year. Paris: privately printed, 1903.

Herman Rudolf and Alastor. *Offener Brief.* Weida: privately printed, 1925.

Olla: An Anthology of Sixty Years of Song. London: OTO, 1946.

Oracles: The Biography of an Art. Foyers: SPRT, 1905.

Orpheus: A Lyrical Legend. Foyers: SPRT, 1905.

The Poem: A Little Drama in Four Scenes. London: privately printed, 1898.

The Revival of Magick and Other Essays. Edited by Hymenaeus Beta and Richard Kaczynski. Tempe, AZ: New Falcon, 1998.

The Rites of Eleusis. London: privately printed, 1910.

Rodin in Rime. See *Seven Lithographs by Clot,* 1907.

H. D. Carr. *Rosa Coeli: A Poem.* London: privately printed, 1907.

Rosa Decidua. Privately printed, 1910.

H. D. Carr. *Rosa Inferni: A Poem.* London: privately printed, 1907.

H. D. Carr. *Rosa Mundi: A Poem.* Paris: Ph. Renouard, 1905.

Vincey, Leo. *The "Rosicrucian" Scandal.* London: privately printed, 1912–1913.

The Late Major Lutiy and Another. *The Scented Garden of Abdullah the Satirist of Shiraz*. London: privately printed, 1910.

Comte de Fénix. *The Scientific Solution to the Problem of Government*. London: privately printed, c. 1937.

The Scrutinies of Simon Iff. Edited by Martin P. Starr. Chicago: Teitan Press, 1987.

Anonymous. *777 vel Prolegomena Symbolica ad Systemam Sceptico-Mysticae Viae Explicande, Fundamentum Hieroglyphicum Sanctissimorum Scientiae Summae*. London: Walter Scott, 1909.

Seven Lithographs by Clot from the Water-colours of Auguste Rodin with a Chaplet of Verse. London: Chiswick Press, 1907.

Ko Yuen. *Shih Yi: A Critical and Mnemonic Paraphrase of the Yi King*. Oceanside, CA: H. P. Smith, 1971.

Snowdrops from a Curate's Garden. Cosmopoli, 1881 [Paris: privately printed, 1904] (rpt. Chicago: Teitan Press, 1986, ed. Martin P. Starr).

Songs for Italy. London: privately printed, 1923.

Songs of the Spirit. London: Kegan Paul, Trench, Trübner & Co., 1898 (rpt. SPRT, 1905).

The Soul of Osiris: A History. London: Kegan Paul, Trench, Trübner & Co., 1901.

The Soul of the Desert. Kings Beach, CA: Thelema Publications, 1974.

The Spirit of Solitude: An Autohagiography. Subsequently Re-Antichristened The Confessions of Aleister Crowley. London: Mandrake Press, 1929 (Only two of six volumes were released; edited version published as *The Confessions of Aleister Crowley*, ed. John Symonds and Kenneth Grant, London: Jonathan Cape, 1969 and New York: Hill and Wang, 1969; an unexpurgated seven-volume edition, ed. Hymenaeus Beta, is forthcoming).

The Star and the Garter. London: Watts & Co., 1903 (rpt. SPRT, 1904).

The Stratagem and Other Stories. London: Mandrake Press, 1930.

Summa Spes. London: privately printed, 1903.

The Sword of Song, Called by Christians the Book of the Beast. Benares: SPRT, 1904.

A Gentleman of the University of Cambridge. *The Tale of Archais: A Romance in Verse*. London: Kegan, Paul, Trench, Trübner & Co., 1898.

Aleister Crowley (words) and Bernard F. Page (music), *The Tango Song*. London: Wieland & Co., 1913.

Tannhauser: A Story of All Time. London: Kegan Paul, Trench, Trübner & Co., 1902 (rpt. SPRT, 1907).

Ko Yuen. *The Tao Teh King*. Kings Beach, CA: Thelema Publications, 1976.

Temperance: A Tract for the Times. London: OTO, 1939.

Anonymous. ΘΕΛΗΜΑ, vol. 1–3. London: privately printed 1909–1910.

Thumbs Up! A Pentagram: A Pantacle to Win the War. London: privately printed, 1941.

Anonymous. 1924. *To Man*. Tunis: privately printed, 1924.

Crowley, Aleister, Victor Neuburg, and Mary Desti. *The Vision and the Voice with Commentary and Other Papers.* Edited by Hymenaeus Beta. Yorke Beach, ME: Samuel Weiser, 1998.

Bishop, George Archibald. *White Stains: The Literary Remains of George Archibald Bishop, a Neuropath of the Second Empire.* Amsterdam: privately printed, 1898.

Why Jesus Wept: A Study of Society and of the Grace of God. London: privately printed, 1904.

The Winged Beetle. Privately printed, 1910.

The Works of Aleister Crowley, vol. 1. Foyers: SPRT, 1905.

The Works of Aleister Crowley, vol. 2. Foyers: SPRT, 1906.

The Works of Aleister Crowley, vol. 3. Foyers: SPRT, 1907.

Ankh-f-n-Khonsu. *The World Teacher to the Theosophical Society.* Tunis: privately printed, 1925.

The World's Tragedy. Paris: privately printed, 1910.

E. G. O. *The Writing on the Ground.* London: privately printed, 1913.

II. Poetry and Fiction in Magazines and Newspapers

"Adonis." *The Equinox* 1912, 1(7): 117–57.

"Anna of Havana." *Vanity Fair,* Jan 1916, 43.

"The Artistic Temperament." *International* 1917, 11(10): 295–301.

"Ballade of a Far Country." *Cambridge Magazine,* 27 Apr 1899, 1(1).

"Ballade of Bad Verses." *Granta,* 30 Apr 1898, 11(233): 271.

"The Ballad of Burdens." *Granta,* 3 Feb 1899, 13.

"Ballade of a Far Country," *Cambridge Magazine* 1899, 1(1).

"Ballade of Criticism." *Cambridge Magazine,* 18 May 1899, 1(4).

"Ballade of Summer Joys." *Cambridge Magazine,* 1 Jun 1899, 1(6).

"Ballade of Ursa and Ursula," *Cambridge Magazine* 1899, 1(3).

"Ballade of Whist." *Cambridge Magazine,* 11 May 1899, 1(3).

"Balzac: To Auguste Rodin." *Weekly Critical Review,* 5 Feb 1903, 1(3): 5 (rpt. *Les Maîtres Artistes,* Oct 1903, 8: 283, trans. Marcel Schwob).

"Big Game." *International* 1917, 11(9): 259–67.

"A Birthday." *The Equinox* 1912, 1(7): 419–24.

"The Burning of Melcarth." *International* 1917, 11(10): 310–2.

"Chants before Battle." *English Review,* Aug 1914, 1–7.

"Chez Sherry: A Prose Poem." *Vanity Fair,* Dec 1916, 168.

"The City of God (Moscow)." *English Review,* Jan 1914, 161–6. Rpt. London: The OTO, 1943.

"The Conduct of John Briggs." *International* 1917, 11(12): 355–60.

"Dawn." *International* 1918, 12(1): 9.

"The Disciples." *The Equinox* 1913, 1(10): 91–2.

"The Drug." *Idler: An Illustrated Monthly Magazine,* Jan 1909, 34(76): 403–8.

"Ezekiel in the Quarter Montparnesse." *Vanity Fair,* 12 Aug 1908, 211.

"The Ghouls." *The Equinox* 1912, 1(7): 159–78.

"The God of Ibreez." *International* 1918, 12(1): 19–24.

"The Heart of Holy Russia." *International* 1918, 12(1): 10–4.

"The Hearth." *International* 1917, 11(11): 334–8.

"The Hermit's Hymn to Solitude." *Weekly Critical Review,* 2 Apr 1903, 1(11): 3–4;

"His Secret Sin." *The Equinox* 1912, 1(8): 49–60.

"Hymn." *International* 1917, 11(11): 333.

"In the Red Room of Rose Croix." *International* 1917, 11(10): 294.

"Ineligible." *International* 1918, 12(2): 35–40.

"Jeremiah in the Quartier Montparnasse." *Vanity Fair,* 3 Jun 1908, 713.

"The King of the Wood." *International* 1918, 12(4): 99–102.

"Knight-errant." *International* 1918, 12(3): 85.

"Le Bourgeois de Calais." *Weekly Critical Review* 1903, v. 2.

"Love is One." *International* 1917, 11(10): 309.

Lévi, Éliphas. "The Magician." Translated by Aleister Crowley. *The Equinox* 1909, 1(1): 109.

"Mantra Yogi." *Vanity Fair,* 3 Mar 1909.

"The Mass of Saint Secaire." *International* 1918, 12(2): 42–6.

Michael Fairfax, "Moon-Wane." *English Review,* Oct 1922, 167: 283–5.

"The Mystic." *Vanity Fair,* 22 Jul 1908, 105.

"Not Good Enough." *International* 1918, 12(1): 3–9.

"Of the Mutability of Human Affairs." *Granta,* 26 Feb 1898, 11: 223.

"The Old Man of the Peepul-tree." *International* 1918, 12(4): 107–10.

"On the Edge of the Desert." *English Review,* Jun 1911, 362–3.

"Outside the Bank's Routine." *International* 1917, 11(11): 323–31.

"Pan to Artemis." *The Equinox* 1910, 1(4): 197–8.

"The Pentagram." *New Age,* 21 Mar 1908, 2(21): 410.

"A Riddle." *International* 1917, 11(12): 379.

Fairfax, Michael. "The Rock." *English Review,* Oct 1922, 167: 285–6.

"Rodin." *Weekly Critical Review,* 21 May 1903, 1(18): 8 (rpt. *Les Maîtres Artistes,* Oct 1903, 8: 283, trans. Marcel Schwob).

"Rodin I: Eve." *Weekly Critical Review,* 5 Nov 1903, 2(42): 374.

"Rodin II: Tête de Femme (Luxembourg)." *Weekly Critical Review,* 28 May 1903, 1(19): 6.

"Rodin III: Syrinx and Pan." *Weekly Critical Review,* 4 Jun 1903, 1(20): 10.

"Rodin IV: Illusion." *Weekly Critical Review,* 11 Jun 1903, 1(21): 3.

"Rodin IX: La Tentation de Saint-Antoine." *Weekly Critical Review,* 16 Jul 1903, 1(26): 8.

"Rodin V: La Fortune." *Weekly Critical Review,* 18 Jun 1903, 1(22): 19.

"Rodin VI: Paolo and Francesca." *Weekly Critical Review,* 25 Jun 1903, 1(23): 16–7.

"Rodin VII: Les deux Génies." *Weekly Critical Review,* 2 Jul 1903, 1(24): 16.

"Rodin VIII: La Vielle Heaulmière." *Weekly Critical Review,* 9 Jul 1903, 1(25): 18.

"Rodin X: La Main de Dieu." *Weekly Critical Review,* 30 Jul 1903, 2(28): 38.

"Rodin XI: An Indicent (Rue de l'Université. 182)." *Weekly Critical Review,* 6 Aug 1903, 2(29): 56.

"A Septennial." *International* 1917, 11(12): 376.

"A Sonnet of Spring Fashions." *Granta,* 21 May 1898, 11(236): 308.

"The Stratagem." *English Review,* Jun 1914, 339–51. Rpt. in *Smart Set,* Sep 1916, 1(1): 229–36.

King, Lavinia. "The Suffragette: A Farce." *New Age,* 30 May 1908, 3(5): 91–2.

"Titanic Disaster." *New York Times,* 26 May 1912, SM4; rpt. *The Equinox* 1913, I(9): 47–8.

"To a Brunette: Addressed to His Beloved, after a Short Absence." *Vanity Fair,* Feb 1916, 63.

Fairfax, Michael. "To a New-Born Child." *English Review,* Oct 1922, 167: 287.

"To America." *English Review,* Oct 1914, 273–9 (see *An Appeal to the American Republic*).

"To Laylah—Eight-and-twenty." *The Equinox* 1913, 1(10): 235–6.

"The Triads of Despair." *Weekly Critical Review,* 12 Mar 1903, 1(8): 6.

"Villon's Apology (On Reading Stevenson's Essay)." *Poetry Review,* Dec 1912, 1(12): 540.

"A Vision of the Eucharist." *International* 1918, 12(2): 62.

"Visions." *International* 1918, 12(4): 117.

"The Woodcutter." *The Equinox* 1912, 1(8): 79–88.

III. Essays in Magazines and Newspapers

"1066: A Study of the Ruling Class of England," *International* 1917, 11(9):272–6.

Jeanne La Goulue. "Absinthe," *International* 1918, 11(10): 306.

"Absinthe, the Green Goddess," *International* 1918, 12(2): 47–51.

"Across the Gulf." *The Equinox* 1911, 1(7): 239–254.

"Aleister Crowley Explains." *Continental Times,* 11 Oct 1915, 22: n.p.

"America's Attitude to the War: Hatred of the People for the Press." *Continental Times,* 6 Oct 1915, 22(42): n.p.

An Englishman. "The American Verdict on the War." *International* 1916, 10(7): 202.

"Another Note on Cabell." *Reviewer* 1923, 3(11–12): 907–14.

"Art and Clairvoyance." *International* 1917, 11(12): 379.

"Art in America." *English Review,* Nov 1913, 578–95.

"The Attainment of Happiness: A Restatement of the Purpose of Mystical Teachings." *Vanity Fair,* Nov 1916, 55, 134.

"Behind the Front: Impressions of a Tourist in Western Europe." *Fatherland,* 29 Dec 1915, 3(21): 365; 5 Jan 1916, 3(22): 383–4.

"(On) A Burmese River: From the Note Book of Aleister Crowley." *Vanity Fair,* 3 Feb 1909, 135; 10 Feb 1909, 169; 17 Feb 1909, 201; 24 Feb 1909, 232; 3 Mar 1909, 269; 31 Mar 1909, 393.

"The Camel: A Discussion of the Value of 'Interior Certainty.'" *Occult Review,* Apr 1911, 13: 208–13.

Crowley, E. A. "Chalk Climbing on Beachy Head." *Scottish Mountaineering Club Journal,* May 1895, 3(17): 288–94.

Ta Dhuibh. "Chess Notes," *Eastbourne Gazette,* 31 Jan 1894; 7 Feb 1894; 14 Feb 1894; 21 Feb 1894; 28 Feb 1894; 7 Mar 1894; 14 Mar 1894; 21 Mar 1894; 28 Mar 1894; 4 Apr 1894; 11 Apr 1894; 18 Apr 1894; 25 Apr 1894.

"Cocaine." *International* 1917, 11(10): 291–4.

Verlaine, Paul. "Colloque Sentimental." Translated by Aleister Crowley. *Vanity Fair,* Sep 1915, 66.

A Past Grand Master. "The Crisis in Freemasonry." *English Review,* Aug 1922, 127–34.

"A Curious Kind of Lightning." *New York Times,* 16 July 1916, E2.

"Das Herz des Meisters." *Pansophia* 1925, 7(1), 93–124 (see *The Heart of the Master*).

"Delenda Est Britannia (Being a Prologue and Epilogue to 'The Vampire of the Continent')." *Fatherland,* 3 Jan 1917, 5(22).

"Der Meister Therion." *Pansophia* 1925, 7(1), 77–92 (see "The Master Therion: A Biographical Note").

"Drama Be Damned." *International* 1918, 12(4): 127–8.

A London Physician. "The Drug Panic." *English Review,* Jul 1922, 65–70.

"Dynamic and Static Concentration," *Occult Review,* Jun 1910, 11: 335.

"Ecclesiæ Gnosticæ Catholicæ Canon Missæ." *International* 1918, 12(3): 70–4.

"Ein Stern in Sicht." *Pansophia* 1925, 7(1), 125–153 (see "One Star in Sight").

"End of England." *Continental Times,* 26 Jul 1915, 22: n.p.

"England on the Brink of Revolution." *Fatherland,* 21 Jul 1915, 2(24): 3– 5.

"England's Blind Spot." *Viereck's The American Weekly,* 18 May 1917, 6(11): 182–3.

"The Expedition to Chogo Ri: Leaves from the Notebook of Aleister Crowley." *Vanity Fair,* 8 Jul 1908, 51–2; 15 Jul 1908, 71–2; 22 Jul 1908, 106–7; 5 Aug 1908, 179–80; 19 Aug 1908, 246–7; 2 Sep 1908, 310–1; and 16 Sep 1908, 372–3.

"Ezekiel in the Quarter Montparnesse." *Vanity Fair,* 12 Aug 1908, 211.

"The Future of the Submarine." *Fatherland,* 6 Oct 1915, 3(9): 152–3.

"The Genius of Mr. James Joyce," *New Pearson's,* Jul 1923, 52–3.

Geomancy." *International* 1918, 12(1): 28–9.

"A Great Climb: Ready to Ascend Kinchinjunga: The Food Supplies," *Daily Mail,* 29 Aug 1905.

"The Great Climb: Four Men Killed on Kinchinjunga: Expedition Abandoned at 21,000 Feet." *Daily Mail,* 11 Sep 1905.

A New York Specialist. "The Great Drug Delusion." *English Review,* Jun 1922, 571–6.

"The Greek Qabalah." *OTO Newsletter* 1979, 2(7–8): 9–44.

"A Hindu at the Polo Grounds: A Letter from Mahatma Sri Paramananda Guru Swamiji (Great Soul Saint Supreme-Bliss Teacher Learned Person) to His Brother in India." *Vanity Fair,* Aug 1915, 63.

Kwaw Li Ya. "The Hokku: A New Verse Form and a Prize Contest for Ambitious American Poets." *Vanity Fair,* Aug 1915, 46.

Kwaw Li Ya. "The Hokku Winners: A Few Comments." *Vanity Fair,* Dec 1915, 47.

"Honesty is the Best Policy." *Fatherland,* January 13, 1915, 1(23): 11–5; 20 Jan 1915, 1(24): 5–6.

Cor Scorpionis. "How Horoscopes Are Faked." *International* 1917, 11(11): 345.

"How to Tell and Englishman from an American." *Liliput,* Aug 1946, 147.

Oliver Haddo. "How to Write a Novel! After W. S. Maugham." *Vanity Fair,* 30 Dec 1908, 838–40.

"An Improvement on Psycho-analysis: The Psychology of the Unconscious—for Dinner-table Consumption." *Vanity Fair,* Dec 1916, 60, 137.

"Introduction." In Stuart X, *A Prophet in His Own Country: Being the Letters of Stuart X to Many Men on Many Occasions* (Washington, D.C.: the author, 1916), 11–27.

"Ireland as Peace Arbiter: Irish Poet Would Have Forgiveness, Not Revenge, Free Erin's Motto." *Washington Post,* 12 May 1916, 9.

Crowley, Alex C. "The Irish Flag." *New York Times,* 21 Jul 1915, 10.

"Jack the Ripper." *Sothis* 1974, 1(4): 62.

A Gentile. "The Jewish Problem Re-stated." *English Review,* Jul 1922, 28–37.

L. P. 33. Y., "Leaves from a Lost Portfolio." *Fatherland,* 8 Mar 1916, 4(5): 67–9.

Letter. *Fatherland,* 11 Aug 1915, 3(1): 9.

"Liber A'ash." *The Equinox* 1911, 1(6): 33–9.

"Liber Astarte." *The Equinox* 1911, 1(7): 37–58.

"Liber B." *The Equinox* 1911, 1(7): 5–9.

"Liber Cheth." *The Equinox* 1911, 1(6): 23–7.

"Liber HAD." *The Equinox* 1911, 1(7): 83–91.

"Liber IOD (inaccurately called TAV)." *The Equinox* 1911, 1(7): 93–100.

"Liber Israfel." *The Equinox* 1911, 1(7): 21–7.

"Liber NV." *The Equinox* 1911, 1(7): 11–20.

"Liber Os Abysmi." *The Equinox* 1911, 1(7): 77–81.

"Liber Resh." *The Equinox* 1911, 1(6): 29–32.

"Liber RV." *The Equinox* 1911, 1(7): 59–67.

"Liber Turris." *The Equinox* 1911, 1(6): 8–15.

"Liber Tzaddi." *The Equinox* 1911, 1(6): 17–22.

"Liber Viarum Viae." *The Equinox* 1911, 1(7): 101–3.

"Lifting the Mask from England." *Fatherland,* 15 Mar 1916, 4(6): 85–6.

"The Master Therion: A Biographical Note." *The Equinox* 1986, 3(10): 16– 7.

"The Message of the Master Therion." *International* 1918, 12(1): 26.

Quiller, A, Jr. "My Crapulous Contemporaries No. VI: An Obituary." *The Equinox* 1912, 1(8): 243–9.

"Mystics and Their Little Ways: One is Nothing, While Two Is—in Reality—One." *Vanity Fair,* Oct 1916, 142, 144.

"A New Heaven and a New Earth: As Foreshadowed in Lord Dunsany's *The Gods of Pegana.*" *Vanity Fair,* Oct 1917, 134, 136.

"A New Parsifal, Wilhelm II: The Vision of an English Poet." *Continental Times,* 20 Aug 1915, 22(22): n.p.

"The New Parsifal: A Study of Wilhelm II." *Open Court* 1915, 29(8): 499– 502.

"The Nonsense about *Vers Libre:* Why Not a Little Free Prose for a Change?" *Vanity Fair,* Dec 1915, 65.

"On the Kinchin Lay: I. Prospect and Retrospect." *Pioneer,* 10 Aug 1905.

"On the Kinchin Lay: II. Bandoblast." *Pioneer,* 17 Aug 1905.

"On the Kinchin Lay: The March." *Pioneer,* 20 Sep 1905.

"On the Kinchin Lay: V. Mountains or Metaphysics?" *Pioneer,* 15 Oct 1905, 3–4.

Dionysus Carr. "On the Management of Blondes: Prolegomena to Any System of Philosophy Devoted to Their Treatment and Care." *Vanity Fair,* May 1916, 85.

"One Star in Sight." In *Magick in Theory and Practice.* Paris: Lecram Press, 1929.

"An Orgy of Cant: Aleister Crowley, the British Poet, Calls a Spade a Spade." *Continental Times,* 24 Feb 1915, 21(23): supplement.

"The Oriental Mind." *Washington Post,* 2 Jun 1916, 6.

"The Origin of the Game of Pirate Bridge." *Vanity Fair,* Jan 1917, 56.

"The Ouija Board." *International* 1917, 11(10): 319.

Prometheus. "Percy Bysshe Shelley." *English Review,* Jul 1922, 16–21.

"Praemonstrance of A∴A∴ and Curriculum of A∴A∴." *The Equinox* 1919, 3(1): 11–38.

Kwaw Li Ya. "The Prize Winners of the Hokku Contest: Their Poetry and an Analysis of It by the Eminent Chinese Poet." *Vanity Fair,* Oct 1915, 70.

"Protests against Normal Way of Giving Anesthetics." *Washington Post,* 4 Sep 1916, 7.

"Protests He Is Not Author of Book by Stuart X." *Washington Post,* 2 Oct 1916, 9.

"The Pseudo-Occultist," *Occult Review,* Jul 1914, 20: 29.

"Ratan Devi: Indian Singer." *Vanity Fair,* May 1916, 79.

"The Revival of Magick." *International* 1918, 11(8): 247–8; 11(9): 280–2; 11(10): 302–4; 11(11): 332–3.

Baudelaire, Charles. "Six Little Poems in Prose." Translated by Aleister Crowley. *Vanity Fair,* Dec 1915, 51.

An Englishman, "Skeletons in the Cabinet." *Fatherland,* 10 Nov 1915, 3(14): 245.

"The Soul of the Desert," *Occult Review,* Jul 1914, 20: 18–24.

"The Star-spangled Banner: An Explanation of Why—with the Best Will in the World—We Cannot Sing Our National Hymn." *Vanity Fair,* Aug 1917, 33, 90.

"Stuart X, The Great Unknown: An Unofficial Adviser to the Universe in General." *Vanity Fair,* Aug 1916, 35.

"A Syllabus of the Official Instructions of A∴A∴ Hitherto Published." *The Equinox* 1913, 1(10): 43–7.

John Frederick Charles Fuller and Aleister Crowley. "The Temple of Solomon the King." *The Equinox* 1909–1913, 1(1): 141–229; 1(2): 217–334; 1(3): 133–280; 1(4): 41–196; 1(5): 65–120; 1(7): 355–400; 1(8): 5–48; 1(9): 1–11; 1(10): 93–125.

"Three Great Hoaxes of the War: Blessed Are They that Have Not Seen and Yet Have Believed." *Vanity Fair,* Jan 1916, 37, 118.

Baudelaire, Charles. "Three Little Poems in Prose." Translated by Aleister Crowley. *Vanity Fair,* Nov 1915, 59.

"Vain Tale: With a Madman on the Alps." *Vanity Fair,* 24 Jun 1908, 823.

"Vanity Fair's Prize Move Scenario: Winner of the Thousand-dollar Reward for the Worst Short Film Story." *Vanity Fair,* Jun 1916, 89.

"Waite's Wet." *The Equinox* 1912, 1(8): 233–42.

"What's Wrong with the Movies? The Industry Seems to Be in a Critical Condition—and Perhaps It Deserves to Be." *Vanity Fair,* Jul 1917, 55, 88.

Verlaine, Paul. "With Muted Strings." Translated by Aleister Crowley. *Vanity Fair,* Oct 1915, 46.

Picture Credits

The publisher thanks those who have given kind permission to reproduce the images listed. Every effort has been made to obtain proper clearances from the owners or heirs of photographs and give proper credit; however, some have not proven possible due to the passage of time. Any holder of copyright is invited to communicate via the publisher about any omissions.

6   Grey, *Crowley's Brewery*, 10, from an unidentified nineteenth-century portrait.

7   Hampshire Record Office, 62M91/1, p139

7   *Proceedings and Transactions of the Croydon Natural History and Scientific Society*, 1903, frontis.

10   NS 74.1, Yorke Collection, Warburg Institute Archives.

13   NS 74.2, Yorke Collection, Warburg Institue Archives.

17   *Confessions*, 1929, v. 1, used with permission of OTO.

23   *Confessions*, 1929, v. 1, used with permission of OTO.

29   *Confessions*, 1929, v. 1, used with permission of OTO.

34   Crowley, *Works* v. 1, frontis.

38   MS Thr 447, Harvard Theatre Collection, Houghton Library.

44   Used by permission of the Royal Asiatic Society of Great Britain and Ireland, catalog number 026.001.

57   *Ars Quatuor Coronatorum* 1894, frontis.

59   *Daily Mirror*, 27 Apr. 1911.

63   *Confessions*, 1929, v. 1, used with permission of OTO.

69   Crowley, *MMM Manifesto*, 1912, from the collection of Helen Parsons Smith.

82   Library of Congress.

88   *Climbers' Club Journal* 1903, v. 5 no. 20.

94   Rámanáthan, *Culture of the Soul*, 1906, frontis.

100   Hess, *Saggi sulla psicologia dell'alpinista*, 1914, 435.

100   Jacot-Guillarmod, *Six Mois dans l'Himalaya*, 1902, frontis.

101   *Confessions*, 1929, v. 2, used with permission of OTO.

104   Jacot-Guillarmod, *Six mois dans l'Himalaya*, 1902, 228.

107   Frater Perdurabo and Soror Virakam, *Book 4*, Part I, 1911, frontis.

114   Reproduced from *British Medical Journal*, 23 June 1951, 1(4720): 1452, with permission from BMJ Publishing Group Ltd.

118   *The Candid Friend and Traveller*, 1902, 399.

121   Aleister Crowley PH:LF1, P21, Harry Ransom Humanities Research Center, the University of Texas at Austin.

125   *The Equinox* 1912, I(7).

140   *Berge der Welt*, 1948, 199. © Swiss Foundation for Alpine Research, used with permission.

141   S0021401, Royal Geographical Society.

144   *Jahrbuch des Schweizer Alpenclub*, 1905.

148   *Jahrbuch des Schweizer Alpenclub*, 1905.

159   Fuller, *The Star in the West*, 1907, from the collection of Clive Harper.

165   *Appleton's Magazine* 1905, 6(1): 47.

166   Courtesy of OTO, with permission from Timothy d'Arch Smith.

169   *What's On*, 31 Aug. 1907, 5.

171   *Pearson's*, Oct. 1907, 344.

174   Used with permission of Francis Wyndham.

187   National Archives, College Park, MD.

190   *Memoirs of Kenneth Martin Ward*, 1929.

195   Crowley, *Rosa Decidua*, 1910, frontis.

209   *Co-Mason*, April 1913, frontis.

213   *Play Pictorial*, Sep. 1911, 81.

215   "The Goddess," *The Rites of Eleusis* promotional booklet, 1910.

220   Radclyffe, *Wealth and Wild Cats*, 1898,

frontis.

226 Unidentified news clipping (private collection) and *Liverpool Courrier,* 28 Oct. 1910.

227 *Bystander,* 12 Oct. 1910, 73.

236 *Journal of the Gypsy Lore Society,* 1911.

239 Photograph by E. O. Hoppé © 2010 E. O. Hoppé Estate Collection/Curatorial Assistance, Pasadena, California.

250 *Vanity Fair,* Feb. 1915, 42.

250 *The Equinox,* Sep. 1911, 1(7), frontis.

253 *Audi Alteram Partem,* 1935, 27, taken from an unidentified biographical guidebook, Zurich, 1918.

275 Library of Congress.

284 Library of Congress.

289 *Vanity Fair,* Sep. 1917, 46.

289 Billy Rose Theatre Collection, the New York Public Library for the Performing Arts, Astor, Lenox and Tilden Foundations.

294 *Fatherland,* 11 Aug. 1915.

294 Library of Congress.

300 Library of Congress.

302 *Vanity Fair,* Aug. 1916, 35.

314 *Atlanta Constitution,* 5 Jan. 1919, D1.

314 *Pearson's Magazine,* October 1917, 168.

321 National Archives, College Park, MD.

326 B2034.25, Vol. 116(3), Widener Library, Harvard University.

327 Howard Johnson (words) and Theodore Morse (music), *M–O–T–H–E–R: A Word that Means the World to Me* (Leo. Feist: New York, 1915), cover.

327 National Archives, College Park, MD.

329 National Archives, College Park, MD.

333 Burton, *City of Detroit,* 1922, v. 3, 243.

338 National Archives, College Park, MD.

343 *The Equinox* 1919, III(1).

348 OTO Archives, with permission from Tony Stansfeld-Jones.

357 National Archives, College Park, MD.

364 National Archives, College Park, MD.

376 Private collection, courtesy of Keith Richmond.

382 NS74.64, Yorke Collection, Warburg Institute Archives.

382 May, *Tiger Woman,* 1929, frontis.

385 *Sunday Express,* 26 Nov. 1922, 1.

387 *New York Times Book Review and Magazine,* 1 Jul. 1923, 29.

393 Unidentified newspaper article.

402 Kenneth Anger Accession, OTO Archives.

404 OTO Archives.

414 National Archives, College Park, MD.

430 From the collection of T. M. Caldwell.

434 Mansell, Time & Life Pictures, Getty Images.

439 *Détective* magazine, 1930.

445 *Oxford Daily Mail,* 3 Feb. 1930.

467 OTO Archives.

478 Unidentified newspaper clippings, private collection.

486 From *Occult Digest,* as cited.

516 Crowley, *Thumbs Up!,* used with permission of OTO.

523 Crowley, *Fun of the Fair,* used with permission of OTO.

526 Crowley, *City of God,* used with permission of OTO.

528 OTO Archives.

533 Courtesy of LAShTAL.com.

540 Courtesy of the Cameron Foundation.

547 OTO Archives.

Index

A. C. S. & H. Crowley 4–8, 38, 567
   See also Crowley & Co.
A∴A∴ 156, 162, 167, 173, 175–176, 183–184,
   186, 188–189, 203–204, 209–211, 216,
   220–221, 223, 229, 234, 236–237, 241, 243,
   249, 258, 260, 266, 268, 295, 313, 342, 347,
   350, 365, 367, 373, 376–377, 395, 413–414,
   419–420, 462, 469, 486, 501–502, 547, 556,
   560, 618
     Probationer 0°=0▫ 185
     Neophyte 1°=10▫ 258
     Adeptus Minor 5°=6▫ 172
     Adeptus Exemptus 7°=4▫ 172, 203, 271
     Babe of the Abyss 461
     Magister Templi 8°=3▫ 162, 167, 172,
       190, 192, 197, 203, 295, 306, 374, 463
     Magus 9°=2▫ 154, 202–203, 237, 277,
       295, 331, 409, 614
     Ipsissimus 10°=1▫ 308, 370, 409
Abbey of Thelema 332, 349–350, 356–359,
   361, 364–366, 369–370, 372–378, 380, 384,
   386–400, 405–406, 408–409, 412–413,
   416–418, 423, 427, 431, 473, 480, 512–513,
   535, 641, 645
Abrahadabra 129, 246, 323, 650
Abramelin operation 54, 69–70, 73–76, 80, 83,
   116, 160, 210, 475, 548, 581, 584
Abuldiz 242–247, 252
Abyss 161–162, 167, 172, 192, 197–199, 202–
   203, 218, 235, 237, 308
Achad. *See* Jones, Charles Stansfeld
Ackerman, Forrest J. 660
Act of Truth 400–401
Adair, Homer W. 334
Adams, Evangeline 304–305
   Astrology: Your Place Among the Stars 628
   Astrology: Your Place in the Sun 628
Adamson, Henry Anthony 33
Adler, Alfred 448
Aeon of Horus 133, 277, 295–296, 400, 517
Agape Lodge 295, 487, 494, 502, 505, 513, 521,
   524, 526–527, 537–539, 553, 555–556
Agnostic Journal 158, 165
Agrippa, Cornelius 134
Ahitha. *See* Minor, Roddie
Aissa, Soliman ben 255

Aiwass 126–129, 155–156, 172, 175, 198, 200,
   242, 323, 325–326, 332, 339, 365, 367, 401–
   402, 421, 490, 536, 562, 594, 650
alchemy 31, 41, 52, 56, 58, 252, 559, 574
Aldington, Richard 256
Alexander VI, Pope 330
Alpine Club 31, 43–44, 50–51, 102, 107, 147,
   149–150, 260, 574
Amalantrah 323–325, 328, 330
American Society for Psychical Research 344,
   637
AMORC 328, 487–489, 502, 561
   Gauge of Amity with OTO 487
Ananda Metteya, Bhikkhu. *See* Bennett, Allan,
   Bhikku Ananda Metteya
Ancient and Mystical Order Rosæ Crucis. *See*
   AMORC.
Ancient and Primitive Rite of Memphis and
   Mizraim. *See* Memphis-Mizraim, Ancient
   and Primitive Rite of
Anhalonium lewinii. *See* peyote
Ankh-f-n-Khonsu 125, 176, 323, 530
Anthroposophical Society 255, 420, 497, 561
Apex Printing 508, 515
Apuleius, *Golden Ass* 559
Aquila Press 440, 447–448
Archer, Ethel (Mrs. Eugene Wieland) 218, 220–
   221, 223, 229, 237, 249–250, 518–519, 611
   Vampire 231
   Whirlpool 223
Arden Press 181
Arkell, Mary 14, 571
Arnold, Margaret 505
Ashburnham, Lord 117
Ashby Jr. Thomas 567
Ashby, Ann 567
Ashby, Catherine Sophia 567
Ashby, Charles 6, 567
Ashby, Thomas 5–6
Ashby, William 567
astral projection 55, 66, 92–93, 154–155, 166,
   342, 347, 368, 372, 410, 504, 534
astrology 58, 73, 305, 410, 541
Atkins, Henry Ernest 33, 575
Atlantis Bookshop 491, 515, 543
atomic bomb 535, 665
Auer, Leopold 212, 609

Augoeides invocation 123, 154, 156, 158, 160, 243, 434, 538
Augustine, Saint 127, 443
Aumont, Gérard 418, 435, 437

Baba, Meher 211
Babalon 202–203, 291, 327, 349, 370, 398, 414–416, 421, 650
Bach, J. S., *Aria for G String* 224
Back, Ivor 113–114, 130, 132, 134–136, 519, 591
Bacon, Roger 265
Bailey, James Gilbert 608
Baker, Julian L. 52–55, 60–61, 63, 76, 86, 580
Ballantyne, Robert Michael, *Martin Rattler* 22
Baphomet. *See* Crowley, Aleister, magical mottoes
Barefoot, Bobby 497
Barrett, Francis, *The Magus* 429
Barron, George 417–418, 421
Barth, Otto Wilhelm 419, 649
Bartlett, Paul Wayland 115
Bass, Kasimira 427, 430–431, 433–434, 436–437, 463
Baudelaire, Charles 204, 625
Baum, L. Frank, *Wonderful Wizard of Oz* 529
Baverstock, James B. 4–6, 566
Bax, Clifford 134, 153, 489, 496–497, 540, 546, 596, 604, 658
Baxter, Beverly 515
Bayley, James Gilbert 209, 211, 428, 517–518, 530, 549, 554
Beardsley, Aubrey 37–39, 47, 50, 130, 576
Beatles 556, 562
Beaton, Mary. *See* Rogers, Mary Alice
Beaverbrook, Lord 409–411, 415, 418, 431, 450, 466
Beckmann, Max 456
Beethoven, Ludwig von 224
beetles 130
Bennet, Charles Augustus 164
Bennet, George Montagu (7th Earl of Tankerville) 164–165, 167–169, 172, 176, 195, 600–601
Bennet, Leonora Sophia (née van Marter) 164
Bennett, Allan 61–65, 67–68, 70–71, 73–74, 90, 93–98, 123, 132, 153–154, 162–163, 183, 214, 228, 232, 237, 250, 258, 360, 497, 559, 584
    Bhikkhu Ananda Metteya 93, 98, 613
    Note on Genesis 191
    Training of the Mind 231
Bennett, Arnold 113, 129–130, 379, 411, 594
    Grand Babylon Hotel 113
Bennett, Frank 209–211, 282–283, 309, 373–377, 399–400, 409, 424, 608, 643
    6°=5° Adeptus Major 376–377
    IX° OTO 376
    X° OTO 376
Bennett, Justice 466
Benson, Edward F., *The Babe B.A.* 39
Bentrovata, Vera (Lola) 160, 192

Beresford, John Davys 380, 471
Bergson, Henri 58, 582
Berkeley, George Bishop 559
Berridge, Edward 61, 77–78, 80, 232
Besant, Annie 129, 262, 310, 323, 423–424, 561, 594, 649
Besant, Walter 594
Bey, Brugsch. *See* Brugsch, Émile
Bey, Vely. *See* Denizli, Vely Bey.
Bhagavad-Gita 559
Bible 15–16, 499
    Genesis 17
    John 135, 271
    Mark 3
    Matthew 46
    Old Testament 545
    Revelation 16, 133, 295–296, 462, 473–474, 561
Bickers, Betty. *See* Sheridan-Bickers, Betty
Bickers, H. Sheridan. *See* Sheridan-Bickers, H.
Biden, Edmund P. 239
Bigelow, William Sturgis 307, 629
Binetti, Margaret 426
Birven, Henri 419–420, 437, 442, 446, 609
Bishop, Ada Jane 14, 267
Bishop, Alma 312
Bishop, Anne 13–14
Bishop, Elizabeth (née Cole) 13
Bishop, Emily. *See* Crowley, Emily Bertha
Bishop, George Archibald. *See* Crowley, Aleister, pseudonyms
Bishop, John 13–14
Bishop, Lawrence 312–313
Bishop, Tom Bond 13–14, 20, 22, 24–26, 30–31, 157, 258, 572, 577, 592
Bishop, William 14
Black Brothers 161, 463
Blackden, Marcus Worsley 74, 76, 585
Blackley, Josephine 503
Blackwood, Algernon 61
Blake, William 156, 345, 368, 410
Blakeney, T. S. 574
Blanche, Leslie 496–497
Blavatsky, H. P. 41, 90, 175, 222, 253–254, 424, 432, 558, 561, 577, 584, 594
    Voice of the Silence 342, 424, 534
Bles, Arthur 115
Bliss, Alma Hirsig 413, 415–416, 421, 636, 648
Bloxham, John Astley 497
Boca de Inferno 450–452
Bogrand, William H. 345–346
Bond, James 507
Bone, Edith Hajós 532
Book of the Dead 126
Booth, Martin 20, 287
Bosanquet, Claud 395
Bott, Percival 130, 132, 134–135, 595
Bourcier, M. 177, 367, 410
Bowman, Frank E. 344–345
Bradbury, Ray 661
Brahms, Johannes 224
Bream, Julian 532

Brescians 212
Bronowski, Jacob 532
Brook, Dorothy C. 319
Brook, Rupert 210
Brooksmith, Pearl 470, 481, 489, 491–493, 498, 517
Brown, Arthur John Henry 572
Browning, Robert 34, 97, 274
Bruce, Arthur Loring. *See* Crowninshield, Frank
Bruce, Bertha 335, 337–338, 353
Bruce, Charles Granville 141
Bruce, Kathleen 111–112, 136, 192, 214, 230
Brugsch, Émile 126
Bryant, Louise 177
Bucknill, Justice 205
Buddhism 36–37, 63, 71, 93, 96–98, 109, 128, 133, 151, 234, 295, 307, 453, 528, 558–560, 613
Buer (Goetic spirit) 68
Bullock, Percy W. 74–75
Bulwer-Lytton, Lord 154
    Zanoni 58
Bunting, John 666
Burgess, Charles Ebeneezer 9–10, 13
Burnett-Rae, Alan 492–493
Burns & Oates 182
Burr, Jane 380, 643
Burrell, Harry Percy 7, 568
Burt, Sophia 511
Burton, Mary Rose 69
Burton, Sir Richard Francis 34, 43, 45, 47, 96, 214, 265
Bury, Henry Pullen 61
Busch, Bertha (Billie) 456–459, 461, 465–466, 481
Butler, Eliza Marian 536–537, 542, 583
Butler, W. E. 559
Butts, Mary 279, 368–369, 372–373, 376, 386, 641, 643, 645
    A∴A∴ Probationer 373
    OTO initiation 368
Byron, Lord 50, 354, 359, 396

Cabell, James Branch 332, 354, 639
    Jurgen 354, 386
Cagliostro, Count 330–331
Calce, Baron la 367, 378, 397, 412, 417–418
Calder-Marshall, Arthur 444–445
Cambridge Boarding School 15, 21
Cambridge Magazine 35, 575
Cambridge Poets, 1900–13 267
Cambridge University 31–33, 35–36, 39–40, 45, 48, 50, 74, 114, 136, 151, 158, 165–166, 175, 186, 189, 191, 216–217, 260, 282, 359, 394, 411, 428, 444, 502, 517, 572
    Chess Club 33
    Freethought Association 189, 217
    Magpie and Stump debate team 33
Cameron, Marjorie 538, 665
Cammell, Charles Richard 489–490, 493, 496, 500–501, 509, 516
Cammell, Ionia 516

Campbell, Joseph 559
Cannon, Alexander 461–462, 492, 654–655
Cantab 35
Capa, Robert 177
Capone, Al 628
Carey, Mary A. 14, 20, 571
Carlos, Don 116–117
Carlyle, Thomas 34
Carpenter, Edward, *Intermediate Sex* 179
Carrière, Eugène 115
Carrington, Hereward 344, 553, 605, 637
Carroll, Luther L. 502
Carter, Edward 339, 637
Carter, John Filis Carré 440, 455, 458, 654
Carus, Paul 292–293, 295, 622, 625
Catullus 519, 661
Cayenne, Louis Eugene de 426
Cefalù. *See* Crowley, Aleister, Places of residence
Celtic Revival 32, 59, 64–65, 292
Celtic-Cornish Society 117, 592
Cephaloedium Working. *See* Crowley, Aleister, magical workings 367
Cerneau, Joseph 254
chalk-cliff climbing 27, 29, 150
Champney, Rev. Henry d'Arcy 18, 21–22, 24, 40, 217, 572
Chanler, Robert 341, 637
Chat Blanc, Le 112, 115, 180, 360, 379
Chaucer, Geoffrey 274
Chéron, Jane 230, 269, 272–274, 290, 357
chess 27, 32–33, 35, 116, 303, 310, 359–360, 369, 388, 410, 432, 442, 461, 510, 532, 541, 545, 575, 628
Chesterton, G. K. 89, 133, 135–136, 379
Chiswick Press 61, 256, 378, 406, 516, 519, 522–523, 525, 527, 542
Chopin, Frédéric 238
Choronzon 198–202
Choronzon Club 377, 485–486
Christensen, Christian P. 344
Churchill, Winston 33, 511, 517
City of the Pyramids 161, 197, 202–203
clairvoyance 67, 166, 184, 265, 316–317, 364, 451, 470
Clarke & Bishop (printers) 109
Clarke, Herbert 410
Clay, Richard 263
Cleugh, James 440
Close, Herbert (Meredith Starr) 209, 211, 249, 608
Cloud upon the Sanctuary. See Eckartshausen, Karl von 41
Clymer, R. Swinburne 487
Coates, Dorothy 280–281
cocaine 63, 354, 362–363, 366, 377–378, 383, 385, 393, 438–439
Coleridge, Samuel Taylor, *Rime of the Ancient Mariner* 22
Collegium Pansophicum. *See* Pansophical Lodge
Collie, J. Norman 31, 35, 574
Collins, Mabel 180, 221–222
    Blossom and the Fruit 221

Collins, William 380, 384, 409, 571
Co-Masonry 210, 262, 390, 424, 497, 502
concentration 86, 108
Conference of Grand Masters 418, 420
Confucianism 558
Conrad, Joseph 273
Constable and Co. 465, 471–472, 481
Constant, Alphonse Louis (Éliphas Lévi) 110, 180, 222, 265, 330, 368, 428–429, 538
    Key of the Mysteries 266, 429
Continental Times 284, 622, 625
Conway, Sir Martin 31, 42, 45, 101–102, 107, 589
Coomaraswamy, Alice Ethel. *See* Devi, Ratan
Coomaraswamy, Ananda K. 298–301, 304, 307, 310
Copnall, Edward Bainbridge 497
Corregio, Antonio Allegri de 180
Cosgrave, John O'Hara 284
Coster, Ian 467, 655
Cowethas Kelto-Kernuak. *See* Celtic-Cornish Society
Cowie, George MacNie 241, 256, 261, 265, 274, 277, 282, 317–319, 355
Cowper, Emma 14, 20, 571
Cowper, Susan 14, 20, 571
Cracknell, Maud 75–79
Cran, George Rose 205, 607
Crane, Walter 141
Cranshaw, C. H. 508, 519–520
Cremers, Vittoria 221–223, 256, 258, 265, 275
Cronin, Edward 11–12
Crow, William Bernard 528–529, 535, 662–663
Crowley & Co. 7, 38
    See also A. C. S. & H. Crowley
Crowley, Abraham 4–6, 566–567
Crowley, Abraham Curtis 6–7, 9, 567
Crowley, Agnes 9, 13, 569
Crowley, Agnes (née Pope) 9
Crowley, Aleister
    0°=0□ Neophyte 1–3, 61
    1°=10□ Zelator 64
    2°=9□ Theoricus 64
    3°=8□ Practicus 64
    4°=7□ Philosophus 64
    5°=6□ Adeptus Minor 71–72, 74, 196
    6°=5□ Adeptus Major 196
    7°=4□ Adeptus Exemptus 153, 162, 196
    8°=3□ Magister Templi 167–169, 172, 176, 196, 202, 271, 357
    9°=2□ Magus 196, 244, 271, 295, 297, 299, 304–306, 308
    10°=1□ Ipsissimus 370–371, 407, 409
    addiction 377–380, 508
    ascents
        Aiguille de la Za 35–36
        Aiguilles Rouges d'Arolla 35
        Am Basteir 26
        Beachy Head 27–31, 35, 51, 150, 177
        Beinn Dubhchraig 573
        Ben A'an 573

Ben Cruachan 573
Ben Lawers 573
Ben Ledi 573
Ben Lui 573
Ben More 573
Ben Nevis 573
Ben Oss 573
Ben Vane 573
Ben Vorlich 573
Bloody Stone 26
Bowfell 573
Brèche de la Meije 36
Broad Crag 573
Bruach na Frìthe 26
Cabeza 87
Carnedd Dafydd 573
Carnedd Llewelyn 573
Citlaltepetl 88
Colima volcano 88–89
Craig Yr Ysfa ridge 573
Crinkle Crags 573
Dent Blanche 50
Dollywaggon Pike 573
Eiger 31
Eissespitze 574
El Espinazo del Diablo 89
Foel Grach 573
Glyder Fach 573
Glyder Fawr 573
Gran Zebrù 30
Great End 573
Great Gable 573
Hanging Knott 573
Harrison Stickle 573
Helvellyn 573
Helvellyn Lower Man 573
High White Stones 573
Ill Crag 573
Ixtacíhuatl 87
Jungfrau 31
K2 95, 98, 101–108, 137–139, 142, 507, 589
Kangchenjunga 44, 138–139, 142–150, 152–154, 195, 277, 355, 440, 597–598
Königspitze 574
Mönch 31, 35
Mont Collon 36
Monte Cevedale 30
Nevado de Colima 88
Nevado de Toluca 89
Ortler 30
Panza 87
Pavey Art 573
Pen yr Helgi 573
Pic Coolidge 36
Pico del Fraile 89
Pike o' Blisco 573
Popocatépetl 90
Rossett Crag 573
Sca Fell 573
Scafell Pike 573

Schönbühl glacier 50
Schrötterhorn 30
Sergeant Man 573
Sgurr a' Ghreadaidh 26
Sgurr a' Mhadaidh 26
Sgurr-nan-Gillean 26
Shelter Crags 573
Skiddaw 573
Snowdon 573
Stickle Pike 573
Suldenspitze 30
Suldenspitzse 574
Thunacar Knott 573
Thurwieserpitze 30
Trift 31
Trifthorn 35
Tryfan 573
Tschengglser Hochwand 30
Twill Ddu cliff 573
Vertainspitze 30
Vuibez Séracs 35
Wastdale Head 35, 41, 44–45, 575
Wetterhorn 31
Y Garn 573
Y Lliwedd 573
Yr Elen 573
asthma 508, 660
attitude toward
    abstinence 95
    anesthesia 304
    black magic 467
    drugs 64, 379
    Grand Canyon 296
    homosexuality 40
    Masonic lineage 263
    New York City 83
    politics 36
    Queen Victoria 87
    religion 20, 23
    San Francisco 90, 296
    sex 26, 360
    Torquay 510
    university degrees 50
bankruptcy 483–484
birth 14
divorce 182, 193–195, 204, 355, 440,
    450, 455
drug use 373
election as Outer Head of OTO 419
funeral 549, 551
inheritance 19, 32, 194, 266, 277, 316,
    355
magical mottoes
    Baphomet (X° M.M.M.) 256, 323, 370
    Christeos Luciftias (Adeptus Minor
        5°=6°) 72–73, 584
    Ol Sonuf Vaoresagi (Adeptus Major
        6°=5°) 270
    OI MH (Adeptus Exemptus 7°=4·)
        162, 342, 601
    Perdurabo (Neophyte 0°=0°) 3, 60, 73,
        76, 158, 162, 185, 250

To Mega Therion (Magus 9°=2°) 275,
    295, 297, 320, 322, 324–326, 343,
    367, 372, 473–474, 486, 498
Vi Veri Vniversum Vivus Vici (Magister
    Templi 8°=3°) 168–169, 173, 175,
    511, 601
magical workings
    Abuldiz Working 242–244, 252, 322
    Amalantrah Working 322–326, 328,
        367
    Cephaloedium Working 367, 371, 493
    John St. John 180, 184
    Paris Working 269, 271–273, 367, 392,
        621
    Rite of Artemis 218–219
    Rites of Eleusis 223–225, 228, 235, 256,
        261, 316, 385
    Vision and the Voice 193, 196–203, 252
painting 309, 331–332, 339–341, 344,
    360, 365, 440, 443, 447–448, 455–456
paintings
    Burmese Lady 340
    Day Dream of Dead Hats 340
    Dead Souls 339–341
    Ella Wheeler Wilcox and the Swami 341
    Equinox of the Gods 365
    *Is This the Face That Launched a Thousand
        Ships?* 341, 637
    La Chambre des Cauchemars 365
    La Femme de Chez Moi 335
    La Nature Malade 365
    May Morn 341, 343–344
    portrait of Eva Tanguay 341
    portrait of Madame Yorska 341
    Portrait of Norman Mudd 402
    *Young Bolshevik Girl with Wart Looking at
        Trotsky* 341
pirate bridge 311–312, 630
places of residence
    93 Jermyn Street 523, 527
    Barton Brow 512–513
    Bell Inn (Aston Clinton, Buckingham-
        shire) 530, 532–533
    Boleskine 68–69, 73–75, 80, 116, 121–
        122, 130, 132, 135, 137–138, 189,
        194, 225, 259, 274, 277, 319, 583,
        612
    Cambridge Boarding School 15, 18, 21
    Cefalù 279, 337, 358–359, 363–366,
        369–370, 384, 386, 462, 473, 480,
        535, 641, 665
    Chancery Lane 54, 62
    Drayton Gardens 22
    Eastbourne 27, 30
    Grange (Redhill, Surrey) 16, 19
    Grange. *See* Crowley, Aleister, places of
        Residence, Surrey
    Leamington Spa 13, 15, 56
    Malvern College 26, 40, 158
    Netherwood (Hastings) 532–533, 535–
        536, 539–540, 542, 547–549, 551
    Richmond 509

Southampton 19
St. Petersburg 35
Tonbridge Schools 15, 26–27
Torquay 15, 24, 509–510
White Rock Boarding School for Young Gentlemen 17
White Rock School (Hastings) 17
pseudonyms
  Bishop, George Archibald 49, 474
  Boleskine, Laird 70–71, 122
  Boleskine, Lord 194
  Carr, Dionysus 626
  Chioa Khan 124, 130, 133
  Fairfax, Michael 379
  Gentleman of the University of Cambridge 46
  Grey, Cyril 297
  Haddo, Oliver 113, 180–181, 191, 429, 603
  King, Lavinia 178
  Kwaw Li Ya 294
  London Physician 379
  Lutiy, The Late Major 213
  MacGregor, Aleister 70
  MacGregor, Count 194
  Marsyas 192
  New York Specialist 379
  Norfolk, Hilda 203
  Prometheus 575
  Shivaji, Mahatma Guru Sri Paramahansa 504
  Svareff, Vladimir 54, 61, 194, 263, 612
  Swamiji, Mahatma Sri Paramananda Guru 294
  Ta Dhuibh 27
  Verey, Rev. C 191
  Vincey, Leo 259
spying 284–288, 385, 388, 437, 506–507, 623–624
Star-Sponge Vision 307
works
  Account of A∴A∴ 184
  Aceldama 46, 48–49, 136, 359, 576, 582
  Across the Gulf 237, 531
  Adept 111
  Adonis 235–237
  After Judgement 179
  Aha! 192–193, 204, 235, 493
  Ahab 98, 109, 122–123
  Aleister Explains Everything. See Crowley, Aleister, works, Magick without Tears
  Alexandra 161
  Ali Sloper, or the 40 Liars 176
  Alice, An Adultery 91, 110, 113, 131, 137, 280
  Almira 337
  Amath 163
  Ambergris 214, 234
  Ambrosii Magi Hortus Rosarum 73, 133, 232
  Amphora. (See also Crowley, Aleister, works, Hail Mary) 181–182, 250

Amrita 465
Anima Lunae 96
Another Note on Cabell 639
Appeal to the American Republic (see also To America) 70, 131, 136, 278, 312, 620
Argonauts 98, 135, 218, 587
Art in America 267
Artistic Temperament 310
Ascension Day 97
Assumpta Canidia 84
At Bordj-an-Nus 203
At Sea 260
At Stockholm 36
At the Fork in the Roads 67, 184
Athanasius Contra Decanum 217, 260
Avenger to the Theosophical Society 425
Bagh-i-Muattar. See Crowley, Aleister, works, Scented Garden
Ballad of Burdens 575
Balzac 115
Banned Lecture 444–446, 514
Belladonna 179
Berashith 109–110
Big Game 310
Birthday 235
Black Mass 111
Book Four 95, 245, 247–248, 250, 260, 279, 347, 372, 426, 428, 432, 496, 559
Book of Lies 251–252, 266
Book of Photographs 412
Book of the Heart Girt with the Serpent. See Crowley, Aleister, works, Liber Cordis Cincti Serpente
Book of the Law 408
Book of the Law (Liber Al vel Legis) 126–130, 133, 155–156, 161, 170, 172–173, 175, 189–191, 195, 203, 237, 241, 243, 246–247, 249–250, 263, 265–266, 305, 308, 324, 339, 347–348, 358–359, 367, 369–370, 372, 375, 379, 387, 395, 398, 401–403, 416, 418–421, 425, 428, 431, 435, 446, 464, 484, 490, 493, 498–501, 517–518, 524, 528, 535–538, 541, 543, 549, 560, 562, 583, 662
Book of Thoth 510, 519, 525–528, 530, 533
Burning of Melcarth 309
Butterfly Net. See Moonchild
Camel 231
Carmen Sæculare 94, 116–117, 131
Challenge 267
Chants before Battle 274, 287
Chicago May 273
Child of Ephraim 133
Chymical Jousting of Brother Perardua 184
City of God 264, 268, 519, 525–526
Clouds without Water 112, 160, 168,

191–192, 449
Cocaine 292, 320
Concerning the Law of Thelema 328
Conduct of John Briggs 310
Confessions of Aleister Crowley 14, 20, 186, 398, 400, 417, 433, 441, 443, 447, 449, 460, 557
Convert 214
Crisis in Freemasonry 379
Crowley on Christ. See Gospel According to St. Bernard Shaw
Crowleymas Day 98
Dance of Shiva 93
Darlings of the Gods 292
Das Herz des Meisters (see also Heart of the Master) 659
Dawn 296
De Arte Magica 275
De Homunculo Epistola 275
De Nuptiis Secretis Deorum Cum Hominibus 275
De Thaumaturgia 305
Death of a Drunkard 18
Descent of the Moench 35
Diary of a Drug Fiend 230, 380, 384, 386–387, 393–394, 409, 431, 456, 466, 643
Disciples 313, 324
Drama be Damned 327
Drug Panic 379
Dumb! 260
Earth 230
Ecclesiae Gnosticae Catholicae Canon Missae. *See* Gnostic Mass
Eight Lectures on Yoga 495–496, 504
Ein Zeugnis 420–421
Electric Silence 230
Empty-Headed Athenians 170
Energized Enthusiasm 250, 260
England, Stand Fast! 506, 515, 522
Equinox 55, 183–187, 189, 191, 193, 203, 205–208, 211, 214, 217, 220–225, 229–231, 235–237, 241–242, 248–252, 258, 260, 263, 265–266, 280, 288, 313, 320, 328–329, 335–337, 342–345, 347–352, 354, 383, 395, 399, 424, 428–429, 432, 439, 456, 490–491, 501, 504, 529–531, 534, 557, 559–561, 577, 581, 639, 659
Equinox of the Gods 248, 490–491, 493, 497–500, 503, 658
Ercildoune 170, 260
Eruption of Aetna 398–399
Ethyl Oxide 398
Excluded Middle 109
Expedition to Chogo Ri 178, 603
Eyes of Dorothy 179
Eyes of the Pharaoh 153
Ezekiel in the Quarter Montparnesse 603
Fun of the Fair 264, 328, 523, 525, 620

Gargoyles 135, 137, 160
Genius of Mr. James Joyce 399
Geomancy 320, 632
Ghouls 221, 236, 238
Giant's Thumb 288, 613, 620
Gilt Mask 112
Gnostic Mass 44, 264–265, 312, 320, 342, 350, 354, 360, 392, 468, 502, 505, 521, 525, 529, 543, 550, 632, 640
Goad 40, 267
God Eater 119, 131
God of Ibreez 309
Golden Rose 296–297
Golden Twigs 320, 441, 446, 449, 547, 553
Gospel According to St. Bernard Shaw (published as *Crowley on Christ*) 308–309, 349, 639
Great Drug Delusion 379–380
Greek Qabalah 614
Green Alps 49–50, 137
Growth of God 84
Hail Mary (see also Crowley, Aleister, works, *Amphora)* 250, 279
Heart of Holy Russia 264
Heart of the Master (see also Das Herz des Meisters) 417, 426, 497, 503
Hearth 309
Hermit 170
High History of Good Sir Palamedes the Saracen Knight 153, 250
Hindu at the Polo Grounds 294
His Secret Sin 235
Honesty is the Best Policy 283
Honourable Adulterers 385
House 96
Household Gods 213, 250
How I Became a Famous Mountaineer 260
How to Write a Novel! After W. S. Maugham 181
Hymn for July 4 495
Hymn to Pan 264, 342, 450, 495, 549
Illusion d'Amoureux 173
Improvement on Psycho-analysis 309
In Memoriam A. J. B. 267
In Neville's Court 267
In Residence 114, 136, 575
Ineligible 310
Interpreter 218
Jack the Ripper 222
Jephthah 53, 66, 131, 582
Jewish Problem Re-Stated 379
Jezebel 45, 61, 122, 136, 280, 582
King Ghost 154
King Khang King 330, 504
King of the Wood 309
Konx Om Pax 167, 170, 176, 178, 181, 280, 456
La Gauloise 522
La Gitana 167–168

Landed Gentry 519, 523
Last Straw 285
Law of Liberty 309, 322
Leah Sublime 363, 412
Liber A'ash 237
Liber Aleph 244, 322, 327, 342, 372,
    446, 460, 541–542, 547, 553, 556
Liber Apotheosis 526–527
Liber Ararita 175, 269
Liber Arcanorum 174
Liber Astarte 237
Liber B 237
Liber Causae 203
Liber Cheth 161, 237
Liber Collegii Sancti 204
Liber Cordis Cincti Serpente 172, 342,
    398, 400
Liber E 184, 249
Liber HAD 237
Liber IOD 237
Liber Israfel 237
Liber Jugorum 167
Liber Liberi vel Lapidis Lazuli 172, 349
Liber Librae 184
Liber LII 342
Liber NV 237
Liber Os Abysmi 237
Liber Oz 517–519, 529
Liber Porta Lucis 175
Liber Pyramidos 160, 180, 269, 560
Liber Resh 237, 361, 391, 511
Liber RV 237
Liber Stellae Rubae 173, 252
Liber Tau 175
Liber Trigrammaton 175
Liber Turris 237
Liber Tzaddi 237
Liber Viae Memoriae 237
Liber XII 349
Lines to a Young Lady Violinist 260
Literatooralooral Treasure-Trove 260
Little Essays Toward Truth 423, 460, 504
Lost Continent 264
Magick in Theory and Practice 44, 275,
    279, 371–373, 428–429, 431, 433,
    435–436, 438–439, 442–443, 463,
    475, 498, 510, 533, 542, 549, 561
Magick without Tears 400, 528, 534, 541,
    556, 666
March in the Tropics 84
Mask of Gilt 167
Mass of Saint Secaire 309
Mass of the Phoenix 266, 274
Master of the Temple 342, 349
Mediterranean Manifesto 414–415,
    417, 423–424
Message of the Master Therion 297, 632
Metempsychosis 84
Moonchild 178, 188, 221, 230, 238, 297,
    310, 320, 441–443, 456, 466, 615,
    629
Moon-Wane 379

Morphia 264
Mortadello 235, 250, 435, 460, 462, 493,
    502, 531
Mother's Tragedy 89, 92, 131, 168, 280
Muse 112
My Crapulous Contemporaries 258
My Wanderings in Search of the
    Absolute 225, 484
Nativity 40
Neophyte 320
New Parsifal 287, 292–293, 625
New Year, 1903 109
Night in the Valley 84, 587
Not Good Enough 310
Not the Life and Adventures of Sir Rog-
    er Bloxham 45
Old Man of the Peepul-Tree 309
Olla 519, 525, 527–528, 537, 541–542,
    546, 613, 661
On a Burmese River 178, 603
On Blasphemy in General 225
On Garrett Hostel Bridge 267
On the Edge of the Desert 230, 235
On Waikiki Beach 90
One Star in Sight 559
Open Letter to Lord Beaverbrook 409–410,
    416
Opium Smoker 154
Oracle of the Corycian Cave 309
Oracles 84, 93, 123, 136
Ordeal of Ida Pendragon 111–112, 178,
    230
Orgy of Cant 292, 622, 625
Oriental Mind 303
Orpheus 90, 92, 98, 135, 137
Ouija Board 320, 632
Outside the Bank's Routine 310
Ovariotomy 112
Palace of the World 267
Pan to Artemis 218
Pentecost 97
Percy Bysshe Shelley 379, 575
Perdurabo 267
Perhaps Germany Should Take Poland?
    292
Philosophy of Magick 464
Pilgrim 230
Poem of Hashish 204
Prayer at Sunset 230
Priest of Nemi. See Crowley, Aleister,
    works, King of the Wood
Psychology of Hashish 179, 191, 442
Quack Painter 260
Quest 320
Return 230
Return of Messalina 167
Revival of Magick 320, 325, 543, 561,
    584, 632
Rite of Artemis 220, 228
Rite of the Phoenix 316
Rites of Eleusis (see also Crowley, Aleister,
    magical workings, Rites of Eleusis)

226–228, 237, 256
Rock 379
Rodin 115
Rodin in Rime 111–112, 168, 178
Rosa Coeli 156, 168
Rosa Decidua 204, 241
Rosa Inferni 135, 168
Rosa Mundi 110, 123, 135, 137
Rose and the Cross 320
Rosicrucian 267
Rosicrucian Scandal 259, 613
Sabbé Pi Dukkham 97
Scented Garden 43, 45, 213, 216, 252, 282, 412, 595
Science and Buddhism 109
Scorpion 230
Sepher Sephiroth 258, 584, 618
777 163, 183, 222, 230, 420, 426, 446, 559, 584
Seven Lithographs by Clot. See Crowley, Aleister, works, *Rodin in Rime*
Sevenfold Sacrament 235, 342
Shadowy Dill-Waters 204
Ship 264, 266, 269, 392, 495, 550
Silence of Columbine 179
Sirenae 587
Slim Gilt Soul 260
Snowdrops from a Curate's Garden 115, 132–133, 137, 170, 251, 259
Snowstorm 230
Soldier and the Hunchback 180, 184
Song 112, 267
Songs for Italy 399
Songs of the Spirit 61, 131, 137, 582
Sonnet for a Picture 94
Soul of Osiris 89, 94, 131, 133, 280
Soul of the Desert 273
Spring Snowstorm in Wastdale 35
St. Patrick's Day 98
Star and the Garter 111, 131, 136–137, 178, 238
Star Sapphire 252
Stone of Cybele 309
Stone of the Philosophers 176
Stratagem 273, 441–443
Suffer the Children 313
Suffragette, A Farce 178
Summa Spes 109–110, 116
Suspicious Earl 168
Swimmer 422
Sword of Song 97, 105, 110, 116, 129, 132–133, 135–136, 151, 176, 280
Tale of Archais 61, 131, 582
Tannhäuser 49, 84, 92, 94, 104, 131, 136, 168
Tao Teh King 330, 362
Telepathy 179
Tell-Tale Heart 170
Temperance 507–508
Temple of Solomon the King (co-authored with J.F.C. Fuller) 184, 191, 204, 206, 229, 237, 249, 260, 342,

495
Tent 213
Terzain 192
Testament of Magdalen Blair 250, 260, 280–281, 379
There is No Other God than He 167
Thien Tao 176
Three Schools of Magick 426
Three Wishes 460, 502, 531
Thumbs Up! 511–512, 515–517
Time 130
Titanic 616
Titanic Disaster 251, 616
To a New-Born Child 379
To America (*see also* Appeal to the American Republic) 287, 620
To Laylah—Eight-and-Twenty 264
To Man. *See* Mediterranean Manifesto
True Greater Ritual of the Pentagram 156
Two Hymns on the Feast of the Nativity 267
Two Secrets 180
Tyrol 400
Vain Tale: With a Madman on the Alps 178, 603
Vampire 111
Venus 84
Villon's Apology 259
Violinist 213
Vision and the Voice 231, 399, 446, 607
Vitriol Thrower 112
Vixen 213
Waite's Wet 258
Wake World 160, 176
Welcome to Jabez 573
White Stains 20, 49, 123, 136, 170, 259, 352, 471, 474, 575, 582
Why Jesus Wept 94, 112, 124, 135–136, 139
Winged Beetle 174, 179–180, 214–215, 260, 422, 607, 610
Wings 179
Wizard Way 170
Woodcutter 235
Works of Aleister Crowley 45, 73, 136, 139, 151, 162, 170, 232, 315
World Teacher to the Theosophical Society 424
World's Tragedy 14, 177, 231, 315
Young Man and the Post Office 541
World Teacher campaign 415, 420–421, 423–425
Crowley, Aleister Ataturk 496, 506, 508, 512, 544–545, 548–549, 658
Crowley, Alfred 6, 9, 566–567
Crowley, Alfred Driver 566
Crowley, Anne (née Higginbotham) 9, 13, 130, 132
variant spellings 569
Crowley, Anne Léa (Poupée) 358, 361–362, 365, 368, 373, 377, 409, 415

Crowley, Astarte Lulu Panthea 366, 407, 415, 417, 423, 441
Crowley, Charles Sedgefield 4, 8–9, 566
Crowley, Charlotte (née Curtis) 4, 6
Crowley, Claude Edmund 9, 569
Crowley, Edward (father) 8–13, 15–17, 19–22, 38, 194, 361, 568–570
Crowley, Edward (grandfather) 7–9, 566
Crowley, Elizabeth 566–567
Crowley, Elizabeth (née Curtis) 4
Crowley, Emily Bertha (née Bishop) 13–15, 19–22, 25, 157, 214, 222, 312, 316, 355, 409, 570, 572, 592
Crowley, Emma (née Curtis) 4, 566
Crowley, Frederick 6–7, 9, 567
Crowley, Gertrude Evelyn 568
Crowley, Grace Mary Elizabeth 16
Crowley, Henry 4, 566
Crowley, Jonathan Edward 9
Crowley, Jonathan Sparrow 8–11, 13, 21–22, 569
Crowley, Lilith 132–134, 151, 153, 156–157, 159–161, 172, 195, 347, 391
    death 157
Crowley, Lola Zaza 160, 163, 194–195, 204, 232, 234, 347, 355, 436, 459–460
Crowley, Maria Teresa (née de Miramar) 434, 436, 438–442, 446, 448, 450–455, 461–462, 566–567
Crowley, Mary (née Sparrow) 7–9, 568
Crowley, Mary Elizabeth 8–10, 13
Crowley, Philip 6–7, 9, 567–568
Crowley, Rose (née Kelly) 48, 109–110, 112, 119–126, 129–130, 132–135, 151–154, 156–157, 159–161, 163, 167, 170, 172, 177–178, 180, 182, 193–195, 204, 214, 241–243, 247, 297, 320, 347, 426–427, 455, 459
Crowley, Sarah Maria 8, 10, 568
Crowley, Thomas (great-grandfather) 4, 7, 565
Crowley, Thomas (great-great-grandfather) 3–4, 564–565
Crowley, White & Crowley 10–11, 570
Crowley's Alton Ale. See A. C. S. & H. Crowley and Crowley & Co.
Crowninshield, Frank 288, 294, 311
Crowther, Arnold 542–544
Cruze, Eddie 471, 482
Culling, Louis T. 502
Curtis, Abraham 567
Curzon, Mary Victoria 141

d'Orléens, Prince Henri 174
Dalton, William 109
Dangerous Drug Act (1920) 355, 379
Darby, John Nelson 11–12
Davies, Mary 316–319, 631–632
    arrest 317–318
    disavows Crowley 318
Day, Arthur 502
de Miramar, Maria Teresa. See Crowley, Maria Teresa
Decadent movement 20, 37, 47, 49, 65

Dee, John 85, 128, 189, 198, 230
Degas, Edgar 105
Degas, Hilaire Germain Edgar 109
deGaulle, Charles 517, 522
Denizli, Vely Bey 240, 615
Desart, Fourth Earl of 174
Desio, Ardito 108
Desti, Mary (Virakam) 238–250, 252, 260, 310, 320, 322, 344, 426, 442, 615
    Doctor Bob 248, 258
    Freedom of the Soul 240
    On—On—Poet 248
    Tango 248
Devi, Ratan (Alice Ethel Coomaraswamy) 298–301, 304–305, 307, 310, 347, 356, 369
DeVinne Press 336
Dhammapada 559
Dickens, Charles 4, 22, 569
Divine Pymander 559
Dix, Otto 456
Dockerill, Marian (née Hirsig) 338, 344, 636–637
Doherty, Randall Gair. See Crowley, Aleister Ataturk
Doinel, Jules 617
Donegall, Lord Edward 519
Dorr, J. 291
Doughty, Joseph Henry 44
Douglas, James 384, 386, 447
Douglas, James Archibald 24, 510, 573
Dowd, Freeman B. 487
Dowson, Ernest, Verses 47
Doyle, Sir Arthur Conan 61, 363, 452, 655
Draper, Inspector 412
Dreiser, Theodore 315
Driberg, Tom 423, 425, 496, 499–500, 507, 515, 649
Duncan, Isadora 238, 240, 247, 310
Duncan, Raymond 238
Duncombe-Jewell, L. C. R. 116–119, 121, 132, 157, 170, 592–593
    Celtic-Cornish Society 117
Dunn, Ernest W. T. 283
Dunne, Finley Peter 90
Dunsany, Lord 183, 191
Duranty, Walter 268–269, 272–274, 290, 357
Dutton, E. P. 342

Eastbourne Gazette 27, 573
Ebor School 572
Ecclesia Gnostica Catholica 264, 529
Eckartshausen, Karl von, Cloud upon the Sanctuary 41–42, 60, 184, 487
Eckenstein Boulder 42
Eckenstein, Lina 42
Eckenstein, Oscar 31, 42–44, 50–53, 73, 83, 86–90, 92, 94–95, 98–99, 101–107, 115, 139, 194, 278, 355–356, 360, 489, 587, 589
    alpenstock 50, 356
    crampons 50, 356
    knot-tying 356
Eddy, John Percy 472–473, 477–480

Eddy, Mary Baker 497
Edwardes, George 212
Egan, Beresford 442
EGC. *See* Ecclesia Gnostica Catholica
Elkin Matthews 214, 234
Ellis, Havelock 115
    Studies in the Psychology of Sex 158
Ellmann, Richard David 546
Emerson, Ralph Waldo 333
Emery, Edward 66
Encausse, Gérard (Papus) 254, 263–264, 617
Engel, Leopold 253–254
Engers, Leon. *See* Kennedy, Leon Engers
English Review 70, 235, 250, 260, 267–268,
    273–274, 278, 281, 283, 379–380, 523, 575,
    620, 643
English, Vincent 117
Enochian 85, 189, 193, 196–197, 229, 231, 265,
    495, 507, 538
Epstein, Jacob 266, 383
Equinox of the Gods 126
ether 304, 328, 367, 383, 534
Evans, Montgomery II 405, 413, 424, 440, 509,
    648

Fanfrolico Press 441–442
Farr, Florence 65, 70, 73–79, 92
Farwell, Justice 205, 207–208, 468
Fatherland 283–284, 286–288, 294, 355, 622–
    624
Feilding, Hon. Everard 185, 187–188, 285, 310,
    318, 344, 605, 623
Feilding, Rudolph Robert Basil Aloysius
    Augustine 188
Feilding, Rudolph William Basil 188
Feininger, Lyonel 314
Felkin, R. L. 265, 620
Felkin, R. W. 61
Fellowship of Eulis 255
Fenton, de Wend 231, 260
Ferguson, J. DeLancey 267
Fielding, Henry 34
Fitzgerald, Edward Noel 530, 544, 553
Flaubert, Gustave 37–38, 49, 447
Fleming, Ian 507, 572
Fontainebleau 262, 279, 356, 358, 368, 377,
    406, 436
Ford, Ford Maddox 177
Forel, Auguste 596–597
Forest, Ione de. *See* Heyse, Jeanne
Fortune, Dion 494, 530, 559
Foster, Jeanne Robert (Hilarion) 289–291, 293,
    295–298, 305, 308, 347, 625
    Answer 297
    Neighbors of Yesterday 290
    Wife to a Husband 293, 297
    Wild Apples 290
Foster, R. F. 311, 630
Fowler, Mick 150
Foyle, Christina 463, 655
Foyle, William Alfred 463
Foyle's (bookseller) 464, 507

Franklin, Benjamin 3–4, 565
Fraser, E. E. 352
Fraser, G. G. Rae. *See* Rae-Fraser, G. G.
Fraternitas Rosae Crucis 255, 487
Fraternitas Saturni 419–420, 484, 649
Fraternity of the Inner Light 559
Fraux, Helen 376
Fraux, Mimi 376
Frazer, James G., *The Golden Bough* 308–310,
    446, 559
Freemasonry 86, 114–115, 205–210, 230, 237,
    252–256, 262–264, 279, 285, 317–318,
    334–337, 344–346, 353, 425, 484, 488, 529,
    558
    Blue Lodge 253
    Pilgrim Lodge No. 238 252, 254
    Quatuor Coronati Lodge 57
    Royal Arch 254
    Scottish Rite 57, 85, 208, 252, 254, 262,
        279, 334–336, 346, 608, 629, 658
    Swedenborgian Rite 57
    York Rite 346
    See also Co-Masonry *and* Memphis-
        Mizraim
Freethinker 175, 222, 448
Freshfield, Douglas 105, 139, 142
Freud, Sigmund 185, 308, 322, 365, 375, 448,
    597
Fuller, J. F. C. 139, 158–159, 165, 170–171,
    173, 178–179, 183–184, 188, 202, 204, 211,
    214–215, 220, 224, 229, 231–235, 237, 260,
    278, 308, 391, 471, 497, 519, 581, 583–585,
    596, 599, 605, 614
    5°=6° Adeptus Minor 619
    A∴A∴ Chancellor 619
    Imperial Fascist League 229
    Secret Wisdom of the Qabalah 234
    Star in the West 158, 168–170, 178, 217,
        601
    Temple of Solomon the King. *See*
        Crowley, Aleister, works, Temple of
        Solomon the King
    Treasure-House of Images 204
    Yoga 234
Fuller, Loie 37

G∴B∴G∴ 485
Gallop, Constantine 468, 472, 482, 656
Gandhi, Mohandas K. 506, 590
Gardner, F. Leigh 183
Gardner, Gerald B. 543–544, 553, 614, 666–
    667
    Book of Shadows similarity to Crowley's
        works 543–544
    High Magic's Aid 543
    VII° in OTO 543
    Witchcraft Today 543
Gauguin, Paul 360–361, 640
Gaunt, Admiral Sir Guy 286, 335, 356, 506,
    623–624
Gautier, Theophile, *Mademoiselle de Maupin* 37
Gebhardi, Otto 420–421, 425–426

geomancy 270, 427
Germer, Cora (née Eaton) 433, 446–447, 457,
    484, 512, 520, 523
Germer, Karl 419–420, 423, 425–427, 432–
    433, 441, 443, 446, 448, 454, 456–458, 471,
    477–478, 481, 484–485, 493, 497, 508, 512,
    517, 519–520, 522–523, 526, 531, 538–539,
    543, 546–549, 553–557, 652, 658
Germer, Maria 423, 426
Germer, Sascha 523, 556
Gibbon, Edward 34
Gibson, William A. 334–336
Gilley, Patrick 291
Gillies, Hugh 137–138
Gleadow, Rupert 540
Goethe, Johann Wolfgang von 265
Goetia 62, 68, 73, 123, 135–136, 154, 198, 269,
    585
Golden Dawn 2–3, 55, 58–65, 69–80, 83, 85,
    90, 92, 109, 126, 135, 139, 155, 158, 161–
    163, 173, 176, 183, 185, 190–191, 203, 205,
    232, 237, 243, 252, 258, 280–281, 424, 487,
    494, 511, 518, 529, 536, 546, 548, 558–560,
    564, 582, 584–585, 607, 617, 632, 641, 659,
    664
    Neophyte 0°=0° 1–3, 60–61, 85, 160,
        564
    Zelator 1°=10° 60
    Theoricus 2°=9° 60
    Practicus 3°=8° 60, 184
    Philosophus 4°=7° 60
    Dominus Liminis (Portal) 60, 64
    Adeptus Minor 5°=6° 71, 74–75, 158,
        160, 511
    Adeptus Exemptus 7°=4° 157, 161
    cipher manuscript 58, 77
Goldman, Emma 411, 648
Goldring, Douglas, *South Lodge* 376
Goldston, Edward 440–443, 446–447
Goldstone, Lou 537
Gonne, Maude. *See* MacBride, Maude Gonne
Goodyear, Frederick 258, 618
Gorman, Herbert 449, 451
Gotch, Thomas Cooper 481
Gough, Mary 15
Gould, Sylvester C. 279
Gounod, Charles-François, *Faust* 82
Gouraud, Aimée 324, 400, 415, 418
Graham, W. W. 139
Grange. *See* Crowley, Aleister, places of
    Residence, Surrey
Grant, Gregor 16, 27–30, 117
Grant, Kenneth 533–535, 549, 555–557, 664,
    668
Grant, Steffi 549
Granta 35, 575
Grau, Albin 419–420, 649
Gray, Eileen 110–111, 116, 238
Great Beast 16, 128–129, 133, 295–296, 428,
    460, 481, 561
Great White Brotherhood 161–162, 202–203

Great Work 65, 72, 74, 158, 161, 167, 175, 185,
    237, 246–247, 249, 272, 277, 297, 328–329,
    349, 356, 361, 366, 387, 389, 397–401, 403,
    409–410, 412, 421, 423, 426–427, 435, 455,
    460–461, 463, 468, 504–505, 513, 517, 520,
    541, 548
Green, Andrew 553
Green, Henry. *See* Yorke, Henry Vincent
Greene, Raymond 395–396
Greenidge, Terence Lucy 382
Greer, Justice 483
Gregg, Frederick James 281
Gregory, Lady 79
Grey, Cyril. *See* Crowley, Aleister, pseudonyms
Grey, Edward 286
Grieg, Edvard 212
Grimble, Arthur F. 204
Grosche, Eugen 419–420
Guardi, Francesco 105
Guillarmod, J. Jacot. *See* Jacot-Guillarmod, Jules
Gunston, William Hewison 33
Gurdjieff, G. I. 259, 406–407, 561, 642
Gyles, Althea 67, 184, 583
Gypsy Lore Society 235

Habershon, Arthur Herbert 17
Habershon, Henry Earnest 17
Habershon, Theodore 17–18
Haddo, Oliver. *See* Crowley, Aleister,
    pseudonyms
Haddon, Olivia 258, 275
Hadit 128, 347
Hain der Isis 420
Haldane, J. B. S. 532
Hall, Frederick 335
Hall, Helen 335
Hall, Henry 278, 284
Hall, Sir John 65
Hamilton, Gerald 457–459, 520, 527
Hammond, Edward Jack 339, 636
Hammond, Hans (Hansi) 339, 356, 359, 361,
    398, 413, 415–416, 421, 636
Hammond, Percy 326
Hamnett, Nina 256–257, 265, 368–369, 376,
    387, 464–465, 472–473, 479, 481
    Laughing Torso 462, 465, 470, 472, 481
Hanad, Elizabeth 15
Hanchant, Mr. 448, 455, 463
Hardy, G. H. 399
Harmsworth, Alfred (Lord Northcliffe) 278,
    283
Harris, Frank 178, 181, 183–184, 214, 274, 280,
    293, 405, 410, 460
Harris, Frieda Lady (née Bloxam) 497, 501–504,
    514–518, 521–523, 527, 530, 536, 541, 548–
    549, 553–554, 658, 667
    Affiliates to OTO 501
    Joins A∴A∴ 501
    VII° in OTO, 658
Harris, Sir Percy 497
Harris, Thomas Lake 71, 252, 584
Harrison, Austin 281, 283, 379, 386, 411

Harryhausen, Ray 661
Hartmann, Franz 180, 254, 487, 649
   Magic, White and Black 254, 347
   Secret Symbols of the Rosicrucians 254
hashish 191, 259, 325
Hathayoga Pradipika 559
Hawayrd, Henry 212
Hayes, Joan. *See* Heyse, Jeanne
Hayward, Charles Flavell 212
Heinlein, Robert, *Stranger in a Strange Land* 556
Helburn, Theresa 289
Hemingway, Ernest 423, 649
Henckels, Pola 456
Henley, William Ernest 113
   Slang and its Analogues 113, 132
Hermetic Brotherhood of Luxor 255, 617
heroin 230, 355, 362, 377–378, 385, 408, 411,
   413, 508, 519, 541–542
Heseltine, Philip 411, 442, 648
Hess, Rudolf 507
Heyse, Jeanne (Joan; Ione de Forest) 222–224,
   256–257, 275–276, 612
Hichens, Robert Smythe, *Felix* 163
Higgins, Godfrey 292
Hilarion. *See* Foster, Jeanne Robert
Hilbery, Malcolm 472–476, 479, 481
Hill, Frank 436
Hill, Gordon W. 334, 345, 635
Hinduism 62–63, 93, 96–98, 135, 158–159,
   305, 558–559
Hirsig, Al 421
Hirsig, Fanny Cristina 339, 637
Hirsig, Leah 324, 338–340, 344, 347, 349, 356–
   358, 361–367, 370, 373–375, 377–378, 380,
   386, 389–392, 396–398, 400–406, 408–410,
   412–418, 421, 425–426, 461, 497, 636
   Hans Hammond (son) 339
Hirsig, Poupée. *See* Crowley, Anne Léa
Hitler, Adolf 234, 484, 487, 503, 505, 507, 511,
   520, 534
Hollis, Helen 624, 658
Holy Books 133, 172–175, 222, 236, 252, 269,
   329, 349, 365, 374, 418, 484, 602
Holy Guardian Angel 126, 152, 154, 156, 160,
   172, 180, 192, 197–198, 242, 325, 371, 375–
   376, 477, 485
Hooker, Sir Joseph 139
Hopfer, Oskar 420, 426, 446
Horner, Grace M. 512
Horniblow, Colonel Frank Herbert 70
Horniblow, Lillian (Laura Grahame) 70–71, 73
Horniman, Annie 60, 118
Horus 124–126, 414
Houdini, Harry 561, 668
Houghton, Michael 491, 515, 533
Hubbard, L. Ron 537–539, 561, 665
Hume, David 559
Humphrys, W. E. H. 73, 76
Hunt, Carl de Vidal 431, 433–436, 438, 651
Hunt, Holman 409
Hunter, E. A. 74–79
Huston, E. N., *A Plea for Polygamy* 158

Huxley, Aldous 369, 448–449
Huysman, Joris-Karl, *A Rebours (Against Nature)*
   38
Hylton, F. W. 519
Hymenaeus Alpha. *See* McMurtry, Grady Louis
Hypocrites Club 382, 644

I Ching 175, 356, 358, 362, 370, 397, 409–410,
   440, 471, 483, 496–497, 504, 509, 512
Iff, Simon 310, 313, 320, 380, 446, 628
Illuminati 253–254, 634
Inches, Dr. James W. 351
Inman, Herbert 185, 188, 210–211
International 304–305, 310, 314–315, 320, 325,
   327–330, 347, 360, 584, 625–626, 629, 632
International Buddhist Society 98, 613
International Magian Society 285, 348
invisibility 85, 152, 162
Irwin, Beatrice 65
Isherwood, Christopher 458
Isis 126, 368, 442, 446, 511

Jack, Hugh 334
Jackson, E. M. 532
Jacobi, Charles Thomas 378, 428, 469, 485,
   487, 494
Jacobitism 117
Jacobs, Samuel A. 325–326, 348
Jacot-Guillarmod, Jules 100–107, 137–139,
   141–149, 589, 596, 598
   Haggis 137–138
   Six Mois dans l'Himalaya 137–138
Jaeger, Hanni 446, 448–454, 463, 653
James, William 290, 559
Jameson, John B. 502–504, 659
Jarvis, George 345–346
Jenner, Henry 116–117
Jennings, Hargrave 596
Joad, C. E. M. 515, 532, 661
John Bull 176, 225, 228, 356, 386, 393–394,
   439–440, 454, 467
John, Augustus 111, 236, 249–250, 280, 383,
   411, 537, 541
John, Gwen 236
Johnson, Jack 326
Johnson, Samuel 41
Jones v. The Looking Glass 231–233, 259, 481
Jones, Charles Stansfeld 185, 188, 260, 268,
   277–278, 283, 295, 308, 328, 334–337, 342,
   344, 347–350, 374, 388, 399–400, 413, 419,
   421, 425–426, 429–430, 555, 608, 668
   1°=10° Neophyte 268
   2°=9° Zelator 268
   Babe of the Abyss 295
   8°=3° Magister Templi 295, 308, 342
   10°=1° Ipsissimus 308
   Anatomy of the Body of God 399
   Crystal Vision through Crystal Gazing 399
   Egyptian Revival 399
   Grand Master of MMM 318
   Liber 31 347–348
   Magister Templi 308

move to Chicago 350
QBL: The Bride's Reception 399
Universal Brotherhood 421
Jones, George Cecil 53–55, 60–63, 68–69, 73–74, 76, 109, 139, 157–160, 162–163, 165–167, 169, 172–173, 176, 183, 194, 214, 228–229, 231–234, 258, 278, 308, 343, 409, 459, 497, 560
Jonson, Ben, *Volpone* 47
Joyce, James 448, 668
Finnegans Wake 562
Ulysses 384
Joyce, William (Lord Haw-Haw) 510, 516
Judde, Sir Andrew 27
Jung, Karl 309, 448
Psychology of the Unconscious 308
Juste, Michael. *See* Houghton, Michael

kabbalah 51, 56, 58, 153, 162, 174, 176, 198, 229, 237, 251, 258, 271, 295, 307, 342, 372, 399, 410, 421, 438, 449, 528
Qlippoth 174
Tree of Life 60, 153, 174–175, 183, 197, 277, 308, 347, 399, 409, 420, 584
Kabbalistic Cross 85
Kahl, Regina 468–469, 487, 494, 502, 505, 524
Kahn, Otto 286, 380, 411, 648
Kant, Immanuel 211, 419, 559
Keasbey, Lindley Miller 328, 634
Keating, James 288, 290, 624
Keats, John 54, 119, 151, 593
Kegan Paul, Trench, Trübner & Co. 61, 89, 94, 123, 131, 440
Kellner, Carl 253–255, 265
Kelly, Blanche (née Bradford) 48, 119, 163
Kelly, Edward 198, 265, 330
Kelly, Eleanor Constance Mary 48
Kelly, Frederic Festus (the elder) 48
Kelly, Rev. Frederic Festus 48, 109, 177
Kelly, Rose Edith. *See* Crowley, Rose
Kelly, Sir Gerald 48–49, 61, 69, 76, 90–92, 95, 109–112, 114, 119, 121–123, 129–130, 132, 134, 151, 178, 183, 194, 204, 260, 359, 436, 459, 519, 582, 603
Kemp, Harry 274–275, 278–279, 284
Kempe, John 150
Kennedy, Leon Engers 258–259, 262, 313–315, 343, 630
psychochromes 314, 340
Kennerley, Mitchell 288
Kerman, Isidore 453, 462, 465, 468, 471, 482, 653
Key of Solomon. See Goetia
Keyes, Roger John Brownlow 519
King, Lavinia. *See* Crowley, Aleister, pseudonyms
Kingsford, Anna 41, 58, 577
Perfect Way 58, 241
Kipling, Rudyard, *If* 481
Klein, Henry 254, 617
Knight, Maxwell 507
Knights Templar. *See* Templar, Knights

Knott, Nora 504
Knowles, Guy 43, 99, 101, 103–106, 108, 507, 589
Knox, Ronald Arbuthnott 444–445, 652
Konody, Paul George 440
Koo, Madame Wellongton 501
Koot Hoomi 222
Koran. *See* Qur'an.
Korbay, Francis 81
Kothek, Gerda Maria von 299, 301, 304, 309, 626
Krafft-Ebing, Richard von 474
Psychopathia Sexualis 49
Kramer, Jacob 383, 385
Krishnamurti, Jiddu 262, 423–425, 650
Krumm-Heller, Arnold 488
Küntzel, Martha 420–421, 426, 429, 441, 457, 484, 503, 505, 530
Kwaw Li Ya. *See* Crowley, Aleister, pseudonyms

Laban, Rudolf 312, 630
Lamb, Euphemia 178–179, 199, 201, 214
Lamb, Henry 178–179
Lambe, Harry 97
Lambert (tutor) 27, 30
Lambert, Isabelle 30
Lamp of Invisible Light (LIL) 86, 587
Langelaan, George 623
Langston, W. Steff 317, 631
Lao Tzu 295, 330
Larden, W. 31
Lavaleye, Victor de 511
Laver, James 542
Lavroff, Marie (née Röhling)(Olun) 327
Lawrence, D. H. 214, 441, 443, 448
A Propos of Lady Chatterley's Lover 447
Lady Chatterley's Lover 214, 441
Lawrence, Justice 465
Leadbeater, C. W. 90, 423, 425, 561, 649
Leamington Spa. *See* Crowley, Aleister, places of residence
Lecram Press 436, 442, 642
Leese, Arnold Spencer 229
Leffingwell, Reea 505
Leffingwell, Roy 505, 521–522, 524, 547, 659
Legge, James 330, 559
Legitimism 116–117
See also Jacobitism
Legros, Alphonse 99
Leslie, Dr. Murray 277
Lesser Banishing Ritual of the Pentagram 55, 85, 198, 210, 218, 243, 297, 340, 374
Leverson, Ada 173–174, 323, 601–602
Lévi, Éliphas. *See* Constant, Alphonse Louis
Lévi-Strauss, Claude 536, 559, 668
Lewis, Ann 570
Lewis, H. Spencer 328, 463, 487–489, 561, 634
honorary VII° in OTO 487, 634
Liberal Club 340, 344
Lilliput 540–541
Lincke, Elsa 328, 634
Lindsay, Jack 433, 441, 449

Ling, Arthur Robert 52
Lister, Sir Joseph 26
Lockhart, Robert Hamilton Bruce 287–288
Lodge, Frank T. 336, 345, 349
London Physician. *See* Crowley, Aleister, pseudonyms
Longstaff, George 51, 579
Looking Glass 225, 228–229, 231–233, 259–260, 481, 613
Lord Haw-Haw. *See* Joyce, William
l'Ordre Kabbalistique de la Rose+Croix 617
Lorenz, Hans 100
Lorria, August 42
Loveday, Raoul 381–384, 387–396, 417, 442, 444, 497, 550, 644–646
    death 391
Lovell, Fenella 235–236
Low, Sir Frederic 205, 207–208
Lowry, Malcolm 555
Lunn, Arnold 51
Lusitania 278, 288, 291
Luther, Martin 330
Lutiy, The Late Major. *See* Crowley, Aleister, pseudonyms
Lykiardopoulos, Michael 287
l'Église Gnostique de France 617

MacAlpine, Deirdre Patricia (née Doherty) 481, 489, 492–493, 496, 506, 508, 544, 548–549, 551, 657
Macaulay, Rose 464
MacBean, Reginald Gambier 390
MacBride, Maude Gonne 60
Machen, Arthur 61
Mackenzie, Compton 474
Maeterlinck, Maurice, *Blue Bird* 222
Maggio, Dr. 389–391
Maitland, Cecil 368–369, 372–373, 376, 380
    A∴A∴ Probationer 373
Maitland, Edward 41, 241, 577
Malvern College 26, 40, 158
Mandrake Press 214, 440–443, 446–449, 454, 460, 490, 629
Mannin, Ethel 468
Mansfield, Katherine 258–259, 298
Maples, Fanny 15
Marlow, Louis. *See* Wilkinson, Louis
Marquard, Leo 395
Marsden, Dora 256
Marsh, Vida 335
Marston, G. M. 209–210, 214, 216, 218
Marston, George A. 353
Martinist Order 254, 502
Mascagni, Pietro, *Cavelleria Rusticana* 238
Mason, Arthur 212
Masonry. *See* Freemasonry
Mathers, Mina 58, 62, 80–81, 122, 268, 281–282, 585
Mathers, S. L. MacGregor 54, 58–62, 64, 66, 70–71, 73–81, 83, 86, 92, 108, 115, 117, 122, 130, 135, 158, 161–162, 176, 180, 183, 196, 205–208, 213, 223, 232, 234, 237, 244, 252, 259–260, 268, 281, 306, 332, 442, 466, 487, 495, 529, 557, 559, 577, 585
    Book of the Sacred Magic of Abramelin the Mage 54, 60, 69–70, 210
    Kaballah Unveiled 51, 54, 58
Mattei, Count Cesare 19, 571
Matulka, Jan 177
Maugham, Frederic 519
Maugham, W. Somerset 112–114, 180–181, 603
    Liza of Lambeth 112
    Magician 112–113, 180–181, 191, 429
    Moon and Sixpence 360–361
    Mrs. Craddock 112
    Of Human Bondage 112–113, 591
May, Betty 381–384, 387–393, 452, 464, 478–483, 644–645
    previous marriages 645
    Tiger Woman 442, 472
Maylard, A. E. 31
McAllan, Major J. C. S. 446
McMurtry, Grady Louis (Hymenaeus Alpha) 513–514, 522, 527, 530–532, 534, 539, 541, 546–547, 556–557, 661, 664
    IX° in OTO 527, 534
    Sovereign Grand Inspector General in OTO 664
McPherson, Aimee Semple 656
Medina-Sidonia, Don Jesus de 85–86, 587
Mellinger, Frederick 535, 541, 546–548, 667
Memphis-Mizraim, Ancient and Primitive Rite of 209, 254–255, 262–263, 313, 390, 488, 529, 634, 645
Mencken, H. L. 515
Mendelssohn, Felix 224
Mengens, Sybil. *See* Meugens, Sybil
Merton, Wilfred 256, 618
Merz, W. 100
Metro-Goldwyn Pictures 429–430
Meugens, Sybil 110–111, 590, 610
Meyer, Henry 262–263, 313
Meynell, Wilfrid 182
Micklewright, Frederick Henry Amphlett 535
Military Order of the Temple 36
Miller, Anna Catherine 320
Minchin, W. C. 265
Minor, Roddie 320–323, 326–327, 329–330, 349, 426, 633
Minter, Mary Miles 352
Miramar, Maria Teresa de. *See* Crowley, Maria Teresa
Mohammed 128, 295, 330
Molay, Jacques de 268
Monet, Claude 109
Montagu, Lady Olivia 164
Moore, George 32, 66, 174
Morden, Grover L. 351–352
Morgan, Lord Evan Frederick (4th Baron Tredegar) 507, 527, 530
morphine 63, 105, 163, 379, 459
Morrice, James Wilson 115
Morris, Elsie 491

Morris, John W. 468
Mortlake, Harold 515, 661
Moulton, Justice John Fletcher 205, 207, 607
Mozart, Wolfgang Amadeus 82, 253
Mudd, Norman 175, 214, 217, 350, 363, 378,
    394–403, 405–406, 408–413, 415–418,
    420–422, 424, 444, 461, 646, 648, 665
    Neophyte 1°=10□ 350
    suicide 422
Mueller, Otto 456
Müller, Max 171
Mummery, Albert Frederick 27, 30–31, 35
Münsterberg, Hugo 506
Murnau, Friedrich Wilhelm 419
Murphy, District Attorney Frank 345, 351
Murray, Adam Gray 400, 405–406, 409, 412–
    413
Murry, John Middleton 258–259
Mussolini, Benito 360, 399–400, 534

Naish, William Vawdrey 33
Naval Intelligence Division (NID) 286–287,
    506–507, 511, 548, 659
Neilson, Alexander 205–206
Neuburg, Victor 165–166, 175, 179–180, 183–
    185, 187, 189, 193, 196–204, 214, 216, 218–
    219, 221–224, 229, 237, 249, 252, 256, 258–
    260, 265, 267–278, 297, 308, 388, 391, 442,
    448, 464, 484, 497, 540, 600, 621
    discovers Dylan Thomas 276
    Lost Shepherd 191
    Nocturne 231
    Probationer 0°=0□ 184, 198
    Sunday Referee. 276
    Three Poems 258
    Triumph of Pan 185, 187, 189, 223, 258,
        276
    Vale Jehovah! 165
    Vine Press 276
New Age 70, 177–178, 182, 184, 214, 302, 443
New York Specialist. See Crowley, Aleister,
    pseudonyms
Newman, Hugh George de Willmott 529, 663
Newton, B. W. 11
Nicholson and Lee, Oxford Book of English
    Mystical Verse 320
Nierendorf, Karl 455–456, 653
Nietzsche, Friedrich 265
Nolde, Emil 456
Norfolk, Hilda. See Crowley, Aleister,
    pseudonyms
Normand, Mabel 352
Northcliffe, Lord. See Harmsworth, Alfred
Northrup, Sara Elizabeth (Betty) 537, 539
Norwood, Joseph W. 285, 348
Nott, C. S. 407
Nuit 127–128, 323, 327

O'Connor, Martin 465, 472, 476–480
O'Flaherty, Liam, Ecstasy of Angus 447
Occult Review 183, 211, 213, 215, 231, 234, 251,
    318, 464, 494, 528, 535, 542

Ogden, Charles Kay 440
Olcott, Henry Steel 93, 650
Olivier, Nina 111, 178, 180, 235, 238
Olsen, Dorothy 413–418, 425–429, 650
Open Court 292–293, 622, 625–626
Ophüls, Max 460
opium 63, 154, 218, 230, 269, 273–274, 322,
    357
Oracles of Zoroaster 559
Orage, Alfred Richard 177–178, 259, 561, 602
Orchard, William Arundel 298
Ordeal of the Abyss. See Abyss
Ordo Templi Orientis 208, 230, 251–252, 254–
    256, 258, 262–265, 274–275, 278, 282–283,
    295, 312, 319, 324, 329, 332, 342, 347, 349,
    351–352, 370, 377, 418, 420–421, 438, 446,
    465, 468, 485, 487–488, 494, 498, 502–504,
    506, 512, 518, 523–525, 530–531, 534–535,
    539, 542–544, 547, 549, 553, 555–557, 620,
    628
    0° Minerval 487, 502
    VI° 543
    VII° 252, 254, 282, 468, 487, 543
    VIII° 274, 291
    IX° 251–252, 255, 268–269, 274–275,
        277–278, 325, 347, 370, 377, 420, 527,
        532, 534, 538, 546–547, 553, 557
    X° 256, 376, 418, 553
    XI° 274, 347
    Anational Congress 312
    Australia 376
    Caliph 531–532, 556–557
    Denmark 502
    Detroit 335–337, 344–345, 349–350, 353
    London (1940s) 543
    London (Mysteria Mystica Maxima) 256,
        258–259, 263, 265, 268, 274, 277, 282,
        312, 316–318
    London temple raided 317–318
    Los Angeles. See Agape Lodge
    Outer Head of the Order 419–421, 488,
        519, 532, 553, 556–557
    South Africa 211
    Vancouver 278, 295, 468, 527
Ordóñez, Ezequiel 86, 587
Oriflamme 254–255, 283, 524, 617
Osiris 89, 124, 126, 295, 306, 414, 511
Otter, Elizabeth Gwendolen 221, 223, 259,
    310, 440, 489, 611
    Writing on the Ground 259
Ouarda. See Crowley, Rose
Ouspensky, Pyotr Demianovich 406
Outer Head of the Order. See Ordo Templi
    Orientis, Outer Head of the Order
Oxford Book of English Mystical Verse 320
Oxford University 33, 45, 47, 258, 381–382,
    441, 444–445, 507, 514–515, 575, 614, 624,
    633, 665
    Poetry Society 444

Pache, Alexis 140–143, 145, 147, 149, 596
    Pache's Grave 147–148

Paganini, Nicolò, *Witches' Dance* 224
Paget, Sir James 19
Pailthorpe, Grace Winifred 446, 449
Pailthrope, Grace Winifred 652
Palladino, Eusapia 188, 344
Pan Society 166, 175, 189
Pansophia 503, 659
Pansophical Lodge 418–420, 503
Papen, Franz von 623
Paramahamsa, Mahatma Sri Agamya Guru 171–172, 255, 504
Parananda, Sri. *See* Rámanáthan, Ponnambalam
Parke-Davis Pharmaceuticals 295, 346
Parker, Elsie Gray 324–325
Parker, Garrett & Co 409
Parry, Dean Reginald St. John 216–217, 260, 610
Parsons, Helen. *See* Smith, Helen Parsons
Parsons, Jack (John Whiteside Parsons) 513–514, 521–522, 524–526, 537–539, 555, 660
    Babalon Working 538
Peachell, Gerald 298
Pearson's 280
Péladan, Joséphin, *Le Vice Suprême* 38
Penny, Major 512
Penzer, N. M. 43
Pessoa, Fernando 449–451
Peters, Alfred Vout 451
peyote 211, 218–219, 259, 295, 315, 325, 346, 609
Pfannl, Heinrich 99–106
Pickford, Mary 347
Pigney, John 395
Pike, Albert, *Morals and Dogma* 558
Pinder, Major Frank 407
Pinsent, G. H. S. 189, 191, 210, 267, 606
Pioneer Picture Company 347
pirate bridge 311–312, 629–630
Pistis Sophia 559
Plato, *Timaeus* 327
Plummer, George Winslow 279–280, 621
Plymouth Brethren 11–12, 18, 20, 30, 510, 560, 570, 647
    books, restrictions on 15, 22
    Christmas 15
    dispensationalism 126
    Exclusive Brethren 12, 15, 19–20
    Open Brethren 12
    Raven Division 19
Poe, Edgar Allan, *Tell-Tale Heart* 170
Pollexfen, George 61
Pollitt, Herbert Charles Jerome 37–41, 45, 47, 50, 55, 71, 197
Pope, Alexander, *Rape of the Lock* 47
Potter's Field 46
Pougy, Liane de 37
Pound, Ezra 222, 256–257, 612
    Dance Figure 222–223
    Dead Iönè 257, 268
Poupée. *See* Crowley, Anne Léa
Powell, Anthony 382, 442, 452, 472
Powter, Geoff 150

Powys, John Cooper 515, 661
Prasad, Rama, *Nature's Finer Forces* 559
Pratapa, Bheema Sena 255
Preston, W. E. Hayter 222, 275, 484
Prestwick, Joseph 9
Price, Harry 465, 655
Prometheus. *See* Crowley, Aleister, pseudonyms
psychochromes 314, 340
Pythagoras, *Golden Verses of* 559

Quakers 3–4, 11, 566
Quinn, John 234, 278, 280–282, 293, 297, 335, 354, 474
Qur'an 176, 196, 202, 499, 607

Rabelais, François 128, 293, 332
Radclyffe, Raymond 214, 218–220, 611
Rae-Fraser, G. G. 258, 618
Raffalovich, George 185–187, 204, 214, 224, 230–231, 234, 237, 260, 316, 605
    Deuce and All 223
    History of a Soul 223, 231
    Man-Cover 191
    Planetary Journeys and Earthly Sketches 187
Ragged Ragtime Girls 261–263, 265, 287, 619
Ra-Hoor-Khuit 125, 128
Rais, Gilles de 444, 514
Rámanáthan, Ponnambalam (Sri Parananda) 93, 298, 588
Randle, Charles 194
Randolph, Paschal Beverly 255, 487
Rauschning, Hermann, *Hitler Speaks* 484
Raven, F. E. 19
Read, H. V. 31
Reese, Bert 323, 325
Regardie, Israel 432–434, 436–439, 441, 446, 449–451, 453–454, 494–495, 533, 584, 653
    Golden Dawn 494
    My Rosicrucian Adventure 494
reincarnation 59, 161, 165, 237, 273, 330
Rembrandt, *Old Woman* 332
Renoir, Pierre 109
Renouard, Philippe 116, 133, 137, 161
Rethy, Joseph Bernard 283
Reuss, Albert 252
Reuss, Theodor 208, 251–256, 261–263, 265, 278, 283–284, 287, 312, 370, 418–419, 468, 487–488, 546, 616, 634
    Parsifal 253
    Pranatherapie 253
Reymond, Charles 140–141, 143, 145–149
Richards, Grant 173, 379
Righi, Alcesti C. Rigo de 141, 143–149, 597
Ringler, Anny 263–264
Rintelen, Franz von 623
Ritchie, David 511
Rite of Isis 81, 585
Robbins, N. H. 33
Robeson, Paul 493
Robinson, John Wilson 35
Roche, Justice 483
Rockmore, Clara 609

Rodin, Auguste 99, 105, 109, 111, 115, 137, 168, 178, 192
  Balzac 115
  Sœur et frère 99
Rodker, John 368
Roehling, Marie 327–328, 335, 634
Rogers, Mary Alice (née Beaton) 90–92, 298, 587
Roosevelt, Theodore 164, 263
Rops, Félicien 37
Rose-Innes, Patrick 205
Rosencreutz, Christian 330
Rosenroth, Knorr von, *Kabbala Denudata* 51, 58, 559
Rosetti, D.G. 274
Rosher, Charles 63, 74
Rosicrucians 57–58, 60, 71–73, 76, 134, 205–208, 232, 237, 252, 254, 449, 487–488, 528, 558, 596, 613
Rubinstein, Anton 609
Ruskin, John 34, 575
Russell, Bertrand 411, 648
Russell, C. F. 329, 342, 350, 366–367, 371, 374, 377, 485–486, 657
  Choronzon Club 485–486
  Expulsion from OTO 486
Russell, Charles 79
Ryerson, Albert W. 287, 332–337, 344–345, 348–351, 353–354, 635
  divorce 335
Ryerson, Mazie (née Mitchell) 353

Saayman, Edmund (Eddie) 399–400, 646, 665
Sabatini, Arturo 406, 408, 412, 416–417
Sacher-Masoch, Leopold Ritter von 49
Saint-Saëns, Camille 212, 224
Salvesen, Lord 194, 204, 214, 606
Sankey, Ira D. 164
Sauret, Émile 212, 609
Scarlet Woman 16, 155, 161, 290, 327, 337, 339–340, 356, 358–359, 363, 367, 370, 373, 386–387, 401–402, 409, 414–418, 426, 433, 450, 456–457, 470
Schauffler, Robert Haven 267
Schiller, Mr. 231–232
Schmidt-Rottluff, Karl 456
Schneider, Jean 531
Schneider, Leota 427, 468–469
Schneider, Max 413, 419, 421, 427, 468, 487, 494, 526
Scholz, Georg 456
Schroeder, Theodore 282
Schumann, Robert 224
Schwann, Edward Bageshott 33
Schwob, Marcel 113, 115
Scientology, Church of 537, 561
Scott, Langston 10–11
Scott, Robert 112, 192
Scott, Walter 176, 183
Scottish Mountaineering Club 30, 35, 574
Scrutinium Chymicum 559
Scrutton, Lord Justice 231–233

Seabrook, William 280, 330–332, 349, 511, 621
Seckler, Paul 502
Seckler, Phyllis 502
Secret Chiefs 59–60, 74–76, 108, 130, 156, 161–162, 191, 222, 234, 241–242, 297, 299, 306, 313, 330, 347, 403, 408, 414, 418, 421, 557
Sen, Sun Yat 303
Servants of the Light 559
sex magick 251–252, 255, 268–269, 274–275, 277–278, 282, 291, 295, 309, 316, 325, 330, 347, 358–359, 365, 370, 376–377, 406, 408, 412, 416, 426, 439, 448, 456, 465, 470, 503, 532, 537–538
Shakespeare, William 25, 34, 120
Shaw, Arthur Pilkington 37
Shaw, George Bernard 66, 290, 299, 380, 411, 460, 463
  Androcles and the Lion 308
Shaw, Harold Batty 355
Sheffield, Eliza Dinah 206
Shelley, Percy Bysshe 33–34, 46, 50, 120, 151, 274, 327, 359, 396, 476, 575
  St. Irvyne; or the Rosicrucian: a Romance 46
Sheridan-Bickers, Betty 186, 383
Sheridan-Bickers, H. 185–186, 214, 347, 352, 383, 604
Sherwill, Capt. J. L. 139
Shirley, Ralph 535
Shivaji, Mahatma Guru Sri Paramahansa. *See* Crowley, Aleister, pseudonyms
Shumway, Howard (Howie) 356–359, 361–362, 391, 398
Shumway, Howard C. 356
Shumway, Mimi 398, 406, 417, 430
Shumway, Ninette 356–358, 361–362, 364–366, 374, 376, 378, 380, 386, 389, 391, 397–398, 405–408, 412–413, 415–418, 423, 427, 430, 461
Shumway, Richard 418
Sibley, Cedric Putnam 345–346, 638
Sieveking, Lance 394, 431
Simmons, Harold 231–232
Simpkin Marshall 184, 491, 497
Simpson, Alice (née Hall) 65, 77–78, 92, 588
Simpson, Elaine 65, 76–78, 90, 92–93, 155, 214, 298
Simpson, Howard R. 177
Sins of the Cities of the Plain 133
666 16, 125, 132–133, 136, 295–296, 325, 342, 473–474, 535
Sjallung, Grunddal 502, 659
Skene, Hener 235, 238, 614–615
Skerrett, Frederick Thomas 119–120
Skerrett, Rose. *See* Crowley, Rose
Slesser, Lord Justice 481, 483
Smith, Charles Yale 345–346
Smith, Helen Parsons 513, 522, 537, 660
Smith, Walter Parry Haskett 27
Smith, Wilfred T. 337, 350, 427–428, 430, 433, 468–469, 485, 487, 489, 494, 505, 521–522, 524–527, 547, 658

Grand Treasurer General of British Columbia 468
Liber Apotheosis 526
Smithers, Leonard C. 38, 47–50, 61, 67, 133, 579
Snepp, Vera (Lola) 159–160
Societas Rosicruciana in America 279–280, 621
Societas Rosicruciana in Anglica 57–59, 71, 278, 487
Societas Rosicruciana in Civitibaus Fœderatis 621
Society for Psychical Research 177, 185, 188, 254, 285, 344, 465
Society for the Propagation of Religious Truth 131, 135–136, 168, 176
Sodin, William 15
Solar, Xul 410, 648
Solly, H. 31
Sophocles, *Oedipus Rex* 22
Spare, Austin Osman 185–186, 191, 214, 265, 348, 557, 604, 668
    Book of Pleasure 185
    Book of Satyrs 185
    Earth Inferno 185
Speaight, George Victor 652
Speaight, Hugh 444–445, 652
Speaight, Robert 652
Spence, Richard, *Secret Agent 666* 284, 286, 288, 335, 624, 646, 659
Spencer-Churchill, E. George 33
Spender, Stephen 458, 540
Spiritual Guide of Molinos 559
spiritualism 165–166, 317, 620, 655
Sprengel, Anna (Sapiens Dominabitur Astris) 58, 243–244
Spring-Rice, Cecil 286
Stael, Henri 211
Starr, Meredith. *See* Close, Herbert
Steadman, Van Praagh and Gaylor 205
Stearns, Harold Edmund 177
Steiner, Rudolf 255, 419–420, 561, 618
Stele of Revealing 125–126, 129, 176, 357, 374, 403, 493, 517
Stephensen, P. R. 132, 392, 440–443, 445–447, 449, 508, 573, 582
    Legend of Aleister Crowley 441–442, 446–447, 456, 466, 583, 625
Stephenson, Robert Louis 113
Stewart, Meum 496–497
Stibbard, Albert A. 345–346
Straus, Oscar, *A Waltz Dream* 212, 261
Straus, Ralph 515, 661
Strong, Demas 81
Strong, Susan 81–84, 586
Stuart, Henry Clifford 301–303
Sturges, Preston 239–240, 245, 247–248
Sturges, Solomon 240
Sullivan, J. W. N. 369–370, 471, 642, 665
Sullivan, Sylvia 369–370, 642
Summers, Frank 120
Summers, Montague 428
Sumner, John 354

Sun Engraving 515, 521
Sunday Express 384–388, 392–394, 397, 406, 409, 411, 447, 467, 584
Sutherland, Cordelia 527, 530
Sutherland, M. A. 510, 660
Svareff, Vladimir. *See* Crowley, Aleister, pseudonyms
Swamiji, Mahatma Sri Paramananda Guru. *See* Crowley, Aleister, pseudonyms
Swedenborg, Emanuel 57
Swift, Jonathan 34
Swift, Justice 472, 476–481, 483
Swinburne, Algernon 32, 34, 50, 66, 219, 327, 359
    Atalanta 219
    Ballad of Burdens 575
    Leper 48
    Tannhauser 49
Swinnerton, Frank Arthur 114
Symonds, E. C. Vernon 532, 534
Symonds, John 540–542, 549, 551, 553–554, 557, 666
Symons, Arthur 38, 47, 235

Tanguay, Eva 326–327, 341, 633
Tankerville, Earl of. *See* Bennet, George Montagu
tantra 556
Tao 175, 295
Tao Teh King 176, 247, 559
tarot 155, 174, 176, 237, 347, 367, 404, 410, 501–504, 509–511, 514–515, 517, 519, 521–522, 525–527, 530–531, 559, 614, 617
Taylor, Walter E. 212
Taylor, William Desmond 352
Tchaikovsky, Pëtr 224
Teleny 47–48, 133, 579
Templar, Knights 256, 268
Tennyson, Lord Alfred 50, 274, 359
Thaelmann, Ernst 458
Thaulow, Frits 115
Thelema 127–128, 203, 263, 265, 295–297, 306, 310, 316, 322, 331, 335, 342, 347, 349, 361, 376, 383–384, 387, 395, 401–402, 404, 409, 414–416, 420–421, 423–425, 431, 460, 469, 484, 487, 499, 505, 514, 517, 521, 536, 541, 560–561, 594, 639, 650
Thelema Verlag 420, 426
Theosophical Society 57–59, 90, 129, 175, 210–211, 221, 253, 262, 282, 289, 296, 342, 390, 414–415, 419–420, 423–424, 449, 560–561, 577, 584, 594, 617, 649
Thomas, Dylan 276, 464–465, 540, 621
Thompson, Basil 286
Thompson, Francis 274
Thomson, Elihu 307, 629
Thomson, Wiliam Brown 549
Thornely, Thomas 48
Thornton, Edward 97, 151–152, 576
Thrupp, John 9–10, 570
Thynne, Major Robert Thompson 440, 446–447, 449, 451, 481, 489

Tillyard, Aelfrida 267
Tillyard, Alfred Isaac 267
Tingley, Katherine 296
Titanic 247, 251, 312
Tonbridge Schools 15, 26–27
Tosti, Francesco Paolo 212
Townshend, Marquis 206
Tracy, Spencer 248
Tränker, Heinrich 418–420, 488, 649
Tredegar, Lord. *See* Morgan, Lord Evan
    Frederick
Trotsky, Leon 399
Troxel, Dorothy 328, 634
True Will. *See* Will
Twain, Mark 141

Unamuno, Miguel de 411
Universal Book Stores 332–337, 342, 345, 348,
    350–353
Universal Brotherhood 421
Upanishads 158, 559
Upham, Alice 517

V for Victory 511–512, 516–517
Vagrancy Act 317, 631
Valiente, Doreen 543
Vanity Fair 178, 181, 183–184, 280–282, 288,
    290, 294–295, 297, 299, 302, 304, 309, 311,
    340, 603, 610, 626
Vedanta 97–98, 295
Vedas 158
vegetarian 58, 165, 241
Verdi, Giuseppe, *Aida* 82
Verey, Rev. C. *See* Crowley, Aleister,
    pseudonyms
Vernstorff, Graf von 506
Verrall, Arthur Woolgar 35
Victoria, Queen 11, 19, 87, 355
Viereck, George Sylvester 283–288, 304, 315,
    320, 325, 328, 379, 506
Vieuxtemps, Henri 224, 609
Villa Caldarazzo 359
Vincey, Leo. *See* Crowley, Aleister, pseudonyms
Virakam. *See* Desti, Mary
Vision of the Demon Crowley 329
Vivian, Herbert 117
Voorheis, Paul W. 351–352

Waddell, Leila 211, 213, 215, 217–219, 223–
    224, 230, 235, 238, 240, 243, 247, 250–252,
    259–261, 263–265, 274–275, 279, 282, 291,
    298, 319, 355, 426, 609, 619, 626
    Thelema: A Tone-Testament 258
    Two Anzacs Meet in London 298
    Two Little Brides 261
    Waltz Dream 212
Wade, Floyd E. 505
Wagner, Richard 224, 252, 254, 265, 278, 616
    Das Rheingold 82
    Die Walküre 81
    Götterdämmerung 82
    Lohengrin 81

    Parsifal 253
    Siegfried 82
    Tannhäuser 82, 84
Waite, A. E. 41, 61, 180, 185, 258, 266, 310,
    352–353, 429, 494, 577, 632
    Book of Black Magic and of Pacts 40
    Real History of the Rosicrucians 595
Waite, Arthur Warren 303, 352–353
Walker, Dorothea 425
Waller, George Stanley 507
Ward, Kenneth Martin 185, 189–190, 217, 224,
    234
Warlock, Peter. *See* Heseltine, Philip
Warren, Richard 185
Waska, Mary 180, 214
Watney, Combe, Reid and Co., Ltd 52
Watson, H. 548
Watts, Charles 131
Waugh, Evelyn 382
Weber, Hans 460
Wedgwood, James Ingall 262, 390, 424
Weekly Critical Review 115, 592
Weiser, Samuel 500, 658
Weishaupt, Adam 330
Welles, Orson 531
Wells, Bettina Borrman 320–321
Wells, H. G. 115, 130, 180, 224, 360, 463, 519
Wessely, Victor 100–101, 103–107
West, Rebecca 256
West, T. J. 212
Westcott, W. Wynn 56–61, 74–75, 77, 80, 162,
    254, 424, 585
    Collectanea Hermetica 57
    Extra Pharmacopœia 56
    Magical Ritual of the Sanctum Regnum 57
    *Numbers: Their Occult Power and Mystic
        Virtue* 57
    Sepher Yetzirah 57
    Suicide 56
    Twelve Years' Experience as a London
        Coroner 56
Westley, Helen 288–290, 293, 347, 624–625
Wetton, Peggy 503
Whateley, William 205–207
Wheatley, Dennis 507, 659
Whineray, Edward 163–164, 183, 237
Whistler, James McNeill 37, 39, 105
White Lotus Day 90
White Rock Boarding School for Young
    Gentlemen 17
White, Robert 10–11
Whitehouse, I. R. 87
Whiteley, Justice 482–483
Whittaker, Norman Tweed 303, 628
Whymper, Edward 27
Wieland & Co. 221, 250, 611
Wieland, Eugene (Bunco) 218, 220–221, 256,
    611
Wieniawski, Henryk 212, 224, 609
Wigman, Mary 312, 630
Wilcox, Ella Wheeler 341, 344, 638
Wilde, Mrs. Oscar (Constance Mary) 61

Wilde, Oscar 38, 45, 47, 130, 133, 173–174, 266, 341, 460, 579
    Ballad of Reading Gaol 48
    Ideal Husband 48
    Importance of Being Earnest 48
Wilkinson, C. E. 77–78
Wilkinson, Louis 186, 213, 280, 315, 320, 489, 512–515, 519, 523, 527, 529, 532, 534–535, 537, 548–549, 551
Wilkinson, Oliver 532–533
Will 69, 127, 129, 190, 378, 380, 405, 429, 560
Williams, Justice Vaughan 205–208, 607
Williams, Ralph Vaughan 607
Windram, James Thomas 209, 211, 265, 282–283, 405
Winslow, Rosalind Mae Guggenheim. *See* Burr, Jane.
Witkowski, Paul Harry 93, 588
Wolfe, Jane 347, 349, 352, 357, 362–365, 367, 371–374, 377–378, 386, 389, 391, 394, 409, 413, 417, 421, 423, 425–428, 431, 468, 486–487, 494, 524, 638
Woodman, W. R. 58–59, 61, 75, 162
Work, Milton Cooper 311
Wyndham, Henry 428
Wyndham, Maud Evelyn 428

X, Stuart. *See* Stuart, Henry Clifford

Yale, Elihu 346
Yarker, John 208–209, 237, 249, 254, 256, 262, 266, 313, 390, 424, 608, 650
    Arcane Schools 209, 237
Yates, Edmund 5
Yeats, John Butler 280–282, 289–290, 293

Yeats, W. B. 32, 38, 58–59, 61, 65–67, 71, 73–75, 77–80, 115, 118, 280–282, 292, 299, 310, 442, 546, 559, 583
    A Vision 80
    Resurrection 583
yoga 62, 93–95, 108, 158, 171, 184, 237, 247, 255, 330, 368, 432, 495–496, 559, 587
    ajna chakra 193
    ananda 192
    asana 95, 199, 273, 330
    atmadarshana 192
    dharana 95
    dhyana 95
    hatha yoga 180, 558
    mantra 62, 95
    nadis 558
    pranayama 95, 237, 347, 398, 558
    samadhi 160, 168, 172, 601
    Shivadarshana 62, 160
    tattvas 558
Yorke, Gerald 65, 279, 363, 392, 407, 412, 427–429, 431–436, 438, 440–442, 446–449, 451–455, 458–462, 483, 497, 499–500, 510–511, 516–517, 527, 530, 537, 549, 553–554, 645, 653, 655, 666, 668
    Neophyte 1°=10□ 460
    Probationer in A∴A∴ 428
    resignation from A∴A∴ 462
Yorke, Henry Vincent
Yorke, Vincent Wodehouse 428
Yorska, Madame 341, 637
Younghusband, Sir Francis 107

Zaehnsdorf (book binders) 280, 622
Zohar 51, 58
Zurbriggen, Matthias 42